This book offers an overview of recent research on the psychology of
judgment and decision making, ᵗʰ ᶠⁱᵉˡᵈ ᵗʰᵃᵗ ⁱⁿᵛᵉˢᵗⁱᵍᵃᵗᵉˢ ᵗʰᵉ processes by which people draw c   nd
make choices.

An introductory, historically   of
viewing the overall structure of   D0000434   its
possible directions. Subsequent   ent
papers by prominent researchers, organized to reveal the currents,
connections, and controversies that animate the field. Current trends
in the field are illustrated with papers from ongoing streams of
research on such topics as anomalies of judgment and choice, the
acquisition and use of knowledge, causal judgment, counterfactual
reasoning, and the temporal context of decision and insight. The
papers on "connections" explore memory, explanation and argument, affect, attitudes, and motivation. Finally, a section on "controversies" presents problem representation, domain knowledge,
content specificity, rule-governed versus rule-described behavior,
and proposals for radical departures and new beginnings in the
field.

Cambridge Series on Judgment and Decision Making

Research on judgment and decision making

Cambridge Series on Judgment and Decision Making

The purpose of the series is to convey the general principles of and findings about judgment and decision making to the many academic and professional fields to which these apply. The contributions are written by authorities in the field and supervised by highly qualified editors and the Publications Board. The series will attract readers from many different disciplines, largely among academics, advanced undergraduates, graduate students, and practicing professionals.

Also in the series

Inside the Juror: The Psychology of Juror Decision Making
Edited by Reid Hastie
Psychological Perspectives on Justice: Theory and Applications
Edited by Barbara A. Mellers and Jonathan Baron
Judgment and Decision-Making Research in Accounting and Auditing
Robert Ashton and Alison Ashton
Organizational Decision Making
Edited by Zur Shapira

Research on judgment and decision making

Currents, connections, and controversies

Edited by

William M. Goldstein
University of Chicago

Robin M. Hogarth
University of Chicago

CAMBRIDGE
UNIVERSITY PRESS

PUBLISHED BY THE PRESS SYNDICATE OF THE UNIVERSITY OF CAMBRIDGE
The Pitt Building, Trumpington Street, Cambridge CB2 1RP, United Kingdom

CAMBRIDGE UNIVERSITY PRESS
The Edinburgh Building, Cambridge CB2 2RU, United Kingdom
40 West 20th Street, New York, NY 10011-4211, USA
10 Stamford Road, Oakleigh, Melbourne 3166, Australia

First published 1997

Printed in the United States of America

Typeset in Palatino

Library of Congress Cataloging-in-Publication Data

Research on judgment and decision making: currents, connections, and
controversies / edited by William M. Goldstein, Robin M. Hogarth.

p.   cm. – (Cambridge series on judgment and decision making)

Includes bibliographical references and indexes.

ISBN 0-521-48302-6 (hardcover). – ISBN 0-521-48334-4 (pbk.)

1. Decision-making.   2. Judgment.   I. Goldstein, William M. (William Mark),
1954–   .   II. Hogarth, Robin M.   III. Series.
BF448.J84   1996
153.8'3 – dc21   96-43490
                                                                      CIP

A catalog record for this book is available from the British Library.

ISBN 0 521 48302 6 hardback
ISBN 0 521 48334 4 paperback

Contents

Series preface

The Society for Judgment and Decision Making first collaborated with Cambridge University Press in 1986 with the publication of *Judgment and Decision Making: An Interdisciplinary Reader*, edited by Hal R. Arkes and Kenneth R. Hammond. The goals of the reader were to (1) outline the core ideas of the field and (2) illustrate their wide applicability. The purpose of each of the subsequent volumes in the series was to explain in far greater detail the relevance of judgment and decision-making research to particular domains. Thus *Inside the Juror*, edited by Reid Hastie, pertained to law; *Psychological Perspectives on Justice*, edited by Barbara A. Mellers and Jonathan Baron, dealt with economic, legal, and policy issues related to fairness; and *Judgment and Decision-Making Research in Accounting and Auditing*, edited by Robert H. Ashton and Alison H. Ashton, highlighted the burgeoning quantity of research in these two areas. With the publication of *Research on Judgment and Decision Making: Currents, Connections, and Controversies*, William M. Goldstein and Robin M. Hogarth return to the core ideas of the field, but at a more advanced level than was done in the 1986 reader. The presentation is as accessible as that of the initial book, but the topics include important research ideas and controversies that did not yet exist when the field was less mature a decade ago.

The Publications Committee of the Society for Judgment and Decision Making is very pleased to proffer this volume, because of both the eminence of the editors and the fine array of articles they have chosen to represent noteworthy developments in our field. Because this volume contains topics not targeted toward specific content domains, the principles and ideas should be of interest to a very broad array of interested persons from psychology, business, public policy, law, and medicine.

Hal R. Arkes
For the Publications Committee

Contributors

James R. Bettman *Fuqua School of Business, Duke University*

Berndt Brehmer *Department of Psychology, University of Uppsala, Sweden*

Colin F. Camerer *Center for Decision Research, Graduate School of Business, University of Chicago*

Patricia W. Cheng *Department of Psychology, University of California at Los Angeles*

Robyn M. Dawes *Department of Social and Decision Sciences, Carnegie Mellon University*

Michael E. Doherty *Department of Psychology, Bowling Green State University*

Brian J. Gibbs *Graduate School of Business, Stanford University*

Gerd Gigerenzer *Max Planck Institute for Psychological Research, Munich, Germany*

William M. Goldstein *Department of Psychology, University of Chicago*

Janet Grassia *Center for Research on Judgment and Policy, University of Colorado at Boulder**

Dale Griffin *School of Cognitive and Computing Sciences, University of Sussex, United Kingdom*

Young-Won Ha *Institute for Business Research, Sogang University, Seoul, Korea*

Robert M. Hamm *Clinical Decision Making Program, Department of Family and Preventive Medicine, Health Sciences Center, University of Oklahoma*

Kenneth R. Hammond *Center for Research on Judgment and Policy, Department of Psychology, University of Colorado at Boulder*

Reid Hastie *Center for Research on Judgment and Policy, Department of Psychology, University of Colorado at Boulder*

Ulrich Hoffrage   *Max Planck Institute for Psychological Research, Munich, Germany*

Robin M. Hogarth   *Center for Decision Research, Graduate School of Business, University of Chicago*

Alice M. Isen   *Samuel Curtis Johnson Graduate School of Management, Cornell University*

Eric J. Johnson   *Wharton School of Business, University of Pennysylvania*

Daniel Kahneman   *Department of Psychology and Woodrow Wilson School of Public and International Affairs, Princeton University*

Gideon Keren   *Technische Universiteit Eindhoven, The Netherlands*

Joshua Klayman   *Center for Decision Research, Graduate School of Business, University of Chicago*

Heinz Kleinbölting   *Max Planck Institute for Psychological Research, Munich, Germany*

Howard Kunreuther   *Wharton School of Business, University of Pennsylvania*

Christopher Langston   *Research Department, Philadephia Geriatric Center, Philadelphia, Pennsylvania*

Sarah Lichtenstein   *Decision Research, Eugene, Oregon*

George Loewenstein   *Department of Social and Decision Sciences, Carnegie Mellon University*

Lola L. Lopes   *College of Business Administration, University of Iowa*

Margaret A. Marquis   *Department of Statistics, North Carolina State University**

Craig R. M. McKenzie   *Department of Psychology, University of California at San Diego*

Richard E. Nisbett   *Research Center for Group Dynamics, Institute for Social Research, University of Michigan*

Laura R. Novick   *Department of Psychology and Human Development, Peabody College, Vanderbilt University*

John M. Orbell   *Department of Political Science, University of Oregon*

Bernadette Park   *Department of Psychology, University of Colorado at Boulder*

John W. Payne   *Fuqua School of Business, Duke University*

Tamra Pearson (now Tamra Pearson d'Estree)   *Department of Psychology, University of Arizona*

Nancy Pennington   *Center for Research on Judgment and Policy, Department of Psychology, University of Colorado at Boulder*

Eldar Shafir   *Department of Psychology, Princeton University*

Itamar Simonson   *Graduate School of Business, Stanford University*

Edward E. Smith   *Department of Psychology, University of Michigan*

Jackie Snell   *College of Business, San Jose State University*

Philip E. Tetlock   *Department of Psychology, Ohio State University*

Richard H. Thaler   *Center for Decision Research, Graduate School of Business, University of Chicago*

Amos Tversky (deceased)   *Department of Psychology, Stanford University**

Alphons J. C. van de Kragt (deceased)   *University of Manitoba, Winnipeg, Canada**

Carol A. Varey   *School of Cognitive and Computing Sciences, University of Sussex, United Kingdom*

Willem A. Wagenaar   *Department of Psychology, University of Leiden, The Netherlands*

Elke U. Weber   *Department of Psychology, The Ohio State University*

* Asterisk indicates affiliation when article was originally published.

Editors' preface

The Judgment and Decision Making Society, in association with Cambridge University Press, has undertaken to publish a series of books on a variety of judgment and decision making (JDM) topics, both to help JDM researchers keep up with developments outside of their immediate focus, and as an enticement to others to take a closer look at the field. The current volume represents our attempt to build on one of the Society's earlier offerings, *Judgment and Decision Making: An Interdisciplinary Reader*, edited by H. R. Arkes and K. R. Hammond. The *Reader* was offered as a broad introduction to judgment and decision research, an invitation to the field. Our aim in this book is to provide an update on the considerable activity that has taken place since the *Reader* appeared in 1986, thus extending the *Reader*'s invitation, but also to speak directly to those ready to accept the invitation. To introduce people to the community of JDM researchers, we have tried to provide newcomers with a way of viewing the overall structure of the field, its recent trends, and its possible directions. Of course, there are many different ways to view a field, and the perspective we provide clearly reflects our own backgrounds and interests. Nevertheless, we hope that having such an overview will help people decide where to concentrate their efforts as they consider possibilities for further study and research, and as they develop their own perspectives on the field. In this way, we hope that our book will not only reflect the field of JDM research, but help to expand it as well.

William M. Goldstein
Robin M. Hogarth

Part I
Introduction

1 Judgment and decision research: Some historical context

William M. Goldstein and Robin M. Hogarth

The topics studied under the heading "judgment and decision research" are broad. Moreover, these topics are studied with methods and from perspectives that can seem puzzling to people with backgrounds in other areas of psychology. In this chapter, we consider some of the recent history of research on judgment and decision making (JDM), covering (only) the last fifty years or so. (For other retrospective treatments, see Fishburn, 1988, 1989a, 1989b; Hogarth, 1993; Kahneman, 1991.) A complete history of the field would have to stretch back several centuries at least, and be situated relative to several neighboring or more inclusive topics, such as emotion, thinking, and perception. Our goal in this chapter is more modest and is more contextual than truly historical. Specifically, our goal is to provide a context that can serve as a scaffold to help newcomers develop their own informed opinions about the currents, connections, and controversies that animate the field.

JDM research is not "paradigmatic." There is no single, universally endorsed, overarching theoretical framework that researchers use to organize and guide their efforts. Rather, there are a number of schools of thought that identify different issues as interesting and deem different methods as appropriate. In addition, the situation is complicated by the fact that these schools overlap and interact. In fact, many researchers participate in several. By sketching the intellectual roots of different research traditions, we aim to help readers understand the commingled sources of current research programs, and why particular sets of issues are considered important. Beyond this, we also hope to explicate the reasonableness, given distinct histories and different sets of background concerns, of conflicting positions.

Two foci of early research

Psychological research on JDM can be traced largely to events that took place in the 1940s and 1950s. (For a sequence of early reviews, see Becker &

McClintock, 1967; Edwards, 1954a, 1961; Rapoport & Wallsten, 1972; Slovic, Fischhoff, & Lichtenstein, 1977.) At that time, two programs of research began that were motivated by different questions, forming two different "foci" of the emerging field. One group of psychologists took notice of the efforts of economists and statisticians to account for and advise people about their decision making. For these psychologists, the central questions were: How do people decide on a course of *action*? How do people *choose* what to do next, especially in the face of uncertain consequences and conflicting goals? Do people make these decisions rationally? If not, by what psychological processes do people make decisions, and can decision making be improved?

A different group of psychologists was motivated by an analogy with perception. Just as, for example, the visual system must rely on fallible cues about the external environment to determine distance, so a judge (e.g., a clinical psychologist) must rely on fallible test results and indicators to draw an inference about a patient's condition. For these psychologists, the central questions were: How do people integrate multiple, probabilistic, potentially conflicting cues to arrive at an *understanding* of the situation, a *judgment*? How accurate are people's judgments? Does judgment improve with training and experience? How does human judgment compare with actuarial prediction? How do people identify relevant cues and the proper weights to assign to them? How does the nature of the task environment affect learning and performance?

The result has been that the two foci of decision research, choice and judgment, have proceeded rather independently until relatively recently, despite the efforts of particular individuals who have contributed to both areas. The integration of the two areas is not complete even today, although they have approached each other as their respective research agendas have evolved in the more cognitive Zeitgeist of current American psychology.

Preferential choice

The precipitating event for this line of research was a development in economics, namely the publication of von Neumann and Morgenstern's (1944) *Theory of Games and Economic Behavior*. This book was seminal in many respects, one being that it launched the field of game theory (see Weintraub, 1992). Its impetus for the study of individual choice, however, derived mainly from its brief but penetrating discussion of utility; the book's second edition (1947) became an immediate classic for its inclusion of an appendix that proved a representation theorem for the measurement of cardinal utility. To appreciate the significance of this technical result, it must be realized that economics had been going through a behaviorist period much like that in psychology. The concept of "utility" had been expunged from economics as too introspective, and as unnecessary for the explanation of riskless exchanges (Hicks & Allen, 1934; see Stigler, 1950). By contrast, von Neumann and Morgenstern needed the concept of utility to avoid having to think of games as necessarily paying off in strictly objective (e.g., monetary) terms, and they needed the concept of expected utility – applicable to single plays of a game – to ground their treatment of game playing with (probabilistically) mixed strategies. The von Neumann–Morgenstern appendix rehabilitated the notion of utility and, in a sense, "made subjectivity respectable again in economics" (von Winterfeldt & Edwards, 1986, p. 561).

The von Neumann–Morgenstern axioms specify constraints on a person's choice behavior that, if satisfied, imply that the person's choices can be modeled as always favoring the alternative with the highest expected utility. By specifying conditions under which utility could be measured objectively, von Neumann and Morgenstern rid utility of the stigma that it was an unscientific concept. Moreover, the approach taken by von Neumann and Morgenstern represented a major step toward "fundamental" measurement in the social sciences – measurement of a psychological variable that does not depend on the prior measurement of other quantities. Naturally, this caught the attention of scholars interested in psychological measurement (e.g., psychophysicists, for whom measurement had been a central issue since the time of Fechner), and it had a profound effect on the approach to measurement and modeling emphasized in the developing field of mathematical psychology (Krantz, Luce, Suppes, & Tversky, 1971; Narens & Luce, 1986; Scott & Suppes, 1958; Suppes & Zinnes, 1963).

In addition to its implications for psychological measurement, the von Neumann–Morgenstern axioms offered a new basis for thinking that an old theory of behavior might represent rationality.[1] Previously, it was claimed that one should act to maximize expected utility, because doing so seemed to capture the essence of behavior that was worldly and prudent (e.g., purchasing insurance, dividing risks, avoiding mathematically "fair" games; Bernoulli, 1738; Laplace, 1812; for historical reviews see Daston, 1988; Gigerenzer et al., 1989; Jorland, 1987). However, a number of thinkers argued that the appropriate assessment of a risky prospect depended on whether the situation was to be repeated or not. (For historical and modern comments on the applicability of probability itself, let alone expectation, to single events, see Gigerenzer, 1994.) After the von Neumann–Morgenstern axiomatization, claims for the rationality of expected utility could appeal to the intuitions of many scholars that the axioms specified compelling principles of rational behavior (e.g., transitivity) that applied to single events as well as repeated situations. A (seemingly) defensible theory of rational behavior was too intriguing to resist, and empirical tests by psychologists (Preston & Baratta, 1948), statisticians (Mosteller & Nogee, 1951), and philosophers (Davidson, Suppes, & Siegel, 1957) were soon conducted to see if people actually behaved in the manner prescribed by expected utility theory. In this way, von Neumann and Morgenstern instigated a pattern of psychological experiments in which behavioral deviations from a presumed standard of rationality are considered the "interesting" phenomena to be explained.

Psychological research in JDM received a tremendous boost in 1954. In that year, Ward Edwards published an influential review of the field in *Psychological Bulletin*, making widely available to psychologists the literature that had appeared in economics and statistics. (An important book by Luce and Raiffa, appearing a few years later in 1957, also helped to make this literature accessible.) The year 1954 also saw the publication of *Decision Processes*, edited by Thrall, Coombs, and Davis, which carried a title carefully chosen to suggest psychological rather than statistical decision theory. It presented papers that emerged from a two-month seminar held in Santa Monica in 1952, in which many influential thinkers discussed their ideas about decision making. These publications established an agenda for psychological research on decision making that was rooted in economics and statistics and was conducted by psychologists whose interests originated in issues of psychophysics, psychological measurement, and mathematical modeling in psychology.

This agenda, and these psychologists, formed one focus of the developing field, with an emphasis on preferential choice in the face of uncertainty, that is, risky decision making. Many experiments were conducted in which people were required to choose among gambles, evaluating trade-offs between the likelihood of a possible event (e.g., chances of winning) and the desirability of the event (e.g., amount to be won). Experiments were also conducted in which people were forced to trade off conflicting goals by making choices among complicated alternatives that had both advantages and disadvantages. Initially, virtually all of these studies attempted to test models of preferential choice that were either inherited from economics or derived from psychophysical models. Later, in keeping with the growing influence of cognitive psychology, researchers came to propose and test models that were constructed to embody hypotheses about the psychological processes underlying decision making.

Judgment

Another seminal book to appear in 1954 was *Clinical Versus Statistical Prediction* by Paul Meehl. This book helped to establish the other main focus of JDM research by drawing attention to an observation that defies conventional wisdom and demands explanation. Meehl reviewed approximately twenty studies, and his provocative finding – still valid today (Dawes, Faust, & Meehl, 1989; but see Yaniv & Hogarth, 1993) – was that intuitive ("clinical") judgments are almost invariably less accurate than a simple statistical combination of the same information available to the judge. This result holds despite the fact that judges may draw on the wisdom of many years of experience, whereas the statistical combination of information is a lifeless, mechanical process that cannot appreciate the unique features of individual cases. By raising this conundrum, Meehl's book stimulated a voluminous literature on the way people intuitively combine information from multiple sources to produce numerical judgments (e.g., likely survival time of a terminal patient) and classifications (e.g., diagnoses).

In particular, a year after the appearance of Meehl's book, an important paper by Hammond (1955) showed that Brunswikian principles of perception were applicable to the study of clinical judgment, thereby setting the tone for one of the main branches of research on judgment. Brunswik (1952, 1956; see Hammond, 1966a, 1966b) posited that an object in the environment (i.e., a "distal" stimulus) stimulates a person's sensory organs to produce multiple cues (i.e., "proximal" stimuli) to the object's identity and properties. However, for a number of reasons (e.g., there is no one-to-one and continuous transformation from three-dimensional space to the two-dimensional retina of the eye), the cues are inherently ambiguous. Therefore, like Helmholtz, Brunswik considered perception to involve the psychological construction or inference of a percept from an incomplete and fallible collection of sensory cues. Hammond (1955) pointed out that clinical judgment is analogous: The clinician makes a judgment about a patient (e.g., neurotic vs. psychotic) on the basis of inferences drawn from incomplete and fallible cues (e.g., MMPI subscales). Hammond (1955) also drew attention to additional aspects of Brunswikian theory that, as later amplified and extended by Hammond and his colleagues, have had a profound effect on judgment research.

This research will be summarized below, but we can convey something of its flavor now by briefly mentioning three principles that are basic to Brunswikian research. First, Brunswik inferred from the inherently ambiguous relation between proximal and distal stimuli that the organism must function in an environment that it can apprehend only with uncertainty. That is, from the organism's point of view, the proximal cues are related only probabilistically to the identity and properties of the distal object. Therefore, Brunswik reasoned, although an organism's responses to proximal stimuli might conceivably be deterministic, the organism's responses to distal stimuli will be describable at best only probabilistically. Consequently, a functional psychology, that is, one concerned with the adaptation of organisms to their (distal) environments, must eschew deterministic models and embrace probabilistic models.

Second, Brunswik argued that an organism's perceptual system, functioning as it must in the face of uncertainty, would act like an "intuitive statistician" to combine information from the available cues. In particular, the perceptual system would adapt to its operating environment, learning the intercorrelations among the cues and capitalizing on the intercorrelations to permit particular cues to substitute for and/or predict one another. Thus, the product of the perceptual system, that is, the conscious perception of the object and of the cues themselves, would reflect the intercorrelations that the organism had learned in its environment. Fox example, in studies of perceptual constancy, Brunswik found that the conscious perception of a single, fixed cue was affected by his manipulation of other cues. In other words, the organism's conscious perceptions were guided by prior learning about the correlations between cues. With these arguments and observations, Brunswik helped to establish the topics of learning and adaptation to a task environment as central and enduring concerns in JDM research.

Third, and related to both of the preceding points, Brunswik advanced a number of arguments concerning the importance of studying natural task environments in themselves and studying behavior as situated in natural task environments. Only by studying task environments could one understand the nature of the relationships between distal and proximal stimuli and hope to decompose the probabilistic relationship between distal stimulus and behavioral response. Only by studying behavior as situated in the natural task environment (or environments faithful to it in important ways) could one understand the nature of the organism's adaptation to its environment. By contrast, the orthogonal manipulation of experimental factors, that is, deliberately destroying the intercorrelations of the organism's operating environment, would result either in the subject's misperception of the experimental stimuli (because the relationships between distal and proximal stimuli had been altered) or in disoriented behavior in the face of strange and unfamiliar combinations of cues (because the relationships among the proximal cues had been altered). In neither case would the experiment be informative about the organism's normal adaptation to its natural environment, which Brunswik took to be the goal of psychology. Instead, Brunswik favored a correlational analysis of the behavior elicited by stimulus situations that were sampled from the organism's natural environment, thereby preserving the natural intercorrelations of the cues in what is called "representative design" (Brunswik, 1956; Hammond & Wascoe, 1980).

As mentioned, Brunswikian research on judgment was inspired by an analogy between judgment and perception. Another important branch of research on judgment grew out of work in social psychology. After World War II, an intensive program of research on attitudes and persuasion was undertaken, particularly by Carl Hovland's group at Yale (Hovland, Janis, & Kelley, 1953; Hovland et al., 1957; Sherif & Hovland, 1961). An initial concern for order effects on the persuasiveness of communications (Anderson & Hovland, 1957; Hovland et al., 1957) led Norman Anderson to reconsider the order effects obtained by Solomon Asch (1946) in his studies of person perception and impression formation (Anderson, 1965; Anderson & Barrios, 1961; Anderson & Norman, 1964). Subsequently, Anderson and his colleagues investigated a large number of judgmental phenomena, including judgmental adding versus averaging of stimulus components, context effects, and the relationship between judgment and memory, culminating in Anderson's Information Integration Theory (Anderson, 1981).

In sum, like the research on preferential choice, research on judgment also examines people's responses to complex and/or uncertain sets of information. However, it does not emphasize either matters of personal preference or overt decisions that have direct consequences for the decision maker. Rather, it emphasizes the psychological appraisal of information. In this tradition, the person's numerical or categorical judgment is interpreted as reflecting his or her state of mind about a matter either of fact (prediction or estimation) or evaluation (preference or opinion). The judgment itself may or may not have direct consequences for the judge, or underlie an overt decision (Einhorn & Hogarth, 1981). Thus, research on judgment tends to focus on what a person understands, believes, or feels, as opposed to what course of action a person will choose. In addition, beyond modeling the appraisal of information, researchers who follow in the Brunswikian tradition also tend to emphasize the accuracy of the judgments (i.e., the appropriateness of the understanding) as a function of learning in task environments.

A middle ground that might have been

A third major book to appear in 1954 was *The Foundations of Statistics* by Leonard J. Savage. Although this book is usually grouped with the work on preferential choice, in some ways it might have bridged the two areas of judgment and decision research. Savage's book is remembered mostly for a theoretical accomplishment that enlarges upon the work of von Neumann and Morgenstern (1947). Savage (anticipated by Ramsey, 1931) specified a list of constraints on a person's choice behavior that, if satisfied, imply that the person's choices can be modeled as always favoring the alternative with the highest *subjectively* expected utility. That is, Savage found an axiomatic basis for the simultaneous measurement of utilities and subjective probabilities. In so doing, Savage enlarged the scope of the theory to include gambles based on arbitrary events (e.g., the weather or the outcome of an election) as well as arbitrary (i.e., nonmonetary) payoffs, and he laid out a basis for true fundamental measurement.

The Ramsey–Savage work also advanced two important claims about subjective probabilities. First, it was argued that subjective probabilities provide the proper measure of a person's degree of belief in a proposition. (See also, de Finetti, 1937. This was also the view taken by early probability theorists, notably Jakob Bernoulli, 1713; see Daston, 1988; Gigerenzer, 1994; Gigerenzer et al., 1989. In the twentieth century, however, the subjectivist interpretation of probability has been the minority view among statisticians.) Thus, within a model of preferential choice, there was space to represent a person's state of mind about uncertain events. In this sense, the Ramsey–Savage approach created some middle ground between the two foci of psychological research.

Second, the Ramsey–Savage position held that subjective probabilities should be inferred from a person's actions, rather than the person's direct judgment, to ensure that the measured values applied to the behavior of interest. Although this argument was influential among scholars of preferential choice, many other psychologists greeted it with less than enthusiasm during this declining period of American behaviorism. Moreover, to the judgment researchers who emphasized the appraisal of information over the choice of action, the Ramsey–Savage argument must have seemed to miss the point.

A third important claim implicit in Savage's (1954) book concerned the general metatheoretic outlook of researchers in preferential choice. One reason that von Neumann and Morgenstern's (1944) work had generated such interest over the preceding decade was that many everyday choices could be seen as choices among gambles. After all, virtually all real-life alternatives have consequences that are not perfectly foreseeable and so can be regarded as risky. By explicitly enlarging the scope of utility theory to include gambles based on events other than outcomes of well-understood random devices, Savage (1954) cemented the metaphor that life is a gamble.

This means two things. First, the gambling metaphor specifies that only two kinds of variables are relevant to decision making: (1) the strength of one's beliefs, that is, subjective probabilities; and (2) the desirability of outcomes, that is, utilities. Because it is the *strength* of belief and the *degree* of desirability that matter, issues surrounding these magnitudes and their combination come to the fore, emphasizing matters of measurement and modeling. Second, the gambling metaphor entails a claim that *all* deliberative decision making can be viewed as choice among gambles.

The theoretical position represented by the gambling metaphor raises the possibility that a truly general theory of behavior might be achievable. Moreover, it suggests that experimental procedures can be simplified without harm to the generalizability of results. After all, if the gambling metaphor is appropriate, it does not really matter what sort of stimulus materials are used in preferential choice experiments, and so one might as well use the simplest: well-defined, monetary gambles. In fact, the gambling metaphor suggests that such stimuli would even enhance the generalizability of experimental findings, because subjects would find it much easier to assess the subjective likelihoods and desirabilities involved and could focus on evaluating the trade-offs.

Some early researchers had doubts about this practice. For example, commenting on an experiment by Coombs and Beardslee (1954), Edwards (1954a, p. 39) wrote, "Coombs is reluctant to use sums of money as the valuable objects in his experiments because of the danger that subjects will respond to the numerical value of the amount of dollars rather than to the psychological value. Therefore he used various desirable objects (e.g., a radio) as stimuli. . . ." However, over time, simple monetary gambles have become so common that Lopes (1983) has compared their use to that of fruit flies in research on genetics. At some point, the gambling metaphor became just one of the background assumptions in the worldview of many choice researchers. (For recent attempts to question the gambling metaphor, see Goldstein & Weber, 1995; Hogarth & Kunreuther, 1995.)

By contrast with choice researchers, judgment researchers, especially those in the Brunswikian tradition, must have been skeptical of this experimental practice and the metatheory behind it. Brunswik (1956) had considered the goal of psychology to be the study of organisms' normal adaptation to their natural environment, and he argued strongly that stimulus situations should be sampled from this environment. Although Brunswikian researchers have made use of simplified, abstract stimuli, they generally have done so with caution, along with experiments to determine if the abstracted content affected behavior (e.g., Adelman, 1981; Hammond & Brehmer, 1973; Koele, 1980; Miller, 1971; Muchinsky & Dudycha, 1975; Sniezek, 1986).

As a result of these disagreements, until fairly recently judgment and choice have been studied relatively independently of one another, by researchers with different intellectual roots and different concerns. The more recent history of judgment and decision research is largely a story of rapprochement and convergence, although there are also streams of research that remain true to their intellectual origins. The integration of the two foci of research, however, is itself a complex story, not just a fusion of two areas. Rather, the two areas have evolved, in the context of changes in psychological research more generally, into new forms that retain elements of what came before.

Having described the general landscape of JDM research in the mid-1950s, the remainder of this chapter is organized as follows. In the next section, we trace developments in research on preferential choice. In the following section we discuss research on probabilistic judgment, an area that grew out of preferential choice. Then we trace developments in judgment research, focusing primarily on the Brunswikian tradition. Finally, we comment briefly on the current state of affairs in JDM research and discuss our selection of readings for this volume.

Developments in preferential choice research

The axiomatic analyses of expected utility (EU) theory (von Neumann & Morgenstern, 1947) and subjective expected utility (SEU) theory (Savage, 1954) were significant intellectual milestones for a number of the social sciences, but these theories (which we refer to generically as utility theory) were received rather differently in different quarters. Economics, and significant parts of political science and sociology, largely accepted utility theory as normatively binding and descriptively valid and took it as a cornerstone of the theoretical edifice (Becker, 1976; Coleman, 1986; Elster, 1986; Hargreaves Heap, Hollis, Lyons, Sugden, & Weale, 1992). By contrast, psychology has not. This has led to tension, especially between economists and psychologists (Hogarth & Reder, 1987). The important point is that much psychological research on preferential choice must be understood against the backdrop of this interdisciplinary tension. For example, a continuing debate about whether or not people are rational has been the stimulus for a great deal of psychological research and has provided the context for much of the focus on utility theory. If this debate is overlooked, the attention to utility theory in particular, and to issues of rationality in general, may seem a strange preoccupation.

In the following subsections, we discuss some of the major lines of this research. First, we discuss some noteworthy early research under the headings: (1) paradoxes, (2) arguments, and (3) experiments. Most of this research was conducted in direct response to utility theory and was highly critical of it. Second, we discuss some of the major responses to this research, under the headings: (1) expand the problem area, (2) expand the explanatory principles, (3) expand the methods, and (4) developments in modeling.

Early criticisms of utility theory as a descriptive model

Paradoxes. Certain decision problems have become famous for their ability to elicit choices that conflict with utility theory. This situation is not paradoxical, except in the sense that it was highly surprising and counterintuitive to early proponents of utility theory. Nevertheless, the decision problems and the behavior patterns they elicit have come* to be known as "paradoxes." Although some investigators have collected data to demonstrate the prevalence of the choice patterns that violate utility theory, the persuasive force of the paradoxes seems to derive mainly from their ability to elicit the forbidden patterns from decision researchers themselves. In this sense, then, it is more appropriate to think of the so-called paradoxes as "thought experiments." The two most famous are due to economists, Allais (1953; see also Allais & Hagen, 1979) and Ellsberg (1961). Descriptions of these paradoxes are widely available (e.g., Hogarth, 1987; Yates, 1990).

Suffice it to say that these paradoxes had three significant effects. First, they convinced some economists that utility theory might need modification. In recent years, a number of generalizations of utility theory have been offered, and researchers invariably feel compelled to demonstrate that their proposed generalizations accommodate at least the Allais paradox. Second, the Ellsberg paradox stimulated considerable interest in the psychology of ambiguous situations (Curley & Yates, 1985, 1989; Curley, Yates, & Abrams, 1986; Einhorn & Hogarth, 1985, 1986a; Heath & Tversky, 1991; Hogarth & Einhorn, 1990; Hogarth & Kunreuther, 1985, 1989; Yates & Zukowski, 1976). Third, by inducing researchers to incorporate decision makers' attitudes toward ambiguity in models of decision making, the Ellsberg paradox contributed to a trend in which matters of psychological representation – how decision makers perceive the situation – were given greater importance.

Arguments. Herbert Simon (1955, 1956, 1978, 1983), an early and persistent critic of utility theory, based his case more on the logical appeal of an argument than on empirical data. Simon argued that researchers should consider how people might implement utility theory, and he argued that the full-blown version of the theory (which he sometimes called the "Olympian" model) was beyond people's cognitive limitations. Simon proposed the notion of "bounded rationality," the intelligent use of one's limited cognitive resources, as providing a more suitable conceptual guide for research on judgment and decision making. He suggested that people use heuristics, that is, rules of thumb, to achieve bounded rationality, and that people select alternatives by "satisficing," that is, accepting the first alternative encountered that meets minimal criteria for acceptability, rather than by optimizing.

Simon's arguments have had a profound, albeit delayed and indirect, impact on JDM research. In the 1950s, JDM researchers paid scant attention to Simon's arguments. However, the 1950s and 1960s were a period of decline for American behaviorism (e.g., Bruner, Goodnow, & Austin, 1956; Chomsky, 1959; Miller, Galanter, & Pribram, 1960; Neisser, 1967), and some psychologists were more receptive to Simon's general outlook. Indeed, Simon's work on problem solving and computer simulation of cognitive processes was seminal in both cognitive psychology and artificial intelligence. His influence specifically on JDM research has taken three forms: (1) a general contribution to a climate in which emphasis is placed on cognitive processes, and the specific argument that theories of behavior must respect people's cognitive limitations, (2) the emphasis on heuristics in research on probabilistic judgment, and (3) the use of methods (e.g., concurrent verbal protocols) and concepts (e.g., search of a problem space) that Simon developed in his research on problem solving.

Experiments. Early experimental tests of utility theory usually took one of two forms: (1) a subset of decisions was used to assess utilities and/or subjective probabilities, which in turn were used to predict new choices, or (2) a goodness-of-fit measure was computed for the entire set of decisions without predicting new choices (e.g., Coombs & Beardslee, 1954; Coombs & Komorita, 1958; Davidson & Marschak, 1959; Davidson et al., 1957; Edwards, 1955; Hurst & Siegel, 1956; Mosteller & Nogee, 1951; Tversky, 1967a, 1967b). Apart from some particular recalcitrant phenomena, such as preferences for bets with particular probabilities (Edwards, 1953, 1954b, 1954c) and subjective probabilities that failed to be independent of events' desirabilities (Irwin, 1953; Marks, 1951; Morlock & Hertz, 1964; Slovic, 1966), utility theory initially obtained a substantial amount of support.

Nevertheless, it was clear that there were some persistent problems, and investigators pressed harder on utility theory's weak points. Researchers shifted efforts away from assessments of overall fit or predictiveness and toward investigations of specific necessary consequences of the theory. This shift was so pronounced that Rapoport and Wallsten commented in their 1972 review, "Almost all the recent experiments concerned with SEU have concentrated on testing one or more necessary axioms (postulates)" (p. 136). As the evidence accumulated that necessary consequences of utility theory were systematically violated, researchers became more convinced that the theory was incorrect. By 1977, Slovic, Fischhoff, and Lichtenstein remarked in their review, "during the past 5 years, the proponents of SEU have been greatly outnumbered by its critics" (p. 9).

Responses to the criticisms of utility theory

Expand the problem area. Some researchers responded to the early experiments on utility theory with a sense of dissatisfaction that more progress had not been forthcoming and a desire to find more fruitful areas of study. Edwards, for example, shifted his attention away from preferential choice and toward probabilistic judgment (see von Winterfeldt & Edwards, 1986, pp. 564–5). Edwards's work on probabilistic judgment stimulated much research and expanded interest in comparisons between people's probabilistic judgments and properties mandated by mathematical statistics (for early reviews see Edwards, 1968; Peterson & Beach, 1967).

In many ways, the history of subsequent work on probabilistic judgment parallels that of research on preferential choice. In both cases, the initial attempts to model people's behavior with normative models were disappointing. Subsequent attempts to modify the prescriptive models to make them more descriptive were overtaken by efforts to explain the deviations from normative performance in terms of psychological representations and processes. Moreover, in both cases researchers have tended to focus on deviations from normative behavior as the "interesting" phenomena, changing this view only gradually.

Despite the parallels between these two areas of study, we will not intertwine our accounts of them. For the moment, we will continue with our description of the research on preferential choice. However, first a few comments are in order. Recall that according to the Ramsey–Savage position, subjective probabilities should be inferred from a person's actions, rather than the person's direct judgment. Curiously, although Edwards's work on this topic originated in his collaboration with Savage, direct probability judgments were studied in this program with relatively little concern about their correspondence with the probabilities that could be inferred from choices (but see Beach, 1974; Beach & Phillips, 1967; Beach & Wise, 1969a, 1969b; DuCharme & Donnell, 1973; Wallsten, 1971).

One might think that this methodological change reflected something of a rapprochement between preferential choice researchers and judgment researchers, but this was not the case. Preferential choice researchers continued to focus on choices. Even though these choices were often hypothetical and had no real consequences, it was felt that choices could, in principle, be made operational as overt behavior with consequences. Because subjects' bids (i.e., stated buying or selling prices for alternatives) could also be tied to overt behavior, they also received study. Evaluative judgments in the form of attractiveness ratings, on the other hand, were still considered by these researchers to be in the realm of "verbal behavior under interrogation" (Savage, 1972, p. 27). As a result, these researchers seemed to take note of only a few judgment studies that were closely related to their interests (e.g., Anderson & Shanteau, 1970; Shanteau, 1974). Greater mutual awareness and acceptance came later, and is still not complete.

Expand the explanatory principles. As it became clearer that utility theory was descriptively inadequate, the key question became, "How, then, *do* people make choices?" This question, however, has a number of facets and can be interpreted in a number of ways. Three interpretations seemed to guide subsequent research: (1) What model(s) can do a better job than utility theory at capturing the trade-offs that people make among conflicting goals? (2) What information are people attending to and using? (3) What is the sequence of mental operations by which people arrive at their choices? The first interpretation was the most conservative in that it retained the goal of finding a model – if not utility theory then something else – that would capture the patterns in people's choices. The latter two interpretations were more radical, at least potentially, in that they did not ask about people's choices per se, but rather about the activity that preceded a choice. Research in the field broadened gradually from the first to the subsequent questions, and research on all three questions thrives today.

Early researchers deemed behavior to be of interest if it contradicted utility theory. In response, a researcher typically would suggest a modification of the theory to accommodate the observed violations. The suggested modification might be offered strictly on the basis of its ability to encompass the behavior (e.g., Edwards's, 1962a, suggestion that subjective probabilities might not sum to 1), or it might be supported by reference to psychological representations and processes (e.g., Ellsberg's, 1961, suggestion that ambiguous information prompts people to employ subjective probabilities that are affected by the associated outcomes).

In the late 1960s a change of emphasis began to take place. The general structure of a research report might still have the familiar form: begin by documenting the occurrence of or giving plausible reasons to expect peculiar behavior (which, not so coincidentally, violates utility theory), provide some discussion of psychological representations and processes to motivate the presentation of a model that accommodates the behavior, report experiments in which the peculiar behavior is exhibited in precisely the way allowed by the model and not in a way that would violate the model. However, there would be some important differences from earlier research. The link between the discussed psychological processes and the proposed model would be tighter than before. Discussions of processes and representations were no longer presented merely to explain the inspiration for hypothesized models. That is, these discussions were not offered merely to report the "context of discovery" that precedes the real business of testing models in the "context of justification" (see Reichenbach, 1951). Rather, the models were offered as scientifically interesting *because* they captured important aspects of the hypothesized processes and representations, and it was these *processes and representations* that were offered as possible *explanations* of the peculiar behavior. That one could elicit peculiar behavior (and thereby violate utility theory) was not the point. That one's model could accommodate the peculiar behavior was also not the point. The point was that violation of the model would permit one to reject the hypothesized *processes* as an explanation of the peculiar behavior (insofar as one's model had done a good job of capturing the processes), and conversely, failure to reject the model could be taken as a measure of support for the hypothesized processes.

For example, as Tversky (1969, p. 46) wrote in his paper on intransitive choice, "The main interest in the present results lies not so much in the fact that transitivity can be violated but rather in what these violations reveal about the choice mechanism. . . ." Tversky constructed his Additive Difference Model as a generalization of the Lexicographic Semiorder, which, in turn, was a model that Tversky offered as a way of capturing two hypotheses about the processes of multidimensional choice: (1) that people compare the alternatives on each dimension in turn, as opposed to evaluating each alternative in its entirety before comparing overall evaluations, and (2) that people neglect dimensions on which the alternatives are "too close to call" even if, in a strict psychophysical sense, the alternatives are discriminable on these dimensions. Tversky's (1969) observation of intransitive choices (subsequently replicated and extended by Budescu & Weiss, 1987; Lindman & Lyons, 1978; Montgomery, 1977; Ranyard, 1977, 1982) supported his process hypotheses, and these two aspects of psychological processing became the subject of separate research efforts (for the former see Rosen & Rosenkoetter, 1976; Russo & Dosher, 1983; Shafir, Osherson, & Smith, 1989, 1990, 1993; for the latter see Beach, Beach, Carter, & Barclay, 1974; Beach & Solak, 1969; Crocker, Mitchell, & Beach, 1978; Laestadius, 1970; Larson & Reenan, 1979).

This example illustrates some of the key aspects of a great deal of subsequent research, showing the liberalizing of theoretical interests. The new focus on psychological representations and processes and the use of models as instruments for refining and testing process hypotheses reflected an antibehavioristic trend. Also, the fact that process hypotheses (and models) were offered to explain specific counterintuitive patterns of choice, and were not offered as explanations of choice behavior in general, signaled a change that was not just a lowering of scientific aspirations. Rather, it was part of a growing awareness of an important issue: the multiplicity of people's decision strategies and their flexibility in selecting and adapting their strategies in response to task conditions. For example, Tversky (1969, p. 42) suggested that people's tendencies to evaluate individual stimuli in their entirety, as opposed to employing intradimensional comparisons, would depend on the manner in which the alternatives were displayed.

In two respects much of this work reflected legacies of the earlier attempts to test utility theory. First, many research projects revolved around patterns of choices that were identified as requiring explanation because they were suboptimal or otherwise counterintuitive. This orientation also guided much of the work on probabilistic judgment that grew out of the research on preferential choice. Second, despite the new emphasis that researchers placed on psychological representations and processes, they usually required that hypotheses be tested in terms of predictions about overt choices, rather than by implications for the sorts of data that were increasingly receiving attention in other parts of cognitive psychology, for example, verbal protocols, information-acquisition behavior, response times, post-choice memory for stimulus components, interference from dual tasks.

These two legacies may well characterize the bulk of research on preferential choice that has been conducted to date. In addition to the example already discussed (Tversky, 1969), a great many investigations could be cited, including studies of: (1) inconsistencies between response modes (i.e., "preference reversal phenomena"; see Goldstein & Einhorn, 1987; Lichtenstein & Slovic, 1971; Lindman, 1971; Mellers, Ordóñez, & Birnbaum, 1992; Tversky, Sattath, & Slovic, 1988); (2) the effects of displaying outcomes as gains relative to small reference points or losses relative to large reference points (among other "framing effects"; see Hogarth, 1982; Kahneman & Tversky, 1979; Tversky & Kahneman, 1981); (3) the effects of unrecoverable investments in particular alternatives (i.e., "sunk cost effects"; see Arkes & Blumer, 1985; Staw, 1976); (4) violations of dominance (Birnbaum, 1992; Mellers, Weiss, & Birnbaum, 1992); (5) the effects of already possessing an alternative (i.e., "endowment effects" or closely related "status quo effects"; see Kahneman, Knetsch, & Thaler, 1990; Knetsch, 1989; Samuelson & Zeckhauser, 1988; Thaler, 1980); (6) effects of presentations that prompt people to consider various outcomes separately versus aggregated, and people's preferences for separating versus aggregating different kinds of outcomes (i.e., "mental accounting"; see Linville & Fischer, 1991; Thaler, 1985; Thaler & Johnson, 1990); (7) inconsistencies between decisions that are repeated independently versus policy decisions that are made only once but applied many times (Redelmeier & Tversky, 1990, 1992); and (8) violations of the property known as "independence of irrelevant alternatives" and a variety of closely related context effects (Huber, Payne, & Puto, 1982; Simonson, 1989; Simonson & Tversky, 1992; Tversky, 1972; Tversky & Shafir, 1992; Tversky & Simonson, 1993; Wedell, 1991). In addition, some attempts have been made to address two or more of these effects in a way that shows them to be unified phenomena (Kahneman et al., 1991; Shafir, Simonson, & Tversky, 1993). Many more references could be given for each of the effects mentioned, and many more effects could be mentioned.

Expand the methods. Although the two legacies of utility theory continue to guide a great deal of research on preferential choice (and probabilistic judgment), alternative approaches have been developing for some time. When researchers in the late 1960s began to emphasize psychological representations and processes, some investigators decided to pursue these matters apart from any particular connections to anomalous patterns of choices, thus breaking with the first legacy. For example, Slovic and Lichtenstein (1968a) introduced so-called duplex gambles so that they could distinguish the probabilities and outcomes that defined a gamble from the probabilities and outcomes that were explicitly displayed, thus enabling them to study the features of the stimuli that people were attending to and using. A duplex gamble is actually a pair of gambles to be played independently, one offering a chance to win either w or 0, and the other offering a chance to lose either l or 0. A standard binary gamble offers a chance to win w or lose l, displaying the same probabilities and (nonzero) outcomes as its "parallel" duplex gamble. However, in terms of final outcomes and probabilities, the parallel standard and duplex gambles are different, for the duplex gamble includes the possibilities of obtaining 0 or w − l, which the standard gamble does not.

Slovic and Lichtenstein (1968a) found that people's bids and choices tended not to differentiate between the standard gamble and its parallel duplex gamble, suggesting that they were responding to the gambles' explicitly displayed "surface structure" rather than to the "deep structure" of final outcomes and probabilities. In a complementary study, Payne and Braunstein (1971) found that subjects had systematic preferences between duplex gambles that differed in terms of their explicitly displayed probabilities and outcomes but were equivalent in terms of their final probabilities and outcomes. Moreover, people's preferences could be captured with a process model whose inputs were the explicitly displayed values. These two studies drew attention to the possibility of applying an information-processing approach to preferential choice and stimulated a program of research to distinguish whether decision makers focused on "risk dimensions" (i.e., explicitly displayed values of probabilities and outcomes) or "moments" (i.e., transformations of the final outcomes and probabilities, such as SEU; see Aschenbrenner, 1984; Lichtenstein, Slovic, & Zink, 1969; Montgomery & Adelbratt, 1982; Payne, 1973; Schoemaker, 1979; Slovic & Lichtenstein, 1968b).

Researchers who were attracted to the information-processing approach studied the effects of task factors such as time pressure (Ben Zur & Bresnitz, 1981; Mano, 1990; Svenson & Edland, 1987; Svenson & Maule, 1993; Wright, 1974; see also Busemeyer, 1985; Busemeyer & Townsend, 1993; Goldstein & Busemeyer, 1992) and the number and complexity of choice alternatives (Einhorn, 1971; Hogarth, 1975; Lindman & Lyons, 1978; Olshavsky, 1979; Payne, 1976; Payne & Braunstein, 1978; Timmermans, 1993). These manipulations were not motivated by hypotheses that they would lead to or explain any particular choice anomalies. Rather, they were considered because the image of human beings as information processors with limited cognitive capacity made it seem likely that variables affecting the cognitive load would have interesting repercussions on psychological processing.

More controversially, much of this research also broke with the second legacy of utility theory: It put primary emphasis on measures of performance other than overt choice (e.g., verbal protocols, information-acquisition sequences, response times). The appropriateness of "process-tracing" methods was the subject of debate and research (Einhorn, Kleinmuntz, & Kleinmuntz, 1979; Ericsson & Simon, 1980; Hogarth, 1974; Nisbett & Wilson, 1977; Payne, Braunstein, & Carroll, 1978; Russo, 1978), as it continues to be (Ford, Schmitt, Schechtman, Hults, & Doherty, 1989; Lopes, 1995; Russo, Johnson, & Stephens, 1989). Nevertheless, it seems fair to say that these methods now enjoy wide, if not universal acceptance. They have been used not only to explore new issues, but also to investigate anomalies and to test proposed explanations in ways that complement the tests that are possible with overt choices alone (Busemeyer, Forsyth, & Nozawa, 1988; Fischer & Hawkins, 1993; Johnson, Payne, & Bettman, 1988; Montgomery, 1977; Ranyard, 1982; Rosen & Rosenkoetter, 1976; Russo & Dosher, 1983; Russo & Rosen, 1975; Schkade & Johnson, 1989).

As the use of process-tracing methods has grown, it has become apparent that processes of preferential choice are affected by task and stimulus manipulations that do not necessarily affect overt choice (e.g., switching from the use of intradimensional comparisons to holistic evaluation of alternatives may or may not change the final decision). The emphasis on the contingency of *processing* was emphasized in an important review paper by Payne (1982). Payne also stressed the need to find an overarching theoretical framework that would let researchers rise above the mere cataloging of effects, and he discussed three possibilities: (1) cost/benefit principles applied to the metadecision of choosing a decision strategy (Beach & Mitchell, 1978), (2) a perceptual framework in which the coding, editing, and framing of stimulus information are central (Kahneman & Tversky, 1979; Tversky & Kahneman, 1981), and (3) the development of context-sensitive rule-based theories known as adaptive production systems (Pitz, 1977). Of these three approaches, the first two have received greater attention by decision researchers. The metadecision framework has been developed extensively by Payne, Bettman, and Johnson (e.g., 1990, 1993), and the perceptual framework has stimulated many studies on framing, mental accounting, and various related effects (e.g., Kahneman et al., 1991; Thaler, 1985; Thaler & Johnson, 1990; Tversky & Kahneman, 1986).

Decision researchers have given much less attention to the third approach, possibly because it has been challenged by cognitive psychologists who believe that connectionist models offer advantages over rule-based systems (McClelland & Rumelhart, 1986; Rumelhart & McClelland, 1986; for possible applications of connectionist approaches in decision making, see Weber,

Goldstein, & Barlas, 1995; Weber, Goldstein, & Busemeyer, 1991). On the other hand, some researchers argue in favor of rule-based models (Nisbett, 1993). Although a single, universally accepted framework has not emerged, such an enormous degree of lability in the processes of judgment and decision making has been documented by now that many researchers have concluded that "preferences for and beliefs about objects or events of any complexity are often constructed – not merely revealed – in the generation of a response to a judgment or choice task . . ." (Payne, Bettman, & Johnson, 1992, p. 89).

Developments in modeling. Experiments indicating the descriptive failure of utility theory did not reduce enthusiasm for the mathematical modeling of behavior. On the contrary, these experiments challenged researchers to find models that would account for the observed choice patterns. As researchers came to emphasize psychological representations and processes, the models were interpreted in terms of or built to capture hypotheses about representations and processes. For example, in Kahneman and Tversky's (1979) Prospect Theory, subjectively transformed probabilities (called "decision weights" to emphasize that they are no longer probabilities) multiply subjectively transformed outcomes, where the latter transformation (called a "value function" rather than a "utility function") is defined on losses and gains relative to a reference point. Because the reference point itself depends on the decision maker's expectation, aspiration, and situation, any particular outcome (e.g., receiving $100) could be evaluated either as a gain (relative to a low reference point) or as a loss (relative to a high reference point). In this respect, Prospect Theory illustrates the introduction of issues related to the decision maker's psychological representation of the alternatives and choice situation. Another feature of Prospect Theory is that it specifies a two-stage process in which decision makers first "edit" alternatives (e.g., code outcomes relative to the reference point, combine probabilities associated with identical outcomes, etc.) and subsequently evaluate them.

Much interest has been expressed in models in which the subjective transformation of a probability p depends, not only on the value of p, but also to some extent on the potential outcomes. (The complementary possibility that the subjective transformation of an outcome might depend in part on the probability of receiving it has been incorporated into theories of achievement motivation, e.g., Atkinson, 1957, and has received some discussion in the decision literature, e.g., Edwards, 1962b, but it has not generated as much interest among decision researchers.) Two special cases of this property that have been the focus of much recent attention are called "sign dependence" and "rank dependence." A sign-dependent model is one in which the subjective transformation of a probability p depends on the sign of the associated outcome (i.e., positive vs. zero vs. negative). In a rank-dependent model, the transformed probability depends on the rank of the associated outcome in the distribution of possible outcomes (i.e., best, 2nd best, etc.). Kahneman and Tversky's (1979) Prospect Theory is both sign- and rank-dependent.

Researchers have been led to rank-dependent utility models by a variety of considerations. Among economists, discussions of how SEU theory might be weakened to accommodate at least some of the observed violations (e.g., Chew, 1983; Dekel, 1986; Machina, 1982) led to (special cases of) rank-dependent utility as a way of constructing models that retain the normatively compelling requirement that preferences should respect first-order stochastic dominance (i.e., gamble A should be preferred to gamble B if, for all x, gamble A offers at least as high a probability as gamble B of winning at least x ; see Chew, Karni, & Safra, 1987; Gilboa, 1987; Quiggin, 1982, 1985; Schmeidler, 1989; Segal, 1989; Yaari, 1987). In these discussions, the weight that multiplies the utility of a possible outcome x typically takes the form of a transformation of the cumulative probability of receiving an outcome no better than x .

Among psychologists, the attraction of rank-dependent utility models has been more closely associated with issues concerning the representation of gambles and the processes of deliberation. One prominent proponent is Lopes, whose argument does not appeal to normative properties of the model, but rather to her empirical findings. Specifically, Lopes found that: (1) when multi-outcome gambles were used as stimuli, instead of the more customary two-outcome gambles, subjects' verbal protocols often described the gambles in terms of the chances of winning *at least* a particular amount, and (2) the relative consistency of subjects' risk and preference judgments for gambles among negative amounts versus gambles among positive amounts can be explained in terms of the following psychological conflict: on the one hand wanting to ensure that *at least* an acceptable minimal amount will be won, and on the other hand wanting to win *at least* as much as one's aspiration level. (For discussion of both points, see Lopes, 1984, 1987, 1990, 1995; Schneider, 1992; Schneider & Lopes, 1986.) Lopes argues that a model expressed in terms of the *de*cumulative probability of receiving an outcome better than x captures these aspects of psychological representation and process.

Another route to the issue of psychological representation has been through analysis of properties that imply rank-dependent utility models, and then analysis of the rank-dependent models themselves. For example, Weber (1994) discusses how dependence of decision weights on associated outcomes might arise from asymmetric concern for overestimating versus underestimating uncertain quantities. Luce and Narens (1985; Luce, 1988, 1990, 1992) established that, within a wide class of utility models for two-outcome gambles and multistage gambles constructed out of two-outcome gambles, the most general model for which the utility function will be an interval scale is, in fact, a model with rank-dependent decision weights that sum to 1 (see also, Miyamoto, 1988, 1992). With attention thus focused on the rank-dependent model as a likely candidate for being descriptively adequate, Luce (1990, 1992) has pointed out that the additional constraints that, if true, would force the (binary) model to reduce to its known-to-be-incorrect special case of SEU are, essentially, matters of psychological representation.

To state the result loosely, if people choose gambles only on the basis of the desirability and the probability of the outcomes, so that they are not affected by single-stage versus multistage arrangements or other display manipulations that leave the outcomes and (final) probabilities unchanged, then (binary) rank-dependent linear utility collapses into SEU.[2] This result has bolstered interest in models that permit display effects (e.g., Luce, 1992; Segal, 1990), research that relates people's violations of normative principles to the manner in which alternatives are displayed (e.g., Keller, 1985; Tversky & Kahneman, 1986), and research into psychological representation more generally. It has also drawn attention to a related debate in economics and philosophy about "consequentialism," that is, the proposition that people (do and/or should) choose only on the basis of probabilities and outcomes without regard for past history or various kinds of embedding context (see, e.g., P. J. Hammond, 1988; Hampton, 1994; Levi, 1991; Machina, 1991).

We have emphasized rank-dependent utility models in our discussion because of their connection with the issues of psychological representation and dynamic processes. However, we should mention that a variety of other generalizations of utility theory have been offered. A number of authors have proposed models that, like Kahneman and Tversky's (1979) Prospect Theory, employ decision weights that are both rank- and sign-dependent (Birnbaum, Coffey, Mellers, & Weiss, 1992; Birnbaum & Sutton, 1992; Luce, 1991; Luce & Fishburn, 1991; Tversky & Kahneman, 1992; Wakker & Tversky, 1993). Some have considered models in which the decision weights depend on the magnitude of the associated outcome (Goldstein, Levi, & Coombs, 1990; Hogarth & Einhorn, 1990), and this by no means exhausts the possibilities. Models have been offered in which the utilities of outcomes depend on the lotteries in which the outcomes appear (Becker & Sarin, 1987, 1989; Daniels & Keller, 1990), as well as models in which the basic bilinear form is modified to accommodate intransitive preferences (Fishburn, 1982, 1983, 1984, 1985; Fishburn & LaValle, 1988a, 1988b). The intense activity in this area is exciting, but it does make it difficult for the nonspecialist to jump in and keep up with developments. A helpful introduction is provided by Weber and Camerer (1987). For other reviews and discussions of general issues, see Fishburn (1989c), Levy (1992), Luce (1992), Luce, Mellers, and Chang (1993), Luce and von Winterfeldt (1994), Machina (1987a, 1987b), as well as papers contained in Edwards (1992). For attempts to discriminate empirically among various generalized utility models, see Battalio, Kagel, and Jiranyakul (1990), Camerer (1989, 1992), Camerer and Ho (1994).

Partial convergence with judgment research . Until the early 1970s, preferential choice researchers and judgment researchers worked rather independently of one anoher. As mentioned earlier, preferential choice researchers were suspicious of attractiveness ratings or other response measures that seemed to represent unverifiable reports on subjective experience. With some notable exceptions (e.g., Anderson & Shanteau, 1970; Shanteau, 1974, 1975; Shanteau & Anderson, 1969), preferential choice researchers' main contact with Anderson's (1981) Information Integration Theory involved disagreements about measurement and modeling (e.g., Anderson, 1971; Krantz & Tversky, 1971). For their part, Information Integration theorists had wide interests, and they devoted most of their efforts to issues other than preferential decision making (see Anderson, 1991a, 1991b, 1991c). However, in the wake of discussions about process-tracing methods, preferential choice researchers have broadened their views about the sorts of responses to which their theories should be held accountable. Especially in recent attempts to model perceived risk and preference, there has been a confluence of people and methods with different intellectual histories.

The relationship between preferential choice researchers and Brunswikian judgment researchers, although somewhat similar, has been more complicated. Brunswikian researchers must have thought that preferential choice research, among many other areas of psychology (including Information Integration Theory), had lost sight of the important questions. Hammond (1966b) explained that Brunswik's Probabilistic Functionalism "is a form of functionalism because its main focus is on the adaptive interrelation of the organism with the environment. As Brunswik saw it, the task of psychology is to study and to understand how these two complex systems come to terms with one another" (p. 16). Unfortunately, ". . . psychology has forgotten that it is a science of organism–environment relationships, and has become a science of the organism" (Brunswik, 1957, p. 6). In particular, although preferential choice researchers evaluated the internal consistency of people's choices (e.g., by seeing whether choices satisfied the axioms of utility theory), they seldom tried to evaluate choices relative to external standards.

Subsequent developments have changed this situation. First, when Edwards began comparing people's probability judgments with the answers prescribed by Bayes's theorem, the relationship between organism and environment (i.e., judged probability and objectively correct answer) became the crux of the matter. The centrality of an external standard in the probability judgment task made it easier to see the relevance of Brunswik's arguments.[3] Moreover, it became apparent that people's performance depended on aspects of the task structure, as Brunswik had maintained it would (e.g., people tend to underestimate the diagnostic impact of data in single-stage inferences, but they overestimate the impact of data in multistage inferences; see Edwards, 1968; Gettys, Kelly, & Peterson, 1973; Peterson & Beach, 1967; Snapper & Fryback, 1971). An important review paper by Slovic and

Lichtenstein (1971) made an explicit comparison between Bayesian and Brunswikian research and drew wide attention to the issues.

Second, even though research on preferential choice proceeded largely without an external criterion (see Kahneman, 1994, for a review of important recent exceptions), the dominant theme of research in the 1970s and 1980s was that cognitive processes depend on aspects of the task and context. This was the message of Payne's (1982) review paper, and in keeping with the spirit of Brunswikian research, investigators have sought to systematize and explain the nature of that dependence ever since. In sum, although divisions among preferential choice and judgment researchers have not been erased, there is much greater interchange than previously and it continues to increase.

Probabilistic judgment

By the mid-1960s, Ward Edwards was conducting experiments in which people were asked to estimate probabilities in "textbook" urn-and-balls problems, but the pallid setting for these problems should not be deceiving. These studies were considered to have broad implications and many experimenters followed Edwards's lead. Recall that the Ramsey–Savage position held subjective probability to be the proper measure of degree of belief – belief in any proposition whatsoever. It is important to realize that from this point of view, "probability" is in the mind of the beholder, characterizing the person's idiosyncratic beliefs. From this perspective, studying how people form and revise (subjective) conditional probabilities in the light of new data is seen as nothing less than a general approach to learning.

The problems that Edwards posed for his subjects typically involved two bookbags, each filled with red and blue poker chips in specified proportions. Edwards would flip a fair coin to select a bag, and people would have to infer which bag had been selected from a sample of poker chips drawn from the selected bag. People would report what they thought was the probability of each bag, and Edwards would compare their estimates with the answer specified by Bayes's rule. The typical finding was termed "conservatism" (Edwards, 1968) to indicate that subjects were not extracting as much information from the sample of poker chips as required by Bayes's rule. Research was conducted to see if subjects misperceived the elements that are the inputs to Bayes's rule (prior probabilities – also called base rates – and likelihoods), whether subjects failed to combine these elements as specified by Bayes's rule, or whether conservatism reflected a response bias.

Heuristics and biases. In the early 1970s, Tversky and Kahneman (1971, 1973, 1974; Kahneman, Slovic, & Tversky, 1982; Kahneman & Tversky, 1972, 1973) changed the nature of the discussion about the psychology of inference. They argued that people are not just "myopic" or "bad" Bayesians who attempt to use Bayes's rule, but misperceive or wrongly combine the base rates and likelihoods. Rather, they argued that people are not Bayesians at all, in that the base rates likelihoods are not the psychologically relevant variables. In one of their striking demonstrations, they performed a bookbag-and-poker-chip experiment in which the bags were symmetric – if the "red" bag contained 70% red chips, then the "blue" bag contained 70% blue chips. In these circumstances, Bayes's rule requires that the revised conditional probability, after seeing a sample of chips from the selected bag, must be a function of the difference between the numbers of red and blue chips in the sample, $r - b$, not the relative proportions (or the ratio) of red and blue chips, r/b. By asking people to judge a series of samples in which $r - b$ and r/b were varied orthogonally, Tversky and Kahneman were able to show that subjects' responses depended on the non-Bayesian variable, r/b, and were insensitive to the Bayesian variable, $r - b$.

Pressing their argument further, Tversky and Kahneman claimed that they could characterize the relevant psychological variable in a way that would generalize beyond bookbag-and-poker-chip experiments. They suggested that people estimate the probability that a sample or datum arose from a particular population or source according to the "representativeness" of the sample, a concept related to the similarity between salient features of the sample and salient features of the population. Tversky and Kahneman did not give an explicit definition of "representativeness," but tried instead to construct situations in which there would be wide intuitive agreement about the relative values involved. Then they conducted experiments to show that subjects' judged probabilities followed "representativeness" and ignored other variables.

Studies of this type induced a paradigm shift in research on probabilistic inference. Bookbag-and-poker-chip experiments became rare, yielding to "word problems" about more concrete situations. Explanations for behavior were no longer couched in terms of Bayes's rule, even if many of the phenomena still were (e.g., ignoring base rates). Subsequent research produced evidence of several heuristics (representativeness, availability, anchoring-and-adjustment, simulation, etc.) and a large and growing collection of biases (insensitivity to sample size, ignoring of base rates, insufficiently regressive predictions, insufficient adjustments, misperceptions of chance, illusion of validity, illusory correlations, overconfidence, conjunction fallacy, hindsight bias, etc.). The success of this line of research bolstered general interest in anomalies of decision making, in choice as well as in probabilistic judgment. Further, this research caught the attention of social psychologists, initially because they saw a parallel between neglect of base rates and neglect of consensus information in causal attribution tasks (Fischhoff, 1976; Nisbett & Borgida, 1975; Nisbett, Borgida, Crandall, & Reed, 1976; Ross, 1977). With the energy contributed by social psychologists (see Nisbett & Ross, 1980), the field reached a new level of visibility within psychology. Moreover, the influence of social cognition researchers led judgment and decision researchers to broaden their interests and methods in studying the relations among cognition, affect, motivation, and evaluation. (This literature is vast. Some helpful edited collections include Bassili, 1989; Clark & Fiske, 1982; Fiedler & Forgas, 1988; Forgas, 1991; Higgins & Sorrentino, 1990; Izard, Kagan, & Zajonc, 1984; Martin & Tesser, 1992; Peterson, Hoyer, & Wilson, 1986; Sorrentino & Higgins, 1986; Uleman & Bargh, 1989; see also the annual series, *Advances in Experimental Social Psychology*. Papers reviewing specific parts of this literature include Blaney, 1986; Bornstein, 1989; Isen, 1993; Kunda, 1990; Showers & Cantor, 1985. Papers showing the participation of, or otherwise of particular interest to, JDM researchers include Anderson & Hubert, 1963; Bower, 1981; Dellarosa & Bourne, 1984; Dreben, Fiske, & Hastie, 1979; Fiske & Neuberg, 1990; Hastie & Park, 1986; Johnson & Tversky, 1983; Lichtenstein & Srull, 1987; Mano, 1994; McClelland, Stewart, Judd, & Bourne, 1987; Pennington & Hastie, 1988; Reyes, Thompson, & Bower, 1980; Tetlock & Levi, 1982; Wright & Bower, 1992; Zajonc, 1980.)

Anomalies aplenty. Research on heuristics and biases, however, has also led to controversy. Originally, the experiments were conducted so that the word problems set up a "trap" that subjects would fall into *if* they were using a particular heuristic. In this way, biased behavior was merely a device used to provide (dramatic) evidence that hypothesized psychological processes were at work. Although research of this sort continues, there is also a good deal of research in which the biases seem to have taken on a life of their own. Studies have been conducted to determine the frequency of a bias, conditions under which a bias will or will not occur, whether the original explanation for a bias is sufficient to explain all its occurrences, whether some decision aid can help people avoid the bias, and so on. In addition, some studies have been conducted purely to produce evidence of some new bias, without using the bias as evidence for any particular psychological process.

As a result, what may have begun as an attempt to shift psychological research on inference from questions of "How well?" to questions of "How?" has bound it all the more tightly to the position that behavioral deviations from a presumed standard of rationality are the "interesting" phenomena requiring explanation. This fact has caused concern among some researchers (Beach, Christensen-Szalanski, & Barnes, 1987; Berkeley & Humphreys, 1982; Christensen-Szalanski & Beach, 1984; Lopes, 1991). A related issue is that it is not always clear that a judgment is in error (Funder, 1987; Gigerenzer, 1991; Hastie & Rasinski, 1988; Hogarth, 1981). Still another line of criticism is that the proliferation of heuristics and biases calls for an overarching framework of the sort that is being sought in work on preferential choice (Wallsten, 1983). In general, preferential choice and probabilistic judgment are areas of intense activity and exciting prospects. Nevertheless, there are signals that many researchers are dissatisfied with the current state of affairs. Some have even called for what amounts to a fresh start (Beach & Mitchell, 1987; Hastie, 1991; Lopes, 1987; Tetlock, 1991).

Developments in judgment research

In this section, we focus primarily on research that grew out of Brunswik's (1956) Probabilistic Functionalism. Although an alternative approach to judgment research is provided by Anderson's (1981, 1991a, 1991b, 1991c) Information Integration Theory, recent efforts to study preference and risk perception have involved the joint participation of Information Integration researchers and choice researchers, bringing these groups much closer together. By contrast, the Brunswikian researchers have retained a more distinctive perspective and program.

Earlier in this chapter, we outlined some of the key concepts of Brunswik's thinking on psychology. Kenneth Hammond and his colleagues have applied Brunswik's ideas specifically to judgment and extended these in various ways to create Social Judgment Theory (Brehmer, 1988; Brehmer & Joyce, 1988; Hammond, Rohrbaugh, Mumpower, & Adelman, 1977; Hammond, Stewart, Brehmer, & Steinmann, 1975). In this section, we review some of the developments that led to Social Judgment Theory as well as related lines of research (whether or not the researchers considered themselves to be engaged in Brunswikian research).

The lens model equation

As mentioned above, Paul Meehl's (1954) *Clinical Versus Statistical Prediction* stimulated a voluminous literature on intuitive ("clinical") judgment by publicizing the surprising finding that human judgment was almost invariably less accurate than a simple – usually linear – combination of the same items of information that were available to the judge. In 1955, Hammond drew attention to the applicability of a Brunswikian approach to the study of clinical judgment. Borrowing a term from Brunswik (e.g., 1952, pp. 23–24), Hammond (1955, p. 255) referred to clinical judgment as "quasi-rational," and proceeded to show how Brunswikian principles could be applied to its explication.

As an illustration, Hammond used data from Todd's (1954) dissertation to examine the ability of judges to estimate patients' Wechsler–Bellevue IQ on the basis of their Rorschach responses. Ten clinical psychologists judging the categorized Rorschach responses of 78 patients produced a median correlation between their judgments and actual IQ of .47. When the clinicians were provided with the patients' full verbal protocol, the median correlation rose to .64.[4] Next, Hammond decomposed the "grand strategy" (Brunswik, 1957, p. 8) by which achievement was reached. Specifically, using the four most valid Rorschach factors as independent variables (i.e., the categorized Rorschach responses), he performed separate multiple regression analyses of the environment (i.e., the patients) and the organism (i.e., a separate multiple regression for each clinician). Then he compared them: (1) with respect to overall predictability (multiple R for the patients' actual IQ was

.479, median cross-validated multiple R for the clinicians' judgments of IQ was .85), and (2) with respect to their use of cues ("Certain clinicians were found to be using invalid cues, others neglecting valid ones," Hammond, 1955, p. 261).

In sum, not only did this paper show the relevance of Brunswikian principles for the analysis of clinical judgment in general terms, but it spelled out many of the details for doing so. Moreover, by using multiple regression analysis as a tool for examining the organism (i.e., the clinician's judgments), as well as the environment (i.e., relations among IQ and Rorschach responses among a population of patients), Hammond (1955) helped to move the field away from its exclusive preoccupation with the accuracy of judgment (clinical versus statistical prediction), and toward the relational question of how the judge manages to achieve the level of accuracy that he or she does reach.[5]

Some years later, Hursch, Hammond, and Hursch (1964) gave further methodological guidance by providing a mathematical decomposition of the achievement coefficient, that is, the correlation between criterion (environmental distal variable) and judgment (organismic central response), for a given set of proximal cues. This decomposition, as modified by Tucker (1964), is known as the lens model equation (LME) and has become a standard tool of Brunswikian research.[6]

Linear models

Whereas Meehl (1954) had drawn attention to the comparison between judgment and a model of the environment (i.e., clinical versus actuarial prediction), Hammond (1955) had urged the comparison between a *model* of the judge and a model of the environment. By contrast with both of these approaches, a program of research popularized by Hoffman (1960) emphasized the attempt to construct mathematical models of judges apart from consideration of the environment and the accuracy of judgment. Espousing a program of research that Brunswik would probably have disapproved of as "encapsulated," Hoffman (1960) drew attention to two issues related to judges' self-insight: (1) linear models may fit a set of judgments well despite the judge's verbal account of his or her reasoning being suggestive of a nonlinear process, and (2) the relative weights of the cues (i.e., indices of relative importance derived from linear regression coefficients) may correspond poorly with judges' verbal reports of the relative importance they accorded to the various cues.

The latter issue, concerning the correspondence of model-derived and verbally reported importance weights, has been the subject of sporadic but continuing attention over the years. Early studies (summarized by Slovic & Lichtenstein, 1971) emphasized the fact that people's subjective (i.e., verbally reported) weights accorded substantial importance to a greater number of factors than objective (i.e., model-derived) weights, overestimating the importance of (objectively) minor factors. Ironically, Nisbett and Wilson (1977) interpreted these early, relatively pessimistic studies as providing virtually the only indication of non-negligible insight into one's own psychological processes. Later studies (e.g., Birnbaum & Stegner, 1981) gave a more favorable assessment of the correspondence between subjective and objective weights, by using new objective indices of importance (e.g., Surber, 1985), new tasks by which people could display their self-insight (Reilly & Doherty, 1989, 1992), or arguments to the effect that the objective weights failed to capture what people meant by "importance" (Goldstein, 1990; Goldstein & Beattie, 1991).

The former issue, concerning the linearity of judges who claim to be using nonlinear processes, stimulated an intensive investigation (for summaries, see Goldberg, 1968; Slovic & Lichtenstein, 1971). In particular, a search was undertaken to find genuinely "configural" judges, who exhibit nonlinearity in the sense that the weight given to a particular cue is not a constant, but depends on the levels of other cues. Such judges do not use each cue independently, as linear models do, but rather are sensitive to the "configuration" shown by an entire profile of cues. Configural judges were sought by first trying to identify tasks that required configural judgment to be done well, and then studying judges who were experienced at those tasks. For example, among the judges studied were (1) radiologists making the diagnosis of benign versus malignant gastric ulcers (Hoffman, Slovic, & Rorer, 1968); (2) physicians, nurses, clinical psychologists, and psychiatric social workers deciding whether or not to grant temporary liberty to patients from a psychiatric hospital (Rorer, Hoffman, Dickman, & Slovic, 1967); and (3) clinical psychologists and graduate students in clinical psychology making the differential diagnosis of neurotic versus psychotic on the basis of patients' Minnesota Multiphasic Personality Inventory (MMPI) profiles (Wiggins & Hoffman, 1968). These studies and others produced numerous examples of configural judges, in the sense that analyses of variance of the judgments revealed significant interaction terms. Despite their significance, however, these interactions rarely accounted for much judgmental variance. The implication seemed to be that judges were not necessarily mistaken when they claimed to use information configurally, but that linear models provided such good approximations to nonlinear processes that the judges' nonlinearity was difficult to detect. This implication was supported by such studies as that of Yntema and Torgerson (1961), who provided examples to suggest that a linear model would closely approximate almost any combination of cues provided that the criterion variable was monotonically related to each of the cues.

Yntema and Torgerson (1961) also appear to be the first to suggest that a simple linear model of a person's judgments might do a better job of predicting a criterion variable than the judgments themselves. They reported a study in which subjects were taught to predict a criterion variable that was nonlinearly related to three cues. After 11 days with outcome feedback, subjects were tested on the 12th day without outcome feedback. The correlation between the judgments and the criterion values on the 12th day averaged .84 for the six subjects. Then, Yntema and Torgerson fit a model to each subject that employed main effects only, ignoring interactions, and correlated the models' predictions with the criterion values. Note that these models were constructed to predict the subjects' judgments, not to predict the criterion values. Surprisingly, the average correlation rose to .89. This led Yntema and Torgerson (1961, p. 24) to suggest the "intriguing possibility" that "[a]rtificial, precomputed judgments may in some cases be better than those the man could make himself if he dealt with each situation as it arose." The procedure of replacing a judge with a model of the judge (and usually a simple, linear model, at that), together with the finding that the model typically outperformed the judge, later came to be known as "bootstrapping" (Bowman, 1963; Dawes, 1971; Dudycha & Naylor, 1966; Goldberg, 1970; Kunreuther, 1969; Wiggins & Kohen, 1971).

Bootstrapping "worked," that is, the linear model of the judge predicted the criterion better than the judge himself or herself, apparently because the judge had some real (possibly nonlinear) wisdom to be applied to the prediction problem, and as reviewed above, linear models can provide excellent approximations to nonlinear processes. Thus, so the argument went, the linear model succeeded in approximating the judge's wisdom, and then improved on the judge by applying that wisdom more consistently than the judge was able to. Unfortunately, this plausible explanation was dashed by Dawes and Corrigan (1974), who showed that when the cues had been converted to standard scores (i.e., with mean 0 and variance 1) and scaled (if necessary) so that each cue had a positive relation to the criterion, then linear models with the weights chosen at random (as the absolute value of an observation from a standard normal distribution) on the average tended to outperform bootstrapped models. Linear models with equal weights did even better. Evidently, bootstrapping worked not by extracting judges' expertise, but for reasons connected with the general success of linear models (see also Einhorn & Hogarth, 1975).

Investigations into the conditions under which linear models perform well showed that the typical task environment in which investigators had compared judges, bootstrapped linear models, and optimal linear models could hardly have been more congenial to linear models. This conclusion served to underscore Brunswik's emphasis on understanding the task environment and added some new twists. In particular, the analyses surrounding the linear model revealed that (1) it is also important to understand how the task environment might render a class of models too robust to detect subtle details of nonrandom variations in subjects' use of cognitive strategies, and (2) achievement might be promoted by task environments in which a great variety of behaviors will be approximately optimal (Dawes, 1975, 1979).

Individual learning

In view of the emphasis that Brunswik placed on the ability of organisms to adapt to their (probabilistically apprehended) environments, it is not surprising that Brunswikian researchers have devoted much study to the way that people learn probabilistic relationships. The literature on this and related issues is vast, and we can do little more than provide readers with some pointers.

In studies of multiple-cue probability learning (MCPL), subjects are presented with a profile of cue values that they must use to predict a criterion value. Studies employing outcome feedback provide subjects with the correct criterion value after they have made their prediction. This task was first studied by Smedslund (1955), and the lens model equation was first used to analyze performance at this task by Hammond and Summers (1965). Since then, investigators have employed this task to study the effects on learning of several factors, including (1) various cue-criterion function forms (Brehmer, 1973; Deane, Hammond, & Summers, 1972; Naylor & Clark, 1968), (2) intercorrelations among cues (Knowles, Hammond, Stewart, & Summers, 1972; Lindell & Stewart, 1974; Naylor & Schenck, 1968; Schmitt & Dudycha, 1975), (3) various rules for combining cues (Brehmer, 1969; Edgell, 1978; Summers, Summers, & Karkau, 1969), (4) dynamic environments (Dudycha, Dumoff, & Dudycha, 1973; Kleinmuntz, 1985; Mackinnon & Wearing, 1985; Peterson, Hammond, & Summers, 1965; Summers, 1969), and (5) world knowledge as prompted by the use of particular labels for the cues and criterion variables (Adelman, 1981; Koele, 1980; Miller, 1971; Muchinsky & Dudycha, 1975; Sniezek, 1986). For a general review of early research, see Slovic and Lichtenstein (1971); for a more recent review, see Klayman (1988a).

One general finding of the research on learning from outcome feedback is that it tends to be slow, and often not as effective as one might hope (e.g., Goldberg, 1968; Klayman, 1988a). Partly as a result of this finding, researchers have sought to investigate other forms of feedback and to understand in greater detail how people make use of feedback. By contrast with outcome feedback, a notion of "cognitive feedback" was suggested by Todd and Hammond (1965), in which subjects are informed, not about the outcomes of individual trials, but about statistical properties over blocks of trials. Specifically, subjects are told how the correlation or regression coefficients that relate the cues to their judgments compare with the correlation or regression coefficients that relate the cues to the criterion. This allows subjects to see whether they are allocating importance to the cues in suboptimal ways, and they generally learn more quickly and effectively than with outcome feedback (Balzer, Doherty, & O'Connor, 1989). An interesting issue concerning the way that subjects do make use of outcome feedback is that the criterion value on a trial often is more than mere information to the subject, but also determines a reward. Thus, the informativeness of outcomes must be disentangled from their incentive value (Hogarth, Gibbs, McKenzie, & Marquis, 1991; Tversky & Edwards, 1966; see also Einhorn, 1980a, 1980b; Einhorn & Hogarth, 1978).

Another approach taken to the problem of outcome feedback was pursued by Berndt Brehmer and his colleagues beginning in the mid-1970s. Brehmer (1974a; Brehmer, Kuylenstierna, & Liljergren, 1974; see also Slovic, 1974) suggested that subjects do not address MCPL tasks as inductive problems to be learned in a purely data-driven, "bottom-up" manner. Rather, they come to the tasks with a preconceived set of hypotheses about the sorts of cue-criterion function forms, combination rules, and cue weights that they are likely to see, and they use the outcome feedback to test their hypotheses. If the correct hypothesis is low in the subject's hierarchy of hypotheses, learning will be slow, if it is accomplished at all. Learning will be impeded by the same factors that impair hypothesis testing, for example, probabilistic feedback that cannot definitively reject a hypothesis, failure of the subjects to understand the logic of seeking information that can falsify hypotheses, and so on. (For a general review of this line of research, see Brehmer, 1980a.) Brehmer's approach helped to explain a number of the findings of MCPL studies (e.g., the effect of cue labels – world knowledge affects the set of hypotheses that subjects bring to the learning task), and it also helped to connect judgment and decision research to areas of study that had been pursued independently by cognitive psychologists in other areas. For example, seen this way, MCPL tasks did not seem different from the tasks that had been used for some time to study the processes of concept formation, hypothesis testing, information gathering, and rule discovery (Bruner et al., 1956; Wason, 1960; Wason & Johnson-Laird, 1972), and judgment researchers began to study these issues from perspectives of their own (Doherty, Mynatt, Tweney, & Schiavo, 1979; Klayman, 1988b; Klayman & Ha, 1987, 1989; Mynatt, Doherty, & Tweney, 1978).

Covariation detection and assessment

To perform well in an MCPL task, a subject must detect covariation between cues and criterion values. The task of detecting and/or estimating the degree of covariation between variables, apart from the use of this relationship in prediction, has been studied by judgment researchers and others. One of the earliest studies of this task was conducted by the same investigator who initiated MCPL studies (Smedslund, 1963), and the ensuing literature has become enormous (e.g., Alloy & Abramson, 1979; Arkes & Harkness, 1983; Chapman, 1991; Chapman & Robbins, 1990; Crocker, 1981; Jenkins & Ward, 1965; Lipe, 1990; McKenzie, 1994; Shaklee, 1983; Ward & Jenkins, 1965; Wasserman, Dorner, & Kao, 1990; Yates & Curley, 1986). One issue within this literature meshes interestingly with the effects of world knowledge and cue labels in MCPL tasks. Specifically, investigators have been interested in the effects of prior knowledge and/or expectations on the detection and assessment of covariation (Alloy & Tabachnik, 1984; Chapman & Chapman, 1967, 1969; Jennings, Amabile, & Ross, 1982; Wright & Murphy, 1984). Another interesting direction has been the assessment of causal relationships between variables (Cheng & Novick, 1990, 1991, 1992; Einhorn & Hogarth, 1986b; Tversky & Kahneman, 1980), as well as the distinction between predictive and diagnostic judgment (Bjorkman & Nilsson, 1982; Einhorn & Hogarth, 1982; Mitchell, Russo, & Pennington, 1989; Nilsson & Bjorkman, 1982; Waldmann & Holyoak, 1992).

Interpersonal learning and conflict

Hammond (1965; Hammond, Wilkins, & Todd, 1966) suggested a way that the MCPL tasks used to study individual learning could be employed in the study of interpersonal learning and conflict. Typically, in the training phase of the experiment, two subjects are separated and taught individually, via an MCPL task with outcome feedback, to use different rules or weights in making predictions. Then, in the test phase of the experiment, the two subjects are brought together and presented with a new set of trials in which they are required to make predictions by consensus. The lens model equation, which is usually used to decompose the correlation between judgments and criterion values, can be adapted for the analysis of this conflict paradigm. The key is to let the judgments of one of the subjects play the role of the "criterion" and to decompose the correlation between the two subjects' judgments (i.e., their "agreement"). An interesting result of applying the LME in this way is to see that the two subjects cannot reach perfect agreement, even if their judgmental strategies are identical, unless both subjects are perfectly reliable in the execution of strategies. In other words, conflict need not necessarily be motivational, in the sense that people want different things (i.e., have different judgmental strategies). Rather, conflict may be cognitive, in the sense that people cannot implement their judgmental strategies with perfect control.

A substantial literature on interpersonal learning and conflict has arisen by considering many of the same factors that have been manipulated in MCPL studies, such as cue-criterion function form and cue validity (Brehmer, 1973) and cue intercorrelations (Brehmer, 1974b; Mumpower & Hammond, 1974). (For general reviews, see Brehmer, 1976, 1980b; see also Hammond & Brehmer, 1973; for applications, see Hammond et al., 1977.)

Cognitive continuum theory

The final area of judgment research we would like to mention concerns Cognitive Continuum Theory (Hammond, Hamm, Grassia, & Pearson, 1987). Cognitive Continuum Theory expands on Brunswik's (1956, pp. 89–

99) attempt to place both perception and deductive thinking in a larger category of "ratiomorphic" processes, to be distinguished on the basis of such markers as the distribution of judgmental errors. Cognitive Continuum Theory rejects a dichotomy between intuition and analysis, and instead posits a continuum of modes of thought, with a collection of "quasi-rational" processes occupying the middle ground between intuition and analysis. The theory also posits a Brunswikian distinction between "surface" and "depth" of the task environment. Surface features are aspects of the overt display (e.g., whether judgmental inputs are displayed pictorially or numerically) and depth characteristics concern aspects of the task that are less apparent. Hammond et al. (1987) used these notions to develop a number of hypotheses about the mode of processing that will be induced by a task with particular surface and depth characteristics, together with hypotheses regarding the consequences for achievement. Contrary to certain traditions, they do not always predict that analysis will outperform other modes of thought.

Currents, connections, and controversies in recent research

With the foregoing as general introduction to the field, we would like to close with some comments about recent developments and the selections included in this book. The 1980s and 1990s have been an exciting period for psychological researchers in general and for JDM researchers in particular. Progress has been made on persistent problems, new lines of inquiry have been opened, and new conceptualizations have been offered. At one end of the field, JDM researchers have expanded their interests to include nearly everything that one might place under the label of higher-order thought processes, thus blurring the line between JDM research and cognitive psychology. In addition to studies of preference, uncertainty, and evaluation, JDM researchers now cite and conduct studies concerning memory, mood, and motivation, learning and language, attention and attitude, reasoning and representation, problem solving and perception, expertise and explanatory coherence. Specific examples include studies of: (1) modes of thinking, including (a) automatic/obligatory versus controlled/optional processes (e.g., Fazio, Sanbonmatsu, Powell, & Kardes, 1986; Langer, 1989; Ronis, Yates, & Kirscht, 1989; Uleman & Bargh, 1989), (b) thinking versus feeling (e.g., Clore, 1992; Hammond et al., 1987; Millar & Tesser, 1992; Mitchell & Beach, 1990; Strack, 1992; Wilson, Dunn, Kraft, & Lisle, 1989), and (c) frames of mind (e.g., Beckmann & Gollwitzer, 1987; Gollwitzer, 1990; Gollwitzer, Heckhausen, & Steller, 1990); (2) subjective experience and the metacognition of decision making, including (a) experienced and predicted utility (e.g., Kahneman, 1994; Kahneman, Fredrickson, Schreiber, & Redelmeier, 1993; Kahneman & Snell, 1990, 1992; Tversky & Griffin, 1991; Varey & Kahneman, 1992), (b) the experienced "difficulty" of making decisions (e.g., Beattie & Barlas, 1993), (c) people's insight into their own decision processes (e.g., Reilly & Doherty,

1989, 1992), and (d) people's evaluation of their own and other people's decisions (e.g., Baron & Hershey, 1988; Boles & Messick, 1995; Lipshitz, 1989); and (3) individual differences in decision styles or expertise (e.g., Hunt, Krzystofiak, Meindl, & Yousry, 1989; MacCrimmon & Wehrung, 1990; Shanteau, 1988).

At another end of the field, JDM researchers have undertaken an intensive study of the social aspects of decision making, thereby blurring lines between JDM research and parts of social psychology, economics, sociology, political science, and anthropology. Researchers have investigated: (1) individual versus group performance (e.g., Argote, Devadas, & Melone, 1990; Harmon & Rohrbaugh, 1990; Kameda & Davis, 1990; Mannix & Loewenstein, 1994; Sniezek & Henry, 1990; Tindale, 1989); (2) processes of group behavior (e.g., Allison & Messick, 1990; Allison, Worth, & King, 1990; Brinberg & Jaccard, 1988; Casey, Gettys, Pliske, & Mehle, 1984; Mannix, 1993; Mannix & White, 1992; Messick & Liebrand, 1995; Messick & Mackie, 1989; Sniezek, May, & Sawyer, 1990); (3) judgments of a social nature (e.g., Bies, Tripp, & Neale, 1993; Blount, 1995; Kahneman, Knetsch, & Thaler, 1986a, 1986b; Mellers, 1982, 1986; Mellers & Baron, 1993; Messick & Allison, 1987; Thompson & Loewenstein, 1992); (4) judgments in a social context (e.g., Hagafors & Brehmer, 1983; Simonson & Nye, 1992; Tetlock, 1985a, 1985b; Tetlock & Boettger, 1989; Tetlock, Skitka, & Boettger, 1989); (5) interpersonal learning and conflict (e.g., Brehmer, 1976, 1980b, 1984); (6) resolution of social dilemmas (e.g., Dawes, 1980, 1991; Liebrand, Messick, & Wilke, 1992; Mannix, 1991; Messick, 1984; Messick & Brewer, 1983; White, 1994; Wilke, Messick, & Rutte, 1986); (7) social utility and negotiation (e.g., Bazerman & Carroll, 1987; Bazerman & Neale, 1992; Carnevale & Isen, 1986; Carroll, Bazerman, & Maury, 1988; Loewenstein, Thompson, & Bazerman, 1989; Lurie, 1987; MacCrimmon & Messick, 1976; Mannix & Innami, 1993; Mannix, Thompson, & Bazerman, 1989; Messick & Sentis, 1985; Neale & Bazerman, 1991, 1992; Northcraft, Neale, & Earley, 1994; Pruitt, 1981; Raiffa, 1982; Thompson, 1990; Thompson & Hastie, 1990; Thompson, Mannix, & Bazerman, 1988; White & Neale, 1994; White, Valley, Bazerman, Neale, & Peck, 1994); (8) behavior in organizational context (e.g., MacCrimmon, Wehrung, & Stanbury, 1986; Mannix & Loewenstein, 1993; March & Olsen, 1986; March & Shapira, 1982, 1987; Mitchell, Rediker, & Beach, 1986; Shapira, 1995); (9) experimental markets and auctions (e.g., Andreassen, 1990; Ball, Bazerman, & Carroll, 1991; Camerer & Kunreuther, 1989; Camerer, Loewenstein, & Weber, 1989; Irwin, McClelland, & Schulze, 1992; Kagel & Levin, 1986); and (10) cross-cultural comparisons of risk perception and probabilistic thinking (e.g., Englander, Farago, Slovic, & Fischhoff, 1986; Goszczynska, Tyszka, & Slovic, 1991; Johnson, 1991; Phillips & Wright, 1977; Teigen, Brun, & Slovic, 1988; Wright & Phillips, 1980; Wright et al., 1978; Yates et al., 1989).

In sum, JDM research is moving rapidly, and it is a daunting task to comprehend its scope. We have tried to organize the selections for this book so that readers can sample from across the field without losing their bearings.

Currents

We have chosen our title, *Research on Judgment and Decision Making: Currents, Connections, and Controversies*, with its tripartite subtitle, to highlight the three themes with which we organize this book. The first theme, "Currents," comprises updates on issues of enduring concern that were addressed in the *Reader* by Arkes and Hammond (1986), as well as areas of new or growing interest within the community of JDM researchers. Among the former, we include (1) anomalies of judgment and choice (Gigerenzer, Hoffrage, & Kleinbölting, 1991; Shafir et al., 1993), (2) decision processes and their adaptiveness (Hammond et al., 1987; Payne, Bettman, & Johnson, 1990), and (3) acquisition and use of knowledge (Hogarth et al., 1991; Klayman & Ha, 1987). Among the latter, we include (1) mental simulation, causal, and counterfactual reasoning (Cheng & Novick, 1992; Kahneman & Varey, 1990), (2) training and expertise (Camerer & Johnson, 1991), (3) temporal context (Loewenstein & Thaler, 1989), (4) behavior in group situations (Dawes, van de Kragt, & Orbell, 1988), and (5) subjective experience, metacognition, and insight (Kahneman & Snell, 1992; Tversky & Griffin, 1991). Our aim in this section is to enable students and researchers to keep abreast of a wider array of developments than they probably follow in their customary reading.

Connections

The second theme, "Connections," is intended to cover the efforts of some researchers to build bridges between decision research and related areas of psychology. Studies of memory bear on the cognitive underpinnings of judgment and decision making (Hastie & Park, 1986). Studies of affect, attitude, and motivation (Isen, 1993), and of reasoning, argument, and explanation (Hogarth & Kunreuther, 1995; Pennington & Hastie, 1988), speak to those parts of decision research that concern the appraisal of desirability and the selection of action. By including papers on these topics, we hope to bolster the work of investigators who seek to expand the horizons of decision research and to integrate it better with one of the sciences that provides its intellectual roots.

Controversies

Our third theme, "Controversies," is motivated by the realization that many decision researchers are discontented with the present state of the field. The methods, levels of analysis, styles of explanation, and even the goals of decision research are being questioned. Our aim in this section is to bring together papers on some of the key controversies, so that readers can be brought into the debates and come to some reasoned opinions about the directions that decision research will and/or should pursue.

Three controversies seem particularly relevant to the future of JDM research. First, what methods are appropriate for studying decision processes (e.g., process-tracing methods vs. inference from decision "errors"), and what kinds of models are appropriate for describing the findings (e.g., paramorphic models vs. computational models; Doherty & Brehmer, 1997)? Second, to what extent can we generalize from laboratory studies of abstract tasks (e.g., choice among monetary gambles) to behavior in familiar real-world domains? That is, are psychological processes so sensitive to the content and context of the situation that we must develop separate theories for career decisions, housing decisions, spousal decisions, and so on, or can we find a level of analysis that permits generalizability across domains (Goldstein & Weber, 1995; Wagenaar, Keren, & Lichtenstein, 1988)? Third, is the concept of "strategy" (i.e., the rule-governed sequence of mental operations by which a person makes a decision) a sufficiently powerful explanatory tool for our purposes, or must we consider processes that are nonstrategic (Smith, Langston, & Nisbett, 1992)? In addition to papers on these controversies, we include papers by researchers who have proposed, in effect, that decision research begin over again (Lopes, 1987; Tetlock, 1991).

Notes

1 The point at which rationality was imputed to the von Neumann–Morgenstern theory of utility is not entirely clear. Savage (1972, p. 97) wrote, "One idea now held by me that I think von Neumann and Morgenstern do not explicitly support, and that so far as I know they might not wish to have attributed to them, is the normative interpretation of the theory."

2 Actually, the collapse occurs even if people are able to recognize only mildly complicated but equivalent forms. To give an explicit example, let $(x,p; y,q; \ldots)$ denote the gamble in which x is received with probability p, y is received with probability q, etc. If there are only two outcomes, use the somewhat simpler notation (x,p,y) to indicate that x is received with probability p and y is received with probability $1 - p$. The two-stage gamble $[(x,p,y), p, z]$ is equivalent to the two-stage gamble $[(x,p,z), p, (y,p,z)]$: both are equivalent to the single-stage gamble $[x, p^2; y, p(1 - p); z, (1 - p)]$. If people were always indifferent between the two equivalent two-stage forms, this would be enough. Luce (1992) refers to this property, stated in terms of gambles based on uncertain events without explicitly given probabilities, as "right autodistributivity."

3 Brunswikians might object that the choice of an external standard is not an arbitrary matter, and in particular that the standard should not be the experimenter's notion of optimality in an artificial setting. Functionalism is about how organisms accomplish *their* goals in *their* environments. Nevertheless, the use of an external standard in the probability judgment task helped to highlight a similarity with Brunswikian research.

4 Hammond (1955) pointed out in a footnote that sophomores in elementary psychology did almost as well, achieving a median correlation of .58. This sort of comparison speaks of a general interest in the effects of learning under different kinds of training conditions, which later became a central focus of much Brunswikian judgment research.

5 Hammond (1955) himself gave credit for "the first application of the multiple correlation approach to the analysis of trait-ratings" (p. 261) to Egon Brunswik's wife, Else Frenkel-Brunswik (1942). Still earlier, linear models were used to analyze judgment, if not trait-ratings, by the future Secretary of Agriculture and Vice President, Henry A. Wallace (1923).

6 The name "lens model" derives from a pictorial representation of Brunswik's theory about the way that organisms use proximal variables to establish a stable relationship between distal (i.e., environmental) and central (i.e., intraorganismic) variables. For perception, the image is one in which a distal stimulus at one "focus" emits a scatter of rays, representing proximal cues, among which the organism selects a subset to be recombined into the central perception at the other "focus." For overt action, a central motivational state is pictured at one "focus" as emitting a scatter of rays, representing possible proximal means (i.e., motor behaviors) among which the organism selects, all of whcih lead to the same distal end (i.e., goal) at the other "focus." On different trials, organisms select different subsets of cues or means, and the composite picture shows the collection of cues or means that are used over a large number of trials. The picture resembles a portrayal of the way a convex lens brings a scatter of light rays into focus.

References

Adelman, L. (1981). The influence of formal, substantive, and contextual task properties on the relative effectiveness of different forms of feedback in multiple-cue probability learning tasks. *Organizational Behavior and Human Performance, 27,* 423–442.

Allais, M. (1953). Le comportement de l'homme rationnel devant le risque: Critique des postulats et axiomes de l'école Americaine. *Econometrica, 21,* 503–546.

Allais, M., & Hagen, O. (Eds.). (1979). *Expected utility hypotheses and the Allais paradox.* Dordrecht, Holland: Reidel.

Allison, S. T., & Messick, D. M. (1990). Social decision heuristics in the use of shared resources. *Journal of Behavioral Decision Making, 3,* 195–204.

Allison, S. T., Worth, L. T., & King, M. W. C. (1990). Group decisions as social inference heuristics. *Journal of Personality and Social Psychology, 58,* 801–811.

Alloy, L. B., & Abramson, L. Y. (1979). Judgment of contingency in depressed and nondepressed students: Sadder but wiser? *Journal of Experimental Psychology: General, 108,* 441–485.

Alloy, L. B., & Tabachnik, N. (1984). Assessment of covariation by humans and animals: The joint influence of prior expectations and current situational information. *Psychological Review, 91,* 112–149.

Anderson, N. H. (1965). Primacy effects in personality impression formation using a generalized order effect paradigm. *Journal of Personality and Social Psychology, 2,* 1–9.

Anderson, N. H. (1971). An exchange on functional and conjoint measurement. *Psychological Review, 78,* 457–458.

Anderson, N. H. (1981). *Foundations of information integration theory.* New York: Academic Press.

Anderson, N. H. (Ed.). (1991a). *Contributions of Information Integration Theory: Vol. 1. Cognition.* Hillsdale, NJ: Erlbaum.

Anderson, N. H. (Ed.). (1991b). *Contributions of Information Integration Theory: Vol. 2. Social.* Hillsdale, NJ: Erlbaum.

Anderson, N. H. (Ed.). (1991c). *Contributions of Information Integration Theory: Vol. 3. Developmental.* Hillsdale, NJ: Erlbaum.

Anderson, N. H., & Barrios, A. A. (1961). Primacy effects in personality impression formation. *Journal of Abnormal and Social Psychology, 63,* 346–350.

Anderson, N. H., & Hovland, C. I. (1957). The representation of order effects in communication research. In C. I. Hovland et al. (Eds.), *The order of presentation in persuasion.* New Haven: Yale University Press.

Anderson, N. H., & Hubert, S. (1963). Effects of concomitant verbal recall on order effects in personality impression formation. *Journal of Verbal Learning and Verbal Behavior*, 2, 379–391.

Anderson, N. H., & Norman, A. (1964). Order effects in impression formation in four classes of stimuli. *Journal of Abnormal and Social Psychology*, 69, 467–471.

Anderson, N. H., & Shanteau, J. C. (1970). Information integration in risky decision making. *Journal of Experimental Psychology*, 84, 441–451.

Andreassen, P. B. (1990). Judgmental extrapolation and market over-reaction: On the use and disuse of news. *Journal of Behavioral Decision Making*, 3, 153–174.

Argote, L., Devadas, R., & Melone, N. (1990). The base-rate fallacy: Contrasting processes and outcomes of group and individual judgment. *Organizational Behavior and Human Decision Processes*, 46, 296–310.

Arkes, H. R., & Blumer, C. (1985). The psychology of sunk cost. *Organizational Behavior and Human Performance*, 35, 129–140.

Arkes, H. R., Hammond, K. R. (Eds.). (1986). *Judgment and decision making: An interdisciplinary reader*. Cambridge: Cambridge University Press.

Arkes, H. R., & Harkness, A. R. (1983). Estimates of contingency between two dichotomous variables. *Journal of Experimental Psychology: General*, 112, 117–135.

Asch, S. E. (1946). Forming impressions of personality. *Journal of Abnormal and Social Psychology*, 41, 258–290.

Aschenbrenner, K. M. (1984). Moment- versus dimension-oriented theories of risky choice: A (fairly) general test involving single-peaked preferences. *Journal of Experimental Psychology: Learning, Memory, and Cognition*, 10, 513–535.

Atkinson, J. W. (1957). Motivational determinants of risk-taking behavior. *Psychological Review*, 64, 359–372.

Ball, S. B., Bazerman, M. H., & Carroll, J. S. (1991). An evaluation of learning in the bilateral winner's curse. *Organizational Behavior and Human Decision Processes*, 48, 1–22.

Balzer, W. K., Doherty, M. E., & O'Connor, R., Jr. (1989). Effects of cognitive feedback on performance. *Psychological Bulletin*, 106, 410–433.

Baron, J., & Hershey, J. C. (1988). Outcome bias in decision evaluation. *Journal of Personality and Social Psychology*, 54, 569–579.

Bassili, J. N. (Ed.). (1989). *On-line cognition in person perception*. Hillsdale, NJ: Erlbaum.

Battalio, R. C., Kagel, J. H., & Jiranyakul, K. (1990). Testing between alternative models of choice under uncertainty: Some initial results. *Journal of Risk and Uncertainty*, 3, 25–50.

Bazerman, M. H., & Carroll, J. S. (1987). Negotiator cognition. *Research in Organizational Behavior*, 9, 247–288.

Bazerman, M. H., & Neale, M. A. (1992). *Negotiating rationally*. New York: Free Press.

Beach, L. R. (1974). A note on the intrasubject similarity of subjective probabilities obtained by estimates and by bets. *Organizational Behavior and Human Performance*, 11, 250–252.

Beach, L. R., Beach, B. H., Carter, W. B., & Barclay, S. (1974). Five studies of subjective equivalence. *Organizational Behavior and Human Performance*, 12, 351–371.

Beach, L. R., Christensen-Szalanski, J. J. J., & Barnes, V. E. (1987). Assessing human judgment: Has it been done, can it be done, should it be done? In G. Wright and P. Ayton (Eds.), *Judgmental forecasting*. London: John Wiley.

Beach, L. R., & Mitchell, T. R. (1978). A contingency model for the selection of decision strategies. *Academy of Management Review*, 3, 439–449.

Beach, L. R., & Mitchell, T. R. (1987). Image theory: Principles, plans, and goals in decision making. *Acta Psychologica, 66,* 201–220.

Beach, L. R., & Phillips, L. D. (1967). Subjective probabilities inferred from estimates and bets. *Journal of Experimental Psychology, 75,* 354–359.

Beach, L. R., & Solak, F. (1969). Subjective judgments of acceptable error. *Organizational Behavior and Human Performance, 4,* 242–251.

Beach, L. R., & Wise, J. A. (1969a). Subjective probability and decision strategy. *Journal of Experimental Psychology, 79*(1, Pt. 1), 133–138.

Beach, L. R., & Wise, J. A. (1969b). Subjective probability revision and subsequent decisions. *Journal of Experimental Psychology, 81,* 561–565.

Beattie, J., & Barlas, S. (1993). Predicting perceived differences in tradeoff difficulty. Unpublished manuscript.

Becker, G. M., & McClintock, C. G. (1967). Value: Behavioral decision theory. *Annual Review of Psychology, 18,* 239–286.

Becker, G. S. (1976). *The economic approach to human behavior.* Chicago: University of Chicago Press.

Becker, J. L., & Sarin, R. K. (1987). Lottery dependent utility. *Management Science, 33,* 1367–1382.

Becker, J. L., & Sarin, R. K. (1989). Decision analysis using lottery dependent utility. *Journal of Risk and Uncertainty, 2,* 105–117.

Beckmann, J., & Gollwitzer, P. M. (1987). Deliberative versus implementational states of mind: The issue of impartiality in predecisional and postdecisional information processing. *Social Cognition, 5,* 259–279.

Ben Zur, H., & Bresnitz, S. J. (1981). The effects of time pressure on risky choice behavior. *Acta Psychologica, 47,* 89–104.

Berkeley, D., & Humphreys, P. (1982). Structuring decision problems and the "bias heuristic." *Acta Psychologica, 50,* 201–252.

Bernoulli, D. (1738). Specimen theoriae novae de mensura sortis. *Commentarii Academiae Scientarum Imperialis Petropolitanae, 5,* 175–192. (English translation by L. Sommer (1954). Exposition of a new theory on the measurement of risk. *Econometrica, 22,* 23–36.)

Bernoulli, J. (1713). *Ars Conjectandi.* Basel.

Bies, R. J., Tripp, T. M., & Neale, M. A. (1993). Procedural fairness and profit seeking: The perceived legitimacy of market exploitation. *Journal of Behavioral Decision Making, 6,* 243–256.

Birnbaum, M. H. (1992). Violations of monotonicity and contextual effects in choice-based certainty equivalents. *Psychological Science, 3,* 310–314.

Birnbaum, M. H., Coffey, G., Mellers, B. A., & Weiss, R. (1992). Utility measurement: Configural-weight theory and the judge's point of view. *Journal of Experimental Psychology: Human Perception and Performance, 18,* 331–346.

Birnbaum, M. H., & Stegner, S. E. (1981). Measuring the importance of cues in judgment for individuals: Subjective theories of IQ as a function of hereditiy and environment. *Journal of Experimental Social Psychology, 17,* 159–182.

Birnbaum, M. H., & Sutton, S. E. (1992). Scale convergence and utility measurement. *Organizational Behavior and Human Decision Processes, 52,* 183–215.

Bjorkman, M., & Nilsson, R. (1982). Prediction and diagnosis: An experimental comparison. *Scandinavian Journal of Psychology, 17,* 17–22.

Blaney, P. H. (1986). Affect and memory: A review. *Psychological Bulletin, 99,* 229–246.

Blount, S. (1995). When social outcomes aren't fair: The effect of causal attributions on preferences. *Organizational Behavior and Human Decision Processes, 63*, 131–144.

Boles, T. L., & Messick, D. M. (1995). A reverse outcome bias: The influence of multiple reference points on the evaluation of outcomes and decisions. *Organizational Behavior and Human Decision Processes, 61*, 262–275.

Bornstein, R. F. (1989). Exposure and affect: Overview and meta-analysis of research, 1968–1987. *Psychological Bulletin, 106*, 265–289.

Bower, G. H. (1981). Mood and memory. *American Psychologist, 36*, 129–148.

Bowman, E. H. (1963). Consistency and optimality in managerial decision making. *Management Science, 9*, 310–321.

Brehmer, B. (1969). Cognitive dependence on additive and configural cue-criterion relations. *American Journal of Psychology, 82*, 490–503.

Brehmer, B. (1973). Effects of cue validity on interpersonal learning of inference tasks with linear and nonlinear cues. *Americal Journal of Psychology, 86*, 29–48.

Brehmer, B. (1974a). Hypotheses about relations between scaled variables in the learning of probabilistic inference tasks. *Organizational Behavior and Human Performance, 11*, 1–27.

Brehmer, B. (1974b). The effect of cue intercorrelation on interpersonal learning in probabilistic inference tasks. *Organizational Behavior and Human Performance, 12*, 397–412.

Brehmer, B. (1976). Social judgment theory and the analysis of interpersonal conflict. *Psychological Bulletin, 83*, 985–1003.

Brehmer, B. (1980a). In one word: Not from experience. *Acta Psychologica, 45*, 223–241.

Brehmer, B. (1980b). Probabilistic functionalism in the laboratory: Learning and interpersonal (cognitive) conflict. In K. R. Hammond & N. E. Wascoe (Eds.), *Realizations of Brunswik's representative design* (pp. 13–24). San Francisco: Jossey-Bass.

Brehmer, B. (1984). The role of judgment in small-group conflict and decision making. In G. M. Stephenson and J. H. Davis (Eds.), *Progress in Social Psychology* (Vol. 2). New York: Wiley.

Brehmer, B. (1988). The development of social judgment theory. In B. Brehmer & C. R. B. Joyce (Eds.). (1988). *Human judgment: The SJT view* (pp. 13–40). Amsterdam: Elsevier Science Publishers B.V. (North-Holland).

Brehmer, B., & Joyce, C. R. B. (Eds.). (1988). *Human judgment: The SJT view*. Amsterdam: Elsevier Science Publishers B.V. (North-Holland).

Brehmer, B., Kuylenstierna, J., & Liljergren, J. (1974). Effects of function form and cue validity on the subjects' hypotheses in probabilistic inference tasks. *Organizational Behavior and Human Performance, 11*, 338–354.

Brinberg, D., & Jaccard, J. (Eds.). (1988). *Dyadic decision making*. New York: Springer-Verlag.

Bruner, J. S., Goodnow, J. J., & Austin, G. A. (1956). *A study of thinking*. New York: Wiley.

Brunswik, E. (1952). *The conceptual framework of psychology*. Chicago: Unversity of Chicago Press. (*International encyclopedia of unified science*, Vol. I, No. 10.)

Brunswik, E. (1956). *Perception and the representative design of psychological experiments* (2nd ed.). Berkeley and Los Angeles: University of California Press.

Brunswik, E. (1957). Scope and aspects of the cognitive problem. In H. E. Gruber, K. R. Hammond, & R. Jessor (Eds.), *Contemporary approaches to cognition: A symposium held at the University of Colorado* (pp. 5–31). Cambridge: Harvard University Press.

Budescu, D. V., & Weiss, W. (1987). Reflection of transitive and intransitive preferences: A test of prospect theory. *Organizational Behavior and Human Decision Processes, 39*, 184–202.

Busemeyer, J. R. (1985). Decision making under uncertainty: A comparison of simple scalability, fixed-sample, and sequential-sampling models. *Journal of Experimental Psychology: Learning, Memory, and Cognition, 11*, 538–564.

Busemeyer, J. R., Forsyth, B., & Nozawa, G. (1988). Comparisons of elimination by aspects and suppression of aspects choice models based on choice response time. *Journal of Mathematical Psychology, 32*, 341–349.

Busemeyer, J. R., & Townsend, J. T. (1993). Decision field theory: A dynamic-cognitive approach to decision making in an uncertain environment. *Psychological Review, 100*, 432–459.

Camerer, C. F. (1989). An experimental test of several generalized utility theories. *Journal of Risk and Uncertainty, 2*, 61–104.

Camerer, C. F. (1992). Recent tests of generalizations of expected utility theory. In W. Edwards (Ed.), *Utility theories: Measurements and applications* (pp. 207–251). Boston: Kluwer Academic.

Camerer, C. F., & Ho, T.-H. (1994). Violations of the betweenness axiom and nonlinearity in probability. *Journal of Risk and Uncertainty, 8*, 167–196.

Camerer, C. F., & Johnson, E. J. (1991). The process-performance paradox in expert judgment: How can experts know so much and predict so badly? In K. A. Ericsson & J. Smith (Eds.), *Toward a general theory of expertise: Prospects and limits* (pp. 195–217). Cambridge: Cambridge University Press.

Camerer, C. F., & Kunreuther, H. (1989). Experimental markets for insurance. *Journal of Risk and Uncertainty, 2*, 265–300.

Camerer, C. F., Loewenstein, G., & Weber, M. (1989). The curse of knowledge in economic settings: An experimental analysis. *Journal of Political Economy, 97*, 1232–1254.

Carnevale, P. J. D., & Isen, A. M. (1986). The influence of positive affect and visual access on the discovery of integrative solutions in bilateral negotiations. *Organizational Behavior and Human Decision Processes, 37*, 1–13.

Carroll, J. S., Bazerman, M. H., & Maury, R. (1988). Negotiator cognition: A descriptive approach to negotiators understanding their opponents. *Organizational Behavior and Human Decision Processes, 41*, 352–370.

Casey, J. T., Gettys, C. F., Pliske, R. M., & Mehle, T. (1984). A partition of small group predecision performance into informational and social components. *Organizational Behavior and Human Performance, 34*, 112–139.

Chapman, G. B. (1991). Trial order affects cue interaction in contingency judgment. *Journal of Experimental Psychology: Learning, Memory, and Cognition, 17*, 837–854.

Chapman, G. B., & Robbins, S. I. (1990). Cue interaction in human contingency judgment. *Memory and Cognition, 18*, 537–545.

Chapman, L. J., & Chapman, J. P. (1967). Genesis of popular but erroneous diagnostic observations. *Journal of Abnormal Psychology, 72*, 193–204.

Chapman, L. J., & Chapman, J. P. (1969). Illusory correlation as an obstacle to the use of valid psychodiagnostic signs. *Journal of Abnormal Psychology, 74*, 271–280.

Cheng, P. W., & Novick, L. R. (1990). A probabilistic contrast model of causal induction. *Journal of Personality and Social Psychology, 58*, 545–567.

Cheng, P. W., & Novick, L. R. (1991). Causes versus enabling conditions. *Cognition, 40*, 83–120.

Cheng, P. W., & Novick, L. R. (1992). Covariation in natural causal induction. *Psychological Review, 99,* 365–382.

Chew, S. H. (1983). A generalization of the quasi-linear mean with applications to the measurement of income inequality and decision theory resolving the Allais paradox. *Econometrica, 57,* 1065–1092.

Chew, S. H., Karni, E., & Safra, Z. (1987). Risk aversion in the theory of expected utility with rank dependent probabilities. *Journal of Economic Theory, 42,* 370–381.

Chomsky, N. (1959). Review of Skinner's *Verbal behavior. Language, 35,* 26–58.

Christensen-Szalanski, J. J. J., & Beach, L. R. (1984). The citation bias: Fad and fashion in the judgment and decision literature. *American Psychologist, 39,* 75–78.

Clark, M. S., & Fiske, S. T. (Eds.). (1982). *Affect and cognition: The 17th annual Carnegie symposium on cognition.* Hillsdale, NJ: Erlbaum.

Clore, G. L. (1992). Cognitive phenomenology: Feelings and the construction of judgment. In L. L. Martin & A. Tesser (Eds.), *The construction of social judgments* (pp. 133–163). Hillsdale, NJ: Erlbaum.

Coleman, J. S. (1986). *Individual interests and collective action.* Cambridge: Cambridge University Press.

Coombs, C. H., & Beardslee, D. (1954). On decision-making under uncertainty. In R. M. Thrall, C. H. Coombs, & R. L. Davis (Eds.), *Decision processes* (pp. 255–285). New York: Wiley.

Coombs, C. H., & Komorita, S. S. (1958). Measuring utility of money through decisions. *American Journal of Psychology, 71,* 383–389.

Crocker, J. (1981). Judgment of covariation by social perceivers. *Psychological Bulletin, 90,* 272–292.

Crocker, O. L. K., Mitchell, T. R., & Beach, L. R. (1978). A further examination of equivalence intervals. *Organizational Behavior and Human Performance, 22,* 253–261.

Curley, S. P., & Yates, J. F. (1985). The center and range of the probability interval as factors affecting ambiguity preferences. *Organizational Behavior and Human Decision Processes, 36,* 273–287.

Curley, S. P., & Yates, J. F. (1989). An empirical evaluation of descriptive models of ambiguity reactions in choice situations. *Journal of Mathematical Psychology, 33,* 397–427.

Curley, S. P., Yates, J. F., & Abrams, R. A. (1986). Psychological sources of ambiguity avoidance. *Organizational Behavior and Human Decision Processes, 38,* 230–256.

Daniels, R. L., & Keller, L. R. (1990). An experimental evaluation of the descriptive validity of lottery dependent utility theory. *Journal of Risk and Uncertainty, 3,* 115–134.

Daston, L. (1988). *Classical probability in the Enlightenment.* Princeton, NJ: Princeton University Press.

Davidson, D., & Marschak, J. (1959). Experimental tests of a stochastic decision theory. In C. W. Churchman & P. Ratoosh (Eds.), *Measurement: Definitions and theories.* New York: Wiley.

Davidson, D., Suppes, P., & Siegel, S. (1957). *Decision making: An experimental approach.* Stanford, CA: Stanford University Press.

Dawes, R. M. (1971). A case study of graduate admissions: Application of three principles of human decision making. *American Psychologist, 26,* 180–188.

Dawes, R. M. (1975). The mind, the model, and the task. In F. Restle, R. M. Shiffrin, N. J. Castellan, H. R. Lindman, & D. B. Pisoni (Eds.), *Cognitive theory* (Vol. 1, pp. 119–129). Hillsdale, NJ: Erlbaum.

Dawes, R. M. (1979). The robust beauty of improper linear models in decision making. *American Psychologist, 34,* 571–582.

Dawes, R. M. (1980). Social dilemmas. *Annual Review of Psychology, 31,* 169–193.

Dawes, R. M. (1991). Social dilemmas, economic self-interest, and evolutionary theory. In D. R. Brown & J. E. K. Smith (Eds.), *Frontiers in mathematical psychology* (pp. 53–79). New York: Springer-Verlag.

Dawes, R. M., & Corrigan, B. (1974). Linear models in decision making. *Psychological Bulletin, 81,* 95–106.

Dawes, R. M., Faust, D., & Meehl, P. E. (1989). Clinical versus actuarial judgment. *Science, 243,* 1668–1674.

Dawes, R. M., van de Kragt, A. J. C., Orbell, J. M. (1988). Not me or thee but we: The importance of group identity in eliciting cooperation in dilemma situations: Experimental manipulations. *Acta Psychologica, 68,* 83–97.

Deane, D. H., Hammond, K. R., & Summers, D. A. (1972). Acquisition and application of knowledge in complex inference tasks. *Journal of Experimental Psychology, 92,* 20–26.

de Finetti, B. (1937/1980). Foresight: Its logical laws, its subjective sources. In H. E. Kyburg, Jr. & H. E. Smokler (Eds.), *Studies in subjective probability.* Huntington, NY: Krieger. (Originally published as "La prévision: Ses lois logiques, ses sources subjectives," *Ann. Inst. H. Poincaré,* 1937, 7, 1–68.)

Dekel, E. (1986). An axiomatic characterization of preferences under uncertainty: Weakening the independence axiom. *Journal of Economic Theory, 40,* 304–318.

Dellarosa, D., & Bourne, L. E., Jr. (1984). Decisions and memory: Differential retrievability of consistent and contradictory evidence. *Journal of Verbal Learning and Verbal Behavior, 23,* 669–682.

Doherty, M. E., & Brehmer, B. (1997). The paramorphic representation of clinical judgment: A thirty year retrospective. In W. M. Goldstein & R. M. Hogarth (Eds.), *Research on Judgment and Decision Making: Currents. Connections, and Controversies* (pp. 537–551). Cambridge: Cambridge University Press.

Doherty, M. E., Mynatt, C. R., Tweney, R. D., & Schiavo, M. D. (1979). Pseudodiagnosticity. *Acta Psychologica, 43,* 111–121.

Dreben, E. K., Fiske, S. T., & Hastie, R. (1979). The independence of evaluative and item information: Impression and recall order effects in behavior-based impression formation. *Journal of Personality and Social Psychology, 37,* 1758–1768.

DuCharme, W. M., & Donnell, M. L. (1973). Intrasubject comparison of four response modes for "subjective probability" assessment. *Organizational Behavior and Human Performance, 10,* 108–117.

Dudycha, A. L., Dumoff, M. G., & Dudycha, L. W. (1973). Choice behavior in dynamic environments. *Organizational Behavior and Human Performance, 9,* 323–338.

Dudycha, L. W., & Naylor, J. C. (1966). Characteristics of the human inference process in complex choice behavior situations. *Organizational Behavior and Human Performance, 1,* 110–128.

Edgell, S. E. (1978). Configural information processing in two-cue probability learning. *Organizational Behavior and Human Performance, 22,* 404–416.

Edwards, W. (1953). Probability-preferences in gambling. *American Journal of Psychology, 66,* 349–364.

Edwards, W. (1954a). The theory of decision making. *Psychological Bulletin, 51,* 380–417. [Reprinted in W. Edwards and A. Tversky (Eds.). (1967) *Decision making* (pp. 13–64). Harmondsworth, Middlesex, England: Penguin. Pagination for quotation is taken from the reprinted article.]

Edwards, W. (1954b). Probability preferences among bets with differing expected values. *American Journal of Psychology, 67,* 56–67.

Edwards, W. (1954c). The reliability of probability preferences. *American Journal of Psychology, 67,* 68–95.

Edwards, W. (1955). The prediction of decisions among bets. *Journal of Experimental Psychology, 50,* 201–214.

Edwards, W. (1961). Behavioral decision theory. *Annual Review of Psychology, 12,* 473–498.

Edwards, W. (1962a). Subjective probabilities inferred from decisions. *Psychological Review, 69,* 109–135.

Edwards, W. (1962b). Utility, subjective probability, their interaction, and variance preferences. *Journal of Conflict Resolution, 6,* 42–51.

Edwards, W. (1968). Conservatism in human information processing. In B. Kleinmuntz (Ed.), *Formal representation of human judgment* (pp. 17–52). New York: Wiley.

Edwards, W. (Ed.). (1992). *Utility theories: Measurements and applications.* Boston: Kluwer Academic Publishers.

Einhorn, H. J. (1971). Use of nonlinear, noncompensatory models as a function of task and amount of information. *Organizational Behavior and Human Performance, 6,* 1–27.

Einhorn, H. J. (1980a). Overconfidence in judgment. In R. A. Shweder & D. W. Fiske (Eds.), *New directions for methodology of social and behavioral science: Vol. 4. Fallible judgment in behavioral research* (pp. 1–16.) San Francisco: Jossey-Bass.

Einhorn, H. J. (1980b). Learning from experience and suboptimal rules in decision making. In T. S. Wallsten (Ed.), *Cognitive processes in choice and decision behavior* (pp. 1–20). Hillsdale, NJ: Erlbaum.

Einhorn, H. J., & Hogarth, R. M. (1975). Unit weighting schemes for decision making. *Organizational Behavior and Human Performance, 13,* 171–192.

Einhorn, E. J., & Hogarth, R. M. (1978). Confidence in judgment: Persistence of the illusion of validity. *Psychological Review, 85,* 395–416.

Einhorn, H. J., & Hogarth, R. M. (1981). Behavioral decision theory: Processes of judgment and choice. *Annual Review of Psychology, 32,* 53–88.

Einhorn, H. J., & Hogarth, R. M. (1982). Prediction, diagnosis, and causal thinking in forecasting. *Journal of Forecasting, 1,* 23–36.

Einhorn, H. J., & Hogarth, R. M. (1985). Ambiguity and uncertainty in probabilistic inference. *Psychological Review, 92,* 433–461.

Einhorn, H. J., & Hogarth, R. M. (1986a). Decision making under ambiguity. *Journal of Business, 59,* S225–S250.

Einhorn, H. J., & Hogarth, R. M. (1986b). Judging probable cause. *Psychological Bulletin, 99,* 3–19.

Einhorn, H. J., Kleinmuntz, D. N., & Kleinmuntz, B. (1979). Linear regression *and* process-tracing models of judgment. *Psychological Review, 86,* 465–485.

Ellsberg, D. (1961). Risk, ambiguity, and the Savage axioms. *Quarterly Journal of Economics, 75,* 643–669.

Elster, J. (Ed.). (1986). *Rational choice.* New York: New York University Press.

Englander, T., Farago, K., Slovic, P., & Fischhoff, B. (1986). A comparative analysis of risk perception in Hungary and the United States. *Social Behavior, 1,* 55–66.

Ericsson, K. A., & Simon, H. A. (1980). Verbal reports as data. *Psychological Review, 87,* 215–251.

Fazio, R. H., Sanbonmatsu, D. M., Powell, M. C., & Kardes, F. R. (1986). On the automatic activation of attitudes. *Journal of Personality and Social Psychology, 50,* 229–238.

Fiedler, K., & Forgas, J. (Eds.), (1988). *Affect, cognition, and social behavior.* Toronto Hogrefe.

Fischer, G. W., & Hawkins, S. A. (1993). Strategy compatibility, scale compatibility, and the prominence effect. *Journal of Experimental Psychology: Human Perception and Performance, 19,* 580–597.

Fischhoff, B. (1976). Attribution theory and judgment under uncertainty. In J. H. Harvey, W. J. Ickes, & R. F. Kidd (Eds.), *New directions in attribution research* (Vol. 1, pp. 421–452). Hillsdale, NJ: Erlbaum.

Fishburn, P. C. (1982). Nontransitive measurable utility. *Journal of Mathematical Psychology, 26,* 31–67.

Fishburn, P. C. (1983). Transitive measurable utility. *Journal of Economic Theory, 31,* 293–317.

Fishburn, P. C. (1984). SSB utility theory: An economic perspective. *Mathematical Social Sciences, 8,* 63–94.

Fishburn, P. C. 1985. Nontransitive preference theory and the preference reversal phenomenon. *Rivista Internazionale di Scienze Economiche e Commerciali, 32,* 39–50.

Fishburn, P. C. (1988). Expected utility: An anniversary and a new era. *Journal of Risk and Uncertainty, 1,* 267–283.

Fishburn, P. C. (1989a). Foundations of decision analysis: Along the way. *Management Science, 35,* 387–405.

Fishburn, P. C. (1989b). Retrospective on the utility theory of von Neumann and Morgenstern. *Journal of Risk and Uncertainty, 2,* 127–158.

Fishburn, P. C. (1989c). Generalizations of expected utility theories: A survey of recent proposals. In P. C. Fishburn & I. H. LaValle (Eds.), *Choice under uncertainty: Annals of operations research* (Vol. 19, pp. 3–28). Basel, Switzerland: Baltzer.

Fishburn, P. C., & LaValle, I. H. (1988a). The structure of SSB utilities for decision under uncertainty. *Mathematical Social Sciences, 15,* 217–230.

Fishburn, P. C., & LaValle, I. H. (1988b). Context-dependent choice with nonlinear and nontransitive preferences. *Econometrica, 56,* 1221–1239.

Fiske, S. T., & Neuberg, S. L. (1990). A continuum of impression formation, from category-based to individuating processes: Influences of information and motivation on attention and interpretation. *Advances in Experimental Social Psychology, 23,* 1–74.

Ford, J. K., Schmitt, N., Schechtman, S. L., Hults, B. M., & Doherty, M. L. (1989). Process tracing methods: Contributions, problems, and neglected research questions. *Organizational Behavior and Human Decision Processes, 43,* 75–117.

Forgas, J. (Ed.). (1991). *Emotion and social judgment.* Oxford: Pergamon.

Frenkel-Brunswik, E. (1942). Motivation and behavior. *Genetic Psychology Monographs, 26,* 121-265.

Funder, D. C. (1987). Errors and mistakes: Evaluating the accuracy of social judgment. *Psychological Bulletin, 101,* 75–90.

Gettys, C. F., Kelly, C. W., III, & Peterson, C. R. (1973). The best guess hypothesis in multistage inference. *Organizational Behavior and Human Performance, 10,* 364–373.

Gigerenzer, G. (1991). How to make cognitive illusions disappear: Beyond "heuristics and biases." In W. Stroebe & M. Hewstone (Eds.), *European review of social psychology* (Vol. 2, pp. 83–115). London: Wiley.

Gigerenzer, G. (1994). Why the distinction between single-event probabilities and frequences is important for psychology (and vice versa). In G. Wright & P. Ayton (Eds.), *Subjective probability* (pp. 129–161). Chichester: Wiley.

Gigerenzer, G., Hoffrage, U., & Kleinbölting, H. (1991). Probabilistic mental models: A Brunswikian theory of confidence. *Psychological Review, 98,* 506–528.

Gigerenzer, G., Swijtink, Z., Porter, T., Daston, L., Beatty, J., & Krüger, L. (1989). *The empire of chance: How probability changed science and everyday life.* Cambridge: Cambridge University Press.

Gilboa, I. (1987). Expected utility with purely subjective non-additive probabilities. *Journal of Mathematical Economics, 16,* 65–88.

Goldberg, L. R. (1968). Simple models or simple processes? Some research on clinical judgments. *American Psychologist, 23,* 483–496.

Goldberg, L. R. (1970). Man versus model of man: A rationale, plus some evidence, for a method of improving on clinical inferences. *Psychological Bulletin, 73,* 422–432.

Goldstein, W. M. (1990). Judgments of relative importance in decision making: Global vs. local interpretations of subjective weight. *Organizational Behavior and Human Decision Processes, 47,* 313–336.

Goldstein, W. M., & Beattie, J. (1991). Judgments of relative importance in decision making: The importance of interpretation and the interpretation of importance. In D. R. Brown & J. E. K. Smith (Eds.), *Frontiers of mathematical psychology: Essays in honor of Clyde Coombs.* New York: Springer-Verlag.

Goldstein, W. M., & Busemeyer, J. R. (1992). The effect of "irrelevant" variables on decision making: Criterion shifts in preferential choice? *Organizational Behavior and Human Decision Processes, 52,* 425–454.

Goldstein, W. M., & Einhorn, H. J. (1987). Expression theory and the preference reversal phenomena. *Psychological Review, 94,* 236–254.

Goldstein, W. M., Levi, K. R., & Coombs, C. H. (1990). Optimistic and pessimistic decisions: Value-biased use of likelihood information. Unpublished manuscript.

Goldstein, W. M., & Weber, E. U. (1995). Content and discontent: Indications and implications of domain specificity in preferential decision making. In J. R. Busemeyer, R. Hastie, & D. L. Medin (Eds.), *The psychology of learning and motivation: Vol. 32. Decision making from a cognitive perspective* (pp. 83–136). San Diego: Academic Press.

Gollwitzer, P. M. (1990). Action phases and mind-sets. In E. T. Higgins, & R. M. Sorrentino (Eds.), *Handbook of motivation and cognition: Foundations of social behavior* (Vol. 2, pp. 53–92). New York: Guilford Press.

Gollwitzer, P. M., Heckhausen, H., & Steller, B. (1990). Deliberative and implementational mind-sets: Cognitive tuning toward congruous thoughts and information. *Journal of Personality and Social Psychology, 59,* 1119–1127.

Goszczynska, M., Tyszka, T., & Slovic, P. (1991). Risk perception in Poland: A comparison with three other countries. *Journal of Behavioral Decision Making, 4*, 179–193.

Hagafors, R., & Brehmer, B. (1983). Does having to justify one's decisions change the nature of the decision process? *Organizational Behavior and Human Performance, 31*, 223–232.

Hammond, K. R. (1955). Probabilistic functioning and the clinical method. *Psychological Review, 62*, 255–262.

Hammond, K. R. (1965). New directions in research on conflict resolution. *Journal of Social Issues, 21*, 44–66.

Hammond, K. R. (Ed.). (1966a). *The Psychology of Egon Brunswik.* New York: Holt, Rinehart and Winston.

Hammond, K. R. (1966b). Probabilistic functionalism: Egon Brunswik's integration of the history, theory, and method of psychology. In K. R. Hammond (Ed.), *The psychology of Egon Brunswik* (pp. 15–80). New York: Holt, Rinehart and Winston.

Hammond, K. R., & Brehmer, B. (1973). Quasi-rationality and distrust: Implications for international conflict. In L. Rappoport & D. A. Summers (Eds.), *Human judgment and social interaction* (pp. 338–391). New York: Holt, Rinehart and Winston.

Hammond, K. R., Hamm, R. M., Grassia, J., & Pearson, T. (1987). Direct comparison of the efficacy of intuitive and analytical cognition in expert judgment. *IEEE Transactions on Systems, Man, and Cybernetics, SMC-17*, 753–770.

Hammond, K. R., Rohrbaugh, J., Mumpower, J., & Adelman, L. (1977). Social judgment theory: Applications in policy formation. In M. Kaplan & S. Schwartz (Eds.), *Human judgment and decision processes in applied settings* (pp. 1–30). New York: Academic Press.

Hammond, K. R., Stewart, T. R., Brehmer, B., & Steinmann, D. (1975). Social judgment theory. In M. Kaplan & S. Schwartz (Eds.), *Human judgment and decision processes.* New York: Academic Press.

Hammond, K. R., & Summers, D. A. (1965). Cognitive dependence on linear and nonlinear cues. *Psychological Review, 72*, 215–224.

Hammond, K. R., & Wascoe, N. E. (Eds.). (1980). *Realizations of Brunswik's representative design.* San Francisco: Jossey-Bass.

Hammond, K. R., Wilkins, M. M., & Todd, F. J. (1966). A research paradigm for the study of interpersonal learning. *Psychological Bulletin, 65*, 221–232.

Hammond, P. J. (1988). Consequentialist foundations for expected utility. *Theory and Decision, 25*, 25–78.

Hampton, J. (1994). The failure of expected-utility theory as a theory of reason. *Economics and Philosophy, 10*, 195–242.

Hargreaves Heap, S., Hollis, M., Lyons, B., Sugden, R., & Weale, A. (1992). *The theory of choice.* Oxford: Blackwell.

Harmon, J., & Rohrbaugh, J. (1990). Social judgment analysis and small group decision making: Cognitive feedback effects on individual and collective performance. *Organizational Behavior and Human Decision Processes, 46*, 34–54.

Hastie, R. (1991). A review from a high place: The field of judgment and decision making as revealed in its current textbooks. *Psychological Science, 2*, 135–138.

Hastie, R., & Park, B. (1986). The relationship between memory and judgment depends on whether the judgment task is memory-based or on-line. *Psychological Review, 93*, 258–268.

Hastie, R., & Rasinski, K. A. (1988). The concept of accuracy in social judgment. In D. Bar-Tal & A. Kruglanski (Eds.), *The social psychology of knowledge* (pp. 193–208). New York: Cambridge University Press.

Heath, C., & Tversky, A. (1991). Preference and belief: Ambiguity and competence in choice under uncertainty. *Journal of Risk and Uncertainty, 4,* 5–28.

Hicks, J. R., & Allen, R. G. D. (1934). A reconsideration of the theory of value. *Economica, 1*(New Series), 52–76, 196–219.

Higgins, E. T., & Sorrentino, R. M. (Eds.). (1990). *Handbook of motivation and cognition: Foundations of social behavior* (Vol. 2). New York: Guilford Press.

Hoffman, P. J. (1960). The paramorphic representation of clinical judgment. *Psychological Bulletin, 47,* 116–131.

Hoffman, P. J., Slovic, P., & Rorer, L. N. (1968). An analysis-of-variance model for the assessment of configural cue utilization in clinical judgment. *Psychological Bulletin, 69,* 338–349.

Hogarth, R. M. (1974). Process tracing in clinical judgment. *Behavioral Science, 19,* 298–313.

Hogarth, R. M. (1975). Decision time as a function of task complexity. In D. Wendt & C. Vlek (Eds.), *Utility, probability, and human decision making.* Dordrecht, Holland: Reidel.

Hogarth, R. M. (1981). Beyond discrete biases: Functional and dysfunctional aspects of judgmental heuristics. *Psychological Bulletin, 90,* 187–217.

Hogarth, R. M. (Ed.). (1982). *Question framing and response consistency. New directions for methodology of social and behavioral science* (Vol. 11). San Francisco: Jossey-Bass.

Hogarth, R. M. (1987). *Judgement and choice* (2nd ed.). Chichester: Wiley.

Hogarth, R. M. (1993). Accounting for decisions and decisions for accounting. *Accounting, Organizations and Society, 18,* 407–424.

Hogarth, R. M., & Einhorn, H. J. (1990). Venture theory: A model of decision weights. *Management Science, 36,* 780–803.

Hogarth, R. M., Gibbs, B. J., McKenzie, C. R. M., & Marquis, M. A. (1991). Learning from feedback: Exactingness and incentives. *Journal of Experimental Psychology: Learning, Memory, and Cognition, 17,* 734–752.

Hogarth, R. M., & Kunreuther, H. (1985). Ambiguity and insurance decisions. *American Economic Review, 75,* 386–390.

Hogarth, R. M., & Kunreuther, H. (1989). Risk, ambiguity, and insurance. *Journal of Risk and Uncertainty, 2,* 5–35.

Hogarth, R. M., & Kunreuther, H. (1995). Decision making under ignorance: Arguing with yourself. *Journal of Risk and Uncertainty, 10,* 15–36.

Hogarth, R. M., & Reder, M. W. (Eds.). (1987). *Rational choice: The contrast between economics and psychology.* Chicago: University of Chicago Press.

Hovland, C. I., Janis, I. L., & Kelley, H. H. (1953). *Communication and persuasion.* New Haven: Yale University Press.

Hovland, C. I., Mandell, W., Campbell, E. H., Brock, T., Luchins, A. S., Cohen, A. R., McGuire, W. J., Janis, I. L., Feierabend, R. L., & Anderson, N. H. (1957). *The order of presentation in persuasion.* New Haven: Yale University Press.

Huber, J., Payne, J. W., & Puto, C. (1982). Adding asymmetrically dominated alternatives: Violations of regularity and the similarity hypothesis. *Journal of Consumer Research, 9,* 90–98.

Hunt, R. G., Krzystofiak, F. J., Meindl, J. R., & Yousry, A. M. (1989). Cognitive style and decision making. *Organizational Behavior and Human Decision Processes, 44,* 436–453.

Hursch, C. J., Hammond, K. R., & Hursch, J. L. (1964). Some methodological considerations in multiple-cue probability studies. *Psychological Review, 71,* 42–60.

Hurst, P. M., & Siegel, S. (1956). Prediction of decisions from a higher ordered metric scale of utility. *Journal of Experimental Psychology, 52,* 138–144.

Irwin, F. W. (1953). Stated expectations as functions of probability and desirability of outcomes. *Journal of Personality, 21,* 329–335.

Irwin, J. R., McClelland, G. H., & Schulze, D. (1992). Hypothetical and real consequences in experimental auctions for insurance against low-probability risks. *Journal of Behavioral Decision Making, 5,* 107–116.

Isen, A. M. (1993). Positive affect and decision making. In M. Lewis & J. M. Haviland (Eds.), *Handbook of emotions* (pp. 261–277). New York: Guilford Press.

Izard, C. E., Kagan, J., & Zajonc, R. B. (Eds.). (1984). *Emotions, cognition, and behavior.* Cambridge: Cambridge University Press.

Jenkins, H. M., & Ward, W. C. (1965). Judgment of contingency between responses and outcomes. *Psychological Monographs: General and Applied, 79*(1, Whole No. 594), 1–17.

Jennings, S., Amabile, T. M., & Ross, L. (1982). Informal covariation assessment: Database vs. theory-based judgments. In D. Kahneman, P. Slovic, & A. Tversky (Eds.), *Judgment under uncertainty: Heuristics and biases.* Cambridge: Cambridge University Press.

Johnson, B. B. (1991). Risk and culture research. *Journal of Cross-Cultural Psychology, 22,* 141–149.

Johnson, E. J., Payne, J. W., & Bettman, J. R. (1988). Information displays and preference reversals. *Organizational Behavior and Human Decision Processes, 42,* 1–21.

Johnson, E. J., & Tversky, A. (1983). Affect, generalization, and the perception of risk. *Journal of Personality and Social Psychology, 45,* 20–31.

Jorland, G. (1987). The Saint Petersburg paradox 1713–1937. In L. Kruger, L. J. Daston, & M. Heidelberger (Eds.), *The probabilistic revolution, Vol. 1: Ideas in history* (pp. 157–190). Cambridge, MA: MIT Press.

Kagel, J. H., & Levin, D. (1986). The winner's curse and public information in common value auctions. *American Economic Review, 76,* 894–920.

Kahneman, D. (1991). Judgment and decision making: A personal view. *Psychological Science, 2,* 142–145.

Kahneman, D. (1994). New challenges to the rationality assumption. *Journal of Institutional and Theoretical Economics, 150/1,* 18–36.

Kahneman, D., Fredrickson, B. L., Schreiber, C. A., & Redelmeier, D. A. (1993). When more pain is preferred to less: Adding a better end. *Psychological Science, 4,* 401–405.

Kahneman, D., Knetsch, J. L., & Thaler, R. (1986a). Fairness and the assumptions of economics. *Journal of Business, 59,* S285–S300.

Kahneman, D., Knetsch, J. L., & Thaler, R. (1986b). Fairness as a constraint on profit seeking: Entitlements in the market. *The American Economic Review, 76,* 728–741.

Kahneman, D., Knetsch, J. L., & Thaler, R. H. (1990). Experimental tests of the endowment effect and the Coase theorem. *Journal of Political Economy, 98*(6), 1325–1348.

Kahneman, D., Knetsch, J. L., & Thaler, R. H. (1991). The endowment effect, loss aversion, and status quo bias. *Journal of Economic Perspectives, 5,* 193–206.

Kahneman, D., Slovic, P., & Tversky, A. (Eds.). (1982). *Judgment under uncertainty: Heuristics and biases.* Cambridge: Cambridge University Press.

Kahneman, D., & Snell, J. (1990). Predicting utility. In R. M. Hogarth (Ed.), *Insights in decision making: A tribute to Hillel J. Einhorn* (pp. 295–310). Chicago: University of Chicago Press.

Kahneman, D., & Snell, J. (1992). Predicting a changing taste: Do people know what they will like? *Journal of Behavioral Decision Making, 5,* 187–200.

Kahneman, D., & Tversky, A. (1972). Subjective probability: A judgment of representativeness. *Cognitive Psychology, 3,* 430–454.

Kahneman, D., & Tversky, A. (1973). On the psychology of prediction. *Psychological Review, 80,* 237–251.

Kahneman, D., & Tversky, A. (1979). Prospect theory: An analysis of decision under risk. *Econometrica, 47,* 263–291.

Kahneman, D., & Varey, C. A. (1990). Propensities and counterfactuals: The loser that almost won. *Journal of Personality and Social Psychology, 59,* 1101–1110.

Kameda, T., & Davis, J. H. (1990). The function of the reference point in individual and group risk decision making. *Organizational Behavior and Human Decision Processes, 46,* 55–76.

Keller, L. R. (1985). The effects of problem representation on the sure-thing and substitution principles. *Management Science, 31,* 738–751.

Klayman, J. (1988a). On the how and why (not) of learning from outcomes. In B. Brehmer & C. R. B. Joyce (Eds.), *Human judgment: The SJT view* (pp. 115–162). Amsterdam: Elsevier Science Publishers B.V. (North-Holland).

Klayman, J. (1988b). Cue discovery in probabilistic environments: Uncertainty and experimentation. *Journal of Experimental Psychology: Learning, Memory, and Cognition, 14,* 317–330.

Klayman, J., & Ha, Y. (1987). Confirmation, disconfirmation, and information in hypothesis testing. *Psychological Review, 94,* 211–228.

Klayman, J., & Ha, Y. (1989). Hypothesis testing in rule discovery: Strategy, structure and content. *Journal of Experimental Psychology: Learning, Memory, and Cognition, 15,* 596–604.

Kleinmuntz, D. N. (1985). Cognitive heuristics and feedback in a dynamic decision environment. *Management Science, 31,* 680–702.

Knetsch, J. L. (1989). The endowment effect and evidence of nonreversible indifference curves. *American Economic Review, 79,* 1277–1284.

Knowles, B. A., Hammond, K. R., Stewart, T. R., & Summers, D. A. (1972). Positive and negative redundancy in multiple-cue probability tasks. *Journal of Experimental Psychology, 93,* 425–427.

Koele, P. (1980). The influence of labeled stimuli on nonlinear multiple-cue probability learning. *Organizational Behavior and Human Performance, 26,* 22–31.

Krantz, D. H., Luce, R. D., Suppes, P., & Tversky, A. (1971). *Foundations of measurement: Vol. 1. Additive and polynomial representations.* New York: Academic Press.

Krantz, D. H., & Tversky, A. (1971). An exchange on functional and conjoint measurement. *Psychological Review, 78,* 457–458.

Kunda, Z. (1990). The case for motivated reasoning. *Psychological Bulletin, 108,* 480–498.

Kunreuther, H. (1969). Extensions of Bowman's theory on managerial decision-making. *Management Science, 15,* 415–439.

Laestadius, J. E. (1970). Tolerance for errors in intuitive mean estimations. *Organizational Behavior and Human Performance, 5,* 121–124.

Langer, E. J. (1989). *Mindfulness.* Reading, MA: Addison-Wesley.

Laplace, P. S. (1812). *Théorie analytique des probabilités.* Troisième édition, revue et augmentée par l'auteur. Paris: Courcies, 1820. [Reprinted in Laplace (1878–1912), *Oeuvres complètes de Laplace,* Vol. 7. Paris: Gauthier-Villars.]

Larson, J. R., & Reenan, A. M. (1979). The equivalence internal as a measure of uncertainty. *Organizational Behavior and Human Performance, 23,* 49–55.

Levi, I. (1991). Consequentialism and sequential choice. In M. Bacharach & S. Hurley (Eds.), *Foundations of decision theory: Issues and advances* (pp. 92–122). Oxford: Basil Blackwell.

Levy, H. (1992). Stochastic dominance and expected utility: Survey and analysis. *Management Science, 38,* 555–593.

Lichtenstein, M., & Srull, T. (1987). Processing objectives as a determinant of the relationship between recall and judgment. *Journal of Experimental Social Psychology, 23,* 93–118.

Lichtenstein, S., & Slovic, P. (1971). Reversals of preference between bids and choices in gambling decisions. *Journal of Experimental Psychology, 89,* 46–55.

Lichtenstein, S., Slovic, P., & Zink, D. (1969). Effect of instruction in expected value on optimality of gambling decisions. *Journal of Experimental Psychology, 79,* 236–240.

Liebrand, W. B. G., Messick, D. M., & Wilke, H. A. M. (Eds.). (1992). *Social dilemmas: Theoretical issues and research findings.* Oxford, England: Pergamon Press.

Lindell, M. K., & Stewart, T. R. (1974). The effects of redundancy in multiple-cue probability learning. *American Journal of Psychology, 87,* 393–398.

Lindman, H. R. (1971). Inconsistent preferences among gambles. *Journal of Experimental Psychology, 89,* 390–397.

Lindman, H. R., & Lyons, J. (1978). Stimulus complexity and choice inconsistency among gambles. *Organizational Behavior and Human Performance, 21,* 146–159.

Linville, P. W., & Fischer, G. W. (1991). Preferences for separating or combining events. *Journal of Personality and Social Psychology, 59,* 5–21.

Lipe, M. G. (1990). A lens model analysis of covariation research. *Journal of Behavioral Decision Making, 3,* 47–59.

Lipshitz, R. (1989). "Either a medal or a corporal": The effects of success and failure on the evaluation of decision making and decision makers. *Organizational Behavior and Human Decision Processes, 44,* 380–395.

Loewenstein, G., & Thaler, R. H. (1989). Intertemporal choice. *Journal of Economic Perspectives, 3,* 181–193.

Loewenstein, G., Thompson, L., & Bazerman, M. H. (1989). Social utility and decision making in interpersonal contexts. *Journal of Personality and Social Psychology, 57,* 426–441.

Lopes, L. L. (1983). Some thoughts on the psychological concept of risk. *Journal of Experimental Psychology: Human Perception and Performance, 9,* 137–144.

Lopes, L. L. (1984). Risk and distributional inequality. *Journal of Experimental Psychology: Human Perception and Performance, 10,* 465–485.

Lopes, L. L. (1987). Between hope and fear: The psychology of risk. In L. Berkowitz (Ed.), *Advances in experimental social psychology* (Vol. 20, pp. 255–295). San Diego: Academic Press.

Lopes, L. L. (1990). Re-modeling risk aversion: A comparison of Bernoullian and rank dependent value approaches. In George M. von Furstenberg (Ed.), *Acting under uncertainty: Multidisciplinary conceptions* (pp. 267–299). Boston: Kluwer Academic Publishers.

Lopes, L. L. (1991). The rhetoric of irrationality. *Theory and Psychology, 1,* 65–82.

Lopes, L. L. (1995), Algebra and process in the modeling of risky choice. In J. R. Busemeyer, R. Hastie, & D. L. Medin (Eds.), *The psychology of learning and motivation: Vol. 32. Decision making from a cognitive perspective* (pp. 177–220). San Diego: Academic Press.

Luce, R. D. (1988). Rank-dependent, subjective expected-utility representations. *Journal of Risk and Uncertainty, 1,* 305–332.

Luce, R. D. (1990). Rational versus plausible accounting equivalences in preference judgments. *Psychological Science, 1,* 225–234.

Luce, R. D. (1991). Rank- and sign-dependent linear utility models for binary gambles. *Journal of Economic Theory, 53,* 75–100.

Luce, R. D. (1992). Where does subjective expected utility fail descriptively? *Journal of Risk and Uncertainty, 5,* 5–27.

Luce. R. D., & Fishburn, P. C. (1991). Rank- and sign-dependent linear utility models for finite first-order gambles. *Journal of Risk and Uncertainty, 4,* 29–59.

Luce, R. D., Mellers, B. A., & Chang, S.-J. (1993). Is choice the correct primitive? On using certainty equivalents and reference levels to predict choices among gambles. *Journal of Risk and Uncertainty, 7,* 115–143.

Luce, R. D., & Narens, L. (1985). Classification of concatenation measurement structures according to scale type. *Journal of Mathematical Psychology, 29,* 1–72.

Luce, R. D., & Raiffa, H. (1957). *Games and decisions.* New York: Wiley.

Luce, R. D., & von Winterfeldt, D. (1994). What common ground exists for descriptive, prescriptive, and normative utility theories? *Management Science, 40,* 263–279.

Lurie, S. (1987). A parametric model of utility for two-person distributions. *Psychological Review, 94,* 42–60.

McClelland, G., Stewart, B., Judd, C., & Bourne, L. (1987). Effects of choice task on attribute memory. *Organizational Behavior and Human Decision Processes, 40,* 235–254.

McClelland, J. L., & Rumelhart, D. E. (Eds.). (1986). *Parallel distributed processing: Explorations in the microstructure of cognition, Vol. 2: Psychological and biological models.* Cambridge, MA: MIT Press.

MacCrimmon, K. R., & Messick, D. M. (1976). A framework for social motives. *Behavioral Science, 21,* 86–100.

MacCrimmon, K. R., & Wehrung, D. A. (1990). Characteristics of risk taking executives. *Management Science, 36,* 422–435.

MacCrimmon, K. R., Wehrung, D. A., & Stanbury, W. T. (1986). *Taking risks: The management of uncertainty.* New York: Free Press.

Machina, M. J. (1982). "Expected utility" analysis without the independence axiom. *Econometrica, 50,* 1069–1079.

Machina, M. J. (1987a). Decision-making in the presence of risk. *Science, 236,* 537–543.

Machina, M. (1987b). Choice under uncertainty: Problems solved and unsolved. *Journal of Economic Perspectives, 1,* 121–154.

Machina, M. J. (1991). Dynamic consistency and non-expected utility. In M. Bacharach & S. Hurley (Eds.), *Foundations of decision theory: Issues and advances* (pp. 39–91). Oxford: Basil Blackwell.

McKenzie, C. R. M. (1994). The accuracy of intuitive judgment: Covariation assessment and Bayesian inference. *Cognitive Psychology, 26,* 209–239.

Mackinnon, A. J., & Wearing, A. J. (1985). Systems analysis and dynamic decision making. *Acta Psychologica, 58,* 159–172.

Mannix, E. A. (1991). Resource dilemmas and discount rates in decision making groups. *Journal of Experimental Social Psychology, 27,* 379–391.

Mannix, E. A. (1993). Organizations as resource dilemmas: The effects of power balance on coalition formation in small groups. *Organizational Behavior and Human Decision Processes, 55,* 1–22.

Mannix, E. A., & Innami, I. (1993). The effects of argument preparation and timing of first offer on negotiators' cognitions and performance. *Group Decision and Negotiation, 2,* 347–362.

Mannix, E. A., & Loewenstein, G. F. (1993). Managerial time horizons and interfirm mobility: An experimental investigation. *Organizational Behavior and Human Decision Processes, 56,* 266–284.

Mannix, E. A., & Loewenstein, G. F. (1994). The effects of interfirm mobility and individual versus group decision making on managerial time horizons. *Organizational Behavior and Human Decision Processes, 59,* 371–390.

Mannix, E. A., Thompson, L. L., & Bazerman, M. H. (1989). Negotiation in small groups. *Journal of Applied Psychology, 74,* 508–517.

Mannix, E. A., & White, S. B. (1992). The impact of distributive uncertainty on coalition formation in organizations. *Organizational Behavior and Human Decision Processes, 51,* 198–219.

Mano, H. (1990). Anticipated deadline penalties: Effects on goal levels and task performance. In R. M. Hogarth (Ed.), *Insights in decision making: A tribute to Hillel J. Einhorn* (pp. 154–172). Chicago: The University of Chicago Press.

Mano, H. (1994). Risk-taking, framing effects, and affect. *Organizational Behavior and Human Decision Processes, 57,* 38–58.

March, J. G., & Olsen, J. P. (1986). Garbage can models of decision making in organizations. In J. G. March and R. Weissinger-Baylon (Eds.), *Ambiguity and command: Organizational perspectives on military decision making.* Cambridge. MA: Ballinger.

March, J. G., & Shapira, Z. (1982). Behavioral decision theory and organizational decision theory. In G. R. Ungson & D. N. Braunstein (Eds.), *Decision making: An interdisciplinary inquiry* (pp. 92–115). Boston: Kent.

March, J. G., & Shapira, Z. (1987). Managerial perspectives on risk and risk taking. *Management Science, 33,* 1404–1418.

Marks, R. W. (1951). The effect of probability, desirability, and "privilege" on the stated expectations of children. *Journal of Personality, 19,* 332–351.

Martin, L. L., & Tesser, A. (Eds.). (1992). *The construction of social judgments.* Hillsdale, NJ: Erlbaum.

Meehl, P. E. (1954). *Clinical versus statistical prediction: A theoretical analysis and a review of the evidence.* Minneapolis: University of Minnesota Press.

Mellers, B. A. (1982). Equity judgment: A revision of Aristotelian views. *Journal of Experimental Psychology: General, 111,* 242–270.

Mellers, B. A. (1986). "Fair" allocations of salaries and taxes. *Journal of Experimental Psychology: Human Perception and Performance, 12,* 80–91.

Mellers, B. A., & Baron, J. (Eds.). (1993). *Psychological perspectives on justice: Theory and applications.* Cambridge: Cambridge University Press.

Mellers, B. A., Ordóñez, L. D., & Birnbaum, M. H. (1992). A change-of-process theory for contextual effects and preference reversals in risky decision making. *Organizational Behavior and Human Decision Processes, 52,* 331–369.

Mellers, B. A., Weiss, R., & Birnbaum, M. H. (1992). Violations of dominance in pricing judgments. *Journal of Risk and Uncertainty, 5,* 73–90.

Messick, D. M. (1984). Solving social dilemmas: Individual and collective approaches. *Representative Research in Social Psychology, 14,* 72–87.

Messick, D. M., & Allison, S. T. (1987). Accepting unfairness: Outcomes and attributions. *Representative Research in Social Psychology, 17,* 39–51.

Messick, D. M., & Brewer, M. B. (1983). Solving social dilemmas: A review. In L. Wheeler & P. Shaver (Eds.), *Review of personality and social psychology* (Vol. 4). Beverly Hills, CA: Sage.

Messick, D. M., & Liebrand, W. B. G. (1995). Individual heuristics and the dynamics of cooperation in large groups. *Psychological Review, 102,* 131–145.

Messick, D. M., & Mackie, D. M. (1989). Intergroup relations. *Annual Review of Psychology, 40,* 45–81.

Messick, D. M., & Sentis, K. P. (1985). Estimating social and nonsocial utility functions from ordinal data. *European Journal of Social Psychology, 15,* 389–399.

Millar, M. G., & Tesser, A. (1992). The role of beliefs and feelings in guiding behavior: The mismatch model. In L. L. Martin & A. Tesser (Eds.), *The construction of social judgments* (pp. 277–300). Hillsdale, NJ: Erlbaum.

Miller, G. A., Galanter, E., & Pribram, K. H. (1960). *Plans and the structure of behavior.* New York: Holt, Rinehart, & Winston.

Miller, P. McC. (1971). Do labels mislead? A multiple cue study, within the framework of Brunswik's probabilistic functionalism. *Organizational Behavior and Human Performance, 6,* 480–500.

Mitchell, D. J., Russo, J. E., & Pennington, N. (1989). Back to the future: Temporal perspective in the explanation of events. *Journal of Behavioral Decision Making, 2,* 25–38.

Mitchell, T. R., & Beach, L. R. (1990). ". . . Do I love thee? Let me count . . ." Toward an understanding of intuitive and automatic decision making. *Organizational Behavior and Human Decision Processes, 47,* 1–20.

Mitchell, T. R., Rediker, K. J., & Beach, L. R. (1986). Image theory and its implications for organizational decision making. In H. P. Sims & D. A. Gioia (Eds.), *The thinking organization.* San Francisco: Jossey-Bass.

Miyamoto, J. M. (1988). Generic utility theory: Measurement foundations and applications in multiattribute utility theory. *Journal of Mathematical Psychology, 32,* 357–404.

Miyamoto, J. M. (1992). Generic analysis of utility models. In W. Edwards (Ed.), *Utility theories: Measurements and applications* (pp. 73–106). Boston: Kluwer Academic Publishers.

Montgomery, H. (1977). A study of intransitive preferences using a think aloud procedure. In H. Jungermann & G. de Zeeuw (Eds.), *Decision making and change in human affairs* (pp. 347–362). Dordrecht, Holland: Reidel.

Montgomery, H., & Adelbratt, T. (1982). Gambling decisions and information about expected value. *Organizational Behavior and Human Performance, 29,* 39–57.

Morlock, H. C., Jr., & Hertz, K. J. (1964). Effect of the desirability of outcomes on decision making. *Psychological Reports, 14,* 11–17.

Mosteller, F., & Nogee, P. (1951). An experimental measurement of utility. *Journal of Political Economy, 59*, 371–404.

Muchinsky, P. M., & Dudycha, A. L. (1975). Human inference behavior in abstract and meaningful environments. *Organizational Behavior and Human Performance, 13*, 377–389.

Mumpower, J. L., & Hammond, K. R. (1974). Entangled task dimensions: An impediment to interpersonal learning. *Organizational Behavior and Human Performance, 11*, 377–389.

Mynatt, C. R., Doherty, M. E., & Tweney, R. D. (1978). Consequences of confirmation and disconfirmation in a simulated research environment. *Quarterly Journal of Experimental Psychology, 30*, 395–406.

Narens, L., & Luce, R. D. (1986). Measurement: The theory of numerical assignments. *Psychological Bulletin, 99*, 166–180.

Naylor, J. C., & Clark, R. D. (1968). Intuitive inference strategies in interval learning tasks as a function of validity magnitude and sign. *Organizational Behavior and Human Performance, 3*, 378–399.

Naylor, J. C., & Schenck, E. A. (1968). The influence of cue redundancy upon the human inference process for tasks of varying degrees of predictability. *Organizational Behavior and Human Performance, 3*, 47–61.

Neale, M. A., & Bazerman, M. H. (1991). *Cognition and rationality in negotiation.* New York: Free Press.

Neale, M. A., & Bazerman, M. H. (1992). Negotiator cognition and rationality: A behavioral decision theory perspective. *Organizational Behavior and Human Decision Processes, 51*, 157–175.

Neisser, U. (1967). *Cognitive psychology.* Englewood Cliffs, NJ: Prentice-Hall.

Nilsson, R., & Bjorkman, M. (1982). Prediction and diagnosis: Task variable revealed. *Scandinavian Journal of Psychology, 23*, 253–262.

Nisbett, R. E. (Ed.). (1993). *Rules for reasoning.* Hillsdale, NJ: Erlbaum.

Nisbett, R. E., & Borgida, E. (1975). Attribution and the psychology of prediction. *Journal of Personality and Social Psychology, 32*, 932–943.

Nisbett, R. E., Borgida, E., Crandall, R., & Reed, H. (1976). Popular induction: Information is not necessarily informative. In J. S. Carroll & J. W. Payne (Eds.), *Cognition and social behavior* (pp. 113–134). Hillsdale, NJ: Erlbaum.

Nisbett, R. E., & Ross, L. (1980). *Human inference: Strategies and shortcomings of social judgment.* Englewood Cliffs, NJ: Prentice-Hall.

Nisbett, R. E., & Wilson, T. D. (1977). Telling more than we can know: Verbal reports on mental processes. *Psychological Review, 84*, 231–259.

Northcraft, G. B., Neale, M. A., & Earley, P. C. (1994). Joint effects of assigned goals and training on negotiator performance. *Human Performance, 7*, 257–272.

Olshavsky, R. W. (1979). Task complexity and contingent processing in decision making: A replication and extension. *Organizational Behavior and Human Performance, 24*, 300–316.

Payne, J. W. (1973). Alternative approaches to decision making under risk: Moments versus risk dimensions. *Psychological Bulletin, 80*, 439–453.

Payne, J. W. (1976). Task complexity and contingent processing in decision-making: An information search and protocol analysis. *Organizational Behavior and Human Performance, 16*, 366–387.

Payne, J. W. (1982). Contingent decision behavior. *Psychological Bulletin, 92*, 382–402.

Payne, J. W., Bettman, J. R., & Johnson, E. J. (1990). The adaptive decision maker: Effort and accuracy in choice. In R. M. Hogarth (Ed.), *Insights in decision making: A tribute to Hillel J. Einhorn* (pp. 129–153). Chicago: The University of Chicago Press.

Payne, J. W., Bettman, J. R., & Johnson, E. J. (1992). Behavioral decision research: A constructive processing perspective. *Annual Review of Psychology, 43,* 87–131.

Payne, J. W., Bettman, J. R., & Johnson, E. J. (1993). *The adaptive decision maker.* Cambridge: Cambridge University Press.

Payne, J. W., & Braunstein, M. L. (1971). Preferences among gambles with equal underlying distributions. *Journal of Experimental Psychology, 87,* 13–18.

Payne, J. W., & Braunstein, M. L. (1978). Risky choice: An examination of information acquisition behavior. *Memory and Cognition, 5,* 554–561.

Payne, J. W., Braunstein, M. L., & Carroll, J. S. (1978). Exploring predecisional behavior: An alternative approach to decision research. *Organizational Behavior and Human Performance, 22,* 17–44.

Pennington, N., & Hastie, R. (1988). Explanation-based decision making: Effects of memory structure on judgment. *Journal of Experimental Psychology: Learning, Memory, and Cognition, 14,* 521–533.

Peterson, C. R., & Beach, L. R. (1967). Man as an intuitive statistician. *Psychological Bulletin, 68,* 29–46.

Peterson, C. R., Hammond, K. R., & Summers, D. A. (1965). Multiple probability learning with shifting cue weights. *American Journal of Psychology, 78,* 660–663.

Peterson, R. A., Hoyer, W. D., & Wilson, W. R. (Eds.). (1986). *The role of affect in consumer behavior: Emerging theories and applications.* Lexington, MA: Lexington Books, D. C. Heath and Co.

Phillips, L. D., & Wright, G. N. (1977). Cultural differences in viewing uncertainty and assessing probabilities. In H. Jungermann & G. de Zeeuw (Eds.), *Decision making and change in human affairs* (pp. 507–519). Dordrecht, Holland: Reidel.

Pitz, G. F. (1977). Decision making and cognition. In H. Jungermann & G. de Zeeuw (Eds.), *Decision making and change in human affairs* (pp. 403–424). Dordrecht, Holland: Reidel.

Preston, M. G., & Baratta, P. (1948). An experimental study of the auction-value of an uncertain outcome. *American Journal of Psychology, 61,* 183–193.

Pruitt, D. G. (1981). *Negotiation behavior.* New York: Academic Press.

Quiggin, J. (1982). A theory of anticipated utility. *Journal of Economic Behavior and Organization, 3,* 324–343.

Quiggin, J. (1985). Subjective utility, anticipated utility and the Allais paradox. *Organizational Behavior and Human Decision Processes, 35,* 94–101.

Raiffa, H. (1982). *The art and science of negotiation.* Cambridge, MA: Harvard University Press.

Ramsey, F. P. (1931). Truth and probability. In R. B. Braithwaite (Ed.), *The foundations of mathematics and other logical essays by Frank Plumpton Ramsey* (pp. 156–198). London: Kegan Paul, Trench, Trubner & Co.

Ranyard, R. H. (1977). Risky decisions which violate transitivity and double cancellation. *Acta Psychologica, 41,* 449–459.

Ranyard, R. H. (1982). Binary choice patterns and reasons given for simple risky choice. *Acta Psychologica, 52,* 125–135.

Rapoport, A., & Wallsten, T. S. (1972). Individual decision behavior. *Annual Review of Psychology, 23*, 131–176.

Redelmeier, D. A., & Tversky, A. (1990). The discrepancy between medical decisions for individual patients and for groups. *New England Journal of Medicine. 322*, 1162–1164.

Redelmeier, D. A., & Tversky, A. (1992). On the framing of multiple prospects. *Psychological Science, 3*, 191–193.

Reichenbach, H. (1951). *The rise of scientific philosophy*. Berkeley and Los Angeles: University of California Press.

Reilly, B. A., & Doherty, M. E. (1989). A note on the assessment of self-insight in judgment research. *Organizational Behavior and Human Decision Processes. 44*, 123–131.

Reilly, B. A., & Doherty, M. E. (1992). The assessment of self-insight in judgment policies. *Organizational Behavior and Human Decision Processes, 53*, 285–309.

Reyes, R., Thompson, W., & Bower, G. (1980). Judgmental biases resulting from differing availabilities of arguments. *Journal of Personality and Social Psychology, 39*, 2–12.

Ronis, D. L., Yates, J. F., & Kirscht, J. P. (1989). Attitudes, decisions, and habits as determinants of repeated behavior. In A. R. Pratkanis, S. J. Breckler, & A. G. Greenwald (Eds.), *Attitude structure and function* (pp. 213–239). Hillsdale, NJ: Erlbaum.

Rorer, L. G., Hoffman, P. J., Dickman, H. D., & Slovic, P. (1967). Configural judgments revealed. *Proceedings of the 75th Annual Convention of the American Psychological Association, 2*, 195–196.

Rosen, L. D., & Rosenkoetter, P. (1976). An eye fixation analysis of choice and judgment with multiattribute stimuli. *Memory and Cognition, 4*, 747–752.

Ross, L. (1977). The intuitive psychologist and his shortcomings: Distortions in the attribution process. In L. Berkowitz (Ed.), *Advances in experimental social psychology* (Vol. 10, pp. 173–221). New York: Academic Press.

Rumelhart, D. E., & McClelland, J. L. (Eds.). (1986). *Parallel distributed processing: Explorations in the microstructure of cognition. Vol. 1: Foundations*. Cambridge, MA: MIT Press.

Russo, J. E. (1978). Eye fixations can save the world: A critical evaluation and a comparison between eye fixations and other information processing methodologies. In H. K. Hunt (Ed.), *Advances in consumer research* (Vol. 5, pp. 561–570). Ann Arbor, MI: Association for Consumer Research.

Russo, J. E., & Dosher, B. A. (1983). Strategies for multiattribute binary choice. *Journal of Experimental Psychology: Learning, Memory, and Cognition, 9*, 676–696.

Russo, J. E., & Rosen, L. D. (1975). An eye fixation analysis of multi-alternative choice. *Memory and Cognition, 3*, 267–276.

Russo, J. E., Johnson, E. J., & Stephens, D. L. (1989). The validity of verbal protocols. *Memory and Cognition, 17*, 759–769.

Samuelson, W., & Zeckhauser, R. (1988). Status quo bias in decision making. *Journal of Risk and Uncertainty, 1*, 7–59.

Savage, L. J. (1954). *The foundations of statistics*. New York: Wiley.

Savage, L. J. (1972). *The foundations of statistics* (2nd rev. ed.). New York: Dover.

Schkade, D. A., & Johnson, E. J. (1989). Cognitive processes in preference reversals. *Organizational Behavior and Human Decision Processes, 44*, 203–231.

Schmeidler, D. (1989). Subjective probability and expected utility without additivity. *Econometrica, 57*, 571–578.

Schmitt, N., & Dudycha, A. L. (1975). A reevaluation of the effect of cue redundancy in multiple-cue probability learning. *Journal of Experimental Psychology: Human Learning and Memory, 104*, 307–315.

Schneider, S. L. (1992). Framing and conflict: Aspiration level contingency, the status quo, and current theories of risky choice. *Journal of Experimental Psychology: Learning, Memory and Cognition, 18*, 1040–1057.

Schneider, S. L., & Lopes, L. L. (1986). Reflection in preferences under risk: Who and when may suggest why. *Journal of Experimental Psychology: Human Perception and Performance, 12*, 535–548.

Schoemaker, P. J. H. (1979). The role of statistical knowledge in gambling decisions: Moment vs. risk dimension approaches. *Organizational Behavior and Human Performance, 24*, 1–17.

Scott, D., & Suppes, P. (1958). Foundational aspects of theories of measurement. *Journal of Symbolic Logic, 23*, 113–128.

Segal, U. (1989). Axiomatic representation of expected utility with rank-dependent probabilities. *Annals of Operations Research, 19*, 359–373.

Segal, U. (1990). Two-stage lotteries without the reduction axiom. *Econometrica, 58*, 349–378.

Shafir, E. B., Osherson, D. N., & Smith, E. E. (1989). An advantage model of choice. *Journal of Behavioral Decision Making, 2*, 1–23.

Shafir, E. B., Osherson, D. N., & Smith, E. E. (1990). Comparative choice and the advantage model. In K. Borcherding, O. I. Larichev, & D. M. Messick (Eds.), *Contemporary issues in decision making*. New York: Elsevier.

Shafir, E. B., Osherson, D. N., & Smith, E. E. (1993). The advantage model: A comparative theory of evaluation and choice under risk. *Organizational Behavior and Human Decision Processes, 55*, 325–378.

Shafir, E., Simonson, I., & Tversky, A. (1993). Reason-based choice. *Cognition, 49*, 11–36.

Shaklee, H. (1983). Human covariation judgment: Accuracy and strategy. *Learning and Motivation, 14*, 433–448.

Shanteau, J. C. (1974). Component processes in risky decision making. *Journal of Experimental Psychology, 103*, 680–691.

Shanteau, J. C. (1975). An information integration analysis of risky decision making. In M. Kaplan & S. Schwartz (Eds.), *Human judgment and decision processes* (pp. 109–137). New York: Academic Press.

Shanteau, J. C. (1988). Psychological characteristics and strategies of expert decision makers. *Acta Psychologica, 68*, 203–215.

Shanteau, J. C., & Anderson, N. H. (1969). Test of a conflict model for preference judgment. *Journal of Mathematical Psychology, 6*, 312–325.

Shapira, Z. (1995). *Risk taking: A managerial perspective*. New York: Russell Sage Foundation.

Sherif, M., & Hovland, C. I. (1961). *Social judgment: Assimilation and contrast effects in communication and attitude change*. New Haven: Yale University Press.

Showers, C., & Cantor, N. (1985). Social cognition: A look at motivated strategies. *Annual Review of Psychology, 36*, 275–305.

Simon, H. A. (1955). A behavioral model of rational choice. *Quarterly Journal of Economics, 69*, 99–118.

Simon, H. A. (1956). Rational choice and the structure of the environment. *Psychological Review, 63*, 129–138.

Simon, H. A. (1978). Rationality as process and as product of thought. *American Economic Review, 68*, 1–16.

Simon, H. A. (1983). Alternative visions of rationality. In H. A. Simon, *Reason in human affairs* (pp. 7–35). Stanford, CA: Stanford University Press.

Simonson, I. (1989). Choice based on reasons: The case of attraction and compromise effects. *Journal of Consumer Research, 16*, 158–174.

Simonson, I., & Nye, P. (1992). The effect of accountability on susceptibility to decision errors. *Organizational Behavior and Human Decision Processes, 51*, 416–446.

Simonson, I., & Tversky, A. (1992). Choice in context: Tradeoff contrast and extremeness aversion. *Journal of Marketing Research, 29*, 281–295.

Slovic, P. (1966). Value as a determiner of subjective probability. *IEEE Transactions on Human Factors in Electronics, HFE-7*, 22–28.

Slovic, P. (1974). Hypothesis testing in the learning of positive and negative linear functions. *Organizational Behavior and Human Performance, 11*, 368–376.

Slovic, P., Fischhoff, B., & Lichtenstein, S. (1977). Behavioral decision theory. *Annual Review of Psychology, 28*, 1–39.

Slovic, P., & Lichtenstein, S. (1968a). The importance of variance preferences in gambling decisions. *Journal of Experimental Psychology, 78*, 646–654.

Slovic, P., & Lichtenstein, S. (1968b). Relative importance of probabilities and payoffs in risk taking. *Journal of Experimental Psychology, 78*(3, Pt. 2), 1–18.

Slovic, P., & Lichtenstein, S. (1971). Comparison of Bayesian and regression approaches to the study of information processing in judgment. *Organizational Behavior and Human Performance, 6*, 649–744.

Smedslund, J. (1955). *Multiple probability learning*. Oslo: Akademisk Forlag.

Smedslund, J. (1963). The concept of correlation in adults. *Scandinavian Journal of Psychology, 4*, 165–173.

Smith, E. E., Langston, C., & Nisbett, R. E. (1992). The case for rules in reasoning. *Cognitive Science, 16*, 1–40.

Snapper, K. J., & Fryback, D. G. (1971). Inferences based on unreliable reports. *Journal of Experimental Psychology, 87*, 401–404.

Sniezek, J. A. (1986). The role of variable labels in cue probability learning tasks. *Organizational Behavior and Human Decision Processes, 38*, 141–161.

Sniezek, J. A., & Henry, R. A. (1990). Revision, weighting, and commitment in consensus groups judgment. *Organizational Behavior and Human Decision Processes, 45*, 66–84.

Sniezek, J. A., May, D. R., & Sawyer, J. E. (1990). Social uncertainty and interdependence: A study of resource allocation decisions in groups. *Organizational Behavior and Human Decision Processes, 46*, 155–180.

Sorrentino, R. M., & Higgins, E. T. (Eds.). (1986). *Handbook of motivation and cognition: Foundations of social behavior*. New York: Guilford Press.

Staw, B. (1976). Knee-deep in the big muddy: A study of escalating commitment to a chosen course of action. *Organizational Behavior and Human Performance, 16*, 27–44.

Stigler, G. J. (1950). The development of utility theory. *Journal of Political Economy*, Part I, *58*, 307–327; Part II, *58*, 373–396. [Reprinted in G. J. Stigler (Ed.). (1965). *Essays in the history of economics* (pp. 66–155). Chicago: University of Chicago Press.]

Strack, F. (1992). The different routes to social judgments: Experiential versus informational strategies. In L. L. Martin & A. Tesser (Eds.), *The construction of social
judgments* (pp. 249–275). Hillsdale, NJ: Erlbaum.

Summers, D. A. (1969). Adaptation to change in mulitple probability tasks. *American
Journal of Psychology, 82,* 235–240.

Summers, S. A., Summers, R. C., & Karkau, V. T. (1969). Judgments based on different
functional relationships between interacting cues and a criterion. *American
Journal of Psychology, 82,* 203–211.

Suppes, P., & Zinnes, J. L. (1963). Basic measurement theory. In R. D. Luce, R. R. Bush,
& E. Galanter (Eds.), *Handbook of mathematical psychology* (Vol. 1, pp. 1–76). New
York: Wiley.

Surber, C. F. (1985). Measuring the importance of information in judgment: Individual differences in weighting ability and effort. *Organizational Behavior and
Human Decision Processes, 35,* 156–178.

Svenson, O., & Edland, A. (1987). Change of preference under time pressure: Choices
and judgments. *Scandinavian Journal of Psychology, 28,* 322–330.

Svenson, O., & Maule, A. J. (Eds.). (1993). *Time pressure and stress in human judgment
and decision making.* New York: Plenum.

Teigen, K. H., Brun, W., & Slovic, P. (1988). Societal risks as seen by a Norwegian
public. *Journal of Behavioral Decision Making, 1,* 111-130.

Tetlock, P. E. (1985a). Accountability: The neglected social context of judgment and
choice. In B. Staw & L. Cummings (Eds.), *Research in organizational behavior* (Vol.
7, pp. 297–332). Greenwich, CT: JAI Press.

Tetlock, P. E. (1985b). Accountability: A social check on the fundamental attribution
error. *Social Psychology Quarterly, 48,* 227–236.

Tetlock, P. E. (1991). An alternative metaphor in the study of judgment and choice:
People as politicians. *Journal of Theory and Psychology, 1,* 451–475.

Tetlock, P. E., & Boettger, R. (1989). Accountability: A social magnifier of the dilution
effect. *Journal of Personality and Social Psychology, 57,* 388–398.

Tetlock, P. E., & Levi, A. (1982). Attribution bias: On the inconclusiveness of the
cognition-motivation debate. *Journal of Experimental Social Psychology, 18,* 68–
88.

Tetlock, P. E., Skitka, L., & Boettger, R. (1989). Social and cognitive strategies for
coping with accountability: Conformity, complexity, and bolstering. *Journal of
Personality and Social Psychology, 57,* 632–640.

Thaler, R. H. (1980). Toward a positive theory of consumer choice. *Journal of Economic
Behavior and Organization, 1,* 39–60.

Thaler, R. H. (1985). Mental accounting and consumer choice. *Marketing Science, 4,*
199–214.

Thaler, R. H., & Johnson, E. J. (1990). Gambling with the house money and trying to
break even: The effects of prior outcomes on risky choice. *Management Science,
36,* 643–660.

Thompson, L. (1990). Negotiation behavior and outcomes: Empirical evidence and
theoretical issues. *Psychological Bulletin, 108,* 515–532.

Thompson, L., & Hastie, R. (1990). Social perception in negotiation. *Organizational
Behavior and Human Decision Processes, 47,* 98–123.

Thompson, L., & Loewenstein, G. (1992). Egocentric interpretations of fairness and
interpersonal conflict. *Organizational Behavior and Human Decision Processes, 51,*
176–197.

Thompson, L. L., Mannix, E. A., & Bazerman, M. H. (1988). Group negotiation: Effects of decision rule, agenda, and aspiration. *Journal of Personality and Social Psychology*, *54*, 86–95.

Thrall, R. M., Coombs, C. H., & Davis, R. L. (Eds.). (1954). *Decision processes.* New York: Wiley.

Timmermans, D. (1993). The impact of task complexity on information use in multi-attribute decision making. *Journal of Behavioral Decision Making*, *6*, 95–111.

Tindale, R. S. (1989). Groups vs. individual information processing: The effects of outcome feedback on decision making. *Organizational Behavior and Human Decision Processes*, *44*, 454–473.

Todd, F. J. (1954). A methodological study of clinical judgment. Unpublished doctoral dissertation, University of Colorado.

Todd, F. J., & Hammond, K. R. (1965). Differential feedback in two multiple-cue probability learning tasks. *Behavioral Science*, *10*, 429–435.

Tucker, L. R. (1964). A suggested alternative formulation in the developments by Hursch, Hammond, and Hursch, and by Hammond, Hursch, and Todd. *Psychological Review*, *71*, 528–530.

Tversky, A. (1967a). Utility theory and additivity analysis of risky choices. *Journal of Experimental Psychology*, *75*, 27–36.

Tversky, A. (1967b). Additivity, utility and subjective probability. *Journal of Mathematical Psychology*, *4*, 175–202.

Tversky, A. (1969). Intransitivity of preferences. *Psychological Review*, *76*, 31–48.

Tversky, A. (1972). Elimination by aspects: A theory of choice. *Psychological Review*, *79*, 281–299.

Tversky, A., & Edwards, W. (1966). Information versus reward in binary choices. *Journal of Experimental Psychology*, *71*, 680–683.

Tversky, A., & Griffin, D. (1991). Endowment and contrast in judgments of well-being. In F. Strack, M. Argyle, & N. Schwarz (Eds.), *Subjective well-being: An interdisciplinary perspective* (pp. 101–118). Oxford: Pergamon Press.

Tversky, A., & Kahneman, D. (1971). The belief in the "law of small numbers." *Psychological Bulletin*, *76*, 105–110.

Tversky, A., & Kahneman, D. (1973). Availability: A heuristic for judging frequency and probability. *Cognitive Psychology*, *5*, 207–232.

Tversky, A., & Kahneman, D. (1974). Judgment under uncertainty: Heuristics and biases. *Science*, *185*, 1124–1131.

Tversky, A., & Kahneman, D. (1980). Causal schemas in judgment under uncertainty. In M. Fishbein (Ed.), *Progress in social psychology* (pp. 49–72). Hillsdale, NJ: Erlbaum.

Tversky, A., & Kahneman, D. (1981). The framing of decisions and the psychology of choice. *Science*, *211*, 453–458.

Tversky, A., & Kahneman, D. (1986). Rational choice and the framing of decisions. *Journal of Business*, *59*, S251–S278.

Tversky, A., & Kahneman, D. (1992). Advances in prospect theory: Cumulative representation of uncertainty. *Journal of Risk and Uncertainty*, *5*, 297–323.

Tversky, A., Sattath, S., & Slovic, P. (1988). Contingent weighting in judgment and choice. *Psychological Review*, *95*, 371–384.

Tversky, A., & Shafir, E. (1992). Choice under conflict: The dynamics of deferred decision. *Psychological Science*, *3*, 358–361.

Tversky, A., & Simonson, I. (1993). Context-dependent preferences. *Management Science, 39*, 1179–1189

Uleman, J. S., & Bargh, J. A. (Eds.). (1989). *Unintended thought*. New York: Guilford Press.

Varey, C., & Kahneman, D. (1992). Experiences extended across time: Evaluation of moments and episodes. *Journal of Behavioral Decision Making, 5*, 169–185.

von Neumann, J., & Morgenstern, O. (1944, 1947, 1953). *Theory of games and economic behavior* (3 eds.). Princeton: Princeton University Press.

von Winterfeldt, D., & Edwards, W. (1986). *Decision analysis and behavioral research*. Cambridge: Cambridge University Press.

Wagenaar, W. A., Keren, G., & Lichtenstein, S. (1988). Islanders and hostages: Deep and surface structures of decision problems. *Acta Psychologica, 67*, 175–189.

Wakker, P., & Tversky, A. (1993). An axiomatization of cumulative prospect theory. *Journal of Risk and Uncertainty, 7*, 147–176.

Waldmann, M. R., & Holyoak, K. J. (1992). Predictive and diagnostic learning within causal models: Asymmetries in cue competition. *Journal of Experimental Psychology: General, 121*, 222–236.

Wallace, H. A. (1923). What is in the corn judge's mind? *Journal of the American Society of Agronomy, 15*, 300–304.

Wallsten, T. S. (1971). Subjectively expected utility theory and subjects' probability estimates: Use of measurement-free techniques. *Journal of Experimental Psychology, 88*, 31–40.

Wallsten, T. S. (1983). The theoretical status of judgmental heuristics. In R. W. Scholz (Ed.), *Decision making under uncertainty* (pp. 21–37). Amsterdam: North-Holland.

Ward, W. C., & Jenkins, H. M. (1965). The display of information and the judgment of contingency. *Canadian Journal of Psychology, 19*, 231–241.

Wason, P. C. (1960). On the failure to eliminate hypotheses in a conceptual task. *Quarterly Journal of Experimental Psychology, 12*, 129–140.

Wason, P. C., & Johnson-Laird, P. N. (1972). *Psychology of reasoning: Structure and content*. London: Batsford.

Wasserman, E. A., Dorner, W. W., & Kao, S. F. (1990). Contributions of specific cell information to judgments of interevent contingency. *Journal of Experimental Psychology: Learning, Memory, and Cognition, 16*, 509–521.

Weber, E. U. (1994). From subjective probabilities to decision weights: The effect of asymmetric loss functions on the evaluation of uncertain outcomes and events. *Psychological Bulletin, 115*, 228–242.

Weber, E. U., Goldstein, W. M., & Barlas, S. (1995). And let us not forget memory: The role of memory processes and techniques in the study of judgment and choice. In J. R. Busemeyer, R. Hastie, & D. L. Medin (Eds.), *The psychology of learning and motivation: Vol. 32. Decision making from a cognitive perspective* (pp. 33–81). San Diego: Academic Press.

Weber, E. U., Goldstein, W. M., & Busemeyer, J. R. (1991). Beyond strategies: Implications of memory representation and memory processes for models of judgment and decision making. In W. E. Hockley & S. Lewandowsky (Eds.), *Relating theory and data: Essays on human memory in honor of Bennet B. Murdock* (pp. 75–100). Hillsdale, NJ: Erlbaum.

Weber, M., & Camerer, C. (1987). Recent developments in modelling preferences under risk. *OR Spektrum, 9*, 129–151.

Wedell, D. H. (1991). Distinguishing among models of contextually induced preference reversals. *Journal of Experimental Psychology: Learning, Memory, and Cognition, 17*, 767–778.

Weintraub, E. R. (Ed.). (1992). *Toward a history of game theory.* Durham, NC: Duke University Press.

White, S. B. (1994). Testing an economic approach to resource dilemmas. *Organizational Behavior and Human Decision Processes, 58*, 428–456.

White, S. B., & Neale, M. A. (1994). The role of negotiator aspirations and settlement expectancies in bargaining outcomes. *Organizational Behavior and Human Decision Processes, 57*, 303–317.

White, S. B., Valley, K. L., Bazerman, M. H., Neale, M. A., & Peck, S. R. (1994). Alternative models of price behavior in dyadic negotiations: Market prices, reservation prices, and negotiator aspirations. *Organizational Behavior and Human Decision Processes, 57*, 430–447.

Wiggins, N., & Hoffman, P. J. (1968). Three models of clinical judgment. *Journal of Abnormal Psychology, 73*, 70–77.

Wiggins, N., & Kohen, E. S. (1971). Man vs. model of man revisited: The forecasting of graduate school success. *Journal of Personality and Social Psychology, 19*, 100–106.

Wilke, H., Messick, D., & Rutte, C. (Eds.). (1986). *Experimental social dilemmas.* Frankfurt am Main: Verlag Peter Lang.

Wilson, T. D., Dunn, D. S., Kraft, D., & Lisle, D. J. (1989). Introspection, attitude change, and attitude-behavior consistency: The disruptive effects of explaining why we feel the way we do. In L. Berkowitz (Ed.), *Advances in experimental social psychology* (Vol. 22, pp. 287–343). New York: Academic Press.

Wright, G. N., & Phillips, L. D. (1980). Cultural variation in probabilistic thinking: Alternative ways of dealing with uncertainty. *International Journal of Psychology, 15*, 239–257.

Wright, G. N., Phillips, L. D., Whalley, P. C., Choo, G. T., Ng, K. O., Tan, I., & Wisudha, A. (1978). Cultural differences in probabilistic thinking. *Journal of Cross-Cultural Psychology, 9*, 285–299.

Wright, J. C., & Murphy, G. L. (1984). The utility of theories in intuitive statistics: The robustness of theory-based judgments. *Journal of Experimental Psychology: General, 113*, 301–322.

Wright, P. (1974). The harassed decision maker: Time pressure, distraction, and the use of evidence. *Journal of Applied Psychology, 59*, 55–61.

Wright, W. F., & Bower, G. H. (1992). Mood effects on subjective probability assessment. *Organizational Behavior and Human Decision Processes, 52*, 276–291.

Yaari, M. E. (1987). The dual theory of choice under risk. *Econometrica, 55*, 95–115.

Yaniv, I., & Hogarth, R. M. (1993). Judgmental versus statistical prediction: Information asymmetry and combination rules. *Psychological Science, 4*, 58–62.

Yates, J. F. (1990). *Judgment and decision making.* Englewood Cliffs, NJ: Prentice-Hall.

Yates, J. F., & Curley, S. P. (1986). Contingency judgment: Primacy effects and attention decrement. *Acta Psychologica, 62*, 293–302.

Yates, J. F., Zhu, Y., Ronis, D. L., Wang, D.-F., Shinotsuka, H., & Toda, M. (1989). Probability judgment accuracy: China, Japan, and the United States. *Organizational Behavior and Human Decision Processes, 43*, 145–171.

Yates, J. F., & Zukowski, L. G. (1976). Characterization of ambiguity in decision making. *Behavioral Science, 21*, 19–25.

Yntema, D. B., & Torgerson, W. S. (1961). Man–computer cooperation in decisions requiring common sense. *IRE Transactions of the Professional Group on Human Factors in Electronics*, HFE-2(1), 20–26.

Zajonc, R. B. (1980). Feeling and thinking: Preferences need no inferences. *American Psychologist*, 35, 151–175.

Part II
Currents

2   Reason-based choice

Eldar Shafir, Itamar Simonson, and Amos Tversky

The result is that peculiar feeling of inward unrest known as *indecision*. Fortunately it is too familiar to need description, for to describe it would be impossible. As long as it lasts, with the various objects before the attention, we are said to *deliberate*; and when finally the original suggestion either prevails and makes the movement take place, or gets definitively quenched by its antagonists, we are said to *decide* . . . in favor of one or the other course. The reinforcing and inhibiting ideas meanwhile are termed the *reasons* or *motives* by which the decision is brought about.

William James (1890/1981)

My way is to divide half a sheet of paper by a line into two columns; writing over the one *Pro*, and over the other *Con*. Then, during three or four days' consideration, I put down under the different heads short hints of the different motives, that at different times occur to me for or against the measure. When I have thus got them all together in one view, I endeavor to estimate the respective weights . . . find at length where the balance lies . . . And, though the weight of reasons cannot be taken with the precision of algebraic quantities, yet, when each is thus considered, separately and comparatively, and the whole matter lies before me, I think I can judge better, and am less liable to make a rash step; and in fact

Reprinted from *Cognition*, Vol. 49, E. Shafir, I. Simonson, & A. Tversky, "Reason-based choice," pp. 11–36, 1993, with kind permission from Elsevier Science B. V., Amsterdam, The Netherlands.
 This research was supported by US Public Health Service Grant No. 1-R29-MH46885 from the National Institute of Mental Health, by Grant No. 89-0064 from the Air Force Office of Scientific Research and by Grant No. SES-9109535 from the National Science Foundation. The paper was partially prepared while the first author participated in a Summer Institute on Negotiation and Dispute Resolution at the Center for Advanced Study in the Behavioral Sciences, and while the second author was at the University of California, Berkeley. Funds for support of the Summer Institute were provided by the Andrew W. Mellon Foundation. We thank Robyn Dawes for helpful comments on an earlier draft.

I have found great advantage for this kind of equation, in what may be called *moral* or *prudential algebra*.

Benjamin Franklin, 1772 (cited in Bigelow, 1887)

Introduction

The making of decisions, both big and small, is often difficult because of uncertainty and conflict. We are usually uncertain about the exact consequences of our actions, which may depend on the weather or the state of the economy, and we often experience conflict about how much of one attribute (e.g., savings) to trade off in favor of another (e.g., leisure). In order to explain how people resolve such conflict, students of decision making have traditionally employed either formal models or reason-based analyses. The formal modeling approach, which is commonly used in economics, management science, and decision research, typically associates a numerical value with each alternative, and characterizes choice as the maximization of value. Such value-based accounts include normative models, like expected utility theory (von Neumann & Morgenstern, 1947), as well as descriptive models, such as prospect theory (Kahneman & Tversky, 1979). An alternative tradition in the study of decision making, characteristic of scholarship in history and the law, and typical of political and business discourse, employs an informal, reason-based analysis. This approach identifies various reasons and arguments that are purported to enter into and influence decision, and explains choice in terms of the balance of reasons for and against the various alternatives. Examples of reason-based analyses can be found in studies of historic presidential decisions, such as those taken during the Cuban missile crisis (e.g., Allison, 1971), the Camp David accords (Telhami, 1990), or the Vietnam war (e.g., Berman, 1982; Batts & Gelb, 1979). Furthermore, reason-based analyses are commonly used to interpret "case studies" in business and law schools. Although the reasons invoked by researchers may not always correspond to those that motivated the actual decision makers, it is generally agreed that an analysis in terms of reasons may help explain decisions, especially in contexts where value-based models can be difficult to apply.

Little contact has been made between the two traditions, which have typically been applied to different domains. Reason-based analyses have been used primarily to explain non-experimental data, particularly unique historic, legal and political decisions. In contrast, value-based approaches have played a central role in experimental studies of preference and in standard economic analyses. The two approaches, of course, are not incompatible: reason-based accounts may often be translated into formal models, and formal analyses can generally be paraphrased as reason-based accounts. In the absence of a comprehensive theory of choice, both formal models and reason-based analyses may contribute to the understanding of decision making.

Both approaches have obvious strengths and limitations. The formal, value-based models have the advantage of rigor, which facilitates the derivation of testable implications. However, value-based models are difficult to apply to complex, real world decisions, and they often fail to capture significant aspects of people's deliberations. An explanation of choice based on reasons, on the other hand, is essentially qualitative in nature and typically vague. Furthermore, almost anything can be counted as a "reason," so that every decision may be rationalized after the fact. To overcome this difficulty, one could ask people to report their reasons for decision. Unfortunately, the actual reasons that guide decision may or may not correspond to those reported by the subjects. As has been amply documented (e.g., Nisbett & Wilson, 1977), subjects are sometimes unaware of the precise factors that determine their choices, and generate spurious explanations when asked to account for their decisions. Indeed, doubts about the validity of introspective reports have led many students of decision making to focus exclusively on observed choices. Although verbal reports and introspective accounts can provide valuable information, we use "reasons" in the present article to describe factors or motives that affect decision, whether or not they can be articulated or recognized by the decision maker.

Despite its limitations, a reason-based conception of choice has several attractive features. First, a focus on reasons seems closer to the way we normally think and talk about choices. When facing a difficult choice (e.g., between schools, or jobs) we try to come up with reasons for and against each option – we do not normally attempt to estimate their overall values. Second, thinking of choice as guided by reasons provides a natural way to understand the conflict that characterizes the making of decisions. From the perspective of reason-based choice, conflict arises when the decision maker has good reasons for and against each option, or conflicting reasons for competing options. Unlike numerical values, which are easy to compare, conflicting reasons may be hard to reconcile. An analysis based on reasons can also accommodate framing effects (Tversky & Kahneman, 1986) and elicitation effects (Tversky, Sattath, & Slovic, 1988), which show that preferences are sensitive to the ways in which options are described (e.g., in terms of gains or losses), and to the methods through which preferences are elicited (e.g., pricing versus choice). These findings, which are puzzling from the perspective of value maximization, are easier to interpret if we assume that different frames and elicitation procedures highlight different aspects of the options and thus bring forth different reasons to guide decision. Finally, a conception of choice based on reasons may incorporate comparative considerations (such as relative advantages, or anticipated regret) that typically remain outside the purview of value maximization.

In this article, we explore the logic of reason-based choice, and test some specific hypotheses concerning the role of reasons in decision making. The article proceeds as follows. Section 1 considers the role of reasons in choice between equally attractive options. Section 2 explores differential reliance on reasons for and against the selection of options. Section 3 investigates the interaction between high and low conflict and people's tendency to seek other alternatives, whereas section 4 considers the relation between conflict and the addition of alternatives to the choice set. Section 5 contrasts the impact of a specific reason for choice with that of a disjunction of reasons. Section 6 explores the role that irrelevant reasons can play in the making of decisions. Concluding remarks are presented in section 7.

1. Choice between equally attractive options

How do decision makers resolve the conflict when faced with a choice between two equally attractive options? To investigate this question, Slovic (1975) first had subjects equate pairs of alternatives, and later asked them to make choices between the equally valued alternatives in each pair. One pair, for example, were gift packages consisting of a combination of cash and coupons. For each pair, one component of one alternative was missing, as shown below, and subjects were asked to determine the value of the missing component that would render the two alternatives equally attractive. (In the following example, the value volunteered by the subject may be, say, $10.)

	Gift package A	Gift package B
Cash	—	$20
Coupon book worth	$32	$18

A week later, subjects were asked to choose between the two equated alternatives. They were also asked, independently, which dimension – cash or coupons – they considered more important. Value-based theories imply that the two alternatives – explicitly equated for value – are equally likely to be selected. In contrast, in the choice between gift packages above, 88% of the subjects who had equated these alternatives for value then proceeded to choose the alternative that was higher on the dimension that the subject considered more important.

As Slovic (1975, 1990) suggests, people seem to be following a choice mechanism that is easy to explain and justify: choosing according to the more important dimension provides a better reason for choice than, say, random selection, or selection of the right-hand option. Slovic (1975) replicated the above pattern in numerous domains, including choices between college applicants, auto tires, baseball players, and routes to work. (For additional data and a discussion of elicitation procedures, see Tversky et al., 1988.) All the results were consistent with the hypothesis that people do not choose between the equated alternatives at random. Instead, they resolve the conflict by selecting the alternative that is superior on the more important dimension, which seems to provide a compelling reason for choice.

2. Reasons pro and con

Consider having to choose one of two options or, alternatively, having to reject one of two options. Under the standard analysis of choice, the two tasks are interchangeable. In a binary choice situation it should not matter whether people are asked which option they prefer, or which they would reject. Because it is the options themselves that are assumed to matter, not the way in which they are described, if people prefer the first they will reject the second, and vice versa.

As suggested by Franklin's opening quote, our decision will depend partially on the weights we assign to the options' pros and cons. We propose that the positive features of options (their pros) will loom larger when choosing, whereas the negative features of options (their cons) will be weighted more heavily when rejecting. It is natural to select an option because of its positive features, and to reject an option because of its negative features. To the extent that people base their decisions on reasons for and against the options under consideration, they are likely to focus on reasons for choosing an option when deciding which to choose, and to focus on reasons for rejecting an option when deciding which to reject. This hypothesis leads to a straightforward prediction: consider two options, an *enriched* option, with more positive and more negative features, and an *impoverished* option, with fewer positive and fewer negative features. If positive features are weighted more heavily when choosing than when rejecting and negative features are weighted relatively more when rejecting than when choosing, then an enriched option could be both chosen and rejected when compared to an impoverished option. Let P_c and P_r denote, respectively, the percentage of subjects who choose and who reject a particular option. If choosing and rejecting are complementary, then the sum $P_c + P_r$ should equal 100. On the other hand, according to the above hypothesis, $P_c + P_r$ should be greater than 100 for the enriched option and less than 100 for the impoverished option. This pattern was observed by Shafir (1993). Consider, for example, the following problem which was presented to subjects in two versions that differed only in the bracketed questions. One half of the subjects received one version, the other half received the other. The enriched option appears last, although the order presented to subjects was counterbalanced.

Problem 1 ($n = 170$):

Imagine that you serve on the jury of an only-child sole-custody case following a relatively messy divorce. The facts of the case are complicated by ambiguous economic, social, and emotional considerations, and you decide to base your decision entirely on the following few observations. [To which parent would you award sole custody of the child?/Which parent would you deny sole custody of the child?]

	Award	Deny
Parent A: average income		
average health		
average working hours		
reasonable rapport with the child		
relatively stable social life	36%	45%
Parent B: above-average income		
very close relationship with the child		
extremely active social life		
lots of work-related travel		
minor health problems	64%	55%

Parent A, the impoverished option, is quite plain – with no striking positive or negative features. There are no particularly compelling reasons to award or deny this parent custody of the child. Parent B, the enriched option, on the other hand, has good reasons to be awarded custody (a very close relationship with the child and a good income), but also good reasons to be denied sole custody (health problems and extensive absences due to travel). To the right of the options are the percentages of subjects who chose to award and to deny custody to each of the parents. Parent B is the majority choice both for being awarded custody of the child and for being denied it. As predicted, $P_c + P_r$ for parent B (64 + 55 = 119) is significantly greater than 100, the value expected if choosing and rejecting were complementary ($z = 2.48$, $p < .02$). This pattern is explained by the observation that the enriched parent (parent B) provides more compelling reasons to be awarded as well as denied child custody.

The above pattern has been replicated in hypothetical choices between monetary gambles, college courses, and political candidates (Shafir, 1993). For another example, consider the following problem, presented to half the subjects in the "prefer" and to the other half in the "cancel" version.

Problem 2 (n = 172):

Prefer:

Imagine that you are planning a week's vacation in a warm spot over spring break. You currently have two options that are reasonably priced. The travel brochure gives only a limited amount of information about the two options. Given the information available, which vacation spot would you prefer?

Cancel:

Imagine that you are planning a week's vacation in a warm spot over spring break. You currently have two options that are reasonably priced, but you can no longer retain your reservation in both. The travel brochure gives only a limited amount of information about the two options. Given the information available, which reservation do you decide to cancel?

		Prefer	Cancel
Spot A:	average weather average beaches medium-quality hotel medium-temperature water average nightlife	33%	52%
Spot B:	lots of sunshine gorgeous beaches and coral reefs ultra-modern hotel very cold water very strong winds no nightlife	67%	48%

The information about the two spots is typical of the kind of information we have available when deciding where to take our next vacation. Because it is difficult to estimate the overall value of each spot, we are likely to seek reasons on which to base our decision. Spot A, the impoverished option, seems unremarkable yet unobjectionable on all counts. On the other hand, there are obvious reasons – gorgeous beaches, an abundance of sunshine, and an ultra-modern hotel – for choosing spot B. Of course, there are also compelling reasons – cold water, winds, and a lack of nightlife – why spot B should be rejected. We suggest that the gorgeous beaches are likely to provide a more compelling reason when we choose than when we reject, and the lack of nightlife is likely to play a more central role when we reject than when we choose. Indeed, spot B's share of being preferred and rejected exceeds that of spot A ($P_c + P_r = 67 + 48 = 115$, $p < .05$). These results demonstrate that options are not simply ordered according to value, with the more attractive selected and the less attractive rejected. Instead, it appears that the relative importance of options' strengths and weaknesses varies with the nature of the task. As a result, we are significantly more likely to end up in spot B when we ask ourselves which we prefer than when we contemplate which to cancel (67% vs. 52%, $z = 2.83$, $p < .001$).

One of the most basic assumptions of the rational theory of choice is the principle of procedure invariance, which requires strategically equivalent methods of elicitation to yield identical preferences (see Tversky et al., 1988, for discussion). The choose–reject discrepancy represents a predictable failure of procedure invariance. This phenomenon is at variance with value maximization, but is easily understood from the point of view of reason-based choice: reasons for choosing are more compelling when we choose than when we reject, and reasons for rejecting matter more when we reject than when we choose.

3. Choice under conflict: seeking options

The need to choose often creates conflict: we are not sure how to trade off one attribute relative to another or, for that matter, which attributes matter to us most. It is a commonplace that we often attempt to resolve such conflict by seeking reasons for choosing one option over another. At times, the conflict between available alternatives is hard to resolve, which may lead us to seek additional options, or to maintain the status quo. Other times, the context is such that a comparison between alternatives generates compelling reasons to choose one option over another. Using reasons to resolve conflict has some non-obvious implications, which are addressed below. The present section focuses on people's decision to seek other alternatives; the next section explores some effects of adding options to the set under consideration.

In many contexts, we need to decide whether to opt for an available option or search for additional alternatives. Thus, a person who wishes to buy a used car may settle for a car that is currently available or continue searching for additional models. Seeking new alternatives usually requires additional time and effort, and may involve the risk of losing the previously available options. Conflict plays no role in the classical theory of choice. In this theory, each option x has a value $v(x)$ such that, for any offered set, the decision maker selects the option with the highest value. In particular, a person is expected to search for additional alternatives only if the expected value of searching exceeds that of the best option currently available. A reliance on reasons, on the other hand, entails that we should be more likely to opt for an available option when we have a convincing reason for its selection, and that we should be more likely to search further when a compelling reason for choice is not readily available.

To investigate this hypothesis, Tversky and Shafir (1992b) presented subjects with pairs of options, such as bets varying in probability and payoff, or student apartments varying in monthly rent and distance from campus, and had subjects choose one of the two options or, instead, request an additional option, at some cost. Subjects first reviewed the entire set of 12 options (gambles or apartments) to familiarize themselves with the available alternatives. In the study of choice between bets some subjects then received the following problem.

Conflict:

Imagine that you are offered a choice between the following two gambles:

(x) 65% chance to win $15
(y) 30% chance to win $35

You can either select one of these gambles or you can pay $1 to add one more gamble to the choice set. The added gamble will be selected at random from the list you reviewed.

Other subjects received a similar problem except that option y was replaced by option x', to yield a choice between the following.

Dominance:

(x) 65% chance to win $15
(x') 65% chance to win $14

Subjects were asked to indicate whether they wanted to add another gamble or select between the available alternatives. They then chose their preferred gamble from the resulting set (with or without the added option). Subjects were instructed that the gambles they chose would be played out and that their payoff would be proportional to the amount of money they earned minus the fee they paid for the added gambles.

A parallel design presented choices between hypothetical student apartments. Some subjects received the following problem.

Conflict:

Imagine that you face a choice between two apartments with the following characteristics:

(x) $290 a month, 25 minutes from campus
(y) $350 a month, 7 minutes from campus

Both have one bedroom and a kitchenette. You can choose now between the two apartments or you can continue to search for apartments (to be selected at random from the list you reviewed). In that case, there is some risk of losing one or both of the apartments you have found.

Other subjects received a similar problem except that option y was replaced by option x', to yield a choice between the following.

Dominance:

(x) $290 a month, 25 minutes from campus
(x') $330 a month, 25 minutes from campus

Note that in both pairs of problems the choice between x and y – the *conflict* condition – is non-trivial because the xs are better on one dimension and the ys are better on the other. In contrast, the choice between x and x' – the *dominance* condition – involves no conflict because the former strictly dominates the latter. Thus, while there is no obvious reason to choose one option over the other in the conflict condition, there is a decisive argument for preferring one of the two alternatives in the dominance condition.

ᶜ On average, subjects requested an additional alternative 64% of the time in the conflict condition, and only 40% of the time in the dominance condition ($p < .05$). Subjects' tendency to search for additional options, in other words, was greater when the choice among alternatives was harder to rationalize, than when there was a compelling reason and the decision was easy.

These data are inconsistent with the principle of value maximization. According to value maximization, a subject should search for additional alternatives if and only if the expected (subjective) value of searching exceeds that of the best alternative currently available. Because the best alternative offered in the dominance condition is also available in the conflict condition, value maximization implies that the percentage of subjects who seek an additional alternative cannot be greater in the conflict than in the dominance condition, contrary to the observed data.

It appears that the search for additional alternatives depends not only on the value of the best available option, as implied by value maximization, but also on the difficulty of choosing among the options under consideration. In situations of dominance, for example, there are clear and indisputable reasons for choosing one option over another (e.g., "This apartment is equally distant and I save $40!"). Having a compelling argument for choosing one of the options over the rest reduces the temptation to look for additional alternatives. When the choice involves conflict, on the other hand, reasons for choosing any one of the options are less immediately available and the decision is more difficult to justify (e.g., "Should I save $60 a month, or reside 18 minutes closer to campus?"). In the absence of compelling reasons for choice, there is a greater tendency to search for other alternatives.

4. Choice under conflict: adding options

An analysis in terms of reasons can help explain observed violations of the principle of independence of irrelevant alternatives, according to which the preference ordering between two options should not be altered by the introduction of additional alternatives. This principle follows from the standard assumption of value maximization, and has been routinely assumed in the analysis of consumer choice. Despite its intuitive appeal, there is a growing body of evidence that people's preferences depend on the context of choice, defined by the set of options under consideration. In particular, the addition and removal of options from the offered set can influence people's preferences among options that were available all along. Whereas in the previous section we considered people's tendency to seek alternatives in the context of a given set of options, in this section we illustrate phenomena that arise through the addition of options, and interpret them in terms of reasons for choice.

A major testable implication of value maximization is that a non-preferred option cannot become preferred when new options are added to the offered set. In particular, a decision maker who prefers *y* over the option to defer the choice should not prefer to defer the choice when both *y* and *x* are available. That the "market share" of an option cannot be increased by enlarging the offered set is known as the *regularity condition* (see Tversky & Simonson, 1993). Contrary to regularity, numerous experimental results indicate that the tendency to defer choice can increase with the addition of alternatives. Consider, for instance, the degree of conflict that arises when a person is presented with one attractive option (which he or she prefers to deferring the choice), compared to two competing alternatives. Choosing one out of two competing alternatives can be difficult: the mere fact that an alternative is attractive may not in itself provide a compelling reason for its selection, because the other option may be equally attractive. The addition of an alternative may thus make the decision harder to justify, and increase the tendency to defer the decision.

A related phenomenon was aptly described by Thomas Schelling, who tells of an occasion in which he had decided to buy an encyclopedia for his children. At the bookstore, he was presented with two attractive encyclopedias and, finding it difficult to choose between the two, ended up buying neither – this, despite the fact that had only one encyclopedia been available he would have happily bought it. More generally, there are situations in which people prefer each of the available alternatives over the status quo but do not have a compelling reason for choosing among the alternatives and, as a result, defer the decision, perhaps indefinitely.

The phenomenon described by Schelling was demonstrated by Tversky and Shafir (1992b) in the following pair of problems, which were presented to two groups of students (*n* = 124 and 121, respectively).

High conflict:

Suppose you are considering buying a compact disk (CD) player, and have not yet decided what model to buy. You pass by a store that is having a 1-day clearance sale. They offer a popular SONY player for just $99, and a top-of-the-line AIWA player for just $169, both well below the list price. Do you?:

(*x*) buy the AIWA player.		27%
(*y*) buy the SONY player.		27%
(*z*) wait until you learn more about the various models.		46%

Low conflict:

Suppose you are considering buying a CD player, and have not yet decided what model to buy. You pass by a store that is having a 1-

day clearance sale. They offer a popular SONY player for just $99, well below the list price. Do you?:

(y) buy the SONY player.   66%
(z) wait until you learn more about the various models.   34%

The results indicate that people are more likely to buy a CD player in the latter, *low-conflict*, condition than in the former, *high-conflict*, situation ($p <$ .05). Both models – the AIWA and the SONY – seem attractive, both are well priced, and both are on sale. The decision maker needs to determine whether she is better off with a cheaper, popular model, or with a more expensive and sophisticated one. This conflict is apparently not easy to resolve, and compels many subjects to put off the purchase until they learn more about the various options. On the other hand, when the SONY alone is available, there are compelling arguments for its purchase: it is a popular player, it is very well priced, and it is on sale for 1 day only. In this situation, having good reasons to choose the offered option, a greater majority of subjects decide to opt for the CD player rather than delay the purchase.

The addition of a competing alternative in the preceding example increased the tendency to delay decision. Clearly, the level of conflict and its ease of resolution depend not only on the number of options available, but on how the options compare. Consider, for example, the following problem, in which the original AIWA player was replaced by an inferior model ($n = 62$).

Dominance:

Suppose you are considering buying a CD player, and have not yet decided what model to buy. You pass by a store that is having a 1-day clearance sale. They offer a popular SONY player for just $99, well below the list price, and an inferior AIWA player for the regular list price of $105. Do you?:

(x′) buy the AIWA player.   3%
(y)   buy the SONY player.   73%
(z)   wait until you learn more about the various models.   24%

In this version, contrary to the previous *high-conflict* version, the AIWA player is dominated by the SONY: it is inferior in quality and costs more. Thus, the presence of the AIWA does not detract from the reasons for buying the SONY, it actually supplements them: the SONY is well priced, it is on sale for 1 day only, *and* it is clearly better than its competitor. As a result, the SONY is chosen more often than before the inferior AIWA was added. The ability of an asymmetrically dominated or relatively inferior alternative, when added to a set, to increase the attractiveness and choice probability of the dominating option is known as the asymmetric dominance effect (Huber, Payne, & Puto, 1982). Note that in both the *high-conflict* and the *dominance* problems subjects were presented with two CD players and an option to delay choice. Subjects' tendency to delay, however, is much greater when they lack clear reasons for buying either player, than when they have compelling reasons to buy one player and not the other ($p < .005$).

The above patterns violate the regularity condition, which is assumed to hold so long as the added alternatives do not provide new and relevant information. In the above scenario, one could argue that the added options (the superior player in one case and the inferior player in the other) conveyed information about the consumer's chances of finding a better deal. Recall that information considerations could not explain the search experiments of the previous section because there subjects reviewed all the potentially available options. Nevertheless, to test this interpretation further, Tversky and Shafir (1992b) devised a similar problem, involving real payoffs, in which the option to defer is not available. Students ($n = 80$) agreed to fill out a brief questionnaire for $1.50. Following the questionnaire, one half of the subjects were offered the opportunity to exchange the $1.50 (the default) for one of two prizes: a metal Zebra pen (henceforth, Zebra), or a pair of plastic Pilot pens (henceforth, Pilot). The other half of the subjects were only offered the opportunity to exchange the $1.50 for the Zebra. The prizes were shown to the subjects, who were also informed that each prize regularly costs a little over $2.00. Upon indicating their preference, subjects received their chosen option. The results were as follows. Seventy-five percent of the subjects chose the Zebra over the payment when the Zebra was the only alternative, but only 47% chose the Zebra *or* the Pilot when both were available ($p < .05$). Faced with a tempting alternative, subjects had a compelling reason to forgo the payment: the majority took advantage of the opportunity to obtain an attractive prize of greater value. The availability of competing alternatives of comparable value, on the other hand, did not present an immediate reason for choosing either alternative over the other, thus increasing the tendency to retain the default option. Similar effects in hypothetical medical decisions made by expert physicians are documented in Redelmeier and Shafir (1993).

In the above study the addition of a competing alternative was shown to increase the popularity of the default option. Recall that the popularity of an option may also be enhanced by the addition of an inferior alternative. Thus, in accord with the asymmetric dominance effect, the tendency to prefer x over y can be increased by adding a third alternative z that is clearly inferior to x but not to y (see Fig. 2.1). The phenomenon of asymmetric dominance was first demonstrated, by Huber, Payne, and Puto (1982), in choices between hypothetical options. Wedell (1991) reports similar findings using monetary gambles. The following example involving real choices is taken from Simonson and Tversky (1992). One group ($n = 106$) was offered a choice between $6 and an elegant Cross pen. The pen was selected by 36% of the subjects, and the remaining 64% chose the cash. A second group ($n = 115$) was given a choice among three options: $6 in cash, the same Cross pen, and

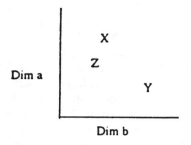

Figure 2.1. A schematic representation of asymmetric dominance. The tendency to prefer x over y can be increased by adding an alternative, z, that is clearly inferior to x but not to y.

a second pen that was distinctly less attractive. Only 2% of the subjects chose the less attractive pen, but its presence increased the percentage of subjects who chose the Cross pen from 36% to 46% ($p < .10$). This pattern again violates the regularity condition discussed earlier. Similar violations of regularity were observed in choices among other consumer goods. In one study, subjects received descriptions and pictures of microwave ovens taken from a "Best" catalogue. One group ($n = 60$) was then asked to choose between an Emerson priced at $110, and a Panasonic priced at $180. Both items were on sale, one third off the regular price. Here, 57% chose the Emerson and 43% chose the Panasonic. A second group ($n = 60$) was presented with these options along with a $200 Panasonic at a 10% discount. Only 13% of the subjects chose the more expensive Panasonic, but its presence increased the percentage of subjects who chose the less expensive Panasonic from 43% to 60% ($p = .05$).[1]

Simonson and Tversky (1992) have interpreted these observations in terms of "trade-off contrast." They proposed that the tendency to prefer an alternative is enhanced or hindered depending on whether the trade-offs within the set under consideration are favorable or unfavorable to that alternative. A second cluster of context effects, called *extremeness aversion*, which refers to the finding that, within an offered set, options with extreme values are relatively less attractive than options with intermediate values (Simonson, 1989). For example, consider two-dimensional options x, y, and z, such that y lies between x and z (see Fig. 2.2). Considerations of value maximization imply that the middle alternative, y, should be relatively less popular in the trinary choice than in either one of the binary comparisons (y compared to x, or y compared to z). Extremeness aversion, on the other hand, yields the opposite prediction because y has small advantages and disadvantages with respect to x and to z, whereas both x and z have more extreme advantages and disadvantages with respect to each other. This pattern was observed in several experiments. For example, subjects

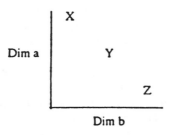

Figure 2.2. A schematic representation of extremeness aversion. Option *y* is relatively more popular in the trinary choice, when both *x* and *z* are available, than in either one of the binary comparisons, when either *x* or *z* is removed.

were shown five 35 mm cameras varying in quality and price. One group ($n = 106$) was then given a choice between two cameras: a Minolta X-370 priced at $170 and a Minolta 3000 i priced at $240. A second group ($n = 115$) was given an additional option, the Minolta 7000 i priced at $470. Subjects in the first group were split evenly between the two options, yet 57% of the subjects in the second group chose the middle option (Minolta 3000 i), with the remaining divided about equally between the two extreme options. Thus, the introduction of an extreme option reduced the "market share" of the other extreme option, but not of the middle option. Note that this effect cannot be attributed to information conveyed by the offered set because respondents had reviewed the relevant options prior to making their choice.

We suggest that both trade-off contrast and extremeness aversion can be understood in terms of reasons. Suppose a decision maker faces a choice between two alternatives, *x* and *y*, and suppose *x* is of higher quality whereas *y* is better priced. This produces conflict if the decision maker finds it difficult to determine whether the quality difference outweighs the price difference. Suppose now that the choice set also includes a third alternative, *z*, that is clearly inferior to *y* but not to *x*. The presence of *z*, we suggest, provides an argument for choosing *y* over *x*. To the extent that the initial choice between *x* and *y* is difficult, the presence of *z* may help the decision maker break the tie. In the pen study, for example, the addition of the relatively unattractive pen, whose monetary value is unclear but whose inferiority to the elegant Cross pen is apparent, provides a reason for choosing the Cross pen over the cash. Similarly, in the presence of options with extreme values on the relevant dimensions, the middle option can be seen as a compromise choice that is easier to defend than either extremes. Indeed, verbal protocols show that the accounts generated by subjects while making these choices involve considerations of asymmetric advantage and compromise; furthermore, asymmetric dominance is enhanced when subjects anticipate having to justify their decisions to others (Simonson, 1989). It is noteworthy that the arguments leading to trade-off contrast and extremeness aversion are comparative in nature; they are based on the positions of the options in the choice set, hence they cannot be readily translated into the values associated with single alternatives.

Tversky and Simonson (1993) have proposed a formal model that explains the above findings in terms of a tournament-like process in which each option is compared against other available options in terms of their relative advantages and disadvantages. This model can be viewed as a formal analog of the preceding qualitative account based on reasons for choice. Which analysis – the formal or the qualitative – proves more useful is likely to depend, among other things, on the nature of the problem and on the purpose of the investigation.

5. Definite versus disjunctive reasons

People sometimes encounter situations of uncertainty in which they eventually opt for the same course of action, but for very different reasons, depending on how the uncertainty is resolved. Thus, a student who has taken an exam may decide to take a vacation, either to reward herself in case she passes or to console herself in case she fails. However, as illustrated below, the student may be reluctant to commit to a vacation while the outcome of the exam is pending. The following problem was presented by Tversky and Shafir (1992a) to 66 undergraduate students.

Disjunctive version:

Imagine that you have just taken a tough qualifying examination. It is the end of the fall quarter, you feel tired and run-down, and you are not sure that you passed the exam. In case you failed you have to take the exam again in a couple of months – after the Christmas holidays. You now have an opportunity to buy a very attractive 5-day Christmas vacation package in Hawaii at an exceptionally low price. The special offer expires tomorrow, while the exam grade will not be available until the following day. Would you?:

(a) buy the vacation package.	32%
(b) not buy the vacation package.	7%
(c) pay a $5 non-refundable fee in order to retain the rights to buy the vacation package at the same exceptional price the day after tomorrow – after you find out whether or not you passed the exam.	61%

The percentage of subjects who chose each option appears on the right. Two additional versions, called *pass* and *fail*, were presented to two different groups of 67 students each. These two versions differed only in the expression in brackets.

Pass/fail versions:

Imagine that you have just taken a tough qualifying examination. It is the end of the fall quarter, you feel tired and run-down, and you find out that you [passed the exam./failed the exam. You will have to take it again in a couple of months – after the Christmas holidays.] You now have an opportunity to buy a very attractive 5-day Christmas vacation package in Hawaii at an exceptionally low price. The special offer expires tomorrow. Would you?:

	Pass	*Fail*
(a) buy the vacation package.	54%	57%
(b) not buy the vacation package.	16%	12%
(c) pay a $5 non-refundable fee in order to retain the rights to buy the vacation package at the same exceptional price the day after tomorrow.	30%	31%

The data show that more than half of the students chose the vacation package when they knew that they passed the exam and an even larger percentage chose the vacation when they knew that they failed. However, when they did not know whether they had passed or failed, less than one third of the students chose the vacation and 61% were willing to pay $5 to postpone the decision until the following day, when the results of the exam would be known.[2] Once the outcome of the exam is known, the student has good – albeit different – reasons for taking the trip: having passed the exam, the vacation is presumably seen as a reward following a hard but successful semester; having failed the exam, the vacation becomes a consolation and time to recuperate before a re-examination. Not knowing the outcome of the exam, however, the student lacks a definite reason for going to Hawaii. Notice that the outcome of the exam will be known long before the vacation begins. Thus, the uncertainty characterizes the actual moment of decision, not the eventual vacation.

The indeterminacy of reasons for going to Hawaii discourages many students from buying the vacation, even when both outcomes – passing or failing the exam – ultimately favor this course of action. Tversky and Shafir (1992a) call the above pattern of decisions a *disjunction effect*. Evidently, a disjunction of different reasons (reward in case of success or consolation in case of failure) is often less compelling than either definite reason alone. A significant proportion of the students above were willing to pay, in effect, for information that was ultimately not going to affect their decision – they would choose to go to Hawaii in either case – but that promised to leave them with a more definite reason for making that choice. The willingness to pay for non-instrumental information is at variance with the classical model, in which the worth of information is determined only by its potential to influence decision.

People's preference for definite as opposed to disjunctive reasons has significant implications in cases where the option to defer decision is not available. Consider the following series of problems presented by Tversky and Shafir (1992a) to 98 students.

Win/lose version:

Imagine that you have just played a game of chance that gave you a 50% chance to win $200 and a 50% chance to lose $100. The coin was tossed and you have [won $200/lost $100]. You are now offered a second identical gamble: 50% chance to win $200 and 50% chance to lose $100. Would you:

	Won	*Lost*
(a) accept the second gamble.	69%	59%
(b) reject the second gamble.	31%	41%

The students were presented with the *win* version of the problem above, followed a week later by the *lose* version, and 10 days after that by the following version that is a disjunction of the previous two. The problems were embedded among other, similar problems so that the relation between the various versions was not transparent. Subjects were instructed to treat each decision separately.

Disjunctive version:

Imagine that you have just played a game of chance that gave you a 50% chance to win $200 and a 50% chance to lose $100. Imagine that the coin has already been tossed, but that you will not know whether you have won $200 or lost $100 until you make your decision concerning a second, identical gamble: 50% chance to win $200 and 50% chance to lose $100. Would you:

(a) accept the second gamble.	36%
(b) reject the second gamble.	64%

The data show that a majority of subjects accepted the second gamble after having won the first gamble and a majority also accepted the second gamble after having lost the first gamble. However, the majority of subjects rejected the second gamble when the outcome of the first was not known. An examination of individual choices reveals that approximately 40% of the subjects accepted the second gamble both after a gain in the first and after a loss. Among these, however, 65% rejected the second gamble in the disjunctive condition, when the outcome of the first gamble was not known. Indeed, this response pattern (accepting in both conditions but rejecting in the disjunction) was the single most frequent pattern, exhibited by 27% of all subjects.

This pattern, which violates Savage's (1954) sure-thing principle, cannot be attributed to unreliability (Tversky & Shafir, 1992a).

The students above were offered a gamble with a positive expected value, and an even chance of a non-trivial loss. Different reasons were likely to arise for accepting the second gamble depending on the outcome of the first. In the *win* condition, the decision maker is already up $200, so even a loss on the second gamble leaves him or her ahead overall, which makes this option quite attractive. In the *lose* condition, on the other hand, the decision maker is down $100. Playing the second gamble offers a chance to "get out of the red," which for many is more attractive than accepting a sure $100 loss. In the *disjunctive* condition, however, the decision maker does not know whether she is up $200 or down $100; she does not know, in other words, whether her reason for playing the second gamble is that it is a no-loss proposition or, instead, that it provides a chance to escape a sure loss. In the absence of a definite reason, fewer subjects accept the second gamble.

This interpretation is further supported by the following modification of the above problem, in which both outcomes of the first gamble were increased by $400 so that the decision maker could not lose in either case.

> Imagine that you have just played a game of chance that gave you a 50% chance to win $600 and a 50% chance to win $300. Imagine that the coin has already been tossed, but that you will not know whether you have won $600 or $300 until you make your decision concerning a second gamble: 50% chance to win $200 and 50% chance to lose $100.

A total of 171 subjects were presented with this problem, equally divided into three groups. One group was told that they had won $300 on the first gamble, a second group was told that they had won $600 on the first gamble, and the third group was told that the outcome of the first gamble – $300 or $600 – was not known (the disjunctive version). In all cases, subjects had to decide whether to accept or to reject the second gamble which, as in the previous problem, consisted of an even chance to win $200 or lose $100. The percentage of subjects who accepted the second gamble in the $300, $600, and disjunctive versions, were 69%, 75%, and 73%, respectively. (Recall that the corresponding figures for the original problem were 59%, 69%, and 36%; essentially identical figures were obtained in a between-subjects replication of that problem.) In contrast to the original problem, the second gamble in this modified problem was equally popular in the disjunctive as in the non-disjunctive versions. Whereas in the original scenario the second gamble amounted to either a no-loss proposition or a chance to avoid a sure loss, in the modified scenario the second gamble amounts to a no-loss proposition regardless of the outcome of the first gamble. The increased popularity of the second gamble in the modified problem shows that it is not the disjunctive situation itself that discourages people from playing. Rather, it is the lack of a specific reason that seems to drive the effect: when the same reason applies regardless of outcome, the disjunction no longer reduces the tendency to accept the gamble.

As illustrated above, changes in the context of decision are likely to alter the reasons that subjects bring to mind and, consequently, their choices. Elsewhere (Shafir & Tversky, 1992) we describe a disjunction effect in the context of a one-shot prisoner's dilemma game, played on a computer for real payoffs. Subjects ($n = 80$) played a series of prisoner's dilemma games, without feedback, each against a different unknown player. In this setup, the rate of cooperation was 3% when subjects knew that the other player had defected, and 16% when they knew that the other had cooperated. However, when subjects did not know whether the other player had cooperated or defected (the standard version of the prisoner's dilemma game) the rate of cooperation rose to 37%. Thus, many subjects defected when they knew the other's choice – be it cooperation or defection – but cooperated when the other player's choice was not known. Shafir and Tversky (1992) attribute this pattern to the different perspectives that underlie subjects' behavior under uncertainty as opposed to when the uncertainty is resolved. In particular, we suggest that the reasons for competing are more compelling when the other player's decision is known and the payoff depends on the subject alone, than when the other's chosen strategy is uncertain, and the outcome of the game depends on the choices of both players.

The above "disjunctive" manipulation – which has no direct bearing from the point of view of value maximization – appears to influence the reasons for decision that people bring to mind. Another kind of manipulation that seems to alter people's reasons without bearing directly on options' values is described in what follows.

6. Non-valued features

Reasons for choice or rejection often refer to specific features of the options under consideration. The positive features of an option typically provide reasons for choosing that option and its negative features typically provide reasons for rejection. What happens when we add features that are neither attractive nor aversive? Can choice be influenced by features that have little or no value?

Simonson and his colleagues have conducted a number of studies on the effects of non-valued features, and tested the hypothesis that people are reluctant to choose alternatives that are supported by reasons that they do not find appealing. In one study, for example, Simonson, Nowlis, and Simonson (1993) predicted that people would be less likely to choose an alternative that was chosen by another person for a reason that does not apply to them. UC Berkeley business students ($n = 113$) were told that, because of budget cuts and in order to save paper and duplicating costs, a questionnaire that they will receive was designed for use by two respondents. Thus, when subjects had to enter a choice, they could see the choice made by the previous "respondent" and the reason given for it. The choices and reasons of the previous respondents were systematically manipulated. One problem, for example, offered a choice between attending the MBA programs at Northwestern and UCLA. In one version of the questionnaire, the previous respondent had selected Northwestern, and provided the (handwritten) reason, "I have many relatives in the Chicago area." Because this reason does not apply to most subjects, it was expected to reduce their likelihood of choosing Northwestern. In a second version, no reason was given for the choice of Northwestern. As expected, those exposed to an irrelevant reason were less likely to choose Northwestern than subjects who saw the other respondent's choice but not his or her reason (23% vs. 43%, p < .05). It should be noted that both Northwestern and UCLA are well known to most subjects (Northwestern currently has the highest ranked MBA program; the UCLA program is ranked high and belongs to the same UC system as Berkeley). Thus, it is unlikely that subjects made inferences about the quality of Northwestern based on the fact that another respondent chose it because he or she had relatives in Chicago.

In a related study, Simonson, Carmon, and O'Curry (1994) showed that endowing an option with a feature that was intended to be positive but, in fact, has no value for the decision maker can reduce the tendency to choose that option, even when subjects realize that they are not paying for the added feature. For example, an offer to purchase a collector's plate – that most did not want – if one buys a particular brand of cake mix was shown to lower the tendency to buy that particular brand relative to a second, comparable cake mix brand (from 31% to 14%, p < .05). Choosing brands that offer worthless bonuses was judged (in a related study) as more difficult to justify and as more susceptible to criticism. An analysis of verbal protocols showed that a majority of those who failed to select the endowed option explicitly mentioned not needing the added feature. It should be noted that sale promotions, such as the one involving the collector's plate offer above, are currently employed by a wide range of companies and there is no evidence that they lead to any inferences about the quality of the promoted product (e.g., Blattberg & Neslin, 1990).

The above manipulations all added "positive," albeit weak or irrelevant, features, which should not diminish an option's value; yet, they apparently provide a reason against choosing the option, especially when other options are otherwise equally attractive. Evidently, the addition of a potentially attractive feature that proves useless can provide a reason to reject the option in favor of a competing alternative that has no "wasted" features.

7. Concluding remarks

People's choices may occasionally stem from affective judgments that preclude a thorough evaluation of the options (cf. Zajonc, 1980). In such cases, an analysis of the reasons for choice may prove unwarranted and, when attempted by the decision maker, may actually result in a different, and possibly inferior, decision (Wilson & Schooler, 1991). Other choices, furthermore, may follow standard operating procedures that involve minimal reflective effort. Many decisions, nonetheless, result from a careful evaluation of options, in which people attempt to arrive at what they believe is the best choice. Having discarded the less attractive options and faced with a choice that is hard to resolve, people often search for a compelling rationale for choosing one alternative over another. In this paper, we presented an analysis of the role of reasons in decision making, and considered ways in which an analysis based on reasons may contribute to the standard quantitative approach based on the maximization of value. A number of hypotheses that derive from this perspective were investigated in experimental settings.

The reasons that enter into the making of decisions are likely to be intricate and diverse. In the preceding sections we have attempted to identify a few general principles that govern the role of reasons in decision making, and thus some of the fundamental ways in which thinking about reasons is likely to contribute to our understanding of the making of decisions. A reliance on the more important dimensions – those likely to provide more compelling reasons for choice – was shown in section 1 to predict preferences between previously equated options. The notions of compatibility and salience were summoned in section 2 to account for the differential weighting of reasons in a choice versus rejection task. Reasons, it appears, lend themselves to certain framing manipulations that are harder to explain from the perspective of value maximization. In section 3, manipulating the precise relationships between competing alternatives was shown to enhance or reduce conflict, yielding decisions that were easier or more difficult to rationalize and justify. Providing a context that presents compelling reasons for choosing an option apparently increases people's tendency to opt for that option, whereas comparing alternatives that render the aforementioned reasons less compelling tends to increase people's tendency to maintain the status quo or search for other alternatives. The ability of the context of decision to generate reasons that affect choice was further discussed in section 4, where the addition and removal of competing alternatives was interpreted as generating arguments for choice based on comparative considerations of relative advantages and compromise. The relative weakness of disjunctive reasons was discussed in section 5. There, a number of studies contrasted people's willingness to reach a decision based on a definite reason for choice, with their reluctance to arrive at a decision in the presence of uncertainty about which reason is actually relevant to the case at hand. Section 6 briefly reviewed choice situations in which the addition of purported reasons for choosing an option, which subjects did not find compelling, was seen to diminish their tendency to opt for that option, even though its value had not diminished.

The nature of the reasons that guide decision, and the ways in which they interact, await further investigation. There is evidence to suggest that a wide variety of arguments play a role in decision making. We often search for a convincing rationale for the decisions that we make, whether for interpersonal purposes, so that we can explain to others the reasons for our decision, or for intrapersonal motives, so that we may feel confident of having made the "right" choice. Attitudes toward risk and loss can sometimes be rationalized on the basis of common myths or clichés, and choices are sometimes made on the basis of moral or prudential principles that are used to override specific cost–benefit calculations (cf. Prelec & Herrnstein, 1991). Formal decision rules, moreover, may sometimes act as arguments in people's deliberations. Thus, when choosing between options x and z, we may realize that, sometime earlier, we had preferred x over y and y over z and that, therefore, by transitivity, we should now choose x over z. Montgomery (1983) has argued that people look for dominance structures in decision problems because they provide a compelling reason for choice. Similarly, Tversky and Shafir (1992a) have shown that detecting the applicability of the sure-thing principle to a decision situation leads people to act in accord with this principle's compelling rationale. Indeed, it has been repeatedly observed that the axioms of rational choice which are often violated in non-transparent situations are generally satisfied when their application is transparent (e.g., Tversky & Kahneman, 1986). These results suggest that the axioms of rational choice act as compelling arguments, or reasons, for making a particular decision when their applicability has been detected, not as universal laws that constrain people's choices.

In contrast to the classical theory that assumes stable values and preferences, it appears that people often do not have well-established values, and that preferences are actually constructed – not merely revealed – during their elicitation (cf. Payne, Bettman, & Johnson, 1992). A reason-based approach lends itself well to such a constructive interpretation. Decisions, according to this analysis, are often reached by focusing on reasons that justify the selection of one option over another. Different frames, contexts, and elicitation procedures highlight different aspects of the options and bring forth different reasons and considerations that influence decision.

The reliance on reasons to explain experimental findings has been the hallmark of social psychological analyses. Accounts of dissonance (Wicklund & Brehm, 1976) and self-perception (Bem, 1972), for example, focus on the reasons that people muster in an attempt to explain their counter-attitudinal behaviors. Similarly, attribution theory (Heider, 1958) centers around the reasons that people attribute to others' behavior. These studies, however, have primarily focused on postdecisional rationalization rather than predecisional conflict. Although the two processes are closely related, there are nevertheless some important differences. Much of the work in social psychology has investigated how people's decisions affect the way they think. The present paper, in contrast, has considered how the reasons that enter into people's thinking about a problem influence their decision. A number of researchers have recently begun to explore related issues. Billig (1987), for example, has adopted a rhetorical approach to understanding social psychological issues, according to which "our inner deliberations are silent arguments conducted within a single self" (p. 5). Related "explanation-based" models of decision making have been applied by Pennington and Hastie (1988, 1992) to account for judicial decisions, and the importance of social accountability in choice has been addressed by Tetlock (1992). From a philosophical perspective, a recent essay by Schick (1991) analyzes various decisions from the point of view of practical reason. An influential earlier work is Toulmin's (1950) study of the role of arguments in ethical reasoning.

In this article, we have attempted to explore some of the ways in which reasons and arguments enter into people's decisions. A reason-based analysis may come closer to capturing part of the psychology that underlies decision and thus may help shed light on a number of phenomena that remain counterintuitive from the perspective of the classical theory. It is instructive to note that many of the experimental studies described in this paper were motivated by intuitions stemming from a qualitative analysis based on reasons, not from a value-based perspective, even if they can later be interpreted in that fashion. We do not propose that accounts based on reasons replace value-based models of choice. Rather, we suggest that an analysis of reasons may illuminate some aspects of reflective choice, and generate new hypotheses for further study.

Notes

1 These effects of context on choice can naturally be used in sales tactics. For example, Williams-Sonoma, a mail-order business located in San Francisco, used to offer a bread-baking appliance priced at $279. They later added a second bread-baking appliance, similar to the first but somewhat larger, and priced at $429 – more than 50% higher than the original appliance. Not surprisingly, Williams-Sonoma did not sell many units of the new item. However, the sales of the less expensive appliance almost doubled. (To the best of our knowledge, Williams-Sonoma did not anticipate this effect.)

2 An additional group of subjects ($n = 123$) were presented with both the fail and the pass versions, and asked whether or not they would buy the vacation package in each case. Two thirds of the subjects made the same choice in the two conditions, indicating that the data for the disjunctive version cannot be explained by the hypothesis that those who like the vacation in case they pass the exam do not like it in case they fail, and vice versa. Note that while only one third of the subjects made different decisions depending on the outcome of the exam, more than 60% of the subjects chose to wait when the outcome was not known.

References

Allison, G. T. (1971). *Essence of decision: explaining the Cuban missile crisis*. Boston: Little Brown.

Bem, D. J. (1972). Self-perception theory. In L. Berkowitz (Ed.), *Advances in experimental social psychology* (Vol. 6). New York: Academic Press.

Berman, L. (1982). *Planning a tragedy*. New York: Norton.

Betts, R., & Gelb, L. (1979). *The irony of Vietnam: the system worked*. Washington, DC: Brookings Institution.

Bigelow, J. (Ed.). (1887). *The complete works of Benjamin Franklin* (Vol. 4). New York: Putnam.

Billig, M. (1987). *Arguing and thinking: a rhetorical approach to social psychology*. New York: Cambridge University Press.

Blattberg, R. C., & Neslin, S. A. (1990). *Sales promotion: concepts, methods, and strategies*. Englewood Cliffs, NJ: Prentice-Hall.

Heider, F. (1958). *The psychology of interpersonal relations*. New York: Wiley.

Huber, J., Payne, J. W., & Puto, C. (1982). Adding asymmetrically dominated alternatives: violations of regularity and the similarity hypothesis. *Journal of Consumer Research*, *9*, 90–98.

James, W. (1981). *The principles of psychology* (Vol. 2). Cambridge, MA: Harvard University Press.

Kahneman, D., & Tversky, A. (1979). Prospect theory: an analysis of decision under risk. *Econometrica*, *47*, 263–291.

Montgomery, H. (1983). Decision rules and the search for a dominance structure: towards a process model of decision making. In P. Humphreys, O. Svenson, & A. Vari (Eds.), *Analyzing and aiding decision processes*. Amsterdam: North-Holland.

Nisbett, R. E., & Wilson, T. D. (1977). Telling more than we can know: verbal reports on mental processes. *Psychological Review*, *84*, 231–259.

Payne, J. W., Bettman, J. R., & Johnson, E. J. (1992). Behavioral decision research: a constructive process perspective. *Annual Review of Psychology*, *43*, 87–131.

Pennington, N., & Hastie, R. (1988). Explanation-based decision making: effects of memory structure on judgment. *Journal of Experimental Psychology: Learning, Memory, and Cognition*, *14*, 521–533.

Pennington, N., & Hastie, R. (1992). Explaining the evidence: tests of the story model for juror decision making. *Journal of Personality and Social Psychology*, *62*, 189–206.

Prelec, D., & Herrnstein, R. J. (1991). Preferences or principles: alternative guidelines for choice. In R. J. Zeckhauser (Ed.), *Strategy and choice*. Cambridge, MA: MIT Press.

Redelmeier, D., & Shafir, E. (1993). Medical decisions over multiple alternatives. Working paper, University of Toronto.

Savage, L. J. (1954). *The foundations of statistics*. New York: Wiley.

Schick, F. (1991). *Understanding action: an essay on reasons*. New York: Cambridge University Press.

Shafer, G. (1986). Savage revisited. *Statistical Science*, *1*, 463–485.

Shafir, E. (1993). Choosing versus rejecting: why some options are both better and worse than others. *Memory & Cognition*, *21*, 546–556.

Shafir, E., & Tversky, A. (1992). Thinking through uncertainty: nonconsequential reasoning and choice. *Cognitive Psychology*, *24*, 449–474.

Simonson, I. (1989). Choice based on reasons: the case of attraction and compromise effects. *Journal of Consumer Research*, *16*, 158–174.

Simonson, I., Carmon, Z., & O'Curry, S. (1994). Experimental evidence on the negative effect of product features and sales promotions on brand choice. *Marketing Science*, *13*, 23–40.

Simonson, I., Nowlis, S. M., & Simonson, Y. (1993). The effect of irrelevant preference arguments on consumer choice. *Journal of Consumer Psychology, 2*, 287–306.

Simonson, I., & Tversky, A. (1992). Choice in context: tradeoff contrast and extremeness aversion. *Journal of Marketing Research, 29*, 281–295.

Slovic, P. (1975). Choice between equally valued alternatives. *Journal of Experimental Psychology: Human Perception and Performance, 1*, 280–287.

Slovic, P. (1990). Choice. In D. Osherson & E. Smith (Eds.), *An invitation to cognitive science* (Vol. 3). Cambridge, MA: MIT Press.

Telhami, S. (1990). *Power and leadership in international bargaining: the path to the Camp David accords.* New York: Columbia University Press.

Tetlock, P. E. (1992). The impact of accountability on judgment and choice: toward a social contingency model. In M. P. Zanna (Ed.), *Advances in experimental social psychology* (Vol. 25). New York: Academic Press.

Toulmin, S. (1950). *The place of reason in ethics.* New York: Cambridge University Press.

Tversky, A., & Kahneman, D. (1986). Rational choice and the framing of decisions. *Journal of Business, 59*, 251–278.

Tversky, A., Sattath, S., & Slovic, P. (1988). Contingent weighting in judgment and choice. *Psychological Review, 95*, 371–384.

Tversky, A., & Shafir, E. (1992a). The disjunction effect in choice under uncertainty. *Psychological Science, 3*, 305–309.

Tversky, A., & Shafir, E. (1992b). Choice under conflict: the dynamics of deferred decision. *Psychological Science, 3*, 358–361.

Tversky, A., & Simonson, I. (1993). Context-dependent preferences. *Management Science, 39*, 1179–1189.

von Neumann, J., & Morgenstern, O. (1947). *Theory of games and economic behavior.* Princeton, NJ: Princeton University Press.

Wedell, D. H. (1991). Distinguishing among models of contextually induced preference reversals. *Journal of Experimental Psychology: Learning, Memory, and Cognition, 17*, 767–778.

Wicklund, R. A., & Brehm, J. W. (1976). *Perspectives on cognitive dissonance.* Hillsdale, NJ: Erlbaum.

Wilson, T. D., & Schooler, J. W. (1991). Thinking too much: introspection can reduce the quality of preferences and decisions. *Journal of Personality and Social Psychology, 60*, 181–192.

Zajonc, R. B. (1980). Preferences without inferences. *American Psychologist, 35*, 151–175.

3 Probabilistic mental models: A Brunswikian theory of confidence

Gerd Gigerenzer, Ulrich Hoffrage, and Heinz Kleinbölting

Do people think they know more than they really do? In the last 15 years, cognitive psychologists have amassed a large and apparently damning body of experimental evidence on over-confidence in knowledge, evidence that is in turn part of an even larger and more damning literature on so-called cognitive biases. The cognitive bias research claims that people are naturally prone to making mistakes in reasoning and memory, including the mistake of overestimating their knowledge. In this article, we propose a new theoretical model for confidence in knowledge based on the more charitable assumption that people are good judges of the reliability of their knowledge, provided that the knowledge is representatively sampled from a specified reference class. We claim that this model both predicts new experimental results (that we have tested) and explains a wide range of extant experimental findings on confidence, including some perplexing inconsistencies.

Moreover, it is the first theoretical framework to integrate the two most striking and stable effects that have emerged from confidence studies – the overconfidence effect and the hard–easy effect – and to specify the conditions under which these effects can be made to appear, disappear, and even invert. In most recent studies (including our own, reported herein), subjects are asked to choose between two alternatives for each of a series of general-knowledge questions. Here is a typical example: "Which city has more

This chapter originally appeared in *Psychological Review*, 1991, *98*(4), 506–528. Copyright © 1991 by the American Psychological Association. Reprinted by permission.

This article was written while Gerd Gigerenzer was a fellow at the Center for Advanced Study in the Behavioral Sciences, Stanford, California. We are grateful for financial support provided by the Spencer Foundation and the Deutsche Forschungsgemeinschaft (DFG 170/2–1).

We thank Leda Cosmides, Lorraine Daston, Baruch Fischhoff, Jennifer Freyd, Kenneth Hammond, Wolfgang Hell, Sarah Lichtenstein, Kathleen Much, John Tooby, Amos Tversky, and an anonymous reviewer for helpful comments on earlier versions of this article.

inhabitants? (a) Hyderabad or (b) Islamabad." Subjects choose what they believe to be the correct answer and then are directed to specify their degree of confidence (usually on a 50%–100% scale) that their answer is indeed correct. After the subjects answer many questions of this sort, the responses are sorted by confidence level, and the relative frequencies of correct answers in each confidence category are calculated. The *overconfidence effect* occurs when the confidence judgments are larger than the relative frequencies of the correct answers; the *hard–easy effect* occurs when the degree of overconfidence increases with the difficulty of the questions, where the difficulty is measured by the percentage of correct answers.

Both effects seem to be stable. Fischhoff (1982) reviewed the attempts to eliminate overconfidence by numerous "debiasing methods," such as giving rewards, clarifying instructions, warning subjects in advance about the problem, and using better response modes – all to no avail. He concluded that these manipulations "have so far proven relatively ineffective," and that overconfidence was "moderately robust" (p. 440). von Winterfeldt and Edwards (1986, p. 539) agreed that "overconfidence is a reliable, reproducible finding." Yet these robust phenomena still await a theory. In particular, we lack a comprehensive theoretical framework that explains both phenomena, as well as the various exceptions reported in the literature, and integrates the several local explanatory attempts already advanced. That is the aim of this article. It consists of four parts: (a) an exposition of the proposed theory of probabilistic mental models (PMM theory), including predictions of new experimental findings based on the theory; (b) a report of our experimental tests confirming these predictions; (c) an explanation of apparent anomalies in previous experimental results, by means of PMMs; and (d) a concluding discussion.

PMM Theory

This theory deals with spontaneous confidence – that is, with an immediate reaction, not the product of long reflection. Figure 3.1 shows a flow chart of the processes that generate confidence judgments in two-alternative general-knowledge tasks.[1] There are two strategies. When presented with a two-alternative confidence task, the subject first attempts to construct what we call a *local mental model* (local MM) of the task. This is a solution by memory and elementary logical operations. If this fails, a PMM is constructed that goes beyond the structure of the task in using probabilistic information from a natural environment.

For convenience, we illustrate the theory using a problem from the following experiments: "Which city has more inhabitants? (a) Heidelberg or (b) Bonn." As explained earlier, the subjects' task is to choose a or b and to give a numerical judgment of their confidence (that the answer chosen is correct).

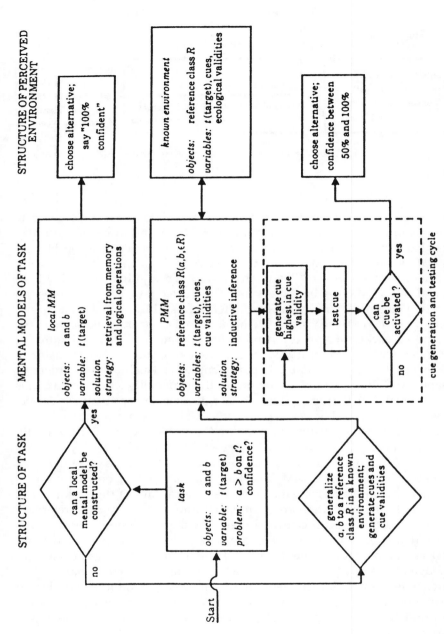

Figure 3.1. Cognitive processes in solving a two-alternative general-knowledge task. (MM = mental model; PMM = probabilistic mental model.)

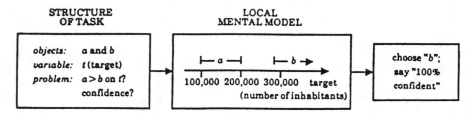

Figure 3.2. Local mental model of a two-alternative general-knowledge task.

Local MM

We assume that the mind first attempts a direct solution that could generate certain knowledge by constructing a local MM. For instance, a subject may recall from memory that Heidelberg has a population between 100,000 and 200,000, whereas Bonn has more than 290,000 inhabitants. This is already sufficient for the answer "Bonn" and a confidence judgment of 100%. In general, a local MM can be successfully constructed if (a) precise figures can be retrieved from memory for both alternatives, (b) intervals that do not overlap can be retrieved, or (c) elementary logical operations, such as the method of exclusion, can compensate for missing knowledge. Figure 3.2 illustrates a successful local MM for the previous example. Now consider a task where the target variable is not quantitative (such as the number of inhabitants) but is qualitative: "If you see the nationality letter P on a car, is it from Poland or Portugal?" Here, either direct memory about the correct answer or the method of exclusion is sufficient to construct a local MM. The latter is illustrated by a subject reasoning "Since I know that Poland has PL it must be Portugal" (Allwood & Montgomery, 1987, p. 370).

The structure of the task must be examined to define more generally what is referred to as a local MM. The task consists of two objects, a and b (alternatives), and a target variable t. First, a local MM of this task is local; that is, only the two alternatives are taken into account, and no reference class of objects is constructed (see the following discussion). Second, it is direct; that is, it contains only the target variable (e.g., number of inhabitants), and no probability cues are used. Third, no inferences besides elementary operations of deductive logic (such as exclusion) occur. Finally, if the search is successful, the confidence in the knowledge produced is evaluated as certain. In these respects, our concept of a local MM is similar to what Johnson-Laird (1983, pp. 134–142) called a "mental model" in syllogistic inference.

A local MM simply matches the structure of the task; there is no use of the probability structure of an environment and, consequently, no frame for inductive inference as in a PMM. Because memory can fail, the "certain" knowledge produced can sometimes be incorrect. These failures contribute to the amount of overconfidence to be found in 100%-confident judgments.

PMM

Local MMs are of limited success in general-knowledge tasks[2] and in most natural environments, although they seem to be sufficient for solving some syllogisms and other problems of deductive logic (see Johnson-Laird, 1983). If no local MM can be activated, it is assumed that a PMM is constructed next. A PMM solves the task by inductive inference, and it does so by putting the specific task into a larger context. A PMM connects the specific structure of the task with a probability structure of a corresponding natural environment (stored in long-term memory). In our example, a natural environment could be the class of all cities in Germany with a set of variables defined on this class, such as the number of inhabitants. This task selects the number of inhabitants as the target and the variables that covary with this target as the cues.

A PMM is different from a local MM in several respects. First, it contains a *reference class* of objects that includes the objects a and b. Second, it uses a network of variables in addition to the target variable for indirect inference. Thus, it is neither local nor direct. These two features also change the third and fourth aspects of a local MM. Probabilistic inference is part of the cognitive process, and uncertainty is part of the outcome.

Reference class

We use Brunswik's (1943, p. 257) term *reference class* to define the class of objects or events that a PMM contains. In our example, the reference class "all cities in Germany" may be generated. To generate a reference class means to generate a set of objects known from a person's natural environment that contains objects a and b.

The reference class determines which cues can function as probability cues for the target variable and what their cue validities are. For instance, a valid cue in the reference class "all cities in Germany" would be the soccer-team cue; that is, whether a city's soccer team plays in the German soccer Bundesliga, in which the 18 best teams compete. Cities with more inhabitants are more likely to have a team in the Bundesliga. The soccer-team cue would not help in the Hyderabad–Islamabad task, which must be solved by a PMM containing a different reference class with different cues and cue validities.

Probability cues

A PMM for a given task contains a reference class, a target variable, probability cues, and cue validities. A variable is a probability cue C_i (for a target variable in a reference class R) if the probability $p(a)$ of a being correct is different from the conditional probability of a being correct, given that the values of a and b differ on C_i. If the cue is a binary variable such as the soccer-team cue, this condition can be stated as follows:

$$p(a) \neq p(a|aC_ib; R),$$

where aC_ib signifies the relation of a and b on the cue C_i (e.g., a has a soccer team in the Bundesliga, but b does not) and $p(a \mid aC_ib; R)$ is the cue validity of C_i in R.

Thus, cue validities are thought of as conditional probabilities, following Rosch (1978) rather than Brunswik (1955), who defined his "cue utilizations" as Pearson correlations. Conditional probabilities need not be symmetric as correlations are. This allows the cue to be a better predictor for the target than the target is for the cue, or vice versa. Cue validity is a concept in the PMM, whereas the corresponding concept in the environment is *ecological validity* (Brunswik, 1955), which is the true relative frequency of any city having more inhabitants than any other one in R if aC_ib. For example, consider the reference class *all cities in Germany with more than 100,000 inhabitants*. The ecological validity of the soccer-team cue here is .91 (calculated for 1988/1989 for what then was West Germany). That is, if one checked all pairs in which one city a has a team in the Bundesliga but the other city b does not, one would find that in 91% of these cases city a has more inhabitants.

Vicarious functioning

Probability cues are generated, tested, and if possible, activated. We assume that the order in which cues are generated is not random; in particular, we assume that the order reflects the hierarchy of cue validities. For the reference class *all cities in Germany*, the following cues are examples that can be generated: (a) the soccer-team cue; (b) whether one city is a state capital and the other is not (state capital cue); (c) whether one city is located in the Ruhrgebiet, the industrial center of Germany, and the other in largely rural Bavaria (industrial cue); (d) whether the letter code that identifies a city on a license plate is shorter for one city than for the other (large cities are usually abbreviated by only one letter, smaller cities by two or three; license plate cue); and (e) whether one has heard of one city and not of the other (familiarity cue). Consider now the Heidelberg–Bonn problem again. The first probability cue is generated and tested to see whether it can be activated for that problem. Because neither of the two cities has a team in the Bundesliga, the first cue does not work.

In general, with a binary cue and the possibility that the subject has no knowledge, there are nine possibilities (see Figure 3.3). In only two of these can a cue be activated. In all other cases, the cue is useless (although one could further distinguish between the four known–unknown cases and the three remaining cases). If a cue cannot be activated, then a further cue is generated and tested. In the Heidelberg–Bonn task, none of the five cues cited earlier can in fact be activated. Finally, one cue may be generated that

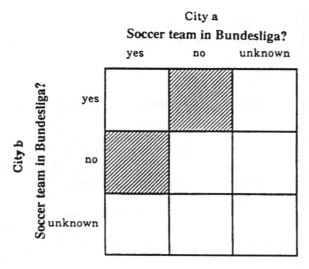

Figure 3.3. Two conditions in which a cue can be activated.

can be activated, such as whether one city is the capital of the country and the other is not (capital cue). This cue has a small probability of being activated – a small activation rate in R (because it applies only to pairs that include Bonn) – and it does not have a particularly high cue validity in R because it is well-known that Bonn is not exactly London or Paris.

The Heidelberg–Bonn problem illustrates that probability cues may have small activation rates in R, and as a consequence, several cues may have to be generated and tested before one is found that can be activated. The capital cue that can be activated for the Heidelberg–Bonn comparison may fail for the next problem, for instance a Heidelberg–Göttingen comparison. Cues can substitute for one another from problem to problem, a process that Brunswik (1955) called "vicarious functioning."

End of cue generation and testing cycle

If (a) the number of problems is large or other kinds of time pressure apply and (b) the activation rate of cues is rather small, then one can assume that the cue generation and testing cycle ends after the first cue that can be activated has been found. Both conditions seem to be typical for general-knowledge questions. For instance, even when subjects were explicitly instructed to produce all possible reasons for and against each alternative, they generated only about three on the average and four at most (Koriat, Lichtenstein, & Fischhoff, 1980). If no cue can be activated, we assume that choice is made randomly, and "confidence 50%" is chosen.

Choice of answer and confidence judgment

Choice of answer and confidence judgment are determined by the cue validity. Choice follows the rule:

$$\text{choose } a \text{ if } p(a|aC_ib; R) > p(b|aC_ib; R).$$

If a is chosen, the confidence that a is correct is given by the cue validity:

$$p(a|aC_ib; R).$$

Note that the assumption that confidence equals cue validity is not arbitrary; it is both rational and simple in the sense that good calibration is to be expected if cue validities correspond to ecological validities. This holds true even if only one cue is activated.

Thus, choice and confidence are inferred from the same activated cue. Both are expressions of the same conditional probability. Therefore, they need not be generated in the temporal sequence choice followed by confidence. The latter is, of course, typical for actual judgments and often enforced by the instructions in confidence studies.

Confidence in the long run and confidence in single events

Until now, only confidence in single events – such as the answer "Bonn" is correct – has been discussed. Confidence in one's knowledge can also be expressed with respect to sequences of answers or events, such as "How many of the last 50 questions do you think you answered correctly?" This distinction is parallel to that between probabilities of single events and relative frequencies in the long run – a distinction that is fundamental to all discussions on the meaning of probability (see Gigerenzer et al., 1989). Probabilities of single events (confidences) and relative frequencies are not the same for many schools of probability, and we argue that they are not evaluated by the same cognitive processes either.

Consider judgments of frequency. General-knowledge tasks that involve a judgment of the frequency of correct answers (frequency tasks) can rarely be answered by constructing a local MM. The structure of the task contains one sequence of N questions and answers, and the number of correct answers is the target variable. Only limiting cases, such as small N (i.e., if only a few questions are asked) combined with the belief that all answers were correct, may allow one to solve this task by a local MM. Again, to construct a local MM of the task means that the mental model consists of only the local sequence of total N answers (no reference class), and because one attempts to solve the task by direct access to memory about the target variable, no network of probability cues is constructed.

Similarly, a PMM of a frequency task is different from a PMM of a confidence task. A confidence task about city size in Germany has "cities in Germany" as a reference class; however, a task that involves judgments of

Table 3.1. *Probabilistic mental models for confidence task versus frequency task: Differences between target variables, reference classes, and probability cues*

PMM	Confidence task	Frequency task
Target variable	Number of inhabitants	Number of correct answers
Reference class	Cities in Germany	Sets of general-knowledge questions in similar testing situations
Probability cues	For example, soccer-team cue or state capital cue	For example, base rates of previous performance or average confidence in N answers

Note: For illustration, questions of the Heidelberg–Bonn type are used. PMM = probabilistic mental model.

frequencies of correct answers in a series of N questions about city size has a different reference class: Its reference class will contain series of similar questions in similar testing situations. Because the target variable also differs (number of correct answers instead of number of inhabitants), the PMM of a frequency task will also contain different cues and cue validities. For instance, base rates of performance in earlier general knowledge or similar testing situations could serve as a probability cue for the target variable. Again, our basic assumption is that a PMM connects the structure of the task with a known structure of the subject's environment.

Table 3.1 summarizes the differences between PMMs that are implied by the two different tasks. Note that in our account, both confidences in a single event and judgments of frequency are explained by reference to experienced frequencies. However, these frequencies relate to different target variables and reference classes. We use this assumption to predict systematic differences between these kinds of judgments.

Adaptive PMMs and representative sampling

A PMM is an inductive device that uses the "normal" life conditions in known environments as the basis for induction. How well does the structure of probability cues defined on R in a PMM represent the actual structure of probability cues in the environment? This question is also known as that of "proper cognitive adjustment" (Brunswik, 1964, p. 22). If the hierarchy of cues and their validities corresponds to that of the ecological validities, then the PMM is well adapted to a known environment. In Brunswik's view, cue validities are learned by observing the frequencies of co-occurrences in an environment.

A large literature exists that suggests that (a) memory is often (but not always) excellent in storing frequency information from various environments and (b) the registering of event occurrences for frequency judgments is a fairly automatic cognitive process requiring very little attention or conscious effort (e.g., Gigerenzer, 1984; Hasher, Goldstein, & Toppino, 1977; Howell & Burnett, 1978; Zacks, Hasher, & Sanft, 1982). Hasher and Zacks (1979) concluded that frequency of occurrence, spatial location, time, and word meaning are among the few aspects of the environment that are encoded automatically and that encoding of frequency information is "automatic at least in part because of innate factors" (p. 360). In addition, Hintzman, Nozawa, and Irmscher (1982) proposed that frequencies are stored in memory in a nonnumerical analog mode.

Whatever the mechanism of frequency encoding, we use the following assumption for deriving our predictions: If subjects had repeated experience with a reference class, a target variable, and cues in their environment, we assume that cue validities correspond well to ecological validities. (This holds true for the average in a group of subjects, but individual idiosyncrasies in learning the frequency structure of the environment may occur.) This is a bold assumption made in ignorance of potential deviations between specific cue validities and ecological validities. If such deviations existed and were known, predictions by PMM theory could be improved. The assumption, however, derives support from both the literature on automatic frequency processing and a large body of neo-Brunswikian research on the correspondence between ecological validities and cue utilization (the latter of which corresponds to our cue validities; e.g., Arkes & Hammond, 1986; K. Armelius, 1979; Brehmer & Joyce, 1988; MacGregor & Slovic, 1986).

Note that this adaptiveness assumption does not preclude that individuals (as well as the average subject) err. Errors can occur even if a PMM is highly adapted to a given environment. For instance, if an environment is changing or is changed in the laboratory by an experimenter, an otherwise well-adapted PMM may be suboptimal in a predictable way.

Brunswik's notion of "representative sampling" is important here. If a person experienced a representative sample of objects from a reference class, one can expect his or her PMM to be better adapted to an environment than if he or she happened to experience a skewed, unrepresentative sample.

Representative sampling is also important in understanding the relation between a PMM and the task. If a PMM is well adapted, but the set of objects used in the task (questions) is not representative of the reference class in the environment, performance in tasks will be systematically suboptimal.

To avoid confusion with terms such as *calibration*, we will use the term *adaptation* only when we are referring to the relation between a PMM and a corresponding environment – not, however, for the relation between a PMM and a task.

Predictions

A concrete example can help motivate our first prediction. Two of our colleagues, K and O, are eminent wine tasters. K likes to make a gift of a bottle of wine from his cellar to Friend O, on the condition that O guesses what country or region the grapes were grown in. Because O knows the relevant cues, O can usually pick a region with some confidence. O also knows that K sometimes selects a quite untypical exemplar from his ample wine cellar to test Friend O's limits. Thus, for each individual wine, O can infer the probability that the grapes ripened in, say, Portugal as opposed to South Africa, with considerable confidence from his knowledge about cues. In the long run, however, O nevertheless expects the relative frequency of correct answers to be lower because K occasionally selects unusual items.

Consider tests of general knowledge, which share an important feature with the wine-tasting situation: Questions are selected to be somewhat difficult and sometimes misleading. This practice is common and quite reasonable for testing people's limits, as in the wine-tasting situation. Indeed, there is apparently not a single study on confidence in knowledge where a reference class has been defined and a representative (or random) sample of general-knowledge questions has been drawn from this population. For instance, consider the reference class "metropolis" and the geographical north–south location as the target variable. A question like "Which city is farther north? (a) New York or (b) Rome" is likely to appear in a general-knowledge test (almost everyone gets it wrong), whereas a comparison between Berlin and Rome is not.

The crucial point is that confidence and frequency judgments refer to different kinds of reference classes. A set of questions can be representative with respect to one reference class and, at the same time, selected with respect to the other class. Thus, a set of 50 general-knowledge questions of the city type may be representative for the reference class "sets of general-knowledge questions" but not for the reference class "cities in Germany" (because city pairs have been selected for being difficult or misleading). Asking for a confidence judgment summons up a PMM on the basis of the reference class "cities in Germany"; asking for a frequency judgment summons up a PMM on the basis of the reference class "sets of general-knowledge questions." The first prediction can now be stated.

1. *Typical general-knowledge tasks elicit both overconfidence and accurate frequency judgments.* By "typical" general-knowledge tasks we refer to a set of questions that is representative for the reference class "sets of general-knowledge questions."

This prediction is derived in the following way: If (a) PMMs for confidence tasks are well adapted to an environment containing a reference class R (e.g., all cities in Germany) and (b) the actual set of questions is not representative for R, but selected for difficult pairs of cities, then confidence judgments exhibit overconfidence. Condition A is part of our theory (the simplifying assumption we just made), and Condition B is typical for the general-knowledge questions used in studies on confidence as well as in other testing situations.

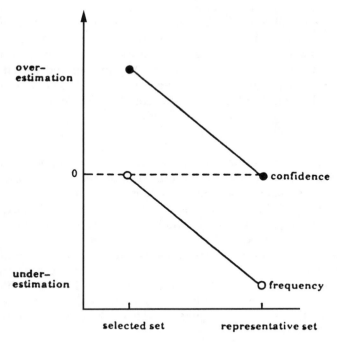

Figure 3.4. Predicted differences between confidence and frequency judgments (confidence-frequency effect).

If (a) PMMs for frequency-of-correct-answer tasks are well adapted with respect to an environment containing a reference class R' (e.g., the set of all general-knowledge tests experienced earlier), and (b) the actual set of questions is representative for R', then frequency judgments are expected to be accurate. Again, Condition A is part of our theory, and Condition B will be realized in our experiments by using a typical set of general-knowledge questions.

Taken together, the prediction is that the same person will exhibit overconfidence when asked for the confidence that a particular answer is correct and accurate estimates when asked for a judgment of frequency of correct answers. This prediction is shown by the two points on the left side of Figure 3.4. This prediction cannot be derived from any of the previous accounts of overconfidence.

To introduce the second prediction, we return to the wine-tasting story. Assume that K changes his habit of selecting unusual wines from his wine cellar, and instead buys a representative sample of French red wines and lets O guess from what region they come. However, K does not tell O about the new sampling technique. O's average confidence judgments will now be close to the proportion of correct answers. In the long run, O nevertheless expects the proportion of correct answers to be less, still assuming the familiar testing situation in which wines were selected, not randomly sampled. Thus, O's frequency judgments will show underestimation.

Consider now a set of general-knowledge questions that is a random sample from a defined reference class in the subject's natural environment. We use the term *natural environment* to denote a knowledge domain familiar to the subjects participating in the study. This is a necessary (although not sufficient) condition to assume that PMMs are, on the average, well adapted. In the experiments reported herein, we used West German subjects and the reference class "all cities with more than 100,000 inhabitants in West Germany." (The study was conducted before the unification of Germany.) The second prediction is about this situation:

2. *If the set of general-knowledge tasks is randomly sampled from a natural environment, we expect overconfidence to be zero, but frequency judgments to exhibit underestimation.* Derivation is as before: If PMMs for confidence tasks are well adapted with respect to R, and the actual set of questions is a representative sample from R, then overconfidence is expected to disappear. If PMMs for frequency-of-correct-answers tasks are well adapted with respect to R', and the actual set of questions is not representative for R', then frequency judgments are expected to be underestimations of true frequencies.

Again, this prediction cannot be derived from earlier accounts. Figure 3.4 shows Predictions 1 and 2. The predicted differences between confidence and frequency judgments is referred to as the *confidence–frequency effect*.

Testing these predictions also allows for testing the assumption of well-adapted PMMs for the confidence task. Assume that PMMs are not well adapted. Then a representative sample of city questions should not generate zero overconfidence but rather over- or underconfidence, depending on whether cue validities overestimate or underestimate ecological validities. Similarly, if PMMs for frequency judgments are not well adapted, frequency judgments should deviate from true frequencies in typical general-knowledge tasks. Independent of the degree of adaptation, however, the confidence–frequency effect should emerge, but the curves in Figure 3.4 would be transposed upward or downward.

We turn now to the standard way in which overconfidence has been demonstrated in previous research, comparing confidence levels with relative frequencies of correct answers at each confidence level. This standard comparison runs into a conceptual problem well-known in probability theory and statistics: A discrepancy between subjective probabilities in single events (i.e., the confidence that a particular answer is correct) and relative frequencies in the long run is not a bias in the sense of a violation of probability theory, as is clear from several points of view within probability theory. For instance, for a frequentist such as Richard von Mises (1928/1957), probability theory is about frequencies (in the long run), not about single events. According to this view, the common interpretation of overconfidence as a bias is based on comparing apples with oranges. What if that conceptual problem is avoided and, instead, the relative frequency of correct answers in each confidence category is compared with the estimated relative frequency in each confidence category? PMM theory makes an interesting prediction for this situation, following the same reasoning as for the frequency judgments in Predictions 1 and 2 (which were estimated frequency-of-correct answers in a series of N questions, whereas estimated relative frequencies in each confidence category are the concern here):

3. *Comparing estimated relative frequencies with true relative frequencies of correct answers makes overestimation disappear.* More precisely, if the set of general-knowledge questions is selected, over- or underestimation is expected to be zero; if the set is randomly sampled, underestimation is expected. Thus, PMM theory predicts that the distinction between confidence and relative frequency is psychologically real, in the sense that subjects do not believe that a confidence judgment of X% implies a relative frequency of X%, and vice versa. We know of no study on overconfidence that has investigated this issue. Most have assumed instead that there is, psychologically, no difference.

Prediction 4 concerns the hard–easy effect, which says that overconfidence increases when questions get more difficult (e.g., Lichtenstein & Fischhoff, 1977). The effect refers to confidence judgments only, not to frequency judgments. On our account, the hard–easy effect is not simply a function of difficulty. Rather, it is a function of difficulty and a separate dimension, selected versus representative sampling. (Note that the terms *hard* and *easy* refer to the relative difficulty of two samples of items, whereas the terms *selected* and *representative* refer to the relation between one sample and a reference class in the person's environment.) PMM theory specifies conditions under which the hard–easy effect occurs, disappears, and is reversed. A reversed hard–easy effect means that overconfidence decreases when questions are more difficult.

In Figure 3.5, the line descending from H to E represents a hard–easy effect: Overconfidence in the hard set is larger than in the easy set. The important distinction (in addition to hard vs. easy) is whether a set was obtained by representative sampling or was selected. For instance, assume that PMMs are well adapted and that two sets of tasks differing in percentage correct (i.e., in difficulty) are both representative samples from their respective reference classes. In this case, one would expect all points to be on the horizontal zero-overconfidence line in Figure 3.5 and the hard–easy effect to be zero. More generally:

4. *If two sets, hard and easy, are generated by the same sampling process (representative sampling or same deviation from representative), the hard–easy effect is expected to be zero.* If sampling deviates in both the hard and the easy set

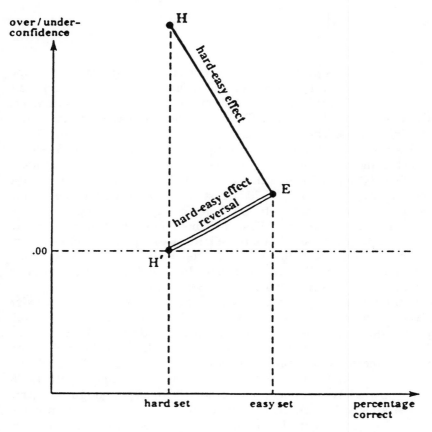

Figure 3.5. Predicted reversal of the hard–easy effect. (H = hard; E = easy.)

equally from representative sampling, points will lie on a horizontal line parallel to the zero-overconfidence line.

Now consider the case that the easy set is selected from a corresponding reference class (e.g., general-knowledge questions), but the hard set is a representative sample from another reference class (denoted as H′ in Figure 3.5). One then would predict a reversal of the hard–easy effect, as illustrated in Figure 3.5 by the double line from E to H′.

5. *If there are two sets, one is a representative sample from a reference class in a natural environment, the other is selected from another reference class for being difficult, but the representative set is harder than the selected set; then the hard–easy effect is reversed.*

In the next section, Predictions 1, 2, and 3 are tested in two experiments; in the Explaining Anomalies in the Literature section, Predictions 4 and 5 are checked against results in the literature.

Experiment 1

Method

Two sets of questions were used, which we refer to as the *representative* and the *selected* set. The representative set was determined in the following way. We used as a reference class in a natural environment (an environment known to our subjects) the set of all cities in West Germany with more than 100,000 inhabitants. There were 65 cities (Statistisches Bundesamt, 1986). From this reference class, a random sample of 25 cities was drawn, and all pairs of cities in the random sample were used in a complete paired comparison to give 300 pairs. No selection occurred. The target variable was the number of inhabitants, and the 300 questions were of the following kind: "Which city has more inhabitants? (a) Solingen or (b) Heidelberg." We chose city questions for two reasons. First, and most important, this content domain allowed for a precise definition of a reference class in a natural environment and for random sampling from this reference class. The second reason was for comparability. City questions have been used in earlier studies on overconfidence (e.g., Keren, 1988; May, 1987).

In addition to the representative set, a typical set of general-knowledge questions, as in previous studies, was used. This selected set of 50 general-knowledge questions was taken from an earlier study (Angele et al. 1982). Two examples are "Who was born first? (a) Buddha or (b) Aristotle" and "When was the zipper invented? (a) before 1920 or (b) after 1920."

After each answer, the subject gave a confidence judgment (that this particular answer was correct). Two kinds of frequency judgments were used. First, after each block of 50 questions, the subject estimated the number of correct answers among the 50 answers given. Because there were 350 questions, every subject gave seven estimates of the number of correct answers. Second, after the subjects answered all questions, they were given an enlarged copy of the confidence scale used throughout the experiment and were asked for the following frequency judgment: "How many of the answers that you classified into a certain confidence category are correct? Please indicate for every category your estimated relative frequency of correct answers."

In Experiment 1, we also introduced two of the standard manipulations in the literature. The first was to inform and warn half of our subjects of the overconfidence effect, and the second was to offer half of each group a monetary incentive for good performance. Both are among a list of "debiasing" methods known as being relatively ineffective (Fischhoff, 1982), and both contributed to the view that overconfidence is a robust phenomenon. If PMM theory is correct, the magnitude of effects resulting from the two manipulations – confidence versus frequency judgment and selected versus representative sampling – should be much larger than those resulting from the "debiasing" manipulations.

Subjects. Subjects were 80 students (43 men and 37 women) at the University of Konstanz who were paid for participation. Eighty-five percent of them grew up in the state of Baden-Württemberg, so the group was fairly homogeneous (knowledge about city populations often depends on the rater's geographical location). Subjects were tested in small groups of a maximum of 12 persons.

Design and procedure. This was a $2 \times 2 \times 2$ design with representative–selected set varied within subjects, and information–no information about over-confidence and monetary incentive–no incentive as independent variables varied between subjects. Half of the subjects answered the representative set first; the other half, the selected set. Order of questions was determined randomly in both sets.

The confidence scale consisted of seven categories, 50%, 51%–60%, 61%–70%, 71%–80%, 81%–90%, 91%–99%, and 100% confident. The 50%- and 100%-confidence values were introduced as separate categories because pre-vious research showed that subjects often tend to use these particular values. Subjects were told first to mark the alternative that seemed to be the correct one, and then to indicate with a second cross their confidence that the answer was correct. If they only guessed, they should cross the 50% category; if they were absolutely certain, they should cross the 100% category. We explained that one of the alternatives was always correct. In the information condition, subjects received the following information: "Most earlier studies found a systematic tendency to overestimate one's knowledge; that is, there were many fewer answers correct than one would expect from the confidence ratings given. Please keep this warning in mind." In the incentive condition, subjects were promised 20 German marks (or a bottle of French champagne), in addition to the payment that everyone received (7.50 marks), for the best performance in the group.

To summarize, 350 questions were presented, with a confidence judgment after each question, a frequency judgment after each 50 questions, and a judgment of relative frequencies of correct answers in each confidence cat-egory at the end.

For comparison with the literature on calibration, we used the following measure:

$$\text{over- or underconfidence} = \frac{1}{n} \sum_{i=1}^{I} n_i \left(p_i - f_i \right) = \bar{p} - \bar{f},$$

where n is the total number of answers, n_i is the number of times the confidence judgment p_i was used, and f_i is the relative frequency of correct answers for all answers assigned confidence p_i. I is the number of different confidence categories used ($I = 7$), and $\bar{p}$ and $\bar{f}$ are the overall mean confidence judgment and percentage correct, respectively. A positive differ-ence is called overconfidence. For convenience, we report over- and under-confidence in percentages ($\times 100$).

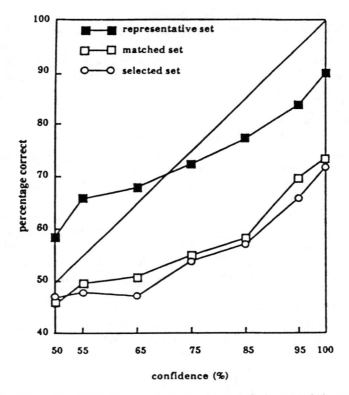

Figure 3.6. Calibration curves for the selected set (open circles), representative set (black squares), and matched set (open squares).

Results

Prediction 1. PMM theory predicts that in the selected set (general-knowledge questions), people show overestimation in confidence judgments (overconfidence) and, simultaneously, accurate frequency judgments.

The open-circle curve in Figure 3.6 shows the relation between judgments of confidence and true relative frequency of correct answers in the selected set – that is, the set of mixed general-knowledge questions.[3] The relative frequency of correct answers (averaged over all subjects) was 72.4% in the 100%-confidence category, 66.3% in the 95% category, 58.0% in the 85% category, and so on. The curve is far below the diagonal (calibration curve) and similar to the curves reported by Lichtenstein, Fischhoff, and Phillips (1982, Figure 2). It replicates and demonstrates the well-known overconfidence effect. Percentage correct was 52.9, mean confidence was 66.7, and overconfidence was 13.8.

Subjects' frequency judgments, however, are fairly accurate, as Table 3.2

Table 3.2. *Mean differences between estimated and true frequencies of correct answers*

Set	No information– no incentive	Incentive only	Information only	Information and incentive
Representative				
1–50	–9.94	–9.42	–8.80	–8.74
51–100	–9.50	–10.37	–11.95	–11.25
101–150	–9.88	–10.89	–10.85	–9.90
151–200	–6.67	–6.70	–9.35	–5.90
201–250	–9.79	–9.84	–7.95	–5.25
250–300	–9.47	–10.84	–9.40	–9.05
Average	–9.21	–9.68	–9.72	–8.35
Selected	–1.75	–.60	–2.65	.30

Note: Negative signs denote underestimation of true number of correct answers.

(last row) shows. Each entry is averaged over the 20 subjects in each condition. For instance, the figure *–1.75* means that , on average, subjects in this condition underestimated the true number of correct answers by 1.75. Averaged across the four conditions, we get –1.2, which means that subjects missed the true frequency by an average of only about 1 correct answer in the set of 50 questions. Quite accurate frequency judgments coexist with overconfidence. The magnitudes of this confidence–frequency effect found is shown in Figure 3.7 (left side). PMM theory predicts this systematic difference between confidence and frequency judgments, within the same person and the same general-knowledge questions.

Prediction 2. PMM theory predicts that in the representative set (city questions) people show zero overconfidence and, at the same time, underestimation in frequency judgments.

The solid-square curve in Figure 3.6 shows the relation between confidence and percentage correct in the representative set – that is, the city questions. For instance, percentage correct in the 100%-confidence category was 90.8%, instead of 72.4%. Overconfidence disappeared (–.9%). Percentage correct and mean confidence were 71.7 and 70.8, respectively.

The confidence curve for the representative set is similar to a regression curve for the estimation of relative frequencies by confidence, resulting in underconfidence in the left part of the confidence scale, overconfidence in the right, and zero overconfidence on the average.

Table 3.2 shows the differences between estimated and true frequencies for each block of 50 items and each of the conditions, respectively. Again, each entry is averaged over the 20 subjects in each condition. For instance, subjects who were given neither information nor incentive underestimated

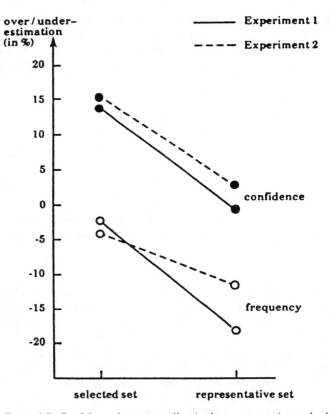

Figure 3.7. Confidence-frequency effect in the representative and selected set. (Solid lines show results of Experiment 1, dotted lines show those of Experiment 2. Frequency judgments are long-run frequencies, $N = 50$.)

their true number of correct answers by 9.94 (on the average) in the first 50 items of the representative set. Table 3.2 shows that the values of the mean differences were fairly stable over the six subsets, and, most important, they are, without exception, negative (i.e., underestimation). For each of the 24 cells (representative set), the number of subjects with negative differences (underestimation) was compared with the number of positive differences (overestimation) by sign tests, and all 24 p values were smaller than .01.

The following is an illustration at the individual level: Subject 1 estimated 28, 30, 23, 25, 23, and 23, respectively, for the six subsets, compared with 40, 38, 40, 36, 35, and 32 correct solutions, respectively. An analysis of individual judgments confirmed average results. Among the 80 subjects, 71 underestimated the number of correct answers, whereas only 8 subjects overestimated it (frequency judgments were missing for 1 subject). Incidentally, 7 of these

8 subjects were male. In the selected set, for comparison, 44 subjects underestimated and 35 subjects overestimated the number of correct answers, and 1 subject got it exactly right.

We have attributed the emergence and disappearance of overconfidence to selection versus use of a representative set. One objection to this analysis is that the difference between the open-circle and the solid-square curve in Figure 3.6 is confounded with a difference in the content of both sets. The selected set includes a broad range of general-knowledge questions, whereas the domain of the representative set (cities) is necessarily more restricted. To check for this possible confound, we determined the item difficulties for each of the 50 general-knowledge questions and selected a subset of 50 city questions that had the same item difficulties. If the difference in Figure 3.6 is independent of content, but results from the selection process, this "matched" subset of city questions should generate the same calibration curves showing overconfidence as the selected set of general-knowledge questions did. Figure 3.6 shows that this is the case (open-square curve). Both content domains produce the same results if questions are selected.

To summarize, in the representative set, overestimation disappears in confidence judgments, and zero-overconfidence coexists with frequency judgments that show large underestimation. Results confirm Prediction 2. Figure 3.7 (right side) shows the magnitude of the confidence–frequency effect found. No previous theory of confidence can predict the results depicted in Figure 3.7.

Prediction 3. PMM theory predicts that overestimation will disappear if the relative frequencies of correct answers (percentage correct) in each confidence category is compared with the estimated relative frequencies. Because subjects estimated percentage correct for all confidence judgments – that is, including both the selected and the representative set – we expect not only that overestimation will disappear (the prediction from the selected set) but also that it will turn into underestimation (the prediction from the representative set).

The solid line in Figure 3.8 shows the results for Experiment 1: Estimated relative frequencies are well calibrated and show underestimation in five out of seven confidence categories. Overestimation of one's knowledge disappears. The only exception is the 100%-confidence category. The latter is the confidence category that contains all solutions by local MMs, and errors in memory or elementary logical operations may account for the difference. Figure 3.8 is a "frequentist" variant of the calibration curve of Figure 3.6. Here, true percentage correct is compared with estimated percentage correct, rather than with confidence. For instance, in the 100%-confidence category, true and estimated percentage correct were 88.8% and 93.0% respectively.

Averaged across experimental conditions, the ratio between estimated frequency in the long run and confidence value is fairly constant, around .87,

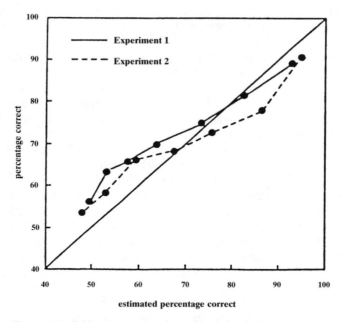

Figure 3.8. Calibration curves for judgments of percentage correct in confidence categories. (Solid lines show results of Experiment 1, dotted lines show those of Experiment 2. Values are averaged across both sets of questions.)

for confidence ratings between 65% and 95%. It is highest in the extreme categories (see Table 3.3).

To summarize, subjects explicitly distinguished between confidence in single answers and the relative frequency of correct answers associated with a confidence judgment. This result is implied by PMM theory, according to which different reference classes are cued by confidence and frequency tasks. As stated in Prediction 3, overestimation disappeared. However, the magnitude of underestimation was not, as might be expected, as pronounced as in the frequency judgments dealt with in Predictions 1 and 2. Except for this finding, results conformed well to Prediction 3. Note that no previous theory of confidence in knowledge we are aware of makes this conceptual distinction and that prediction. Our results contradict much of what has been assumed about how the untutored mind understands the relation between confidence and relative frequency of correct answers.

Information about overconfidence and monetary incentive. Mean confidence judgments were indistinguishable between subjects informed about overconfidence and those uninformed. None of seven *t* tests, one for each confidence category, resulted in *p* values smaller than .05. If a monetary incentive was announced, overconfidence was more pronounced with

Table 3.3. *Estimated and true percentage correct in each confidence category (summarized over the representative and the selected sets)*

Confidence category	No. of confidence judgments	% correct		Over-/under-estimation
		Estimated	True	
100	5,166	93.0	88.8	4.2
91–99	1,629	82.7	81.6	1.1
81–90	2,534	73.1	74.6	−1.5
71–80	2,950	64.3	70.1	−5.8
61–70	3,506	57.3	65.6	−8.3
51–60	4,036	53.7	63.3	−9.6
50	8,178	49.8	56.3	−6.5
Σ or M	27,999	64.8	69.1	−4.2

incentive than without incentive in five categories (65%–100%) and less in the 50% category (all $ps < .05$), with an average increase of 3.6%.

The monetary incentive effect resulted from the incentive/no-information group, in which confidence judgments were higher than in all three other groups (but we found the same percentage correct in all groups). One reason for this interaction could be that we did not specify in the instructions a criterion for best performance. If warned of overconfidence, subjects could easily infer that the incentive was for minimizing overconfidence. If not warned, at least some subjects could also have attempted to maximize percentage correct. None of these attempts, however, was successful, consistent with PMM theory and earlier studies (e.g., Fischhoff, Slovic, & Lichtenstein, 1977). The effort to raise the percentage correct seems to have raised confidence instead, an outcome that cannot be accounted for by PMM theory. The size of this effect, however, was small compared with both the confidence–frequency effect and that of selected versus representative sampling.

To summarize, neither warning of overconfidence nor associated monetary incentive decreased overconfidence or increased percentage correct, replicating earlier findings that knowledge about overconfidence is not sufficient to change confidence. An incentive that subjects seem to have interpreted as rewarding those who maximize the percentage correct, however, increased confidence.

Order of presentation and sex. Which set (representative vs. selected) was given first had no effect on confidences, neither in Experiment 1 nor in Experiment 2. Arkes, Christensen, Lai, and Blumer (1987) found an effect of the difficulty of one group of items on the confidence judgments for a second when subjects received feedback for their performance in the first set. In our experiment, however, no feedback was given. Thus, subjects had no reason to correct their confidence judgments, such as by subtracting a constant value. Sex differences in degree of overconfidence in knowledge have been claimed by both philosophy and folklore. Our study, however, showed no significant differences between the sexes in either overconfidence or calibration, in either Experiment 1 or in Experiment 2. (The men's confidence judgments were on the average 5% higher than women's, but so was their percentage correct. This replicates Lichtenstein and Fischhoff's, 1981, findings about students at the University of Oregon.)

To summarize, as predicted by PMM theory, we can experimentally make overconfidence (overestimation) appear, disappear, and invert. Experiment 1 made our subjects consistently switch back and forth among these responses. The key to this finding is a pair of concepts that have been neglected by the main previous explanations of confidence in one's knowledge – confidence versus frequency judgment and representative versus selected sampling.

Experiment 2

We tried to replicate the facts and test several objections. First, to strengthen the case against this theory, we instructed the subjects both verbally and in written form that confidence is subjective probability, and that among all cases where a subjective probability of X% was chosen, X% of the answers should be correct. Several authors have argued that such a frequentist instruction could enhance external calibration or internal consistency (e.g., Kahneman & Tversky, 1982; May, 1987). According to PMM theory, however, confidence is already inferred from frequency (with or without this instruction) – but from frequencies of co-occurrences between, say, number of inhabitants and several cues, and not from base rates of correct answers in similar testing situations (see Table 3.1). Thus, in our view, the preceding caution will be ineffective because the base rate of correct answers is not a probability cue that is defined on a reference class such as cities in Germany.

Second, consider the confidence–frequency effect. We have shown that this new effect is implied by PMM theory. One objection might be that the difference between confidence and frequency judgments is an artifact of the response function, just as overconfidence has sometimes been thought to be. Consider the following interpretation of overconfidence. If (a) confidence is well calibrated but (b) the response function that transforms confidence into a confidence judgment differs from an identity function, then (c) overconfidence or underconfidence "occurs" on the response scale. Because an identity function has not been proven, Anderson (1986), for instance, denoted the overconfidence effect and the hard–easy effect as "largely meaningless" (p. 91): They might just as well be response function artifacts.

A similar objection could be made against the interpretation of the confidence–frequency effect within PMM theory. Despite the effect's stability across selected and representative sets, it may just reflect a systematic difference between response functions for confidence and frequency judgments. This conjecture can be rephrased as follows: If (a) the difference between "internal" confidence and frequency impression is zero, but (b) the response functions that transform both into judgments differ systematically, then (c) a confidence–frequency effect occurs on the response scales. We call this the *response-function conjecture*.

How can this conjecture be tested? According to PMM theory, the essential basis on which both confidence and frequency judgments are formed is the probability cues, not response functions. We assumed earlier that frequency judgments are based mainly on base rates of correct answers in a reference class of similar general-knowledge test situations. If we make another cue available, then frequency judgments should change. In particular, if we make the confidence judgments more easily retrievable from memory, these can be used as additional probability cues, and the confidence–frequency effect should decrease. This was done in Experiment 2 by introducing frequency judgments in the short run, that is, frequency judgments for a very small number of questions. Here, confidence judgments can be more easily retrieved from memory than they could in the long run. Thus, if PMM theory is correct, the confidence–frequency effect should decrease in the short run. If the issue were, however, different response functions, then the availability of confidence judgments should not matter because confidence and frequency impression are assumed to be identical in the first place. Thus, if the conjecture is correct, the confidence–frequency effect should be stable.

In Experiment 2, we varied the length N of a series of questions from the long run condition $N = 50$ in Experiment 1 to the smallest possible short run of $N = 2$.

Third, in Experiment 1 we used a response scale ranging from 50% to 100% for confidence judgments but a full-range response scale for frequency judgments ranging from 0 to 50 correct answers (which corresponds to 0% to 100%). Therefore one could argue that the confidence–frequency effect is an artifact of the different ranges of the two response scales. Assume that (a) there is no difference between internal confidence and frequency, but (b) because confidence judgments are limited to the upper half of the response scale, whereas frequency judgments are not, (c) the confidence–frequency effect results as an artifact of the half-range response scale in confidence judgments. We refer to this as the *response-range conjecture*. It can be backed up by at least two hypotheses.

1. Assume that PMM theory is wrong and subjects indeed use base rates of correct answers as a probability cue for confidence in single answers. Then confidence should be considerably lower. If subjects anticipate misleading questions, even confidences lower than 50% are reasonable to expect on this conjecture. Confidences below 50%, however, cannot be expressed on a scale

with a lower boundary at 50%, whereas they can at the frequency scale. Effects of response range such as those postulated in range–frequency theory (Parducci, 1965) or by Schönemann (1983) may enforce the distorting effect of the half-range format. In this account, both the overconfidence effect and the confidence–frequency effect are generated by a response-scale effect. With respect to overconfidence, this conjecture has been made and has claimed some support (e.g., May, 1986, 1987; Ronis & Yates, 1987). We call this the *base rate hypothesis*.

2. Assume that PMM theory is wrong in postulating that choice and confidence are essentially one process and that the true process is a temporal sequence: choice, followed by search for evidence, followed by confidence judgment. Koriat et al. (1980), for instance, proposed this sequence. Assume further, contrary to Koriat, that the mind is "Popperian," searching for disconfirming rather than for confirming evidence to determine the degree of "corroboration" of an answer. If the subject is successful in retrieving disconfirming evidence form memory, but is not allowed to change the original answer, confidence judgments less than 50% will result. Such disconfirmation strategies, however, can hardly be detected using a 50%–100% format, whereas they could in a full-scale format. We call this the *disconfirmation strategy hypothesis*.

To test the response-range conjecture, half of the subjects in Experiment 2 were given full-range response scales, whereas the other half received the response scales used in Experiment 1.

Method

Subjects. Ninety-seven new subjects at the University of Konstanz (not enrolled in psychology) were paid for participation. There were 59 male and 38 female subjects. As in Experiment 1, subjects were tested in small groups of no more than 7 subjects.

Design and procedure. This was a $4 \times 2 \times 2$ design, with length of series (50, 10, 5, and 2) and response scale (half range vs. full range) varied between subjects and type of knowledge questions (selected vs. representative set) varied within subjects.

The procedure and the materials were like that in Experiment 1, except for the following. We used a new random sample of 21 (instead of 25) cities. This change decreased the number of questions in the representative set from 300 to 210. As mentioned earlier, we explicitly instructed the subjects to interpret confidences as frequencies of correct answers: "We are interested in how well you can estimate subjective probabilities. This means, among all the answers where you give a subjective probability of X%, there should be X% of the answers correct." This calibration instruction was orally repeated and emphasized to the subjects.

The response scale contained the means (50%, 55%, 65%, . . . , 95%, 100%)

of the intervals used in Experiment 1 rather than the intervals themselves to avoid the problematic assumption that means would represent intervals. Endpoints were marked *absolutely certain that the alternative chosen is correct* (100%), *both alternatives equally probable* (50%), and, for the full-range scale, *absolutely certain that the alternative chosen is incorrect* (0%). In the full-range scale, one reason for using confidences between 0% and 45% was explained in the following illustration: "If you think after you have made your choice that you would have better chosen the other alternative, do not change your choice, but answer with a probability smaller than 50%."

After each set of $N = 50$ (10, 5, or 2) answers, subjects gave a judgment of the number of correct answers. After having completed $50 + 210 = 260$ confidence judgments and 5, 26, 52, or 130 frequency judgments (depending on the subject's group), subjects in both response-scale conditions were presented the same enlarged copy of the 50%–100% response scale and asked to estimate the relative frequency of correct answers in each confidence category.

Results

Response-range conjecture. We tested the conjecture that the systematic difference in confidence and frequency judgments stated in Predictions 1 and 2 (confidence–frequency effect) and shown in Experiment 1 resulted from the availability of only a limited response scale for confidence judgments (50% to 100%).

Forty-seven subjects were given the full-range response scale for confidence judgments. Twenty-two of these never chose confidences below 50%; the others did. The number of confidence judgments below 50% was small. Eleven subjects used them only once (in altogether 260 judgments), 5 did twice, and the others 3 to 7 times. There was one outlier, a subject who used them 67 times. In total, subjects gave a confidence judgment smaller than 50% for only 1.1% of their answers (excluding the outlier: 0.6%). If the response-range conjecture had been correct, subjects would have used confidence judgments below 50% much more frequently.

In the representative set, overconfidence was 3.7% ($SE_M = 1.23$) in the full-range scale condition and 1.8% ($SE_M = 1.15$) in the half-range condition. In the selected set, the corresponding values were 14.4 ($SE_M = 1.54$) and 16.4 ($SE_M = 1.43$). Averaging all questions, we got slightly larger overconfidence in the full-range condition (mean difference = 1.2). The response–range conjecture, however, predicted a strong effect in the opposite direction. Frequency judgments were essentially the same in both conditions. Hence, the confidence–frequency effect can also be demonstrated when both confidence and frequency judgments are made on a full-range response scale.

To summarize, there was (a) little use of confidences below 50% and (b) no decrease of overconfidence in the full-range condition. These results contradict the response–range conjecture.

A study by Ronis and Yates (1987) seems to be the only other study that has compared the full-range and the half-range format in two-alternative choice tasks, but it did not deal with frequency judgments. These authors also reported that only about half their subjects used confidence judgments below 50%, although they did so more frequently than our subjects. Ronis and Yates concluded that confidences below 50% had only a negligible effect on overconfidence and calibration (pp. 209–211). Thus, results in both studies are consistent. The main difference is that Ronis and Yates seem to consider only "failure to follow the instructions" and "misusing the probability scale" (p. 207) as possible explanations for confidence judgments below 50%. In contrast, we argue that there are indeed plausible cognitive mechanisms – the base rate and disconfirmation strategy hypotheses – that imply these kind of judgments, although they would contradict PMM theory.

Both Experiment 2 and the Ronis and Yates (1987) study do not rule out, however, a more fundamental conjecture that is difficult to test. This argument is that internal confidence (not frequency) takes a verbal rather than a numerical form and that it is distorted on any numerical probability rating scale, not just on a 50%–100% response scale. Zimmer (1983, 1986) argued that verbal expressions of uncertainty (such as "highly improbable" and "very likely") are more realistic, more precise, and less prone to overconfidence and other so-called judgmental biases than are numerical judgments of probability. Zimmer's fuzzy-set modeling of verbal expressions, like models of probabilistic reasoning that dispense with the Kolmogoroff axioms (e.g., Cohen, 1989; Kyburg, 1983; Shafer, 1978), remains a largely unexplored source of alternative accounts of confidence.

For the remaining analysis, we do not distinguish between the full-range and the half-range response format. For combining the data, we recoded answers like "alternative *a*, 40% confident" as "alternative *b*, 60% confident," following Ronis and Yates (1987).

Predictions 1 and 2: Confidence–frequency effect. The question is whether the confidence–frequency effect can be replicated under the explicit instruction that subjective probabilities should be calibrated to frequencies of correct answers in the long run. Calibration curves in Experiment 2 were similar to those in Figure 3.6 and are not shown here for this reason. Figure 3.7 shows that the confidence–frequency effect replicates. In the selected set, mean confidence was 71.6%, and percentage correct was 56.2. Mean estimated number of correct answers (transformed into percentages) in the series of N = 50 was 52.0%. As stated in Prediction 1, overconfidence in single answers coexists with fairly accurate frequency judgments, which once again show slight underestimation.

In the representative set, mean confidence was 78.1% and percentage correct was 75.3%.[4] Mean estimated number of correct answers per 50 answers was 63.5%. As forecasted in Prediction 2, overconfidence largely disappeared (2.8%), and frequency judgments showed underestimation (−11.8%).

An individual analysis produced similar results. The confidence–frequency effect (average confidence higher than average frequency judgment) held for 82 (83) subjects in the selected (representative) set (out of 97). Answering the selected set, 92 respondents showed overconfidence, and 5 showed underconfidence. In the representative set, however, 60 exhibited overconfidence and 37, underconfidence.

Prediction 3: Estimated percentage correct in confidence categories. After the subjects answered the 260 general-knowledge questions, they were asked what percentage they thought they had correct in each confidence category. As shown by the dashed line in Figure 3.8, results replicated well. Average estimated percentage correct differed again from confidence and was close to the actual percentage correct.

Despite the instruction not to do so, our subjects still distinguished between a specific confidence value and the corresponding percentage of correct responses. Therefore *confidence* and *hypothesized percentage correct* should not be used as synonyms (e.g., Dawes, 1980, pp. 331–345). As suggested by this experiment, an instruction alone cannot override the cognitive processes at work.

In the 100%-confidence category, for instance, 67 subjects gave estimates below 100%. In a postexperimental interview, we pointed out to them that these judgments imply that they assumed they had not followed the calibration instruction. Most subjects explained that in each single case, they were in fact 100% confident. But they also knew that, in the long run, some answers would nonetheless be wrong, and they did not know which ones. Thus, they did not know which of the 100% answers they should correct. When asked how they made the confidence judgments, most subjects answered by giving examples of probability cues, such as "I know that this city is located in the Ruhrgebiet, and most cities there are rather large." Interviews provided evidence for several probability cues, but no evidence that base rate expectations, as reported in frequency judgments, were also used in confidence judgments.

Response-function conjecture: Frequency judgments in the short and long runs. We tested the conjecture that the confidence–frequency effect stated in Predictions 1 and 2 and shown in Experiment 1 might be due to different response functions for confidence and frequency judgments, rather than to different cognitive processes as postulated by PMM theory. If the conjecture were true, the availability of confidence judgments in the short run should not change the confidence–frequency effect (see the previous discussion).

Contrary to the response–function conjecture, the length of series showed a significant effect on the judgments of frequency of correct answers in each series ($p = .025$) as well as on the difference between judged and true fre-

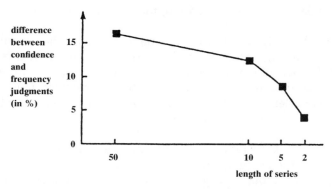

Figure 3.9. Decrease of the confidence-frequency effect in short runs ($N = 50$, 10, 5, and 2). (Values are differences between mean confidence and estimated percentage correct in a series of length N. Values are averaged across all questions.)

quency ($p = .012$). Figure 3.9 shows the extent of the disappearance of the confidence–frequency effect in the short run. The curve shows that the effect decreased from $N = 50$ to $N = 2$, averaged across both sets of items. The decrease was around 12%, an amount similar in the selected set (from 18.9% to 6.9%) and in the representative set (from 15.7% to 3.3%).

As would be expected from both the response–function conjecture and PMM theory, an analysis of variance over all 260 questions showed no significant effect of length of series (short vs. long runs) on either confidence judgment ($p = .39$) or number of correct answers ($p = .40$). (Similar results were obtained when the selected and representative sets were tested separately.)

The breakdown of the confidence–frequency effect in the short run is inconsistent with the objection that the effect can be reduced to a systematic difference in response functions. This result is, however, consistent with the notion that the shorter the run, the more easily are confidence judgments available from memory, and, thus, the more they can be used as probability cues for the true number of correct answers.

Discussion

Our starting point was the overconfidence effect, reported in the literature as a fairly stable cognitive illusion in evaluating one's general knowledge and attributed to general principles of memory search, such as confirmation bias (Koriat et al., 1980), to general motivational tendencies such as fear of invalidity (Mayseless & Kruglanski, 1987), to insensitivity to task difficulty (see von Winterfeldt & Edwards, 1986, p. 128), and to wishful thinking and other "deficits" in cognition, motivation, and personality. Our view, in contrast, proposes that one evaluates one's knowledge by probabilistic mental models. In our account, the main deficit of most cognitive and motivational explanations is that they neglect the structure of the task and its relation to the structure of a corresponding environment known to the subjects. If people want to search for confirming evidence or to believe that their answers are more correct than they are because of some need, wish, or fear, then overestimation of accuracy should express itself independently of whether they judge single answers or frequencies, a selected or representative sample of questions, and hard or easy questions.

Our experiments also do not support the explanation of overconfidence and the hard–easy effect by assuming that subjects are insensitive to task difficulty: In frequency tasks we have shown that subjects' judgments of their percentage correct in the long run are in fact close to actual percentage correct, although confidences are not. Overconfidence does not imply that subjects are not aware of task difficulty. At least two more studies have shown that estimated percentage correct can correspond closely to true percentage correct in general-knowledge tasks. Allwood and Montgomery (1987) asked their subjects to estimate how difficult each of 80 questions was for their peers and found that difficulty ratings ($M = 57\%$) were more realistic (percentage correct = 61%) than confidence judgments ($M = 74\%$). May (1987) asked her subjects to estimate their percentage of correct answers after they completed an experiment with two-alternative questions. She found that judgments of percentage correct accorded better with the true percentage correct than did confidences.

On our account, overconfidence results from one of two causes, or both: (a) A PMM for a task is not properly adapted to a corresponding environment (e.g., cue validities do not correspond to ecological validities), or (b) the set of objects used is not a representative sample from the corresponding reference class in the environment but is selected for difficulty. If a is the true cause, using a representative sample from a known environment should not eliminate overconfidence. If b is true, it should. In both experiments, overconfidence in knowledge about city populations was eliminated, as implied by b. Thus, experimental results are consistent with both PMM theory and the assumption that individual PMMs are on the average well adapted to the city environment we used.[5] Overconfidence resulted in a set of questions that was selected for difficulty. Underconfidence, conversely, would result from questions selected to be easy.

The foregoing comments do not mean that overestimation of knowledge is just an artifact of selected questions. If it were, then judgments of frequency of correct answers should show a similar degree of overestimation. What we have called the confidence–frequency effect shows that this is not the case.

Several authors have proposed that judgments in the frequency mode are more accurate, realistic, or internally consistent than probabilities for single events (e.g., Teigen, 1974, p. 62; Tversky & Kahneman, 1983). Our account is different. PMM theory states conditions under which mean judgments of confidence are systematically larger than judgments of relative frequency. PMM theory does not, however, imply that frequency judgments are generally better calibrated. On the contrary, frequency judgments may be miscalibrated for the same reasons as confidence judgments. The set of tasks may not be representative for the reference class from which the inferences are made.

The experimental control of overestimation – how to make overestimation appear, disappear, and invert – gives support to PMM theory. These predictions, however, do not exhaust the inferences that can be derived from PMM theory.

Explaining anomalies in the literature

In this section, we explain a series of apparently inconsistent findings and integrate these into PMM theory.

Ronis and Yates (1987). We have mentioned that the Ronis and Yates (1987) study is the only other study that tested a full-range response scale for two-alternative tasks. The second purpose of that study was to compare confidence judgments in situations where the subject knows that the answers are known to the experimenter (general-knowledge questions) with outcomes of upcoming basketball games, where answers are not yet known. In all three (response-scale) groups, percentage correct was larger for general-knowledge questions than for basketball predictions. Given this result, what would current theories predict about overconfidence? The insensitivity hypothesis proposes that people are largely insensitive to percentage correct (see von Winterfeldt & Edwards, 1986, p. 128). This implies that overconfidence will be larger in the more difficult (hard) set: the hard–easy effect. (The confirmation bias and motivational explanations are largely mute on the difficulty issue.) PMM theory, in contrast, predicts that overconfidence will be larger in the easier set (hard–easy effect reversal, see Prediction 5) because general-knowledge questions (the easy set) were selected and basketball predictions were not; only with clairvoyance could one select these predictions for percentage correct.

In fact, Ronis and Yates (1987) reported an apparent anomaly: three hard–easy effect reversals. In all groups, overconfidence was larger for the easy general-knowledge questions than for the hard basketball predictions (Figure 3.10). Ronis and Yates seem not to have found an explanation for these reversals of the hard–easy effect.

Koriat et al. (1980). Experiment 2 of Koriat et al.'s (1980) study provided a direct test of the confirmation bias explanation of overconfidence. The explanation is this: (a) Subjects first choose an answer based on their knowledge, then (b) they selectively search for confirming memory (or for evidence disconfirming the alternative not chosen), and (c) this confirming

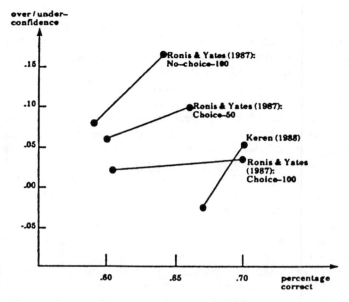

Figure 3.10. Reversal of the hard–easy effect in Ronis and Yates (1987) and Keren (1988).

evidence generates overconfidence. Between the subjects' choice of an answer and their confidence judgment, the authors asked the subjects to give reasons for the alternative chosen. Three groups of subjects were asked to write down one confirming reason, one disconfirming reason, or one of each, respectively. Reasons were given for half of the general-knowledge questions; otherwise, no reasons were given (control condition). If the confirmation bias explanation is correct, then asking for a contradicting reason (or both reasons) should decrease overconfidence and improve calibration. Asking for a confirming reason, however, should make no difference "since those instructions roughly simulate what people normally do" (Koriat et al., 1980, p. 111).

What does PMM theory predict? According to PMM theory, choice and confidence are inferred from the same activated cue. This cue is by definition a confirming reason. Therefore, the confirming-reason and the no-reason (control) tasks engage the same cognitive processes. The difference is only that in the former the supporting reason is written down. Similarly, the disconfirming-reason and both-reason tasks involve the same cognitive processes. Furthermore, PMM theory implies that there is no difference between the two pairs of tasks.

This result is shown in Table 3.4. In the first row we have the no-reason and confirming-reason tasks, which are equivalent. Here, only one cue is activated, which is confirming. There is no disconfirming cue. Now consider the second row, the disconfirming-reason and both-reason tasks, which are again equivalent. Both tasks are solved if one additional cue, which is disconfirming, can be activated. Thus, for PMM theory, the cue generation and testing cycle is started again, and cues are generated according to the hierarchy of cue validities and tested whether they can be activated for the problem at hand. The point is that the next cue that can be activated may turn out to be either confirming or disconfirming.

For simplicity, assume that the probability that the next activated cue turns out to be confirming or disconfirming is the same. If it is disconfirming, the cycle is stopped, and two cues in total have been activated, one confirming and one disconfirming. This stopping happens with probability .5, and it decreases both confidence and overconfidence. (Because the second cue activated has a smaller cue validity, however, confidence is not decreased below 50%.) If the second cue activated is again confirming, a third has to be activated, and the cue generation and testing cycle is entered again. If the third cue is disconfirming, the cycle stops with two confirming cues and one disconfirming cue activated, as shown in the third row of Table 3.4. This stopping is to be expected with probability .25. Because the second cue has higher cue validity than the third, disconfirming, cue, overall an increase in confidence and overconfidence is to be expected. If the third cue is again confirming, the same procedure is repeated. Here and in all subsequent cases confidence will increase. As shown in Table 3.4, the probabilities of an increase sum up to .5 (.25 + .125 + .125), which is the same as the probability of a decrease.

Thus, PMM theory leads to the prediction that, overall, asking for a disconfirming reason will not change confidence or overconfidence. As just shown, the confirmation-bias hypothesis, in contrast, predicts that asking for a disconfirming reason should decrease confidence and overconfidence.

What were the results of the Koriat study? In both crucial conditions, disconfirming reason and both reasons, the authors found only small and non-significant decreases of overconfidence (2% and 1%, respectively) and similar small improvements in calibration (.006 each, significant only in the disconfirming-reason task). These largely insignificant differences are consistent with the prediction by PMM theory that asking for a disconfirming reason makes no difference and are inconsistent with the confirmation-bias explanation. Further evidence comes from a replication of the Koriat study by Fischhoff and MacGregor (1982), who reported zero effects of disconfirming reasons.

To summarize, the effects on confidence of giving confirming and disconfirming reasons in the Koriat study can be both explained by and integrated into PMM theory. There is no need to postulate a confirmation bias.

Dawes (1980). Overconfidence has been attributed to people's tendency to "overestimate the power of our 'intellect' as opposed to that of our coding

Table 3.4. *Predictions of PMM theory for the effects of asking for a disconfirming reason*

Task	No. of cues activated	Cues activated	CON	DIS	Probability	Predicted change in confidence
No: CON	1	CON	1	0	—	—
DIS: both	2	DIS CON	1	1	.5	Decrease
DIS: both	3	DIS CON	2	1	.25	Increase
DIS: both	4	DIS CON	3	1	.125	Increase
DIS: both	>4	. . .	>3	1	.125	Increase

Note: CON = confirming reason; DIS = disconfirming reason; No = no reason; both = both reasons.

abilities." Such overestimation "has been reinforced by our realization that we have developed a technology capable of destroying ourselves" (Dawes 1980, p. 328). Dawes (1980) proposed that overconfidence is characteristic for general-knowledge questions but absent in perceptual tasks; he designed a series of experiments to test this proposal. PMM theory, however, gives no special treatment to perceptual tasks. On the contrary, it predicts overconfidence if perceptual tasks are selected for perceptual illusions – that is, for being misleading – whereas zero overconfidence is to be expected if tasks are not selected. Pictures in textbooks on visual illusions are probably the set of items that produces the most extreme overconfidence yet demonstrated. Nevertheless, in a natural environment, perception is generally reliable.

Dawes reported inconsistent results. When perceptual stimuli were systematically constructed from a Square × Circle matrix, as in the area task, and no selection for stimuli that generated perceptual illusions took place, overconfidence was close to zero (perception of areas of squares is quite well adapted in adults; see Gigerenzer & Richter, 1990). This result is predicted by both accounts. The anomaly arises with the second perceptual task used – judging which of two subsequent tones is longer.[6] If the second tone was longer, Dawes reported almost perfect calibration, but if the first tone was longer, subjects exhibited large overconfidence.

PMM theory predicts that in the inconsistent acoustic task, perceptual stimuli have been selected (albeit unwittingly) for a perceptual illusion. This is in fact the case. From the literature on time perception, we know that of two subsequently presented tones, the tone more recently heard appears to be longer. This perceptual illusion is known as the *negative presentation effect* (e.g., Fraisse, 1964; Sivyer & Finlay, 1982). It implies a smaller percentage of correct answers in the condition where the tone presented first was longer, because this tone is perceived to be shorter. A decrease in percentage correct in turn increases overconfidence. In Dawes's (1980) experiments, this is exactly the inconsistent condition where overconfidence occurred. Thus, from the perspective we propose, this inconsistent result can be reconciled.

Keren (1988). A strict distinction between perceptual judgment and intellectual judgment cannot be derived from many views of perception, such as signal-detection theory (Tanner & Swets, 1954). Reflecting on this fact, Keren (1988) proposed a slightly modified hypothesis: The more perceptionlike a task is, the less overconfident and the better calibrated subjects will be. "As a task requires additional higher processing and transformation of the original sensory input, different kinds of possible cognitive distortions may exist (such as inappropriate inferences) that may limit the ability to accurately monitor our higher cognitive processes" (Keren, 1988, p. 99).

Keren (1988, Experiment 1) used general-knowledge questions and two kinds of perceptual tasks, one of them more difficult than the general-knowledge task, the other less difficult. Keren tested the hypothesis that confidence judgments in perceptual tasks are better calibrated than in general-knowledge tasks. He could not support it, however. Instead, he found an anomaly: The comparison between the general-knowledge task and the more difficult perceptual task reversed the hard–easy effect (see Figure 3.10). As derived in Prediction 5, this puzzling reversal is implied by PMM theory if the Landolt rings used in the more difficult perceptual task were not selected for perceptual illusions, as seems to be the case (Keren, 1988, p. 100).

Note that the kind of general-knowledge questions used (population of cities or countries, and distances between cities) would easily permit defining a reference class in a known environment and obtaining representative samples. But no representative sample of general-knowledge questions was generated. This lack makes the other predictions from PMM theory coincide with Keren's (1988): overconfidence in general-knowledge, and zero overconfidence in the two perceptual tasks. Results show this outcome, except for the large-gap Landolt rings condition, which generated considerable underconfidence. PMM theory cannot account for the latter, nor can the notion of degree of perception-likeness.

A second perceptual task was letter identification. In Experiment 3, Keren (1988) used two letter-identification tasks, which were identical except that the exposure time of the letters to be recognized was either short or long. Mean percentages correct were 63.5 for short and 77.2 for long exposures. According to earlier explanations such as subjects' insensitivity to task difficulty, a hard–easy effect should result. According to PMM theory, however, the hard–easy effect should be zero, because both tasks were generated by the same sampling process (Prediction 4). In fact, Keren (1988, p. 112) reported that in both tasks, overconfidence was not significantly different from zero. He seems to have found no explanation for this disappearance of the hard–easy effect in a situation where differences in percentage correct were large.[7]

Mental models as probabilistic syllogisms

To the best of our knowledge, there is only one other mental models approach to confidence. May (1986, 1987) emphasized the role of mental models to understand the mechanism of confidence judgments and the role of misleading questions to cause overconfidence. Consider again the following question: "Which city has more inhabitants? (a) Hyderabad or (b) Islamabad." May proposed that subjects answer this question by constructing a mental model that can be expressed as a "probabilistic syllogistic inference" (May, 1986, p. 21):

> "Most capitals have quite a lot of inhabitants.
> Islamabad is a capital.
> _____
> Presumably, Islamabad has quite a lot of inhabitants."

Replacing "most" by the probability p(large|capital) = 1 − alpha, that is, the probability that a city has a large population if it is a capital, she made the following argument:

The subjective probability therefore has to be "1 − alpha." Given that the perception of that percentage is correct, the observed frequency of correct answers will be 1 − alpha. Even if there was random fluctuation of subjective probability and task difficulty, in the long run calibration is expected. (May, 1986, p. 20)

May (1986, 1987) did highly interesting analyses of individual general-knowledge questions – among others, direct tests of the use of the capital cue and the familiarity cue in questions of the Hyderabad–Islamabad type. Both May and PMM theory share an emphasis on the mental models subjects use to construe their tasks. We discuss here two issues where we believe that May's position could be strengthened: the kind of mental model she proposed and the role of misleading questions.

First, we show that the probabilistic syllogism does not work in the sense she specified, that is, generating long-run calibration. We propose a working version. The general reason why the syllogism mental model does not work in a two-alternative task is that it does not deal with information about the alternative, that is, whether Hyderabad is known as a capital or noncapital or whether its status is unknown. Specifically, assume that the subject knows nothing about Hyderabad, as May did (1986, p. 19). The syllogism produces the choice a and the confidence judgment $p(a = \text{large}|a = \text{capital})$, where a stands for Islamabad. However, this confidence judgment is not equal to the long-run frequency of correct answers. The long-run frequency of correct answers $p(a$ larger than $b \mid a = \text{capital})$ depends on both $p(a = \text{large}|a = \text{capital})$

and $p(b = \text{large}|b = \text{city})$, where b stands for Hyderabad and "city" means no knowledge of whether b is a capital or a noncapital. For instance, the larger $p(b = \text{large}|b = \text{city})$, the smaller the long-run frequency of correct answers.

A mental model that generates confidence judgments that are well calibrated with long-run frequencies of correct answers can be constructed in at least two ways. First, the probabilistic syllogism can be supplanted by a second syllogism that uses our knowledge about the alternative – capital, noncapital, or just city (no knowledge of whether it is a capital or noncapital). Here is a numerical illustration of what can be called the *double-syllogism model*:

> 80% of capitals have a large population.
> Islamabad is a capital.
> ―――――――――――――――――――――――――――――――――――
> The probability is .80 that Islamabad has a large population.
> 40% of cities have a large population.
> Hyderabad is a capital.
> ―――――――――――――――――――――――――――――――――――
> The probability is .40 that Hyderabad has a large population.

What is the long-run frequency of correct answers? There are four possible classes of events: $a = \text{large}$ and $b = \text{not large}$; $b = \text{large}$ and $a = \text{not large}$; $a = \text{large}$ and $b = \text{large}$; and $a = \text{not large}$ and $b = \text{not large}$. Given the choice a, the first class of events signifies correct choices; the second, incorrect choices; and the third and fourth do not contain discriminating information. The long-run frequency of correct answers consists of the first class of events and of half of the third and fourth – on the assumption that half of the nondiscriminating cases will be correct and the other half incorrect. Thus, the long-run frequency of correct answers is $p(a = \text{large}, b = \text{not large}|a = \text{capital}) + \frac{1}{2}(p[a = \text{large}, b = \text{large}|a = \text{capital}] + p[a = \text{not large}, b = \text{not large}|a = \text{capital}])$. We denote the probabilities from the first and the second syllogism as α and β, respectively. Then, the long-run frequency of correct answers is $\alpha(1 - \beta) + \frac{1}{2}(\alpha\beta + [1 - \alpha][1 - \beta])$, which is $\frac{1}{2}(\alpha - \beta + 1)$. For instance, if $\alpha = \beta$, this probability is .50. Therefore, in the above double-syllogism model, the (calibrated) confidence that α is correct is $\frac{1}{2}(\alpha - \beta + 1)$. May (1986), in contrast, proposed α. For the double syllogism, we get $\frac{1}{2}(80 - .40 + 1) = .70$.

A second solution would be to dispense with the dichotomy of large versus small population and to use the cue validities as defined in PMM theory. Both changes would make May's mental models work and would lead to a mechanism that differs in an interesting way from that illustrated in Figure 3.3. In contrast to what we have proposed, May (1986) assumed that cues are activated even if knowledge from memory can be retrieved only for one alternative.

May (1986, 1987) also proposed that overconfidence is due to misleading items. The Islamabad–Hyderabad question is one example of a misleading item with less than 50% correct answers. Most subjects chose Islamabad, whereas Hyderabad has a much larger population. An extreme example is "Three fourths of the world's cacao comes from (a) Africa or (b) South America" for which Fischhoff et al. (1977) reported only 4.8% correct answers. Fischhoff et al. showed that extreme overconfidence, such as odds greater than 50:1, are prevalent in what they called *deceptive* items (more than 73%) but still exist in nondeceptive items (less than 9%). Because of the latter finding, among other grounds, they concluded that misleading items "are not responsible for the extreme overconfidence effect" (p. 561). In contrast, May (1986, 1987) seems to have held that if misleading items were eliminated, overconfidence would be, too. But she also emphasized, as we do, the role of representative sampling.

We propose that the issue of misleading questions can be fully reduced to the issue of representative sampling from a reference class, which provides a deeper understanding of confidence in knowledge. As we have pointed out before, the same set of general-knowledge questions can be nonrepresentative with respect to one reference class (e.g., all cities in Germany), but representative with respect to a different reference class (e.g., sets of typical general-knowledge questions). The notion of misleading items does not capture this distinction, which is both essential to PMM theory as well as to an explanation for when and why overconfident subjects can quite realistically estimate their true relative frequencies of correct responses.

The Brunswikian perspective

PMM theory draws heavily on the Brunswikian notions of a natural environment known to an individual, reference classes in this environment, and representative sampling from a reference class. We went beyond the Brunswikian focus on achievement (rather than process) by providing a theoretical framework of the processes that determine choice, confidence, and frequency judgment.

Choice and confidence are a result of a cue-testing and activation cycle, which is analogous to Newell and Simon's (1972) postulate that "problem solving takes place by search in a problem space" (p. 809). Furthermore, the emphasis on the structure of the task in PMM theory is similar to Newell and Simon's proposition that "the structure of the task determines the possible structures of the problem space" (p. 789). Unlike PMM theorists, however, Newell and Simon also assumed in the tasks they studied (cryptarithmetic, logic, and chess) a relatively simple mapping between the external structure of the task and the internal representation in a problem space (see Allport, 1975). Although it is cued by the task structure, we assume that a PMM (the functional equivalent of a problem space) has a large surplus structure (the reference class and the cues), which is taken from a known structure in the problem solver's natural environment. The emphasis on the structure of everyday knowledge or environment (as distinguished from the task environment) has been most forcefully defended by Brunswik (see Gigerenzer,

1987). Although Newell and Simon (1972, p. 874) called Brunswik and Tolman "the real forerunners" of their work, they seem not to distinguish clearly between the notions of a probabilistic everyday environment and a task environment. This theory is an attempt to combine both views. Brunswik's focus on achievement (during his behavioristic phase; see Leary, 1987) corresponds more closely to the part of research on probabilistic judgment that focuses on calibration, rather than on the underlying cognitive processes.

The importance of the cognitive representation of the task was studied by the Würzburg school and emphasized in Gestalt theoretical accounts of thinking (e.g., Duncker, 1935/1945), and this issue has recently regained favor (e.g., Brehmer, 1988; Hammond, Stewart, Brehmer, & Steinman, 1975). In their review, Einhorn and Hogarth (1981) emphasized that "the cognitive approach has been concerned primarily with *how* tasks are represented. The issue of *why* tasks are represented in particular ways has not yet been addressed" (p. 57). PMM theory addresses this issue. Different tasks, such as confidence and frequency tasks, cue different reference classes and different probability cues from known environments. It is these environments that provide the particular representation, the PMM, of a task.

Many parts of PMM theory need further expansion, development, and testing. Open issues include the following: (a) What reference class is activated? For city comparisons, this question has a relatively clear answer, but in general, more than one reference class can be constructed to solve a problem. (b) Are cues always generated according to their rank in the cue validity hierarchy? Alternative models of cue generation could relax this strong assumption, assuming, for instance, that the first cue generated is the cue activated in the last problem. The latter would, however, decrease the percentage of correct answers. (c) What are the conditions under which we may expect PMMs to be well adapted? There exists a large body of neo-Brunswikian research that, in general, indicates good adaptation but also points out exceptions (e.g., K. Armelius, 1979; Brehmer & Joyce, 1988; Björkman, 1987; Hammond & Wascoe, 1980). (d) What are the conditions under which cue substitution without cue integration is superior to multiple cue integration? PMM theory assumes a pure cue substitution model – a cue that cannot be activated can be replaced by any other cue – without integration of two or more cues. We focused on the substitution and not the integration aspect of Brunswik's vicarious functioning (see Gigerenzer & Murray, 1987, pp. 66–81), in contrast to the multiple regression metaphor of judgment. Despite its simplicity, the substitution model produces zero overconfidence and a large number of correct answers, if the PMM is well adapted. There may be more reasons for simple substitution models. B. Armelius and Armelius (1974), for instance, reported that subjects were well able to use ecological validities, but not the correlations between cues. If the latter is the case, then multiple cue integration may not work well.

We briefly indicate here that features emphasized by PMM theory, such as representative sampling and the confidence–frequency distinction, can also be crucial for probabilistic reasoning in other tasks.

In several Bayesian-type studies of revision of belief, representative (random) sampling from a reference class is a crucial issue. For instance, Gigerenzer, Hell, and Blank (1988) showed that subjects' neglect of base rates in Kahneman and Tversky's (1973) engineer–lawyer problem disappeared if subjects could randomly draw the descriptions from an urn. Similar results showing people's sensitivity to the issue of representative versus selected sampling have been reported by Cosmides and Tooby (1990), Ginossar and Trope (1987), Grether (1980), Hansen and Donoghue (1977), and Wells and Harvey (1977), but see Nisbett and Borgida (1975).

This study has also demonstrated that judgments of single events can systematically differ from judgments of relative frequencies. Similar differences were found for other kinds of probabilistic reasoning (Gigerenzer, 1991a, 1991b). For instance, the "conjunction fallacy" has been established by asking subjects the probabilities of single events, such as whether "Linda" is more likely to be (a) a bank teller or (b) a bank teller and active in the feminist movement. Most subjects chose the latter, because the description of Linda was constructed to be representative of an active feminist. This judgment was called a conjunction fallacy because the probability of a conjunction (bank teller and feminist) is never larger than the probability of one of its constituents. As in the engineer–lawyer problem, the representativeness heuristic was proposed to explain the "fallacy." Fiedler (1988) and Tversky and Kahneman (1983), however, showed that the conjunction fallacy largely disappeared if people were asked for frequencies (e.g., "There are 100 persons like Linda. How many of them are . . . ?") rather than probabilities of single events. Cosmides and Tooby (1990) showed a similar striking difference for people's reasoning in a medical probability revision problem. The subjects' task was to estimate the probability that people have a disease, given a positive test result, the base rate of the disease, the false-alarm rate, and the hit rate of the test. Originally, Casscells, Schoenberger, and Grayboys (1978) reported only 18% Bayesian answers when Harvard medical students and staff were asked for a single-event probability (What is the probability that a person found to have a positive result actually has the disease?). When Cosmides and Tooby changed the task into a frequency task (How many people who test positive will actually have the disease?), 76% of subjects responded with the Bayesian answer. These results suggest that the mental models subjects construe to solve these reasoning problems were highly responsive to information crucial for probability and statistics – random versus selected sampling and single events versus frequencies in the long run.

Is overconfidence a bias according to probability theory?

Throughout this article, we have avoided classifying judgments as either rational or biased, but instead focused on the underlying cognitive processes and how these explain extant data. Overconfidence is, however, usually classified as a bias and dealt with in chapters on "cognitive illusions" (e.g., Edwards & von Winterfeldt, 1986). Is overconfidence a bias according to probability theory?

Mathematical probability emerged around 1660 as a Janus-faced concept with three interpretations: observed frequencies of events, equal possibilities based on physical symmetry, and degrees of subjective certainty or belief. Frequencies originally came from mortality and natality data, sets of equiprobable outcomes from gambling, and the epistemic sense of belief proportioned to evidence from courtroom practices (Daston, 1988). Eighteenth-century mathematicians used "probability" in all three senses, whereas latter-day probabilists drew a bold line between the first 2 "objective" senses and the third "subjective" one. Today, mathematicians, statisticians, and philosophers are still wrangling over the proper interpretation of probability: Does it mean a relative frequency, a propensity, a degree of belief, a degree of evidentiary confirmation or yet something else? Prominent thinkers can still be found in every camp, and it would be bold unto foolhardy to claim that any interpretation had a monopoly on reasonableness (Gigerenzer et al., 1989).

Overconfidence is defined as the difference between degrees of belief (subjective probabilities) and a relative frequency (percentage correct). Is a deviation between the probability that a particular answer is correct and the relative frequency of correct answers a bias or error, according to probability theory?

From the point of view of dedicated frequentists such as von Mises (1928/1957) and Neyman (1977), it is not. According to the frequentist interpretation (which is the dominant interpretation in statistics departments today), probability theory is about relative frequencies in the long run; it does not deal with degrees of beliefs concerning single events. For instance, when speaking of "the probability of death":

[One] must not think of an individual, but of a certain class as a whole, e.g., "all insured men forty-one years old living in a given country and not engaged in certain dangerous occupations." . . . The phrase "probability of death," when it refers to a single person, has no meaning at all for us. (von Mises, 1928/1957, p. 11)

For a frequentist, one cannot properly speak of a probability until a reference class has been defined. The statistician Barnard (1979), for instance, suggested that if one is concerned with the subjective probabilities of single events, such as confidence, one "should concentrate on the works of Freud and perhaps Jung rather than Fisher and Neyman" (p. 171). Thus, for frequentists, probability theory does not apply to single-event judgments like confidences, and therefore no statement about confidences can violate probability theory.

Moreover, even subjectivists would not generally think of a deviation between probabilities for single events and relative frequencies as a bias. The problem is whether and when a subjectivist, who rejects the identification of probability with objective frequency, should nonetheless make frequency the yardstick of good reasoning (for a discussion of conditions, see Kadane & Lichtenstein, 1982). The subjectivist Bruno de Finetti, for instance, emphatically stated in his early work that subjective probabilities of single events cannot be validated by objective probabilities:

> However an individual evaluates the probability of a particular event, no experience can prove him right, or wrong; nor in general, could any conceivable criterion give any objective sense to the distinction one would like to draw, here, between right and wrong. (de Finetti, 1931/1989, p. 174)

We thus have to face a problem: Many cognitive psychologists think of overconfidence as a bias of reasoning, pointing to probability theory as justification. Many probabilists and statisticians, however, would reply that their interpretation of probability does not justify this label (see Hacking, 1965; Lad, 1984; Stegmüller, 1973).

PMM theory can offer a partial solution to this problem. First, it clarifies the distinction between confidence and frequency judgments and therewith directs attention to the comparison between estimated and true frequencies of correct answers. The latter avoids the previously stated problem. This comparison has not received much attention in research on confidence in knowledge. Second, PMM theory proposes a frequentist interpretation of degrees of belief: Both confidence and frequency judgments are based on memory about frequencies. Our view links both types of judgment but does not equate them. Rather, it specifies when to expect confidence and frequency judgments to diverge, and in what direction, and when they will converge. PMM theory integrates single-event probabilities into a frequentist framework: the Bayesian is Brunswikian.

Conclusions

We conjecture that confidence in one's knowledge of the kind studied here – immediate and spontaneous rather than a product of long-term reflection – is largely determined by the structure of the task and the structure of a corresponding, known environment in a person's long-term memory. We provided experimental evidence for this hypothesis by showing how changes in the task (confidence vs. frequency judgment) and in the relationship between task and environment (selected vs. representative sampling) can make the two stable effects reported in the literature – overconfidence and the hard–easy effect – emerge, disappear, and invert at will. We have demonstrated a new phenomenon, the confidence–frequency effect. One cannot speak of a general overconfidence bias anymore, in the sense that it relates to deficient processes of cognition or motivation. In contrast, subjects seem to be able to make fine conceptual distinctions – confidence versus frequency – of the same kind as probabilists and statisticians do. Earlier attempts postulating general deficiencies in information processing or motivation cannot account for the experimental results predicted by PMM theory and confirmed in two experiments. PMM theory seems to be the first theory in this field that gives a coherent account of these various effects by focusing on the relation between the structure of the task, the structure of a corresponding environment, and a PMM.

Notes

1 For convenience, the theory is presented here in its complete form, although parts of it were developed after Experiment 1 was performed. All those parts were subjected to an independent test in Experiment 2.
2 Allwood and Montgomery (1987, pp. 369–370) estimated from verbal protocols that about 19% of their general-knowledge questions were solved by "full recognition," which seems to be equivalent to memory and elementary logical operations only.
3 In Figure 3.6, we have represented the confidence category (91%–99%) by 95%, and similarly with the other categories. This choice can be criticized because numerical judgments of confidence often cluster around specific values in an interval. (If there is a difference, however, we may expect that it affects the three curves in a similar way, without altering the differences between curves.) In Experiment 2, we used precise values instead of these intervals.
4 Confidence and percentage correct are averaged across all four conditions (series length) because these do not differ systematically among conditions. For comparison, the corresponding values for confidence and percentage correct in the $N = 50$ condition are 71.0 and 56.8 in the selected set and 79.2 and 74.5 in the representative set.
5 After finishing this article, we learned about a study by Juslin (1991), in which random samples were drawn from several natural environments. Overall, overconfidence in general knowledge was close to zero, consistent with this study.
6 Dawes's eye-color task is not dealt with here because it is a memory task, not a perceptual task.
7 Keren (1987, 1988; Wagenaar & Keren, 1985) also distinguished tasks in which the items are related (e.g., repeated weather forecasting) versus unrelated (e.g., typical general-knowledge questions). A similar distinction was made by Ronis and Yates (1987). PMM theory can connect Keren's distinction between two kinds of tasks with a model of cognitive processes involved in different tasks. In a set of unrelated items, a new PPM has to be constructed for each new item that cannot be answered by a local MM. This new PMM includes a new reference class, new target variable, and new cues and cue validities. This holds for reasoning about a set of typical general-knowledge questions. In contrast, the representative set of city questions used in our experiments implies that the PMMs for subsequent items include the same reference class, same target value, and same hierarchy of cues and cue validities but that different cues will be activated in different questions. Thus, in this framework, the distinction between related and unrelated items is neither a dichotomy nor a single continuum, but multidimensional. In general, a set of items can cue a series of PMMs that have (a) the same–different reference class, (b) the same–different target variable, (c) the same–different set of cues and cue validities, and (d) the same–different activated cues. Thus, at the other extreme of the typical general-knowledge task, there is a series of tasks that implies the construction of a succession of PMMs that are identical with respect to all four dimensions. An example is the repeated judgment of the frequency of correct answers in our experiments.

References

Allport, D. A. (1975). The state of cognitive psychology. *Quarterly Journal of Experimental Psychology, 27*, 141–152.
Allwood, C. M., & Montgomery, H. (1987). Response selection strategies and realism

of confidence judgments. *Organizational Behavior and Human Decision Processes*, *39*, 365–383.

Anderson, N. H. (1986). A cognitive theory of judgment and decision. In B. Brehmer, H. Jungermann, P. Lourens, & G. Sevón (Eds.), *New directions in research on decision making* (pp. 63–108). Amsterdam: North-Holland.

Angele, U., Beer-Binder, B., Berger, R., Bussmann, C., Kleinbölting, H., & Mansard, B. (1982). *Über- und Unterschätzung des eigenen Wissens in Abhängigkeit von Geschlecht und Bildungsstand.* [Overestimation and underestimation of one's knowledge as a function of sex and education]. Unpublished manuscript, University of Konstanz, Constance, Federal Republic of Germany.

Arkes, H. R., Christensen, C., Lai, C., & Blumer, C. (1987). Two methods of reducing overconfidence. *Organizational Behavior and Human Decision Processes*, *39*, 133–144.

Arkes, H. R., & Hammond, K. R. (Eds.). (1986). *Judgment and decision making: An interdisciplinary reader*. Cambridge, England: Cambridge University Press.

Armelius, B., & Armelius, K. (1974). The use of redundancy in multiple-cue judgments: Data from a suppressor–variable-task. *American Journal of Psychology*, *87*, 385–392.

Armelius, K. (1979). Task predictability and performance as determinants of confidence in multiple-cue judgments. *Scandinavian Journal of Psychology*, *20*, 19–25.

Barnard, G. A. (1979). Discussion of the paper by Professors Lindley and Tversky and Dr. Brown. *Journal of the Royal Statistical Society of London*, *142*(Series A), 171–172.

Björkman, M. (1987). A note on cue probability learning: what conditioning data reveal about cue contrast. *Scandinavian Journal of Psychology*, *28*, 226–232.

Brehmer, B. (1988). The development of social judgment theory. In B. Brehmer & C. R. B. Joyce (Eds.), *Human judgment: The SJT view* (pp. 13–40). Amsterdam: North-Holland.

Brehmer, B., & Joyce, C. R. B. (Eds.). (1988). *Human judgment: The SJT view*. Amsterdam: North-Holland.

Brunswik, E. (1943). Organismic achievement and environmental probability. *Psychological Review*, *50*, 255–272.

Brunswik, E. (1955). Representative design and probabilistic theory in a functional psychology. *Psychological Review*, *62*, 193–217.

Brunswik, E. (1964). Scope and aspects of the cognitive problem. In *Contemporary approaches to cognition* (pp. 4–31). Cambridge, MA: Harvard University Press.

Casscells, W., Schoenberger, A., & Grayboys, T. (1978). Interpretation by physicians of clinical laboratory results. *New England Journal of Medicine*, *299*, 999–1000.

Cohen, L. J. (1989). *The philosophy of induction and probability*. Oxford, England: Clarendon Press.

Cosmides, L., & Tooby, J. (1990, August). *Is the mind a frequentist?* Paper presented at the 31st Annual Meeting of the Psychonomics Society, New Orleans, LA.

Daston, L. J. (1988). *Classical probability in the Enlightenment*. Princeton, NJ: Princeton University Press.

Dawes, R. M. (1980). Confidence in intellectual judgments vs. confidence in perceptual judgments. In E. D. Lantermann & H. Feger (Eds.), *Similarity and choice: Papers in honor of Clyde Coombs* (pp. 327–345). Bern, Switzerland: Huber.

de Finetti, B. (1989). Probabilism. *Erkenntnis*, *31*, 169–223. (Original work published 1931.)

Duncker, K. (1945). On problem solving (L. S. Lees, trans.). *Psychological Monographs, 58*(5, Whole No. 270). (Original work published 1935.)

Edwards, W., & von Winterfeldt, D. (1986). On cognitive illusions and their implications. In H. R. Arkes & K. R. Hammond (Eds.), *Judgment and decision making: An interdisciplinary reader* (pp. 642–679). Cambridge, England: Cambridge University Press.

Einhorn, H. J., & Hogarth, R. M. (1981). Behavioral decision theory: Processes of judgment and choice. *Annual Review of Psychology, 32*, 53–88.

Fiedler, K. (1988). The dependence of the conjunction fallacy on subtle linguistic factors. *Psychological Research, 50*, 123–129.

Fischhoff, B. (1982). Debiasing. In D. Kahneman, P. Slovic, & A. Tversky (Eds.), *Judgment under uncertainty: Heuristics and biases* (pp. 422–444). Cambridge, England: Cambridge University Press.

Fischhoff, B., & MacGregor, D. (1982). Subjective confidence in forecasts. *Journal of Forecasting, 1*, 155–172.

Fischhoff, B., Slovic, P., & Lichtenstein, S. (1977). Knowing with certainty: The appropriateness of extreme confidence. *Journal of Experimental Psychology: Human Perception and Performance, 3*, 552–564.

Fraisse, P. (1964). *The psychology of time*. London: Eyre & Spottiswoode.

Gigerenzer, G. (1984). External validity of laboratory experiments: The frequency–validity relationship. *American Journal of Psychology, 97*, 185–195.

Gigerenzer, G. (1987). Survival of the fittest probabilist: Brunswik, Thurstone, and the two disciplines of psychology. In L. Krüger, G. Gigerenzer, & M. S. Morgan (Eds.), *The probabilistic revolution, Vol. 2: Ideas in the sciences*. Cambridge, MA: MIT Press.

Gigerenzer, G. (1991a). From tools to theories: A heuristic of discovery in cognitive psychology. *Psychological Review, 98*, 254–267.

Gigerenzer, G. (1991b). How to make cognitive illusions disappear: Beyond "heuristics and biases." *European Review of Social Psychology, 2*, 83–115.

Gigerenzer, G., Hell, W., & Blank, H. (1988). Presentation and content: The use of base rates as a continuous variable. *Journal of Experimental Psychology: Human Perception and Performance, 14*, 513–525.

Gigerenzer, G., & Murray, D. J. (1987). *Cognition as intuitive statistics*. Hillsdale, NJ: Erlbaum.

Gigerenzer, G., & Richter, H. R. (1990). Context effects and their interaction with development: Area judgments. *Cognitive Development, 5*, 235–264.

Gigerenzer, G., Swijtink, Z., Porter, T., Daston, L. J., Beatty, J., & Krüger, L. (1989). *The empire of chance. How probability changed science and everyday life*. Cambridge, England: Cambridge University Press.

Ginossar, Z., & Trope, Y. (1987). Problem solving in judgment under uncertainty. *Journal of Personality and Social Psychology, 52*, 464–474.

Grether, D. M. (1980). Bayes rule as a descriptive model: The representativeness heuristic. *The Quarterly Journal of Economics, 95*, 537–557.

Hacking, I. (1965). *Logic of statistical inference*. Cambridge, England: Cambridge University Press.

Hammond, K. R., Stewart, T. R., Brehmer, B., & Steinmann, D. O. (1975). Social judgment theory. In M. F. Kaplan & S. Schwartz (Eds.), *Human judgment and decision processes*. San Diego, CA: Academic Press.

Hammond, K. R., & Wascoe, N. E. (Eds.). (1980). Realizations of Brunswik's representative design. *New Directions for the Methodology of Social and Behavioral Science, 3,* 271–312.

Hansen, R. D., & Donoghue, J. M. (1977). The power of consensus: Information derived from one's own and others' behavior. *Journal of Personality and Social Psychology, 35,* 294–302.

Hasher, L., Goldstein, D., & Toppino, T. (1977). Frequency and the conference of referential validity. *Journal of Verbal Learning and Verbal Behavior, 16,* 107–112.

Hasher, L., & Zacks, R. T. (1979). Automatic and effortful processes in memory. *Journal of Experimental Psychology: General, 108,* 356–388.

Hintzman, D. L., Nozawa, G., & Irmscher, M. (1982). Frequency as a nonpropositional attribute of memory. *Journal of Verbal Learning and Verbal Behavior, 21,* 127–141.

Howell, W. C., & Burnett, S. (1978). Uncertainty measurement: A cognitive taxonomy. *Organizational Behavior and Human Performance, 22,* 45–68.

Johnson-Laird, P. N. (1983). *Mental models.* Cambridge, MA: Harvard University Press.

Juslin, P. (1991). *Well-calibrated general knowledge: An ecological inductive approach to realism of confidence.* Manuscript submitted for publication. Uppsala, Sweden.

Kadane, J. B., & Lichtenstein, S. (1982). *A subjectivist view of calibration* (Rep. No. 82–86). Eugene, OR: Decision Research.

Kahneman, D., & Tversky, A. (1973). On the psychology of prediction. *Psychological Review, 80,* 237–251.

Kahneman, D., & Tversky, A. (1982). On the study of statistical intuitions. In D. Kahneman, P. Slovic, & A. Tversky (Eds.), *Judgment under uncertainty: Heuristics and biases* (pp. 493–508). Cambridge, England: Cambridge University Press.

Keren, G. (1987). Facing uncertainty in the game of bridge: A calibration study. *Organizational Behavior and Human Decision Processes, 39,* 98–114.

Keren, G. (1988). On the ability of monitoring non-veridical perceptions and uncertain knowledge: Some calibration studies. *Acta Psychologica, 67,* 95–119.

Koriat, A., Lichtenstein, S., & Fischhoff, B. (1980). Reasons for confidence. *Journal of Experimental Psychology: Human Learning and Memory, 6,* 107–118.

Kyburg, H. E. (1983). Rational belief. *Behavioral and Brain Sciences, 6,* 231–273.

Lad, F. (1984). The calibration question. *British Journal of the Philosophy of Science, 35,* 213–221.

Leary, D. E. (1987). From act psychology to probabilistic functionalism: The place of Egon Brunswik in the history of psychology. In M. G. Ash & W. R. Woodward (Eds.), *Psychology in twentieth-century thought and society* (pp. 115–142). Cambridge, England: Cambridge University Press.

Lichtenstein, S., & Fischhoff, B. (1977). Do those who know more also know more about how much they know? The calibration of probability judgments. *Organizational Behavior and Human Performance, 20,* 159–183.

Lichtenstein, S., & Fischhoff, B. (1981). *The effects of gender and instruction on calibration* (Tech. Rep. No. PTR-1092-81-7). Eugene, OR: Decision Research.

Lichtenstein, S., Fischhoff, B., & Phillips, L. D. (1982). Calibration of probabilities: The state of art to 1980. In D. Kahneman, P. Slovic, & A. Tversky (Eds.), *Judgment under uncertainty: Heuristics and biases* (pp. 306–334). Cambridge, England: Cambridge University Press.

MacGregor, D., & Slovic, P. (1986). Perceived acceptability of risk analysis as a decision-making approach. *Risk Analysis, 6,* 245–256.

May, R. S. (1986). Overconfidence as a result of incomplete and wrong knowledge. In

R. W. Scholz (Ed.), *Current issues in West German decision research* (pp. 13–30). Frankfurt am Main, Germany: Lang.

May, R. S. (1987). *Realismus von subjektiven Wahrscheinlichkeiten: Eine kognitionspsychologische Analyse inferentieller Prozesse beim Overconfidence-Phänomen* [Calibration of subjective probabilities: A cognitive analysis of inference processes in overconfidence]. Frankfurt, Federal Republic of Germany: Lang.

Mayseless, O., & Kruglanski, A. W. (1987). What makes you so sure? Effects of epistemic motivations on judgmental confidence. *Organizational Behavior and Human Decision Processes, 39*, 162–183.

Newell, A., & Simon, H. A. (1972). *Human problem solving.* Englewood Cliffs, NJ: Prentice-Hall.

Neyman, J. (1977). Frequentist probability and frequentist statistics. *Synthese, 36*, 97–131.

Nisbett, R. E., & Borgida, E. (1975). Attribution and the psychology of prediction. *Journal of Personality and Social Psychology, 32*, 932–943.

Parducci, A. (1965). Category judgment: A range–frequency model. *Psychological Review, 72*, 407–418.

Ronis, D. L., & Yates, J. F. (1987). Components of probability judgment accuracy: Individual consistency and effects of subject matter and assessment method. *Organizational Behavior and Human Decision Processes, 40*, 193–218.

Rosch, E. (1978). Principles of categorization. In E. Rosch & B. B. Lloyd (Eds.), *Cognition and categorization* (pp. 27–48). Hillsdale, NJ: Erlbaum.

Schönemann, P. H. (1983). Some theory and results for metrics for bounded response scales. *Journal of Mathematical Psychology, 27*, 311–324.

Shafer, G. (1978). Non-additive probabilities in the work of Bernoulli and Lambert. *Archive for the History of Exact Sciences, 19*, 309–370.

Sivyer, M., & Finlay, D. (1982). Perceived duration of auditory sequences. *Journal of General Psychology, 107*, 209–217.

Statistisches Bundesamt. (1986). *Statistisches Jahrbuch 1986 für die Bundesrepublik Deutschland* [Statistical yearbook 1986 for the Federal Republic of Germany]. Stuttgart, Germany: Kohlhammer.

Stegmüller, W. (1973). *Probleme und Resultate der Wissenschaftstheorie und Analytischen Philosophie. Bd. IV: Personelle und Statistische Wahrscheinlichkeit. Teil E.* [Problems and results of philosophy of science and analytical philosophy. Vol. IV: Personal and statistical probability. Part E]. Berlin, Federal Republic of Germany: Springer.

Tanner, W. P., Jr., & Swets, J. A. (1954). A decision-making theory of visual detection. *Psychological Review, 61*, 401–409.

Teigen, K. H. (1974). Overestimation of subjective probabilities. *Scandinavian Journal of Psychology, 15*, 56–62.

Tversky, A., & Kahneman, D. (1983). Extensional versus intuitive reasoning: The conjunction fallacy in probability judgment. *Psychological Review, 90*, 293–315.

von Mises, R. (1928). *Wahrscheinlichkeit, Statistik und Wahrheit.* Berlin, Germany: Springer. (Translated and reprinted as *Probability, statistics, and truth.* New York: Dover, 1957.)

von Winterfeldt, D., & Edwards, W. (1986). *Decision analysis and behavioral research.* Cambridge, England: Cambridge University Press.

Wagenaar, W., & Keren, G. B. (1985). Calibration of probability assessments by professional blackjack dealers, statistical experts, and lay people. *Organizational Behavior and Human Decision Processes, 36,* 406–416.

Wells, G. L., & Harvey, J. H. (1977). Do people use consensus information in making causal attributions? *Journal of Personality and Social Psychology, 35,* 279–293.

Zacks, R. T., Hasher, L., & Sanft, H. (1982). Automatic encoding of event frequency: Further findings. *Journal of Experimental Psychology: Learning, Memory, and Cognition, 8,* 106–116.

Zimmer, A. C. (1983). Verbal vs. numerical processing by subjective probabilities. In R. W. Scholz (Ed.), *Decision making under uncertainty* (pp. 159–182). Amsterdam: North-Holland.

Zimmer, A. C. (1986). What uncertainty judgments can tell about the underlying subjective probabilities. *Uncertainty in Artificial Intelligence,* 249–258.

4 Direct comparison of the efficacy of intuitive and analytical cognition in expert judgment

Kenneth R. Hammond, Robert M. Hamm,
Janet Grassia, and Tamra Pearson

Research in the field of judgment and decision making often compares the rationality of a person's intuitive judgments under uncertainty with analytically derived answers produced by a formal model such as Bayes's theorem, a multiple regression equation, or other rules from the conventional probability calculus (for reviews see [16], [30], [39], [40], and [52]). Such comparisons are *indirect*: they compare a *person's* intuitive efforts with *person-independent* operations. That is, they compare a person's intuitive processes and judgments with those of an analytically derived rule or equation put forward as a standard of rationality. Indirect comparisons are undeniably important, but they are necessarily restricted in three ways. First, because indirect comparisons evaluate intuition with respect to a standard of rationality, researchers must choose one standard from among the many offered. However, agreement on which standard of rationality is correct has never been achieved. The choice of any standard, therefore, is subject to dispute, and any conclusions that subjects have failed to achieve the standard chosen are sure to be criticized by those who prefer a different standard (as indeed they have been; see [2], [11], [44], [49], and also [16]), thus leaving the comparison between intuitive judgments and rationality unresolved.

Second, indirect comparisons cannot fail to show that analytical cognition is equal or superior to intuitive cognition because analytical models, however chosen, provide the standard to be achieved by persons. If intuition

Manuscript received January 25, 1987; revised May 18, 1987. This work was supported in part by the Engineering Psychology Programs, Office of Naval Research, Contract N00014-81-C-0591, Work Unit Number NR 197-073, and by BRSG Grant RR07013-14, awarded by the Biomedical Research Support Program, Division of Research Resources, NIH. Reproduction in whole or in part is permitted for any purpose of the United States Government. Approved for public release; distribution unlimited.

offers an advantage over analysis, as many have argued it does, its putative advantage cannot be demonstrated in indirect comparisons because the analytical model provides a ceiling for performance. Therefore, it is not altogether surprising that populational studies find that few persons' intuitive efforts achieve the standard [40] and none exceed it. (See also [63].)

Third, when indirect comparisons are made, the analytical models are always provided with all the correct (and only the correct) substantive information each model requires, and such models are almost always executed without error – at least in academic journals. In practice, however, the analytical cognition of persons, in contrast to analytical computation by formal models, is vulnerable to substantive failures (insufficient information, incorrect information, incorrect substantive theory) and to procedural failures (incorrect assignment of numbers to the symbols of the equation, computational errors, use of an incorrect model, insufficient time). In short, valuable as indirect comparisons may be, these restrictions prevent them from informing us about the relative efficacy of the intuitive and analytical cognition of people.

Therefore, *direct* comparisons between a person's use of intuition and the same person's use of analysis are also needed. Direct comparisons will inform us about the *relative efficacy* of these modes of cognition in terms of empirical achievement or correctness. Comparisons of relative efficacy, however, require the presence of an empirical criterion with which judgments are compared, rather than a standard of rationality. When a criterion is available, direct comparisons enable us to address the age-old question: does a person's intuitive or analytical cognition produce more empirically accurate answers? (See [16] for parallel remarks; see also [17] for a stimulating discussion of "accuracy versus truth"; see [19] for a recent direct comparison of intuitive and analytical cognition across subjects.) The work to be described directly compares the efficacy of intuitive and analytical modes of cognition in the context of a study of expert judgment.

Direct comparison of the efficacy of intuitive and analytical cognition by experts, particularly engineers, is important because such experts (and others) frequently must choose between these modes of cognition. The choice is made difficult by contrasting and contradictory folk beliefs about each. For example, good intuition is often said to be the mark of a true expert, yet intuition is often despised as mere guesswork hiding behind analytical laziness. Good analytical ability is often praised as high competence, yet often dismissed as nothing more than slavish "going by the book."

Always a controversial topic in management, this antinomy was addressed by Simon [56] in relation to "styles of management":

It is a fallacy to contrast "analytic" and "intuitive" styles of management. Intuition and judgment – at least good judgment – are simply analyses frozen into habit and into the capacity for rapid response through recognition. Every manager needs to be able to analyze problems systematically (and with the aid of the modern arsenal of analytical tools provided by management science and operations research). Every manager needs also to be able to respond to situations rapidly, a skill that requires the cultivation of intuition and judgment over many years of experience and training. The effective manager does not have the luxury of choosing between "analytic" and "intuitive" approaches to problems. Behaving like a manager means having command of the whole range of management skills and applying them as they become appropriate [56, p. 63].

However, the term "appropriate" begs the question. Exactly when is intuition appropriate but analysis inappropriate? When is the reverse true? What are the consequences of mistakenly using one "style" instead of the other? Finally, what is the criterion for appropriateness? Research based on *indirect* comparisons would lead to the conclusion that one should always use an analytical approach – an algorithm – when one is available, and Simon's remarks seem to suggest that. However, Bayes's theorem and similar algorithms may not be applicable, and intuition, as Simon notes, is obviously faster. Research that *directly* compares intuitive cognition and analytical cognition in the same person under carefully specified conditions is the only way we can adequately determine which mode of cognition should be applied to which conditions and thus discover which mode is "appropriate" for which conditions. However, such direct comparisons within the same subject have not yet been made. Our study is an attempt to remedy this omission. Before describing the study, however, we specify our premises and describe our theory of cognition.

Premises

Our approach rejects the traditional *dichotomy* between intuition and analysis. It is based on the premise that both cognitive processes and task conditions can be arranged on a *continuum* that runs from intuition to analysis ([27, p. 340], see also [7], [20], [22], [23], [25], [36]). Furthermore, once cognitive processes are defined in terms of their location on a cognitive continuum, they will be found to interact in predictable ways with various task conditions located on a similar continuum.

This premise follows directly from the systems-oriented argument that specification and variation of the formal properties of tasks are essential to the generalization of results, an argument that is receiving increasing support. For example, Beach and Mitchell [3], Einhorn and Hogarth [16], Payne [51], and Howell and Kerkar [37] have emphasized the need for further theoretical analysis of the effects of task properties on cognitive processes. Recent examples are provided by Keller [42], who shows that violation of the sure thing and substitution principles varies as a function of problem representation, and by Hoch and Tschirgi [35], who show that the "confirmation bias" produced when subjects attempt to solve deductive problems presented in abstract form [62] largely disappears when the task is designed to include cue redundancy (an important aspect of Brunswik's [7] representative design). Klayman and Ha [43], moreover, have shown that under certain task conditions the "confirmation bias" will be useful rather than detrimental. Such studies at once restrict previous overgeneralizations and extend our knowledge. Nevertheless, a general theory of task conditions remains absent; therefore, in what follows we provide such a theory and test it.

Theoretical background: A systems approach

As early as 1957 Brunswik [8] introduced the systems approach to the study of cognition. He asserted that

Both organism and environment will have to be seen as systems, each with properties of its own. . . . Each has surface and depth, or overt and covert regions. It follows that much as psychology must be concerned with the texture of the organism . . . it must also be concerned with the texture of the environment [8, p. 5].

Thus comparisons of different forms of cognition require not only a theory of cognition but a theory of environmental context as well, unless the cognitive theory claims universal generality over all conditions. Since we reject the traditional premise of a dichotomy between intuition and analysis and posit a continuum instead, the continuum theory must first provide a set of descriptive terms that will make it possible to determine the location of a person's cognitive activity on the cognitive continuum; second, it must provide a set of descriptive terms that will enable us to determine the location of a task on a task continuum according to the hypothesized ability of the task to activate cognition in a predicted region on the cognitive continuum; and third, it must indicate the consequences of the correspondence between task location and cognitive location for various behaviors, such as the accuracy of judgments. The theory also specifies when (under what task conditions) each mode of cognition, defined as a location on the cognitive continuum, is appropriate. If a cognitive theory does not provide a priori a reasonably complete set of descriptors of both task properties and cognitive properties, the predictions of behavior that are derived from that theory are liable to be context vague, difficult to falsify, and thus misleading.

Cognitive properties

Although researchers in cognition take great pains to differentiate precisely among formal analytical models of cognition, they almost never explain what they mean by intuition. As a result, it is customary to define intuition in terms of what it is not. Brooks [5], for example, compares "analytical and *non*analytical concept formation," and Beach and Mitchell [3] refer to "*non*analytical [italics added] strategies." Kahneman and Tversky [41, p. 124] indicate that a "judgment is called intuitive if it is reached by an informal and

Table 4.1. *Properties of intuition and analysis*

	Intuition	Analysis
Cognitive control	low	high
Rate of data processing	rapid	slow
Conscious awareness	low	high
Organizing principle	weighted average	task specific
Errors	normally distributed	few, but large
Confidence	high confidence in answer; low confidence in method	low confidence in answer; high confidence in method

unstructured mode of reasoning, *without* [italics added] the use of analytic methods or deliberate calculation." Even philosophers (e.g., [11]) who criticize psychological research on judgment fail to say what they mean by intuition. (Von Winterfeldt and Edwards [60] describe four types of intuition and thus are the rare and recent exception. They also concur with our conclusion that researchers have generally taken a negative approach toward defining intuitive cognition, see [60, p. 550]. See also [14], which is laudatory but vague about intuition, and [21].)

In Table 4.1 we provide a list of cognitive properties that make it possible to differentiate intuition from analysis. (For further distinctions, see [25].) The *compromise* form of cognition, quasi-rationality or common sense, lies in between these polar forms of cognition and includes properties from both types of cognition. Some applications of quasi-rationality will lie closer to intuition, some closer to analysis. (See [7]; see [22], [23] for early discussions of compromise and quasi-rationality; see also [25] for a comparison of quasi-rationality with *bounded rationality* introduced by Simon [54, pp. 196–206]; see [50], [64] for examples of compromise among probability estimates; see [53] for a general treatise on "three ways of knowing.")

Task properties

In his 1982 review, Payne indicated that research shows that "decision-making . . . is highly contingent on the demands of the task" [51, p. 382]. We agree with Payne's conclusion, and in an effort to further our understanding of the demands of the task, we offer a systematic approach to the construction and analysis of task conditions. First, tasks used for research should be constructed and presented in terms of *packages* that include many task properties (see, e.g., [7, pp. 69, 115]), as tasks ordinarily do, rather than two or three orthogonal variables that represent, for statistical convenience, the deliberate reduction and diseggregation of naturally cooccurring and covarying task properties. (ANOVA is an example of the latter approach; see

Table 4.2. *Inducement of intuition and analysis by task conditions*

Task characteristic	Intuition-inducing state of task characteristic	Analysis-inducing state of task characteristic
1. Number of cues	large (>5)	small
2. Measurement of cues	perceptual measurement	objective reliable measurement
3. Distribution of cue values	continuous highly variable distribution	unknown distribution; cues are dichotomous; values are discrete
4. Redundancy among cues	high redundancy	low redundancy
5. Decomposition of task	low	high
6. Degree of certainty in task	low certainty	high certainty
7. Relation between cues and criterion	linear	nonlinear
8. Weighting of cues in environmental model	equal	unequal
9. Availability of organizing principle	unavailable	available
10. Display of cues[a]	simultaneous display	sequential display
11. Time period	brief	long

[a] Applicable to surface conditions only.

[28]; [55] directly rejects this methodology). Second, the inclusion of properties in the task package presented to the subjects should be justified in terms of their presence within naturally occurring tasks. Meeting this requirement increases the likelihood of achieving ecological generalization to environmental systems. Third, the number of task properties included in the task package should be sufficiently high to allow for intersubstitutability. Intersubstitutability, a feature of naturally occurring tasks, permits a low value of one task property to be compensated for by a high value of another and also enhances generalization over environmental systems [6], [7], [23], [33]. Fourth, the investigator should provide a reasonably complete list of task properties that are anticipated, on theoretical or empirical grounds, to affect cognitive activity. Otherwise, there will be no end to the introduction of new task properties, usually one or two at a time, as investigators seek to test the generality of results previously obtained. Therefore, we present a reasonably complete list of task properties predicted to affect cognitive activity and indicate how these are grouped and quantified and how each task is located on the task continuum.

The task properties that differentially induce intuition and analysis are displayed in Table 4.2. Degrees of quasi-rationality are induced to the extent that a task contains properties from both sets, or properties whose values lie between the polar values (see [25] for further elaboration).

Inducement of cognitive properties

A specific theoretical prediction is that each package of task properties will induce a corresponding package of cognitive properties. For example, if (a) the task presents *many redundant* cues (attributes), (b) the cue values are *continuous*, (c) the cues are displayed *simultaneously*, (d) the cues are measured *perceptually*, and (e) the subject has available no *explicit* principle, scientific theory, or method for organizing cues into a judgment, then the subject will employ intuitive cognition. That is, subjects will observe and use many redundant cues (because of their simultaneous display), measure their values perceptually (because there is no alternative), and, therefore, assign unreliable subjective cue values to each cue. The unreliability of the cue values, exacerbated by the continuous nature of the cues, lead to inconsistency or low cognitive control. Moreover, if the subject cannot employ the appropriate organizing principle either because he or she knows of none or because time will not permit its application, then the subject will implicitly apply a weighted sum or weighted averaging method of organizing the information.

We predict that a summative weighted average organizing principle will be used in intuitive cognition because it has been shown to be the most robust of all aggregation methods [13]. Robustness in this context means high accuracy in spite of (a) incorrect assignments of weights, (b) poor approximations to the correct function forms between cue and criterion, and (c) poor approximation to the correct organizing principle in the task. Such robustness would provide a cognitive evolutionary advantage for any organism capable of multiple cue usage in tasks that induce intuition, particularly when time is limited. Therefore, a weighted averaging or simple summation method should be a strong candidate for an intuitive method of organizing information under the intuition-inducing conditions. (See [19] for evidence that task properties induce corresponding modes of cognition; see [61] for empirical support for a similar conceptual link between additive processes and intuitive (nonexpert) cognition; see [1] for examples of studies in which weighted averages frequently appear and for a detailed technical treatment of *cognitive algebra*; see [7, pp. 89–99] and [24] for a discussion of the advantages of intuitive cognition for survival; see also [15], [45].) The rationale for the task properties that induce analysis is opposite in substance but similar in form.

We say that certain task properties *induce* intuitive or analytical cognition to avoid implying that the relation between task properties and cognitive properties is inevitable or fully deterministic. Certainly, analysis can be applied to intuition-inducing tasks (e.g., if there is time), and intuition can be applied to analysis-inducing tasks (e.g., if time is limited). Moreover, as the concept of quasi-rationality implies, task conditions may include some properties from each end of the continuum, and therefore, some of the properties of both modes of cognition can be induced in a single task. Tasks with both intuitive and analytical properties may induce a compromise between intuition and analysis. (See [6], [7], [22], [23], [27]; [4] demonstrates the role of task properties in producing compromise in interpersonal conflict; see also [59] for the use of the concept of cognitive *trade-offs*, which imply compromise between one mode of cognition and another.)

The precise location of cognitive activity on the cognitive continuum will depend upon (a) how many task properties are present, (b) which task properties are present, and (c) the amount of a property present. Unfortunately, we do not yet know the relative power of various task properties to induce the activation of cognition at one location or another on the continuum. The study to be described in this article takes an initial step toward the acquisition of such knowledge.

Differentiation between surface and depth in cognitive tasks. In addition to the distinction between intuitive and analytical task conditions, the *surface* and *depth* characteristics of tasks must also be specified. The distinction between surface and depth is particularly important to systems engineering because it pertains to the different forms in which information about the same system may be displayed. It has been developed by Hammond et al. [31, p. 275] and has also been used in problem-solving research [55] (see also [10]). In both cases the term *depth* refers to the covert relationships among the variables within the task, whereas *surface* refers to the overt display of the task variables to the subject.

Congruence between surface and depth characteristics. Since both the depth and surface characteristics of tasks can be described in terms of the same set of task properties, they may also be described in terms of their *congruence* with one another. The degree of congruence can be measured by the respective locations of these characteristics on the task continuum. For example, a logical problem will by definition have covert depth properties that place it at the analysis-inducing pole of the continuum. However, the surface materials that inform the subject about the problem may be displayed in a variety of ways, some of which may also be analysis inducing (and thus congruent with the depth characteristics of the task) and some of which may be intuition inducing (and thus incongruent with them). The range of possible surface displays for a logical problem includes (in order of decreasing congruence) (a) symbolic logic, (b) the languages for computer programs, (c) natural languages, (d) diagrams, or (e) pictures. At the other extreme, surface displays for tasks in which depth characteristics are intuition inducing may also vary along the intuition–analysis continuum. The overt surface materials for a pictorial work of art may be (in order of decreasing congruence) (a) displayed visually, (b) diagrammed to show its form (as da Vinci's "Last Supper" has been diagrammed), (c) described in natural language, or (d) described in the language of a computer program (in the case of computer-produced art).

Various combinations of intuition- and analysis-inducing surface characteristics are often used in both types of tasks, thus rendering these tasks
quasi-rational in character. For example, art teachers induce quasi-rational
cognition when they point to various visual features of a work of art, ask
students to appreciate them by use of visual perception, and then systematically verbally analyze the features that justify the work's classical status. An
opposite example is provided by the physics teacher who displays a set of
relations first as an equation, and then as a pictorial schematic model. In this
case the schematic model is used to appeal, via visual perception, to intuitive
cognition and thereby to convince students that the abstract equation is true.
(It is shown in [48] that early quantum theorists engaged in disputes about
whether visual, and thus intuitively appealing, representations of the relations among concepts should be allowed to supplement mathematical, and
thus fully analytical, representations.)

Although surface–depth relations are an intrinsic, inescapable, and
highly apparent component of every cognitive task presented to experts, no
systematic treatment of their relative effects on cognition has yet appeared.
Payne [51, pp. 390–391], for example, describes the importance of "information display," but none of the studies he reviews examines systematically
the effects of various surface displays across tasks with different depth
characteristics. As a result, we know little about the effect of the relation
between surface and depth characteristics on cognition and the judgments
of experts. (However, in [58], it is reported that students and faculty
in accounting and finance who were "given information in the form of
[schematic] multidimensional *faces* [italics added] were able to classify
bonds . . . more accurately than those given tables of financial ratios" [58,
p. 201].)

Method

Our study of highway engineers is based on three tasks that can be located
according to their depth characteristics at three positions on the task
continuum: the intuition-inducing pole, the analysis-inducing pole, and a
position in between. Three different sets of surface characteristics, or displays, were used with each of the three tasks (see Fig. 4.1). The surface
characteristics also were constructed so that the properties of one display
represented the intuition-inducing pole, those of another represented the
analysis-inducing pole, and those of the third represented conditions in
between. Since we wished to examine the effect of the surface and depth
properties of tasks on the cognitive activity of the same subject over these
task conditions, each subject (with one exception, noted later) was tested in
all nine cells of Figure 4.1. (See [28] in which we place this research approach
in the context of the multitrait–multimethod methodology introduced by
Campbell and Fiske [9], and thus develop a new measure of *competence* in
expert judgment.)

		SURFACE TASK CHARACTERISTICS		
		Film Strips (Intuition Inducing) I	Bar Graphs (Quasi-Rationality Inducing) Q	Formulas (Analysis Inducing) A
D E P T H T A S K C H A R A C T E R I S T I C S	Aesthetics (Intuition Inducing) E	IE	QE	AE
	Safety (Quasi-Rationality Inducing) S	IS	QS	AS
	Capacity (Analysis Inducing) C	IC	QC	AC

Figure 4.1. Design of study.

Subjects

Twenty-one expert highway engineers (male, 30–70 years of age) were chosen as subjects because of their trained capacity to engage in analytical cognition, as well as the other two modes of cognition. Each expert volunteered approximately 20 hours to the project. One engineer did not make judgments of highway capacity.

Depth characteristics of tasks

Three tasks were selected on the a priori judgment (to be tested subsequently) that the package of characteristics inherent in these tasks would induce cognition to be located at three different points on the cognitive continuum. The tasks required predictions of (a) highway aesthetics (intuition inducing), (b) highway safety (quasi-rationality inducing), and (c) highway capacity (analysis inducing). Each task is described in turn; objective measures of task location on the cognitive continuum are described later.

Intuition. Judgments of highway aesthetics were used because many of the depth properties of this task are intuition inducing. For example, no known algorithm exists for organizing the cues used to judge the aesthetic value of highways, and no delimited specification of which cues are relevant; indeed, no indication exists of how aesthetics-related information (whatever it may be) should be used. Consequently, judgments of highway aesthetics depend largely on the use of perceptual material provided by the visual inspection of a highway and are never arrived at by calculation. The intuition-inducing properties of this task are illustrated in the remarks of the engineers. For example, one engineer stated: "My confidence will be zero. When you . . . ask me how I did this I will say, 'I don't know.'"

Quasi-rationality. Judgments of highway safety were used as a quasi-rationality-inducing task. This task is between intuition and analysis because some of its depth properties are intuition inducing, some are analysis inducing, and some are midway between the two. Although there is no established theory, algorithm, or equation for calculating the safety of a highway and no single official or professionally approved set of cues is used for measuring or judging the safety of highways (thus allowing for some degree of intuition as described earlier), nevertheless there is general agreement about what dimensions or cues (e.g., lane width) should be used, and what their functional relationships with safety are. In addition, engineers can provide more or less defensible explanations for using certain dimensions in the form given, thus indicating that some degree of analysis occurs. For example, one engineer stated: "I will . . . select the most important points that have a tendency to constitute accidents. . . . Probably, the most important would be the curves per mile. . . . Shoulder width is the next most important thing."

Analysis. Judgments of highway capacity were used as an analysis-inducing task because its depth properties include many of the analysis-inducing properties in Table 4.2. That is, it is generally agreed that the capacity of a highway can be calculated using a nonstochastic nonlinear algorithm based on well-known dimensions. The relations between these dimensions and capacity are well known to highway engineers, the process is analytically and technically defensible, and it is in regular use in the design of highways. One engineer said: "The idea of taking a maximum capacity . . . and then multiplying it by factors is the *Highway Capacity Manual* way of doing it. And so I knew it was a legal way to go about it, but I didn't remember the process exactly, or the numbers especially."

Surface characteristics of tasks

Three forms of displaying information were constructed, in accordance with cognitive continuum theory, to induce cognition to be located at three different points on the cognitive continuum within each task. Each of the three display forms is described in turn; objective measures are described later.

Intuition. The engineers were induced to employ intuitive cognition for each task (aesthetics, safety, and capacity) by being required to judge 40 two-lane rural Colorado highways from film strips representing one- to three-mile segments of these highways. The film strip presentation is intuition-inducing because all the information must be processed by visual perception. Moreover, the cues displayed in the film strips are numerous, frequently redundant, and contemporaneously displayed, the values of the cues are generally continuous and normally distributed, and the cue values must be measured solely by visual examination. Furthermore, no time was provided to organize the information according to an analytical principle.

Quasi-rationality. The engineers were induced to employ quasi-rational cognition for each task by being required to judge bar graphs representing the same highway segments as in the film strips. The bar graphs induce both intuition and analysis.They induce intuition because the cues are displayed visually and contemporaneously; the cues are redundant and are generally continuous and normally distributed. The bar-graph presentation also induces analysis, however, because the number of cues is reduced from a large unknown number to a specific set (aesthetics is 8, safety is 10, capacity is 9), each cue is visually separated from the others, and its numerical value is clearly indicated. The cue values are also numerically presented, thus facilitating brief comparison.

Analysis. The engineers were given the names of the same variables that were provided in the bar-graph presentation for each task. They were induced to employ analytical cognition by being required to devise mathematical formulas for calculating aesthetics, safety, and capacity for all two-lane rural highways. The engineers were told that although a certain amount of time had been targeted for this task, they could work until their formulas were completed. They were provided with paper, pencils, and a calculator to facilitate the use of whatever "intellectual tools" (see [60]) might seem appropriate.

Independent variables

No attempt is made to break each of the nine task conditions down into their constituent properties and to examine the relationship of each task property to each of the four cognitive properties to be described for each of the 21 engineers. This approach was not taken because analyses of the thousands of relationships thus engendered would defy interpretation, and because, as we argued before, behavior is best understood in relation to the molar level of packages of many task properties. The location of each task package on the task continuum is indicated in terms of a task continuum index.

Task continuum index. Eight of the task characteristics predicted by cognitive continuum theory to induce cognition at different locations were used to construct a task continuum index (TCI). The TCI includes measure of (a) the number of cues presented, (b) the redundancy among the cues, (c) the reliability of cue measurement, (d) the degree to which the task is decomposed for the subject, (e) the availability to the subject of an organizing principle, (f) the degree of nonlinearity in the optimal organizing principle, (g) the extent to which the cues are weighted equally in the optimal organizing principle for the task, and (h) the degree of certainty in the criterion (see Appendix I). Scores on the eight measures were aggregated by assigning equal weights and adding them. In the absence of any information about the relative power of task properties to induce cognitive properties, or about the possible interactions between them, equal weights and the additive function were chosen because they constitute the simplest and most robust theory of task systems under the circumstances.

The TCI is a measure that permits each of the nine task conditions to be located on the task continuum for both surface and depth conditions. The TCI values for the nine task conditions (IE: 1.84; QE: 3.53; AE: 4.09; IS: 5.38; QS: 6.90; AS: 7.58; IC: 6.96; QC: 8.56; AC: 9.13) are graphed in Figure 4.2. The surface and depth condition means of Figure 4.2 indicate that although equal distances were not established among the task conditions employed, they were found to be in the appropriate order, with one exception.

Dependent variables

The effects of the independent variables described earlier were examined with respect to (a) the location of each subject's cognitive activity on the cognitive continuum index, (b) each engineer's degree of empirical achievement in predicting each criterion accurately in the nine conditions.

Cognitive continuum index. Four cognitive properties predicted by cognitive continuum theory to discriminate between intuitive and analytical cognition could be measured in the present study and were combined in a cognitive continuum index (CCI). The four properties were measures of (a) cognitive control, (b) organizing principle, (c) error distribution, and (d) differential confidence.

Cognitive control [32], expected to be higher in analytical cognition, is measured by R_s, the linear predictability of the engineer's judgments in the film-strip and bar-graph conditions. This correlation was deemed an acceptable approximation to cognitive control due to the low nonlinear use of cues that was observed in the data. In the formula condition, cognitive control was measured by the correlation between the answers produced by the

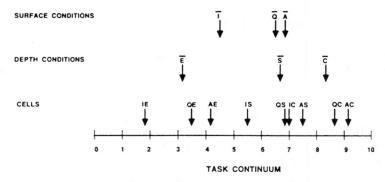

Figure 4.2. Location of task conditions on task continuum.

formula the engineer intended to present to the research team and the formula he actually presented (see Appendix II).

The extent to which the engineer's judgments are produced by a *nonlinear organizing principle* is a second subindex of the CCI. Analytical cognition is expected to be nonlinear, in contrast to intuitive cognition, which is expected to be linear. This property is measured by the difference between the R^2 of a nonlinear model of the judgments (whose predictors include squared cue measures and selected interaction terms) and the R^2 of the linear model.

Error distribution is measured by the kurtosis of the distribution of errors, that is, differences between the engineer's judgments and the criterion after the judgments have been rescaled onto the same range as the criterion. A positive kurtosis denotes the peaked distributions in which answers are frequently very accurate yet occasionally highly inaccurate, a pattern predicted to be characteristic of analytical cognition.

The fourth measure included in the CCI is the difference between the engineer's confidence in his *method* and his confidence is his *answers*. Since method confidence is expected to be high in analysis and answer confidence to be high in intuition, the greater the difference between these measures, the more analytic the subject's cognitive activity.

The CCI was calculated so that if in any task condition an engineer exhibited (a) high cognitive control, (b) a highly nonlinear organizing principle, (c) high kurtosis (peaked, with high tails) in his error distribution (thus indicating a great number of nearly correct answers and a large number of large errors), and (d) a great difference between method and answer confidence, then he would receive a high analytical score on the CCI. If the reverse conditions held, the subject would receive a low analytical (and thus high intuitive) score on the CCI. Each raw measure was rescaled within each engineer to a common scale and the subscores were combined by a simple additive (equal weights) procedure. Therefore, each score was relative to *each engineer's own performance*, not to an absolute score.

Note that both the CCI and the TCI are compensatory measures; a low score on one subindex may be compensated for by a high score on another subindex. This form was chosen because it represents the intersubstitutability of cognitive activities as well as task properties, an essential part of the general theory of probabilistic functionalism put forward by Brunswik [6], [7] and Hammond [23], [25].

Achievement. The correlation (r_a) between an engineer's judgments over the set of highways and the appropriate criterion (to be described) was measured in each task in each display mode, using the methods described in Appendix II. *Knowledge* is measured in the intuitive and quasi-rational surface conditions by G (from the lens model equation; see Appendix II). In analytical cognition the correlation between the criterion and the answers produced by the engineer's intended formula serves as a measure of knowledge, that is, of what the engineer could have achieved if he had expressed his formula as he intended. The distinction between the degree of accuracy achieved with the intended formula and with the formula actually used is essential in any effort to compare the *use* of analytical cognition with the use of intuition. (See [31] for a detailed discussion of the distinction between *consistency* and *cognitive control*; see also the literature on the discrepancy between mental models and task properties in [55].)

Statistical analysis

Hypotheses are tested by examining the conformance of each subject's behavior to the behavior predicted by the theory. Aggregation over subjects is carried out by counting the number of subjects whose behavior conforms to the prediction. (See Appendix III for the distinction between this methodology and that ordinarily used by psychologists.)

Procedure

Task materials

The same set of 40 highway segments was used in all nine cells of the study.

Statistical properties of the intuition-inducing (aesthetics judgment) task. The aesthetics criterion was produced by a group of 91 highway users who judged the 40 highways. To vary methods, some of the citizens viewed the film strips, some viewed slides, and some viewed photocopies of one or four frames from the film strip. The slides and film strips were rated, and the photocopies were rated or rank ordered. The 91 citizens' judgments were factor analyzed. Only one factor was identified; there was no evidence of method factors. The score for each highway on this factor served as the criterion measure of its aesthetic value. The engineers were told that their task was to predict the aesthetic judgments of this group of citizens.

Eight aesthetics cues (attributes) were presented to the engineers in the bar-graph and formula tasks. The cues were attractiveness of design, road condition, scenery, amount of roadside culture, amount of reparative landscaping, color, vegetation, and type of terrain. The cue values were determined by averaged ratings of the cue values from 14 of the citizens, who rated the cues for each of the 40 highways upon viewing the film strips.

A linear model of the task yielded an R_e^2 of .937 (corrected for estimated shrinkage, .920). The correlation between each cue and the criterion, as well as the intercorrelations among the cues, is given in [29, table 4]. The average intercorrelation among cues is .56.

Statistical properties of the quasi-rationality-inducing (safety judgment) task. The criterion for the accuracy of judgments is the accident rate, averaged over seven years, for each of the 40 highways. Accident rate is defined as the total number of accidents (involving fatalities, injuries, or only property damage) divided by the number of vehicle miles traveled. One highway with an extremely high accident rate was considered to be an unrepresentative outlier and was not used in the analysis of safety judgments.

Highways were measured on ten dimensions, chosen for inclusion in the study on the basis of discussions with highway safety experts who indicated the information they considered essential for evaluating the safety of a road. The dimensions were lane width, shoulder width, percent no passing zone, curves per mile, percent with substantial grade, traffic volume, traffic mix, intersections per mile, average speed limit, and obstacles per mile. Eight of these measures were available from highway department records; two measures, number of curves per mile and number of obstacles per mile, had to be counted by the experimenters from visual inspection of film strips of each highway segment. The beta weights for each dimension or cue in predicting accident rate are also presented in [29, table 5]. Visual examination of the scatterplots of the relations between each cue and the criterion indicated little if any nonlinear covariation. This finding was supported by the results from calculation of the contribution of squared terms and interactions to accident rates, which is negligible.

An optimally weighted linear multiple regression model of the task indicates that $R_e = .863$; corrected for estimated shrinkage, $R_e = .809$. Application of equal weights and linear functions, each cue given the sign that appeared in the best fit equation, yields an R_e of .769 (corrected for shrinkage $R_e = .667$). The intercorrelations among the ten cues and the criteria are presented in [29, table 5].

Statistical properties of the analysis-inducing (capacity judgment) task. The criterion for the accuracy of judgments of capacity is the maximum number of vehicles that the road could carry in both directions in one hour under ideal conditions. Each highway's capacity was determined by applying a standard procedure from the *Highway Capacity Manual* [34] to the measured features of the highway (see [29, appendix D]).

The highways were measured on nine dimensions, each of which was chosen for inclusion either because it was involved in the formal procedure that highway departments typically use for determining capacity, or because it was plausibly related to capacity. The dimensions were lane width, lateral clearance, side obstacles, intersections per mile, traffic mix (percent trucks), type of terrain, angle of steepest grade, length of steepest grade, and average speed limit. These measures were available from the Colorado Department of Highways records.

Because the capacity criterion is a fully determined function of the set of highway dimensions, the procedure also serves as the model of the environment. Thus, there is no environmental error, and the model of the environment is neither linear nor additive. The formulas in [29, appendix D] show the approximate degree of nonlinearity in the model. Additionally, the function forms have steplike discontinuities rather than being linear or smooth because the procedure involves tables. The model of the subject, on the other hand, is estimated by linear regression. Since the models of environment and subject are of different kinds, the generalization of the lens model equation described by Stewart [57] was used for this situation (see Appendix II for further detail).

Rating scales

Rating scales were constructed to be appropriate to the cognitive activity induced. An abstract rating scale from 1 (low) to 10 (high) was used for judging aesthetics, safety, or capacity from the film strips, to induce intuitive cognition. In the bar-graph presentation and in the task requiring the construction of a formula, scales specific to the task were used because this specificity is compatible with calculation and thus with analytical cognition. Thus in the capacity judgment task a scale from 750 to 2500 vehicles per hour was used, and in the safety judgment task a scale from 0 to 32 accidents per million vehicles miles traveled was used. The 1–10 scale was used in all three surface task conditions for the aesthetics judgment task. Transformations to a common scale were made for purposes of data analysis.

Order of presentation

All engineers were presented with the surface task conditions in the same order: first, the film strips, second, the bar graphs, third, the materials for formula construction. Surface conditions were deliberately not counterbalanced because it has been demonstrated that analytical work requiring use of certain cues in an explicit fashion influences subsequent intuitive judgments, whereas the reverse is not true [38]. The order of depth conditions within each surface condition was counterbalanced across all engineers. Participation in each surface condition was separated by at least a week.

In the intuition-inducing surface condition, ten of the 40 highways were shown twice; in the quasi-rationality-inducing surface condition 16 highways were shown twice. These repetitions permitted calculation of repeated trials reliability for each engineer. These data were not used for comparison, however, because the values for the intuition-inducing conditions were inflated due to recognition of the highways in the film strips.

Time

Response times in the nine conditions were determined by surface task conditions and thus are not dependent variables; that is, presentation of a film strip necessarily required more of a subject's time than presentation of a bar graph. The mean response time in the film-strip condition (where the engineer saw approximately 100 separate exposures for each of 40 highway segments) was 64 seconds, and in the bar-graph condition (where the engineer was shown one bar graph for each highway segment), it was 19 seconds.

In the formula-producing condition, response time varied within two subgroups (see [29] for explanation of the subgroups). Eighteen engineers were encouraged to complete their formulas within 45 minutes and their mean response time was 51 minutes. The remaining three engineers had a mean response time of 2 hours and 40 minutes.

Hypotheses

Five auxiliary hypotheses are tested in order of their importance to cognitive continuum theory. The first hypothesis predicts that surface and depth task properties, combined or taken separately, induce corresponding cognitive properties. The second hypothesis predicts that analytical cognition carried out by a person, rather than a model, is a fallible process and therefore will not always provide a ceiling for performance. The third hypothesis asserts that analytical cognition is apt to produce extreme errors. The fourth hypothesis takes into account the correspondence between the properties of each task and the cognitive properties each subject applies to it; it predicts that the greater the correspondence, the better performance will be. *Correspondence* may be the theoretical counterpart to what Simon [56] referred to as the "appropriate" method of cognition. Thus it is important to discover whether performance is better when a person employs cognitive properties that correspond to the properties of the task. The fifth hypothesis asserts that knowledge of the congruence between the surface and depth characteristics of tasks is necessary and sufficient to predict performance (i.e., knowledge of the subject's cognitive activity is unnecessary).

Results

Two statistical methods were used for analyzing the data: correlational analysis and order table analysis. The correlational analysis examines the covariation between the TCI (task properties combined into an index of task location) and the CCI (cognitive properties combined into an index of cognitive location) over the nine task conditions. The order table analysis ascertains whether the predicted order of behavior occurs for each engineer for each of the surface and depth task conditions separately. Both procedures provide specific and precise tests of each hypothesis for the behavior of each engineer over the nine conditions.

Task inducement of cognitive properties

H_1. Task properties induce corresponding cognitive properties.

Correlational analysis. Each engineer's cognitive location on the CCI for each of the nine task conditions was correlated with the location of each task condition on the TCI. These correlations were positive for 19 of the 21 engineers ($\chi^2 = 12.91, p < .001$). Nine of the positive relations were significant at $p < .05$ (degrees of freedom (DF) = 7, one tailed). The mean correlation (z transformed) is .51, which is significantly different from zero ($t = 6.63, p < .001$, DF = 20). These results support the hypothesis that task properties induce corresponding cognitive properties.

The CCI for each engineer was separately correlated with measures of depth task characteristics and surface task characteristics (the average value of each row and column in Table 4.3, respectively). The correlation between CCI and the surface TCI was positive for 18 engineers ($\chi^2 = 9.33, p < .01$), and six of these relations were significant at $p < .05$ (DF = 7, one tailed). The mean correlation (z transformed) was .38 ($t = 3.89, p < .001$, DF = 20, one tailed). Similarly, the correlation between CCI and the depth TCI was positive for 20 engineers ($\chi^2 = 15.43, p < .001$) and five were significant. The mean correlation was .39 ($t = 5.36, p < .001$). These results indicate that both surface and depth characteristics of tasks induce corresponding cognitive properties.

The CCI for each engineer was separately correlated with measures of depth task characteristics and surface task characteristics (the average value of each row and column in Table 4.3, respectively). The correlation between CCI and the surface TCI was positive for 18 engineers ($\chi^2 = 9.33$, $p < .01$), and six of these relations were significant at $p < .05$ (DF = 7, one tailed). The mean correlation (z transformed) was .38 ($t = 3.89, p < .001$, DF = 20, one tailed). Similarly, the correlation between CCI and the depth TCI was positive for 20 engineers ($\chi^2 = 15.43, p < .001$) and five were significant. The mean correlation was .39 ($t = 5.36, p < .001$). These results indicate that both surface and depth characteristics of tasks induce corresponding cognitive properties.

Table 4.3. *Effect of surface condition on cognitive continuum index (CCI)*[a]

		Aesthetics		Depth task conditions safety		Capacity		Cognitive continuum index averaged across all depth conditions for each engineer	
		Expected	Observed	Expected	Observed	Expected	Observed	Expected	Observed
Predicted order	$A > Q > I$	3.5	8	3.5	8	3.33	10	3.33	9
One departure from predicted order	$A > I > Q$	3.5	8	3.5	5	3.33	4	3.33	6
	$Q > A > I$	3.5	1	3.5	5	3.33	3	3.33	1
Two departures from predicted order	$Q > I > A$	3.5	1	3.5	0	3.33	1	3.33	2
	$I > A > Q$	3.5	2	3.5	0	3.33	1	3.33	1
Three departures from predicted order	$I > Q > A$	3.5	1	3.5	3	3.33	1	3.33	1
Test of predicted order		$x^2 = 5.49, p < .02$		$x^2 = 5.49, p < .02$		$x^2 = 13.71, p < .001$		$x^2 = 9.63, p < .01$	
Test of 0 or 1 departures from predicted order		$x^2 = 6.86, p < .01$		$x^2 = 9.33, p < .01$		$x^2 = 8.45, p < .01$		$x^2 = 6.05, p < .02$	

[a]Cell values are expected and observed numbers of engineers exhibiting each possible CCI order among the formula (*A*), bar graph (*Q*), and film strip (*I*) surface task conditions.

Order table analyses. This analysis provides a more rigorous test of the hypothesis because it demands that the location of each engineer's cognitive activity on the CCI be in exactly the order required by the order of the task conditions on the TCI. Table 4.3 shows that in the aesthetic judgment task the three surface task conditions induced cognition to be activated in exactly the predicted order on the cognitive continuum (formula (A) > bar graph (Q) > film strip (I)) for eight engineers $(\chi^2 = 5.5, p < .02)$. An additional nine engineers had two of the three predicted orders $(A > Q, Q > I,$ and $A > I)$. Three engineers had two departures from the predicted order, and one engineer had three (i.e., a complete reversal of the predicted order). Thus 17 of the 21 engineers were more consistent with the prediction than chance; that is, 17 had at least two of the three predicted pairwise relationships $(\chi^2 = 6.86, p < .01)$. The pattern of results for the safety and capacity tasks is similar. The same result appears when each engineer's CCI scores are averaged across the three depth tasks (right column of Table 4.3).

Table 4.4 shows that in the film strip surface task condition (left column of Table 4.4), the three depth task conditions induced eight engineers' cognition to be activated on the cognitive continuum in exactly the predicted order (capacity (C) > safety (S) > aesthetics (E)) $(p < .02)$, six engineers to have one deviation, five engineers to have two deviations, and one engineer to have three deviations (i.e., a complete reversal of the predicted order). Within the bar-graph condition, the number of engineers having the predicted order or at least two of the three relationships was significant. Within the formula condition (column 3), and when the engineers' CCI was averaged across all three surface task conditions (column 4), there was a greater than expected number of engineers who had exactly the predicted order, although this number was not statistically significant. However, for each of these columns 18 engineers had at least two of the three predicted relations $(\chi^2 = 11.25, p < .001)$.

Thus both correlational analysis and order analysis showed that (a) although the location of the task on the task continuum did not induce cognitive activity to be located at a corresponding point on the cognitive continuum for all engineers in every condition, (b) task location did induce the location of cognitive activity in the predicted order for most engineers in most conditions.

Relative efficacy of intuition, quasi-rationality, and analysis

H_2. Analytical cognition by persons does not provide a ceiling for performance.

Is analytical cognition, in practice, always superior to intuitive and quasi-rational cognition employed by the same person? The answer is clearly no. When judging capacity, 11 of the 20 engineers had higher achievement in the intuitive (film-strip) or quasi-rational (bar-graph) condition than in the analytical (formula-producing) condition (Table 4.5 part A, first column, all

Table 4.4. *Effect of depth condition on cognitive continuum index for each surface condition*[a]

		Film strip		Surface task conditions bar graph		Formula		Cognitive continuum index averaged across all surface conditions for each engineer	
		Expected	Observed	Expected	Observed	Expected	Observed	Expected	Observed
Predicted order	$C > S > E$	3.33	8	3.33	9	3.33	6	3.33	5
One departure	$C > E > S$	3.33	3	3.33	0	3.33	3	3.33	2
from predicted order	$S > C > E$	3.33	3	3.33	6	3.33	9	3.33	11
Two departures	$S > E > C$	3.33	3	3.33	3	3.33	1	3.33	1
from predicted order	$E > C > S$	3.33	2	3.33	1	3.33	0	3.33	0
Three departures from predicted order	$E > S > C$	3.33	1	3.33	1	3.33	1	3.33	1
Test of predicted order		$x^2 = 6.25, p < .02$		$x^2 = 9.63, p < .01$		$x^2 = 1.70$, n.s.		$x^2 = 0.49$, n.s.	
Test of 0 or 1 departures from predicted order		$x^2 = 2.45$, n.s.		$x^2 = 4.05, p < .05$		$x^2 = 11.25, p < .001$		$x^2 = 11.25, p < .001$	

[a] Cell values are expected and observed numbers of engineers exhibiting each possible CCI order among the capacity (C), safety (S) and aesthetics (E) depth task conditions.

Table 4.5. *Effect of surface-depth congruence on performance as measured by achievement* (r_a) *and knowledge* (G)

| | | (A) Capacity | | |
		r_a	G	
Three predicted relations	$A > Q > I$	9	7	for
Two of three predicted	$A > I > Q$	0	1	hypothesis
relations	$Q > A > I$	8	9	
One of three predicted	$Q > I > A$	3	2	against
relations	$I > A > Q$	0	0	hypothesis
Zero of three predicted	$I > Q > A$	0	1	
relations				
Test of predicted order		$\chi^2 = 9.63$	$\chi^2 = 3.62$	
		$p < .01$	$p < .10$	
Test of zero or one departure from		$\chi^2 = 8.45$	$\chi^2 = 8.45$	
predicted order		$p < .01$	$p < .01$	

| | | (B) Safety | | |
		r_a	G	
Both predicted	$Q > A > I$	2	0	for
relations	$Q > I > A$	6	6	hypothesis
One predicted	$I > Q > A$	2	8	neutral
relation	$A > Q > I$	9	0	
Neither predicted	$A > I > Q$	0	0	against
relation	$I > A > Q$	2	7	hypothesis
Test of predicted order		$\chi^2 = .054$	$\chi^2 = .054$	
		n.s.	n.s.	

| | | (C) Aesthetics | | |
		r_a	G	
Three predicted relations	$I > Q > A$	0	2	for
Two of three predicted	$I > A > Q$	0	2	hypothesis
relations	$Q > I > A$	1	3	
One of three predicted	$Q > A > I$	2	7	
relations	$A > I > Q$	4	2	against
Zero of three predicted	$A > Q > I$	14	5	hypothesis
relations				
Test of predicted order		$\chi^2 = 3.09$ (reversed direction) $p < .10$	$\chi^2 = .34$ (reversed direction) n.s.	
Test of zero or one departure from		$\chi^2 = 15.43$ (reversed direction) $p < .001$	$\chi^2 = 1.71$ (reversed direction) n.s.	
predicted order				

cases not in first or second row). The same was true for 12 of the 21 engineers when judging safety (Table 4.5 part B, first column, all cases not in fourth or fifth row). However, this was true for only three of the 21 engineers when judging aesthetics (Table 4.5 part C, first column, all cases not in fifth or sixth row), a result treated separately next.

Clearly, when direct comparisons are made between the same person's actual use of intuitive, quasi-rational, or analytical cognition, the latter does not provide a ceiling that other forms of cognition cannot exceed. This finding has long been suspected by students of cognition but, so far as we can determine, has never been demonstrated heretofore.

The extreme errors of analytical cognition

H_3. Analytical cognition is apt to produce extreme errors.

Because (a) errors of judgment are commonly emphasized in research on judgment and decision making, (b) various types of errors are not differentiated, and (c) this hypothesis carries considerable practical significance, we provide further detail regarding these engineers' errors. Figure 4.3 illustrates, in the analytical (formula) surface condition, that the range of achievement scores increases dramatically from intuition to analysis. Thus the worst as well as the best performances are produced by analytical cognition.

Detailed analysis of each engineer's performance shows how such errors come about. Engineer 2, for example, made a careless arithmetic error in producing the weights in his safety formula. He first assigned a weight of .10 to each of the ten cues. Next he adjusted the weights of important cues to .12. Finally, intending to assign weights of .08 to cues he felt were slightly less important, he wrote instead .8. Thus he gave the greatest weight to the cues to which he wished to give least weight. The effects of his error were serious: his achievement (r_a) was only .07, and his mean error was 44.2 on a scale he intended to run from 0 to 32. Similarly, on the capacity task Engineer 8 intended to subtract a set of factors from the maximum capacity, 2500, but used an extra minus sign. His formula therefore produced answers that correlated negatively with the capacity criterion (−.57). Correcting this error and another minor one produced a formula that performed at .88, moving him from being the worst performing engineer to the best performing engineer on this task. Errors of this type, capable of affecting the engineer's entire performance, appeared more often in the formula condition than in the filmstrip or bar-graph conditions.

Further, among the three formula conditions the errors became more serious as the depth task condition became more analytical (as the TCI increased). The seriousness of an error can be evaluated by the correlations of the answers produced by the erroneous formula with the answers produced by a corrected formula. Among the eight engineers with erroneous aesthetics formulas, the median correlation between corrected and uncor-

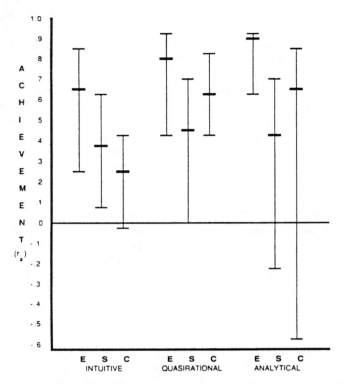

Figure 4.3. Medians and ranges of achievement in each condition. *E* is aesthetics judgment, *S* is safety judgment, and *C* is capacity judgment.

rected formulas is .997, indicating that the errors in this intuition-inducing depth task were not at all serious. The median correlation between corrected and uncorrected formulas for the seven engineers who made errors on their safety formulas is .72, and the median for the nine engineers with capacity formula errors is .67. Thus the most serious errors in the formula condition were produced in the most analysis-inducing depth task, capacity judgment.

Errors in substance versus errors in process. Accidental errors that have systematic effects such as those just described are not the only reason that analytical cognition is frequently outperformed by the engineers' intuitive and quasi-rational cognition. Removing the effects of *nonsystematic* errors by using the measure *G* from the lens model equation (see Appendix II) shows that performance in the analytical surface task is exceeded by performance in the intuitive or quasi-rational condition for 12 of the 20 engineers on the capacity task (Table 4.5 part A, second column), for all 21 engineers on the safety task (Table 4.5 part B, second column), and for 14 of the 21 engineers on the aesthetics task (Table 4.5 part C, second column). These results indicate that intuitive and quasi-rational cognition are frequently superior to analytical cognition because they are substantively more correct, a finding that was wholly unanticipated. This result implies that current methods of building expert systems that consist only of rules derived from experts' verbal reports may be overlooking an important aspect of expertise. For the empirical examination of intuitive or quasi-rational judgments, such as those obtained from these highway engineers, evidently can provide new and useful information about the content of the expert's knowledge, as well as his or her process of applying it.

In practice, then, a person's analytical cognition does not always represent an upper bound for that person's performance, even when the occasional large accidental errors in its execution have been corrected. (Practitioners are beginning to appreciate the risk of analytical cognition; see, for example, the cautions expressed in *The Wall Street Journal* [18] about the risk of large errors produced by the incorrect use of computer spread sheets.)

Correspondence between task properties and cognitive properties and its effect on performance

The hypothesis that the correspondence between the overall task location (TCI) and the location of each engineer's cognitive activity (CCI) is a determinant of the accuracy of judgment was investigated by (a) measuring the absolute difference between the location of each engineer's cognitive activity on the cognitive continuum and the location of the task on the task continuum, |TCI-CCI|, and (b) correlating this measure and r_a for each engineer, resulting in the following.

H_4. The greater |TCI-CCI|, the lower the engineer's achievement (r_a).

The mean of the distribution of each engineer's z-transformed correlation between his |TCI-CCI| score and his r_a is $-.37 \pm .07$, significantly different from zero ($p < .001$, DF = 20, two tailed). Since both the TCI and the CCI are composites of unreliable measures, this result is almost certainly an underestimate of the true relation. Thus we conclude that the engineer's accuracy is higher when the cognitive activity induced by the task more closely corresponds to the overall task location on the cognitive continuum. In short, performance is better when cognitive properties correspond to task properties, a result also found by Friedman et al. [19].

One further result illustrates the importance of distinguishing between the surface and depth characteristics of tasks. In the case of H_2 we noted the superiority of aesthetic achievement in the formula construction task. Twenty of the 21 engineers achieved greater accuracy in the aesthetics task by constructing a formula than by directly observing film strips of the highways (Table 4.5, part C, rows 4–6). Moreover, the accuracy of the formulas was very high in absolute as well as relative terms (mean $r_a = .91$). The apparent oddity of this result disappears when surface and depth task characteristics are distinguished. The depth characteristics of the aesthetics task induced all but three of the engineers to rely on intuitive cognitive activity in the construction of their formulas. This result is particularly notable because these engineers used a linear weighted-sum organizing principle. The interview material from the formula-writing sessions shows that the engineers resorted to linear weighted-sum formulas because they had no professional or analytical experience on which to base construction of any other type of formula. High accuracy, that is, high correlation with citizens' panel judgments, occurred because the perceptual judgments of the citizens' panel were also produced (implicitly) by similar cognitive activity in a task with rather highly intercorrelated cues (mean $r_a = .55$). In short, the engineers were induced to use explicitly the same cognitive approach the citizens' panel used implicitly with the consequence that the robustness of both the explicit and implicit linear equations produced high accuracy (cf. [13]). These results show why it is important to distinguish between the surface and depth characteristics of cognitive tasks and to examine their differential effects on the inducement of cognitive properties. In addition, they illustrate how cognitive activities are induced and how the properties of the task on which they are brought to bear interact to produce accuracy of judgment.

Relations between the congruence of task properties and performance

H_5. The greater the congruence between surface and depth task characteristics, the higher the engineer's achievement.

The hypothesis that congruence between surface and depth task characteristics enhances performance was tested by creating a variable in which a 2 was assigned to the cells on the descending diagonal (in Figure 4.1), a 1 to the adjacent cells, and a 0 to the corner cells. This variable is orthogonal to surface and depth task conditions.

The mean of the distribution of each engineer's (z-transformed) correlation between r_a and the measure of congruence is .18 (with a standard error of ±.06), which is significantly different from zero ($p < .01$, DF = 20, two tailed). These results suggest that congruence between surface and depth task characteristics only weakly enhances achievement. Although this result might be thought an underestimation because of the coarse grouping (3-point scale), an order table analysis similar to those reported previously confirms this weak relationship (and, therefore, it is not presented here).

This result is important because it indicates that, contrary to theoretical prediction, performance is not significantly related to the congruence of surface and depth properties of the task system. However, this result does not mean that congruence is an empirically unimportant task condition. Rather, it suggests that the empirical significance of congruence for performance needs to be examined in terms of whether the subject was induced to develop the cognitive activity *corresponding* to the related task condition, as demonstrated in relation to H_4.

Summary

Treating both environment and organism as systems, each with surface and depth, enabled us to break with the long tradition of assuming that a dichotomy exists between analysis and intuition and to treat analysis and intuition as endpoints of a cognitive continuum. The systems approach also made it possible to place environmental tasks on a parallel continuum, thus enabling us to investigate the cognitive consequences of the relation between these systems. We directly examined the effect of various forms of tasks, defined in terms of system properties, on various forms of cognition, also defined in terms of system properties. The systems approach also enabled us to distinguish between the surface properties and depth properties of task systems, and thus to introduce the concepts of (a) the congruence between the surface displays of information and the depth properties of tasks and (b) the correspondence between task properties and cognitive properties. The research reported here investigates the effect of congruence and correspondence on the efficacy of various forms of human judgment. We directly compare the efficacy of intuitive, quasi-rational, and analytical cognition as these modes are actually employed by the same person in relation to an empirical criterion. Many indirect comparisons between persons and normative models have been made (see [40]), but despite a long history of dispute over the relative efficacy of intuitive and analytical cognition, we can find no previous scientific efforts to compare them directly.

Direct comparisons were made of the efficacy of 21 expert highway engineers' use of intuition, quasi-rationality, and analysis in predicting an empirical criterion. Each engineer was studied individually over nine task conditions. Both the surface and depth characteristics of the task were measured and located on a task continuum index (TCI) defined in terms of eight measures selected a priori. Each engineer's cognitive activity in each task condition was located on a cognitive continuum index (CCI) defined in terms of four measures of the subject's cognitive activity, also selected a priori. Although surface and depth characteristics of tasks are obviously separable, researchers have never separated them and ascertained their differential effects on cognition. There are six main results.

First, both surface and depth properties of tasks tend to induce corresponding cognitive properties. This result confirms the importance of specifying task properties as well as distinguishing between surface and depth characteristics of tasks, not only in studies of cognition but also in the display of information generally.

Second, comparison of the efficacy of three forms of cognition within the same person across three tasks, each displayed in three different ways, indicates not only that intuitive and quasi-rational cognition can perform as well as analytical cognition, but that intuitive or quasi-rational cognition can outperform analytical cognition by the same person.

Third, analytical cognition is more likely than intuitive cognition to produce extreme errors.

Fourth, the greater the correspondence between task properties and cognitive properties, the greater the subject's achievement. This result indicates the task circumstances for which each form of cognition is likely to be most efficacious and therefore "appropriate" (see also [19]).

Fifth, the degree of congruence between the surface and depth characteristics of tasks had only a marginally positive relation to performance. The synergistic function of congruence did not appear to enhance performance significantly.

Sixth, eight objective measures, selected a priori and combined into an index (TCI) for locating the nine task conditions on the task continuum, produced perfect orderings of both surface and depth task conditions (Fig. 4.2). In addition, the four measures selected a priori for describing cognitive activity produced an index (CCI) that bore a definite relation to the TCI under a stringent test of the predicted performance of each of 21 experts. This result suggests that further research on the differential effects of task properties will markedly increase our ability to predict the form of a person's cognitive activity from a knowledge of task properties. Further, the relation between the two should predict performance.

Discussion

We discuss first what is likely to be the most controversial finding and then examine its practical implications. The conclusion that the greater the correspondence between task properties and cognitive properties the better or more accurate the judgments of the experts is controversial because it contradicts current arguments that intuition produces biased incorrect judgments and should be replaced whenever possible by analytical methods (see [40] for numerous examples). In our view, the contradiction is not an artifact. It occurs for two reasons: (a) the tendency to use multiple definitions of intuition and (b) the reliance on indirect comparisons, between persons and equations, for example, rather than on direct comparisons of intuition and analysis within persons.

Definitions of intuition are important. Because researchers currently allow the term *intuition* to be anything that analysis is not, they have described intuitive cognitive activity in many ways – even as a form of analysis, as in Simon's remark that "intuition and judgment – at least good judgment – are simply analyses frozen into habit and into the capacity for rapid response through recognition" [56, p. 63]. On the other hand, as noted previously, Kahneman and Tversky emphasize nonanalytical features of intuition when they argue that "a judgment is called intuitive if it is reached by an informal and unstructured mode of reasoning *without* [italics added] the use of analytic methods or deliberate calculation" [41, p. 124]. Indeed, many examples of contradictory definitions could be cited. Because it is difficult to know exactly which cognitive processes have been studied under the rubric of intuition (cf. [60]), it is difficult to ascertain whether the results of our study contradict current conclusions about the widespread fallibility of intuition.

Indirect comparisons should not be substituted for direct comparisons. Current conclusions incorrectly lead us to believe that intuitive cognition has been compared with analytical cognition because the results of indirect comparison (person versus model) are surreptitiously treated as direct comparisons (a person's intuitive processes versus a person's analytical processes). That is, the demonstration that normative models outperform persons' cognitive efforts is considered a demonstration of the superiority of one form of cognitive activity over another. Our finding that greater correspondence leads to greater achievement is based on a comparison different from the one on which previous conclusions are based. Nevertheless, this finding should be accepted with caution for several reasons. Our definitions of intuition and analysis are new and will undoubtedly be revised. The data are scanty, although the number of experts and tasks in our study is far larger than is ordinarily the case. The range of individual differences among tasks has hardly been touched, and therefore the study of direct comparisons of intuitive and analytical cognition within the same person has just begun. For these reasons we cannot at present be certain which mode of cognition is appropriate for which task.

Implications for practice

Engineers and other experts cannot, however, withhold their expert judgment until this question is settled. Until it is settled, we offer the following suggestions.

1. Experts should increase their awareness of the correspondence between task and cognition. Experts should examine task display features to determine whether the form in which data are presented is primarily intuition inducing or analysis inducing. From this examination they should anticipate the form of cognition likely to be applied to the problem.

2. When the display features of the task are not susceptible to alteration, the expert should estimate the location of the task on the task continuum. Having made this estimation, the expert can then maximize the probability of accurate judgments by adapting his or her cognitive activity to the (unalterable) display features of the task. In other words, the expert should try to use that mode of cognition likely to be induced by the task condition. The results from our study suggest that accuracy will vary as an inverted U curve function of the mode of cognition. At some point on the cognitive continuum, performance will be best and accuracy will fall off as the expert becomes either more analytical or more intuitive.

3. When the mode of cognitive activity to be used on a task is unalterable, task displays should be those likely to correspond with the anticipated cognitive activity. Cognitive activity is unalterable when, for example, administrative rules demand evidence of analytical cognition, or when intuitive cognition will be used because of insufficient time (as in control room emergencies). In such conditions, accuracy should be expected to vary as a single-peaked function of the task's location on the task continuum.

In short, maximizing accuracy in any judgment task will require that the expert carefully attend to both task conditions and the cognitive activity to be applied to them.

Appendix I: Construction of the task continuum index

The eight subindices of the task continuum index are measured as follows:

1. *number of cues presented*: measured by counting the cues explicitly presented in the bar-graph and formula conditions and the total number of cues available in the film-strip condition;
2. *redundancy among the cues*: measured by the mean intercorrelation among all the relevant cues;
3. *reliability of cue measurement*: measured by the mean intercorrelation among the cue judgments of several experts (safety, $n = 5$; capacity, $n = 5$; aesthetics, $n = 14$) for the film-strip condition, and by assigning a value of 1 in the bar-graph and formula conditions;
4. *degree to which the task is decomposed for the subject*: measured by assigning the cells in the film-strip, bar-graph, and formula surface conditions values of 1, 2, and 3, respectively, reflecting the extent to which the task presentation decomposes the task for the subject;
5. *availability to the subject of an organizing principle*: measured by assigning the cells in the aesthetics, safety, and capacity depth conditions values of 1, 2, and 3, respectively, reflecting the general availability of explicit organizing principles for these judgment tasks;
6. *degree of nonlinearity in the optimal organizing principle*: measured by using the difference between the R^2 of the appropriate nonlinear model of the relation between cues and criterion (the environment) and the R^2 of the best fit linear model of the environment;
7. *extent to which the cues are weighted equally in the optimal organizing principle for the task*: measured by using the standard deviation of the beta weights from the environmental model;

8. *degree of certainty in the task system*: measured by the R^2 of the environmental model.

To produce a task continuum index value for a given task, these subindices are combined according to the following procedure. Each of the subindices is rescaled (by linear transformation) onto a 1–10 scale, in which 1 is the most intuition-inducing and 10 the most analysis-inducing end of the scale. (The rescaling reversed the scales for subindices 1 and 2.) The eight rescaled subindices are averaged with equal weights to produce the task continuum index score for the task. To produce TCI scores for each depth condition or surface condition, the mean of the three cell scores in its row or column, respectively, is calculated.

Appendix II: Derivation of measures of achievement, knowledge, and cognitive control from the lens model

The lens model

Achievement can be decomposed into several components by means of the lens model equation [31] as follows:

$$r_a = GR_eR_s + C\sqrt{1 - R_e^2}\sqrt{1 - R_s^2}$$

where

r_a	achievement, the correlation between the engineer's judgments and criterion values,
G	correlation between judgments and criterion values corrected for attenuation due to less than perfect linear predictability in each,
R_e	predictability (linear form) of criterion from cues,
R_s	predictability (linear form) of subject's judgments from cues,
C	correlation between residuals from linear predictions of criterion and residuals from linear predictions of subject's judgments.

The lens model for capacity judgments is a variant of this.

Capacity

In the capacity judgment task the environmental model derived from the *Highway Capacity Manual* [34] involves nonlinear cue use, while the engineer's judgments are fit with a linear model. Since the models are different, it cannot be assumed that the residuals of one model are uncorrelated with the predictions of the other. There must now be four terms in the lens model equation [57, pp. 114, 115]. Thus,

$$r_a = GR_eR_s + r\left(\hat{Y}_e, Z_s\right)R_e\sqrt{\left(1 - R_s^2\right)}$$
$$+ r\left(Z_e, \hat{Y}_s\right)\sqrt{\left(1 - R_e^2\right)}R_s + C\sqrt{\left(1 - R_e^2\right)}\sqrt{\left(1 - R_s^2\right)}$$

where the observed judgment Y_s is decomposed into the portion predicted by the judgment model $\hat{Y}_s$ and the residual Z_s; therefore, $r(\hat{Y}_e, Z_s)$ is the correlation between the *prediction* of the environmental model and the *residual* of the model of the engineer's judgments. However, since environmental prediction is perfect (due to the fact that the capacity criterion was produced by the environmental model from the cue values), $R_e = 1$ and $\sqrt{(1 - R_e^2)} = 0$. Two terms thus drop out of this equation, leaving the formula

$$r_a = GR_eR_s + r\left(\hat{Y}_e, Z_s\right)R_e\sqrt{\left(1 - R_s^2\right)}$$

Knowledge and cognitive control

In the absence of significant correlations between residuals (trivial values of C in the lens model equation) then $r_a = GR_eR_s$. Under these conditions G represents the engineer's *knowledge* because it indicates what the subject's achievement would have been if he had executed his judgment policy with perfect *cognitive control* (i.e., $R_s = 1.00$) and if the environmental task criterion were perfectly predictable from the cues (i.e., $R_e = 1.00$).

Cognitive control [31], [32] is appropriately measured by R_s in the equation (and thus used in the CCI) since there was little evidence in this study of lack of fit in the linear model in either the intuition-inducing film-strip presentation or in the quasi-rationality-inducing bar-graph presentation.

In the analysis-inducing formula-construction situation, however, the engineers' judgments are produced by formulas; no "error" exists in the sense of random variation about a policy, as occurs in the intuitive and quasi-rational surface task conditions, because the formula produces the answers deterministically. Thus in the analytical condition, R_s, the measure of cognitive control, equals 1.0, and G, the measure of knowledge, differs from r_a only because of R_e, the environmental unpredictability – a factor that is independent of the engineer's behavior.

Using R_s to measure cognitive control thus ignores the fact that errors could be made by the engineers in the analytical mode. Errors were made in *constructing formulas* rather than in *executing judgments*. A subject's cognitive control in the analytical surface task condition can, however, be ascertained by a careful comparison of his verbalized intentions (transcribed) of what his formula should be with the formula he actually constructed. This step results in two formulas for each engineer: the one presented to the researcher, the other constructed by the researcher to reflect the engineer's intentions. The correlation between the answers produced by these two formulas provides a measure of the discrepancy between what was *intended* and what was *executed*; thus it is a measure of cognitive control comparable to the measure employed in the intuitive and quasi-rational surface task conditions.

Appendix III: Methodology

The present paper departs from the usual null hypothesis testing procedure used by psychologists in favor of the more rigorous approach used by physical scientists. Meehl [47] summarized his argument against the standard null hypothesis approach by stating that "I believe that the almost universal reliance on merely refuting the null hypothesis as the standard method for corroborating substantive theories in the soft areas [of psychology] is a terrible mistake, is basically unsound, poor scientific strategy, and one of the worst things that ever happened in the history of psychology" [47, p. 817], a conclusion with which we agree (see [12] for a recent defense of Meehl's views). Therefore, we believe that we should point out that the test of the cognitive continuum theory presented here did not involve the usual weak ANOVA procedure of testing group means within the nine-cell design described in the text (see Fig. 4.1). Rather, we tested auxiliary hypotheses *directly* by predicting the *exact* order of appearance of a specific type of cognitive activity for each engineer separately, over a set of nine conditions, each of which included a sample of 40 highways. Thus there were in effect 21 individual experiments, each of which tested the auxiliary hypotheses of the theory, a step which Meehl [46] declares rarely occurs in conventional theory testing. A further example of the value of the procedure can be found in [28] where a multiconcept–multimethod matrix is created separately for each engineer, thus enabling us to develop a new measure of expert *competence*. (See also [26] which asserts that the conventional ANOVA design of experiments is appropriate for applied, but not basic, research in psychology.)

References

[1] N. H. Anderson, *Foundations of Information Integration Theory*. New York: Academic, 1981.

[2] H. R. Arkes and K. R. Hammond, *Judgment and Decision Making: An Interdisciplinary Reader*. Cambridge, UK: Cambridge Univ. Press, 1986.

[3] L. R. Beach and T. R. Mitchell, "A contingency model for the selection of decision strategies," *Academy Management Rev.*, vol. 3, pp. 439–449, 1978.

[4] B. Brehmer, "Response consistency in probabilistic inference tasks," *Organizat. Behavior Human Perform.*, vol. 22. pp. 103–115, 1978.

[5] L. Brooks, "Nonanalytic concept formation and memory for instances," in *Cognition and Categorization*, E. Rosch and B. Lloyd, Eds. New York: Erlbaum, 1978, pp. 170–211.

[6] E. Brunswik, *The Conceptual Framework of Psychology*. Chicago, IL: Univ. of Chicago Press, 1952.

[7] ——, *Perception and the Representative Design of Psychological Experiments*, 2nd ed. Berkeley, CA: Univ. of California Press, 1956.

[8] ——, "Scope and aspects of the cognitive problem," in *Cognition: The Colorado Symposium*, H. Gruber, K. Hammond, and R. Jessor, Eds. Cambridge, MA: Harvard Univ. Press. 1957, pp. 5–31.

[9] D. T. Campbell and D. W. Fiske. "Convergent and discriminant validation by the multitrait-multimethod matrix," *Psych. Bull.*, vol. 56, pp. 81–105, 1959.

[10] M. T. H. Chi, R. Glaser, and E. Rees, "Expertise in problem solving," *Advan. Psych. Human Intell.*, vol. 1, pp. 7–75, 1982.

[11] L. J. Cohen, "Can human irrationality be experimentally demonstrated?," *Behavioral, Brain Sci.*, vol. 43, pp. 317–370, 1981.

[12] R. Dar, "Another look at Meehl, Lakatos, and the scientific practices of psychologists," *Amer. Psych.*, vol. 42, pp. 145–151, 1987.

[13] R. M. Dawes and B. Corrigan, "Linear models in decision making." *Psych. Bull.*, vol. 81, pp. 95–106, 1974.

[14] H. L. Dreyfus, S. E. Dreyfus, and T. Athanasiou, *Mind over Machine: The Power of Human Intuition and Expertise in the Era of the Computer*. New York: The Free Press, 1986.

[15] H. J. Einhorn, "Cue definition and residual judgment," *Organizat. Behavior Human Perform.*, vol. 12, pp. 30–49, 1974.

[16] H. J. Einhorn and R. M. Hogarth, "Behavioral decision theory: Processes of judgment and choice," *Ann. Rev. Psych.*, vol. 32, pp. 53–88, 1981.

[17] ——, "Reply to commentaries," in *Decision Making: An Interdisciplinary Inquiry*, G. R. Ungson and D. N. Braunstein, Eds. Boston, MA: Kent, 1982, pp. 53–56.

[18] R. M. Freeman, "A slip of the chip on computer spread sheets can cost millions," *Wall Street J.*, p. 10, Aug. 20, 1984.

[19] L. Friedman, W. C. Howell, and C. R. Jensen, "Diagnostic judgment as a function of the preprocessing of evidence," *Human Factors*, vol. 27, pp. 665–673, 1985.

[20] B. S. Goldsberry, "Induced judgment decrements," Rice Univ., Department of Psychology, Houston, TX, Rep. 83-3, 1983.

[21] R. M. Hamm, "Clinical intuition and clinical analysis: Expertise and the cognitive continuum," in *Professional Judgment*, J. Dowie and A. Elstein, Eds. Cambridge, UK: Cambridge Univ. Press, 1988, pp. 78–105.

[22] K. R. Hammond, "Probabilistic functioning and the clinical method," *Psych. Rev.*, vol. 62, pp. 255–262, 1955.

[23] ——, Ed., *The Psychology of Egon Brunswik*. New York: Holt, Rinehart, Winston, 1966.

[24] ——, "The integration of research in judgment and decision theory," Univ. Colorado, Center for Research on Judgment and Policy, Boulder, CO, Rep. 226, 1980.

[25] ——, "Unification of theory and research in judgment and decision making," Univ. Colorado, Center for Research on Judgment and Policy, Boulder, CO, unpublished, 1982.

[26] ——, "Generalization in operational contexts: What does it mean? Can it be done?," *IEEE Trans. Syst., Man, Cybern.*, vol. SMC-16, pp. 428–433, 1986.

[27] K. R. Hammond and B. Brehmer, "Quasi-rationality and distrust: Implications for international conflict," in *Human Judgment and Social Interaction*, L. Rappoport and D. Summers, Eds. New York: Holt, Rinehart, Winston, 1973, pp. 338–391.

[28] K. R. Hammond, R. M. Hamm, and J. Grassia, "Generalizing over conditions by combining the multitrait–multimethod matrix and the representative design of experiments," *Psych. Bull.*, vol. 100, pp. 257–269, 1986.

[29] K. R. Hammond, R. M. Hamm, J. Grassia, and T. Pearson, "The relative efficacy of intuitive and analytical cognition," Univ. Colorado, Center for Research on Judgment and Policy, Boulder, CO, Rep. 252, 1984.

[30] K. R. Hammond, G. H. McClelland, and J. Mumpower, *Human Judgment and Decision Making: Theories, Methods, and Procedures*. New York: Praeger, 1980.

[31] K. R. Hammond, T. R. Stewart, B. Brehmer, and D. O. Steinmann, "Social judgment theory," in *Human Judgment and Decision Processes*, M. F. Kaplan and S. Schwartz, Eds. New York: Academic, 1975, pp. 271–312.

[32] K. R. Hammond and D. A. Summers, "Cognitive control," *Psych. Rev.*, vol. 79, pp. 58–67, 1972.

[33] K. R. Hammond and N. E. Wascoe, Eds., *New Directions for Methodology of Social and Behavioral Science: Realizations of Brunswik's Representative Design*. San Francisco, CA: Jossey-Bass, 1980.

[34] Highway Research Board, *Highway Capacity Manual 1965*, Highway Research Board Special Rep. 87, National Research Council Publication 1328, National Research Council, Washington, DC, 1965.

[35] S. J. Hoch and J. E. Tschirgi, "Cue redundancy and extra logical inferences in a deductive reasoning task," *Memory, Cognition.* vol. 11, pp. 200–209, 1983.

[36] W. C. Howell, "Task influences in the analytic-intuitive approach to decision making," Rice University, Department of Psychology, Research Report Series, Houston, TX, Final Rep., 1984.

[37] W. Howell and S. Kerkar, "A test of task influence in uncertainty measurement," *Organizat. Behavior Human Perform.*, vol. 30, pp. 365–390, 1982.

[38] C. Jones and P. Harris, "Insight into the law of large numbers: A comparison of Piagetian and judgment theory," *Quart. J. Experiment. Psych. Sec. A: Human Experiment. Psych.*, vol. 34A, pp. 479–488, 1982.

[39] H. Jungermann, "The two camps on rationality," in *Decision Making under Uncertainty*, R. Scholz, Ed. Amsterdam, The Netherlands: North-Holland, 1983, pp. 63–86.

[40] D. Kahneman, P. Slovic, and A. Tversky, Eds., *Judgment under Uncertainty: Heuristics and Biases*. Cambridge, UK: Cambridge Univ. Press, 1982.

[41] D. Kahneman and A. Tversky, "On the study of statistical intuitions," *Cognition*, vol. 11, pp. 123–141, 1982.

[42] L. R. Keller, "The effects of problem representation on the sure-thing and substitution principles," *Management Sci.*, vol. 31, pp. 738–751, 1985.

[43] J. Klayman and Y.-W. Ha, "Confirmation, disconfirmation, and information in hypothesis-testing," *Psych. Rev.*, vol. 94, pp. 211–228, 1977.

[44] H. Kyburg, "Rational belief," *Behavioral, Brain Sci.*, vol. 6, pp. 231–274, 1983.

[45] K. Lehrer, "Rationality as weighted averaging," *Syntheses*, vol. 57, pp. 283–295, 1983.

[46] P. E. Meehl, "Theory testing in psychology and in physics: A methodological paradox," *Phil. Sci.*, vol. 34, pp. 103–115, 1967.

[47] ———, "Theoretical risks and tabular asterisks: Sir Karl, Sir Ronald, and the slow progress of soft psychology," *J. Consulting, Clinical Psych.*, vol. 46, pp. 806–834, 1978.

[48] A. I. Miller, "Visualization lost and regained: The genesis of the quantum theory in the period 1913–27," in *On Aesthetics in Science*, J. Wechsler, Ed. Cambridge, MA: MIT Press, 1978, pp. 73–102.

[49] D. Navon, "The importance of being conservative: Some reflections on human Bayesian behavior," *Brit. J. Math. Statist. Psych.*, vol. 31, pp. 33–48, 1978.

[50] J. Payne, "Task complexity and contingent processing in decision making: An information search and protocol analysis," *Organizat. Behavior, Human Perform.*, vol. 16, pp. 366–387, 1976.

[51] ———, "Contingent decision behavior," *Psych. Bull.*,vol. 92, pp. 382–402, 1982.

[52] G. F. Pitz and N. J. Sachs, "Judgment and decision: Theory and applications," *Ann. Rev. Psych.*, vol. 35, pp. 139–163, 1984.

[53] J. R. Royce, "Three ways of knowing, and the scientific world view," *Method. Sci.*, vol. 11, pp. 146–164, 1978.

[54] H. A. Simon, *Models of Man*. New York: Wiley, 1957.

[55] ———, *Models of Thought*. New Haven, CT: Yale Univ. Press, 1979.

[56] ———, "Making management decisions: The role of intuition and emotion," *Acad. Management Exec.*, vol. 1, pp. 57–63, 1987.

[57] T. R. Stewart, "Components of correlation and extensions of the lens model equation," *Psychometrika*, vol. 41, pp. 101–120, 1976.

[58] D. Stock and C. J. Watson, "Human judgment accuracy, multidimensional graphics, and humans versus models," *J. Account. Res.*, vol. 22, pp. 192–206, 1984.

[59] A. Tversky and D. Kahneman, "Extensional versus intuitive reasoning: The conjunction fallacy in probability judgment," *Psych. Rev.*, vol. 90, pp. 293–315, 1983.

[60] D. von Winterfeldt and W. Edwards, *Decision Analysis and Behavioral Research*. Cambridge, UK: Cambridge Univ. Press, 1986.

[61] T. S. Wallsten and D. V. Budescu, "Additivity and nonadditivity in judging MMPI profiles," *J. Experiment. Psych.: Human Perception, Perform.*, vol. 7, pp. 1096–1109, 1981.

[62] P. C. Wason and P. N. Johnson-Laird, *Psychology of Reasoning: Structure and Content*. Cambridge, MA: Harvard Univ. Press, 1972.

[63] J. C. Wright and G. L. Murphy, "The utility of theories in intuitive statistics: The robustness of theory-based judgments," *J. Experiment. Psych.: General*, vol. 113, pp. 301–322, 1984.

[64] R. Wyer, "An investigation of the relations among probability estimates," *Organizat. Behavior, Human Perform.*, vol. 15, pp. 1–18, 1976.

5 The adaptive decision maker: Effort and accuracy in choice

John W. Payne, James R. Bettman,
and Eric J. Johnson

In his dissertation research, Hillel Einhorn examined a question that is central to behavioral decision research and of substantial applied interest. How do people evaluate and choose among a set of multiattribute alternatives (Einhorn, 1970, 1971)? Einhorn concluded that no single model such as additive utility was likely to be an adequate general representation of evaluative decision making. He proposed that conditions should be specified under which various models apply as representations of human decision making. The work described in this chapter follows Einhorn's suggestion and considers why decision makers, given a particular decision task, select one particular decision strategy instead of others.

Contingent strategy selection reflects the fascinating ability of individuals to adapt to a wide variety of environmental conditions. The issue of strategy selection also reflects a growing concern in cognitive psychology with the regulation of cognition, or metacognition (Brown et al., 1983). The research program described in this chapter emphasizes the adaptivity of human decision behavior to task demands and the cognitive control question of how one decides how to decide.

Deciding how to decide

The most frequently advocated approach to explaining strategy selection is to assume that strategies have differing advantages and disadvantages and to hypothesize that an individual selects the strategy that is best for the task (Beach and Mitchell, 1978). Several factors, such as the chance of making an

This chapter originally appeared in R. M. Hogarth (Ed.), *Insights in Decision Making: A Tribute to Hillel J. Einhorn* (pp. 129–153). Chicago: The University of Chicago Press, 1990. Copyright © 1990 by the University of Chicago. All rights reserved. Reprinted by permission.

The research reported in this chapter was supported by a contract from the Perceptual Science Programs, Office of Naval Research. Each author contributed equally to all phases of this project.

error (Thorngate, 1980), avoidance of conflict (Hogarth, 1987), and justifiability (Tversky, 1972), can affect decision makers' perceptions of the appropriateness of a strategy for a particular task and hence can affect strategy selection. However, our research has focused on the role played in strategy choice by the cognitive effort (mental resources) required to execute a strategy in a specific task environment.

The idea that decision making is influenced by considerations of cognitive effort is an old one (e.g., Simon, 1955; Marschak, 1968). It seems obvious, for example, that different strategies require different amounts of computational effort. Expected-utility maximization, for instance, requires a person to process all relevant problem information and to trade off values and beliefs. The lexicographic choice rule (Tversky, 1969), on the other hand, chooses the alternative that is best on the most important attribute, ignoring much of the potentially relevant problem information.

At a more precise level of analysis, however, a comparison among decision strategies in terms of cognitive effort is more difficult. In part, this is because decision strategies proposed in the literature have varied widely in terms of their formal expression. Some have been proposed as formal mathematical models (e.g., elimination by aspects; Tversky, 1972) and others as verbal process descriptions (e.g., the majority-of-confirming-dimensions rule; Russo and Dosher, 1983). The research described here developed a language that could be used to express a diverse set of decision strategies in terms of a common set of elementary information processes. That language allows strategy selection to be investigated at a detailed information-processing level rather than at a more general level of analysis, such as comparisons of analytic versus nonanalytic (Beach and Mitchell, 1978) or analytic versus intuitive strategies (Hammond, 1986). One can examine, for instance, how cognitive effort is affected by both the amount of information to be processed and the specific mix of elementary information processes used.

In addition to cognitive effort, we have been concerned with how the use of simplified decision rules affects the accuracy of decisions. For example, a simple equal-weighting strategy can closely approximate the accuracy of an optimal-weighting rule in some task environments (Einhorn and Hogarth, 1975).

The rest of this chapter is organized as follows. First, studies that test and elaborate the implications of an effort–accuracy framework for strategy selection are briefly reviewed. The studies include Monte Carlo simulations of how the effort and accuracy of different strategies might vary across task environments, an empirical test of various models of subjects' effort using different decision strategies in different choice environments, and experiments that examine whether the actual decision behaviors exhibited by subjects across different task environments are consistent with the efficient processing patterns identified by the simulation. Some unresolved issues relating to the effort–accuracy framework are then considered, such as the extent to which strategies may be not so much selected as they are constructed throughout the decision process. Such construction may allow individuals to notice and exploit structure in the choice set in ways that reduce effort (Bettman, 1979). Finally, some implications of our research for decision aiding are described.

Effort, accuracy, and choice environments

As typically formulated, decision problems consist of three basic components: the alternatives available to the decision maker; events or contingencies that relate actions to outcomes as well as their associated probabilities; and the values associated with the outcomes. These informational elements, along with a goal statement (such as "choose the preferred alternative"), represent the task environment presented to a decision maker. The decision maker's internal representation of this task environment is the individual's problem space, containing the solution (i.e., the preferred alternative), which must be identified (Newell and Simon, 1972). Generally, decision tasks become more difficult with more alternatives, multiple contingencies, and multiple conflicting dimensions of value.

Much research supports Einhorn's suggestion (1970, 1971) that an individual will utilize a number of different information-processing strategies to solve decision tasks (Abelson and Levi, 1985). Sometimes the strategies involve an exhaustive use of the available information in a form of compensatory processing. However, often the strategies used are heuristics that simplify search through the problem space either by disregarding some problem information or simplifying the processing done on particular elements of the problem. Examples of the latter are within-attribute comparison as opposed to the combining of information across attributes (Russo and Dosher, 1983). Alternative heuristics such as elimination by aspects (EBA), satisficing (SAT), lexicographic choice (LEX), and equal weighting (EQW) represent different simplification strategies for search through the problem space. For example, the EQW rule reduces processing by ignoring any different weights for the decision outcomes while still examining the values for all outcomes. The LEX rule, on the other hand, uses the weights to limit search to one or a few of the most important attributes and simplifies processing by using only comparisons of one outcome value to another. More generally, people seem to react to the discrepancy between information-processing demands and information-processing capacity in decision making by selectively processing a subset of the available information and/or selectively applying to that information operations that are easier to perform.

The use of heuristics that save effort can also lead to serious decision errors (Tversky, 1969). However, some cognitive simplifications can both save effort and maintain reasonably high levels of accuracy in a given task environment (Einhorn and Hogarth, 1975). This point is crucial; we do not believe that heuristics and biases should be viewed as synonymous. Rather, we argue that the use of heuristics often represents intelligent, if not optimal, decision making. Given this perspective, characterizing the effort required to use various heuristics and the accuracy of those heuristics in various task environments is essential. In the next section, we report Monte Carlo simulation experiments that provide estimates of accuracy and effort for several heuristics in different decision-task environments. Decision makers can potentially use such estimates to both save effort and maintain accuracy by selecting different heuristics for different task environments. In later sections, we examine whether decision makers in fact adapt to different tasks in ways that the simulations suggest are relatively efficient (i.e., that maintain accuracy with savings in effort).

Monte Carlo simulations of effort and accuracy in choice

The two main purposes of the simulation studies were to characterize the effort and accuracy of various strategies in different decision environments and to develop insights into how processing might change if efficient effort–accuracy trade-offs were desired in selecting decision strategies. The simulations provide a task analysis of the problem of strategy selection in decision making. Additional details on the simulations can be found in Johnson and Payne (1985) and Payne, Bettman, and Johnson (1988).

Measuring strategy effort

Building on the ideas of Newell and Simon (1972), 10 decision strategies were decomposed into elementary information processes (EIPs). The set of strategies included weighted additive (WADD), EBA, EQW, LEX, majority of confirming dimensions (MCD), SAT, lexicographic semiorder (LEXSEMI), two combined strategies, and a random-choice rule. Each decision strategy was viewed as a specific sequence of EIPs, such as reading the values of two alternatives on an attribute, comparing them, and so forth. The set of EIPs used in the simulations included operators to *read* an alternative's value on an attribute into working memory, *compare* two alternatives on an attribute, *add* the values of two attributes in working memory, calculate the size of the *difference* of two alternatives for an attribute, weight one value by another (*product*), *eliminate* an alternative from consideration, *move* to the next element of the task environment, and *choose* the preferred alternative and end the process.

A count of the total number of EIPs used by a strategy to reach a decision in a particular choice environment provides a straightforward measure of the effort associated with the use of that decision strategy in that environment.[1] Several areas of cognitive research use EIP counts to measure processing load (e.g., Card, Moran, and Newell, 1983).

To illustrate how EIP counts of effort would be determined, consider the set of EIPs given above and a simple decision problem involving two options (A and B), two events with probabilities (weights), and two payoff values per option (one payoff for each of the two possible outcomes). For an elimination-by-aspects rule, the process might proceed as follows. First, the decision maker finds the most probable outcome (most important attribute; throughout this chapter we use the terms *outcome* and *attribute* interchangeably). This involves reading the two probability values and comparing the two values to determine which is larger (two *reads* and one *compare*). Next, the decision maker might acquire an explicit cutoff value and then compare the payoff values on the most probable outcome for each option against that cutoff value. If the first option (A) failed the cutoff and the second option (B) passed, then a choice of B would be made. This process of comparing options to the cutoff involves three *reads*, two *compares*, one *elimination*, and one *choice*. Thus, the entire decision process consists of five *reads*, three *compares*, one *elimination*, and one *choice*, for a total EIP count of 10.

In contrast, if the WADD rule were used on the same size decision problem (two options, two events, and four payoff values), one might proceed as follows. First, the probability of event 1 and the payoff of option A given event 1 would be acquired (two *reads*). Next, the payoff would be multiplied by the probability (one *product*). The process would be repeated for the next probability and payoff, and the two products would be added, for a total of four *reads*, two *products*, and one *addition*. The same process would be repeated for option B. Finally, the overall values for A and B would be compared (one *compare*) and the option with the largest value chosen (one *choice*). The total EIP count would be 16 (eight *reads*, four *products*, two *additions*, one *compare*, and one *choice*).

A particular set of EIPs, like the one given above, requires a theoretical judgment regarding the appropriate level of decomposition. For instance, the product operator might itself be decomposed into more elementary processes. We hypothesized, however, that a reasonable approximation of the cognitive effort associated with a strategy could be obtained from the level of decomposition outlined above. An experimental test of this hypothesis is reported below.

The strategies examined in the simulations differed in several ways, for example, amount of information processed, selectivity in processing, and form of processing. For example, the WADD process involves no selectivity in processing. The values of each alternative on all the relevant attributes and all the relative importances (weights) of the attributes are considered. The WADD strategy also uses alternative-based processing: all information about the multiple attribute values of a single alternative is processed before information about a second alternative is considered. In contrast, EBA selectively attends to a subset of the available information. The processing of information is also attribute based. That is, information about the values of several alternatives on a single attribute is processed before information about a second attribute is processed. When the results of the simulation are presented in Table 5.1 below, the form of processing and selectivity are indicated for each rule as an aid in interpreting those results.

Table 5.1. *Simulation results for accuracy and effort of heuristics*

Strategy	Processing form	Processing selectivity	Time pressure absent				Severe time pressure			
			Dominance possible		Dominance not possible		Dominance possible		Dominance not possible	
			Low dispersion	High dispersion	Low dispersion	High dispersion	Low dispersion	High dispersion	Low dispersion	High dispersion
WADD	Alternative	No								
RA			1.0	1.0	1.0	1.0	.28	.28	.12	.24
UOC			160	160	160	160	NA	NA	NA	NA
EQW	Alternative	No								
RA			.89	.67	.41	.27	.72	.55	.26	.18
UOC			85	85	85	85	NA	NA	NA	NA
LEX	Attribute	Yes								
RA			.69	.90	.67	.90	.47	.59	.48	.60
UOC			60	60	60	60	NA	NA	NA	NA
LEXSEMI	Attribute	Yes								
RA			.71	.87	.64	.77	.40	.49	.43	.51
UOC			87	78	79	81	NA	NA	NA	NA
EBA	Attribute	Yes								
RA			.67	.66	.54	.56	.49	.65	.48	.61
UOC			87	88	82	82	NA	NA	NA	NA
SAT	Alternative	Yes								
RA			.32	.31	.03	.07	.30	.23	.06	.04
UOC			49	49	61	61	NA	NA	NA	NA
MCD	Attribute	No								
RA			.62	.48	.07	.09	.23	.17	-.02	.02
UOC			148	148	141	140	NA	NA	NA	NA
EBA + WADD	Mixed	Yes								
RA			.84	.79	.69	.66	.43	.48	.27	.43
UOC			104	106	102	102	NA	NA	NA	NA
EBA + MCD	Attribute	Yes								
RA			.69	.59	.29	.31	.44	.49	.27	.36
UOC			89	89	86	86	NA	NA	NA	NA

Note: RA = relative accuracy (95 percent confidence interval width = ±.029). UOC = unweighted operations count (95 percent confidence interval width = ±2.75). WADD = weighted-additive strategy. EQW = equal weighing strategy. LEX = lexicographic choice strategy. LEXSEMI = lexicographic semiorder strategy. EBA = elimination-by-aspects strategy. SAT = satisficing strategy. MCD = majority-of-confirming-dimensions strategy. EBA + WADD = combined elimination-by-aspects plus weighted-additive strategy. EBA + MCD = combined elimination-by-aspects plus majority-of-confirming-dimensions strategy. The UOC is marked NA in the severe time-pressure conditions because the operations count was constrained to be approximately 50 for all rules in these conditions.

Measuring accuracy

Accuracy of choice could be defined by basic principles of coherence, such as avoiding selection of dominated alternatives or intransitive patterns of preferences. However, more specific criteria for choice accuracy can be developed in certain types of task environments. For instance, the expected-utility (EU) model is generally suggested as a normative decision procedure for risky choice because it can be derived from more basic principles. A special case of the EU model, the maximization of expected value (EV), has been used as a criterion to investigate the accuracy of decision heuristics via computer simulation (Thorngate, 1980). A similar model, the WADD rule, is often used as a criterion for decision effectiveness in multiattribute choice (Zakay and Wooler, 1984).

In our research, we have emphasized a measure of accuracy that considers the performance of a heuristic relative to the upper and lower baseline strategies of maximization of EV (or the equivalent WADD value) and of random choice. The accuracy measure provides an indication of the relative performance of heuristics:

$$\text{relative accuracy} = \frac{\text{EV}_{\text{heuristic-rule choice}} - \text{EV}_{\text{random-rule choice}}}{\text{EV}_{\text{expected-value choice}} - \text{EV}_{\text{random-rule choice}}}.$$

This measure is bounded by a value of 1.0 for the EV rule and an average value of 0 for the random rule. While we have relied primarily on this measure of relative accuracy, we have used other measures with similar results (Johnson and Payne, 1985). Note, incidentally, that an EV strategy represents a complete use of the information in the problem statement. A random-choice rule, in contrast, uses none of the information.

Task and context environments

Several aspects of choice tasks were investigated in the simulations, including number of alternatives, number of attributes (outcomes), time pressure, dispersion of probabilities within each gamble, and the possibility or absence of dominated alternatives. Task size (i.e., the number of alternatives and the number of attributes) was included in the simulation because variations in choice-problem size have produced some of the clearest examples of contingent decision behavior (Payne, 1982). Time pressure was of particular interest since the use of a normative decision strategy like EV maximization may be less attractive or infeasible under time constraints (Simon, 1981). Under time pressure, deciding how to choose becomes a selection of the best of the available heuristics, not a choice between using some heuristic or the optimal normative rule. To illustrate the dispersion-of-probabilities variable, a four-outcome gamble with a low degree of dispersion might have probabilities of .30, .20, .22, and .28 for the four outcomes. In contrast, a gamble with a high degree of dispersion might have probabilities of, for example, .68, .12, .05, and .15. This variable was included because Thorngate (1980) had suggested that probability information may be relatively unimportant in making accurate risky choices (see also Beach, 1983). Finally, the absence or possibility of dominated alternatives was included because McClelland (1978), among others, has suggested that the use of certain simplification procedures, such as the EQW strategy, is dependent on the presence of dominated alternatives.

Time constraints, number of alternatives, and number of attributes represent task variables, which are variables associated with general characteristics of the decision problem and not dependent on the particular values of the alternatives. Dominance possible or absent and dispersion of probabilities, on the other hand, represent context variables, which are variables associated with the particular values of the alternatives (Payne, 1982).

Results

Table 5.1 summarizes the results of our simulations for the two context variables and the two extreme time-pressure conditions (absent and severe). These results support four major conclusions. First, the simulations show that heuristics, in at least some task environments, can approximate the accuracy of normative rules with substantial savings in effort. For example, in an environment characterized by high dispersion in probabilities, dominance possible, and no time constraint, the LEX strategy achieved a 90 percent relative accuracy score, with only about 40 percent of the effort that would be needed to use a normative strategy like EV (i.e., 60 as opposed to 160 EIPs).

Second, no single heuristic did well across all decision environments. For instance, in the no-time-pressure condition, when the dispersion in probabilities varied from high to low, the accuracy of the LEX rule dropped from 90 to 69 percent. In contrast, the alternative simplification represented by the EQW strategy produced an increase in accuracy from 67 to 89 percent as dispersion in probabilities went from high to low. The existence of efficient heuristics and the sensitivity of heuristics to changes in task environments are highlighted by Figure 5.1, which shows the relative effort and accuracy associated with different strategies in two different environments. One prediction that can be drawn from Figure 5.1 concerns the relative effort and accuracy of the EQW and LEX strategies as a function of dispersion in probabilities. Note that, for the EQW strategy in a low-dispersion environment and the LEX strategy under high dispersion, the accuracy obtained is roughly equal. However, less effort is required in the high-dispersion condition. Thus, a decision maker desiring relatively high levels of accuracy could maintain that accuracy across contexts through a shift in strategies, but with a substantial savings in effort in the high-dispersion environment. More generally, Figure 5.1 and other results reported in Johnson and Payne (1985)

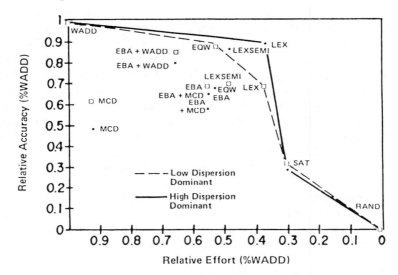

Figure 5.1. Effort-accuracy trade-offs for various decision strategies in the low-dispersion (□) and high-dispersion (*) environments in which dominance is possible. The lines join the most efficient pure strategies for each environment.

and Payne, Bettman, and Johnson (1988) suggest that, in order to achieve both a reasonably high level of accuracy and low effort, a decision maker would have to use a repertoire of strategies, with strategy selection contingent on situational demands.

A third conclusion was that both the effort and the accuracy of strategies were differently affected by number of alternatives, number of attributes, and the possibility or absence of dominance. For example, the effort required to use heuristics such as EBA increased much more slowly than the effort required to use the WADD rule as the number of alternatives increased. This simulation result is compatible with substantial empirical research showing strategy shifts due to the number of alternatives (Payne, 1982). The decision task characterized by dominance absent and low dispersion in probabilities was one in which no heuristic did particularly well in terms of accuracy. The accuracy score of the best simple heuristic, LEX, was only .67, or .22 less than the accuracy score for the best heuristic in the other environments. Since a decision maker would not be able to reduce effort appreciably without suffering a substantial loss in accuracy in this type of task environment, such an environment should be perceived as particularly difficult. In fact, when asked, subjects report that decisions in the dominance absent, low-dispersion choice environments are more difficult. Subjects also take longer to make decisions in this environment than in the other three environments, representing combinations of dominance possible or absent and dispersion.

Fourth, time constraints were shown to have different effects on the various decision strategies. The WADD rule, for example, showed a reduction in accuracy from the baseline value of 1.0 under no time pressure to an average accuracy of only .12 under the most severe time constraint in the dominance absent, low-dispersion environment. Strategies that require many EIPs show degraded performance under time pressure because such procedures must be truncated when time runs out.[2] In contrast, the EBA heuristic was relatively unaffected by time pressure. The average accuracy across environments was only reduced from .69 under no time pressure to .56 with severe time pressure. More generally, under high time pressure, strategies that process at least some information about all alternatives as soon as possible performed best.

The simulation results indicated what a decision maker could do to adapt to various decision environments. The results clearly suggested that a decision maker could maintain a high level of accuracy and minimize effort by using a diverse set of heuristics, changing rules as context and task characteristics change.

Note, however, that the simulation results alone do not identify which particular strategy a decision maker will select in a given decision task. That would depend on the degree to which a decision maker was willing to trade decreases in accuracy for savings in effort. This trade-off might depend on factors such as the decision maker's goal structure, the size of the payoffs, and the need to justify a decision. We will discuss the role of such factors in strategy selection in more detail below, but it is important to recognize that the simulation indicates general changes in processing that might be expected regardless of any particular trade-off between effort and accuracy, for example, the effect of dispersion on the attractiveness of a LEX versus an EQW strategy.

Thus, the results of the simulation yield interesting predictions about the general patterns of processing that might characterize decision makers desiring to make efficient accuracy–effort trade-offs. However, the simulation work itself would remain only suggestive without further validation. For example, the simulation makes the crucial assumption that EIP counts represent reasonable measures of effort. Both this assumption and the predicted patterns of processing can be examined experimentally with actual decision makers. The next two sections report this empirical work.

Cognitive effort in choice

The research reported in this section examined the assumption that EIP counts provide a measure of cognitive effort. Decision makers made choices using different prescribed strategies for choice sets varying in size. Both decision latencies and self-reports of decision difficulty were obtained as measures of strategy-execution effort. The crucial question was whether models based on EIP counts could predict these two indicators of cognitive effort in choice. In addition, we characterized how the effort required by subjects to use different decision strategies varied as task size (number of alternatives and number of attributes) varied. Given space constraints, the following description of our methods and results is necessarily limited (for more details, see Bettman, Johnson, and Payne, 1990).

Overview of method

Seven subjects were trained to use six different decision strategies: WADD, EQW, LEX, EBA, SAT, and MCD. Each strategy was used by each subject in a separate session to make 20 decisions ranging in problem size from two to six alternatives and from two to four attributes. The decision problems involved selection among job candidates. For each session, subjects were to use the prescribed rule exactly as given to them to make their selections. Subjects used the MOUSELAB computer-based information acquisition system to acquire information and make their decisions (Johnson et al., 1988). Subjects used a mouse as a pointing device to move a cursor around a screen containing the probabilities and outcome values in a matrix format. When the cursor pointed to a cell of the matrix, the information in that cell was displayed, and all other information remained concealed. The computer-based acquisition system monitored the subjects' information sequences and recorded latencies for each acquisition, the overall time for each problem, any errors made by the subject (i.e., departures from the prescribed search pattern or choice), and the choice. In addition, subjects rated the difficulty of each choice and the effort each choice required on two response scales presented at the end of each decision problem. Subjects also provided data in a seventh session for 12 choice problems of various sizes on which the subject was free to use any strategy desired.

Results

As expected, decision problems of increasing complexity (i.e., more alternatives and/or more attributes) took longer and were viewed as more effortful. Of greater interest, the effects of task complexity varied by strategy. Compared to other strategies, the WADD rule showed much more rapid increases in response time and somewhat more rapid increases in self-reports of effort as a function of increased task complexity. Thus, there was evidence of a strategy × task interaction in terms of these two indicators of cognitive effort.

The central question of interest, however, was whether the EIP framework could predict the effort required by each strategy in the various task environments. To answer this question, we used regression analyses to assess the degree to which four alternative models of effort based on EIPs fit the observed response times and self-reports of effort. The simplest model treated each EIP as equally effortful and summed the numbers of each component EIP to get an overall measure of effort (the *equal-weighted EIP* model). The second model allowed the effort required by each individual EIP to vary by using counts for each of the individual EIPs as separate independent variables (the *weighted EIP* model). A third model allowed the effortfulness of the individual EIPs to vary across rules (the *weighted EIP by rule* model). While such a variation is possible, of course, the goal of developing a unifying framework for describing the effort of decision strategies would be much more difficult if the sequence of operations or the rule used affected the effort required for individual EIPs. The fourth model allowed the required effort for each EIP to vary across individuals but not rules (the *weighted EIP by individual* model) on the basis of the expectation that some individuals would find certain EIPs relatively more effortful than other individuals would. A fifth model based simply on the amount of information processed was also assessed as a baseline model of decision effort (the *information acquisition* model). This last model implies that the specific type of processing done on the information acquired makes little or no difference in determining decision effort.

Overall, the results yielded strong support for the EIP approach to strategy effort. A model of effort based on weighted EIP counts provided good fits for response times ($R^2 = .84$) and self-reports of effort ($R^2 = .59$). In addition, the fit of the weighted EIP model to the data was statistically superior to that of the baseline model of information acquisition and to that of the equal-weighted EIP model. Thus, it appears that a model of cognitive effort in choice requires not only concern for the amount of information processed but also different weighting of the particular processes (EIPs) applied to that information. Interestingly, the estimates of the time taken for each EIP were mostly in line with prior cognitive research. For example, the *read* EIP combines encoding information with the motor activity of moving the mouse. Its estimated latency is 1.19 seconds. This estimate is plausible since it might consist of the movement of the mouse, estimated to be in the range of .2–.8 seconds by Johnson et al. (1988), and an eye fixation, estimated to require a minimum of .2 seconds (Russo, 1978). *Additions* and *subtractions* both take less than 1 second, with estimates of .84 and .32, respectively. These values are not significantly different and are consistent with those provided by Dansereau (1969), Groen and Parkman (1972), and others (see Chase 1978, table 3, p. 76). Our estimate for the *product* EIP, 2.23 seconds, is larger than that commonly reported in the literature. The time for *compares* is very short, .08 seconds, and that for *eliminations*, 1.80 seconds, is relatively long. This may reflect the collinearity of *compares* and *eliminations*.

The weights for the various EIPs were essentially the same regardless of the decision strategy used. That is, the fits for the more complex weighted EIP by rule model were essentially the same as the fits for the weighted EIP model. This supports the assumption of independence of EIPs across rules.

The results showed significant individual differences in the effort associated with individual EIPs, suggesting that individuals may choose different decision strategies in part because component EIPs may be relatively more or less effortful across individuals. In fact, Bettman, Johnson, and Payne (1990) show that the processing patterns used by subjects in an unconstrained choice environment were related to the relative costs of certain EIPs, although the limited number of subjects in that study precluded any strong conclusions. Subjects for whom arithmetic operators were relatively more difficult, as indicated by the coefficients for the various EIPs, showed greater selectivity in processing.

To summarize, we found strong support for the EIP approach to conceptualizing and measuring the effort of executing a particular choice strategy in a specific task environment. Next, we examine whether the general patterns of processing predicted by the simulation agree with the processing patterns exhibited by decision makers adapting to variations in dispersion of probabilities and time pressure. Such a match, together with the success of the EIP approach to measuring effort reported above, would provide powerful support for our proposed approach to contingent strategy selection. In the next section, therefore, we consider adaptivity in strategy selection when both effort and accuracy may be valued and when subjects are free to use any information-processing strategy they wish in making a choice.

Adaptive strategy selection

The experiments asked the following two questions. To what extent do people vary their information-processing behavior as a function of context effects, such as the dispersion of probabilities, and task effects, such as time pressure? Are these changes in processing in the directions suggested by the simulation work described earlier? Again, the method and results can only be summarized. Details can be found in Payne, Bettman, and Johnson (1988).

Method

Two experiments were conducted in which subjects were asked to make a series of choices from sets of risky options. Each choice set contained four risky options, with each option offering four possible outcomes (attributes). For any given outcome, the probability was the same for all four options. Thus, there was only one set of probabilities for each set of four alternatives. The payoffs ranged from $.01 to $9.99. Dominated options were possible. At the end of an experiment, subjects actually played one gamble and received the amount of money that they won. The sets varied in terms of two factors: presence or absence of time pressure and high or low dispersion in probabilities. In terms of the simulation, the no-time-pressure conditions correspond to the dominance possible, low- and high-dispersion conditions shown in Figure 5.1. The high-time-pressure sets correspond to conditions not shown in Figure 5.1, but the general patterns of results for such conditions were briefly discussed in the section describing the simulation results. In the first experiment, the time-pressure condition involved a 15-second time constraint. In the second experiment, half the subjects had a 15-second constraint. The other half had a more moderate 25-second time constraint. Also, in the second experiment, subjects returned for a second experimental session that was similar to the first except that the time constraint was at the level they had not yet experienced; that is, the time pressure for the second session was set at 25 seconds if the subject was in the 15-second condition on the first day, and vice versa. For comparison, the average response time for the no-time-pressure conditions was 44 seconds.

The design was a complete within-subjects procedure, with a total of 40 randomly ordered decision problems in an experimental session, 10 in each of the four dispersion by time pressure conditions. This design was motivated by the desire to provide the strongest possible test of adaptivity in decision making (i.e., the same subject would be expected to switch strategies from one trial to the next). The subjects were not provided any accuracy feedback in these experiments for two reasons. It is the exception, rather than the rule, for probabilistic decision problems to provide immediate and clear outcome feedback (Einhorn, 1980). To the extent that adaptivity is exhibited in such situations, it suggests that adaptivity is crucial enough to decision makers that they will guide themselves to it without the need for explicit feedback.

Information acquisitions, response times, and choices were monitored using the MOUSELAB system (Johnson, Payne, et al., 1988). For the time-constrained trials, the MOUSELAB system ensured that subjects could not collect any additional information once the available time had expired. A clock on the display screen was used to indicate the time left as it counted down.

Results

Overall, the results for subjects' actual decision behaviors validated the patterns predicted by the simulation. Subjects showed a substantial degree of adaptivity in decision making, although this adaptivity was not perfect.

More specifically, subjects processed less information, were more selective in processing, and tended to process more by attribute when dispersion in probabilities was high rather than low. Moreover, accuracy was equivalent for the two dispersion conditions. Thus, subjects showed an ability to take advantage of changes in the structure of the available alternatives so as to reduce processing load while maintaining accuracy. Recall that this prediction was drawn from the simulation results.

At the level of individual subject behavior, there was evidence that subjects who were more adaptive in their patterns of processing (i.e., relatively more selective and attribute-based processors in high-dispersion environments) also performed better in terms of relative accuracy scores. What is important, this increase in performance was not accompanied by a significant increase in effort. Hence, more adaptive subjects also appeared to be more efficient decision makers.

Several effects of time pressure were also demonstrated. First, under severe time pressure, people accelerated their processing (i.e., less time was spent per item of information acquired), selectively focused on a subset of the more important information, and changed their pattern of processing in the direction of relatively more attribute-based processing. This general pattern of results is consistent with the simulation, which suggested that an efficient strategy under severe time pressure was one that involved selective and attribute-based processing.

The effects of time pressure were substantially less for those subjects with a 25- as opposed to a 15-second constraint. In the more moderate condition, subjects showed evidence of acceleration in processing and some selectivity in processing but no evidence of a shift in the pattern of processing. These results suggested a possible hierarchy of responses to time pressure. First, people may try to respond to time pressure simply by working faster. If this is insufficient, people may then focus on a subset of the available information. Finally, if that is still insufficient, people may change processing strategies, for example, from alternative-based processing to attribute-based processing.

Although these results suggest high adaptivity, there was evidence to suggest that the adaptivity to time pressure was not perfect on a trial-by-trial basis. When the responses to the no-time-pressure condition were compared for the two groups of subjects in the second experiment, some carryover from behavior generated in response to the time-pressure trials to performance on the no-time-pressure trials was detected. Specifically, subjects who had the more severe 15-second time constraint showed comparatively more attribute-based processing, even in the no-time-pressure trials.

To summarize, the results provided strong evidence of adaptivity in decision making. While not perfectly adaptive, our subjects were able to change processing strategies in ways that the simulation indicated were appropriate. Taken together, the results of the simulation, models of cognitive effort, and experiments in adaptive decision making provide strong and consistent support for the proposed EIP approach to strategy selection. We believe that this approach provides a more systematic approach to characterizing effort and accuracy for decision strategies than any other currently available. It is our belief that further application of this conceptualization to problems of contingent strategy selection would be very fruitful.

Although we are excited by the progress made thus far, there are several incomplete aspects of our framework. The next section examines several of these issues.

Some unresolved issues

Implicit in our approach is a top-down view of strategy selection. When deciding how to decide, a decision maker is assumed to evaluate the costs and benefits of the various strategies known to him or her and to select that strategy that is in some sense best for the environment. We now believe that this view is too restrictive. While we still espouse an effort–accuracy view-point and the idea of multiple strategy use, we have begun to consider several broader concerns that lead to a more complex view of contingent decision behavior.

Assessing how well one is doing

In order to adapt to task demands, it seems reasonable that individuals must determine, even if roughly, how well they are doing. The notion of adjust-ment via effort–accuracy trade-offs, in particular, implies the ability to gen-erate ideas about the degree of effort and accuracy characterizing one's decision process. Our data on adaptivity in strategy use suggest that people can learn to change behavior as a function of task and context variables. Yet none of the experiments provided subjects with explicit accuracy or outcome feedback. Thus, how do people learn when and how to change decision strategies?

In the absence of explicit feedback, individuals must somehow generate their own feedback about effort and accuracy. This is not too difficult to imagine for effort. In the course of solving a decision problem, the decision maker has a fairly rich data base available about how effortful or difficult he or she is finding the decision. This process feedback (Anzai and Simon, 1979) could provide the basis for a change in strategy. To illustrate, consider a faculty member asked to identify a small number (three) of job candidates to be brought in for an interview. Assume that over 100 applications have been received. Also assume that the faculty member is inexperienced at this task and that he or she wants to do a good job. Initially, we suspect that the faculty member would try to evaluate each application in great depth. How-ever, at some point that person would likely recognize that the process is becoming increasingly effortful and would think about a change in process-ing strategy. One implication of such readily available process feedback on effort is that considerations of effort will play a prominent role in strategy selection.

Self-generation of accuracy feedback is not as obvious. One possibility is that, along with process feedback, people have some general knowledge of the properties of a reasonable strategy. For example, decision makers might believe that a good strategy involves looking first at the most important information for all alternatives and then looking at other information as desired or as time allows. Some data supporting such general beliefs about good decision strategies are reported in Payne, Bettman, and Johnson (1988). With such knowledge, the individual could not only ascertain the effort required during the course of making a decision but also determine how closely this decision process resembled his or her notion of what a good strategy should entail. In the absence of environmental constraints the match between the strategy used and notions of a good strategy should presumably be close, and the individual's accuracy assessment would be high. However, if there were severe environmental constraints (e.g., great time pressure), the individual may feel that the strategy, either as executed or while executing, did not match his or her notion of a reasonable strategy. For example, important information may not have been examined before time ran out. Klein (1983) reports data supporting this kind of learning about the task during decision making. The individual could then adjust the decision process to be more in line with his or her notion of reasonableness, either on line or the next time such a decision is faced.

Recently, Reder (1987) has considered strategy changes without explicit feedback in a task dealing with question-answering strategies and proposed a "feeling of knowing" process that is related to our ideas. She argues that people may develop strategies that are adaptive to different problem environments by trying to minimize effort while maintaining a feeling of knowing that a reasonable answer is being produced. An interesting issue is how well calibrated such feelings of knowing may be in the area of decision making and how they are affected by decision-task properties.

The possibility that process feedback provides information about both the effort and the accuracy of making a decision raises another question. Under what conditions will explicit feedback about effort and accuracy be used by decision makers? Creyer, Bettman, and Payne (1990) found that explicit feedback on the time used to make a decision (a measure of effort used) had no effect on decision processes. Of greater interest, explicit accuracy feedback also had little effect on decision problems similar to the high dispersion in probabilities (weights) choice problems used in Payne, Bettman, and Johnson (1988) and discussed above. On the other hand, explicit accuracy feedback did change processing and improve performance for those decision problems involving low dispersion in weights (probabilities). One explanation of these results is that explicit accuracy feedback is needed only to supplement process feedback for those situations in which the decision maker is faced with more difficult problems. When asked to rate decision problems according to degree of difficulty, subjects rated low-dispersion problems as more difficult than high-dispersion problems.

Although there is a large literature on feedback, learning, and judgment (Brehmer, 1980; Einhorn, 1980), issues regarding learning and contingent strategy selection in decision making are just beginning to be explored.

However, a better understanding of the role of process feedback and strategy selection seems crucial for building a more complete model of the adaptive use of heuristics in decision making. As discussed in Johnson and Payne (1985), learning mechanisms in decision making also offer a solution to the infinite-regress difficulty associated with the hypothesis that people decide how to choose. Such strategy decisions are not made often, but the relation between task and context variables and the efficiency of a decision strategy is learned over time. Finally, as discussed next, process feedback may also be important in understanding the construction of decision processes (Bettman, 1979) as well as their selection.

A constructive view of choice and editing

As noted above, effort–accuracy frameworks for strategy selection often implicitly assume a top-down process. That is, information about the task is used to assess the costs and benefits of various strategies, and the best strategy is then selected and applied to solving the choice problem. There are data supporting such a goal-directed process of strategy selection (Payne, 1976). Nonetheless, heuristic problem solvers not only use information extracted from the initial problem definition in deciding how to search but also utilize information from states already explored in the problem space to identify promising paths for search (Langley et al., 1987). That is, as people learn about the problem structure during the course of making a decision, they may change their processing to exploit this structure. This view of strategy selection as an opportunistic process (Hayes-Roth and Hayes-Roth, 1979) also suggests that editing processes (Kahneman and Tversky, 1979) are a crucial component of adaptivity.

Editing processes have been proposed as an important component of choice (Kahneman and Tversky, 1979; Goldstein and Einhorn, 1987), with individuals supposedly editing choice problems into simpler forms before choosing. Editing could involve cancellation of outcomes that are identical across alternatives, eliminating dominated alternatives, or combining of equal payoff outcomes, for example. To the extent that editing can simplify choice, it is potentially a major component in understanding the role of cognitive effort and adaptivity to different decision environments.

Whereas Kahneman and Tversky (1979) and Goldstein and Einhorn (1987) argue that editing processes come first, with alternatives edited and then the simplified options evaluated, we argue instead that editing occurs throughout a choice, whenever individuals notice some structure in the choice environment that can be exploited. Hence, editing can be a bottom-up process, driven by the data, as well as a priori or top down. Thus, one might not decide a priori to eliminate dominated alternatives but might eliminate such alternatives only if noticed during the course of processing.

The editing process itself may be adaptive in that the particular editing operations used may be a function of problem states already explored. Different types of processing will leave different traces in working memory, and these traces will be more or less compatible with different editing operations. For example, processing a pair of alternatives using an attribute-based form of processing will facilitate the detection of dominance, whereas an alternative-based form of processing would discourage such detection. Hence, different choice strategies enable different editing operations during the course of processing. Therefore, different choice environment properties will affect editing because they affect strategy selection. This is likely to be particularly true for the effects of information display. Slovic (1972), for example, has argued for a principle of concreteness, which states that individuals tend to use information in the form in which it is displayed. To the extent that this is true, display should exert a strong influence on editing processes by encouraging or discouraging various types of processing.

This opportunistic view of editing implies a more constructive view of choice (Bettman, 1979) – that people develop simplifications and strategies as they progress in a decision process rather than invoking them a priori. Which regularities in the task environment (if any) are noted and exploited can profoundly affect the course of the decision process, so the sequence of editing operations can have a major effect on the resultant process and decision (Tversky and Kahneman, 1986).

Amazingly, almost nothing is known about editing processes. Such research topics as what features of a decision task are noticed and exploited, how this changes with display format, and studies of the determinants of focus of attention in decision making are badly needed. We agree with Yates, Jagacinski, and Faber (1978) that events affecting attention in the real world are likely to be numerous and powerful and that such events are not just experimental nuisance factors.

Incentives and strategy selection

As stated at the beginning of this chapter, the major focus of our research has been on the role of cognitive effort in strategy selection. Questions of strategy accuracy have played an important, but secondary, role in our research. In particular, we have not emphasized the direct role of incentives in strategy selection, although subjects in our studies do receive compensation tied to performance. However, it is clear that an effect–accuracy framework for strategy selection must deal with incentive effects more directly.

The effort–accuracy framework implies that people should utilize strategies that provide greater accuracy at the cost of greater effort when the incentives associated with accuracy are increased. However, as pointed out by several authors (Tversky and Kahneman, 1986; Wright and Aboul-Ezz, 1988), incentives sometimes enhance performance and other times have no effect. We have obtained similar mixed results in our own research. Sometimes incentive effects are in the direction predicted by our framework, in that people increase the amount of processing, are less selective in processing, and process more by alternative than by attribute when goals and incentives are structured to emphasize accuracy more than effort (Creyer, Bettman, and Payne, 1990). At other times, however, we have found incentive effects either difficult to detect or in directions opposite from those predicted. For example, Simonson (1987) found that the frequency with which the context variable of asymmetric dominance relations (Huber, Payne, and Puto, 1982) affects choice is *larger* with an increased need to justify one's decision. To the extent that the need to justify or be accountable for a decision affects the desire to make a good decision (Beach and Mitchell, 1978; Tetlock, 1985), this finding seems contrary to what one would expect.

One solution to the ambiguity of this research is the common distinction between working harder and working smarter. Tversky and Kahneman (1986), for example, argue that incentives work by focusing attention and prolonging deliberation. That is, incentives cause people to work harder but not necessarily smarter (see also Einhorn and Hogarth, 1986). However, if people do not change strategies but just work harder, this may have the paradoxical effect of increasing error in decisions through increased effort applied to executing a flawed strategy (Arkes, Dawes, and Christensen, 1986). It is also important to recognize that incentives will not eliminate errors if a normative strategy is impossible to use because of information-processing limitations or environmental factors such as severe time pressure (Simon, 1981). Finally, any shift in strategy due to incentives would seem to require awareness of alternative strategies. In some cases, incentives may have limited effect because of a lack of awareness of any better decision strategy than the one currently being used. Thus, one important direction for research on strategy selection is to understand better when and how incentives will affect processing and choice.

To this point, we have reviewed basic questions in the area of behavioral decision research. However, as indicated in the theme of this volume,[3] the work of Hillel Einhorn was concerned with both theory and application. Consequently, we will end this chapter with a discussion of one implication of our program of research for improving decisions.

Designing decision displays

An exciting application of the effort–accuracy approach is guiding the design of information displays to facilitate better decision making. By designing displays that make more effective processing easier, decision performance should be improved. Like Slovic (1972), we suspect that decision makers are greatly influenced by the form of the information presented and are unlikely to transform information so that it will fit strategies. By making better strategies easier to use, the application of more efficient decision heuristics can be encouraged.

An excellent demonstration of decision aiding through information display changes is provided by Russo (1977). Russo argued that using unit-price information in the supermarket was unduly effortful, requiring that consumers locate the various unit-price tags spread throughout the shelf and remember these values until other brands could be located. He reduced the required effort by combining all unit-price tags into a single list, sorted by unit price. A field study comparing the existing shelf tags and the list showed that the list produced a 2 percent decrease in the average price paid, representing 11 percent of the savings possible by always buying the least expensive brand. More generally, encouraging the use of efficient strategies by making them easier to execute has important implications for providing product information to the public (Bettman, Payne, and Staelin, 1986).

Johnson, Payne, and Bettman (1988) show that the design of information displays can have important consequences on the frequency of one of the most dramatic decision errors, the preference reversal (Lichtenstein and Slovic, 1971). In the preference reversal paradigm, subjects choose among and give monetary equivalents for two gambles. Preference reversals occur when a subject indicates a choice of one gamble but gives a higher monetary equivalent for the other gamble in the pair. In the typical preference reversal experiment, the probabilities are described as fractions, a consequence of using a roulette wheel to determine outcomes. Johnson, Payne, and Bettman suggested that these fractions ($^{29}/_{36}$, e.g.) discouraged the use of expectation strategies and facilitated the use of heuristic strategies, producing reversals. They manipulated the way identical probabilities were displayed, ranging from simple decimals (.8) to quite complex fractions ($^{284}/_{355}$). The complex fractions produced almost twice as many reversals as the decimals. Further, process-tracing measures, collected with MOUSELAB, were consistent with the notion that the simpler displays encouraged using expectation strategies.

Together, these examples illustrate the principle of passive decision support. In contrast to more active approaches that replace human cognitive processes to aid decisions, better decisions can be encouraged by designing displays that passively encourage more accurate strategies by making them easier to execute. Such reductions in execution effort can be achieved by using formats that make operations such as comparisons easier or by making individual pieces of data easier to process, for example.

Conclusion

A major finding of the last 20 years of decision research is that an individual will use many different strategies in making a decision, contingent on task demands (Einhorn and Hogarth, 1981; Payne, 1982; Abelson and Levi, 1985). The use of multiple strategies raises the fundamental issue of how people decide to decide. This chapter reviews a program of research directed at understanding the adaptive use of strategies in decision making. While people clearly sometimes make decisions that violate certain principles of rationality (Tversky, 1969), it is also becoming clear that decision makers often adapt in directions representing efficient effort–accuracy trade-offs.

Notes

1 Different EIPs may require different levels of effort. For example, comparing two values may be easier than adding or multiplying them. Hence, the operator counts could be weighted by some measure of the effort required for each individual operator, such as the time estimates mentioned below. The results remain essentially the same whether a weighted or an unweighted EIP count is used to measure effort.
2 Depending on the definition of the particular strategy, the alternative selected when time ran out was either the best alternative processed up to the point time ran out or an alternative randomly chosen from those alternatives not yet eliminated when time ran out.
3 Editors' note: This reference is to Hogarth (1990); see acknowledgements.

References

Abelson, R. P., and A. Levi. 1985. Decision making and decision theory. In *The handbook of social psychology*, Vol. 1, ed. G. Lindzey and E. Aronson. New York: Random House.

Anzai, Y., and H. A. Simon. 1979. The theory of learning by doing. *Psychological Review 86*:124–40.

Arkes H. R., R. M. Dawes, and C. Christensen. 1986. Factors influencing the use of a decision rule in a probabilistic task. *Organizational Behavior and Human Decision Processes 37*:93–110.

Beach, L. R. 1983. Muddling through: A response to Yates and Goldstein. *Organizational Behavior and Human Performance 31*:47–53.

Beach, L. R., and T. R. Mitchell. 1978. A contingency model for the selection of decision strategies. *Academy of Management Review 3*:439–49.

Bettman, J. R. 1979. *An information processing theory of consumer choice*. Reading, Mass.: Addison-Wesley.

Bettman, J. R., E. J. Johnson, and J. W. Payne. 1990. A componential analysis of cognitive effort in choice. *Organizational Behavior and Human Decision Processes 45*:111–139.

Bettman, J. R., J. W. Payne, and R. Staelin. 1986. Cognitive considerations in designing effective labels for presenting risk information. *Journal of Marketing and Public Policy 5*:1–28.

Brehmer, B. 1980. In a word: Not from experience. *Acta Psychologica 45*:223–41.

Brown, A. L., J. D. Bransford, R. A. Ferrara, and J. C. Campioni. 1983. Learning, remembering, and understanding. In *Handbook of child psychology*, ed. P. H. Mussen, Vol. 3, *Cognitive development*, ed. J. H. Flavell and E. M. Markman. New York: Wiley.

Card, S. K., T. P. Moran, and A. Newell. 1983. *The psychology of human–computer interaction*. Hillsdale, N.J.: Erlbaum.

Chase, W. G. 1978. Elementary information processes. In *Handbook of learning and cognitive processes*, Vol. 5, ed. W. K. Estes. Hillsdale, N.J.: Erlbaum.

Creyer, E. H., J. R. Bettman, and J. W. Payne. 1990. The impact of accuracy and effort feedback and goals on adaptive decision behavior. *Journal of Behavioral Decision Making* 3:1–16.

Dansereau, D. F. 1969. An information processing model of mental multiplication. Ph.D. diss., Carnegie-Mellon University.

Einhorn, H. J. 1970. Use of nonlinear, noncompensatory models in decision making. *Psychological Bulletin* 73:221–30.

———. 1971. Use of nonlinear, noncompensatory models as a function of task and amount of information. *Organizational Behavior and Human Performance* 6:1–27.

———. 1980. Learning from experience and suboptimal rules in decision making. In *Cognitive processes in choice and decision behavior*, ed. T. S. Wallsten. Hillsdale, N.J.: Erlbaum.

Einhorn, H. J., and R. M. Hogarth. 1975. Unit weighting schemes for decision making. *Organizational Behavior and Human Performance* 13:171–92.

———. 1981. Behavioral decision theory: Processes of judgment and choice. *Annual Review of Psychology* 32:53–88.

———. 1986. Decision making under ambiguity. *Journal of Business* 59:S225–S250.

Goldstein, W. M., and H. J. Einhorn. 1987. Expression theory and the preference reversal phenomena. *Psychological Review* 94:236–54.

Groen, G. J., and J. M. Parkman. 1972. A chronometric analysis of simple addition. *Psychological Review* 79:329–43.

Hammond, K. R. 1986. A theoretically based review of theory and research in judgment and decision making. Report no. 260. University of Colorado, Institute of Cognitive Science, Center for Research on Judgment and Policy.

Hayes-Roth, B., and F. Hayes-Roth. 1979. A cognitive model of planning. *Cognitive Science* 3:275–310.

Hogarth, R. M. 1987. *Judgement and choice*, 2d ed. New York: Wiley.

Huber, J., J. W. Payne, and C. Puto. 1982. Adding asymmetrically dominated alternatives: Violations of regularity and the similarity hypothesis. *Journal of Consumer Research* 9:90–98.

Johnson, E. J., and J. W. Payne. 1985. Effort and accuracy in choice. *Management Science* 31:395–414.

Johnson, E. J., J. W. Payne, and J. R. Bettman. 1988. Information displays and preference reversals. *Organizational Behavior and Human Decision Processes* 42:1–21.

Johnson, E. J., J. W. Payne, D. A. Schkade, and J. R. Bettman. 1988. Monitoring information processing and decisions: The MOUSELAB system. Duke University, Fuqua School of Business, Center for Decision Studies, Working Paper.

Kahneman, D., and A. Tversky. 1979. Prospect theory: An analysis of decision making under risk. *Econometrica* 47:263–91.

Klein, N. M. 1983. Utility and decision strategies: A second look at the rational decision maker. *Organizational Behavior and Human Performance* 31:1–25.

Langley, P., H. A. Simon, G. L. Bradshaw, and J. M. Zytkow. 1987. *Scientific discovery*. Cambridge, Mass.: MIT Press.

Lichtenstein, S., and P. Slovic. 1971. Reversals of preference between bids and choices in gambling decisions. *Journal of Experimental Psychology* 89:46–55.

McClelland, G. H. 1978. Equal versus differential weighting for multiattribute decisions. University of Colorado, Boulder. Typescript.

Marschak, J. 1968. Decision making: Economic aspects. In *International encyclopedia of the social sciences*, Vol. 4, ed. D. L. Stills. New York: Macmillan.

Newell, A., and H. A. Simon. 1972. *Human problem solving*. Englewood Ciffs, N.J.: Prentice-Hall.

Payne, J. W. 1976. Task complexity and contingent processing in decision making: An information search and protocol analysis. *Organizational Behavior and Human Performance* 16:366–87.

———. 1982. Contingent decision behavior. *Psychological Bulletin* 92:382–402.

Payne, J. W., J. R. Bettman, and E. J. Johnson. 1988. Adaptive strategy selection in decision making. *Journal of Experimental Psychology: Learning, Memory, and Cognition* 14:534–52.

Reder, L. M. 1987. Strategy selection in question answering. *Cognitive Psychology* 19:90–138.

Russo, J. E. 1977. The value of unit price information. *Journal of Marketing Research* 14:193–201.

———. 1978. Eye fixations can save the world: Critical evaluation and comparison between eye fixations and other information processing methodologies. In *Advances in consumer research*, Vol. 5, ed. H. K. Hunt. Ann Arbor, Mich.: Association for Consumer Research.

Russo, J. E., and B. A. Dosher. 1983. Strategies for multiattribute binary choice. *Journal of Experimental Psychology: Learning, Memory, and Cognition* 9:676–96.

Simon, H. A. 1955. A behavioral model of rational choice. *Quarterly Journal of Economics* 69:99–118.

———. 1981. *The sciences of the artificial*, 2d ed. Cambridge, Mass.: MIT Press.

Simonson, I. 1987. Justification processes in choice. Ph.D. diss., Duke University.

Slovic, P. 1972. From Shakespeare to Simon: Speculations – and some evidence – about man's ability to process information. *Oregon Research Institute Research Bulletin*, Vol. 12, No. 12.

Tetlock, P. E. 1985. Accountability: The neglected social context of judgment and choice. *Research in Organizational Behavior* 7:297–332.

Thorngate, W. 1980. Efficient decision heuristics. *Behavioral Science* 25:219–25.

Tversky, A. 1969. Intransitivity of preferences. *Psychological Review* 76:31–48.

———. 1972. Elimination by aspects: A theory of choice. *Psychological Review* 79:281–99.

Tversky, A., and D. Kahneman. 1986. Rational choice and the framing of decisions. *Journal of Business* 59:S251–S278.

Wright, W. F., and M. E. Aboul-Ezz. 1988. Effects of extrinsic incentives on the quality of frequency assessments. *Organizational Behavior and Human Decision Processes* 41:143–52.

Yates, J. F., C. M. Jagacinski, and M. D. Faber. 1978. Evaluation of partially described multiattribute options. *Organizational Behavior and Human Performance* 21:240–51.

Zakay, D., and S. Wooler. 1984. Time pressure, training and decision effectiveness. *Ergonomics* 27:273–84.

6 Confirmation, disconfirmation, and information in hypothesis testing

Joshua Klayman and Young-Won Ha

A substantial proportion of the psychological literature on hypothesis testing has dealt with issues of confirmation and disconfirmation. Interest in this topic was spurred by the research findings of Wason (e.g., 1960, 1968) and by writings in the philosophy of science (e.g., Lakatos, 1970; Platt, 1964; Popper, 1959, 1972), which related hypothesis testing to the pursuit of scientific inquiry. Much of the work in this area, both empirical and theoretical, stresses the importance of disconfirmation in learning and reasoning. In contrast, human reasoning is often said to be prone to a "confirmation bias" that hinders effective learning. However, confirmation bias has meant different things to different investigators, as Fischhoff and Beyth-Marom point out in a recent review (1983). For example, researchers studying the perception of correlations have proposed that people are overly influenced by the co-occurrence of two events and insufficiently influenced by instances in which one event occurs without the other (e.g., Arkes & Harkness, 1983; Crocker, 1981; Jenkins & Ward, 1965; Nisbett & Ross, 1980; Schustack & Sternberg, 1981; Shaklee & Mims, 1982; Smedslund, 1963; Ward & Jenkins, 1965). Other researchers have suggested that people tend to discredit or reinterpret information counter to a hypothesis they hold (e.g., Lord, Ross, & Lepper, 1979; Nisbett & Ross, 1980; Ross & Lepper, 1980) or they may conduct biased tests that pose little risk of producing disconfirming results (e.g., Snyder, 1981; Snyder & Campbell, 1980; Snyder & Swann, 1978).

The investigation of hypothesis testing has been concerned with both

This chapter originally appeared in *Psychological Review*, 1987, 94(2), 211–228. Copyright © 1987 by the American Psychological Association. Reprinted by permission.

This work was supported by Grant SES-8309586 from the Decision and Management Sciences program of the National Science Foundation. We thank Hillel Einhorn, Ward Edwards, Jackie Gnepp, William Goldstein, Steven Hoch, Robin Hogarth, George Loewenstein, Nancy Pennington, Jay Russo, Paul Schoemaker, William Swann, Tom Trabasso, Ryan Tweney, and three anonymous reviewers for invaluable comments on earlier drafts.

descriptive and prescriptive issues. On the one hand, researchers have been interested in understanding the processes by which people form, test, and revise hypotheses in social judgment, logical reasoning, scientific investigation, and other domains. On the other hand, there has also been a strong implication that people are doing things the wrong way and that efforts should be made to correct or compensate for the failings of human hypothesis testing. This concern has been expressed with regard to everyday reasoning (e.g., see Bruner, 1951; Nisbett & Ross, 1980) as well as professional scientific endeavor (e.g., Mahoney, 1979; Platt, 1964).

In this article, we focus on hypotheses about the factors that predict, explain, or describe the occurrence of some event or property of interest. We mean this broadly, to include hypotheses about causation ("Cloud seeding increases rainfall"), categorization ("John is an extrovert"), prediction ("The major risk factors for schizophrenia are . . ."), and diagnosis ("The most diagnostic signs of malignancy are . . ."). We consider both descriptive and prescriptive issues concerning information gathering in hypothesis-testing tasks. We include under this rubric tasks that require the acquisition of evidence to determine whether or not a hypothesis is correct. The task may require the subject to determine the truth value of a given hypothesis (e.g., Jenkins & Ward, 1965; Snyder & Campbell, 1980; Wason, 1966), or to find the one true hypothesis among a set or universe of possibilities (e.g., Bruner, Goodnow, & Austin, 1956; Mynatt, Doherty, & Tweney, 1977, 1978; Wason, 1960, 1968).

The task known as rule discovery (Wason, 1960) serves as the basis for the development of our analyses, which we later extend to other kinds of hypothesis testing. We first examine what "confirmation" means in hypothesis testing. Different senses of confirmation have been poorly distinguished in the literature, contributing to misinterpretations of both empirical findings and theoretical prescriptions. We propose that many phenomena of human hypothesis testing can be understood in terms of a general *positive test strategy*. According to this strategy, you test a hypothesis by examining instances in which the property or event is expected to occur (to see if it does occur), or by examining instances in which it is known to have occurred (to see if the hypothesized conditions prevail). This basic strategy subsumes a number of strategies or tendencies that have been suggested for particular tasks, such as confirmation strategy, verification strategy, matching bias, and illicit conversion. As some of these names imply, this approach is not theoretically proper. We show, however, that the positive test strategy is actually a good all-purpose heuristic across a range of hypothesis-testing situations, including situations in which rules and feedback are probabilistic. Under commonly occurring conditions, this strategy can be well suited to the basic goal of determining whether or not a hypothesis is correct.

Next, we show how the positive test strategy provides an integrative frame for understanding behavior in a variety of seemingly disparate domains, including concept identification, logical reasoning, intuitive personality testing, learning from outcome feedback, and judgment of contingency or correlation. Our thesis is that when concrete, task-specific information is lacking, or cognitive demands are high, people rely on the positive test strategy as a general default heuristic. Like any all-purpose strategy, this may lead to a variety of problems when applied to particular situations, and many of the biases and errors described in the literature can be understood in this light. On the other hand, this general heuristic is often quite adequate, and people do seem to be capable of more sophisticated strategies when task conditions are favorable.

Finally, we discuss some ways in which our task analysis can be extended to a wider range of situations and how it can contribute to further investigation of hypothesis-testing processes.

Confirmation and disconfirmation in rule discovery

The rule-discovery task

Briefly, the rule-discovery task can be described as follows: There is a class of objects with which you are concerned; some of the objects have a particular property of interest and others do not. The task of rule discovery is to determine the set of characteristics that differentiate those with this target property from those without it. The concept identification paradigm in learning studies is a familiar example of a laboratory rule-discovery task (e.g. Bruner, Goodnow, & Austin, 1956; Levine, 1966; Trabasso & Bower, 1968). Here, the objects may be, for example, visual stimuli in different shapes, colors, and locations. Some choices of stimuli are reinforced, others are not. The learner's goal is to discover the rule or "concept" (e.g., red circles) that determines reinforcement.

Wason (1960) was the first to use this type of task to study people's understanding of the logic of confirmation and disconfirmation. He saw the rule-discovery task as representative of an important aspect of scientific reasoning (see also Mahoney, 1976, 1979; Mynatt et al., 1977, 1978; Simon, 1973). To illustrate the parallel between rule discovery and scientific investigation, consider the following hypothetical case. You are an astrophysicist, and you have a hypothesis about what kinds of stars develop planetary systems. This hypothesis might be derived from a larger theory of astrophysics or may have been induced from past observation. The hypothesis can be expressed as a rule, such that those stars that have the features specified in the rule are hypothesized to have planets and those not fitting the rule are hypothesized to have no planets. We will use the symbol R_H for the hypothesized rule, H for the set of instances that fit that hypothesis, and $\bar{H}$ for the set that do not fit it. There is a domain or "universe" to which the rule is meant to apply (e.g., all stars in our galaxy), and in that domain there is a target set (those stars that really do have planets). You would like to find the rule that exactly specifies which members of the domain are in the target set (the rule that describes exactly what type of stars have planets). We will use T for the target set, and R_T for the "correct" rule, which specifies the target set exactly. Let us assume for now that such a perfect rule exists. (Alternate versions of the rule might exist, but for our purposes, rules can be considered identical if they specify exactly the same set T.) The correct rule may be extremely complex, including conjunctions, disjunctions, and trade-offs among features. Your goal as a scientist, though, is to bring the hypothesized rule R_H in line with the correct rule R_T and thus to have the hypothesized set H match the target set T. You could then predict exactly which stars do and do not have planets. Similarly, a psychologist might wish to differentiate those who are at risk for schizophrenia from those who are not, or an epidemiologist might wish to understand who does and does not contract AIDS. The same structure can also be applied in a diagnostic context. For example, a diagnostician might seek to know the combination of signs that differentiates benign from malignant tumors.

In each case, an important component of the investigative process is the testing of hypotheses. That is, the investigator wants to know if the hypothesized rule R_H is identical to the correct rule R_T and if not, how they differ. This is accomplished through the collection of evidence, that is, the examination of instances. For example, you might choose a star hypothesized to have planets and train your telescope on it to see if it does indeed have planets, or you might examine tumors expected to be benign, to see if any are in fact malignant.

Wason (1960, 1968) developed a laboratory version of rule discovery to study people's hypothesis-testing strategies (in particular, their use of confirmation and disconfirmation), in a task that "simulates a miniature scientific problem" (1960, p. 139). In Wason's task, the universe was made up of all possible sets of three numbers ("triples"). Some of these triples fit the rule, in other words, conformed to a rule the experimenter had in mind. In our terms, fitting the experimenter's rule is the target property that subjects must learn to predict. The triples that fit the rule, then, constitute the target set, T. Subjects were provided with one target triple (2, 4, 6), and could ask the experimenter about any others they cared to. For each triple the subject proposed, the experimenter responded *yes* (fits the rule) or *no* (does not fit). Although subjects might start with only a vague guess, they quickly formed an initial hypothesis about the rule (R_H). For example, they might guess that the rule was "three consecutive even numbers." They could then perform one of two types of hypothesis tests (Htests): they could propose a triple they expected to be a target (e.g., 6, 8, 10), or a triple they expected not to be (e.g., 2, 4, 7). In this paper, we will refer to these as a positive hypothesis test (+Htest) and a negative hypothesis test (−Htest), respectively.

Wason found that people made much more use of +Htests than −Htests. The subject whose hypothesis was "consecutive evens," for example, would try many examples of consecutive-even triples and relatively few others. Subjects often became quite confident of their hypotheses after a series of

+Htests only. In Wason's (1960) task this confidence was usually unfounded, for reasons we discuss later. Wason described the hypothesis testers as "seeking confirmation" because they looked predominantly at cases that fit their hypothesized rule for targets (e.g., different sets of consecutive even numbers). We think it more appropriate to view this "confirmation bias" as a manifestation of the general hypothesis-testing strategy we call the positive test (+test) strategy. In rule discovery, the +test strategy leads to the predominant use of +Htests, in other words, a tendency to test cases you think will have the target property.

The general tendency toward +testing has been widely replicated. In a variety of different rule-discovery tasks (Klayman & Ha, 1985; Mahoney, 1976, 1979; Mynatt et al., 1977, 1978; Taplin, 1975; Tweney et al., 1980; Wason & Johnson-Laird, 1972) people look predominantly at cases they expect will have the target property, rather than cases they expect will not. As with nearly all strategies, people do not seem to adhere strictly to +testing, however. For instance, given an adequate number of test opportunities and a lack of pressure for a quick evaluation, people seem willing to test more widely (Gorman & Gorman, 1984; Klayman & Ha, 1985). Of particular interest is one manipulation that greatly improved success at Wason's 2, 4, 6 task. Tweney et al. (1980) used a task structurally identical to Wason's but modified the presentation of feedback. Triples were classified as either DAX or MED, rather than *yes* (fits the rule) or *no* (does not fit). The rule for DAX was Wason's original ascending-order rule, and all other triples were MED. Subjects in the DAX/MED version used even fewer −Htests than usual. However, they treated the DAX rule and the MED rule as two separate hypotheses, and tested each with +Htests, thereby facilitating a solution.

The thrust of this work has been more than just descriptive, however. There has been a strong emphasis on the notion that a +test strategy (or something like it) will lead to serious errors or inefficiencies in the testing of hypotheses. We begin by taking a closer look at this assumption. We examine what philosophers of science such as Popper and Platt have been arguing, and how that translates to prescriptions for information gathering in different hypothesis-testing situations. We then examine the task characteristics that control the extent to which a +test strategy deviates from those prescriptions. We begin with rule discovery as described above, and then consider what happens if additional information is available (examples of known targets and nontargets), and if an element of probabilistic error is introduced. The basic question is, if you are trying to determine the truth or falsity of a hypothesis, when is a +test strategy unwise and when is it not?

The logic of ambiguous versus conclusive events

As a class, laboratory rule-discovery tasks share three simplifying assumptions. First, feedback is deterministically accurate. The experimenter provides the hypothesis tester with error-free feedback in accordance with an

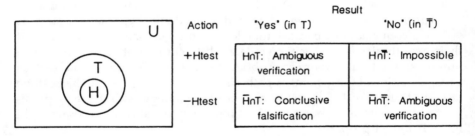

Figure 6.1. Representation of a situation in which the hypothesized rule is embedded within the correct rule, as in Wason's (1960) "2, 4, 6" task. (U = the universe of possible instances [e.g., all triples of numbers]; T = the set of instances that have the target property [e.g., they fit the experimenter's rule: increasing]; H = the set of instances that fit the hypothesized rule [e.g., increasing by 2].)

underlying rule. Second, the goal is to determine the one correct rule (R_T). All other rules are classified as incorrect, without regard to *how* wrong R_H may be, although the tester may be concerned with *where* it is wrong in order to form a new hypothesis. Third, correctness requires both sufficiency and necessity: A rule is incorrect if it predicts an instance will be in the target set when it is not (false positive), or predicts it will not be in the target set when it is (false negative). We discuss later the extent to which each of these assumptions restricts generalization to other tasks.

Consider again Wason's original task. Given the triple (2, 4, 6), the hypotheses that occur to most people are "consecutive even numbers," "increasing by 2," and the like. The correct rule, however, is much broader: "increasing numbers." Consider subjects whose hypothesized rule is "increasing by 2." Those who use only +Htests (triples that increase by 2, such as 6, 8, 10) can never discover that their rule is incorrect, because all examples of "increasing by 2" also fit the rule of "increasing." Thus, it is crucial to try −Htests (triples that do not increase by 2, such as 2, 4, 7). This situation is depicted in Figure 6.1. Here, U represents the universe of instances, all possible triples of numbers. T represents the target set, triples that fit the experimenter's rule ("increasing"). H represents the hypothesized set, triples that fit the tester's hypothesized rule (say, "increasing by 2"). There are in principle four classes of instances, although they do not all exist in this particular example:

1. H ∩ T: instances correctly hypothesized to be in the target set (positive hits).
2. H ∩ T̄: instances incorrectly hypothesized to be in the target set (false positives).
3. H̄ ∩ T̄: instances correctly hypothesized to be outside the target set (negative hits).
4. H̄ ∩ T: instances incorrectly hypothesized to be outside the target set (false negatives).

Instances of the types H ∩ T̄ and H̄ ∩ T *falsify* the hypothesis. That is, the occurrence of either shows conclusively that H ≠ T, thus R_H ≠ R_T; the hypothesized rule is not the correct one. Instances of the types H ∩ T and H̄ ∩ T̄ *verify* the hypothesis, in the sense of providing favorable evidence. However, these instances are ambiguous: The hypothesis may be correct, but these instances can occur even if the hypothesis is not correct. Note that there are only conclusive falsifications, no conclusive verifications. This logical condition is the backbone of philosophies of science that urge investigators to seek falsification rather than verification of their hypotheses (e.g., Popper, 1959). Put somewhat simplistically, a lifetime of verifications can be countered by a single conclusive falsification, so it makes sense for scientists to make the discovery of falsifications their primary goal.

Suppose, then, that you are the tester in Wason's task, with the hypothesis of "increasing by 2." If you try a +Htest (e.g., 6, 8, 10) you will get either a *yes* response, which is an ambiguous verification of the type H ∩ T, or a *no*, which is a conclusive falsification of the type H ∩ T̄. The falsification H ∩ T̄ would show that meeting the conditions of your rule is not sufficient to guarantee membership in T. Thus, +Htests can be said to be tests of the rule's sufficiency. However, unknown to the subjects in the 2, 4, 6, task (Figure 6.1) there are no instances of H ∩ T̄, because the hypothesized rule is sufficient: Any instance following R_H ("increasing by 2") will in fact be in the target set T ("increasing"). Thus, +Htests will never produce falsification. If you instead try a −Htest (e.g., 2, 4, 7) you will get either a *no* answer which is an ambiguous verification (H̄ ∩ T̄) or a *yes* answer which is a conclusive falsification (H̄ ∩ T). The falsification H̄ ∩ T shows that your conditions are not necessary for membership in T. Thus, −Htests test a rule's necessity. In the 2, 4, 6 task, −Htests can result in conclusive falsification because R_H is sufficient but not necessary (i.e., there are some target triples that do not increase by 2).

In the above situation, the Popperian exhortation to seek falsification can be fulfilled only by −Htesting, and those who rely on +Htests are likely to be misled by the abundant verification they receive. Indeed, Wason deliberately designed his task so that this would be the case, in order to show the pitfalls of "confirmation bias" (Wason, 1962). The hypothesis-tester's situation is not always like this, however. Consider the situation in which the hypothesized set merely overlaps the target set, as shown in Figure 6.2, rather than being *embedded* within it, as shown in Figure 6.1. This would be the case if, for example, the correct rule were "three even numbers." There would be some members of H ∩ T̄, instances that were "increasing by 2" but not "three evens" (e.g., 1, 3, 5), and some members of H̄ ∩ T, "three evens" but not "increasing by 2" (e.g., 4, 6, 2). Thus, conclusive falsification could occur with either +Htests or −Htests. Indeed, it is possible to be in a situation just the opposite of Wason's, shown in Figure 6.3. Here, the hypothesis is too broad and "surrounds" the target set. This would be the case if the correct rule were, say, "consecutive even numbers." Now a tester who did only −Htests

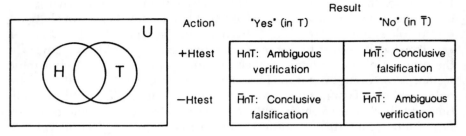

Figure 6.2. Representation of a situation in which the hypothesized rule overlaps the correct rule.

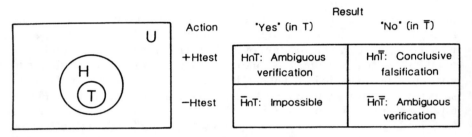

Figure 6.3. Representation of a situation in which the hypothesized rule surrounds the correct rule.

could be sorely misled, because there are no falsifications of the type $\overline{H} \cap T$; any instance that violates "increasing by 2" also violates "consecutive evens." Only +Htests can reveal conclusive falsifications ($H \cap \overline{T}$ instances such as 1, 3, 5).

Aside from these three situations, there are two other possible relationships between H and T. When H and T are disjoint (Figure 6.4), any +Htest will produce conclusive falsification, because nothing in H is in T; –Htests could produce either verification or falsification. This is not likely in the 2, 4, 6 task, because you are given one known target instance to begin with. In the last case (Figure 6.5), you have finally found the correct rule, and H coincides with T. Here, every test produces ambiguous information; a final proof is possible only if there is a finite universe of instances and every case is searched.

In naturally occurring situations, as in Wason's (1960) task, one could find oneself in any of the conditions depicted, usually with no way of knowing which. Suppose, for example, that you are a manufacturer trying to determine the best way to advertise your line of products, and your current hypothesis is that television commercials are the method of choice. For you, the universe, U, is the set of possible advertising methods; the target set, T, is the set of methods that are effective, and the hypothesized set, H, is

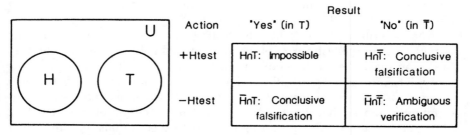

Figure 6.4. Representation of a situation in which the hypothesized rule and the correct rule are disjoint.

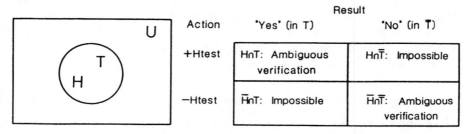

Figure 6.5. Representation of the situation in which the hypothesized rule coincides with the correct rule.

television commercials. Suppose that in fact the set of effective advertising methods for these products is much broader: any visual medium (magazine ads, etc.) will work. This is the situation depicted in Figure 6.1. If you try +Htests (i.e., try instances in your hypothesized set, television commercials) you will never discover that your rule is wrong, because television commercials will be effective. Only by trying things you think will not work (−Htests) can you obtain falsification. You might then discover an instance of the type $\overline{H} \cap T$: nontelevision advertising that is effective.

Suppose instead that the correct rule for effectively advertising these products is to use humor. This is the situation in Figure 6.2. You could find a (serious) television commercial that you thought would work, but does not ($H \cap \overline{T}$), or a (humorous) nontelevision ad that you thought would not work, but does ($\overline{H} \cap T$). Thus, conclusive falsification could occur with either a +Htest or a −Htest. If instead the correct rule for these products is more restricted, say, "prime-time television only," you would have an overly broad hypothesis, as shown in Figure 6.3. In that case, you will never obtain falsification if you use −Htests (i.e., if you experiment with methods you think will not work), because anything that is not on television is also not on prime time. Only +Htests can reveal conclusive falsifications, by finding instances of $H \cap \bar{T}$ (instances of television commercials that are not effective).

What is critical, then, is not the testing of cases that do not fit your hypothesis, but the testing of cases that are most likely to prove you wrong. In Wason's task these two actions are identical, but as shown in Figures 6.2 through 6.5, this is not generally so. Thus, it is very important to distinguish between two different senses of "seeking disconfirmation." One sense is to examine instances that you predict will not have the target property. The other sense is to examine instances you most expect to falsify, rather than verify, your hypothesis. This distinction has not been well recognized in past analyses, and confusion between the two senses of disconfirmation has figured in at least two published debates, one involving Wason (1960, 1962) and Wetherick (1962), the other involving Mahoney (1979, 1980), Hardin (1980), and Tweney, Doherty, and Mynatt (1982). The prescriptions of Popper and Platt emphasize the importance of falsification of the hypothesis, whereas empirical investigations have focused more on the testing of instances outside the hypothesized set.

Confirmation and disconfirmation: Where's the information?

The distinction between −testing and seeking falsification leads to an important question for hypothesis testers: Given the choice between +tests and −tests, which is more likely to yield critical falsification? As is illustrated in Figures 6.1 through 6.5, the answer depends on the relation between your hypothesized set and the target set. This, of course, is impossible to know without first knowing what the target set is. Even without prescience of the truth, however, it is possible for a tester to make a reasoned judgment about which kind of test to perform. Prescriptions can be based on (at least) two considerations: (a) What type of errors are of most concern, and (b) Which test could be expected, probabilistically, to yield conclusive falsification more often. The first point hinges on the fact that +Htests and −Htests reveal different kinds of errors (false positives and false negatives, respectively). A tester might care more about one than the other and might be advised to test accordingly. Although there is almost always some cost to either type of error, one cost may be much higher than the other. For example, a personnel director may be much more concerned about hiring an incompetent person ($H \cap \bar{T}$) than about passing over some potentially competent ones ($\bar{H} \cap T$). Someone in this position should favor +Htests (examining applicants judged competent, to find any failures) because they reveal potential false positives. On the other hand, some situations require greater concern with false negatives than false positives. For example, when dealing with a major communicable disease, it is more serious to allow a true case to go undiagnosed and untreated ($\bar{H} \cap T$) than it is to mistakenly treat someone ($H \cap \bar{T}$). Here the emphasis should be on −Htests (examining people who test negative, to find any missed cases), because they reveal potential false negatives.

It could be, then, that a preference for +Htests merely reflects a greater concern with sufficiency than necessity. That is, the tester may simply be more concerned that all chosen cases are true than that all true cases are chosen. For example, experiments by Vogel and Annau (1973), Tschirgi (1980), and Schwartz (1981, 1982) suggest that an emphasis on the sufficiency of one's actions is enhanced when one is rewarded for each individual success rather than only for the final rule discovery. Certainly, in many real situations (choosing an employee, a job, a spouse, or a car) people must similarly live with their mistakes. Thus, people may be naturally inclined to focus more on false positives than on false negatives in many situations. A tendency toward +Htesting would be entirely consistent with such an emphasis. However, it is still possible that people retain an emphasis on sufficiency when it is inappropriate (as in Wason's task).

Suppose that you are a tester who cares about both sufficiency and necessity: your goal is simply to determine whether or not you found the correct rule. It is still possible to analyze the situation on the basis of reasonable expectations about the world. If you accept the reasoning of Popper and Platt, the goal of your testing should be to uncover conclusive falsifications. Which kind of test, then, should you expect to be more likely to do so? Assume that you do not know in advance whether your hypothesized set is embedded in, overlaps, or surrounds the target. The general case can be characterized by four quantities:[1]

$p(t)$	The overall base-rate probability that a member of the domain is in the target set. This would be, for example, the proportion of stars in the galaxy that have planets.
$p(h)$	The overall probability that a member of the domain is in the hypothesized set. This would be the proportion of stars that fit your hypothesized criteria for having planets.
$z^+ = p(\bar{t}|h)$	The overall probability that a positive prediction will prove false, for example, that a star hypothesized to have planets will turn out not to.
$z^- = p(t|\bar{h})$	The overall probability that a negative prediction will prove false, for example, that a star hypothesized not to have planets will turn out in fact to have them.

The quantities z^+ and z^- are indexes of the errors made by the hypothesis. They correspond to the false-positive rate and false-negative rate for the hypothesized rule R_H (cf. Einhorn & Hogarth, 1978). In our analyses, all four of the above probabilities are assumed to be greater than zero but less than one.[2] This corresponds to the case of overlapping target and hypothesis sets, as shown in Figure 6.2. However, other situations can be regarded as boundary conditions to this general case. For example, the embedded, surrounding, and coincident situations (Figures 6.1, 6.3, and 6.5) are cases in which $z^+ = p(\bar{t}|h) = 0$, $z^- = p(t|\bar{h}) = 0$, or both, respectively, and in the disjoint situation (Figure 6.4), $z^+ = 1$.

Recall that there are two sets of conclusive falsifications: $H \cap \bar{T}$ (your hypothesis predicts planets, but there are none), and $\bar{H} \cap T$ (your hypothesis predicts no planets, but there are some). If you perform a +Htest, the probability of a conclusive falsification, $p(\text{Fn}|+\text{Htest})$, is equal to the false positive rate, z^+. If you perform a −Htest, the chance of falsification, $p(\text{Fn}|-\text{Htest})$, is equal to the false negative rate, z^-. A Popperian hypothesis-tester might wish to perform the type of test with the higher expected chance of falsification. Of course, you cannot have any direct evidence on z^+ and z^- without obtaining some falsification, at which point you would presumably form a different hypothesis. However, the choice between tests does not depend on the values of z^+ and z^- per se, but on the relationship between them, and that is a function of two quantities about which an investigator might well have some information: $p(t)$ and $p(h)$. What is required is an estimate of the base rate of the phenomenon you are trying to predict (e.g., what proportion of stars have planets, what proportion of the population falls victim to schizophrenia or AIDS, what proportion of tumors are malignant) and an estimate of the proportion your hypothesis would predict. Then

$$z^+ = p(\bar{t}|h) = 1 - p(t|h)$$
$$= 1 - p(t \cap h)/p(h)$$
$$= 1 - \left[p(t) - p(t \cap \bar{h}) \right]/p(h)$$
$$= 1 - \frac{p(t)}{p(h)} + \frac{p(t|\bar{h}) \cdot p(\bar{h})}{p(h)}$$
$$z^+ = z^- \cdot \frac{p(\bar{h})}{p(h)} + \left(1 - \frac{p(t)}{p(h)} \right). \tag{6.1}$$

According to Equation 6.1, even if you have no information about z^+ and z^-, you can estimate their relationship from estimates of the target and hypothesis base rates, $p(t)$ and $p(h)$. It is not necessarily the case that the tester knows these quantities exactly. However, there is usually some evidence available for forming estimates on which to base a judgment. In any case, it is usually easier to estimate, say, how many people suffer from schizophrenia than it is to determine the conditions that produce it.

It seems reasonable to assume that in many cases the tester's hypothesis is at least about the right size. People are not likely to put much stock in a hypothesis that they believe greatly overpredicts or underpredicts the target phenomenon. Let us assume, then, that you believe that $p(h) \approx p(t)$. Under these circumstances, Equation 6.1 can be approximated as

$$z^+ = \frac{p(\bar{t})}{p(t)} \cdot z^- \tag{6.2}$$

Thus, if $p(t) < .5$, then $z^+ > z^-$, which means that $p(\text{Fn}|+\text{Htest}) > p(\text{Fn}|-\text{Htest})$. In other words, if you are attempting to predict a minority phenomenon, you are more likely to receive falsification using +Htests than −Htests. We would argue that, in fact, real-world hypothesis testing most often concerns minority phenomena. For example, a recent estimate for the proportion of stars with planets is $\frac{1}{3}$ (Sagan, 1980, p. 300), for the prevalence of schizophrenia, less than 1% (American Psychiatric Association, 1980), and for the incidence of AIDS in the United States, something between 10^{-4} and 10^{-5} (Centers for Disease Control, 1986). Even in Wason's original task (1960), the rule that seemed so broad (any increasing) has a $p(t)$ of only $\frac{1}{6}$, assuming one chooses from a large range of numbers. Indeed, if $p(t)$ were greater than .5, the perception of target and nontarget would likely reverse. If 80% of the population had some disease, immunity would be the target property, and $p(t)$ would then be .2 (cf. Bourne & Guy, 1968; Einhorn & Hogarth, 1986).

Thus, under some very common conditions, the probability of receiving falsification with +Htests could be much greater than with −Htests. Intuitively, this makes sense. When you are investigating a relatively rare phenomenon, $p(t)$ is low and the set $\bar{\text{H}}$ is large. Finding a t in $\bar{\text{H}}$ (obtaining falsification with −Htests) can be likened to the proverbial search for a needle in a haystack. Imagine, for example, looking for AIDS victims among people believed not at risk for AIDS. On the other hand, these same conditions also mean that $p(\bar{t})$ is high, and set H is small. Thus, finding a $\bar{t}$ in H (with +Htests) is likely to be much easier. Here, you would be examining people with the hypothesized risk factors. If you have a fairly good hypothesis, $p(\bar{t}|h)$ is appreciably lower than $p(\bar{t})$, but you are still likely to find healthy people in the hypothesized risk group, and these cases are informative. (You might also follow a strategy based on examining *known* victims; we discuss this kind of testing later.)

The conditions we assume above (a minority phenomenon, and a hypothesis of about the right size) seem to apply to many naturally occurring situations. However, these assumptions may not always hold. There may be cases in which a majority phenomenon is the target (e.g., because it was unexpected); then $p(t) > .5$. There may also be situations in which a hypothesis is tested even though it is not believed to be the right size, so that $p(h) \neq p(t)$. For example, you may not be confident of your estimate for either $p(t)$ or $p(h)$, so you are not willing to reject a theoretically appealing hypothesis on the basis of those estimates. Or you may simply not know what to add to or subtract from your hypothesis, so that a search for falsification is necessary to suggest where to make the necessary change. In any case, a tester with some sense of the base rate of the phenomenon can make a reasoned guess as to which kind of test is more powerful, in the sense of being more likely to find critical falsification. The conditions under which +Htests or −Htests are favored are summarized in Table 6.1.

There are two main conclusions to be drawn from this analysis. First, it is important to distinguish between two possible senses of "seeking disconfirmation": (a) testing cases your hypothesis predicts to be nontargets,

Table 6.1. *Conditions favoring +Htests or −Htests as means of obtaining conclusive falsification*

Target and hypothesis base rates	Comparison of probability of falsification (Fn) for +Htests and −Htests[a]
$p(t) < .5$	
$\quad p(t) > p(h)$	Depends on specific values of z^+ and z^-
$\quad p(t) = p(h)$	$p(Fn\,|+Htest) > p(Fn\,|-Htest)$
$\quad p(t) < p(h) \leq .5$	$p(Fn\,|+Htest) > p(Fn\,|-Htest)$
$\quad p(t) < .5 < p(h)$	Depends on specific values of z^+ and z^-
$p(t) \geq .5$	
$\quad p(t) \geq .5 > p(h)$	Depends on specific values of z^+ and z^-
$\quad p(t) > p(h) \geq .5$	$p(Fn\,|+Htest) < p(Fn\,|-Htest)$
$\quad p(t) = p(h)$	$p(Fn\,|+Htest) \leq p(Fn\,|-Htest)$
$\quad p(t) < p(h)$	Depends on specific values of z^+ and z^-

[a] See Equation 6.1 for derivation.

and (b) testing cases that are most likely to falsify the hypothesis. It is the latter that is generally prescribed as optimal. Second, the relation between these two actions depends on the structure of the environment. Under some seemingly common conditions, the two actions can, in fact, conflict. The upshot is that, despite its shortcomings, the +test strategy may be a reasonable way to test a hypothesis in many situations. This is not to say that human hypothesis testers are actually aware of the task conditions that favor or disfavor the use of a +test strategy. Indeed, people may not be aware of these factors precisely because the general heuristic they use often works well.

Information in target tests

The 2, 4, 6 task involves only one-half of the proposed +test strategy, that is, the testing of cases hypothesized to have the target property (+Htesting). In some tasks, however, the tester may also have an opportunity to examine cases in which the target property is *known* to be present (or absent) and to receive feedback about whether the instance fits the hypothesis. For example, suppose that you hypothesize that a certain combination of home environment, genetic conditions, and physical health distinguishes schizophrenic individuals from others. It would be natural to select someone diagnosed as schizophrenic and check whether the hypothesized conditions were present. We will call this a positive target test (+Ttest), because you select an instance known to be in the target set. Similarly, you could examine the history of someone judged not to be schizophrenic to see if the hypothesized conditions were present. We call this a negative target test (−Ttest). Generally,

Ttests may be more natural in cases involving diagnostic or epidemiological questions, when one is faced with known effects for which the causes and correlates must be determined.

Ttests behave in a manner quite parallel to the Htests described above. A +Ttest results in verification (T ∩ H) if the known target turns out to fit the hypothesized rule (e.g., someone diagnosed as schizophrenic turns out to have the history hypothesized to be distinctive to schizophrenia). A +Ttest results in falsification if a known target fails to have the features hypothesized to distinguish targets (T ∩ H̄). The probability of falsification with a +Test, designated x^+, is $p(\bar{h}|t)$. This is equivalent to the miss rate of signal detection theory (Green & Swets, 1966). The falsifying instances revealed by +Ttests (missed targets, T ∩ H̄) are the same kind revealed by −Htests (false negatives, H̄ ∩ T). Note, though, that the miss rate of +Ttests is calculated differently than the false negative rate of −Htests [$x^+ = p(\bar{h}|t)$; $z^- = p(t|\bar{h})$]. Both +Ttests and −Htests assess whether the conditions in R_H are *necessary* for schizophrenia.

With −Ttests, verifications are of the type T̄ ∩ H̄ (nonschizophrenics who do not have the history hypothesized for schizophrenics), and falsifications are of the type T̄ ∩ H (nonschizophrenics who do have that history). The probability of falsification with −Ttests, designated x^-, is $p(h|\bar{t})$. This is equivalent to the false alarm rate in signal detection theory. −Ttests and +Htests reveal the same kinds of falsifying instances (false alarms or false positives). The rate of falsification with −Ttests is $x^- = p(h|\bar{t})$ compared to $z^+ = p(\bar{t}|h)$ for +Htests. Both −Ttests and +Htests assess whether the conditions in R_H are *sufficient*.

We can compare the two types of Ttests in a manner parallel to that used to compare Htests. The values x^+ and x^- (the miss rate and false alarm rate, respectively) can be related following the same logic used in Equation 6.1:

$$x^+ = x^- \frac{p(\bar{t})}{p(t)} + \left(1 - \frac{p(h)}{p(t)}\right). \tag{6.3}$$

If we again assume that $p(t) < .5$ and $p(h) = p(t)$, then $x^+ > x^-$. This means that +Ttests are more likely to result in falsification than are −Ttests. The full set of conditions favoring one type of Ttest over the other are shown in Table 6.2. Under common circumstances, it can be normatively appropriate to have a second kind of "confirmation bias," namely, a tendency to test cases known to be targets rather than those known to be nontargets.

It is also interesting to consider the relations between Ttests and Htests. In some situations, it may be more natural to think about one or the other. In an epidemiological study, for example, cases often come presorted as T or T̄ (e.g., diagnosed victims of disease vs. normal individuals). In an experimental study, on the other hand, the investigator usually determines the presence or absence of hypothesized factors and thus membership in H or H̄ (e.g.,

Table 6.2. *Conditions favoring +Ttests or −Ttests as means of obtaining conclusive falsification*

Target and hypothesis base rates	Comparison of probability of falsification (Fn) for +Ttests and −Ttests[a]
$p(t) < .5$	
$\quad p(t) > p(h)$	$p(\text{Fn}|+\text{Ttest}) > p(\text{Fn}|-\text{Ttest})$
$\quad p(t) = p(h)$	$p(\text{Fn}|+\text{Ttest}) > p(\text{Fn}|-\text{Ttest})$
$\quad p(t) < p(h)$	Depends on specific values of x^+ and x^-
$p(t) \geq .5$	
$\quad p(t) > p(h)$	Depends on specific values of x^+ and x^-
$\quad p(t) = p(h)$	$p(\text{Fn}|+\text{Ttest}) \leq p(\text{Fn}|-\text{Ttest})$
$\quad p(t) < p(h)$	$p(\text{Fn}|+\text{Ttest}) < p(\text{Fn}|-\text{Ttest})$

[a] See Equation 6.3 for derivation.

treatment vs. control group). Suppose, though, that you are in a situation where all four types of test are feasible. There are then two tests that reveal falsifications of the type H ∩ T̄ (false positives or false alarms), namely +Htests and −Ttests. These falsifications indicate that the hypothesized conditions are not *sufficient* for the target phenomenon. For example, suppose a team of meteorologists wants to test whether certain weather conditions are sufficient to produce tornadoes. The team can look for tornadoes where the hypothesized conditions exist (+Htests) or they can test for the conditions where tornadoes have not occurred (−Ttests). The probability of discovering falsification with each kind of test is as follows:

$$p\left(\text{Fn}|+\text{Htest}\right) = z^+ = p\left(\bar{t}|h\right) = \frac{p\left(h \cap \bar{t}\right)}{p(h)}$$

$$p\left(\text{Fn}|-\text{Ttest}\right) = x^- = p\left(h|\bar{t}\right) = \frac{p\left(h \cap \bar{t}\right)}{p\left(\bar{t}\right)}$$

$$z^+ = x^- \cdot \frac{p\left(\bar{t}\right)}{p(h)}. \tag{6.4}$$

Thus, if we assume, as before, that $p(t) < .5$, and $p(h) = p(t)$, then $z^+ > x^-$: the probability of finding a falsifying instance (h ∩ t̄) is higher with +Htests than with −Ttests.

There are also two tests that reveal falsifications of the type H̄ ∩ T (false negatives or misses): +Ttests and −Htests. These falsifications indicate that the hypothesized conditions are not *necessary* for the target phenomenon. The meteorologists can test whether the hypothesized weather conditions are necessary for tornadoes by looking at conditions where tornadoes are sighted (+Ttests) or by looking for tornadoes where the hypothesized conditions are lacking (–Htests). The probability of falsification with these two tests can be compared, parallel to Equation 6.4, above:

$$x^+ = z^- \cdot \frac{p(\bar{h})}{p(t)}. \tag{6.5}$$

Thus, the probability of finding $\bar{H} \cap T$ falsifications is higher with +Ttests than with –Htests.

These relationships reinforce the idea that it may well be advantageous in many situations to have two kinds of "confirmation bias" in choosing tests: a tendency to examine cases hypothesized to be targets (+Htests) and a tendency to examine cases known to be targets (+Ttests). Taken together, these two tendencies compose the general +test strategy. Under the usual assumptions $[p(t) < .5$ and $p(t) \approx p(h)]$, +Htests are favored over –Htests, and +Ttests over –Ttests, as more likely to find falsifications. Moreover, if you wish to test your rule's sufficiency, +Htests are better than –Ttests; if you wish to test the rule's necessity, +Ttests are better than –Htests. Thus, it may be advantageous for the meteorologists to focus their field research on areas with hypothesized tornado conditions and areas of actual tornado sighting (which, in fact, they seem to do; see Lucas & Whittemore, 1985). Like many other cognitive heuristics, however, this +test heuristic may prove maladaptive in particular situations, and people may continue to use the strategy in those situations nonetheless (cf. Hogarth, 1981; Tversky & Kahneman, 1974).

Hypothesis testing in probabilistic environments

Laboratory versions of rule discovery usually take place in a deterministic environment: There is a correct rule that makes absolutely no errors, and feedback about predictions is completely error-free (see Kern, 1983, and Gorman, 1986, for interesting exceptions). In real inquiry, however, one does not expect to find a rule that predicts every schizophrenic individual or planetary system without error, and one recognizes that the ability to detect psychological disorders or celestial phenomena is imperfect. What, then, is the normative status of the +test heuristic in a probabilistic setting?

Irreducible error. In a probabilistic environment, it is somewhat of a misnomer to call any hypothesis correct, because even the best possible hypothesis will make some false-positive and false-negative predictions. These irreducible errors might actually be due to imperfect feedback, but from the tester's point of view they look like false positives or false negatives. Alternatively, the world may have a truly random component, or the problem may be so complex that in practice perfect prediction would be beyond human reach. In any case, the set T can be defined as the set of instances that the feedback indicates are targets. A best possible rule, R_B, can be postulated that defines the set B. B matches T as closely as possible, but not exactly. Because of probabilistic error, even the best rule makes false-positive and false-negative prediction errors (i.e., $p(\bar{t}|b) > 0$ and $p(t|\bar{b}) > 0$). The probabilities of these errors, designated ε^+ and ε^-, represent theoretical or practical minimum error rates.[3]

Qualitatively, the most important difference between deterministic and probabilistic environments is that both verification and falsification are of finite value and subject to some degree of probabilistic error. Thus, falsifications are not conclusive but merely constitute some evidence against the hypothesis, and verifications must also be considered informative, despite their logical ambiguity. Ultimately, it can never be known with certainty that any given hypothesis is or is not the best possible. One can only form a belief about the probability that a given hypothesis is correct, in light of the collected evidence.

Despite these new considerations, it can be shown that the basic findings of our earlier analyses still apply. Although the relationship is more complicated, the relative value of +tests and −tests is still a function of estimable task characteristics. In general, it is still the case that +tests are favored when $p(t)$ is small and $p(h) \approx p(t)$, as suggested earlier. Although we discuss only Htests here, a parallel analysis can be performed for Ttests as well.

Revision of beliefs. Assume that your goal is to obtain the most evidence you can about whether or not your current hypothesis is the best possible. Which type of test will, on average, be more informative? This kind of problem calls for an analysis of the expected value of information (e.g., see Edwards, 1965; Raiffa, 1968). Such analyses are based on Bayes's equation, which provides a normative statistical method for assessing the extent to which a subjective degree of belief should be revised in light of new data. To perform a full-fledged Bayesian analysis of value of information, it would be necessary to represent the complete reward structure of the particular task and compute the tester's subjective expected utility of each possible action. Such an analysis would be very complex or would require a great many simplifying assumptions. It is possible, though, to use a simple, general measure of "impact," such as the expected change in belief (EΔP).

Suppose you think that there is some chance your hypothesis is the best possible, $p(R_H = R_B)$. Then, you perform a +Htest, and receive a verification (Vn). You would now have a somewhat higher estimate of the chance that your hypothesis is the best one $p(R_H = R_B|Vn, +H)$. Call the impact of this test $\Delta P_{vn,+H}$, the absolute magnitude of change in degree of belief. Of course, you might have received a falsification (Fn) instead, in which case your belief that $R_H = R_B$ would be reduced by some amount, $\Delta P_{Fn,+H}$. The expected change in belief for a +Htest, given that you do not know in advance whether you will receive a verification or a falsification, would thus be

$$E\Delta P_{+H} = p(Fn|+Htest) \cdot \Delta P_{Fn,+H} + p(Vn|+Htest) \cdot \Delta P_{Vn,+H}. \qquad (6.6)$$

In the Appendix, we show that

$$\Delta P_{Fn,+H} = 1 - \frac{\varepsilon^+}{z^+}, \tag{6.7}$$

$$\Delta P_{Vn,+H} = \frac{1-\varepsilon^+}{1-z^+} - 1, \tag{6.8}$$

$$p(Fn|+Htest) \cdot \Delta P_{Fn,+H} = (z^+ - \varepsilon^+) \cdot p(R_H = R_B), \tag{6.9}$$

and

$$p(Vn|+Htest) \cdot \Delta P_{Vn,+H} = (z^+ - \varepsilon^+) \cdot p(R_H = R_B). \tag{6.10}$$

Thus

$$E\Delta P_{+H} = 2(z^+ - \varepsilon^+) \cdot p(R_H = R_B). \tag{6.11}$$

Similarly,

$$E\Delta P_{-H} = 2(z^- - \varepsilon^-) \cdot p(R_H = R_B). \tag{6.12}$$

This probabilistic analysis looks different from its deterministic counterpart in one respect. Before, the emphasis was strictly on falsification. Here, verification can sometimes be more informative than falsification. Using +Htests to illustrate, Equations 6.7 and 6.8 imply that if $z^+ > .5$, then $\Delta P_{vn,+H} > \Delta P_{Fn,+H}$. A hypothesis with $z^+ > .5$ is a weak hypothesis; you believe the majority of predicted targets will prove wrong. Perhaps this is an old hypothesis that is now out of favor, or a new shot-in-the-dark guess. The ΔP measure captures the intuition that surprise verification of a longshot hypothesis has more impact than the anticipated falsification.

In considering the expected impact of a test, you must balance the greater impact of unexpected results against the fact that you do not think such results are likely to happen. With the $E\Delta P$ measure, the net result is that verifications and falsifications are expected to make equal contributions to changes in belief, overall (as shown in Equations 6.9 and 6.10). Verifications and falsifications have equal expected impact even in a deterministic environment, according to this definition of impact. The deterministic environment is merely a special case in which $\varepsilon^+ = \varepsilon^- = 0$.

Given this probabilistic view of the value of verification and falsification, where should one look for information? The answer to this question, based on the comparison between +Htests and −Htests, changes very little from the deterministic case. It would be a rational policy for a tester to choose the type of Htest associated with the greatest expected change in belief. In that case, according to Equations 6.11 and 6.12, you want to choose the test for which $z - \varepsilon$ is greatest: +Htests if $(z^+ - \varepsilon^+) > (z^- - \varepsilon^-)$. In other words, choose the test for which you believe the probability of falsification (z) is most above the level of irreducible error (ε). This prescription is obviously very similar to the conditions specified for the deterministic environment. Indeed, if the two εs are equal (even if nonzero) the rule is identical: Choose the test with the higher z. Thus, the prescriptions shown in Table 6.1 hold in a probabilistic environment, as long as irreducible error is also taken into account. In the Appendix we also present an alternative measure of informativeness (a measure of "diagnosticity" often used in Bayesian analyses); the basic premises of our comparison remain intact. Qualitatively similar results obtain even when using a non-Bayesian analysis, based on statistical information theory (see Klayman, 1986).

Information in hypothesis testing: Conclusions

The foundation of our analysis is the separation of disconfirmation as a goal from disconfirmation as a search strategy. It is a widely accepted prescription that an investigator should seek falsification of hypotheses. Our analyses show, though, that there is no correspondingly simple prescription for the search strategy best suited to that goal. The optimal strategy is a function of a variety of task variables such as the base rates of the target phenomenon and the hypothesized conditions. Indeed, even attempting falsification is not necessarily the path to maximum information (see also Klayman, 1986).

We do not assume that people are aware of the task variables that determine the best test strategies. Rather, we suggest that people use a general, all-purpose heuristic, the positive test strategy, which is applied across a broad range of hypothesis-testing tasks. Like any all-purpose heuristic, this +test strategy is not always optimal and can lead to serious difficulties in certain situations (as in Wason's 2, 4, 6 task). However, our analyses show that +testing is not a bad approach in general. Under commonly occurring conditions, the +test strategy leads people to perform tests of both sufficiency and necessity (+Htests and +Ttests), using the types of tests most likely to discover violations of either.

Beyond rule discovery: The positive test strategy in other contexts

The main point of our analysis is not that people are better hypothesis testers than previously thought (although that may be so). Rather, the +test strategy can provide a basis for understanding the successes and failures of human hypothesis testing in a variety of situations. In this section, we apply our approach to several different hypothesis-testing situations. Each of the tasks we discuss has an extensive research literature of its own. However, there has been little cross-task generality beyond the use of the common "confirmation bias" label. We show how these diverse tasks can be given an integrative interpretation based on the general +test strategy. Each task has its unique requirements, and ideally, people should adapt their strategies to the characteristics of the specific task at hand. People may indeed respond appropriately to some of these characteristics under favorable conditions (when there is concrete task-specific information, light memory load, adequate time, extensive experience, etc.). We propose that, under less friendly conditions, hypothesis testers rely on a generally applicable default approach based on the +test strategy.

Concept identification

At the beginning of this paper, we described the concept-identification task (Bruner et al., 1956) as a forerunner of Wason's rule-discovery task (Wason, 1960). In both tasks, the subject's goal is to identify the rule or concept that determines which of a subset of stimuli are designated as correct. In concept identification, however, the set of possible instances and possible rules is highly restricted. For example, the stimuli may consist of all combinations of four binary cues (letter X or T, large or small, black or white, on the right or left), with instructions to consider only simple (one-feature) rules (e.g., Levine, 1966). The hypothesis set, then, is restricted to only eight possibilities. Even when conjunctions or disjunctions of features are allowed (e.g., Bourne, 1974; Bruner et al., 1956), the hypothesis set remains circumscribed.

A number of studies of concept identification have documented a basic win–stay, lose–shift strategy (e.g., see Levine, 1966, 1970; Trabasso & Bower, 1968). That is, the learner forms an initial hypothesis about which stimuli are reinforced (e.g., "Xs on the left") and responds in accordance with that hypothesis as long as correct choices are produced. If an incorrect choice occurs, the learner shifts to a new hypothesis and responds in accordance with that, and so on. In our terms, this is +Htesting. It is what we would expect to see, especially since total success requires a rule that is sufficient for reward, only. In the concept-identification task +Htesting alone could lead to a successful solution. However, because there are only a finite number of instances (cue combinations), and a finite number of hypotheses, +testing is not the most effective strategy. A more efficient strategy is to partition the hypotheses into classes and perform a test that will eliminate an entire class of hypotheses in a single trial. For example, if a small, black X on the left is correct on one trial, the rules "large," "white," "T," and "right" can all be eliminated at once. If on the next trial a large, black X on the right is correct, only "black" and "X" remain as possibilities, ignoring combinations. This "focusing" strategy (Bruner et al., 1956) is mathematically optimal but requires two things from subjects. First, they must recognize that having a circumscribed hypothesis set means it is possible to use a special efficient strategy not otherwise available. Second, focusing requires considerable cognitive effort to design an efficient sequence of tests and considerable memory demands to keep track of eliminated sets of hypotheses. Subjects sometimes do eliminate more than one hypothesis at a time, but considering the mental effort and memory capacity required by the normative strategy, it is not surprising that a basic +test heuristic predominates instead (Levine, 1966, 1970; Millward & Spoehr, 1973; Taplin, 1975).

The four-card problem

As suggested earlier, the +test strategy applies to both Htests and Ttests. Thus, tasks that allow both are of particular interest. One example is the four-card problem (Wason, 1966, 1968; Wason & Johnson-Laird, 1972) and its descendants (e.g., Cox & Griggs, 1982; Evans & Lynch, 1973; Griggs, 1983; Griggs & Cox, 1982, 1983; Hoch & Tschirgi, 1983, 1985; Yachanin & Tweney, 1982). In these tasks, subjects are asked to determine the truth-value of the proposition "if P then Q" (P → Q). For example, they may be asked to judge the truth of the following statement: "If a card has a vowel on the front, it has an even number on the back" (Wason, 1966, 1968). They are then given the opportunity to examine known cases of P, $\overline{P}$, Q, and $\overline{Q}$. For example, they can look at a card face-up with the letter E showing, face-up with the letter K, face-down with the number 4 showing, or face-down with the number 7. In our terms, this is a hypothesis-testing task in which "has an even number on the back" is the target property, and "has a vowel on the front" is the hypothesized rule that determines the target set. However, the implication P → Q is not logically equivalent to the if-and-only-if relation tested in rule discovery: P is required only to be sufficient for Q, not also necessary. Subjects nevertheless use the same basic +test approach.

From our point of view, to look at a vowel is to do a +Htest. The card with the consonant is a –Htest, the even number a +Ttest, and the odd number a –Ttest. If the +test heuristic is applied to problems of the form P → Q, we would expect to find a tendency to select the +Htest and the +Ttest (P and Q), or the +Htest only (P). Indeed, these choice patterns (P and Q, or P only) are the most commonly observed in a number of replications (Evans & Lynch, 1973; Griggs & Cox, 1982; Wason, 1966, 1968; Wason & Johnson-Laird, 1972). However, there is a critical difference between the rule to be evaluated in the four-card problem and those in rule discovery. The implication P → Q is subject to only one kind of falsification, P ∩ $\overline{Q}$. As a result, the +test strategy is inappropriate in this task. The only relevant tests are those that find false positives: +Htests and –Ttests (P and $\overline{Q}$, e.g., E and 7).

Earlier, we proposed that people would be able to move beyond the basic +test strategy under favorable conditions, and research on the four-card problem has demonstrated this. In particular, a number of follow-up studies have shown that a concrete context can point the way for subjects. Consider, for example, the casting of the problem at a campus pub serving beer and cola, with the proposition "if a person is drinking beer, then the person must be over 19" (Griggs & Cox, 1982). Here the real-world context alerts subjects to a critical feature of this specific task: The error of interest is "beer-drinking and not-over-19" (P ∩ $\overline{Q}$). The presence of people over 19 drinking cola ($\overline{P}$ ∩ Q) is immaterial. In this version, people are much more likely to examine the appropriate cases, P and $\overline{Q}$ (beer drinkers and those under 19). Hoch and Tschirgi (1983, 1985) have shown similar effects for more subtle and general contextual cues as well.

Although there have been many explanations for the presence and absence of the P and Q choice pattern, a consensus seems to be emerging. The if/then construction is quite ambiguous in natural language; it often approximates a biconditional or other combination of implications (e.g., see Legrenzi, 1970; Politzer, 1968; Rumain, Connell, & Braine, 1983; Tweney & Doherty, 1983). A meaningful context disambiguates the task by indicating the practical logic of the situation. Some investigators have suggested that in an abstract or ambiguous task, people resort to a degenerate strategy of merely matching whatever is mentioned in the proposition, in other words, P and Q (Evans & Lynch, 1973; Hoch & Tschirgi, 1985; Tweney & Doherty, 1983). We suggest, however, that this heuristic of last resort is not a primitive refuge resulting from confusion or misunderstanding, but a manifestation of a more general default strategy (+testing) that turns out to be effective in many natural situations. People seem to require contextual or "extra logical" information (Hoch & Tschirgi, 1983) to help them see when this all-purpose heuristic is not appropriate to the task at hand.

Intuitive personality testing

Snyder, Swann, and colleagues have conducted a series of studies demonstrating that people tend to seek confirmation of a hypothesis they hold about the personality of a target person (Snyder, 1981; Snyder & Campbell, 1980; Snyder & Swann, 1978; Swann & Giuliano, 1987). For example, in some studies (Snyder, 1981; Snyder & Swann, 1978), one group of subjects was asked to judge whether another person was an extrovert, and a second group was asked to determine whether that person was an introvert. Given a list of possible interview questions, both groups tended to choose "questions that one typically asks of people already known to have the hypothesized trait" (Snyder, 1981, p. 280). For example, subjects testing the extrovert hypothesis often chose the question "What would you do if you wanted to liven things up at a party?"

This behavior is quite consistent with the +test heuristic. Someone's personality can be thought of as a set of behaviors or characteristics. To understand person A's personality is, then, to identify which characteristics in the universe of possible human characteristics belong to person A and which do not. That is, the target set (T) is the set of characteristics that are true of person A. The hypothesis "A is an extrovert" establishes a hypothesized set of characteristics (H), namely those that are true of extroverts. The goal of the hypothesis tester is, as usual, to determine if the hypothesized set coincides well with the target set. In other words, to say "A is an extrovert" is to say: "If it is characteristic of extroverts, it is likely to be true of A, and if it is not characteristic of extroverts, it is likely not true of A." Following the +test strategy, you test this by examining extrovert characteristics to see if they are true of the target person (+Htests).

The +test strategy fails in these tasks because it does not take into account an important task characteristic: Some of the available questions are nondiagnostic. The question above, for example, is not very conducive to an answer such as "Don't ask me, I never try to liven things up." Both introverts and extroverts accept the premise of the question and give similar answers (Swann, Giuliano, & Wegner, 1982). Subjects would better have chosen neutral questions (e.g., "What are your career goals?") that could be more diagnostic. However, it is not +Htesting that causes problems here; it is the mistaking of nondiagnostic questions for diagnostic ones (Fischhoff & Beyth-Marom, 1983; Swann, 1984). All the same, it is not optimal for testers to allow a general preference for +Htests to override the need for diagnostic information.

A series of recent studies suggest that, given the opportunity, people do choose to ask questions that are reasonably diagnostic; however, they still tend to choose questions for which the answer is *yes* if the hypothesized trait is correct (Skov & Sherman, 1986; Strohmer & Newman, 1983; Swann & Giuliano, 1987; Trope & Bassok, 1982, 1983; Trope, Bassok, & Alon, 1984). For example, people tend to ask a hypothesized introvert questions such as "Are you shy?" Indeed, people may favor +Htesting in part because they believe +Htests to be more diagnostic in general (cf. Skov & Sherman, 1986; Swann & Giuliano, 1987). Interestingly, Trope and Bassok (1983) found this +Htesting tendency only when the hypothesized traits were described as extreme (e.g., extremely polite vs. on the polite side). If an extreme personality trait implies a narrower set of behaviors and characteristics, then this is consistent with our normative analysis of +Htesting: As $p(t)$ becomes smaller, the advantage of +Htesting over −Htesting becomes greater (see Equations 6.1 and 6.2). Although only suggestive, the Trope and Bassok results may indicate that people have some salutary intuitions about how situational factors affect the +test heuristic (see also Swann & Giuliano, 1987).

Learning from outcome feedback

So far we have only considered tasks in which the cost of information gathering and the availability of information are the same for +tests and −tests. However, several studies have looked at hypothesis testing in situations where tests are costly. Of particular ecological relevance are those tasks in which one must learn from the outcomes of one's actions. As mentioned earlier, studies by Tschirgi (1980) and Schwartz (1982) suggest that when test outcomes determine rewards as well as information, people attempt to replicate good results (reinforcement) and avoid bad results (nonreinforcement or punishment). This encourages +Htesting, because cases consistent with the best current hypothesis are believed more likely to produce the desired result.

Einhorn and Hogarth (1978; see also Einhorn, 1980) provide a good analysis of how this can lead to a conflict between two important goals: (a) acquiring useful information to revise one's hypothesis and improve long-term success, and (b) maximizing current success by acting the way you think works best. Consider the case of a university admissions panel that must select or reject candidates for admission to graduate school. Typically, they admit only those who fit their hypothesis for success in school (i.e., those who meet the selection criteria). From the point of view of hypothesis testing, the admissions panel can check on selected candidates to see if they prove worthy (+Htests). It is much more difficult to check on rejected candidates (–Htests) because they are not conveniently collected at your institution and may not care to cooperate. Furthermore, you would really have to admit them to test them, because their outcome is affected by the fact that they were rejected (Einhorn & Hogarth, 1978). In other words, –Htests would require admitting some students hypothesized to be unworthy. However, if there is any validity to the admissions committee's judgment, this would have the immediate effect of reducing the average quality of admitted students. Furthermore, it would be difficult to perform either kind of Ttest in these situations. +Ttests and –Ttests would require checking known successes and known failures, respectively, to see whether you had accepted or rejected them. As before, information about people you rejected is hard to come by and is affected by the fact that you rejected them.

The net result of these situational factors is that people are strongly encouraged to do only one kind of tests: +Htests. This limitation is deleterious to learning, because +Htests reveal only false positives, never false negatives. As in Wason's 2, 4, 6 task, this can lead to an overly restrictive rule for acceptance as you attempt to eliminate false-positive errors without knowing about the rate of false negatives.

On the other hand, our analyses suggest that there are situations in which reliance on +Htesting may not be such a serious mistake. First, it might be the case that you care more about false positives than false negatives (as suggested earlier). You may not be too troubled by the line you insert in rejection letters stating that "Regrettably, many qualified applicants must be denied admission." In this case, +Htests are adequate because they reveal the more important errors, false positives. Even where both types of errors are important, there are many circumstances in which +Htests may be useful because false positives are more likely than false negatives (see Table 6.1). When $p(t) = p(h)$ and $p(t) < .5$, for example, the false-positive rate is always greater than the false-negative rate. In other words, if only a minority of applicants is capable of success in your program, and you select about the right proportion of applicants, you are more likely to be wrong about an acceptance than a rejection. As always, the effectiveness of a +test strategy depends on the nature of the task. Learning from +Htests alone is not an optimal approach, but it may often be useful given the constraints of the situation.

Judgments of contingency

There has been considerable recent interest in how people make judgments of contingency or covariation between factors (e.g., see Alloy & Tabachnik, 1984; Arkes & Harkness, 1983; Crocker, 1981; Nisbett & Ross, 1980; Schustack

& Sternberg, 1981; Shaklee & Mims, 1982), and one often-studied class of contingency tasks is readily described by the theoretical framework proposed in the present paper. These are tasks that require the subject to estimate the degree of contingency (or its presence or absence) between two dichotomous variables, on the basis of the presentation of a number of specific instances. For example, Ward and Jenkins (1965) presented subjects with the task of determining whether there was a contingency between the seeding of clouds and the occurrence of rainfall on that day. Subjects based their judgments on a series of slides, each of which indicated the state of affairs on a different day: (a) seeding + rain, (b) seeding + no rain, (c) no seeding + rain, or (d) no seeding + no rain.

In our terms, the dichotomous-contingency task can be characterized as follows: The subject is presented with a target property or event and a set of conditions that are hypothesized to distinguish occurrences of the target from nonoccurrences. In the Ward and Jenkins (1965) example, the target event is rain, and the condition of having seeded the clouds is hypothesized to distinguish rainy from nonrainy days. This task is different from rule discovery in two ways. First, the hypothesized rule is not compared to a standard of "best possible" prediction, but rather to a standard of "better than nothing." Second, the information search takes place in memory; the tester determines which information to attend to or keep track of rather than controlling its presentation. (A similar characterization is presented by Crocker, 1981.)

Despite these differences, we propose that the basic +test strategy is manifested in covariation judgment much as it is in other, more external tasks. The event types listed above can be mapped onto our division of instances into H and $\overline{H}$, T and $\overline{T}$ (see Table 6.3). The labels given the cells, A, B, C, and D, correspond to the terminology commonly used in studies of contingency. One possible evaluation strategy in such a problem is to think of cases in which the conditions were met (days with cloud seeding), and estimate how often those cases possessed the target property (rain). This is +Htesting: examining instances that fit the hypothesized conditions (H: cloud seeding) to see whether they are target events (T: rain) or nontargets ($\overline{T}$: no rain). In other words, +Htesting is based on instances in cells A and B. Similarly, one could think of cases in which the target property occurred (it rained) to see whether the hypothesized conditions were met (clouds had been seeded). This is equivalent to +Ttesting, based on instances in cells A and C.

We expect, as usual, that people will favor +Htests and +Ttests over –Htests and –Ttests. We also expect that there may be a tendency toward +Htesting in particular, because of greater attention to the sufficiency of rules than to their necessity (e.g., you do not mind if it rains sometimes without seeding). Also, many contingency tasks are framed in terms of the relation between causes and effects. Htests may be more natural then, because they are consistent with the temporal order of causation, moving from known causes to possible results (cf. Tversky & Kahneman, 1980).

Table 6.3. *The relationship of hypothesis-testing terms to contingency judgments*

	Target event or property	
Proposed cause or condition	Present (T)	Absent ($\bar{\text{T}}$)
Present (H)	Cell A: H ∩ T	Cell B: H ∩ $\bar{\text{T}}$
Absent ($\bar{\text{H}}$)	Cell C: $\bar{\text{H}}$ ∩ T	Cell D: $\bar{\text{H}}$ ∩ $\bar{\text{T}}$

These hypotheses lead to some specific predictions about people's judgments of contingency. On a group level, judgments will be most influenced by the presence or absence of A-cell instances, because they are considered in both +Htests and +Ttests. B-cell and C-cell data will have somewhat less influence, because B-cell data are considered only with +Htests and C-cell only with +Ttests. If +Htests are the most popular tests, then B-cell data will receive somewhat more emphasis than C-cell data. Finally, D-cell data will have the least effect, because they are not considered in either of the favored tests. On an individual-subject level, there will be extensive use of strategies comparing cell A with cell B (+Htesting) and comparing cell A with cell C (+Ttesting).

The data from a variety of studies support these predictions. Schustack and Sternberg (1981), for example, found that the contingency judgments of subjects taken as a group were best modeled as a linear combination of the number of instances of each of the four types, with the greatest emphasis placed on A-cell, B-cell, C-cell, and D-cell data, in that order. Similar results were reported in an experiment by Arkes and Harkness (1983, Experiment 7), and in a meta-analysis of contingency–judgment tasks by Lipe (1982).

A number of studies have also examined data from individual subjects. Although some studies indicate that people are influenced almost entirely by A-cell data (Jenkins & Ward, 1965; Nisbett & Ross, 1980; Smedslund, 1963), there is now considerable evidence for the prevalence of an A − B strategy (Arkes & Harkness, 1983; Shaklee & Mims, 1981, 1982; Ward & Jenkins, 1965). This label has been applied to strategies that compare the number of H ∩ T instances with the number of H ∩ $\bar{\text{T}}$ (Cell A vs. Cell B) as well as strategies that compare T ∩ H (Cell A) with T ∩ $\bar{\text{H}}$ (Cell C). The first comparison is consistent with our idea of +Htesting, the second with +Ttesting. These two kinds of comparison have not been clearly distinguished in the literature. For example, Arkes and Harkness (1983) sometimes label the condition-but-no-event cell as B, and sometimes the event-but-no-condition cell as B. However, in one study, Shaklee and Mims (1981) were able to distinguish A − B and A − C patterns in their data and found evidence of both.

Further evidence of a +test approach is found in a recent study by Doherty and Falgout (1985). They presented the Ward and Jenkins (1965) cloud-seeding task on a computer screen and enabled subjects to save instances in computer memory for later reference. Although there were large individual differences, the most common pattern was to save a record of instances in cells A and B (the results of +Htests). The second most common pattern was to save A-, B-, and C-cell instances (+Htests and +Ttests), and the third most common pattern was B and C (the falsifications from +Htests and +Ttests). Together, these 3 patterns accounted for 32 of 40 data-saving patterns in two experiments.

In contingency judgment as in rule discovery, the +test strategy can often work well as a heuristic for hypothesis testing. However, this approach can deviate appreciably from statistical standards under some circumstances. Most statistical indexes (e.g., chi-square or correlation coefficient) put equal weight on all four cells, which +testing does not. Are people capable of more sophisticated strategies? Shaklee and Mims (1981, 1982) and Arkes and Harkness (1983) describe a sum-of-diagonals strategy that generally fares well as a rough estimate of statistical contingency. However, a simple combination of +Htests and +Ttests would result in a pattern of judgments very similar to the sum-of-diagonals strategy. A stimulus set could be carefully constructed to discriminate the two, but in the absence of such studies, we suspect that many sum-of-diagonals subjects may actually be using a combination of A versus B (+Htests) and A versus C (+Ttests). This may explain why individual analyses indicate frequent use of sum-of-diagonals strategies whereas group analyses often indicate that D-cell data are given little weight. On the other hand, we would expect that subjects might use more sophisticated strategies under favorable circumstances. There is some evidence that reduced memory demands have such an effect. Contingency judgments are more sophisticated when data are presented in summary form, rather than case by case (Arkes & Harkness, 1983; Shaklee & Mims, 1981, 1982; Shaklee & Tucker, 1980; Ward & Jenkins, 1965). Also, the problem context and the wording of the question may direct attention to relevant sources of data (Arkes & Harkness, 1983; Crocker, 1982; Einhorn & Hogarth, 1986).

Further theoretical and empirical questions

The concept of a general +test strategy provides an integrative interpretation for phenomena in a wide variety of hypothesis-testing tasks. This interpretation also prompts a number of new theoretical and empirical questions. There are several ways our analyses can be extended to explore further the nature of hypothesis-testing tasks and the strategies people use to accomplish them. We present a few examples here.

In this article we discuss tasks in which the goal is to determine the correctness of a single hypothesis. This is a common situation, since people (including scientists) tend to view hypothesis testing in terms of verifying or

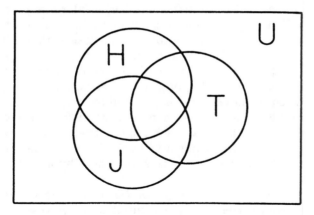

Figure 6.6. Representation of hypothesis testing situation involving two alternate hypotheses, R_H and R_J, specifying sets H and J, respectively.

falsifying one particular hypothesis (Mitroff, 1974; Tweney, 1984, 1985; Tweney & Doherty, 1983; Tweney et al., 1980). On the other hand, it would be interesting to analyze the use of simultaneous alternate hypotheses in obtaining informative tests of hypotheses (see Figure 6.6). The importance of specific alternatives has been emphasized in laboratory hypothesis-testing studies (e.g., Wason & Johnson-Laird, 1972, chap. 16) and in philosophical discussions (e.g., Platt, 1964). An analysis like ours could be used to examine how alternate hypotheses can increase the expected information from tests, under what circumstances an alternative is not useful (e.g., with a straw-man hypothesis), and when it would be better to simultaneously verify or falsify two alternatives rather than perform a test that favors one over the other. From a theoretical perspective, it might also be interesting to examine a situation in which a larger set of alternate hypotheses are evaluated simultaneously. This may not be representative of ordinary scientific thought, but could provide an interesting normative standard (cf. Edwards, 1965; Raiffa, 1968). It is also akin to problems commonly faced by artificial intelligence researchers in designing expert systems to perform diagnostic tasks (see, e.g., Duda & Shortliffe, 1983; Fox, 1980).

Another possible extension of these analyses is to consider standards of comparison other than "correct" or "best possible." In many situations, it may be more appropriate to ask whether or not your hypothesis is "pretty good," or "good enough," or even "better than nothing." Then, instead of comparing error rates to irreducible minima (ε^+ and ε^-), you are comparing them to other standards (s^+ and s^-). Similarly, it would be possible to consider the testing of a rule for estimating a continuous variable rather than for predicting the presence or absence of a property. What you want to know then is the expected amount of error, rather than just the probability of error.

Our theoretical analyses also suggest a number of interesting empirical questions concerning the ways in which people adapt their strategies to the task at hand. For example, we indicate that certain task variables have a significant impact on how effective the +test strategy is in different situations. We do not know the extent to which people respond to these variables, or whether they respond appropriately. For example, do people use −Htests more when the target set is large? Will they do so if the cost of false negative guesses is made clear? Our review of existing research suggests that people may vary their approach appropriately under favorable conditions. However, there is still much to learn about how factors such as cognitive load and task-specific information affect hypothesis-testing strategies.

Finally, there is a broader context of hypothesis formation and revision that should be considered as well. We have focused on the process of finding information to test a hypothesis. The broader context also includes questions about how to interpret your findings (e.g., see Darley & Gross, 1983; Hoch & Ha, 1986; Lord et al., 1979). The astrophysicist must decide if the blur in the picture is really a planet; the interviewer must judge whether the respondent has given an extroverted answer. Moreover, questions about how hypotheses are tested are inevitably linked to questions about how hypotheses are generated. The latter sort of questions have received much less attention, however, possibly because they are harder to answer (but see, e.g., Gettys, 1983; Gettys & Fisher, 1979). Obtaining falsification is only a first step. The investigator must use that information to build a new hypothesis and must then do further testing. Thus, analyses of hypothesis testing and hypothesis generation will be mutually informative.

Conclusions

Over the past 30 years, there have been scores of studies on the nature of hypothesis testing in scientific investigation and in everyday reasoning. Many investigators talk about confirmation bias, but this term has been applied to many different phenomena in a variety of contexts. In our review of the literature, we find that different kinds of "confirmation bias" can be understood as resulting from a basic hypothesis-testing heuristic, which we call the positive test strategy. That is, people tend to test hypotheses by looking at instances where the target property is hypothesized to be present or is known to be present.

This +test strategy, in its various manifestations, has generally been regarded as incompatible with the prescription to seek disconfirmation. The central idea of this prescription is that the hypothesis tester should make a deliberate attempt to find any evidence that would falsify the current hypothesis. As we show, however, +testing does not necessarily contradict the goal of seeking falsification. Indeed, under some circumstances, +testing may be the only way to discover falsifying instances (see Figure 6.3). Furthermore, in probabilistic environments, it is not even necessarily the case that falsification provides more information than verification. What is best depends on the characteristics of the specific task at hand.

Our review suggests that people use the +test strategy as a general default heuristic. That is, this strategy is one that people use in the absence of specific information that identifies some tests as more relevant than others, or when the cognitive demands of the task preclude a more carefully designed strategy. Our theoretical analyses indicate that, as an all-purpose heuristic, +testing often serves the hypothesis tester well. That is probably why it persists, despite its shortcomings. For example, if the target phenomenon is relatively rare, and the hypothesis roughly matches this base rate, you are probably better off testing where you do expect the phenomenon to occur or where you know the phenomenon occurred rather than the opposite. This situation characterizes many real-world problems. Moreover, +tests may be less costly or less risky than −tests when real-world consequences are involved (Einhorn & Hogarth, 1978; Tschirgi, 1980).

Like most general-purpose heuristics, however, +testing can lead to problems when applied inappropriately. In rule discovery, it can produce misleading feedback by failing to reveal a whole class of important falsifications (violations of necessity). In propositional reasoning (e.g., the four-card problem), +testing leads to superfluous tests of necessity (+Ttests) and neglect of some relevant tests of sufficiency (−Ttests). In a variety of tasks, including concept indentification, intuitive personality testing, and contingency judgment, a +test strategy can lead to inefficiency or inaccuracy by overweighting some data and underweighting others. The consequences of using a +test strategy vary with the characteristics of the task.

Our task analyses serve two major functions. First, they highlight some of the structural similarities among diverse tasks in the broad domain of hypothesis testing. This permits integration of findings from different subareas that have so far been fairly isolated from each other. Second, our approach provides a framework for analyzing what each task requires of the subject, why people make the mistakes they do, and why changes in the structure and content of tasks sometimes produce significant changes in performance. These questions are central to understanding human hypothesis testing in the larger context of practical and scientific reasoning.

Appendix

Two measures of the expected impact of a test

Assume that you have a hypothesized rule, R_H, and some subjective degree of belief that this rule is the best possible, $p(R_H = R_B)$. Your goal is to achieve the maximum degree of certainty that $R_H = R_B$ or $R_H \neq R_B$. Suppose that you perform a +Htest, and receive a falsification (Fn, +H). Then, according to Bayes's equation, your new degree of belief should be

$$p(R_H = R_B | Fn, +H) = \frac{p(Fn, +H | R_H = R_B)}{p(Fn, +H)} \cdot p(R_H = R_B). \tag{A1}$$

According to earlier definitions, $p(Fn, +H | R_H = R_B) = p(\bar{t}|b) = \varepsilon^+$, and $p(Fn, +H) = p(\bar{t}|h) = z^+$. Thus

$$p(R_H = R_B | Fn, +H) = \frac{\varepsilon^+}{z^+} \cdot p(R_H = R_B). \tag{A2}$$

Similarly, if your +Htest yields verification,

$$p(R_H = R_B | Vn, +H) = \frac{1 - \varepsilon^+}{1 - z^+} \cdot p(R_H = R_B). \tag{A3}$$

By definition, $\varepsilon^+ \le z^+$, so verifications produce an increased degree of belief that $R_H = R_B$ (or no change) and falsification a decrease in belief (or no change). For −Htests, revisions are equivalent but depend on ε^- and z^- rather than ε^+ and z^+.

Using the expected change in belief (EΔP) as a measure of informativeness (as defined in the text),

$$\Delta P_{Fn, +H} = \left| p(R_H = R_B) - \frac{\varepsilon^+}{z^+} p(R_H = R_B) \right|$$

$$= p(R_H = R_B) \cdot \left[1 - \frac{\varepsilon^+}{z^+} \right],$$

$$\Delta P_{Vn, +H} = \left| p(R_H = R_B) - \frac{1 - \varepsilon^+}{1 - z^+} \cdot p(R_H = R_B) \right|$$

$$= p(R_H = R_B) \cdot \left[\frac{1 - \varepsilon^+}{1 - z^+} - 1 \right], \text{ and}$$

$$E\Delta P_{+H} = p(Fn| + H) \cdot \Delta P_{Fn, +H} + p(Vn| + H) \cdot \Delta P_{Vn, +H}$$

$$= z^+ \left[1 - \frac{\varepsilon^+}{z^+} \right] \cdot p(R_H = R_B)$$

$$+ (1 - z^+) \left[\frac{1 - \varepsilon^+}{1 - z^+} - 1 \right] \cdot p(R_H = R_B)$$

$$= (z^+ - \varepsilon^+) \cdot p(R_H = R_B) + (z^+ - \varepsilon^+) \cdot p(R_H = R_B)$$

$$= p(R_H = R_B) \cdot 2(z^+ - \varepsilon^+). \tag{A4}$$

Similarly,

$$E\Delta P_{-H} = p(R_H = R_B) \cdot 2(z^- - \varepsilon^-). \tag{A5}$$

An alternate measure of impact, diagnosticity, is frequently used in Bayesian analyses. An alternate form of Bayes's theorem states that

$$\frac{p(R_H = R_B|Result)}{p(R_H \neq R_B|Result)} = \frac{p(Result|R_H = R_B)}{p(Result|R_H \neq R_B)} \cdot \frac{p(R_H = R_B)}{p(R_H \neq R_B)} \qquad (A6)$$

$$\Omega' = \qquad LR \qquad \cdot \Omega$$

The likelihood ratio (LR) is the basis of the diagnosticity measure. It is equal to the ratio of revised odds (Ω') to prior odds (Ω). A likelihood ratio of 1 means the result has no impact on your beliefs; it is nondiagnostic. The further from 1 the likelihood ratio is, the greater the event's impact.

Edwards (1968; Edwards & Phillips, 1966) suggests that subjective uncertainty may be better represented by log odds than by probabilities or raw odds, based on evidence that subjective estimates made on such a scale tend to conform better to normative specifications. Following this suggestion, diagnosticity can be measured as the magnitude of the change in log-odds (ΔL) that an event would engender, which is equivalent to the magnitude of the log likelihood ratio, $|\log LR|$. If, for instance, you performed a +Htest and received falsification, the diagnosticity of this datum would be

$$\Delta L_{Fn,+H}$$

$$= \log\frac{p(R_H = R_B)}{1 - p(R_H = R_B)} - \log\frac{p(R_H = R_B|Fn,+H)}{1 - p(R_H = R_B|Fn,+H)}. \qquad (A7)$$

For ease of exposition, we will use the letter C to stand for the subjective probability $p(R_H = R_B)$. Following equations A2 and A3 above,

$$\Delta L_{Fn,+H} = \log\frac{C}{1-C} - \log\frac{\varepsilon^+/z^+ \cdot C}{1 - (\varepsilon^+/z^+ \cdot C)} \qquad (A8)$$

and

$$\Delta L_{Vn,+H} = \log\frac{\dfrac{1-\varepsilon^+}{1-z^+} \cdot C}{1 - \left(\dfrac{1-\varepsilon^+}{1-z^+} \cdot C\right)} - \log\frac{C}{1-C} \qquad (A9)$$

Parallel to our earlier analyses, we can define the expected change in log-odds (EΔL) for a +Htest as $p(Fn|+Htest).\Delta L_{Fn,+H} + p(Vn|+Htest)\cdot\Delta L_{Vn,+H}$. That is,

$$E\Delta L_{+H} = z^+\Delta L_{Fn,+H} + (1 - z^+)\Delta L_{Vn,+H}. \qquad (A10)$$

Accordingly, the expected change in log-odds for −Htests can be calculated by substituting ε^- for ε^+ and z^- for z^+ in Equations A8, A9, and A10.

EΔL increases monotonically with increasing z, except for some small, local violations when C is very low, z is very high, and ε is near .5 (rather degraded conditions). EΔL decreases monotonically with increasing ε. Thus, as in earlier analyses, more information is expected from the test with the higher z and the lower ε. The exact trade-off between z and ε is complex, however. Under most circumstances, the component due to falsifications ($z^{+}\Delta L_{Fn,+H}$ for +Htests or $z^{-}\Delta L_{Fn,-H}$ for −Htests) is greater than the component due to verification [$(1 - z^{+})\Delta L_{Vn,+H}$ or $(1 - z^{-})\Delta L_{vn,-H}$, respectively]. That is, more information is expected to come from falsification, overall, than from verification with this measure.

Notes

1 We use a lowercase letter to designate an instance of a given type: t is an instance in set T, t̄ is an instance in T̄, and so on.
2 Our analyses treat the sets U, T, and H as finite, but also apply to infinite sets, as long as T and H designate finite, nonzero fractions of U. In Wason's task (1960), for example, if U = all sets of three numbers and H = all sets of three even numbers, then we can say that H designates $\frac{1}{8}$ of all the members of U, in other words, $p(h) = \frac{1}{8}$.
3 For simplicity, we ignore the possibility that a rule might produce, say, fewer false positives but more false negatives than the best rule. We assume that the minimum ε^{+} and ε^{-} can both be achieved at the same time. The more general case could be analyzed by defining a joint function of ε^{+} and ε^{-} which is to be minimized.

References

American Psychiatric Association (1980). *Diagnostic and statistical manual of mental disorders* (3rd ed.). Washington, DC: Author.

Alloy, L. B., & Tabachnik, N. (1984). Assessment of covariation by humans and animals: The joint influence of prior experience and current situational information. *Psychological Review, 91*, 112–149.

Arkes, H. R., & Harkness, A. R. (1983). Estimates of contingency between two dichotomous variables. *Journal of Experimental Psychology: General, 112*, 117–135.

Bourne, L. E., Jr. (1974). An inference model for conceptual rule learning. In R. L. Solso (Ed.), *Theories in cognitive psychology: The Loyola symposium* (pp. 231–256). New York: Erlbaum.

Bourne, L. E., Jr., & Guy, D. E. (1968). Learning conceptual rules II: The role of positive and negative instances. *Journal of Experimental Psychology, 77*, 488–494.

Bruner, J. S. (1951). Personality dynamics and the process of perceiving. In R. R. Blake & G. V. Ramsey (Eds.), *Perception: An approach to personality* (pp. 121–147). New York: Ronald Press.

Bruner, J. S., Goodnow, J., & Austin, G. A. (1956). *A study of thinking.* New York: Wiley.

Centers for Disease Control (1986). Cases of specific notifiable diseases, United States. *Morbidity and Mortality Weekly Report, 34*, 775–777.

Cox, J. R., & Griggs, R. A. (1982). The effect of experience on performance in Wason's selection task. *Memory and Cognition, 10*, 496–502.

Crocker, J. (1981). Judgment of covariation by social perceivers. *Psychological Bulletin, 90*, 272–292.

Crocker, J. (1982). Biased questions in judgment of covariation studies. *Personality and Social Psychology Bulletin, 8*, 214–220.

Darley, J. M., & Gross, P. H. (1983). A hypothesis confirming bias in labeling effects. *Journal of Personality and Social Psychology, 44*, 20–33.

Doherty, M. E., & Falgout, K. (1985, November). *Subjects' data selection strategies for assessing covariation.* Paper presented at the meeting of the Psychonomics Society, Boston, MA.

Duda, R. O., & Shortliffe, E. H. (1983). Expect systems research. *Science, 220,* 261–268.

Edwards, W. (1965). Optimal strategies for seeking information: Models for statistics, choice reaction times, and human information processes. *Journal of Mathematical Psychology, 2,* 312–329.

Edwards, W. (1968). Conservatism in human information processing. In B. Kleinmuntz (Ed.), *Formal representations of human judgment* (pp. 17–52). New York: Wiley.

Edwards, W., & Phillips, L. D. (1966). Conservatism in a simple probability inference task. *Journal of Experimental Psychology, 72,* 346–354.

Einhorn, H. J. (1980). Learning from experience and suboptimal rules in decision making. In T. S. Wallsten (Ed.), *Cognitive processes in choice and decision behavior* (pp. 1–20). Hillsdale, NJ: Erlbaum.

Einhorn, H. J., & Hogarth, R. M. (1978). Confidence in judgment: Persistence of the illusion of validity. *Psychological Review, 85,* 396–416.

Einhorn, H. J., & Hogarth, R. M. (1986). Judging probable cause. *Psychological Bulletin, 99,* 3–19.

Evans, J. St. B. T., & Lynch, J. S. (1973). Matching bias in the selection task. *British Journal of Psychology, 64,* 391–397.

Fischhoff, B., & Beyth-Marom, R. (1983). Hypothesis evaluation from a Bayesian perspective. *Psychological Review, 90,* 239–260.

Fox, J. (1980). Making decisions under the influence of memory. *Psychological Review, 87,* 190–211.

Gettys, C. F. (1983). *Research and theory on predecisional processes* (Rep. No. TR-11-30-83). Norman: University of Oklahoma, Decision Processes Laboratory.

Gettys, C. F., & Fisher, S. D. (1979). Hypothesis generation and plausibility assessment. *Organizational Behavior and Human Performance, 24,* 93–110.

Gorman, M. E. (1986). How the possibility of error affects falsification on a task that models scientific problem-solving. *British Journal of Psychology, 77,* 85–96.

Gorman, M. E., & Gorman, M. E. (1984). A comparison of disconfirmatory, confirmatory, and a control strategy on Wason's 2-4-6 task. *Quarterly Journal of Experimental Psychology, 36A,* 629–648.

Green D. M., & Swets, J. A. (1966). *Signal detection theory and psychophysics.* New York: Wiley.

Griggs, R. A. (1983). The role of problem content in the selection task and the THOG problem. In J. St. B. T. Evans (Ed.), *Thinking and reasoning: Psychological approaches* (pp. 16–43). London: Routledge & Kegan Paul.

Griggs, R. A., & Cox, J. R. (1982). The elusive thematic-materials effect in Wason's selection task. *British Journal of Psychology, 73,* 407–420.

Griggs, R. A., & Cox, J. R. (1983). The effect of problem content on strategies in Wason's selection task. *Quarterly Journal of Experimental Psychology, 35,* 519–533.

Hardin, C. L. (1980). Rationality and disconfirmation. *Social Studies of Science, 10,* 509–514.

Hoch, S. J., & Ha, Y.-W. (1986). Consumer learning: Advertising and the ambiguity of product experience. *Journal of Consumer Research, 13,* 221–233.

Hoch, S. J., & Tschirgi, J. E. (1983). Cue redundancy and extra logical inference in a deductive reasoning task. *Memory & Cognition, 11,* 200–209.

Hoch, S. J., & Tschirgi, J. E. (1985). Logical knowledge and cue redundancy in deductive reasoning. *Memory & Cognition, 13,* 453–462.

Hogarth, R. M. (1981). Beyond discrete biases: Functional and dysfunctional aspects of judgmental heuristics. *Psychological Bulletin, 90,* 197–217.

Jenkins, H. M., & Ward, W. C. (1965). Judgment of contingency between responses and outcomes. *Psychological Monographs: General and Applied, 79* (1, Whole No. 594).

Kern, L. H. (1983, November). *The effect of data error in inducing confirmatory inference strategies in scientific hypothesis testing.* Paper presented at the meeting of the Society for the Social Studies of Science, Blacksburg, VA.

Klayman, J. (1986). *An information-theory analysis of the value of information in hypothesis testing* (Working Paper No. 119a). Chicago, IL: University of Chicago, Graduate School of Business, Center for Decision Research.

Klayman, J., & Ha, Y.-W. (1985, August). *Strategy and structure in rule discovery.* Paper presented at the Tenth Research Conference of Subjective Probability, Utility and Decision Making, Helsinki, Finland.

Lakatos, I. (1970). Falsification and methodology of scientific research programmes. In I. Lakatos & A. Musgrave (Eds.), *Criticism and the growth of scientific knowledge* (pp. 91–196). New York: Cambridge University Press.

Legrenzi, P. (1970). Relations between language and reasoning about deductive rules. In G. B. Flores d'Arcais & W. J. M. Levelt (Eds.), *Advances in psycholinguistics* (pp. 322–333). Amsterdam: North Holland.

Levine, M. (1966). Hypothesis behavior by humans during discrimination learning. *Journal of Experimental Psychology, 71,* 331–338.

Levine, M. (1970). Human discrimination learning: The subset-sampling assumption. *Psychological Bulletin, 74,* 397–404.

Lipe, M. G. (1982). *A cross-study analysis of covariation judgments* (Working Paper No. 96). Chicago, IL: University of Chicago, Graduate School of Business, Center for Decision Research.

Lord, C., Ross, L., & Lepper, M. (1979). Biased assimilation and attitude polarization: The effect of prior theories on subsequently considered evidence. *Journal of Personality and Social Psychology, 37,* 2098–2109.

Lucas, T., & Whittemore, H. (1985). *Tornado!* (NOVA program No. 1217). Boston: WGBH Transcripts.

Mahoney, M. J. (1976). *Scientist as subject: The psychological imperative.* Cambridge, MA: Ballinger.

Mahoney, M. J. (1979). Psychology of the scientist: An evaluative review. *Social Studies of Science, 9,* 349–375.

Mahoney, M. J. (1980). Rationality and authority: On the confusion of justification and permission. *Social Studies of Science, 10,* 515–518.

Millward, R. B., & Spoehr, K. T. (1973). The direct measurement of hypothesis-testing strategies. *Cognitive Psychology, 4,* 1–38.

Mitroff, I. (1974). *The subjective side of science.* Amsterdam: Elsevier.

Mynatt, C. R., Doherty, M. E., & Tweney, R. D. (1977). Confirmation bias in a simulated research environment: An experimental study of scientific inference. *Quarterly Journal of Experimental Psychology, 29,* 85–95.

Mynatt, C. R., Doherty, M. E., & Tweney, R. D. (1978). Consequences of confirmation and disconfirmation in a simulated research environment. *Quarterly Journal of Experimental Psychology, 30,* 395–406.

Nisbett, R., & Ross, L. (1980). *Human inference: Strategies and shortcomings of social judgment.* Englewood Cliffs, NJ: Prentice-Hall.

Platt, J. R. (1964). Strong inference. *Science, 146,* 347–353.

Politzer, G. (1986). Laws of language use and formal logic. *Journal of Psycholinguistic Research, 15,* 47–92.

Popper, K. R. (1959). *The logic of scientific discovery.* New York: Basic Books.

Popper, K. R. (1972). *Objective knowledge.* Oxford, England: Clarendon.

Raiffa, H. (1968). *Decision analysis.* Reading, MA: Addison-Wesley.

Ross, L., & Lepper, M. R. (1980). The perseverance of beliefs: Empirical and normative considerations. In R. A. Shweder (Ed.), *Fallible judgment in behavioral research: New directions for methodology of social and behavioral science* (Vol. 4, pp. 17–36). San Francisco: Jossey-Bass.

Rumain, B., Connell, J., & Braine, M. D. S. (1983). Conversational comprehension processes are responsible for reasoning fallacies in children as well as adults: *If* is not the biconditional. *Developmental Psychology, 19,* 471–481.

Sagan, C. (1980). *Cosmos.* New York: Random House.

Schustack, M. W., & Sternberg, R. J. (1981). Evaluation of evidence in causal inference. *Journal of Experimental Psychology: General, 110,* 101–120.

Schwartz, B. (1981). Control of complex, sequential operants by systematic visual information in pigeons. *Journal of Experimental Psychology: Animal Behavior Processes, 7,* 31–44.

Schwartz, B. (1982). Reinforcement-induced behavioral stereotypy: How not to teach people to discover rules. *Journal of Experimental Psychology: General, 111,* 23–59.

Shaklee, H., & Mims, M. (1981). Development of rule use in judgments of covariation between events. *Child Development, 52,* 317–325.

Shaklee, H., & Mims, M. (1982). Sources of error in judging event covariations: Effects of memory demands. *Journal of Experimental Psychology: Learning, Memory & Cognition, 8,* 208–224.

Shaklee, H., & Tucker, D. (1980). A rule analysis of judgments of covariation between events. *Memory & Cognition, 8,* 459–467.

Simon, H. A. (1973). Does scientific discovery have a logic? *Philosophy of Science, 40,* 471–480.

Skov, R. B., & Sherman, S. J. (1986). Information-gathering processes: Diagnosticity, hypothesis confirmatory strategies and perceived hypothesis confirmation. *Journal of Experimental Social Psychology, 22,* 93–121.

Smedslund, J. (1963). The concept of correlation in adults. *Scandinavian Journal of Psychology, 4,* 165–173.

Snyder, M. (1981). Seek and ye shall find: Testing hypotheses about other people. In E. T. Higgins, C. P. Heiman, & M. P. Zanna (Eds.), *Social cognition: The Ontario symposium on personality and social psychology* (pp. 277–303). Hillsdale, NJ: Erlbaum.

Snyder, M., & Campbell, B. H. (1980). Testing hypotheses about other people: The role of the hypothesis. *Personality and Social Psychology Bulletin, 6,* 421–426.

Snyder, M., & Swann, W. B., Jr. (1978). Hypothesis-testing in social interaction. *Journal of Personality and Social Psychology, 36,* 1202–1212.

Strohmer, D. C., & Newman, L. J. (1983). Counselor hypothesis-testing strategies. *Journal of Counseling Psychology, 30,* 557–565.

Swann, W. B., Jr. (1984). Quest for accuracy in person perception: A matter of pragmatics. *Psychological Review, 91,* 457–477.

Swann, W. B., Jr., & Giuliano, T. (1987). Confirmatory search strategies in social interaction: How, when, why and with what consequences. *Journal of Social and Clinical Psychology, 5,* 511–524.

Swann, W. B., Jr., Giuliano, T., & Wegner, D. M. (1982). Where leading questions can lead: The power of conjecture in social interaction. *Journal of Personality and Social Psychology, 42,* 1025–1035.

Taplin, J. E. (1975). Evaluation of hypotheses in concept identification. *Memory & Cognition, 3,* 85–96.

Trabasso, T., & Bower, G. H. (1968). *Attention in learning.* New York: Wiley.

Trope, Y., & Bassok, M. (1982). Confirmatory and diagnosing strategies in social information gathering. *Journal of Personality and Social Psychology, 43,* 22–34.

Trope, Y., & Bassok, M. (1983). Information gathering strategies in hypothesis-testing. *Journal of Experimental Social Psychology, 19,* 560–576.

Trope, Y., Bassok, M., & Alon, E. (1984). The questions lay interviewers ask. *Journal of Personality, 52,* 90–106.

Tschirgi, J. E. (1980). Sensible reasoning: A hypothesis about hypotheses. *Child Development, 51,* 1–10.

Tversky, A., & Kahneman, D. (1974). Judgment under uncertainty: Heuristics and biases. *Science, 185,* 1124–1131.

Tversky, A., & Kahneman, D. (1980). Causal schemas in judgments under uncertainty. In M. Fishbein (Ed.), *Progress in social psychology* (Vol. 1, pp. 49–72). Hillsdale, NJ: Erlbaum.

Tweney, R. D. (1984). Cognitive psychology and the history of science: A new look at Michael Faraday. In H. Rappard, W. van Hoorn, & S. Bem (Eds.), *Studies in the history of psychology and the social sciences* (pp. 235–246). The Hague: Mouton.

Tweney, R. D. (1985). Faraday's discovery of induction: A cognitive approach. In D. Gooding & F. James (Eds.), *Faraday rediscovered* (pp. 159–209). London: Macmillan.

Tweney, R. D., & Doherty, M. E. (1983). Rationality and the psychology of inference. *Synthese, 57,* 139–161.

Tweney, R. D., Doherty, M. E., & Mynatt, C. R. (1982). Rationality and disconfirmation: Further evidence. *Social Studies of Science, 12,* 435–441.

Tweney, R. D., Doherty, M. E., Worner, W. J., Pliske, D. B., Mynatt, C. R., Gross, K. A., & Arkkelin, D. L. (1980). Strategies of rule discovery in an inference task. *Quarterly Journal of Experimental Psychology, 32,* 109–123.

Vogel, R., & Annau, Z. (1973). An operant discrimination task allowing variability of response patterning. *Journal of the Experimental Analysis of Behavior, 20,* 1–6.

Ward, W. C., & Jenkins, H. M. (1965). The display of information and the judgment of contingency. *Canadian Journal of Psychology, 19,* 231–241.

Wason, P. C. (1960). On the failure to eliminate hypotheses in a conceptual task. *Quarterly Journal of Experimental Psychology, 12,* 129–140.

Wason, P. C. (1962). Reply to Wetherick. *Quarterly Journal of Experimental Psychology, 14,* 250.

Wason, P. C. (1966). Reasoning. In B. M. Foss (Ed.), *New horizons in psychology* (pp. 135–151). Harmondsworth, Middlesex, England: Penguin.

Wason, P. C. (1968). On the failure to eliminate hypotheses – A second look. In P. C. Wason & P. N. Johnson-Laird (Eds.), *Thinking and reasoning* (pp. 165–174). Harmondsworth, Middlesex, England: Penguin.

Wason, P. C., & Johnson-Laird, P. N. (1972). *Psychology of reasoning: Structure and content*. London: Batsford.

Wetherick, N. E. (1962). Eliminative and enumerative behavior in a conceptual task. *Quarterly Journal of Experimental Psychology, 14,* 246–249.

Yachanin, S. A., & Tweney, R. D. (1982). The effect of thematic content on cognitive strategies in the four-card selection task. *Bulletin of the Psychonomic Society, 19,* 87–90.

7 Learning from feedback: Exactingness and incentives

Robin M. Hogarth, Brian J. Gibbs,
Craig R. M. McKenzie, and Margaret A. Marquis

The manner in which different types of feedback affect learning has long been of central concern in psychological studies of decision making (see, e.g., Balzer, Doherty, & O'Connor, 1989). In this article, we examine learning within the context of a repetitive decision-making task, and we examine a dimension of feedback that has received little attention to date, namely, the effects of differences in the severity with which performance is evaluated.

Central to our work is recognition of the inherent ambiguity of feedback. In particular, we note that feedback from the outcomes of decisions can serve two functions that are often confounded. One function is inferential. Feedback informs the decision maker about the structure of the underlying task. For example, when a student writes a paper, feedback in the form of a grade provides information about how to write a good paper. The second function is evaluative. Feedback provides information about the student's performance. It tells us whether the performance was good or bad. Note, however, that the feedback – in this case a grade – is confounded. To what extent does the grade reflect the student's ability to write papers, and to what extent does it reflect the teacher's grading policy?

Evaluation of decision-making performance can differ on a dimension that we term the *exactingness* of the environment and that reflects the severity of penalties imposed for errors. Tasks are exacting to the extent that deviations from optimal decisions are heavily punished and lenient to the extent that they are not.

This chapter originally appeared in the *Journal of Experimental Psychology: Learning, Memory, and Cognition*, 1991, 17(4), 734–752. Copyright © 1991 by the American Psychological Association. Reprinted by permission.

This work was funded by a contract from the Office of Naval Research as well as by special funds from the Graduate School of Business, University of Chicago. We are grateful to Colin Camerer, Terry Connolly, Joshua Klayman, George Loewenstein, and Kenneth Hammond as well as several excellent referees for critical comments on earlier drafts.

In addition to exactingness, decision-making tasks can vary in the extent to which different levels of performance have consequences for the decision maker. In the case of the student essay, for example, the student may or may not perceive the grade as consequential (e.g., by affecting chances of admission to graduate school). In other words, tasks can vary in the extent to which decision makers have incentives to perform well.

There are several reasons for studying the effects of exactingness together with the effects of incentives. First, knowing when and how exactingness and incentives affect learning is important at a practical level. In business or in the military, for example, what levels of exactingness implied by different evaluation schemes promote efficient learning? Do real consequences in terms of money or lives help people learn to make decisions more effectively? If exactingness or incentives are detrimental, how can learning be structured to overcome these impediments? Second, despite the importance of exactingness in many real world tasks, little theoretical attention has been directed toward understanding its effects. Third, and also from a theoretical viewpoint, controversy exists as to whether incentives necessarily improve performance. For example, one could argue from naive behaviorist or economic viewpoints that incentives will always improve performance, and much evidence is consistent with this contention. However, there is also evidence that under some conditions incentives can be detrimental (see, e.g., Lepper & Greene, 1978).

The article is organized as follows. We first elaborate on the concept of exactingness and comment on the literature that has considered the link between incentives and performance. Next, we outline the theoretical framework, arguing that exactingness induces forces that both help and hinder learning as measured by performance and that incentives accentuate the effects of these opposing forces. This leads to predictions about how exactingness will affect learning and about the nature of interactions between exactingness and incentives. The theoretical framework is then tested in a series of five experiments. Finally, we discuss the results of our experimental work from both theoretical and practical perspectives and make suggestions for further research.

Evaluation and incentive schemes

Evaluation as feedback

The task used in our experiments is similar to many real world situations in that subjects learn from outcome feedback. Although the ambiguity, and even the misleading nature of outcome feedback, has long been recognized (see, e.g., Brehmer, 1980; Einhorn & Hogarth, 1978; Hammond, Summers, & Deane, 1973), we wish to emphasize a specific aspect of this ambiguity, namely, that outcome feedback simultaneously conveys and confounds information concerning both the structure of the underlying task and how well the subject is performing. Thus, on receiving feedback a person may make inferences both about the structure of the task (e.g., how two variables are related), and the level of his or her performance (e.g., better than expected, better than a rival).

We conceive of feedback as being a function of three variables: (a) the specific action taken by the decision maker, (b) the nature of the underlying system governing outcomes, and (c) the manner in which these outcomes are evaluated. To illuminate the distinction between (b) and (c), note that if two otherwise identical tasks differed only in how outcomes were evaluated, a person making the same decisions in both tasks could receive different feedback. However, if the person was ignorant a priori of both the nature of the underlying tasks and how outcomes were evaluated, it would be difficult to attribute differences in feedback to the different evaluation functions as opposed to possible differences in the structures of the underlying tasks.

Incentives

It is common to classify incentives as *internal* or *external*. Internal incentives are any intrinsic motivations that people have to perform well in a task, the source of which can have various origins including, for example, a need to exhibit mastery (White, 1959), pride, or a wish to impress others (for a review, see Deci & Ryan, 1985). External incentives are explicit rewards, such as money, that depend on performance. Our major concern is with external incentives, although we do manipulate internal incentives in one study.

It would be naive to assert that incentives always improve performance. For example, when external incentives are removed for performing a task that people find intrinsically interesting, subsequent interest and performance in the task can decrease (Lepper, Greene, & Nisbett, 1973; Levine & Fasnacht, 1974). In addition, the presence of incentives has been found to reduce the amount of incidental learning that people acquire in cognitive tasks, presumably because attention is focused on the central task that is rewarded (Bahrick, 1954; Bahrick, Fitts, & Rankin, 1952).

The role of incentives has been examined in several different types of decision-making tasks. For our purposes, studies can be categorized as to whether subjects did or did not receive feedback after their decisions. Because the latter provide no opportunity for learning, we consider the former.

One well-studied task is the binary outcome prediction paradigm in which subjects are required to predict which of two signals will appear on each of a series of trials (for an overview, see Luce & Suppes, 1965). Incentives have produced mixed results. Siegel (1961) used two levels of monetary incentives and found that, with the greater level of incentives, the proportion of the time that subjects chose the more frequent signal became quite extreme (.95, which is still not the optimal value of 1). Edwards (1956) also found more extreme responses under incentives, and Tversky and Edwards (1966) found that although incentives changed behavior, behavior was still far from optimal. In general, the results of these and similar experiments are that payoffs affect subjects' behavior in the appropriate direction, but subjects still do not behave as the normative models prescribe.

Arkes, Dawes, and Christensen (1986) used a probabilistic task in which subjects were given a rule that would have enabled them to choose correctly 70% of the time. They found that, with incentives, subjects were more willing to abandon the rule. The result was that they performed worse than those without incentives. (See also Ashton, 1990.)

The literature does not reveal a simple relation between incentives and performance. For tasks that are understood, incentives appear to improve performance. For example, in summarizing many studies, McCullers (1978) pointed out that incentives enhance performance when the latter depends on making "simple, routine, unchanging responses and when circumstances favor the making of such responses quickly, frequently, and vigorously" (p. 14). He continued, however, by noting that the role of incentives is far less clear in tasks that require flexible, open-ended and creative responses. A similar distinction was made by McGraw (1978) between tasks requiring algorithmic or heuristic, problem-solving, mental strategies, on the one hand, and tasks that subjects find attractive or aversive, on the other. McGraw concluded that incentives are detrimental to performance in tasks that subjects find attractive and that require heuristic, problem-solving, mental strategies (cf. Amabile, 1982; McGraw & McCullers, 1979).

In reviewing work on processes of social facilitation, Zajonc (1965) offered the hypothesis that conditions of arousal tend to enhance the emission of dominant responses. Thus, although incentives should lead people to perform well at tasks with which they are familiar, they can accentuate the probability of producing incorrect responses in unfamiliar settings. Similarly, Easterbrook (1959) summarized a vast psychological literature showing that under high drive states people restrict attention to limited ranges of available cues and that this can inhibit performance in cognitive tasks (see also Kahneman, 1973).

More recently, several researchers have adopted a similar explanation as to why incentives may lead to worse performance when learning complex tasks (Humphreys & Revelle, 1984; Kanfer & Ackerman, 1989; Wood, Bandura, & Bailey, 1990). This is that, in the presence of incentives, complex tasks divert needed attention from inference to evaluation, that is, from a concern about *how* to do the task to *how well* one is doing. In tasks that are understood, however, attention can be more profitably allocated to executing known strategies.

Theoretical framework

The specific task

The structure of our task is similar to that used in many single- and multiple-cue probability learning studies (see, e.g., Klayman, 1988). Over a series of trials, subjects are presented with information in the form of cues or predictor variables and are asked to predict a criterion that is probabilistically related to the cues. Following each prediction, feedback is provided. In our task, subjects observed a value of a variable, W, and then chose a value of a decision variable, Q. Feedback, however, did not consist of observing the correct value of Q. Instead, feedback was provided in the form of evaluation points. Subjects were instructed that their objective was to maximize the number of evaluation points but were given no explanation as to how these were calculated. (More detailed information about the task is provided below in the experimental section of the paper.)

Evaluation points for each trial were calculated according to the formula

$$\text{Evaluation points} = 500 - \alpha(Q - D)^2, \tag{7.1}$$

in which Q was the subject's response and D was the correct value of the criterion. D had a strong but imperfect correlation with W, the variable observed by subjects before each trial, and can be characterized by the equation

$$D = \beta_0 + \beta_1 W + \varepsilon, \tag{7.2}$$

in which β_0 (= –1020) and β_1 (= 20) are parameters and ε is a random error term.

As illustrated by Equation 7.1, evaluation points for a given trial are a negative, linear function of the squared error of the subject's decision for that trial. The slope coefficient, α, makes operational the concept of exactingness, that is, as α increases, so does the penalty associated with erroneous decisions. Lenient environments are therefore characterized by small values of α, and exacting environments by large values.[1]

To compare performance (P) across different levels of exactingness, we measure observed performance (P) on a given trial i by

$$P_i = 500 - |Q_i - D_i|, \tag{7.3}$$

and consider mean performance, π, across a series of n trials, that is,

$$\pi = \left(\frac{1}{n}\right)\sum_{i=1}^{n} P_i. \tag{7.4}$$

Exactingness

We hypothesize that exactingness (α) induces forces that have both positive and negative effects on mean performance (π).

The positive aspect of increases in exactingness (α) lies in the opportunities that they provide for learning. To see this, imagine a situation where $\alpha = 0$. In this case, subjects always receive perfect scores of 500 no matter what values they select for Q (see Equation 7.1). They can therefore never learn what values of Q to associate with W. As α increases, evaluation points become more sensitive to differences between D and Q, thereby providing greater possibilities for learning the relation between W and Q. Learning, however, would not be expected to increase linearly with α. Instead, we hypothesize that the positive aspect of learning (as measured by performance, π) is an increasing, concave function of exactingness (α).

The main negative aspect associated with increases in exactingness (α) lies in the interpretation of feedback and subsequent reactions to this. Specifically, as exactingness (α) increases, feedback in terms of evaluation points is increasingly liable to be negative and, in the absence of alternative points of reference, perceived as such.[2] For example, in a lenient environment with α = .01, a difference of 50 between Q and D yields +475 evaluation points (see Equation 7.1). In an exacting environment with α = .50, the same performance translates into –750 evaluation points. In learning environments, people are likely to react differently to positive and negative feedback. Whereas positive feedback reinforces maintaining and refining existing behavior or response strategies (cf. Schwartz, 1982), negative feedback encourages shifting strategies and seeking alternatives that may work better. Because the subset of response strategies that work in exacting environments is much smaller than those that do not, continual shifting of strategies results in lower performance (π) – at least in the short run.[3] We hypothesize that as exactingness (α) increases, the rate at which this negative factor affects learning does not decrease. Thus, the negative aspect of learning (as measured by performance, π) is a nonconcave decreasing function of exactingness (α).

Incentives

We propose that incentives accentuate both the positive and the negative forces of exactingness. More specifically, when feedback is generally positive, as in lenient environments, incentives will induce more consistent application of apparently successful response strategies, and performance will improve (cf. Hammond & Summers, 1972). When feedback is generally negative, as in exacting environments, incentives will induce a more intensive search for alternatives, and performance will degrade, at least in the short run.

A formal model

To clarify implications of the above arguments, we use the heuristic device of a simple, algebraic model. Let

$$\pi = k \, [b\alpha^{\lambda} - c\alpha], \tag{7.5}$$

where k is a constant of proportionality, b and c are coefficients ($b, c > 0$) representing the extent to which the presence of incentives accentuates, respectively, the positive and negative aspects of exactingness (α) on performance (π), and λ $(0 < \lambda < 1)$ determines the degree of concavity of the function that represents the positive aspect of exactingness (α) on performance.[4]

We draw two general implications from this model. First, the form of Equation 7.5 is such that performance will be a single-peaked (inverted-U-shaped) function of exactingness (α) (cf. Coombs & Avrunin, 1977). This means that performance will be better when exactingness (α) is at intermediate rather than at extreme values.

Second, we can enquire about how incentives interact with exactingness. To do so, assume that Equation 7.5 represents performance with no incentives and denote performance with incentives by

$$\pi' = k[b'\alpha^\lambda - c'\alpha], \tag{7.6}$$

where $b' > b$ and $c' > c$. Next, ask when performance with incentives exceeds that without incentives, that is, when $\pi' > \pi$. Simple algebraic manipulation leads to the condition

$$(b' - b)/(c' - c) > \alpha^{1-\lambda}. \tag{7.7}$$

The general implication of Equation 7.7 is that there is a critical value of exactingness (α) below which incentives lead to superior performance but above which incentives are dysfunctional.[5]

Predictions

The model implied by Equation 7.5 and its underlying assumptions lead to several predictions concerning observed performance (π):

1. Environments characterized by intermediate levels of exactingness (α) will lead to better performance (π) than will lenient or exacting environments. (This is implied by the fact that π is a single-peaked or inverted-U-shaped function of α.)
2. There will be an interaction between incentives and exactingness. Whereas incentives will lead to improved performance in lenient environments, they will become less beneficial as exactingness increases.

Our third prediction is intended as a test of the assumption that exactingness (α) has both positive and negative effects on performance.

3. If the negative effects of exactingness (α) on performance (π) are eliminated, performance (π) should increase as a function of exactingness (α).[6]

In addition to these predictions, our theoretical model suggests other observable implications concerning the process by which exactingness and incentives affect performance. Of particular interest are the effects of these variables on the consistency with which subjects execute response strategies. First, because subjects in exacting environments are more likely to observe negative feedback than those in lenient environments, their strategies should exhibit more inconsistency as they search for strategies that work better. Second, there should be an interaction between exactingness and incentives. When feedback is positive (lenient environments), subjects should exhibit less inconsistency in the presence of incentives because they will be more motivated to take care in executing successful strategies. On the other hand, when facing negative feedback (exacting environments), the search for better strategies should be intensified in the presence of incentives, thereby resulting in even greater inconsistency.

Experimental evidence

We conducted five experiments to test the above predictions and related issues. In Experiment 1, we investigated three levels of exactingness both with and without incentives. This study used what we call a *sharp* incentive scheme in which subjects were rewarded if their mean evaluation points over a series of trials were positive, but not otherwise. This allowed us to test Predictions 1 and 2.

In Experiment 2, we did not use explicit monetary rewards. Instead, arguing that self-determined aspirations are incentives, we manipulated subjects' aspirations of performance. This allowed us to test Prediction 2.

In Experiment 3, we tested the limits of our theoretical scheme by using an incentive scheme that did not make clear distinctions between successful and unsuccessful performance.

Because we were intrigued by the question of whether different mental sets during learning could lead to different levels of subsequent performance, we also ran a condition in which subjects were explicitly instructed to learn how to make decisions in the task as opposed to maximizing evaluation points. In Experiment 4, we compared the performance of these subjects with those in Experiments 1 and 2 under conditions in which all subjects' performance was evaluated by the same sharp evaluation scheme and when all had experience in the task. Finally, Experiment 5 tested Prediction 3 by having subjects perform the experimental task under conditions designed to mitigate the negative aspects of exactingness.

Experiment 1

Method

Subjects. The subjects in this and in our other experiments were all recruited in the same manner through advertisements placed around the University of Chicago. They were offered between $5 and $15 for participating in an experiment on decision making. Their mean age was 22.4 years, and their mean educational level was 2.9 years beyond high school. One hundred and twenty-one subjects participated in this experiment.

Task. The task, which was individually administered by microcomputer, involved making a series of decisions. As described above, subjects were shown a value of a predictor variable, W, and then required to give a response, Q. Immediate feedback on each decision was provided by way of a score labeled *evaluation points.* Subjects were told that the object of the game was to maximize evaluation points. Evaluation points were linearly related (negatively) to the squared difference between their response, Q, and the unobservable criterion, D (see Equation 7.1), though this was not known to subjects.

More specifically, subjects were told that they were to set a value of a "DECISION VARIABLE that can vary between 1 and 1000." Moreover, "At the time you make this decision you will see the value of another variable called W. Your performance in each period of the game will be measured by a variable called EVALUATION POINTS." As part of the feedback, subjects were also told that they would "see the values of 2 other variables that could be useful to you in your decision making. These are called A and B." A and B were variables that could have provided limited but useful information for subjects who achieved a more advanced understanding of the way the underlying system worked.[7] Subjects were permitted to take notes and were also given the ability to scroll back the computer screen and examine data from past decisions.

The relation between the unobservable criterion, D, and W was subject to a small random disturbance so that the same evaluation points would not necessarily be observed if subjects repeated a response to the same W – see Equation 7.2. (The correlation between W and D was high, $r = .99$.) W was normally distributed with a mean of 70 and a standard deviation of 7.

Design and procedure

Each subject was allocated at random to one of six groups created by crossing two levels of incentives (incentives vs. no incentives) by three types of environment (lenient, intermediate, and exacting) so that there were 20 subjects in each group. (One group had 21 subjects.) Subjects in the no-incentives condition were informed, "Your pay for this part of the experiment will not depend on how well you do in the game." In contrast, subjects in the incentives condition were told that their pay would depend on how well they performed. Specifically, their pay would depend on the mean evaluation points achieved over 30 trials with one cent for each point above zero. Thus remuneration could vary between $0.00 and $5.00. Feedback concerning mean evaluation points earned to date was continually updated and displayed on the screen of the microcomputer used for administering the task for all subjects. We specifically maintained this information on the screen so that subjects would be aware of how well they were doing and whether they were likely to be paid for participating in this part of the experiment (i.e., whether their mean score was above or below zero).

Differences in exactingness of the environment were manipulated by changing the constant of proportionality, α, in Equation 7.1. For the lenient environment, $\alpha = .01$; for the intermediate environment, $\alpha = .05$; and for the exacting environment, $\alpha = .50$. We chose these values after observing outcomes associated with simulated strategies that differed in accuracy as measured by π (see Equation 7.4).

At the outset of the experiment, subjects were told that they would make 30 decisions. This was Round 1. After completing this task, they were first asked to rank themselves in percentile terms regarding how well they thought they had performed in the task relative to other University of Chicago students. They were then told that they were to play a second series of 30 trials under exactly the same conditions. This was Round 2. Next, subjects were asked to complete a questionnaire that quizzed them about their understanding of the model underlying the task (i.e., relations between variables, and so on). They were then asked to complete a further series of 30 trials for Round 3. For this round, however, subjects who had previously been in the no-incentives condition were required to make their decisions under the same incentives conditions as the other subjects. The question on self-ranking of performance was also repeated after Rounds 2 and 3. In this experiment we consider only responses for Rounds 1 and 2. Round 3 responses form part of the data for Experiment 4.

In short, the design of Experiment 1 involved two between-subject variables, one with two levels (incentives vs. no incentives), and the other with three (lenient, intermediate, and exacting environments). There were two rounds each involving 30 trials, and subjects completed a questionnaire about their understanding of the task after the second round.

Results

As discussed above, the differential effects of positive and negative feedback are an important element of our theoretical model. A check on whether subjects did observe mainly positive, mixed, or negative feedback in the different environments is provided by the proportions of subjects in each condition whose mean evaluation points were greater than zero in Round 2 (when subjects were more experienced in the task). These were. .68, .46, and .05 for the lenient, intermediate, and exacting environments, respectively.

Performance (π). Table 7.1 and Figures 7.1 and 7.2 provide overviews of the results. For all six experimental conditions, the top two sections of Table 7.1 report means and standard deviations by rounds regarding performance (π) and evaluation points (i.e., the penalty functions actually experienced by the subjects).

Table 7.1. *Experiment 1: Performance (π), evaluation points, and inconsistency in lenient, intermediate, and exacting environments*

	Incentives			No incentives		
Round	Lenient	Intermediate	Exacting	Lenient	Intermediate	Exacting
Performance (π)						
1						
M	331	309	274	263	317	287
SD	73	89	77	77	67	71
2						
M	386	393	328	314	394	351
SD	74	98	93	84	66	87
Evaluation points						
1						
M	−10	−2812	−40,569	−390	−2455	−36,809
SD	362	1977	18,853	451	1747	18,907
2						
M	230	−1098	−27,065	−80	−787	−21,537
SD	267	2137	21,719	427	1340	20,393
Inconsistency (σ_z)						
1						
M	167	209	229	229	206	222
2						
M	74	92	150	140	99	137

Figure 7.1 shows performance (π) achieved by subjects in the three different environments for both rounds. The upward sloping lines indicate that performance (π) improved across rounds, that is, learning occurred. Subjects in the intermediate condition outperformed those in both the lenient and the exacting environments – Prediction 1.

Figure 7.2 displays the overall mean performance (π) across both rounds for each of the six experimental conditions and, in particular, the effects of incentives. There is clear evidence of an Incentives × Exactingness interaction – Prediction 2. Subjects in the lenient–incentives condition outperformed those in the lenient–no-incentives condition, mean of 359 versus 289; and subjects in the exacting–no-incentives condition outperformed those in the exacting–incentives condition, mean of 319 versus 301. Finally, there was essentially no difference between the mean scores of the incentives and the no-incentives groups in the intermediate environment, 351 versus 356.

As for formal tests of our predictions using performance (π) as the dependent variable, a repeated measures analysis of variance (ANOVA) (with round as the repeated measure) showed main effects for round, $F(1, 115) = 142.8$, $MS_e = 1748$, $p < .001$, and exactingness, $F(2, 115) = 3.56$, $MS_e = 11,209$, $p = .03$, as well as a significant Incentives × Exactingness interaction, $F(2, 115)$

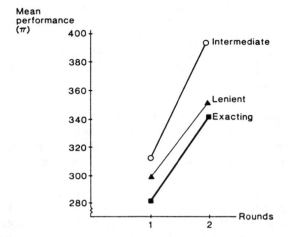

Figure 7.1. Experiment 1: Mean performance (π) by types of environment (lenient, intermediate, and exacting) across rounds.

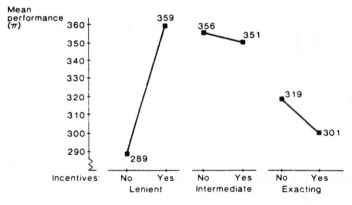

Figure 7.2. Experiment 1: Mean performance (π) for Rounds 1 and 2 by experimental conditions.

= 4.00, MS_e = 11,209, p = .02. Round did not interact with any of the other variables.

Looking at the results in terms of planned comparisons, mean performance (π) of the intermediate condition in Round 1, 313, was not significantly greater than that of the lenient and exacting conditions, 297 and 281, respectively. However, the Round 2 performance (π) measures of 394 for intermediate versus 350 for lenient, and 339 for exacting, were significant, $t(79)$ = 2.31, p = .02, for the former, and $t(79)$ = 2.82, p = .006, for the latter. In addition, separate ANOVAs on the data in the lenient and exacting conditions showed that the predicted Incentives × Exactingness interactions were significant both in Round 1, $F(1, 76) = 5.81$, $MS_e = 5574$, $p = .018$, and Round 2, $F(1, 76) = 6.29$, $MS_e = 7202$, $p = .014$.

Further insight into these interactions can be gleaned by contrasts between the two incentives conditions within each of the three types of environment. Within the lenient environment, subjects in the incentives condition had superior performance (π) to the others in both Rounds 1 and 2, with respectively, means of 331 versus 263, $t(38) = 2.84$, $p = .007$, and 386 versus 314, $t(38) = 2.90$, $p = .006$. The differences between the mean performance (π) of incentives and no-incentives subjects in both the intermediate and exacting conditions were not statistically significant in either Round 1 or Round 2.

Parenthetically, we note that subjects in all experimental conditions were unbiased in that the average error of their decisions was not significantly different from zero in any of the rounds. This suggests that subjects responded appropriately to the nature of the symmetric penalty functions in their feedback.

Inconsistency of response strategies. Underlying our theoretical model is the notion that, after negative feedback, subjects shift response strategies, whereas after positive feedback, they persist with and refine the same strategies. Moreover, the impact of incentives is to accentuate these effects. Before examining this, we first define inconsistency in operational terms.

Imagine that subjects' response strategies can be modeled by the regression of their responses, Q, on W, that is,

$$Q = \beta'_0 + \beta'_1 W + z. \tag{7.8}$$

A measure of the inconsistency of response strategy implied by this model is σ_z, that is, the conditional standard deviation of Q given W. This measures the variance in subjects' responses that is not systematically related to W and can be thought of as indicating the extent to which subjects varied their response strategies.[8] We note, however, that observed inconsistency in strategies can have two sources. One is inconsistent use of valid strategies as a result of, for example, lack of attention. The second is the result of experimentation or deliberately trying out alternative strategies. Mean values of estimates of σ_z are reported at the foot of Table 7.1 by experimental condition.

Because the level of perceived negative feedback increases with exactingness (see above), strategies would be expected to be more inconsistent as exactingness increases. Analysis of variance on measures of σ_z for both rounds of Experiment 1 reveals a significant effect for exactingness in Round 2, $F(2, 115) = 3.15$, $MS_e = 7894$, $p = .047$ but not for Round 1. For Round 2, mean estimates of inconsistency are 107, 96, and 144 for the lenient, intermediate, and exacting environments, respectively. Thus, inconsistency in the exacting environment ($\alpha = .50$) is greater than in the lenient ($\alpha = .01$) and intermediate ($\alpha = .05$) conditions.

It is important to note, however, that this pattern does not match performance (π), which, as reported above, was superior in the intermediate environment. Indeed, that performance in the intermediate condition is greater than in the lenient and, yet, inconsistency does not differ significantly between conditions, accords well with the assumption that exactingness exerts both positive and negative effects on performance (see Equation 7.5). In particular, even though subjects in the intermediate condition are just as inconsistent as subjects in the lenient condition, they are able to learn better strategies.

As for incentives, the pattern of inconsistency would be expected to mirror that of performance, that is, there should be an interaction between incentives and exactingness. This follows from the assumption that incentives accentuate the effects of exactingness by both reinforcing the consistent use of successful strategies (i.e., causing subjects to take more care in execution) and intensifying changes in strategy following the observation of negative feedback. To test this, we performed ANOVAs on both the 3×2 design of the experiment (i.e., 3 levels of Exactingness $\times$ 2 levels of Incentives) and a 2×2 design that omitted the intermediate level of exactingness. For the full design, a repeated measures analysis shows a main effect for round, $F(1, 115) = 217.4$, $MS_e = 2493$, $p < .001$, indicating a significant decrease in inconsistency across rounds (see Table 7.1), but the predicted Incentives $\times$ Exactingness interaction is only marginally significant $F(2, 115) = 2.69$, $MS_e = 11,947$, $p = .07$. For the reduced design, however, in addition to the effect for round, $F(1, 76) = 108.4$, $MS_e = 2744$, $p < .001$, the predicted interaction is significant, $F(1, 76) = 4.44$, $MS_e = 12,505$, $p = .038$.

Further results. Other sources of data shed light on the processes that gave rise to the observed effects. One datum collected by the microcomputer was time (in minutes) taken by subjects to complete each round. These averaged 22.4 and 14.6 for Rounds 1 and 2, respectively. A repeated measures ANOVA (with round as the repeated measure) showed a significant main effect for round, $F(1, 115) = 96.7$, $MS_e = 38.5$, $p < .001$, but no significant effects for either incentives or environment and no Incentive $\times$ Environment interaction. In addition, round did not interact with the other variables. On the other hand, performance (π) was correlated at the individual level with time spent on the task, $r = .21$, $p < .05$, and .29, $p < .01$, for Rounds 1 and 2, respectively. We therefore reanalyzed performance (π) with time as a covariate using a repeated measures analysis (with round as the repeated measure and on the complete 3×2 design). Once again, main effects were observed for round, $F(1, 114) = 87.7$, $MS_e = 1752$, $p < .001$, and for exactingness, $F(2, 114) = 3.30$, $MS_e = 10,545$, $p = .04$. In addition, the predicted Incentives $\times$ Exactingness interaction was significant, $F(2, 114) = 3.72$, $MS_e = 10,545$, $p = .03$.

Recall that at the end of each round, subjects were asked to rank their performance in percentile terms vis-à-vis other University of Chicago students. Overall, the mean rankings were at the 45.1 and 54.9 percentiles for Rounds 1 and 2, respectively. A repeated measures ANOVA showed the difference between Rounds 1 and 2 to be significant, $F(1, 115) = 49.8$, $MS_e = 114.8$, $p < .001$, as well as a Round $\times$ Exactingness interaction, $F(2, 115) = 5.59$, $MS_e = 114.8$, $p = .005$. (Mean rankings increased more between rounds for subjects in the intermediate as opposed to other conditions.) At the individual level, it is of interest to note that whereas there was essentially no relation between self-assessed rank and feedback (i.e., evaluation points) for Round 1, $r = .10$, ns, this was not the case for Round 2, where the analogous correlation was .42, $p < .001$. Experience with the task apparently helped subjects assess their own performance more accurately in relative terms.

The questionnaire completed after Round 2 contained two kinds of questions. The first were direct questions concerning which variables subjects deemed most important as well as whether they thought that "the outcomes of the game (i.e., evaluation points) are determined according to some systematic set of rules." With regard to the latter, there was an interesting effect for exactingness. Subjects in the intermediate condition (who performed best) rated outcomes as being determined by a more systematic set of rules than subjects in the other conditions, mean of 5.41 on a 7-point scale versus 4.40 for lenient and 3.89 for exacting, $F(2, 113) = 6.96$, $MS_e = 3.49$, $p = .001$. The contrast of intermediate versus lenient was significant, $t(79) = 2.58$, $p = .01$, as was the contrast of intermediate versus exacting, $t(77) = 3.66$, $p < .001$.

Subjects were also asked to write "How does the game work?" by specifying the roles played by the different variables and their interrelations, and while imagining having "to explain to an agent how to play the game in your behalf," to give "a simple description of the system to convey a general sense of how it works" as well as "any specific tips you might have to achieve high evaluation points." The answers to these questions were graded like an examination using a preestablished checklist of criteria. Of particular interest was whether subjects articulated both the sign and slope of the critical relation between W and the decision variable. Each subject's questionnaire was scored on 4-point scales for both variables. We also gave each subject a total understanding score which, in addition to the scores for sign and slope, took into account their understanding that there were two types of error (i.e., setting the decision variable too high as well as too low), recognizing an identity between the decision variable and the sum of A and B (the two secondary feedback variables, see above), and whether they gave any valid tips to an "agent." The total score was calculated by summing the scores of the components (Einhorn & Hogarth, 1975). The ratings of the questionnaires were made independently by two of the authors and their judgments were averaged. As an indication of reliability, the correlation between the scores of the two judges on the total index was .85, $p < .001$.

Statistical analyses of the various indices revealed effects due to exactingness whereby subjects in the intermediate condition showed superior understanding to those in the lenient and exacting environments in a manner paralleling Prediction 1. The appropriate means for the slope index were .91 for intermediate versus .53 and .26 for the lenient and exacting, respectively, $F(2, 115) = 5.46$, $MS_e = .79$, $p = .005$; the analogous figures for the sign index were 1.40 versus .95 and .78, ns; for appreciation of errors, .88 versus .22 and .28, $F(2, 115) = 11.72$, $MS_e = .47$, $p < .001$; and for the total index, 4.03 versus 2.49 and 2.22, $F(2, 115) = 6.42$, $MS_e = 6.04$, $p = .002$.

The indices were also related to performance (π) at the individual subject level. Across all subjects, the correlations between performance (π) and the sign index in Rounds 1 and 2 were .38, and .51, respectively, $p < .001$ for both. The corresponding figures for the slope index were .40 and .55, $p < .001$ for both. In addition, the correlations between performance across rounds and the index of total knowledge were .47, and .64, $p < .001$ for both.

Finally, we found no significant differences when we analyzed results by demographic variables (e.g., age, gender, mathematics and science background vs. nonmathematics and science background).

Discussion

In short, the results of Experiment 1 validate two of our theoretical predictions. First, performance was seen to have an inverted-U-shaped relation with exactingness, that is, performance was better in the intermediate as opposed to the lenient or the exacting environments (Prediction 1).

Second, incentives interacted with exactingness in their effects on performance (Prediction 2). In lenient environments, incentives improved performance; however, incentives were ineffective in intermediate and exacting environments. Indeed, the data suggest deleterious effects of incentives in exacting environments.

In addition to performance, other data supported the main results. First, a measure of inconsistency in strategy use showed that this varied with exactingness. In addition, inconsistency mirrored the Incentives × Exactingness interaction.

Second, subjects in the intermediate condition reported finding the task as having been generated by a more systematic set of rules. Their written analyses also showed greater understanding of the task. Related to this were the strong correlations between measures of understanding and performance at the individual level. These are important findings and speak to the issue of whether and when verbalizable knowledge and performance are related. In some studies, Broadbent and his colleagues have found no relation between the ability to verbalize understanding of relations between variables learned through taking decisions and performance (Berry & Broadbent, 1984; Broadbent, 1977; Broadbent & Aston, 1978). However, more recent work suggests that when the relation between decision and action is salient (as in the case of simple tasks), performance and verbalizable knowledge could well be related (Berry & Broadbent, 1988; Broadbent, FitzGerald, & Broadbent, 1986).

Finally, this study employed a sharp incentive scheme whereby subjects in the incentives condition were only remunerated if they had positive mean scores for evaluation points. Thus, it is tempting to argue that the lack of a positive effect for incentives in the exacting environment was due to subjects giving up when they realized that they had little chance of achieving a positive score. (In the exacting condition, discerning subjects who had made bad errors could realize that it would be impossible for them to break even by the end of the round.) Two arguments mitigate against this explanation. First, as reported above, we found no significant time differences by experimental conditions. Second, we reanalyzed the data to check for trends in learning by experimental conditions, both across the 30 trials and blocks of 5 trials within rounds, paying particular attention to behavior toward the end of each round (where giving up would be most likely to occur). We found no evidence of giving up.

Experiment 2

Rationale

As noted in our review of the literature, incentives can take many forms. In this experiment we consider the incentives implicit in targets or aspirations that people set for themselves. Our argument is the following: Aspirations are a form of incentives and therefore, like monetary payments, should accentuate both the positive and the negative aspects of exactingness. Thus, in terms of the model in Equation 7.5, high aspirations imply larger b and c coefficients than low aspirations. This, in turn, implies an interaction between aspirations and exactingness: In lenient environments, high aspirations should lead to better performance than low aspirations; as exactingness increases, however, this difference should reverse. In other words, the use of aspirations permits a further test of Prediction 2.

Method

Subjects. There were 80 subjects recruited in the same manner and from the same population as Experiment 1.

Task. The task was identical to the no-incentives condition used in Experiment 1 except that we modified the instructions and the information display to manipulate aspirations.

Design and procedure. Each subject was allocated at random to one of four groups created by crossing two levels of aspirations (high vs. low) by two types of environment (lenient vs. exacting) so that there were 20 subjects in each group. (We did not include an intermediate exactingness condition in this experiment.) Assuming that subjects like to compare their performance with that of similar others, we manipulated aspirations by informing subjects of the median average score achieved by other University of Chicago students who had participated in the experiment before them. This figure was provided in the instructions (on the microcomputer screen) before subjects began Rounds 1 and 2 and remained on the screen throughout each round. In fact, the actual median was not used. Instead, subjects in the low-aspirations condition were given the score corresponding to the .10 fractile of the empirical distribution of scores in the appropriate lenient or exacting conditions of Experiment 1. For subjects in the high-aspirations condition, it was the score corresponding to the .90 fractile. Consistent with the data from Experiment 1, these medians showed improvement for Round 2 over Round 1.

As in Experiment 1, there were two rounds consisting of 30 decisions each. After each round, subjects were asked to rank themselves in percentile terms regarding how well they thought they had performed the task relative to other University of Chicago students. After Round 2, subjects completed the same questionnaire used in Experiment 1. After this, subjects completed a third round that differed from the others in that no aspirations were provided, and all subjects played under an incentives condition in exactly the same manner as Round 3 of Experiment 1. The data from this third round are reported below as part of Experiment 4.

Because of the deception involved in the experimental manipulation, subjects were contacted individually after the experiment was completed and were thoroughly debriefed. This involved providing full details concerning the underlying rationale for the study and the nature of the deception. Subjects were also offered a written summary of the study and results.

Results

Because aspirations were manipulated by providing the median performance of other University of Chicago students, subjects' rankings of their own performance relative to the same population provide a check on the effectiveness of the manipulation. Specifically, subjects in the high-aspirations condition would be expected to assess their relative rank lower than those in the low-aspirations condition. This was the case. Mean percentile ranks, for high versus low, were 34 versus 64, and 41 versus 69 for Rounds 1 and 2, respectively. These differences were statistically significant, $F(1, 76) = 69.7$, $MS_e = 267$, $p < .001$ for Round 1, and $F(1, 76) = 41.2$, $MS_e = 423$, $p < .001$ for Round 2.

Performance (π). Table 7.2 reports means and standard deviations by rounds for performance (π) and evaluation points.

Table 7.2. *Experiment 2: Performance (π) and evaluation points among subjects with high and low aspirations in lenient and exacting environments*

	High		Low	
Round	Lenient	Exacting	Lenient	Exacting
Performance (π)				
1				
M	299	250	280	298
SD	64	67	73	87
2				
M	364	337	315	345
SD	60	93	84	91
Evaluation points				
1				
M	−180	−47,196	−247	−35,148
SD	339	18,249	394	22,589
2				
M	152	−26,390	−55	−22,326
SD	245	21,192	484	19,023

A repeated measures ANOVA on performance (π) (with round as the repeated measure) reveals a single main effect for round (thereby indicating learning), $F(1, 76) = 96.0$, $MS_e = 1419$, $p < .001$, an Incentives × Round interaction, $F(1, 76) = 8.77$, $MS_e = 1419$, $p = .004$, and a marginally significant Aspiration Level × Exactingness interaction, $F(1, 76) = 3.46$, $MS_e = 10,947$, $p = .067$. These two interactions are illuminated by separate ANOVAs for each round that show a significant Aspiration Level × Exactingness interaction for Round 1, $F(1, 76) = 4.02$, $MS_e = 6924$, $p = .049$, but not for Round 2. Moreover, the nature of the interaction supports Prediction 2, that is, in the lenient environment, high aspiration subjects outperform those with low aspirations; in the exacting environment, it is the reverse.

Inconsistency of response strategies. There were neither significant main effects nor interactions involving the measure of inconsistency of response strategies.

Further results. Time spent on the task was similar to that in Experiment 1 with means of 21.0 and 15.0 min for Rounds 1 and 2, respectively. Across experimental conditions, the only statistically significant difference on time was between rounds, $F(1, 76) = 48.3$, $MS_e = 29.7$, $p < .001$. As in Experiment 1, time spent on the task was significantly correlated at the individual level with performance (π) for both Round 1, $r = .30$, $p < .01$, and Round 2, $r = .38$, $p = .001$.

With respect to the questionnaire administered after Round 2, there were no significant main effects or interactions for the sign and slope indices. (Recall that unlike Experiment 1 there was no intermediate exactingness condition.) However, the indices did correlate significantly with performance (π) at the individual level. For sign, the correlations for Rounds 1 and 2 were, respectively, .51, and .62; for slope, .48 and .54; and for the index of total knowledge, .58 and .71, $p < .001$ for all.

Discussion

These data provide further support for Prediction 2 in that there was a significant Incentives × Exactingness interaction when incentives were operationalized by aspirations as opposed to cash rewards. In addition, there were significant correlations between the ability to articulate understanding of the task and performance.

The main result, however, is weaker than that of Experiment 1 in that although the predicted Incentives × Exactingness interaction was significant in Round 1, it was not significant in Round 2. A possible reason for the weaker effect is that subjects might have been uncertain as to whether feedback should be interpreted as positive or negative. On the one hand, one can imagine subjects coding outcomes as successes or failures relative to the aspiration levels implicit in the task instructions. On the other hand, subjects could also have been responding to whether outcomes yielded positive or negative scores for evaluation points. For example, whereas 29 (of 40) and 2 (of 40) subjects achieved positive mean evaluation point scores for Round 2 in the lenient and exacting environments, respectively, only 1 (out of 20) subjects in the lenient–high-aspirations condition achieved a score above the aspiration level, and 18 (out of 20) achieved a score above the aspiration level in the exacting–low-aspirations condition. This weaker effect of the Incentives × Exactingness interaction, and the possible confusion in interpreting feedback as positive or negative, was further evidenced by the fact that there were no significant effects for inconsistency in strategy use.

Our manipulation of aspirations inevitably leads to comparisons with work on goal setting. One of the most consistent results from this literature is the comparison between situations where people are given high, explicit goals as opposed to being told to do their best. High, explicit goals, it is claimed, lead to better performance than more vague "do your best" goals (Locke, Shaw, Saari, & Latham, 1981). In a recent study, Earley, Connolly, and Ekegren (1989) demonstrated limits to this empirical regularity. Specifically, in a prediction task subjects who were given high, explicit goals in terms of stringent conditions on allowable prediction error performed worse than subjects who were given "do your best" goals. If we equate Earley et al.'s stringent conditions with our exacting environment, the results are consistent and support the notion that when subjects fail to reach high goals, subsequent changes in strategy can lead to lower performance. Earley et al.

further point out that in the tasks on which the empirical regularity summarized by Locke et al. is based, performance is typically measured by quantity of outputs (e.g., number of judgments) as opposed to quality (e.g., mean predictive accuracy). Whereas a direct relation may be expected between effort and quantity of outputs, it is not clear that effort and quality would be related in the same way.

In fact, by combining experimental conditions from Experiments 1 and 2, it is possible to test directly the differential effects of high, explicit versus "do your best" goals. Specifically, consider the comparison between subjects in the high-aspirations group of Experiment 2 and the no-incentives condition of Experiment 1. Using a repeated measures ANOVA (with round as the repeated measure), there was a significant Instructions (no incentives vs. high aspirations) × Exactingness interaction, $F(1, 76) = 4.79$, $MS_e = 9802$, $p = .03$. In the lenient environment, high aspirations led to better performance in accordance with the goal-setting literature, mean of 332 versus 289; in the exacting environment, however, the relation was reversed, mean of 294 versus 319. In addition, although there was a main effect for round (indicating improvement from Round 1 to Round 2), $F(1, 76) = 97.1$, $MS_e = 1832$, $p < .001$, round did not interact with the other variables. Finally, in terms of contrasts within conditions of exactingness, the only statistically significant main effect was within the lenient environment, where the high-aspirations group outperformed the no-incentives subjects in Round 2, mean performance (π) of 364 versus 314, $t(38) = 2.17$, $p = .037$.

Experiment 3

Rationale

The incentive scheme used in Experiment 1 contained an important discontinuity in that subjects were remunerated only if their scores on mean evaluation points were positive. In Experiment 2, where incentives took the form of induced aspirations, effects were weaker. Moreover, we speculated that this might have been due to ambiguity concerning the positive or negative nature of feedback. Taken together, these results (as well as our theoretical framework) suggest limitations on the types of incentives that are likely to have an impact. Specifically, if feedback from incentive schemes does not clearly distinguish between positive and negative outcomes, incentives are far less likely to affect performance in the form of an Incentives × Environment interaction (Prediction 2).[9] Experiment 3 was designed to test this issue.

Method

Subjects. There were 80 subjects recruited in the same manner and from the same population as Experiments 1 and 2.

Task. The task was identical to that used in Experiment 1 except that we modified the payment scheme in the incentives condition. On the basis of the distribution of mean evaluation scores in Experiment 1, we created a function linking mean evaluation points to remuneration so that even though the function always indicated greater rewards for better performance, poor performance would always receive some reward. To make the reward associated with a perfect score the same as in Experiment 1, we restricted payment from $0 to $5. The range of evaluation points remunerated was from −58,900 to +500, and the function was nonlinear in that it was flatter for low scores (e.g., a 100-point improvement at the high end of the evaluation points scale brought greater incremental rewards than at the low end). So that subjects would clearly understand the relation between performance and payment, each was provided with a chart that showed how remuneration varied with mean evaluation points.

Design and procedure. Each subject was allocated at random to one of four groups created by crossing two levels of incentives (incentives vs. no incentives) by two types of environment (lenient vs. exacting) so that there were 20 subjects in each group. Subjects completed two rounds of 30 trials and completed a questionnaire after Round 2. (As in the previous experiments, subjects also completed a third round of 30 trials in which all subjects were in the same incentives condition.)

Results

Performance. There were no statistically significant effects in terms of performance (π). Averaged across both rounds, mean scores (π) in the lenient environment were 325 and 316 for the incentives and no-incentives conditions, respectively. For the exacting environment, the corresponding figures were 316 and 324. A repeated measures ANOVA (with round at the repeated measure) showed main effects only for round, mean of 289 for Round 1 and 352 for Round 2, $F(1, 77) = 102.13$, $MS_e = 1543$, $p < .001$, and no significant interactions.

Inconsistency of response strategies. The data revealed a main effect within both rounds whereby subjects in the lenient environment exhibited less inconsistency, mean of 188 versus 222 for Round 1, $F(1, 77) = 4.60$, $MS_e = 5152$, $p = .039$; and 95 versus 138 for Round 2, $F(1, 77) = 5.17$, $MS_e = 7235$, $p = .026$.

Further results. Despite the lack of effects in performance (π) between experimental conditions, subjects' experiences with the task differed. First, subjects in the incentives condition spent more time, means of 28.7 min versus 21.1 min in Round 1, $F(1, 77) = 6.26$, $MS_e = 186.8$, $p = .015$; and 16.9 min versus 13.4 min in Round 2, $F(1, 77) = 4.33$, $MS_e = 55.5$, $p = .041$. However, using time as a covariate did not alter the results for performance (π).

Second, subjects in the lenient condition ranked their own performance higher after both Round 1 and Round 2, means of 53.8 versus 41.2, $F(1, 77) = 7.78$, $MS_e = 392$, $p = .007$, and 64.9 versus 47.6, $F(1, 77) = 13.99$, $MS_e = 430$, $p < .001$.

On the basis of the questionnaire administered after Round 2, subjects in the lenient condition also rated outcomes as being determined by a more systematic set of rules with a mean of 5.16 versus 4.18 on a 7-point scale, $F(1, 77) = 6.27$, $MS_e = 3.13$, $p = .014$. Relative to the questionnaire administered in Experiment 1, this questionnaire contained some additional questions (also on 7-point scales) about the process. Mean scores on this questionnaire revealed that, relative to the exacting environment, subjects in the lenient condition found the task more enjoyable, 3.95 versus 3.08, $F(1, 77) = 7.59$, $MS_e = 2.05$, $p = .007$; less frustrating, 4.05 versus 5.35, $F(1, 77) = 13.7$, $MS_e = 2.50$, $p = .004$; less challenging, 4.77 versus 5.80, $F(1, 77) = 13.6$, $MS_e = 1.58$, $p < .001$; and less discouraging, 3.40 versus 5.25, $F(1, 77) = 27.7$, $MS_e = 2.51$, $p < .001$. They also stated that they put less effort into the task, 4.17 versus 4.96, $F(1, 53) = 5.74$, $MS_e = 1.52$, $p = .020$, and fewer reported thinking about giving up, 25% versus 60%, $F(1, 77) = 11.5$, $MS_e = .022$, $p = .001$. However, there was no difference between the proportions of subjects reporting having given up.

Analyses of subjects' descriptions of how the game worked revealed only one statistically significant result. This was an interaction between incentives and environment concerning subjects' appreciation that there were two types of error in the task. Within the lenient environment, this was better understood by subjects in the incentives condition, mean of .80 versus .50, whereas the relation reversed in the exacting environment, .24 versus .65, $F(1, 77) = 2.56$, $MS_e = 0.60$, $p = .040$.

Once again, indices of understanding were correlated with performance (π) at the individual level. Across all subjects, the correlations between performance (π) and the sign index in Rounds 1 and 2 were, respectively, .22, $p = .05$, and .42, $p < .001$. The corresponding figures for the slope index were .21, ns, and .38, $p = .001$. In addition, the correlations between performance across rounds and the index of total knowledge were .38, $p = .001$, and .53, $p < .001$.

Discussion

Experiment 3 was similar to Experiment 1 except that (a) there was no intermediate exactingness condition, and (b) we changed the nature of the incentives scheme so that there was no longer a discontinuity between performance that was rewarded and performance that was not rewarded. Underlying this manipulation was the hypothesis that incentives are more likely to have an effect on performance (π) if they clearly discriminate between positive and negative feedback, a hypothesis that is consistent with these results.

Despite the lack of an Incentives × Environment interaction on performance (π) with this incentive scheme, supplementary evidence indicated that subjects in the different experimental conditions did not have the same experience of the task. Under incentives, subjects took longer to perform the task. In the lenient environment, subjects' use of strategies showed less inconsistency, and they generally found the task less aversive than in the exacting environment.

Experiment 4

Rationale

There are two major, practical questions for the present line of research. First, what combinations of incentives and exactingness are most effective for learning? Second, once people have acquired a certain level of expertise, does performance reflect carryover effects from conditions experienced during learning (cf. Schwartz, 1982)? Recall that an important conceptual consideration underlying our work is the notion that outcome feedback confounds two kinds of information. One is information concerning the structure of the underlying system in which decisions are being made (i.e., how variables are related). The second relates to how well the decision maker is performing the task. Given this ambiguity, it is reasonable to assume that concentrating attention only on the structure of the task during learning should improve subsequent performance. Experiment 4 was designed to test this hypothesis. During two 30-trial rounds subjects were instructed to concentrate only on learning the task used in Experiments 1 and 2 (instead of maximizing evaluation points). They were then switched to an incentives condition in a third round, and their performance was compared with the Round 3 incentives performance of the subjects in Experiments 1 and 2 who had learned the task under different conditions.

Method

Subjects. There were 201 subjects, 80 of whom had participated in Experiment 1 and 80 of whom had participated in Experiment 2. The 41 subjects who participated only in this experiment came from the same population as the other experiments and were recruited in the same manner.

Task. For the 41 subjects participating uniquely in Experiment 4, the task was the same as Experiment 1 with two exceptions. First, instructions differed in that subjects were told, "The object of this game is to maximize EVALUATION POINTS. However, in playing the game you should not be concerned with how well you do. Instead, your objective is to learn how the game works." In addition, half of the subjects were specifically told to expect to be asked how the game worked and to make their understanding explicit. Second, after Rounds 1 and 2 subjects did not rank their own performance. Instead they ranked how well they thought that they had understood the task relative to other University of Chicago students.

Design and procedure. The design of the study involved two between-subjects variables. These were prior learning conditions (with six levels) and exactingness of the environment (with two levels, lenient and exacting). Two levels of the prior learning conditions involved the 41 Experiment 4-only subjects, whom we shall refer to as the inference group and who were allocated at random to four subgroups. These were level of instructions (explicitly told to expect to have to explain their understanding of the game vs. not explicitly told) and exactingness of the task environment (lenient vs. exacting, using the same parameters as Experiments 1 and 2). Thus, inference group subjects had two rounds of 30 trials in which their task was to discover how the system worked; they then completed the same questionnaire used in Experiments 1 and 2 before being switched in Round 3 to the same incentives condition experienced by subjects in those experiments. Apart from the differences in the task noted above, procedures for these subjects were exactly the same as in Experiment 1.

Two other levels of prior learning conditions were for incentives and no incentives and involved the 80 Experiment 1 subjects who had been exposed to the lenient and exacting environments. The final two levels of prior learning were the high- and low-aspirations conditions from Experiment 2.[10]

Results

We first note that there were no significant main effects or interactions involving the difference in the levels of the instructions given to inference group subjects concerning whether they would be asked later on to explain their understanding of the game. We therefore ignore this experimental manipulation and analyze the results as arising from a 5 × 2 design (i.e., 5 prior Learning Conditions × 2 Levels of Exactingness).

Before discussing the results of performance in Round 3, it is important to note that subjects in the inference group took, on average, 54% longer than the others to complete the experimental tasks, $t(199) = 5.64$, $p < .001$. Mean times were 33.2 min versus 21.5 min in Round 1, 23.6 versus 14.2 in Round 2, and 18.0 versus 13.0 in Round 3. This result is particularly interesting because subjects in all experiments were given the same expectations concerning remuneration for participation and had identical incentives in Round 3. In addition, neither group was told how much time to spend on the experimental tasks. Apparently giving subjects a set to learn induced a more careful approach (evidenced by time spent) that also carried over to the incentives condition in Round 3.

Table 7.3. *Selected results from Experiment 4*

		Prior condition				
				Aspirations		
Outcome	Inference	Incentives	No incentives	High	Low	M
Mean performance (π) for Round 3						
Lenient environment	389	399	347	384	313	366
Exacting environment	405	372	372	363	350	372
M	397	385	359	374	332	—
Indices of understanding						
Sign						
Lenient environment	1.74	1.43	.48	.93	.80	1.08
Exacting environment	1.33	.90	.65	.76	1.20	.97
M	1.54	1.17	.57	.35	1.00	—
Slope						
Lenient environment	.93	.83	.23	.33	.18	.50
Exacting environment	.80	.23	.30	.34	.88	.51
M	.87	.53	.27	.34	.53	—

The first panel of Table 7.3 summarizes data on mean accuracy scores for Round 3 in which all subjects were in the same incentives condition. The other panels report mean indices of understanding in respect of the sign and slope of the important predictive relation determining outcomes. These means are based on the questionnaire completed at the end of Round 2.

For performance (π), Table 7.3 shows little difference for the effect of exactingness of the environment, 366 versus 372. However, differences due to prior experimental treatments are large. Overall, the inference condition has the highest mean score, 397, compared with the poor showing of the low-aspirations group, 332. A 5×2 ANOVA only reveals a significant main effect for prior learning condition, $F(4, 191) = 3.37$, $MS_e = 7680$, $p = .011$, and no significant Prior Learning Condition $\times$ Exactingness interaction.

Contrasts between prior learning conditions permit more refined analyses. The inference group outperformed the no-incentives subgroup, 397 versus 359, $t(79) = 1.96$, $p = .053$, but there was no significant difference between the inference and incentive groups, 397 versus 385, $t(79) = .619$, $p = .538$. Similarly, the inference group significantly outperformed the low-aspirations group, 397 versus 332, $t(79) = 3.15$, $p = .002$, but not the high-aspirations group, 397 versus 374, $t(79) = 1.35$, $p = .181$.

In other words, averaged across both lenient and exacting environments, subjects who either learned under incentives in Rounds 1 and 2 or who were given high aspirations performed as well in Round 3 as the inference subjects who had been given a set to learn despite the fact that the latter took much longer to perform the task. The inference subjects did, however, perform better than subjects who, during the first two rounds were either in the no-incentives condition or who were given low aspirations.

Concerning the prior-aspirations conditions (high vs. low), there is a large difference in Round 3 performance of subjects who were previously exposed to high aspirations, 374, as opposed to those who were previously exposed to low aspirations, 332, $F(1, 76) = 4.00$ $MS_e = 8692$, $p = .049$, but no main effect for exactingness nor a significant interaction between exactingness and prior-aspirations conditions. Subjects in the low-aspirations group showed relatively poor performance in Round 2 (mean score of 330) and did not improve when switched to incentives in Round 3 (mean score of 332).

The inference group had the highest scores on the indices of understanding for both sign and slope. An ANOVA shows main effects for prior learning in respect of sign, $F(4, 190) = 3.64$, $MS_e = 1.45$, $p = .007$, and slope, $F(4, 190) = 3.28$, $MS_e = .67$, $p = .013$. In terms of contrasts, the mean score achieved by the inference group for sign of 1.54 was significantly greater than that achieved by the others, .89, $t(198) = 3.04$, $p = .003$. For slope, the analogous figures were .87 vs. .41, $t(198) = 3.10$, $p = .002$. Thus, in addition to more time spent on the task, the set to learn was accompanied by a greater ability to articulate the appropriate predictive relation.

Finally, correlations between individual scores on the understanding indices and performance were also high for the inference group. For Round 3, these were .69 for sign, .59 for slope, and .73 for the index of total knowledge, $p < .001$ for all. In addition, there was a relation between how well inference group subjects thought they had performed in the task after Round 3 and actual performance in evaluation points, $r = .51$, $p < .001$.

Discussion

The results of Experiment 4 show that performance in Round 3 (in which all subjects were in an incentives condition) reflects subjects' prior exposure to the decision-making task. The inference subjects outperformed those in the no-incentives and low-aspirations conditions but did no better on average than the incentives and high-aspirations groups. On the other hand, the inference subjects took on average 54% longer to complete the experimental tasks, which suggests that gains in performance should be measured against additional costs in time. Subjects who had previously been provided with low aspirations performed at a lower level than those who were given high aspirations. Finally, subjects in the inference condition were more capable of articulating an accurate understanding of the task.

Although the inference subjects were instructed to learn the game in Rounds 1 and 2 and thus ignore the evaluative dimension of feedback, it is unclear whether people can ignore the evaluative implications of any feedback. Two pieces of evidence support this notion. First, if exacting feedback has greater potential for learning, one would expect subjects in the exacting condition to have learned more effectively in the absence of evaluation. However, mean performance in Round 3 between inference subjects in the lenient and the exacting environments did not differ significantly, 389 versus 405. Second, whereas from our viewpoint scoring performance of the inference subjects lacks meaning for Rounds 1 and 2, these subjects still observed the evaluation points that they would have achieved. Moreover, their performance (π) was comparable with subjects in the other conditions, 283 versus 285 for Round 1, and 359 versus 342 for Round 2, thereby suggesting that they had not been penalized for experimenting more than subjects who had been instructed to maximize evaluation points.

A further interesting Round 3 comparison can be made between the level of performance (π) obtained by the inference group and subjects in the intermediate exactingness environment of Experiment 1. These were 397 for the former and 415 for the latter but did not differ significantly. In addition, there were no significant differences between the scores that both groups achieved on the sign and slope indices. In short, there were no significant differences in either performance or understanding between the inference subjects, averaging over lenient and exacting environments, and subjects in an environment of intermediate exactingness, averaging over conditions of incentives and no incentives. The data show that there are different paths to the same levels of performance and understanding.

Experiment 5

Rationale

Prediction 3 states that if the negative effects of exactingness (α) on performance (π) are eliminated, performance (π) should increase as a function of exactingness (α) – see Equation 7.5. Experiment 5 was designed to test this hypothesis. Further, because eliminating the negative effects of exactingness reduces the impact of negative feedback, inconsistency of response strategies should not be expected to increase with exactingness.

Method

Subjects. Subjects were recruited in the same manner and from the same population as in the other experiments. The plan was to have 80 subjects in the experiment but, because after running several subjects, it became clear that there were "outliers," a total of 90 subjects were finally recruited to participate in the task (see below).

Task. The task was identical to that used in Experiment 1 (using the same discontinuous incentive function) except that subjects were provided with feedback both in the form of evaluation points and the correct value of the decision variable, that is, D – see Equations 7.1 and 7.2. The rationale was that correct outcome feedback would eliminate the negative effects of exactingness because there would no longer be any ambiguity concerning the meaning of feedback expressed in evaluation points, that is, subjects could also measure performance by differences between Q, the decision variable, and D, the outcome.

Design and procedure. Each subject was allocated at random to one of four groups created by crossing two levels of incentives (incentives vs. no incentives) by two types of environment (lenient vs. exacting). As in previous experiments, there were three rounds each involving 30 trials. After Round 2, subjects completed a questionnaire, and in Round 3 all subjects faced the same incentives condition.

Results

Distributions of scores on individual performance (π) indicated several outliers. To eliminate outliers, we used two criteria based on performance achieved in Round 3 and time taken on the task. Subjects were eliminated if their performance was greater than five standard deviations from the mean of the distributions of their experimental conditions (excluding outliers), or if total time taken for the whole task was either under 20 min or over 3 hr. This left the data of 79 subjects for subsequent analysis, 20 in each of the lenient–incentives and exacting–no-incentives conditions, 18 in the exacting–incentives conditions, and 21 in the lenient–no-incentives conditions. Ten of the 11 subjects eliminated were in the exacting conditions.

Performance (π). Results by experimental conditions and rounds are presented in Table 7.4. Subjects in the exacting conditions outperformed those in the lenient conditions in all three rounds. Moreover, this difference in performance (π) is statistically significant in both Rounds 2 and 3, $F(1, 75) = 5.05$, $MS_e = 1987$, $p = .027$, and $F(1, 75) = 5.34$, $MS_e = 1547$, $p = .023$. The only other statistically significant effects for performance (π) are in respect of round, between Rounds 1 and 2, overall means of 427 and 471, $F(1, 73) = 128.9$, $MS_e = 62,381$, $p < .001$, but not between Rounds 2 and 3, means of 471 versus 476.

Inconsistency of response strategies. Subjects in the exacting environment were not more inconsistent in their use of response strategies than those in the lenient condition. If anything, their measures of inconsistency were smaller, with means averaged over Rounds 1 and 2 of 64 versus 84 for those in the lenient condition. This difference, however, was not statistically significant.

Further results. One important difference between subjects in the lenient and the exacting conditions was that the latter took more time to complete the task. Mean times by rounds were, for lenient and exacting, respectively, 30.1

Table 7.4. *Experiment 5: Performance (π) and evaluation points in lenient and exacting environments*

	Incentives		No incentives	
Round	Lenient	Exacting	Lenient	Exacting
Performance (π)				
1				
M	423	430	405	449
SD	62	79	93	38
2				
M	466	481	454	484
SD	46	32	66	18
3				
M	468	483	463	489
SD	50	22	54	6
Evaluation points				
1				
M	278	−10,075	210	−5397
SD	257	16,914	373	5919
2				
M	442	−594	398	−471
SD	151	2,823	210	1633
3				
M	445	−171	432	196
SD	146	1,614	141	606

versus 37.8 for Round 1, *ns*; 17.0 versus 21.0 for Round 2, $F(1, 75) = 4.74$, MS_e = 66.6, $p = .03$; and 15.0 versus 20.0 for Round 3, $F(1, 75) = 7.45$, $MS_e = 67.5$, p = .008. Using time as a covariate, reanalysis of the data showed no main effect for exactingness on performance (π) in any of the rounds. Time, however, was only weakly correlated with performance (π) at the individual level, $r =$ .21, *ns*, .29, $p < .05$, and .12, *ns*, for Rounds 1, 2, and 3, respectively.

In terms of the questionnaire administered after Round 2, the only statistically significant differences revealed for either attitudes toward the task or understanding of how the underlying system worked were that, in the exacting environment, subjects found the experience more discouraging than those in the lenient environment, means of 4.04 versus 2.43 on a 7-point scale, $F(1, 75) = 19.4$, $MS_e = 2.63$, $p < .001$. This was also true of subjects in the incentives as opposed to the no-incentives condition, means of 3.74 versus 2.73, $F(1, 75) = 7.64$, $MS_e = 2.63$, $p = .007$.

At the individual subject level, correlations between the indices of understanding and performance (π) were significant. For example, the correlation between the index of total understanding and performance was .38, $p = .001$, .53, $p < .001$, and .50, $p < .001$ for Rounds 1, 2, and 3, respectively.

Discussion

The main result from Experiment 5 was that subjects in the exacting environment outperformed those in the lenient environment, thereby validating Prediction 3. Another difference was that subjects in the exacting environment took more time to complete the task.

In addition to superior performance, further evidence that the provision of correct outcome feedback mitigated the negative aspect of exactingness was that inconsistency in strategy use was not significantly greater in the exacting condition.

Total time taken on the task by subjects in this experiment exceeded that in Experiments 1, 2, and 3, mean of 70.5 min versus 50.0, 49.0, and 53.4 min, respectively, $t(198) = 5.16$, $t(157) = 4.77$, and $t(159) = 3.94$, $p < .001$, for all. In fact, the total time taken in this experiment was similar to that in the inference condition of Experiment 4, mean of 74.8 min. That subjects in this experiment took more time than those in Experiments 1–3 might be rationalized by the fact that they had more information to consider, that is, revealed values of the D variable. On the other hand, this information also made the task easier to understand. Perhaps what these data suggest is that the presence of correct outcome feedback gave subjects more to think about when they were planning their decisions than in situations in which this information was absent. In the latter, one can imagine that because of ignorance, subjects put more emphasis on learning through taking action and observing, as opposed to thinking more about outcomes that were already observed.

We believe that caution should be exercised in interpreting our results because most of the outliers excluded from the data analysis were in the exacting conditions. For the most part, these subjects rushed through the task (in under 20 min) and their performance (π) showed little or no improvement from Rounds 1 to 3. Their data were so different from the majority of subjects in the exacting conditions that we had few scruples in eliminating them from analysis. On the other hand, they do also suggest that, for a minority of subjects, provision of the "correct" amount to be predicted, D, did not eliminate the negative aspect of exactingness on performance.

The astute reader will have noticed an additional implication of the model in Equation 7.5 with respect to the effects of incentives. When there are no negative effects of exactingness, incentives should improve performance (because $b' > b$). Why, then, was there no effect for incentives in the present experiment? The reason, we believe, is that because most subjects received positive feedback following their decisions, they did not experience a discontinuity between being rewarded and not being rewarded. In other words, for subjects the incentive function was experienced as being more like that in Experiment 3 than Experiment 1. For example, in Round 2 the percentages of subjects who received positive mean evaluation points were 85% and 74% in the lenient and exacting conditions, respectively. Thus, given the levels of performance achieved, the presence or absence of incentives did not differentially accentuate exactingness.

General discussion

We first review the major findings of our experiments, distinguishing between effects of exactingness, effects of incentives, and other issues. Subsequently, we discuss these results from both theoretical and practical perspectives. We also suggest topics for further study.

Effects of exactingness

Our experiments demonstrated that exactingness (α) has both positive and negative effects on performance. First, consistent with our theoretical model, we showed in Experiment 1 that an intermediate level of exactingness ($\alpha = .05$) resulted in superior performance to lenient ($\alpha = .01$) and exacting ($\alpha = .50$) environments – Prediction 1. Second, when the negative effects of exactingness were mitigated by using correct outcome feedback in addition to evaluation points (Experiment 5), performance (π) was better in the exacting environment – Prediction 3.

Critical to our underlying model was the assumption that, during learning, people react differently to positive and negative feedback. Positive feedback reinforces the use of existing strategies, negative feedback encourages the search for other strategies that might work better. Because positive feedback is likely in lenient environments, and negative feedback is likely in exacting environments, we postulated greater inconsistency in strategy use in exacting environments. This implication was validated in Experiments 1 and 3 but not in Experiment 2, in which incentives took the form of manipulated aspirations. On the other hand, as noted in the discussion of that experiment, whether feedback was encoded as positive or negative was ambiguous in that subjects could attend to aspiration levels, the sign of evaluation points achieved, or both. In Experiment 5, we provided correct outcome feedback to mitigate the negative effects of exactingness. Thus, in this case the lack of an effect for exactingness on inconsistency in strategy use was consistent with our theoretical expectations.

Based on work within the lens model tradition (Hammond & Summers, 1972), one might imagine that performance (π) would always be inversely related to inconsistency in strategy use so that measures of these variables would be redundant. However, it is important to state that this is not the case. In Experiment 1, for example, subjects in both the lenient ($\alpha = .01$) and intermediate ($\alpha = .05$) conditions did not have significantly different levels of inconsistency in strategy use, and yet, performance in the intermediate was better than in the lenient. In other words, although subjects in both conditions were equally inconsistent, those in the intermediate environment learned better strategies. Note also that in this experiment, although subjects in the lenient condition were less inconsistent than those in the exacting environment, their performance was not significantly different.

Questionnaires constructed to determine subjects' attitudes toward the experimental task as well as their understanding of the underlying task structure revealed some differences that were caused by exactingness. For example, subjects found the lenient task to be more enjoyable than the exacting (Experiment 3), and less discouraging (Experiment 5). Measures of understanding (e.g., the sign and slope indices) were largest in the intermediate environment (Experiment 1). An interesting finding was that, in all of our experiments, subjects' ability to articulate their understanding of the task was highly correlated with performance.

Effects of incentives

Our theoretical model stated that incentives would accentuate the effects of exactingness, thereby leading to an Incentives × Exactingness interaction on performance – Prediction 2. We investigated this prediction under three conditions. In Experiment 1, we employed an incentive function with a discontinuity in which subjects could easily discriminate successful (cash reward) versus unsuccessful (no cash reward) performance. In Experiment 3, on the other hand, we employed an incentive function that effectively guaranteed that all subjects would receive some cash reward (although the better they did, the more they earned). The predicted interaction was validated in Experiment 1 but not in Experiment 3, thereby suggesting that, to have an effect, external incentive schemes need to be "sharp." We also induced differential incentive conditions in Experiment 2 by manipulating subjects' aspirations and, although we obtained the predicted interaction, the effect was weaker than in Experiment 1. As noted above, we have reason to believe that the aspiration-level manipulation did not necessarily lead subjects to make clear distinctions between successful and unsuccessful performance, and this may have induced the weaker effect.

We obtained no effects for incentives in Experiment 5 (with correct outcome feedback), but we noted that almost all subjects received positive feedback following their decisions. Thus, incentives had little opportunity to accentuate the effects of exactingness.

Other issues

Experiment 4 addressed the issue of how different conditions experienced during learning affect subsequent performance. This was achieved by seeing how all subjects performed in a third round of 30 trials administered under incentive conditions. Results showed no effects between lenient and exacting environments, but there were differences caused by prior incentive conditions. Subjects who learned either under no incentives or with low aspirations (Experiment 2) performed less well. Of particular interest were subjects who, during the first two rounds, were instructed to learn the task as opposed to maximize evaluation points. Their performance was at the same level as that of subjects who learned under incentives. They differed, however, in that they took more time and were capable of expressing a better understanding of the underlying task. On the other hand, the performance of these inference subjects on both the task and indices of understanding was matched by the subjects in Experiment 1, who had been exposed to the intermediate level of exactingness ($\alpha = .05$). In other words, in terms of performance, training in the intermediate environment (with or without incentives) was just as effective as training in a learning mode in the lenient and exacting environments. The effectiveness of an intermediate level of exactingness, however, can be measured by the fact that it took one third less time to achieve the same measures of performance.

Other differences in time were also noted. In Experiment 5 (with correct outcome feedback), subjects took more time in the exacting as opposed to the lenient conditions. Moreover, we interpreted these findings as indicating that the differential levels of exactingness induced these differences. Of additional interest was the finding that the total time taken by the subjects in Experiment 5 matched that taken by the inference subjects in Experiment 4. In one sense, because of the additional feedback, subjects in Experiment 5 had an easier task than did those in the other experiments (their performance was also better). We speculate that this additional feedback led to a more reflective style of decision making as opposed to learning "through doing" that was more characteristic of subjects who only received feedback in the form of evaluation points.

Theory

From a theoretical viewpoint, our studies break new ground in that we explicitly consider the possible effects of exactingness on learning in a decision-making task. Central to our model is the notion that there are positive and negative effects of exactingness that trade off so that learning (as measured by performance, π) is an inverted-U-shaped function of exactingness. On the positive side, as exactingness increases, so do opportunities for learning. The negative aspect reflects how people react to feedback. If feedback is interpreted as negative (which is increasingly likely with greater levels of exactingness), we argued that inconsistency in responses induced by trying out alternative strategies would lead to lower levels of performance. Exactingness therefore influences learning because people react differently to positive and negative feedback.

An issue that we have not addressed in this article is the relation between exactingness and task complexity (for discussions of the latter concept, see Hammond, 1988; Wood, 1986). Conceptually, we propose that these concepts be treated as distinct in that whereas exactingness reflects the evaluative dimension of feedback (how well one is performing), complexity reflects the difficulty of the inferential dimension (how the underlying system works). However, because feedback is confounded, it is likely that exactingness and complexity are also confounded in the mind of the decision maker. This suggests, therefore, that because different levels of task complexity will affect the extent to which decision makers receive positive or negative feedback, task complexity and exactingness might have similar effects on performance (see, e.g., Wood, Bandura, & Bailey, 1990). Future research should explicitly address the effects of both complexity and exactingness and the extent to which they might have independent or interactive effects on performance.

As to incentives, our model suggests that these accentuate both the positive and the negative aspects of exactingness. Interestingly, this leads to an implication similar to data observed in several studies – albeit with respect to tasks that vary in complexity. This is that for tasks that are not well understood, incentives can be dysfunctional. As noted earlier, the main theoretical argument in the literature is that, in the presence of incentives, more complex tasks divert needed attention from inference to evaluation, that is, from a concern about how to do the task to how well one is doing (Humphreys & Revelle, 1984; Kanfer & Ackerman, 1989; Wood, Bandura, & Bailey, 1990).

These theories and findings are consistent within our conceptual scheme if one makes the distinction between the subtasks of developing an appropriate response strategy, on the one hand, and executing it, on the other. When tasks are relatively simple or understood, more effort can be devoted to execution, and this leads to improved performance. However, for more complex tasks, the chances of having or developing the appropriate strategy are smaller. Thus, if because of negative feedback, incentives induce greater inconsistency in execution, performance is degraded. The key, therefore, lies in how people react to positive and negative feedback.

When we talk about incentives, it is easy to overlook the fact that these can take many forms. For example, even within the class of external incentives, schemes for rewarding performance can vary greatly. One hint provided by our data is that incentive functions have to be sharp enough so that people can distinguish between good and bad performance. At the theoretical level, therefore, this point links nicely to the fact that people react differently to positive and negative feedback.

Practical implications

Our results raise many practical issues. First, however, it is appropriate to consider the limitations of our experimental paradigm and the extent to which the findings might be expected to generalize to a wider range of situations. In many ways, our experiments provided almost ideal opportunities for learning compared with more realistic settings. Feedback after decisions was immediate. Subjects could take notes and consult their histories of past decisions. The tasks did not involve a large number of variables, and there was a limited number of relations between variables in the system that were important. Moreover, the system that generated observations did not change over time.

There are many real world tasks that exhibit similar characteristics, such as production and inventory scheduling decisions, predictions of economic and financial indicators, and weather forecasts. These tasks may differ from ours, however, in that people would typically not make so many decisions in such a short period of time. (Experiments tend to collapse experience in terms of time.) In one sense, real world tasks may also be more inferentially complex than ours; on the other hand, this complexity may be offset by having more time to think through issues before making decisions. Moreover, whereas our task involved abstract variables, the context of real world tasks engages knowledge that facilitates inference. Nonetheless, there are other real world tasks that are similar to ours and in which people do experience much feedback within fairly short periods of time. These tasks include learning how to handle mechanical or electronic devices that require frequent decisions and provide almost immediate feedback. Word processing systems are a good example.

Two important dimensions of real world tasks are whether people are aware of the exactingness of the environment and whether they or others have the ability to control or manipulate it. In many situations in which outcomes and rewards are the same (as in financial transactions), people are typically ignorant of the effects of exactingness. Thus, incentives may or may not promote effective learning. In this case, it would be advisable to learn to make decisions within an inference set (as in Experiment 4) before having to deal with real payoffs. On the other hand, in situations in which it is possible to control how decisions are evaluated (as in our experiments), this may be used deliberately in training decision makers. The implications from our results are clear. Intermediate environments induce more effective learning than do lenient or exacting ones, and in this kind of environment incentives make little difference. If one is forced into using a lenient evaluation function, however, use incentives; with an exacting function, do not use incentives.

Finally, in our task subjects were not told how they were evaluated, that is, how decisions and outcomes were translated into evaluation points. An argument could be made that learning would be fostered if people were aware of the exact nature of the evaluation function because this would reduce one source of ambiguity in feedback and, indeed, this was shown to be the case by the results of Experiment 5. On the other hand, because different evaluation functions induce different rates of learning, it is not clear that it would always be advantageous to reveal these functions to learners. We believe that this issue should be explored further in future studies.

Issues for further study

Because, to the best of our knowledge, the effects of exactingness and incentives have not previously been studied together, the present research suggests many issues for further investigation. We mention a few.

First, the penalty functions used in our tasks were symmetric. Subjects received the same penalty if they overshot or undershot the appropriate setting of the decision variable. It would also be interesting to investigate different types of asymmetric penalty functions. In particular, with highly skewed functions subjects would experience large variations in penalties that might be similar in effect to exacting environments with symmetric functions. However, they would probably also learn to adjust responses to avoid the larger penalties. In our work, we adopted a simple mechanism to model exactingness in the environment. It is possible that this could be achieved in other ways.

Second, although we examined the effects of different types of incentive functions (i.e., sharp vs. continuous) the present work ignored the fact that there could be many different levels of incentives. Thus, although the level of incentives used with the sharp function was sufficient to induce effects, we have no information concerning the relation between size of incentives and effects. We suspect that in a laboratory task relatively small differences in real money paid to subjects do have motivational effects (see also Arkes et al., 1986; Edwards, 1956; Hogarth & Einhorn, 1990), but we are uncertain about how this might generalize outside the psychological laboratory.

Third, our studies have been based on a single experimental task. We believe that it is important to investigate the effects of incentives over a wider range of experimental tasks but, in doing so, we see the necessity of developing an appropriate taxonomy of tasks. In particular, whereas our studies explored the effect of different penalty functions, feedback could also prove more or less frustrating to subjects, depending on the complexity of the underlying causal model generating outcomes. We therefore need to understand how complexity interacts with exactingness. Recently, Hammond et al. (1987) have elaborated a theory of how characteristics of tasks map into different modes of cognition that vary on a continuum from analysis to intuition. Hammond et al. would classify our task as *analysis inducing* so that it would best be handled by an analytic mode of cognition. Whether our theoretical framework and results would also apply in tasks that could be defined as *intuition inducing* is an open and important issue.

Fourth, we noted above that by informing people of the nature of penalty functions, one should, in principle, reduce the ambiguity of outcome feedback. However, because feedback still implies an evaluation, it is not clear that people are able to separate the informational content of feedback concerning the inferential structure of the task from its evaluative component (cf. Experiment 5). This suggests conducting studies similar to those reported above in which the nature of the penalty function is made explicit to subjects.

The question asked is whether it is necessarily better to inform people how they are being evaluated.

Fifth, a central premise of this work is that feedback is ambiguous. Given this ambiguity, it is legitimate to ask whether people might learn more effectively if they received less rather than more information about the effectiveness of past decisions. For example, instead of providing feedback for each decision, would subjects perform better by the end of the experimental session if they only received feedback in the form of average statistics over small blocks of trials? Advantages are that subjects might be forced to experiment with particular strategies over specific blocks of trials and the effects of random error would be mitigated by the averaging process.

To conclude, we have demonstrated that changes in the parameter of the function that evaluates outcomes of decisions can induce significant changes in performance as well as reverse the sign of the effects of incentives. Such sensitivity to a single task feature merits more detailed attention.

Notes

1 Although we have chosen to operationalize differences in exactingness by manipulating α within the context of a squared error loss function, there are other ways to do this. Exactingness could, for example, be represented by different forms of asymmetric loss functions.

2 Whether feedback is negative also depends on the constant of 500 in Equation 7.1. It is important to note, therefore, that by choice of appropriate constants it would be possible to design lenient environments in which actual feedback is predominantly negative or exacting enviroments in which actual feedback is predominantly positive. What matters, however, is whether feedback is perceived by subjects to be positive or negative.

3 Whereas shifting strategies can result in lower performance in the short run, we note that this behavior may often be generally adaptive. For example, if a subject's initial hypothesis about the nature of the underlying system is incorrect, then shifting strategies in attempts to test alternative hypotheses is quite appropriate.

4 Although our model could be developed using general functional forms, we have used specific functions to make the presentation more concrete. In particular, whereas we have modeled the negative aspect of exactingness in Equation 7.5 by a linear function, the implications of our model would also hold for nonlinear functions that are nonconcave decreasing functions of exactingness.

5 Recalling that $(b' - b)$ and $(c' - c)$ represent, respectively, the increases in the extent to which incentives accentuate the positive and negative aspects of exactingness, it is instructive to examine the precise implications of our model when α is restricted to the range from 0 to 1. First, note that if $(b' - b) > (c' - c)$, incentives will always improve performance regardless of exactingness (α). In other words, if the effect of incentives is to accentuate the positive aspects of exactingness (α) more than the negative, incentives will always increase performance. Second, if $(b' - b) < (c' - c)$, there is a critical point of exactingness (α) on the 0 to 1 range below which incentives are functional but above which they are dysfunctional. In other words, even if incentives have more influence on the negative as opposed to the positive aspects of exactingness, they can aid performance provided that exactingness is low. As exactingness increases, however, incentives become less beneficial.

6 If there is no negative aspect of exactingness, the $c\alpha$ term in Equation 7.5 is assumed not to exist.

7 A and B were defined as follows (see Equation 7.1). If $Q < D$, then $A = Q$ and $B = 0$; if $Q \geq D$, then $A = D$ and $B = Q - D$.

8 The R^2 from the regression implied by Equation 7.8 is typically used to measure the consistency of response strategies within the lens model paradigm (Hammond & Summers, 1972) and is, of course, a function of σ_z (within each individual regression). However, we do not

use R^2 here because (a) conventional lens model analysis does not apply to single-cue situations, (b) the variance in Q is relevant to our theoretical analyses and differs across experimental conditions, and (c) W and D (the criterion) are so highly correlated that consistency as measured by R^2 would not provide an independent measure of the contribution of consistency to performance.

9 In terms of Equation 7.7, the fact that feedback from incentives schemes does not distinguish clearly between positive and negative outcomes can be modeled by setting $b = b'$ and $c = c'$, that is, incentives have no differential effect on the positive and negative aspects of exactingness.

10 We do not include subjects from Experiment 3 in these comparisons because these subjects faced a different incentive scheme in Round 3.

References

Amabile, T. M. (1982). Children's artistic creativity: Detrimental effects of competition in a field setting. *Personality and Social Psychology Bulletin, 8*, 573–578.

Arkes, H. R., Dawes, R. M., & Christensen, C. (1986). Factors influencing the use of a decision rule in a probabilistic task. *Organizational Behavior and Human Decision Processes, 37*, 93–110.

Ashton, R. H. (1990, April). *Paradoxical effects of incentives, feedback, and justification in accounting decision settings.* Unpublished manuscript, Fuqua School of Business, Duke University.

Bahrick, H. P. (1954). Incidental learning under two incentive conditions. *Journal of Experimental Psychology, 47*, 170–172.

Bahrick, H. P., Fitts, P. M., & Rankin, R. E. (1952). Effects of incentives upon reactions to peripheral stimuli. *Journal of Experimental Psychology, 44*, 400–406.

Balzer, W. K., Doherty, M. E., & O'Connor, R., Jr. (1989). Effects of cognitive feedback on performance. *Psychological Bulletin, 106*, 410–433.

Berry, D. C., & Broadbent, D. E. (1984). On the relationship between task performance and associated verbalizable knowledge. *The Quarterly Journal of Experimental Psychology, 36A*, 209–231.

Berry, D. C., & Broadbent, D. E. (1988). Interactive tasks and the implicit–explicit distinction. *British Journal of Psychology, 79*, 251–272.

Brehmer, B. (1980). In one word: Not from experience. *Acta Psychologica, 45*, 223–241.

Broadbent, D. E. (1977). Levels, hierarchies, and the locus of control. *Quarterly Journal of Experimental Psychology, 29*, 181–201.

Broadbent, D. E., & Aston, B. (1978). Human control of a simulated economic system. *Ergonomics, 21*(12), 1035–1043.

Broadbent, D. E., FitzGerald, P., & Broadbent, M. H. P. (1986). Implicit and explicit knowledge in the control of complex systems. *British Journal of Psychology, 77*, 33–50.

Coombs, C. H., & Avrunin, G. S. (1977). Single-peaked functions and the theory of preference. *Psychological Review, 84*(2), 216–230.

Deci, E. L., & Ryan, R. M. (1985). *Intrinsic motivation and self-determination in human behavior.* New York: Plenum Press.

Earley, P. C., Connolly, T., & Ekegren, G. (1989). Goals, strategy development, and task performance: Some limits on the efficacy of goal setting. *Journal of Applied Psychology, 74*(1), 24–33.

Easterbrook, J. A. (1959). The effect of emotion on cue utilization and the organization of behavior. *Psychological Review, 66*(3), 183–201.

Edwards, W. (1956). Reward probability, amount, and information as determiners of sequential two-alternative decisions. *Journal of Experimental Psychology, 52,* 177–188.

Einhorn, H. J., & Hogarth, R. M. (1975). Unit weighting schemes for decision making. *Organizational Behavior and Human Performance, 13,* 171–192.

Einhorn, H. J., & Hogarth, R. M. (1978). Confidence in judgment: Persistence of the illusion of validity. *Psychological Review, 85,* 395–416.

Hammond, K. R. (1988). Judgment and decision making in dynamic tasks. *Information and Decision Technologies, 14,* 3–14.

Hammond, K. R., Hamm, R. M., Grassia, J., & Pearson, T. (1987). Direct comparison of the efficacy of intuitive and analytical cognition in expert judgment. *IEEE Transactions on Systems, Man, and Cybernetics,* SMC-17(5), 753–770.

Hammond, K. R., & Summers, D. A. (1972). Cognitive control. *Psychological Review, 79,* 58–67.

Hammond, K. R., Summers, D. A., & Deane, D. H. (1973). Negative effects of outcome-feedback in multiple-cue probability learning. *Organizational Behavior and Human Performance, 9,* 30–34.

Hogarth, R. M., & Einhorn, H. J. (1990). Venture theory: A model of decision weights. *Management Science, 36,* 780–803.

Humphreys, M. S., & Revelle, W. (1984). Personality, motivation, and performance: A theory of the relationship between individual differences and information processing. *Psychological Review, 91*(2), 153–184.

Kahneman, D. (1973). *Attention and effort.* Englewood Cliffs, NJ: Prentice-Hall.

Kanfer, R., & Ackerman, P. L. (1989). Motivation and cognitive abilities: An integrative/aptitude-treatment interaction approach to skill acquisition. *Journal of Applied Psychology, 74*(4), 657–690.

Klayman, J. (1988). On the how and why (not) of learning from outcomes. In B. Brehmer & C. R. B. Joyce (Eds.), *Human judgment: The SJT view* (pp. 115–162). Amsterdam: North-Holland.

Lepper, M. R., & Greene, D. (Eds.). (1978). *The hidden costs of reward.* Hillsdale, NJ: Erlbaum.

Lepper, M. R., Greene, D., & Nisbett, R. E. (1973). Undermining children's intrinsic interest with extrinsic reward: A test of the "overjustification" hypothesis. *Journal of Personality and Social Psychology, 28,* 129–137.

Levine, F. M., & Fasnacht, G. (1974). Token rewards may lead to token learning. *American Psychologist, 29,* 816–820.

Locke, E. A., Shaw, K. N., Saari, L. M., & Latham, G. P. (1981). Goal setting and task performance: 1969–1980. *Psychological Bulletin, 90,* 125–152.

Luce, R. D., & Suppes, P. (1965). Preference, utility, and subjective probability. In R. D. Luce, R. R. Bush, & E. Galanter (Eds.) *Handbook of mathematical psychology* (Vol. III, pp. 249–410). New York: Wiley.

McCullers, J. C. (1978). Issues in learning and motivation. In M. R. Lepper & D. Greene (Eds.), *The hidden costs of reward* (pp. 5–18). Hillsdale, NJ: Erlbaum.

McGraw, K. O. (1978). The detrimental effects of reward on perfomance: A literature review and a prediction model. In M. R. Lepper & D. Greene (Eds.), *The hidden costs of reward* (pp. 33–60). Hillsdale, NJ: Erlbaum.

McGraw, K. O., & McCullers, J. C. (1979). Evidence of a detrimental effect of extrinsic incentives on breaking a mental set. *Journal of Experimental Social Psychology, 15,* 285–294.

Schwartz, B. (1982). Reinforcement-induced behavioral stereotypy: How not to teach people to discover rules. *Journal of Experimental Psychology: General, 111*(1), 23–59.

Siegel, S. (1961). Decision making and learning under varying conditions of reinforcement. *Annals of the New York Academy of Sciences, 89*, 766–783.

Tversky, A., & Edwards, W. (1966). Information versus reward in binary choices. *Journal of Experimental Psychology, 71*, 680–683.

White, R. W. (1959). Motivation reconsidered: The concept of competence. *Psychological Review, 66*, 297–333.

Wood, R. E. (1986). Task complexity: Definition of the construct. *Organizational Behavior and Human Decision Processes, 37*, 60–82.

Wood, R., Bandura, A., & Bailey, T. (1990). Mechanisms governing organizational performance in complex decision-making environments. *Organizational Behavior and Human Decision Processes, 46*, 181–201.

Zajonc, R. B. (1965). Social facilitation. *Science, 149*, 269–274.

*Causation, mental simulation, and
counterfactual reasoning*

8   Covariation in natural
causal induction

Patricia W. Cheng and Laura R. Novick

We do not perceive the visual world as a two-dimensional mosaic of bits of
light patches. Instead, these data from the retina are processed by our central
visual system to yield a coherent perception of the world, reflecting its visual
and spatial structures. Similarly, we do not perceive our lives or the world
beyond as a stream of unconnected elemental events. Here, too, central
processes act on the data to yield an organized view, structured in terms of
commonsensical and scientific theories. Causal induction is an example of
such organizing processes. When a government resorts to violent suppression of its people or yields to peaceful reform, when a couple decides to date
or a marriage breaks up, or when an epidemic strikes or a new vaccine
controls it, we seek out causes.

How do ordinary people induce the causes of events? Moreover, given
that the primary goals of causal induction are the recovery of the causal
structure of the world and the prediction of future events, is the mechanism
underlying natural causal induction adequate for satisfying these goals?
Covariation – the change in the probability of an effect given the presence
versus the absence of a potential cause – has generally been regarded as a
necessary (although insufficient) criterion of normative causal induction.[1]
The computation of covariation has generated a considerable body of research in the cognitive and social literatures, both of which have presented

This chapter originally appeared in *Psychological Review*, 1992, 99(2), 365–382. Copyright © 1992
by the American Psychological Association. Reprinted by permission.

The preparation of this article was supported by National Science Foundation Research Grant
BNS87-10305 and by the Committee on Research of the Academic Senate of the Los Angeles
Division of the University of California on behalf of Patricia W. Cheng. It was also supported
by a National Institute of Mental Health Individual Postdoctoral Fellowship and by the dean's
office of Peabody College of Vanderbilt University on behalf of Laura R. Novick.

We thank Angela Fratianne, Rochel Gelman, Keith Holyoak, Richard Nisbett, Michael
Waldmann, Bernard Weiner, and three anonymous reviewers for their valuable comments on
an earlier draft.

rather messy pictures of the psychological mechanism. These literatures suggest that the covariation component in natural causal induction is non-normative in many ways. Deviation from normative covariation has also received considerable attention in philosophy. In this article, we evaluate the biases and models discussed in these three domains with respect to focal sets: contextually selected sets of events over which covariation is computed. Moreover, we compare these models to our *probabilistic contrast model* (Cheng & Novick, 1990a, 1990b, 1991).

Deviations from normative covariation

Linear-combination heuristics

Cognitive psychologists have described a variety of nonnormative heuristics based on linear combinations of the frequencies of the four cells of a 2×2 contingency table formed by crossing the presence and absence of a potential cause with the presence and absence of a target effect (e.g., Arkes & Harkness, 1983; Downing, Sternberg, & Ross, 1985; Einhorn & Hogarth, 1986; Jenkins & Ward, 1965; Schustack & Sternberg, 1981; Shaklee, 1983). Arkes and Harkness (1983) reported that their subjects used a variety of heuristics depending on task characteristics. They concluded that "a search for *the* heuristic that people use will be a futile search" (p. 132). Similarly, Shaklee and Tucker (1980, p. 466) concluded that "the variety of rules evident in our results indicates that characterization of group judgment by any single rule would be inappropriate." Other researchers concluded that normal people untrained in statistics typically do not have any concept corresponding to statistical contingency or contrast (Jenkins & Ward, 1965; Smedslund, 1963; Ward & Jenkins, 1965), the putatively normative basis of the concept of covariation (e.g., see Alloy & Abramson, 1979; Jenkins & Ward, 1965; Rescorla, 1968; Salmon, 1984; Skyrms, 1986).

Kelley's analysis of variance model

The causal attribution literature in social psychology has largely measured performance against an apparently different normative standard: namely, variations of Kelley's (1967, 1973) influential proposal that people are "intuitive scientists" who use a mechanism of causal induction analogous to the analysis of variance (ANOVA) (Cheng & Novick, 1990a; Försterling, 1989; Hewstone & Jaspars, 1987; Hilton, 1988, 1990; Jaspars, 1983; Orvis, Cunningham, & Kelley, 1975; Pruitt & Insko, 1980). This literature has, until recently, presented a chaotic picture of causal induction not unlike that in cognitive psychology: Causal induction sometimes conforms to the normative standard but often deviates from it. Such deviations include a bias against using consensus information (which has been regarded as a tendency to ignore base-rate information), a bias toward attributing effects to a person, a tendency for actors and observers to make different causal attributions for the same event, and a tendency to make a variety of unpredicted attributions to conjunctions of factors (for reviews, see Cheng & Novick, 1990a; Jaspars, Hewstone, & Fincham, 1983; Kelley & Michela, 1980; Nisbett & Ross, 1980).

Causes, enabling conditions, and causally irrelevant factors

A deviation from normative covariation that has received considerable attention in philosophy and related fields concerns the intuitive distinction people make between causes and enabling conditions (e.g., Einhorn & Hogarth, 1986; Hart & Honoré 1959/1985; Hesslow, 1983, 1988; Hilton, 1990; Kahneman & Miller, 1986; Mackie, 1965, 1974; Mill, 1843/1973; Taylor, 1983; White, 1965). In response to the question "What caused the airplane to crash?" investigators are unlikely to reply, "The gravitational pull of the earth." Rather, they are likely to reserve the title of "cause" for factors such as the malfunctioning of a critical component of the aircraft, pilot error, or wind shear. Gravity, they might say, was merely a condition that enabled the crash to occur. In contrast to all of these factors, which an investigator would (or could) perceive as causally relevant, the color of the airplane seats or the number of infants on board, for example, would be perceived as causally irrelevant.

It has long been recognized that the distinction between causes and enabling conditions cannot be explained by accounts of inference formulated purely in terms of necessary and sufficient conditions. Mill (1843/1973, p. 329), for example, thought that everyday explanation diverged from scientific explanation in the "capricious manner in which we select from among the conditions which we choose to denominate the cause." Consider a particular airplane crash for which the malfunctioning of the airplane's guidance system and gravity were necessary factors. These two factors hold the same logical relationship to the effect in terms of necessity and sufficiency: The crash would not have occurred either if the component had not malfunctioned or if there had been no gravity: moreover, the malfunctioning of the component and gravity, along with other necessary factors such as the failure of a backup system, were jointly sufficient to have produced that crash.[2]

To compound the puzzlement, the perception of what is a cause or an enabling condition may vary depending on context. For example, Hart and Honoré (1959/1985, p. 35) noted that the presence of oxygen typically would be considered an enabling condition rather than the cause of a fire; the cause might be an event such as the dropping of a lighted cigarette. However, "if a fire breaks out in a laboratory or in a factory, where special precautions are taken to exclude oxygen during part of an experiment or manufacturing process . . . there would be no absurdity at all in saying that the presence of oxygen was the cause of the fire."

To make sense of the distinction between causes and enabling conditions, a number of theorists argued that a causal question invariably implies comparisons among a selected set of events (Einhorn & Hogarth, 1986; Hart & Honoré, 1959/1985; Hastie, 1983; Hesslow, 1983, 1988; Hilton, 1990; Kahneman & Miller, 1986; Mackie, 1965, 1974; McGill, 1989). McGill (1989, p. 189), for example, hypothesized that "individuals structure the to-be-explained event as the difference or deviation between a target episode and a contrasting causal background." On this view, a question such as "What caused the forest to be on fire?" can be understood as, "What made the difference between this occasion in the forest on which there was a fire and other occasions in the forest on which there was no fire?" Note that the selected set of events is often only a subset of the events related to an effect. The expanded question, for example, does not include all events in one's knowledge base that are related to fires: It does not include events in which oxygen is absent, for instance, even though such events (at least in an abstract form) are in a typical educated adult's knowledge base. On this view, shifts in the perception of an event as a cause or an enabling condition are due to the adoption of different contrasting causal backgrounds (i.e., focal sets in our terminology).

Overview

Our probabilistic contrast model may be regarded as a modification of Kelley's (1967) analogy between causal induction and the ANOVA or as an extension of the contingency rule discussed in the cognitive psychology, animal conditioning, and philosophy literatures (e.g., Jenkins & Ward, 1965; Rescorla, 1968; Salmon, 1984). Extending these models by analogy to statistical contrasts, our model proposes that everyday causal inference is based on contrasts (i.e., differences or differences between differences) between the probability of the effect conditional on the presence versus the absence of (single or multiple) potential causal factors. These contrasts are computed for selected factors in a focal set.

The question we address is this: Considering a focal set for selected discrete variables describing the event to be explained, what do ordinary people compute to induce the causes of an event? In this article, we first review our model and its explanation of the distinction among causes, enabling conditions, and causally irrelevant factors (Cheng & Novick, 1991). In this section, we also derive Kelley's (1971) *discounting* principle as a corollary of our model. Second, we review our explanation of the myriad well-documented deviations from Kelley's ANOVA model. To support our explanations, we (a) review two experiments that test our reinterpretations of many of the biases reported in the social psychology literature (Cheng & Novick, 1990a; Novick, Fratianne, & Cheng, 1991) and (b) extend our reinterpretation to reported biases based on different paradigms in that literature. We end the first two parts with a discussion of the theoretical implications of the constraints imposed by a consideration of phenomena observed in philosophy and social psychology for previous theories in these domains. Third, we present a theoretical refutation, in view of such constraints, of all alternative current models in cognitive psychology and philosophy. We discuss (a) the linear combination heuristics proposed by cognitive psychologists, (b) Suppes's model (1970, 1984), and (c) a probabilistic extension of Mill's (1843/1973) method of difference. In addition, we review our analysis (Cheng & Novick, 1991) of the normality criterion, a dominant criterion according to which the distinction between causes and enabling conditions is based on the prevalence of potential causes (e.g., Einhorn & Hogarth, 1986; Hart & Honoré, 1959/1985; Hilton & Slugoski, 1986; Kahneman & Miller, 1986; Mackie, 1965, 1974; Turnbull & Slugoski, 1988). We specify how this criterion and formulations of causality in terms of necessity and sufficiency may be regarded as special cases of our model. Finally, we review and extend the interpretation of an earlier experiment (Cheng & Novick, 1991, Experiment 2) in support of our model against competing models.

The covariation component of everyday causal inference has been depicted as heterogeneous and prone to either systematic or capricious biases. To account for these biases, numerous models and heuristics have been proposed. In contrast with the previous depiction, our assessments converge on a single normative mechanism that underlies this essential component of causal induction.

Scope of the article

Although covariation is a necessary criterion for causal induction, it is not a sufficient one. There clearly are innate and acquired constraints on the selection of potential causal factors with respect to a given effect. On theoretical grounds, the problem of combinatorial explosion in covariation computation surely requires that there be some innate biases in the inductive process. Empirically, it is clear that animals have such innate biases (Garcia, McGowan, Ervin, & Koelling, 1968; Garcia, McGowan, & Green, 1972). Other biases may be acquired through learning (e.g., Bullock, Gelman, & Baillargeon, 1982; Mendelson & Shultz, 1976).

To reduce the number of variables for which covariation is computed, one plausible criterion is that covariation is evaluated only for factors that are psychologically prior to the target effect. Psychological priority may be established by manipulation, potential manipulation, or perceived temporal priority. Adding this criterion, however, fails to eradicate the following problem: Whereas one normatively defined covariational relation may be designated as causal (e.g., that between touching a red-hot poker and burning one's hand), another may not (e.g., that between a drop in the barometric reading and a subsequent storm). A possible extension of the covariation view to deal with this problem of differentiating between genuine and spurious causes (covariational relations that are causal and noncausal, respectively, following Suppes's, 1970, 1984, terminology) is to adopt a criterion of conditional independence (e.g., Reichenbach, 1956; Salmon, 1980, 1984; Suppes, 1970, 1984). In terms of our model, the adoption of such a criterion involves computing contrasts separately for focal sets that are restricted to events in which a psychologically prior covariational factor (e.g., a drop in atmospheric pressure for the storm example – a factor that is psychologically prior to a drop in the barometric reading) is (a) present and (b) absent. If the contrast for a factor does not noticeably differ from zero in both focal sets, the factor is a spurious cause. Our model adopts the psychological priority criterion and allows the use of the conditional-independence criterion (Cheng & Novick, 1990a, 1991). An alternative potential solution is to assume that some understanding of an underlying causal mechanism is necessary (e.g., Bullock et al., 1982; Salmon, 1984; Shultz, 1982).

A full discussion of the problem of differentiating between genuine and spurious causes would go far beyond the scope of this article. We therefore remove from our discussion normatively defined covariations that are judged to be noncausal. Inference regarding such factors is not accounted for by any of the covariational rules discussed here.

Probabilistic contrast model

In our model, causal inferences to explain a target event are determined by contrasts computed over events in a focal set for selected discrete variables describing the target event.

Main-effect contrasts

A main-effect contrast, Δp_i, which specifies a cause involving a single factor i, is defined by the contrast (i.e., contingency) rule described earlier:

$$\Delta p_i = p_i - p_{\bar{i}}, \tag{8.1}$$

where p_i is the proportion of events for which the effect occurs when factor i is present and $p_{\bar{i}}$ is the proportion of events for which the effect occurs when factor i is absent. (A bar above a letter denotes the absence of the represented factor.) If Δp_i is noticeably different from zero (by some empirically determined criterion), factor i is a cause.[3] Otherwise, i is causally irrelevant. A positive contrast specifies a facilitatory cause; a negative contrast specifies an inhibitory cause (also see Kelley, 1973, on this distinction).

Because a contrast cannot be computed for a factor that is constantly present in a focal set (due to division by zero in the computation of the probability of the effect in the absence of the factor), the causal status of such a factor cannot be determined by events in the focal set; instead, its status is determined by events in other focal sets. Such a factor is (a) an enabling condition if its contrast value is noticeably different from zero (i.e., it covaries with the effect) in another focal set, but (b) causally irrelevant if its contrast value is not noticeably different from zero in other focal sets (Cheng & Novick, 1991).

To illustrate our model with the forest fire example, assume that lightning struck the forest where the fire started immediately before it started. Applying our model to the focal set, we see that the proportion of cases for which fire occurs in the presence of lightning is greater than the proportion of cases for which fire occurs in the absence of lightning. Lightning is therefore a cause. (Notice that our model does *not* require that fire always occur in the presence of lightning to covary with it.) In contrast, the corresponding difference in proportions cannot be computed for oxygen, because oxygen is constantly present in every event in the set. Oxygen is therefore merely an enabling condition. It is not causally irrelevant because people (at least those educated in chemistry) do have a focal set for which oxygen does covary with fire. Finally, the presence of stones in the forest, which does not covary with forest fire in any focal set, is considered causally irrelevant.

Interaction contrasts

A cause may involve not just a single factor but a conjunction of factors (e.g., the simultaneous presence of positively charged clouds and negatively charged clouds as the cause of thunder; the combination of talent, hard work, and opportunity as the cause of success). In our model, an interaction contrast specifies a cause involving a conjunction of factors. Whereas a main-effect contrast specifies a difference between the proportions of events in which the effect occurs in the presence of a factor and in the absence of it, a two-way interaction contrast specifies a difference between such differences for levels of an orthogonal factor (i.e., a second-order difference; Cheng & Novick, 1990a). A two-way interaction contrast, Δp_{ij}, involving potential causal factors i and j, is defined as follows:

$$\Delta p_{ij} = \left(p_{ij} - p_{i\bar{j}} \right) - \left(p_{\bar{i}j} - p_{\bar{i}\bar{j}} \right), \tag{8.2}$$

where p, as before, denotes the proportion of cases in which the effect occurs when a potential contributing factor is either present or absent, as denoted by its subscripts. More generally, interaction contrasts involving n factors are defined as nth-order differences, where n is any positive integer.[4] Like main-effect contrasts, interaction contrasts can be facilitatory or inhibitory, depending on whether they are positive or negative. Our model distinguishes multiple alternative causes (corresponding to multiple main-effect and/or interaction contrasts) from a conjunctive cause (corresponding to a contrast involving multiple factors, i.e., an interaction contrast).[5]

Illustration of contrasts computed over various focal sets

Figure 8.1 illustrates contrasts specifying causes, enabling conditions, and causally irrelevant factors. It also illustrates the effect of varying focal sets.

UNIVERSAL SET

$$\Delta p_q = p_q - p_{\bar{q}} = 8/32 - 0/12 = .25 \qquad\qquad \Delta p_s = p_s - p_{\bar{s}} = 4/22 - 4/22 = 0$$

$$\Delta p_r = p_r - p_{\bar{r}} = 8/12 - 0/32 = .67 \qquad\qquad \Delta p_t = p_t - p_{\bar{t}} = 2/11 - 6/33 = 0$$

$$\Delta p_{qr} = (p_{qr} - p_{q\bar{r}}) - (p_{\bar{q}r} - p_{\bar{q}\bar{r}}) = (8/8 - 0/4) - (0/24 - 0/8) = 1 - 0 = 1$$

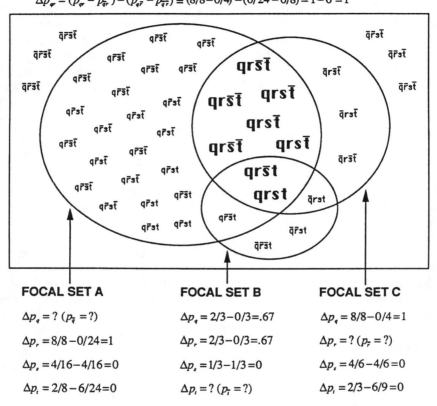

FOCAL SET A

$$\Delta p_q = ?\ (p_{\bar{q}} = ?)$$

$$\Delta p_r = 8/8 - 0/24 = 1$$

$$\Delta p_s = 4/16 - 4/16 = 0$$

$$\Delta p_t = 2/8 - 6/24 = 0$$

FOCAL SET B

$$\Delta p_q = 2/3 - 0/3 = .67$$

$$\Delta p_r = 2/3 - 0/3 = .67$$

$$\Delta p_s = 1/3 - 1/3 = 0$$

$$\Delta p_t = ?\ (p_{\bar{t}} = ?)$$

FOCAL SET C

$$\Delta p_q = 8/8 - 0/4 = 1$$

$$\Delta p_r = ?\ (p_{\bar{r}} = ?)$$

$$\Delta p_s = 4/6 - 4/6 = 0$$

$$\Delta p_t = 2/3 - 6/9 = 0$$

Figure 8.1. Computation of covariation within focal sets according to the probabilistic contrast model as an explanation of the distinction among causes, enabling conditions, and causally irrelevant factors. (Each letter [e.g., q] represents a potential causal factor. A bar above a letter [e.g., $\bar{q}$] denotes the absence of that factor. An event is represented by a sequence of letters (e.g., $\bar{q}rst$) denoting the conjunct of those factors in the event. The presence of the effect for an event is represented by larger bold type. The absence of the effect for an event is represented by regular, nonbold letters. Finally, loops and the rectangle enclose events in focal sets.)

The figure is assumed to represent the entire set of events that are relevant to a particular effect in a hypothetical person's knowledge base (labeled *universal set* in the figure).

As can be seen in the figure, with respect to the universal set of events, factors q and r are individually necessary (i.e., $p_{\bar{q}} = p_{\bar{r}} = 0$) and jointly sufficient (i.e., $p_q < 1$, $p_r < 1$, but $p_{qr} = 1$) for the occurrence of the effect. According to our model, q and r are the factors in the two-way interaction contrast, Δp_{qr}, which has a value of 1 ($p_{qr} = 1$, $p_{\bar{q}r} = p_{q\bar{r}} = p_{\bar{q}\bar{r}} = 0$). Previous formulations of causality in terms of necessity and sufficiency may be regarded as special extreme cases of our model in which (a) the focal set is the universal set and (b) the proportions are expressed in relation to 0 (i.e., equal to or greater than 0) or 1 (i.e., equal to or less than 1; see preceding example) rather than as proportions.[6]

Now consider Focal Set A. In this set, $p_r = 1$ (i.e., r is sufficient for the occurrence of the effect in that context), and $p_{\bar{r}} = 0$ (i.e., r is necessary for the effect in that context). Because p_r is greater than $p_{\bar{r}}$ (i.e., $\Delta p_r > 0$), r should be perceived as a cause of the effect for this subset. Factor q, however, is constantly present. A difference in probabilities conditional on the presence versus the absence of q, therefore, cannot be computed for this subset. Thus, q should not be selected as a cause. However, it is an enabling condition, because it does covary with the effect in another focal set: Set C (and to a lesser extent in Set B as well). Notice that q and r, which have the same status in terms of necessity and sufficiency with respect to the universal set, differ in their status with respect to Focal Set A. Factor q, unlike r, is insufficient ($p_q < 1$), and its necessity is undetermined ($p_{\bar{q}}$ is undefined) in that context. Designating r as a cause and q as an enabling condition, therefore, does not conflict with the logical status of these factors within this focal set.

Our model explains the effects of shifting contexts on the distinction between causes and enabling conditions by the selection of different focal sets over which covariation is computed. Consider q and r in Set C. Unlike in Set A, q covaries with the effect, but r is constantly present. Only q, therefore, should be perceived as the cause of the effect for that set. In sum, both q and r covary with the effect in some focal set. These factors should be perceived as (a) causes when the focal set of events selected for a particular context is one in which the factors covary with the effect and (b) enabling conditions when the selected focal set is not one in which the factors covary with the effect. Varying the relevant focal set thus alters which factor should be considered a cause and which should be considered an enabling condition.

Focal Sets A and C illustrate the extreme case of our model in which a cause is necessary and sufficient for the effect. Focal Set B illustrates probabilistic covariations. In this set, both q and r would be considered causes because both yield substantial positive contrasts. The contrast values for these factors are different from those in Sets A and C as a result of the different frequencies with which other necessary factors are present in the two focal sets. In contrast, t is causally irrelevant: It is constantly present in Set B, and it does not covary with the effect in either of the other sets.

Finally, notice that although s is sometimes present and sometimes absent in each of the three focal sets, its presence or absence does not covary with the effect in any focal set. Therefore, this factor, like t, is causally irrelevant to the effect. In sum, computing covariation over different focal sets accounts for the distinctions among causes, enabling conditions, and causally irrelevant factors.

Multiple independent causes

We have only considered the situation in which there is a single cause of effect E within a focal set. Now consider the situation in which there are multiple independent causes of E. Let C be a potential cause in the presence of which E occurs with probability $P(E|C)$. When the other causes often produce E, then $P(E|\bar{C})$ will be relatively large. Accordingly, Δp_c will be relatively small. Conversely, when the other causes rarely produce E, Δp_c will be relatively large. That is, Δp_c is an inverse function of how often the other causes produce E.

This prediction may be considered an extension of Kelley's (1971) discounting principle, which is a corollary of Equation 8.1 if the independence of causes is assumed. According to this principle, "the role of a given cause in producing a given effect is discounted if other plausible causes are also present" (Kelley, 1971, p. 8).[7] Evidence supporting this principle has been reported in numerous experiments (e.g., Jones, Davis, & Gergen, 1961; Lepper, Greene, & Nisbett, 1973; Thibaut & Riecken, 1955). (See the Appendix for a proof of this prediction from Equation 8.1.)

Deviations from Kelley's model

Our model may be regarded as a modification of Kelley's (1967, 1973) ANOVA model. Because myriad deviations from his model have been reported in the social psychology literature, the question of how these deviations are to be reconciled with our model no doubt arises. We argue that these deviations, rather than representing irrational biases in the inductive process per se, could be due to discrepancies between the set of events specified by the researcher and the subject's focal set.

Interpretation of biases based on experiments specifying configurational information

Many experiments testing Kelley's (1967, 1973) model specified the stimulus input in terms of the variables of consensus (the amount of agreement between the target person and other people in their responses to the target stimulus on the target occasion), distinctiveness (the amount of disagreement between the target person's response to the target stimulus and his or her responses to other stimuli on the target occasion), and consistency (the amount of agreement between the target person's response to the target stimulus on the target occasion and his or her responses to that stimulus on other occasions). The subject's task is to explain what caused a target person to have a certain reaction to a target stimulus on a target occasion. These three information variables measure covariation along the three dimensions of persons, stimuli, and time, which Kelley (1967, 1973) proposed as independent variables in his ANOVA analogy and which he illustrated in his cube.[8] Following Cheng and Novick (1990a, 1990b), we use the term *configuration* to denote the pattern of information specified by consensus, distinctiveness, and consistency. For example, one configuration specifies high consensus, low distinctiveness, and low consistency (HLL).

As noted by several investigators (Cheng & Novick 1990b; Försterling, 1989; Hilton, 1988, 1990; Jaspars et al., 1983; Pruitt & Insko, 1980), information on these variables, often assumed to represent all the data relevant to making causal attributions, actually covers only a subset of the potentially relevant information: specifically, one row, column, and beam of the cube. Previous researchers apparently often made the plausible but erroneous assumption that nonconfigurational information, which includes information on how other people react to other stimuli on other occasions, is *irrelevant* for explaining why a particular person has a certain reaction to a particular stimulus on a particular occasion. (An analogous assumption was made by learning theorists before Rescorla, 1968, demonstrated that the frequency of association between the unconditioned stimulus and the *absence* of the conditioned stimulus is critically important in conditioning.) However, recent evidence in the causal attribution literature indicates that subjects do make use of their assumptions regarding the occurrence of the effect in the nonconfigurational part of the cube. For example, Hilton and Slugoski (1986) insightfully demonstrated that causal attributions were influenced by people's implicit knowledge of norms (i.e., "presuppositions about what a class of persons generally does to a class of stimuli"; Hilton, Smith, & Alicke, 1988, p. 531). Such knowledge homogeneously fills the nonconfigurational (i.e., unspecified) part of Kelley's cube.

We (Cheng & Novick, 1990a, 1990b) hypothesized that because causal attribution is a joint function of the data on which the inference rules operate and the rules themselves, the apparent biases found in previous experiments – rather than being due to the inferential process – may reflect the subjects' assumptions regarding the pattern of information for the unspecified part of the cube. In experiments specifying only configurational information, it is typically not known what assumptions subjects might have spontaneously made regarding the occurrence of the effect in the remainder of the cube. If some subjects do use information in the entire cube as the basis for causal induction, then when this focal set is identified, causal attributions may reveal an unbiased assessment of covariation.

Our hypothesis is supported by several studies in which nonconfigurational information was manipulated or assessed independently of configurational information (Cheng & Novick, 1990a; Hilton & Slugoski, 1986; Novick et al., 1991; Pruitt & Insko, 1980). Here we briefly describe the results of two of our experiments. In one experiment, we explicitly varied the pattern of information in the nonconfigurational part of the cube while keeping configurational information constant (Cheng & Novick, 1990a). Thus, we provided subjects with information that completely filled Kelley's (1967) cube. In a second experiment (Novick et al., 1991), we gave subjects only configurational information and assessed both assumptions concerning the unspecified cells of the cube and causal attributions.

Specifying complete information. With the complete information problems used in the first experiment, we tested our hypothesis in two ways. First, across problems, we counterbalanced presence or absence of the effect over the three dimensions of the cube so that any bias toward a dimension (or an information variable) could not be attributed to asymmetries in the input. Second, for each of four configurations, we constructed a set of problems that shared that configuration but differed in the pattern of information over the nonconfigurational part of the cube. The patterns of nonconfigurational information were chosen such that for some of the problems our model predicts main-effect and interaction attributions that are not predicted by any previous models, including attributions that previously have been reported as biases (e.g., attributions to person, stimulus, or the conjunction of person and stimulus for the high-consensus, low-distinctiveness, high-consistency (HLH) configuration; attributions to the conjunction of person and occasion and to the conjunction of stimulus and occasion for the HLL configuration). Obtaining such attributions would demonstrate that these apparent biases can, in fact, be explained by a normative covariational model. Furthermore, the patterns of nonconfigurational information were constructed such that, over our entire set of problems, our model predicts all possible types of main-effect and interaction attributions that are unpredicted by previous models.

Our results, reported in detail in Cheng and Novick (1990a), showed that the predicted attributions were obtained. For each of the four configurations tested, the various problems sharing a configuration differed reliably in the causal attributions they elicited, as predicted by our model. In particular, for every configuration, the problem for which a particular pattern of responses was predicted by our model showed a reliably higher percentage of such responses than did problems with the same configuration for which those responses were not predicted. Moreover, our counterbalanced set of problems showed no evidence for either a bias toward making a person attribution (or any other attribution) or a tendency to ignore consensus information (or any other type of information) when such information was redefined in terms of probabilistic contrasts to capture covariation over the entire cube rather than over the configuration only.

Besides addressing the issue of bias, our experiment also allowed a comparison between our model and previous models in the social literature. All previous models (Jaspars et al., 1983; Kelley, 1967, 1973; Orvis et al., 1975), with the exception of those of Försterling (1989) and Hilton and Slugoski (1986), made predictions that were based on configurations. One interpretation of all configuration-based models is that they predict the same attributions for all of our problems that shared a configuration. In contrast, our model predicts different attributions for each of these problems. It is possible to separate principles underlying configuration-based models from the literal predictions previously made. An alternative set of predictions for those models may be derived by applying the underlying principles to information over the entire cube. Even under this approach, none of the previous models (configuration based or otherwise) can account for our data. For at least three of the four configurations we tested, all of these models predict either no causal attribution possible or the same attribution for some if not all of the problems sharing a configuration. Our results show that for every configuration tested, every problem sharing the configuration elicited a reliably different pattern of response, as predicted by our model but not by any previous model.

Assessing assumptions about the unspecified part of the cube. Just as we were able to vary the information given for the nonconfigurational part of the cube, subjects in previous experiments also might have varied their assumptions regarding that region from problem to problem or from one person to another for a given problem, thus producing what appeared to be capricious biases. We tested this hypothesis more directly in our second experiment by giving subjects configurational information only and assessing both their assumptions and causal attributions (Novick et al., 1991). For each of two configurations, we constructed scenarios in two content domains (e.g., expertise at dancing vs. music appreciation) that we expected would lead to quite different assumptions concerning the occurrence of the effect in the unspecified cells of the cube because of people's world knowledge about these domains. The resulting patterns of information in the cube (configuration plus subjects' assumptions) were predicted to lead to different causal attributions as determined by probabilistic contrasts computed for the two patterns for each configuration. Both our expectations concerning the dominant assumptions for each scenario and our predictions for the resulting causal attributions were confirmed. Furthermore, our assessment of individual subjects' assumptions allowed us to predict individual differences in subjects' causal attributions. The various causal attributions of a large majority of the subjects were consistent with the probabilistic contrasts computed over the focal sets consisting of the configuration plus subjects' individual patterns of assumptions in the nonconfigurational part of the cube. Thus, what may appear as capricious biases that differ from subject to subject in fact follow from a normative model.

In sum, our results with both complete-information and configurational-information problems indicate that people compute covariation over events in a focal set, which often consists of events in the entire cube. The computed covariation then determines causal inferences.

An interpretation of other results indicating bias

Biases have been reported not only in experiments using materials framed in the rather artificial format summarizing configurational information but also in studies that used apparently less artificial formats. In many of these studies (e.g., Chapman & Chapman, 1967, 1969; Jones & Harris, 1967), subjects' implicit assumptions in their focal sets were not manipulated or measured; an interpretation of these findings according to our model (e.g., in terms of subjects' prior assumptions) would therefore be speculative. However, some of these studies did manipulate and, at least partially, measure subjects' assumptions. We present our interpretation of two findings reported in such studies.[9]

Bias against using consensus information. A controversial piece of evidence against the use of consensus information was reported by Nisbett and Borgida (1975). In one of their studies, they asked subjects to read a description of an experiment by Darley and Latané (1968), in which one of the participants was heard, over an intercom, having what sounded like a seizure; the other participants faced the decision of whether to help him. Some subjects (the consensus group) were told the rather surprising results of the study (that most participants helped only after considerable delay or never), whereas other subjects (control) were not. All subjects were then asked to explain the behavior of a (male) participant who never helped. One of the questions asked was "Was the behavior of the participant due to his personality or the situation?" Because most control subjects were found to assume that most people would have helped, Nisbett and Borgida interpreted the covariation principle to predict that the surprising consensus information should generate more situational responses: Whereas the control group should perceive the target participant as an exception among others who would have helped (and thus should attribute the failure to help to the target participant), the consensus group should perceive no variation across the participants with respect to helping (and thus should attribute the behavior to the situation rather than to any particular person). Nisbett and Borgida's results showed that consensus information had no effect on attribution, leading them to conclude that, contrary to common sense and prescriptive norms, people almost totally ignore consensus information.

Notice that none of Nisbett and Borgida's (1975) subjects were told whether the participants behaved similarly in situations other than the seizure situation. Without this information, subjects were presumably free to assume that they did. If subjects made this assumption, in addition to assuming that most people typically would help (as was reported), a main-effect contrast for the target participant would be predicted for the focal set (consisting of subjects' assumptions in addition to the respective experimenter-specified information) for both the consensus group and the control group. In fact, a main-effect contrast would be predicted for the entire group of participants in the consensus condition. That is, the effect (not helping) is more likely for the target person in the control condition and for the entire group of participants (including the target person) in the consensus condition than for the population in general.

Wells and Harvey (1977) found that, when it was emphasized to subjects in a similar experiment that the participants were randomly selected from the general population, subjects in the consensus group did produce more situational attributions, indicating that they did not ignore the consensus information. The effect of emphasizing the representativeness of the sample is to supply additional information concerning how the participants probably behaved in other situations (namely, that they typically would help). With this additional information, a main-effect contrast for the seizure situation would be predicted for the consensus group (one is less likely to help in that situation than in other situations) but not for the control group (one is likely to help both in the seizure situation and in other situations). Thus, the differing results reported by Nisbett and Borgida (1975) and Wells and Harvey (1977) are both consistent with the unbiased use of covariation.

Actor–observer differences. Jones and Nisbett (1972) suggested that, whereas actors tend to attribute their own behavior to characteristics of the situation, observers tend to attribute an actor's behavior to personal characteristics of the actor. The proposed divergent perceptions of the actor and the observer have been documented in a number of studies (see Watson, 1982, for a review). One explanation offered for this divergence was in terms of the ambiguity of causal questions, which allows the adoption of different contrasting backgrounds (Einhorn & Hogarth, 1986; Hilton, 1990; Kahneman & Miller, 1986; McGill, 1989). For example, a question Nisbett, Caputo, Legant, and Maracek (1973) asked their subjects, "Why did you [your best friend] choose this major?", may be interpreted as (a) "Why did you [your best friend] choose this major in particular?" or (b) "Why did you [your best friend] in particular choose this major?" Hilton (1990) and McGill (1989) proposed that actors are likely to presuppose their own presence as a constant background factor and ask themselves what is special about the situation that caused the behavior, thus adopting the first interpretation in this example. In contrast, observers are likely to treat the situation as background and ask what is special about the actors that differentiates them from other people in the same situation, thus adopting the second interpretation in this example. Such a view predicts that if the causal question is disambiguated, the actor–observer differences should disappear.

The results of an experiment by McGill (1989) support this hypothesis, which she tested by comparing ambiguous causal questions to disambiguated versions as just illustrated. Actor–observer differences have been explained in terms of the adoption of differing contrasting backgrounds (Einhorn & Hogarth, 1986; Hilton, 1990; Jones & Nisbett, 1972; Kahneman & Miller, 1986; McGill, 1989). This explanation previously has been interpreted in terms of normality (Einhorn & Hogarth, 1986; Kahneman & Miller, 1986), conversational pragmatics (Hilton, 1990), or Mill's (1843/1973) method of difference (Hilton, 1990; McGill, 1989). We note that computing probabilistic contrasts over events in these differing backgrounds also predicts actor–observer differences. We discuss the alternative explanations later.

Implications of phenomena observed in social psychology and philosophy

We have shown that the computation of contrasts over events in a focal set can explain deviations form normative predictions discussed in philosophy and social psychology. We believe that simultaneously considering phenomena in both domains imposes constraints on model construction that are not entirely satisfied by any previous mode of causal induction proposed in either literature. On the one hand, the social causal-attribution literature underscores the fact that attributions are often based on probabilistic stimuli (e.g., "Ralph has almost always tripped over Joan's feet while dancing with her"). On the basis of such probabilistic stimuli, subjects are able to make conjunctive attributions as well as simple (i.e., single-factor) attributions. On the other hand, the philosophical literature convincingly shows that the concept of a focal set is central in explaining the distinction between causes and enabling conditions as well as the effects of shifting context on that distinction.

What is missing in previous accounts of causal induction in both social psychology and in philosophy – and what our model provides – is an account of probabilistic causal induction that specifies conjunctive as well as simple causes. Many models proposed in the literature on causes versus enabling conditions are deterministic (Hesslow, 1983, 1988; Hilton, 1990; Mackie, 1965, 1974). It is not obvious how these models can be generalized to account for conjunctive probabilistic causes, even if the probabilistic generalization for simple causes is straightforward. In social psychology, in which the phenomena to be explained are clearly probabilistic, some of the models are nonetheless deterministic (e.g., Försterling, 1989; Hewstone & Jaspars, 1987; Jaspars, 1983; the covariation principle in Kelley, 1967, 1973). Of those that are not, none provides a formal definition of conjunctive causes (e.g., Hilton & Slugoski, 1986; the ANOVA analogy in Kelley, 1967, 1973; McGill, 1989; see Cheng & Novick, 1990a, for a discussion of these models).

Table 8.1. *Event frequencies in a contingency table formed by the presence and absence of a causal factor and of the effect*

Causal factor	Effect	
	Present	Absent
Present	a	b
Absent	c	d

Moreover, models in social psychology lack an explicit and generalized concept of the focal set. The focal sets discussed in the literature on causes versus enabling conditions explain the distinction by being subsets of the universal set. Social theorists do implicitly assume that their subjects' focal sets are subsets of the universal set; for example, the condition of the target person being alive is never included as one of the potential causal factors despite the necessity of it for the person's reaction to a stimulus (the event to be explained). These theorists therefore circumvent the puzzle posed by the distinction. However, they have failed to generalize the concept of the focal set. In social causal attribution experiments, the actual focal set (i.e., the one used by subjects) often happens to be a *superset* of the subset assumed by the theorist. The implicitly assumed subsets, therefore, create rather than explain the reported biases in the social literature.

Our model builds on the previous work. It aims at satisfying the constraints imposed by phenomena in both literatures. Using the formal concept of probabilistic contrast, our model is able to account for simple and conjunctive attributions for probabilistic causal relations. Adopting the concept of a focal set, our model is able to explain the deviations in the social literature as well as the distinction among causes, enabling conditions, and causally irrelevant factors.

Other competing models of causal induction have been proposed in cognitive psychology and philosophy. In the following sections, we apply these constraints to our evaluation of these models. None of these models specify a formal account of the induction of conjunctive causes. We argue that these models do not provide an adequate account of the induction of even simple causes.

Linear heuristics in everyday causal reasoning

All linear-combination heuristics that have been proposed in the cognitive literature may be regarded as special cases of Schustack and Sternberg's (1981) model. Schustack and Sternberg (1981) described causal inference as a linear function of five variables. The variables have weights that are determined empirically by multiple regression. The first four variables involve information about covariation: a, the frequency of the joint presence of a potential cause and the effect; b, the frequency of the presence of the potential cause coupled with the absence of the effect; c, the frequency of the absence of the potential cause coupled with the presence of the effect; and d, the frequency of the joint absence of a potential cause and the effect (see Table 8.1). The fifth variable in their model is a measure of the strength of competing causes. Schustack and Sternberg's regression modeling showed that the weights for a and d were positive, whereas those for b and c were negative.

Their model is not normative in two respects. First, the four types of frequency information received different weights. Subjects showed a bias toward giving more weight to a and b (potential cause present) than to c and d (potential cause absent). Second, regardless of whether the weights are equal, their model makes anomalous predictions, as we explain.

A variety of specific linear heuristics apparently used by college students to assess covariation have been identified (e.g., Arkes and Harkness, 1983; Jenkins & Ward, 1965; Nisbett & Ross, 1980; Shaklee, 1983; Shaklee & Elek, 1988; Shaklee & Goldston, 1989; Shaklee & Hall, 1983; Shaklee & Mims, 1981, 1982; Shaklee & Tucker, 1980; Smedslund, 1963; Ward & Jenkins, 1965). We state next the four that have been reported to be used by a substantial proportion of subjects. The $a - c$ rule assesses the strength and direction of covariation by comparing a and c. That is, for cases in which the effect is present, if a potential cause is present more often than it is absent, the covariation is judged to be positive; conversely, if the potential cause is absent more often than it is present, the covariation is judged to be negative. This rule, which was used by 18% of Shaklee and Tucker's (1980) subjects and 36% of Shaklee and Hall's (1983) subjects, has weights of 1 and −1, respectively, for variables a and c and a weight of 0 for each of the other three variables in Schustack and Sternberg's model described previously. The a rule assesses covariation between two factors according to the magnitude of a (i.e., the joint presence of the two target factors). Jenkins and Ward (1965) reported that a was the best predictor of their subjects' responses. This rule has a weight of 1 for variable a and a weight of 0 for each of the remaining variables. The $a + d$ rule assesses covariation on the basis of the frequency of confirming cases (weights of 1 for a and d and a weight of 0 for each of the remaining variables). Ward and Jenkins (1965) reported the dominant usage of this rule for subjects receiving trial-by-trial information and those receiving trial-by-trial information in addition to summary information. The difference in sums of diagonal cells rule assesses the direction and strength of covariation by computing the difference between the sum of a and d and the sum of b and c. This rule, which was used by 35% of Shaklee and Tucker's subjects and 16% of Shaklee and Hall's subjects, has weights of 1 for both variables a and d, −1 for both variables b and c, and 0 for the competing-causes variable.

What do the linear-combination heuristics predict?

Is causal induction, fundamental as it intuitively seems, based on nothing more than a frail set of heuristics? We challenge this position in view of the intuitive distinction among causes, enabling conditions, and causally irrelevant factors.

Schustack and Sternberg's (1981; also see Downing et al., 1985) model was proposed to describe how people make causal inferences when given incomplete information about complex problems involving multiple factors. Although situations involving causes, enabling conditions, and causally irrelevant factors fall within the purview of their theory, predictions of linear models for such situations have not been considered previously. We derive such predictions here.

Let us examine the predictions of linear heuristics for a focal set in which one of the potential causal variables is constantly present. It is clear that, without the assumption of a focal set, these heuristics cannot account for the effects of changing contexts on causal inference. Even with such an assumption, these heuristics make anomalous predictions. Consider, for example, an answer to the question "What causes it to rain today?" for the focal set in which gravity is constantly present. For this factor in this focal set, because c and d both equal 0, the result of a linear combination of cell frequencies would be solely determined by a and b. The relative magnitudes of a and b will depend on the prevalence of other necessary conditions for rain in the events in one's knowledge base. For a resident of Edinburgh, for whom the other necessary conditions for rain are frequently present, a is much larger than b. In contrast, for a resident of Los Angeles, where it hardly ever rains, the opposite is true.

The output of a linear combination of cell frequencies is a number that may be positive, zero, or negative, corresponding, respectively, to a facilitatory cause, a causally irrelevant factor, and an inhibitory cause. Therefore, Schustack and Sternberg's (1981) linear-combination rule (for which the weights for a and b were roughly equal) and the difference in the sums of diagonal cells rule predict that a resident of Edinburgh would reply, "Gravity is a cause of rain," whereas a resident of Los Angeles would reply, "Gravity inhibits rain." For the a rule, the $a - c$ rule, and the $a + d$ rule, because c and d for gravity both equal 0 in this focal set, the causal strength of gravity is equal to a. Because a is always positive and is higher for a resident of Edinburgh than of Los Angeles, each of these rules predicts that residents of both cities would think gravity is a cause of rain and that a resident of Edinburgh would believe that it is a stronger cause than would a resident of Los Angeles.

These predictions clearly contradict an ordinary person's intuition that gravity is not a cause of rain but merely a condition that enables rainfall *regardless* of the frequency of rain in one's experience. In sum, our analysis reveals that there is no theoretical construct in the output of a linear-combination rule that could correspond to an enabling condition. According to linear heuristics, an enabling condition has the same status as a cause (either facilitatory or inhibitory depending on the prevalence of the effect).[10]

More detrimental yet to these heuristics than the previously mentioned anomalous predictions, none of these heuristics can distinguish the causal status of a factor such as gravity from causally irrelevant factors that are nearly always present in one's experience, such as houses and automobile exhaust for the inhabitants of Edinburgh and Los Angeles. The virtually constant presence of such factors implies that c and d would be much smaller than a and b and, therefore, that the result of a linear combination of cell frequencies would be largely determined by a and b. Thus, the same predictions would be made for the presence of houses or automobile exhaust as for gravity according to any of these rules! Clearly, no one would consider the presence of either of these factors to be a cause or an inhibitor of rain or the extent to which either factor causes or inhibits rain to be dependent on the frequency of rainfall in one's experience.

In sum, even with the assumption that linear combinations are computed over a focal set of events, the linear heuristics proposed in the cognitive literature erroneously predict that enabling conditions and causally irrelevant factors that are always present (or nearly always present) in one's experience have the same status as either facilitatory or inhibitory causes depending on the prevalence of the effect.

Arguments in defense of linear heuristics

A number of arguments may be made in defense of these heuristics. First, it may be argued that such heuristics should apply only to factors that are attended to. Because factors that are virtually constantly present in one's experience are not salient (although one might argue that the constant presence of automobile exhaust in Los Angeles is quite salient), causal heuristics are not likely ever to be applied to them. In the special case of Schustack and Sternberg's (1981) model, it may in addition be argued that, because of the fifth variable in their model (the strength of competing causes), a normatively covarying competing factor (which is predicted to have greater causal strength than constant factors) would reduce the causal strengths of the constant factors, rendering the predictions for the constant factors less important.

However, these arguments do not explain why, among factors that are virtually constantly present, people differentiate between enabling conditions (e.g., gravity with respect to rain) and causally irrelevant factors (e.g., the presence of automobile exhaust or houses with respect to rain), a differentiation that clearly is made. Moreover, counter to the argument based on salience, even when attention is deliberately brought to the cell frequencies for these factors, people are quite unlikely to be persuaded that these factors are indeed causes and inhibitors.

A second argument is that normatively irrelevant (i.e., noncovariational) factors that are constantly present, such as houses and automobile exhaust in the rain example, are considered to be spurious causes despite the perceived covariation according to linear heuristics. One weakness of this argument is that people probably would not acknowledge any covariational relation at all between rain and causally irrelevant factors such as houses. (In contrast, it seems that people would readily acknowledge a covariational, but noncausal, relation between a drop in the barometric reading and the approach of a storm.) Moreover, this argument cannot be applied to the predictions of linear models regarding constant factors that are normatively causally relevant (gravity is not a spurious cause of rain). Whereas normatively covariational but noncausal relations pose a problem for all purely covariational accounts of causal induction, normatively *noncovariational* relations that are constantly present pose a unique problem for linear models.

A third argument might be that the distinction between a cause and an enabling condition reflects the conversational principle of being *informative* to the inquirer given assumptions about his or her state of knowledge. Thus, whereas a cause is always a condition assumed to be unknown to the hypothetical inquirer (otherwise there would be no reason for asking), an enabling condition is typically a condition assumed to be already known to the inquirer (Hilton, 1990; Mill, 1843/1973; Turnbull, 1986; Turnbull & Slugoski, 1988; cf. Grice, 1975). For example, a competent adult inquiring about an airplane crash presumably does not know about the malfunctioning of the critical component in the airplane but does know that the gravity of the earth exerts a downward force. On this hypothesis, causes and enabling conditions do not reflect differences in underlying beliefs about the true causes of events but rather differences in the informativeness of a covarying factor with respect to an inquirer.

This hypothesis cannot absolve linear heuristics of their transgression in predicting normatively causally irrelevant factors that are constantly present to be either facilitatory or inhibitory causes depending on the prevalence of the effect (e.g., houses inhibit rain in Los Angeles) – the facilitatory or inhibitory status of these factors can hardly be assumed to be already known to the inquirer. For the same reason, neither can this hypothesis prevent such heuristics from predicting a constantly present necessary condition to be an inhibitory cause when the target effect is rare (e.g., gravity inhibits rain in Los Angeles).

This hypothesis can potentially amend linear heuristics only for those cases in which the target effect is prevalent, when a constantly present necessary condition is predicted by these heuristics to be a facilitatory cause (e.g., gravity with respect to rain in Edinburgh). In these cases, it might be argued that the causal status of such a condition is already known to the inquirer. Even for such cases, however, we (Cheng & Novick, 1991) reported evidence showing that the distinction between causes and enabling conditions cannot be explained by conversational pragmatics.

A fourth argument might be that knowledge such as gravity as an enabling condition for rain or oxygen as an enabling condition for fire is based
on academic instruction rather than natural computation. Although it is
dubious that the concept of an enabling condition is part of formal instruction, one potential explanation is that academic knowledge is perceived to be
less intuitively compelling, albeit more reliable, than naturally computed
covariations. Being from a more authoritative source, such knowledge over-
rides naturally computed covariations; but being less intuitively compelling,
it yields the status of merely enabling conditions. Note, however, that because academic instruction remains constant for an individual across contexts at any particular time, this argument cannot account for the effects of
context on causal judgments. We review later one of our experiments (Cheng
& Novick, 1991, Experiment 2) in which subjects' perceptions of an enabling
condition shifted across two contexts because of a manipulation of the focal
set, indicating that the status of an enabling condition was not due to academic training.

Explanation of evidence supporting linear heuristics

If linear heuristics do not describe natural causal induction, why were a
variety of them reported to be used by college students to assess covariation?
Crocker (1981) and Beyth-Marom (1982) observed that the phrasing of a
covariation question seems to influence the particular heuristic used. More
specifically, Beyth-Marom noted that the instructions given to subjects regarding the task often emphasized certain aspects of covariation, with the
emphasis differing from experiment to experiment. For example, in a task
involving the relationship between cloud seeding and rainfall, Ward and
Jenkins (1965) told their subjects, "At the end of the experiment . . . you are to
judge how much control seeding the clouds had over the occurrence of
rainfall. . . . Complete control means that whenever you seed, it rains, and
whenever you don't seed, it does not rain" (p. 235). These instructions
emphasized the confirming cases (Cells *a* and *d*), exactly those on which their
subjects based their judgments. Similarly, emphases on various cell frequencies reflected in the instructions given in the experiments reported by Alloy
and Abramson (1979), Jenkins and Ward (1965), Shaklee and Tucker (1980),
and Smedslund (1963) were found to closely mirror the biases, or lack of
biases, observed in the respective studies. Consistent with Beyth-Marom's
analysis, Schustack and Sternberg's (1981) finding regarding higher weights
for *a* and *b* (causal factor present) compared with *c* and *d* (causal factor
absent) may reflect their instructions to "determine the likelihood that a
particular one of the possible causes, in isolation, leads to the outcome" (p.
106). To explain their subjects' emphasis on sufficiency rather than necessity
(*a* and *b* rather than *c* and *d*), Schustack and Sternberg (1981) noted, "In our
experiments . . . the task was more specific than that of evaluating 'causality';
our subjects were evaluating the probability of the occurrence of the outcome

in the *presence* [italics added] of the target" (p. 116). (In terms of our model, the latter assessment concerns p_i, only *one* of the two proportions in our definition of a main-effect contrast.) As Beyth-Marom suggested, subjects in these experiments "appear to do what they are told to do" (p. 513). Because the issue of how causality is related to the dependent variables in these experiments is left unaddressed, the biases reported in this literature are difficult to interpret.

Suppes's model

According to Suppes (1984), an event C is a cause (a "prima facie cause" in his terminology) of an event E (the effect) if and only if (a) C occurs earlier than E, (b) $P(C) > 0$, and (c) $P(E|C) > P(E)$, where $P(E)$ is the unconditional probability of E occurring. Let ΔP_C represent the difference between $P(E|C)$ and $P(E)$. Because $P(E|C)$ is compared with the baseline defined by $P(E)$, it follows that for a potential cause C with any given $P(E|C)$, ΔP_C will be larger when $P(E)$ is small than when it is large. That is, C will be a stronger or more likely cause when E is rare than when it is prevalent. An exception to this, which we discuss later, is the case in which C is constantly present.

Consider the following two ways in which $P(E)$ may vary for C. Either there is a single cause of E or there are multiple causes. When E has the single cause C, $P(E)$ is a function of $P(C)$. When there are multiple causes of E, $P(E)$ is again a function of $P(C)$. In addition, $P(E)$ may vary depending on how often other causes produce E.

We argue that the predicted variation in ΔP_C as a result of variations in $P(C)$ is anomalous in the case in which C is the only cause (i.e., $P(E \cap \bar{C}) = 0$). We see that in this case

$$\Delta P_C = P(E|C) - P(E) = P(E|C) - P(E \cap C) = P(E|C) \cdot [1 - P(C)].$$

Therefore, ΔP_C is larger when C is rare than when it is prevalent. To take a concrete example, consider the strength of the cause of Down's syndrome for children born of older women and those born of younger women. It is known that the genetic defect that deterministically leads to the syndrome occurs vastly more often among infants of older women than among those of younger women. Thus, Suppes's model predicts that the relevant genetic defect should be perceived as a stronger cause of the syndrome for infants of younger women (for whom the cause is rare) than for those of older women (for whom the cause is more prevalent).

In contrast, the probabilistic contrast for the genetic defect is equal for the two groups of children. For either group, $\Delta p_c = p_c - p_{\bar{c}} = 1.0$. Our model, therefore, correctly predicts that the genetic defect has identical causal strength for the two groups of children.

Let us now consider the case in which there are multiple independent causes of E. In this case, the prevalence of E varies not only as a function of $P(C)$ but also as a function of how often causes other than C produce E. When these other causes often produce E, $P(E)$ will be relatively large. Therefore, for any given C, ΔP_C will be relatively small. Conversely, when other causes rarely produce E, ΔP_C will be relatively large. Like Equation 8.1, then, Suppes's rule also predicts a reduced contrast as a result of the prevalence of the effect due to other causes (see the Appendix).

In sum, both Suppes's rule and Equation 8.1 in our model correctly predict that the prevalence of other causes influences the strength of a potential cause. However, Suppes's rule erroneously predicts that a particular cause should be perceived as stronger when it is rare than when it is prevalent.

Probabilistic extension of Mill's method of difference

Several theorists hypothesized that causal explanation involves the application of Mill's (1843/1973) method of difference to a target episode and a contrasting causal background; that is, a cause is the difference between a target episode in which the to-be-explained effect is present and a contrasting causal background in which that effect is absent (Hilton, 1990; Mackie, 1965, 1974; McGill, 1989). Notice that events are partitioned according to the presence versus the absence of the effect. If one were to recast this hypothesis probabilistically, it would therefore seem most natural and accurate to formulate it in terms of the probability of a potential causal factor conditional on the presence versus the absence of the effect; that is, the contrast rule for potential cause C and effect E is

$$\Delta P_C = P(C|E) - P(C|\overline{E}).\tag{8.3}$$

In a focal set in which C is constantly present, $P(C|E) = P(C|\overline{E}) = 1$. Therefore, this extension of Mill's method of difference predicts that the factor will have a contrast of 0. Note that for this focal set, regardless of the prevalence of E, $P(E|C) = P(E)$. Therefore, Suppes's model also predicts that C will have a contrast of 0.

One potential interpretation of this result is that C is causally irrelevant in such cases. This interpretation does not permit the prediction of an enabling condition, which seems appropriate when C is causally relevant in some other focal set. These models, however, can be amended by defining an enabling condition as a factor that has a contrast of 0 within the current focal set but a positive contrast in another focal set. This amendment, however, implies that an enabling condition involves conflicting information from two focal sets, one indicating it to be a cause and the other indicating it to be causally irrelevant.

Let C_1 be a factor that is constantly present in the current focal set (e.g., a suspect's being alive at the time a crime was committed in the context of the question "Who caused the disappearance of a wallet from its owner's pocket?") but is causally relevant (i.e., is a cause in another focal set). Now, let C_2 be a cause in some focal set but, within the current focal set, occur with equal nonzero probability when the effect is present as when it is absent. Simple algebra shows that within the current focal set, according to both Suppes's model and Equation 8.3, C_2 should have a contrast of 0 (likewise according to our model). Note that according to Suppes's model and Equation 8.3, because C_1 and C_2 each have a contrast of 0 within the current focal set and is a cause in another focal set, the causal statuses of C_1 and of C_2 are indistinguishable. This is true with or without the amendment.

C_1 and C_2 do not seem indistinguishable to us. Consider the previous question about the disappearance of the wallet and the potential causal factor of the suspects "being alive." Let this factor be constantly present in the set of potential suspects (Focal Set 1) but known to be necessary for the effect (guilt in a crime) judging from another focal set (Focal Set 2). Imagine arriving at a world (Focal Set 3) in which being alive at the time a crime was committed is irrelevant for guilt in that crime (e.g., suppose there are ghosts who can steal). The causal status of "being alive" in our world and in this novel world do not seem indistinguishable. Indeed, one might find the change quite disconcerting: "Being alive," something that is a constant condition for theft in our world (Focal Set 1), becomes causally irrelevant in this novel world (Focal Set 3). Whereas juxtaposing information from Focal Sets 1 and 2 to arrive at the integrative status of an enabling condition is undisturbing, juxtaposing information from Focal Sets 3 and 2 produces a clear conflict.

In sum, we judge C_1 (e.g., the factor of "being alive" with respect to theft in Focal Set 1) to be neither causally irrelevant nor indistinguishable from C_2 (e.g., "being alive" in Focal Set 3). These intuitions contradict the predictions made by Suppes's model and by our probabilistic extension of Mill's method of difference.

Normality criterion

The normality criterion is a prominent explanation of the distinction between causes and enabling conditions that has held sway ever since it was first proposed by the philosophers Hart and Honoré (1959/1985) and Mackie (1965, 1974). A number of psychologists who have considered the distinction concurred with this explanation (Einhorn & Hogarth, 1986; Hilton & Slugoski, 1986; Kahneman & Miller, 1986; Turnbull & Slugoski, 1988; see Cheng & Novick, 1991, for a review). Hart and Honoré maintained that central to the commonsensical concept of cause, and at least as essential as the notions of invariable or constant sequence stressed by Mill and Hume, is the notion of human intervention in a course of events that would normally take place. Postulating the generalization of this notion to cases in which there is no literal human intervention, they suggested that a cause is "a *difference* from the normal course which accounts for the difference in the outcome" (p. 29). On this view, among the set of factors that are individually necessary and jointly sufficient to produce an effect (e.g., an airplane crash, a couch on fire), an abnormal factor (e.g., the malfunctioning of a component in the airplane, a dropped cigarette) will be designated as the cause, whereas normal factors (e.g., the gravitational pull of the earth, the combustibility of the couch) are merely enabling conditions. Here we limit our discussion of this criterion to its interpretation in terms of the statistical sense of prevalence. (See Cheng & Novick, 1991, for tests of two other interpretations of this criterion: namely, Kahneman & Miller's, 1986, default value interpretation and Mackie's, 1974, interpretation of normality in its ethical sense of a correct standard.) Under the statistical interpretation, normality is defined by the prevalence of the causal factor in the context (i.e., focal set) under consideration.

Cheng and Novick (1991) noted that one of the limitations of the normality view is that it does not account for the perception of the causes of prevalent events (e.g., objects staying in place instead of floating weightlessly), which have prevalent factors (e.g., the mass of the object, the gravitational pull of the earth, and so on) that are individually necessary and jointly sufficient to produce the effect. Although people in everyday life typically ask about the causes of only rare events (e.g., Kahneman & Miller, 1986; Lehnert, 1978; Weiner, 1985), leaving it to scientists to ask questions about prevalent events and discover (or invent) concepts such as gravity, ordinary people do perceive and understand such concepts when they are used in everyday contexts. For example, even though gravity is ubiquitous on the surface of the earth, the statement "The earth's gravity causes objects near its surface to fall" does not sound anomalous (even though a physicist might not put it that way). It clearly carries the usual causal implication that without the cause (e.g., in a special gravity-free chamber) the effect would not occur (i.e., objects would not fall). The statement might be made, for example, in answer to a child's question. It seems to us, then, that a major weakness of the normality position is that it cannot account for ordinary people's perception of causality regarding prevalent events, thereby implying that two distinct mechanisms underlie people's concepts of causality in everyday versus scientific situations.

We propose here that the normality criterion should be regarded as a special case of our model, which can account for causal induction involving either prevalent or rare events with a single mechanism. As illustrated in Figure 8.1, factors that have a noticeable probabilistic contrast with respect to an effect can be either prevalent or rare. In Focal Set A, the factor that has a large contrast (r) is rare. However, in Set C, the factor that has a large contrast (q) is prevalent. The normality criterion corresponds to the case in which the probabilistic contrast is computed for an effect that is rare in the context in question (as in Set A of Figure 8.1), with the exception of cases in which the cause of a rare effect (e.g., skin cancer) is prevalent (sunlight). These exceptions involve factors whose contrast values are small but nonetheless noticeable.

Our model overcomes the inability of the normality criterion to account for the perception of causality regarding prevalent events by differentiating between two concepts that are conflated in the normality view – the constant presence of a potential factor and the prevalence of such factors. We predict that people do differentiate between the two.

Manipulating the prevalence of the cause and the effect

Linear heuristics, Suppes's (1984) model, and the normality criterion all predict an impact of the prevalence of a potential causal factor or the prevalence of the effect, or both. In contrast, our model predicts that although the constancy of a potential causal factor will influence causal judgments, the prevalence of neither the factor nor the effect will have any impact in situations in which the effect is not simultaneously produced by multiple alternative causes.

We (Cheng & Novick, 1991, Experiment 2) manipulated (a) the constancy of causal factors and (b) the prevalence of the causal factors and of the effect. More specifically, we manipulated which factor covaried with an effect (plant growth) and which remained constant in two scenarios. One scenario was about the blooming of dandelions, and the other was about the maturation of corn plants. For each scenario, the effect was prevalent in one version and rare in another. In each scenario, one factor covaried with the effect. This factor differed across the scenarios (sunlight in the dandelion scenario versus nutrients in the soil in the corn scenario). The remaining three factors were held constant in each scenario: two were necessary for the effect according to subjects' prior knowledge (water in both scenarios plus nutrients or sunlight) and one was not (the presence of a house next to the plants). Within each scenario, the covarying factor was either prevalent or rare in accord with the prevalence of the effect.

Prevalence was defined for the effect and the positive value of the covarying factor by describing them as occurring in either most of or a few of the cases in the given context. For example, in the prevalent-corn scenario, many corn plants matured (i.e., the effect occurred) in four of the five cornfields tended by a farmer. There four fields had virgin soil (the positive value of the covarying factor), whereas the fifth field had its soil depleted of nutrients by previous farming.

At the end of each scenario was a question on what caused the growth of the relevant plants (e.g., what caused the corn plants to mature in the four recently cleared fields?). Subjects were asked to indicate the causal status (cause, enabling condition, causally irrelevant factor, or inhibitor) of each of the four factors in each scenario. To test the linear heuristics against our model, a second question asked whether each of four items inhibited the growth of the plants. Two of these items were constantly present in the specified focal set – one a necessary factor (e.g., sunlight in the corn scenario), the other unnecessary (the house in both scenarios). The other two items were negative values of two necessary factors – one the covarying factor (e.g., lack of nutrients for the corn scenario), the other a constant factor (e.g., lack of water in the corn scenario).

Before subjects read the scenarios, we introduced our terminology by giving a brief explanation of the distinction between causes and enabling conditions in terms of an example, chosen so as to be neutral with respect to all alternative models that allow the construct of an enabling condition. To measure the focal sets perceived by the subjects, after they made judgments on the causal status of the various factors, they were asked to rate how accurately each of three expanded questions that specified different focal sets reflected their interpretation of the causal question in the scenario. This question served to ensure that our manipulation of focal sets was effective (and it was).

Our model predicts that a potential causal factor that covaries with the effect in the focal set will be considered a cause and will be distinguished from necessary factors that are constantly present in that set. In particular, it predicts that the two scenarios will produce shifts in judgments concerning causes and enabling conditions: Factors that yield a large positive probabilistic contrast in the focal set (sunlight in the dandelion scenario vs. nutrients in the corn scenario) will be perceived as causes; conversely, those that yield a large negative contrast (lack of sunlight vs. lack of nutrients in the respective scenarios) will be perceived as inhibitors. It also predicts that necessary factors that are constant in that set (nutrients and water in the dandelion scenario vs. sunlight and water in the corn scenario) will be perceived as enabling conditions, whereas unnecessary factors that are constant in that set (the house in both scenarios) will be perceived as causally irrelevant. These predictions are independent of the prevalence of the covarying factor (e.g., whether most or few areas have rich soil) and of the effect (e.g., whether most or few corn plants matured) in the focal set.

In contrast, the normality view predicts that, within each scenario (dandelion or corn), the prevalence of the factors should influence causal judgments. In particular, only in the rare versions should necessary factors be considered causes; in the prevalent versions, necessary factors should be considered enabling conditions despite high probabilistic contrasts for those factors within the focal set. Like the normality view (but for a different reason), Suppes's (1970, 1984) contrast rule predicts that a rare necessary factor will be more likely to be considered a cause than a prevalent one, if one assumes that a factor with a large contrast is more likely to be considered a cause than a factor with a much smaller contrast.

The linear-combination heuristics predict that the prevalence of the effect should influence causal judgments on all factors that remain constant in the focal set regardless of whether they are necessary for the effect. According to heuristics that have a positive weight for a and a negative weight for b, when the effect is prevalent, these constant factors should be considered causes; when the effect is rare, these factors should be considered inhibitors. For example, in the prevalent-corn scenario, the house, sunlight, and water should be identified as causing the corn plants to mature, whereas in the rare version of the scenario, these factors should be seen as inhibiting maturation.

In support of our model, the results indicated that manipulating which factor has a large probabilistic contrast across scenarios had a huge effect on causal judgments. The effect of shifting scenarios also indicates that subjects based their judgments on the focal sets they perceived in the scenarios we constructed rather than merely on their prior knowledge, including book-learned knowledge. Within each scenario, causal judgments were just as predicted by our model but contrary to what were predicted by the normality criterion, the linear-combination heuristics, and Suppes's contrast rule. In particular, varying the prevalence of either the potential causes or the effect had absolutely no impact on judgments of causal status.

Summary and conclusion

Our probabilistic contrast model integrates normative models of covariation proposed in the cognitive and social psychology literatures and the animal behavior literature, extending them by developing formal definitions of simple and conjunctive causes and by adding an explicit assumption of computation of covariation over focal sets (an idea adapted from the philosophical literature). The present review of our explanations of deviations from normative covariation in the disparate domains of philosophy and social psychology shows that the same concept of computation of probabilistic contrasts over events in a focal set underlies causal induction in both domains. Adding to our previous theoretical analyses (Cheng & Novick, 1990a, 1991), we evaluate alternative theories of causal induction in view of the constraints imposed by a simultaneous consideration of phenomena in the two domains. Our analysis reveals that no alternative model of causal induction in cognitive and social psychology and in philosophy satisfies those constraints. Moreover, we note that (a) Suppes's (1984) model erroneously predicts that the assessment of a potential cause is a function of its prevalence, (b) the class of heuristics based on linear combinations of cell frequencies erroneously predicts that the assessment of a potential cause is a function of the prevalence of the target effect, and (c) the clear difference between a causally irrelevant factor and a constant but relevant condition favors our contrast rule over both an amended version of Suppes's rule and a probabilistic extension of Mill's (1843/1973) method of difference. Furthermore, we derive Kelley's (1971) discounting principle as a corollary of our modification of his ANOVA model. We also specify how the normality criterion and previous explanations of the distinction between causes versus enabling conditions in terms of necessity and sufficiency may be regarded as special cases of our model.

In addition to extending our previous theoretical analyses, we extend our interpretation of previous empirical results. We show that (a) our (Cheng &

Novick, 1991, Experiment 2) findings contradict the predictions made by the linear-combination rules and Suppes's (1984) model, (b) the differing results reported by Nisbett and Borgida (1975) and Wells and Harvey (1977) in their controversial debate regarding the use of consensus information are both consistent with our model, and (c) the differing attributions of actors and observers are also consistent with our model.

It seems that causal induction is the proverbial elephant. Many researchers reported on various of the multiple facets of covariation computation, a component of causal induction that has been regarded as essential. These seemingly inconsistent, nonoptimal, shifting facets of this putatively essential component have led some to conclude that a coherent elephant of causality does not exist. We by no means claim that we have a complete view of the beast; as we mentioned, there are important aspects of causality that we skirt. On the basis of our own work and our interpretation of others' reports, however, we believe we have put together enough pieces to suggest that an elephant is indeed there and that it shows signs of being an adaptive animal.

Appendix

Role of a given cause in the context of independent alternative causes

We derive the contrast for a potential cause according to our probabilistic contrast model in the cases in which independent alternative causes (a) could be present, (b) are known to be present, and (c) are known to be absent in the event to be explained. We compare these contrasts with the situation in which only a single cause is present in the target event.[11]

Let M denote the event in which potential cause m is present and $\overline{M}$ denote the event in which m is absent for the situation in which there is a single cause. Let m denote the event in which m is present and $\bar{m}$ denote the event in which m is absent for the situation in which alternative causes, $n_1, \ldots, n_k$, could be present. Assume that $P(M) = P(m)$ and that the effect does not occur when no causes are present. Let e denote the presence of the effect, and $P_{n_i}(e)$ denote the probability of a single cause n_i producing e.

Because e does not occur if none of the causes present produces e,

$$P(e|m) = 1 - P(\bar{e}|m)$$

$$= 1 - \left[1 - P(e|M)\right] \prod_{i=1}^{k} \left[1 - P_{n_i}(e)\right];$$

$$P(e|\bar{m}) = 1 - P(\bar{e}|\bar{m})$$

$$= 1 - \prod_{i=1}^{k} \left[1 - P_{n_i}(e)\right].$$

For the case in which the presence of n_i is unknown,

$$P_{n_i}(e) = P(n_i)P(e|n_i).$$

For the case in which n_i is known to be present,[12]

$$P_{n_i}(e) = P(e|n_i). \qquad \text{(A1)}$$

For the case in which all n_i are known to be absent,

$$P_{n_i}(e) = 0. \qquad \text{(A2)}$$

Probabilistic contrast model. For event M,

$$\Delta p_{\text{M}} = P(e|\text{M}) - P(e|\overline{\text{M}}),$$

where $P(e|\overline{\text{M}}) = 0$.
  For event m,

$$
\begin{aligned}
\Delta p_m &= P(e|m) - P(e|\overline{m}) \\
&= 1 - [1 - P(e|\text{M})]\prod_{i=1}^{k}[1 - P_{n_i}(e)] \\
&\quad - \left\{ 1 - \prod_{i=1}^{k}[1 - P_{n_i}(e)] \right\} \\
&= P(e|\text{M})\prod_{i=1}^{k}[1 - P_{n_i}(e)] = \Delta p_{\text{M}}\prod_{i=1}^{k}[1 - P_{n_i}(e)].
\end{aligned}
$$

Because $[1 - P_{n_i}(e)] < 1$ if n_i is a cause of e, $\Delta p_m < \Delta p_{\text{M}}$. That is, the probabilistic contrast for m is decreased by the addition of n_i, as stated by Kelley's discounting principle. The magnitude of the decrement from Δp_{M} to Δp_m is (a) proportional to both $p(e|n_i)$ and the prevalence of n_i when the presence of n_i is unknown and (b) proportional to $p(e|n_i)$ when n_i is known to be present. For the special case in which one or more alternative causes always produces e when it is present and it is known to be present whenever m is present (see Equation A1 and Footnote 12), $\prod_{i=1}^{k}[1 - P_{n_i}(e)] = 0$; therefore, $\Delta p_m = 0$. For the case in which all n_i are known to be absent, $\Delta p_m = \Delta p_{\text{M}}$.

Suppes's model. Similar predictions follow from Suppes's model. For event M,

$$\Delta P_{\text{M}} = P(e|\text{M}) - P(e),$$

where

$$P(e) = P(e \text{ and } \text{M}) + P(e \text{ and } \overline{\text{M}}).$$

Therefore,

$$\Delta P_M = P(e|M) - P(e|M)P(M) - P(e|\overline{M})P(\overline{M})$$

$$= [1 - P(M)][P(e|M) - P(e|\overline{M})] = [1 - P(M)]\Delta p_M.$$

Similarly, for event m,

$$\Delta P_m = [1 - P(m)]\Delta p_m$$

$$= [1 - P(m)]\Delta p_M \prod_{i=1}^{k}[1 - P_{n_i}(e)] = \Delta P_M \prod_{i=1}^{k}[1 - P_{n_i}(e)].$$

Because $[1 - P_{n_i}(e)] < 1$ if n_i is a cause of e, $\Delta P_m < \Delta P_M$ if $P(M) < 1$. That is, when m is not constantly present, the contrast for m is decreased by the addition of n_i. The magnitudes of the decrements from ΔP_M to ΔP_m in the cases in which (a) the presence of n_i is unknown, (b) n_i is known to be present, and (c) n_i is known to be absent parallel those for the probabilistic contrast model.

Notes

1 Even when adaptive learning apparently occurs on the basis of a single trial, covariation of the cause and the effect exists. For example, assuming that rats learn to avoid a new-tasting food after a single ingestion of that food is followed by gastrointestinal illness, the probability of the effect (gastrointestinal illness) in the presence of the potential causal factor (the new-tasting food) is 1, whereas the probability of the effect in its absence (based on prior experience) is presumably substantially less than 1. There is, therefore, a positive covariation between the events.

2 For types of effects rather than particular instances of an effect, the logical relationship between a factor and the effect is more complicated, because there are often alternative ways of producing a type of effect (e.g., there are multiple ways of producing forest fires). Developing Mill's ideas, the philosopher Mackie (1965, 1974) proposed that an individual condition (e.g., lightning) is an insufficient but necessary part of an unnecessary but sufficient (INUS) conjunctive set of factors (e.g., lightning, the presence of combustible material, and the presence of oxygen) making up a cause of a type of effect (e.g., forest fire). Although more complicated in the case of types rather than instances of effects, the logical relation between an individual condition and the effect remains equivalent for all conditions in the set.

3 The proportions are estimates of the corresponding conditional probabilities. We assume that the magnitude of the criterion should reflect the role of sample size in people's interpretations of random sampling fluctuations, but we leave the elucidation of the exact role of sample size in causal induction to future research (see Nisbett, Krantz, Jepson, & Kunda, 1983).

4 People will no doubt have greater difficulty with interaction contrasts involving greater complexity, and at some maximum level of complexity computation presumably will become impossible. However, because our model is a computational model (in Marr's, 1982, sense of the term) that specifies what is computed, rather than a process model that specifies how the computation is carried out, it leaves the issue of such limitations to a general model of processing limitations. It seems reasonable to expect that a model of processing limitations should apply across many different types of tasks rather than being specific to inference tasks. Although our model does not specify the algorithm whereby contrasts are computed, abundant evidence shows that people and other animals are indeed sensitive to probabilities and changes in probabilities (Estes, 1964; Gallistel, 1990).

5 Our model applies to dichotomous events but potentially can be generalized to continuous

effects (a model in terms of contrasts between means) or continuous causes as well as effects (a model in terms of regressions of the effect on potential causes).

6 According to our model, a cause consisting of INUS conditions (Mackie, 1965, 1974; see footnote 2) corresponds to an interaction contrast (among other sufficient contrasts, including other INUS conditions), for which the effect occurs (a) with probability of 1 in the universal set when all of its contributing factors are present and (b) with probability of 0 in a focal set in which no other sufficient cause is present when one (or more) of the contributing factors of the INUS conditions is absent. Suppose that a two-way interaction contrast, Δp_{qr}, is such a contrast. It follows that (a) $p_{qr} = 1$ in the universal set (i.e., the conjunction of q and r is sufficient for the effect), (b) $p_{\bar{q}\bar{r}} > 0$, $p_{\bar{q}r} > 0$, or $p_{q\bar{r}} > 0$ in the universal set (i.e., the conjunction is unnecessary for the effect), and (c) $p_{q\bar{r}} < 1$ and $p_{\bar{q}r} < 1$ in the focal set in which no other sufficient cause is present (i.e., q and r are insufficient under those circumstances), but (d) $p_{\bar{q}} = 0$ and $p_{\bar{r}} = 0$ in that focal set (i.e., q and r are necessary under those circumstances).

7 The discounting principle concerns the situation in which multiple alternative causal factors are present in the event to be explained. In such situations, the criterion of conditional independence requires computing contrasts for a focal set that is restricted to events in which prior known covariational factors are held constant. If the criterion is applied in these situations, the following refinement of our earlier definition of an enabling condition becomes necessary. Let i be a factor that is constantly present in the current focal set. Factor i is merely an enabling condition for a cause j in that focal set if i covaries with the effect in another focal set, and j no longer covaries with the effect in a focal set in which i is constantly absent. In contrast, i is an alternative to cause j if i covaries with the effect in another focal set, and there exists a focal set in which i is constantly absent, but j continues to covary with the effect in this set. Note that whereas an enabling condition is, by our definition, constant within the current focal set, an alternative cause can be either constant or not.

8 Materials in these experiments have sometimes been described as providing "prepackaged" covariational information (e.g., Alloy & Tabachnik, 1984; Crocker, 1981). We note that, with respect to our model, these materials – although in summary form – do not give prepackaged covariational information, even for the relatively simple case in which the focal set consists solely of events in the configuration. Consider computing a main-effect contrast for a target person for this focal set. Computing this contrast involves taking the difference between the proportion of times the effect occurs in the presence and in the absence of that person. In turn, computing the former proportion involves integrating information across the target event, distinctiveness information, and consistency information and computing the latter proportion involves consensus information. This partitioning of the given information is not prepackaged and neither is the integration nor the subtraction.

9 Many before us have argued that the selection of information is a source of bias. None, however, has argued and demonstrated that the process of causal induction per se is unbiased.

10 For the special case in which the weighted sum happens to be zero, the enabling condition has the same status as a causally irrelevant factor.

11 We thank Thomas Wickens for his valuable comments on an earlier draft of our derivations. In particular, we thank him for generalizing our derivations to apply to an indefinite number of alternative causes.

12 Equations A1 and A2, respectively, imply the restriction of the focal set to events in which n_i is present and events in which n_i is absent.

References

Alloy, L. B., & Abramson, L. Y. (1979). Judgment of contingency in depressed and nondepressed students: Sadder but wiser? *Journal of Experimental Psychology: General*, *108*, 441–485.

Alloy, L. B., & Tabachnik, N. (1984). Assessment of covariation by humans and animals: The joint influence of prior expectations and current situational information. *Psychological Review*, *91*, 112–149.

Arkes, H. R., & Harkness, A. R. (1983). Estimates of contingency between two dichotomous variables. *Journal of Experimental Psychology: General, 112,* 117–135.

Beyth-Marom, R. (1982). Perception of correlation reexamined. *Memory & Cognition, 10,* 511–519.

Bullock, M., Gelman R., & Baillargeon, R. (1982). The development of causal reasoning. In W. J. Friedman (Ed.), *The developmental psychology of time* (pp. 209–254). San Diego, CA: Academic Press.

Chapman, L. J., & Chapman, J. P. (1967). Genesis of popular but erroneous psychodiagnostic observations. *Journal of Abnormal Psychology, 73,* 193–204.

Chapman, L. J., & Chapman, J. P. (1969). Illusory correlations as an obstacle to the use of valid psychodiagnostic signs. *Journal of Abnormal Psychology, 74,* 271–280.

Cheng, P. W., & Novick, L. R. (1990a). A probabilistic contrast model of causal induction. *Journal of Personality and Social Psychology, 58,* 545–567.

Cheng, P. W., & Novick, L. R. (1990b). Where is the bias in causal attribution? In K. Gilhooly, M. Keane, R. Logie, & G. Erdos (Eds.), *Lines of thought: Reflections on the psychology of thinking* (pp. 181–197). Chichester, England: Wiley.

Cheng, P. W., & Novick, L. R. (1991). Causes versus enabling conditions. *Cognition, 40,* 83–120.

Crocker, J. (1981). Judgment of covariation by social perceivers. *Psychological Bulletin, 90,* 272–292.

Darley, J. M., & Latané, B. (1968). Bystander intervention in emergencies: Diffusion of responsibility. *Journal of Personality and Social Psychology, 8,* 377–383.

Downing, C. J., Sternberg, R. J., & Ross, B. H. (1985). Multicausal inference: Evaluation of evidence in causally complex situations. *Journal of Experimental Psychology: General, 114,* 239–263.

Einhorn, H. J., & Hogarth, R. M. (1986). Judging probable cause. *Psychological Bulletin, 99,* 3–19.

Estes, W. K. (1964). Probability learning. In A. W. Melton (Ed.), *Categories of human learning* (pp. 89–128). San Diego, CA: Academic Press.

Fösterling, F. (1989). Models of covariation and attribution: How do they relate to the analogy of analysis of variance? *Journal of Personality and Social Psychology, 57,* 615–625.

Gallistel, C. R. (1990). *The organization of learning.* Cambridge, MA: MIT Press.

Garcia, J., McGowan, B., Ervin, F., & Koelling, R. (1968). Cues: Their relative effectiveness as reinforcers. *Science, 160,* 794–795.

Garcia, J., McGowan, B., & Green, K. F. (1972). Sensory quality and integration: Constraints on conditioning. In A. H. Black & W. F. Prokasy (Eds.), *Classical conditioning II: Current research and theory.* New York: Appleton-Century-Crofts.

Grice, H. P. (1975). Logic and conversation. In P. Cole & J. L. Morgan (Eds.), *Syntax and semantics* (Vol. 3, pp. 41–58). San Diego, CA: Academic Press.

Hart, H. L., & Honoré, A. M. (1985). *Causation in the law* (2nd ed.). Oxford, England: Oxford University Press. (Original work published 1959)

Hastie, R. L. (1983). Social inference. *Annual Review of Psychology, 34,* 511–542.

Hesslow, G. (1983). Explaining differences and weighting causes. *Theoria, 49,* 87–111.

Hesslow, G. (1988). The problem of causal selection. In D. Hilton (Ed.), *Contemporary science and natural explanation: Commonsense conceptions of causality* (pp. 11–32). Brighton, England: Harvester Press.

Hewstone, M. R. C., & Jaspars, J. M. F. (1987). Covariation and causal attribution: A logical model of the intuitive analysis of variance. *Journal of Personality and Social Psychology, 53*, 663–672.

Hilton, D. J. (1988). Logic and causal attribution. In D. Hilton (Ed.), *Contemporary science and natural explanation: Commonsense conceptions of causality* (pp. 33–65). Brighton, England: Harvester Press.

Hilton, D. J. (1990). Conversational processes and causal explanation. *Psychological Bulletin, 107*, 65–81.

Hilton, D. J., & Slugoski, B. R. (1986). Knowledge-based causal attribution: The abnormal conditions focus model. *Psychological Review, 93*, 75–88.

Hilton, D. J., Smith, R. H., & Alicke, M. D. (1988). Knowledge-based information acquisition: Norms and the functions of consensus information. *Journal of Personality and Social Psychology, 55*, 530–540.

Jaspars, J. M. F. (1983). The process of causal attribution in common sense. In M. R. C. Hewstone (Ed.), *Attribution theory: Social and functional extensions* (pp. 28–44). Oxford, England: Basil Blackwell.

Jaspars, J. M. F., Hewstone, M. R. C., & Fincham, F. D. (1983). Attribution theory and research: The state of the art. In J. M. F. Jaspars, F. D. Fincham, & M. R. C. Hewstone (Eds.), *Attribution theory: Essays and experiments* (pp. 3–36). San Diego, CA: Academic Press.

Jenkins, H., & Ward, W. (1965). Judgment of contingency between responses and outcomes. *Psychological Monographs, 79*, 1–17.

Jones, E. E., Davis, K. E., & Gergen, K. J. (1961). Role playing variations and their informational value for person perception. *Journal of Abnormal and Social Psychology, 63*, 302–310.

Jones, E. E., & Harris, V. A. (1967). The attribution of attitudes. *Journal of Experimental Social Psychology, 3*, 1–24.

Jones, E. E., & Nisbett, R. E. (1972). The actor and the observer: Divergent perceptions of the causes of behavior. In E. E. Jones, D. E. Kanouse, H. H. Kelley, R. E. Nisbett, S. Valins, & B. Weiner (Eds.), *Attribution: Perceiving the causes of behavior* (pp. 79–94). Morristown, NJ: General Learning Press.

Kahneman, D., & Miller, D. T. (1986). Norm theory: Comparing reality to its alternatives. *Psychological Review, 93*, 136–153.

Kelley, H. H. (1967). Attribution theory in social psychology. In D. Levine (Ed.), *Nebraska symposium on motivation* (Vol. 15, pp. 192–238). Lincoln: University of Nebraska Press.

Kelley, H. H. (1971). *Attribution in social interaction*. Morristown, NJ: General Learning Press.

Kelley, H. H. (1973). The processes of causal attribution. *American Psychologist, 28*, 107–128.

Kelley, H. H., & Michela, J. L. (1980). Attribution theory and research. *Annual Review of Psychology, 31*, 457–501.

Lehnert. W. (1978). *The process of question answering*. Hillsdale, NJ: Erlbaum.

Lepper, M. R., Greene, D., & Nisbett, R. E. (1973). Undermining children's intrinsic interest with extrinsic reward: A test of the overjustification hypothesis. *Journal of Personality and Social Psychology, 28*, 129–137.

Mackie, J. L. (1965). Causes and conditions. *American Philosophical Quarterly, ii*, 245–264.

Mackie, J. L. (1974). *The cement of the universe: A study of causation*. Oxford, England: Clarendon Press.

Marr, D. (1982). *Vision*. New York: Freeman.

McGill, A. L. (1989). Context effects in judgments of causation. *Journal of Personality and Social Psychology, 57*, 189–200.

Mendelson, R., & Shultz, T. R. (1976). Covariation and temporal contiguity as principles of causal inference in young children. *Journal of Experimental Child Psychology, 22*, 408–412.

Mill, J. S. (1973). A system of logic ratiocinative and inductive. In J. M. Robson (Ed.), *Collected works of John Stuart Mill* (Vols. 7, 8). Toronto, Canada: University of Toronto Press. (Original work published 1843)

Nisbett, R. E., & Borgida, E. (1975). Attribution and the psychology of prediction. *Journal of Personality and Social Psychology, 32*, 932–943.

Nisbett, R. E., Caputo, C., Legant, P., & Maracek, J. (1973). Behavior as seen by the actor and as seen by the observer. *Journal of Personality and Social Psychology, 27*, 154–164.

Nisbett, R. E., Krantz, D. H., Jepson, C., & Kunda, Z. (1983). The use of statistical heuristics in everyday inductive reasoning. *Psychological Review, 90*, 339–363.

Nisbett, R. E., & Ross, L. (1980). *Human inference: Strategies and shortcomings of social judgment*. Englewood Cliffs, NJ: Prentice-Hall.

Novick, L. R., Fratianne, A., & Cheng, P. W. (1991). *Knowledge-based assumptions in causal induction*. Unpublished manuscript, Vanderbilt University.

Orvis, B. R., Cunningham, J. D., & Kelley, H. H. (1975). A closer examination of causal inference: The roles of consensus, distinctiveness, and consistency information. *Journal of Personality and Social Psychology, 32*, 605–616.

Pruitt, D. J., & Insko, C. A. (1980). Extension of the Kelley attribution model: The role of comparison-object consensus, target-object consensus, distinctiveness, and consistency. *Journal of Personality and Social Psychology, 39*, 39–58.

Reichenbach, H. (1956). *The direction of time*. Berkeley: University of California Press.

Rescorla, R. A. (1968). Probability of shock in the presence and absence of CS in fear conditioning. *Journal of Comparative and Physiological Psychology, 66*, 1–5.

Salmon, W. C. (1980). Probabilistic causality. *Pacific Philosophical Quarterly, 61*, 50–74.

Salmon, W. C. (1984). *Scientific explanation and the causal structure of the world*. Princeton, NJ: Princeton University Press.

Schustack, M. W., & Sternberg, R. J. (1981). Evaluation of evidence in causal inference. *Journal of Experimental Psychology: General, 110*, 101–120.

Shaklee, H. (1983). Human covariation judgment: Accuracy and strategy. *Learning and Motivation, 14*, 433–448.

Shaklee, H., & Elek, S. (1988). Cause and covariate: Development of two related concepts. *Cognitive Development, 3*, 1–13.

Shaklee, H., & Goldston, D. (1989). Development in causal reasoning: Information sampling and judgment rule. *Cognitive Development, 4*, 269–281.

Shaklee, H., & Hall, L. (1983). Methods of assessing strategies for judging covariation between events. *Journal of Educational Psychology, 75*, 583–594.

Shaklee, H., & Mims, M. (1981). Development of rule use in judgment of covariation between events. *Child Development, 52*, 317–325.

Shaklee, H., & Mims, M. (1982). Sources of error in judging event covariations: Effects of memory demands. *Journal of Experimental Psychology: Learning, Memory, and Cognition, 8*, 208–224.

Shaklee, H., & Tucker, D. (1980). A rule analysis of judgments of covariation between events. *Memory & Cognition, 8*, 459–467.

Shultz, T. R. (1982). Rules of causal attribution. *Monographs of the Society for Research in Child Development, 47* (Serial No. 194).

Skyrms, B. (1986). *Choice and chance: An introduction to inductive logic* (3rd ed.). Belmont, CA: Wadsworth.

Smedslund, J. (1963). The concept of correlation in adults. *Scandinavian Journal of Psychology, 4,* 165–173.

Suppes, P. (1970). *A probabilistic theory of causality.* Amsterdam: North-Holland.

Suppes, P. (1984). *Probabilistic metaphysics.* Oxford, England: Basil Blackwell.

Taylor, A. J. P. (1983). *The origins of the second world war* (2nd ed.). New York: Athenaeum.

Thibaut, J. W., & Riecken, H. W. (1955). Some determinants and consequences of the perception of social causality. *Journal of Personality, 24,* 113–133.

Turnbull, W. (1986). Everyday explanation: The pragmatics of puzzle resolution. *Journal for the Theory of Social Behaviour, 16,* 141–160.

Turnbull, W., & Slugoski, B. R. (1988). Conversational and linguistic processes in causal attribution. In D. Hilton (Ed.), *Contemporary science and natural explanation: Commonsense conceptions of causality* (pp. 66–93). Brighton, England: Harvester Press.

Ward, W., & Jenkins, H. (1965). The display of information and the judgment of contingency. *Canadian Journal of Psychology, 19,* 231–241.

Watson, D. (1982). The actor and the observer: How are their perceptions of causality different? *Psychological Bulletin, 92,* 682–700.

Weiner, B. (1985). "Spontaneous" causal thinking. *Psychological Bulletin, 97,* 74–84.

Wells, G. L., & Harvey, J. H. (1977). Do people use consensus information in making causal attribution? *Journal of Personality and Social Psychology, 35,* 279–293.

White, M. (1965). *Foundations of historical knowledge.* New York: Harper & Row.

9 Propensities and counterfactuals: The loser that almost won

Daniel Kahneman and Carol A. Varey

The question of how people think of things that could have happened but did not has attracted increasing interest among psychologists in recent years (J. T. Johnson, 1986; Kahneman & Miller, 1986; Kahneman & Tversky, 1982a; Landman, 1987; D. T. Miller, Turnbull, & MacFarland, 1990; Wells & Gavanski, 1989; Wells, Taylor, & Turtle, 1987). As philosophers have long known, the study of counterfactuals cannot be separated from a conception of causality, and an understanding of causality requires a conception of possibility and conditional probability. Counterfactual assertions rest on causal beliefs, and causal attributions invoke counterfactual beliefs, for example, about what would have happened in the absence of a putative cause. Some counterfactual assertions assign degrees of probability or plausibility to unrealized outcomes, many causal beliefs are probabilistic, and judgments of probability often draw on impressions of causal tendencies or propensities. The present article is concerned with a psychological analysis of this nexus of issues.

Our study began with an attempt to understand the psychology of assertions of the form "*X* almost happened," which we call *close counterfactuals*. An important characteristic of such assertions is that they are not expressed as a conditional with a specified antecedent, as counterfactual conditionals

This chapter originally appeared in the *Journal of Personality and Social Psychology*, 1990, 59(6), 1101–1110. Copyright © 1990 by the American Psychological Association. Reprinted by permission.

This article is based on a talk presented at the Conference on Counterfactual Thinking and Other Forms of Mental Simulation, Brown County, Indiana, April 1989. The research was supported by the Air Force Office of Scientific Research, Air Force Systems Command, U.S. Air Force, under Grant A FOSR-88-0206 to Daniel Kahneman.

We are grateful to Maya Bar-Hillel, Baruch Fischhoff, Dale Griffin, Lenore Kahneman, Igal Kvart, Dale Miller, and Amos Tversky for helpful comments and conversations; to Anne Treisman for her insights throughout the project; and to three anonymous reviewers for useful suggestions.

are. The close counterfactual does not invoke an alternative possible world, but states a fact about the history of this world – namely that things were close to turning out differently than they did.

Our approach combines some elementary phenomenological observations and an equally elementary linguistic inquiry into the conditions under which close counterfactual assertions are appropriate. The genre is not unknown in psychology: Heider (1958) and Schank and Abelson (1977), in particular, have successfully carried out ambitious exercises in this vein. Studies of what people mean when they say that "John went to the restaurant" or when they use the words *can* and *try* have contributed significantly to an understanding of how people think about events and actions. In this article we examine the use of the word *almost* in a speculative attempt to explore how people think about counterfactuals, probability, and causation.[1] The present analysis is restricted to cases in which "X almost happened" implies that X could have happened. We ignore figurative uses of *almost* in which it is used to denote "coming close" without implication of possibility, as in "at that bend the train almost touches the embankment." We also restrict our discussion of *almost* to cases in which either the actual outcome or the close counterfactual is an achievement (see Lyons, 1977; G. A. Miller & Johnson-Laird, 1976; Vendler, 1967) – a change of state that occurs at a particular moment, usually as the culmination of a longer causal episode. We analyze the beliefs that a speaker expresses by the assertion that an individual almost died, or almost missed a deadline, and examine what such beliefs imply to us about the cognitive representation of uncertain events and of causal propensities.

This article develops the following ideas: (a) Counterfactuals, causes, and (some) probabilities are treated as facts about the world, not as constructions of the mind. (b) The absence of perfect hindsight indicates that people attribute inherent uncertainty to causal systems – what happened is not treated as necessary or inevitable. (c) The perception and representation of causal episodes is organized around possible outcomes of the episode. (d) Probabilities of outcomes can be assessed on the basis of advance knowledge (dispositions) or of cues gained from the causal episode itself (propensities). The distinction is critical to the use of *almost*, which requires the attribution of a strong propensity to the counterfactual outcome. (e) Cues to propensity are the temporal or causal proximity of the focal outcome and indications of rapid progress through a causal script. (f) A general schema of causal forces competing over time is applicable to many achievement contexts. (g) There are characteristic differences between a psychological and a philosophical approach to the analysis of probability, causality, and counterfactuals.

The counterfactual stance

The statement "X almost happened" implies several ancillary beliefs. It commits the speaker to the belief that another observer with the same information would agree with the counterfactual assertion, as would be the case with public, objective facts. The close counterfactual also implies that X could have happened, denying the necessity or inevitability of what actually happened and implicitly denying the deterministic character of the situation. We examine these beliefs in the following sections.

Objective reference

By definition, counterfactual statements refer to events that did not, in fact, occur. However, there is a compelling intuition that some counterfactuals are treated as having an objective character, not as mere mental constructions. Refuting the possible-worlds analysis of counterfactuals, Goodman (1983) put the point strongly: "We have come to think of the actual as one among many possible worlds. We need to repaint that picture. All possible worlds lie within the actual one" (p. 57). In ascribing objective status to counterfactuals, we intend to contrast the attitude toward these objects of thought from the attitude toward imaginings, fantasies, and desires, which are normally tagged as subjective (M. K. Johnson, 1988). The discrimination of what actually happened from what almost did is, of course, essential in the monitoring of reality – the counterfactual event is not perceived as real, but it is not treated as subjective. The "fact" is that the outcome truly is close, or is not close, independently of anyone's beliefs.

The distinction between beliefs that have objective or subjective status recalls an earlier discussion of alternative cognitive representations of probability (Kahneman & Tversky, 1982b). Two main interpretations of that notion were identified, which respectively assign it subjective or objective status. In the subjective interpretation, which is standard in Bayesian philosophy, a probability judgment describes the subject's degree of belief in a proposition. "The probability that the Nile is longer than the Amazon is p" is usually understood as describing the speaker's beliefs, not as a fact about these rivers. The attribution of subjective status to a belief is often marked by the possessive pronoun: "My probability that the Nile is longer than the Amazon . . ." is more natural than "the probability that the Nile. . . ." In contrast, the probability that a thumbtack will land on its point if tossed and the probability that Team A will defeat Team B are normally understood as descriptions of the causal dispositions of the thumbtack or of the competing teams. A speaker who wishes to indicate a subjective interpretation of probability will use the possessive pronoun: "My probability that Team A will win is . . ." acknowledges the possibility of valid alternatives, a stance that is not usually adopted in factual statements.

The two types of representation of uncertainty are most clearly distinguished when the uncertainty is removed. The possessive pronoun is then obligatory if the probability has subjective status. "The probability that the Nile is longer than the Amazon was . . ." is simply anomalous. In contrast, it is reasonable to maintain that the probability that the thumbtack would land on its point was .55 even when it is known that it did not do so on a particular instance. More interestingly, the statement that "the probability that Team A would win was high . . ." is acceptable even if that team is known to have lost. The statement of past probability need not refer to anyone's beliefs at the time of the episode. The statement could be made, for example, by a speaker who learned, after the game had ended, that a player of Team B had undertaken to throw the game if he had an opportunity to do so. As this example illustrates, current knowledge of the relevant causal factors may allow a speaker to say retrospectively that an event that did not take place had high probability – and as a special and rather extreme case to assert that the event almost occurred.

Although in this article we often appeal to the reader's intuitions in the expectation that they match ours, we also tested some of our conclusions by collecting judgments of appropriateness from native speakers of English. Subjects were recruited on the Berkeley campus by a poster offering students a small payment in return for a completed questionnaire. Respondents were given instructions and several questions as illustrated by the examples below.

In the following questions you are asked to rate statements on a scale from "appropriate" to "very peculiar." One or more statements are presented for each question. You are to rate whether the statement in italics is appropriate, given the information in the rest of the question.

1. *Tom almost died* but in fact he was never in real danger.

   Appropriate 7%   Somewhat peculiar   27%
   Very peculiar 66% $(n = 29)$[2]

2. *Everyone thought Phil almost died* but in fact he was never in real danger.

   Appropriate 69%   Very peculiar 10% $(n = 29)$

3. The autopsy showed that when he was a child, Sid had suffered from a rare childhood disease. The pathologist said that if the disease had lasted a few days longer, it would have killed him. No one knew about it at the time; they thought he had a mild case of measles. *Sid almost died* as a *child from that rare disease.*

   Appropriate 61%   Very peculiar 0% $(n = 18)$

These examples illustrate that the close counterfactual has the status of a historical fact. As is generally true when such facts are asserted, everything known to the speaker at the time of the utterance can be relevant, but the beliefs of observers of the actual event are not. As shown by Example 2, the objective status of close counterfactuals allows them to be believed erroneously. Indeed, counterfactuals can be faked. Professional wrestlers on television have perfected the art of appearing almost to kill one another, but they avoided regulation by demonstrating that their occupation is actually quite safe.

Like counterfactuals and (some) probabilities, causal attributions are also treated as objective facts about the world. This is true of causality directly observed, as in the perception of a collision and in Michotte's (1946) demonstrations of launching. It is also true of the more abstract causes that are judged to raise the (objective) probabilities of events or, in some contexts, render them inevitable (Mackie, 1974). The counterfactual assertion that an effect would not have occurred in the absence of the cause, the sine qua non condition of necessity, has the same objective character.

Inherent uncertainty

The frequent mentions of counterfactual possibilities in everyday discourse demonstrate a prevailing intuition that things could have been different, and in some cases almost were. This intuition commits the speaker to a particular set of beliefs about causality. Specifically, X is neither necessary nor inevitable if it can properly be said that Y almost happened instead of it. Naive intuitions are evidently not dominated by a pervasive belief in strict determinism. Kvart (1986) reached a similar conclusion in his discussion of counterfactual conditionals.

There is an intriguing tension between the intuition that things could have been otherwise and the well-known hindsight effect, in which the inevitability of events that actually took place tends to be exaggerated. The evidence is compelling that retrospective assessments of the probability of events are affected by knowledge of whether or not these events have taken place (Fischhoff, 1975, 1982). The term *creeping determinism* has been used in this context. Two distinct forms of hindsight effects are associated, respectively, with subjective and objective interpretations of probability. The most common test of hindsight effects requires the retrieval of a past state of belief: "What was your probability at the end of 1988 that the Berlin Wall would be opened within a year?" A hindsight bias is revealed in such questions by a tendency to exaggerate the past subjective probabilities of whatever is now known to be true. An example of an objective hindsight question could be "In the light of current knowledge, what was the probability in 1988 that the Berlin Wall would be opened within a year?" A discrepancy between prospective and retrospective probabilities is typically observed in tests of objective as well as subjective hindsight (Fischhoff, 1975).

Unlike the subjective case, hindsight with an objective interpretation of probability is not necessarily a mistake. It is entirely reasonable for an observer to make inferences about a causal system from the knowledge that it produced a particular outcome. Indeed, what is most puzzling in this context is the limited extent of creeping determinism in retrospective evaluations of outcomes.

Of course, not all causal systems are uncertain. As illustrated by most people's attitudes toward the mechanical and electronic devices that surround them, a belief in strict determinism does not require much understanding of how the system works; it cannot be ignorance about the causal system that precludes determinism about close counterfactuals. It is an important fact about causal reasoning that a sense of the necessity of consequences is often absent. In particular, there is no sense of necessity or inevitability in considering games of chance, many contests and competitions, some physical systems (e.g., weather and chance devices), or intentional actions.

The representation of causal episodes

The idea that perceived goals serve to organize the representation of action and imbue events with meaning was articulated by Heider (1958), and is at the core of the more recent treatments of scripts and story grammars (Black & Bower, 1979; Kintsch & van Dijk, 1978; Rumelhart, 1977; Schank, 1975; Trabasso, Secco, & van den Broek, 1984) and treatments of decision making and causal reasoning that rely on a story-based account (Pennington & Hastie, 1988; Read, 1987). Our conception of causal episodes generalizes this idea to achievements. The class of achievements contains the outcomes of intentional action but is much richer: Dying from a disease, a river overflowing its bank, and the Dow–Jones index rising 1,000 points in a year are all achievements. Many achievements are associated with particular causal scripts. The representation of an episode as an instantiation of a causal script is therefore organized in terms of its possible *focal outcomes*, and attention to different achievements will alter the representation. The storm that could fill the reservoirs could also ruin the cherry crop, and its representation will be different if attention is directed to one of these outcomes rather than the other.

To illustrate the function of focal outcomes, we introduce a thought experiment to which we shall repeatedly return. Imagine observing a sequence of red and blue balls as they are drawn from an urn, or the representation of such a process on a computer screen. Note the potent effects of an intention to watch for a particular outcome, such as the color that is most frequent after 11 draws, or an excess of four red balls or six blue balls – whichever happens first. Although these focal outcomes are not goals, they serve the same function in organizing the impression of the sequence. Most important, watching the same sequence with different outcomes in mind alters the experience. Although our thought experiment involves real-time observation and uncertainty, neither of these elements is essential: A designated outcome will affect the interpretation of a story, and the effect is not reduced when thinking of an episode whose outcome is already known.

The probability of the focal outcome may fluctuate in the course of a causal episode. Changes of probability are always involved in close counterfactuals: Perhaps the most compelling intuition about the statement "X almost happened" is that the probability of X must have been quite high at some point before it dropped – all the way to zero if another outcome eventually terminated the episode.[3]

There are several reasons for probability changing in the course of an episode. We turn again to the urn example to illustrate two types of probability change. If there was initial uncertainty about the composition of the urn, beliefs about the urn will change to accommodate observed events – by Bayes's rule for an ideal observer – and the probability of the focal outcome will change accordingly. In addition, the actual probability of the focal outcome also changes *because* of the intervening events. Every red ball drawn makes it more probable that the aggregate outcome will be an excess of red over blue balls. The probability of the focal outcomes will change, more or less regularly and perhaps with large fluctuations, until a decisive event brings about an outcome that terminates the episode. Note that this situation can support a close counterfactual: It is easy to imagine a sequence of draws of which it can appropriately be said that the focal outcome almost occurred (red almost won), or almost did not.

The same types of changes of probability will also be found in observing (or hearing about) a storm that could cause a flood or a couple deciding on a joint future. The events that constitute the episode reveal the strength of an underlying causal process, and also contribute to bring about or retard the outcome. They also indicate possible changes in the causal system – changes that could be modeled by an urn whose composition is modified after each draw, perhaps in response to the draw.

Propensities and dispositions

The discussion so far has been in terms of "objective" probabilities – in the chance example these are probabilities that could be computed precisely, given some initial beliefs about the composition of the urn. It is evident from this example that an account of *almost* in terms of probability has some appeal: The probability of the counterfactual outcome must have been high at some point. It turns out, however, that an account that relies exclusively on objective probabilities will not work. Some aspects of the puzzle to be solved are illustrated by the following examples:

4. Mark tried to register for the chess tournament. Because of a problem in mailing the form he missed the registration deadline by one day. Mark is a much stronger player than all the participants in the tournament. *Mark almost won the tournament.*

   Appropriate 0%   Very peculiar 97% ($n = 33$)

5. At the end of a long game of chance, John could have won the whole pot if a die that he rolled showed a six. The die that he rolled was loaded to show six 80% of the time. John rolled it and it showed a two. *The die almost showed six.*

Appropriate 0%   Very peculiar 77% ($n = 31$)

6. At the end of a long game of chance, John could have won the whole pot if a die that he rolled showed a six. The die that he rolled was loaded to show six 80% of the time. John rolled it and it showed a two. *John almost won the whole pot.*

Appropriate 43%   Very peculiar 20% ($n = 31$)

The close counterfactual is decisively rejected in Examples 4 and 5 but not in Example 6, although the prior probability of the focal outcome was high in all cases. Before it was rolled, the probability of the die showing six was .80 in Examples 5 and 6, and the prior probability of Mark winning the tournament was also high, though unspecified. Despite this, the intuition that *almost* is inappropriate in the first two examples is so strong that they seem almost absurd. A strong belief in the counterfactual conditional "Mark would have won if he had played" is not sufficient to support the close counterfactual "Mark almost won," even if it is also accepted that he almost played in the tournament. Why is this the case? And what else is required for the close counterfactual to be appropriate?

The answer to the first question is that the close counterfactual is never appropriate if it is only supported by indications of likelihood or causal force that were available before the onset of the relevant causal episode. Achievements, such as winning a tournament, getting married, or a die showing six, are associated with causal scripts that usually have a definite starting point: when play begins, when the couple start dating, when the die is rolled. Probabilities can be assigned to possible outcomes of a causal process before it is initiated: Mark may be a rated player, the couple could appear severely mismatched, the die could be loaded. We shall refer to the cognitive representation of such prior probabilities as the (perceived) *disposition* of a causal system to yield particular outcomes. Examples 4 and 5 show that dispositions, however strong, do not suffice to support the assertion of a close counterfactual.

A close counterfactual must be supported by the evidence of event cues, as these accumulate in the course of the causal episode. We use the term *propensity* for what is learned about the probability of an outcome from observing event cues or from hearing about them. Mark had a disposition to win his chess tournament and probably would have won it if he had registered, but the causal episode for his victory never began, and there was therefore no opportunity to establish a propensity for that outcome. The standard example of propensity in a chance event is the cinematic cliché of the roulette wheel that slows down as it approaches a critical number, slows down even more, leans against the spring, then finally trips it and stops on a neighboring number. To be described as almost showing six, a die must display a propensity to stop its roll in that position.

The contrasting responses to Examples 5 and 6 illustrate the need to distinguish propensity from probability. We suppose that our respondents would have assigned a probability of .8 both to the die showing six and to John winning the whole pot. However, the propensities of the two outcomes clearly differ. Example 6 illustrates a common structure in which one achievement (the die showing six) is nested inside another (John winning the pot). Because the focal outcome of winning the pot invokes a more inclusive causal episode that had begun long before the critical play, John can be said to have had a propensity to win, even if it is not established that the die had a propensity to show six. Thus, although the two statements have the same probability before the throw, the differential effects of propensity and disposition allow "John almost won" to be appropriate although "the die almost showed six" is not.

We should now review the rather subtle relations among the concepts of disposition, propensity, and probability, as they are used in this article. Disposition has been defined as the cognitive representation of the probability of a focal outcome, before the beginning of the relevant causal episode. A disposition can be assessed either prospectively or in hindsight, depending on whether or not the outcome is known. Disposition is a psychological construct, not a logical or mathematical one, and in view of what is known about intuitive judgment there is little reason to expect dispositions to obey the standard axioms of probability (Kahneman, Slovic, & Tversky, 1982). Dispositions represent knowledge about the particular causal system that will (or will not) produce the focal outcome of current concern. Dispositions are inferred from the base rates of outcomes previously produced by that system (Mark has won most of his tournaments) or from structural knowledge that supports causal inferences (the die was loaded in a particular fashion). Thus, the concept of disposition has causal as well as statistical implications.

Our concept of propensity is even more imbued with causal content. Event cues reveal the causal system in action. They indicate advance toward the focal outcome, or regression away from it. They suggest changes in the momentary state of the causal system – changes that may be real or illusory, as when a player is seen to have a "hot hand" (Gilovich, Vallone, & Tversky, 1985). Perhaps most important, propensities depend on the proximity of the outcome, on the possibility of quickly achieving a decisive advance to it. In sharp contrast to probability, the propensities for all competing outcomes of a process may be low early in a causal episode, and more than one propensity can be high at once when the end is close. These ideas are elaborated in subsequent sections.

Our main interest in the remainder of this article is to use close counterfactuals to learn about propensity. We consider propensity to be a dimension of the experience and cognitive representation of events, just as pitch is a dimension of auditory experience. There should be no presuppositions about the determinants of propensity; in particular, propensity could reflect causality as well as probability, just as pitch depends on both the frequency and the intensity of sound. To anchor this speculative analysis in observables, we assume that the appropriateness of *almost*, in its literal meaning, provides a usable indication of high propensity.

Disposition neglect

Dispositions and propensities are differentially susceptible to revision in hindsight. Consider two cases in which the observer of the last lap of a footrace might assign a high probability of victory to a particular runner: (a) a runner who is in contention and is known to have a strong finish, or (b) a runner who has been catching up rapidly with the leader. The real-time expectations are equally strong in both cases, we assume, but they are based on different cues – dispositional knowledge in (a) and event cues in (b). Now imagine that the two runners both fail to win, by the same amount: The first did not show a strong finish and the second never quite caught up. Note that it will not do to say of the runner who usually has a strong finish that he or she almost won the race with a strong finish, if in fact he or she showed no evidence of talent on that particular occasion. The close counterfactual that the loser almost won is more applicable to (a) than to (b), although a counter-factual conditional could be appropriate in (a). The general hypothesis is that dispositional expectations that are not confirmed by event cues become irrelevant in hindsight.

The differential weighting of event cues and dispositional expectations in retrospective judgments will be called *disposition neglect*; the effect bears an intriguing resemblance to the relative neglect of base-rate information that has been observed in some prospective judgments. For example, the judged probability that a short personality sketch describes a lawyer rather than an engineer is not much affected by the proportion of engineers and lawyers in the sample from which it was drawn. The information about the individual case largely supersedes the information about the base rate instead of com-bining with it according to Bayes's rule (Kahneman & Tversky, 1973). Simi-larly, Ajzen (1977) found that people predicting exam success for a student based their predictions on a descriptive sketch and gave little weight to the information that the student was drawn at random from a set selected by a researcher to include 75% failures. As Ajzen observed, however, the ne-glected base rate in these examples is merely statistical. There is no causal connection between the composition of the student sample and the factors that would make a particular student succeed or fail. The situation changes when such a causal connection is provided: The information that 75% of students taking the test failed it leads readily to the inference that the test was a difficult one, and the information has much more impact on the judgment of the probable success of an individual (Ajzen, 1977). There have been other demonstrations of the general principle that causally relevant base-rate information will not be neglected (Gigerenzer, Hell, & Blank, 1988; Tversky & Kahneman, 1980, 1982; see also Bar-Hillel, 1990, for a discussion of these issues).

Ajzen's (1977) experiment demonstrated that dispositional information tends to dominate statistical base rates, and that dispositional information from two sources (the difficulty of the exam and the student's ability) tends to be integrated. A variation of this experiment would demonstrate disposition neglect: Evidence that a student is extremely able does not support the inference that the student almost passed an exam that he failed, nor does the knowledge that a test was very hard support the conclusion that a student who passed almost failed it. In assessing close counterfactuals, event cues dominate causal base rates and other dispositional information.

The neglect of statistical base rates leads to violations of Bayes's rule in prospective judgments. The neglect of dispositional expectations in hindsight is not necessarily an error, but the psychology of the two effects may well reflect a single general principle. In both cases the data that bear most directly on the causal forces at work in the individual case have the greatest impact.

Correlates of propensity

In this section we develop the concept of propensity by examining two of its close correlates: shrinking distance and increasing impact. The role of distance and motion in the close counterfactual is evident in the near synonymy of "X almost happened," "X nearly happened," and "X was close to happening." These expressions invoke a rich metaphor in which an extended causal process is represented as movement in space (e.g., see the "source–path–goal" kinesthetic image schema analyzed in Lakoff, 1987; the various "journey" metaphors in Lakoff & Johnson, 1980; and the force and space images in Talmy, 1981, 1983). This metaphor imposes a metric of causal distance between situations and suggests the closest approach to an outcome as a measure of its propensity. The second correlate of increasing propensity is an escalation in the apparent causal significance of events as the outcome is approached.

Causal proximity

The present analysis has emphasized causal processes that extend over time, but close counterfactuals can be asserted on the basis of a measure of proximity or similarity even when the process is instantaneous. For example, the statement "The house was almost struck by lightning" is appropriate when lightning struck nearby. The actual outcome is the only event cue in such cases, and it induces a gradient of propensity in its spatial and temporal vicinity. From the fact that lightning struck in a particular place at a particular time, a propensity is inferred to strike in neighboring places, and at about the same time. Similarly, it is appropriate to say that Tom almost got six sixes in rolling dice if he got five sixes and a two. Indeed, it would be even more appropriate to say that Tom almost got six sixes if he rolled five sixes and a five.

Scripts for achievements often specify a series of landmarks that provide a provisional metric of proximity to the outcome. Getting a wedding license, for example, is one of the last landmarks in the script for marriage. It will usually be appropriate to say of a couple that came that far but did not marry that they almost got married. However, although high propensity for an outcome can be inferred from the near completion of the script for that outcome, such inferences are tentative and dependent on default assumptions about the causal system. Thus, it is not correct to say of a tethered mountain climber who falls that he or she "almost fell to the bottom of the cliff," or even was close to doing so, although the script for a fall to the bottom was almost completely satisfied. Nor will it be correct to say that Tom almost rolled six sixes if one of the dice has been altered to make that outcome impossible. The propensity for a counterfactual outcome cannot be reduced to a superficial assessment of the similarity of the actual episode to the completed script for that outcome.

Intentions can contribute to an impression of propensity. For example, it is more appropriate to say that the escaping murderer was almost killed by a shot that went six inches above his or her head if the shot was intended to kill than if it was intended to warn. Intentions do not suffice, however, when there are significant obstacles to be overcome. For an individual to "consider doing X" is sometimes sufficient to support the inference that the individual "almost did X," but not always. Selected examples follow:

7. Martin considered getting married to Meg. *Martin almost married Meg.*

   Appropriate 14%   Very peculiar 34% ($n = 29$)

8. Neil considered not getting married to Amanda. *Neil almost didn't marry Amanda.*

   Appropriate 62%   Very peculiar 19% ($n = 32$)

9. Fred considered stealing his child's savings. *Fred almost stole his child's savings.*

   Appropriate 30%   Very peculiar 15% ($n = 75$)

10. Ned considered breaking into a bank vault. *Ned almost broke into a bank vault.*

    Appropriate 18%   Very peculiar 44% ($n = 75$)

Mere consideration of a marriage is not sufficient (at least in this culture) to support the assertion that the marriage almost took place. The situation is somewhat different in Example 8, because either party (again in this culture) has the power single-handedly to put a stop to plans to marry. Responses to Examples 9 and 10 show that subjects are sensitive to the fact that much more remains to be done, beyond mere consideration, for the project of breaking into a bank vault than for stealing one's child's savings.

Decisiveness

Many outcomes are produced by a conjunction of events, all contributing to making the outcome necessary. It is useful to distinguish two privileged roles of events in multiple causation: *Critical events* are those that initiate a causal episode, potentiate subsequent causal events, or both; *decisive events* are those that rule out all alternatives, and ensure (or almost ensure) a particular outcome. The special role of critical events that initiate coherent causal episodes has been confirmed in studies of blame (J. T. Johnson, Ogawa, Delforge, & Early, 1989) and studies of mental simulations that "undo" outcomes (Wells et al., 1987). The person who starts a quarrel will get much of the blame for its consequences. However, the decisive and irreversible events that terminate causal episodes are also important, especially when the events in the causal sequence are not themselves causally related (D. T. Miller & Gunasegaram, 1990). Hart and Honoré (1959) proposed that a cause is found by "tracing back" from the effect to the nearest plausible candidate in the causal chain. They also discussed the legal doctrine of the last clear chance: The last person who had a good chance to avoid harm is alone held responsible (see also Wells & Gavanski, 1989). The responsible individual is the one whose actions cannot be reversed by anyone else. The same intuition shows up in the context of blackjack; many players believe that the player on the seventh box, who receives cards immediately prior to the dealer's draw that all players are trying to beat, determines the outcomes for all players (Keren & Wagenaar, 1985). By the time the cards are dealt, the sequence of cards is fixed, though unknown, and the seventh player, by refusal or acceptance of a card, decisively determines its allocation.

It is instructive to analyze decisiveness in terms of probability. Consider an urn game that ends whenever the excess of balls of one color reaches a critical value. Suppose the prior probability of red being the "winning" color is high, because there are more red than blue balls in the urn. Now imagine another scenario, which involves a balanced urn and a majority of red balls in early draws. When the objective probabilities of a red victory are matched in these two scenarios, the probabilities of two more specific events will be higher in the case favored by event cues: (a) the probability of the outcome occurring *soon*, and (b) the probability that the current lead will be preserved until the end of the game. We suggest that impressions of propensity are related to the probability of the next favorable event being decisive, and of current progress not being reversed before the outcome is reached.

The intuition that causal impact increases in the course of the episode is especially compelling when the episode terminates at a fixed time. Obviously, the probability that a team that leads by a touchdown will win the ball game must increase as time remaining to play diminishes. A score that changes the lead is accordingly perceived as more likely to be decisive if it comes late rather than early in the game. Correspondingly, the close counterfactual is most compelling if the propensity for the unrealized outcome peaked late in the causal episode. An early event may support a counterfactual such as "Team A could have won if Fred had not missed that touchdown in the first quarter," but the description "Team A almost won" is much more convincing if the missed touchdown happened in the closing minutes of the game.

Propensities for all outcomes will be weak in the early phases of a causal episode, if no decisive advantage can be gained at that time. Early in a football game, neither team has a strong propensity to win, although one of them may have a strong disposition to do so. Later on, propensities to win will be attributed to a team to the extent that it already has, or appears on its way to achieving, a lead that is likely to be maintained to the end. Toward the end of the game, a team with a large lead has an overwhelming propensity to win, and both teams have a significant propensity if the game is close. On the usual interpretation of probability, of course, the sums of the probabilities of victory for the two teams (barring ties) should add to one at all stages of the game. A formal representation of propensities should incorporate the attribute of noncomplementarity, which is admissible in some nonstandard models of probability (Shafer, 1976).

Competitive causation

The psychological concept of propensity that was introduced in the preceding section has a dual meaning as a probabilistic and as a causal notion. We have interpreted propensity as an intuitive assessment of the current probability of the focal outcome based on event cues, and also as an assessment of the current probability of particular cases of the focal outcome – for example, the event of this outcome occurring soon. But the term *propensity* was chosen because it also denotes a direct expression of causal force – *Webster's Dictionary* defines propensity as "an urgent and often intense natural inclination." Urgency and intensity are not part of the meaning of probability in theoretical discourse. We suggest, however, that these dynamic features are important aspects of the cognitive representation of many causal processes, including, in particular, the processes that have achievements as outcomes.

The probabilistic and the causal aspects of propensity suggest different representations of the relation between the alternative outcomes of a causal process. In the language of probability, this relation is expressed by complementarity: Changes in the probability of the focal outcome are mirrored by compensating changes in the aggregate probability of other outcomes. In the language of causal dynamics, the relation between alternative outcomes is best described as competition and conflict. The competition metaphor is evident in many phrases chosen to describe episodes and their outcomes (e.g., "They had to admit defeat and gave up hope of beating the deadline" or "The Harvard job offer won out"). A competitive model of causation is particularly appealing for close counterfactuals, where the strongest propensity is associated first with one outcome, then with another – suggesting a shifting balance between variable opposing forces.

A schema of competing and interacting propensities is most obviously applicable to athletic contests, from which several of our examples have been drawn, but is not restricted to these situations. Displays of the chance games that we have discussed invite a competitive interpretation, much as the figures in the famous Heider and Simmel (1944) animation evoke impressions of intentionality and meaningful interaction. We propose the general hypothesis that the competitive schema is commonly evoked by situations in which the focal outcome is an achievement. These include such varied cases as the making of a difficult individual decision, the vicissitudes of a couple that may or may not break up or get married, the struggle of a firm threatened with bankruptcy, the story of a life-threatening illness, the construction of a building under time constraints, and the wrecking of a building by a tropical storm. Each of these situations is defined by one or more focal achievements. Causal episodes that produce such achievements, or fail to produce them, are naturally described as a struggle of conflicting and variable forces favoring alternative outcomes, or in some cases as a struggle between a single variable force and a series of obstacles.

The notion of conflict between opposing forces is not new to psychological analyses of causality, at least in the context of explaining action. Lewin (1936) introduced motion in a force field as a model of action under conflict. His theory influenced Heider's subsequent analysis of the naive theory of action, in which action is the resultant of the effective personal force and the effective environmental force (Heider, 1958). Both models explain action as a vectorial combination of forces. Lewin's famous theory of conflict also incorporated a dynamic element: The forces acting on the individual change predictably as the individual moves toward sources of attraction or away from aversive states. In general, however, applications of force field analysis have been static. There has been little emphasis on time or on the possibility of causal forces interacting and changing in the course of an event.

A model of competing propensities would extend Lewinian force field analysis in several ways. First, the concept of focal achievement applies to outcomes that are not goals, such as someone dying from a disease, and to situations that do not involve intentions at all, such as a storm destroying a building. Second, the focus of the competitive model is on extended causal episodes. Third, the competitive model attributes inherent uncertainty to causal systems and describes causal episodes in terms of propensities that may change and interact.

Psychology – or philosophy?

The present study occupies a somewhat uncomfortable middle ground between psychology and philosophy. We have attempted to identify the conditions under which a particular class of counterfactual assertions would be considered true, or appropriate, and we have introduced a notion of propensity to account for these observations. The questions we addressed are similar to those modern philosophers often raise: Philosophical analyses of counterfactuals, for example, focus on the truth conditions or assertability conditions for counterfactual conditionals. Furthermore, some elements of the method are similar: Persuasive philosophical arguments commonly draw on compelling examples that evoke strong shared intuitions. Although the final product of philosophical analysis often has the form of a formal deductive system, induction from intuitions about particular examples is clearly an important part of philosophical endeavor. However, there are important differences between the aims and assumptions of the two disciplines. Philosophers try to understand causality, probability, or counterfactual conditionals, whereas psychologists try to understand how people think about these topics. These different aims have important consequences in the attitude toward logical consistency: Understanding a matter involves imposing a consistent logical structure on it, but the study of human thinking should neither assume nor impose consistency on its subject matter.

There is a large and interesting philosophical literature on counterfactuals (e.g., Adams, 1976; Goodman, 1954; Lewis, 1973, 1979; Nute, 1980; Pollock, 1976; Skyrms, 1980; Stalnaker, 1968).[4] After developing our notions of causal episodes and changing propensities, we encountered similar ideas in Kvart's treatment of counterfactuals and in his later work on causality (Kvart, 1986, 1989). Kvart (1986) described the truth conditions for counterfactual conditionals on the basis of causal processes diverging from actual historical processes at a particular point in time. He introduced a notion of causal paths, explicated by reference to conditional probabilities changing over time. Kvart also emphasized that the commonsense view of the world is nondeterministic, involving a concept of an open future. As might be expected in a philosophical analysis, Kvart treated counterfactuals as objects of thought, not as constructions of the mind. He also had recourse to formal notions of probability and to formal constraints on causal paths, which we have avoided.

Psychologists have drawn most heavily on the tools and concepts of logical and philosophical analysis in studies of deductive reasoning (Braine, 1978; Johnson-Laird, 1983; Rips, 1990). The costs of such borrowing could be high in studies of causality, probability, and counterfactuals. The intensity of current philosophical debate regarding these topics suggests the existence of compelling but mutually inconsistent intuitions. The concepts that have been developed in attempts to resolve these inconsistencies are sometimes quite remote from the naive categories of thought with which psychologists are concerned. Just as an understanding of naive physics may benefit more from acquaintance with Aristotelian physics than with the modern variety, psychological studies of causality, probability, and counterfactuals may do well to avoid exaggerated dependence on the categories of modern philosophical thought.

The dominant approach to causality in psychology, perhaps reflecting a similar dominance in philosophy, treats causation as a particular relationship of dependency between events – expressed by necessary or sufficient conditions or by increased conditional probabilities (Einhorn & Hogarth, 1986; Kelley, 1967; Mackie, 1974). There is another view, however, which treats causality as a directly perceived link between events or as an emergent property of a patterned sequence of events. The main sources of this approach to causality in psychology are still the classic works by Michotte (1946) and Heider and Simmel (1944), which, respectively, explored variations on the themes of spatiotemporal contiguity and of schemas of intentional action. Ducasse (1969) has developed a philosophical analysis that draws on similar intuitions. The notion of propensity that has been presented here belongs to this tradition of research in causality.

In our use of the term, the representation of propensity is inherently causal, and inherently predictive, much like the perception of an object in motion (Freyd & Finke, 1984). Our emphasis on event cues to propensity deliberately straddled the standard distinction between causes and effects as well as the distinction between causal force and probability. Is there a justification for a concept that blurs accepted distinctions between important categories of thought? There may be. We have described propensity as a perceived attribute with objective reference, much like the perceived length of a line or the perceived distance of an object. Even in the case of lengths and distances, the crude correspondence of the dimensions of percepts to the dimensions of physical description of the world does not guarantee correspondence of the geometries that describe the space people perceive and the space in which they move. The more general point is that the mental representations of events and their relations may not correspond to any logical analysis of causality or probability, and that intuitions about these matters may not be internally consistent. The student of lay intuitions faces a problem that is familiar to cultural anthropologists: How does one make sense of a system of thought without imposing alien categories on it?

Notes

1 The importance of the word *almost* as an indication of cognitively and emotionally relevant alternatives to outcomes that actually materialized was pointed out by Heider (1958, pp. 141–144), who drew attention to an instructive passage in Henry Fielding's *Tom Jones* (1749/1975, Vol. 2, p. 691); see also Hofstadter (1979, pp. 634–643).

2 The number in parentheses refers to the number of respondents answering the question. In later examples, results will be reported only for the two extreme categories of response.

3 Kvart (1986) has offered a treatment for a broad class of counterfactual conditionals in which causality is explicated by probabilities that change over time.

4 Skyrms (1980) has a treatment of counterfactual conditionals that relies on what he calls "prior propensities." However, the meaning of his term more closely resembles our usage of dispositions.

References

Adams, E. W. (1976). Prior probabilities and counterfactual conditionals. In W. L. Harper & C. A. Hooker (Eds.), *Foundations of probability theory, statistical inference, and statistical theories of science* (Vol. 1, pp. 1–21). Dordrecht, Holland: Reidel.

Ajzen, I. (1977). Intuitive theories of events and the effects of base-rate information on prediction. *Journal of Personality and Social Psychology, 35,* 303–314.

Bar-Hillel, M. (1990). Back to base rates. In R. M. Hogarth (Ed.), *Insights in decision making: A tribute to Hillel J. Einhorn* (pp. 200–216). Chicago: University of Chicago Press.

Black, J. B., & Bower, G. H. (1979). Episodes as chunks in narrative memory. *Journal of Verbal Learning and Verbal Behavior, 18,* 309–318.

Braine, M. D. S. (1978). On the relation between the natural logic of reasoning and standard logic. *Psychological Review, 85,* 1–21.

Ducasse, C. J. (1969). *Causation and the types of necessity.* New York: Dover.

Einhorn, H., & Hogarth, R. (1986). Judging probable cause. *Psychological Bulletin, 99,* 3–19.

Fielding, H. (1975). *The History of Tom Jones, a foundling* (Vol. 2). Oxford, England: Wesleyan University Press/Oxford University Press. (Original work published 1749.)

Fischhoff, B. (1975). Hindsight ≠ foresight: The effect of outcome knowledge on judgment under uncertainty. *Journal of Experimental Psychology: Human Perception and Performance, 1,* 288–299.

Fischhoff, B. (1982). For those condemned to study the past. In D. Kahneman, P. Slovic, & A. Tversky (Eds.), *Judgment under uncertainty: Heuristics and biases* (pp. 422–444). Cambridge, England: Cambridge University Press.

Freyd, J., & Finke, R. (1984). Representational momentum. *Journal of Experimental Psychology: Learning, Memory and Cognition, 10,* 126–132.

Gigerenzer, G., Hell, W., & Blank, H. (1988). Presentation and content: The use of base rates as a continuous variable. *Journal of Experimental Psychology: Human Perception and Performance, 14,* 513–525.

Gilovich, T., Vallone, R., & Tversky, A. (1985). The hot hand in basketball: On the misperception of random sequences. *Cognitive Psychology, 17,* 295–314.

Goodman, N. (1954). *Fact, fiction and forecast* (1st ed.). London: Athlone Press.

Goodman, N. (1983). *Fact, fiction and forecast* (4th ed.). Cambridge, MA: Harvard University Press.

Hart, H. L. A., & Honoré, A. M. (1959). *Causation in the law.* London: Oxford University Press.

Heider, F. (1958). *The psychology of interpersonal relations.* New York: Wiley.

Heider, F., & Simmel, M. (1944). An experimental study of apparent behavior. *American Journal of Psychology, 57,* 243–259.

Hofstadter, D. (1979). *Godel, Escher, Bach: An eternal golden braid.* New York: Basic Books.

Johnson, J. T. (1986). The knowledge of what might have been: Affective and attributional consequences of near outcomes. *Personality and Social Psychology Bulletin, 12*, 51–62.

Johnson, J. T., Ogawa, K. H., Delforge, A., & Early, D. (1989). Causal primacy and comparative fault: The effect of position in a causal chain on judgments of legal responsibility. *Personality and Social Psychology, 15*, 161–174.

Johnson, M. K. (1988). Discriminating the origin of information. In T. F. Oltmanns & B. A. Maher (Eds.), *Delusional beliefs: Interdisciplinary perspectives* (pp. 34–65). New York: Wiley.

Johnson-Laird, P. N. (1983). *Mental models: Towards a cognitive science of language, inference, and consciousness*. Cambridge, MA: Harvard University Press.

Kahneman, D., & Miller, D. T. (1986). Norm theory: Comparing reality to its alternatives. *Psychological Review, 93*, 136–153.

Kahneman, D., Slovic, P., & Tversky, A. (Eds.). (1982). *Judgment under uncertainty: Heuristics and biases*. New York: Cambridge University Press.

Kahneman, D., & Tversky, A. (1973). On the psychology of prediction. *Psychological Review, 80*, 237–251.

Kahneman, D., & Tversky, A. (1982a). The simulation heuristic. In D. Kahneman, P. Slovic, & A. Tversky (Eds.), *Judgment under uncertainty: Heuristics and biases* (pp. 201–208). New York: Cambridge University Press.

Kahneman, D., & Tversky, A. (1982b). Variants of uncertainty. *Cognition, 11*, 143–157.

Kelley, H. H. (1967). Attribution theory in social psychology. In D. Levine (Ed.), *Nebraska Symposium on Motivation* (Vol. 15, pp. 192–240). Lincoln: University of Nebraska Press.

Keren, G., & Wagenaar, W. A. (1985). On the psychology of playing blackjack: Normative and descriptive considerations with implications for decision theory. *Journal of Experimental Psychology: General, 114*, 133–158.

Kintsch, W., & van Dijk, T. A. (1978). Toward a model of text comprehension and production. *Psychological Review, 85*, 363–384.

Kvart, I. (1986). *A theory of counterfactuals*. Indianapolis: Hackett.

Kvart, I. (1989). *Causal independence*. Unpublished manuscript.

Lakoff, G. (1987). *Women, fire, and dangerous things: What categories reveal about the mind*. Chicago: University of Chicago Press.

Lakoff, G., & Johnson, M. (1980). *Metaphors we live by*. Chicago: University of Chicago Press.

Landman, J. (1987). Regret and elation following action and inaction. *Personality and Social Psychology Bulletin, 13*, 524–536.

Lewin, K. (1936). *Principles of topological psychology* (F. Heider & G. M. Heider, Trans.). New York: McGraw-Hill.

Lewis, D. (1973). *Counterfactuals*. Cambridge, MA: Harvard University Press.

Lewis, D. (1979). Counterfactual dependence and time's arrow. *Noûs, 13*, 455–476.

Lyons, J. (1977). *Semantics* (Vol. 2). Cambridge, England: Cambridge University Press.

Mackie, J. L. (1974). *The cement of the universe: A study of causation*. Oxford, England: Clarendon Press (Oxford University Press).

Michotte, A. E. (1946). *La perception de la causalité* [The perception of causality]. Louvain, Belgium: University of Louvain Publications.

Miller, D. T., & Gunasegaram, S. (1990). Temporal order and the perceived mutability of events: Implications for blame assignment. *Journal of Personality and Social Psychology, 59*, 1111–1118.

Miller, D. T., Turnbull, W., & McFarland, C. (1990). Counterfactual thinking and social perception: Thinking about what might have been. In M. Zanna (Ed.), *Advances in experimental social psychology* (Vol. 23, pp. 305–331). Orlando, FL: Academic Press.

Miller, G. A., & Johnson-Laird, P. L. (1976). *Language and perception.* Cambridge, England: Cambridge University Press.

Nute, D. (1980). *Topics in conditional logic.* Boston: Reidel.

Pennington, N., & Hastie, R. (1988). Explanation-based decision making: Effects of memory structure on judgment. *Journal of Experimental Psychology: Learning, Memory and Cognition, 14,* 521–533.

Pollock, J. L. (1976). *Subjunctive reasoning.* Dordrecht, Holland: Reidel.

Read, S. J. (1987). Constructing causal scenarios: A knowledge structure approach to causal reasoning. *Journal of Personality and Social Psychology, 52,* 288–302.

Rips, L. (1990). Reasoning. *Annual Review of Psychology, 41,* 321–353.

Rumelhart, D. E. (1977). Understanding and summarizing brief stories. In D. Laberge & J. Samuels (Eds.), *Basic processes in reading, perception and comprehension* (pp. 265–303). Hillsdale, NJ: Erlbaum.

Schank, R. C. (1975). The structure of episodes in memory. In D. G. Bobrow & A. Collins (Eds.), *Representation and understanding: Studies in cognitive science* (pp. 237–272). New York: Academic Press.

Schank, R. C., & Abelson, R. P. (1977). *Scripts, plans, goals, and understanding.* Hillsdale, NJ: Erlbaum.

Shafer, G. (1976). *A mathematical theory of evidence.* Princeton, NJ: Princeton University Press.

Skyrms, B. (1980). The prior propensity account of subjunctive conditionals. In W. L. Harper, R. Stalnaker, & G. Pearce (Eds.), *Ifs: Conditionals, belief, decision, chance and time* (Vol. 1, pp. 125–162). Dordrecht, Holland: Reidel.

Stalnaker, R. C. (1968). A theory of conditionals. In N. Rescher (Ed.), *Studies in logical theory: American Philosophical Quarterly monograph series 2* (pp. 98–112). Oxford, England: Blackwell.

Talmy, L. (1981, May). *Force images.* Paper presented at the Conference on Language and Mental Imagery, University of California, Berkeley.

Talmy, L. (1983). How language structures space. In H. Pick & L. Acredolo (Eds.), *Spatial orientation: Theory, research and application* (pp. 219–282). New York: Plenum Press.

Trabasso, T., Secco, T., & van den Broek, P. (1984). Causal cohesion and story coherence. In H. Mandl, N. L. Stein, & T. Trabasso (Eds.), *Learning and comprehension of text* (pp. 83–111). Hillsdale, NJ: Erlbaum.

Tversky, A., & Kahneman, D. (1980). Causal schemas in judgments under uncertainty. In M. Fishbein (Ed.), *Progress in social psychology* (Vol. 1, pp. 153–160). Hillsdale, NJ: Erlbaum.

Tversky, A., & Kahneman, D. (1982). Evidential impact of base rates. In D. Kahneman, P. Slovic, & A. Tversky (Eds.), *Judgment under uncertainty: Heuristics and biases* (pp. 201–208). New York: Cambridge University Press.

Vendler, Z. (1967). *Linguistics in philosophy.* Ithaca, NY: Cornell University Press.

Wells, G. L., & Gavanski, I. (1989). Mental simulation of causality. *Journal of Personality and Social Psychology, 56,* 161–169.

Wells, G. L., Taylor, B. R., & Turtle, J. W. (1987). The undoing of scenarios. *Journal of Personality and Social Psychology, 53,* 421–430.

10 The process–performance paradox in expert judgment: How can experts know so much and predict so badly?

Colin F. Camerer and Eric J. Johnson

1. Introduction

A mysterious fatal disease strikes a large minority of the population. The disease is incurable, but an expensive drug can keep victims alive. Congress decides that the drug should be given to those whose lives can be extended longest, which only a few specialists can predict. The experts work around the clock searching for a cure; allocating the drug is a new chore they would rather avoid.

In research on decision making there are two views about such experts. The views suggest different technologies for modeling experts' decisions so that they can do productive research rather than make predictions. One view, which emerges from behavioral research on decision making, is skeptical about the experts. Data suggest that a wide range of experts like our hypothetical specialists are not much better predictors than less expert physicians, or interns. Furthermore, this view suggests a simple technology for replacing experts – a simple linear regression model (perhaps using medical judgments as inputs). The regression does not mimic the thought process of an expert, but it probably makes *more* accurate predictions than an expert does.

The second view, stemming from research in cognitive science, suggests that expertise is a rare skill that develops only after much instruction, prac-

This chapter originally appeared in K. A. Ericsson & J. Smith (Eds.), *Toward a General Theory of Expertise: Prospects and Limits* (pp. 195–217). Cambridge: Cambridge University Press, 1991. Copyright © Cambridge University Press 1991. Reprinted with the permission of Cambridge University Press.

The authors contributed equally; the order of authors' names is purely alphabetical. We thank Helmut Jungermann, as well as Anders Ericsson, Jaqui Smith, and the other participants at the Study of Expertise conference in Berlin, 25–28 June 1989, at the Max Planck Institute for Human Development and Education, for many helpful comments. Preparation of this chapter was supported by a grant from the Office of Naval Research and by NSF grant SES 88-09299.

tice, and experience. The cognition of experts is more sophisticated than that of novices; this sophistication is presumed to produce better predictions. This view suggests a model that strives to mimic the decision policies of experts – an "expert (or knowledge-based) system" containing lists of rules experts use in judging longevity. An expert system tries to match, not exceed, the performance of the expert it represents.

In this chapter we describe and integrate these two perspectives. Integration comes from realizing that the behavioral and cognitive science approaches have different goals: Whereas behavioral decision theory emphasizes the *performance* of experts, cognitive science usually emphasizes differences in experts' *processes* (E. Johnson, 1988).

A few caveats are appropriate. Our review is selective; it is meant to emphasize the differences between expert performance and process. The generic decision-making task we describe usually consists of repeated predictions, based on the same set of observable variables, about a complicated outcome – graduate school success, financial performance, health – that is rather unpredictable. For the sake of brevity, we shall not discuss other important tasks such as probability estimation or revision, inference, categorization, or tradeoffs among attributes, costs, and benefits.

The literature we review is indirectly related to the well-known "heuristics and biases" approach (e.g., Kahneman, Slovic, & Tversky, 1982). Our theme is that experts know a lot but predict poorly. Perhaps their knowledge is biased, if it comes from judgment heuristics or they use heuristics in applying it. We can only speculate about this possibility (as we do later, in a few places) until further research draws the connection more clearly.

For our purposes, an expert is a person who is experienced at making predictions in a domain and has some professional or social credentials. The experts described here are no slouches: They are psychologists, doctors, academics, accountants, gamblers, and parole officers who are intelligent, well paid, and often proud. We draw no special distinction between them and extraordinary experts, or experts acclaimed by peers (cf. Shanteau, 1988). We suspect that our general conclusions would apply to more elite populations of experts,[1] but clearly there have been too few studies of these populations.

The chapter is organized as follows: In section 2 we review what we currently know about how well experts perform decision tasks, then in section 3 we review recent work on expert decision processes. Section 4 integrates the views described in sections 2 and 3. Then we examine the implications of this work for decision research and for the study of expertise in general.

2. Performance of experts

Most of the research in the behavioral decision-making approach to expertise has been organized around performance of experts. A natural measure of expert performance is predictive accuracy; later, we discuss other aspects. Modern research on expert accuracy emanates from Sarbin (1944), who drew an analogy between clinical reasoning and statistical (or "actuarial") judgment. His data, and the influential book by Meehl (1954), established that in many clinical prediction tasks experts were *less* accurate than simple formulas based on observable variables. As Dawes and Corrigan (1974, p. 97) wrote, "the statistical analysis was thought to provide a floor to which the judgment of the experienced clinician could be compared. The floor turned out to be a ceiling."

2.1. A language for quantitative studies of performance

In many studies, linear regression techniques are used to construct statistical models of expert judgments (and to improve those judgments) and distinguish components of judgment accuracy and error.[2] These techniques are worth reviewing briefly because they provide a useful language for discussing accuracy and its components.

A subject's judgment (denoted Y_s) depends on a set of informational cues (denoted $X_1, \ldots, X_n$). The cues could be measured objectively (college grades) or subjectively by experts (evaluating letters of recommendation). The actual environmental outcome (or "criterion") (denoted Y_e) is also assumed to be a function of the same cues.

In the comparisons to be described, several kinds of regressions are commonly used. One such regression, the "actuarial" model, predicts outcomes Y_e based on observable cues X_i. The model naturally separates Y_e into a predictable component $\hat{Y}_e$, a linear combination[3] of cues weighted by regression coefficients $b_{i,e}$, and an unpredictable error component Z_e. That is,

$$Y_e = \sum b_{i,e} X_i + z_e \quad \text{(actuarial model)}$$
$$= \hat{Y}_e + z_e$$

(10.1)

Figure 10.1 illustrates these relationships, as well as others that we shall discuss subsequently.

2.2. Experts versus actuarial models

The initial studies compared expert judgments with those of actuarial models. That is, the correlation between the expert judgment Y_s and the outcome Y_e (often denoted r_a, for "achievement") was compared with the correlation between the model's predicted outcome $\hat{Y}_e$ and the actual outcome Y_e (denoted R_e).[4]

Meehl (1954) reviewed about two dozen studies. Cross-validated actuarial models outpredicted clinical judgment (i.e., R_e was greater than r_a) in all but one study. Now there have been about a hundred studies; experts did better in only a handful of them (mostly medical tasks in which well-developed

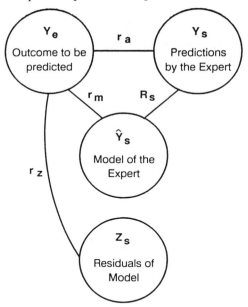

Figure 10.1. A quantitative language for describing decision performance.

theory outpredicted limited statistical experience; see Dawes, Faust, & Meehl, 1989). The studies have covered many different tasks – university admissions, recidivism or violence of criminals, clinical pathology, medical diagnosis, financial investment, sports, weather forecasting. Thirty years after his book was published, Meehl (1986, p. 373) suggested that "there is no controversy in social science that shows such a large body of qualitatively diverse studies coming out so uniformly in the same direction."

2.3. Experts versus improper models

Despite their superiority to clinical judgment, actuarial models are difficult to use because the outcome Y_e must be measured, to provide the raw data for deriving regression weights. It can be costly or time-consuming to measure outcomes (for recidivism or medical diagnosis), or definitions of outcomes can be ambiguous (What is "success" for a Ph.D.?). And past outcomes must be used to fit cross-validated regression weights to predict current outcomes, which makes models vulnerable to changes in true coefficients over time. Therefore, "improper"[5] models – which derive regression weights without using Y_e – might be more useful and nearly as accurate as proper actuarial models.

In one improper method, regression weights are derived from the Y_s judgments themselves; then cues are weighted by the derived weights and summed. This procedure amounts to separating the overall expert judgment Y_s into two components, a modeled component $\hat{Y}_s$ and a residual component z_s, and using only the modeled component $\hat{Y}_s$ as a prediction.[6] That is,

$$Y_s = \sum b_{is}X_i + z_s$$
$$= \hat{Y}_s + z_s \tag{10.2}$$

If the discarded residual z_s is mostly random error, the modeled component $\hat{Y}_s$ will correlate more highly with the outcome than will the overall judgment, Y_s. (In standard terminology, the correlation between $\hat{Y}_s$ and Y_e, denoted r_m, will be higher than r_a.)

This method is called "bootstrapping" because it can improve judgments without any outcome information: It pulls experts up by their bootstraps. Bowman (1963) first showed that bootstrapping improved judgments in production scheduling; similar improvements were found by Goldberg (1970) in clinical predictions based on MMPI scores[7] and by Dawes (1971) in graduate admissions. A cross-study comparison showed that bootstrapping works very generally, but usually adds only a small increment to predictive accuracy (Camerer, 1981a). Table 10.1 shows some of those results. Accuracy can be usefully dissected with the lens-model equation, an identity relating several interesting correlations. Einhorn's (1974) version of the equation states

$$r_a = r_m R_s + r_z \left(1 - R_s^2\right)^{1/2} \tag{10.3}$$

where R^2_s is the bootstrapping model R^2 (how closely the judge resembles the linear model), and r_z is the correlation between bootstrapping-model residuals z_s and outcomes Y_e (the "residual validity"). If the residuals z_s represent only random error in weighing and combining the cues, r_z will be close to zero. In this case, r_m will certainly be larger than r_a, and because $R_s \leq 1$, bootstrapping will improve judgments. But even if r_z is greater than zero (presumably because residuals contain some information that is correlated with outcomes), bootstrapping works unless

$$r_z \geq r_m \left(\frac{1 - R_s}{1 + R_s}\right)^{1/2} \tag{10.4}$$

For $R_s = .6$ (a reasonable value; see Table 10.1), residual validity r_z must be about half as large as model accuracy for experts to outperform their own bootstrapping models. This rarely occurs.

When there are not many judgments, compared with the number of variables, the regression weights in a bootstrapping model cannot be estimated reliably. Then one can simply weight the cues equally[8] and add them up. Dawes and Corrigan (1974) showed that equal weights worked remarkably well in several empirical comparisons (the accuracies of some of these

Table 10.1. *Examples of regression-study results*

Study	Prediction task	Model fit, R_s	Judge, r_a	Bootstrapping model, r_m	Bootstrapping residuals, r_z	Equal-weight model, r_{ew}	Actuarial model,[a] R_c
				Mean accuracy of:			
Goldberg (1970)	Psychosis vs. neurosis	.77	.28	.31	.07	.34	.45
Dawes (1971)	Ph.D. admissions	.78	.19	.25	.01	.48	.38
Einhorn (1972)	Disease severity	.41	.01	.13	.06	n.a.	.35
Libby (1976)[b]	Bankruptcy	.79	.50	.53	.13	n.a.	.67
Wiggens & Kohen (1971)	Grades	.85	.33	.50	.01	.60	.57

[a] All are cross-validated R_c except Einhorn (1972) and Libby (1976).
[b] Figures cited are recalculations by Goldberg (1976).
Source: Adapted from Camerer (1981a) and Dawes & Corrigan (1974).

are shown in the column r_{ew}, in Table 10.1). Simulations show that equal weighting generally works as well as least squares estimation of weights unless there are twenty times as many observations as predictors (Einhorn & Hogarth, 1975). As Dawes and Corrigan (1974) put it, "the whole trick is to decide what variables to look at and then to know how to add" (p. 105).

2.4. Training and experience: Experts versus novices

Studies have shown that expert judgments are less accurate than those of statistical models of varying sophistication. Two other useful comparisons are those between experts and novices and between experienced and inexperienced experts.

Garb (1989) reviewed more than fifty comparisons of judgments by clinical psychologists and novices. The comparisons suggest that (academic) training helps but additional experience does not. Trained clinicians and graduate students were more accurate than novices (typically untrained students, or secretaries) in using the MMPI to judge personality disorders. Students did better and better with each year of graduate training. The effect of training was not large (novices might classify 28% correctly, and experts 40%), but it existed in many studies. Training, however, generally did *not* help in interpreting projective tests (drawings, Rorschach inkblots, and sentence-completion tests); using such tests, clinical psychologists probably are no more accurate than auto mechanics or insurance salesmen.

Training has some effects on accuracy, but experience has almost none. In judging personality and neurophysiological disorders, for example, clinicians do no better than advanced graduate students. Among experts with varying amounts of experience, the correlations between amount of clinical experience and accuracy are roughly zero. Libby and Frederick (1989) found that experience improved the accuracy of auditors' explanations of audit errors only slightly (although even inexperienced auditors were better than students).

In medical judgments too, training helps, but experience does not. Gustafson (1963) found no difference between residents and surgeons in predicting the length of hospital stay after surgery. Kundel and LaFollette (1972) reported that novices and first-year medical students were unable to detect lesions from radiographs of abnormal lungs, but fourth-year students (who had had some training in radiography) were as good as full-time radiologists.

These tasks usually have a rather low performance ceiling. Graduate training may provide all the experience one requires to approach the ceiling. But the myth that additional experience helps is persistent. One of the psychology professors who recently revised the MMPI said that "anybody who can count can score it [the MMPI], but it takes expertise to interpret it" (*Philadelphia Inquirer*, 1989). Yet Goldberg's (1970) data suggest that the only expertise required is the ability to add scores with a hand calculator or paper and pencil.

If a small amount of training can make a person as accurate as an experienced clinical psychologist or doctor, as the data imply, then lightly trained paraprofessionals could replace heavily trained experts for many routine kinds of diagnoses. Citing Shortliffe, Buchanan, and Feigenbaum (1979), Garb (1989) suggested that "intelligent high school graduates, selected in large part because of poise and warmth of personality, can provide competent medical care for a limited range of problems when guided by protocols after only 4 to 8 weeks of training."

It is conceivable that outstanding experts are more accurate than models and graduate students in some tasks. For instance, in Goldberg's (1959) study of organic brain damage diagnoses, a well-known expert (who worked very slowly) was right 83% of the time, whereas other Ph.D. clinical psychologists got 65% right. Whether such extraordinary expertise is a reliable phenomenon or a statistical fluke is a matter for further research.

2.5. Expert calibration

Whereas experts may predict less accurately than models, and only slightly more accurately than novices, they seem to have better self-insight about the accuracy of their predictions. Such self-insight is called "calibration." Most people are poorly calibrated, offering erroneous reports of the quality of their predictions, and these reports systematically err in the direction of overconfidence: When they say a class of events are 80% likely, those events occur less than 80% of the time (Lichtenstein, Fischhoff, & Phillips, 1977). There is some evidence that experts are less overconfident than novices. For instance, Levenberg (1975) had subjects look at "kinetic family drawings" to detect whether the children who drew them were normal. The results were, typically, a small victory for training: Psychologists and secretaries got 66% and 61% right, respectively (a coinflip would get half right). Of these cases about which subjects were "positively certain," the psychologists and secretaries got 76% and 59% right, respectively. The psychologists were better calibrated than novices – they used the phrase "positively certain" more cautiously (and appropriately) – but they were still overconfident.

Better calibration of experts has also been found in some other studies (Garb, 1989). Expert calibration is better than novice calibration in bridge (Keren, 1987), but not in blackjack (Wagenaar & Keren, 1985). Doctors' judgments of pneumonia and skull fracture are badly calibrated (Christensen-Szalanski & Bushyhead, 1981; DeSmet, Fryback, & Thornbury, 1979). Weather forecasters are extremely well calibrated (Murphy & Winkler, 1977). Experiments with novices showed that training improved calibration, reducing extreme overconfidence in estimating probabilities and numerical quantities (Lichtenstein et al., 1977).

2.6. Summary: Expert performance

The depressing conclusion from these studies is that expert judgments in most clinical and medical domains are no more accurate than those of lightly trained novices. (We know of no comparable reviews of other domains, but we suspect that experts are equally unimpressive in most aesthetic, commercial, and physical judgments.) And expert judgments have been worse than those of the simplest statistical models in virtually all domains that have been studied. Experts are sometimes less overconfident than novices, but not always.

3. Expert decision processes

The picture of expert performance painted by behavioral decision theorists is unflattering. Why are experts predicting so badly? We know that many experts have special cognitive and memory skills (Chase & Simon, 1973; Ericsson & Polson, 1988; Larkin, McDermott, Simon, & Simon, 1980). Do expert *decision makers* have similar strategies and skill? If so, why don't they perform better? Three kinds of evidence help answer these questions: process analyses of expert judgments, indirect analyses using regression models, and laboratory studies in which subjects become "artificial experts" in a simple domain.

3.1. Direct evidence: Process analyses of experts

The rules and cues experts use can be discovered by using process tracing techniques – protocol analysis and monitoring of information acquisition. Such studies have yielded consistent conclusions across a diverse set of domains.

Search is contingent. If people think like a regression model, weighting cues and adding them, then cue search will be simple – the same variables will be examined, in the same sequence, in every case. Novices behave that way. But experts have a more active pattern of contingent search: Subsets of variables are considered in each case, in different sequences. Differences between novice and expert searches have been found in studies of financial analysts (Bouman, 1980; E. Johnson, 1988), auditors (Bedard & Mock, 1989), graduate admissions (E. Johnson, 1980), neurologists (Kleinmuntz, 1968), and physicians (Elstein, Shulman, & Sprafka, 1978; P. Johnson, Hassebrock, Duran, & Moller, 1982).

Experts search less. A common finding in studies of expert cognition is that information processing is less costly for experts than for novices. For example, expert waiters (Ericsson & Chase, 1981) and chess players (Chase & Simon, 1973) have exceptional memory skills. Their memory allows more efficient encoding of task-specific information; if they wanted to, experts could search and sift cheaply through more information. But empirical studies show that experts use *less* information than novices, rather than more, in auditing (Bedard, 1989; Bedard & Mock, 1989), financial analysis (Bouman, 1980; E. Johnson, 1988), and product choice (Bettman & Park, 1980; Brucks, 1985; E. Johnson & Russo, 1984).

Experts use more knowledge. Experts often search contingently, for limited sets of variables, because they know a great deal about their domains (Bouman, 1980; Elstein et al., 1978; Libby & Frederick, 1989). Experts perform a kind of diagnostic reasoning, matching the cues in a specific case to prototypes in a casual brand of hypothesis testing. Search is contingent because different sets of cues are required for each hypothesis test. Search is limited because only a small set of cues are relevant to a particular hypothesis.

3.2. Indirect evidence: Dissecting residuals

The linear regression models described in section 2 provide a simple way to partition expert judgment into components. The bootstrapped judgment is a linear combination of observed cues; the residual is everything else. By dissecting the residual statistically, we can learn how the decision process experts use deviates from the simple linear combination of cues. It deviates in three ways.

Experts often use configural choice rules. In configural rules, the impact of one variable depends on the values of other variables. An example is found in clinical lore on interpretation of the MMPI. Both formal instruction and verbal protocols of experienced clinicians give rules that note the state of more than one variable. A nice example is given by an early rule-based system constructed by Kleinmuntz (1968) using clinicians' verbal protocols.

Many of the rules in the system reflect such configural reasoning: "Call maladjusted if $P_a \geq 70$ unless $M_t \leq 6_r$ and $K \geq 65$." Because linear regression models weight each cue independently, configural rules will not be captured by the linear form, and the effects of configural judgment will be reflected in the regression residual.

Experts use "broken-leg cues." Cues that are rare but highly diagnostic often are called broken-leg cues, from an example cited by Meehl (1954; pp. 24–25): A clinician is trying to predict whether or not Professor A will go to the movies on a given night. A regression model predicts that the professor will go, but the clinician knows that the professor recently broke his leg. The cue "broken leg" probably will get no weight in a regression model of past cases, because broken legs are rare.[9] But the clinician can confidently predict that the professor will not go to the movies. The clinician's recognition of the broken-leg cue, which is missing from the regression model, will be captured by the residual. Note that while the frequency of any one broken-leg cue is rare, in "the mass of cases, there may be *many (different) rare kinds of factors*" (Meehl, 1954, p. 25).

Note how the use of configural rules and broken-leg cues is consistent with the process data described in section 3. To use configural rules, experts must search for different sets of cues in different sequences. Experts also can use their knowledge about cue diagnosticity to focus on a limited number of highly diagnostic broken-leg cues. For example, in E. Johnson's (1988) study of financial analysts, experts were much more accurate than novices because they could interpret the impact of news events similar to broken-leg cues.

Experts weight cues inconsistently and make errors in combining them. When experts do combine cues linearly, any inconsistencies in weighting cues, and errors in adding them, will be reflected in the regression residual. Thus, if experts use configural rules and broken-leg cues, their effects will be contained in the residuals of a linear bootstrapping model. The residuals also contain inconsistencies and error. By comparing residual variance and test–retest reliability, Camerer (1981b) estimated that only about 40% of the variance in residuals was error,[10] and 60% was systematic use of configural rules and broken-leg cues. (Those fractions were remarkably consistent across different studies.) The empirical correlation between residuals and outcomes, r_z, however, averaged only about .05 (Camerer, 1981a) over a wider range of studies. Experts are using configural rules and broken-leg cues systematically, but they are not highly correlated with outcomes. Of course, there may be some domains in which residuals are more valid.[11]

3.3. Artificial experts

A final kind of process evidence comes from "artificial experts," subjects who spend much time in an experimental environment trying to induce accurate judgmental rules. A lot of this research belongs to the tradition of multiple-cue probability learning (MCPL) experiments that stretches back decades, with the pessimistic conclusion that rule induction is difficult, particularly when outcomes have random error. We shall give three more recent examples that combine process analysis with a rule induction task.

Several studies have used protocol analysis to determine *what* it is that artificial experts have learned. Perhaps the most ambitious attempts to study extended learning in complex environments were Klayman's studies of cue discovery (Klayman, 1988; Klayman & Ha, 1985): Subjects looked at a complex computer display consisting of geometric shapes that affected the distance traveled by ray traces from one point on the display to another. The true rule for travel distance was determined by a complex linear model consisting of seven factors that varied in salience in the display. None of Klayman's subjects induced the correct rule over 14 half-hour sessions, but their performances improved steadily. Some improvement came from discovering correct cues (subjects correctly identified only 2.83 of 7 cues, on average). Subjects who systematically experimented, by varying one cue and holding others fixed, learned faster and better than others. Because the cues varied greatly in how much they affected distance, it was important to weight them differently, but more than four-fifths of the rules stated by subjects did not contain any numerical elements (such as weights) at all. In sum, cue discovery played a clear role in developing expertise in this task, but learning about the relative importance of cues did not.

In a study by Meyer (1987), subjects learned which attributes of a hypothetical metal alloy led to increases in its hardness. As in Klayman's study, subjects continued to learn rules over a long period of time. The true rule for hardness (which was controlled by the experimenter) was linear, but most subjects induced configural rules. Subjects make only fairly accurate predictions, because the true linear rule could be mimicked by nonlinear rules. Learning (better performance) consisted of adding more elaborate and baroque configural rules, rather than inducing the true linear relationships.

In a study by Camerer (1981b), subjects tried to predict simulated wheat-price changes that depended on two variables and a large interaction between them (i.e., the true rule was configural). Subjects did learn to use the interaction in their judgments, but with so much error that a linear bootstrapping model that omitted the interaction was more accurate. Similarly, in E. Johnson's (1988) financial-analyst study, even though expert analysts used highly diagnostic news events, their judgments were inferior to those of a simple linear model.

3.4. Summary: Expert decision processes

Studies of decision processes indicate that expert decision makers are like experts in other domains: They know more and use their knowledge to guide search for small subsets of information, which differ with each case.

Residuals from bootstrapping models and learning experiments also show that experts use configural rules and cues not captured by linear models (but these are not always predictive). The process evidence indicates that experts know more, but what they know does not enable them to outpredict simple statistical rules. Why not?

4. Reconciling the performance and process views of expertise

One explanation for the process–performance paradox is that prediction is only one task that experts must perform; they may do better on other tasks. Later we shall consider this explanation further. Another explanation is that experts are quick to develop configural rules that often are inaccurate, but they keep these rules or switch to equally poor ones. (The same may be true of broken-leg cues.) This argument raises three questions, which we address in turn: Why do experts develop configural rules? Why are configural rules often inaccurate? Why do inaccurate configural rules persist?

4.1. Why do experts develop configural rules?

Configural rules are easier. Consider two common classes of configural rules, conjunctive (hire Hope for the faculty if she has glowing letters of recommendation, good grades, *and* an interesting thesis) and disjunctive (draft Michael for the basketball team if he can play guard *or* forward *or* center extremely well). Configural rules are easy because they bypass the need to trade off different cues (Are recommendations better predictors than grades?), avoiding the cumbersome weighting and combination of information. Therefore, configural rules take much less effort than optimal rules and can yield nearly optimal choices (E. Johnson & Payne, 1985).[12]

Besides avoiding difficult trade-offs, configural rules require only a simple categorization of cue values. With conjunctive and disjunctive rules, one need only know whether or not a cue is above a cutoff; attention can be allocated economically to categorize the values of many cues crudely, rather than categorizing only one or two cues precisely.

Prior theory often suggests configural rules. In his study of wheat prices, Camerer (1981b) found that subjects could learn of the existence of a large configural interaction only when cue labels suggested the interaction a priori. Similarly, cue labels may cause subjects to learn configural rules where they are inappropriate, as in Meyer's (1987) study of alloy hardness. These prior beliefs about cue–outcome correlations often will be influenced by the "representativeness" (Tversky & Kahneman, 1982) of cues to outcomes; the representativeness heuristic will sometimes cause errors.

Besides their cognitive ease and prior suggestion, complex configural rules are easy to learn because it is easy to weave a causal narrative around a configural theory. These coherent narratives cement a dependence between variables that is easy to express but may overweight these "causal" cues, at the cost of ignoring others. Linear combinations yield no such coherence. Meehl (1954) provides the following example from clinical psychology, describing the case of a woman who was ambivalent toward her husband. One night the woman came home from a movie alone. Then:

Entering the bedroom, she was terrified to see, for a fraction of a second, a large black bird ("a raven, I guess") perched on her pillow next to her husband's head. . . . She recalls "vaguely, some poem we read in high school." (p. 39)

Meehl hypothesized that the woman's vision was a fantasy, based on the poem "The Raven" by Edgar Allen Poe: "The [woman's] fantasy is that like Poe's Lenore, she will die or at least go away and leave him [the husband] alone." Meehl was using a configural rule that gave more weight to the raven vision because the woman knew the Poe poem. A linear rule, simply weighting the dummy variables "raven" and "knowledge of Poe," yields a narrative that is much clumsier than Meehl's compelling analysis. Yet such a model might well pay attention to other factors, such as the woman's age, education, and so forth, which might also help explain her ambivalence.

Configural rules can emerge naturally from trying to explain past cases. People learn by trying to fit increasingly sophisticated general rules to previous cases (Brehmer, 1980; Meyer, 1987). Complicated configural rules offer plenty of explanatory flexibility. For example, a 6-variable model permits 15 two-way interactions, and a 10-variable model allows 45 interactions.[13] In sports, for instance, statistics are so plentiful and refined that it is easy to construct subtle "configuralities" when global rules fail. Bucky Dent was an average New York Yankee infielder, except in the World Series, where he played "above his head," hitting much better than predicted by his overall average. (The variable "Dent" was not highly predictive of success, but adding the interaction "Dent" × "Series" was.)[14] Because people are reluctant to accept the possibility of random error (Einhorn, 1986), increasingly complicated configural explanations are born.

Inventing special cases is an important mechanism for learning in more deterministic environments, where it can be quite effective. The tendency of decision makers to build special-case rules mirrors more adaptive processes of induction (e.g., Holland, Holyoak, Nisbett, & Thagard, 1986, chapter 3, esp. pp. 88–89) that can lead to increased accuracy. As Holland and associates pointed out, however, the validity of these mechanisms rests on the ability to check each specialization on many cases. In noisy domains like the ones we are discussing, there are few replications. It was unlikely, for example, that Dent would appear in many World Series, and even if he did, other "unique" circumstances (opposing pitching, injuries, etc.) could always yield further "explanatory" factors.

In sum, configural rules are appealing because they are easy to use, have plausible causal explanations, and offer many degrees of freedom to fit data. Despite these advantages, configural rules may have a downfall, as detailed in the next section.

4.2 Why are configural rules often inaccurate?

One reason configural rules may be inaccurate is that whereas they are induced under specific and often rare conditions, they may well be applied to a larger set of cases. Often, people induce such rules from observation, they will be overgeneralizing from a small sample (expecting the sample to be more "representative" of a population than it is; Tversky & Kahneman, 1982). This is illustrated by a verbal protocol recorded by a physician who was chair of a hospital's admissions committee for house staff, interns, and residents. Seeing an applicant from Wayne State who had very high board scores, the doctor recalled a promising applicant from the same school who had perfect board scores. Unfortunately, after being admitted, the prior aspirant had done poorly and left the program. The physician recalled this case and applied it to the new one: "We have to be quite careful with people from Wayne State with very high board scores. . . . We have had problems in the past."

Configural rules may also be wrong because the implicit theories that underlie them are wrong. A large literature on "illusory correlation" contains many examples of variables that are thought to be correlated with outcomes (because they are similar) but are not. For example, most clinicians and novices think that people who see male features or androgynous figures in Rorschach inkblots are more likely to be homosexual. They are not (Chapman & Chapman, 1967, 1969). A successful portfolio manager we know refused to buy stock in firms run by overweight CEOs, believing that control of one's weight and control of a firm are correlated. Because variables that are only illusorily correlated with outcomes are likely to be used by both novices and experts, the small novice–expert difference suggests that illusory correlations may be common.

Configural rules are also likely to be unrobust to small errors, or "brittle."[15] Linear models are extremely robust; they fit nonlinear data remarkably well (Yntema & Torgerson, 1961). That is why omitting a configural interaction from a bootstrapping model does not greatly reduce the accuracy of the model.[16] In contrast, we suspect that small errors in measurement may have great impacts on configural rules. For example, the conjunctive rule "require good grades *and* test scores" will lead to mistakes if a test score is not a predictor of success or if the cutoff for "good grades" is wrong; the linear rule that weights grades and scores and combines them is less vulnerable to either error.

4.3. Why do inaccurate configural rules persist?

One of the main lessons of decision research is that feedback is crucial for learning. Inaccurate configural rules may persist because experts who get slow, infrequent, or unclear feedback will not learn that their rules are wrong. When feedback must be sought, inaccurate rules may persist because people tend to search instinctively for evidence that will confirm prior theories (Klayman & Ha, 1985). Even when feedback is naturally provided, rather than sought, confirming evidence is more retrievable or "available" than disconfirming evidence (Tversky & Kahneman, 1973). The disproportionate search and recall of confirming instances will sustain experts' faith in inaccurate configural rules. Even when evidence does disconfirm a particular rule, we suspect that the natural tendencies to construct such rules (catalogued earlier) will cause experts to refine their rules rather than discard them.

4.4. Nonpredictive functions of expertise

The thinking of experts is rich with subtle distinctions, novel categories, and complicated configural rules for making predictions. We have given several reasons why such categories and rules might arise, and persist even if they are inaccurate. Our arguments provide one possible explanation why knowledgeable experts, paradoxically, are no better at making predictions than novices and simple models.

Another explanation is that the knowledge that experts acquire as they learn may not be useful for making better predictions about important long-range outcomes, but it may be useful for other purposes. Experts are indispensable for measuring variables (Sawyer, 1966) and discovering new ones (E. Johnson, 1988).

Furthermore, as experts learn, they may be able to make more kinds of predictions, even if they are no more accurate; we speculate that they mistake their increasing fertility for increasing accuracy. Taxi drivers know lots of alternative routes when they see traffic on the Schuylkill Expressway (cf. Chase, 1983), and they probably can predict their speeds on those alternative routes better than a novice can. But can the experts predict whether there will be heavy traffic on the expressway better than a statistical model can (using time of day, day of week, and weather, for example)? We doubt it.

There are also many social benefits of expertise that people can provide better than models can. Models can make occasional large mistakes that experts, having common sense, would know to avoid (Shanteau, 1988).[17] Experts can explain themselves better, and people usually feel that an expert's intuitive judgments are fairer than those of a model (cf. Dawes, 1971).

Some of these attitudes toward experts stem from the myth that experts are accurate predictors, or the hope that an expert will never err.[18] Many of these social benefits should disappear with time, if people learn that models are better; until then, experts have an advantage. (Large corporations have learned: They use models in scoring credit risks, adjusting insurance claims, and other activities where decisions are routine and cost savings are large. Consumers do think that such rules are unfair, but the cost savings overwhelm their objections.)

5. Implications for understanding expert decision making

Our review produces a consistent, if depressing, picture of expert decision makers. They are successful at generating hypotheses and inducing complex decision rules. The result is a more efficient search of the available information directed by goals and aided by the experts' superior store of knowledge. Unfortunately, their knowledge and rules have little impact on experts' performance. Sometimes experts are more accurate than novices (though not always), but they are rarely better than simple statistical models.

An inescapable conclusion of this research is that experts do some things well and others poorly. Sawyer (1966) found that expert measurement of cues, and statistical combination of them, worked better than expert combination or statistical measurement. Techniques that combine experts' judgments about configural and broken-leg cues with actuarial models might improve performance especially well (Blattberg & Hoch, 1990; E. Johnson, 1988).

Of course, expert performance relative to models depends critically on the task and the importance of configural and broken-leg cues. There may be tasks in which experts beat models, but it is hard to think of examples. In pricing antiques, classic cars, or unusual real estate (e.g., houses over $5 million), there may be many broken-leg cues that give experts an advantage, but a model including the expert-rated cue "special features" may also do well.

Tasks involving pattern recognition, like judging the prospective taste of gourmet recipes or the beauty of faces or paintings, seem to involve many configural rules that favor experts. But if one adds expert-rated cues like "consistency" (in recipes) or "symmetry" (in faces) to linear models, the experts' configural edge may disappear.

Another class of highly configural tasks includes those in which variable weights change across subsamples or stages. For instance, one should play the beginning and end of a backgammon or chess game differently. A model that picks moves by evaluating position features, weighting them with fixed weights, and combining them linearly will lose to an expert who implicitly changes weights. But a model that could shift weights during the game could possibly beat an expert, and one did: Berliner's (1980) backgammon program beat the 1979 world champion.

There is an important need to provide clearer boundaries for this dismal picture of expert judgment. To what extent, we ask ourselves, does the picture provided by this review apply to the other domains discussed in this volume? Providing a crisp answer to this question is difficult, because few of these domains provide explicit comparisons between experts and linear models. Without such a set of comparisons, identifying domains in which experts will do well is speculation.

We have already suggested that some domains are inherently richer in broken-leg and configural cues. The presence of these cues provides the opportunity for better performance but does not necessarily guarantee it. In addition, the presence of feedback and the lack of noise have been suggested as important variables in determining the performances of both experts and expert systems (Carroll, 1987). Finally, Shanteau (1988) has suggested that "good" experts are those in whom the underlying body of knowledge is more developed, providing examples such as soil and livestock judgment.

6. Implications for the study of expertise

Expertise should be identified by comparison to some standard of performance. Random and novice performances make for natural comparisons. The linear-model literature suggests that simple statistical models provide another, demanding comparison.

The results from studies of expert decision making have had surprisingly little effect on the study of expertise, even in related tasks. For instance, simple linear models do quite well in medical-judgment tasks such as the hypothetical task discussed at the beginning of this chapter. Yet most of the work in aiding diagnosis has been aimed at developing expert systems that can mimic human expert performance, not exceed or improve upon it.

Expert systems may predict less accurately than simple models because the systems are *too much* like experts. The main lesson from the regression-model literature is that large numbers of configural rules, which knowledge engineers take as evidence of expertise, do not necessarily make good predictions; simple linear combinations of variables (measured by experts) are better in many tasks.

A somewhat ironic contrast between rule-based systems and linear models has occurred in recent developments in connectionist models. Whereas these models generally represent a relatively low level of cognitive activity, there are some marked similarities to the noncognitive "paramorphic" regression models we have discussed. In many realizations, a connectionist network is a set of units with associated weights that specify constraints on how the units combine the input received. The network generates weights that will maximize the goodness of fit of the system to the outcomes it observes in training (Rumelhart, McClelland, & PDP Research Group, 1986).

In a single-layer system, each unit receives its input directly from the environment. Thus, these systems appear almost isomorphic to simple regressions, producing a model that takes environmental cues and combines them, in a linear fashion, to provide the best fit to the outcomes. Much like regressions, we would expect simple, single-layer networks to make surprisingly good predictions under uncertainty (Jordan, 1986; Rumelhart et al., 1986).

More complex, multilayer systems allow for the incorporation of patterns of cues, which resemble the configural cues reported by experts. Like human experts, we suspect that such hidden units in these more complex systems will not add much to predictive validity in many of the domains we have discussed. The parallel between regression models and connectionist networks is provocative and represents an opportunity for bringing together two quite divergent paradigms.

Finally, we note that this chapter stands in strong contrast to the chapters that surround it: Our experts, while sharing many signs of superior expert processing demonstrated in other domains, do not show superior performance. The contrast suggests some closing notes. First, the history of the study of expert decision making raises concerns about how experts are to be identified. Being revered as an expert practitioner is not enough. Care should be given to assessing actual performance. Second, the case study of decision making may say something about the development of expertise in general and the degree to which task characteristics promote or prevent the development of superior performance. Experts fail when their cognitive abilities are badly matched to environmental demands.

In this chapter we have tried to isolate the characteristics of decision tasks that (1) generate such poor performance, (2) allow experts to believe that they are doing well, and (3) allow us to believe in them. We hope that the contrast between these conditions and those provided by other domains may contribute to a broader, more informed view of expertise, accounting for experts' failures as well as their successes.

Notes

1 While presenting a research seminar discussing the application of linear models, Robyn Dawes reported Einhorn's (1972) classic finding that three experts' judgments of Hodgkin's disease severity were uncorrelated with actual severity (measured by how long patients lived). One seminar participant asked Dawes what would happen if a certain famous physician were studied. The questioner was sure that Dr. So-and-so makes accurate judgments. Dawes called Einhorn; the famous doctor turned out to be subject 2.

2 Many regression studies use the general "lens model" proposed by Egon Brunswik (1952) and extended by Hammond (1955) and others. The lens model shows the interconnection between two systems: an ecology or environment, and a person making judgments. The notation in the text is mostly lens-model terminology.

3 Although the functions relating cues to the judgment and the outcome can be of any form, linear relationships are most often used, because they explain judgments and outcomes surprisingly well, even when outcomes are known to be nonlinear functions of the cues (Dawes & Corrigan, 1974).

4 The correlation between the actuarial-model prediction and the outcome Y_e is the square root of the regression R^2, and is denoted R_e. A more practical measure of actuarial-model accuracy is the "cross-validated" correlation, when regression weights derived on one sample are used to predict a new sample of Y_e values.

5 By contrast, actuarial models often are called "optimal linear models," because by definition no linear combination of the cues can predict Y_e more accurately.

6 Of course, such an explanation is "paramorphic" (Hoffman, 1960): It describes judgments in a purely statistical way, *as if* experts were weighing and combining cues in their heads; the process they use might be quite different. However, Einhorn, Kleinmuntz, and Kleinmuntz (1979) argued persuasively that the paramorphic regression approach might capture process indirectly.

7 Because suggested Minnesota Multiphasic Personality Inventory (MMPI) cutoffs were originally created by statistical analysis, it may seem unsurprising that a statistical model beats a judge who tries to mimic it. But the model combines scores *linearly*, whereas judges typically use various scores in configural nonlinear combinations.

8 Of course, variables must be standardized by dividing them by their sample standard deviations. Otherwise, a variable with a wide range would account for more than its share of the variation in the equally weighted sum.

9 Unless a broken leg has occurred in the sample used to derive regression weights, the cue "broken leg" will not vary and will get no regression weight.

10 These data correct the presumption in the early bootstrapping literature (e.g., Dawes, 1971; Goldberg, 1970) that residuals were entirely human error.

11 A recent study with sales forecasters showed a higher r_z, around .2 (Blattberg & Hoch, 1990). Even though their residuals were quite accurate, the best forecasters only did about as well as the linear model. In a choice between models and experts, models will win, but a mechanical combination of the two is better still: Adding bootstrapping residuals to an actuarial model increased predictive accuracy by about 10%.

12 Configural rules are especially useful for narrowing a large set of choices to a subset of candidates for further consideration.

13 A linear model with k cues has only k degrees of freedom, but the k variables offer $k(k-1)/2$ multiplicative two-variable interactions (and lots of higher-order interactions).

14 We cannot determine whether Dent was truly better in the World Series or just lucky in a limited number of Series appearances. Yet his success in "big games" obviously influenced the Yankees' owner, George Steinbrenner (who has not otherwise distinguished himself as an expert decision maker). He named Dent manager of the Yankees shortly after this conference was held, citing his ability as a player "to come through when it mattered." Dent was later fired 49 games into the season (18 wins, 31 losses), and the Yankees had the worst record in Major League baseball at the time.

15 Although the robustness of linear models is well established, we know of no analogous work on the *un*robustness of configural rules.

16 Linear models are robust to nonlinearities provided the relationship between each predictor and outcome has the same direction for any values of the other predictors (although the relationship's magnitude will vary). This property is sometimes called "conditional monotonicity."

17 This possibility has been stressed by Ken Hammond in discussions of analytical versus intuitive judgment (e.g., Hammond, Hamm, Grassia, & Pearson, 1987). For example, most of the unorthodox moves generated by the leading backgammon computer program (which beat a world champion in 1979) are stupid mistakes an expert would catch; a few are brilliant moves that might not occur to an expert.

18 A model necessarily errs, by fixing regression coefficients and ignoring many variables. It "accepts error to make less error" (Einhorn, 1986). An expert, by changing regression coefficients and selecting variables, conceivably could be right every time. This difference is made dramatic by a medical example. A statistician developed a simple linear model to make routine diagnoses. Its features were printed on a card doctors could carry around; the card showed several cues and how to add them. Doctors wouldn't use it because they couldn't defend it in the inevitable lawsuits that would result after the model would have made a mistake.

References

Bedard, J. (1989). Expertise in auditing: Myth or reality? *Accounting, Organizations and Society, 14,* 113–131.

Bedard, J., & Mock, T. J. (1989). *Expert and novice problem-solving behavior in audit planning: An experimental study.* Unpublished paper, University of Southern California.

Berliner, H. J. (1980). Backgammon computer program beats world champion. *Artificial Intelligence, 14*, 205–220.

Bettman, J. R., & Park, C. W. (1980). Effects of prior knowledge and experience and phase of the choice process on consumer decision processes: A protocol analysis. *Journal of Consumer Research, 7*, 234–248.

Blattberg, R. C., & Hoch, S. J. (1990). Database models and managerial intuition: 50% database + 50% manager. *Management Science, 36*, 887–899.

Bouman, M. J. (1980). Application of information-processing and decision-making research, I. In G. R. Ungson & D. N. Braunstein (Eds.), *Decision making: An interdisciplinary inquiry* (pp. 129–167). Boston: Kent Publishing.

Bowman, E. H. (1963). Consistency and optimality in management decision making. *Management Science, 10*, 310–321.

Brehmer, B. (1980). In one word: Not from experience. *Acta Psychologica, 45*, 223–241.

Brucks, M. (1985). The effects of product class knowledge on information search behavior. *Journal of Consumer Research, 12*, 1–16.

Brunswik, E. (1952). *The conceptual framework of psychology.* University of Chicago Press.

Camerer, C. F. (1981a). The validity and utility of expert judgment. Unpublished Ph.D. dissertation, Center for Decision Research, University of Chicago Graduate School of Business.

Camerer, C. F. (1981b). General conditions for the success of bootstrapping models. *Organizational Behavior and Human Performance, 27*, 411–422.

Carroll, B. (1987). Expert systems for clinical diagnosis: Are they worth the effort? *Behavioral Science, 32*, 274–292.

Chapman, L. J., & Chapman, J. P. (1967). Genesis of popular but erroneous psychodiagnostic observations. *Journal of Abnormal Psychology, 73*, 193–204.

Chapman, L. J., & Chapman, J. P. (1969). Illusory correlation as an obstacle to the use of valid psychodiagnostic signs. *Journal of Abnormal Psychology, 46*, 271–280.

Chase, W. G. (1983). Spatial representations of taxi drivers. In D. R. Rogers & J. H. Sloboda (Eds.), *Acquisition of symbolic skills* (pp. 391–405). New York: Plenum.

Chase, W. G., & Simon, H. A. (1973). Perception in chess. *Cognitive Psychology, 4*, 55–81.

Christensen-Szalanski, J. J. J., & Bushyhead, J. B. (1981). Physicians' use of probabilistic information in a real clinical setting. *Journal of Experimental Psychology: Human Perception and Performance, 7*, 928–935.

Dawes, R. M. (1971). A case study of graduate admissions: Application of three principles of human decision making. *American Psychologist, 26*, 180–188.

Dawes, R. M., & Corrigan, B. (1974). Linear models in decision making. *Psychological Bulletin, 81*, 97.

Dawes, R. M., Faust, D., & Meehl, P. E. (1989). Clinical versus actuarial judgment. *Science, 243*, 1668–1674.

DeSmet, A. A., Fryback, D. G., & Thornbury, J. R. (1979). A second look at the utility of radiographic skull examination for trauma. *American Journal of Radiology, 132*, 95–99.

Einhorn, H. J. (1972). Expert measurement and mechanical combination. *Organizational Behavior and Human Performance, 7*, 86–106.

Einhorn, H. J. (1974). Expert judgment: Some necessary conditions and an example. *Journal of Applied Psychology, 59*, 562–571.

Einhorn, H. J. (1986). Accepting error to make less error. *Journal of Personality Assessment, 50*, 387–395.

Einhorn, H. J., & Hogarth, R. M. (1975). Unit weighting schemas for decision making. *Organizational Behavior and Human Performance, 13*, 171–192.

Einhorn, H. J., Kleinmuntz, D. N., & Kleinmuntz, B. (1979). Linear regression and process tracing models of judgment. *Psychological Review, 86*, 465–485.

Elstein, A. S., Shulman, A. S., & Sprafka, S. A. (1978). *Medical problem solving: An analysis of clinical reasoning*. Cambridge, MA: Harvard University Press.

Ericsson, K. A., & Chase, W. G. (1981). Exceptional memory. *American Scientist, 70*(6), 607–615.

Ericsson, K. A., & Polson, P. G. (1988). An experimental analysis of the mechanisms of a memory skill. *Journal of Experimental Psychology: Learning, Memory, and Cognition, 14*, 305–316.

Ericsson, K. A., & Simon, H. A. (1987). Verbal reports as data. *Psychological Review, 87*, 215–251.

Garb, H. N. (1989). Clinical judgment, clinical training, and professional experience. *Psychological Bulletin, 105*, 387–396.

Goldberg, L. R. (1959). The effectiveness of clinicians' judgments: The diagnosis of organic brain damage from the Bender–Gestalt test. *Journal of Consulting Psychology, 23*, 25–33.

Goldberg, L. R. (1968). Simple models or simple processes? *American Psychologist, 23*, 483–496.

Goldberg, L. R. (1970). Man versus model of man: A rationale, plus some evidence, for a method of improving on clinical inferences. *Psychological Bulletin, 73*, 422–432.

Goldberg, L. R. (1976). Man versus model of man: Just how conflicting is that evidence? *Organizational Behavior and Human Performance, 16*, 13–22.

Gustafson, J. E. (1963). The computer for use in private practice. In *Proceedings of Fifth IBM Medical Symposium*, pp. 101–111. White Plains, NY: IBM Technical Publication Division.

Hammond, K. R. (1955). Probabilistic functioning and the clinical method. *Psychological Review, 62*, 255–262.

Hammond, K. R. (1987). Toward a unified approach to the study of expert judgment. In J. Mumpower, L. Phillips, O. Renn, & V. R. R. Uppuluri (Eds.), *NATO ASI Series F: Computer & Systems Sciences: Vol. 35, Expert judgment and expert systems* (pp. 1–16). Berlin: Springer-Verlag.

Hammond, K. R., Hamm, R. M., Grassia, J., & Pearson, T. (1987). Direct comparison of the efficacy of intuitive and analytical cognition in expert judgment. *IEEE Transactions on Systems, Man, and Cybernetics, SMC-17*, 753–770.

Hoffman, P. J. (1960). The paramorphic representation of clinical judgment. *Psychological Bulletin, 57*, 116–131.

Holland, J. H., Holyoak, K. J., Nisbett, R. E., & Thagard, P. R. (1986). *Induction: Processes of inference, learning, and discovery*. Cambridge, MA: MIT Press.

Johnson, E. J. (1980). Expertise in admissions judgment. Unpublished doctoral dissertation, Carnegie-Mellon University.

Johnson, E. J. (1988). Expertise and decision under uncertainty: Performance and process. In M. T. H. Chi, R. Glaser, & M. J. Farr (Eds.), *The nature of expertise* (pp. 209–228). Hillsdale, NJ: Erlbaum.

Johnson, E. J., & Payne, J. (1985). Effort and accuracy in choice. *Management Science, 31*, 395–414.

Johnson, E. J., & Russo, J. E. (1984). Product familiarity and learning new information. *Journal of Consumer Research, 11*, 542–550.

Johnson, P. E., Hassebrock, F., Duran, A. S., & Moller, J. (1982). Multimethod study of clinical judgment. *Organizational Behavior and Human Performance, 30*, 201–230.

Jordan, M. I. (1986). An introduction to linear algebra in parallel distributed processing. In D. Rumelhart, J. McClelland, & PDP Research Group (Eds.), *Parallel distributed processing: Explorations in the microstructure of cognition: Vol. 1. Foundations* (pp. 365–422). Cambridge, MA: MIT Press.

Kahneman, D., Slovic, P., & Tversky, A. (1982). *Judgment under uncertainty: Heuristics and biases.* Cambridge University Press.

Keren, G. B. (1987). Facing uncertainty in the game of bridge: A calibration study. *Organizational Behavior and Human Decision Processes, 139*, 98–114.

Klayman, J. (1988). Cue discovery in probabilistic environments: Uncertainty and experimentation. *Journal of Experimental Psychology: Learning, Memory, and Cognition, 14*, 317–330.

Klayman, J., & Ha, Y. (1985). Confirmation, disconfirmation, and information in hypothesis testing. *Psychological Review, 94*, 211–228.

Kleinmuntz, B. (1968). *Formal representation of human judgment.* New York: Wiley.

Kundel, H. L., & LaFollette, P. S. (1972). Visual search patterns and experience with radiological images. *Radiology, 103*, 523–528.

Larkin, J., McDermott, J., Simon, D. P., & Simon, H. A. (1980). Expert and novice performance in solving physics problems. *Science, 208*, 1335–1342.

Levenberg, S. B. (1975). Professional training, psychodiagnostic skill, and kinetic family drawings. *Journal of Personality Assessment, 39*, 389–393.

Libby, R. (1976). Man versus model of man: Some conflicting evidence. *Organizational Behavior and Human Performance, 16*, 1–12.

Libby, R., & Frederick, D. M. (1989, February). *Expertise and the ability to explain audit findings* (University of Michigan Cognitive Science and Machine Intelligence Laboratory Technical Report No. 21).

Lichtenstein, S., Fischhoff, B., & Phillips, L. D. (1977). Calibration of probabilities: The state of the art. In H. Jungermann & G. de Zeeuw (Eds.), *Decision making and change in human affairs.* Amsterdam: D. Reidel.

Meehl, P. E. (1954). *Clinical versus statistical prediction: A theoretical analysis and a review of the evidence.* Minneapolis: University of Minnesota Press.

Meehl, P. E. (1986). Causes and effects of my disturbing little book. *Journal of Personality Assessment, 50*, 370–375.

Meyer, R. J. (1987). The learning of multiattribute judgment policies. *Journal of Consumer Research, 14*, 155–173.

Murphy, A. H., & Winkler, R. L. (1977). Can weather forecasters formulate reliable probability forecasts of precipitation and temperature? *National Weather Digest, 2*, 2–9.

Philadelphia Inquirer. (1989, August 15). Personality test gets revamped for the '80s, pp. 1-D, 3-D.

Rumelhart, D., McClelland, J., & PDP Research Group (Eds.). (1986). *Parallel distrib-*

uted processing: Explorations in the microstructure of cognition: Vol. 1. Foundations.
Cambridge, MA: MIT Press.

Sarbin, T. R. (1944). The logic of prediction in psychology. *Psychological Review, 51,* 210–228.

Sawyer, J. (1966). Measurement and prediction, clinical and statistical. *Psychological Bulletin, 66,* 178–200.

Shanteau, J. (1988). Psychological characteristics and strategies of expert decision makers. *Acta Psychologica, 68,* 203–215.

Shortliffe, E. H., Buchanan, B. G., & Feigenbaum, E. A. (1979). Knowledge engineering for medical decision making: A review of computer-based decision aids. *Proceedings of the IEEE, 67,* 1207–1224.

Tversky, A., & Kahneman, D. (1973). Availability: A heuristic for judging frequency and probability. *Cognitive Psychology, 4,* 207–232.

Tversky, A., & Kahneman, D. (1982). Judgments of and by representativeness. In D. Kahneman, P. Slovic, & A. Tversky (Eds.), *Judgment under uncertainty: Heuristics and biases* (pp. 84–98). Cambridge University Press.

Voss, J. F., & Post, T. A. (1988). On the solving of ill-structured problems. In M. T. H. Chi, R. Glaser, & M. J. Farr (Eds.), *The nature of expertise* (pp. 261–285). Hillsdale, NJ: Erlbaum.

Wagenaar, W. A., & Keren, G. B. (1985). Calibration of probability assessments by professional blackjack dealers, statistical experts, and lay people. *Organizational Behavior and Human Decision Processes, 36,* 406–416.

Wiggens, N., & Kohen, E. S. (1971). Man vs. model of man revisited: The forecasting of graduate school success. *Journal of Personality and Social Psychology, 19,* 100–106.

Yntema, D. B., & Torgerson, W. J. (1961). Man–computer cooperation in decision requiring common sense. *IRE Transactions of the Professional Group on Human Factors in Electronics, 2,* 20–26.

11   Intertemporal choice

George Loewenstein and Richard H. Thaler

Introduction

Intertemporal choices, decisions in which the timing of costs and benefits are spread out over time, are both common and important. How much schooling to obtain, whom to marry, whether to have children, how much to save for retirement, how to invest, whether to buy a house, and if so which house to buy – all these vital decisions have strong intertemporal components. As examples of individual decision making, intertemporal choices are also interesting because the relevant economic theory makes unusually testable predictions. In many contexts, economic theories of individual behavior are untestable because the predictions are too vague. Almost any choice, no matter how bizarre, can be rationalized by finding some utility function for which the choice represents an optimal solution. In contrast, for decisions involving choices between time streams of money (receipts and payments), economic theory makes a precise and testable prediction, namely that (at the margin) people should discount money streams at the (after-tax) market rate of interest (r).

The existence of capital markets creates what amounts to an internal arbitrage opportunity for the consumer. If presented with an investment option that pays off at a rate higher than r, the consumer can enjoy greater consumption in every period by accepting the option and borrowing appropriately at rate r. Options that pay less than r should be rejected since they are dominated by lending in the capital market. The implication is that consumers should make intertemporal trade-offs so that their marginal rate

This chapter originally appeared in the *Journal of Economic Perspectives*, Fall 1989, 3(4), 181–193. Copyright © 1989 by the American Economic Association. Reprinted by permission.

The authors wish to thank without implicating George Ainslie, Colin Camerer, John Campbell, Werner De Bondt, Jon Elster, William Lang, and Nachum Sicherman for helpful comments, and Concord Capital Management and the Russell Sage Foundation for financial support.

of time preference equals the interest rate. Furthermore, consumers should be consistent in their intertemporal choices. The discount rate used should be constant across situations and over time. However, research shows that depending on the context examined, the implied discount rates of observed behavior can vary from negative to several hundred percent per year.

A well-known example of apparent negative discount rates is the fact that a large majority of U.S. taxpayers receive refunds every year from the Internal Revenue Service. These interest-free loans to the government are easily avoidable by adjusting the withholding rate. Similarly, many school teachers are given the choice between being paid in 9 monthly installments (September–June) or 12 (September–August). Most of those given this choice elect the latter option. Finally, studies of life-cycle consumption choices reveal that consumption tends to increase over time until retirement. In the absence of binding borrowing constraints, this pattern can only be consistent with the life-cycle theory if people have negative discount rates (see, Courant, Gramlich, and Laitner, 1986).

Examples of extremely high discount rates are also easy to find. A recent change in West Virginia law provides an example. Students under the age of 18 who drop out of school lose their driving permits. The first year results indicate that this law has reduced the dropout rate by one-third. It seems implausible that one-third of the high school dropouts were so close to the margin that the loss of driving privileges for a year or two (or more precisely, the expected costs of driving illegally for this period) could tip a rational human capital investment decision toward completing high school. Rather, the behavior seems to reveal extremely myopic preferences. A similar myopia is evident in the lament of a dermatologist that her warnings about the risk of skin cancer have little effect, but "My patients are much more compliant about avoiding the sun when I tell them that it can cause large pores and blackheads."

It is not just teenagers and sun lovers who display high discount rates. Most homeowners have too little insulation in their attics and walls, and fail to buy more expensive energy-efficient appliances even when the pay-back period for the extra expense is less than a year. Hausman's (1979) study of air conditioner purchases, which examined consumer trade-offs between purchase price and delayed energy payments, estimated an average consumer discount rate of about 25 percent. A subsequent study by Gately (1980) comparing pairs of refrigerators differing only in energy use and initial purchase price revealed that the implicit discount rates associated with purchasing the cheaper models were incredibly high: from 45 to 130 percent assuming an electricity cost of 3.8 cents per kilowatt hour, and from 120 to 300 percent at 10 cents per kilowatt hour. Most recently, Ruderman, Levine, and McMahan (1986) computed the discount rates implicit in several different kinds of appliances (for the average model on the market, relative to the most efficient): space heaters, air conditioners, water heaters, refrigerators, and freezers. They found that the implicit discount rate for room air conditioners was 17 percent, somewhat lower than Hausman's estimate. However, the discount rates for other appliances were much higher, e.g., gas water heater, 102 percent; electric water heater, 243 percent; and freezer, 138 percent. Economic theory has a clear prediction about these inefficient appliances – they will not be produced. But they are produced, and purchased.[1]

So, as usual, where there are testable predictions, there are anomalies. The remainder of this column examines a number of situations in which people do not appear to discount money flows at the market rate of interest or any other single discount rate. Discount rates observed in both laboratory and field decision-making environments are shown to depend on the magnitude and sign of what is being discounted, on the time delay, on whether the choice is cast in terms of speed-up or delay, on the way in which a choice is framed, and on whether future benefits or costs induce savoring or dread.

Variations in the discount rate for an individual

An experiment that investigated the first three of these effects was presented in Thaler (1981). Subjects (mostly students) were asked to imagine that they had won some money in a lottery conducted by their bank. They could take the money now or wait until later. They were asked how much they would need to be paid to make waiting as attractive as immediate payment. Each subject received a 3×3 table to fill in with amounts of money varied along one dimension and length of time along the other. Four versions of the questionnaires were used, three involving gains, and one involving losses. In the losses version, subjects were asked to imagine that they had been issued a traffic fine that could either be paid at face value now or at an increased price later. In all cases subjects were asked to assume that there was no risk of not getting the reward (or of avoiding the fine) if they waited. All amounts were to be received (or paid) by mail.[2] The experiment thus manipulated the three variables of interest: the length of time to be waited; the magnitude of the outcome; whether the outcome is a gain or loss.

Three strong patterns emerged from the subjects' responses. First, discount rates declined sharply with the length of time to be waited, consistent with earlier findings for animals (Herrnstein, 1961; Ainslie, 1975). Second, discount rates declined with the size of the reward. Discount rates for small amounts (under $100) were very high, while those for larger amounts were more reasonable. Third, discount rates for gains were much higher than for losses. Subjects needed to be paid a lot to wait for a reward, but were unwilling to pay very much to delay a fine.

These three findings have been replicated in a much larger study by Benzion, Rapoport, and Yagil (1989). They used a $4 \times 4 \times 4$ design which manipulated the time delay (.5, 1, 2, and 4 years), amount of money ($40, $200, $1000, and $5000), and scenario (postponing a gain; postponing a loss; expediting a gain; and expediting a loss). The subjects were undergraduate

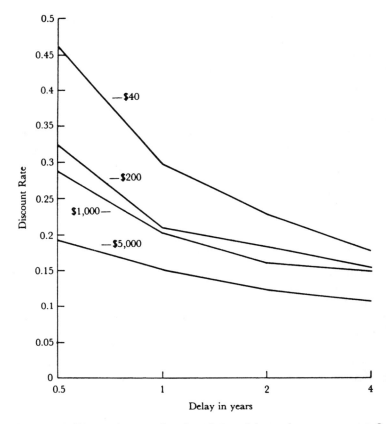

Figure 11.1. Discounting as a function of time delay and money amount. Source: Benzion et al. (1989).

and graduate students in economics and finance at two Israeli universities, a relatively sophisticated subject pool. Their results are shown in Figure 11.1 (averaging across the four scenarios). As can be seen clearly, discount rates again decline sharply with the length of time to be waited and the size of the prize.[3]

We will discuss each of these three strong patterns of discount rate variations in turn.

Dynamic inconsistency

The negative relationship between discount rates and time delay has important consequences for the dynamic consistency of behavior. Suppose, as illustrated in Figure 11.2, that an individual must choose between two rewards, a small early reward S, which occurs at t_1, and a bigger later reward

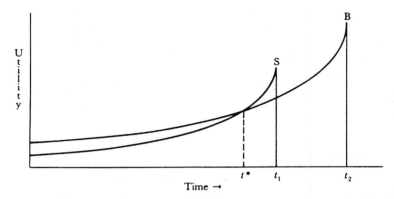

Figure 11.2. Non-exponential discounting. Source: Ainslie (1975).

B, which occurs at t_2.[4] The lines represent the present utility of the rewards as perceived by the individual at different points in time. If the individual discounts the future at a constant rate, that is, if discounting is constant for different time delays, then the curves will never cross. However, if discounting decreases as a function of time delay, as the empirical research suggests, then the curves may cross, leading to a reversal of preference. When both rewards are sufficiently distant, the individual prefers B, but as S becomes more proximate, its relative value increases until at t^*, S abruptly comes to dominate B in terms of present utility. The significance of the crossing curves is that behavior will not generally be consistent over time. In the morning, when temptation is remote, we vow to go to bed early, stick to our diet, and not have too much to drink. That night we stay out until 3:00 A.M., have two helpings of chocolate decadence, and sample every variety of Aquavit at a Norwegian restaurant. Applied to saving, as Strotz (1956) demonstrated, if the discount rate declines over time, then people will always consume more in the present than called for by their previous plans.

The problem of dynamic inconsistency raises questions about consumer sovereignty. Who is sovereign, the self who sets the alarm clock to rise early, or the self who shuts it off the next morning and goes back to sleep? It is instructive that we normally see the far-sighted self take actions which constrain or alter the behavior of the myopic self. Dieters pay money to stay on "fat farms" whose main appeal is that they guarantee to underfeed their guests; alcoholics take Antabuse, which causes nausea and vomiting if they take a drink; smokers buy cigarettes by the pack (rather than by the carton, which is cheaper). And, though no longer fashionable, for many years Christmas clubs were extremely popular in the United States. These savings plans offered the unusual combination of inconvenience (deposits were made in person every week), illiquidity (funds could not be withdrawn until late November), and low interest (in some cases, zero interest). Of course, illiquidity was the Christmas club's raison d'être since customers wanted to assure themselves of funds to pay for Christmas presents. Recognizing the limited ability of conventional decision models to account for self-binding behavior and other forms of intrapersonal conflict, a number of authors have proposed models that view economic behavior as an internal struggle between multiple selves with conflicting preferences (Ainslie 1975, 1992; Elster, 1979; Schelling, 1984; Thaler and Shefrin, 1981; Winston, 1980).

Magnitude effects

The effect of magnitude on the discount rate is as strong as the effect of time delay. In both the Thaler and Benzion et al. studies using hypothetical questions, the implicit discount rates declined sharply with the size of the purchase. A similar result has been observed by Holcomb and Nelson (1989) over a small range of actual payoffs, $5–$17. Also, the very high discount rates observed for relatively small hypothetical rewards were obtained by Horowitz (1988) for an actual payoff of $50.

There are two plausible behavioral explanations for the magnitude effect. The first is based on the psychology of perception (psychophysics): people are sensitive not only to relative differences in money amounts, but also to absolute differences (Loewenstein and Prelec, 1989b). The perceptual difference between $100 now and $150 in a year, for example, appears greater than the difference between $10 now and $15 in one year, so that many people are willing to wait for the extra $50 in the first instance, but not for the $5 in the second. The second explanation relies on notions of mental accounting (Shefrin and Thaler, 1988). Suppose that small windfalls are entered into a mental checking account and are largely consumed, while larger amounts are entered into a mental savings account, with a much smaller propensity to consume. Then the cost of waiting for a small windfall may be perceived to be forgone consumption, while in contrast, the opportunity cost of waiting for a large windfall is perceived as simply forgone interest. If forgone consumption is more tempting than forgone interest, the magnitude effect will be observed.[5] (Thaler, 1990, discusses these issues in more detail.)

Sign effects

The third strong empirical regularity in the discounting surveys is that the discount rate for gains is much greater than for losses. People are quite anxious to receive a positive reward, especially a small one, but are less anxious to postpone a loss. Part of this preference comes from a simple "debt aversion." Many people pay off mortgages and student loans more quickly than they have to, even when the rate they are paying is less than they earn on safe investments.

Reference points

In descriptive theories of decision making under uncertainty, the distinction between gains and losses has received considerable attention. Decision makers do not appear to integrate outcomes with their wealth or existing consumption level, as normally assumed in expected utility theory. Rather individuals appear to react to events as changes, relative to some natural reference point. This observation was first made by Markowitz (1952), and more recently Kahneman and Tversky (1979) used changes in wealth relative to a reference point as the carriers of value in their prospect theory.

Reference points are also important in intertemporal choice (Loewenstein and Prelec, 1989a). Loewenstein (1988) offers the following demonstration of a reference point effect. An experiment was conducted using 105 high school sophomores and juniors. All subjects received a $7 gift certificate for a local record shop. The expected time at which the students would receive the certificates was varied among one, four, and eight weeks. The students were then given a series of binary choices between keeping their certificates at the originally appointed times, or trading them either for smaller certificates to be received earlier, or for larger certificates to be received later. For example, subjects who expected to receive a four week certificate were asked whether they would trade it for an eight week certificate, the value of which was varied between $7.10 and $10.00. They were told that the experimenter would select and implement one of their choices at random.

The design of this experiment allows the role of the reference point to be empirically tested. Some subjects were asked to make a trade-off between the size of the reward and its *delay* from week 1 to week 4, while other subjects were making a trade-off between the size of the reward and its *speed-up* from week 4 to week 1. If subjects were not influenced by reference points, then this manipulation would have no effect. The results of the experiment are shown in Table 11.1. The figures shown are the mean minimum amounts to speed up or delay consumption, depending on the condition. For all three comparisons, the mean delay premium is at least twice the mean speed-up cost, with all differences being statistically significant. Subjects demand more to wait past the expected arrival date than they are willing to pay to speed up its expected arrival. (Similar results are obtained by Benzion et al., 1989.) The result is compatible with Kahneman and Tversky's notion of *loss aversion*, the idea that the disutility of losing a given amount of money is significantly greater in absolute value than the utility of gaining the same amount.

Loss aversion also induces preferences for particular patterns of consumption over time. In situations when past consumption levels set reference points for future consumption, individuals may prefer an increasing consumption profile. For example, Loewenstein and Prelec (1989a) asked 95 Harvard undergraduates three questions. First, the students were asked to choose between two free dinners to be consumed on a Friday night in one

Table 11.1. *Mean amounts to speed-up and delay consumption ($7 record store gift certificate)*

Time interval	Delay	Speed-up	Significance
1 week versus 4 weeks	$1.09	$.25	.001
4 weeks versus 8 weeks	$ .84	$.37	.005
1 week versus 8 weeks	$1.76	$.52	.001

month: a dinner at a fancy French restaurant, or a dinner at a local Greek restaurant. Most had the good sense to prefer the French dinner. Then, they were asked whether they would rather have the French dinner in one month or two months. Of those who selected the French dinner originally, 80 percent preferred to have it in one month rather than two, implying a positive discount rate. The third question offered subjects two hypothetical meals, the first in one month, the second in two months. Subjects were asked which order they preferred: Greek in one month, and French in two months; or French in one month, and Greek in two months. Here, 57 percent of the French food lovers elected to have the Greek meal first. In a standard utility framework, this latter response implies a negative rate of time preference, inconsistent with the answer to the second question. There is no inconsistency, however, if people evaluate current consumption relative to past consumption and are loss averse. They simply prefer a pattern of increasing utility over time.

The preference for a rising consumption profile helps explain an anomaly in labor markets, namely that wages rise with age even when productivity does not (Medoff and Abraham, 1980). In many academic departments, for example, the highest paid faculty are the oldest, even if they are no longer the most productive. The two most important standard explanations for this pattern involve specific human capital and agency costs. The human capital argument is that firms offer the increasing age–earnings profile to encourage workers to stay in the firm long enough to make firm-specific training pay off. The agency cost argument, due to Lazear (1981), suggests that firms offer wages above marginal product for older workers to prevent workers from cheating and shirking. (A worker who gets caught risks losing the present value of the difference between pay and productivity.) While both of these explanations have merit in some occupations (see the articles by Carmichael, 1989, and by Hutchens, 1989), Frank and Hutchens (1990) show that the same pattern of wages is observed for two occupations in which neither traditional explanation is plausible, namely airline pilots and inter-city bus drivers. In the case of pilots, Frank and Hutchens show that wages increase sharply with age while productivity does not. Yet, virtually all the training pilots receive is general, and pilots who shirk on (say) safety are amply punished by nature. Rather, in this case, it seems that the upward sloping age–earnings profile must be due to a preference for income growth, per se.

Evidence for such a pattern of preferences comes from a survey of 100 adults polled at the Museum of Science and Industry in Chicago (Loewenstein and Sicherman, 1989). Respondents were asked to choose between several hypothetical jobs which lasted six years and were identical except in the wage profile they offered. All jobs paid the same total *undiscounted* wages but differed in slope. For one job, wages decreased yearly. For another, they remained constant, and for the remaining five they increased at varying rates. In addition to interest, virtually every economic consideration favored the job with declining wages. For example, if the subject didn't like the job and quit, or was fired before the end of the six years, the declining wage option would provide greater total payments. Despite the incentives for selecting the decreasing wage profile, only 12 percent of the subjects liked it best. Another 12 percent preferred the flat profile, with all other subjects selecting one of the increasing profiles as their favorite.

A result such as this one always makes an economist wonder whether the subjects were just confused. Certainly, if the subjects had the logic of the economic argument explained to them (that the downward sloping wage profile plus saving dominates the others) they would come to their senses, right? To check on this, subjects were asked their preferences again, but after they had been presented with the economic argument favoring the declining profile, and with psychological arguments in favor of increasing profiles. The effect of these arguments was minimal. The number of subjects preferring the increasing profile fell from 76 to 69 percent.

The preference for an increasing income stream can be understood by using two concepts discussed above: loss aversion and self-control. Loss aversion explains why workers prefer an increasing *consumption* profile (since the utility of current consumption will depend on previous consumption). Costly self-control explains why workers want an increasing *income* profile, because they cannot rely on themselves to save enough from a flat income (or declining) profile to produce the desired increasing consumption profile.

Savoring and dread

The standard discounted utility model assumes that the discount rate is constant and, normally, positive. Are there any circumstances in which people prefer to have gains postponed or losses expedited? Marshall (1891, p. 178) suggested one negative influence on the discount rate for gains: "When calculating the rate at which a future benefit is discounted, we must be careful to make allowance for the pleasures of expectation." We will use the terms *savoring* to refer to the positive utility derived from anticipating

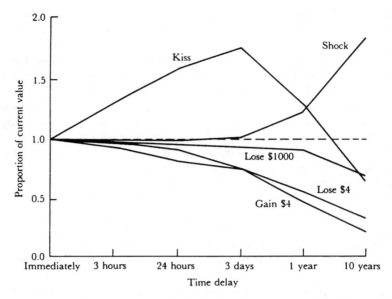

Figure 11.3. Maximum payment to obtain/avoid outcomes at selected times. Proportion of current value (N = 30). Source: Loewenstein (1987).

future pleasant outcomes and *dread* to refer to the negative contemplation of unpleasant outcomes.

The influence of both savoring and dread is demonstrated in the following experiment conducted by Loewenstein (1987). Subjects were asked to specify "the most you would pay now" to obtain (avoid) each of five outcomes, immediately, and following delays of: 3 hours, 1 day, 3 days, 1 year, and 10 years. The five outcomes were: gain $4; lose $4; lose $1000; receive a (nonlethal) 110 volt shock; receive a kiss from the movie star of your choice. The results are plotted in Figure 11.3.

Discounted utility predicts that the value of a gain and the aversiveness of a loss should decline monotonically with delay before the event occurs. People should want to consume gains as soon as possible and postpone losses as long as possible. As can be seen, however, the two non-monetary outcomes yielded quite different patterns of time preference. For the kiss from the movie star, subjects preferred to delay the outcome for three days, presumably to savor its anticipation. For the electric shock, subjects were willing to pay substantially more to avoid a shock to be received in one or ten years than one in the immediate future. In this case subjects seemed to be willing to pay to avoid having to worry about the event over an extended period of time.

While a kiss from a movie star and an electric shock are rather exotic experiences, Loewenstein (1987) has also obtained similar results for more mundane items. In a demonstration of the utility of savoring, 84 percent of his subjects indicated that they would prefer to receive a dinner at a fancy French restaurant on the second of three weekends rather than the first. To demonstrate dread, subjects were asked: (p. 674) "What is the least amount of money you would accept for cleaning 100 hamster cages at the Psychology Department's animal laboratory? You will be paid immediately. . . . The job is unpleasant but takes only three hours. How much would you need to be paid to clean the cages: (1) once during the next 7 days; (2) once during the week beginning one year from now?" The mean reservation wage for cleaning the cages next week was $30 while the reservation wage for doing the task in a year was $37. In fact, only 2 of 37 subjects gave a smaller response to question (2) than question (1).

Commentary

The policy implications of this line of research are both interesting and treacherous. At a micro level, the high discount rates observed in some contexts (such as appliance purchases) and by some groups (such as teenagers) raise serious questions about consumer rationality. (As mentioned above, in many intertemporal situations involving self-control, individuals question *their own* ability to make rational, long-term choices.) How can it be rational for a consumer to choose a refrigerator that costs $50 less than another equivalent model but consumes $50 more in electricity every year? While such cases do not establish a need for government intervention, the presumption that consumers choose best for themselves is rather weakened.

At a macro level, the psychology of intertemporal choice complicates the already complicated question of selecting the proper social rate of discount. The standard view is that the market rate of interest, corrected for tax distortions, represents an aggregation of individual time preferences, and is the appropriate social rate of time discounting. However, correcting for tax distortions is far from trivial, and the situation is further complicated by the internationalization of capital markets, which obscures the relationship between time preferences and interest rates in a particular country. Lind (1990) argues that given these complications, the only reasonable way to determine the social rate of time preference is to elicit time preferences at the individual level. But if individuals do not discount everything at a single rate, then which rate is the one that is appropriate for social discounting? Suppose that an individual's freezer purchase implies a discount rate of 50 percent, but that the same person is indifferent between saving 10 lives this year and 10 lives in 20 years? How then should we decide between building another power plant and improving highway safety?

Many economists view the research on the psychology of decision making as a nuisance. The research often provides evidence that individuals violate certain assumptions of rational choice without offering alternative assumptions that can easily be incorporated into economic models. However, psychology can be constructive as well as destructive. For example, in the case of increasing wage profiles, the psychologists' observation that people care about changes in as well as absolute levels of income and consumption (which should be noncontroversial since economists don't argue about tastes) can reconcile the preference for increasing wage profiles with the standard economic assumption that people discount the future. The advantage of drawing on empirical research to suggest modifications in the utility function is that the proposed modifications are less ad hoc. A good example of this kind of reasoning is offered by Constantinides (1988) in his paper on the "equity premium puzzle" (why are returns on stocks so much higher than on bonds?). Constantinides bases his explanation on the assumption that the utility of current consumption depends on past levels of consumption, or as he calls it, habit formation. A cynic might argue that if you try enough utility functions, you can explain anything. However, here that criticism would be misplaced. The habit formation assumption seems to fit intuitions about behavior, and is consistent with a great deal of empirical research. It is even testable. Explanations that rely on assumptions that are testable (or even better, true!) are more attractive than those based on assumptions which are untestable or implausible, for example those which depend on time-varying changes in the unobservable risk of economic catastrophe.

Notes

1 Two other explanations might be offered for the purchase of inefficient appliances: ignorance and illiquidity. According to the ignorance hypothesis, customers do not know, or bother to find out, the advantages of buying a more efficient model even though that information is plainly displayed on government mandated labels. According to the illiquidity argument, customers are so short of cash that they cannot afford to buy the more efficient model. (Of course, these are precisely the customers who cannot afford to buy the cheaper model!) Since most appliances are probably purchased on credit, and since the extra cost of the energy efficient model is relatively small, it seems unlikely that borrowing constraints are really the answer.

2 In this study, and some others described here, the questions asked were hypothetical. Of course, all things being equal it would be better to study actual choices. However, there are serious trade-offs between hypothetical and real money methods. Using hypothetical questions one can ask subjects to consider options that incorporate large amounts of money, both gains and losses, and delays of a year or more. In studies using real choices, the experimenter must reduce the size of the stakes and the length of the delay, and it is difficult to investigate actual losses. Also, in a hypothetical question, one can ask the subject to assume that there is no risk associated with future payments, while in experiments using real stakes, subjects must assess the experimenter's credibility. It is reassuring that in this domain, as well as many others, the phenomena discovered using hypothetical choices have been reproduced in studies using actual choices, see for example, Horowitz (1988) and Holcomb and Nelson (1989).

3 It is obvious that whatever pattern of choices subjects indicate in these experiments, market interest rates do not depend (greatly) on either magnitude or time delay, but this does not imply that the experimental evidence is irrelevant for economics. Economics is concerned with predicting both market prices and individual behavior. Though arbitrageurs may assure that one cannot earn (much) more interest from buying and selling a series of 12 one-month treasury bills than a single one-year bond, this does not guarantee that predictions at the individual level will be accurate. If car customers elect financing over more attractive rebates,

no (costless) arbitrage opportunity exists for anyone else. A bank could try to convince car buyers that they would be better off taking the rebate and financing the purchase at their bank, but such campaigns are expensive, and consumers may be skeptical regarding the impartiality of the advice they are being given.

4 This analysis is based on Ainslie (1975).

5 It seems likely that there are also differential discount rates by type of consumption good. One might be more impatient to receive a new car than a new (energy-efficient) furnace, as long as the old furnace works. More research is needed on this question.

References

Ainslie, George, "Specious Reward: A Behavioral Theory of Impulsiveness and Impulse Control," *Psychological Bulletin*, 1975, *82*, 463–509.

Ainslie, George, *Picoeconomics: The Strategic Interaction of Successive Motivational States Within the Person*. Cambridge: Cambridge University Press, 1992.

Benzion, Uri, Amnon Rapoport, and Joseph Yagil, "Discount Rates Inferred from Decisions: An Experimental Study," *Management Science*, March 1989, *35*, 270–84.

Carmichael, H. Lorne, "Self-Enforcing Contracts, Shirking, and Life Cycle Incentives," *Journal of Economic Perspectives*, 1989, *3*(4), 65–83.

Constantinides, George, "Habit Formation: A Resolution of the Equity Premium Puzzle," unpublished working paper, University of Chicago, Graduate School of Business, 1988.

Courant, Paul, Edward Gramlich, and John Laitner, "A Dynamic Micro Estimate of the Life-Cycle Model." In Aaron, Henry G., and Gary Burtless, eds., *Retirement and Economic Behavior*. Washington D.C.: Brookings Institution, 1986.

Elster, Jon, *Ulysses and the Sirens*. New York: Cambridge University Press, 1979.

Frank, Robert, and Robert Hutchens, "Feeling Better vs. Feeling Good: A Life-Cycle Theory of Wages," Working Paper, Department of Economics, Cornell University, 1990.

Gately, Dermot, "Individual Discount Rates and the Purchase and Utilization of Energy-Using Durables: Comment," *Bell Journal of Economics*, 1980, *11*, 373–374.

Hausman, Jerry, "Individual Discount Rates and the Purchase and Utilization of Energy-Using Durables," *Bell Journal of Economics*, 1979, *10*, 33–54.

Herrnstein, Richard J., "Relative and Absolute Strength of Response as a Function of Frequency of Reinforcement," *Journal of Experimental Analysis of Behavior*, 1961, *4*, 267–272.

Holcomb, John H., and Paul S. Nelson, "An Experimental Investigation of Individual Time Preference," unpublished working paper, 1989.

Horowitz, John K., "Discounting Money Payoffs: An Experimental Analysis." Working paper, Department of Agricultural and Resource Economics, University of Maryland, 1988.

Hutchens, Robert M., "Seniority, Wages and Productivity: A Turbulent Decade," *Journal of Economic Perspectives*, 1989, *3*(4), 49–64.

Kahneman, Daniel, and Amos Tversky, "Prospect Theory: An Analysis of Decision Under Risk," *Econometrica*, 1979, *47*, 363–391.

Lazear, Edward, "Agency, Earnings Profiles, Productivity, and Hours Restrictions," *American Economic Review*, 1981, *61*, 606–620.

Lind, Robert, "Reassessing the Government's Discount Rate Policy in Light of New Theory and Data in a World Economy with a High Degree of Capital

Mobility," *Journal of Environmental Economics and Management*, 1990, *18*(2), Part 2, S8–S28.

Loewenstein, George, "Anticipation and the Valuation of Delayed Consumption," *Economic Journal*, 1987, *97*, 666–684.

Loewenstein, George, "Frames of Mind in Intertemporal Choice," *Management Science*, 1988, *34*, 200–214.

Loewenstein, George, and Drazen Prelec, "Anomalies in Intertemporal Choice: Evidence and Interpretation," Russell Sage Foundation Working Paper, 1989a.

Loewenstein, George, and Drazen Prelec, "Decision Making Over Time and Under Uncertainty: A Common Approach," Working paper, University of Chicago, Center for Decision Research, 1989b.

Loewenstein, George, and Nachum Sicherman, "Do Workers Prefer Increasing Wage Profiles?" working paper, University of Chicago, Center for Decision Research, 1989.

Marshall, Alfred, *Principles of Economics*, 2nd ed. London: Macmillian, 1891.

Markowitz, Harry, "The Utility of Wealth," *Journal of Political Economy*, 1952, *60*, 151–158.

Medoff, James L., and Katharine G. Abraham, "Experience, Performance and Earnings," *Quarterly Journal of Economics*, December 1980, *95*, 703–736.

Ruderman, Henry, Mark Levine, and James McMahon, "Energy-Efficiency Choice in the Purchase of Residential Appliances." In Kempton, Willett, and Max Neiman, eds., *Energy Efficiency: Perspectives on Individual Behavior*. Washington D.C.: American Council for an Energy Efficient Economy, 1986.

Schelling, Thomas, "Self-Command in Practice, in Policy, and in a Theory of Rational Choice," *American Economic Review*, 1984, *74*, 1–11.

Shefrin, Hersh, and Richard H. Thaler, "The Behavioral Life-Cycle Hypothesis," *Economic Inquiry*, October 1988, *26*, 609–643.

Strotz, Robert H., "Myopia and Inconsistency in Dynamic Utility Maximization," *Review of Economic Studies*, 1956, *23*, 165–180.

Thaler, Richard H., "Some Empirical Evidence on Dyanmic Inconsistency," *Economics Letters*, 1981, *8*, 201–207.

Thaler, Richard H., "Saving, Fungibility, and Mental Accounts," *Journal of Economic Perspectives*, 1990, *4*(1), 193–205.

Thaler, Richard H., and Hersh M. Shefrin, "An Economic Theory of Self-Control," *Journal of Political Economy*, *89*, 1981, 392–410.

Winston, Gordon, "Addiction and Backsliding," *Journal of Economic Behavior and Organization*, December 1980, *1*, 295–324.

12   Not me or thee but we: The importance of group identity in eliciting cooperation in dilemma situations: Experimental manipulations

*Robyn M. Dawes, Alphons J. C. van de Kragt,
and John M. Orbell*

Theoretical background

Social dilemmas occur when payoffs to each participant yield dominating decision strategies that converge on a deficient equilibrium. Examples abound: decisions of whether to donate to public radio and television, decisions of whether to ride a bicycle rather than drive a car during a pollution alert, decisions of whether to publish yet another paper (which changes the adaptation level of deans and promotion committees who never have the time to read them anyway), decisions of whether to dispose of industrial waste in the atmosphere or rivers when no laws prohibit doing so, decisions of whether to add to the earth's already strained, if not overstrained, carrying capacity by adding the most exploitive and polluting agent yet known – another human being.

Historically, theorists have concentrated on four proposals to resolve such dilemmas – i.e., to encourage people to forgo dominating strategies in dilemma situations in favor of dominated cooperative ones that result in outcomes preferred by all to the deficient one.

Reprinted from *Acta Psychologica*, Vol. 68, R. M. Dawes, A. J. C. van de Kragt, & J. M. Orbell, "Not me or thee but we: The importance of group identity in eliciting cooperation in dilemma situations: Experimental manipulations," pp. 83–97, 1988, with kind permission from Elsevier Science B. V., Amsterdam, The Netherlands.

Earlier versions have been presented at the Public Choice Meeting, Tucson, Arizona, March 28, 1987 and the Midwestern Psychological Association Meeting (Invited Address), Chicago, Illinois, May 8, 1987.

This work was supported by NSF grant SES 8605284 Decision-Making under Laissez Faire Collective Decision Rules.

(1) *Leviathan* (Hobbs, 1651/1947). However it is established, a central state mandates cooperation by punishing defection. People accept this state's authority because the alternative is the dilemma situation of the "warre of alle against alle". They accept it even if the state consists of a hated minority using the cooperation of others primarily for its own benefit.

(2) *Reciprocal altruism* (Axelrod, 1984). Through some mechanism – perhaps biological (Trivers, 1971) – cooperation on the part of one individual in a dilemma situation enhances the probability that others will cooperate later in that same situation or a similar one. Thus, an individual's "enlightened self-interest" is to cooperate in hopes of eliciting reciprocity. In computer tournaments, Axelrod has studied the success of Anatol Rapoport's TIT-FOR-TAT strategy (Rapoport and Chammah, 1965) (cooperate on trial 1 and then make the same choice that the other interacting individual did on the previous trial) and demonstrated that it garners more profit for itself "in the long run" than do any competing strategies; moreover, Axelrod has demonstrated that in an evolutionary context in which strategies' probability of replication is positively related to profit, TIT-FOR-TAT can become predominant.

(3) Mutual coercion mutually agreed upon (Hardin, 1968). Rather than being punished for defection by a (potentially arbitrary) central authority, freely choosing people agree to provide punishments to each other for choosing a dominating defecting choice. While the coercive agent itself may consist of a centralized authority, its existence is maintained through the consent of the governed, rather than their mere acquiescence.

(4) *Socially instilled conscience and self-esteem* (Campbell, 1975). While externally provided payoffs may define a social dilemma, social training can lead to such a "bad" conscience for choosing a dominating defecting strategy – or to such heightened self-esteem for eschewing such strategies in favor of cooperation – that the individual is better off cooperating, irrespective of external consequences. While not widely publicized outside psychology, Campbell's solution was quite controversial within it, in part because it supported traditional morality and constraint in contrast to challenging these as irrational and urging people to "do your own thing". (In fact, for reasons unrelated to Campbell's theorizing, psychology as a field and psychologists as people have become much more conservative in the years since 1975 than in the years previous.) According to Campbell, "social evolution" – through moral teachings and the resulting cooperative behavior – keeps "biological evolution" from running amok only to drain into a sink of universal defection.

These four "solutions" have one characteristic in common; they turn an apparent dilemma into a non-dilemma by manipulation (conscious or automatic) of the consequences *accruing to the individual* for cooperation or defection. Manipulation of behavior through the egoistic payoffs resulting from such consequences is compatible with: (i) psychoanalytic beliefs in the preeminence of primitive drives, (ii) behaviorist beliefs in the automatic and omnipotent effects of reward and punishment (circularly defined as "reinforcement" by all but a few theorists), (iii) conservative economic theory, (iv) social exchange theory, (v) the insistence of sociobiologists that altruism be compatible with "inclusive fitness", and (vi) the obvious success in U.S. current society of appeals to personal payoffs (e.g., "are *you* better off than you were four years ago?" – italics added). The first three proposals concentrate on external payoffs *per se*, while the fourth postulates the development of an individual utility for "doing the right thing" that overwhelms the utility from the social rewards of defection.

We do not claim that any or all of the mechanisms postulated above do not encourage cooperation; certainly, for example, beliefs that one will go to jail or be tortured by guilt for defection will enhance a tendency to cooperate, as will the social rewards accruing to an individual with a reputation for being cooperative and trustworthy (Taylor, 1976; Axelrod, 1984). What we do claim is that a series of experiments over the past ten years have led us, somewhat reluctantly at first, to conclude that none of these are *necessary* to promote cooperation – in particular to promote it above a base rate that can be ascribed to a habit of cooperating in situations outside our experiments similar to those within them. Our experiments have led us to conclude that cooperation rates can be radically affected by one factor in particular that is independent of the consequences for the choosing individual. That factor is group identity. Such identity – or solidarity – can be established and consequently enhance cooperative responding in the absence of any expectation of future reciprocity, or current reward or punishment, or even reputational consequences among other group members; moreover, this identity operates independently of the dictates of conscience. In other words, our experiments indicate that group solidarity increases cooperation independently of the side payments – either external or internal – often associated with such identity.

While rewards, punishments, expectations of reciprocity, moralizing and lack of anonymity have all been shown to "work", these variables have in general been manipulated in others' experiments without a comparison with what happens *in their absence*. The clearest example of this lack can be found in the experimentation on 2-person dilemmas (estimated to consist of at least 2000 studies). In almost all of these prisoner's dilemma games the subjects' play has been *iterated*. (In fact, we have been able to find only two instances in the literature prior to our own work in which players make a single choice: Deutsch, 1960, and Wrightsman, 1966.) The hypothesis supposedly supported by numerous results is that cooperation is *due to* the successful or attempted establishment of reciprocal altruism through engaging in such strategies as TIT-FOR-TAT. But in the absence of any evidence that people do *not* cooperate when the games are *not* iterated, this interpretation is dubious.[1] Moreover, claims that cooperation results from the rewards accruing to individuals *qua* individuals approach vacuity given the standard instructions to subjects to "get as many points for yourself as you can". Experimental subjects tend to be cooperative – with the experimenter at least – and solve the problem this experimenter presents to them in the best manner that they can. It follows of necessity that behavior given such instructions is in large part determined by the egoistic consequences for the subjects. (The argument is saved from complete vacuity by the empirical fact that experimental manipulations often don't work at all.)

Methodological considerations

In contrast, our experimental work makes self-conscious use of the "subtractive procedure" by systematically comparing the presence of factors with their absence. Moreover, we have eliminated all side payments by simply prohibiting them, we have eliminated concern with reputation by having all choices be anonymous, and we have eliminated the possibility of reciprocal altruism by having our subjects make a choice in our dilemma situations only once. We nevertheless obtain substantial rates of cooperation. Could these simply be due to factors affecting egoistic payoffs that are usually present outside our experiments and that lead some subjects to cooperate out of habit? The answer is no, because we can manipulate a variable having nothing to do with any of these factors in a way that will yield cooperation rates – given the same egoistic payoffs – ranging from 25% to 100%. That variable is, as mentioned above, group identity. In this paper, we will describe conditions from the three most recent series of experiments in which such identity is manipulated. Let us first mention, however, that our standard way of manipulating it is to allow subjects in groups to talk for up to 10 minutes about the dilemma with which we present them (and, of course, in line with our "subtractive" philosophy, such groups are compared with those who cannot communicate). We do *not* allow our subjects in our discussion conditions to make deals, agreements to meet later, or even agreements to tell each other what they choose; moreover, we make every effort to use groups of strangers. We are not claiming that our discussion manipulation is the *only* way to create a group identity – but that it is one way that works, and does so in the absence of the factors listed at the beginning of this paper. (For example, Kramer and Brewer (1986) have shown that they can create a group identity between subjects by simply having the magnitude of their payoffs determined by the same coin flip.)

Experimental results: I

In the first series of studies (van de Kragt, Dawes, and Orbell with Braver and Wilson, 1986), using monetary incentives, we discovered that discussion between group members not only enhanced cooperation when people had at least a mild egoistic incentive to contribute but also enhanced cooperation when people *didn't*. Specifically, we found that allowing discussion in an assurance game – where all receive $10 if all contribute $5 – enhances cooperation. But we later discovered that discussion enhanced cooperation when the subject's own contribution had only a probabilistic relationship to the subject's outcome. Later, we found the same pattern of the beneficial effects of discussion when a subject's own contribution had *no* effect on the subject's own outcome – that is in *"non-contingent"* games in which subjects received or didn't receive a bonus only on the basis of *others'* rates of contribution.

Let us explain the method used in these studies in some detail. First, subjects were recruited for a one-hour "group decision-making experiment" from advertisements in local student and town newspapers promising "from $4 to $19 depending upon what you and the other group members decide". Only those responding who were over 18 years of age (by self-report and judgment of telephone voice) were invited to participate. Subjects who called indicating interest for groups were scheduled for separate experimental sessions, and a list was maintained to make sure that all subjects participated in only one.

Upon arrival, subjects were run in groups of size nine. All were paid $4 for "showing up," including any extra subjects we had scheduled to make sure that we would have nine participants in each group. At the beginning of the experiment itself, all were given a "promissory note" for $5, which was theirs to keep if they chose. They were also told that there was the possibility of receiving a $10 bonus depending upon how many people chose to "give away" their $5 to the group. At the time of the initial instructions, subjects were told that the choice of whether or not to give away the $5 was anonymous; to assure anonymity, they would make their choice by placing a check mark on one of two lines in a "response form" that others couldn't see, and we would pay each subject one at a time, making certain that the previous subject had left the area before the next was paid – which we did.

One factor in our design was defined by the rule according to which each subject received or did not receive the $10 bonus.

- *Contingent* rule: If five or more subjects including the choosing subject himself or herself gave away the $5, all received the $10 bonus.
- *Non-contingent* rule: If four or more of the *remaining* subjects gave away the $5, the subject received the $10 bonus.

According to both rules, a subject who gave away the $5 lost it. Such a subject received $10 according to both rules if four or more of the remaining subjects gave the $5 away, otherwise 0 (except for the flat $4 for attending the experiment). A subject who kept the $5 received either $15 or $5, depending on whether enough of the remaining subjects gave away the $5. The crucial difference between the two rules was that in the contingent condition subjects could "help themselves" by giving away the money; for if exactly four others did, a subject giving away the $5 received $10 rather than $5. In the non-contingent condition, a subject always received $5 more for keeping the money than for giving it away – $15 rather than $10 if four or more others gave it away, and $5 rather than 0 if not. Thus, the non-contingent condition confronted subjects with a strict social dilemma (all would receive $10 if all gave away, $5 if none did, yet not giving away was a dominating strategy). In contrast, exactly five subjects giving away the money was an equilibrium outcome in the contingent rule condition (in which case those who gave it away received $10 and those who didn't $15).

In half of the groups in each rule condition we let the subjects discuss the choice for up to 10 minutes, and in half they had to remain silent. Previous research (van de Kragt, Orbell, and Dawes, 1983) has demonstrated that subjects develop an awareness of the equilibrium in the contingent condition, and when allowed to discuss will determine – by a combination of volunteering and lot – exactly *which* five should give away the $5 (thereby creating an "assurance game" for these five individuals; see Sen, 1967). To prevent subjects in the discussion condition from doing so, we told them how many give-away choices were required for the bonus only after they had completed their discussion. Most groups hit upon the idea of numbering themselves and requiring people numbered 1 through k to give away the $5 after the experimenters announced the number k necessary to provide the bonus. The experimenters simply told subjects in such groups that "you can't do that", and being thus prohibited they were unable to implement the idea.

Figure 12.1 shows the percent contributing in each of the four conditions defined by the contingent versus non-contingent rule and discussion versus silence. Both effects of the rule and of discussion are significant,[2] ($p < .04$ and $p < .001$ respectively; for more details, see the original paper). What is striking, however, is that the effect of discussion *per se* is the stronger of the two. While the results show an effect of self-interest (the contingent rule elicits higher cooperation rates), such interest cannot explain the relatively high rates of giving away the $5 in the non-contingent condition after discussion, a condition in which subjects *always* receive the higher payoff for keeping the $5.

Experimental results: II

In a subsequent series of studies (Orbell, van de Kragt, and Dawes, 1988), we addressed the question of whether the discussion effects we have previously found to be important may have served to arouse "conscience" and its associated payoffs, or whether the results can be better accounted for by concern with others' actual outcomes – and if so, how that concern relates to group identity.

To pit conscience against caring, we varied the identity of the beneficiaries of cooperation: other group members versus strangers. If discussion triggers conscience, and our contributing subjects are acting to satisfy its demands, then discussion should enhance contribution to strangers. If, however, dis-

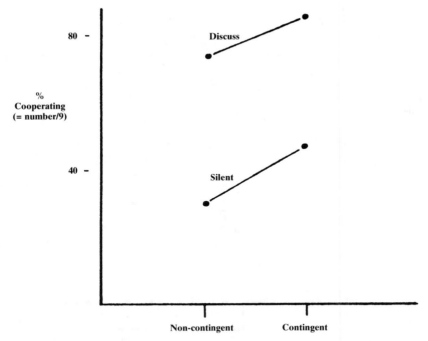

Figure 12.1. Results: experiment 1.

cussion elicits caring about group members, then it should enhance contributions only to people in the group with whom one interacts.

Our basic condition was a *give-away* dilemma game involving seven people. Subjects began with promissory notes for $6, which they could either keep or give away (anonymously, again) for the group benefit. Each $6 given away was augmented to $12 by the experimenters, with a $2 bonus going to each of the other six group members. The situation is a dilemma, because each subject is $6 better off keeping the money, but if all give it away all receive $12 while all receive $6 if all keep.

We recruited groups of 14 subjects, using the same methods as in the previous experiment, who were then randomly divided into groups of seven which met in separate rooms. Again, we crossed discussion with no discussion. We varied the games, however, by telling half the groups that the $12 would go to the other six members of their own group and half that it would go to six comparable members of the other group – with subjects' own potential bonuses being dependent, respectively, upon what members of their own or the other group did. In all conditions, the $6 was kept by the subjects themselves if they chose not to give it away.

Finally, three minutes before the final choice, we switched the group membership of the relevant others in half the conditions. For example, in a

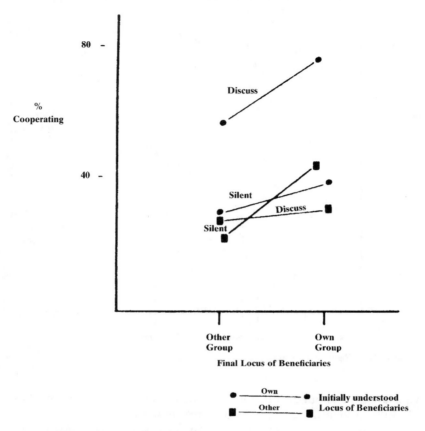

Figure 12.2. Results: experiment 2.

switch condition, a subject discussed the choice believing the $12 would go
to the subjects in his or her own group and that he or she might receive
money from them, but was subsequently told it would go to subjects in the
other group – and that money would (might) come from choices in this other
group. In an equal number of instances subjects believed that the relevant
subjects were in the other group, and were then told that they were their own
group members. Half the time we made no such switch. No further discussion in the discussion conditions was allowed after the switch.

We thus crossed three factors: the initially understood locus of relevant
others (own group versus other group), interaction (discussion versus no
discussion), and actual locus of relevant others (own group versus other
group). We ran eight groups in each of the resulting eight conditions
(number of groups = 64; number of subjects = 448). The results are presented
in Figure 12.2.

With group cooperation rate as the unit of analysis, all main effects are significant beyond the .001 level. Of greatest importance, however, is the interaction of discussion with belief about locus of benefit. With discussion, cooperation rate averaged 69% when people first believed that relevant others would be in their own group, but only 31% when they believed they would be in the other. The comparable figures for the no discussion conditions were 34% and 33%. Thus, discussion does *not* enhance contribution when beneficiaries are strangers, counter to the clear conscience hypothesis. Moreover, there is *no* ingroup–outgroup effect in the absence of discussion. Also, the believed locus of relevant others when the subjects first considered their choices was more important than the actual (subsequent) locus (est. ω^2 = 30% vs. 10%).

Because discussion does promote cooperation vis-à-vis the parochial group but not the group with which there was no contact, we had to consider the importance of group identity as a factor. (Recall, again, that choices were single ones made in total anonymity.) Also, however, we noted a great deal of promising to give the money away in the high cooperation condition, and it *appeared* to be effective. Slightly over 11 percent of coded subject–predicate utterances across all conditions were commitments to give (as opposed to 3.1% commitments to keep, which most often occurred when the beneficiaries of giving were believed to be in the other group), and the product moment correlation between number of commitments to give and cooperation rate in the group was .59 ($p < .01$, using groups as the unit of measurement). Thus, we were led in a subsequent experiment to investigate the importance of three other factors.

(1) *Group identity.* Research in the "minimal group" paradigm (e.g., Tajfel and Turner, 1979; Tajfel, 1974, 1978; Turner, 1975; and the papers contained in Turner and Giles, 1981) has repeatedly demonstrated that allocative decisions can be sharply altered by manipulations substantially weaker than ten minutes of discussion. For example, a "common fate" group identity – amount of payoff dependent on the same coin toss – can lead subjects to attempt to "compensate" for defecting people in their own group by increasing cooperation, while simultaneously decreasing cooperation when the defecting people are believed to be in the other group, even when the identities of all people are unknown (Kramer and Brewer, 1986).

(2) *The desirable and binding nature of promising.* Even though subjects' choices are anonymous, similar choices in the world outside our experiments typically aren't. In general, it is to a promiser's long-term best interests to develop a reputation for cooperativeness and reliability (Axelrod, 1984; Taylor, 1976). Thus, while there are no reputational effects of not promising or reneging on promises made in our particular experimental situation, it may be psychologically similar to situations in which there are such effects – similar enough that it does not elicit clearly distinct behavior. Alternatively, subjects may adopt cooperative promising and fulfillment of promises as a good "rule of thumb" ("heuristic"), given that in most situations such

behavior is desirable from the perspective of future conseqences. Irrationalities in a particular situation may appear less irrational when the situation is viewed as one of a class of situations that might require too much "mental accounting" to distinguish among (Thaler, 1985).

(3) *Expectations derived from others' promises.* A single individual who keeps the $6 while all others give away $12 receives $18; if that individual likewise gives away the $12 the payoff is $12. In contrast, an individual who keeps the $6 when no others give away $12 receives only that $6, while the payoff for giving away the $6 under these circumstances is 0. Perhaps, consistent with Fechner's Law, the difference between $18 and $12 is psychologically less than the difference between $6 and 0. And in general, while there is a constant $6 incentive to defect, this incentive may become less psychologically dominant as more others are expected to give away the $12. But other incentives, for example, "desire to do the right thing," may simultaneously remain constant. Perhaps, as Dawes (1980: 191) has speculated, "if others cooperate, then the expected payoff for cooperation will not be too low, even though – in a uniform game [as this one was], for example – the *difference* between the payoff for cooperation and that for defection is still quite large. People may be greedy, may prefer more to less, but their greed is not 'insatiable' when other utilities are involved." The more other people expected to cooperate, according to this hypothesis, the less important the $6 incentive. Promises may, then, perform the self-exacerbating role of leading to expectations that a sufficient number of others will cooperate that the choosers themselves are motivated to cooperate. The .59 correlation between promises made and cooperation appears to support this interpretation, but it is important to note that these promises are not equivalent to the number of *people* who promised, because we did not identify individuals.

Experimental results: III

A third series of experiments (Orbell, van de Kragt, and Dawes, 1988) assessed the impact of these factors. (It also concerned others not relevant here, which is why it is quite complex.) Subjects meeting in groups of 14 were informed that they would be subsequently divided at random into two subgroups of seven and then faced with a *trinary* choice: (i) keep $5 for themselves, (ii) give away $12, with $2 going to each of the other people in their seven-person subgroup, (iii) give away $21, with $3 going to each of the people in the other subgroup. After being told that both subgroups would either be allowed to discuss the choice or would have to remain silent, all 14-person groups were given up to 10 minutes to discuss the problem. This 14-person discussion was monitored by two experimenters who coded whether or not *each subject* made at least one promise – or otherwise indicated a commitment – to give away the $21 to the members of the other subgroup once the groups were divided.

What is of importance for this paper is that in almost precisely half (13 of

24) of the 14-person groups all subjects made a verbal commitment to give away the $21 to the other subgroup members. Eighty-four percent of the subjects in these *universal promising* groups actually did so. In contrast, only 58% of the subjects from the other eleven groups gave away the $21. The difference (again using groups as the unit of analysis) was highly significant, $p < .01$.

That finding was not surprising, because it follows from all three factors listed above. In contrast, the relationship between promising and actual choice in the eleven groups without universal promising was striking. There wasn't any. First, the correlation across groups between the number of people who promised to give away the $21 and the number who subsequently did was only .09. Second, the contingency at the individual level between promising to give away the $21 and actually doing so was only .03. Finally, the correlation between each individual's choice to give away the $21 or not and the number of others in the group who promised to give away the $21 was, again, .03. The hypothesis that promises are binding implies a positive correlation between commitment and choice. The hypothesis that cooperation is due to expectations of a "reasonable" payoff if others are expected to cooperate implies a positive correlation between choice and the number of commitments made by others in the group. Neither correlation occurs in the data.

Conclusions

What is left are two hypotheses: (i) group identity is indicated in a step level manner by universal promising, but it is the solidarity – not commitments *per se* – that leads to the higher level of cooperation in the universal promising groups, and (ii) promises are effective, but only in a context of universal promising.

The present data do not distinguish between these interpretations. Nor do they address the question of whether solidarity elicits promising or *vice versa* (or – more likely – whether the relationship between the two variables is one of reciprocal augmentation). Cooperation is a function of group interactions.

Even the quickest glance at the transcripts of this and other experiments supports our group identity hypothesis (and we have done more thorough analyses as well that are compatible). People immediately start discussing what "we" should do, and spend a great deal of time and effort to persuade others in their own group to cooperate (or defect!), even in situations where these others' behavior is irrelevant to the speaker's own payoffs. In fact, in the first experiment reported in this paper there were frequent statements that the best results would occur if *we* all keep and *they* all give to *us*. In contrast, in all our experiments not allowing discussion our results can be explained on the purely egoistic basis of external gain or satisfaction of conscience (as indicated by post-experimental questionnaires not reported here). That generalization has held true over the last 10 years for 27 different no discussion conditions with 1188 subjects in 178 groups, and for 12 different discussion conditions with 637 subjects in 95 groups. All 39 variations we have developed lead to the same conclusion: With no discussion, egoistic motives explain cooperation; with discussion, group identity – alone or in interaction with verbal promises – explains its dramatic increase.

Can that generalization fit into an evolutionary framework in which *individual* inclusive fitness must be correlated with whatever evolves? Yes, provided we postulate, as does Caporael (1987), that *sociality* is primary for humans and historically precedes other changes. Then it is clear that ease in forming group identity could be of individual benefit. It is not just the successful group that prevails, but the individuals who have a propensity to form such groups. Moreover, we need not be too concerned with the problem of hypocrisy (i.e., positive selection for those only faking group identity within groups, see Wilson, 1983). As the late Senator Sam Irvin once pointed out: "The problem with lying is that you have to have a perfect memory to remember exactly what you said." None of us do.

Instead, theorists have been concerned with speculating about what leads to sociality – usually in the form of some individual incentives for becoming social ("All D [defection] is the primeval state . . ." – Axelrod, 1984: 99). In contrast, we don't speculate – but do point out that there have been no findings indicating that humans ever *weren't* social. It's fun and somewhat romantic to speculate about how isolates developed our most cherished characteristic – our ties to other humans. But once again, such speculations must be evaluated in terms of our knowledge of how humans behaved without such ties, and there is no evidence we ever did.

Finally, we wish to point out that group identity does not equal morality. It is fragile, easily manipulated, and at times draconian – as when the good group member Rudolf Hoess, the commandant at Auschwitz, systematically murdered 2,900,000 members of an outgroup – despite claims in his autobiography (Hoess, 1959) that he himself suffered great emotional pain from the suffering he inflicted on others. For the greater good of his national socialist group, he claims, he "stifled all softer emotions". Group identity can do that, as well as lead to self-sacrificial acts that we regard as moral.

The casual observer of modern economic theory might conclude that the major motivation of us humans is supplied by a short looped tape cycling in our heads continually asking the question "have you improved your asset position today?" Modern psychological theory is worse; the tape asks "have you raised your self-esteem today?" Love, sex, friendship, beauty, art, knowledge, contentment, peak experiences, and even the joy of doing something well for its own sake are all what behaviorists used to term "secondary reinforcers" – the primary one being the ability to supply an affirmative answer to the nagging question. We interpret our experimental results as implying that there are other primary motivations – in particular the parochial one of contributing to one's group of fellow humans. We do not, for example, deny that an affirmative answer to the question "are *you* better off than you were four years ago?" (italics added) provides a powerful incentive for such actions as voting. What we question – or rather, what our data question – is whether all, or even a majority, of group regarding behaviors can be "ultimately" related to such egoistic concerns.

Notes

1 As part of a class project at Carnegie Mellon in an empirical research methods course, Alphons van de Kragt and Dawes have conducted a 2-person dilemma experiment with payoffs of from 0 to $12 with and without iteration. The proportion of subjects cooperating on the first trial of the iterated game condition was 66% (21/32) *but* 50% (16/32) also cooperated in the condition where they knew they would only play once. The standard game theory prediction is that *no one* should cooperate in this condition except those for whom the utility of such behavior itself is more important than the utility of the money. (The games were uniform ones with a $4 incentive for defection.) But if 50% cooperate for such reasons, they are more important than the anticipation of reciprocal altruism, which accounts for an augmentation of only 16%. Whether actual reciprocity would enhance cooperation rate was not addressed in this study.
2. Percentages are simply equal to (1/9) of the number of people who opted to give away the $5; the analyses are based on these simple numbers, one characterizing each group. The significance levels are determined by standard ANOVA procedures, given equal cell size and no a priori reason to believe these numbers violate the normality assumption (which is a sufficient justification for the reported levels – but not necessary given the equal cell sizes). The actual experiments involved four additional conditions not presented here.

References

Axelrod, R., 1984. The evolution of cooperation. New York: Basic Books.

Campbell, D. T., 1975. On the conflicts between biological and social evolution and between psychology and the moral tradition. American Psychologist 30, 1103–1126.

Caporael, L. R., 1987. "Homo sapiens, homo faber, homo socians: technology and the social animal". In: W. Callebaut and R. Pinxten (eds.), Evolutionary epistemology: a multiparadigm program. Dordrecht: Reidel. pp. 233–244.

Dawes, R. M., 1980. Social dilemmas. Annual Review of Psychology 31, 169–193.

Deutsch, M., 1960. The effect of motivational orientation upon trust and suspicion. Human Relations 13, 123–139.

Hardin, G. R., 1968. The tragedy of the commons. Science 162, 1243–1248.

Hobbs, T., 1651/1947. Leviathan. London: J. M. Dent & Sons.

Hoess, R., 1959. Commandant at Auschwitz: autobiography. London: Weidenfeld and Nicholson.

Kramer, R. M. and M. B. Brewer 1986. "Social group identity and the emergence of cooperation in resource conservation dilemmas". In: H. Wilke, D. Messick and C. Rutte (eds.), Experimental social dilemmas. Frankfurt am Main: Verlag Peter Lang. pp. 205–234.

Orbell, J. M., A. J. C. van de Kragt and R. M. Dawes, 1988. Explaining discussion-induced cooperation. Journal of Personality and Social Psychology 54, 811–819.

Rapoport, Anatol and A. M. Chammah, 1965. Prisoner's dilemma. Ann Arbor, MI: University of Michigan Press.

Sen, A., 1967. Isolation, assurance and the social rate of discount. Quarterly Journal of Economics 80, 112–124.

Tajfel, H., 1974. Social identity and intergroup behavior. Social Science Information 13, 65–93.

Tajfel, H. (ed.), 1978. Differentiation between social groups: studies in the social psychology of intergroup relations. London: Academic Press.

Tajfel, H. and J. Turner, 1979. "An integrative theory of intergroup conflict". In: W. Austin and S. Worchel (eds.), The social psychology of intergroup relations, Monterey, CA: Brooks/Cole. pp. 33–47.

Taylor, M., 1976. Anarchy and cooperation. London: Wiley.

Thaler, R., 1985. Mental accounting and consumer choice. Marketing Science 4, 199–214.

Trivers, R. L., 1971. The evolution of reciprocal altruism. Quarterly Review of Biology 46, 35–57.

Turner, J., 1975. Social comparison and social identity: some prospects for intergroup behavior. European Journal of Social Psychology 5, 5–34.

Turner, J. and H. Giles, 1981. Intergroup behavior. Chicago, IL: University of Chicago Press.

Van de Kragt, A. J. C., J. M. Orbell and R. M. Dawes 1983. The minimal contributing set as a solution to public goods problems. American Political Science Review 77, 112–122.

Van de Kragt, A. J. C., J. M. Orbell and R. M. Dawes with S. R. Braver and L. A. Wilson, II (1986). "Doing well and doing good as ways of resolving social dilemmas". In: H. Wilke, D. Messick and C. Rutte (eds.), Experimental social dilemmas. Frankfurt/Main: Lang Gmbh. pp. 177–203.

Wilson, D. S., 1983. The group selection controversy: history and current status. Annual Review of Ecology Systematics 14, 159–187.

Wrightsman, L. S., 1966. Personality and attitudinal correlates of trusting and trustworthiness in a two-person game. Journal of Personality and Social Psychology 4, 328–332.

Subjective experience, metacognition, and insight

13 Predicting a changing taste: Do people know what they will like?

Daniel Kahneman and Jackie Snell

Although students of decision-making behavior often view themselves as critics of the rational model of economics and pure decision theory, that model has a pervasive influence on the agenda of behavioral research. In particular, the positivistic methodology of economics and the powerful myth of economic rationality have contributed to a severely impoverished conception of utility, the central variable of decision theory. Utility is generally interpreted, even by behavioral researchers, as an intervening variable that is derived from observed choices and has no surplus meaning of its own. This may be one of the few surviving examples of rigid operationalism in current behavioral research. The focus on revealed preferences as the sole measure of utility is not only a methodological choice; it also reflects the standard assumption that economic agents are rational, and therefore make the choices that are most likely to turn out best for them. Little is left in this usage of the original sense of utility in the writings of Bernoulli, Bentham, and Mills, where it was identified with the hedonic quality of experience (Stigler, 1950). In the classic usage, still current in discussion of utilitarian philosophy (Glover, 1990), utility is a characteristic of experienced outcomes, not an inference from observed decisions.

A straightforward suggestion is to distinguish two basic concepts of utility (Kahneman and Snell, 1990). The *decision utility* of a possible outcome is defined by the sign and weight of that outcome in the context of a choice. The *experienced utility* of an outcome is defined by the quality and intensity of the

This chapter originally appeared as "Predicting a changing taste: Do people know what they will like?" by D. Kahneman and J. Snell, in the *Journal of Behavioral Decision Making*, 1992, 5, 187–200. Copyright © 1992 by John Wiley & Sons, Ltd. Reprinted by permission of John Wiley & Sons, Ltd.

The research reported in this article was supported by the Office of Naval Research and by the Sloan Foundation. The second author was supported by the Alfred P. Sloan Foundation grant to the Institute of Cognitive Studies, University of California, Berkeley. We thank Carol E. Nickerson for her unstinting help and advice on statistical matters.

QUESTIONS ABOUT UTILITY

VALIDITY   Predicted   ------------->   Experienced
                Utility   Utility
                Do people know what will be good for them?

RATIONALITY   Predicted   ------------->   Decision
                Utility   Utility
                Do people use their hedonic knowledge?

EFFICIENCY   Decision   ------------->   Experienced
                Utility   Utility
                Do people choose what will be good for them?

Figure 13.1. An agenda of research on utility.

hedonic experience associated with that outcome. An additional notion must be introduced along with that of experienced utility: the *predicted utility* of an outcome is defined by the individual's beliefs about the experienced utility of that outcome some time in the future.

The distinction between decision utility and experienced utility suggests a reformulation of the concept of utility maximization: we now ask whether an individual's decision maximizes the (expected) experienced utility of outcomes. Decisions that do not maximize expected experienced utility can come about in several ways. First, people do not live for pleasure alone, and they sometimes *want* to be guided by values and principles rather than by hedonic considerations (Sen, 1987). Less admirably, people may wish to maximize their (expected) experienced utility, yet fail to do so. In particular, the decision maker may not *know*, when making a decision at time t_0, how much he or she will enjoy the consumption of its consequences at time t_1 (Kreps, 1979; March, 1978). Furthermore, even when beliefs about future hedonic experiences are accurate, a decision maker may fail to weigh these beliefs appropriately in making choices (Varey and Kahneman, 1992).

The distinctions we draw among variants of utility suggest a research agenda, which is summarized in Figure 13.1 (see Kahneman and Snell, 1990, p. 297). In the framework of Figure 13.1 high efficiency is the traditional assumption of economics and decision theory. However, we note that decision makers can only achieve efficient choices if their predicted utilities are valid and their decision utilities are rational. Some aspects of rational weighting are explored in a companion article (Varey and Kahneman, 1992). The experiments reported here address the issue of validity, the relation between predicted and experienced utility.

Much hangs on the accurate prediction of future experiences of pleasure or discomfort. Expectations about the hedonic quality of future experience are critical to many decisions, ranging in importance from the choice of a flavor at an ice cream parlor to the rejection of a surgical operation that would destroy one's vocal cords. The attitude to a proposed change of life-style, such as the cessation of smoking or the adoption of a regime of diet or exercise, also depends on expectations about future tastes. Even the decision of whether the choice of bedroom curtains is worth a marital quarrel depends, or should rationally depend, on one's anticipated adaptation to an object that is now hateful. Thus, the ability to predict the intensity of one's future likes and dislikes appears to be an essential element of rational decision making (March, 1978). Indeed, there would be little point in carefully evaluating options if future utilities could not be ordered.

Predicting future tastes is evidently a useful skill. How good are we at it? In spite of its importance, the question has not been much studied directly, although hints can be found in several bodies of literature. Predictions of future pain and fear have been studied in related research programs by Rachman and by Arntz, with their respective collaborators (Arntz et al., 1990; Arntz and Lousberg, 1990; Arntz and van den Hout, 1988; Hunter et al., 1979; Rachman and Arntz, 1991; Rachman and Bichard, 1988; Rachman and Eyrl, 1989; Rachman and Lopatka, 1988).

However, the focus of these studies was on the affective and hedonic consequences of overprediction and underprediction, and they were not designed to assess the accuracy of predictions. There has been research on various aspects of taste change, especially in the contexts of adaptation to food (Crandall, 1985; Hill et al., 1984; Hrboticky and Krondl, 1984; Rolls et al., 1981, 1982; Rozin and Schiller, 1980; Schutz and Pilgrim 1958; Siegel and Pilgrim 1958), the effects of mere exposure on liking (Birch and Marlin, 1982; Bornstein, 1989; Harrison, 1977; Pliner, 1982; Zajonc, 1968), effects of dissonance on tastes (Carlsmith and Aronson, 1963; Cooper and Fazio, 1984; Greenwald and Ronis, 1978), and the opponent process theory of motivation (Solomon, 1977, 1980). Several of these theoretical models are commonly recognized as non-intuitive, suggesting that people may not be able to antici-pate the taste consequences of repeated exposure, dissonance, or initially intense positive or negative affect (Kahneman and Snell, 1990). There is also a literature on the accuracy of self-prediction of future behavior and out-comes (Osberg and Shrauger, 1986; Scheier and Carver, 1983; Shrauger and Osberg, 1981, 1982), and on the self-fulfilling character of some of these predictions (Greenwald et al., 1987; Sherman, 1980). These studies, which were not directly concerned with the forecast of future tastes, provide no indication that people are particularly adept at self-prediction.

The decision literature is generally silent on the issue of the accuracy of taste prediction, and the few mentions of it (Kreps, 1979; March, 1978) mainly note the theoretical importance of the question. There has been more discussion of intertemporal inconsistency, observed when people who make choices about outcomes in the distant future change their minds as the critical time approaches (Ainslie, 1985; Loewenstein, 1988; Strotz, 1956). The present analysis suggests that intertemporal inconsistency could arise either from improper weighting of future consequences or from inaccurate forecasts of future tastes. For example, both effects could exist in the case of one well-known study of intertemporal inconsistency: Christensen-Szalanski (1984) documented the incidence of cases in which women in labor reversed a long-standing preference for delivery without anesthetics. Did these women fail to predict the intensity of their pain? Or did they have accurate predictions, but improperly discount future pain in their initial preferences? Simonson (1990) reported a study in which subjects who chose in advance three snacks to be consumed at intervals of one week did not duplicate the decisions of other subjects who chose snacks for immediate consumption on three separate occasions. The discrepancies were reduced when subjects were explicitly instructed to predict choices they would make later, a result which suggests that simple choices for future consumption may not consult predictions at all. Snell (1991) showed that predictions of future tastes can be volatile, and suggested that the dominant heuristic is to consult current desires.

In summary, little is known about the question of how accurately people predict their future tastes, or about the more specific question of the factors that control accuracy. Indeed, formal research on this topic is so scarce that it is difficult even to judge whether the validity of predicted utility is a problem that deserves the attention of students of decision making. Intrigued by this issue, we decided to carry out an exploratory study of people's ability to predict their changing tastes, in a relatively favorable context. We chose students as our subjects, food and pop music as the objects of preferences, and frequent repetition as a means of inducing changes of hedonic responses. Our reasoning was that many students have experience not only with both pop music and ice cream but also with the effect of frequently repeated exposure to such stimuli. Frequent repetition is known to induce accelerated change of hedonic response, in both the positive and the negative directions (Rozin and Vollmecke, 1986). We wanted to find out if the individual participants in our experiment would accurately predict the direction in which their taste would change, and the extent of the change. The present article reports our attempts to answer this question.

We describe a pilot study and a fairly large experiment. Participants in both studies consumed a particular food while listening to a particular piece of music, once each day for a period of about a week. In the pilot study the food was a preferred flavor of ice cream and the music was initially unfamiliar. In the main experiment the food was plain yogurt, which was fairly unfamiliar and mildly aversive, and the music was chosen by the subject. Thus each experiment included a very familiar stimulus and a relatively foreign stimulus within a familiar domain. The participants rated their enjoyment of the experiences after each exposure. On the first day of the experiment, they predicted how they would evaluate the experience on the next day and on the last day of the experiment, a week later.

Our intent was to examine the accuracy of these predictions, and our main findings are easily summarized: tastes were sometimes predictable by projection from current tastes, but changes were not well predicted; the average decline in liking for two initially attractive familiar stimuli was anticipated, but the individuals who deviated from the modal pattern did not predict they would do so; the progressive increase in liking for a neutral or mildly aversive stimulus was generally not anticipated, and individual deviations from the average pattern were again not predicted. The main message to be drawn from this preliminary study is that the task of predicting changing tastes turned out to be surprisingly difficult even under highly favorable conditions.

Pilot study

Method

Subjects. Volunteers were contacted by phone from a pool of regular participants in attention and perception experiments. They were told they would be paid $20 at the completion of the experiment if they missed no appointments, $15 if they missed one, and nothing if they missed more than one. They were also told that they would eat a serving of ice cream while listening to assigned music each day. There were no refusals to participate. Of the 18 people who agreed to participate, 16 (seven males and nine females) completed the experiment.

Procedure. The experiment started on a Monday for all participants. The experimenter greeted each subject individually, explained that we were interested in people's tastes over time, and described the terms of the experiment. Each subject was informed that he or she would get the same flavor of ice cream every day of the experiment, and was given a choice of chocolate, strawberry, coffee, or vanilla Hägen Dazs ice cream, or Dole tangerine sherbet. The subject was then led to the "ice cream" room, a small office furnished with a refrigerator, a table and chair, and a small tape player. The experimenter gave the subject a serving (two scoops or about 4 oz) of the chosen flavor of ice cream, a tape which had about ten minutes of unfamiliar French–Canadian rock music, and a brief questionnaire requesting a rating of how much the subject wanted to eat the ice cream, and separate ratings of how much he or she liked the ice cream and the music. The ice cream question read:

You should now be eating your chosen flavor of ice cream and listening to the music which we have provided. We would like to know how pleasurable eating this ice cream is for you. After about two minutes of eating and listening please take a bite of the ice cream and take a moment to just taste the ice cream without thinking about the questionnaire. Then rate on the scale below how much you enjoy the taste of the ice cream.

A 13-point scale, anchored with "dislike very much" and "like very much", was shown immediately below each question. The subject was left alone to eat the ice cream while listening to the tape. The experimenter then administered an oral questionnaire asking for separate predictions of "how much you will want to eat ice cream (listen to the music)" and "how much you will enjoy eating the ice cream (listening to the music)". Predictions were requested for "tomorrow, day 2 of the experiment" and for "the last day, day 8". The same 13-point scale was used, and was displayed visually for reference during the interview.

On the remaining seven days of the experiment subjects came to the lab at an individually scheduled time, picked up a questionnaire, and went to the ice cream room on their own. Individual servings of ice cream were prepared in advance and placed in the freezer in styrofoam cups labelled by subject number. Subjects rated how much they wanted the ice cream and the music at the beginning of the brief session, and how much they had liked these experiences at its end.

Results and discussion

Our analysis of the accuracy of self-predictions is adapted from a model that Gage and Cronbach (1955) offered many years ago for the analysis of accuracy in interpersonal judgments. The accuracy of predictions in our design can be analyzed into two components, which are both logically and statistically independent:

(1) The discrepancy between the average prediction and the average outcome is a measure of the accuracy of an implicit stereotype. In the present context, the accuracy of the mean prediction of a future taste, or change of taste, can be taken as an indication of the validity of implicit knowledge about taste dynamics.

(2) The discrepancies (or, equivalently, the correlation) between individual predictions and the corresponding individual outcomes provide an indication of specific knowledge or discriminative ability. In the present context, the validity coefficient for individual predictions of future tastes, or of changes of tastes, reflects the specific knowledge that individuals have about what distinguishes them from others.

The data relevant to the two analyses are presented respectively in Tables 13.1 and 13.2. Table 13.1 presents the mean predictions of liking and wanting for days 2 and 8 (labelled P for predicted), and the mean ratings of liking and wanting on days 1, 2, and 8 (labelled A for actual). A measure of change was

Table 13.1. *Pilot study: predicted and actual ratings*

	Day 1	Day 2	Day 8	Change Mean	Change S.D.
Like ice cream					
Actual	4.50	4.75	2.94	-1.81^b	1.94
Predicted		4.31	1.19	-3.12^b	2.50
Want ice cream					
Actual	3.00	4.37	1.62	-2.75^b	3.07
Predicted		3.69	.19	-3.50^b	2.48
Like unfamiliar music					
Actual	2.94	2.81	1.25	-1.56^a	2.48
Predicted		2.37	-.94	-3.31^b	2.98
Want unfamiliar music					
Actual		2.06	.37	-1.69	3.28
Predicted		2.81	-.25	-3.06^b	2.72

$N = 16$.
$^a p < .05$.
$^b p < .01$.

Table 13.2. *Selected correlations – ice cream and music*

	Actual stability A1–A2	Actual stability A1–A8	Actual stability A2–A8	Predicted stability A1–P2	Predicted stability A1–P8	Validity Raw scores P2–A2	Validity Raw scores P8–A8	Validity Change A–P
Ice cream								
Like	$.52^a$	-.02	-.24	.30	-.19	.15	-.14	.11
Want^c	.26	.28	-.44	.23	.44	$.72^b$	-.24	.02
Music								
Like	$.64^b$	.43	.49	$.83^b$	.42	.44	.24	-.16
Want^c			.19			$.73^b$	.33	-.05

Note: A = actual, P = predicted, followed by the number of the day. Change scores (last column) are measured from day 2 to day 8.
$^a p < .05$.
$^b p < .01$.
^{c}Students were not asked on the first day how much they wanted to listen to the music since they did not yet know what kind of music they would hear. Note also that "want" ratings for the ice cream on the first day were based on a less well-defined understanding of what was to follow than later "want" ratings.

defined for each variable by the difference between the values predicted (or observed) on days 8 and 2.

The subjects overwhelmingly agreed in predicting that their ratings of liking and wanting for both the ice cream and the music would decline between days 2 and 8 of the experiment. Of the 64 predicted change scores (four for each of the 16 participants) 53 were strictly negative and the remaining 11 were predictions of no change. There was rather less consistency in actual changes: for example, actual changes in "wanting" ice cream ranged from −8 to +2. Of the total of 64 measures of actual change, 20 were either positive ($n = 12$) or showed no change ($n = 8$). The general trend of actual change was negative for all variables, but the average of actual changes was somewhat smaller than the average of predictions. The difference between predicted and actual changes approaches significance for the "like" measures of ice cream ($t(15) = 1.76$) and of music ($t = 1.68$).

The results in Table 13.1 suggest a stereotyped prediction of declining liking for an initially liked stimulus, which, on average, may overpredict the actual decline. Table 13.2 presents the second component of predictive accuracy: the correlation between individual predicted and actual changes. These correlations are negligible for all four measures, averaging −.02. The implication is that, on average, the predictions that subjects made about their own changes of liking or wanting were no more valid to predict these particular changes than to predict changes in the ratings made by a random stranger. There is no indication that subjects have any "privileged access" to whether their tastes will change more or less than those of others (Nisbett and Wilson, 1977). In 18 of the 20 cases in which ratings remained constant or improved between days 2 and 8, the subject had predicted a decrease.

Table 13.2 includes selected correlations between the measures of the study. The first three columns present correlations between ratings on days 1, 2, and 8 for both ice cream and music. A somewhat surprising result is the total lack of consistency of the ratings of ice cream early and late in the experiments. Correlations between "like" responses on immediately consecutive days (not shown in Table 13.2) averaged .37, but the drift from day to day quickly eliminated any correlation with the initial attitude. The restricted range of responses may be a factor in this apparent instability of taste; all subjects started with positive and rather similar attitudes to their chosen ice cream flavor. The responses to the music showed more variability across subjects, and more consistency over time: the correlations between "like" responses on consecutive days averaged 0.67 and the responses on day 8 were still somewhat predictable from the responses on day 1.

The next two columns relate the predictions that subjects made on day 1 to the ratings of their experiences on that day. These correlations are high when subjects implicitly predict that their tastes will remain stable. Correlations between predictions and the initial rating appear to be higher for music than for ice cream. The suggested inference is that the current experience played a more important part in predictions for music than for ice cream. The last three columns in the table present information about the validity of predictions. The only significant correlations are between predictions of "want" made on day 1 and actual ratings of "want" made on day 2, for both music and ice cream (.71 and .72, respectively). The high accuracy of these predictions is not surprising, since no relevant experience intervened between the prediction made at the end of the first session and the "want" rating made at the beginning of the second. The result is welcome, however, because it suggests that the low validities observed in other cases cannot be attributed simply to response noise.

The high validity of predicted "want" ratings for day 2 is the only significant discrepancy between the results for "want" and for "like". The "want" measure was used in the study because we speculated that a dissociation between wanting and liking might occur if the repeated experience yielded a mild form of addiction to the ice cream or the music. Solomon's (1977, 1980) opponent-process theory of adaptation suggests that in some cases an individual may crave an initially positive experience progressively more but like it progressively less. Clinical studies of addiction also suggest that liking and wanting may be independent (Orford, 1985). There is no evidence of dissociation in our data. Across subjects, the correlation between the measures of actual change in liking and wanting was .72 for ice cream and .78 for music. Within-subject correlations (computed over the ratings made on the eight days of the experiment) were also consistently positive.

The main conclusion of this pilot study is that the participants showed little ability to predict changes in their hedonic responses, beyond a generally valid expectation of diminishing enjoyment. The only clear success was observed when subjects predicted at the end of one day how much they would want the experience at the beginning of the next. Some constancy in the attitude to the music enabled moderately valid predictions of future hedonic responses, but individual differences in hedonic *change* were not predicted.

Main study

One obvious limitation of the pilot study was the small size of the sample, a serious matter in a study in which the main finding was a null result. Another limitation was the restricted range of the responses to ice cream. Finally, the strange situation of the experiment could have contributed to subjects' difficulties; even the laboratory setting itself may have influenced the enjoyment or the predictions. Perhaps participants could do better in their natural surroundings. The main experiment was designed to avoid these problems: the number of subjects was large, plain low-fat yogurt was used instead of ice cream, and the repeated experience occurred in the subjects' homes.

The study also includes two control groups: a *no-prediction* group and a *no-rating* group. One control group made no predictions, to permit a test of whether the prediction task was intrusive. Sherman (1980) and Greenwald et al. (1987) have shown that asking people to predict their own behavior can change that behavior, because the predictions tend to be self-fulfilling, at least in the context of the socially desirable behaviors they studied. The no-prediction control provides a test of the hypothesis that taste predictions are similarly self-fulfilling, and of the competing conjecture that explicit predictions could yield a contrast effect. The second control group made no initial rating of the stimuli. Some pilot results in our laboratory had suggested that individuals might anchor their predictions on initial ratings. We tested the possibility that predictions might be more accurate when the subjects were not required to make such a rating.

Method

Subjects. The study was run in three phases. The first included only subjects who performed the prediction task ($N = 35$). The second phase included 34 subjects in the prediction condition and 33 subjects in the no-prediction one. The third phase included 10 prediction subjects and 42 subjects in the no-rating control condition. For each phase, notices were posted in the Psychology Department, offering $15 for doing a simple experiment at home, with no mention of what the experiment would involve. Of 182 people who came to the information meetings, nine decided not to participate in the experiment for a variety of reasons, and 19 others did not return at the end of the week, for an overall compliance rate of 85%. The subjects who did not return did not differ from others in their initial ratings or predictions. Three subjects returned questionnaires in which one or more of the main responses were missing.

Procedure. Subjects who came to the laboratory were given written instructions describing the experiment. The instructions required a commitment to eat a serving (three-quarters of a cup or about 6 oz) of plain low-fat yogurt while listening to the same piece of music, chosen by the subject, for seven consecutive evenings at home (eight consecutive evenings in the first phase). Each daily session was to be held at least 2 hours after the last meal of the day. Participants were requested not to talk to friends or have television playing in the room during the experiment. After reading the instructions, they were given one teaspoon of plain low-fat yogurt and asked to specify the music that they would play. Experimental subjects rated the yogurt they had tasted, indicated their memory of liking for the music they had chosen, and made predictions of how much they would want and like the yogurt and the music on the first and on the last days of the experiment. Control subjects either rated their current impression or predicted future responses.

Responses were made on 13-point scales ranging from –6 to +6. Each subject was given a supply of yogurt and a packet of questionnaires to

Table 13.3. *Main study: predicted and actual ratings*

	In lab	Day 1	Day 8	Change Mean	S.D.
Yogurt					
Experimental (*N* = 76)					
Predicted		−.62	−1.09	−.47	2.32
Actual	−.84	−2.13	−.51	1.62	3.48
No-rating (*N* = 42)					
Predicted		−.76	−1.60	−.83	2.92
Actual		−3.29	−1.17	2.12	4.28
No-prediction (*N* = 33)					
Actual	−1.27	−2.48	−.82	1.67	3.42
Favorite music					
Experimental (*N* = 76)					
Predicted		4.71	2.79	−1.92	2.38
Actual		3.74	2.95	−.79	2.12
No-rating (*N* = 42)					
Predicted		4.70	2.50	−2.19	2.45
Actual		3.24	2.36	−.88	2.92
No-prediction (*N* = 33)					
Actual		3.15	2.58	−.58	2.94

complete at home. Participants were promised $15 upon returning the completed questionnaires to the lab, even if they had missed one day.

Results. Subjects who either missed or changed the time of the experiment on only one day were included in the analysis. One subject reported playing a piece of music other than the one she had specified on the first day. This subject was excluded from all analyses. Subsequent debriefing indicated that subjects did not think the predictions were the main point of the study. Most did not remember the predictions they had made; some did not remember that they had made predictions. Our impression from the debriefing was that the subjects had taken the task seriously and that the great majority of the responses were likely to be valid. The similarity of the results to those obtained under controlled conditions in the pilot study also contributed to our confidence in the overall validity of the data, as did several features of the results listed below.

The predicted and actual measures for the "like" and "want" ratings were highly correlated, and yielded results that were very similar in all important respects. Only "like" results are reported. Table 13.3 presents the means and standard deviations of predicted and of actual responses to plain yogurt and to a freely chosen piece of music. We analyze the two experiences in turn.

In the case of yogurt, the predictions of the experimental group for the first day were similar to their ratings of the initial spoonful they had just tasted: the majority of subjects (67%) predicted a rating identical to the one they had just given. For the longer term, most subjects in the experimental and the no-rating groups predicted either a decline (50% of subjects) or no change (23%) in their liking for yogurt between days 1 and 8 of the experiment. The declining trend of predictions was significant in an analysis of variance ($F(1,116) = 7.10$, $p < .01$), which indicated no overall difference between the experimental and the no-rating groups ($F < 1$) and no interaction between groups and days ($F < 1$). Thus, the subjects generally expected their first experience of a full serving of yogurt to resemble their recent experience of a spoonful, and, on average, they expected repetition to make the experience of yogurt more aversive. As we see next, these expectations were not confirmed.

The actual ratings of liking for the yogurt show two trends that the subjects had not anticipated: there was a marked drop of liking between the initial spoonful in the laboratory and the first full serving at home, and a pronounced increase of liking between days 1 and 8. The drop in liking between days 0 and 1 was highly significant ($F(1,107) = 18.02$, $p < .0001$), in an analysis that indicated no difference between the experimental and the no-prediction groups and no group by day interaction ($F < 1$). The ratings of yogurt on day 1 were also much lower than subjects had predicted ($F(1,116) = 47.37$, $p < .0001$); the difference between the experimental and no-rating groups and the group by day interaction were both non-significant ($F = 1.56$ and $F = 2.97$, respectively). The subjects' failure to predict how much they were going to dislike their first full serving of yogurt at home provides some reassurance about the role of demand characteristics in this study: participants were evidently not intent on making their predictions come true.

Contrary to the expectations of most subjects, the trend between days 1 and 8 was one of increased liking (decreasing dislike) for yogurt. Most participants (92 of 151, with 16 showing no change) came to like the yogurt more, or dislike it less. The favorable change was significant ($F(1,148) = 31.59$, $p < .0001$); there was no main effect of groups, and no group by day interaction. A planned comparison of the experimental group against the two controls also yielded no significant effect. The discrepancy between predicted and actual changes was significant ($F(1,116) = 7.50$, $p < .01$); an ANOVA indicated no significant difference between the experimental and the no-rating groups.

The apparently non-intuitive results, both for the first full serving and for the trend over the week, also suggests that participants fulfilled their commitments to eat yogurt. If they had completed the questionnaires without consuming the yogurt it seems unlikely that they would report results differing much from their intuitive predictions.

The results for ratings of music were similar to those observed for ice cream in the pilot study. Not surprisingly, the initial ratings of the piece that the subjects had chosen were high on day 1. Most subjects (79 of 118) predicted a decline in their rating of the music between day 1 and day 8; only four subjects predicted an increase. A decline of liking occurred for 63 of the 118 students, with 34 showing an increase. The effect of days was the only significant result in an ANOVA of actual ratings ($F(1,148) = 11.53$, $p < .001$), which indicated no significant difference between experimental and control groups and no group by day interaction. Confirming a result that was marginally significant in the case of ice cream in the pilot study, the actual decline in the ratings was significantly smaller than predicted ($F(1,116) = 9.37$, $p < .01$); an ANOVA again showed no differences between the experimental and no-rating groups.

The results summarized in Table 13.3 indicate rather poor performance in this hedonic forecasting task. The subjects overestimated the effect of repetition in reducing their liking for a piece of music, erroneously believed that their liking for a full serving of yogurt would match their liking for a teaspoonful, and generally failed to anticipate the effect of repetition in increasing the palatability of yogurt. Table 13.3 also provides no evidence that the prediction task was intrusive, or that the initial ratings provided an anchor for subsequent ones, two hypotheses we had entertained.

We now turn to the correlation analysis of the "like" responses, to examine the relationship between the *deviations* of subjects' predictions from average predictions and the corresponding deviations of their actual ratings from average ratings. Again, the most important results are in the right-hand column of Table 13.4, which shows the correlations between predicted and actual change scores. The correlations are low, and only one is significant. The correlations for the "want" measure were similarly low: the coefficients corresponding to the entries in the right-hand column of Table 13.4 are .10, .21, .06, and −.26 (all non-significant). The low validity of change predictions confirms the negative conclusions of the pilot study. The results are not due to restricted variability of the change scores: the standard deviations of these scores (see Table 13.3) indicate that the effects of repetition on taste were quite variable across subjects, but this variation was not accurately predicted. However, it is important to remember in interpreting the low validities that response noise attenuates all correlations, and that measures based on differences between noisy responses are particularly susceptible to reliability problems (Cohen and Cohen, 1975).

The correlations between actual ratings indicate substantial stability of tastes across the week: the response to the initial teaspoonful of yogurt correlated .36 with the rating given to a serving of yogurt 8 days later, and ratings of the music also showed significant consistency. Stable tastes can be forecast by using current ratings as predictions of future ratings. The question of interest is whether the subjects' predictions contain *any* information that is not already implicit in their initial ratings. The predictions of liking for yogurt on day 8 provide an opportunity to answer this question. Subjects' predictions for that day (P8) strayed substantially from their ratings of the

Table 13.4. *Selected correlations: Yogurt and music*

	Actual stability			Predicted stability		Validity		
						Raw scores		Change
	A0–A1	A0–A8	A1–A8	A0–P1	A0–P8	P1–A1	P8–A8	A–P
Like yogurt								
Experimental	$.55^b$	$.36^b$	$.48^b$	$.92^b$	$.63^b$	$.53^b$	$.36^b$	.04
No-rating	$.76^b$	$.44^b$	$.45^b$					
No-prediction			.18			$.49^b$	.26	.25
Like music[c]								
Experimental			$.41^b$			$.37^b$	$.41^b$	$.22^a$
No-rating			.27					
No-prediction			$.37^a$			$.32^a$	.20	−.10

[a] $p < .05$.
[b] $p < .01$.
[c] Music ratings in lab before beginning of experiment (A0) were made from memory.
A0 = rating of initial taste of yogurt in the lab.
Ratings at home are numbered by day and labeled A for actual and P for predicted.

first teaspoonful (the correlation between P8 and A0 was only .63), but did exceed the validity of the early rating taken without modification. The partial correlation between P8 and A8, controlling for the initial rating A0, is positive (.19), though its significance is marginal ($t(76) = 1.58$). Thus, we find no compelling evidence that deliberate attempts to forecast future tastes add valid information to current ratings.

General discussion

These experiments were not primarily concerned with the question of how people make hedonic predictions, when they do. However, the results are compatible with the idea that the current hedonic response provides a powerful anchor in predicting future tastes in the relatively short term (see also Snell, 1991). When predicting for a longer horizon, however, our subjects were as likely to overestimate as to underestimate the changes in their hedonic ratings. The shared trend of the predictions reflected a stereotyped hypothesis that repetition is detrimental to liking. We speculate that other circumstances might elicit a theory of learning, and thus, predictions of enhanced liking, but the present study hints at the difficulty people have in choosing between conflicting beliefs. Neither did this study suggest the source of individual deviations from shared stereotypes: it only illustrated a few cases in which the validity of these deviations was low. A conservative conclusion is that subjects do not show impressive ability to predict changes in their tastes.

There are several variants of hedonic prediction. First, people may be asked about their general expectations of the conditions under which tastes will change, to discover the explicit folk theory of this matter. We have described elsewhere some preliminary results of a study conducted with Carol Varey and Brian Gibbs, in which intuitions about the determinants of hedonic change were compared to relevant conclusions of psychological research (Kahneman and Snell, 1990). Performance was unimpressive, and there was little consensus on questions that went beyond commonplaces such as Weber's law or habituation to pleasurable stimuli. There is also an applied folk theory of taste change, which is embodied in practices that cultures and individuals adopt in deliberate attempts to educate preferences. Casey and Rozin (1989) studied this theory by asking parents what methods they would use to get their children to like – not just eat – certain foods. Here again, consensus was often both weak and incorrect.

The average of the predictions that people make about changes in their own tastes also expresses an implicit folk theory of this domain. By this measure, the subjects of the present studies believed that repetition generally decreases liking and either increases dislike (at least for yogurt) or leaves it unaffected. These stereotypes were wide of the mark in the case of yogurt. There is no indication in these results that subjects' expectations, or their public statements of these expectations, had a major impact on their ratings of actual experiences as Sherman's (1980) and Greenwald's (1987) results might suggest. Neither does it appear, as Stang (1974) has suggested, that participants had correct intuitions, or lay theories, about which stimuli would elicit a "mere exposure" effect. Rather, it appears that intuition strongly favors predictions of satiation. Even though broadly correct when applied to pleasant experiences of music and ice cream, predictions of change were no better than a simple prediction of no change would have been: both correlations were .36.

Finally, the correlational study of the accuracy of individual self-prediction answers the question of what people know about future changes in their own tastes, beyond what they could forecast about a random stranger. In the particular context of our experiment, the answer was "not much". Individual differences in initial attitudes allowed some accuracy in the prediction of future tastes, but changes were not accurately predicted. This negative result is significant because the conditions of the present experiment were rather favorable for accurate prediction: the tasks of taste prediction that our subjects performed were surely easier than those which must be confronted in choosing a roommate or a job. It would be absurd to conclude from the present data that people have no ability to predict their future tastes, but it appears reasonable to conclude that the problem of predicting changing tastes is more serious than its customary neglect might suggest.

The implications of individual ignorance about future tastes are significant, both for the individuals themselves and for theorists of choice and welfare. To take but one example, problems of commitment and self-control are often formulated in terms of a subject who knows the path of his future desires and therefore resists transient changes of preference. Thus, Ulysses knows that the song of the Sirens will later tempt him to the depths, and also that if his sailors tie him to the mast he will later be pleased they did (Elster, 1977; Schelling, 1980). Different normative and ethical issues arise if the possibility of hedonic ignorance is considered. For example, it might be right for others to tie Ulysses to the mast against his will if they consider him unable to forecast his future attitudes. In the same spirit, the value that is attached to "informed consent" to surgery is surely limited if patients are incapable of assessing the quality of their post-surgical lives. There is an urgent need for more knowledge on this neglected aspect of decision making.

References

Ainslie, G. "Beyond Microeconomics. Conflict Among Interests in a Multiple Self as a Determinant of Value", in J. Elster (ed.), The *Multiple Self*, Cambridge: Cambridge University Press, 1985.

Arntz, A. and Lousberg, R. "The Effects of Underestimated Pain and Their Relationship to Habituation", *Behaviour Research and Therapy*, **28**(1990), 15–28.

Arntz, A., van Eck, M. and Heijmans, M. "Predictions of Dental Pain: The Fear of Any Expected Evil Is Worse Than the Evil Itself", *Behaviour Research and Therapy*, **28**(1990), 29–41.

Arntz, A. and van den Hout, M. "Generalizability of the Match/Mismatch Model of Fear", *Behaviour Research and Therapy*, **26**(1988), 207–23.

Birch, L. L. and Marlin, D. W. "I Don't Like It; I Never Tried it: Effects of Exposure on Two-Year-Old Children's Food Preferences", *Appetite*, **3**(1982), 353–60.

Bornstein, R. F. "Exposure and Affect: Overview and Meta-analysis of Research, 1968–1987", *Psychological Bulletin*, **106**(1989), 265–89.

Carlsmith, J. M. and Aronson, E. "Some Hedonic Consequences of the Confirmation and Disconfirmation of Expectancies", *Journal of Abnormal and Social Psychology*, **66**(1963), 151–6.

Casey, R. and Rozin, P. "Changing Children's Food Preferences: Parent Opinions", *Appetite*, **12**(1989), 171–82.

Christensen-Szalanski, J. J. "Discount Functions and the Measurement of Patient's Values: Women's Decisions During Child Birth", *Medical Decision Making*, **4**(1984), 47–58.

Cohen, J. and Cohen, P. *Applied Multiple Regression/Correlation Analysis for the Behavioural Sciences*, Hillsdale, NJ: Erlbaum, 1975.

Cooper, J. and Fazio, R. H. "A New Look at Dissonance Theory", In L. Berkowitz (ed.), *Advances in Experimental Social Psychology*, **17**(1984), 229–66, San Diego, CA: Academic Press.

Crandall, C. S. "The Liking of Foods as a Result of Exposure: Eating Doughnuts in Alaska". *The Journal of Social Psychology*, **125**(1985), 187–94.

Elster. J. "Ulysses and the Sirens: a Theory of Imperfect Rationality", *Social Science Information*, **16**(1977), 469–526.

Gage, N. L. and Cronbach, L. J. "Conceptual and Methodological Problems in Interpersonal Perception", *Psychological Review*, **62**(1955), 441–22.

Glover, J. (ed.), *Utilitarianism and its Critics*, New York: Macmillan, 1990.

Greenwald, A. G., Carnot, C. G., Beach, R. and Young, B. "Increasing Voting Behavior by Asking People If They Expect to Vote", *Journal of Applied Psychology*, **72**(1987), 315–18.

Greenwald, A. G. and Ronis, D. L. "Twenty Years of Cognitive Dissonance: Case Study of the Evolution of a Theory", *Psychological Review*, **85**(1978), 53–7.

Harrison, A. A. "Mere Exposure", in L. Berkowitz (ed.), *Advances in Experimental Social Psychology*, **10**(1977), 39–83.

Hill, A. J., Magson, L. D. and Blundell, J. E. "Hunger and Palatability: Tracking Ratings of Subjective Experience Before, During and After the Consumption of Preferred and Less Preferred Food", *Appetite*, **5**(1984), 361–71.

Hrboticky, N. and Krondl, M. "Acculturation to Canadian Foods by Chinese Immigrant Boys: Changes in the Perceived Flavor, Health Value and Prestige of Foods", *Appetite*, **5**(1984), 117–26.

Hunter, M., Philips, C. and Rachman, S. "Memory for Pain", *Pain*, **6**(1979), 35–46.

Kahneman, D. and Snell, J. S. "Predicting Utility", in R. M. Hogarth (ed.), *Insights in Decision Making*, Chicago, IL: University of Chicago Press, 1990.

Kreps, D. M. "A Representation Theorem for Preferences for Flexibility", *Econometrica*, **147**(1979), 565–78.

Loewenstein, G. "Frames of Mind in Intertemporal Choice", *Management Science*, **34**(1988), 200–14.

March, J. "Bounded Rationality, Ambiguity, and the Engineering of Choice", *Bell Journal of Economics*, **9**(1978), 587–608.

Nisbett, R. E. and Wilson, T. D. "Telling More Than We Can Know: Verbal Reports on Mental Processes", *Psychological Review*, **84**(1977), 231–74.

Orford, J. *Excessive Appetites: A Psychological View of Addictions*, New York: John Wiley, 1985.

Osberg, T. M. and Shrauger, J. S. "Self-prediction: Exploring the Parameters of Accuracy", *Journal of Personality and Social Psychology*, **51**(1986), 1044–57.

Pliner, P. "The Effects of Mere Exposure on Liking for Edible Substances", *Appetite*, **3**(1982), 283–90.

Rachman, S. and Arntz, A. "The Overprediction and Underprediction of Pain", *Clinical Psychology Review*, **11**(1991), 339–55.

Rachman, S. and Bichard, S. "The Overprediction of Fear", *Clinical Psychology Review*, **8**(1988), 303–12.

Rachman, S. and Eyrl, K. "Predicting and Remembering Recurrent Pain", *Behaviour Research and Therapy*, **27**(1989), 621–35.

Rachman, S. and Lopatka, C. "Accurate and Inaccurate Predictions of Pain", *Behaviour Research and Therapy*, **26**(1988), 291–6.

Rolls, B. J., Rolls, E. T. and Rowe, E. A. "The Influence of Variety on Human Food Selection and Intake", in L. M. Barker (ed.), *The Psychobiology of Human Food Selection*, Westport, CT: AVI Publishing, 1982.

Rolls, B. J., Rolls, E. T., Rowe, E. A. and Sweeney, K. "Sensory Specific Satiety in Man", *Physiology and Behavior*, **27**(1981), 137–42.

Rozin, P. and Schiller, D. "The Nature and Acquisition of a Preference for Chili Pepper by Humans", *Motivation and Emotion*, **4**(1980), 77–101.

Rozin, P. and Vollmecke, T. A. "Food Likes and Dislikes", *Annual Review of Nutrition*, **6**(1986), 433–56.

Schelling, T. C. "The Intimate Contest for Self-Command", *Public Interest*, **60**(1980), 94–118.

Scheier, M. F. and Carver, C. S. "Self-directed Attention and the Comparison of Self with Standards", *Journal of Experimental Social Psychology*, **19**(1983), 205–22.

Schutz, H. G. and Pilgrim, F. J. "A Field Study of Food Monotony", *Psychological Reports*, **4**(1958), 559–65.

Sen, A. *On Ethics and Economics*. Oxford: Blackwell, 1987.

Sherman, S. J. "On the Self-erasing Nature of Errors of Prediction", *Journal of Personality and Social Psychology*, **39**(1980), 211–21.

Shrauger, J. S. and Osberg, T. M. "The Relative Accuracy of Self-predictions and Judgments by Others in Psychological Assessment", *Psychological Bulletin*, **90**(1981), 322–51.

Shrauger, J. S. and Osberg, T. M. "Self-awareness: The Ability to Predict One's Future Behavior", in G. Underwood (ed.), *Aspects of Consciousness*, New York: Academic Press, 1982.

Siegel, P. S. and Pilgrim, F. J. "The Effect of Monotony on the Acceptance of Food", *American Journal of Psychology*, **71**(1958), 756–9.

Simonson, I. "The Effect of Purchase Quantity and Timing on Variety-seeking Behavior", *Journal of Marketing Research*, **27**(1990), 150–62.

Snell, J. S. *A Bias in Hedonic Self-prediction*, Doctoral dissertation, University of California, Berkeley, 1991.

Solomon, R. "An Opponent-process Theory of Motivation: V. Affective Dynamics of Eating", in L. Barker, M. Best and M. Domjan (eds), *Learning Mechanisms in Food Selection*, Waco, TX: Baylor University Press, 1977.

Solomon, R. "An Opponent-process Theory of Acquired Motivation: The Costs of Pleasure and the Benefits of Pain", *American Psychologist*, **35**(1980), 691–712.

Stang, D. J. "Intuition as Artifact in Mere Exposure Studies", *Journal of Personality and Social Psychology*, **30**(1974), 647–53.

Stigler, G. J. "The Development of Utility Theory", *Journal of Political Economy*, **58**(1950), 373–96.

Strotz, R. H. "Myopia and Inconsistency in Dynamic Utility Maximization", *Review of Economic Studies*, **23**(1956), 165–80.

Varey, C. and Kahneman, D. "Experiences Extended Across Time: Evaluation of Moments and Episodes", *Journal of Behavioral Decision Making*, **5**(1992), 169–85.

Zajonc, R. "Attitudinal Effects of Mere Exposure", *Journal of Personality and Social Psychology: Monograph Supplement*, **9**(1968), (2, part 2), 1–27.

14 Endowment and contrast in judgments of well-being

Amos Tversky and Dale Griffin

Introduction

In a recent educational television programme, an amnesic patient was asked about his childhood and high-school experiences. Verbally fluent, he was able to converse about daily events, but could not remember any details about his past. Finally, the interviewer asked him how happy he was. The patient pondered this question for a few seconds before answering, "I don't know."

Clearly, memory plays a crucial role in the assessment of well-being. The present evidently does not provide enough information to define happiness without reference to the past. Yet memories have a complex effect on our current sense of well-being. They represent a direct source of happiness or unhappiness, and they also affect the criteria by which current events are evaluated. In other words, a salient hedonic event (positive or negative) influences later evaluations of well-being in two ways: through an *endow-ment* effect and a *contrast* effect. The endowment effect of an event represents its direct contribution to one's happiness or satisfaction. Good news and positive experiences enrich our lives and make us happier; bad news and hard times diminish our well-being. Events also exercise an indirect contrast effect on the evaluation of subsequent events. A positive experience makes us happy, but it also renders similar experiences less exciting. A negative experience makes us unhappy, but it also helps us appreciate subsequent experiences that are less bad. The hedonic impact of an event, we suggest, reflects a balance of its endowment[1] and contrast effects. The present chapter explores some descriptive and prescriptive implications of this notion.

This chapter originally appeared in F. Strack, M. Argyle, and N. Schwarz (Eds.), *Subjective Well-Being: An Interdisciplinary Perspective* (pp. 101–118). Oxford: Pergamon Press, 1991. Copyright © by Fritz Strack, Michael Argyle, and Norbert Schwarz. Reprinted by permission.

This work was supported by a grant from the Alfred P. Sloan Foundation. It has benefited from discussions with Daniel Kahneman and Lee Ross.

A few examples illustrate the point. Consider a professor from a small midwestern town who attends a conference in New York and enjoys having dinner at an outstanding French restaurant. This memorable event contributes to her endowment – she is happier for having had that experience – but it also gives rise to a contrast effect. A later meal in the local French restaurant becomes somewhat less satisfying by comparison with the great meal she had in New York. Similarly, exposure to great theatre is enriching, but makes it harder to enjoy the local repertory company. The same principle applies to accomplishments. A successful first novel contributes a great deal to the author's endowment and self-esteem, but it also reduces the satisfaction derived from future novels if they are less good.

The effects of endowment and contrast also apply to negative events. Some people, dominated by a negative endowment, become depressed and unable to enjoy life in the aftermath of a bad experience; others are elated by the contrast between the present and the bleak past. People may vary in the degree to which their reactions are dominated by endowment or by contrast. Note that the endowment–contrast dimension of individual differences is orthogonal to the more familiar dimension of optimism–pessimism. Both endowment and contrast, of course, are memory based. The stronger the memory of the past, the greater its impact on present well-being. With no memory, there can be no endowment and no contrast, just immediate pleasures and pains.

There is little novelty in suggesting that well-being depends both on the nature of the experience that is being evaluated and on the standard of evaluation. Furthermore, many authors have observed that satisfaction is directly related to the quality of the experience, or its endowment, and inversely related to the evaluation standard, which serves as a contrast. What is perhaps less obvious is the observation that the same (past) event makes a dual contribution to well-being – a direct contribution as endowment and an inverse contribution as contrast. Although these effects have been discussed in the well-being literature (under various names), we know of no explicit attempt to integrate them.

The distinction between endowment and contrast has nothing to do with the character of the event itself; any hedonic experience affects our well-being both through the endowment it generates and through the contrast to which it gives rise. The endowment depends primarily on the quality and the intensity of the event, whereas the contrast depends primarily on its similarity or relevance to subsequent events. A great meal at a French restaurant in New York will probably not reduce your ability to enjoy a Chinese meal back home; similarly, while a great theatre performance may spoil your taste for the local repertory company, you will probably continue to take pleasure in concerts or even high-school plays.

Because the contrast effect depends on similarity or perceived relevance, it is susceptible to framing and other cognitive manipulations. The same sequence of events can produce varying degrees of satisfaction depending on whether an early event is viewed as similar or relevant to the evaluation of later events. Thus, happiness should be maximized by treating positive experiences as endowments and negative experiences as contrasts. To achieve this goal, one should find ways to treat the positive experiences of the past as different from the present (to avoid comparisons with the glorious past). By the same token, one should compare present conditions to worse situations in the past (to enjoy the benefits of a positive contrast). This prescription raises some intriguing questions that lie beyond the scope of this chapter. Are people who emphasize the endowment of positive events and the contrast of negative events generally happier than those who do not? And how much freedom do people have in the framing of hedonic events?

The present chapter reports some preliminary explorations based on experimental manipulations of endowment and contrast. In the next section we vary the quality and the relevance of past events and investigate their effects on judgments of well-being. We develop a simple method for assessing the relative contributions of endowment and contrast in these studies, and we apply this analysis to some experiments of Schwarz, Strack and their colleagues (see Schwarz and Strack, 1991), and to the study of expectation effects. In the last section of the chapter, we discuss the use of choice and of judgment for the assessment of well-being, illustrate the discrepancy between the two procedures, and relate it to the relative contribution of endowment and contrast.

Studies of endowment and contrast

The following two experiments employ the same design to study the impact of a past event on present judgments of happiness. In the first study, we use fictitious scripts to investigate the role of endowment and contrast in judgments regarding the well-being of another person. In the second study, subjects rated their own satisfaction following an actual experience.

In our first study, subjects were given a "story" – a description of two events, allegedly taken from an interview with a student – and were asked to rate the happiness of that student. In each case, the earlier event was either positive or negative, and the later event was neutral. Four types of events were used in the study: a date, a term paper, a party, and a movie. The two events presented to the subject could be of the same type (e.g., two term papers or two parties) or of different types (e.g., a date followed by a party or vice versa). This arrangement gives rise to a 2 × 2 (between-subjects) design in which a neutral event is preceded by either a positive or a negative event that could be of the same type or of a different type.

Because the second event is always neutral, we can focus on the endowment and the contrast effects produced by the first event. For events of different types, we expect an endowment effect, with little or no contrast. Judged happiness, therefore, should be high when the first event is positive and low when the first event is negative. For events of the same type, however, both contrast and endowment effects are expected. As a consequence, a related positive event should produce less happiness than an unrelated positive event, whereas a related negative event should produce greater happiness than an unrelated negative event. For example, an excellent paper followed by an average paper should produce less satisfaction than an excellent paper followed by an average party because the original paper makes a subsequent paper (but not a subsequent party) somewhat disappointing by contrast. On the other hand, a bad paper followed by an average paper should produce more satisfaction than a bad paper followed by an average party.

Sixty-four students participated in our first experiment, which was administered in a class setting in four groups of approximately sixteen students each. All subjects received the following instructions:

On the next few pages you will find several descriptions of life events experienced by high-school students. These are everyday sorts of events that you or your friends have probably experienced some time in your high-school career.

Your task will be to read these stories carefully and try to understand how the person felt during these episodes. Each individual narrator will present two vignettes from his or her own high-school experience. The vignettes were all gathered during the narrator's junior year in high school. After each pair of stories, you will be asked to rate the feelings of the narrator.

Each storyteller was asked to recount two experiences. First, they were asked to describe an experience from the week before, and then they were asked to describe something that had happened that very day. These narratives were given orally, so the grammar and prose are not perfect.

Each story is very short, so please take your time and try to imagine what the scene looked like and felt like to the narrator. Especially try to imagine how the narrator was feeling as he or she recounted the story.

The stories refer to four domains: a date with a young woman, performance in a course, the planning of a party, and the reaction to an Australian movie. Three events were constructed for each domain: positive, neutral, and negative. Recall that for each pair of events, the present event was always neutral and it was preceded either by a positive or a negative event that was either related or unrelated. Each respondent evaluated four stories, one in each quality/relation condition (i.e., positive/related, positive/unrelated, negative/related, and negative/unrelated). The following story describes a negative event regarding class performance followed by a related neutral event; an unrelated neutral event is also given for comparison.

Tim's Story

(Past, Negative)

What happened last week? Last week, let's see. I had a bad day. A really, really bad day. In the morning, I had a quiz in French. I was so tired and I just couldn't keep my mind on the problems. And then with about 10 minutes to go in the period, I sort of woke up and realized that I was in bad trouble. I had sort of puttered on the first page of a three-page quiz and there was no way I was going to finish. I almost broke out in a cold sweat; the quiz wasn't very important or anything, but it was like a dream where I was racing against time and my heart was pounding and there was no way I was going to get finished. So I felt bad about that all morning, not to mention embarrassed at blowing the quiz, and then in the afternoon I got a test back in Chemistry. I had almost failed it; it was a pretty hard test and everything, but it just made me want to give up. I was just stunned, not to mention tired. Good grades in Chemistry are important to me because I want to take sciences in college. So I skipped track practice that day and just went home. I didn't want to deal with anything else bad that could happen to me.

(Present, Related)

What happened today? I had three classes this morning, but since one of them is Civics, it wasn't too bad. In Civics, we discussed political issues that have been in the news. That was o.k., mostly a break from taking notes in other classes. First period I had Geometry, and we had a substitute teacher so we just did our homework in class. Before lunch I had French, which I am taking instead of Spanish this year. We practiced our conversations, which we have to present next week. That's pretty much it, I think.

Story 2 (Present, Unrelated)

What happened today? Well, I had another lunch with Susan. We had a pretty good time. We talked most of the time, about classes and some people we both know. Mostly we talked about the English class, though, and the way that exams were given. We argued some about whether the professor was fair, but we both agreed that the exams were aimed more at trivial detail than were the lectures. We ate pretty slowly, but both made it to our one o'clock classes. It was hard to get a feeling for what was going on, but I think she liked me well enough.

The dependent variable was a rating of happiness on a scale ranging from one (very unhappy) to ten (very happy). Subjects were asked "On the day that Tim answered these questions: how happy do you think he was with his life overall?" Because there were no significant differences between the responses to the stories, the results were pooled. Figure 14.1 displays the average rating of happiness in each of the four conditions, averaged across subjects and stories. The results confirmed our predictions. There was a significant interaction between the quality of the past event (positive or negative) and its relation (related, unrelated) to the present event, $F(1,60) = 6.71$, $p < .02$. As expected, we observed a significant endowment effect: in both the related and unrelated conditions, judged satisfaction was higher for the positive than for the negative prior event. Furthermore, there was a significant contrast effect: for the positive event, satisfaction was higher in the unrelated ($M = 7.1$) than in the related condition ($M = 6.8$), whereas for the negative event, the pattern was reversed ($M = 4.9$ for the unrelated condition, and $M = 5.5$ for the related condition). For example, the memory

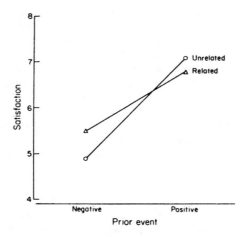

Figure 14.1. The effect of prior events.

of a good date last week diminished the satisfaction with a neutral date this week, but it enhanced the satisfaction with a neutral movie this week. The memory of a painful date, on the other hand, enhanced the satisfaction with a neutral date this week, while it diminished the satisfaction with a neutral movie this week.

To aid in the interpretation of experimental data, we find it useful to express judgments of satisfaction as an additive combination of endowment and contrast effects. We assume that the endowment effect E_{12} is given by the sum of the endowments of the first and second events denoted E_1 and E_2, respectively, and that the contrast effect C_{12} is expressible as the signed hedonic discrepancy between the two events d_{12}, weighted by their degree of relatedness r_{12}. Thus, we obtain the form

$$\begin{aligned} \text{Satisfaction} &= \text{Endowment} + \text{Contrast} \\ &= E_{12} + C_{12} \\ &= E_1 + E_2 + r_{12}d_{12}. \end{aligned}$$

To apply this scheme to the results of our first study, let S denote the rating of satisfaction. For simplicity, we suppose that the grand mean has been subtracted from all observations, so S is expressed as a deviation score. Let S^+ and S^- be respectively the responses in a condition where the first event was positive or negative, and let S_r and S_u denote the responses in a condition where the two events were related or unrelated. Let E^+ and E^- denote the endowment associated with a positive or negative event, and let C^+ and C^- denote the contrast associated with a positive or negative event, respectively. Because the second event in this study was always neutral we can neglect its endowment, and set $E_2 = 0$. Naturally, the contrast associated with a prior positive event is negative, $C^+ < 0$, and the contrast associated with a prior negative event is positive, $C^- > 0$. We also assume that, for unrelated events, $r_{12} = 0$, hence the contrast term vanishes in that case. Judgments of satisfaction in the present design can be represented as:

	Negative	Positive
Unrelated	$S_u^- = E^-$	$S_u^+ = E^+$
Related	$S_r^- = E^- + C^-$	$S_r^+ = E^+ + C^+$

We use this model to estimate the effect of contrast and endowment. The total endowment effect is:

$$E = E^+ - E^- = S_u^+ - S_u^- = 7.1 - 4.9 = 2.2.$$

As we assume the unrelated events involve no contrast, the overall endowment effect is simply the difference between mean satisfaction in the cells representing positive versus negative unrelated events. The contrast associated with the positive first event is:

$$C^+ = S_r^+ - S_u^+ = 6.8 - 7.1 = -.3.$$

Similarly, the contrast associated with the negative first event is:

$$C^- = S_r^- - S_u^- = 5.5 - 4.9 = .6.$$

Thus, the total contrast effect in this experiment is $C^- - C^+ = .9$, which is considerably smaller than the endowment effect, as can be seen in Figure 14.1.

In our second study, subjects rated their own satisfaction with actual experiences. Seventy-two subjects took part in a computer-controlled stock-market game played for real money. Subjects were given information about different stocks and were instructed to construct a portfolio from these stocks. They were told that the computer would simulate the market and that their actual payoffs would depend on the performance of their portfolios. Each session included an initial game (with a payoff of $2 or $6) and a later game (with a payoff of $4) separated by a filler task involving no gains or losses. As in the first study, we manipulated two variables: (a) the payoff in the first game and (b) the similarity or relatedness between the first and the second games. In the related condition, subjects played essentially the same game with different stocks. In the unrelated condition, the games involved different markets (stocks versus commodities) and used different procedures for portfolio construction. After subjects played both games, they were asked to rate their overall satisfaction with the experience, using a 10-point scale.

This design allows us to test the following hypotheses regarding judged satisfaction. First, the difference between the low ($2) and the high ($6) payoffs will be greater in the unrelated than in the related condition. This prediction follows from the assumption that for the unrelated games, the

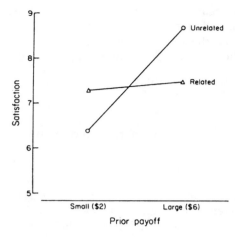

Figure 14.2. The effect of prior payoffs.

difference reflects a pure endowment effect. In the related games, however, the positive endowment will be reduced by the negative contrast, whereas the negative endowment will be reduced by the positive contrast. Second, the negative contrast effect following the high payoff (when $d_{12} > 0$) will be larger than the positive contrast effect following the low payoff (when $d_{12} < 0$), as suggested by the notion of loss aversion in prospect theory (Kahneman and Tversky, 1979).

The pattern of results displayed in Figure 14.2 supported the endowment-contrast analysis. In the unrelated condition, where there is pure endowment and no contrast, those who received the larger payoff in the first game were generally more satisfied ($M = 8.7$) than those who received the smaller payoff in the first game ($M = 6.4$), $t(33) = 1.95$, $p < .05$, one-tailed. However, in the related condition, where contrast and endowment worked in the opposite directions, there was essentially no difference between the satisfaction of those who received the larger reward in the first game ($M = 7.5$) and those who received the smaller reward in the first game ($M = 7.3$).

The decomposition scheme introduced in the first study is applicable to the results of the present study. In this study too, E_2 is a constant, and hence can be ignored in the analysis. To simplify matters, we also assume that the difference between the satisfaction derived from the high prior payoff and the low prior payoff in the unrelated games yields an estimate of the total endowment effect:

$$E = S_u^+ - S_u^- = 8.7 - 6.4 = 2.3.$$

The positive contrast (the increase in satisfaction caused by a low expectation) was:

$$C^- = S_r^- - S_u^- = 7.3 - 6.4 = .9;$$

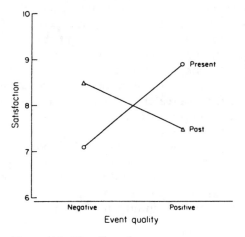

Figure 14.3. The effect of past versus present events.

and the negative contrast (the decrease in satisfaction caused by a large expectation) was:

$$C^+ = S_r^+ - S_u^+ = 7.5 - 8.7 = -1.2.$$

Note that the overall endowment effect was about the same in the two experiments, but the overall contrast effect, $C = C^- - C^+ = 2.1$, was doubled in the present study. As implied by loss aversion, people's disappointment with a "loss" of \$2 was greater than their satisfaction with a "gain" of \$2.

Applications of the endowment–contrast scheme

Our conceptual scheme for the integration of endowment and contrast effects, described above, can be applied to two studies conducted by Schwarz, Strack and their colleagues (see Schwarz and Strack, 1991). In one experiment, Strack, Schwarz, and Gschneidinger (1985) instructed subjects in one group to recall and write down a very negative event in their lives; subjects in another group were instructed to recall and write down a very positive event in their lives. Within each group, half of the subjects were asked to recall a present event, and half were asked to recall a past event. Subjects were then asked to rate their well-being on a 10-point scale. This procedure yields a 2 × 2 (between-subjects) design in which the recalled event was either positive or negative, in the present or in the past. For the events in the present, the results were hardly surprising. Recalling a positive present event made people feel good, whereas thinking about a negative present event made people feel less happy. The results for past events were more surprising: ratings of well-being were higher for those who recalled a past negative event than for those who recalled a past positive event (see Figure 14.3). We have replicated this result at Stanford.

The endowment–contrast scheme provides a natural account of these findings. For the events in the present, there is no room for contrast; hence we get a positive endowment effect for the positive event and a negative endowment effect for the negative event. The recall of past events, however, introduces a contrast with the present, which is positive for negative events and negative for positive ones. Because present events are more salient than past events, the endowment effect is greater for present than past events. Thus, for past events, the contrast component offsets the endowment component and produces the observed reversal.

Again, let S^+ and S^- refer to judged satisfaction when a positive or negative event, respectively, has been brought to mind. (As before, we first subtract the grand mean from each observation and operate on deviation scores.) Let S_c and S_p refer to the judgments associated with a current and a past event, respectively. We can represent the average judgment in each cell as follows:

	Negative	Positive
Current	$S_c^- = E^-$	$S_c^+ = E^+$
Past	$S_p^- = E^- + C^-$	$S_p^+ = E^+ + C^+$

The total endowment effect is:

$$E = E^+ - E^- = S_c^+ - S_c^- = 8.9 - 7.1 = 1.8.$$

The contrast associated with the positive first event is:

$$C^+ = S_p^+ - S_c^+ = 7.5 - 8.9 = -1.4.$$

The contrast associated with the negative first event is:

$$C^- = S_p^- - S_c^- = 8.5 - 7.1 = 1.4.$$

The total contrast effect in this experiment is thus $C = C^- - C^+ = 2.8$. In this study, therefore, the contrast effect is considerably greater than the endowment effect.

More generally, thinking about positive events in the past (e.g., a tour of the Greek islands, or a happy time at summer camp) calls attention to the less exciting present. This is the stuff of which nostalgia is made. On the other hand, recalling some bad times in the past (e.g., failing a test or being lonely) reminds us that the present, although imperfect, could be a great deal worse. While Strack et al. (1985) see mood as the carrier of endowment, we do not regard mood as a necessary condition for an endowment effect. We shall address this difference in emphasis at the conclusion of this section.

In another study, Schwarz, Strack, Kommer, and Wagner (1987) required subjects to spend an hour either in an extremely pleasant room (spacious, nicely furnished, and decorated with posters and flowers) or in an extremely unpleasant room (small, dirty, smelly, noisy, and overheated). After the session, subjects were asked to assess general satisfaction as well as satisfaction with regard to their current housing situation. The room influenced the

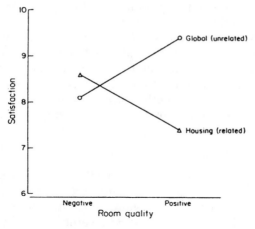

Figure 14.4. The effect of room quality.

rating of overall satisfaction; subjects who were placed in the pleasant room reported higher overall life satisfaction than those in the unpleasant room. However, subjects' rating of their normal living conditions exhibited the opposite pattern (see Figure 14.4). Those placed in the unpleasant room reported higher satisfaction with their housing than those who had been in the pleasant room. This pattern is naturally interpreted as a contrast effect. One's own room appears less attractive when compared with the pleasant room than when compared with the unpleasant room. Because contrast depends on the relevance or the similarity of the standard to the target, the contrast effect of the experimental room was confined to the evaluation of housing, and did not extend to the rating of life satisfaction. A specific event, therefore, is likely to have a significant contrast effect in the domain to which it belongs, and little or no contrast effect in others.

Using the notation introduced earlier, let S^+ and S^- denote, respectively, judgments of satisfaction for the pleasant and unpleasant rooms, and let S_r and S_u denote, respectively, judgments of satisfaction for the related (housing) and unrelated (life satisfaction) domains. The analysis of these results is then identical to the analysis of Study 1. In particular, the total endowment effect is:

$$E = S_u^+ - S_u^- = E^+ - E^- = 9.4 - 8.1 = 1.3.$$

The contrast effect associated with the positive first event is:

$$C^+ = S_r^+ - S_u^+ = 7.4 - 9.4 = -2.0.$$

The contrast effect associated with the negative first event is:

$$C^- = S_r^- - S_u^- = 8.6 - 8.1 = .5.$$

As one might expect, the contrast effect produced by the room is considerably larger ($C = C^- - C^+ = 2.5$) than its endowment effect.

Although different in focus, our analysis is generally compatible with that offered by Schwarz and Strack (see Schwarz and Strack, 1991). They assume the operation of contrast effects and focus on the role of emotion or mood in generating endowment. Our account assumes the existence of endowment effects, produced through either mood or other processes, and focuses on the factors that control the relative strength of endowment and contrast.

Expectations as contrast and endowment

Much psychological research on the assessment of well-being has focused on the role of expectations. It has been shown in many contexts that the same event can be perceived as more or less satisfying, depending on whether a positive or negative expectation has been induced (Feather, 1966; Shrauger, 1975). Whether a given test score is pleasing or disappointing will depend on whether the student was led to expect a low or a high score (Schul, 1989). Expectation effects are generally interpreted as contrast. Indeed, people are commonly advised to lower their expectations in order to avoid disappointment. In line with our previous analysis, we propose that expectations produce endowment as well as contrast. We are relieved when a dreaded event does not happen, but the memory of anxiety and fear still haunts us long afterward. Imagine that you have been living two weeks with the possibility that your child has leukemia. Further tests now prove your worries unfounded. Despite your elation at this news, we suspect that you are worse off for the experience. In such circumstances, the endowment effect of a negative expectation has a strong impact on your well-being long after the specific worry has been relieved.

Much as unrealized fears can generate negative endowment, unrealized hopes can give rise to positive endowment. Consider the experience of someone who owns a lottery ticket. Because the probability of winning is very small, the failure to win does not cause much disappointment. However, the dream of becoming an overnight millionaire could produce enough pleasure to offset the mild disappointment of not winning the lottery. Indeed, it appears that many people enjoy playing the lottery even when they do not win. Probability plays here a critical role. As the probability of winning increases, the costs of disappointment seem to increase faster than the benefits of hope. Holding expected value constant, therefore, playing long odds should be more pleasurable than playing short odds. Losers on long odds had sweeter dreams than losers on short odds; and their disappointment was also less bitter. This analysis suggests another reason for the attractiveness of long shots, in addition to the overweighting of small probabilities (Kahneman and Tversky, 1979).

The present treatment adopts a symbolic rather than a consummatory conception of well-being. We derive pleasure and pain not merely from the positive and the negative events we experience, but also from the memory of past events and the anticipation of future events (Schelling, 1984). Like the memories of past events, expectations of future events, we suggest, serve both as endowment and as contrast. Expectations not only control the evaluation of future events, they have a hedonic impact of their own – whether or not the event they refer to actually comes to pass. Our hedonic portfolio encompasses memories and expectations: successes and failures of the past, hopes and fears of the future.

The assessment of well-being: Choice versus judgment

The preceding studies were concerned, like most of the empirical work discussed in this volume, with judgments of satisfaction or happiness, which have served as a major source of data for students of well-being (Argyle, 1987; Diener, 1984). Another paradigm for the study of welfare, dominant in economics, focuses on choice rather than on judgment. In this paradigm, a person is said to be better off in State A than in State B if he or she chooses State A over State B. Indeed, the concept of utility has been used in economics and decision theory in two different senses: (a) experience value, the degree of pleasure or pain associated with the actual experience of an outcome, and (b) decision value, the contribution of an anticipated outcome to the overall attractiveness of an option (Kahneman and Tversky, 1984). Experience values are generally measured by judgmental methods (e.g., self-reports or judgments by observers), although physiological measures (e.g., blood pressure or heart rate) are occasionally used. Decision values are inferred from choices using an appropriate model such as expected utility theory or the theory of revealed preference. The distinction between experience and decision values is rarely made explicit because, with a few notable exceptions (e.g., March, 1978; Schelling, 1984; Sen, 1982), it is commonly assumed that judgment and choice yield the same ordering. In many situations, however, experience values, as expressed in self-ratings, appear to diverge from decision values, as inferred from choice.

First, choice and judgment may yield different results because of moral considerations and problems of self-control. We commonly avoid certain pleasurable experiences because they are immoral, illegal, or fattening. On the other hand, there are times we cannot resist experiences that will ultimately make us unhappy, because of a lack of self-control. Choice, therefore, could conceal rather than reveal one's "true preferences." Second, a choice–judgment discrepancy is likely to arise if the decision maker's prediction of the consequences of choice is inaccurate or biased. A common bias in the prediction of utility is a tendency to overweight one's present state or mood. Some perceptive consumers have learned to avoid doing their weekly grocery shopping either when they are very hungry (because they would buy too much) or after a very large meal (because they would not buy enough). A related source of error is the failure to anticipate our remarkable ability to adapt to new states. People tend to overestimate the long-term impact of both positive events, such as winning a lottery or receiving tenure, and negative events, such as injury or personal loss (Brickman, Coates, and Janoff-Bulman, 1978). The ability to predict future well-being depends largely on the nature of the experience. People generally have a reasonable idea of what it is like to lose money or to have a bad cold, but they probably do not have a clear notion of what it means to go bankrupt, or to lose a limb. For illuminating discussions of the role of adaptation and the problems of predicting one's own future satisfaction, see Kahneman and Snell (1990), and Kahneman and Varey (1991).

But even if the judgment, like the choice, precedes the experience of the consequence, the two tasks can give rise to different answers because they highlight different aspects of the problem. When people are asked to assess the hedonic value of some future states (e.g., job offers) they try to imagine what it would feel like to experience those states. But when asked to choose among these states, they tend to search for reasons or arguments to justify their choice. Consequently, the two procedures could lead to different results. For example, Tversky, Sattath, and Slovic (1988) have shown that the most important attribute of a multi-dimensional decision problem is weighted more heavily in choice than in judgment, presumably because it provides a convenient rationale for choice. Recall the stock-market study, presented in the first section of this chapter. Given a choice, subjects would surely elect to participate in the negative contrast condition, where they earn $10, rather than in the positive contrast condition, where they earn $6. Yet subjects who had a lower total endowment ($6) and a positive contrast were just as satisfied as subjects who had a higher total endowment ($10) and a negative contrast. It appears that the choice depends primarily on the payoffs whereas judgments of satisfaction are more sensitive to the contrast.

To explore the choice–judgment discrepancy, we presented the following information to some sixty-six undergraduate students.

Imagine that you have just completed a graduate degree in Communications and you are considering one-year jobs at two different magazines.

(A) At Magazine A, you are offered a job paying $35,000. However, the other workers who have the same training and experience as you do are making $38,000.

(B) At Magazine B, you are offered a job paying $33,000. However, the other workers who have the same training and experience as you do are making $30,000.

Approximately half the subjects were asked, "Which job would you choose to take?" while the other half were asked, "At which job would you be happier?" The results confirmed our prediction that the comparison with others would loom larger in judgment, and that the salary would dominate the choice. Eighty-four per cent of the subjects (twenty-seven out of thirty-two) preferred the job with the higher absolute salary and lower relative position, while sixty-two per cent (twenty-one out of thirty-four) of the subjects anticipated higher satisfaction in the job with the lower absolute salary and higher relative position ($\chi^2(1) = 14.70$, $p < .01$).

We further explored the relation between choice and judgment in the assessment of an actual experience using a within-subjects design. Thirty-eight undergraduate students participated in a study of "verbal creativity" involving two different tasks. One was described as a test of "cognitive production": the ability to come up with many words that fit a sentence. The other task was described as a test of "grammatical production": the ability to produce many words of a particular grammatical type. Subjects were told that their payoffs would depend on their performance in these tasks.

All subjects performed both tasks, each of which consisted of a practice trial followed by a payoff trial. In one task, subjects were told that their performance was below average on the practice trial, and about average on the payoff trial. In the other task, subjects were told that they performed above average on the practice trial, and about average on the payoff trial. Thus, the performance of each subject "improved" on one task and "declined" on the other task. The order and type of task were counterbalanced. The payoff in the declining condition ($3) was higher than the payoff in the improving condition ($1). Thus, one task paired a larger payoff with an unfavourable comparison. The other task paired a smaller payoff with a favourable comparison. After each task, subjects were asked to rate their satisfaction with their performance on a 10-point scale. Following the completion of both tasks, subjects were asked, "If you could do just one task, which would you choose to do?"

As predicted, the payoffs loomed larger in choice than in judgment, or (equivalently) the contrast was weighted more heavily in judgment than in choice. Of the twenty-eight subjects whose ratings were not identical on the two tasks, 75 per cent chose the high-payoff task while 54 per cent expressed greater satisfaction with the low-payoff task. This reversal pattern is significant ($p < .05$ by a McNemar test of symmetry).

These studies show that judgments of satisfaction and choice can yield systematically different orderings. Furthermore, it appears that choice is determined primarily by the payoffs, which reflect the endowment effect, whereas the judgment is more sensitive to comparison or contrast. The salary or payoff one receives provides a more compelling reason for choice than the contrast between one's own salary and the salary of others. This contrast, however, is a very salient feature of the anticipated experience, as reflected in the judgment task. Note that the present use of *contrast* is consistent with, but considerably broader than, the concept invoked in the first part of the chapter. There the term refers to the indirect contribution of a past event to current well-being, whereas here it refers to the standard of reference by which the relevant outcomes are evaluated, which may be determined by prior experience or by other factors, such as the salary of colleagues.

The choice–judgment discrepancy raises an intriguing question: which is the correct or more appropriate measure of well-being? This question cannot be readily answered, and perhaps it cannot be answered at all, because we lack a gold standard for the measurement of happiness. We believe that both choice and judgment provide relevant data for the assessment of well-being, although neither one is entirely satisfactory. Since, as we argue below, the two methods seem to be biased in opposite directions, a compromise between them may have some merit.

Perhaps the most basic principle of welfare economics is Pareto optimality: an allocation of resources is acceptable if it improves everybody's lot. Viewed as a choice criterion, this principle is irresistible. It is hard to object to a policy that improves your lot just because it improves the lot of someone else even more. This is a pure endowment argument that neglects contrast altogether. Policies that ignore contrast effects can create widespread unhappiness. Consider, for example, a policy that doubles the salary of a few people in an organization and increases all other salaries by 5 percent. Even though all salaries rise, it is doubtful that this change will make most people happier. There is a great deal of evidence (e.g., Brickman, 1975; Brickman and Campbell, 1971; Crosby, 1976) that people's reported satisfaction depends largely on their relative position, not only on their objective situation.

Both experimental and survey research on happiness have shown that judgments of well-being are highly sensitive to comparison or contrast and relatively insensitive to endowment effects. Perhaps the most dramatic illustration of this phenomenon concerns the effect of windfall gains and tragedies. Judged by their ratings, lottery winners are no happier than normal controls, and quadriplegics are only slightly less happy than healthy people and no less happy than paraplegics (Brickman et al., 1978). Surveys indicate that wealthier people are slightly happier than people with less money, but substantial increases in everyone's income and standard of living do not raise the reported level of happiness (Easterlin, 1974).

Do these data reflect rapid adaptation that negates the immediate impact of any endowment – as implied by the treadmill theory of happiness (Brickman & Campbell, 1971)? Or do they reflect a normalization of the response scale that makes the ratings of ordinary people and paraplegics essentially incomparable? (As if the paraplegic answers the question: how do I feel relative to other paraplegics?) There are no simple answers to these questions. Obviously, everyone would choose to be healthy rather than paraplegic, and rich rather than poor. But it is not obvious how to demonstrate that the rich are actually happier than the poor if both groups report the same level of well-being. At the same time, it is clear that an adequate measure of well-being must distinguish between rich and poor, and between paraplegic and quadriplegic.

It seems that judgments of well-being are insufficiently sensitive to endowment, whereas choice is insufficiently sensitive to contrast. The exclusive reliance on either method can lead to unreasonable conclusions and unsound recommendations. Welfare policy derived from Pareto optimality could result in allocations that make most people less happy because it ignores the effect of social comparison. On the other hand, a preoccupation with judgment has led some psychologists to the view that "persons with a few ecstatic moments in their lives may be doomed to unhappiness" (Diener, 1984, p. 568), hence, "if the best can come only rarely, it is better not to include it in the range of experiences at all" (Parducci, 1968, p. 90). These conclusions are justified only if endowment effects are essentially ignored. A few glorious moments could sustain a lifetime of happy memories for those who can cherish the past without discounting the present.

Note

1 Our use of this term to denote a component of hedonic experience should be distinguished from the endowment effect demonstrated by Thaler (1980), which refers to the impact of acquiring material goods on subsequent choices.

References

Argyle, M. *The psychology of happiness*. London: Methuen, 1987.

Brickman, P. Adaptation level determinants of satisfaction with equal and unequal outcome distributions in skill and chance situations. *Journal of Personality and Social Psychology*, 1975; **32**, 191–198.

Brickman, P. and Campbell, D. T. Hedonic relativism and planning the good society. In M. H. Appley (ed.), *Adaptation level theory: A symposium* (pp. 287–302). New York: Academic Press, 1971.

Brickman, P., Coates, D. and Janoff-Bulman, R. Lottery winners and accident victims: Is happiness relative? *Journal of Personality and Social Psychology*, 1978; **36**, 917–927.

Crosby, F. A model of egoistical relative deprivation. *Psychological Review*, 1976; **83**, 85–113.

Diener, E. Subjective well-being. *Psychological Bulletin*, 1984; **95**(3), 542–575.

Easterlin, R. A. Does economic growth improve the human lot? Some empirical evidence. In P. A. David and M. W. Reder (eds.), *Nations and households in economic growth* (pp. 89–125). New York: Academic Press, 1974.

Feather, N. T. Effects of prior success and failure on expectations of success and failure. *Journal of Personality and Social Psychology*, 1966; **3**, 287–298.

Kahneman, D. and Snell, J. Predicting utility. In R. Hogarth (ed.), *Insights in decision making: A tribute to Hillel J. Einhorn* (pp. 295–310). Chicago, IL: University of Chicago Press, 1990.

Kahneman, D. and Tversky, A. Prospect theory: An analysis of decision under risk. *Econometrica*, 1979; **47**, 263–291.

Kahneman, D. and Tversky, A. Choices, values and frames. *American Psychologist*, 1984; **39**, 341–350.

Kahneman, D. and Varey, C. Notes on the psychology of utility. In J. Elster & J. Roemer (eds.), *Interpersonal comparisons of well-being* (pp. 127–163). Chicago, IL: University of Chicago Press, 1991.

March, J. G. Bounded rationality, ambiguity, and the engineering of choice. *The Bell Journal of Economics*, 1978; **9**(2), 587–608.

Parducci, A. The relativism of absolute judgments. *Scientific American*, 1968; **219**, 84–90.

Schelling, T. A. *Choice and consequence.* Cambridge, MA: Harvard University Press, 1984.

Schul, Y. *Expectations, performance, and satisfaction.* Unpublished manuscript, The Hebrew University of Jerusalem, 1989.

Schwarz, N. and Strack, F. Evaluating one's life: A judgment model of subjective well-being. In F. Strack, M. Argyle, & N. Schwarz (eds.), *Subjective well-being: An interdisciplinary perspective* (pp. 27–47). Oxford: Pergamon Press, 1991.

Schwarz, N., Strack, F., Kommer, D. and Wagner, D. Soccer, rooms, and the quality of your life: Mood effects on judgments of satisfaction with life in general and with specific domains. *European Journal of Social Psychology*, 1987; **17**, 69–79.

Sen, A. *Choice, welfare and measurement.* Cambridge, MA: MIT Press, 1982.

Shrauger, J. S. Responses to evaluation as a function of initial self-perception. *Psychological Bulletin*, 1975; **82**, 581–596.

Strack, F., Schwarz, N. and Gschneidinger, E. Happiness and reminiscing: The role of time perspective, affect, and mode of thinking. *Journal of Personality and Social Psychology*, 1985; **49**(6), 1460–1469.

Thaler, R. Toward a positive theory of consumer choice. *Journal of Economic Behavior and Organization*, 1980; **1**, 39–60.

Tversky, A., Sattath, S. and Slovic, P. Contingent weighting in judgment and choice. *Psychological Review*, 1988; **95**(3), 371–384.

Part III
Connections

15 The relationship between memory and judgment depends on whether the judgment task is memory-based or on-line

Reid Hastie and Bernadette Park

There ought to be a relationship between memory and judgment. Our intuition tells us that we should be able to generate more arguments and information in support of a favored position than against it, that evaluations of people should be related to the amounts of good and bad information we have about them. When a person is able to remember many arguments against a belief, or to cite many good characteristics of an acquaintance, we are surprised if they endorse the belief or dislike the person. In support of intuitions like these, names have been given to the idea that memory and judgment have a simple direct relationship, including "availability," "dominance of the given," "salience effect," and so forth.

However, empirical studies of the relationship between memory and judgment with subject matter as diverse as social impressions, personal attitudes, attributions of causes for behavior, evaluations of legal culpability, and a variety of probability and frequency estimates have not revealed simple relations between memory and judgment. Some relationships have been found, but strong empirical relations are rare and results are often contradictory.

Some examples seem to support the expectation of a direct relationship between memory and judgment. Tversky and Kahneman (1973) demonstrated that many judgments of numerosity were directly correlated with the "ease with which instances or associations could be brought to mind" (p. 208). In an illustrative series of experiments, they showed that judgments of the frequency of words in English text were correlated with the ease of

This chapter originally appeared in *Psychological Review*, 1986, 93(3), 258–268. Copyright © 1986 by the American Psychological Association. Reprinted by permission.

This research was supported by funds from the Trout Foundation. Nancy Pennington provided extensive and valuable advice at all stages of this research. Ebbe B. Ebbesen, David L. Hamilton, G. Daniel Lassiter, and Thomas M. Ostrom made helpful comments on the research plan and on the manuscript.

remembering the words. Beyth-Marom and Fischhoff (1977) provided more definite evidence on the strength of the memory–judgment relationship, and Gabrielcik and Fazio (1984) demonstrated that ease of retrieval exerts a causal (not just correlational) influence on the frequency estimates.

Similar demonstrations have been provided in research studying memory–judgment relationships for more complex naturally occurring events. Lichtenstein, Slovic, Fischhoff, Layman, and Combs (1978; Combs & Slovic, 1979) obtained large correlations between judged frequencies of deaths and the frequencies of reports of causes of death in newspaper articles. For these events, reporting rates were not correlated with actuarial frequencies, supporting the conclusion that newspaper reporting rates biased memory availability, which in turn influenced the frequency estimates. Another neat everyday example is provided by Ross and Sicoly (1979) in their research on the attribution of responsibility. They found simple, direct relationships in joint tasks such as home improvement projects, writing scientific papers, and competing in team sports between subjects' judgments of responsibility for themselves and others and the subjects' ability to remember relevant evidence. These examples imply a direct relationship between memory and judgment: The more a subject can remember and the more easily it comes to mind, the higher the estimates of frequency, probability, or responsibility.

However, there is another side to the literature on memory–judgment relationships. Although researchers almost invariably expect to find the direct relationships illustrated by the first set of examples, this has not always been the case. In a classic experiment by Anderson and Hubert (1963), subjects made likableness ratings of a hypothetical character on the basis of ensembles of trait adjectives. In some conditions of the experiment, subjects were also asked to recall the adjectives. Anderson and Hubert noted that when the recall data were summarized as serial position curves, a recency effect was obtained; however, the likableness rating data showed that early adjectives in the sequence had the greatest impact on subjects' final impressions, a primacy effect. Anderson and Hubert concluded that "the impression memory is distinct from the verbal memory for the adjectives" (p. 391).

Another frequently cited study of memory–judgment relationships is an experiment by Reyes, Thompson, and Bower (1980) in which subjects were asked to make judgments of the apparent guilt of a defendant briefly described in a drunken driving case. These experimenters manipulated information about the defendant's character and the memorability of items of evidence favoring defense or prosecution sides of the case. The authors did not find a relationship between memory and judgment at short delays; however, after a 48-hour delay a significant but low correlation (+.31) was obtained. The authors concluded that "such a low correlation suggests that judgments of apparent guilt were not made simply on the basis of the differential availability of the arguments" (p. 7).

Finally, there is a third relationship between memory and judgment that appears in some person impression formation tasks. Hastie and Kumar (1979; replicated by many others, most notably Srull, 1981) found that when subjects studied sentences describing the behavior of a hypothetical character while making judgments of the character's personality, behaviors that were incongruent with the final trait ratings were the best recalled on a subsequent memory test. This reversal of the commonly expected direct memory–judgment relationship has been explained as resulting from "special processing" accorded to the incongruent acts when they were attributed to a single character in the context of an impression formation task (Hastie, 1984). Empirical results suggest that this special processing involves the subject's effort to explain why the surprising, incongruent actions were performed by the character, a plausible subtask within the larger impression formation task.

The scope of the literature from which these examples were culled is large. We have identified more than 50 published experiments that report correlational or treatment effect findings relevant to the memory–judgment relationship in judgment tasks. The variety of judgment task domains included in these studies is remarkably diverse even within the social judgment area: impression formation involving traits, behaviors, likability, and ability judgments; occupation suitability judgments; attitude formation and change; judgments of historical events' antecedents and consequences; predictions of sports events; psychodiagnosis of clinical cases; causal attribution for individual behavior; statistical decision making; and deductive reasoning.

Theoretical analysis

The contrast between our expectations that memory–judgment relationships should be direct and pervasive and the mixed results of research on the relationship is puzzling. We believe that a careful analysis of the cognitive processes that could produce or obscure a memory–judgment relationship can explain why the relationship appears or does not appear across experimental tasks. Several specific models for the perception, memory, and judgment processes that could produce correlations between memory and judgment measures have been presented by researchers studying social judgment. To resolve the enigma concerning when memory and judgment will be directly related, we need to clarify the alternate process models and identify the empirical conditions under which each model will apply.

Our theoretical analysis is nested in the context of an information processing approach to social cognition (Hastie & Carlston, 1980; Smith, 1984; Wyer & Srull, 1980). Briefly, we assume that when a person is presented with a judgment task, either in an experimental or natural situation, evidence information is processed by a judgment operator that performs its function to generate a conclusion on which a response is based. Traditionally, judgment researchers have described these operators as algebraic combination rules (e.g., Anderson, 1981; Edwards, 1968; Hammond, Stewart, Brehmer, & Steinmann, 1975), stochastic processes (e.g., Thomas & Hogue, 1976), or cognitive heuristics (e.g., Kelley, 1973; Tversky & Kahneman, 1974).

The judgment operator is limited by working-memory capacities constraining the complexity of elementary information processes that can be executed at any point in time. The same limits apply to the activation of memory representations and constrain the amount of evidence that can be input into the operator at any moment. Information processing researchers have identified many information formats and structures that might characterize the evidence that is input into the operator. They have also described many potential judgment operators that have been learned over a person's life span and are stored in long-term memory along with other cognitive skill procedures.

Five information processing models

The current social cognition literature provides several examples of memory–judgment models. They can be separated into three classes according to the causal priority of memory or judgment processes: no-priority–independence, memory causes judgment, and judgment causes memory. The most populated class comprises judgment-causes-memory models (biased retrieval, biased encoding, and incongruity-biased encoding), with one example each of an independence model (two-memory hypothesis) and a memory-causes-judgment model (availability-biased judgment). Note that the establishment of a direct or indirect correlation between memory and judgment measures will not answer the question of whether memory has causal priority and causes judgment or the reverse, judgment causes memory. Furthermore, most research has not attempted to go beyond correlational analysis to resolve the ambiguity and establish causal relationships (Dellarosa & Bourne, 1984; and Gabrielcik & Fazio, 1984, are possibly the only exceptions). However, we will review the alternate theoretical models before we turn to the tough questions of empirical prediction and identifiability.

Independence. First, there is a basic model that postulates independence between judgment and memory processes, with no relationship expected between measures of memory and judgments. Norman Anderson (1981; Anderson & Hubert, 1963) has probably stated this position most clearly in his articles on the two-memory hypothesis in trait-adjective-based impression formation tasks:

The judgment was based on a memory system different from the recall. . . . As each adjective was received, the valuation operation extracted its implications for the task at hand. Further processing, especially the integration, was performed on these implications. The verbal material itself, no longer necessary, was transferred to a verbal memory or forgotten. (Anderson, 1981, pp. 95–96)

Thus, the valuation and integration operations involved in the execution of the judgment operator (usually summarized as an algebraic weighted averaging calculation) and the encoding of evidence information into long-term memory traces occur simultaneously and independently.

Availability. Second is the currently popular family of availability models which assume that memory availability causes judgment. The model has many precedents, but a seminal article by Tversky and Kahneman (1973) on the "availability heuristic" is its most common source. This model can be stated as follows: (a) During the time when evidence information is available in the external environment, the subject encodes that information in working memory. The judgment is not made at this time; usually the subject is unaware that the information is relevant to a future judgment. (b) At this time only one process operates that is relevant to the later memory–judgment relationship, namely, the further encoding of the evidence information by transforming it from working-memory codes into long-term memory traces. (c) At some later point in time when a judgment is called for (by the experimenter or "spontaneously"), the subject initiates the judgment process and retrieves information from long-term memory to use as input into a judgment operator. (d) A judgment is generated and reported to the experimenter at this point on the basis of evidence retrieved from long-term memory. (e) When the experimenter tests memory, the memory retrieval process is repeated (in essentially the same fashion as it occurred to generate input for the judgment operator) and the subject responds on the memory test. A relationship is produced between judgment and memory because any tendency that the subject may have to selectively remember information will be reflected both in biased input to the judgment operator and in the biased sample of information reported on the memory test.

The availability process model we have described is slightly more limited than the original Tversky and Kahneman (1973) heuristic. We exclude cases of perceptual availability and restrict the model to memory availability. We also exclude consideration of the availability of previously made inferences and judgments to focus on memory availability of relatively raw evidence information (see Lingle & Ostrom, 1979, for a different opinion). These more complex cases involving judgments based on the retrieval of other judgments and principles of perceptual salience are treated as derived from our five elementary models (see discussion below).

In the introduction to this article we gave examples of experiments by Tversky and Kahneman, Ross and Sicoly, Lichtenstein et al., and others who reported correlational results consistent with the availability heuristic memory-causes-judgment hypothesis. The memory-causes-judgment process model that we sketched above is surely correct in many applications.

However, one point of the present article is that the availability heuristic model has been generalized to many tasks to which it does not apply. The evidence for overgeneralization appears in many articles in which a strong correlation between memory and judgment is not obtained, although the authors often persist with the availability heuristic interpretation in their discussion sections (e.g., Fiske, Kenny, & Taylor, 1982; Reyes et al., 1980).

Biased retrieval. A second set of causal models assumes that judgment causes memory. The most common process model assumes that the judgment and memory-encoding processes go on at about the same time, independently, but the judgment, once completed, has the potential to bias retrieval. (a) Evidence information occurs in the environment and is encoded into a representation in working memory. (b) During its stay in working memory, the information serves as input for two independent processes; information is transformed and written into long-term memory traces and information is operated on to produce a unitary judgment conclusion. (c) When the experimenter asks the subject to report his or her judgment, the subject responds by considering the judgment conclusion that is stored in working memory or, if time has passed, in long-term memory. (d) When the experimenter tests the subject's memory for the evidence, the subject searches long-term memory to find trace information to respond on the memory test. At this point the subject's judgment plays a special role in that it biases access to traces stored in long-term memory or serves to edit the traces as they are output in the form of responses on the memory test. Thus, the judgment serves a selective function such that traces that "fit" the judgment are likelier to be found in the memory search or to be reported at the memory decision stage. Common names for this class of biases include "selective recall," "confirmatory memory," and "access-biased memory" (Leamer, 1974, 1975; Snyder & Uranowitz, 1978). The selective influence of the judgment during the retrieval phase of a memory task biases recall in a fashion that produces a correlation between the judgment (c) and the memory (d) responses.

There is some controversy in the literature about exactly what mechanism at retrieval produces the bias. Snyder and Uranowitz (1978) suggested that the search phase of retrieval was the locus of the bias, but subsequent studies by Bellezza and Bower (1981) and Clark and Woll (1981) favored an editing or response threshold mechanism to explain the relevant findings. For present purposes it will suffice to cite the Snyder and Uranowitz results as illustrating the basic retrieval bias phenomenon because either biased search or biased responses would fit the slightly more general model we are describing.

Biased encoding. The fourth model assumes that judgment causes memory by biasing the encoding of evidence information. (a) Evidence information enters working memory and is used as input to the judgment operator in the formation of an initial judgment. (b) The initial judgment filters subsequent evidence information by guiding information search, encoding, and comprehension in such a way that information that fits the initial judgment (or that can be interpreted to fit) has an advantage in subsequent transfer to long-term memory. (c) When the experimenter asks the subject to report his or her judgment, the subject responds by considering the judgment conclusion that is stored in working memory or, if time has passed, in long-term memory. (d) When the experimenter tests the subject's memory for the evidence, the subject searches long-term memory to find trace information to respond on the memory test. Because the evidence stored in long-term memory was filtered through the lens of the initial judgment, memory search will locate a biased sample of information reflecting the encoding bias.

Oddly enough, although this is the most frequently mentioned judgment–memory model, there is the least support for its applicability to social judgment phenomena (Alba & Hasher, 1983; Hastie, 1981). In our view, the social psychological findings that have been cited as examples of the model are more plausibly interpreted as biased-retrieval phenomena (see Taylor & Crocker, 1981, for a typical review). We must admit, however, that some examples are ambiguous and could represent either biased-encoding or biased-retrieval processes (e.g., Berman, Read, & Kenny, 1983).

Incongruity-biased encoding. Finally, there is a model which assumes that judgment causes memory during the encoding stage, but the hypothesized memory–judgment relationship is the reverse of the common filtered encoding bias: we call this the incongruity-biased-encoding model. Hastie (1980, 1984) and Srull (1981) have given this model its clearest statement in interpreting the results of a series of studies of impression formation and recall tasks in which judgment-incongruent evidence was better recalled than judgment-congruent evidence (see also Woll & Graesser, 1982, for an interpretation that emphasizes incongruity-biased-encoding processes). (a) Evidence information is encoded in working memory and is input to a judgment operator where an initial judgment is formed. (b) Later incoming information is reviewed in the context of the initial judgment, and information that is incongruent (contradictory) is given special processing that enhances its memorability (e.g., it receives more associative links to other information in working memory, or it receives "special tags" that strongly attach it to a knowledge structure that organizes current events in long-term memory). (c) When the experimenter asks the subject to report a final judgment, the subject responds by considering the judgment that is stored in working memory or in long-term memory. (d) When the experimenter tests the subject's memory for the evidence, the subject searches long-term memory and is especially likely to find incongruent information. The incongruent information advantage accrues from the rich network of associative links or the special tags that were attached to incongruent evidence during encoding. The most frequently cited examples of this model are found in the Hastie and Kumar (1979) and Srull (1981) person memory experiments cited above.

Given that information processing can plausibly follow one of several alternate models, the derivation of unequivocal predictions concerning the direction and strength of memory–judgment relationships, even at the gross correlational level, will not be a simple matter. Furthermore, it is likely that in many laboratory and naturally occurring judgment tasks more than one of the theoretical process models may apply to a single subject's performance (e.g., both encoding and retrieval biases may operate or both judgment-causes-memory and memory-causes-judgment processes may apply; Hastie, 1981). We should not be surprised that empirical results are mixed, given theoretical hypotheses to account for either direct or indirect relationships. We believe that careful thought about the task conditions that elicit each model can resolve some of the theoretical and empirical confusions.

On-line versus memory-based judgment tasks

The key distinction we would like to make concerns the source of inputs to the judgment operators. In essence our hypothesis is that in some tasks the judgment is necessarily memory based and the subject must perforce rely on the retrieval of relatively concrete evidence from long-term memory in order to render a judgment. Under these memory-based conditions, direct relationships between memory for the evidence and the judgment will be obtained. The direct relationships would be predicted from either of the availability process models that would apply to memory-based tasks. However, these conditions are rare, both in natural and laboratory environments, and ingenuity must be exercised to design tasks that will produce simple, direct memory–judgment relationships. The alternative, more common, class of on-line judgment tasks is associated with several process models that do not all yield predictions of a direct memory–judgment relationship.

In many judgment tasks, information for the operator follows a path from the stimulus environment external to the subject into working memory and directly to the judgment operator. We call tasks of this type on-line judgment tasks because the subject is forming the judgment "on-line" as evidence information is encountered. For example, in most research on impression formation (Anderson & Hubert, 1963; Asch, 1946), adjectives are presented to subjects as the basis for an impression and they are used by the judgment operator to update the impression almost immediately after they are perceived by the subject.

A second example of an on-line, perception-based task is the abbreviated legal judgment task employed by Reyes et al. (1980), which was also described in the introduction to this article. Another well-known on-line judgment task was introduced by Ward Edwards (1968) and has been used to study judgments that can be characterized as dynamic probability revision judgments. One version of this judgment task involved subjects' inductive inferences concerning which of two bookbags was the source of a sample of poker chips. The bags differed in the composition of chips, of distinctive colors, that they contained, and a random sample of chips from the bag would be informative about which bag had been selected by the experimenter. Lopes (1982; see also Einhorn & Hogarth, 1985) proposed what we believe is the most plausible judgment operator for performance in this task. Her "anchoring and adjustment" model for opinion revision is a prototype of an on-line judgment procedure. In all of these cases, our assumption is that subjects making the judgment revise, on-line, as items of evidence are encountered. Furthermore, the evidence items are used directly, with few intervening inferences, as inputs into the judgment operator.

Our review of the five theoretical processing models implies that it will not be possible to unequivocally predict the relationship that will be obtained between memory and judgment measures when the judgment is made on-line. It should be clear that four of the five models could apply; thus, direct, indirect, or no relationship might be observed. Because previous research has not been sensitive to the possible variety of process models and relationships that might apply in on-line judgment tasks, it is difficult to definitely identify the appropriate process model in most experiments.

The judgment procedure can take a different, memory-based course, with the input to the operator coming from long-term memory into working memory rather than directly from the external environment. The clearest examples of this condition in the judgment literature appear in the Tversky and Kahneman (1973) demonstrations of availability effects. For example, when subjects were asked to estimate the frequency of occurrence of words with certain characteristics (e.g., k as the first letter), they had to rely on information that had been stored in long-term memory to make estimates of frequencies. In addition, in the introduction to the present article we described research on risk judgments by Lichtenstein et al. (1978) and responsibility judgments by Ross and Sicoly (1979) in which subjects appeared to rely on their ability to retrieve instances that were directly relevant to a judgment from long-term memory.

If our theoretical review is valid, prediction of the memory–judgment relationship is possible in memory-based tasks. Only the availability processing model is applicable, and it predicts that there will be a direct relationship between memory and judgment measures.

The on-line versus memory-based distinction has many precedents in the social cognition literature. Two series of experiments, one directed by Lingle (Lingle, Dukerich, & Ostrom, 1983; Lingle, Geva, Ostrom, Lieppe, & Baumgardner, 1979; Lingle & Ostrom, 1979) and one by Carlston (1980), simultaneously introduced the notion of memory-based judgments to the social literature. These authors studied the case in which a subject made an initial judgment and then retrieved the first judgment from memory to serve as the basis for a second judgment. Perhaps McArthur (1980) most clearly distinguished between direct, perception-based judgment and indirect, recall-mediated judgment in the same terms as our distinction between perception and memory sources of input (see also Taylor & Thompson, 1982). Finally, Sherman and his colleagues (Sherman, Zehner, Johnson, & Hirt, 1983) and Lichtenstein and Srull (1985) have also reached the conclusion that direct memory–judgment relationships are likeliest to be found in memory-based tasks.

Why is the on-line versus memory-based task difference the key to understanding the mixed results from empirical research on the memory–judgment relationship? If we can arrange conditions to insure that a subject makes a memory-based judgment, the memory–judgment relationship should fit the availability process model, which predicts a direct relationship between evidence memorability and the judgment conclusion. However, if the judgment task is on-line, four of the five models may apply. Therefore the memory–judgment relationship can be either direct, indirect, or null, and unequivocal prediction is not possible.

Because so many conditions are likely to instigate perception-based, on-line judgments, the difficult question for experimenters on the memory–judgment relationship is how to produce memory-based judgments. Memory-based judgments are usually more effortful than on-line judgments, and people realize that memory processes are less reliable than the perceptual processes involved in on-line judgments. Hence, subjects make on-line judgments when they believe that a judgment is likely to be required at a later point in time.

What are the conditions that will produce memory-based judgments? Probably the most reliable method to produce memory-based judgments is to surprise subjects with a novel judgment that is unlikely to be preceded by a relevant on-line judgment. Everyday examples of memory-based "surprise judgments" abound. A university professor returns from a professional meeting and learns that her department has a position open. Relatively effortful memory-based judgments are made of prospective candidates who had been encountered at the meeting. Similarly, a student might discover that he is looking for a roommate and then review acquaintances on the basis of memory to make preliminary judgments of compatibility. In these examples it is obvious that if the judgments had been anticipated before the evidence was encountered, the judgments would have been on-line.

On-line spontaneous judgments

Normally people make many judgments spontaneously, without waiting for an instruction from one of life's experimenters. We often make spontaneous inferences about other people, particularly in the first encounter situations so frequently simulated in laboratory and field research on impression formation, stereotyping, attribution, moral evaluation, and persuasion. Essentially we assume that most judgments studied by social psychologists are perception-based, on-line processes. Even the reader who believes that people are mindless drones in most natural social interactions (Langer, Blank, & Chanowitz, 1978) will admit that psychology experiments on social judgment are an exception to the norm of mental inactivity. In these experiments judgments of interest to the experimenter are almost always being made on-line by subjects because of the nature of the situation (e.g., "This is a hypothetical acquaintance situation"; "We are interested in your first impressions"; "Suppose that you are a personnel officer"); the task (e.g., "You will make judgments of the likability of 12 individuals"); or specific instructions (e.g., "Attempt to evaluate the relative degrees of responsibility . . .").

Recently social psychologists have conducted research that identifies some of the major types of social judgments that will tend to be made spontaneously, on-line, "in the absence of an investigator's instructions" (Winter & Uleman, 1984, p. 237). In accord with our above assumption, trait (Winter & Uleman, 1984) and causal (Weiner, 1985) inferences are likely to be made spontaneously. Furthermore, several additional classes of factors have been found to elicit spontaneous social judgments.

First are a set of individual difference factors that are frequently referred to as "schematicism" or "chronicity" in the social psychology literature. For example, Markus (1977) demonstrated that people exhibit differential tendencies to make judgments of other people along certain dimensions or with reference to certain attributes. Some people appear to be constantly concerned with the masculinity–femininity of others, some people with the dependence–independence of others, some people with the intelligence of others, and so forth. These individual differences lead subjects to spontaneously make inferences about almost everybody they meet, although the specific dimensions will differ across subjects (see also Bargh, 1982; Higgins, King, & Mavin, 1982).

Second, Hastie (1980, 1984) has speculated that unexpected events will tend to elicit certain types of social judgments, particularly causal attribution judgments. Third, it seems that other stimulus conditions can also invoke spontaneous judgments: stimulus properties that are strikingly and distinctively associated with certain social categories or activities. For example, it is difficult to look at Arnold Schwarzenegger without making a judgment of his athletic prowess. Fourth, there is considerable speculation about the relationships between social goals (e.g., to form a clear impression of another person, to induce another to like oneself, to persuade another to comply with one's desires, to inform another about one's [self-conceived] identity, etc.) and judgment. Weiner (1985) concluded that a goal of "mastery" is the primary instigating condition for causal attribution judgments. Similarly, Jones and Pittman (1982) hypothesized that many types of judgments would be made to facilitate "strategic self presentation" in the service of a motive to exert power over others. More specific social goals have been identified by other theorists (e.g., Hamilton, Katz, & Leirer, 1980; Hoffman, Mischel, &

Mazze, 1981; Swann, 1984), but little empirical research on the goal–judgment link has been conducted.

In fact, there is a further complication: Even when subjects have not spontaneously made the judgment requested by an experimenter, they seem reluctant to consult long-term memory for evidence on which to base a novel judgment. Rather, they appear to prefer to make a new judgment on the basis of earlier judgments and inferences without retrieving specific evidence from memory (Lingle, Dukerich, & Ostrom, 1983; Lingle & Ostrom, 1979). Thus, true memory-based judgments may be rare because so many judgments are made on-line (spontaneously) and because when a new judgment must be made in the absence of perceptually available evidence, subjects rely on previous judgments rather than remembered evidence.

To summarize, we started with the empirical enigma of the rarity of direct memory–judgment relationships in the results of experiments designed to obtain them. Five models for the information processes that might underlie memory–judgment relationships were abstracted from the social cognition literature: the two-memory independence hypothesis, availability, retrieval bias, encoding bias, and incongruity-biased encoding. The independence model predicts no correlation between memory and judgment measures, the incongruity-biased-encoding model predicts a negative correlation, and the remaining models predict a positive correlation. A distinction was introduced between on-line and memory-based judgment tasks, and we hypothesized that the availability model was the only candidate to apply in memory-based tasks. However, most laboratory and real-world judgments probably occur under on-line task conditions where there is uncertainty about which of the remaining four process models apply, and thus the memory–judgment relationship is equivocal.

The bottom line of our analysis is that to guarantee a direct relationship between memory and judgment measures, we must study memory-based judgment tasks that occur (a) when no previous relevant judgment has been made and (b) when the subject is motivated to use evidence retrieved from memory as input at the time of judgment. In the next section we will summarize the results of four experiments that vary task conditions to produce the predicted direct relationship between memory and judgment.

Empirical research

The most convincing argument we can make in support of our conceptual analysis is to conduct research showing that empirical phenomena fit our predictions. Results from four experiments that investigated the memory–judgment relationship are summarized in Table 15.1.[1] In each experiment, task conditions were arranged to force subjects to adopt a memory-based judgment strategy, where we would predict substantial correlations between memory and judgment measures. In the last three experiments we added task conditions that would either encourage on-line judgment strategies or

Table 15.1. *Correlations between memory and judgment measures from four experiments*

	Task							
	Total recall				First five recall			
	On-line		Memory		On-line		Memory	
Judgment	r	n	r	n	r	n	r	n
Experiment 1								
Job suitability	−.14	35	.46	33	.14	35	.42	33
Experiment 2								
Job suitability (nonspontaneous)	.24	20	.39	23	.21	20	.44	23
Gender (spontaneous)	.37	20	.20	22	.26	20	.47	22
Experiment 3								
Exercise (nonspontaneous)	.09	64	.56	65				
Sociability (spontaneous)	.11	65	−.09	64				
Experiment 4								
Intelligence	.15	53	.67	39				
Friendliness	.29	53	.73	41				
Likability	.10	53	.56	43				

would allow subjects to make the final judgment based on a previous spontaneous judgment retrieved from memory. In these conditions we did not predict correlations between memory and judgment. We will briefly sketch the methods and results from each experiment.

In Experiment 1 subjects were asked to make a judgment of a man's suitability for a job as a computer programmer after hearing a 5-min conversation between two men. Half of the subjects were told of the judgment before hearing the conversation (on-line task condition), and half learned of the judgment only after the conversation (memory-based task condition). Pretesting assured us that the job suitability judgment would not be made spontaneously by subjects in the memory-based task. After the tape-recorded conversation, all subjects made the job suitability judgment (on a 10-point rating scale) and recalled as much information from the conversation as they could. Order of the rating and recall tasks was varied, but it did not affect the results. Experimental instructions, identical except for timing in on-line and memory-based conditions, stressed accuracy in judgment and completeness of recall to counter any tendencies that subjects might have to follow an unspoken experimental demand for agreement between recall and judgment.

Several indices of the strength of recall of items favoring or opposing the job candidate were calculated, and all supported the same conclusions. The measure we will report is a ratio (calculated for each subject) of the number of items recalled favoring suitability divided by the number of items recalled favoring and opposing suitability. A ratio of .50 corresponds to recall of an equal number of items favoring and opposing, greater than .50 indicates more favoring items recalled, and less than .50 indicates more opposing items recalled. A similar ratio was calculated on the basis of only the first five items recalled, on the assumption that in a memory-based judgment process, primacy in retrieval would determine item impact on the judgment (i.e., the subject would probably not recall more than five items before rendering one of our experimental judgments, and the earliest items retrieved would have the greatest impact on the judgment).

The measures of the relationship between memory and judgment reported in Table 15.1 are simple correlation coefficients calculated across subjects in each judgment condition (on-line vs. memory-based) between the subjects' recall ratios and judgments of job suitability. In all cases where a relationship was discernible, the function relating judgment and recall measures appeared to be linear, based on an inspection of the residuals from a fitted line. Our prediction was confirmed: The correlations between memory and judgment measures are substantial in the memory-based task (+.46 and +.42, $ps < .05$) but not in the on-line task (−.14 and +.14, ns).

Experiment 2 provides a replication of these results for the same job suitability judgment but with new evidence items presented in a written format. A second judgment task was included in the Experiment 2 design, with subjects judging the gender of a respondent interviewed in a national survey of leisure time activities. Subjects in the gender judgment condition were either told before reading the written interview that their task would be to infer the gender of the respondent (on-line), or they were given a general "form an impression" instruction before and the gender judgment instruction only after reading the interview (memory). A single written interview containing items relevant to the job judgment (favoring or opposing) and items relevant to the gender judgment (implying the respondent was male or female) was read by all subjects. Our hypothesis was that the on-line versus memory-based task differences obtained in Experiment 1 would be replicated in the job judgments of Experiment 2. However, the gender judgment would be made spontaneously by all subjects whether or not they received the experimenter's instruction before reading the interview. Thus, we would not predict a substantial correlation between recall ratio and judgment measures in either on-line or memory-based tasks for the gender judgment.

The results from Experiment 1 are replicated in the job judgment condition of Experiment 2 (rs of .39 and .44, $ps < .05$, for memory-based judgments; rs of .24 and .21, ns, for on-line judgments). Results for the gender judgment are not exactly in line with our predictions, although they do not strictly contradict our hypothesis. Essentially there is no clear difference between on-line and memory-based tasks in the strength of the memory–judgment correlations. The total recall ratio analysis suggests that the relationship in the on-line condition is stronger (.37 vs. .20), whereas the first five recall ratio yields the reverse order (.26 vs. .47). However, although our theoretical analysis left us uncertain about what, if any, relationship to expect in spontaneous conditions, we were surprised to obtain substantial recall ratio–judgment correlations.

Experiment 3 shifts to a new content domain and to judgments of numerosity rather than suitability or category membership. Subjects listened to a tape-recorded monologue attributed to another undergraduate describing his activities during the past week. Two judgment conditions were used: (a) one selected to be spontaneous, a judgment of the frequency with which the speaker interacted with women (sociability and gender were the judgments most commonly cited as spontaneous by pretest subjects) and (b) one selected to be nonspontaneous, a judgment of the frequency with which the speaker engaged in cardiovascular exercise (none of the pretest subjects cited this type of judgment as occurring spontaneously). As before, half of the subjects were given instructions for the judgment task before the tape (on-line) and half only after the tape (memory). In this experiment every subject received one judgment before the tape and both after, so that each subject provided data for one on-line task (sociability or exercise) and one memory-based task (exercise or sociability). Note that because we have identified the sociability judgment as spontaneous, we do not expect to obtain differences between on-line and memory-based subjects for this judgment.

The results from Experiment 3 confirm our predictions for the exercise judgment; a relationship between memory and judgment measures was observed in the memory-based but not in the on-line task conditions (rs of .56, $p < .05$, and .09, ns). The results for the sociability judgment were also in line with our prediction: no relationship between memory and judgment measures in either memory-based or on-line tasks (rs of +.11 and −.09, both ns).

Experiment 4 provides new materials, judgment tasks, and a new operationalization of the on-line versus memory-based task distinction. Subjects listened to a tape-recorded list of 30 sentences describing a person engaged in everyday actions that had implications for the person's intelligence and friendliness (see Hastie & Kumar, 1979, for a description of the materials). Previous research (Winter & Uleman, 1984) and our pretest ratings suggested that personality and ability judgments would usually be made spontaneously by our undergraduate subjects. Thus, the problem of operationalizing the on-line versus memory-based difference becomes the problem of turning a spontaneously made (on-line) judgment into a memory-based judgment. Note that in the previous experiments our problem was to turn a rarely made nonspontaneous judgment into an on-line judgment. In those studies, we used experimenter instructions before presenting evidence to make the nonspontaneous judgment on-line. In Experiment 4 we attempted to interfere with the subjects' tendency to make personality and ability judgments spontaneously by presenting a novel judgment task that we expected would divert the subjects' mental processes from their normal spontaneous judgments. The task we used required subjects to make a judgment of the grammaticality of each sentence as it was presented on the tape recorder. We believed that making the grammaticality judgment would prevent the subjects from spontaneously integrating information from the sentences into impressions of the person's personality, abilities, or likability. Thus, the interfering grammaticality judgments would make impression judgments, after the tape recording, memory based. The on-line task was established by instructing subjects that they would make personality judgments at the end of the list of sentences and by requiring a likability judgment of the person after each sentence was presented.

Ratings of intelligence, friendliness, and likability from Experiment 4 subjects revealed the predicted pattern: substantial recall ratio–judgment correlations in the memory-based task (rs of .67, .63, and .56, all $ps < .05$) but not in the on-line (grammaticality) task (rs of .15, .29, and .10, ns). We should note that differences in the variances associated with the variables entered into any of these correlational analyses do not account for differences in the magnitudes of the coefficients. For example, there was no tendency for variances to be lower in the on-line task conditions in comparison with memory-based conditions for either recall ratio or judgment measures.

Results from some secondary analyses also fit the theoretical account we have advanced to explain the on-line versus memory-based task differences. Evidence items in Experiments 1 and 2 were separated into judgment-relevant and judgment-irrelevant sets to explore the effects of task (on-line versus memory-based) on the relative recall of these two types of items. One prediction from our initial theoretical account is that relevant and irrelevant items will receive differential attention and encoding in on-line tasks, where relevant items should be well remembered in comparison with irrelevant items. However, under memory-based task conditions there would be no reason to expect differential treatment of the two sets of items until after the judgment task is presented. Thus, there should be little or no difference in the recall of relevant and irrelevant items in memory-based tasks. The pattern of means of proportion recalled measures predicted by this hypothesis was observed in the results from Experiments 1 and 2: distinctively high recall of judgment-relevant items in the on-line task and no advantage in recall of relevant items in the memory-based task (all Task × Item Type interactions significant at the .05 level, means in Table 15.2).

One series of analyses, concerned with subjects' tendency to interpret evidence in a manner biased to fit their final judgments, did not find support for biased interpretation effects. In several of the experiments, subjects were asked, after making their judgments and recalling the evidence, to review each evidence item and to rate its implication for the judgment. We had thought that these ratings might be correlated with the final judgments (e.g.,

Table 15.2. *Proportion recalled measures of memory for evidence from experiments 1 and 2*

	Task			
	On-line		Memory based	
Judgment	Relevant	Irrelevant	Relevant	Irrelevant
Experiment 1				
Job suitability judgment	.36	.26	.26	.28
Experiment 2				
Job suitability judgment	.40	.34	.18	.33
Gender judgment	.25	.12	.17	.15

a subject who judged the job candidate as unsuited would also rate the evidence items as more strongly implying unsuited than a subject who judged the candidate to be suited). We also speculated that the biased inter-pretation effect would be more pronounced in on-line tasks in comparison with memory-based tasks. However, our results did not show significant or consistent correlations between final judgments and postjudgment item rat-ings under any of our experimental conditions. (Of course, these results may merely indicate that our materials were relatively unambiguous and did not permit much variance in individual interpretations.)

A recipe for memory–judgment correlations?

At times our research program has seemed like a quest for conditions suffi-cient to produce a significant correlation between recall ratio and judgment measures. Our theoretical clue was to seek task conditions in which subjects would be forced to rely on evidence previously stored in long-term memory and where no previously made judgment (also stored in memory) was available on which to base the judgment. In fact, our quest has been mostly successful; we did find several experimental tasks in which sizable memory–judgment relationships were reliably obtained.

The goal of our analysis is to find useful fundamental categories that classify the subject's cognitive processing strategies (five models) and to find judgment tasks (two tasks) that can serve as the building blocks to describe behavior in more complex tasks. Predictive power in the system comes from the links we have hypothesized between process models and tasks. How-ever, we should attach a warning that several of our attempts to obtain memory–judgment correlations were not successful. Most of these failures occurred early in our research program, before we realized the importance of preventing subjects from making spontaneous on-line judgments relevant to the final judgment (in memory-based tasks). The best advice we can give researchers who extend our methods to new domains is to carefully study the types of judgments that subjects make spontaneously in their experimental tasks and then to insure that these judgments are not related to the final judgment of interest to the experimenter.

This warning is not simply a methodological note. The implication is that most judgments, laboratory and real world, do not take the simple forms of the availability and independence models we identified at the start of our analysis. Rather, conditions that invoke the biased-retrieval, biased-encoding, and incongruity-biased-encoding models associated with on-line tasks are quite common, making predictions of memory–judgment relationships difficult or impossible. We would go a step further and warn that most important judgments occur in an extended time frame and no not depend on the application of a simple operator like those identified in the algebraic, stochastic, and heuristic traditions that dominate the psychological literature. For example, even in the present experiments (2 and 3), talk-aloud reports suggest that our spontaneous judgment conditions (gender and sociability) are treated as both on-line and memory-based tasks by the subjects. They both induce an initial impression on-line, spontaneously, and rejudge in a memory-based fashion when the experimenter explicitly requests a judgment at the end of the experiment. Of course, even this complication seems trivial when compared to the duration and complexity of real-world legal (Pennington & Hastie, 1981); medical (Elstein, Shulman, & Sprafka, 1978); or diplomatic (Axelrod, 1976; Jervis, 1976) judgments. Nonetheless, simple models such as the five we begin with here constitute the proper starting point for a reduction of the complex cases to their tractable theoretical components.

Conclusion

In this article we have made the case for a distinction between two types of judgment tasks: on-line and memory-based. In support of the distinction we outlined a theoretical, information processing framework for memory–judgment relationships and identified five alternate models for processing that differed in the causal relations among memory and judgment events. The alternate models were linked to the on-line versus memory-based task distinction. The most persuasive argument for the distinction was the predicted pattern of memory–judgment relationships that we found in the results of four experiments in which on-line and memory-based tasks were presented to subjects in several social judgment domains.

Traditional theories of human judgment do not provide useful concepts to describe memory–judgment relationships. For example, cognitive algebra approaches to judgment have yielded considerable progress in our understanding of process but have not illuminated memory–judgment relationships (Anderson, 1981). Linear statistical models of judgment policies are also mute on the memory–judgment relationship (Hammond & Summers, 1965). Similarly, approaches based on normative mathematical models would not distinguish between the memory-based and on-line task conditions that affected our subjects' behavior (Edwards, 1968).

The judgment heuristics approach was one inspiration for our information processing analysis (Tversky & Kahneman, 1974). We believe that the general form of the judgment heuristics approach provides the best current characterization of the judgment information processing system. However, the description of judgment operators, memory processes, and memory structures is extremely abstract, and specific hypotheses about the task conditions under which availability heuristics will be activated are not included in recent statements of the heuristics and biases approach (Kahneman, Slovic, & Tversky, 1982). This makes the formulation too abstract to yield a priori, testable predictions or even to describe many phenomena in the judgment literature.

The on-line versus memory-based distinction is based on differences in the sources of the information that is entered as input to the hypothetical judgment operator. Research in our laboratory suggests that the two types of tasks may affect performance in ways that are not obvious from the memory–judgment results reported here. In our experiments, talk-aloud protocols suggest that our subjects are using judgment operators that can best be described (within the larger information processing system) as algebraic combination rules similar to the weighted average or weighted sum principles identified by Anderson (1981), Hammond (1955; Hammond & Summers, 1965), and their colleagues. We believe that our subjects' operators are closest to the anchor and adjust procedures proposed by Lopes (1982) and Einhorn and Hogarth (1985) in recent extensions of the algebraic modeling approach. However, subjects do not adopt the anchor and adjust operator as frequently in memory-based tasks as in on-line tasks. Thus, there is a suggestion that the heart of the judgment process, the operator, is affected by on-line versus memory-based task conditions. A second, suggestive observation is that when evidence information is unbalanced to favor one side of the judgment, the final judgment will be both more polarized and held with more confidence in on-line as compared to memory-based tasks.

For the moment, the on-line versus memory-based distinction has made one important contribution to our understanding of human judgment. It is a mistake to look for simple memory–judgment relationships in on-line judgment tasks. Memory and judgment will be directly related, though, when the judgment is based directly on the retrieval of evidence information in memory-based judgment tasks.

Note

1 A detailed report, which has been submitted for publication, is available from the authors.

References

Alba, J. W., & Hasher, L. (1983). Is memory schematic? *Psychological Bulletin, 93,* 203–231.

Anderson, N. H. (1981). *Foundations of information integration theory.* New York: Academic Press.

Anderson, N. H., & Hubert, S. (1963). Effects of concomitant verbal recall on order effects in personality impression formation. *Journal of Verbal Learning and Verbal Behavior, 2,* 379–391.

Asch, S. (1946). Forming impressions of personality. *Journal of Abnormal and Social Psychology, 41,* 258–290.

Axelrod, R. (1976). *Structure of decision.* Princeton, NJ: Princeton University Press.

Bargh, J. A. (1982). Attention and automaticity in the processing of self-relevant information. *Journal of Personality and Social Psychology, 43,* 425–436.

Bellezza, F. S., & Bower, G. H. (1981). Person stereotypes and memory for people. *Journal of Personality and Social Psychology, 41,* 856–865.

Berman, J. S., Read, S. J., & Kenny, D. A. (1983). Processing inconsistent social information. *Journal of Personality and Social Psychology, 45,* 1211–1224.

Beyth-Marom, R., & Fischhoff, B. (1977). Direct measures of availability and judgments of category frequency. *Bulletin of the Psychonomic Society, 9,* 236–238.

Carlston, D. E. (1980). The recall and use of traits and events in social inference processes. *Journal of Experimental Social Psychology, 16,* 303–328.

Clark, L. F., & Woll, S. B. (1981). Stereotype biases: A reconstructive analysis of their role in reconstructive memory. *Journal of Personality and Social Psychology, 41,* 1064–1072.

Combs, B., & Slovic, P. (1979). Newspaper coverage of causes of death. *Journalism Quarterly, 56,* 837–849.

Dellarosa, D., & Bourne, L. E., Jr. (1984). Decisions and memory: Differential retrievability of consistent and contradictory evidence. *Journal of Verbal Learning and Verbal Behavior, 23,* 669–682.

Edwards, W. (1968). Conservatism in human information processing. In B. Kleinmuntz (Ed.), *Formal representation of human judgment* (pp. 17–52). New York: Wiley.

Einhorn, H. J., & Hogarth, R. M. (1985). Ambiguity and uncertainty in probabilistic inference. *Psychological Review, 92,* 433–461.

Elstein, A. S., Shulman, L. S., & Sprafka, S. A. (1978). *Medical problem solving.* Cambridge, MA: Harvard University Press.

Fiske, S. T., Kenny, D. A., & Taylor, S. E. (1982). Structural models for the mediation of salience effects on attribution. *Journal of Experimental Social Psychology, 18,* 105–127.

Gabrielcik, A., & Fazio, R. H. (1984). Priming and frequency estimation: A strict test of the availability heuristic. *Personality and Social Psychology Bulletin, 10,* 85–89.

Hamilton, D. L., Katz, L. B., & Leirer, V. O. (1980). Cognitive representation of personality impressions: Organizational processes in first impression formation. *Journal of Personality and Social Psychology, 39,* 1050–1063.

Hammond, K. R. (1955). Probabilistic functioning and the clinical method. *Psychological Review, 62,* 255–262.

Hammond, K. R., Stewart, T. R., Brehmer, B., & Steinmann, D. (1975). Social judgment theory. In M. Kaplan & S. Schwartz (Eds.), *Human judgment and decision processes* (pp. 2–27). New York: Academic Press.

Hammond, K. R., & Summers, D. A. (1965). Cognitive dependence on linear and nonlinear cues. *Psychological Review, 72*, 215–224.

Hastie, R. (1980). Memory for behavioral information that confirms or contradicts a personality impression. In R. Hastie, T. M. Ostrom, E. B. Ebbesen, R. S. Wyer, Jr., D. L. Hamilton, & D. E. Carlston (Eds.), *Person memory: The cognitive basis of social perception* (pp. 155–178). Hillsdale, NJ: Erlbaum.

Hastie, R. (1981). Schematic principles in human memory. In E. T. Higgins, C. P. Herman, & M. P. Zanna (Eds.), *Social cognition: The Ontario Symposium* (Vol. 1, pp. 39–88). Hillsdale, NJ: Erlbaum.

Hastie, R. (1984). Causes and effects of causal attribution. *Journal of Personality and Social Psychology, 46*, 44–56.

Hastie, R., & Carlston, D. E. (1980). Theoretical issues in person memory. In R. Hastie, T. M. Ostrom, E. B. Ebbesen, R. S. Wyer, Jr., D. L. Hamilton, & D. E. Carlston (Eds.), *Person memory: The cognitive basis of social perception* (pp. 1–54). Hillsdale, NJ: Erlbaum.

Hastie, R., & Kumar, A. P. (1979). Person memory: Personality traits as organizing principles in memory for behavior. *Journal of Personality and Social Psychology, 37*, 25–38.

Higgins, E. T., King, G. A., & Mavin, G. H. (1982). Individual construct accessibility and subjective impressions and recall. *Journal of Personality and Social Psychology, 43*, 35–47.

Hoffman, C., Mischel, W., & Mazze, K. (1981). The role of purpose in the organization of information about behavior: Trait-based versus goal-based categories in person cognition. *Journal of Personality and Social Psychology, 40*, 211–225.

Jervis, R. (1976). *Perception and misperception in international politics.* Princeton: Princeton University Press.

Jones, E. E., & Pittman, T. S. (1982). Towards a general theory of strategic self-presentation. In J. Suls (Ed.), *Psychological perspectives on the self* (pp. 141–184). Hillsdale, NJ: Erlbaum.

Kahneman, D., Slovic, P., & Tversky, A. (1982). *Judgment under uncertainty: Heuristics and biases.* New York: Cambridge University Press.

Kelley, H. H. (1973). The processes of causal attribution. *American Psychologist, 28*, 107–128.

Langer, E. J., Blank, A., & Chanowitz, B. (1978). The mindlessness of ostensibly thoughtful action: The role of "placebic" information in interpersonal interaction. *Journal of Personality and Social Psychology, 36*, 635–642.

Leamer, E. E. (1974). False models and post-data model construction. *Journal of the American Statistical Association, 69*, 122–131.

Leamer, E. E. (1975). "Explaining your results" as access-biased memory. *Journal of the American Statistical Association, 70*, 88–93.

Lichtenstein, M., & Srull, T. K. (1985). Conceptual and methodological issues in examining the relationship between consumer memory and judgment. In L. F. Alwitt & A. A. Mitchell (Eds.), *Psychological processes and advertising effects: Theory, research, and application.* Hillsdale, NJ: Erlbaum.

Lichtenstein, S., Slovic, P., Fischhoff, B., Layman, M., & Combs, B. (1978). Judged frequency of lethal events. *Journal of Experimental Psychology: Human Learning and Memory, 4*, 551–578.

Lingle, J. H., Dukerich, J. M., & Ostrom, T. M. (1983). Accessing information in memory-based impression judgments: Incongruity versus negativity in retrieval selectivity. *Journal of Personality and Social Psychology, 44*, 262–272.

Lingle, J. H., Geva, N., Ostrom, T. M., Lieppe, M. R., & Baumgardner, M. H. (1979). Thematic effects of person judgments on impression formation. *Journal of Personality and Social Psychology, 37*, 674–687.

Lingle, J. H., & Ostrom, T. M. (1979). Retrieval selectivity in memory-based impression judgments. *Journal of Personality and Social Psychology, 37*, 180–194.

Lopes, L. L. (1982). Toward a procedural theory of judgment. *Wisconsin Human Information Processing Program, Technical Report, 17*, 1–49.

Markus, H. (1977). Self-schemata and the processing of information about the self. *Journal of Personality and Social Psychology, 35*, 63–78.

McArthur, L. Z. (1980). Illusory causation and illusory correlation: Two epistemological accounts. *Personality and Social Psychology Bulletin, 6*, 507–519.

Pennington, N., & Hastie, R. (1981). Juror decision-making: The generalization gap. *Psychological Bulletin, 89*, 246–287.

Reyes, R. M., Thompson, W. C., & Bower, G. H. (1980). Judgmental biases resulting from differing availabilities of arguments. *Journal of Personality and Social Psychology, 39*, 2–12.

Ross, M., & Sicoly (1979). Egocentric biases in availability and attribution. *Journal of Personality and Social Psychology, 37*, 322–336.

Sherman, S. J., Zehner, K. S., Johnson, J., & Hirt, E. R. (1983). Social explanation: The role of timing, set, and recall on subjective likelihood estimates. *Journal of Personality and Social Psychology, 44*, 1127–1143.

Smith, E. R. (1984). Model of social inference processes. *Psychological Review, 91*, 392–413.

Snyder, M., & Uranowitz, W. (1978). Reconstructing the past: Some cognitive consequences of person perception. *Journal of Personality and Social Psychology, 36*, 941–950.

Srull, T. K. (1981). Person memory: Some tests of associative storage and retrieval models. *Journal of Experimental Psychology: Human Learning and Memory, 7*, 440–463.

Swann, W. B., Jr. (1984). Quest for accuracy in person perception: A matter of pragmatics. *Psychological Review, 91*, 457–477.

Taylor, S. E., & Crocker, J. (1981). Schematic bases of social information processing. In E. T. Higgins, C. P. Herman, & M. P. Zanna (Eds.), *Social cognition: The Ontario Symposium* (Vol. 1, pp. 89–134). Hillsdale, NJ: Erlbaum.

Taylor, S. E., & Thompson, S. C. (1982). Stalking the elusive "vividness" effect. *Psychological Review, 89*, 155–181.

Thomas, E. A. C., & Hogue, A. (1976). Apparent weight of evidence, decision criteria, and confidence ratings in juror decision making. *Psychological Review, 83*, 442–465.

Tversky, A., & Kahneman, D. (1973). Availability: A heuristic for judging frequency and probability. *Cognitive Psychology, 5*, 207–232.

Tversky, A., & Kahneman, D. (1974). Judgment under uncertainty: Heuristics and biases. *Science, 185*, 1124–1131.

Weiner, B. (1985). "Spontaneous" causal thinking. *Psychological Bulletin, 97*, 74–84.

Winter, L., & Uleman, J. S. (1984). When are social judgments made? Evidence for the spontaneousness of trait inferences. *Journal of Personality and Social Psychology,* *47*, 237–252.

Woll, S. B., & Graesser, A. C. (1982). Memory discrimination for information typical or atypical of person schemas. *Social Cognition, 1*, 287–310.

Wyer, R. S., Jr., & Srull, T. K. (1980). The processing of social stimulus information: A conceptual integration. In R. Hastie, T. M. Ostrom, E. B. Ebbesen, R. S. Wyer, Jr., D. L. Hamilton, & D. E. Carlston (Eds.), *Person memory: The cognitive basis of social perception* (pp. 227–300). Hillsdale, NJ: Erlbaum.

16 Explanation-based decision making: Effects of memory structure on judgment

Nancy Pennington and Reid Hastie

A central question in decision making research concerns how people evaluate available evidence. We have argued that evidence evaluation in complex diagnostic decisions is *explanation based* (Pennington & Hastie, 1986). By this we mean that decision makers begin the decision process by constructing a causal model to explain the available facts and then base subsequent decisions on the causal interpretation imposed on the evidence.

In explanation-based decision making, the decision maker constructs a causal explanation of the evidence by combining evidence with related world knowledge and expectations about what constitutes an adequate explanation in the decision domain. This process results in a mental representation of the evidence that constitutes an interpretation of what the evidence is about, incorporating inferred events and causal connections between events in addition to relevant evidentiary events. Our conception of this intermediate summary representation of the evidence is analogous to the "situation model" proposed by van Dijk and Kintsch (1983) in text comprehension research or the "mental models" proposed by investigators conducting research on problem solving (e.g., Gentner & Stevens, 1983; Johnson-Laird, 1983). The structure of the causal model will be domain specific. For example, we have proposed that a juror uses story structures to organize and interpret evidence in criminal trials (Pennington & Hastie, 1981, 1986), but different causal rules and structures would underlie an internist's causal model of a patient's condition (Pople, 1982), a merchant's

This chapter originally appeared in the *Journal of Experimental Psychology: Learning, Memory, and Cognition*, 1988, *14*(3), 521–533. Copyright © 1988 by the American Psychological Association. Reprinted by permission.

This research was supported by National Science Foundation Law and Social Sciences Program Grant SES-80-12002, by University of Chicago Graduate School of Business Faculty Research Support, and by funding from the Alfred P. Sloan Foundation to Reid Hastie at the Center for Advanced Study in the Behavioral Sciences.

image of the economic factors in a resort town (Hogarth, Michaud, & Mery, 1980), a diplomat's cognitive map of political forces in the Middle East (Axelrod, 1976), or an engineer's mental model of an electrical circuit (de Kleer & Brown, 1983).

The purpose of the present research is to test three claims of our explanation-based decision approach. First, we propose that the explanation structure is constructed by the decision maker spontaneously and stored in memory. Second, we claim that the causal explanation imposed on the evidence and stored in memory determines the decision alternative chosen. Third, we claim that the coherence of the explanation the decision maker is able to construct influences the confidence associated with the decision. Tests of these claims depend on understanding the causal structure of explanations within a particular decision domain. In the present research, we concentrate on decisions similar to those a juror would make when presented with evidence in a criminal trial because specific proposals have been made concerning explanation structures in this domain (Pennington & Hastie, 1981, 1986; Bennett & Feldman, 1981).

Explanation-based decision making in judicial decisions

The juror's decision task is a prototype of the tasks to which the explanation-based model should apply: First, a massive "database" of evidence is input at trial, frequently requiring several days to present. Second, the evidence comes in a scrambled sequence; usually several witnesses and exhibits convey pieces of a historical puzzle in a jumbled temporal sequence. Third, the evidence is piecemeal and full of gaps in its depiction of the historical events that are the focus of reconstruction: Event descriptions are incomplete, usually some critical events were not observed by the available witnesses, and information about personal reactions and motivations is not presented (often because of the rules of evidence). Finally, subparts of the evidence (e.g., individual sentences or statements) are interdependent in their probative implications for the verdict. The meaning of one statement cannot be assessed in isolation because it depends on the meanings of several related statements.

Explanation structure

Empirical research has demonstrated that the juror's explanation of legal evidence takes the form of a "story" in which causal and intentional relations among events are prominent (Pennington, 1981; Pennington & Hastie, 1986). For this reason we have called our application of the explanation-based framework to individual juror decisions the Story Model. The explanation structure, the story, is constructed from information explicitly presented at trial and knowledge possessed by the juror. Two kinds of knowledge are critical: (a) expectations about what makes a complete story and (b) knowledge about events similar in content to those that are the topic of dispute.

It is well established that people have knowledge about the kinds of information necessary to form a story (Kintsch & van Dijk, 1978; Mandler, 1984; Rumelhart, 1977; Stein & Glenn, 1979), and that these expectations influence the cognitive processing of narrative texts (e.g., Haberlandt, Berian, & Sandson, 1980) and the mental representation of story information (e.g., Kintsch, Mandel, & Kozminsky, 1977). An important aspect of this knowledge is that stories are expected to consist of a set of interrelated *episodes*, and each episode should contain *initiating events*, *goals*, *actions*, *consequences*, and accompanying *states*, in a particular causal configuration (see Mandler, 1984; Pennington & Hastie, 1986; Trabasso & van den Broek, 1985). Each component of an episode may consist of an episode so that the story structure can be represented as a hierarchy of embedded episodes (see Trabasso & van den Broek, 1985).

In decision-making tasks, this general knowledge about the structure of human purposive action sequences and of stories, characterized as an episode schema, serves several important functions. First, these expectations organize evidentiary events according to the causal and intentional relations among them as perceived by the juror. Expectations about the kinds of information necessary to make a story tell the juror when important pieces of the explanation structure are missing and when inferences must be made. Second, the hierarchical nature of the story representation helps the juror identify the most important story events such that the highest level story episode characterizes the most important features of "what happened." Finally, knowledge about the structure of stories allows the juror to form an opinion concerning the *completeness* of the evidence, the extent to which a story has all its parts.

More than one story may be constructed by the juror, but one story will usually be accepted as more coherent than the others. *Coherence* comprises judgments of completeness, consistency, and plausibility. Consistency is the extent to which the story does not contain contradictions and the plausibility of a story may be assessed by comparing story sequences to known or imagined events in the real world. If more than one story is judged to be coherent, then the story will not be unique and uncertainty will result. If there is one coherent story, this story will be accepted as the explanation of the evidence and will be instrumental in reaching a decision.

Choice set

Concomitant with or subsequent to the construction of a causal model of the evidence, the decision maker is engaged in a separate activity to learn or create a set of alternatives from which an action will be chosen. In some decision tasks the potential actions are given to the decision maker (instructions from the trial judge on verdict alternatives) or known beforehand (treatment options available to a physician). In others, creation of alternatives is a major activity of the decision maker (e.g., drafting alternate regulations for industrial waste disposal, planning alternate marketing strategies, or negotiating alternate acceptable trade contracts). These solution design tasks may invoke their own embedded decision tasks.

In criminal trials the decision maker receives information about the set of potential solutions at the end of the trial in the judge's instructions on the law. The process of learning the verdict categories is a one-trial learning task in which the material to be learned is very abstract. Interference may occur from jurors' prior knowledge of concepts such as first degree murder, manslaughter, armed robbery, and so on. The juror attempts to learn the defining features (elements of the crime) of each verdict alternative and a decision rule specifying their appropriate combination. We hypothesize that the conceptual unit is a category (frame) defined by a list of critical features referring to *identity, mental state, circumstances,* and *actions* required for the verdict alternative (Kaplan, 1978; Pennington & Hastie, 1981).

Match process

A decision is made when the causal model of the evidence is successfully matched to an alternative in the choice set. Confidence in the final decision will be partly determined by the goodness of fit of the evidence–solution pairing and whether there is more than one winning combination. For example, a juror may have to decide whether a story circumstance such as "pinned against a wall" is a good match to a required circumstance, "unable to escape," for a verdict of not guilty by reason of self-defense. The classification process in the juror's task is aided by relatively direct relations between attributes of the decision categories and the components of the episode schema. The criminal law has evolved so that the main attributes of the decision categories suggested by legal experts (Kaplan, 1978) – identity, mental state, circumstances, and actions – correspond closely to the central features of human action sequences represented as episodes – initiating events, goals, actions, and accompanying states.

Alternative models

All of the major types of models that have appeared in the mathematical, economic, and psychological literatures on decision making have been applied to the juror decision-making task. Pennington and Hastie (1981) distinguished four primary classes of models. *Information integration* models (Kaplan & Kemmerick, 1974; Ostrom, Werner, & Saks, 1978) describe the juror's decision process as a series of independent evaluations of evidence items on a single dimension of culpability, culminating in a calculation in which all of the item values are weighted and summed to determine a final judgment of probability of guilt. *Bayesian probability* models (Marshall &

Wise, 1975; Schum & Martin, 1982) describe the decision process as a sequence of multiplicative products of the prior opinion and diagnosticity of each evidence item. Most applications of the Bayesian model treat the evidence items as independent sources of information, but recent work by Schum and his colleagues has incorporated conditional dependencies among the implications of the items. *Poisson process* models (Thomas & Hogue, 1976) describe the decision as a constant accumulation of the weight of the evidence until a critical stochastic event occurs that fixes the weight at a final value. The final value is compared to a decision criterion and a decision is made to convict or acquit. *Sequential weighting* models (N. H. Anderson, 1959; Einhorn & Hogarth, 1985; Lopes, 1982) describe the process as a series of opinion revision, where each revision is the weighted average of the previous judgment and the value of the current evidence item.

The traditional models have contributed to our understanding of decision-making processes, but there are many phenomena associated with decision making in realistic legal tasks that lie beyond these approaches. For example, our research finds that jurors' decisions do not show a continuous updating pattern across evidence presentation; that interdependencies among evidence items are pervasive and important to jurors; that inferences about missing or unstated events are common; that reasoning about uncertainty does not follow the rules of conventional probability theory; and that the penultimate step in the decision process involves reasoning about multiattribute verdict categories, rather than a single dimension of "guiltiness" (Pennington & Hastie, 1986, 1987; Schum & Martin, 1982). A distinctive assumption in our explanation-based approach to decision making is the hypothesis that decision makers construct an intermediate memory representation of the evidence and that this representation, rather than the original "raw" evidence, is the basis of the final decision (see also Medin, Altom, Edelson, & Freko, 1982; Tversky & Kahneman, 1983; Wallsten & Barton, 1982). Moreover, we propose that this representation is organized according to causal relations between events that "explain" the evidence. Interposition of this organization facilitates evidence comprehension, directs the inferences drawn, enables the decision maker to reach a decision, and determines the confidence assigned to the accuracy or success of the decision. In the present article we report research that supports these assumptions and that is inconsistent with the traditional models in the sense that we identify reliable patterns of memory, evidence evaluation, and decision behavior that are not anticipated by the traditional formulations.

Research

Our previous research on the Story Model provided descriptions of mental representations of evidentiary information and verdict information at one point in time during the decision process (Pennington & Hastie, 1986). Two results were established that support the Story Model as a viable theory of decision making in the juror context. First, the evidence summaries constructed by jurors had story structure and verdict structures looked like category structures. Second, jurors who chose different verdicts had constructed different stories such that there was a distinct causal configuration of events that constituted a story corresponding to each verdict category. Moreover, jurors choosing different verdicts did not have systematically different verdict representations, nor did they apply different classification criteria. Thus, verdict decisions covaried with story structures but did not covary with verdict learning or story classification.

Although previous research provided strong descriptive support for the idea that jurors' representations of evidence take the form of stories, the interview methodology used in the research precluded strong inferences concerning the functional role of stories in the decision phase. Data were obtained by interviewing jurors drawn from jury pools after they had watched a 3-hr videotaped trial. Interviews may have created a demand for a story as a conversational form, a justification of their decisions (Clark, 1983; Tetlock & Manstead, 1985). In the following experiments, we directly test whether or not subjects *spontaneously* construct causal explanations for the evidence in the form of stories and whether or not this causal explanation mediates the subsequent decision.

Experiment 1

In this study we extend the conclusions of our previous interview study (Pennington & Hastie, 1986) by using conventional laboratory methods with college students. The major motivation for this first experiment was to determine whether or not mental representations that resemble stories are constructed *spontaneously* in the course of the juror's performance, that is, without the prompt of an experimenter's requests to discuss the evidence or the decision. We also tested our theoretical proposition that the perceived importance of evidence items can be predicted from the role of each evidence item in the story structure.

In the interview study, we obtained detailed descriptions of each juror's mental representation of the evidence at a particular point in time. As noted earlier, these representations were characterized by causally connected sequences of events, including events referred to in trial testimony as well as events inferred by the jurors, and these causal sequences were in the form of stories. Among jurors who chose a particular verdict there was substantial overlap of their story structures. Therefore, for each verdict group, we developed a causal network, designated the *verdict story*, which included those events and causal connections that were present in 80% of the individual juror stories within that verdict group. In the following description of the present research, we refer to evidence items as associated with or not associated with the different verdict stories derived from the earlier interview study. By this we mean that a particular evidence item refers to an event that was included in or not included in a particular verdict story.

In the present experiment subjects' responses to sentences presented in a recognition memory task were used to draw conclusions about their postdecision representations of evidence (Bransford & Franks, 1971; Brewer & Dupree, 1983; Kintsch, 1974). Our predictions were derived from the Story Model and from recent research by Kintsch and his colleagues concerning memory representations in text comprehension and their relation to recognition memory task performance (van Dijk & Kintsch, 1983; Kintsch, 1986; Perrig & Kintsch, 1985; Schmalhofer & Glavanov, 1986). On the basis of this research, we assume that when evidence is presented, the subject constructs a verbatim representation of the surface structure of the evidence (in the present experiment the evidence was presented as a written text), a semantic representation of the evidence in the form of a propositional textbase, and a situation model that represents an interpretation of what the evidence is about (in our terms, this is the juror's story that we hypothesize is a determinant of the juror's decision). When subjects are presented with a recognition test sentence, they are asked to judge whether or not that sentence was presented as evidence, that is, whether it occurred in the text verbatim. However, a vast amount of research supports the claim that subjects respond to recognition judgments by using information from all three representations: verbatim, propositional, and situational (e.g., Bower, Black, & Turner, 1979; Bransford, Barclay, & Franks, 1972; Bransford & Franks, 1971; Brewer & Dupree, 1983; Garnham, 1981; Kintsch, 1974, 1986; Perrig & Kintsch, 1985; Reder, 1982; Schmalhofer & Glavanov, 1986; Sulin & Dooling, 1974). Therefore, the test sentences most likely to be "recognized" as evidence will be those for which the subject can potentially find corresponding information in all three memory representations.

Specific Story Model predictions for the recognition memory task following from these assumptions were as follows. First, subjects should be most likely to recognize test sentences that had been presented as evidence ("old" items) *and* referred to events that were part of the story corresponding to the subject's verdict decision (i.e., referred to events that were in the juror's situation model as well as in the textbase). Note that the test sentences for which we predicted the highest rates of correct recognitions (hit rates) were from different sets (verdict stories) for subjects making different decisions. A similar argument led to predictions concerning false recognitions ("recognizing" a new test sentence that was not presented as evidence) for subjects choosing different verdicts. Subjects were expected to falsely recognize test sentences not presented as evidence when the sentence referred to an event associated with the story corresponding to the subject's verdict decision more often than when the sentence referred to an event associated with a rejected verdict story or to an event not associated with any story. Thus, we also predicted different patterns of false alarm rates for subjects making different decisions. If these predictions are confirmed, then we can conclude that predicted story inferences and elaborations supporting such inferences were made *spontaneously*, because there was no experimental requirement to discuss the decision.

Subjects' ratings of the importance of each evidence item for their decisions were also used as indicants of the nature of their postdecision representations of evidence. Trabasso has shown (Trabasso & Sperry, 1985; Trabasso & van den Broek, 1985) that importance ratings of story statements are predicted by the statement's causal and logical relations to other statements in the text. Analogously we have claimed that the role of the evidence item in the explanation structure will index its importance in the decision. Therefore, we expected that importance ratings of evidence items would be predicted by (a) whether or not the item was in the verdict story for subjects choosing that verdict and (b) the hierarchical and causal role of the evidence item in the story. If these results are obtained, then additional support is gained for the spontaneous construction of a story and for the role of the explanation structure in indexing the relative importance of evidentiary information.

Method

Materials. In our previous research subjects watched a realistic, 3-hr videotaped reenactment of a criminal trial, *Commonwealth v. Johnson*, and subsequently provided think-aloud protocols relevant to their decisions. In this stimulus trial, the defendant, Johnson, was charged with stabbing another man, Caldwell, to death in a barroom fight. In the present study a shorter, written version of the *Commonwealth v. Johnson* trial was prepared, consisting of an indictment, 119 evidence items (sentences) attributed to a series of witnesses, and instructions on the two verdict alternatives and on standards of proof. The two verdict alternatives were *guilty of murder* and *not guilty* (by reason of self-defense). The order of witnesses and the order of evidence items within witnesses were the same for all subjects and were similar to that of the original videotaped trial. A sample of the evidence items from three witnesses is shown in Table 16.1.

In order to understand how we constructed recognition test materials and analyzed importance ratings of evidence items, it is important to understand the distinction between the evidence presented at trial and our concept of verdict stories. The evidence is a series of assertions by witnesses that certain events occurred. The juror chooses to believe only some of these assertions and will make inferences that other events occurred, events that are never stated explicitly in the evidence, as well as inferences concerning causal connections between events. This activity on the part of the juror results in a mental structuring of the evidence that is the "juror's story." Moreover, among jurors who choose the same verdict, there is a substantial similarity among their individual stories. Thus, a verdict story consists of events (including some referred to in evidence and some inferred by jurors) and causal

Table 16.1. *Sample evidence items from written version of stimulus trial: Experiment 1*

Item no.	Evidence item
1	The first witness is a police officer: Sergeant Robert Harris
2	I was on my usual foot patrol at 9:00 p.m.
3	I heard loud voices from the direction of Gleason's Bar
4	Johnson and Caldwell were outside the bar
5	Johnson laughed at Caldwell
6	Caldwell punched Johnson in the face
7	Johnson raised a knife over his head
8	I yelled, "Johnson, don't do it"
9	Johnson stabbed Caldwell in the chest
10	I handcuffed Johnson and called an ambulance
11	Johnson's knife had an eight inch blade
12	There are no streetlights near Gleason's Bar
13	I could see everything clearly from my position across the street
14	The second witness is a medical examiner: Dr. Richard Katz
15	I performed the autopsy examination of Caldwell's body
16	Caldwell died at 9:30 p.m. from a knife wound in the heart
17	Considerable force was required to drive the knife into his chest
18	Caldwell was very intoxicated when he died
19	There was a razor in Caldwell's rear pants pocket
20	The weapon was a sharp kitchen type knife
21	Caldwell was a big man, weighing about 220 pounds
.	
.	
.	
63	The seventh witness is the defendant: Frank Johnson
64	I work as a janitor
65	I suffer from chronic asthma
66	I was in Borda's Lunchroom that morning
67	Caldwell made some loud comments about my wife
68	I wanted to get out of Caldwell's way
69	I got up to leave Borda's
70	Caldwell walked over to me
71	Caldwell threatened to hit me
72	I was very frightened of Caldwell
73	I went to Gleason's Bar that night to watch TV
74	I left Gleason's when Caldwell came in
75	Caldwell followed me out the door
76	Caldwell knocked me down to the ground
77	Then Caldwell pulled his razor out
78	That night I was carrying my fishing knife
79	I held my knife out in front of me
80	Caldwell lunged at me right onto the knife blade
81	I often carry my fishing knife with me
82	I may not have had my knife with me in Borda's

connections between events viewed as "likely to be true" by 80% of subjects who *chose that verdict* in previous research (Pennington & Hastie, 1986).

We can therefore classify each of the 119 evidence items presented to subjects according to whether or not the evidence item is an assertion about events included in the guilty of murder verdict story, the not guilty (self-defense) verdict story, both stories, or neither story. Thirty-nine evidence items referred to events that were in the guilty story only, for example, "Johnson stabbed Caldwell in the chest" (Table 16.1, item 9). Thirty-seven evidence items referred to events that were in the not guilty story only, for example, "Johnson held his knife out in front of himself" (Table 16.1, item 79). Twenty-one evidence items referred to events that were in both stories, for example, "Johnson and Caldwell were outside Gleason's Bar" (Table 16.1, item 4). Twenty-two evidence items referred to events that were in neither story, for example, "There are no streetlights near Gleason's Bar," "Johnson works as a janitor" (Table 16.1, items 12 and 64). Thus, 60 evidence items (39 guilty story only plus 21 both stories) referred to events in the guilty story and 58 evidence items (37 not guilty story only plus 21 both stories) referred to events in the not guilty story.

The recognition test contained 93 test sentences. Sixty-three were "old" sentences selected from the 119 evidence items that subjects would study in the course of making a decision. These were classified according to their relation to the verdict-stories: 21 were evidence items referring to events in the not guilty story, 21 were evidence items referring to events in the guilty story, 16 were evidence items referring to events in both stories, and 5 were evidence items referring to events that were in neither story. The remaining 30 recognition test sentences were "new" sentences, not included in the evidence, that were descriptions of plausible case-relevant events. These were also classified according to their roles in the verdict stories. Eight sentences referred to inferred events in the not guilty story (i.e., not presented as evidence), for example, "Johnson was trying to protect himself" and "Johnson was stunned by Caldwell's punch." Eight sentences referred to inferred events in the guilty story, for example, "Johnson was looking for Caldwell" and "Johnson and Keating were waiting for Caldwell at Gleason's Bar." Fourteen sentences referred to plausible events that were not a part of either verdict story, for example, "Johnson didn't want to lose face by staying home," "The waitress told Keating to stop the fight," and "Borda ordered Johnson and Caldwell to leave his lunchroom." As can be seen from the examples, lure sentences (new sentences not included in the evidence) were not paraphrases or rearrangements of surface orders of evidence items; they always introduced a new but plausible action carried out by the characters who were involved in the events referred to by the evidence. In the case of lure sentences referring to events in verdict stories, they were derived from the statements made by subjects in the prior interview study that had been generated as "intrusions," statements the interview subjects believed were true, although they had not been presented as evidence.

For those evidence items and inferred events in the guilty story (60 evidence items and 8 inferred events), and separately for those evidence items and inferred events in the not guilty story (58 evidence items and 8 inferred events), a causal network was derived (according to procedures outlined by Trabasso & Sperry, 1985; see also Graesser, 1981; Graesser, Robertson, & Anderson, 1981; Pennington, 1981; Schank, 1975, for details of similar analyses) that represented the *causal structure* of each of the verdict stories. On the basis of the causal structure of the verdict story, each evidence item can be described according to two criteria: (a) its degree of causal connectedness and (b) whether or not it is on the causal chain (Trabasso & Sperry, 1985; Trabasso & van den Broek, 1985). Causal connectedness refers to the number of direct causal connections an evidence item has to all other events in the story structure; each evidence item in the story was assigned this number for later analysis. The causal chain is that subset of story events that have causes and consequences leading from the story's opening initiating events to its closing consequences. The chain effectively identifies the highest level story episode and those events causally connected to it. Each evidence item was designated according to whether or not it referred to an event that was on the story causal chain. Forty of the 60 guilty story evidence items were in the guilty causal chain. For example, "Johnson stabbed Caldwell in the chest" (Table 16.1, item 9) is an evidence item in the guilty story *and* in the guilty story causal chain, but "Police Officer Harris yelled, 'Johnson, don't do it'" (Table 16.1, item 8) is an evidence item in the guilty story but *not* in the causal chain. Thirty-four of the 58 not guilty story evidence items were in the not guilty causal chain. For example, "Johnson held his knife out in front of himself" (Table 16.1, item 79) is an evidence item in the not guilty story *and* in the not guilty story causal chain, but "Johnson often carries his fishing knife" (Table 16.1, item 81), is an evidence item in the not guilty story but *not* in the causal chain.

Subjects. Thirty-four college students from the Northwestern University Psychology subject pool participated in the 1-hr experiment, one at a time.

Procedure. All instructions and stimulus materials were presented to subjects individually on the video display of an IBM/PC microcomputer. The experimental session began with general instructions to subjects that they were going to view evidence from a legal trial and to make a decision about the case. A practice case was presented that included an indictment, 10 evidence items, instructions on the law, and the decision question. Subjects then paced themselves through the *Commonwealth v. Johnson* case materials, reading the indictment, the 119 evidence items, and the judge's instructions on the law. Evidence items were presented one at a time and subjects pressed the keyboard space bar to advance to each new sentence. Subjects then indicated the proper verdict for the *Commonwealth v. Johnson* case: Thirteen subjects selected not guilty and 21 selected guilty of murder. Note that, up to this point in the session, subjects did not anticipate memory tests, interviews, or any activity beyond judgments of the verdict.

Following the verdict decision, subjects received instructions for the recognition memory task. If subjects recognized a sentence from the original evidence, they were told to "... respond to each sentence as quickly as possible" by pressing the key labeled "yes" on the IBM keyboard to indicate "yes–old" or the key labeled "no" to indicate "no–new." The instructions made clear that the "yes" response was to indicate they had *seen the sentence*, not that they merely believed the sentence was "true" about the crime events – whether or not it had been presented. Subjects were given recognition items from the practice case as examples and feedback was given explaining when lures were plausible but not actually presented. They then completed the recognition memory test for the *Commonwealth v. Johnson* materials, in which the 93 target and lure sentences were presented in one of three randomly scrambled sequences.

The final task performed by subjects was to rate each sentence presented as evidence for its importance to their decision. These ratings were made on a 65-unit scale labeled according to the verdict selected by each subject: "Important Evidence Against [verdict]" ... "Not Important" ... "Important Evidence For [verdict]."

Results

The hit rates (rate of responding "yes" to an item presented as evidence) and false alarm rates (rate of responding "yes" to an item not presented as evidence) from the recognition memory test are presented in Table 16.2. It is obvious on inspection that verdict decisions predict the higher hit and false alarm rates found for sentences in the stories corresponding to subjects' chosen verdicts. Consistent with Story Model predictions, subjects correctly recognized test sentences that referred to evidence *and* referred to events in their "own" verdict story 85% of the time, compared with 79% correct recognition of test sentences that had been presented as evidence but referred to events in the "other" (rejected) verdict story. Even more significant for the Story Model, subjects falsely recognized lure test sentences that referred to predicted inferences in their own verdict story 29% of the time, to events in the "other" verdict story 18% of the time, and to events in neither story only 7% of the time.

A 2 (guilty/not guilty verdict choice) × 2 (old/new test sentence) × 2 (guilty/not guilty story membership of the test item) analysis of variance (ANOVA) on proportion of "yes–old" responses to test items revealed that the appropriate Verdict × Story Membership interaction effect was reliable, $F(1, 32) = 13.03$, $MS_e = 172.8$, $p < .001$. It is also clear that the truth (old/new) of an item is a major determinant of subject recognition memory, $F(1, 32) = 529.89$, $MS_e = 209.5$, $p < .001$, although increased delay between study and test would be likely to diminish this effect (J. R. Anderson & Bower, 1973; Kintsch, 1974;

Table 16.2. *Percentage of "yes" responses to recognition memory test sentences by subject's verdict choice and the story membership of the test sentence, for old test sentences presented as evidence and new test sentences not presented as evidence: Experiment 1*

Subject's verdict choice	Old items referring to events in		New items referring to events in	
	Guilty story	Not guilty story	Guilty story	Not guilty story
Guilty[a]	84.2	83.9	28.6	16.7
RT (in ms)	265	246	345	278
Not guilty[b]	74.4	86.2	19.2	28.8
RT (in ms)	296	246	327	245

[a] $n = 21$. [b] $n = 13$.

Reder, 1982; Sulin & Dooling, 1974). Response times to recognition test items (transformed to ms per syllable) in each category are also shown in Table 16.2. Response times for correct recognitions ($M = 263$ ms) were not reliably different from response times for false recognitions ($M = 299$ ms), $F(1, 52) = 2.88$, $MS_e = .009$, $p < .10$, although there was a trend for subjects to respond "yes" correctly somewhat faster than to respond "yes" incorrectly.

Subjects' ratings of the importance to their decisions of each evidence item were scaled to range from 0 to 32, with all ratings from the center of the displayed scale (*not important*) to the far left anchor (*against [verdict]*) collapsed to the value of 0. Thus, items that were perceived as supporting the subject's decision would receive positive scale values and items perceived as unimportant (undiagnostic) or opposing the subject's verdict would receive values of zero. This rescaling was performed to allow an analysis of the determinants of perceived positive implicational support for the subject's verdict.[1] The importance ratings are presented in Table 16.3 for subjects in each verdict-choice group. It is clear that items that are in the story corresponding to the subject's chosen verdict received the highest ratings (8.54 for guilty subjects, 9.06 for not guilty subjects), and items in the opposition story are given the lowest ratings (1.99 and 1.65, respectively). Statistical analyses support the conclusion that story membership is a powerful determinant of perceived importance of evidence items, $F(1, 32) = 84.11$, $MS_e = 7.2$, $p < .001$ (Verdict × Story Membership interaction).

A second analysis revealed that causal chain membership and causal connectedness also contributed to subjects' evaluations of the importance of evidence items. Regression analyses on the three factors (whether or not an item was in the verdict story, whether or not the item was in the verdict story causal chain, and number of causal connections) were performed for impor-

Table 16.3. *Mean importance ratings for evidence items by subject's verdict choice and the story membership of the evidence item: Experiment 1*

Subject's verdict choice	Evidence items referring to events in	
	Guilty story	Not guilty story
Guilty[a]	8.54	1.99
Not guilty[b]	1.65	9.06

Note: Responses range from 0 (*not important*) to 32 (*important*).
[a] $n = 21$. [b] $n = 13$.

tance rating measures by subjects choosing a guilty verdict and for importance rating measures by subjects choosing a not guilty verdict. Story status was coded nominally as 0/1 and was entered into the regression analysis first (because causal chain status and causal connectedness are always coded zero if the item is not a story item and therefore include story status). Causal chain status was coded nominally as 0/1 and was entered into the regression analysis second because items on the causal chain are also highly causally connected (Trabasso & Sperry, 1985) and we wished to examine causal connectedness only after causal connectedness accounted for by the causal chain had been entered. Causal connectedness was coded on an interval scale and was entered last into the regression analysis. For importance ratings by subjects choosing a guilty verdict, story status accounted for 31% of the variance in their importance ratings, causal chain status accounted for an additional 9% of the variance, and causal connectedness accounted for an additional 12% of the variance. For importance ratings by subjects choosing a not guilty verdict, story status accounted for 24% of the variance in importance ratings, causal chain status accounted for an additional 27%, and causal connectedness added an additional 5%. Considering these three aspects of story structure together, we can say that approximately 54% of the variance in evaluations of an evidence item's importance can be accounted for by whether or not the item is in the story, whether or not it is in the main episode or causally connected to it, and its causal connectedness above and beyond causal chain status.

Discussion

The key implication of the recognition memory experiment, when considered together with our previous research (Pennington & Hastie, 1986), is that jurors spontaneously, without the prompting of interview questions, construct a story structure summary of the evidence. Evidence is presented at trial by testimony from various witnesses in an order that only partially preserves the causal and temporal sequence of the events to which the testimony refers. Our subjects' ability to discriminate between evidence items that had and had not been presented shows that subjects retain some information about the "surface structure" of the evidence as it was originally presented, under conditions of short delay. However, jurors also construct a chronological representation of the event sequence referred to by testimony, the situation model (van Dijk & Kintsch, 1983) or in our terms the elaborated explanation that gives the evidence meaning, that is the effective mental representation in subsequent decision making. Furthermore, this chronologically ordered causal explanation also serves as a retrieval system when subjects are confronted with a memory task (Brewer & Dupree, 1983). The strongest support for this claim is derived from subjects' responses to lure sentences that had not been presented as evidence. For these items, the effect of the subject's verdict choice is especially dramatic: Subjects are nearly twice as likely to falsely "recognize" lures from their own verdict-story structure as they are to "recognize" lures from the alternative verdict-story structure.

It could be argued that subjects are not retrieving memories at all in these instances, but are assessing only the plausibility of the test item (Reder, 1982, 1987). In the strictest sense, this is probably true in that it is unlikely that subjects are finding in memory exact propositional matches for the test sentences. However, the situational elaborations on which such judgments must be based (Reder, 1982; Schmalhofer & Glavanov, 1986) imply the particular proposition so strongly that subjects believe they have seen the statement as evidence (remember that subjects were given extensive instructions, practice, and feedback concerning the recognition versus plausibility distinction). Moreover, subjects make false recognition judgments almost as fast as they make judgments about sentences that they have seen, and they make them systematically. Even though lures that were not in either story were plausible behaviors that were consistent with evidence presented, the false alarm rate is only 7% for these lures compared to a rate of 29% for lures in verdict stories for subjects' chosen verdicts. Thus, the causal explanation seems to provide a retrieval system for memory for evidence and results in the elevated "yes" response rates to story items associated with the verdict chosen.

Importance rating results corroborate conclusions from previous research that the evidence summary structure was in the form of a story and that structures differed between verdict groups. Our analysis shows that subjects' ratings of the importance of evidence items to their decisions can be predicted from the items' story membership and from the position of the item in the story's causal structure. Moreover, importance ratings correspond to the "effective weights" associated with evidence items that play central roles in many algebraic models for judgment (cf. N. H. Anderson,

1959, 1981; Hammond, Stewart, Brehmer, & Steinmann, 1975; Pennington & Hastie, 1981; Slovic, 1972). Thus, the Story Model directly addresses the question "Where do the weights come from?" that is frequently raised in critical evaluations of the popular linear models for information integration in judgment. The perceived importance of a piece of evidence is determined by its place in the explanatory structure imposed by the decision maker during the evidence evaluation stage of the decision process.

Even though causal explanations are constructed spontaneously in the course of decision making, as indicated by the present and past results, these results are correlational in the sense that subjects determine their assignments to conditions in the experimental design by their verdict decisions. Therefore, we have still not demonstrated that the story constructed by the juror determines the verdict decision. It is possible that story construction is a justification process that occurs after the decision is made. In the next experiment we address the questions of whether or not the story structure evidence summaries are true mediators (i.e., cause) of the final verdict decisions and the extent to which confidence in decisions is affected by story coherence and uniqueness.

Experiment 2

In Experiment 2 we manipulated the order of evidence presentation in the trial so that the underlying prosecution and defense stories were either easy or difficult to construct. We predicted that when the prosecution story was easy to construct but the defense story was not, subjects would be more likely to return guilty verdicts and conversely, that not guilty verdicts would predominate when the defense story was easier to construct. If the difficulty of story construction influences verdicts, it implies that stories are constructed before verdicts are chosen rather than as postdecision justifications.

Stories were considered easy to construct when evidence was presented in "story order," with trial presentation order preserving temporal and causal order between evidence items (Baker, 1978). Stories were considered difficult to construct when the evidence presentation order did not preserve the underlying causal and temporal order. A typical order for evidence presentation that disrupts the natural causal and temporal ordering of events is "witness by witness" (as shown in Table 16.1), so we used this "witness" order for comparison. Thus, the guilty story should be easier to construct when the prosecution evidence follows story order but the defense evidence follows witness order; the not guilty story should be easier to construct when the defense evidence follows story order but the prosecution evidence follows witness order.

In Experiment 2, we also examined subjects' perceptions of the strength of prosecution and defense evidence and their confidence in their decisions. We assume that difficulty in story construction makes it less likely that the story will be fully constructed and will therefore be judged as less complete. For this reason we expected that ratings of prosecution and defense evidence strength would be greater when evidence had been presented in story order compared with when it had been presented in witness order. We have also proposed that subjects' level of certainty or confidence in their decisions will be influenced by the coherence of the constructed story. Thus, we expected to see greater confidence in a verdict when the evidence has been presented in story order than when it has not. We also hypothesized that whether or not the constructed story was perceived as unique would affect confidence. Thus, confidence should be influenced by the coherence of the opposing verdict's story.

Method

Materials. The 119-sentence version of the *Commonwealth v. Johnson* stimulus trial created for Experiment 1 was adapted for use in Experiment 2. One hundred of the 119 evidence items from Experiment 1 were used. The 100 evidence items were divided into two sets: (a) the prosecution evidence comprised the 39 guilty of murder evidence items plus 11 of the items from both and neither story; and (b) the defense evidence comprised the 37 not guilty items plus 13 both and neither items. For each set of evidence, prosecution and defense, two evidence orders were created. In the *story order*, evidence items (within prosecution and defense sets of evidence) were arranged in their natural temporal and causal order, for example, beginning with testimony about events preceding the fatal encounter, followed by testimony concerning the fight that resulted in the victim's death, followed by testimony about the arrest and the autopsy. In the *witness order*, evidence items (within prosecution and defense sets of evidence) were arranged in an order close to their occurrence in the original trial. For example, the policeman testifies about the fight in the evening, the medical examiner testifies about the time of death and the nature of the wound, a friend testifies about events in the morning preceding the fatal encounter, and so forth. The two versions of the defense evidence and the two versions of the prosecution evidence were identical in every way except for the order of the 50 evidence items within the prosecution and within the defense evidence sets. To ensure that any efforts of our order manipulation could not be accounted for by primacy or recency of "important" evidence, we computed the correlations between presentation order of the evidence item and the importance rating of the item (from Experiment 1) for defense and prosecution evidence sets in each of the two orders. None of the four correlations were reliably different from zero, indicating that in both orders of both evidence sets, "strong" evidence was distributed evenly across the 50 serial positions.

The two prosecution versions were combined with the two defense versions to make four different orders of identical evidence items: one in which both prosecution and defense evidence were ordered as stories; one in which the prosecution evidence was in story but the defense evidence was in witness order; one in which the defense evidence was in story order but the prosecution evidence was in witness order; and one in which both prosecution and defense evidence were in witness order. In all four versions, the stimulus trial materials began with an indictment, followed by an opening summary statement that was impartial with respect to prosecution or defense perspectives, followed by the evidence items with prosecution evidence always preceding defense evidence as is usual in legal trials, and concluded with instructions on the law and on standards of proof. All instructions and case materials were tape recorded for presentation to subjects.

Procedure. Subjects were instructed that their task was to listen to evidence from an actual murder trial, to come to a verdict decision, and to answer some questions about the case. They listened to the tape-recorded stimulus trial materials and then responded to written questions. Verdict choice was a dichotomous variable since subjects indicated a decision of guilty of murder or not guilty. Confidence in the verdict choice was assessed by responses on a 5-point scale (1 = *pure guess*, 5 = *very certain*); ratings of prosecution case strength and defense case strength were also obtained on 5-point rating scales (1 = *very weak*, 5 = *very strong*).

Subjects. Subjects were 130 undergraduate and graduate students at Northwestern University (42 subjects) and University of Chicago (88 subjects) who were paid for participation in the experiment. Subjects participated in groups of 2 to 10 subjects in experimental sessions lasting approximately 1 hr. Subject groups were assigned to one of the four experimental conditions in a manner designed to keep cell sizes approximately equal as the experiment progressed. This resulted in about 32 subjects per experimental condition, with Northwestern and University of Chicago subjects represented proportionately in all conditions. Although subjects were run in groups, they were separated by wooden partitions and did not interact. Therefore, individual subject scores were treated as independent observations.

Results

As predicted, subjects were most likely to decide that the defendant was guilty of murder when the prosecution evidence was presented in story order and the defense evidence was presented in witness order (78% chose guilty of murder) and they were least likely to choose the guilty verdict when the defense was presented as a story and the prosecution evidence was not (31% chose guilty of murder) as shown in Table 16.4. Conditions in which both or neither side was presented in story order resulted in intermediate levels of guilty verdicts. To test for all main and interaction effects, the

Table 16.4. *Percentage of subjects choosing a verdict of guilty of murder by prosecution and defense order conditions: Experiment 2*

	Defense evidence		
Prosecution evidence	Story order	Witness order	M
Story order	59	78	69
Witness order	31	63	47
M	45	70	58

dichotomous judgments were analyzed by fitting a (hierarchical) log-linear model to the cell frequencies, with fit determined by a likelihood goodness-of-fit chi-square statistic (Fienberg, 1977). The simplest model that described the observed frequencies included the two-way interactions between verdict and defense evidence order and between verdict and prosecution evidence order, $\chi^2(2, N = 130) = .42, p > .80$. No other model added explanatory power to this model. Put another way, the pattern of verdict choices was accounted for by main effects of defense evidence order and prosecution evidence order with no interaction.

We expected that story order would also affect the perceived strength of the prosecution and defense evidence. As shown in Table 16.5, prosecution evidence was perceived as stronger when presented in story order than it was when presented in witness order, $F(1, 126) = 4.09, MS_e = .53, p < .05$. Moreover, whether or not the *defense* evidence was presented in story order affected the perceived strength of the *prosecution* case, $F(1, 126) = 4.13, MS_e = .53, p < .05$; prosecution evidence was perceived as less strong when the defense evidence was presented in story order than when it was not. An identical pattern of results was obtained for perception of defense evidence strength although statistical reliability was marginal in this analysis. Defense evidence strength was perceived as greater in story order than in witness order, $F(1, 126) = 2.40, MS_e = .62, p < .13$, and the order of the *prosecution* evidence influenced perceptions of the *defense* evidence strength, $F(1, 126) = 3.45, MS_e = .62, p < .07$; the defense evidence was rated as less strong when the prosecution evidence was in story order.

We also predicted that confidence in a chosen verdict would be greater when a more complete story could be constructed. Thus, a person who decided that the defendant was guilty of murder and had heard the prosecution evidence in story order was expected to express more confidence in a guilty verdict than the person who decided that the defendant was guilty but had heard the prosecution evidence in witness order. Similarly, greater confidence was expected from the person choosing not guilty who had heard

Table 16.5. *Mean ratings of strength of prosecution and defense evidence by prosecution and defense order conditions: Experiment 2*

	Defense evidence		
Prosecution evidence	Story order	Witness order	M
Ratings of prosecution evidence			
Story order	3.6	3.7	3.7
Witness order	3.2	3.6	3.4
M	3.4	3.7	
Ratings of defense evidence			
Story order	2.9	2.6	2.8
Witness order	3.1	2.9	3.0
M	3.0	2.8	

Note: Responses range from 1 (*very weak*) to 5 (*very strong*).

Table 16.6. *Mean confidence ratings by verdict choice and by prosecution and defense evidence order conditions: Experiment 2*

Subject's verdict choice	Evidence in story order				
	Both prosecution defense	Prosecution only	Defense only	Neither prosecution defense	M
Guilty[a]	3.69	3.54	3.36	3.30	3.47
Not guilty[b]	3.36	3.13	3.08	3.08	3.16
M	3.53	3.34	3.22	3.19	

Note: Confidence ratings range from 1 (*pure guess*) to 5 (*very certain*).
[a] $n = 75$. [b] $n = 55$.

the defense evidence in story order when compared with a person choosing not guilty having heard the defense evidence in witness order. This prediction was based on the assumption that both persons in the comparison were trying to construct stories but that this endeavor would be more successful and more complete when the evidence was ordered for them. A partially constructed story would be perceived as less complete (as indicated in the evidence strength ratings above) and this was expected to lead to reduced confidence in the verdict.

To test this, subjects were classified according to their verdict choice and according to their evidence-order condition, and confidence ratings were analyzed in a 4 (order conditions) × 2 (guilty/not guilty verdict choice) ANOVA. Subjects choosing guilty verdicts exhibited greater confidence, $F(1, 125) = 4.21$, $MS_e = .60$, $p < .05$, as shown in Table 16.6. The order of evidence also influenced confidence ratings, $F(3, 125) = 4.24$, $MS_e = .60$, $p < .05$, but not as we had predicted. The greatest confidence is expressed by those who heard both prosecution and defense evidence in story order, followed by those who heard the prosecution evidence in story order (but defense in witness order), by those who heard the defense evidence in story order (prosecution in witness order), and by those who heard neither set of evidence in story order (see Table 16.6). Only the contrast between the extremes (both and neither) is statistically reliable ($p < .05$) although the similarity in patterns across order conditions within verdict groups is striking.

Discussion

Story coherence as determined by the presentation order of evidence affects perceptions of evidence strength, verdict decisions, and confidence in decisions. Subjects were more than twice as likely to find the defendant guilty of murder in our stimulus case when prosecution evidence was ordered in story form and defense evidence was not, compared to when defense evidence was presented in story form and prosecution evidence was not (Table 16.4). Subjects rated both the prosecution and defense evidence as stronger when presented in story order than when not presented in story order, even though the evidence items were identical (Table 16.5). These effects cannot be accounted for by differential primacy or recency of strong evidence because (a) in terms of gross order, prosecution evidence preceded defense evidence for all subjects, and (b) within prosecution and defense evidence sets, serial position and the importance of evidence (as rated by subjects in Experiment 1) were uncorrelated.

Our results also provide evidence that it is not just the coherence of one story that affects decisions and perceptions of evidence strength, but rather it is the strength of one story compared with the alternative that is important (Einhorn & Hogarth, 1986). Ratings of the strength of the prosecution evidence were influenced not only by the story order of the prosecution evidence but also by the story order of the defense evidence; perceptions of defense evidence strength were also affected by both (Table 16.5). However, these effects were noticeably weaker for assessments of defense evidence strength. There are two plausible explanations for different patterns of ratings for prosecution and defense evidence. It is possible that having a coherent defense story is less critical than having a coherent prosecution story because the burden of proof is on the prosecution and therefore subjects are less influenced by coherence in their perceptions of defense evidence strength. However, this explanation is hard to reconcile with the large effect of defense story order on decisions. A second explanation, that we prefer, is specific to our stimulus trial. Even when the defense story is easily constructed, subjects do not always consider it to be highly plausible (the defendant claims that the victim was drunk, coming at him with a razor, and in the process lunged onto his knife). This difference in plausibility is supported in the present study by a greater proportion of guilty verdicts when subjects heard both stories (Table 16.4), and the greater overall strength ratings for the prosecution evidence (Table 16.5), and in previous research using this trial (Hastie, Penrod, & Pennington, 1983; Pennington & Hastie, 1986). Differential plausibility could account for the weaker effects of story order on perceptions of strength of the defense evidence by contributing to greater variability in the ratings as well as a diminished increment for the story order versus witness order manipulation.

The effect of the strength of alternative stories also emerged in the pattern of results for the confidence ratings (Table 16.6), but in a different way. Subjects were most confident of their decisions, regardless of direction of the decision, when both prosecution and defense evidence were presented in story order and least confident when neither prosecution nor defense was presented in story order. This suggests a "clarity" factor that we had not anticipated. That is, confidence will be greater when subjects feel that they have a clear view of the competing interpretations of the evidence. Considering the intermediate conditions, in which subjects heard either prosecution or defense evidence in story order, but not both, we see the predicted direction of the effect for prosecution story order but not for defense story order. Again, we appeal to the burden-of-proof and/or differential-plausibility explanations offered earlier; that is, any advantage in confidence in a not guilty verdict that might arise from having the complete defense story may have been offset by its level of plausibility, even though knowing the complete story was sufficient to move verdict decisions substantially in the not guilty direction. Further research that varies plausibility *and* ease of story construction independently could serve to clarify these issues.

In sum, our results strongly support the conclusion that story construction is an essential part of evidence comprehension, which in turn determines the verdict choice. Thus, an interpretation of the Story Model of evidence evaluation in which stories are constructed as post-decision justifications is rejected. Furthermore, the construction of alternative stories plays an important role in evidence evaluation and an important but different role in determining confidence in decisions. That is, the strength of one interpretation of the evidence will be influenced by the coherence of that interpretation contrasted with the coherence of alternative interpretations. Confidence will be affected by strength of evidence but also by global clarity; by whether or not alternative possible interpretations can be established.

Our results, along with other work demonstrating strong order effects in judgment, are inconsistent with a Bayesian updating model of evidence evaluation (Schum & Martin, 1982). We also know that primacy and recency order effects predicted by various algebraic updating models in which a judgment accumulates and is adjusted as each new piece of evidence is heard

(N. H. Anderson, 1959, 1981; Einhorn & Hogarth, 1985) cannot account for the story order effects. We believe that such models would have difficulty accounting for these results without additional theoretical propositions describing intermediate memory products. We do not claim that linear combination rules such as the anchor and adjust model never apply; indeed in certain tasks in which the evidence is simple, its constituents are independent in their implications for the decision, and in which the judgment criteria are clear from the outset, anchor and adjust strategies will be used (Hastie & Park, 1986; Pennington & Hastie, 1987).

General discussion

The research we have reported continues our exploration of explanation-based decision making in the juror decision domain. Our application of the explanation-based approach to the juror's task yields the Story Model for juror decisions. Our previous research (Pennington & Hastie, 1986) provided evidence that jurors construct explanations of the evidence that take the form of stories, that decision alternatives are represented as categories, and that variability in the stories constructed corresponds to variability in decisions. In the present research we have further demonstrated that story inferences are made spontaneously and that explanation summaries of the evidence, in the form of stories, play a causal role in determining verdict decisions. Other implications of the Story Model were examined and confirmed: The causal role of an evidence item predicts its rated importance for the decision. Story coherence mediates global perceptions of evidence strength and judgments of confidence. The coherence of alternative stories also mediates perceptions of evidence strength and judgments of confidence. However, future research should be conducted to investigate the possible interactive effects of completeness and plausibility on perceptions of evidence strength and on confidence.

The present research was not designed to test our model in competition with alternative models described earlier (see also Pennington & Hastie, 1981). This is because our theory has, in part, been developed to account for phenomena that lie beyond traditional decision making models based on algebraic or stochastic operators. From this point of view, our explanation-based approach could be viewed as complementary to these other models. For example, we propose that the importance of particular evidence items for the decision will be determined by their position in the explanation structure. This may be viewed as an account of where the weights in information integration models "come from," or alternatively, as an account of which conditional dependencies between evidence items will be considered in Bayesian calculations. However, there are aspects of our results that are inconsistent with traditional models. None of the traditional models would predict the specific story-order effects we found, nor do they contain theoretical constructs to account for them.

The fundamental difference between our explanation-based approach and traditional algebraic operator approaches is that we view *reasoning about the evidence* to be a central process in decision making, in contrast to an emphasis on the computation that occurs once evidence has been selected, augmented, and evaluated. Our direction in this regard parallels recent work demonstrating the role of explanation and the insufficiency of similarity computations to account for categorization behavior (Murphy & Medin, 1985; Rips, 1989), and analogous work in category learning (e.g., Schank, Collins, & Hunter, 1986).

The question of the generality of the present results can be divided into two parts, one concerned with the pervasiveness of explanation-based decision-making strategies and the other concerned with the extent to which story structures will serve as explanation frames in other explanation-based decision tasks. In the introduction to the present research we outlined the explanation-based decision strategy and suggested that it applied to several complex natural decision tasks from the domains of law, business, diplomacy, medicine, and engineering. To date we have only conducted research in the legal domain, where we have shown it does apply. Furthermore, we would not expect the explanation-based strategy to apply to many typical laboratory decision tasks. For example, in the popular research tasks where subjects are asked to assess the attractiveness of lottery gambles, it is difficult to see why a subject would be motivated to construct a complex intermediate model of the evidence or to reason about causal relations concerning outcomes that are explicitly determined by mechanized random generators such as game spinners or bingo cages. In other laboratory tasks where a decision is made on a relatively small set of independent evidence items, and where the required judgment dimension is unidimensional and known prior to hearing evidence, we believe that algebraic models such as those based on anchor-and-adjust updating processes provide an adequate picture of the judgment strategy (N. H. Anderson, 1981; Einhorn & Hogarth, 1985; Lopes, 1982). Indeed, in other experiments we have shown that with appropriate instructions and rating task requirements, simple legal decisions can be shifted from an explanation-based strategy to an anchor-and-adjust process (Pennington & Hastie, 1987).

Explanations of the evidence in juror decisions take the form of stories because stories and legal trials are about human goals and actions in everyday physical environments. This explanation form is therefore likely to apply to many areas of decision making in which decision-relevant evidence concerns motivated human behavior. Unexpected but interesting support for this claim was provided in a recent study (Patel, Arocha, & Groen, 1987) in which physicians from different specialties provided diagnostic protocols for a single case. All physicians' protocols showed that they constructed causal models to explain the evidence (symptoms) but one physician's causal model showed clear story structure. This protocol was provided by the lone psychiatrist in the sample, who provided a psychosocial explanation rather than a biomedical explanation.

The most general conclusion from our research is that the explanation-based decision model is supported as a description of juror decision making. The key precept of the explanation-based approach is that a summary representation of decision-relevant evidence is constructed, is retained in memory, and serves as the intermediate input to the ultimate stage of the decision process. Furthermore, the summary representation is not usefully described as an algebraic or probabilistic quantity, but rather as a semantic structure comprising key causal relations among important events. Assessments of confidence and uncertainty may be expressed as quantitative ratings, but they are "computed" by reasoning about essentially semantic properties of the summary evidence representation such as its completeness, consistency, plausibility, and uniqueness.

Note

1 Analyses identical to the ones reported were also conducted on the importance rating raw scale values ranging from −32 to +32 and on the absolute values of the raw scale values (e.g., an item rated as −10, moderately important evidence against the chosen verdict, would be counted the same as +10, moderately important evidence for the chosen verdict). Although the numerical values of the means reported in Table 16.1 were quite different, the direction of mean differences between cells and results of the statistical analyses were identical to those reported here.

References

Anderson, J. R., & Bower, G. H. (1973). *Human associative memory.* Washington, DC: Winston.

Anderson, N. H. (1959). Test of a model for opinion change. *Journal of Abnormal and Social Psychology, 59*, 371–381.

Anderson, N. H. (1981). *Foundations of information integration theory.* New York: Academic Press.

Axelrod, R. (1976). *Structure of decision: The cognitive maps of political elites.* Princeton, NJ: Princeton University Press.

Baker, L. (1978). Processing temporal relationships in simple stories: Effects of input sequence. *Journal of Verbal Learning and Verbal Behavior, 17*, 559–572.

Bennett, W. L., & Feldman, M. (1981). *Reconstructing reality in the countroom.* New Brunswick, NJ: Rutgers University Press.

Bower, G. H., Black, J. B., & Turner, T. J. (1979). Scripts in memory for text. *Cognitive Psychology, 11*, 177–220.

Bransford, J. D., Barclay, J. R., & Franks, J. J. (1972). Sentence memory: A constructive versus interpretive approach. *Congnitive Psychology, 3*, 193–209.

Bransford, J. D., & Franks, J. J. (1971). The abstraction of linguistic ideas. *Cognitive Psychology, 2*, 331–350.

Brewer, W. F., & Dupree, D. A. (1983). Use of plan schemata in the recall and recognition of goal-directed actions. *Journal of Experimental Psychology: Learning, Memory, and Cognition, 9*, 117–129.

Clark, H. H. (1983). Language use and language users. In G. Lindzey & E. Aronson (Eds.), *Handbook of social psychology* (Vol. 2, pp. 179–231). New York: Random House.

van Dijk, T. A., & Kintsch, W. (1983). *Strategies of discourse comprehension*. New York: Academic Press.

Einhorn, H. J., & Hogarth, R. M. (1985). *A contrast/surprise model for updating beliefs* (Tech. Rep. No. 13). Chicago: University of Chicago, Center for Decision Research.

Einhorn, H. J., & Hogarth, R. M. (1986). Judging probable cause. *Psychological Bulletin, 99*, 3–19.

Fienberg, S. E. (1977). *The analysis of cross-classified categorical data*. Cambridge, MA: MIT Press.

Garnham, A. (1981). Mental models as representations of text. *Memory & Cognition, 9*, 560–565.

Gentner, D., & Stevens, A. L. (Eds.). (1983) *Mental models*. Hillsdale, NJ: Erlbaum.

Graesser, A. C. (1981). *Prose comprehension beyond the word*. New York: Springer-Verlag.

Graesser, A. C., Robertson, S. P., & Anderson, P. A. (1981). Incorporating inferences in narrative representations: A study of how and why. *Cognitive Psychology, 13*, 1–26.

Haberlandt, K., Berian, C., & Sandson, J. (1980). The episode schema in story processing. *Journal of Verbal Learning and Verbal Behavior, 19*, 635–650.

Hammond, K. R., Stewart, T. R., Brehmer, B., & Steinmann, D. O. (1975). Social judgment theory. In M. F. Kaplan & S. Schwartz (Eds.), *Human judgment and decision processes* (pp. 271–312). New York: Academic Press.

Hastie, R., & Park, B. (1986). The relationship between memory and judgment depends on whether the judgment task is memory-based or on-line. *Psychological Review, 93*, 258–268.

Hastie, R., Penrod, S., & Pennington, N. (1983). *Inside the jury*. Cambridge, MA: Harvard University Press.

Hogarth, R. M., Michaud, C., & Mery, J. L. (1980). Decision behavior in urban development: A methodological approach and substantive considerations. *Acta Psychologica, 45*, 95–117.

Johnson-Laird, P. N. (1983). *Mental models*. Cambridge, MA: Harvard University Press.

Kaplan, J. (1978). *Criminal justice: Introductory cases and materials* (2nd ed.). Mineola, NY: Foundation Press.

Kaplan, M. F., & Kemmerick, G. D. (1974). Juror judgment as information integration: Combining evidential and nonevidential information. *Journal of Personality and Social Psychology, 30*, 493–499.

Kintsch, W. (1974). *The representation of meaning in memory*. Hillsdale, NJ: Erlbaum.

Kintsch, W. (1986). Learning from text. *Cognition and Instruction, 3*, 87–108.

Kintsch, W., & van Dijk, T. A. (1978). Toward a model of text comprehension and production. *Psychological Review, 85*, 363–394.

Kintsch, W., Mandel, T. S., & Kozminsky, E. (1977). Summarizing scrambled stories. *Memory and Cognition, 5*, 547–552.

de Kleer, J., & Brown, J. S. (1983). Assumptions and ambiguities in mechanistic mental models. In D. Gentner & A. L. Stevens (Eds.), *Mental models* (pp. 155–190). Hillsdale, NJ: Erlbaum.

480   PENNINGTON AND HASTIE

Lopes, L. L. (1982). *Toward a procedural theory of judgment.* Unpublished manuscript, University of Wisconsin – Madison.

Mandler, J. M. (1984). *Stories, scripts and scenes: Aspects of schema theory.* Hillsdale, NJ: Erlbaum.

Marshall, C. R., & Wise, J. A. (1975). Juror decisions and the determination of guilt in capital punishment cases: A Bayesian perspective. In D. Wendt & C. Vlek (Eds.), *Utility, probability, and human decision making* (pp. 257–269). Dordrecht, The Netherlands: Reidel.

Medin, D. L., Altom, M. W., Edelson, S. M., & Freko, D. (1982). Correlated symptoms and simulated medical classification. *Journal of Experimental Psychology: Learning, Memory, and Cognition, 8*, 37–50.

Murphy, G. L., & Medin, D. L. (1985). The role of theories in conceptual coherence. *Psychological Review, 92*, 289–316.

Ostrom, T. M., Werner, C., & Saks, M. J. (1978). An integration theory analysis of jurors' presumptions of guilt or innocence. *Journal of Personality and Social Psychology, 36*, 436–450.

Patel, V. L., Arocha, J. F., & Groen, G. J. (1987). Domain specificity and knowledge utilization in diagnostic explanation. *Proceedings of the Ninth Annual Conference of The Cognitive Science Society* (pp. 187–202). Hillsdale, NJ: Erlbaum.

Pennington, N. (1981). *Causal reasoning and decision making: The case of juror decisions.* Unpublished doctoral dissertation, Harvard University.

Pennington, N., & Hastie, R. (1981). Juror decision making models: The generalization gap. *Psychological Bulletin, 89*, 246–287.

Pennington, N., & Hastie, R. (1986). Evidence evaluation in complex decision making. *Journal of Personality and Social Psychology, 51*, 242–258.

Pennington, N., & Hastie, R. (1987). *Explaining the evidence: Further tests of the Story Model for juror decision making.* Unpublished manuscript, University of Chicago.

Perrig, W., & Kintsch, W. (1985). Propositional and situational representations of text. *Journal of Memory and Language, 24*, 503–518.

Pople, H. E., Jr. (1982). Heuristic methods for imposing structure on ill-structured problems: The structuring of medical diagnostics. In P. Szolovits (Ed.), *Artificial intelligence in medicine* (pp. 119–190). Boulder, CO: Westview Press.

Reder, L. M. (1982). Plausibility judgments versus fact retrieval: Alternative strategies for sentence verification. *Psychological Review, 89*, 250–280.

Reder, L. M. (1987). Strategy selection in question answering. *Cognitive Psychology 19*, 90–138.

Rips, L. J. (1989). Similarity, typicality, and categorization. In S. Vosniadou & A. Ortony (Eds.), *Similarity and analogical reasoning* (pp. 21–59). Cambridge: Cambridge University Press.

Rumelhart, D. E. (1977). Understanding and summarizing brief stories. In D. LaBerge & S. J. Samuels (Eds.), *Basic processes in reading: Perception and comprehension* (pp. 265–303). Hillsdale, NJ: Erlbaum.

Schank, R. C. (1975). The structure of episodes in memory. In D. G. Bobrow & A. M. Collins (Eds.), *Representation and understanding: Studies in cognitive science* (pp. 237–272). New York: Academic Press.

Schank, R. C., Collins, G. C., & Hunter, L. E. (1986). Transceding inductive category formation in learning. *The Behavioral and Brain Sciences, 9*, 639–686.

Schmalhofer, F., & Glavanov, G. (1986). Three components of understanding of a programmer's manual: Verbatim, propositional, and situational representations. *Journal of Memory and Language, 25,* 279–294.

Schum, D. A., & Martin, A. W. (1982). Formal and empirical research on cascaded inference in jurisprudence. *Law and Society Review, 17,* 105–151.

Slovic, P. (1972). Psychological study of human judgment: Implications for investment decision making. *Journal of Finance, 27,* 779–799.

Stein, N. L., & Glenn, C. G. (1979). An analysis of story comprehension in elementary school children. In R. O. Freedle (Ed.), *New directions in discourse processing* (Vol. 2, pp. 53–120). Norwood, NJ: Ablex.

Sulin, R. A., & Dooling, D. J. (1974). Intrusion of a thematic idea in retention of prose. *Journal of Experimental Psychology, 103,* 255–262.

Tetlock, P. E., & Manstead, A. S. R. (1985). Impression management versus intrapsychic explanations in social psychology: A useful dichotomy. *Psychological Review, 92,* 59–77.

Thomas, E. A. C., & Hogue, A. (1976). Apparent weight of evidence, criteria, and confidence ratings in juror decision making. *Psychological Review, 83,* 442–465.

Trabasso, T., & van den Broek, P. (1985). Causal thinking and the representation of narrative events. *Journal of Memory and Language, 24,* 612–630.

Trabasso, T., & Sperry, L. L. (1985). Causal relatedness and importance of story events. *Journal of Memory and Language, 24,* 595–611.

Tversky, A., & Kahneman, D. (1983). Extensional versus intuitive reasoning: The conjunction fallacy in probability judgment. *Psychological Review, 90,* 293–315.

Wallsten, T. S., & Barton, C. (1982). Processing probabilistic multidimensional information for decisions. *Journal of Experimental Psychology: Learning, Memory, and Cognition, 8,* 361–384.

17 Decision making under ignorance: Arguing with yourself

Robin M. Hogarth and Howard Kunreuther

1. Introduction

Consider the following scenario: you are the proud owner of a VCR that you have just purchased at a local store. On completion of the sale, you are suddenly confronted with a question by the salesperson as to whether you want to buy a warranty at a particular price. However, you have essentially no information on the chances that the machine will fail and the likely costs of repair. How do you decide?

The standard paradigm of choice requires individuals to state their preferences between alternatives characterized by well-specified probabilities and outcomes (Kleindorfer, Kunreuther, and Schoemaker, 1993). Thus, the decision should be based on a comparison of the price of the warranty with the expected cost of repairs (i.e., the chance of a breakdown and the resulting repair bill). However, what happens when you have no real notions of the probability of breakdown or the cost of repairs?

In this article, we explore choices similar to these where people have very little information about the economically relevant variables. We refer to these situations as involving states of *ignorance*, even though we acknowledge that true states of ignorance are rare, because individuals typically have some information about the likelihood and consequences of specific events (see also Coombs, Dawes, and Tversky, 1970).

We propose that, under ignorance, people determine choices by using arguments that do not quantify the economic risks and may reflect concerns that are not part of standard choice theory. For example, in the warranty

This chapter originally appeared in the *Journal of Risk and Uncertainty*, 1995, 10, 15–36. Copyright © 1995 by Kluwer Academic Publishers. Reprinted by permission.

This work was funded by a grant from the Russell Sage Foundation. We wish to thank Craig McKenzie, Barry Blecherman, Cynthia Sherman, Klaus Wertenbroch, and Mike Ziolkowski for most able assistance, and William Goldstein, Steve Kimbrough, Craig McKenzie, and two anonymous referees for many useful comments.

Knowledge: Probabilities

		Precise	Ambiguous	None (Ignorance)
Losses				
Precise		1 Precise-Precise	2 Precise -Ambiguous	3 Precise -Ignorance
Ambiguous		4 Ambiguous-Precise	5 Ambiguous -Ambiguous	6 Ambiguous -Ignorance
None (Ignorance)		7 Ignorance-Precise	8 Ambiguous -Precise	9 Ignorance -Ignorance

Figure 17.1. Characterization of decision-making situations.

scenario, a person might focus solely on the reputation of the manufacturer ("A good manufacturer doesn't need to give a warranty"), a desire for peace of mind ("I'd sleep easier with a warranty"), or fear that the salesperson is taking unfair advantage of the customer ("If they charge that much, they must be making money, so I guess it's overpriced").

Recently, there has been growing interest in enriching the standard paradigm by considering situations in which subjects are provided with vague or ambiguous information about probabilities and/or outcomes. In fact, the literature now contains many examples of the effects of ambiguous probabilities in both laboratory tasks and real-world contexts (Camerer and Weber, 1992). In this article, we propose to extend this work, as illustrated in Figure 17.1.

Figure 17.1 depicts the conceptual differences between decision making under risk, ambiguity, and ignorance. The information on probabilities and outcomes possessed by an individual can be characterized on a continuum ranging from precise (i.e., risk or knowledge of probabilities and outcomes) to none (i.e., ignorance or lack of knowledge about probabilities and outcomes). To simplify this representation, we have divided the probability and outcome dimensions into three zones denoted "Precise," "Ambiguous," and "None (Ignorance)," respectively. By crossing the two dimensions, we obtain nine different situations.

Cell 1 ("Precise-Precise")[1] has been the most widely studied. Both explicit probabilities and payoffs are provided to decision makers.[2] Cell 2 ("Precise-Ambiguous") has been the focus of recent studies on ambiguity of probabilistic information where outcomes are well specified. This has been made operational in experimental studies by providing subjects with probabilistic information in the form of ranges of values (see, e.g., Curley and Yates, 1985), point estimates with considerable uncertainty surrounding the value (Einhorn and Hogarth, 1986; Hogarth and Kunreuther, 1989), and predictive tasks where people believe they possess specific competence for making estimates (Heath and Tversky, 1991).

Recently, a study of insurer behavior where both the probabilities and the losses are ambiguous (Cell 5) has been completed (Kunreuther et al., 1995).[3] We are not aware of other studies which have looked at the impact on choice in Cell 5 or the other six cells in Figure 17.1, even though they may be representative of many real-world decisions.

In this article, we focus on comparisons between Cells 1 and 9 through controlled experiments on warranty purchases such as the scenario described at the outset of this article. Our studies were designed to investigate three issues:

1. Does the likelihood of individuals purchasing warranties differ under conditions of ignorance (Cell 9) and risk (Cell 1)?
2. Do people use different decision processes under conditions of ignorance and risk?
3. What types of arguments do subjects use in their decision process when presented with either no information or precise data on the risks?

With respect to the first issue, we conjectured that the greater uncertainty associated with Cell 9 would lead to a higher probability of purchasing the warranty than in Cell 1. Because ignorance represents an extreme form of ambiguity, this hypothesis follows from the work on ambiguity which documents greater aversion to taking risks under ambiguity (Camerer and Weber, 1992). A sub-issue related to this question was how the price of the warranty and the reliability of the product affect the probability of purchasing the warranty under conditions of ignorance and risk. We hypothesized that both cheaper prices (for warranties) and lower reliability (of the products) would increase the likelihood of purchasing warranties.

As to the second question, we reasoned that under risk (Cell 1), people's choices could be well modeled by standard economic cost–benefit models. However, under ignorance (Cell 9), if choices are governed by arguments involving considerations that are not economically appropriate, this should not be the case.

Turning to the third question, the notion that decision makers use arguments or reasons to justify choices to themselves is not new (see, e.g., Slovic, 1975). Indeed, Montgomery (1983) has suggested that people engage in considerable cognitive activity so that reasons in favor of a particular alternative are not contradicted by other arguments. More recently Shafir, Simonson, and Tversky (1993) have shown through a series of experiments that decision makers utilize reasons and arguments to justify their choices to both themselves and others.

Under risk, we hypothesize that the explicit trade-offs between expected benefits and costs are salient to the decision maker, since information on the probability of a loss and its consequences are available to the individual. Under ignorance, decision makers are *not* presented with these data and would be more likely to consider justificatory processes that are not quantified (e.g., "I bought this warranty for peace of mind").

The next section of this article describes the experimental design of the two studies comparing behavior in Cells 1 and 9. Section 3 presents the results from these studies, and section 4 then discusses implications and directions for future research.

2. Experimental design

2.1. General overview

We designed two experiments for examining individual choices. In Experiment 1, subjects first faced a series of four decisions involving the purchase of warranties for consumer durables. This was done in Cell 9 conditions ("Ignorance-Ignorance"). After answering questions about the likelihood of purchasing these warranties, subjects were again shown the stimuli and asked to estimate the probability of breakdowns and the costs of repair.

The following week, the same subjects returned to the experimental laboratory and faced the same situations which they had met the previous week, but this time in Cell 1 conditions ("Precise-Precise"). More specifically, the subjects' stimuli were individually tailored by giving them the same probabilities and costs for each stimulus which they had estimated the previous week. Thus, in the first stage of the experiment, subjects made choices under ignorance; in the second stage (a week later), they faced the same choice under risk.

In Experiment 2, the conditions of ignorance and risk were reversed. At the first stage, subjects faced decisions in Cell 1 conditions ("Precise-Precise"). At the second stage (one week later), subjects faced the same choices in Cell 9 ("Ignorance-Ignorance"), i.e., with no information about probabilities and costs of breakdowns. Because it was not possible to elicit subjects' personal estimates of probabilities and costs prior to their first choices (in the risk conditions), we supplied subjects with probabilities and costs of breakdowns. These were the mean estimates from Experiment 1 (see below).

In both experiments, we investigated the role of arguments by two means. After the first of four choices (at both stages), subjects were asked to express, in writing, why they had made their particular choice. (Subjects typed their responses at a computer terminal.) After their second choice, subjects reviewed a list of 20 arguments and assessed the extent to which each argument played a role in their decision by providing a rating between 0 and 10.

Except for the ignorance-risk ordering noted above, both experiments involved identical procedures, and we describe them together.

2.2. Subjects

The subjects were recruited by campus advertisements from the graduate (mainly MBA) and undergraduate student populations at the Universities of Chicago and Pennsylvania. They were offered $10 for participating in experiments on decision making that would require two sessions involving a one-week interval between sessions. There were 62 subjects in Experiment 1 and 65 in Experiment 2, with almost equal numbers from the two universities within each experiment.

2.3. Task

The task was individually administered by microcomputer. At both stages of the experiment, each subject was presented with scenarios involving the possible purchase of consumer warranties for a personal computer, a stereo system, a VCR, and a CD player that he/she was to imagine he/she had just acquired.[4]

The four scenarios (corresponding to each of the four products) were presented sequentially, i.e., subjects had to respond to the questions concerning each product when they appeared on the computer screen. Subjects were told the price that they had paid for the item as well as the cost of the warranty which offered "one year's protection against all types of mechanical breakdown." They were asked: "How likely is it that you would buy the warranty?" In addition, they were requested to express their answer on a percentage scale (from "Certain not to buy" to "Sure to buy").[5] For the first item, subjects were asked the following question:

"In assessing how likely you were to buy the warranty, you undoubtedly considered various reasons to guide your decision. What were these reasons or arguments? Type in your reasons or arguments in the box below. Please try to enumerate them – you may type in as many reasons as you wish."

For the second product, subjects were again asked for their arguments but this time they were presented with a list of items and asked "how much weight" each had played in their decision. The instructions were:

"In assessing how likely you were to buy the warranty, you doubtlessly raised arguments with yourself as to why you would or would not buy the warranty. On the next two screens, you will find a list of 20 such arguments – 11 reasons to buy the warranty and 9 reasons not to buy it. You will be asked to determine how much weight (if any) each of these arguments played in your decision." The arguments were rated on a 10-point scale (from 0 – "not considered," to 10 – "critical").

No arguments were elicited for the third and fourth scenarios.

In Experiment 1, the scenarios in stage 1 (the first seen by subjects) contained no information about probabilities and costs of breakdowns. After responding to the fourth item, subjects were shown each scenario again (sequentially) and asked to estimate their subjective probabilities and estimated costs of breakdowns by specifying maximum, minimum, and most likely values. In addition, they also specified indifference prices for the warranties, i.e., prices that would leave them indifferent between buying and not buying.

In stage 2 of Experiment 1 (a week later), subjects faced the same four scenarios, but were given additional information on probabilities and costs of breakdowns. Specifically, each person was provided with the "most likely" estimates of the probabilities and costs of breakdowns which he/she had supplied at the end of the first experimental session. For the first two products, subjects had to provide arguments in exactly the same way as for the first experimental session. No arguments were elicited for the third and fourth scenarios. Subjects did not have to make estimates of costs and probabilities at the end of the task, since these had already been provided.

In Experiment 2, the procedures were reversed. At stage 1, subjects encountered stimuli with information on costs and probabilities. At stage 2 (a week later), these data were not provided, so that at the end of this session subjects were asked to provide the same estimates as subjects at the end of stage 1 in Experiment 1. The data on costs and probabilities provided in stage 1 of Experiment 2 were mean figures, by scenarios and experimental conditions, of the data from Experiment 1.

2.4. Design

The four scenarios presented to subjects involved a personal computer, a stereo set, a VCR, and a CD player that cost $1,600, $800, $400, and $200, respectively. Within each of these scenarios, two factors were varied: warranty price, set at either 5% or 10% of product cost; and product reliability, set at either low or high.

The low reliability description of the personal computer, for example, included the statement: "It is a new model that incorporates several innovative but relatively unknown design features and is produced by a small computer manufacturer who was previously unknown to you." The high reliability version of the stereo scenario included the words: "This is a well-known model produced by a large Japanese manufacturer with a good reputation in consumer electronics."

Subjects were allocated at random to four groups that formed a Latin square involving two levels of cost (5% and 10%) and two levels of reliability (low and high). Each subject saw each of the four scenarios but with different combinations of warranty cost (5% or 10% of product cost) and reliability (low or high). Scenarios were presented to each subject in random order. Thus, product scenarios for which arguments were elicited were randomized across subjects.

3. Experimental results

3.1. General overview

We present the results of three types of analyses that correspond to the three issues that motivated this research (see above). The first focuses on expressed intentions to purchase warranties, broken down by products and experimental conditions. It also investigates whether the order in which subjects made their choices (i.e., going from Cell 9 to Cell 1 as compared to going from Cell 1 to Cell 9) affected the likelihood of purchasing a warranty.

The second analysis investigates whether cost–benefit models can account for the subjects' responses in either conditions of risk or ignorance.

The third analysis explores the types of arguments which individuals use in making decisions when presented with either no or precise information on the risks.

3.2. Analysis 1: Purchase intentions

Tables 17.1 and 17.2 report effects of the different experimental manipulations for Experiments 1 and 2, respectively, when the dependent variable was "probability of purchasing a warranty." For the statistical analysis, each product was treated as a separate experiment.[6] Analyses of variance were performed with a single within-subject factor (stage 1 versus stage 2), and two between-subjects factors, price (5% and 10%), and reliability (high and low).

Overall, the data support the notion that people are more likely to purchase warranties under conditions of ignorance. When no information is given to subjects, there is a greater probability of purchasing the warranty than when precise data on probabilities and potential costs are furnished. This is particularly true for Experiment 1 (Table 17.1) where the mean probability of purchase decreases for each of the four products from stage 1 (ignorance) to stage 2 (risk). To illustrate, the mean probability of purchasing a warranty for a computer in stage 1 is .63; it decreases to .46 in stage 2. The differences are statistically significant at least at the .005 level for all four scenarios.

In Experiment 2 (Table 17.2) the results are not as strong. The only statistically significant effects of stage are for the computer and stereo (.47 versus .36 and .51 versus .41, respectively). One reason for this asymmetry may be that it is more "natural" to move from a state of ignorance to a state of risk than the reverse. This might lead one to question the relevance of Experiment

Table 17.1. *Experiment 1: Stated probability of purchase (×100)*

	Stage 1 (Ignorance) Reliability		Stage 2 (Risk) Reliability		Main effects*		
	High	Low	High	Low	Stage	Price	Reliability
Computer ($1600)							
Price 5%	49	88	49	65	$F(1,55)$	$F(1,55)$	$F(1,55)$
10%	44	71	23	47	$= 8.65$	$= 5.67$	$= 14.71$
		63		46	$p = .005$	$p = .021$	$p < .001$
Stereo ($800)							
Price 5%	68	80	52	57	$F(1,51)$	$F(1,51)$	$F(1,51)$
10%	40	60	30	42	$= 12.25$	$= 7.30$	$= 2.21$
		62		45	$p = .001$	$p = .009$	$p = .143$
VCR ($400)							
Price 5%	67	69	45	48	$F(1,57)$	$F(1,57)$	$F(1,57)$
10%	61	60	40	54	$= 11.73$	$= .34$	$= .29$
		64		47	$p = .001$	$p = .562$	$p = .591$
CD player ($200)							
Price 5%	70	88	59	71	$F(1,56)$	$F(1,56)$	$F(1,56)$
10%	59	63	43	46	$= 13.77$	$= 7.71$	$= 1.60$
		70		45	$p < .001$	$p = .008$	$p = .211$

*There were no significant interactions.

Table 17.2. *Experiment 2: Stated probability of purchase (×100)*

	Stage 2 (Ignorance) Reliability			Stage 1 (Risk) Reliability			Main effects*		
	High	(mean)	Low	High	(mean)	Low	Stage	Price	Reliability
Computer ($1600)									
Price 5%	51	47	45	47	36	41	$F(1,61)$ = 6.10 p = .016	$F(1,61)$ = 1.92 p = .171	$F(1,61)$ = .87 p = .356
10%	40		54	16		39			
Stereo ($800)									
Price 5%	42	51	62	32	41	73	$F(1,61)$ = 5.93 p = .018	$F(1,61)$ = 4.09 p = .048	$F(1,61)$ = 8.28 p = .006
10%	44		51	25		34			
VCR ($400)									
Price 5%	58	57	81	56	57	79	$F(1,61)$ = .01 p = .920	$F(1,61)$ = 11.80 p = .001	$F(1,61)$ = 15.30 p < .001
10%	36		53	24		66			
CD player ($200)									
Price 5%	60	63	64	53	62	63	$F(1,61)$ = .05 p < .820	$F(1,61)$ = .10 p = .754	$F(1,61)$ = 3.07 p = .085
10%	66		62	72		60			

*For the stereo scenario, there was an interaction between stage and price, $F(1,61) = 6.29$, $p = .015$; otherwise there were no other significant interactions ($p < .05$).

2. However, we feel that Experiment 2 was necessary to test whether effects due to ignorance were induced solely by the order in which the stimuli were processed. This was clearly not the case.

Another factor which may have caused less of a difference between ignorance and risk in Experiment 2 is that the data on probabilities and losses presented to individuals in stage 1 were mean estimates for the subject population in Experiment 1, rather than figures derived from the individuals themselves. If some subjects had very different estimates of the risk of product failure, then these average estimates may have affected responses.

Significant main effects for price (5% or 10% of the costs of the products) obtain in Experiment 1 for all products except the VCR and are in the direction that one would expect. People are more prepared to buy the warranty when it is cheaper. In Experiment 2, price is significant for two of the products, namely, the stereo and VCR.

One way of summarizing these results is to note that the decrease in the "probability of purchase" when the price is increased from 5% to 10% of the product cost is about the same as going from a condition of ignorance to one of risk. In Experiment 1, the grand means across products for the low (5%) and high (10%) prices were .64 and .49, respectively; for the "ignorance" and "risk" conditions, the grand means were .65 and .46, respectively. In Experiment 2, the corresponding figures were .57 and .46 for the two price conditions, and .55 and .49 for the ignorance and risk conditions.

As to the effects of product reliability, there were no systematic statistically significant effects. In Experiment 1, the mean probability of purchase for each of the four products was always greater when the scenario indicated that the particular item had low rather than high reliability, but the only statistically significant difference was for the computer. In Experiment 2, there was no systematic pattern for either the computer or CD player; the stereo and VCR both showed significant effects in the expected direction.

3.3. Impact of memory on responses

An open question regarding the two-stage experiment is whether subjects remembered their responses from one week to the next and the extent to which memory interacted with the type of information presented to the individual in Experiments 1 and 2. Given the large number of judgments required at each experimental session, we believe it is highly unlikely that subjects could have remembered their previous responses.

One possibility is that subjects might have remembered the general direction of their responses (e.g., more likely to buy than not buy) but not their precise probability estimates. No matter what interpretation is correct, it is clear that there were differences between risk and ignorance in the same direction in both experiments.[7]

3.4. Analysis 2: Cost-benefit analyses

Recall that we hypothesized that when subjects had precise data on probabilities and losses, their decisions would be determined by comparing the expected cost of repairs to the cost of the warranty. More specifically, we expected the "probability of purchasing a warranty" (y) to be an increasing function of the difference between these two quantities. That is

$$y = f(q \cdot r - c) \tag{17.1}$$

where q is the probability of product failure, r is the repair cost, and c is the cost of the warranty.

Under conditions of ignorance, where q and r were not initially provided to subjects, we did not expect such a model to hold unless subjects were behaving as if they had estimates of these values. Equation 17.1 could nonetheless still be estimated in the ignorance condition, because subjects were required to estimate q and r after they had made their choices.

Using economic reasoning, the intention to purchase should increase monotonically with both q and r, but decrease in c. A simple way to test the explanatory power of any such model is to build a multiple-regression model with y as the dependent variable and q, r, and c as the independent variables.

Table 17.3 depicts the results of these regressions by summarizing the t-statistics and coefficients of determination (R^2) that were found to be significant for average repair cost, probability, and warranty cost. In Experiment 1, the regression results are "significant" under risk for the computer and stereo but not for the other two products. In Experiment 2, significant regressions under risk obtain only in the cases of the stereo and VCR. With respect to conditions of ignorance, probability is significant in five out of the eight possible cases (including all four products in Experiment 2). Overall, the cost–benefit model does not account for much variance in purchasing intentions under conditions of either risk or ignorance.[8]

3.5. Analysis 3a: Analysis of free-form arguments

A principal purpose of these experiments was to analyze the types of arguments provided by subjects. More specifically, we were interested in determining whether subjects used more nonquantifiable arguments to justify their decisions under conditions of ignorance than under risk.

In both Experiments 1 and 2, subjects typed free-form arguments directly onto computer screens without any restrictions as to length or form. We therefore adopted certain conventions concerning (a) the definition of an argument, and (b) the categories to which arguments should be allocated. The key elements of the coding system involved identifying meaningful units within subjects' statements which were the focus of the arguments. For example, did subjects specify the price of the warranty and/or the product

Table 17.3. *Summary statistics of regression analyses*

			t-statistics		
		Average repair cost	Probability of loss	Warranty cost	R^2
Experiment 1					
Computer	Stage 1 (Ignorance)	—	—	—	.059 ns
	Stage 2 (Risk)	—	2.85**	—	.185**
Stereo	Stage 1 (Ignorance)	—	2.34*	—	.146*
	Stage 2 (Risk)	2.23*	3.29**	—	.332***
VCR	Stage 1 (Ignorace)	−2.26*	—	—	.104 ns
	Stage 2 (Risk)	—	—	—	.070 ns
CD player	Stage 1 (Ignorance)	—	—	—	.091 ns
	Stage 2 (Risk)	—	2.17*	—	.084 ns
Experiment 2					
Computer	Stage 2 (Ignorance)	—	2.10*	—	.090 ns
	Stage 1 (Risk)	2.08*	—	—	.082 ns
Stereo	Stage 2 (Ignorance)	—	3.07**	—	.173**
	Stage 1 (Risk)	—	2.30*	—	.314***
VCR	Stage 2 (Ignorance)	2.38*	2.67**	−3.25**	.275***
	Stage 1 (Risk)	—	3.37**	−2.84*	.300***
CD Player	Stage 2 (Ignorance)	—	2.62*	—	.144*
	Stage 1 (Risk)	2.11*	—	—	.116 ns

Note: * implies $p < .05$, ** for $p < .01$, and *** for $p < .001$. ns means "not significant" ($p > .05$).

when making their decisions? Did they focus on the probability of break-down? Did they consider two or more dimensions of the problem within the same argument, e.g., by comparing the warranty price directly to the product price?

To categorize the arguments, a set of rules was written reflecting the above concerns.[9] Two judges then used the rules to categorize the arguments independently of each other. These independent assignments to categories were the same in 92.8% and 94.1% of cases for Experiments 1 and 2, respectively. The two judges discussed cases where there was disagreement and came to a consensus as to how they should be classified.

3.6. Differences between risk and ignorance conditions

Table 17.4 reports the distribution of free-form arguments by categories for both experiments as well as for both stages (ignorance and risk) within experiments. The mean numbers of arguments provided by each subject were slightly more than two in each condition as noted at the foot of the table.

Examination of Table 17.4 reveals two important trends. First, the patterns of distributions of arguments by categories are similar across both experiments. Second, there is considerable similarity between the distributions of arguments in the ignorance conditions of both experiments, as well as between the distributions of arguments in the risk conditions. To operationalize the concept of similarity, consider the correlations between distributions by conditions both across and within experiments.[10] Across experiments, the correlations (not shown in Table 17.4) are .909 and .926 for the ignorance and risk conditions, respectively. However, within experiments, correlations between ignorance and risk conditions (also not shown in Table 17.4) are low, −.040 and .122 in Experiments 1 and 2, respectively.[11]

A second measure of differences between the risk and ignorance conditions is the number of single- to multi-attribute arguments (where "sundry" arguments are classified as single-attribute). This is shown at the foot of Table 17.4. The ratio of single- to multi-attribute arguments under ignorance is 3.1 and 3.0 for Experiments 1 and 2, respectively. The corresponding figures for risk are 1.3 and 1.7. One interpretation of the differences between these ratios is that arguments under ignorance are less complex than those under risk, because individuals have less information.

A more detailed look at the arguments used by subjects illustrates these points. Under conditions of ignorance, individuals were provided with neither the probability of breakdown nor the loss associated with product failure, and Table 17.4 reveals few arguments concerning these two elements. In Experiments 1 and 2, six and four individuals, respectively, volunteered "breakdown probability" as a reason for purchasing or not purchasing a warranty. Few individuals mentioned "repair cost" either as a single argument or as part of a multi-attribute argument.

Table 17.4. *Experiments 1 and 2: Distribution of free-form arguments*

		Experiment 1		Experiment 2	
		Ignorance Stage 1	Risk Stage 2	Ignorance Stage 2	Risk Stage 1
I.	Single-attribute arguments				
	a. Price of product	7	4	10	4
	b. Price of warranty	7	6	12	7
	c. Length/comprehensiveness of coverage	14	1	14	4
	d. Breakdown probability	6	28	4	19
	e. Absolute repair cost	0	3	5	6
II.	Multi-attribute arguments				
	a. Warranty price and product price	21	7	20	5
	b. Warranty price and expected or absolute repair costs	5	34	11	37
	c. Repair cost and product price	0	1	0	1
	d. Breakdown probability and warranty price	1	3	5	1
	e. Breakdown probability and repair cost	0	2	1	4
III.	Sundry				
	a. Reliability	26	4	28	8
	b. General meta-rules	5	5	6	9
	c. Regret/peace of mind	5	6	10	6
	d. Availability arguments	7	0	5	4
	e. Other	8	6	17	13
Mean number of arguments per subject		2.20	2.16	2.26	1.97
Numbers of single-attribute arguments (I & III)		85	63	111	80
Numbers of multiple-attribute arguments (II)		27	47	37	48
Ratio of single to multiple arguments		3.1	1.3	3.0	1.7

On the other hand, a large number of individuals used these arguments as a basis for their decisions in the risk condition where they were explicitly provided. "Breakdown probability" was by far the most common single-attribute argument in both experiments.

The lack of explicit probabilistic information in the ignorance condition also seems to lead to a different framing of the problem than in the risk condition. Simultaneous consideration of "Warranty price and product price" (IIa) is a frequent response under ignorance and reflects the nature of the concrete information provided. Subjects compare the cost of the warranty to the cost of the product, because this represents the available, concrete information. In this case, the cost of the product can probably be thought of as providing some information about the possible costs of repairs in the event of a breakdown. Under risk, however, the nature of the concrete information provided is different and enables a direct comparison of the "Warranty cost to expected repair costs" (IIb) – 5 versus 34, and 11 versus 37.

Concern about product "Reliability" (IIIa) is much more frequent under ignorance than risk, 25 versus 6, and 28 versus 8, perhaps because it served as a proxy for "Breakdown probability." In other words, subjects are likely to see probability of breakdown as an important factor under conditions of both risk and ignorance, but express this concern in different ways. It is also striking that, in both experiments, "Length/comprehensiveness of coverage" is more frequent under ignorance as opposed to risk, 14 versus 1, and 14 versus 4. One explanation could be that the lack of precise information makes this issue salient in the former condition.

In summary, different types of free-form arguments are used under conditions of ignorance and risk. In particular, the types of arguments used tend to reflect the concrete information provided in the problem descriptions. Under ignorance, many subjects consider both the cost of the warranty and the cost of the product, i.e., the cost of the warranty is compared in some way to the cost of the product. Under risk, a comparison of concrete information is also made, but this time between the cost of the warranty and the expected cost of repairs.

3.7. Impact of arguments on purchase intentions

To what extent was the use of particular types of argument predictive of subjects' purchase intentions? In answering this question, it is important to distinguish between two types of arguments. The first are those that, by their nature, are specific to the situation and determine the decision. For example, if subjects' reasoning stressed regret that could be experienced if they failed to buy a warranty, it would not be surprising to find them expressing a high likelihood to purchase. The second type of argument is more general in nature, e.g., centered on the cost of the warranty or the issue of product reliability.

To examine whether certain general types of arguments tend to be more associated with intentions to buy or not to buy, we classified expressed probabilities of purchase into three groups: "buy" for expressed probabilities >.5; "not buy" for expressed probabilities <.5; and "undecided" for expressed probabilities =.5. In fact, there were few undecided, so we ignored this category in the subsequent analysis.[12]

Examining the four arguments with the greatest frequencies in Table 17.4 (Id, IIa, IIb, and IIIa), we found some evidence that particular types of arguments were predictive of purchase intentions. Under conditions of risk, "Breakdown probability" (Id) was heavily associated with "not buy" decisions in Experiment 2 (14 versus 2 with 3 "undecideds"), but not in Experiment 1 (13 versus 12 with 3 "undecideds"). "Warranty price and expected or absolute repair costs" (IIb) was used about twice as frequently by "not buys" than "buys" in both Experiments 1 and 2 (20 versus 12, and 25 versus 11).[13]

3.8. Types of processing strategies

It is typically assumed in many studies of decision making that subjects use a specific rule or strategy for making decisions. However, considerations of the range of arguments summarized in Table 17.4 suggests that different types of rules could have been used. After studying the arguments provided by subjects, we formed the hypothesis that two general types of strategies were being used.

One is what we call a "meta-strategy." This takes little account of the specific characteristics of stimuli, but, instead, uses some higher-order rule to solve the choice problem. An example would be the use of a regret argument such as "I would regret not buying the warranty should a breakdown occur," or a principle a person has formed to handle these kinds of situations such as "I never buy these types of warranties." An important feature of a meta-strategy is that, although the use of the strategy is triggered by the stimulus encountered, it is not responsive to detailed features of the stimulus. The following is an example of a meta-argument provided by one subject: "I seldom buy warranties, particularly if I trust the model enough to buy it in the first place."

In operational terms, the meta-arguments are those classified under "General meta-rules" and "Regret/peace of mind" (IIIb and IIIc) in Table 17.4. Moreover, as can be seen from Table 17.4, the use of meta-strategies did not vary between conditions of ignorance and risk. The frequencies are 10 versus 11 in Experiment 1, and 16 versus 15 in Experiment 2. The numbers of subjects using these kinds of arguments were 16 out of 62 in Experiment 1, and 22 out of 65 in Experiment 2. We classified these subjects as "meta-users."

In contrast, a non-meta-strategy is more responsive to the detailed features of the stimulus. For example, it may take specifically into account the estimated probability of a breakdown and/or the cost of repairs. An example of this reasoning provided by one subject was "Expected repair expense was less than $20, but price of insurance was $80." In operational terms, these strategies are exemplified by all the argument classifications in Table 17.4 except IIIb and IIIc. The numbers of subjects who were non-meta-strategy users were 46 (out of 62) and 43 (out of 65) in Experiments 1 and 2, respectively.

Did the fact that someone was a meta-user affect purchase intentions? Our data show that this did occur in Experiment 1, but not in Experiment 2. Specifically, in Experiment 1 the overall mean probability of purchase (averaging across both products and stages) was .73 for the meta-users and .51 for the non-meta-users. For each product across both conditions of ignorance and risk, means for the meta-users were larger and significant in five out of eight cases ($p < .05$). As noted, this pattern did not replicate in Experiment 2.

3.9. Analysis 3b: Responses to structured arguments

In addition to the free-form arguments discussed above, we also asked subjects to specify the extent to which they had used arguments that we explicitly provided.[14] These arguments were presented after subjects indicated their choices for the second of the four scenarios at each experimental session, the free-form arguments having been provided after information was elicited on purchasing a warranty for the first product.

Whereas analyzing the ratings of arguments provided by the experimenters should be regarded with caution when trying to assess subjects' underlying decision processes, it is instructive to see whether these data are consistent with the free-form arguments. Table 17.5 shows the 20 arguments rated by subjects and the mean ratings associated with the two stages (ignorance and risk) of the two experiments. In the experiments, "reasons to buy" were presented before "reasons not to buy." In Table 17.5, we have reordered the arguments to create groups of meta- and non-meta-arguments both for and against buying the warranty. The numbers associated with each argument indicate the order in which they were presented.

From Table 17.5, it can be seen that different weights are given to some of the arguments between conditions of ignorance and risk in Experiment 1. In particular, the regret argument for buying warranty (4) is rated much higher under ignorance as opposed to risk (6.39 versus 4.98, $t = 3.61$, $p < .001$); there are also significant differences for arguments 15 and 18 (meta-arguments not to buy), as well as some differences on non-meta-arguments to buy.

A particularly interesting difference is provided by argument 17, where it is seen that the trade-off argument ("The cost of the warranty is high relative to the chance of something going wrong") is rated much higher under risk than under ignorance (5.95 versus 4.40, $t = -3.24$, $p < .01$). This suggests that when information on probability of failure is presented to subjects, they are much more likely to use this information in their reasoning process than under conditions of ignorance.

As for Experiment 2, there is only one statistically significant difference (argument 1), and this involves the comparison between the cost of the warranty and the price, information that is present under both ignorance and risk.

Table 17.6 examines the differences in weights given to structured arguments by meta- and non-meta-users (as defined above). There is more consistency between the two experiments when this classification scheme is used.

Table 17.5. *Mean ratings given to arguments provided*

		Experiment 1		Experiment 2	
		Ignorance	Risk	Ignorance	Risk
Reasons to buy the warranty					
Meta-arguments:					
2. I typically buy these types of warranty.		3.03	3.10	2.23	1.85
4. I'd regret not having the warranty if there was a breakdown.		6.39	4.98***	4.91	5.37
9. I'd sleep a lot more securely with the insurance.		2.73	2.31	2.28	2.34
10. I'm unlucky. My products always seem to break down.		1.79	1.76	1.54	1.68
	(mean)	(3.49)	(3.04)*	(2.74)	(2.81)
Non-meta-arguments:					
1. The cost of the warranty is small relative to the price (of the product).		6.66	6.34	6.09	5.00**
3. The cost of repairs (or replacement) would be much higher than the cost of the warranty.		6.97	5.98*	6.18	6.00
5. The premium is not expensive.		5.73	5.77	5.26	5.66
6. The nature of the product is such that it is particularly likely to break down.		5.68	5.24	4.92	4.60
7. Even though the risk of loss is small, I don't want to chance it.		4.58	3.81*	3.35	3.46
8. The cost of the warranty is not high relative to the chance of something going wrong.		6.10	4.94*	4.97	5.26
11. This product is worth a lot to me.		5.74	5.10*	4.89	4.48
	(mean)	(5.92)	(5.31)*	(5.09)	(4.92)
Reasons not to buy the warranty					
Meta-arguments:					
12. I'm lucky. Things like breakdowns don't seem to happen to me.		2.00	2.05	2.00	1.86

Table 17.5. (cont.)

		Experiment 1		Experiment 2	
		Ignorance	Risk	Ignorance	Risk
15. I don't trust insurance and warranties. They don't always cover everything and one has to keep track of lots of paper, etc.		3.48	2.45**	3.15	3.15
18. I usually don't buy warranties of this type.		3.53	2.52**	3.40	3.75
20. I'd regret "wasting money" on the warranty if there was no breakdown.		3.94	4.00	3.22	3.45
	(mean)	(3.24)	(2.76)*	(2.94)	(3.05)
Non-meta-arguments:					
13. The nature of the product is such that it is not likely to break down.		4.40	4.42	4.29	3.68
14. The warranty is expensive relative to the cost of the product.		5.03	4.73	3.85	3.62
16. The product is not worth a lot to me.		2.90	2.53	2.22	2.58
17. The cost of the warranty is high relative to the chance of something going wrong.		4.40	5.95**	4.45	4.65
19. The premium is expensive.		4.65	4.77	4.11	3.85
	(mean)	(4.28)	(4.48)	(3.78)	(3.68)

Note: *implies $p < .05$, **for $p < .01$, and ***for $p < .001$.

As might be expected, meta-users place greater weight on meta-arguments to buy a warranty than do non-meta-users, as shown by the mean scores for this category, 2.78 versus 4.70 and 2.37 versus 3.57, for Experiments 1 and 2, respectively ($t = -4.04$, $p < .001$, and $t = -2.63$, $p < .05$). In Experiment 2, there is also a statistically significant difference (2.50 versus 3.97) between the use of meta-arguments for not buying the warranty ($t = -2.74$, $p < .01$). In addition, in Experiment 1, non-meta-users rate non-meta-arguments "not to buy a warranty" higher than meta-users (4.73 versus 3.20, $t = 2.52$, $p < .05$). Taken as a whole, the weights given to the rated arguments support the analysis of the free-form arguments.

Table 17.6. *Mean ratings given to arguments by non-meta- and meta-users*

	(n =)	Experiment 1		Experiment 2	
		Non-meta (46)	Meta (16)	Non-meta (43)	Meta (22)
Reasons to buy the warranty					
Meta-arguments:					
2. I typically buy these types of warranty.		2.38	5.22***	1.99	2.13
4. I'd regret not having the warranty if there was a breakdown.		4.95	7.75***	4.58	6.23*
9. I'd sleep a lot more securely with the insurance.		2.35	3.19	1.67	3.55**
10. I'm unlucky. My products always seem to break down.		1.47	2.66	1.22	2.36
	(mean)	(2.78)	(4.70)***	(2.37)	(3.57)*
Non-meta-arguments:					
1. The cost of the warranty is small relative to the price (of the product).		6.40	6.81	5.80	5.05
3. The cost of repairs (or replacement) would be much higher than the cost of the warranty.		6.32	6.66	6.24	5.80
5. The premium is not expensive.		5.63	6.41	5.84	4.73
6. The nature of the product is such that it is particularly likely to break down.		5.57	5.03	4.72	4.84
7. Even though the risk of loss is small, I don't want to chance it.		3.66	5.78**	3.06	4.09
8. The cost of the warranty is not high relative to the chance of something going wrong.		5.48	5.81	5.37	4.61
11. This product is worth a lot to me.		5.16	6.03	4.50	5.05
	(mean)	(5.46)	(6.08)	(5.08)	(4.88)

Table 17.6. (*cont.*)

	($n =$)	Experiment 1		Experiment 2	
		Non-meta (46)	Meta (16)	Non-meta (43)	Meta (22)
Reasons not to buy the warranty					
Meta-arguments:					
12. I'm lucky. Things like breakdowns don't seem to happen to me.		2.02	1.81	1.53	2.70
15. I don't trust insurance and warranties. They don't always cover everything and one has to keep track of lots of paper, etc.		2.82	2.94	2.66	4.11
18. I usually don't buy warranties of this type.		2.94	3.00	3.03	4.64*
20. I'd regret "wasting money" on the warranty if there was no breakdown.		4.07	3.63	2.77	4.43*
	(mean)	(2.96)	(2.84)	(2.50)	(3.97)**
Non-meta-arguments:					
13. The nature of the product is such that it is not likely to break down.		4.70	3.19	4.30	3.36
14. The warranty is expensive relative to the cost of the product.		5.27	3.66	3.73	3.73
16. The product is not worth a lot to me.		2.68	2.63	2.59	2.02
17. The cost of the warranty is high relative to the chance of something going wrong.		5.63	3.72*	4.66	4.32
19. The premium is expensive.		5.38	2.81**	3.85	4.23
	(mean)	(4.73)	(3.20)*	(3.83)	(3.53)

Note: *implies $p < .05$, **for $p < .01$, and ***for $p < .001$.

3.10. Summary of experimental evidence

Our results support the hypothesis that people make different decisions under risk and ignorance. In both experiments, the increase in mean purchase intentions due to lack of knowledge of probabilities and outcomes was about the same as that induced by halving the price of the warranties from 10% to 5% of the cost of the products.

Contrary to our expectations, cost–benefit models did not explain subjects' choices well under conditions of risk. There are several possible explanations. First, subjects' judgments were not reliable. Indeed, purchase intentions in the risk conditions correlated only .27 and .54 with subsequently expressed indifference prices in Experiments 1 and 2, respectively.

Second, studies in which subjects' judgments are modeled by regression techniques typically involve within-subject designs using many stimuli. In our experiments, the models involved many subjects and few stimuli. The predictability of our models would therefore be attenuated by between-subject variance. Moreover, one could argue that because subjects were dealing with only a few stimuli embedded within a rich context, they might not have evolved "strategies" for use across a larger series of cases. The analysis of arguments associated with the decision process suggests that subjects facing real-world tasks, as opposed to well-designed laboratory gambles, make decisions in ways that are more idiosyncratic than previously imagined. Subjects used a variety of arguments to describe their choices.

As originally hypothesized, arguments under ignorance tend to focus on more nonquantifiable reasons than those used under risk. For example, trade-offs and other multiple-attribute arguments were more common under risk even though the numbers of arguments used were about the same under both conditions. It is perhaps ironic that, under ignorance, when people should probably think harder when making decisions, they do not. In fact, they may be swayed by the availability of simple arguments that serve to resolve the conflicts of choice.

Examination of the free-form arguments suggests that subjects had at least two different ways of approaching their choices, a meta-strategy that took little account of specific characteristics of stimuli and a non-meta-strategy that was more stimulus specific. Moreover, the distinction between subjects who used meta- and non-meta-strategies was upheld by our examination of weights given to specific arguments for subsequent choices.

The use of specific arguments was not predictive of actual choices unless they were of the meta type. For example, a statement that a subject did not believe that consumer warranties were worthwhile would clearly indicate not buying the warranty. On the other hand, a comparison of the cost of the warranty with, say, the cost of the product or the expected cost of repairs did not predict direction of choice.

Finally, because subjects in the ignorance condition of our experiments did make estimates of probabilities and costs (after their choices), it could be argued that their decisions were made under ambiguity as opposed to ignorance. We do not intend to join this debate, because our stimuli under ignorance were far more "ambiguous" than the stimuli used in studies of decision making under ambiguity (Camerer and Weber, 1992). However, we do wish to address a methodological criticism made by Heath and Tversky (1991) of previous studies of ambiguity effects. Heath and Tversky raised the possibility that differences in responses to ambiguous and non-ambiguous stimuli may, at least in part, reflect regression effects rather than ambiguity per se. In the present article, recall that each subject in Experiment 1 was faced with his or her own estimates of probabilities and outcomes at stage 2, and thus these values were equated. We did not rely on subjects inferring equality between probabilities and either (a) best estimates of values provided by a third party or (b) the midpoint of a range of probability. In other words, the objections raised by Heath and Tversky were ruled out in this study and, yet, large ambiguity – or ignorance – effects still obtained.[15]

4. Implications and future research

Our work provides insight into descriptive models of choice, normative theories of choice, and prescriptive guidelines for helping people make better decisions.

4.1. Descriptive models

Figure 17.1 suggests that decisions modeled as though they are in Cell 1 ("Precise-Precise") are the exception rather than the rule. Moreover, our results suggest that even when individuals have precise information on probabilities and outcomes, their behavior does not necessarily conform to the dictates of rational models such as cost–benefit analysis.

In this study, we assumed that people were using arguments to make their decisions and, in fact, asked them to state and rate arguments used. This differs from other studies. In the work of Simonson (1989) and Shafir et al. (1989), for example, subjects are not asked to express arguments. Instead, the arguments are inferred from choices made between alternatives with specific configurations of arguments.

Our results suggest that one-sided arguments or justificatory processes may be more likely to occur in situations of ignorance as opposed to risk. Under risk, explicit trade-offs are salient. Under ignorance, decision makers are free to recruit arguments to support their intuitions and to ignore conflicting arguments.

Our work also implies that people can approach choices in two ways –

namely, with predetermined meta-rules or by being sensitive to the particular features of choice alternatives. In most decision research, investigators typically postulate that subjects use one kind of strategy for particular choices. The distinction between meta- and non-meta-strategies reported here is similar to a distinction made by Fiske and Pavelchak (1986) between "category-based" and "piecemeal-based" responses in the domain of affect. That is, when making affective responses to stimuli, people sometimes react to the whole pattern of the stimulus (i.e., by recognizing categories) or by processing its component parts. As in our work, it will be important to determine when people use one kind of rule or the other.

4.2. Normative choice theory

Our results provide further evidence of the importance of ambiguity in choice but relate to the more general topic of "decision making under ignorance." Relatively little has been written in this area. Arrow and Hurwicz (1972) and Cohen and Jaffray (1980) have suggested that under complete ignorance, people should act as though they are completely sure or unsure about events affecting outcomes. In our task, this would mean assuming that a breakdown either would or would not occur. Had subjects in our experiments behaved in this manner, we would have expected to have seen many more extreme probability of purchase intentions in the ignorance conditions.

4.3. Prescriptive implications

Our results suggest that it would be helpful to provide consumers with information on the probability of breakdowns and costs of repairs. When consumers have knowledge of these values (admittedly "provided" by third parties), this does change their decisions. One idea is to provide consumers with a simple form or card that prompts them to estimate the relevant quantities prior to making a decision. Alternatively, these kinds of questions could be generated by a computer program that consumers could consult prior to making important household purchases.

Consumer decision making could also be improved if arguments focused on relevant trade-offs. For example, an argument under ignorance that takes trade-offs explicitly into account is the realization that firms will typically not offer warranties at prices below expected value. A relevant argument for consumers would therefore focus on whether they are sufficiently risk averse (financially and psychologically) to let the firm have their profit for the kind of item under consideration. For some, this may translate into how much they are prepared to pay over expected value to justify "peace of mind." For others, a warranty may be treated as a form of financial insurance: paying a small premium to protect oneself against a potentially large loss.

4.4. Future research

Our paradigm and results raise the issue of whether the standard gamble (as represented by Cell 1 of Figure 17.1) can be enriched in future research, since it does not capture much of the variety of choices faced by people in the real world. A useful analogy is to think of the laboratory gamble's role in choice theory as being akin to the use of nonsense syllables in the psychological study of memory (Goldstein and Weber, 1995).

Nonsense syllables have been useful for studying limited aspects of how memory works, e.g., variations in short-term memory span and so on. However, because human memory is a phenomenon that is so dependent on context, the nonsense syllable paradigm has proven inadequate. Similarly, the effects of context have been demonstrated as critical to the study of choice over the last two decades (Einhorn and Hogarth, 1981; Payne et al., 1992).

Will the study of choice finally show that the standard laboratory gamble was an oversimplification of individual decision making in much the same way that nonsense syllables proved inadequate for studying memory? The findings reported in this article suggest the need to expand the treatment of decision making under risk, ambiguity, and ignorance. Thinking of choice as an argument with oneself may help to enrich the standard paradigm.

Notes

1 Cell names are given first by row and then by column, i.e., the outcome dimension followed by the probability dimension.
2 For example, Kahneman and Tversky (1979) used a wide range of such standard gambles to develop and test the concepts of prospect theory.
3 The ambiguous loss estimates were operationalized by giving subjects a range of possible values bounded by minimum and maximum loss estimates.
4 The four items were chosen after discussions with students. They were familiar to almost everyone, since most of the students and/or their families owned several of the items.
5 A percentage scale was used to avoid a sense of commitment to a definite answer that might have been engendered by a Yes or No response. We did this, because, following a pilot study, we wished to avoid having subjects feel that they had to justify their answers (i.e., to buy or not buy) when we subsequently asked them for the arguments which they had used in determining their responses.
6 In theory, one could combine all data into one experimental analysis. We feel, however, that the results are more interpretable when each stimulus is treated as a separate experiment. We note, parenthetically, that the analysis used here leads to more conservative estimates of experimental effects.
7 When debriefing Experiment 2, we specifically asked 13 subjects whether they remembered their responses from the previous week. Only one of these subjects claimed to be able to remember his responses. However, he was able to recall accurately only one of his four responses concerning the likelihood of purchasing the warranty.
8 There is a large literature showing that regression techniques capture much variance of judgments made by individuals across a series of cases (see, e.g., Slovic and Lichtenstein, 1971). We are reluctant to believe, however, that this difference in unit of analysis can account for the poor regression results reported here. In addition to the regression results reported in Table 17.3, we also investigated various nonlinear models to account for the fact that y is constrained between 0 and 1. However, overall, these models did not provide better fits to our data.

9 We are grateful to Klaus Wertenbroch for developing the argument coding scheme, a copy of which can be obtained from the authors.
10 The intuition behind using correlation as a measure of similarity is expressed in the following question: If you knew the values within each category for one distribution, could you predict another?
11 Across experiments, risk and ignorance also have low correlations, namely, .003 and −.003.
12 Across all products, the average percentage of subjects that gave responses of .50 were six in Experiment 1 and 7.5 in Experiment 2. Similarly, the percentages of probabilities <.50 were 27 and 38 for the ignorance conditions of Experiments 1 and 2, respectively. The corresponding figures for the risk conditions were 50 and 48.
13 Of the two types of arguments that were more frequent under conditions of ignorance – IIa: "Warranty price and product price"; and IIIa: "Reliability" – there was little evidence that the type of argument used was related to purchasing decisions. One exception occurred in Experiment 1 where "Warranty price and product price" was used in a ratio of 14:4 by "buys" versus "not buys."
14 The specific arguments were generated by us following an analysis of data from a pilot experiment.
15 We also note that our study demonstrated the existence of ambiguity/ignorance effects for values of probabilities that were not equal to .5.

References

Arrow, K. J., and L. Hurwicz (1972). "An Optimality Criterion for Decision Making Under Ignorance." In C. F. Carter and J. L. Ford (eds.), *Uncertainty and Expectations in Economics*. Oxford: Basil Blackwell & Mott Ltd.

Camerer, C. F., and M. Weber (1992). "Recent Developments in Modeling Preferences: Uncertainty and Ambiguity," *Journal of Risk and Uncertainty* 5, 325–370.

Cohen, M., and J.-Y. Jaffray (1980). "Rational Behavior under Complete Ignorance," *Econometrica* 48(5), 1281–1299.

Coombs, C. H., R. M. Dawes, and A. Tversky (1970). *Mathematical Psychology: An Elementary Introduction*. Englewood Cliffs, NJ: Prentice-Hall.

Curley, S. P., and J. F. Yates (1985). "The Center and the Range of the Probability Interval as Factors Affecting Ambiguity Preferences," *Organizational Behavior and Human Decision Processes* 36, 273–287.

Einhorn, H. J., and R. M. Hogarth (1981). "Behavioral Decision Theory: Processes of Judgment and Choice," *Annual Review of Psychology* 32, 53–88.

Einhorn, H. J., and R. M. Hogarth (1986). "Decision Making under Ambiguity," *Journal of Business* 59(4), Part 2, S225–S250.

Fiske, S. T., and M. A. Pavelchak (1986). "Category-based versus Piecemeal-based Affective Responses: Developments in Schema-triggered Affect." In R. M. Sorrentino and E. T. Higgins (eds.), *Handbook of Motivation and Cognition: Foundations of Social Behavior*. New York: Guilford Press, pp. 167–203.

Goldstein, W. M., and E. U. Weber (1995). "Content and Discontent: Indications and Implications of Domain Specificity in Preferential Decision Making." In J. R. Busemeyer, R. Hastie, and D. L. Medin (eds.), *The Psychology of Learning and Motivation: Vol. 32. Decision Making from a Cognitive Perspective*. San Diego: Academic Press, pp. 83–136.

Heath, C., and A. Tversky (1991). "Preference and Belief: Ambiguity and Competence in Choice under Uncertainty," *Journal of Risk and Uncertainty* 4, 5–28.

Hogarth, R. M., and H. C. Kunreuther (1989). "Risk, Ambiguity, and Insurance," *Journal of Risk and Uncertainty* 2, 5–35.

Kahneman D., and A. Tversky (1979). "Prospect Theory: An Analysis of Decision under Risk," *Econometrica* 47, 263–291.

Kleindorfer, P. R., H. C. Kunreuther, and P. J. H. Schoemaker (1993). *Decision Sciences: An Integrative Perspective*. New York: Cambridge University Press.

Kunreuther, H., J. Meszaros, R. M. Hogarth, and M. Spranca (1995). "Ambiguity and Underwriter Decision Processes," *Journal of Economic Behavior and Organization* 26(3), 337–352.

Montgomery, H. (1983). "Decision Rules and the Search for a Dominance Structure: Towards a Process Model of Decision Making." In P. C. Humphreys et al. (eds.), *Analyzing and Aiding Decision Processes*. Amsterdam: North-Holland, pp. 343–369.

Payne, J. W., J. R. Bettman, and E. J. Johnson (1992). "Behavioral Decision Research: A Constructive Process Perspective," *Annual Review of Psychology* 43, 87–131.

Shafir, E., D. N. Osherson, and E. E. Smith (1989). "An Advantage Model of Choice," *Journal of Behavioral Decision Making* 2(1), 1–23.

Shafir, E., Simonson, I., and Tversky, A. (1993). "Reason-based Choice," *Cognition* 49, 11–36.

Simonson, I. (1989). "Choice Based on Reasons: The Case of Attraction and Compromise Effects," *Journal of Consumer Research* 16, 158–174.

Slovic, P. (1975). "Choice between Equally-valued Alternatives," *Journal of Experimental Pyschology: Human Perception and Performance* 1(3), 280–287.

Slovic, P., and S. Lichtenstein (1971). "Comparison of Bayesian and Regression Approaches to the Study of Information Processing in Judgment," *Organizational Behavior and Human Performance* 6, 649–744.

18 Positive affect and decision making

Alice M. Isen

Introduction

Most people seem to have a sense that affect (feelings, emotion) can influence their decisions, at least under certain circumstances. However, it is usually assumed that such influence is something irregular or unusual; that only strong and infrequent feelings would have such effects; and that most often only negative feelings such as anger, sadness, or fear would have an impact on thinking processes. Furthermore, most people assume that when affect plays a role in their decision processes, such influences are disruptive and tend to make their decisions "irrational" and less appropriate than otherwise.

Interestingly, however, a growing body of research indicates that even mild and even positive affective states can markedly influence everyday thought processes, and do so regularly. For example, the presence of positive feelings has been found to cue positive material in memory, making access to such thoughts easier and thus making it more likely that positive material will "come to mind" (e.g., Isen, Shalker, Clark, & Karp, 1978; Nasby & Yando, 1982; Teasdale & Fogarty, 1979). This reflects the fact that material in mind is organized and accessible in terms of its positive affective tone, and that people spontaneously use positive affect as a way to organize their thoughts. Thus, far from being an infrequent influence on thought processes, common positive feelings are fundamentally involved in cognitive organization and processing.

This chapter originally appeared in M. Lewis and J. M. Haviland (Eds.), *Handbook of Emotions* (pp. 261–277). New York: Guilford Press, 1993. Copyright © 1993 by Guilford Press. Reprinted by permission.

I wish to thank Mark Chen, John Condry, Jeannette Haviland, Barbara E. Kahn, Carol Krumhansl, and Margaret G. Meloy for their helpful comments on an earlier draft of this chapter.

Positive affect has also been found to promote creativity in problem solving and negotiation, and both efficiency and thoroughness in decision making (Carnevale & Isen, 1986; Isen, Daubman, & Nowicki, 1987; Isen, Johnson, Mertz, & Robinson, 1985; Isen & Means, 1983; Isen, Rosenzweig, & Young, 1991). Thus, under many circumstances,the influence of mild positive feelings on thinking and decision making has been found to be not only substantial but facilitative, leading to improved decision making and problem solving. How can these two views – people's intuitions and the findings of such studies – be reconciled? Most likely, the resolution is in the details. It is these details that are considered in this chapter.

To put the findings regarding positive affect in context, it should be pointed out first that from the very outset of the work on affect and memory, an asymmetry was noted in the influence of positive and negative affect on memory for compatible material (e.g., Isen et al., 1978; Nasby & Yando, 1982; Teasdale & Fogarty, 1979): Whereas positive affect was found to be an effective retrieval cue for positive material in memory, induced negative affect was not found to be an effective cue for negative material, or was seen to be less effective as a cue for negative material than was positive affect for positive material (e.g., Isen et al., 1978; Teasdale, Taylor, & Fogarty, 1980). Thus, although some authors have reported symmetrical effects of positive and negative affect (e.g., Bower, 1981), it seems likely that those findings may be attributable to something about the type of affect induction employed (e.g., hypnosis with instructions to maintain the state at the induced level), because the preponderance of the studies report asymmetrical findings for positive and negative affect and material – that is, less marked cueing effects for negative than for positive affect (see Isen, 1984, 1985, 1987, 1990, for discussion). This asymmetry may have implications for our understanding of the influence of positive affect itself. Moreover, it suggests that we should not necessarily expect the influence of negative affect on cognitive processing in any task to be the inverse of, or parallel to, that of positive affect.

Even when we are dealing with only positive induced affect, there is reason to expect an asymmetry of influence if the *materials* are affectively valenced (e.g., Isen et al., 1985). The fact that positive affect preferentially cues positive material means that the valence of the material in any cognitive task may well make a difference in the effect of thinking about or performing the task (and, in particular, in positive affect's influence on that effect). That is, as has been found in many studies (and will be discussed more fully later), positive affect may have different effects on the cognitive processing of material of different valence, because it cues positive material as contrasted with other material.

Another matter that involves the valence of the material, and that I discuss in more detail later, is that, all else being equal, positive affect appears to give rise to a motive to try to maintain the positive feeling state (e.g., Isen & Simmonds, 1978). Thus, if there is not a good reason to focus on negative material, people in whom positive affect has been induced may avoid difficult or unpleasant tasks or material, or may choose to work on more pleasant items instead (e.g., Isen & Reeve, 1992). This may be another reason that the impact of positive affect may not be the same for negative material as for other material.

In addition, as we shall see, the impact of positive affect appears to depend on the type of task or decision being made and on specific aspects of the decision situation besides valence of the material. For example, whether the choice is about something interesting or important to subjects, as opposed to uninteresting, trivial, or hypothetical, seems to play a role in determining the precise effect that feelings have (e.g., Isen & Patrick, 1983). People in whom positive affect has been induced have been found to elaborate and think more thoroughly, but usually only about relatively interesting or pleasant (or at least neutral) material (e.g., Isen et al., 1985, 1991; Kraiger, Billings, & Isen, 1989).

Furthermore, these factors (task importance, valence, and the motive to maintain the positive state) may interact to influence the ultimate impact of positive affect: If the task is unimportant and promises to be dull or unpleasant, those in a positive feeling state may decline to work on it or may work on it with as little effort as possible; in contrast, if the material is important to the person, or if there is another reason to work carefully on the task, then positive-affect subjects will do so (Isen et al., 1991; Isen & Reeve, 1992). Consequently, negatively valenced material itself may not produce the same effects in positive-affect subjects across all circumstances; and use of negative material presents a complicating factor that should not be minimized. Thus, the effects of positive feelings will depend on many aspects of the situation, resolved and integrated through the person's judgment and goals in the situation.

In emphasizing the importance of the person's goals and choices (motivation) in determining the impact of positive feelings, I do not mean to imply that the effect can be attributed to a concerted effort to *overcome* some more fundamental tendency to avoid negative material or to avoid systematic processing. Instead, I am emphasizing here the multifacetedness of the influence of positive affect; the flexibility of people who are feeling happy; and the importance of plans, goals, and strategies in people's behavior, even in the context of emotional states.

Another factor that must be considered is that mild positive affect appears to influence the way material is organized in mind – what is seen as related to what – so that the context is different, more complex or rich, for people in whom positive affect has been induced (e.g., Isen & Daubman, 1984; Isen et al., 1985; Isen, Niedenthal, & Cantor, 1992; Kahn & Isen, 1993; Kraiger et al., 1989). This is because, as noted earlier, positive affect cues positive material in memory, and positive material is more extensive and diverse than other material (e.g., Cramer, 1968). Thus, the cognitive context is more complex when a person is feeling happy, as a broader range of ideas is cued (Isen et al., 1985). In this way, thoughts that do not usually come to mind in the context of each other do come to mind at the same time, when a person is feeling happy, to form a new and more complex context at that time.

Thus, positive affect appears to influence the context itself, which in its own right has been shown to influence thinking and decision making (e.g., Bransford, 1979; Cramer, 1968; Huber, Holbrook, & Kahn, 1986; Kahneman & Tversky, 1979; Simonson, 1990; Tversky & Kahneman, 1981). This effect, too, can be expected to occur more for certain kinds of tasks, situations, or materials than for others (e.g., it would not be expected with negative material, under most circumstances); thus, the influence of affect on cognitive organization and context needs to be explored.

These points all indicate that the influence of positive affect is complexly determined and will be different in different situations, rather than characterizable by broad, global statements. Determinants of the kinds of tasks that will be affected by feeling states, or the kinds of materials that people experiencing positive affect will prefer, and determinants of the motivations that will guide the behavior of people who are feeling happy, need to be investigated. Although there is still much to be done, some generalizations are emerging from studies on these topics.

A general guideline that can be drawn from this work is that the influence of positive affect on cognitive processes such as judgment and decision making depends on what the affect, together with the task and other aspects of the context, leads the person to think about (e.g., Arkes, Herren, & Isen, 1988; Isen & Geva, 1987; Isen et al., 1985). This in turn depends not only on the impact of affect on memory and on motivation, but also on the context more generally. Moreover, as noted above, context itself is also influenced by affect, through affect's influence on memory and cognitive organization; this, then, can play a role in the way the person sees the situation and the kinds of activities he or she is motivated to undertake.

The impact of affect on thought will thus depend to some extent on particular circumstances and idiosyncratic thought processes of individuals. Yet there are commonalities of thought that can be expected among members of the same culture. For example, any two individuals may have different particular memories or thoughts associated with positive affect, as with any cognitive category. Yet there will also be some overlap in the thoughts they have categorized in that way (i.e., as "positive"). This would be especially true for members of the same or similar cultures (and there may even be some near-universals that one might expect to be common to all people as components of the positive-affect category). Thus, there are regularities in the data, and there is reason to anticipate the discovery of more.

This chapter presents some of the findings regarding the impact of mild positive affect on thinking and motivation, and explores the processes underlying them and the circumstances under which they are likely to be observed. The focus is on decision making, but in order to understand affect's influence on decisions, it is helpful to consider its impact on cognitive organization (or the way material is thought about and related to other material) and on motivation. This is because organization or context, including the person's goals, plays a crucial role in decision making (e.g., Bransford, 1979; Simonson, 1990; Tversky & Kahneman, 1981). I begin, then, by considering the influence of positive affect on cognitive organization.

Positive affect and cognitive organization

A growing body of literature indicates that positive affect influences the way in which stimuli are thought about or related to other ideas in mind. For example, studies have shown that people in whom positive affect has been induced in any of a variety of simple ways (e.g., watching 5 minutes of a comedy film, receiving a small bag of candy, or giving associates to positive words) have a broader range of associates, and more diverse associates, to neutral material (Isen et al., 1985).

Similarly, people in such conditions are able to categorize material more flexibly, seeing ways in which nontypical members of categories can fit or be viewed as members of the categories (Isen & Daubman, 1984; Kahn & Isen, 1993; Isen et al., 1992). This has been found for items in natural categories, such as those used by Rosch (1975; Isen & Daubman, 1984); for products in the mildly pleasant class of snack foods (Kahn & Isen, 1993); and for person types in positive, but not in negative, person categories (Isen et al., 1992). Thus, positive affect has been shown to enable people to see more similarities among items.

It has also been found that if people are specifically asked to focus on differences and find ways in which items differ from one another, positive affect can result in more perceived *difference* as well (Isen, 1987, p. 234; Murray, Sujan, Hirt, & Sujan, 1990). Together, these studies can be interpreted as indicating that positive affect promotes cognitive flexibility: People who are feeling happy become more able to make associations among ideas and see different, multiple relations (similarities *or* differences) among stimuli than people in a neutral feeling state.

It is important to note again in this context that the impact of positive feelings on thought processes, and especially on the results of assigned tasks (such as judgments, ratings, sortings, categorizations, etc.), depends on particulars of the task and the situation. Nonetheless, the effect is regular, predictable, and understandable. If asked to judge similarity among items, people in positive-affect conditions indicate greater similarity than do control subjects; if asked to find differences, they may indicate more difference. As will be explained below, this may not be as irrational as it sounds, nor is it the result of simple response bias.

The process that underlies these effects, as suggested by the word-association findings reported above (Isen et al., 1985), may be that people experiencing positive affect may engage in greater elaboration about the material. Thus, they see more aspects of the items and have more, and more diverse, associations to the items, as those studies reported. Then, as explained by Tversky and Gati (1978) for knowledge about material in general (i.e., not affective material or induced affect in particular), the context supplied by the task (searching for differences vs. searching for similarities) will determine whether this greater elaboration (greater knowledge, in the work by Tversky & Gati) results in a judgment of greater similarity or of greater difference. Those authors found that people rated pairs of items about which they knew more (e.g., the United States and the Soviet Union) as more similar to each other than pairs about which they knew less (e.g., Bolivia and Ceylon) when the task required a similarity judgment, but that people rated the pairs about which they knew more as more *different* from each other when the task focused attention on differences. Thus, to return to the affect situation, if people in positive-affect conditions have more information (elaboration) about material, more thoughts about it, or more associations to it, then they would be expected to indicate more perceived similarity or difference among the items than control subjects would, depending on the context created by the question posed.

However, as noted in the introduction, an aspect of the context that is critically important in determining the impact that positive affect will have is the nature, including the valence, of the materials being considered. Thus, one cannot expect positive affect to influence the categorization of, or to increase the perceived similarity (or difference) of, *all* stimuli automatically.

To illustrate this point, let us examine the results of a recent study that extended the work on affect's impact on categorization to the area of person categorization (Isen et al., 1992). In that study, subjects were asked to rate the degree to which nonprototypic examples of positive or negative categories of people (e.g., "bartender" as a member of the category "nurturant people," or "genius" as a member of the negative category "unstable people") fit as members of the category. Compared with control subjects, positive-affect subjects rated the weakly related members of the positive categories as fitting better in the category, but this was not observed for the negative person categories. That is, people in the positive-affect condition rated "bartender" as a better exemplar of the category "nurturant people" than did control subjects, but they did not rate "genius" as a better exemplar of the category "unstable people." In accord with results of studies showing that positive affect cues positive material in memory, and enables more ready access to such material and to a broader range of such associates (e.g., Isen et al., 1978, 1985), people in the positive-affect condition could presumably see more positive aspects of the relatively neutral type "bartender"; however, nothing in their affective state would be expected to prompt their seeing the person type "genius" as better fitting a negative superordinate category, in that situation.

This interaction illustrates the importance of the type of material with which the subject is asked to work, in determining the effects of feelings.

Although an underlying process (increased elaboration) is postulated to occur, this process is expected to be different for different kinds of material in the situation described. Since positive affect cues positive material, the elaborative process would be expected to occur with positive material (for all subjects) or for positive-affect subjects working with neutral material (see Isen et al., 1985). There is no reason in this situation to expect negative material to be elaborated, or to expect the elaboration of negative material to be facilitated by the induction of a positive affective state.

In addition, as pointed out in the introduction, presentation of sufficiently negatively valenced material may also result in people's not dealing with the material; this tendency may be more notable among people in whom positive affect has been induced, who may be seeking to maintain that positive state (e.g., Isen & Simmonds, 1978). This will probably depend on the degree of negativity in the materials, the importance of the task, and so forth, as noted earlier. It should also be pointed out that if the negative materials are bad enough, they may go so far as actually to overturn the affect induction itself. Moreover (as will be discussed more fully later, in the section on decision making), in a negative frame, where the task requires subjects to focus on possible meaningful loss, people in a positive-affect state may actually have more thoughts about losing than controls (e.g., Isen & Geva, 1987) and may behave conservatively so as to protect themselves from the loss (Isen & Geva, 1987; Isen, Nygren, & Ashby, 1988; Isen & Simmonds, 1978). In the study described here (Isen et al., 1992), however, there was no negative frame (loss or danger) to the task; therefore, such motivational and methodological additional complications were probably not in evidence, and the effect of positive affect simply did not extend to the negative material, as often it does not. However, the point illustrated is that use of negative material in studies of the influence of positive affect can make for complexity in formulating predictions.

A methodological point is worth noting here as well. The interaction observed in the person-categorization study (Isen et al., 1992) between induced affect and the valence of the materials also indicates that the impact of affect on categorization is not an artifact of such processes as response bias, nonsystematic thinking, or reduction in cognitive capacity. This is because the interaction between affect and category valence shows that positive affect influences the categorization of one type of material (positive), but, in comparison with the control group, does not change the way the other type of material (negative) is organized; by contrast, the alternative interpretation (global effects, such as carelessness or reduced cognitive capacity) involves processes that should result in all categories' or stimulus materials' being affected equally.

Compatibly, a study of the impact of positive affect on job perceptions and satisfaction also found that people in whom positive affect had been induced perceived an interesting task that they had been assigned, but not a meaningless one, as richer and more satisfying than did control subjects (Kraiger et al., 1989). Again, this can be seen as reflecting an ability on the part of the positive-affect subjects to see additional associations and aspects of interesting things. At the same time, the interaction with type of task again indicates that a substantive process related to elaboration and thinking, rather than an artifact such as response bias or nonsystematic processing, is responsible for the observed effects.

Another series of studies reflecting affect's influence on cognitive organization indicates that positive affect promotes creative or innovative responding, as would be expected from the kinds of findings described above. Such responding can be seen as involving cognitive flexibility or the ability to put ideas together in new, but useful, ways. For example, people in whom positive affect was induced in any of several ways were better able to solve tasks usually thought to require creativity (Isen et al., 1987). In one of these, the "candle problem" (Duncker, 1945), a person is presented with a candle, a box of tacks, and a book of matches, and is asked to affix the candle to the wall so that it will burn without dripping wax on the table or floor. To solve the problem, the person can empty the box of tacks, tack the box to the wall, and place the candle in it so that it can be lit and won't drip onto the table or floor. Thus, the person must use one of the items (the box) in an unaccustomed way. People in whom positive affect had been induced performed significantly better than controls on this task. A second task that has been used to study the influence of positive affect on cognitive flexibility or creativity is based on the Remote Associates Test (Mednick, Mednick, & Mednick, 1964). In this test, which in its full form was designed to measure individual differences in creativity, subjects are presented with three words and a blank line and are asked to respond with a word that relates to each of the three words given in the problem. An example of a Remote Associates Test item is the following:

MOWER   ATOMIC   FOREIGN   _____

(In this example, POWER would be the correct answer.) Seven items of moderate difficulty are used in the research on the influence of affect. These studies using this dependent measure of cognitive flexibility or creativity also confirm that positive affect increases such ability, and is distinct from negative affect and affectless "arousal" in doing so.

In the studies that examined the influence of negative affect and affectless arousal, negative affect was induced by having subjects view a few minutes of the film *Night and Fog*, a French documentary about the World War II German death camps. People in this condition did not perform better than controls on the Remote Associates Test items (Isen et al., 1987).

Affectless "arousal" was induced by having subjects step up and down on a cinderblock for 2 minutes, so that their heart rates were increased by 66%. Theoretically, arousal should not be expected to increase creativity, since it is thought to facilitate the *dominant* response in a person's response repertoire rather than an innovative one. Nonetheless, its effect was investigated because people sometimes have the hunch that it is "arousal," rather than or as a component of positive affect, that is responsible for the facilitative effect of positive feelings. Results indicated, however, that subjects in this condition did not perform better than controls on the Remote Associates Test (Isen et al., 1987; see also Isen, 1990, and Isen & Daubman, 1984, for discussion). Moreover, reconceptualizations of the "arousal" concept suggest that it may not be a unitary construct and may need to be investigated differently from the way it has been addressed in the past (e.g., Lacey, 1967, 1975; Neiss, 1990; Venables, 1984).

Most recently, tests of these effects of positive feelings on creative problem solving have been extended to include investigation of performance on routine tasks, in order to examine whether there is evidence for an alternative interpretation having to do with effort or global motivation. That is, it is possible that positive affect does not facilitate creative problem solving per se, or seeing connections among things, but rather that it simply raises motivation – that these subjects are simply trying harder. (In some ways, this may be related to the hunches about "arousal," mentioned above, but it can be seen as distinct.) In order to address this alternative interpretation, in some studies we examined positive affect's influence on the performance of two types of routine tasks – circling the letter *a* every time it appeared in pages of randomly ordered letters, and long division – while also examining its influence on creative problem solving, represented by two tasks (the Remote Associates Test and a logical problem-solving task, meant to represent something like scientific creativity). These studies indicated a facilitative influence of positive affect on the Remote Associates Test and the logical problem-solving task, but not on either of the routine tasks, on which performance of the positive-affect subjects and control subjects did not differ (Isen & Berg, 1991). This suggests that it is not just an increase in overall motivation that is responsible for the positive-affect subjects' improved performance on creative tasks.

Another study has found that positive affect, induced by means of receipt of a small gift and by reading funny cartoons, can facilitate the process of negotiation and result in improved outcomes in an integrative bargaining situation (Carnevale & Isen, 1986). An "integrative bargaining" task is one in which, in order to reach the optimal agreement, people must make trade-offs on different issues, of differing value to them, about which they are bargaining. Reaching agreement on such a task requires seeing possibilities, thinking innovatively, and reasoning flexibly about how trade-offs might be made. Obvious compromises or simple yielding will not result in satisfactory outcomes (for greater detail, see, e.g., Pruitt, 1983).

In this study, people in the positive-affect condition who bargained face to face were significantly less likely to break off negotiation, and more likely to reach agreement and to reach the optimal agreement possible in the situation, than were face-to-face bargainers in the control condition, in which positive affect had not been induced. They were also less likely to engage in aggressive tactics during the negotiation, and reported more enjoyment of the session (Carnevale & Isen, 1986). And they were better able than control subjects to figure out the other person's payoff matrix (schedule of profit for each component of the agreement) in the negotiation, which differed for the two bargainers. These results support the suggestion that positive affect facilitates a problem-solving approach and improves people's ability to integrate ideas and see ways of relating aspects of situations to one another, in order to come up with a good solution to a problem.

Thus, in summary of this section, positive affect appears to influence the way in which cognitive material is organized – how ideas are related to one another in mind. In particular, it has been found in most situations to give rise to greater elaboration in response to neutral or positive material (but not negative material) and a richer context, which in turn promotes flexibility in thinking. (It should be noted that depending on the task, with positive *material*, although the elaboration effect is occurring, the difference between positive-affect subjects and control subjects may not be apparent: The material itself induces positive affect, and this produces the effect even in the "control" condition. See Isen et al., 1985.)

This means that in any task (that deals with material of neutral or positive valence) undertaken while a person is feeling happy, one should expect unusual and innovative, though reasonable and logical, thoughts and responses. It is a mistake to assume that people in whom positive affect has been induced will think only those arguments and thoughts about the experimental materials that are provided by the experimenters, in the standard way. On the basis of the research reviewed here, we should expect people in the positive-affect condition to think about the materials in a more elaborated, extensive, flexible, responsible, and positive way – provided that the materials are not negative or boring. Thus, in attitude-change studies, for example, people in the positive-affect conditions may think of their own arguments pro or con and may behave accordingly.

In the case of negative material, it is more difficult to predict the behavior of positive-affect subjects. We would expect these subjects not to elaborate the negative material more than controls; in some tasks (e.g., categorization, word association), this will result in their responses' not differing from those of control subjects (e.g., Isen et al., 1985, 1992). On other tasks, we would expect positive-affect subjects actively to avoid, or show caution with, the materials. Issues related to these distinctions are discussed in the next two sections.

Thus, in sum, positive feelings have been shown to have complex but largely facilitative effects on the thoughts generated, the way these thoughts are organized, and the cognitive context that results, in response to most material. Although ideas are elaborated, and more thoughts (and more nontypical thoughts) come to mind, thinking is flexible, so that both usual *and* unusual aspects and senses of concepts are accessible. And this has a fundamental influence on the performance of many kinds of tasks.

Positive affect and motivation

All of the work described thus far indicating that positive affect promotes enjoyment and enrichment of potentially enjoyable, though serious, tasks (e.g., Carnevale & Isen, 1986; Kraiger et al., 1989) suggests that positive affect may influence task motivation (because richer tasks are also more motivating). I have already discussed two other kinds of possible effects of feelings on motivation: one on global motivation or trying harder, and one on specific motivations or direction of effort that may be thought to result from the presence of happy feelings (the tendency to behave so as to maintain the positive state).

Regarding global motivation, recall that there is no evidence as yet to suggest that positive affect simply raises effort on all tasks (e.g., Isen & Berg, 1991). In addition, other studies, such as those investigating the influence of affect on creativity, have reported effects of positive feelings that differ from those resulting from mere "arousal" (e.g., Isen et al., 1987). Therefore, it seems more promising to investigate specific aspects of tasks that are facilitated by positive feelings.

As noted earlier, several reports suggest that positive affect may introduce a motive to maintain the positive state (e.g., Isen & Simmonds, 1978; see also Isen, 1987, for discussion). One early study showed, for example, that people in whom positive affect had been induced (by receipt of a coin in the coin-return slot of a public telephone) were *less* likely than control subjects to help a stranger, when the helping task was one that was portrayed as virtually certain to make them feel depressed (Isen & Simmonds, 1978). This contrasts with the often-obtained finding that in general, people who are feeling happy are more likely than controls to help in any of a variety of ways (e.g., Cunningham, 1979; Isen, 1970; Isen & Levin, 1972). Thus, the results of the study by Isen and Simmonds (1978) were interpreted as indicating that positive affect engenders a motive to avoid loss of the positive state.

On the basis of various studies' results, such a motive would not be expected to be absolute in its effects, nor to result in blind, irrational bias or in distortion of negative stimuli or tasks (e.g., Isen et al., 1985; Isen & Shalker, 1982; Schiffenbauer, 1974). Nonetheless, it can be expected to introduce a tendency to leave more negative topics for another time, or at least to consider doing so. Thus, it could influence responses, or latency of responding, on tasks involving negative material. Such a motive may also be related to positive-affect subjects' relative risk aversion that has been observed under certain circumstances (e.g., Isen & Geva, 1987; Isen et al., 1988; Isen & Patrick, 1983) and that is discussed in the section on decision making.

In parallel, several lines of investigation suggest that positive affect leads to increased enjoyment or pleasure from potentially positive material and situations (e.g., Isen et al., 1978; Kraiger et al., 1989). This work, then, points to two other kinds of motives that appear to be fostered by positive affect: (1)

intrinsic motivation, and (2) variety seeking (stimulation seeking) among safe, enjoyable alternatives.

For example, one series of studies suggests that positive affect promotes variety seeking among safe and pleasant products (Kahn & Isen, 1993). Three studies reported that people in whom positive affect had been induced, when given the opportunity to make several choices in a food category (such as soup or snacks), showed more switching among alternatives than controls and included a broader range of items in their choice sets, as long as the circumstances did not make unpleasant or negative potential features of the items salient. In contrast, when a negative but not risky feature (e.g., the possibility that a low-salt product would taste less good than the regular) was salient, there was no difference between affect groups in variety seeking, the tendency to switch around among the items in making their choices. Thus, there is evidence that positive affect promotes stimulation seeking – that is, enjoyment of variety and of a wider range of possibilities – but only when the situation does not prompt the person to think of unpleasant outcomes.

Another interesting possibility regarding the impact of affect on motivation, suggested by the results of three recent studies, is that positive affect may promote intrinsic motivation (Estrada, Young, & Isen, 1992; Isen & Reeve, 1992). In one study, people in whom positive affect had been induced by receipt of a small bag of candy spent more time, relative to controls, working on a task that promised to be interesting (a puzzle) than on a task on which they could earn money but that promised to be boring and involved time pressure (finding particular combinations of numbers in three pages of randomly ordered numbers during a limited time period). Thus, people in the positive-affect condition appeared relatively less influenced by the extrinsic motivator (money) and more influenced by the intrinsic motivator (interest in the task) than people in the control condition. They also reported more liking for the puzzle task after working on it than did controls, which is another indicator of intrinsic motivation. In this study, subjects were free to choose whichever task they preferred to work on. A follow-up study conceptually replicated this finding, but also showed that when positive-affect subjects knew that the more boring task had to be completed (not for money this time), they were as likely as controls to work on it (Isen & Reeve, 1992).

These findings directly support the observation made earlier that positive affect promotes enjoyment (in particular, enjoyment of tasks in which the subject is interested) and increases the likelihood of engaging in activities that are enjoyable or expected to be fun. They are also compatible with the findings that positive affect increased the perception of task enrichment and satisfaction in regard to interesting jobs (Kraiger et al., 1989). At the same time, they show that people in positive-affect conditions will not avoid work tasks, or more boring, unpleasant, or difficult tasks, if it is clear that those tasks need to be done or if there is some potential benefit in doing them. People who feel good prefer pleasant things and enjoy them more when they do them; however, relative to control subjects, they do not shirk, irrationally "defend against," or irresponsibly refuse to engage in less pleasant tasks.

Another series of studies, investigating the influence of positive affect on physicians' decision making, suggests that positive affect may influence the relative strength of intrinsic (humanistic), as opposed to extrinsic (money and status), sources of practice satisfaction among physicians (Estrada et al., 1992). That is, relative to a control group, physicians in whom positive affect had been induced (by receipt of candy) attributed greater importance to humanistic sources of satisfaction than to extrinsic sources, on a questionnaire asking about the sources of their satisfaction from practicing medicine. (It should be noted that, overall, the physicians gave higher endorsement to the humanistic motives than to the extrinsic. But the difference was more pronounced in the positive-affect condition.)

It should also be mentioned, in the context of motivations induced by positive affect, that a large body of evidence indicates that under normal circumstances positive affect promotes helpfulness, generosity/responsibility, and friendliness/sociability (see Isen, 1987, for a review and discussion). Of course, as we have seen, this tendency can be overridden by such factors as the potential affective consequences of the helping task (e.g., Isen & Simmonds, 1978), or by other factors, such as dislike of the person or organization in need, that might cause the person not to want to help (e.g., Forest, Clark, Mills, & Isen, 1979). These findings may also indicate that people who are happy may feel more free to behave as they want to behave. Moreover, these latter effects may themselves depend on such factors as the amount of harm that might come to the person in need if the potential helper did not help, and so on (see Isen, 1987, for discussion). The point to be made here is that positive affect in general promotes not selfishness, but a tendency to be kind to both self and others; social connectedness and responsibility; and the ability to see situations from another person's perspective.

Thus, in summary of this section, positive affect appears to produce a variety of behaviors that may be seen as resulting not only from the cognitive effects that have been discussed (increased elaboration and access to positive material, increased integration of concepts and ability to see connections among ideas, etc.), but also from apparent motivational changes. On the basis of the data presented here, it seems reasonable to propose that positive affect gives rise to two broad classes of motives: (1) enjoyment, interest, and graciousness in neutral or positive situations (or where negatives or uninteresting things can be ignored safely); and (2) self-protection in clearly negative situations in which the person must, for some reason, respond to the negative material. The relevance of these findings for decision making of various kinds is considered in the next section.

Positive affect and decision making

All of these findings relate to the influence of affect on decision making and suggest that positive affect, in conjunction with the type of task, the framing of the situation, the importance or utility of the task, and other aspects of the situation, may influence decision making of various kinds.

At the outset, it should be noted that the processes described are not postulated to be automatic, but rather are seen as resulting from appraisal of the requirements of the situation. This suggests that processes such as decision making and problem solving may be hierarchically organized rather than monolithic – that before the problem is actually addressed, some command decisions or evaluations may be made regarding how important the task is, what its utility may be, or whether the person has any control over its eventual outcome, as well as what its hedonic consequences may be, how disruptive of ongoing feelings it may prove to be, and so on. These decisions may influence the way in which the problem is addressed. Furthermore, the person may also sometimes go back and re-evaluate such decisions during solving of the task problem.

To state this a bit differently, perhaps the person makes a series of decisions in deciding or solving the problem, and perhaps the first one in the series relates to the domain of the task, with regard to both valence and importance. A helpful way of viewing this first level of decision may be in terms of the framing of the problem. That is, the person may derive a sense of whether this is a situation that is safe, in which he or she can enjoy himself or herself (gain something, share, etc.), or is a situation in which the person must be concerned not to be harmed (not to lose what he or she already has or needs), as well as a sense of what his or her options are.

A conceptualization in terms of the framing of the situation has been useful in the decision-making and risk-taking literature, where differences have been found in people's decisions according to whether the problem was framed as a potential gain or as a potential loss (e.g., Kahneman & Tversky, 1979; Tversky & Kahneman, 1981). Although the parallel may not be exact, a distinction like this (or at least related to safety in contrast to danger) seems to correspond to the two motives resulting from positive affect that have been discussed, and there may be some benefit in thinking about the effects in this way. Issues related to the framing of the experimental situation, and to the possibility of the kind of hierarchical evaluation or decision process proposed, need to be explored more fully in their own right. However, this view may be of some help in understanding the findings that have been obtained.

Risk

One kind of decision that has been studied as a function of positive affect is risk preference (e.g., Arkes et al., 1988; Dunn & Wilson, 1990; Isen & Geva,

1987; Isen et al., 1988; Isen & Patrick, 1983; Isen, Pratkanis, Slovic, & Slovic, 1984). In one series of studies, Dunn and Wilson (1990) suggested that the "illusion of control" effect (the tendency to behave as if one can control random events) might be limited to safe low-cost situations. They noted that positive affect resulting from induced feelings of control promoted wagering where the cost was low but not where the stakes were high.

In another series of studies, people in whom positive affect had been induced were more risk-averse, compared with subjects in control conditions, when the risk situation about which they were reasoning was a realistic one that made them focus on the probability of a real, meaningful loss (e.g., Arkes et al., 1988; Isen & Patrick, 1983; Isen & Geva, 1987). Otherwise, they appeared more risk-prone than controls (Arkes et al., 1988; Isen & Patrick, 1983). For example, when subjects were betting chips representing their credit for participating in the study, those in whom positive affect had been induced bet less (Isen & Patrick, 1983) and required a higher probability of winning before agreeing to a substantial bet (Isen & Geva, 1987), compared with subjects in control conditions. They also showed more thoughts about losing in a thought-listing task following this assessment. Interestingly, when asked just to indicate their likelihood of taking a risk on a hypothetical task (such as starting up a business in an unstable foreign land), without having to wager anything of value to themselves on their assessment, people in the positive-affect conditions indicated greater riskiness (Isen & Patrick, 1983). Similarly, when people were asked, without an affect induction, to estimate what effect they *thought* positive affect would have on their risk preference, they intuited that it would increase their riskiness (Isen et al., 1984). This difference between response in hypothetical, as contrasted with more real, situations has been noted in the experimental literature before (e.g., Feather, 1959; Slovic, 1969).

The relative risk aversion observed in positive-affect subjects considering real risks can be interpreted in terms of affect maintenance: People who are feeling happy risk losing that state, as well as any tangible stake, if they lose a gamble. Therefore, with more to lose than controls, they are more risk-averse than controls. This interpretation is supported by the results of the study described next, which examined the utility associated with various outcomes, as a function of induced positive affect (Isen et al., 1988).

This study used a technique devised by Davidson, Suppes, and Siegel (1956) to estimate utilities, over a series of gambles, by inference from gambles preferred. Subjects were told that they were wagering fractions of their credit for participating in the study, so that the risk situation was a real one. Affect was induced by means of a small bag of candy. Results showed that in this situation, people in whom positive affect had been induced displayed a greater sensitivity to loss than control subjects, indicating that the same loss had greater negative utility for them than it did for controls (Isen et al., 1988). These results, showing that a loss seems worse to people who are feeling happy, support the suggestion that positive affect may result in a tendency or motive to protect the induced positive state. Together with the rest of the findings regarding positive affect and risk preference, they illustrate in the area of risk perception (as noted in other areas) that the influence of positive affect does not appear to be simple, but interacts with task and setting characteristics in the situation.

Complex decision making

Another type of decision making that has been studied as a function of positive affect is what might be called "complex decision making," in which people are asked to choose the best item from among several alternatives (e.g., to choose a car for purchase) or to solve a complex problem (e.g., to make a medical diagnosis). All of the findings reported thus far suggest that positive affect, in conjunction with other aspects of the task and decision situation, may influence the way people go about making complex decisions, and perhaps even their skill in doing so or their thoroughness in considering alternatives and possibilities. In fact, several interesting effects of feelings on these decision processes have been reported.

Results of two studies suggest that people in whom positive affect has been induced are more efficient in decision making, but at the same time may also be more thorough if the task lends itself to increased effort or care (Isen & Means, 1983; Isen et al., 1991). In the first study, in which positive affect was induced by report of success on a task unrelated to the decision problem, the affect and control groups did not differ in their choices; however, people in the positive-affect condition took significantly less time than those in the control condition to reach a decision (about 11 minutes, in contrast with the control group's average of about 19 minutes). These subjects also displayed significantly less redundancy in their search pattern, compared with controls, and tended significantly more than controls to eliminate unimportant dimensions from consideration (Isen & Means, 1983). In this study the decision task was to choose a hypothetical car for purchase from among six alternatives, differing along nine dimensions (fuel economy, purchase price, etc.).

The second study (Isen et al., 1991) used materials patterned on those of the car-choice experiment, but different in topic. In this study, the subjects were medical students who had completed their third year of medical training and had finished a rotation in either pediatrics or internal medicine; the task was to choose, from among six descriptions of patients varying with regard to each of nine health-relevant descriptors (e.g., cough, chest X-ray, and so on), the one most likely to have lung cancer. Affect was induced by report of success on a task unrelated to the decision problem or to medicine at all (anagrams). As in the car-choice study, control subjects were shown the task materials but received no performance feedback.

The results of this study were compatible with those of the car-choice study, but particular measures produced different results because of the contextual differences. As had been found in the earlier study, people in the positive-affect condition reached the same answer (a correct one) to the assigned question as did control subjects, but they did so significantly earlier in their protocols. In this study, however, they then went on to do more with the materials – suggesting diagnoses for the other patients, and in some cases thinking about treatments. Their protocols also revealed significantly less confusion and greater integration of information, in the decision process. Thus, in this study the two affect groups did not differ on the specific measures that had been examined in the car-choice study (total time, amount of redundancy in the search, and number of dimensions eliminated). However, this was because those in the positive-affect condition were significantly more likely than controls to go beyond the assigned task and attempt to diagnose the remaining cases or determine treatments for the patients represented in the materials. Consequently, they continued to work on the materials after reaching the decision on the assigned task; they went back over material already considered in solving the original problem; and they did not eliminate any dimensions from consideration completely.

The differences between these two studies, which were designed to use similar materials, illustrate the importance of attention to the specifics of the situation in anticipating the influence of positive affect on particular measures. Although the results of the two studies are conceptually compatible, they indicate differences in particular measures. They also show that understanding the situation from the perspective of the *subject*, rather than from that of the experimenter, is important. Positive-affect participants in both studies were more efficient in reaching a decision; however, the measures that reflected this efficiency were different in the two situations. In the car-choice study, in which there was no point in working with the materials further, positive-affect subjects simply stopped working on the task once the choice was made; thus, total time on task revealed the difference between the groups. In the medical-diagnosis situation, where working with the materials after the decision was made could be interesting and helpful, those in the positive-affect condition went beyond the assigned task and did *more* than control subjects. Thus, their total time on task did not reflect the greater efficiency with which they had solved the assigned task.

These results suggest another possible influence of positive affect on decision making: greater integration of cognitive material. Subjects in the positive-affect condition in the medical-diagnosis study showed significantly less confusion and a significantly greater tendency to integrate material with which they were working. Thus, as has been discussed earlier regarding the cognitive impact of positive affect, it appears that under conditions of positive affect, people integrate material used in decision processes. This enables them to be less overwhelmed by the task, to show less confusion, and to work faster. Then they can either finish sooner, as in the car-choice task, or turn their attention to other details or tasks within the materials, as in the medical-diagnosis situation.

The findings of the medical decision-making study suggest that positive affect may promote not only more efficiency but also more thoroughness in a person's approach to a decision task. It should also be noted, however, that such an effect may be observed only where the materials allow for this possibility. Moreover, compatibly with similar points made earlier in this chapter, this may be true only for material that people experiencing positive affect *want* to think about or in which they are interested. A similar point has been made recently by Forgas (1991), who also found that positive affect increased the efficiency of decision making under some, but not all, circumstances. Results of the medical decision study indicate, notably, that such material includes tasks requiring complex consideration of serious topics of interest to the subjects, and is not limited to stereotypically "positive" or fun topics.

Heuristics

One question that has arisen recently is whether positive affect results in the use of heuristics, as contrasted with systematic cognitive processing, in decision making and problem solving. Two early studies in our laboratory (cited in Isen, Means, Patrick, & Nowicki, 1982) suggested that positive affect might sometimes promote use of heuristics. Even at that time, however, it was thought that the effect might be limited to certain kinds of situations, and it was suggested that the sparseness of the context (e.g., lack of performance feedback or unexpected testing) might have been playing a role in the observed effect. These ideas were proposed because it was recognized, even then, that the most striking effects of mild positive affect on cognitive processing were facilitative. However, those studies did not actually explore the circumstances under which people experiencing positive affect might be more likely to use heuristics.

At that time, it was suggested that perhaps people in whom positive affect had been induced might rely on heuristic processing *instead of* on systematic processing. This suggestion was based on the assumption that people in whom positive affect had been induced would seek, more than would others, to avoid "cognitive strain" (e.g., Isen et al., 1982). However, the studies were preliminary and did not test those particular propositions (absence of systematic processing, avoidance of "cognitive strain") specifically, either. As the other work reviewed in this chapter has shown, it now appears that the suggestion that positive affect leads to avoidance of "cognitive strain" may be too sweeping.

Furthermore, even if problem simplification does occur, the particular way in which it is accomplished can vary, and it need not involve use of heuristics or nonsystematic thinking. Recent studies suggest, for example, that people in positive-affect conditions integrate material more than those in control conditions do, while nonetheless working systematically on the problem (e.g., Isen et al., 1991). As has been discussed in an earlier paper

(Isen, 1987), there is reason to expect processes such as increased differentiation or elaboration, which has been found among people who are feeling happy, to be accompanied by greater integration as well. This is because seeing more dimensions may enable seeing more bases for combination or integration. This kind of two-part process involving both elaboration and integration has been suggested before – in the literature on cognitive style, for example, where it has been related to a style termed "integrative complexity" (e.g., Harvey, Hunt, & Schroder, 1961). It is interesting to note that this style has also been associated with the kinds of flexible processing described here as resulting from positive affect. The greater integration may allow for apparently simplified processing, but this method of simplification is based on elaboration and greater differentiation, better understanding of the issues. Although it may reduce cognitive strain, it may not be the same as use of a heuristic and does not necessarily imply nonsystematic processing. In fact, this kind of processing has been identified in the literature as typical of the way experts, as contrasted with novices, solve problems.

Thus, it can be seen that a person's using a heuristic does not necessarily mean that he or she will not also use systematic processing. But this possibility was not addressed in the earlier studies. Consequently, although those studies showed increased use of heuristics or problem simplification, they do not speak to the matter of whether positive affect reduces systematic processing, because they did not allow discovery of any simultaneous systematic processing that might also have been present.

In sum, there is no substantial evidence in the experimental literature to justify the general conclusion that in most situations, positive affect promotes use of heuristics *as opposed to* systematic processing, or interferes with systematic processing in decision making. Indeed, the preponderance of the evidence suggests just the opposite: that most often positive affect facilitates efficient, but thorough, problem solving.

On the other hand, some studies – for example, in the attitude-change literature – have suggested that positive affect can disrupt systematic processing (or at least can appear to do so), and at least one article has even proposed that this occurs because positive affect drains the limited cognitive capacity store available for performing cognitive functions (Mackie & Worth, 1989). How can these conflicting pictures be reconciled? There is insufficient space here to address this question fully; however, a few thoughts on the topic may be appropriate. Again, the resolution may be in the details and specifics of the situations.

For example, many of the differences may come from aspects of the materials used in the studies, and may result from motivational differences engendered by those. As noted throughout this chapter, if boring or unpleasant material is presented to people in positive-affect conditions, and they are not told that it is important to pay attention to those tasks, they may not be motivated to do their utmost in working on them. This may be reflected in the amount of effort or attention they expend on them, or in their latency in beginning to work on them.

Indeed, some variant of this "motivational" interpretation is the argument suggested by a number of authors who start from the premise that positive affect does disrupt systematic processing, but that the disruption comes as a result of insufficient motivation (or insufficient motivation to process systematically), rather than as a result of loss of cognitive capacity (e.g., Bless, Bohner, Schwarz, & Strack, 1990; Kuykendall & Keating, 1990; Smith & Shaffer, 1991).

However, the evidence that, as a rule, mild positive affect disrupts systematic processing actually does not itself seem substantial or convincing. This is because the studies attempting to show this are difficult to interpret, either because they did not include an affect control group (positive and negative affect were contrasted), or because they used materials allowing for an alternative interpretation, such as ones involving negative topics or matters over which subjects have no control (see Schwarz, Bless, & Bohner, 1991, for a review of these studies and a somewhat contrasting view). Further, when evidence for a disruptive influence of positive affect on systematic processing has been obtained, it has been under a severely limited set of conditions (e.g., Mackie & Worth, 1989), and therefore would not justify a sweeping global statement that positive affect decreases systematic processing.

Another problem in interpreting the studies that discuss interference with systematic processing is that such interference has often been inferred indirectly – from the relative effectiveness of weak versus strong arguments in producing attitude change, for example (e.g., Mackie & Worth, 1989). The problem is that attitude change may be reported by subjects for reasons unrelated to their processing of the messages: They may want to be more agreeable, for example, or they may think of good arguments themselves, as noted earlier in this chapter. Consequently, the attitude-change paradigm may not be the best one for assessing the influence of positive affect on the capacity or motivation for systematic cognitive processing.

Thus, the evidence that positive affect per se disrupts systematic processing per se is not yet clear. In cases where it appears to do so, this may be the result of a lack of motivation *for the task presented*; however, this kind of motivational effect is different from one that postulates general interference with motivation to process systematically, or with motivation overall.

This is not to say that positive affect, no matter how intense and no matter what the circumstances, cannot interfere with performance on any task. Certainly it may be true that intensely positive events or interesting good news may sometimes interfere with performance (or may do so for at least certain kinds of tasks). And this may be the source of the sense that people have, as noted at the beginning of this chapter, that affect, even positive affect, is disrupting. For example, news of winning an important prize or victory may distract a person and interfere with performance of a more mundane task. But the reason may be exactly that – that it distracts the person from the other task, or changes what he or she wants to think about – not that it necessarily drains the person's capacity or interferes with systematic cognitive processing, in general. However, this effect would not be unique to positive affect, but would apply to intense negative affect as well or, indeed, to any important or interesting information introduced. In addition, even in the case of intense affect, it may be that the person would not allow a *very important* task to be disrupted. That is, although it might be better not to tell a prize-winning surgeon the news of the prize during a surgery, let us hope that he or she could finish a complicated surgery successfully, even if notified then (and feeling happy about the prize). This, of course, remains to be seen; but in this illustration, in any case, we are speaking of intense positive affect, not the mild affect inductions that have been the subject of this chapter.

Regarding the matter of whether mild, everyday positive affect reduces cognitive capacity, other authors have noted recently that there is not yet substantial enough support to warrant acceptance of that position (e.g., Schwarz et al., 1991). Much of the evidence presented in this chapter further undermines the suggestion that positive affect generally drains a person's cognitive capacity and therefore leaves the person unable to process information clearly or effectively. Furthermore, when the capacity-reduction hypothesis is addressed more fully, proponents of that view will have to delineate the conditions under which capacity-reduction would be expected to occur; in addition, there will have to be differentiation between effects that may stem from distraction and those stemming from true reduction in capacity.

Conclusion

In summary of the work presented in this chapter, it seems appropriate to emphasize once again that the influence of affect depends on what it makes the person think about, and that this is determined not by the affective state alone, but by the affect in conjunction with several aspects of the situation that together influence the person's goals, judgments, and expectations.

All else being equal, positive affect tends to promote exploration and enjoyment of new ideas and possibilities, as well as new ways of looking at things. Therefore, people who are feeling good may be alert to possibilities and may solve problems both more efficiently and more thoroughly than controls. However, people who are feeling good respond cautiously in dangerous situations or when caution is otherwise appropriate. They may avoid unpleasant material or situations where possible. However, in situations in which they must think about possible losses, they may be expected to be self-protective and to consider the negative possibilities thoroughly.

Regarding systematic thinking, the most accurate general characterization of the impact of positive affect might be to say that if people who are happy can be expected to want to think about the topic or task that is presented to them (and this will include tasks involving serious topics in which they are competent and interested), then, compared with controls, they will elaborate on the task more and deal with it effectively and efficiently. In contrast, if people in whom positive affect has been induced can be expected to prefer not to focus on the materials or topic (for whatever reason), and there is nothing in the situation that requires, recommends, or alerts them that they should attend to the boring task, then they may not perform that task, may do so with as little effort as possible, or may show reluctance to engage in it. This should not be taken as evidence that positive feelings disrupt systematic thinking as a rule, or that positive-affect subjects *cannot* perform the task. Rather, it only reflects the sensible behavior of free individuals. For, if there is a reason for positive-affect subjects to work on a less preferred task, evidence suggests that they will also do that.

However, these considerations should alert us to the fact that if we expect people to be happy at the time of performing a task, depending on the circumstances we may want to inform them of the importance of the task or the necessity of getting it done, especially if this is not clear from the situation itself. It might be added that this may be more of a necessity in experimental settings, where the meaningfulness of the tasks is not always apparent, than in everyday life.

Thus, common positive feelings seem generally to promote activities that foster enjoyment and maintenance of those feelings, but in rational, responsible, adaptive ways. In addition, they provide many benefits (apart from the happiness inherent in them): They can facilitate creative problem solving, enabling people to come up with solutions to difficult problems that others find extremely hard to solve (while at the same time not detracting from performance on routine tasks, such as long division); and in some instances they enable negotiated solutions to interpersonal disputes. Positive affect has been found to give rise to elaboration and a wide range of cognitive associations in response to neutral stimulus material (while not reducing association to negatively toned words). It increases preference for variety and acceptance of a broader range of options in people's choice sets, when the choice is among safe, enjoyable alternatives, but does not promote risk taking in situations of genuine risk. Happy feeling can lead to efficient and thorough decision making; it stimulates enjoyment of enjoyable tasks and the perception of interesting tasks as even more enriched (but not at the cost of working on less interesting things if these need to be done). When less interesting or slightly negative things are presented, those things may be deferred if that is an option, but will be addressed effectively if not. Socially, of course, positive affect is known to promote generosity, helpfulness, and responsibility under most circumstances.

This chapter has examined some of the evidence regarding ways in which positive affect influences decision making. Yet much remains to be explored about these relationships, the circumstances under which they occur, and the processes that are involved in producing them. Given the importance of positive feelings in our lives, and the great advantages to social behavior and problem solving that result from people's feeling happy, this seems a worthwhile topic for continued investigation.

References

Arkes, H. R., Herren, L. T., & Isen, A. M. (1988). Role of possible loss in the influence of positive affect on risk preference. *Organizational Behavior and Human Decision Processes, 42*, 181–193.

Bless, H., Bohner, G., Schwarz, N., & Strack, F. (1990). Mood and persuasion: A cognitive response analysis. *Personality and Social Psychology Bulletin, 16*, 331–345.

Bower, G. H. (1981). Mood and memory. *American Psychologist, 36*, 129–148.

Bransford, J. D. (1979), *Human cognition*. Belmont, CA: Wadsworth.

Carnevale, P. J. D., & Isen, A. M. (1986). The influence of positive affect and visual access on the discovery of integrative solutions in bilateral negotiation. *Organizational Behavior and Human Decision Processes, 37*, 1–13.

Cramer, P. (1968). *Word association*. New York: Academic Press.

Cunningham, M. R. (1979). Weather, mood, and helping behavior: Quasi-experiments in the sunshine Samaritan. *Journal of Personality and Social Psychology, 37*, 1947–1956.

Davidson, D., Suppes, P., & Siegel, S. (1956). *Decision making: An experimental approach*. Stanford, CA: Stanford University Press.

Duncker, K. (1945). On problem-solving. *Psychological Monographs, 58*(Whole No. 5).

Dunn, D. A., & Wilson, T. D. (1990). When the stakes are high: A limit to the illusion-of-control effect. *Social Cognition, 8*, 305–323.

Estrada, C. A., Young, M. J., & Isen, A. M. (1992). Positive affect influences reported source of practice satisfaction in physicians. *Clinical Research, 40*(3), 768A. (Abstract)

Feather, N. T. (1959). Subjective probability and decision under certainty. *Psychological Review, 66*, 150–164.

Forest, D., Clark, M., Mills, J., & Isen, A. M. (1979). Helping as a function of feeling state and nature of the helping behavior. *Motivation and Emotion, 3*(2), 161–169.

Forgas, J. P. (1991). Affective influences on partner choice: Role of mood in social decisions. *Journal of Personality and Social Psychology, 61*, 708–720.

Harvey, O. J., Hunt, D. E., & Schroder, H. M. (1961). *Conceptual systems and personality organization*. New York: Wiley.

Huber, J., Holbrook, M. B., & Kahn, B. (1986). Effects of competitive context and of additional information on price sensitivity. *Journal of Marketing Research, 23*, 250–260.

Isen, A. M. (1970). Success, failure, attention, and reactions to others: The warm glow of success. *Journal of Personality and Social Psychology, 15*, 294–301.

Isen, A. M. (1984). Toward understanding the role of affect in cognition. In R. Wyer & T. Srull (Eds.), *Handbook of social cognition* (Vol. 3, pp. 179–236). Hillsdale, NJ: Erlbaum.

Isen, A. M. (1985). The asymmetry of happiness and sadness in effects on memory in normal college students. *Journal of Experimental Psychology: General, 114*, 388–391.

Isen, A. M. (1987). Positive affect, cognitive processes, and social behavior. In L. Berkowitz (Ed.), *Advances in experimental social psychology* (Vol. 20, pp. 203–253). New York: Academic Press.

Isen, A. M. (1990). The influence of positive and negative affect on cognitive organization: Some implications for development. In N. Stein, B. Leventhal, & T. Trabasso (Eds.), *Psychological and biological approaches to emotion* (pp. 75–94). Hillsdale, NJ: Erlbaum.

Isen, A. M., & Berg, J. W. (1991). *The influence of affect on creative vs. routine tasks.* Unpublished manuscript, Cornell University.

Isen, A. M., & Daubman, K. A. (1984). The influence of affect on categorization. *Journal of Personality and Social Psychology, 47*, 1206–1217.

Isen, A. M., Daubman, K. A., & Nowicki, G. P. (1987). Positive affect facilitates creative problem solving. *Journal of Personality and Social Psychology, 52*, 1122–1131.

Isen, A. M., & Geva, N. (1987). The influence of positive affect on acceptable level of risk: The person with a large canoe has a large worry. *Organizational Behavior and Human Decision Processes, 39*, 145–154.

Isen, A. M., Johnson, M. M. S., Mertz, E., & Robinson, G. F. (1985). The influence of positive affect on the unusualness of word associations. *Journal of Personality and Social Psychology, 48*, 1413–1426.

Isen, A. M., & Levin, P. F. (1972). Effect of feeling good on helping: Cookies and kindness. *Journal of Personality and Social Psychology, 21*, 384–388.

Isen, A. M., & Means, B. (1983). The influence of positive affect on decision-making strategy. *Social Cognition, 2*, 18–31.

Isen, A. M., Means, B., Patrick, R., & Nowicki, G. P. (1982). Some factors influencing decision-making strategy and risk-taking. In M. S. Clark & S. T. Fiske (Eds.), *Affect and cognition: The 17th Annual Carnegie Symposium on Cognition* (pp. 243–261). Hillsdale. NJ: Erlbaum.

Isen, A. M., Niedenthal, P., & Cantor, N. (1992). An influence of positive affect on social categorization. *Motivation and Emotion, 16*, 65–78.

Isen, A. M., Nygren, T. E., & Ashby, F. G. (1988). The influence of positive affect on the subjective utility of gains and losses: It is just not worth the risk. *Journal of Personality and Social Psychology, 55*, 710–717.

Isen, A. M., & Patrick, R. (1983). The effect of positive feelings on risk-taking: When the chips are down. *Organizational Behavior and Human Performance, 31*, 194–202.

Isen, A. M., Pratkanis, A. R., Slovic, P., & Slovic, L. M. (1984). *An influence of affect on risk preference.* Paper presented at the meeting of the American Psychological Association, Washington, DC.

Isen, A. M., & Reeve, J. M. (1992). *The influence of positive affect on intrinsic motivation.* Unpublished manuscript, Cornell University.

Isen, A. M., Rosenzweig, A. S., & Young, M. J. (1991). The influence of positive affect on clinical problem solving. *Medical Decision Making, 11*(3), 221–227.

Isen, A. M., & Shalker, T. E. (1982). Do you "accentuate the positive, eliminate the negative" when you are in a good mood? *Social Psychology Quarterly, 45*, 58–63.

Isen, A. M., Shalker, T., Clark, M. S., & Karp, L. (1978). Affect, accessibility of material and behavior: A cognitive loop? *Journal of Personality and Social Psychology, 36*, 1–12.

Isen, A. M., & Simmonds, S. F. (1978). The effect of feeling good on a helping task that is incompatible with good mood. *Social Psychology Quarterly, 41*, 345–349.

Kahn, B. E., & Isen, A. M. (1993). The influence of positive affect on variety-seeking among safe, enjoyable products. *Journal of Consumer Research, 20*(2), 257–270.

Kahneman, D., & Tversky, A. (1979). Prospect theory: An analysis of decision under risk. *Econometrica, 47*, 263–291.

Kraiger, K., Billings, R. S., & Isen, A. M. (1989). The influence of positive affective states on task perceptions and satisfaction. *Organizational Behavior and Human Decision Processes, 44*, 12–25.

Kuykendall, D., & Keating, J. P. (1990). Mood and persuasion: Evidence for the differential influence of positive and negative states. *Psychology and Marketing, 7*(1), 1–9.

Lacey, J. I. (1967). Somatic response patterning and stress: Some revisions of activation theory. In M. H. Appley & R. Trumball (Eds.), *Psychological stress: Issues in research* (pp. 14–44). New York: Appleton-Century-Crofts.

Lacey, J. I. (1975). Psychophysiology of the autonomic nervous system. In J. R. Nazarrow (Ed.), *Master lectures on physiological psychology.* Washington, DC: American Psychological Association. (Audiotape).

Mackie, D. M., & World L. T. (1989). Processing deficits and the mediation of positive affect in persuasion. *Journal of Personality and Social Psychology, 57*, 27–40.

Mednick, M. T., Mednick, S. A., & Mednick, E. V. (1964). Incubation of creative performance and specific associative priming. *Journal of Abnormal and Social Psychology, 69*, 84–88.

Murray, N., Sujan, H., Hirt, E. R., & Sujan, M. (1990). The influence of mood on categorization: A cognitive flexibility interpretation. *Journal of Personality and Social Psychology, 59*, 411–425.

Nasby, W., & Yando, R. (1982). Selective encoding and retrieval of affectively valenced information. *Journal of Personality and Social Psychology, 43*, 1244–1255.

Neiss, R. (1990). Ending arousal's reign of error: A reply to Anderson. *Psychological Bulletin, 107*, 101–105.

Pruitt, D. G. (1983). Strategic choice in negotiation. *American Behavioral Scientist, 27*, 167–194.

Rosch, E. (1975). Cognitive representations of semantic categories. *Journal of Experimental Psychology: General, 104*(3), 192–233.

Schiffenbauer, A. (1974). Effects of observer's emotional state on judgments of the emotional state of others. *Journal of Personality and Social Psychology, 30*(1), 31–36.

Schwarz, N., Bless, H., & Bohner, G. (1991). Mood and persuasion: Affective states influence the processing of persuasive communications. In M. Zanna (Ed.), *Advances in experimental social psychology* (Vol. 24, pp. 161–199). New York: Academic Press.

Simonson, I. (1990). The effect of purchase quantity and timing on variety-seeking behavior. *Journal of Marketing Research, 27*, 150–162.

Slovic, P. (1969). Differential effects of real versus hypothetical payoffs on choices among gambles. *Journal of Experimental Psychology, 80*, 434–437.

Smith, S. M., & Shaffer, D. R. (1991). The effects of good moods on systematic processing: "Willing but not able, or able but not willing?" *Motivation and Emotion, 15*, 243–279.

Teasdale, J. D., & Fogarty, S. J. (1979). Differential effects of induced mood on retrieval of pleasant and unpleasant events from episodic memory. *Journal of Abnormal Psychology, 88*, 248–257.

Teasdale, J. D., Taylor, R., & Fogarty, S. J. (1980). Effects of induced elation–depression on the accessibility of memories of happy and unhappy experiences. *Behaviour Research and Therapy, 18,* 339–346.

Tversky, A., & Gati, I. (1978). Studies of similarity. In E. Rosch & B. B. Lloyd (Eds.), *Cognition and categorization* (pp. 79–98). Hillsdale, NJ: Erlbaum.

Tversky, A., & Kahneman, D. (1981). The framing of decisions. *Science, 211,* 453–458.

Venables, P. H. (1984). Arousal: An examination of its status as a concept. In M. G. H. Coles, J. R. Jennings, & J. A. Stern (Eds.), *Psychophysiological perspectives: Festschrift for Beatrice and John Lacey* (pp. 134–142). New York: Van Nostrand Reinhold.

Part IV

Controversies

19 The paramorphic representation of clinical judgment: A thirty-year retrospective

Michael E. Doherty and Berndt Brehmer

In an article published in *Psychological Bulletin*, Hoffman (1960) introduced the expression "paramorphic representation" into the jargon of judgment and decision theorists. This remarkable paper has had, in the intervening thirty years, a profound effect on the field of judgment and decision making, as evidenced by the fact that it has been cited numerous times, and for many purposes. While it is this broad impact on judgment and decision making that occasioned this retrospective, the proximal stimulus for the review was a conversation in which the second author commented to the first that the term "paramorphic representation" had long been an "albatross around the neck of judgment theorists."

In the present paper we first provide illustrations of the variety of uses to which Hoffman's "The Paramorphic Representation of Clinical Judgment" has been put, with a fairly comprehensive literature review. The main focus of the literature review will be those publications that have adverted to the scientific status of regression models of judgment. After doing so we will quote Hoffman (1960) directly to ascertain exactly what Hoffman's paper said about that central issue. The next section is a more general discussion of models in science, relying primarily on expositions by Black (1962) and Hesse (1966). In the final section we return to the scientific status of regression models of human judgment.

Review of citations to Hoffman (1960)

The variety of citations

In preparing this retrospective we scanned over 200 citations to Hoffman's paper, only some of which will be cited herein. The variety of uses to which "The Paramorphic Representation of Clinical Judgment" has been put defies simple categorization. Citations include those which identify it as one of the starting points of policy capturing (Brehmer & Brehmer, 1988), which use it as a source for the relative weight index (Ashton, 1974, 1980; Dalgleish, 1988; Holzworth, 1980; Stewart, 1988), as evidence for limitations on or methods of assessing self-insight (Adelman & Mumpower, 1979; Brehmer & Brehmer, 1988; Blevins, 1975; Doherty & Balzer, 1988; Faust, 1986; Taylor & Wilsted, 1976), and for differential cue use by subjects (Permut, 1973). It has been used to support the use of a linear model (Royce & Weiss, 1975), to substantiate that linear models work well with intuitive cognition (Hamm, 1988), to dismiss problems resulting from violations of independence of predictors (Holmstrom & Beach, 1973), and to argue that cues bearing a monotonic relation to the judgment will be integrated in a simple linear fashion (Salancik & Conway, 1975).

While the paper is obviously multifaceted, this retrospective will focus on the fundamental scientific issue raised by Hoffman, and by many of the references to his paper, the issue that prompted the albatross comment. That issue is the scientific status of regression models.

Citations pertaining to the scientific status of regression models

In this section we illustrate four categories of references to Hoffman (1960) that are more directly relevant to the interpretation of statistical models of judgment. These are presented in generally ascending order of what we perceive as criticism of the imputation of psychological import to statistical models of judgment, and often explicitly to regression models.

Regression models as converging operations. Some authors have simply posited that regression models might best be considered as converging operations in multimethod attempts to discover something about the cognitive processes under investigation. The paper by Einhorn, Kleinmuntz, and Kleinmuntz (1979) epitomizes this category. Other statements to this effect include Brehmer (1973), Hogarth (1974), and Schoemaker (1979).

Regression models as predictors of behavior. Many authors have cited Hoffman in support of some assertion to the effect that policy capturing "... can be used to predict *what* a decision maker might do, but it does not necessarily indicate *how* the decision was made" (Allen & Muchinsky, 1984, p. 3; see also Monahan & Muchinsky, 1985; Romano & Bellack, 1980; Rynes, Schwab, & Heneman, 1983; Schwartz & Griffin, 1986). Others make a similar use of Hoffman's paper but go on to expand on the simple assertion. Grunert (1982), for example, notes that a regression model may be such that it "describes the behavior of the subjects well, just as a chemical formula may describe a substance well ..." (p. 32). He also cites Hoffman to the effect that "alternative formulations" are possible (see also Chan & Jackson, 1982; Einhorn, 1971; Einhorn et al., 1979; Green, 1968; Jago, 1978; Payne, 1973; Payne, Braunstein, & Carroll, 1978).

Regression models as explanations. A number of authors directly address the question whether a regression model is an "explanation." Citations of two will illustrate the diversity of the interpretations of Hoffman's paper. Goldberg (1972) notes that "the regression model has been utilized (probably inappropriately) to explain the manner in which experts combine cues in making their diagnostic and prognostic decisions ..." (p. 557), while Westmeyer (1975) concludes that, compared to a variety of other descriptive and prescriptive approaches, the approach represented by Hoffman, Hammond, and others is "more explanatory" (p. 57).

Regression models as contrasts with other models. Another thread runs through the literature. Many authors assert that a regression model is only a paramorphic representation, that it does not represent the "actual" or "underlying" cognitive process. Since this seems to say what a regression model is *not*, they then try to indicate what it *is*. One conclusion is that it is a simulation of the psychological processes underlying the decisions (Ashton, 1975; Boster, 1984; Dawes, 1979; Hobson & Gibson, 1983; Parker & Srinivasan, 1976; Schmidt, Johnson, & Gugel, 1978; Srinivasan, Shocker, & Weinstein, 1973). Werner, Rose, and Yesavage (1983) referred to statistical models as "analogies or similes" (p. 823) while Fischhoff and Beyth-Marom (1983) contented themselves with interpreting paramorphic models in terms of the less theoretically implicative phrase, "capturing stimulus–response relationships" (p. 252). Similarly, Goldberg (1968) noted that the strategy taken by Hoffman and also by Hammond and his colleagues was "diametrically opposite" to that of investigators who were developing complex, hierarchical representations of clinicians' verbal reports. Hoffman's strategy was, Goldberg posited, to start simple and then add complications only so far as necessary to "reproduce the inferential responses of a particular judge" (p. 486).

A number of investigators have used Hoffman's article as a means of making distinctions between regression models as paramorphic, as compared to other, preferred models which are supposed to be more faithful to the actual cognitive processes. These include Azuma and Cronbach (1966), Borko and Cadwell (1982), Elstein and Bordage (1979, but not pejoratively with respect to regression models), Elstein, Shulman, and Sprafka (1978), Lamiell, Foss, Trierweiler, and Leffel (1983), Payne et al. (1978), Reed and Jackson (1975), Rock, Bransford, Maisto, and Morey (1987), and Ungson, Braunstein, and Hall (1981). Perhaps the most explicit statement of this position is by Ramaprasad (1987):

The many models of cognitive information processing can be broadly classified into isomorphic models and paramorphic models. Isomorphic models seek to replicate the input, process and outcomes of cognitive information processing, whereas paramorphic models seek only to replicate the "input–output relationships ... without guarantee of fidelity to the underlying process." (Fischhoff, Goitein, & Shapira, 1983, p. 188; Hoffman, 1960). Computer simulation models such as General

Problem Solver (Newell, Shaw, & Simon, 1960) and EPAM (Feigenbaum, 1961) are two well-known examples of isomorphic models. (p. 142)

This position is cited and adopted by Walker and Weber (1984). Whereas the above citations are rather direct, other authors, after making the basic point that a regression model is "only" a paramorphic representation, imply that alternative models may be something more than paramorphic models (Aldag & Stearns, 1988; Bell, 1984; Srinivasan & Shocker, 1973; Zakay, 1985), simply by not making a similar critical comment about the model next discussed.

While an explicit contrast between regression models as paramorphic and other models as isomorphic is not stated quite so baldly in print by many investigators, it is implicitly so by many. This contrast reflects the conception of many scholars in the community of judgment and decision researchers. It is this contrast that is the albatross to which we referred above.

What did Hoffman say?

In "The Paramorphic Representation of Clinical Judgment" Hoffman wrote:

Even in the hypothetical situation in which prediction is perfect, one cannot conclude that the mental process has been "discovered." By definition, of course, this point should be obvious, but it is well to point out that even among sets of mathematical relationships (models) which are ostensibly different, there may be some which are in fact equivalent with respect to explanatory power.

An example may serve to clarify this point. Let us assume that for a given judge, and for two information variables, X and Y, the judgments can be independently predicted from X and Y with 95% accuracy by the following equation:

$$J' = +\sqrt{X^2 + Y^2 + 2XY}$$

. . . the equation $J' = X + Y$ will account for the judgments equally as well. . . . It is therefore no more reasonable to conclude that the judge is in fact "using" one particular combination of the information than it is to conclude that he is using the other. One would have to establish different criteria before a choice between two such representations may be intelligently made. (p. 124)

The last two sentences are by no means unexceptionable. If one were to accept this position without reservation, then of course one could restore humankind once more to the privileged position of the center of the universe, for the Copernican revolution will have been for naught. The only mathematical difference between a sophisticated Ptolemaic, earth-centered conception and a Copernican, heliocentric one lies in the complexity of the equations. But scientists do not take lightly the differences between the cumbersome equations demanded by a geocentric model and the simpler ones permitted by the heliocentric conception. In fact scientists use such differences as one of the fundamental criteria of what science takes to be the nature of reality. That criterion for scientific truth goes under different names. A prosaic name is "parsimony." Another is "elegance." A more poetic name is "beauty"! Recall the widely quoted statement by Dirac: ". . . a theory that has some mathematical beauty is more likely to be correct than an ugly one that gives a detailed fit to some experiments" (Holton, 1973, p. 26).

There are other, perhaps even more powerful arguments in the general case of theories making the same predictions of a data set. One is that, given some not too unreasonable assumptions, two such alternative theories should be able to be extended to make some non-identical predictions. For example the more complicated form of the equation Hoffman gave (for the sake of illustration) would assume that people routinely make complex scale transformations. Such an assumption should have empirical consequences. These reservations evidently reflect what Hoffman referred to as "different criteria." Hoffman went on:

But this should not be a troublesome point. Mathematical models are designed to provide a scheme whereby one set of events may be satisfactorily predicted from another, and whereby testable derivations may lead to more complete theoretical understanding of the phenomena. Such models therefore constitute a level of description and explanation which suffices for scientific purposes. It is not required of models that they bear any semblance of some "actual" state of affairs, either within the organism or elsewhere, nor would this necessarily lead to a better understanding of nature. . . .

We have borrowed the term *paramorphic* from mineralogy and employ it in relation to representations of human judgment. The analogy may not be complete, but its limitations are not serious. The mathematical representation of the judgment process is a level of description that approaches the chemical description of minerals. The formula helps to account for or "explain" what is observed concerning certain properties or characteristics of the judge, just as the chemical formula "explains" many, though not all, properties or characteristics of the substance. In addition, the formulae are useful in making predictions concerning the outcomes of certain other tests which may later be employed. But as with chemical analysis, the mathematical description of judgment is inevitably incomplete, for there are other properties of judgment still undescribed, and it is not known how completely or how accurately the underlying process has been represented. The term "paramorphic representation," used in relation to judgment, would seem adequately to indicate this state of affairs. (pp. 124–125)

Hoffman is clearly *not* implying that a mathematical model is a *merely* paramorphic representation of some underlying judgment process. While he asserts that models need not bear even a semblance of any actual state of affairs (a position with which we will take issue), he attributes to policy models a status approaching that of *chemical representations* – hardly an uninteresting, trivial, or *mere* level of representation!

The use of the term *model* in scientific discourse

Scientists use the term *model* in a wide variety of ways. Among psychologists it is used to denote representations of supposed structures (as in brain models), processes (as in information-processing models, attention models, computer simulation models), research methods (as in operant-conditioning model), statistical techniques (as in fixed-effects model, regression model, model of randomness), and others. In order to specify the meaning of the term *model* that is of immediate interest, we list some characteristics of models, adapted largely from the philosophers Black (1962) and Hesse (1966). While we have borrowed ideas heavily from the philosophers mentioned, and have borrowed words freely from Black's exposition, we have not maintained some of the distinctions that Black drew in his book, nor reported all of the characteristics he described.

1. A model is a member of the class of tools for thought by which people attempt to gain insight into something they do not understand by relating it to something they understand better. This class includes metaphors, analogies, and metonyms as well as physical and mathematical models. Sharp distinctions among the members of the class are hard to draw. All of the members share the quality of having an asymmetric directionality of base-to-target: if A is a model of B, then B is not normally a model of A. This is related to Tversky's (1977) analysis of the asymmetry of similarity.

2. "There is no such thing as a perfectly faithful model; only by being unfaithful in *some* way can a model represent its original" (Black, 1962, p. 220).

3. There are agreed-upon conventions of interpretation that rest upon partial identity of properties. That is, there must be rules for translating the terminology of the model domain to the target domain. In discussing this attribute of what he calls an analogue model, Black refers to this as isomorphism.

4. The model is generally simpler than the target. In the special case of mathematical models, the model is also more abstract than the target.

5. A model is intended to reproduce as faithfully as possible a structure or web of relationships in the original. That is, it will manifest a point-by-point correspondence between the relations embodied in the model and those embodied in the original.

It is in light of this fifth characteristic that an objection is raised to Hoffman's comment that models need not bear even a "semblance of some 'actual' state of affairs." While the issue may turn on one's definition of "semblance," it seems imperative that models must bear partial identities in important ways to their targets; else they would be pointless.

In short, a model is a tool for thought, one that entails knowledge borrowed from one domain to help us think about another domain to which the model is imperfectly but usefully related. Models should provide the user a sense of understanding, facilitate communication, and help the user generate testable hypotheses about the target domain. Both Black and Hesse take a strong position that metaphors, models, and analogies are indeed tools for thought, not merely pedagogical devices, as some have argued. Black puts it nicely:

The existential use of models seems to me characteristic of the practice of the great theorists in physics. Whether we consider Kelvin's "rude mechanical models," Rutherford's solar system, or Bohr's model of the atom, we can hardly avoid concluding that these physicists conceived themselves to be describing the atom *as it is* and not merely offering mathematical formulas in fancy dress. In using theoretical models, they were not comparing two domains from a position neutral to both. They used language appropriate to the model in thinking about the domain of application: they worked not *by* analogy, but *through* and by means of an underlying analogy. Their models were conceived to be more than expository or heuristic devices. (pp. 228–229)

And a few pages later he says:

A memorable metaphor has the power to bring two separate domains into cognitive and emotional relation by using language directly appropriate to the one as a lens for seeing the other; the implications, suggestions, and supporting values entwined with the literal use of the metaphorical expression enable us to see a new subject matter in a new way. The extended meanings that result, the relations between initially disparate realms created, can neither be antecedently predicted nor subsequently paraphrased in prose. We can comment *upon* the metaphor, but the metaphor itself neither needs nor invites explanation and paraphrase. Metaphorical thought is a distinctive mode of achieving insight, not to be construed as an ornamental substitute for plain thought. (pp. 236–237)

Metaphors, analogies, and models are part of the very stuff of which science is made. Scientific models may be embodied in literal three-dimensional models, as in Watson and Crick's tinkertoy double helix (Watson, 1968) or Bohr's compound nucleus model made of shallow trays and steel balls (French & Kennedy, 1985). They may take the form of pictures (Ziman, 1978, ch. 4) or even visual images (Miller, 1986). They very often take the form of equations, graphs, flow charts, computer programs, etc. Certainly a regression equation, or policy equation, is a model in the sense described above, which is the sense in which Hoffman used the term.

The status of regression models qua models

Do regression models reveal anything about judgment processes?

Is a policy model a sort of revivification of dust bowl empiricism that lets us predict behavior without any commitment to or interest in the understanding of that behavior, as Anderson (1982) suggests? Should we accept without reservation the propositions of proponents of other methodologies in which they contrast regression models with models that yield the "correct" analysis, or those that contrast regression models with "process" models? Or do we argue that a policy equation does mirror, with varying degrees of distortion, some structure or process of interest?

As Black implied when he wrote that "we can hardly avoid concluding that these physicists conceived themselves to be describing the atom *as it is* . . ." (cf. supra), scientists behave as naive realists. If so, then the question stands, does a policy model have any interesting epistemological implications? Specifically, does it have any interesting relation to the structure or process of judgment?

A policy equation gives us evidence concerning what cues, predictor variables, or dimensions of utility are influencing a person's judgments. Various terms for the attributes of the object of judgment are used, since a policy model can be used for a variety of cognitive tasks. In the case that some model of structure or process stipulates that some attribute ought not to affect judgment, then the presence of significant cue usage as evidenced by a regression analysis falsifies such a model. A policy model might also be used to falsify, though less convincingly, a conceptual model by showing that an attribute is not used. Arguing from the failure to find a significant effect for a variable or interaction entails accepting the null hypothesis, and therefore permits at best a weak form of inference. By the same logic (i.e., the logical asymmetry between falsification and confirmation; Popper, 1963), policy models may support, though not prove, process models. We turn now to some data that we believe bear directly on the scientific status of regression models. The first set of data clearly falsifies a process hypothesis, and at the same time suggests that regression models reflect psychological reality beyond that implied by the ability to replicate input–output relations.

Regression models as instruments for studying insight. Perhaps the most common use of regression models is simply as a method for determining those attributes that are influencing a person's judgments. In one investigation, Reilly and Doherty (1989) had 40 senior accounting students rate the desirability of 160 jobs. Eleven returned for personal feedback and were first shown a matrix of 40 columns and rows. The columns represented subjects, and the rows represented attributes. The cell entries were usefulness indices (Darlington, 1968). The subjects were asked to identify their own policies and were able to do so far beyond chance. This investigation has subsequently been replicated with 72 nontechnical subjects, varying numbers of attributes, and even with correlated attributes (Reilly & Doherty, 1992). This outcome is evidence that people have better insight into their judgment processes than had been thought (Balke, Hammond, & Meyer, 1973; Slovic & Lichtenstein, 1971). Since the subjects selected their own policies from among those of students similar to themselves, it is also a conclusive refutation of Nisbett and Wilson's (1977) substantive hypothesis that the modest insight that people do show in judgment tasks is due to culturally learned rules that produce common variance in statistical and subjective weights. The subjects' ability to identify themselves from a set of statistically derived weights yields evidence about self-insight, and in doing so, shows that policy models mirror psychological reality closely enough to permit self-recognition.

Regression models as instruments for assessing weights people place on variables. One might postulate that regression models are successful at prediction because of the sheer predictive power of the linear model (Dawes & Corrigan, 1974). What is the result of comparing a linear model based on regression weights with one based on subjective weights? If an investigator obtains enough data from a given subject, then that subject's judgment model, based on only a subset of judgments, can be subjected to cross validation. That is, the model can be used to predict a holdout sample of judgments, and the predictive power of the model can be compared without prejudice with the predictive power of a linear model composed of subjective weights. We have now made such comparisons for 157 subjects; 40 in an unpublished reanalysis of faculty salary judgments made by Ph.D.s (Roose & Doherty, 1978), 40 in the analysis of the accounting students' job choice data (Reilly & Doherty, 1989), and 77 in undergraduate females' judgments of potential roommates (Reilly & Doherty, 1992). All such comparisons, save those for two students in the roommate study who had nonsignificant multiple correlation coefficients in the validation sample, resulted in higher correlations for the regression weighted equations. Note, of course, that the cross-validation operation removes the advantage due to capitalization on chance that regression models normally have. These results are consistent with the hypothesis that regression models can isolate the variables that are influencing subjects' judgments and can give the investigator information about the weights that the subjects are attributing to each variable.

Is a regression model a paramorphic representation?

The immediately preceding discussion has argued for the utility of the regression model, not as a tool for prediction but as a tool for making scientifically valid inferences about reality. As such, its ultimate value will be determined on a variety of grounds. In order to address the question just posed, we must adopt a philosophically more sophisticated stance than the naive realism that shaped the prior discussion. For thousands of years, philosophers have wrestled with issues of the nature of knowledge, and one's conception of the nature of knowledge is at the very root of the question of whether a regression model is a paramorphic representation.

As early as the fourteenth century, William of Ockham had worked through some of the fundamental ideas underlying the modern conception of knowledge, and even specifically of scientific knowledge. In fact, the historian of science Pierre Duhem identified the Ockhamist school as the "earliest starting point of our modern scientific era" (Duhem, 1909, cited in Tornay, 1938, p. 51). Ockham's empiricist orientation allied to his nominalist conception of the nature of scientific knowledge is astonishingly contemporary. In expanding upon Thomas Aquinas and Duns Scotus, he concluded that while science may be about the world, scientific knowledge is *knowledge of propositions* (Boehner, 1957). Ockham's words, in Boehner's translation, were: "Properly speaking, the science of nature is about mental contents which are common to such things [i.e., sensible things or substances – M.E.D. & B.B.] and which stand precisely for such things in many propositions . . ." (p. 11).

It is but a short step from Ockham's insight that scientific knowledge is knowledge of propositions to the modern insight that ought to be so obvious that it ought not need saying: *all scientific models are paramorphic representations. All models of judgment are paramorphic representations.* Of course Hoffman was right. A regression model is a paramorphic representation of human judgment. So also is an ANOVA model based on a factorial design. So also is a flow chart based on a set of reaction time data or on the sequence of selections from an information board. And so also is a computer program based upon a protocol analysis.

Conclusion

This retrospective is not intended as a criticism of those other models. It is simply a belated effort to address a criticism that has often been directed specifically at regression models. It may also have the effect of getting competing camps in the judgment and decision arena (Hammond, McClelland, & Mumpower, 1980) to recognize common ground, to see each others' methods as potentially converging operations (Garner, Hake, & Eriksen, 1956), and to use multiple methods in the service of understanding the nature of human judgment and decision making (Einhorn et al., 1979). Brehmer (1979) stated this position clearly:

A common misunderstanding is that SJT [social judgment theory] holds that the judgment process itself operates according to the principles of multiple regression. . . . [R]esearchers following SJT do not believe that the judgment process works according to the principles of multiple regression or the analysis of variance just because they use these methods for investigating the judgment process. . . . Instead, the methods are used to test a series of hypotheses about the nature of the judgment process, hypotheses about the nature of cue weights, function forms, combination rules, and predictability. (p. 199)

The results from numerous studies show that these concepts are useful for describing, predicting, and understanding human judgment. The conception that emerges from these investigations is that human judgment entails a set of imperfectly reliable processes by which the person identifies relevant variables, gives weights to these variables according to their perceived importance, and combines them into a judgment. The combination rule may well depend upon the task (Hammond, 1986), but in a great many task environments the combination rule appears to be well-described by a linear model. If there is to be a challenge to the use of linear models in the scientific study of human judgment, that challenge should be directed at this *conception* of the judgment process, rather than at the use of regression analysis or the analysis of variance. The conception of human judgment emerging from regression studies of human judgment can be refuted only by evidence that shows that judgment is something other than a matter of combining pieces of information that are weighted according to their importance. So far, such evidence has failed to materialize.

References

Adelman, L., & Mumpower, J. (1979). Analysis of expert judgment. *Technological Forecasting and Social Change, 15*, 191–204.

Aldag, R. J., & Stearns, T. M. (1988). Issues in research methodology. *Journal of Management, 14*, 253–276.

Allen, J. S., & Muchinsky, P. M. (1984). Assessing raters' policies in evaluating proposed services for transporting the physically handicapped. *Journal of Applied Psychology, 69*, 3–11.

Anderson, N. H. (1982). *Methods of information integration theory.* New York: Academic Press.

Ashton, R. H. (1974). Cue utilization and expert judgments: A comparison of independent auditors with other judges. *Journal of Applied Psychology, 59*, 437–444.

Ashton, R. H. (1975). User prediction models in accounting: An alternative use. *Accounting Review, 50*, 710–722.

Ashton, R. H. (1980). Sensitivity of multiattribute decision models to alternative specifications of weighting parameters. *Journal of Business Research, 8*, 341–359.

Azuma, H., & Cronbach, L. J. (1966). Cue-response correlations in the attainment of a scalar concept. *American Journal of Psychology, 79*, 38–49.

Balke, W. M., Hammond, K. R., & Meyer, G. D. (1973). An alternate approach to labor-management relations. *Administrative Science Quarterly, 18*, 311–327.

Bell, J. (1984). The effect of presentation form on the use of information in annual reports. *Management Science, 30*, 169–185.

Black, M. (1962). *Models and metaphors: Studies in language and philosophy.* Ithaca, NY: Cornell University Press.

Blevins, D. E. (1975). Claimed vs. calculated cue-weighting systems for screening employee applicants. *Journal of Vocational Behavior, 7*, 327–336.

Boehner, P. (1957). *Ockham: Philosophical writings.* London: Thomas Nelson and Sons Ltd.

Borko, H., & Cadwell, J. (1982). Individual differences in teachers' decision strategies: An investigation of classroom organization and management decisions. *Journal of Educational Psychology, 74*, 598–610.

Boster, J. (1984). Inferring decision making from preferences and behavior: An analysis of Aguaruna Jivaro Manioc selection. *Human Ecology, 12*, 343–358.

Brehmer, A., & Brehmer, B. (1988). What have we learned about human judgment from thirty years of policy capturing? In B. Brehmer & C. R. B. Joyce (Eds.), *Human judgment: The SJT view* (pp. 75–114). Amsterdam: North-Holland.

Brehmer, B. (1973). Single-cue probability learning as a function of the sign and magnitude of the correlation between cue and criterion. *Organizational Behavior and Human Performance, 9*, 377–395.

Brehmer, B. (1979). Preliminaries to a psychology of inference. *Scandinavian Journal of Psychology, 20*, 193–210.

Chan, D. W., & Jackson, D. N. (1982). Individual differences in the perception and judgment of psychopathology. *Multivariate Behavioral Research, 17*, 3–32.

Dalgleish, L. I. (1988). Decision making in child abuse cases: Applications of social judgment theory and signal detection theory. In B. Brehmer & C. R. B. Joyce (Eds.), *Human judgment: The SJT view* (pp. 317–360). Amsterdam: North-Holland.

Darlington, R. B. (1968). Multiple regression in psychological research and practice. *Psychological Bulletin, 69*, 161–182.

Dawes, R. M. (1979). The robust beauty of improper linear models in decision making. *American Psychologist, 34*, 571–582.

Dawes, R. M., & Corrigan, B. (1974). Linear models in decision making. *Psychological Bulletin, 81*, 95–106.

Doherty, M. E., & Balzer, W. K. (1988). Cognitive feedback. In B. Brehmer & C. R. B. Joyce (Eds.), *Human judgment: The SJT view* (pp. 163–197). Amsterdam: North-Holland.

Duhem, P. (1909). *Études sur Léonard de Vinci, Vol. II.* Paris: A. Hermann.

Einhorn, H. J. (1971). Use of nonlinear, noncompensatory models as a function of task and amount of information. *Organizational Behavior and Human Performance, 6*, 1–27.

Einhorn, H. J., Kleinmuntz, D. N., & Kleinmuntz, B. (1979). Linear regression *and* process-tracing models of judgment. *Psychological Review, 86*, 465–485.

Elstein, A. S., & Bordage, G. (1979). Psychology of clinical reasoning. In G. Stone, F. Cohen, & N. Adler (Eds.), *Health psychology: A handbook* (pp. 333–367). San Francisco: Jossey-Bass.

Elstein, A. S., Shulman, L. S., & Sprafka, S. A. (1978). *Medical problem solving: An analysis of clinical reasoning.* Cambridge, MA: Harvard University Press.

Faust, D. (1986). Research on human judgment and its application to clinical practice. *Professional Psychology – Research and Practice, 17*, 420–430.

Feigenbaum, E. A. (1961). The simulation of verbal learning behavior. *Proceedings of the Western Joint Computer Conference, 19*, 121–132.

Fischhoff, B., & Beyth-Marom, R. (1983). Hypothesis evaluation from a Bayesian perspective. *Psychological Review, 90*, 239–260.

Fischhoff, B., Goitein, B., & Shapira, Z. (1983). Subjective expected utility: A model of decision-making. In R. W. Scholz (Ed.), *Decision making under uncertainty* (pp. 183–207). Amsterdam: North-Holland.

French, A. P., & Kennedy, P. J. (1985). *Niels Bohr: A centenary volume.* Cambridge, MA: Harvard University Press.

Garner, W. R., Hake, H. W., & Eriksen, C. W. (1956). Operationism and the concept of perception. *Psychological Review, 63*, 149–159.

Goldberg, L. R. (1968). Simple models or simple processes? Some research on clinical judgments. *American Psychologist, 23*, 483–496.

Goldberg, L. R. (1972). Some recent trends in personality assessment. *Journal of Personality Assessment, 36*, 547–560.

Green, B. F. (1968). Descriptions and explanations: A comment on papers by Hoffman and Edwards. In B. Kleinmuntz (Ed.), *Formal representation of human judgment* (pp. 91–98). New York: Wiley.

Grunert, K. G. (1982). Linear processing in a semantic network: An alternative view of consumer product evaluation. *Journal of Business Research, 10*, 31–42.

Hamm, R. M. (1988). Clinical intuition and clinical analysis: Expertise and the cognitive continuum. In J. Dowie & A. Elstein (Eds.), *Professional judgment: A reader in clinical decision making* (pp. 78–105). Cambridge: Cambridge University Press.

Hammond, K. R. (1986). *A theoretically based review of theory and research in judgment and decision making.* Report No. 260. Boulder: University of Colorado, Center for Research on Judgment and Policy.

Hammond, K. R., McClelland, G. H., & Mumpower, J. (1980). *Human judgment and decision making: Theories, methods, and procedures.* New York: Praeger.

Hesse, M. B. (1966). *Models and analogies in science.* Notre Dame, IN: University of Notre Dame Press.

Hobson, C. J., & Gibson, F. W. (1983). Policy capturing as an approach to understanding and improving performance appraisal: A review of the literature. *Academy of Management Review, 8,* 640–649.

Hoffman, P. J. (1960). The paramorphic representation of clinical judgment. *Psychological Bulletin, 57,* 116–131.

Hogarth, R. M. (1974). Process tracing in clinical judgment. *Behavioral Science, 19,* 298–313.

Holmstrom, V. L., and Beach, L. R. (1973). Subjective expected utility and career preferences. *Organizational Behavior and Human Performance, 10,* 201–207.

Holton, G. (1973). *Thematic origins of scientific thought: Kepler to Einstein.* Cambridge, MA: Harvard University Press.

Holzworth, R. J. (1980). Reversal of order of information in a multiple-cue probability learning task. *Journal of General Psychology, 102,* 211–223.

Jago, A. G. (1978). Configural cue utilization in implicit models of leader behavior. *Organizational Behavior and Human Performance, 22,* 474–496.

Lamiell, J. T., Foss, M. A., Trierweiler, S. J., & Leffel, G. M. (1983). Toward a further understanding of the intuitive personologist: Some preliminary evidence for the dialectical quality of subjective personality impressions. *Journal of Personality, 51,* 213–235.

Miller, A. I. (1986). *Imagery in scientific thought: Creating 20th-century physics.* Cambridge, MA: The MIT Press.

Monahan, C. J., & Muchinsky, P. M. (1985). Intrasubject predictions of vocational preference: Convergent validation via the decision theoretic paradigm. *Journal of Vocational Behavior, 27,* 1–18.

Newell, A., Shaw, J. C., & Simon, H. A. (1960). Report on a general problem solving program for a computer. In *Information Processing: Proceedings of the International Conference on Information Processing* (pp. 256–264). UNESCO, Paris.

Nisbett, R. E., & Wilson, T. D. (1977). Telling more than we can know: Verbal reports on mental processes. *Psychological Review, 84,* 231–259.

Nystedt, L., & Murphy, K. R. (1979). Some conditions affecting the utility of subjectively weighted models in decision making. *Perceptual and Motor Skills, 49,* 583–590.

Parker, B. R., & Srinivasan, V. (1976). Consumer preference approach to planning of rural primary health-care facilities. *Operations Research, 24,* 991–1025.

Payne, J. W. (1973). Alternative approaches to decision making under risk: Moments vs. risk dimensions. *Psychological Bulletin, 80,* 439–453.

Payne, J. W., Braunstein, M. L., & Carroll, J. S. (1978). Exploring predecisional behavior: An alternative approach to decision research. *Organizational Behavior and Human Performance, 22,* 17–44.

Permut, S. E. (1973). Cue utilization patterns in student–faculty evaluation. *Journal of Psychology, 83*, 41–48.

Popper, K. R. (1963). *Conjectures and refutations: The growth of scientific knowledge.* London: Routledge and Kegan Paul.

Ramaprasad, A. (1987). Cognitive process as a basis for MIS and DSS design. *Management Science, 33*, 139–148.

Reed, P. L., & Jackson, D. N. (1975). Clinical judgment of psychopathology: A model for inferential accuracy. *Journal of Abnormal Psychology, 84*, 475–482.

Reilly, B. A., & Doherty, M. E. (1989). A note on the assessment of self-insight in judgment research. *Organizational Behavior and Human Decision Processes, 44*, 123–131.

Reilly, B. A., & Doherty, M. E. (1992). The assessment of self-insight in judgment policies. *Organizational Behavior and Human Decision Processes, 53*, 285–309.

Rock, D. L., Bransford, J. D., Maisto, S. A., & Morey, L. (1987). The study of clinical judgment: An ecological approach. *Clinical Psychology Review, 7*, 645–661.

Romano, J. M., & Bellack, A. S. (1980). Social validation of a component model of assertive behavior. *Journal of Consulting and Clinical Psychology, 48*, 478–490.

Roose, J. E., & Doherty, M. E. (1978). A social judgment theoretic approach to sex discrimination in faculty salaries. *Organizational Behavior and Human Performance, 22*, 193–215.

Royce, W. S., & Weiss, R. L. (1975). Behavioral cues in the judgment of marital satisfaction: A linear-regression analysis. *Journal of Consulting and Clinical Psychology, 43*, 816–824.

Rynes, S. L., Schwab, D. P., & Heneman, H. G. (1983). The role of pay and market pay variability in job application decisions. *Organizational Behavior and Human Performance, 31*, 353–364.

Salancik, G. R., & Conway, M. (1975). Attitude inferences from salient and relevant cognitive content about behavior. *Journal of Personality and Social Psychology, 32*, 829–840.

Schmidt, F. L., Johnson, R. H., & Gugel, J. F. (1978). Utility of policy capturing as an approach to graduate admissions decision-making. *Applied Psychological Measurement, 2*, 347–359.

Schoemaker, P. J. H. (1979). The role of statistical knowledge in gambling decisions: Moment vs. risk dimension approaches. *Organizational Behavior and Human Performance, 24*, 1–17.

Schwartz, S., & Griffin, T. (1986). *Medical thinking: The psychology of medical judgment and decision making.* New York: Springer-Verlag.

Slovic, P., & Lichtenstein, S. (1971). Comparison of Bayesian and regression approaches to the study of information processing in judgment. *Organizational Behavior and Human Performance, 6*, 649–744.

Srinivasan, V., & Shocker, A. D. (1973). Estimating the weights for multiple attributes in a composite criterion using pairwise judgments. *Psychometrika, 38*, 473–493.

Srinivasan, V., Shocker, A. D., & Weinstein, A. G. (1973). Measurement of a composite criterion of management success. *Organizational Behavior and Human Performance, 9*, 147–167.

Stewart, T. R. (1988). Judgment analysis: Procedures. In B. Brehmer & C. R. B. Joyce (Eds.), *Human judgment: The SJT view* (pp. 41–74). Amsterdam: North-Holland.

Taylor, R. L., & Wilsted, W. D. (1976). Capturing judgment policies in performance rating. *Industrial Relations, 15*, 216–224.

Tornay, S. C. (1938). *Ockham: Studies and selections*. La Salle, IL: The Open Court Publishing Co.

Tversky, A. (1977). Features of similarity. *Psychological Review, 84*, 327–352.

Ungson, G. R., Braunstein, D. N., & Hall, P. D. (1981). Managerial information processing: A research review. *Administrative Science Quarterly, 26*, 116–134.

Walker, G., & Weber, D. (1984). A transaction cost approach to make-or-buy decisions. *Administrative Science Quarterly, 29*, 373–391.

Watson, J. D. (1968). *The double helix*. New York: Atheneum Press.

Werner, P. D., Rose, T. L., & Yesavage, J. A. (1983). Reliability, accuracy, and decision-making strategy in clinical predictions of imminent dangerousness. *Journal of Consulting and Clinical Psychology, 51*, 815–825.

Westmeyer, H. (1975). The diagnostic process as a statistical-causal analysis. *Theory and Decision, 6*, 57–86.

Zakay, D. (1985). Expected loss ratio model and the notion of psychological distances. *American Journal of Psychology, 98*, 305–309.

Ziman, J. (1978). *Reliable knowledge: An exploration of the grounds for belief in science*. Cambridge: Cambridge University Press.

20 Islanders and hostages: Deep and surface structures of decision problems

Willem A. Wagenaar, Gideon Keren, and Sarah Lichtenstein

Many theories of decision making assume that every decision problem can be represented as a choice among bets. Prescriptive theories based on this notion, such as subjective expected utility (SEU) theory, take into account only those elements of a decision problem that remain after reduction to a choice-among-bets representation. According to SEU theory, the choice-among-bets formulation forms the *deep structure* of the decision problem. That is, all information that could determine the decision is contained in this reduced representation. Most often decision problems are not presented to decision makers in a deep structure fashion, but by a cover story, which we will call the *surface structure*. Surface structures contain a number of elements that are supposed to be irrelevant for the decision-making process. Tversky and Kahneman (1981), for instance, presented their subjects with the following surface structure:

Imagine that the US is preparing for the outbreak of an unusual Asian disease, which is expected to kill 600 people. Two alternative programs to combat the disease have been proposed. Assume that the exact scientific estimate of the consequences of the program are as follows:
If Program A is adopted, 200 people will be saved.
If Program B is adopted, there is 1/3 probability 600 people will be saved, and 2/3 probability that no people will be saved.
Which of the two programs would you favor? (1981: 453)

Reprinted from *Acta Psychologica*, Vol. 67, W. A. Wagenaar, G. Keren, & S. Lichtenstein, "Islanders and hostages: Deep and surface structures of decision problems," pp. 175–189, 1988, with kind permission from Elsevier Science B.V., Amsterdam, The Netherlands.

All three authors contributed equally to this paper; the order of authorship should not be interpreted otherwise. We thank Paul Slovic for his helpful comments on this paper. This research was supported by the Institute for Perception TNO and by Decision Research, a Branch of Perceptronics, Inc.

Tversky and Kahneman translated the problem to a deep structure, containing a choice between:

(A) a sure saving of 200,
(B) $p = 1/3$ to save 600,
      $p = 2/3$ to save nothing.

It is irrelevant to the deep structure that the problem is located in the U.S., that the loss is of lives rather than money or any other commodity, that people will die from an Asian disease instead of manslaughter, or that the story indicates how many out of 600 will be saved instead of the complementary number of people who will die. Pursuing the latter point, Tversky and Kahneman presented the same deep structure in another fashion. They used the same cover story but presented the two programs as:

If Program C is adopted, 400 people will die.
If Program D is adopted, there is 1/3 probability that nobody will die, and 2/3 probability that 600 people will die. (1981: 453)

Of 152 subjects faced with the choice between A and B, 72% favored program A. However, of another 155 subjects given the choice between C and D, 78% preferred the uncertain outcome of program D. Apparently the two problem representations as analyzed by the subjects are not equal. People derive different deep structures whereas the logic of SEU theory does not.

For the Asian disease problem the SEU logic could be replaced by the logic of prospect theory (Kahneman and Tversky 1979). This logic stipulates that saving lives implies gain relative to the prospect of losing 600 lives first introduced in the cover story. In contrast, mentioning the number of people dying would be seen as a loss relative to the offered prospect that no one may die. Since people are usually risk averse when gains are involved but risk prone when forced to choose among losses, the prospect logic would lead to problem representations that correctly predict subjects' preferences.

Further examples of the effect of changing surface structure in ways to which prospect theory is sensitive are given by Slovic et al. (1982). For example, given a choice between a small sure loss and a gamble offering either a larger loss or no loss, people change their preferences when the sure loss is described as an "insurance premium."

Any descriptive theory of human decision making that has predictive power will for its major part consist of a logic specifying how a subject's understanding of the problem surface structure is transformed into the deep structure analyzed by the decision maker. In this paper we will present examples illustrating the difficulties in making the link between surface structure and deep structure. Changes of a single problem's surface structure will appear to have dramatic effects on subjects' preferences. We conclude that generalization of results obtained with a limited set of surface structures is highly speculative if their correspondence to deep structure is verified only intuitively.

Experiment 1

In 1982, Hammerton et al., published data showing that decision makers were risk averse when faced with a choice that involved losses of lives. The cover story ran as follows:

1. One hundred people live on an island. They all visit the mainland once a week.
2. There is an epidemic of a serious disease on the mainland, and it is known that one islander has returned carrying the disease. Unfortunately, no one (not even the carrier) knows who it is.
3. If nothing is done, everybody on the island has an equal chance of 1% of dying from the disease.
4. If the Medical Officer of Health injects everybody on the island, none of them will get the disease, but the injection itself will cause the carrier to drop dead the next day.

Which course of action would you take if you were the Medical Officer of Health? (1982: 204)

Approximately 83% of the subjects favored injection, which would cause the certain death of one person. Doing nothing, implying an uncertain outcome of zero to many casualties, was rejected by most subjects.

The deep structure of such problems according to SEU theory has been explicated by Keeney (in press). He represented independent risks to many people as a risk profile, that is, a vector, r, specifying the risk to each person. In this formulation, for the islander problem, if nothing is done, the deep structure is a single risk profile with 100 elements showing that each islander has 1% chance of dying:

$$r = (0.01, \ 0.01, \ \ldots \ , \ 0.01).$$

In contrast, if the injection is given, the deep structure according to SEU theory is a lottery among 100 risk profiles, as represented in Figure 20.1. In the lottery, there is a probability, $p_1 = 0.01$, that the first risk profile, in which only the first person dies and all others live, will occur, a probability $p_2 = 0.01$ that the second risk profile will occur, and so forth.

Keeney proposed that a preference for the single risk profile (do nothing) is consistent with a preference for risk equity and risk seeking whereas a preference for the lottery across 100 risk profiles (inject) is consistent with risk aversion.

However, the deep structure assumed by SEU theory is not an obvious one. Subjects may not base their decisions on it, but on one or more elements of the surface structure omitted in the SEU representation. Subjects may wonder how it can be known that exactly one islander got infected, or how

$p_1 = 0.01 \qquad r_1 = (1, 0, \ldots, 0, 0)$

$p_2 = 0.01 \qquad r_2 = (0, 1, \ldots, 0, 0)$

$\vdots \qquad\qquad\qquad \vdots$

$p_{99} = 0.01 \qquad r_{99} = (0, 0, \ldots, 1, 0)$

$p_{100} = 0.01 \qquad r_{100} = (0, 0, \ldots, 0, 1)$

Figure 20.1. A representation according to SEU theory of the "do nothing" option in Hammerton et al.'s (1982) islander problem. The p's are the probabilities of a lottery; the r's are risk profiles.

it was determined that exactly 1% of the infected islanders will die from the disease. One conspicuous element of the surface structure not represented in the deep structure is the pictorial display used by Hammerton et al. to illustrate the choice. This display showed the island with 99 upright black stylized figures and one horizontal red (dead) figure for the inject condition. The do-nothing condition was illustrated by 100 black figures "threatened" by a scattering of red dots. Another element is that subjects were asked to play the role of the medical officer. It is not obvious that the problem would look the same if they identified with the islanders themselves. In fact, Hammerton et al. tested this hypothesis, but they administered role as a within-subjects variable, medical officer always being the first role. It is not surprising that under such conditions only two out of 120 subjects changed their decision. A third element is the omission of the probabilities of different possible outcomes in the do-nothing option. Subjects were told that "possible outcomes included no deaths, one death (the most likely outcome), 2 deaths, and so on up to the highly improbable 100 deaths" (1982: 25), but the probability, for example, that no deaths would occur was not given. The large number of "threatening" red dots, the responsibility attached to the role of medical officer, or the explicit mention of 100 deaths are just three out of many other potential elements that could have shaped the deep structure of the do-nothing condition into something quite different from the structure presented above. These possibilities were checked in this experiment.

Method

Stimuli. Six versions of the islander problem were used. In one condition (Exact) the Hammerton et al. study was replicated as closely as possible, including the pictorial displays. In a second condition (No Display) the written cover story was the same, but the pictorial display was omitted. The other four conditions used expanded versions of the story, with special care taken to describe the role of Medical Officer or islander. The cover story in the Role Officer condition was:

You are the Public Health Officer for a particular region of the country. As such, you are responsible not only for carrying out the public health policies of the country, but also, on occasion, for making independent decisions regarding public health problems that unexpectedly arise. Your superiors recognize that you sometimes must make these tough decisions; afterwards, they always ask you to justify your decision to them. Like you, they are concerned for the best welfare of the community, but you know that, whatever your decision, they will later question it closely.

Such a problem, about which you alone must make a decision, has now arisen. It concerns an island within your jurisdiction. You do not live on the island.

One hundred people live on the island. They have all just returned from a visit to the mainland. There is an epidemic of a serious disease on the mainland, and it is known that *one* of the 100 islanders has been infected with the disease during the visit. Unfortunately, no one, not even the infected person, knows the identity of the infected person.

You could decide to give an injection to everyone on the island. This injection will prevent anyone else from contracting the disease. However, the injection is fatal for the one islander already infected. The injections will fully protect 99 of the islanders but cause the sure death of one of them.

Alternatively, if nothing is done, everyone on the island will become infected with the disease. The disease has no symptoms, but each person who has the disease stands a 1% chance of dying.

As the Public Health Officer for the island, what do you decide?

In the Role Islander condition the cover story was:

You are one of one hundred people who live on an island. You have all just returned from a visit to the mainland, and it is known that *one* of the 100 islanders has been infected with the disease during the visit. Unfortunately, no one, not even the infected person, knows the identity of the infected person.

The authorities could decide to give an injection to everyone on the island. This injection will prevent anyone else from contracting the disease. However, the injection is fatal for the one islander already infected. The injections will fully protect 99 of the islanders, but cause the sure death of one of them. Alternatively, if nothing is done, everyone on the island will become infected with the disease. The disease has no symptoms, but each person who has the disease stands a 1% chance of dying.

As one of the 100 islanders, which option is your own personal preference?

The fifth and sixth conditions were labelled Binomial Officer–C and Binomial Islander–C because the exact binomial probabilities in the do-nothing condition were presented in a chart. (The addition of the code "–C" will be explained in a later section.) In both conditions the do-nothing option was further described by:

For the island as a whole, the most likely outcome in this situation is that one person will die (chances of this are 37%). However, other outcomes are also possible. For example, it is almost as likely that no one will die (the chances of this are 36%). At the other extreme, it is possible, but unlikely, that many people will die. The chart below, labeled "do nothing," shows the chances associated with the possible outcomes of no deaths, one death, two deaths, three deaths, four deaths, and more than four deaths (from 5 to 100).

Inject	Do nothing	
	Number of deaths	Chances
	0	36%
One person will die for sure	1	37%
	2	19%
	3	6%
	4	1.5%
	More than 4	0.5%

In all conditions the cover stories were written in Dutch.

Procedure and subjects. The decision problems were presented to subjects during one-hour sessions in which a number of paper-and-pencil tasks were administered. No time limit was imposed.

The subjects were 622 student volunteers from different Dutch universities. They were paid for their participation.

Results and discussion

The results are presented in Table 20.1. The Exact condition, although eliciting the most "inject" responses, did not show as much risk aversion as did the original Hammerton et al. study, $\chi^2(1) = 14.6$, $p < 0.01$.

As a rule of thumb we can state that, since in all conditions the number of subjects (shown in Table 20.1) approximates 100, differences in a column are significant when they are above 14% (cf. Rümke, 1976). With this criterion in mind we can draw the following conclusions:

1. The absence of the pictorial illustration in the No Display condition did not change the results.
2. The expanded story led to less risk aversion, significantly so for the Officer Conditions.
3. The two Islander instructions led to more risk aversion than the Officer instructions but significance was reached only in the Binomial condition.
4. Addition of the binomial numbers hardly changed the subjects' preferences.

Clearly, we were not successful at replicating the risk-aversion effect of Hammerton et al. In only three of our six conditions was risk aversion the majority choice. There are several possible explanations for the differences. For example, the subjects for the Hammerton et al. study were a representative sample of the British adult population, whereas our subjects were Dutch

Table 20.1. *Results of experiment 1: Percentage of subjects choosing the injection*

Condition	n	Inject
Exact	99	61
No Display	99	52
Role Officer	94	37
Role Islander	96	45
Binomial Officer–C	115	37
Binomial Islander–C	119	55

college students. Hammerton et al. presented their task as a poll, at the door, whereas we presented it as one of several paper-and-pencil tasks in a classroom setting.

More illustrative of the difficulties one engages in when rich surface structures are translated into deep structures is the change in preference resulting from an increased emphasis on role responsibilities. The Exact, No Display, Role Officer, and Binomial Officer conditions all asked for a response based on the role of a Medical Health Officer. But the two short versions (Exact and No Display) received about 20 percentage points more risk-averse choices than did the two longer versions. This suggests that the conclusions about the form of utility curves put forward by Hammerton et al. are unwarranted. If risk-averse utility curves are the basis for decisions, changes in the surface structure should not have had such extreme changes in choice.

Experiment 2

One element of Hammerton's islander problem not represented in the deep structure derived by using SEU logic is the fact that the certain outcome is reached through action, the uncertain outcome through inaction. The 63% of our Officer subjects who appeared to be risk seeking might instead be stating a preference for taking no action. Perhaps it is worse if people die from an injection you gave than if people die from a disease they caught themselves. Would the preferences be the same if, instead, the certain death outcome were linked to doing nothing? Testing this possibility requires the construction of a cover story radically different from the stories of experiment 1. Yet the logic of SEU theory does not allow us to model an action-certainty relation in the deep structure problem representation unless strong assumptions are made about the utility of action. Since Hammerton et al. did not put forward such assumptions, it seems worthwhile investigating the extent to which this neglected aspect of the problem's surface structure determines the deep structure of the problem representation.

In addition, in this experiment we used both Dutch and American college students, to explore the generalization of effects across different populations.

Method

Stimuli. Two new cover stories were written that complemented the two Binomial stories of experiment 1. In the two previous Binomial stories, action was associated with the *certain* outcome of one death. Hence, those conditions were labeled –C. In the new stories action is associated with an *uncertain* number of deaths and coded –U.

The new cover stories were identical with the Binomial stories in experiment 1 except for the two paragraphs describing the two decision alternatives. For the Binomial Officer [Islander]–U group, these two paragraphs said:

> If nothing is done, the infected person will surely die. However, the other 99 islanders are safe because the disease can no longer spread (it is not contagious any more).
>
> Alternatively, you [the authorities] could decide to give an injection to everyone on the island. This injection will halt the course of the disease in the infected person, so that person will not die from the disease. However, the injection itself is risky: each person who is injected (including the infected person) stands a 1% chance of dying from the injection. For the island as a whole, the most likely outcome in this situation is that exactly one person will die (the chances of this are 37%). However, other outcomes are also possible. For example, it is almost as likely that no one will die (the chances of this are 36%). At the other extreme, it is possible, but unlikely, that many people will die. The chart below, labeled "Inject," shows the chances associated with the possible outcomes of no deaths, one death, two deaths, three deaths, four deaths, and more than four deaths (from 5 to 100).

(The accompanying chart was relabeled appropriately.)

Procedure and subjects. The subjects were 223 students from a Dutch university and 326 Americans, volunteers who responded to an ad in the student newspaper of the University of Oregon. The Dutch students each received one of two –U forms. Each American subject received one of the four Binomial forms. The procedure was the same as used in experiment 1.

Results and discussion

The results are summarized in Table 20.2, together with the Dutch Binomial–C conditions of experiment 1.

For the Dutch subjects, when action was associated with the uncertain outcome subjects were more likely to prefer action. This was true for both the officers, $\chi^2(1) = 6.28$, $p < 0.01$, and the islanders, $\chi^2(1) = 4.48$, $p < 0.05$. This pattern was also found, but not significantly, for the American subjects.

For the Dutch students, in both the –C (as previously noted) and the –U conditions islanders were more inclined to action than were officers. This was not found for the American students.

Table 20.2. *Results of experiment 2: Percentage of subjects choosing the injection and percentage choosing the one-certain-death outcome*

Condition	Dutch			American		
	n	Inject	Certain	n	Inject	Certain
Binomial Officer–C	115[a]	37	37	83	40	40
Binomial Islander–C	119[a]	55	55	81	37	37
Binomial Officer–U	107	54	46	81	42	58
Binomial Islander–U	116	68	32	81	49	51

Note: C means injection led to one certain death: U means injection led to an uncertain number of deaths.
[a] These subjects were from experiment 1.

When the choices were coded in terms of risk propensity instead of action preparedness a curious, and highly significant, interaction was revealed for the Dutch subjects: linking action to uncertainty made officers *less* risk seeking but islanders *more* risk seeking. In other words, officers disliked the certain-death outcome more when it was a result of their own injections, whereas islanders disliked the certain death more when it was the result of the authorities' inaction. However, this interaction was completely lacking in the American data. There, both islanders and officers disliked the certain-death outcome more when it was a result of action (although this result fell just short of traditional, $p = 0.05$, significance for the islanders).

Taking experiments 1 and 2 together, we can discern only one possible regularity: In four of the five pairs of conditions that varied role, holding all else equal (that is, for the pairs labeled "Role," "Dutch Binomial–C," "Dutch Binomial–U," and "American Binomial–U"), islanders were more likely to choose the action alternative than were medical officers. Intriguing explanations of this possible finding spring readily to mind. Such theorizing, however, would be a rewarding enterprise only if the phenomenon possessed some generality. It would be unsatisfactory to develop a theory of the effect of role on decision making if the theory is restricted to islanders threatened with infectious diseases. Hence experiment 3.

Experiment 3

Method

In this experiment the four Binomial conditions were repeated using an entirely new cover story, a hostage problem, in which all the previously mentioned possible components of deep structure were identical to the islander problem.

The subjects were 205 Dutch university students. The procedure was identical to the procedure in the first two experiments.

The cover story for the Hostage Authority–C condition was as follows:

At this moment 100 children are kept hostage in a kindergarten. You are the authority who is responsible for all decisions taken in this situation. Although you are assisted by a crisis team that can suggest some solutions, the final responsibility for raiding or not raiding the school resides with you.

The children have now been kept in the school for ten days, and the winterly conditions are appalling. The terrorists request a discussion with an important personality from abroad. This talk is being organized but it cannot take place for two days. The terrorists have agreed to surrender after the talk and refuse any further communication. If the school is not raided within two days, medical experts estimate that every child has a 1% chance of dying from dehydration, hunger, and cold. For the group as a whole, the most likely outcome of deferring the raid is that exactly one child will die (the chances of this are 37%). However, other outcomes are also possible. For example, it is almost as likely that no one will die (the chances of this are 36%). At the other extreme it is possible, but unlikely, that many children will die.

The chart below, labeled "do nothing," shows the chances associated with the possible outcomes of no deaths, one death, two deaths, three deaths, four deaths, and more than four deaths (from 5 to 100). If the school is raided one child will certainly be killed, but not more than one. The terrorists have mounted explosives that will ignite automatically as soon as the school is raided. One of the children is tied to the explosives, and it is unknown which child it is. The military experts agree that the life of the child cannot be saved. There is no reason to doubt the information of the medical and military experts.

[The chart was then presented.]

What would you, being the responsible authority, decide?

In the Hostage Parent–U condition the cover story was:

You are the parent of one of 100 children who are kept hostage in a kindergarten. During the terrorist action one child was critically wounded, but it is not known which child. The child needs medical treatment urgently, but the terrorists refuse treatment until their requests are fulfilled. They want a discussion with an important personality from abroad. This talk is being organized but it cannot take place for two days. The terrorists have agreed to surrender after this talk and refuse any further communication. According to the medical experts the child is certain to die within two days without medical treatment.

In order to save the child the school must be raided. Military experts tell us that every child has a 1% chance to be killed during the raid. For the group as a whole the most likely outcome of the raid is that exactly one child will die (the chances of this are 37%). However, other outcomes are also possible. For example, it is almost as likely that no one will die (the chances of this are 36%). At the other extreme, it is possible, but unlikely, that many children will die. The chart below, labeled "raid," shows the chances associated with the possible outcomes of no deaths, one death, two deaths, three deaths, four deaths, and more than four deaths (from 5 to 100).

[The chart was then presented.]

Which decision would you prefer, being the parent of one of the children?

Table 20.3. *Results of experiment 3: Percentage of subjects choosing the raid and percentage choosing the one-certain-death outcome*

Condition	n	Raid	Certain
Hostages Authority–C	50	8%	8%
Hostages Parent–C	50	13%	13%
Hostages Authority–U	52	86%	14%
Hostages Parent–U	53	85%	15%

Note: C means the raid led to one certain death;
U means the raid led to an uncertain number of deaths.

The other two stories (Hostage Authority–U and Hostage Parent–C) were variations of the two stories presented above. The stories were presented in Dutch.

Results and discussion

The results are summarized in Table 20.3. These results differ dramatically from those obtained in the previous experiments. All groups preferred the uncertain choice, independent of either role or association with the action variable.

In order to test the robustness of these results, experiment 3 was replicated with 151 Dutch managers and 165 Israeli university students. The percentage of responses favoring the certain choice was 17% and 27% respectively and these numbers were independent of the four conditions.

Many possible reasons exist for this large effect of context change. It is possible that the degree of reality is much higher in the hostage study. After all, such a terrorist action really occurred in The Netherlands in the late seventies. The malevolent agent is human instead of a virus. The victims are children instead of islanders of unspecified age. Public interest in the hostages' situation might be much higher because dying in the hands of a terrorist is much more unusual than dying from a disease. Whatever the explanation is, it is abundantly clear that change of cover story affected the deep structure of the problem as it was analyzed by subjects. Even if we had proposed a theory that would account for all results obtained with the islander cover story, it is not clear how such a theory would predict these dramatically different results for the hostages problem.

General discussion

Starting from Hammerton et al.'s result of 83% preference for the certain outcome we have, after a number of changes in the problem's surface structure, finally come to 92% preference for the uncertain outcome. Figure 20.2 shows how much our results, in terms of preference for the certain outcome, spread along the percentage axis (in Figure 20.2 the Dutch and American data from experiment 2 have been combined).

The shifts in preference are brought about by three types of variations in the surface structure of the problem formulation: variations of presentation, variations within confounding variables, and variations of context. Hammerton et al. interpreted their results in terms of the shape of utility curves. Since SEU theory has nothing to say about the variations that appeared to determine the decisions to such a great extent, such an interpretation was hasty.

Any descriptive theory of human decision making should specify how a problem's surface structure is transformed into deep structure that is analyzed by the decision maker. The theory would then specify how this deep structure is evaluated in order to reach a decision. Most decision theories are explicit with respect to the evaluation function but uninformative about the earlier, transformation phase, which is left to the imagination of the researcher. Ignoring the transformation stage can lead to a habit of stating conclusions in terms of an assumed deep structure without testing the researchers' intuitions that gave rise to this structure.

A strictly formal theory, like SEU theory, does not pretend to describe the transformation from surface to deep structure and cannot be blamed for the transformations proposed by others. But the absence of transformation rules could finally prove to be a basic obstacle for application of the theory, which is why richer theories, encompassing transformation prescriptions, should be preferred. A good example of such a theory is Kahneman and Tversky's (1979; Tversky and Kahneman 1981) prospect theory:

Prospect theory describes two phases in the choice process: an early phase of editing and a subsequent phase of evaluation. The editing phase consists of preliminary analysis of the offered prospects. . . . (Kahneman and Tversky 1979: 274)

As summarized by Fischhoff (1983), six editing operations have been identified in prospect theory: (a) coding (describing each outcome in terms of a reference point), (b) segregation (isolating the riskless from the risky components of a prospect), (c) cancellation (discarding the components that are shared by all prospects), (d) combination (adding probabilities that are associated with identical outcomes), (e) simplification (rounding probabilities or outcomes), and (f) detection of dominance (eliminating dominated prospects).

We laud this effort to develop a theory of framing; however, this list of editing operations does not help us in understanding the present data. The list refers to operations on probabilities and outcomes, yet these were the very aspects that were kept constant in the change from islanders to hostages.

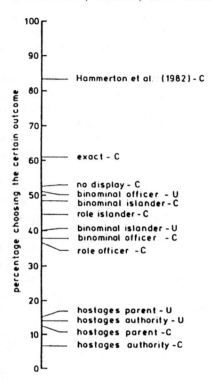

Figure 20.2. Degree of preference for the certain outcome for our three experiments and for Hammerton et al. (1982).

The islander and hostage cover stories illustrate that the jump from surface structure to deep structure might be tricky. The reason is, of course, that the surface structures were chosen to resemble realistic situations of everyday life. In that manner a richness is tapped which ensures the realism of the tasks performed by the subjects but which at the same time undermines the construct validity of the research. Using unrealistic tasks is misleading; using tasks without construct validity is pointless. The only narrow path through this Scylla and Charybdis is to vary the surface structures of realistic decision problems systematically along all dimensions that are deemed irrelevant by the theory being tested. As soon as inconsistencies are found the theory will need to be reformulated or expanded, especially with respect to the rules that govern the transformation from surface to deep structure. Expansion of theories could be guided by the reasons subjects provide for their choices. Such experimental programs are time consuming and expensive. But who said that decision theory should be completed by the turn of the century?

References

Fischhoff, B., 1983. Predicting frames. Journal of Experimental Psychology: Learning, Memory and Cognition, 9, 103–116.

Hammerton, M., M.W., Jones-Lee and V. Abbott, 1982. Equity and public risk: some empirical results. Operations Research 30, 203–207.

Kahneman, D. and A. Tversky, 1979. Prospect theory: an analysis of decision under risk. Econometrica 47, 263–292.

Keeney, R.L., in press. "The analysis of risks of fatalities." In: J. Menkes, V. Covello and J. Mumpower (eds.), Contemporary issues in risk analysis. New York: Plenum.

Rümke, C.L., 1976. Nomogrammen voor de toetsing van het verschil tussen twee percentages of kansen. Nederlands Tijdschrift voor Geneeskunde 120, 2205–2211.

Slovic, P., B. Fischhoff and S. Lichtenstein, 1982. "Response mode, framing, and information-processing effects in risk assessment." In: R. Hogarth (ed.), New directions for methodology of social and behavioral science: question framing and response consistency, Vol. 11. San Francisco, CA: Jossey-Bass. pp. 21–36.

Tversky, A. and D. Kahneman, 1981. The framing of decisions and the psychology of choice. Science 211, 453–458.

21 Content and discontent: Indications and implications of domain specificity in preferential decision making

William M. Goldstein and Elke U. Weber

I. Introduction

Research on preferential decision making has been and largely continues to be dominated by the use of a particular kind of stimulus material: simple monetary gambles. Sometimes other highly structured stimuli are used (e.g., apartments described in terms of monthly rent and distance from work), but almost always the stimuli have an incomplete and schematic form that conveys a generic quality to the choice alternatives. Although research has also been conducted on moral decision making (Baron, 1993; Mellers & Baron, 1993), legal decision making (Hastie, 1993; Lloyd-Bostock, 1989), medical decision making (Bursztajn, Feinbloom, Hamm, & Brodsky, 1990; Schwartz & Griffin, 1986), and political decision making (Sniderman, Brody, & Tetlock, 1991), as well as some other content-specific forms of decision making, the fact remains that the vast majority of studies on preferential choice and judgment have employed simple monetary gambles or other highly structured and content-impoverished stimuli. This state of affairs contrasts sharply with several other areas of psychology, where the *semantic content* of the stimuli, that is, what the task is "about," has been found to influence behavior, and where energetic research has been undertaken to identify functionally distinct domains of content, to isolate the affected stages of psychological processing, and to delineate the responsible psychological mechanisms (Hirschfeld & Gelman, 1994).

Our impression is that decision researchers have regarded these develop-

This chapter originally appeared in J. R. Busemeyer, R. Hastie, & D. L. Medin (Eds.), *The Psychology of Learning and Motivation, Volume 32. Decision Making from a Cognitive Perspective* (pp. 83–136). San Diego: Academic Press, 1995. Copyright © 1995 by Academic Press, Inc. Reprinted by permission.

The authors thank Jerome Busemeyer, Jeanne Enders, Gerd Gigerenzer, Reid Hastie, Douglas Medin, and especially Miriam Bassok for valuable comments on an earlier draft of this chapter.

ments in neighboring fields with considerable suspicion, but for reasons that may not be readily apparent to others. It may appear that decision researchers fear a loss of parsimony. It may indeed seem a poor trade to exchange familiar content-free taxonomies of decision problems (e.g., decisions under uncertainty, risk, and certainty) for an explosion of content-specific categories of decisions (e.g., career decisions, housing decisions, animal, mineral, and vegetable decisions, etc.), each of which may require a different theory. However, in addition to a desire for parsimony, we believe that decision researchers have reservations that are theoretically based. The prevalent use of simple gambles as stimuli is sanctioned by fundamental metatheoretical assertions about the "essence" of decision making, coupled with the belief that generalizability is enhanced by studying decision making in its "essential" form. If the metatheory of decision research has been underappreciated by others, we believe that decision researchers often reciprocate by failing to appreciate the reasons why many researchers have come to accept content specificity as a fact and as a research topic. Various areas of psychology have had their own metatheories to contend with, and have given up the dream of content-free accounts of behavior only when forced to by the data.

The purpose of this chapter is to critique the metatheory that guides most research on preferential judgment and choice, which we call the *gambling metaphor*, but to do so specifically with respect to the issue of content effects. Others have voiced concerns at the level of general metatheory, but these have related mainly to other issues (which will be discussed later). Some possible exceptions notwithstanding (Beach & Mitchell, 1987; Hastie, 1991), these criticisms need not be interpreted as questioning the content-impoverished nature of the stimuli that are used almost universally in studies of preferential decision making. Such a critique is the burden of this chapter.

It should be emphasized that we are restricting our scope to the study of preference and evaluation, that is, to decisions about what is "good." Although judgment and decision researchers collectively have devoted less attention to the possibility that behavior may depend on the semantic content of the stimuli than have researchers in other areas of psychology, within decision research, attention (or inattention) to the issue has been uneven. Researchers interested in learning have shown the most concern toward content, those studying probabilistic judgment have shown less (these areas of research will be discussed later), and investigators of preference and evaluation appear to have shown the least concern. Although research on probabilistic judgment has shifted from reliance on bookbag-and-poker-chip problems to word problems, an analogous shift has not taken place in research on preferential judgment and choice. In this area of decision research, simple monetary gambles remain as important to researchers as fruit flies to geneticists (Lopes, 1983).

The use of gambles as stimuli in psychological experiments is a reasonable extension of some time-honored lines of thought. We review this background to show how compelling the use of gambles can be. Then, we critique the gambling metaphor in two ways. First, we briefly review several areas of psychology in which the semantic content of stimuli has been found to be an important determinant of behavior: in memory, animal learning, categories and concepts, deductive reasoning, problem solving and expertise, and cognitive development. The psychological mechanisms underlying preferential decision making overlap sufficiently with those in other areas of psychology that decision researchers *should* draw from the substantive results concerning the effects of semantic content. We also find interesting historical parallels between developments in decision research and those in some of the other areas we discuss (especially memory), suggesting that thinking in decision research may evolve in similar ways. Our second line of criticism is more direct. We review the research on preferential decision making that bears on the issue of content dependence. We find a number of studies that might be interpreted as supporting the view that content effects are present and interesting, but they do not necessarily impugn the core theory of the gambling metaphor. Other recent studies, however, are much more damaging. They provide evidence that the central variables of the gambling metaphor – degree of belief and degree of desirability – cannot support generalizations at the level of analysis to which the gambling metaphor aspires. Finally, we sketch our views of what a theory of content effects in preferential decision making might look like if it is to maintain a reasonable degree of parsimony.

II. Metatheory of preferential decision research: History of the gambling metaphor

In the late 1940s and 1950s, a number of psychologists became aware of work in economics and statistics that had direct implications for psychological measurement. The view that psychological measurement is central to the establishment of a scientific psychology goes back to Immanuel Kant, who concluded that psychological measurement was unattainable and that psychology therefore could never be more than a "merely" empirical science. Gustav Fechner (1860) proposed a method of psychological measurement, but because it relied on the prior measurement of response probabilities, it failed to achieve the goal of "fundamental" measurement, that is, measurement without any prior measurement of any kind. Nevertheless, Fechner's work was extremely influential and, as developed further (especially by Thurstone, e.g., 1927; see Thurstone, 1959), became the basis for much of the work on psychological measurement in the first half of this century.

In 1947, von Neumann and Morgenstern published the second edition of their book, *Theory of Games and Economic Behavior*, in which they listed conditions under which a person's choices among gambles could be used to infer a "utility function" for the outcomes of the gambles, which in turn could be used to describe the person's choices. That is, if the conditions were satisfied, people's choices could be described as if they were choosing so as to maximize the expected utility of choice outcomes. Expected utility was seen by psychologists as an interesting model of individual choice behavior, and they (and others) soon undertook to test it (Preston & Baratta, 1948; Mosteller & Nogee, 1951). Even more exciting was the fact the von Neumann and Morgenstern were a hair's breadth away from fundamental measurement of a psychological variable: utility. However, because von Neumann and Morgenstern required the prior measurement of the probabilities with which events occurred in the gambles offered to subjects, they did not quite achieve fundamental measurement. Nevertheless, von Neumann and Morgenstern's approach was quite different from Fechner's, and it generated much interest. By 1954, Leonard J. Savage had extended the von Neumann and Morgenstern approach to gambles whose payoffs depended on the results of uncertain events, for example, the result of an election or the weather, without prior measurement of the probabilities. In his book, *The Foundations of Statistics*, Savage provided conditions under which a person's choices could be used to infer a "subjective probability function" as well as a "utility function," and thus Savage spelled out conditions for true fundamental measurement of these psychological variables.

Psychologists then began to test whether these conditions were satisfied, and this stream of psychological research on decision making was off and running (Edwards, 1954; Thrall, Coombs, & Davis, 1954). In this research, one of the presuppositions that psychologists adopted is what we call the gambling metaphor. The examples in Savage's book make it clear that gambling decisions were believed to be prototypical of virtually *all* decisions. Almost any contemplated action, for example, where to go to school, what job to take, or whom to marry, will have consequences that cannot be predicted with certainty but which vary in their likelihood and desirability. In this sense, then, real-life decisions have the same structure as gambles. Moreover, because this applies to virtually all decisions, *life is a gamble*. The generality of this metaphor leads directly to an argument for a simplification in reasearch practice: if all interesting real-life decisions are fundamentally like gambling decisions, then real-life decision processes can be studied in the laboratory by asking people to make gambling choices. Bolstered by this argument, simple monetary gambles have become the primary stimulus material used in research on preferential decision making. Also, because of the appeal of the argument that all decisions can be reduced to the same structure, decision researchers have resisted the implications of recent findings on domain specificity, namely that *content* influences psychological processes.

Although the metaphor of life as a gamble apparently came to psychology via von Neumann and Morgenstern (1947) and Savage (1954), its origins are considerably older, dating back to Jakob Bernoulli's (1713) *Ars Conjectandi*. Discussions of gambling figured heavily in the mid-seventeenth century correspondence between Pascal and Fermat, but unlike Bernoulli, these early probabilists did not consider gambles to be representative of all decision problems. Rather, the very early probabilists turned to the law, both for a source of ideas (about degrees of certainty) and for a source of applications (e.g., aleatory contracts in matters of insurance, annuities, fair shares of uncertain profits, and games of chance; see Daston, 1988). By contrast Bernoulli made it clear that he was pursuing probability as "a general theory of rational decision under uncertainty, not just a mathematization of legal practice" (Daston, 1988, p. 44). He was seeking a theory that would apply to "choices about which witness (or creed) to believe, which venture to invest in, which candidate to elect, what insurance premium to charge, which scientific theory to endorse" (Daston, 1988, p. 50).

The generality of the gambling metaphor was reinforced by Bernoulli's interpretation of probability. Daston (1988) says:

We owe to Bernoulli the classical interpretation of probability as a state of mind rather than a state of the world. . . . Bernoulli insists that the throw of a die is "no less necessary (*non minus necessario*)" than an eclipse. The only difference between the gambler and the astronomer lies in the relative completeness of their respective knowledge of dice and eclipses, and a people ignorant of astronomy might well gamble on the occurrence of eclipses. "Contingent" events only exist relative to our ignorance, so that one man's contingency might easily be another's necessity. (pp. 34–35)

This view of probability as a degree of knowledge is entirely consistent with Savage's (1954) notion (anticipated by Ramsey, 1931) of "personal probability" as a degree of belief. Moreover, by so enlarging the scope of events to which the concept of probability applies, this view strengthens the position that all of life's decisions have the same structure as games of chance.

The generality of the gambling metaphor was supported in an analogous way by Jakob Bernoulli's nephew, Daniel. Daniel Bernoulli (1738), although preceded by Gabriel Cramer (1728) as Bernoulli himself states, is usually credited with the idea that people do not (and should not) deliberate directly about the monetary amounts that might accrue to them in a game of chance (or from an insurance contract, etc.) (correspondence of Gabriel Cramer to Nicolas Bernoulli in a letter dated May 21, 1728). Instead, people deliberate about the *worth* of that money to them, its *utility*, which depends on people's individual circumstances (e.g., their wealth). As Cramer (1728) put it, "Mathematicians value money in proportion to its quantity, commonsense men in proportion to its use" (quoted by Jorland, 1987, p. 159). Bernoulli's detailed examples referred to the utility of money, and the specific (logarithmic) utility function that Bernoulli proposed is only defined for a quantitative argument (e.g., money). Nevertheless, in his discussion, Bernoulli at least implied that the concept of utility was to be applied to other "items" as well, including the abstract notion of a person's "productive capacity" (D. Bernoulli, p. 25; see Daston, 1988, p. 74, for links to contemporary economic theory). In this way, Daniel Bernoulli's work can be seen as enlarging the scope of the "outcomes" that must be addressed by a theory of behavior under uncertainty. Whether a gamble paid off in monetary amounts or in another "currency" was immaterial. What mattered was the subjective *value* placed on the potential outcomes by the decision maker.

In laying out the logic and history behind the gambling metaphor's position that monetary gambles may be taken as emblematic of all of life's decisions, we have implicitly relied on another assumption. So far, the argument has proceeded roughly as follows. Monetary gambles are characterized by two sorts of variables: (1) the amounts of money that might be won or lost, and (2) the probabilities with which these outcomes actually occur. Through Daniel Bernoulli's treatment of utility, we are led to think of the monetary outcomes merely as representatives of any valued consequences that might result from the choice of an alternative. What counts is that people place more or less *value* (desire, want, hope, fear, etc.) on different outcomes. By using Jakob Bernoulli's interpretation of probability, we are led to think of the probabilities of the monetary gamble merely as representatives of the degrees of *belief* that a person might hold about the prospects that ensuing events will actually produce the valued outcomes. The implicit assumption in this approach, the gambling metaphor's *reductionist* aspect, is that all of the considerations involved in a decision can be reduced to two types of variables: (1) (degree of) value and (2) (degree of) belief.

The position that people evaluate their alternatives in terms of beliefs and values – that people take deliberate actions (and only those deliberate actions) that they *believe* will advance their *valued* goals – is a position that stretches back to antiquity. Schick (1991) traces this view to Aristotle in *De Motu Animalium* and *Nicomachean Ethics*. Some philosophers have held that it is necessary to assume some form of this view (characterized as assuming that people are rational in a very general sense) to be able to infer someone's beliefs from his or her behavior, or indeed to infer that the person has any beliefs at all (Cherniak, 1986; Davidson, 1973, 1974, 1975; Dennett, 1978, 1987; Stich, 1990, chap. 2, traces all variants of this idea to a passage in Quine, 1960). The view that people evaluate alternatives in terms of beliefs and values is so intuitive and so entrenched in Western culture that philosophers tend to refer to it as "folk psychology," and the connection to decision theory has not gone unnoticed (Pettit, 1991). (It should be noted that philosophers sometimes use the term in what seems to be a derogatory way. The claim is that a belief–value theory of behavior is a naive "folk" theory in much the same way that naive, intuitive, untutored physics is a "folk" theory, and moreover that both theories are empirically false. See Christensen and Turner, 1993, for papers on various aspects of these issues.)

The gambling metaphor is a special case of belief–value "folk" psychology that directs attention not to beliefs and values in themselves, but to the *degree* of belief and the *degree* of value. From this perspective, one's *reasons* for liking something or for thinking that an event is likely to happen, or more generally the *processes* by which one determines one's beliefs and values, are immaterial to the final choice among alternatives. Thus, the gambling metaphor is positioned at a level of analysis where the semantic content of the choice alternatives is irrelevant. It does not mandate the use of simple monetary gambles as stimuli, but it can be taken as theoretical justification.

It is important to note that the psychologists who drew inspiration from the work of von Neumann and Morgenstern (1947) and Savage (1954) didn't immediately, or unreflectively or exclusively, begin employing simple monetary gambles as stimuli. For example, Coombs and Beardslee (1954) reported an experiment in which the prizes in an imaginary lottery consisted of a rattan chair, an electric broiler, a typewriter, a radio, and a portable phonograph. Edwards commented in his well-known *Psychological Bulletin* paper (1954) that "Coombs is reluctant to use sums of money as the valuable objects in his experiments because of the danger that subjects will respond to the numerical value of the amount of dollars rather than to the psychological value. Therefore he used various desirable objects (e.g., a radio) as stimuli, ..." Nevertheless, simple monetary gambles soon came to predominate.[1]

III. Content and its discontents

A. *Nonsense syllables and British associationism*

The prototypical example of the use of content-impoverished stimuli in psychological research is provided by Ebbinghaus' (1964) study of memory. Among the many important contributions for which he is remembered, Ebbinghaus was the originator of stimulus materials known as "nonsense syllables." Although the use of nonsense syllables has since lost its popularity, we think the use of nonsense syllables by memory researchers provides an illuminating and provocative analogy to the use of simple monetary gambles by decision researchers. This comparison is not meant to be disparaging (to either party). On the contrary, we think this comparison helps to illustrate why the use of content-impoverished stimuli can be so appealing. For both nonsense syllables and monetary gambles, the choice of stimulus materials was backed by theoretical frameworks that strongly suggested that the generalizability of results would be enhanced, not limited, by the use of these stimuli. In neither case were stimulus materials chosen lightly, or merely for convenience. Moreover, their use enabled researchers to make significant progress, discovering results and developing methods of enduring importance. Nevertheless, in the case of memory research, as well as in the other areas that we review later, the recurring finding is that behavior is affected by the semantic content of the stimulus materials employed. In these areas, the data force the conclusion that the exclusive use of content-impoverished stimuli simply cannot support theory at the level of generality implied by the metatheory. Similar data are beginning to become available in work on preferential decision making.

Ebbinghaus (1964) described his reasons for employing content-impoverished materials as follows:

The nonsense material, just described, offers many advantages, in part because of this very lack of meaning. First of all, it is relatively simple and relatively homogeneous. In the case of the material nearest at hand, namely poetry or prose, the content is now narrative in style, now descriptive, or now reflective; it contains now a phrase that is pathetic, now one that is humorous; its metaphors are sometimes beautiful, sometimes harsh; its rhythm is sometimes smooth and sometimes rough. There is thus brought into play a multiplicity of influences which change without regularity and are therefore disturbing. Such are associations which dart here and there, different degrees of interest, lines of verse recalled because of their striking quality or their beauty, and the like. All this is avoided with our syllables. (p. 23)

Ebbinghaus goes on to say that nonsense syllables can be used to generate an endless supply of new series that are comparable with each other, "while different poems, different prose pieces always have something incomparable" (p. 24). Also, series of nonsense syllables can be varied quantitatively, "whereas to break off before the end or to begin in the middle of the verse or the sentence leads to new complications because of various unavoidable disturbances of the meaning" (p. 24). Thus, Ebbinghaus used meaningless materials because they conferred certain practical advantages, and because their use reduced response variability caused by factors outside the main focus of his study.

It is good experimental practice to reduce error variance by careful selection of stimuli and by control of extraneous factors. However, this by itself is not enough to account for the popularity of nonsense syllables and gambles. In both cases, the stimulus materials were sanctioned by widely respected *theoretical frameworks* that (1) provided guidance about exactly which factors should be regarded as "extraneous" (e.g., meaningful content), and (2) provided a rationale for believing that the simplified stimuli retained exactly the structure required to get to the bottom of issues at the very foundation of psychology.

To understand this in the case of Ebbinghaus' meaningless materials and his experimental task of serial recall, one must consider a combination of the following beliefs: (1) empiricism (i.e., the assumption that all knowledge comes from experience), (2) sensationist atomism (i.e., the assumption that elementary sensations and memories of sensations form the indivisible "atoms" of experience which are combined to form "complex ideas" and which occur in sequences to form the "train of thought"), and (3) associationism (i.e., the assumption that ideas or sensations experienced in contiguity, at the same time or in quick succession, become "associated" and are thereby capable of eliciting one another in sequence or of coalescing into "complex ideas"). Given such a position, a study of the way that new materials without prior associations (e.g., nonsense syllables) come to be associated as a result of exposure to sequences (as in the serial recall task) is nothing less than a study of the ontogeny of mind. Titchener, who was perhaps the most outspoken and influential proponent of this theoretical position, considered "the recourse to nonsense syllables, as the means to the study of (conscious) association, . . . the most considerable advance in this chapter of psychology, since the time of Aristotle" (Titchener, 1909, pp. 380–381; quoted by Verhave & van Hoorn, 1987, p. 89). (To be fair, it should be noted that Ebbinghaus himself did not subscribe to any simple version of associationist theory; see Hoffman, Bamberg, Bringmann, & Klein, 1987; Verhave & van Hoorn, 1987. In fact, some of Ebbinghaus' own experiments demonstrated that a simple chaining of associations between adjacent items in a list could not account for the observed behavior. Moreover, Ebbinghaus *was* concerned with meaningful material as well as nonsense syllables; throughout his book, Ebbinghaus made comparisons between the learning of nonsense syllables and the learning of poetry.)

Simple gambles are as prevalent in decision research as nonsense syllables ever were in memory research (see Newman, 1987). In both cases, the content-impoverished stimuli, and the associated theoretical frameworks, have facilitated the discovery of many important phenomena and the development of many important methods. Our concern in this chapter, however, is with the limitations. Although neither early memory researchers nor current decision researchers have devoted all their efforts to the study of meaning-free materials, and although many insights have resulted from studies employing such materials, it is also true that the exclusive study of nonsense syllables would have prevented memory researchers from learning about such intrinsically content-based phenomena as: (1) the distinction between verbatim memory and memory for gist (Sachs, 1967), (2) distinctions among semantic, episodic, and procedural memory (Anderson, 1976; Tulving, 1972), (3) semantic priming effects (Meyer & Schvaneveldt, 1971), and (4) schema-based intrusions, deletions, and reorganizations (Bransford & Franks, 1971; Jenkins, 1974).

The point is not merely that the experimental practice of using content-impoverished stimuli would have failed to discover a number of interesting phenomena, but that the particular phenomena that would have been overlooked are those that *conflict* with the overarching theoretical framework. The demonstration that the *meaning* of material exerts a causal influence on psychological processing violates associationism. Fodor (1992) put it this way:

. . . precisely because the mechanisms of mental causation were assumed to be associationistic (and the conditions for association to involve preeminently spatio-temporal propinquity), the [British] Empiricists had no good way of connecting the *contents* of a thought with the effects of entertaining it. They therefore never got close to a plausible theory of thinking, and neither did the associationistic psychology that followed in their footsteps. (p. 20, emphasis in original)

By analogy, our concern is not only that decision researchers may be overlooking a similarly rich set of phenomena, but that the gambling metaphor may be supporting an experimental practice that makes it impossible to detect its limitations. To be clear about this, we do not object to the use of gambles as stimuli per se, but we argue that the predominant use of these stimuli may impede the *theoretical* advance of recognizing the limited circumstances in which degree of belief and degree of value (rather than the beliefs and valued goals in themselves and the knowledge base in which they are embedded) suffice to account for behavior.

B. The general climate in psychology

In this section, we briefly review a number of areas of psychology in which initially content-independent accounts of behavior have been forced to change in the face of content-dependent effects. We believe these reviews are relevant for two reasons. First, we think decision researchers should draw from the substantive findings of researchers in related areas. Second, we think it is useful to see how researchers in neighboring fields have dealt with the often unwelcome prospect that behavior depends on the semantic content of the stimuli.

1. Learning. Contrary to Plato's doctrine of formal discipline, according to which study in abstract fields (e.g., arithmetic) provides general training for reasoning in all domains, early research on the transfer of learning (Thorndike & Woodworth, 1901) indicated remarkably little generality in the matter of *what* is learned. As a consequence, regularities in an organism's overt behavior were taken to depend on the historical accident of its specific experiences (i.e., its reinforcement history). No particular behavioral regularities could be expected on theoretical grounds to generalize across situations or organisms. Nevertheless, the matter of *how* learning takes place was considered to be entirely different. Behaviorists' refusal to distinguish among stimuli or responses on the basis of their content indicated a commitment to extremely general, abstract, content-independent laws of learning. However, the *how* of learning turned out to be not entirely independent of *what* was being learned, and the commitment to content-independent laws of learning could not be maintained. In a historical review of learning studies, Kimble (1985) chided himself for having failed to see this sooner. Commenting on his earlier opinion that "just about any activity of which the organism is capable can be conditioned, and these responses can be conditioned to any stimulus that the organism can perceive" (Kimble, 1956, p. 195), he remarked:

Kimble should have known better. As early as 1930, C. W. Valentine had reported being unable to repeat Watson's demonstration of fear conditioning in children, using a pair of opera glasses instead of a white rat as the conditioned stimulus. It was well-known laboratory lore that training a rat to press a bar or a pigeon to peck a key to turn off shock was next to impossible. More formal evidence along these lines was soon to accumulate to prove that the assumption of *equipotentiality* is wrong: animals are *prepared* to form certain associations and counterprepared to form others (Seligman & Hager, 1972). (Kimble, 1985, pp. 60–61, emphasis in original.)

Results indicating violations of equipotentiality (e.g. Garcia & Koelling, 1966) were slow to win acceptance (Lubek & Apfelbaum, 1987). However, behaviorists did eventually take steps toward content dependence in the laws of learning.

2. Categories and concepts. Categories were classically conceived to be collections of entities that satisfy individually necessary and collectively sufficient conditions of membership (e.g., an "even" number is an integer that is divisible by 2 with no remainder). However, the discovery that natural categories have graded structure, that some members are considered "better" or more "typical" members than others, contradicted the classical conception, at least as a psychological model of category representation (Rosch & Mervis, 1975; Smith, Shoben, & Rips, 1974; people even discriminate among different examples of even numbers, see Armstrong, Gleitman, & Gleitman, 1983). In subsequent research conducted to account for typicality and related effects, debate has arisen as to whether categories are represented abstractly (e.g., by prototypes; Posner & Keele, 1968) or by storage of specific categorized instances (Brooks, 1978; Medin & Schaffer, 1978). Although it can be difficult to distinguish between prototype and exemplar models (Barsalou, 1990), the weight of evidence seems to favor the specific over the abstract (see Medin & Ross, 1989, for a review).

Exemplar models are specific in that they posit that categories are represented by memory traces of the particular instances encountered, and therefore they posit that regularities in people's categorization *behavior* depend on the historical accident of their specific experiences (i.e., history of encounters with exemplars). Nevertheless, they portray the matter of *how* categorization takes place as being entirely different, proceeding according to general, abstract, content-independent laws. However, a recent program of research on the coherence of people's categories appears to be forcing a modification of this view (Medin & Ortony, 1989; Murphy & Medin, 1985; Wattenmaker, Dewey, Murphy, & Medin, 1986; Wattenmaker, Nakamura, & Medin, 1988). These investigators found that the "structure" of encountered exemplars (i.e., the pattern of presences and absences among abstractly coded features of the exemplars) is insufficient to account for category learning. Rather, the identity of the features according to the cover story – and the activated knowledge structure – is crucial to the behavior. For example, Wattenmaker et al. (1986) found that they could facilitate the learning of linearly separable categories, or the learning of nonlinearly separable categories, depending on the knowledge structures they made salient. Wattenmaker et al. (1988) observed that "it is not the case that ease of learning can be specified in terms of the configuration of independent features inherent in the category structure" (p. 220). Rather, these investigators emphasize a knowledge-based approach to conceptual coherence and an explanation-based approach to categorization. In other words: (knowledge about) content matters.

3. *Deductive reasoning.* Some of the earliest and most sustained interest in the role of semantic content has been shown by researchers who study deductive reasoning. One line of research concerns the effects of stimulus material that arouses people's emotions or prejudices (Janis & Frick, 1943; Kaufmann & Goldstein, 1967; Lefford, 1946). This research might be seen as a precursor to recent work on "motivated" cognition (Kunda, 1990; Larrick, 1993). A second line of research, stretching back nearly 70 years (Wilkins, 1928), compares the effect of material that is (1) abstract and symbolic, versus (2) concrete but unfamiliar, versus (3) concrete and familiar. A still energetic wave of research on this topic was begun some 23 years ago by Wason and Shapiro (1971) and by Johnson-Laird, Legrenzi, and Legrenzi (1972). These studies investigated Wason's (1966) well-known "four-card problem." Subjects are shown a deck of cards, each of which says on one side either "p" or "not p," and on the other side says either "q" or "not q." Four cards are dealt on the table so that the sides facing the subject read "p," "not p," "q," and "not q." Subjects are then asked to indicate exactly those cards that must be turned over in order to test whether the rule "if p then q" is satisfied by the deck. When the problem is given to people in the abstract form just described, they do spectacularly badly at it. However, the studies by Wason and Shapiro (1971) and by Johnson-Laird et al. (1972) showed that when the task is fleshed out with understandable content, there is remarkable improvement. Wason and Johnson-Laird (1972) commented that "Taken together, these two experiments force on us a radical reconsideration of the role of content in reasoning. The nature of the material would seem to be decisive in terms of whether the subjects exercise rational thought" (p. 193).

A great deal of research on the four-card problem ensued, and it was found that concrete stimulus materials did not always produce marked improvement in performance (e.g., Manktelow & Evans, 1979). This led to the proposal (Griggs & Cox, 1982) that it is not the concreteness of the material per se that improves performance, but sufficient *familiarity* with the domain to allow the recall of specific instances that could falsify the rule. Once more, people's behavior was described as depending on the historical accident of their specific experiences. Thus, *behavior* could be content-dependent while relying on general, abstract, content-independent *mechanisms* of memory storage and retrieval. This version of content independence was, however, also challenged. In papers that provided the source for much of our own interest in content effects, Cheng and Holyoak (1985; Cheng, Holyoak, Nisbett, & Oliver, 1986) argued that "people often reason using neither syntactic, context-free rules of inference, nor memory of specific experiences. Rather, they reason using abstract knowledge structures induced from ordinary life experiences, such as 'permissions,' 'obligations,' and 'causations'" (Cheng & Holyoak, 1985, p. 395). Cheng and Holyoak argued that people reason according to *pragmatic reasoning schemas* that stand at an intermediate level of abstraction and relate to people's goals.

In one striking example that shows that improvement on the four-card problem relies on the cuing of an appropriate *schema* which is neither purely syntactic nor bound to any particular domain-specific content, Cheng and Holyoak (1985, Experiment 2) asked subjects to imagine themselves as authorities checking to see whether people were obeying regulations of the form, "If one is to take action A, then one must first satisfy precondition P." In contrast with only 19% who correctly verified an arbitrary rule ("If a card has an *A* on one side, then it must have a 4 on the other side."), 61% of the subjects correctly verified the regulation. Although there is debate about the origin and identity of the reasoning schemas that people use (Cheng & Holyoak, 1989; Cosmides, 1989; Gigerenzer, 1996; Gigerenzer & Hug, 1992), there seems to be consensus about the appropriateness of an intermediate level of abstraction.

4. *Problem solving and expertise.* In the 1960s and early 1970s, work on problem solving and expertise focused on general heuristics (e.g., means–ends analysis) by which a person could limit search through an abstract problem space (Newell, Shaw, & Simon, 1958; Newell & Simon, 1972). Soon thereafter, it became apparent that expertise was not driven by superior general-purpose search heuristics so much as by domain-specific knowledge that could enhance memory and promote specialized inference patterns within the domain (Anderson, 1987; Chase & Simon, 1973a, 1973b; Chi, Feltovich, & Glaser, 1981; Larkin, McDermott, Simon, & Simon, 1980; however, see Holyoak, 1991, for an argument that superior domain knowledge does not explain all phenomena of expertise).

One particular line of research that directly addresses the role of content in the acquisition of expertise is concerned with the way that people access and use previously learned (base) problems in constructing analogies to help solve new (target) problems (for reviews, see Medin & Ross, 1989; Reeves & Weisberg, 1994). The evidence indicates that spontaneous transfer from base problems is affected by similarities and differences in both the overall content domains of the cover stories (Gick & Holyoak, 1980; B. H. Ross, 1984) as well as by the content of particular objects appearing in important relationships in the problems (Bassok, 1990; Holyoak & Koh, 1987). When people are told that the base problem is relevant to the target problem, so that the use and not the access of the base problem is the issue, people are affected by content in a way that appears to indicate a conflict between mapping structurally analogous objects from base to target, on the one hand, and mapping superficially similar objects to corresponding relational roles in the two problems, on the other hand (Bassok, 1990; Gentner & Toupin, 1986; B. H.

Ross, 1987, 1989). Of course, if people *knew* which features of the base problem reflected structural (i.e., solution-relevant) properties and which reflected merely superficial content, they would map only the structural features. The apparent conflict is thought to result from the attempt to map as many features as possible, in the absence of knowledge about what really is and is not relevant.

This theoretical approach to content effects in analogical problem solving may or may not be yet another example in which content-dependent behavior is thought to depend on content-independent mechanisms. If the processes of feature matching are hypothesized to be domain-general, then this issue hinges on whether the primitive "features" themselves are thought to originate in ways that are independent of the content of the base and target problems. This matter is usually considered to be outside the scope of the theories, and in practice, the experiments are generally conducted under the assumption that the features are known. However, recent research by Bassok, Wu, and Olseth (1995) addresses this issue directly. Bassok et al. (1995) argue that naive subjects, who do not have the experimenter's understanding of the problem structure, use the content of the base problem together with its worked-out solution to abstract an *interpreted* structure which may or may not match the objective structure that the experimenter has in mind. Then subjects try to map from the base to the target problem on the basis of the features that are structural, given *their* interpretations.

To test their theory, Bassok et al. (1995, Experiment 2) first trained subjects on a base problem in which the manager of a country club assigned caddies at random to golfers and subjects had to compute the probability that the three most experienced caddies would be assigned to the three newest members, respectively. The correct answer depends on the total size of the "assigned" set (caddies) and not on the total size of the "receiving" set (golfers). Bassok et al. then tested subjects on target problems in which either carts were assigned to caddies (and so the correct answer depends on the number of carts) or caddies were assigned to carts (the correct answer depends on the number of caddies). If subjects transfer by mapping similar objects to similar roles, they should perform better on the caddies-assigned-to-carts problem because mapping caddies to caddies would give the correct answer. However, Bassok et al. predicted the reverse. They reasoned that the asymmetry in status between golfers and caddies would induce subjects to interpret the base problem in terms of a "get" relation rather than an "assign" relation: no matter who assigns what to whom, golfers "get" caddies and not the other way around. Likewise, for the target problems, caddies "get" carts (i.e., people "get" objects). Therefore, subjects should do better on the carts-assigned-to-caddies problem, because the "get" relation directs subjects to the number of to-be-gotten objects, carts, in this case the correct answer. In fact, 94% of the subjects answered correctly on the carts-assigned-to-caddies problem, and only 24% answered correctly on the caddies-assigned-to-carts problem. The results strongly support Bassok et al.'s argument that subjects map *what they interpret to be* structural features and that their interpretations are influenced by the *content* of the base problems.

5. *Cognitive development.* Finally, we will briefly mention one more area of psychology in which content has come to be considered an important determinant of behavior. Because children begin as novices at virtually everything and become relative experts as they grow up, the literature on cognitive development has come to overlap that on the acquisition of expertise. In fact, the cognitive development literature shows a similar shift in emphasis from domain-general hypotheses (e.g., Piagetian stages of development, maturational increases in speed and capacity of the central processor) to an emphasis on the acquisition of knowledge. For example, Chi (1978) compared 10-year-olds and adults on two memory tasks: a digit-span task and a chess memory task of the sort studied by Chase and Simon (1973a, 1973b). The adults were superior to the children on the digit-span task, replicating a well-known result. However, the results of the chess task contradicted the hypothesis of a domain-general difference in memory capacity. The children, all experienced chess players, remembered the positions of more chess pieces than the adults, all of whom were chess novices. (See Chi & Ceci, 1987, for a review of the role of content knowledge in memory development.) More generally, as remarked by Carey (1990):

It now seems unlikely that the grand simplifying description of universal developmental stages that Piaget proposed is correct – especially if the stages are interpreted as reflecting domain-general changes in the representational or computational capacity of the information processor. It seems that cognitive development is mainly the result of acquiring knowledge in particular content domains. (pp. 161–162)

(See also Hirschfeld & Gelman, 1994; Wellman & Gelman, 1992.)

6. *Summary and interpretation.* It seems to us that a great deal of the reviewed research can be summarized in broad strokes as exhibiting one or more of four reactions to the prospect of content dependence, which can be arranged more or less in the following sequence. First, various areas of psychology initially sought to describe behavior at a level of analysis abstract enough to achieve generalizability across people, stimuli, conditions, and, in particular, semantic content (e.g., organisms strive to maximize reinforcement). However, because overt behavior and psychological mechanisms need not be analyzed at the same level of abstraction, it was a short step to the second stage. Specifically, by describing behavior in somewhat more concrete terms, researchers acknowledged that overt behavior depends on the individual, the stimuli, the conditions, and so on, while maintaining that this nongeneralizability of behavior was consistent with general, abstract, content-independent psychological mechanisms. Thus, differences in

behavior were attributed to idiosyncratic factors of no particular interest to psychological theory (e.g., reinforcement histories, past encounters with exemplars, idiosyncratic utility functions, etc.). Third, particular psychological mechanisms of theoretical interest were deemed to be affected by content (e.g., encoding of stimulus information, retrieval of information, manipulation of encoded stimulus and/or retrieved information), but not the mechanisms considered to be of core interest (e.g., one could maintain that people employ content-independent rules of deductive inference, but that they systematically misinterpret the premises; see Henle, 1962). Fourth, content effects were acknowledged as potential influences on core mechanisms, and research was undertaken to determine the mechanisms affected and to identify functionally distinct domains of content.

A succinct, if somewhat crude rendition of this sequence takes the following form: (1) behavior is thought to be content-independent, (2) behavior is acknowledged to be content-dependent for "uninteresting" reasons that can safely be ignored, (3) behavior is thought to be content-dependent for reasons that are somewhat interesting but not central to core theory, and (4) content-dependent phenomena are seen to have important implications for theory that cannot be ignored.[2] In the next section, we will see that research on preferential decision making can be characterized as mostly falling in the second or third stage of this sequence, but that there are some indications that it may be moving into the fourth stage.

IV. Content effects in research on preferential judgment and choice

Although simple monetary gambles have been the predominant stimulus material for studies in preferential decision research, the use of gambles has not been completely exclusive, and there is some research that is relevant to the issue of content effects. However, with the exception of a few studies to be discussed later, the issue of content has arisen only indirectly in (1) studies of phenomena that are attributed broadly to the way people encode decision inputs, and (2) studies of the way people deal with missing or degraded information.

A. Framing effects

A number of phenomena attributed to encoding are sometimes referred to collectively as "framing" effects (Tversky & Kahneman, 1981). Studies of framing address the influence of people's perspectives, that is, whether, so to speak, it makes a difference to look at the glass as half empty or half full. To manipulate people's perspectives, the studies all involve manipulation of decision inputs apart from net final outcomes and probabilities, and can be viewed as manipulating (aspects of) content. However, as far as we are aware, only a few studies (Schneider, 1992; Wagenaar, Keren, & Lichtenstein, 1988; discussed later) have been concerned with semantic content as such. Probably the most studied issue concerns the coding of outcomes as losses or gains relative to different reference points or aspiration levels (e.g., Kahneman & Tversky, 1979; Levin & Gaeth, 1988; McNeil, Pauker, Sox, & Tversky, 1982; Payne, Laughhunn, & Crum, 1980; Schneider, 1992; see also Lopes, 1987). Related phenomena include sunk-cost effects (i.e., failure to restrict focus to future incremental outcomes without regard for unrecoverable costs already invested in particular alternatives; Arkes & Blumer, 1985; Staw, 1976), status quo effects (i.e., privileged standing accorded to whichever choice alternative represents the status quo or default alternative; Samuelson & Zeckhauser, 1988), endowment effects (i.e., greater value placed on an object that is "owned" rather than on an identical object that is not owned; Kahneman, Knetsch, & Thaler, 1990; Thaler, 1980), and loss aversion (subjective pleasure of gaining an object exceeded by the subjective pain of losing the same object; Tversky & Kahneman, 1991) (see Kahneman, Knetsch, & Thaler, 1991, for a review of the last three effects). A set of issues known collectively as *mental accounting* concerns people's preferences for and the effects of combining versus separating events (Linville & Fischer, 1991; Thaler, 1985; Thaler & Johnson, 1990) and decisions (Luce, 1995; Redelmeier & Tversky, 1992). An additional issue that relates to the way people encode decision inputs concerns problem formats that make the applicability of a decision principle transparent versus opaque (Tversky & Kahneman, 1986).

Each of the above "perspectival" effects is well established, but contains little or no reference to content *domain*, that is, what the decision is "about." Possibly, content domain exerts an influence via perspectival effects by inducing people to look at things in a particular way (cf. Bassok et al., 1995, discussed earlier). None of the preceding studies systematically examined content domain in this way. The following effect, however, suggests that there may be some validity to this hypothesis: in choosing between a sure loss and the risk of incurring a larger loss, people are affected by whether the problem is described as a gambling decision or an insurance decision (Hershey, Kunreuther, & Schoemaker, 1982; Hershey & Schoemaker, 1980; Schoemaker & Kunreuther, 1979; Slovic, Fischhoff, Lichtenstein, Corrigan, & Combs, 1977). This effect is well known, but it seems to have been interpreted as demonstrating the general importance of framing, rather than as indicating a need to study the influence of content domain on preferential decision making.

B. Missing or degraded information

A good deal of research has been conducted on decision behavior in the face of incomplete or degraded information (e.g., Fischhoff, Slovic, & Lichtenstein, 1978; Slovic & MacPhillamy, 1974; Yates, Jagacinski, & Faber,

1978). One branch of this research examines whether, when, and how people draw inferences about the missing or degraded items of information (Davidson, Yantis, Norwood, & Montano, 1985; Einhorn & Hogarth, 1985; Ford & Smith, 1987; Huber & McCann, 1982; Jaccard & Wood, 1988; Johnson & Levin, 1985; Levin, Chapman, & Johnson, 1988; Simmons & Lynch, 1991; Yamagishi & Hill, 1983). Also relevant is research on the construal of information (Griffin, Dunning, & Ross, 1990; L. Ross, 1987, 1989; L. Ross & Nisbett, 1991). Although most of this research has not directly addressed the content domain of the decision problem, inferences about missing or degraded information presumably rely on knowledge about the domain. Recent research by Sanbonmatsu, Kardes, and Herr (1992; see also Kardes & Sanbonmatsu, 1993) has shown that domain experts and novices respond differently to missing information. Experts are likelier to notice that information is missing and to infer likely values for the missing items.

In sum, although the research on perspectival effects and the processing of incomplete information is voluminous, and although these topics lend themselves to the study of content effects, scholars of preferential judgment and choice have given relatively little attention to content domain as such. Perspectives taken and inferences drawn are occasionally discussed as depending on the *amount* of knowledge or *aspects* of content, but even then it is rare to connect these aspects of knowledge to what the decision is about. Our impression is that decision researchers view these streams of research as efforts to flesh out rather than test the gambling metaphor; these studies are thought to indicate how people go about arriving at their degrees of belief and degrees of value, but they do not challenge the sufficiency of these variables to account for behavior. In this sense, we think these studies represent what we refer to as a "stage 3" reaction to content effects: interesting, but not of central importance to core theory (or metatheory). Of course, challenges to a content-independent metatheory cannot be discovered if researchers rely only on content-impoverished stimuli or stimuli from a single domain. Although the results of gambling studies may well replicate in other settings, and indeed often have, we think there is reason to be cautious about the generalizability of gambling studies, and therefore reason to be dubious of the gambling metaphor.

C. Challenges to the generalizability of gambling behavior

Wagenaar et al. (1988) presented subjects with a variety of cover stories, all of which had the same deep structure, namely, versions of Tversky and Kahneman's (1981) well-known Asian disease problem. Manipulating such aspects as the identity of the potential victims (e.g., islanders subject to a disease vs. children held hostage by terrorists) and the role of the subject as decision maker (e.g., islander vs. public health officer for the islander version; parent vs. authority for the hostage version) had a profound effect on the choices of subjects who were all considering the "same" problem. In a sense, as Wagenaar et al. (1988) suggest, this result is a matter of framing (Tversky & Kahneman, 1981). In any case, generalizability across content domains is problematic, even when attempts have been made to hold constant the deep structure of the stimuli. Schneider (1992) obtained similar results, in that the magnitude of framing effects varied widely across scenarios that differed "only" in content (see also Frisch, 1993).

Heath and Tversky (1991) studied subjects' choices among gambles with identical potential outcomes, but whose payoffs were contingent on different sorts of events: a random event with stated probability, having one's answer to a general-knowledge question turn out to be correct, or giving a correct prediction for a football game or political election. Heath and Tversky (1991) found that subjects' choices were determined not solely by the perceived likelihood of the event yielding the favorable outcome and the precision with which this likelihood could be estimated, but also by the subject's self-perceived knowledge and "competence" in the domain of events. In one experiment, subjects predicted the results of various football games and the results of the (then future) 1988 presidential election in various states. Later, subjects rank ordered their preferences among gambles that were matched to have the same probability of winning on the basis of: (1) a chance device, (2) the subject's own prediction in his or her strong domain (politics or football), and (3) the subject's own prediction in his or her weak domain. Only when the probability of winning was 100% did subjects prefer to bet on the chance device. Otherwise, independent of the numerical probability of winning, subjects preferred to bet on their strong domain, the chance device, and their weak domain, in that order. In a sense, subjects were indicating that they had definite preferences among "identical" gambles; probabilities and outcomes did not capture all the relevant factors: domain still mattered.

Hogarth and Kunreuther (1995) asked subjects to assess the probability that they would buy 1-year maintenance contracts for various consumer durables (personal computer, stereo, VCR, CD player). Subjects were given the price of the product, the price of the maintenance contract, and a description of the manufacturer implying either high or low product reliability. After judging their purchase intentions for all four products, subjects considered each product again, this time judging their subjective probabilities and the likely costs of breakdowns should they occur. In a second session, subjects again rated their intentions to buy maintenance contracts for the same products, but this time subjects were given additional information about the probabilities and costs of breakdowns, specifically the same values that the subjects themselves previously had said were most likely. The result was that self-rated probability of purchase was reduced by the explicit information by approximately the same amount as increasing the price of the maintenance contract from 5 to 10% of the product price. Again, probabilities and outcomes did not capture all the relevant factors; subjects responded differently to "identical" gambles.

In addition to these results, indicating that subjects' purchase intentions did not generalize as one might have expected, Hogarth and Kunreuther (1995) also provided evidence that the decision *processes* did not generalize. At particular points in the experiment, they asked their subjects (1) to give free-form explanations of the reasons and arguments they had considered in judging their purchase intentions, and (2) to evaluate how much weight they had given to specific arguments listed by the experimenters. Hogarth and Kunreuther (1995) found that the kinds of arguments subjects reported depended on the information that was explicitly displayed in the problem description. Among other differences, the ratio of single-attribute arguments to multiple-attribute arguments was much smaller when probabilities and repair costs were explicitly displayed (in the neighborhood of 1.5) than when probabilities and repair costs were not explicitly displayed (approximately 3). Also, there was a subset of subjects whose arguments, independent of the display conditions, were insensitive to the attributes of the maintenance contracts or products (e.g., "I never buy these types of warranties."). Although subjects using these "meta" strategies, as Hogarth and Kunreuther called them, did not vary their strategies across display conditions, we speculate that subjects might vary their use of attribute-insensitive strategies across content domains.

In sum, despite numerous other areas of psychology in which content domain has been found to affect behavior, despite the evidence that neither behavior *nor* underlying processes may generalize from studies of gambling to other decisions, and with only a nod in the direction of "amount" of knowledge and "aspects" of content, decision researchers have continued to rely almost exclusively on simple monetary gambles or highly schematic stimuli that are just barely fleshed out with content, and to rely on the gambling metaphor as justification for this practice. It may not *always* be incorrect to think that decisions are mediated (only) by degree of belief and degree of desirability, but we think the evidence contradicts the universality to which the gambling metaphor aspires. Indeed, the gambling metaphor has proved inadequate even when applied to games of chance (Heath & Tversky, 1991).

D. Influence of content domain on judgment and decision making

In this section, we briefly summarize selected results from two experiments that we conducted for three purposes: (1) to gather additional evidence that semantic content influences the psychological processes underlying preferential judgment and choice, (2) to test some hypotheses about the way that processing is affected by content, and (3) to begin an exploration of the distinguishing characteristics of content domains that elicit different modes of processing. The experiments will be reported more fully elsewhere (Goldstein & Weber, in preparation).

In Experiment 1, we examined whether people would be differentially sensitive to an experimental manipulation when making evaluative judgments of stimuli from different content domains. We decided to contrast judgments about social relationships with judgments about inanimate objects (e.g., consumer items) in order to explore a broad distinction between the evaluation of people and things. Specifically, the two domains were (1) people with whom one might pursue a long-term romantic relationship potentially leading to marriage, and (2) compact disk (CD) players. We expected that people would evaluate CD players by weighing the advantages and disadvantages of the models. By contrast, for potential spouses, the work of Pennington and Hastie (1988, 1992, 1993; discussed later) suggested to us that people might try to construct stories or story fragments about what life might be like if they were to pursue the relationship.

It should be emphasized that we hypothesized the semantic content of the domain to affect only people's *preferred* mode of processing. We do not suppose that people are incapable of implementing unpreferred modes of processing. Certainly, people *could* evaluate potential spouses by enumerating and weighing their separate features, but doing so seems depersonalizing and inappropriate. Also, people *could* evaluate CD players by trying to imagine how life would unfold if the CD player were obtained, but this seems unlikely. The thrust of our hypothesis was that people have preferences for the type of decision strategy to be used, and that these preferences are affected by the semantic content of the decision domain. We hypothesized that people would tend to use the mode of processing they preferred in the content domain, unless we made it difficult for them to do so by our experimental manipulation, which is exactly what we tried to do.

A crucial difference between constructing a story and tallying up advantages and disadvantages is that story construction requires that one possess an overarching knowledge structure or schema (i.e., knowledge of what constitutes a coherent story; see Schank & Abelson, 1977; Stein & Glenn, 1979; Trabasso & van den Broek, 1985), which is used to draw inferences and to organize the information into a unified whole. That is, for people to construct a story, they must augment the presented information by filling in gaps and going "beyond the information given," to use Bruner's (1957) famous phrase. We expected people's inferences to be both semantically and evaluatively consistent with the information that was presented, thereby *accentuating* the attractiveness or unattractiveness of the stimuli relative to the evaluation produced by weighing (only) the presented information (without augmenting inferences). With this in mind, two stimuli in each content domain (marriage partners and CD players) were designed to be relatively attractive overall, and two were relatively unattractive.

Each stimulus was described by a set of "schema items," intended to promote the inference of interitem relations and the construction of an integrated representation, and a set of "nonschema items" that were more akin to isolated features. For the potential spouses, the nonschema items consisted of a list of personality traits. The schema items consisted of sentences describing how the decision maker had met the person, how the relationship had developed so far, and how things had been left. (To make it more plausible that the subject might be deciding which of several relationships to pursue, each relationship was described as having ended relatively amicably and on a somewhat ambiguous note.) For each potential spouse, we targeted a recognizable (stereotypical) story. The targeted stories could be labeled: (1) childhood sweetheart, (2) college friend turned lover, (3) intense and stormy romance, and (4) stagnant relationship.

To make the CD players a more comparable domain, we tried to design these stimuli with a structure parallel to that of the potential spouses. However, in a sense, the very difficulty of doing this helps to make our larger point: people are not inclined to use the same processes in evaluating CD players and potential spouses. People are capable of constructing a story of what life would be like with a CD player, but it seems unlikely that they would do so. More plausible, and still requiring the use of an overarching knowledge structure to draw inferences and organize the information, is that people would construct and decide on the basis of an image associated with a CD player (as in, "We don't sell a product, we sell an image") and/or a story of the act of purchasing the item. As with the potential spouses, we targeted a recognizable (stereotypical) image for each stimulus. The targeted images could be labeled: (1) Rolls Royce of CD players, (2) good-value-for-money model, (3) basic no-frills model, and (4) low-quality-but-cheap model. For each CD player, the schema items described the reputation/prestige of the brand, the reputation/prestige of the store and service, the reliability and standards of an acquaintance recommending the model, and the convenience of the store location. The nonschema items related the CD player's price, its capacity to hold multiple CDs, the manufacturer's warranty and availability of an extended warranty from the store, and the availability and features of a remote control.

Taking our cue from manipulations used by Pennington and Hastie (1988, 1992), we manipulated the order in which subjects received the items of information describing each stimulus. Specifically, we varied whether the schema items or the nonschema items were presented early in the description of each stimulus. The rationale for this manipulation is that people with foreknowledge of the task are likely to process the information on-line as they encounter each item of information (Hastie & Park, 1986). Presenting nonschema items early (personality traits for the potential spouses and product features for the CD players) encourages people to begin with an attribute-weighing decision strategy and may make it difficult for them to switch in midstream to a schema-based decision strategy when they later encounter the schema items, even if they are so inclined. Pennington and Hastie (1988, 1992) found analogous effects by presenting items in the sequence versus out of the sequence that would be required by a narrative.

As predicted, we found a three-way interaction between content domain, order of information, and attractiveness of stimuli. The differences in ratings given to attractive versus unattractive potential spouses were responsive to the order manipulation. When schema items were presented early, making it easy to implement the preferred (schema-based) mode of processing, we obtained a relatively large difference between attractive and unattractive spouses (4.91 rating points on a scale from −10 to +10). When the schema items were presented late, making it difficult to implement the preferred mode of processing, we obtained a relatively small difference between attractive and unattractive spouses (2.61 rating points). This difference between differences is as expected, because people using schemas (i.e., stories, images) to draw inferences beyond the information presented were predicted to accentuate the differences between attractive and unattractive stimuli. By contrast, the differences between ratings given to attractive and unattractive CD players were unresponsive to the order manipulation, presumably because subjects were *not* inclined to use schema-based (i.e., image) processing even when it was easy (mean differences of 3.21 and 4.02 rating points for schema items presented early and late, respectively). This pattern supports our hypothesis that people are inclined to employ schema-based processing when thinking about potential spouses, provided that conditions make it easy to do so (schema items early), but not when it is hard (schema items late). By contrast, when thinking about CD players, people seem predisposed to employ an attribute-weighing strategy of evaluation, irrespective of the order manipulation.

Experiment 2 was designed to compare the effect of content domain with another factor, apart from content per se, which might drive a shift in decision strategy. To state the obvious, choosing a spouse is more important than choosing a CD player. Payne, Bettman, and Johnson's (1993) theory of meta-decision making predicts that important decisions induce people to use decision strategies that are more effortful and more likely to reach the correct conclusion. Experiment 2 was designed in part to separate the effects of decision importance and content domain to see whether we could obtain evidence of a strategy shift that would be more clearly related to content per se.

In addition, we tried to push our notions about content domain and preferred decision strategy a bit further. In Experiment 1, we tested the hypothesis that decisions about social relationships tend to elicit a version of Pennington and Hastie's (1988, 1992, 1993) story model, in which people tell themselves story fragments about what life would be like if they were to pursue a course of action. Narratives describe events, actions. and reactions as they unfold over *time*. The basic temporality of narratives suggested to us that people might construct story fragments for a wider class of issues than social relationships. In some decisions, it is a salient fact that the chosen course of action will require monitoring and tending, unforeseeable subsidiary decisions and adjustments, all of which will evolve over time and be experienced as an ongoing stream of events and actions. For example, choosing a profession, weighing a permanent job offer, considering whether to have a child, all involve actions that will produce a flow of consequences to be experienced and managed over a lengthy period of time. In a sense, these are decisions about whether to embark on a "journey" or to undertake an "endeavor." For lack of a better label, we will refer to these as decisions about "endeavors," stressing the activity and ongoing experience that will follow after having made a choice, in contrast to decisions about "objects." We hypothesized that decisions about endeavors would tend to elicit the construction of story fragments. In contrast, for decisions about objects whose consequences do not require monitoring and tending, we predicted people to use schemas other than narratives, if they used schema-based processing at all, or to use a strategy in which attributes are weighed against each other directly, that is, without drawing inferences to construct an integrated, mediating representation of the alternative.

To test these ideas, we asked people their opinions about the strategies they thought they would use for various decision problems, and the strategies they thought typical, appropriate, and inappropriate. Despite concerns that people may not be in a position to report accurately on the decision strategies they would (or did) use (Ericsson & Simon, 1980; Nisbett & Wilson, 1977), inferring people's strategies from their decision patterns (as in Experiment 1) involves its own set of assumptions, and we thought we should seek converging evidence from a procedure with different assumptions. We constructed four decision problems in a 2 × 2 design. Two problems concerned matters that we thought undergraduates would construe as decisions about "endeavors" (roommates and jobs) and two concerned matters that we thought they would construe as decisions about "objects" (stereo systems and houses). Within each domain, one decision was more important than the other (jobs are more important than roommates, and houses are more important than stereo systems). This design let us examine the importance of the decision and the domain of the decision independently.

Each respondent was asked to consider all four decision problems, which were about: (1) a prospective roommate, (2) a postgraduation job offer, (3) the purchase of a house, and (4) the purchase of a stereo system. In each case, a short paragraph fleshed out a scenario to give some context to the decision problem. For example, in the roommate problem, respondents were asked to imagine that they were single, unattached, and continuing next year at the University of Chicago. After mentioning to a same-sex acquaintance, a fellow student, that an apartment would be needed, the acquaintance suggests looking for an apartment to share. The decision was whether or not to accept the suggestion.

After reading the description of a decision problem, people were shown descriptions of six decision "methods." (We avoided the word *strategy*, unsure of the connotations this word might have for undergraduates.) For each decision problem, people were asked to make four judgments about the listed decision methods. Specifically, they were asked to indicate the single decision method that best described: (1) the method they would use, (2) the most typical decision method for that problem, (3) the most appropriate method, and (4) the most inappropriate method. Although decision methods were described procedurally and not labeled for respondents, the six methods might be labeled: (1) follow gut feeling, (2) seek and follow advice, (3) social comparison, (4) feature-focused processing, (5) similarity to ideal, and (6) story-based processing. For our present purposes, we will concentrate on whether people said that they would use feature-focused processing ("Try to think it through 'rationally.' . . . See if the favorable points are more numerous and/or more important than the unfavorable points.") or story-based processing ("Try to think about what life would be like. . . . Picture how your life would unfold, and construct a story about the way things would go.").

The average respondent reported that he or she would use 2.3 distinct strategies across the four problems. Evidently, people believe that they would engage in considerable strategy shifting. For each decision problem, people most frequently said they would use the feature-focused strategy, with story-based processing running a not-too-distant second for the decisions involving endeavors (roommate and job decisions). Consistent with our hypothesis about domain-dependent processing, significantly more respondents said they would use story-based processing for at least one endeavor decision (roommate and job) than said they would use it for at least one object decision (stereo and house; 17/38 vs. 7/38 respondents; $p = .021$ by binomial test for equality of correlated proportions). The popularity of the feature-focused strategy, however, was not so sensitive to the domain. The proportion of respondents saying they would use feature-focused processing for at least one endeavor decision (25/38) did not differ significantly from the proportion saying they would use this strategy for at least one object decision (28/38). Evidently, the greater popularity of the story-based strategy for the endeavors than for the objects comes at the expense of strategies other than feature-focused processing (see Goldstein & Weber, in preparation).

In contrast to the domain of the decision, the importance of the decision seemed to have little impact. Although there was a slightly greater tendency for the story-based approach to be used in the *more* important decision of each domain (job vs. roommate and house vs. stereo), the proportion of respondents saying they would use story-based processing for at least one relatively important decision (16/38) did not differ significantly from the proportion saying they would use it for at least one relatively unimportant decision (11/38). Neither did the proportion saying they would use the feature-focused strategy for at least one relatively important decision (30/38) differ from the proportion saying they would use it for at least one relatively unimportant decision (26/38). Thus, the content of these decisions seems to exert a greater influence on the decision strategy that people say they would use than does the importance of the decision.

In sum, Experiment 2 provides additional evidence that decision strategies are influenced by the content domain of the decision problem. Although story-based processing was never the most frequently selected strategy, people believed themselves more likely to use it for decisions involving endeavors rather than objects. The importance of the decision problem did not affect the strategies people thought themselves likely to use. (Both content domain and decision importance marginally affected the strategies that people thought were typical; see Goldstein & Weber, in preparation.)

V. Toward an outline of a theory of domain-specific decision making

A. Level of analysis

The gambling metaphor represents an austere parsimony with its insistence that any decision whatsoever, in any content domain, can be explained with reference to only two relevant variables: degree of belief and degree of value. We have argued, however, that the evidence accumulated in neighboring fields of study, and in a number of studies specifically on judgment and decision making, demonstrates that psychological processing and overt responses are often sensitive to the semantic content of the stimuli used in the tasks. Therefore, we think that the gambling metaphor must be rejected as a general theory.

In defense, one might object that the issue is one of the level of analysis, and that choosing a level of analysis is to some extent a matter of strategy and of taste. It is legitimate to decide, for the sake of parsimony, to look first for highly general, content-independent results, and to put off until later the pursuit of more specialized content-specific phenomena. It is also legitimate to decide that one's scientific interests as a decision researcher focus on matters that transcend the semantic content of the choice alternatives and generalize across content domains.

Although we acknowledge the cogency of this objection as an argument in support of research at a content-independent level of analysis, we do not think it works as a defense of the gambling metaphor. The gambling metaphor does not merely assert that behavioral regularities are to be found at a content-independent level of analysis, but it also makes a powerful statement about the nature of those regularities, namely, that they depend only on degree of belief and degree of value. In fact, there is a trade-off to be faced between the *generality* or scope of a theory, that is, its applicability across people, alternatives, and conditions, and its *power* to make detailed state-ments about the cases to which it specifically applies (Coombs, 1983, chap. 5). Theories with extremely general applicability can be obtained at the price of vagueness and triviality (e.g., "people generally choose whatever seems best to them at the time"). Conversely, extremely rich and powerful descriptions may be obtained for the decision processes of particular individuals on specific occasions (e.g., President Kennedy's 1962 decision to impose a naval blockade on Cuba; see Allison, 1971), but the lessons to be drawn from these descriptions are unclear. It is entirely legitimate to choose a level of generality (e.g., content independence) and then pursue research to obtain the most powerful theory possible at that level. The gambling metaphor, however, presupposes a degree of power at the content-independent level of generality that we think is contradicted by the evidence (e.g., Heath & Tversky, 1991; Hogarth & Kunreuther, 1995).

If the gambling metaphor is rejected, then what? Do we have another metaphor or an alternative theoretical framework to offer? Unfortunately not. At present, we are in a position only to sketch what we see as possible directions and to take a few steps in a direction that seems promising. In very general terms, we see only two possibilities. On the one hand, one can continue the search for content-independent regularities of decision making, but do so with variables other than the two identified by the gambling metaphor's reductionist aspect, the degrees of belief and value. On the other hand, one can change the level of analysis and aim for a collection of theories of more limited scope.

Pursuing the first possibility, Shafir, Simonson, and Tversky (1993) have reviewed a number of studies that reveal violations of traditional models of value maximization, and they interpret these violations in terms of the reasons (e.g., *number* of reasons) that a person might offer in support of a decision. For example, a richly described alternative, with both good and bad aspects, provides many reasons why it should be chosen over a more neutral or sparsely described alternative. However, it also provides many reasons why it should be rejected. Shafir (1993) found that subjects instructed to choose, chose the rich alternative, and that subjects instructed to reject, rejected it. The concept of "number of reasons" can explain this effect. In another example, the fact that alternative A dominates alternative B, whereas alternative C does not, provides a reason for selecting A over C (Tversky & Shafir, 1992). Because the reasons under discussion by Shafir et al. (1993) are rather abstract and content-independent, we view them as shifting the focus away from degrees of belief and value as the key explanatory variables while retaining the goal of a content-independent level of analysis of the psychological mechanisms.

By contrast, we view the study of Hogarth and Kunreuther (1995) as pursuing the other alternative to the gambling metaphor, namely, changing the level of analysis. By shifting their focus toward a study of the *types* of reasons and arguments that subjects entertain, Hogarth and Kunreuther (1995) have opened the door for content to become a central matter in the explanation of psychological mechanisms. For the moment, we prefer to explore this latter possibility. However, we do not propose to go from one extreme to the other. The extreme opposite of content-independence, that is, the position that each decision is unique and cannot be explained without detailed information about the decision maker's content knowledge, is antithetical to the development of theoretical principles. Instead, we are seeking: (1) an intermediate level of analysis, neither content-free nor completely dependent on the minutiae of the content (cf. Cheng & Holyoak, 1985), and (2) a principled way of coordinating the various domain-specific theories that will result. To see how it might be possible to satisfy these criteria, we consider how content effects might exert their influence.

The semantic content of stimuli can affect psychological processing in various ways. In the literature we reviewed earlier, some of the content effects are attributed to the encoding and representation of information (e.g., Bassok et al., 1995). Some are attributed to the use of domain-specific rules for manipulating encoded information (e.g., Cheng & Holyoak, 1985). Still others may be attributable to attentional mechanisms (e.g., Garcia & Koelling, 1966), in that people or animals may be predisposed to notice certain kinds of events or contingencies between certain kinds of events. One striking feature of the explanations that have been proposed for content effects, with the possible exception of innate mechanisms (Cosmides & Tooby, 1994), is the reliance on *prior knowledge* to guide the encoding, organization, and manipulation of information. In the remainder of this chapter, we explore the way that prior knowledge might affect psychological processes relevant to decision making.

B. Domain knowledge and representation

Any theory of decision making, including the gambling metaphor, must leave room for domain knowledge to affect certain psychological processes. Knowledge is required for a person to identify and encode the relevant aspects of a situation, to extract the relevant implications, and to organize the information in a manner conducive for subsequent processing. From the perspective of the gambling metaphor, this is to say that people must use their knowledge to assess the subjective likelihood and desirability of possible events. It is even consistent with the gambling metaphor to assert that developing expertise in a content domain might change the way a person perceives this "deep structure" (i.e., subjective likelihood and desirability) in the domain (cf. Chi et al., 1981). Thus, domain knowledge might affect the reference points people use to frame outcomes as gains versus losses, or the manner in which people combine or separate events in their "mental accounting."

From our perspective, the undue limitation of the gambling metaphor is its assumption that all content domains are transduced through the same deep structure. We think that content knowledge permits people to organize situation-specific information in a variety of ways, and that different organizations of information are conducive to different modes of deliberation about the choice alternatives. We will consider next how processes of delib-eration relate to different ways of representing and organizing knowledge. Then, we will discuss how semantic content influences knowledge represen-tation and organization, thus constraining the applicable repertoire of deci-sion strategies within the given circumstances. We will also consider how the semantic content of the decision problem might exert a direct influence on the selection of a decision strategy, in addition to its indirect influence via knowledge organization.

C. Knowledge structures and deliberation

We briefly describe four broad categories of decision making, distinguished according to the way knowledge is used (or not used) to evaluate alterna-tives: nondeliberative, associative, rule-based, and schema-based. The boundaries between categories are not entirely sharp, however, and we acknowledge that hybrids and combinations of strategies from different categories are also possible.

1. Nondeliberative decision making. For a decision that is repeated and routinized (Ronis, Yates, & Kirscht, 1989), procedural memory might direct the overt behavior in much the same way that it directs overlearned motor tasks. For example, one might select the same brand of milk from the grocer's shelf time after time without so much as looking at the price. Habitual behavior may barely deserve to be called decision making, but it illustrates the fact that choices may be made in nondeliberative ways (cf. Langer, 1989). Additional examples of *nondeliberative* decision making include choosing at random or by whim, and "passing the buck" (i.e., giving decision making authority – and responsibility – to someone else). For an example of nondeliberative decision making that is driven by distributed representation of information and composite memory storage, see the chapter by Weber, Goldstein, and Barlas (1995; see also Weber, Goldstein, & Busemeyer, 1991).

A particularly noteworthy nondeliberative decision strategy draws on declarative memory. In a strategy we call *category-based* decision making, the decision maker recognizes the alternative or situation as a member of a category for which a judgment or action has already been stored. There may have been deliberation on previous occasions, but if judgment or action is required subsequently, it is only retrieved. For example, consider a decision maker who responds to others on the basis of stereotypes. In this case, a judgment is already stored in memory in association with the category (the stereotyped group), and if needed, it is retrieved rather than computed (cf. Fiske, 1982; Fiske & Pavelchak, 1986). Despite the negative connotations of stereotyping, having a large repertoire of categories whose members can be recognized quickly, together with associated and easily retrieved judgments or actions, is one way to characterize expertise (Chase & Simon, 1973a,

1973b). Such expertise could be driven by a rich episodic memory, in which the current situation reminds the expert of similar situations encountered in the past (i.e., situations in the same category), the actions taken then, and their consequences (Weber, Bockenholt, Hilton, & Wallace, 1993). If this reminding is unconscious (cf. Logan, 1988), episodic memory may provide a basis for the "intuitive" decision making of the expert.

2. Associative deliberation. By *associative deliberation* we refer to a process of deliberation that was described by William James (1890):

At every moment of it [i.e., deliberation] our consciousness is of an extremely complex object, namely the existence of the whole set of motives and their conflict . . . Of this object, the totality of which is realized more or less dimly all the while, certain parts stand out more or less sharply at one moment in the foreground, and at another moment other parts, in consequence of the oscillations of our attention, and of the "associative" flow of our ideas. (Vol. II, pp. 528–529)

If habitual behavior barely deserves to be called decision making, it may be something of a stretch to refer to associative deliberation as a decision strategy. In associative deliberation, the decision maker is not actively guiding the process of deliberation by following a well-defined procedure so much as he or she is being buffeted by the stream of considerations that come to mind. Each successive consideration inclines the decision maker toward a particular course of action, either augmenting or counteracting the effects of previous considerations. The decision is resolved when the cumulative effects of the considerations sufficiently incline the decision maker toward a course of action.

When applied to very simple stimuli (e.g., monetary gambles), fluctuations in attention to the various probabilities and outcomes drive the fluctuations in the decision maker's inclinations. When applied to complex alternatives that are not completely described in explicit detail, the process of associative deliberation is driven by knowledge as represented in a semantic associative network and retrieved by spreading activation (Anderson, 1984). For these stimuli, the successive considerations can be regarded as inferences about the implications of a course of action, occurring in a stream-of-consciousness flow. A sophisticated mathematical model of associative deliberation that accounts for choice latency as well as choice probability has been offered by Busemeyer and Townsend (1993).

3. Rule-based deliberation. Whenever deliberation follows a plan, that is, a set of rules for acquiring and using relevant information, procedural memory is required to guide the implementation of the plan. For example, if a lexicographic strategy is to be implemented, the decision maker must have the procedural knowledge to direct his or her attention to the most important attribute of the alternatives, select the subset of alternatives that are tied at the best level of this attribute, examine the second most important attribute for alternatives in this selected subset, select the subset of these that are tied at the best level of this attribute, and so on, continuing until a single alternative remains or picking nondeliberatively from the tied set that remains after the attributes have been exhausted.

Several comments about this example are in order. First, we mean the example of lexicographic decision making to indicate behavior that is actually under the guidance and direction of a plan (i.e., following the plan) and not merely a sequence of behaviors that happens to be describable by a plan (see Smith, Langston, & Nisbett, 1992, for a discussion of this distinction). Second, it is clear in the example that the lexicographic strategy, as a generally applicable strategy, is not purely procedural. Declarative knowledge, namely the importance ordering of attributes and the relative desirability of levels within attributes, is required to implement the strategy. If the lexicographic strategy were applied repeatedly in a particular content domain, in which the orderings of attributes and levels could themselves be brought under the governance of rules, the entire strategy could be proceduralized or "compiled" (cf. Anderson, 1987). Thus, the experience and expertise of the decision maker is virtually certain to affect the interplay of declarative and procedural memory in following a plan. Third, especially if the plan has been proceduralized, the decision maker may have little conscious awareness of the rules that are being followed; experts are often unable to describe the procedures they follow. Following rules that are inaccessible to consciousness may be one of the bases for intuitive decision making. By contrast, the relatively slow, laborious following of rules that are stored in explicit declarative form is probably a large component of analytic decision making (see Weber et al., 1995).

So far, we have implied, perhaps, that our third category of decision processes consists of rule-following or plan-following decision making. However, upon thinking about how a person might select a decision strategy, it seems to us that it would be more useful to employ a somewhat broader notion. Suppose that a person focuses on each alternative and considers which procedures in his or her repertoire would sanction the selection of that alternative. Suppose also that the person chooses the alternative that is sanctioned by the plan the decision maker deems most satisfactory (rational, defensible, justifiable, explicable, etc.). In such a case, rules and plans have influenced the decision in more than an incidental way, and yet the rules have not been "followed" in a strict sense. To include such instances of rule-sanctioned, but not quite rule-followed, decision making in our third category of deliberation processes, we will use the term *rule-based* deliberation. Our purpose in including this strategy in our third category is to capture the collection of strategies that rely heavily on procedural memory or on declarative knowledge of procedures.

4. Schema-based deliberation. Our remaining category, *schema-based* deliberation, to which we alluded in describing our experimental results earlier, focuses more fundamentally on the uses of declarative knowledge in decision making. Much of our thinking about schema-based decision making was inspired by the work of Pennington and Hastie (1988, 1992, 1993) on explanation-based decision making. Explanation-based decision making, proposed by Pennington and Hastie and investigated intensively as applied to juror decisions in criminal trials, has three parts: (1) the decision maker constructs a causal model to explain available facts (e.g., a narrative story is constructed from witness testimony and attorney argument to explain the actions of the defendant and others in the case), (2) the decision maker endeavors to learn, create, or discover choice alternatives (e.g., the judge instructs the jury about the possible verdicts and the conditions for their appropriateness), and (3) the decision is made when the causal model is successfully matched to an available choice alternative.

The key property of explanation-based decision making is that it depends crucially on the construction of a mediating representation, namely, the causal model. The causal model organizes much (ideally all) of the information into a whole by promoting and guiding the inference of both supplemental items of information that were not presented explicitly (e.g., that the defendant formed a goal to harm the victim) and relations between items (e.g., various actions of the defendant are interpreted as efforts to achieve an overarching goal). Evidence for such inferences was provided by systematic intrusions into people's memories for presented items of information (Pennington & Hastie, 1988). Moreover, people's choices of action and the confidence they placed in those choices were shown to be mediated by their *evaluations of* the causal models they constructed (Pennington & Hastie, 1988, 1992, 1993). That is, causal models are subject to internal structural constraints (e.g., a story must be composed of related episodes that make reference to the goals and beliefs of the participants, the obstacles they face, their plans to overcome obstacles, etc.). The extent to which a person's causal model respects these constraints, accounts for a large portion of the information, and does so in the absence of competing causal models affects both the likelihood that the person will accept the causal model as the basis for a choice and the confidence placed in that choice (Pennington & Hastie, 1988, 1992, 1993).

Our notion of schema-based decision making relaxes some of the restrictions that Penningtion and Hastie explicitly place on explanation-based decision making, and some that are merely implicit in the studies they have conducted to date. We retain the central ideas of explanation-based decision making: (1) that judgments and choices proceed by fitting a preexisting knowledge structure to the available information and by fleshing it out with inferred information and relations, and (2) that the judgments and choices themselves depend partly on an assessment of the adequacy of the resulting instantiated structure as an organization of the information. (The requirements that inferences must fit into an overarching knowledge structure and that the assessed adequacy of the instantiated structure influences the deci-

sion, both distinguish schema-based processing from associative deliberation.) Our main relaxation of explanation-based decision making is that we
do not require the mediating cognitive structure to be a *causal* model.
Although Pennington and Hastie allow different sorts of causal models to
be invoked in different content domains, they make it clear that they
intend explanations to implicate causation, albeit with a liberal construal of
causation. By referring to decision making as schema-based rather than
explanation-based, we want to draw attention to the possibility that mediating cognitive structures may guide inferences and organize information
by reference to relations that are typical, stereotypical, conventional,
appropriate, meaningful, exemplary, ideal, and so on, as well as causal.[3]

We employ the notion of "schema" as an overarching or generic knowledge structure that provides the mental representation and organization of
declarative information of all types. We regard as special cases the knowledge structures that represent categories (i.e., concepts; Smith & Medin,
1981),[4] events and activities (i.e., scripts, plans, and narratives; Schank &
Abelson, 1977; Stein & Glenn, 1979; Trabasso & van den Broek, 1985), and
various other physical and social structures (e.g., mental models; Johnson-
Laird, 1983). Nevertheless, schemas are not completely unconstrained
(Barsalou, 1992).

D. Semantic content, knowledge representation, and modes of deliberation

1. Amount of knowledge. Within each of the preceding categories of decision
processes, there are ways of implementing particular strategies that require
relatively more or less knowledge of the content domain of the decision
problem. Category-based and schema-based decision making can be
implemented with categories and schemas that are relatively abstract and
content-general or relatively concrete and content-specific. Similarly, rule-
based strategies can be geared to abstract attributes of alternatives (e.g.,
subjective probability and utility) or to relatively domain-specific aspects
and relations (e.g., a prospective graduate student's glowing letters of
recommendation should not be taken to compensate for mediocre grades or
test scores unless you have personal knowledge of the recommenders' high
standards).

We hypothesize, however, that the relative appeal of different categories
of decision processes depends partly on the decision maker's experience and
expertise in the content domain of the decision problem. Strategy selection
clearly depends on a variety of factors. Nevertheless, category-based and
schema-based strategies presumably are more attractive to decision makers
who have rich, well-articulated sets of categories and schemas, whereas
(non-category-based) nondeliberative strategies (e.g., passing the buck) and
relatively abstract (and justifiable) rule-based approaches must appeal to less
knowledgeable decision makers. Therefore, it is important to recognize that

expertise in a content domain does not grow merely by increasing the number of facts in declarative memory, the number of associations in a semantic network, or the number of rules in procedural memory. Overarching knowledge structures emerge. New categories and schemas are developed. Because the various decision processes just discussed require knowledge to be represented and organized in different ways, growing expertise permits a broader array of strategies to be implemented and, we think, affects the relative attractiveness of the different strategies.

Given the prevalence within judgment and decision research of experiments that employ fairly abstract stimuli (e.g., explicit monetary gambles or sparsely described consumer items), it is not surprising that the typical findings indicate the use of rule-based strategies, albeit different rule-based strategies under different conditions. Even when the stimuli employed are not so abstract, the attributes of the stimuli are often varied orthogonally or otherwise without regard for the sorts of stimuli that people might experience outside the laboratory. This can easily create stimuli that appear "strange" and which cannot be approached with the categories and schemas that people have developed, with the result that people are forced to rely on less knowledge-demanding strategies than they might otherwise have preferred (cf. Brunswik, 1956). These considerations argue once more not only that researchers may have unwittingly conducted their experiments in a way that is likely to overlook interesting decision processes, but that the overlooked processes are exactly the ones that contradict the gambling metaphor by failing to reduce the problem (merely) to the variables of degree of belief and degree of value.

2. Semantic content per se. If expertise in a content domain affects the variety of ways a person can represent information and thereby affects the relative attractiveness of different decision strategies, it does not necessarily follow that semantic content per se should be regarded as anything more than a variable that interacts with individual differences in expertise. One might take the position that content expertise produces variance akin to individual differences in the shapes of utility functions. These individual differences may be of some interest, but they are not of fundamental significance to core theory. By contrast, we argue that people's predilections for particular modes of deliberation in particular content domains are not idiosyncratic and are not merely the accidental product of idiosyncratic learning histories that have no bearing on core theory. We think the connections between semantic content, on the one hand, and representations of information and modes of deliberation, on the other hand, are more systematic and more significant than that. We have two classes of reasons for this belief.

First, there are intrinsic constraints on the types of content and the types of representations that are suited to each other. For example, story schemas have figured prominently in our earlier discussion. However, stories are necessarily about the way things unfold over *time*. This is the observation that led us to our notion of endeavors. Decision domains that do not involve a temporal dimension (e.g., aesthetic preferences for different styles of architecture) cannot be represented in story schemas. Because different decision processes require knowledge to be represented differently, constraints on the representations that *can* be used in particular content domains in turn constrain the repertoire of applicable decision processes.

Second, there is a cluster of considerations having to do with social norms and culture. In many domains, the nature of the knowledge that is considered expertise is socially constrained, or even socially constituted. Consequently, people do not become more idiosyncratic as they acquire expertise. Rather, they become socialized into a system of categories and schemas and rules, ways of organizing information about items in the domain, and ways of deliberating about items and options. Thus, experts may become *less* idiosyncratic in the ways they organize information and deliberate about alternatives. It is probably easiest to appreciate that experts may become more uniform in their decision processes (if not in their final decisions) in arcane areas of knowledge, where it is obvious to the novice that the expert has specialized ways of thinking about the issues. What may be overlooked by concentrating too much on arcane knowledge is that we are all relatively expert, that is, thoroughly socialized, in the ways of our culture. Culture provides us with ways of organizing information in spheres of life both large and small, with constraints on the applicability and relative attractiveness of different modes of deliberation. Beyond this, culture also carries prescriptions: (1) for *appropriate* ways of representing information for certain kinds of decisions in certain domains, thus indirectly constraining deliberation processes, and (2) for *appropriate* modes of deliberation, thus affecting these processes directly as well as indirectly. For example, in making personnel decisions, it may be mandated that job applicants be represented and evaluated "objectively," for example, via a profile of test scores, whereas it would be considered depersonalizing and inappropriate to represent and evaluate close personal relationships in this manner.

3. Construal. Despite the fact that we think semantic content is often connected in nonarbitrary ways to representation of information and to modes of deliberation, there is still room for people to *construe* domains and situations in ways that are sensitive to their idiosyncratic knowledge, preferences, and immediate goals (cf. Griffin et al., 1990; L. Ross, 1987, 1989). It is mainly for this reason that we emphasized earlier that we do not think people are compelled to use particular decision processes. We think that people's deliberations about decision alternatives, and the knowledge they bring to bear on these deliberations, are guided by the way they *interpret* the alternatives and the implications of the decision (Bassok et al., 1995). Within limits, interpretations themselves can be matters of choice, or habit, or whim. One may or may not be inclined to regard the purchase of a house, for example, as initiating a long-term flow of events and constraints to be understood in terms of a narrative. One could construct a story about what life would be like in the house. On the other hand, one could evaluate the house in terms of relevant features (e.g., cost, location, size), either with inferences drawn to flesh out a (nonnarrative) schematic understanding of the house (e.g., as a flawed example of the Second Empire style of architecture) or without drawing these sorts of inferences at all. It seems clear that some of these possibilities depend on the decision maker's expertise (e.g., knowledge about architecture), and that a decision maker's inclinations to interpret the decision one way or another may also depend on his or her resources (financial and otherwise) and goals (e.g., planning horizon).

In sum, by focusing on the relationships among semantic content, ways of representing and organizing information, and ways of deliberating, we think that room can be found for an approach to research on judgment and decision making that satisfies the criteria we listed earlier. Because the emphasis is on the *types* of representations and *modes* of deliberation that are related to content, the approach is positioned at an intermediate level of analysis, neither content-free nor completely dependent on the minutiae of the content. Moreover, by developing taxonomies of representation types and deliberation modes, researchers can avoid a chaotic proliferation of domain-specific theories. Rather, the taxonomies can provide a principled means of relating domain-specific theories to one another.

VI. Discussion and conclusions

In the final paragraphs of this chapter, we would like to offer some additional context for the issues we have raised here by relating our concerns to the work of others in judgment and decision research and to some other research projects we have been involved with.

A. Other areas of judgment and decision research

We have restricted our scope in this chapter to the study of preferential decision making. We did so because it is researchers in this area who have been particularly dedicated to the use of content-impoverished stimuli and to content-independent analyses. It seems only fair to point out that researchers who study learning and probabilistic judgment have not shown the same reluctance to address issues of semantic content. Studies of learning have examined the influence of content with tasks involving (1) multiple cue probability learning (e.g., Hammond & Brehmer, 1973; Miller, 1971; Sniezek, 1986; see Klayman, 1988, for a general review not limited to content effects), (2) covariation detection and estimation (e.g., Billman, Bornstein, & Richards, 1992; Chapman & Chapman, 1967, 1969; Jennings, Amabile, & Ross, 1982; Wright & Murphy, 1984; for general reviews see Alloy & Tabachnik, 1984; Crocker, 1981), and (3) induction (e.g., see Klayman &

Ha, 1989, for investigation of a rule discovery task; see Nisbett, Krantz, Jepson, & Kunda, 1983, for investigation of a task requiring subjects to generalize from a sample to a population; see Holyoak & Nisbett, 1988, for a general review).

Research on probabilistic judgment has come into contact with issues of content in some indirect ways, all traceable to the seminal work of Tversky and Kahneman (1971, 1973, 1974; Kahneman & Tversky, 1972, 1973). First, work in this area has shifted away from content-impoverished bookbag-and-poker-chip tasks and toward the use of "word problems" about concrete situations. However, the typical use of word problems has been to demonstrate that a finding replicates across a variety of content domains – chosen intuitively for their diversity rather than for any theoretical distinction among the domains – suggesting that content domain is merely a nuisance variable that can safely be ignored. Second, Tversky and Kahneman's work prompted a search for the heuristics underlying judgments (Kahneman, Slovic, & Tversky, 1982). Although the hypothesized heuristics generally transcend any particular content domain as such, some of them do require knowledge of content. For example, the availability heuristic rests on a search of memory and therefore is affected by the organization of knowledge. The representativeness heuristic rests on a judgment of similarity or typicality, which itself is affected by knowledge about the domain (Tversky & Gati, 1978). In these ways, then, research on probabilistic judgment opened a door for the study of content-specific effects. Third, some researchers have stepped through this door. In particular, the phenomenon of base-rate neglect (Kahneman & Tversky, 1973) has led researchers to consider extrastatistical factors such as (1) the salience or concreteness of information (Borgida & Nisbett, 1977; Fischhoff, Slovic, & Lichtenstein, 1979; Nisbett, Borgida, Crandall, & Reed, 1976), (2) the "relevance" of the base rate or the specificity of the group to which it applies (Bar-Hillel, 1980; Carroll & Siegler, 1977), and (3) whether the event described by the base rate is perceived to be causally related to the target event (Ajzen, 1977; Tversky & Kahneman, 1980; see also Einhorn & Hogarth, 1986). Some investigators have argued explicitly that content domain is important to the use of base rates (Gigerenzer, Hell, & Blank, 1988).

It is evident that judgment and decision researchers have not all been equally averse to investigations of content effects. Nevertheless, it seems to us that judgment and decision researchers as a group are a few steps behind the rest of cognitive psychology in recognizing the importance of semantic content in influencing the processes by which people represent, retrieve, organize, and manipulate information.

B. Criticisms of metatheory

Researchers who study preferential judgment and decision making have been the least concerned with issues of content effects. We think this is largely because the gambling metaphor offers a theoretical framework that encourages the belief that generalizability is enhanced by studying preferential decision making with simple monetary gambles or similar content-impoverished stimuli. We have argued at great length in this chapter against the general applicability of this metatheory and against this experimental practice. However, we are far from the first to argue that decision research should rethink its general metatheory.

For example, Simon's (1955, 1956) pioneering work on bounded rationality stressed the need for psychological theory to respect people's cognitive limitations. Payne et al. (1993) have emphasized the multiplicity of people's decision strategies and their ability to adapt them to the circumstances. Lopes (1987) has argued that research on risky decision making has overemphasized a psychophysical approach and neglected the way that stimuli raise motivational concerns and conflicts. Beach and Mitchell (1987) have argued that too much importance is placed on the selection of an optimal member of a choice set, as opposed to the way people screen individual alternatives for compatibility with their values, goals, and plans, and the way people monitor the progress of their ongoing plans-in-operation. Busemeyer and Townsend (1993) have urged researchers to put aside their static and deterministic perspectives and to face up to the time-dependent and inconsistent aspects of decision making with models that are dynamic and probabilistic. Tetlock (1991) criticizes the standard approach for its neglect of the social context of decision making. (For additional high-level reflections on decision research, see Hastie, 1991; Kahneman, 1991; Kleinmuntz, 1991.)

In view of the relatively large number of recent discussions about the general metatheory of decision research, it appears that the area is experiencing some dissatisfaction with the prospect of business as usual. We are sympathetic to many of the criticisms that have been offered. The criticism that we add implicates the prevalent use of content-impoverished stimuli and the general reliance on content-independent analyses (see also Beach & Mitchell, 1987; Hastie, 1991). We have argued that issues of semantic content should not be ignored in a rethinking of the metatheory of decision research, and we have tried to illustrate an approach that avoids the excesses of the opposite extreme.

C. Selection of decision strategies

Elsewhere we have argued that researchers may have focused too narrowly on decision "strategy" as virtually the sole explanatory concept for a theory of judgment and decision making, and we urged that concepts drawn from the study of memory be included (Weber et al., 1995). To support that argument, we demonstrated that content-independent aspects of memory, specifically having to do with distributed representation of information and composite memory storage, may account for some phenomena that are usually attributed to information combination strategies (see also Weber et al., 1991). Our present emphasis that the repertoire of strategies (or modes of deliberation) is constrained by the way the decision problem is represented may seem to be inconsistent with our other arguments. However, we believe that the concepts of decision strategy and strategy selection should be supplemented, not replaced. For example, we have argued (Weber et al., 1995) that distributed representation and parallel processing have implications for processes which, in turn, influence strategy selection (e.g., the assessment of the cognitive "effort" that a particular strategy will require; see Payne, Bettman, & Johnson 1988, 1990, 1993). Thus, our contention that semantic content influences the selection of a decision strategy, both directly and indirectly via the organization of knowledge, is not inconsistent with the position taken by Weber, Goldstein, and Barlas (1995). In fact, because memory is the repository of knowledge about content, our current chapter also draws on concepts from memory research. Therefore, we view this chapter as complementing our other work, in that it attempts to bring additional aspects of memory within the orbit of decision research, specifically content-dependent aspects of the way that knowledge is represented, organized, stored, and retrieved.

D. History and future

In closing, we would like to point out one more wrinkle in our historical analogy between associationism and the gambling metaphor: the robustness of these theoretical frameworks. Frederic Bartlett, the best-known early opponent of associationist psychology, the psychologist who characterized "every human cognitive reaction – perceiving, imaging, remembering, thinking and reasoning – as an *effort after meaning*" (Bartlett, 1932, p. 44, emphasis in original) once asked, "Why is it that, although everybody now admits the force of the criticism of associationism, the associationist principles still hold their ground and are constantly employed?" (Bartlett, 1932, p. 307). In summarizing his own answers to this question, Bartlett said, "It [associationism] tells us something about the characteristics of associated details, when they are associated, but it explains nothing whatever of the activity of the conditions by which they are brought together" (p. 308). In other words, laws of association help to describe the products of thought, if not the processes of thought. Bartlett concluded that "therefore, associationism is likely to remain, though its outlook is foreign to the demands of modern psychological science" (p. 308).

We foresee a similar robustness for the gambling metaphor, and for similar reasons. In broad strokes, people generally prefer alternatives that offer them higher probabilities of obtaining more highly valued outcomes; the gambling metaphor helps to describe people's final judgments and choices, at least approximately. However, we are also a bit more optimistic than Bartlett was about the prospects for the future. Most researchers who study judgment and decision making do feel the need to explain psychological processes as well as overt behavioral products. Although we think the gambling metaphor fails on both accounts, it is somewhat easier to make the case on process grounds that the gambling metaphor cannot be sustained: people do not transduce all their decision processes through the variables of degree of belief and degree of value. We have tried to outline an approach to decision research that would acknowledge this fact without opening a Pandora's box of unrelated domain-specific theories. We think this approach is promising.

Notes

1 One of the present authors (W. M. G.) was a student of Coombs and recalls Coombs saying that he gave up the use of nonmonetary objects because monetary amounts seemed not to present the difficulty he had anticipated and because nonmonetary objects presented difficulties of their own. As an example, Coombs described a subject who placed high value on a pair of binoculars during football season, but low value on the binoculars after football season ended.

2 It has been said that there is a typical sequence of reactions to most new ideas. First, it's not true. Later, it's true but unimportant. Finally, it's true and important but it's old news. (This joke may contain an important truth, but it's an old joke.)

3 Three additional differences between schema-based and explanation-based decision making should be mentioned briefly, although we think they may reflect matters of emphasis and interest rather than theoretical disagreement. First, Pennington and Hastie have used explanation-based decision making to account for people's constructions of belief (i.e., about "what really happened" in the matters concerning a criminal trial). By contrast, we are using the idea of schema-based decision making to account for people's constructions of value, that is, for preferential evaluations of various alternatives. Second, and related, Pennington and Hastie portray their subjects as constructing stories to explain events in the past. By contrast, we hypothesize that people instantiate schemas (including stories or story fragments) to project events into the future (cf. Schoemaker, 1993). Third, Pennington and Hastie have examined their model in the context of choice among alternatives (i.e., selection of a verdict), whereas we apply the notion of schema-based decision strategies to evaluations of single stimuli as well as choice.

4 The use of categories in schema-based decision making should not be confused with (nondeliberative) category-based decision making. The key property of category-based decision making is that an action or evaluation is merely retrieved from memory when an instance is categorized, and implemented or acted upon without deliberation. ("Oh, it's one of *those*. Well, I know how much I like *them*.") By contrast, categories may be used in schema-based decision making to guide nonevaluative inferences ("It's a sports car; it probably has a manual transmission."), to ground an assessment of one's understanding of the situation ("This thing is 'neither fish nor fowl.' I'm not sure *what* to do with it."), and to guide an assessment of gradation (via graded category membership).

References

Ajzen, I. (1977). Intuitive theories of events and the effects of base-rate information on prediction. *Journal of Personality and Social Psychology, 35*, 303–314.

Allison, G. T. (1971). *Essence of decision: Explaining the Cuban Missile Crisis*. Boston: Little, Brown.

Alloy, L. B., & Tabachnik, N. (1984). Assessment of covariation by humans and animals: The joint influence of prior expectations and current situational information. *Psychological Review, 91*, 112–149.

Anderson, J. R. (1976). *Language, Memory, and Thought*. Hillsdale, NJ: Erlbaum.

Anderson, J. R. (1984). Spreading activation. In J. R. Anderson & S. M. Kosslyn (Eds.), *Tutorials in learning and memory: Essays in honor of Gordon Bower* (pp. 61–90). San Francisco: W. H. Freeman.

Anderson, J. R. (1987). Skill acquisition: Compilation of weak-method problem solutions. *Psychological Review, 94*, 192–210.

Arkes, H. R., & Blumer, C. (1985). The psychology of sunk cost. *Organizational Behavior and Human Performance, 35*, 129–140.

Armstrong, S. L., Gleitman, L. R., & Gleitman, H. (1983). What some concepts might not be. *Cognition, 13*, 263–308.

Bar-Hillel, M. (1980). The base-rate fallacy in probability judgments. *Acta Psychologica, 44*, 211–233.

Baron, J. (1993). *Morality and rational choice*. Boston: Kluwer.

Barsalou, L. W. (1990). On the indistinguishability of exemplar memory and abstraction in category representation. In T. K. Srull & R. S. Wyer (Eds.), *Advances in social cognition: Vol. 3. Content and process specificity in the effects of prior experiences* (pp. 61–88). Hillsdale, NJ: Erlbaum.

Barsalou, L. W. (1992). Frames, concepts, and conceptual fields. In A. Lehrer & E. Kittay (Eds.), *Frames, fields, and contrasts: New essays in semantic and lexical organization*. Hillsdale, NJ: Erlbaum.

Bartlett, F. C. (1932). *Remembering: A study in experimental and social psychology*. Cambridge: Cambridge University Press.

Bassok, M. (1990). Transfer of domain-specific problem solving procedures. *Journal of Experimental Psychology: Learning, Memory, and Cognition, 16*, 522–533.

Bassok, M., Wu, L.-L., & Olseth, K. L. (1995). Judging a book by its cover: Interpretative effects of content on problem-solving transfer. *Memory and Cognition, 23*, 354–367.

Beach, L. R., & Mitchell, T. R. (1987). Image theory: Principles, plans, and goals in decision making. *Acta Psychologica, 66*, 201–220.

Bernoulli, D. (1954). Specimen theoriae novae de mensura sortis. *Commentarii Academiae Scientarum Imperialis Petropolitaneae, 5*, (1730–1733) 175–192 (L. Sommer, Trans.). (Original work published 1738) [Exposition of a new theory on the measurement of risk.] *Econometrica, 22*, 23–36.

Bernoulli, J. (1969–1975). *Ars Conjectandi*. In *Die Werke von Jakob Bernoulli* (Vol. 3, pp. 107–259). Basel, Switzerland: Basel Naturforschende Gesellschaft. (Original work published 1713)

Billman, D., Bornstein, B., & Richards, J. (1992). Effects of expectancy on assessing covariation in data: "Prior belief" versus "meaning." *Organizational Behavior and Human Decision Processes, 53*, 74–88.

Borgida, E., & Nisbett, R. E. (1977). The differential impact of abstract versus concrete information. *Journal of Applied Social Psychology, 7*, 258–271.

Bransford, J. D., & Franks, J. J. (1971). The abstraction of linguistic ideas. *Cognitive Psychology, 2*, 331–350.

Brooks, L. R. (1978). Nonanalytic concept formation and memory for instances. In E. Rosch & B. B. Lloyd (Eds.), *Cognition and categorization* (pp. 169–211). Hillsdale, NJ: Erlbaum.

Bruner, J. S. (1957). Going beyond the information given. In H. Gruber, K. Hammond, & R. Jessor (Eds.), *Contemporary approaches to cognition* (pp. 41–70). Cambridge, MA: Harvard University Press.

Brunswik, E. (1956). *Perception and the representative design of psychological experiments* (2nd ed.). Berkeley and Los Angeles: University of California Press.

Bursztajn, H. J., Feinbloom, R. I., Hamm, R. M., & Brodsky, A. (1990). *Medical choices, medical chances*. New York: Routledge.

Busemeyer, J. R., & Townsend, J. T. (1993). Decision field theory: A dynamic–cognitive approach to decision making in an uncertain environment. *Psychological Review, 100*, 432–459.

Carey, S. (1990). Cognitive development. In D. N. Osherson & E. E. Smith (Eds.), *An Invitation to Cognitive Science: Vol. 3, Thinking* (pp. 147–172). Cambridge, MA: MIT Press.

Carroll, J. S., & Siegler, R. S. (1977). Strategies for the use of base-rate information. *Organizational Behavior and Human Performance, 19*, 392–402.

Chapman, L. J., & Chapman, J. P. (1967). Genesis of popular but erroneous diagnostic observations. *Journal of Abnormal Psychology, 72*, 193–204.

Chapman, L. J., & Chapman, J. P. (1969). Illusory correlation as an obstacle to the use of valid psychodiagnostic signs. *Journal of Abnormal Psychology, 74*, 271–280.

Chase, W. G., & Simon, H. A. (1973a). Perception in chess. *Cognitive Psychology, 4*, 55–81.

Chase, W. G., & Simon, H. A. (1973b). The mind's eye in chess. In W. G. Chase (Ed.), *Visual information processing*. New York: Academic Press.

Cheng, P. W., & Holyoak, K. J. (1985). Pragmatic reasoning schemas. *Cognitive Psychology, 17*, 391–416.

Cheng, P. W., & Holyoak, K. J. (1989). On the natural selection of reasoning theories. *Cognition, 33*, 285–313.

Cheng, P. W., Holyoak, K. J., Nisbett, R. E., & Oliver, L. M. (1986). Pragmatic versus syntactic approaches to training deductive reasoning. *Cognitive Psychology, 18*, 293–328.

Cherniak, C. (1986). *Minimal rationality*. Cambridge, MA: MIT Press.

Chi, M. T. H. (1978). Knowledge structures and memory development. In R. S. Siegler (Ed.), *Children's thinking: What develops?* (pp. 73–96). Hillsdale, NJ: Erlbaum.

Chi, M. T. H., & Ceci, S. J. (1987). Content knowledge: Its role, representation, and restructuring in memory development. *Advances in Child Development and Behavior, 20*, 91–142.

Chi, M. T. H., Feltovich, P. J., & Glaser, R. (1981). Categorization and representation of physics problems by experts and novices. *Cognitive Science, 5*, 121–152.

Christensen, S. M., & Turner, D. R. (Eds.). (1993). *Folk psychology and the philosophy of mind*. Hillsdale, NJ: Erlbaum.

Coombs, C. H. (1983). *Psychology and mathematics: An essay on theory*. Ann Arbor: University of Michigan Press.

Coombs, C. H., & Beardslee, D. (1954). On decision-making under uncertainty. In R. M. Thrall, C. H. Coombs, & R. L. Davis (Eds.), *Decision processes* (pp. 255–285). New York: Wiley.

Cosmides, L. (1989). The logic of social exchange: Has natural selection shaped how humans reason? Studies with the Wason selection task. *Cognition, 31*, 187–276.

Cosmides, L., & Tooby, J. (1994). Origins of domain specificity: The evolution of functional organization. In L. A. Hirschfeld & S. A. Gelman (Eds.), *Mapping the mind: Domain specificity in cognition and culture* (pp. 85–116). New York: Cambridge University Press.

Crocker, J. (1981). Judgment of covariation by social perceivers. *Psychological Bulletin*, *90*, 272–292.

Daston, L. (1988), *Classical probability in the Enlightenment*. Princeton, NJ: Princeton University Press.

Davidson, A. R., Yantis, S., Norwood, M., & Montano, D. E. (1985). Amount of information about the attitudinal object and attitude–behavior consistency. *Journal of Personality and Social Psychology*, *49*, 1184–1198.

Davidson, D. (1973). Radical interpretation. *Dialectica*, *27* 313–328.

Davidson, D. (1974). On the very idea of a conceptual scheme. *Proceedings and Addresses of the American Philosophical Association*, *47*, 5–20.

Davisdon, D. (1975). Thought and talk. In S. Guttenplan (Ed.), *Mind and language*. Oxford: Oxford University Press.

Dennett, D. (1978). *Brainstorms*. Cambridge, MA: MIT Press.

Dennett, D. (1987). *The intentional stance*. Cambridge, MA: MIT Press.

Ebbinghaus, H. (1964). *Memory: A contribution to experimental psychology*. (H. A. Ruger & C. E. Bussenius, Trans.), New York: Dover. (Reprint of book published in 1913, New York: Columbia University, Teacher's College; original work published 1885, Leipzig: Duncker and Humblot.)

Edwards, W. (1954). The theory of decision making. *Psychological Bulletin*, *51*, 380–417. [Reprinted in W. Edwards and A. Tversky (Eds.). (1967). *Decision making* (pp. 13–64). Harmondsworth, UK: Penguin. Pagination taken from the reprinted article.]

Einhorn, H. J., & Hogarth, R. M. (1985). Ambiguity and uncertainty in probabilistic inference. *Psychological Review*, *92*, 433–461.

Einhorn, H. J., & Hogarth, R. M. (1986). Judging probable cause. *Psychological Bulletin*, *99*, 3–19.

Ericsson, K. A., & Simon, H. A. (1980). Verbal reports as data. *Psychological Review*, *87*, 215–251.

Fechner, G. T. (1860). *Elemente der psychophysik*. Leipzig: Breitkopf and Hartel.

Fischhoff, B., Slovic, P., & Lichtenstein, S. (1978). Fault trees: Sensitivity of estimated failure probabilities to problem representation. *Journal of Experimental Psychology: Human Perception and Performance*, *4*, 330–344.

Fischhoff, B., Slovic, P., & Lichtenstein, S. (1979). Subjective sensitivity analysis. *Organizational Behavior and Human Performance*, *23*, 339–359.

Fiske, S. T. (1982). Schema-triggered affect: Applications to social perception. In M. S. Clark and S. T. Fiske (Eds.), *Affect and cognition: The seventeenth Annual Carnegie Symposium on Cognition* (pp. 55–78). Hillsdale, NJ: Erlbaum.

Fiske, S. T., & Pavelchak, M. A. (1986). Category-based versus piecemeal-based affective responses: Developments in schema-triggered affect. In R. M. Sorrentino & E. T. Higgins (Eds.), *Handbook of motivation and cognition: Foundations of social behavior* (pp. 167–203). New York: Guilford Press.

Fodor, J. A. (1992). Fodor's guide to mental representation: The intelligent auntie's vade-mecum. In J. A. Fodor, *A theory of content and other essays* (pp. 3–29). Cambridge, MA: MIT Press.

Ford, G. T., & Smith, R. A. (1987). Inferential beliefs in consumer evaluations: An assessment of alternative processing strategies. *Journal of Consumer Research*, *14*, 363–371.

Frisch, D. (1993). Reasons for framing effects. *Organizational Behavior and Human Decision Processes*, *54*, 399–429.

Garcia, J., & Koelling, R. (1966). Relation of cue to consequence in avoidance learning. *Psychonomic Science, 4,* 123–124.

Gentner, D., & Toupin, C. (1986). Systematicity and surface similarity in the development of analogy. *Cognitive Science, 10,* 277–300.

Gick, M. L., & Holyoak, K. J. (1980). Analogical problem solving. *Cognitive Psychology, 12,* 306–355.

Gigerenzer, G. (1996). Why social context matters to rationality. In P. B. Baltes & U. Staudinger (Eds.), *Interactive minds: Life-span perspectives on the social foundation of cognition.* Cambridge: Cambridge University Press.

Gigerenzer, G., Hell, W., & Blank, H. (1988). Presentation and content: The use of base rates as a continuous variable. *Journal of Experimental Psychology: Human Perception and Performance, 14,* 513–525.

Gigerenzer, G., & Hug, K. (1992). Domain-specific reasoning: Social contracts, cheating, and perspective changes. *Cognition, 43,* 127–171.

Goldstein, W. M., & Weber, E. U. (in preparation). Effects of content domain on preferential decision making. Unpublished manuscript. Center for Decision Research, Graduate School of Business, University of Chicago.

Griffin, D. W., Dunning, D., & Ross, L. (1990). The role of construal processes in overconfident predictions about the self and others. *Journal of Personality and Social Psychology, 59,* 1128–1139.

Griggs, R. A., & Cox, J. R. (1982). The elusive thematic-materials effect in Wason's selection task. *British Journal of Psychology, 73,* 407–420.

Hammond, K. R., & Brehmer, B. (1973). Quasi-rationality and distrust: Implications for international conflict. In L. Rappoport & D. A. Summers (Eds.), *Human judgment and social interaction* (pp. 338–391). New York: Holt, Rinehart, and Winston.

Hastie, R. (1991). A review from a high place: The field of judgment and decision making as revealed in its current textbooks. *Psychological Science, 2,* 135–138.

Hastie, R. (Ed.). (1993). *Inside the juror: The psychology of juror decision making.* Cambridge: Cambridge University Press.

Hastie, R., & Park, B. (1986). The relationship between memory and judgment depends on whether the judgment task is memory-based or on-line. *Psychological Review, 93,* 258–268.

Heath, C., & Tversky, A. (1991). Preference and belief: Ambiguity and competence in choice under uncertainty. *Journal of Risk and Uncertainty, 4,* 5–28.

Henle, M. (1962). On the relation between logic and thinking. *Psychological Review, 69,* 366–378.

Hershey, J. C., Kunreuther, H. C., & Schoemaker, P. J. H. (1982). Sources of bias in assessment procedures for utility functions. *Management Science, 28,* 936–954.

Hershey, J. C., & Schoemaker, P. J. H. (1980). Risk taking and problem context in the domain of losses: An expected-utility analysis. *Journal of Risk and Insurance, 47,* 111–132.

Hirschfeld, L. A., & Gelman, S. A. (Eds.). (1994). *Mapping the mind: Domain specificity in cognition and culture.* New York: Cambridge University Press.

Hoffman, R. R., Bamberg, M., Bringmann, W., & Klein, R. (1987). Some historical observations on Ebbinghaus. In D. S. Gorfein & R. R. Hoffman (Eds.), *Memory and learning: The Ebbinghaus centennial conference* (pp. 57–75). Hillsdale, NJ: Erlbaum.

Hogarth, R. M., & Kunreuther, H. (1995). Decision making under ignorance: Arguing with yourself. *Journal of Risk and Uncertainty, 10*, 15–36.

Holyoak, K. J. (1991). Symbolic connectionism: Toward third-generation theories of expertise. In K. A. Ericsson & J. Smith (Eds.), *Toward a general theory of expertise: Prospects and limits* (pp. 301–355). Cambridge: Cambridge University Press.

Holyoak, K. J., & Koh, K. (1987). Surface and structural similarity in analogical transfer. *Memory and Cognition, 15*, 332–340.

Holyoak, K. J., & Nisbett, R. E. (1988). Induction. In R. J. Sternberg & E. E. Smith (Eds.), *The psychology of human thought* (pp. 50–91). Cambridge: Cambridge University Press.

Huber, J., & McCann, J. (1982). The impact of inferential beliefs on product evaluations. *Journal of Marketing Research, 19*, 324–333.

Jaccard, J., & Wood, G. (1988). The effects of incomplete information on the formation of attitudes toward behavioral alternatives. *Journal of Personality and Social Psychology, 54*, 580–591.

James, W. (1980). *The principles of psychology*. New York: Henry Holt & Co. (Reprinted by Dover, 1950.)

Janis, I. L., & Frick, F. (1943). The relationship between attitudes toward conclusions and errors in judging logical validity. *Journal of Experimental Psychology, 33*, 73–77.

Jenkins, J. J. (1974). Remember that old theory of memory? Well, forget it! *American Psychologist, 29*, 785–795.

Jennings, D. L., Amabile, T. M., & Ross, L. (1982). Informal covariation assessment: Data-based versus theory-based judgments. In D. Kahneman, P. Slovic, & A. Tversky (Eds.), *Judgment under uncertainty: Heuristics and biases* (pp. 211–230). Cambridge: Cambridge University Press.

Johnson, R. D., & Levin, I. P. (1985). More than meets the eye: The effect of missing information on purchase evaluations. *Journal of Consumer Research, 12*, 169–177.

Johnson-Laird, P. N. (1983). *Mental models*. Cambridge, MA: Harvard University Press.

Johnson-Laird, P. N., Legrenzi, P., & Legrenzi, M. (1972). Reasoning and a sense of reality. *British Journal of Psychology, 63*, 395–400.

Jorland, G. (1987). The Saint Petersburg paradox 1713–1937. In L. Kruger, L. J. Daston, & M. Heidelberger (Eds.), *The probabilistic revolution: Vol. 1. Ideas in history* (pp. 157–190). Cambridge, MA: MIT Press.

Kahneman, D. (1991). Judgment and decision making: A personal view. *Psychological Science, 2*, 142–145.

Kahneman, D., Knetsch, J. L., & Thaler, R. H. (1990). Experimental tests of the endowment effect and the Coase theorem. *Journal of Political Economy, 98*(6), 1325–1348.

Kahneman, D., Knetsch, J. L., & Thaler, R. H. (1991). The endowment effect, loss aversion, and status quo bias. *Journal of Economic Perspectives, 5*, 193–206.

Kahneman, D., Slovic, P., & Tversky, A. (Eds.). (1982). *Judgment under uncertainty: Heuristics and biases*. Cambridge: Cambridge University Press.

Kahneman, D., & Tversky, A. (1972). Subjective probability: A judgment of representativeness. *Cognitive Psychology, 3*, 430–454.

Kahneman, D., & Tversky, A. (1973). On the psychology of prediction. *Psychological Review, 80*, 237–251.

Kahneman, D., & Tversky, A. (1979). Prospect theory: An analysis of decision under risk. *Econometrica, 47*, 263–291.

Kardes, F. R., & Sanbonmatsu, D. M. (1993). Direction of comparison, expected feature correlation, and the set-size effect in preference judgment. *Journal of Consumer Psychology, 2*, 39–54.

Kaufmann, H., & Goldstein, S. (1967). The effects of emotional value of conclusions upon distortion in syllogistic reasoning. *Psychonomic Science, 7*, 367–368.

Kimble, G. A. (1956). *Principles of general psychology.* New York: Ronald.

Kimble, G. A. (1985). Conditioning and learning. In G. A. Kimble & K. Schlesinger (Eds.), *Topics in the history of psychology* (Vol. 1, pp. 21–67). Hillsdale, NJ: Erlbaum.

Klayman, J. (1988). On the how and why (not) of learning from outcomes. In B. Brehmer & C. R. B. Joyce (Eds.), *Human judgment: The SJT view* (pp. 115–162). Amsterdam: North-Holland.

Klayman, J., & Ha, Y.-W. (1989). Hypothesis testing in rule discovery: Strategy, structure, and content. *Journal of Experimental Psychology: Learning, Memory, and Cognition, 15*, 596–604.

Kleinmuntz, D. N. (1991). Decision making for professional decision makers. *Psychological Science, 2*, 135, 138–141.

Kunda, Z. (1990). The case for motivated reasoning. *Psychological Bulletin, 108*, 480–498.

Langer, E. J. (1989). *Mindfulness.* Reading, MA: Addison-Wesley.

Larkin, J. H., McDermott, J., Simon, D., & Simon, H. A. (1980). Expert and novice performance in solving physics problems. *Science, 208*, 1335–1342.

Larrick, R. P. (1993). Motivational factors in decision theories: The role of self-protection. *Psychological Bulletin, 113*, 440–450.

Lefford, A. (1946). The influence of emotional subject matter on logical reasoning. *Journal of General Psychology, 30*, 127–151.

Levin, I. P., Chapman, D. P., & Johnson, R. D. (1988). Confidence in judgments based on incomplete information: An investigation using both hypothetical and real gambles. *Journal of Behavioral Decision Making, 1*, 29–41.

Levin, I. P., & Gaeth, G. J. (1988). How consumers are affected by the framing of attribute information before and after consuming the product. *Journal of Consumer Research, 15*, 374–378.

Linville, P. W., & Fischer, G. W. (1991). Preferences for separating or combining events. *Journal of Personality and Social Psychology, 59*, 5–21.

Lloyd-Bostock, S. M. A. (1989). *Law in practice: Applications of psychology to legal decision making and legal skills.* Chicago: Lyceum.

Logan, G. D. (1988). Toward an instance theory of automatization. *Psychological Review, 95*, 492–527.

Lopes, L. L. (1983). Some thoughts on the psychological concept of risk. *Journal of Experimental Psychology: Human Perception and Performance, 9*, 137–144.

Lopes, L. L. (1987). Between hope and fear: The psychology of risk. In L. Berkowitz (Ed.), *Advances in experimental social psychology* (Vol. 20, pp. 255–295). San Diego: Academic Press.

Lubek, I., & Apfelbaum, E. (1987). Neo-behaviorism and the Garcia effect: A social psychology of science approach to the history of a paradigm clash. In M. G. Ash & W. R. Woodward (Eds.), *Psychology in twentieth-century thought and society* (pp. 59–91). Cambridge: Cambridge University Press.

Luce, R. D. (1995). Joint receipt and certainty equivalents of gambles. *Journal of Mathematical Psychology, 39,* 73–81.

Manktelow, K. I., & Evans, J. St. B. T. (1979). Facilitation of reasoning by realism: Effect or noneffect? *British Journal of Psychology, 70,* 477–488.

McNeil, B. J., Pauker, S. G., Sox, H. C., & Tversky, A. (1982). On the elicitation of preferences for alternative therapies. *New England Journal of Medicine, 306,* 1259–1262.

Medin, D. L., & Ortony, A. (1989). Psychological essentialism. In S. Vosniadou & A. Ortony (Eds.), *Similarity and analogical reasoning* (pp. 179–195). Cambridge: Cambridge University Press.

Medin, D. L., & Ross, B. H. (1989). The specific character of abstract thought: Categorization, problem solving, and induction. In R. J. Sternberg (Ed.), *Advances in the psychology of human intelligence* (Vol. 5, pp. 189–223). Hillsdale, NJ: Erlbaum.

Medin, D. L., & Schaffer, M. M. (1978). A context theory of classification learning. *Psychological Review, 85,* 207–238.

Mellers, B. A., & Baron, J. (Eds.). (1993). *Psychological perspectives on justice: Theory and applications.* Cambridge: Cambridge University Press.

Meyer, D. E., & Schvaneveldt, R. W. (1971). Facilitation in recognizing pairs of words: Evidence of a dependence between retrieval operations. *Journal of Experimental Psychology, 90,* 227–234.

Miller, P. McC. (1971). Do labels mislead? A multiple-cue study, within the framework of Brunswik's probabilistic functionalism. *Organizational Behavior and Human Performance, 6,* 480–500.

Mosteller, F., & Nogee, P. (1951). An experimental measurement of utility. *Journal of Political Economy, 59,* 371–404. [Reprinted in W. Edwards and A. Tversky (Eds.). (1967). *Decision making* (pp. 124–169). Harmondsworth, UK: Penguin.]

Murphy, G.L., & Medin, D. L. (1985). The role of theories in conceptual coherence. *Psychological Review, 92,* 289–316.

Newell, A., Shaw, J. C., & Simon, H. A. (1958). Elements of a theory of human problem solving. *Psychological Review, 65,* 151–166.

Newell, A., & Simon, H. A. (1972). *Human problem solving.* Englewood Cliffs, NJ: Prentice-Hall.

Newman, S. E. (1987). Ebbinghaus' *On Memory:* Some effects on early American research. In D. S. Gorfein & R. R. Hoffman (Eds.), *Memory and learning: The Ebbinghaus centennial conference* (pp. 77–87). Hillsdale, NJ: Erlbaum.

Nisbett, R. E., Borgida, E., Crandall, R., & Reed, H. (1976). Popular induction: Information is not necessarily informative. In J. S. Carroll & J. W. Payne (Eds.), *Cognition and social behavior* (pp. 113–134). Hillsdale, NJ: Erlbaum.

Nisbett, R. E. Krantz, D. H., Jepson, D., & Kunda, Z. (1983). The use of statistical heuristics in everyday reasoning. *Psychological Review, 90,* 339–363.

Nisbett, R. E., & Wilson, T. D. (1977). Telling more than we can know: Verbal reports on mental processes. *Psychological Review, 84,* 231–259.

Payne, J. W., Bettman, J. R., & Johnson, E. J. (1988). Adaptive strategy selection in decision making. *Journal of Experimental Psychology: Learning, Memory, and Cognition, 14,* 534–552.

Payne, J. W., Bettman, J. R., & Johnson, E. J. (1990). The adaptive decision maker: Effort and accuracy in choice. In R. M. Hogarth (Ed.), *Insights in decision making: A tribute to Hillel J. Einhorn* (pp. 129–153). Chicago: University of Chicago Press.

Payne, J. W., Bettman, J. R., & Johnson, E. J. (1993). *The adaptive decision maker.* Cambridge: Cambridge University Press.

Payne, J. W., Laughhunn, D. J., & Crum, R. (1980). Translation of gambles and aspiration level effects in risky choice behavior. *Management Science, 26,* 1039–1060.

Pennington, N., & Hastie, R. (1988). Explanation-based decision making: The effects of memory structure on judgment. *Journal of Experimental Psychology: Learning, Memory, and Cognition, 14,* 521–533.

Pennington, N., & Hastie, R. (1992). Explaining the evidence: Tests of the story model for juror decision making. *Journal of Personality and Social Psychology, 62,* 189–206.

Pennington, N., & Hastie, R. (1993). Reasoning in explanation-based decision making. *Cognition, 49,* 123–163.

Pettit, P. (1991). Decision theory and folk psychology. In M. Bacharach and S. Hurley (Eds.), *Foundations of decision theory: Issues and advances* (pp. 147–175). Oxford: Basil Blackwell.

Posner, M. I., & Keele, S. W. (1968). On the genesis of abstract ideas. *Journal of Experimental Psychology, 77,* 353–363.

Preston, M. G., & Baratta, P. (1948). An experimental study of the auction value of an uncertain outcome. *American Journal of Psychology, 61,* 183–193.

Quine, W. (1960). *Word and object.* Cambridge, MA: MIT Press.

Ramsey, F. P. (1931). Truth and probability. In R. B. Braithwaite (Ed.), *The foundations of mathematics and other logical essays by Frank Plumpton Ramsey* (pp. 156–198). London: Kegan Paul, Trench, Trubner.

Redelmeier, D. A., & Tversky, A. (1992). On the framing of multiple prospects. *Psychological Science, 3,* 191–193.

Reeves, L. M., & Weisberg, R. W. (1994). The role of content and abstract information in analogical transfer. *Psychological Bulletin, 115,* 381–400.

Ronis, D. L., Yates, J. F., & Kirscht, J. P. (1989). Attitudes, decisions, and habits as determinants of repeated behavior. In A. R. Pratkanis, S. J. Breckler, & A. G. Greenwald (Eds.), *Attitude structure and function* (pp. 213–239). Hillsdale, NJ: Erlbaum.

Rosch, E., & Mervis, C. B. (1975). Family resemblances: Studies in the internal structure of categories. *Cognitive Psychology, 7,* 573–605.

Ross, B. H. (1984). Remindings and their effects in learning a cognitive skill. *Cognitive Psychology, 16,* 371–416.

Ross, B. H. (1987). This is like that: The use of earlier problems and the separation of similarity effects. *Journal of Experimental Psychology: Learning, Memory, and Cognition, 13,* 629–639.

Ross, B. H. (1989). Distinguishing types of superficial similarities: Different effects on the access and use of earlier problems. *Journal of Experimental Psychology: Learning, Memory, and Cognition, 15,* 456–468.

Ross, L. (1987). The problem of construal in social inference and social psychology. In N. E. Grunberg, R. E. Nisbett, J. Rodin, & J. E. Singer (Eds.), *A distinctive approach to psychological research: The influence of Stanley Schachter* (pp. 118–130). Hillsdale, NJ: Erlbaum.

Ross, L. (1989). Recognizing construal processes. In I. Rock (Ed.), *The legacy of Solomon Asch: Essays in cognition and social psychology* (pp. 77–96). Hillsdale, NJ: Erlbaum.

Ross, L., & Nisbett, R. E. (1991). *The person and the situation: Perspectives of social psychology.* New York: McGraw-Hill.

Sachs, J. D. S. (1967). Recognition memory for syntactic and semantic aspects of connected discourse. *Perception and Psychophysics, 2,* 437–442.

Samuelson, W., & Zeckhauser, R. (1988). Status quo bias in decision making. *Journal of Risk and Uncertainty, 1,* 7–59.

Sanbonmatsu, D. M., Kardes, F. R., & Herr, P. M. (1992). The role of prior knowledge and missing information in multiattribute evaluation. *Organizational Behavior and Human Decision Processes, 51,* 76–91.

Savage, L. J. (1954). *The foundations of statistics.* New York: Wiley.

Schank, R. C., & Abelson, R. (1977). *Scripts, plans, goals, and understanding.* Hillsdale, NJ: Erlbaum.

Schick, F. (1991). *Understanding action: An essay on reasons.* Cambridge: Cambridge University Press.

Schneider, S. L. (1992). Framing and conflict: Aspiration level contingency, the status quo, and current theories of risky choice. *Journal of Experimental Psychology: Learning, Memory, and Cognition, 18,* 1040–1057.

Schoemaker, P. J. H. (1993). Multiple scenario development: Its conceptual and behavioral foundation. *Strategic Management Journal, 14,* 193–213.

Schoemaker, P. J. H., & Kunreuther, H. C. (1979). An experimental study of insurance decisions. *Journal of Risk and Insurance, 46,* 603–618.

Schwartz, S., & Griffin, T. (1986). *Medical thinking: The psychology of medical judgment and decision making.* New York: Springer-Verlag.

Seligman, M. E. P., & Hager, J. L. (Eds.). (1972). *Biological boundaries of learning.* New York: Appleton-Century-Crofts.

Shafir, E. (1993). Choosing versus rejecting: Why some options are both better and worse than others. *Memory and Cognition, 21,* 546–556.

Shafir, E., Simonson, I., & Tversky, A. (1993). Reason-based choice. *Cognition, 49,* 11–36.

Simmons, C. J., & Lynch, J. G., Jr. (1991). Inference effects without inference making? Effects of missing information on discounting and use of presented information. *Journal of Consumer Research, 17,* 477–491.

Simon, H. A. (1955). A behavioral model of rational choice. *Quarterly Journal of Economics, 69,* 99–118.

Simon, H. A. (1956). Rational choice and the structure of the environment. *Psychological Review, 63,* 129–138.

Slovic, P., Fischhoff, B., Lichtenstein, S., Corrigan, B., & Combs, B. (1977). Preference for insuring against probable small losses: Implications for the theory and practice of insurance. *Journal of Risk and Insurance, 44,* 237–258.

Slovic, P., & MacPhillamy, D. (1974). Dimensional commensurability and cue utilization in comparative judgment. *Organizational Behavior and Human Performance, 11,* 172–194.

Smith, E. E., Langston, C., & Nisbett, R. E. (1992). The case for rules in reasoning. *Cognitive Science, 16,* 1–40.

Smith, E. E., & Medin, D. L. (1981). *Categories and concepts.* Cambridge, MA: Harvard University Press.

Smith, E. E., Shoben, E. J., & Rips, L. J. (1974). Structure and processes in semantic memory: A featural model for semantic decisions. *Psychological Review, 81,* 214–241.

Sniderman, P. M., Brody, R., & Tetlock, P. E. (1991). *Reasoning and choice: Explorations in political psychology*. Cambridge: Cambridge University Press.

Sniezek, J. A. (1986). The role of variable labels in cue probability learning tasks. *Organizational Behavior and Human Decision Processes, 38*, 141–161.

Staw, B. (1976). Knee-deep in the big muddy: A study of escalating commitment to a chosen course of action. *Organizational Behavior and Human Performance, 16*, 27–44.

Stein, N. L., & Glenn, C. G. (1979). An analysis of story comprehension in elementary school children. In R. O. Freedle (Ed.), *New directions in discourse processing* (Vol. 2, pp. 53–120). Norwood, NJ: Ablex.

Stich, S. P. (1990). *The fragmentation of reason*. Cambridge, MA: MIT Press.

Tetlock, P. E. (1991). An alternative metaphor in the study of judgment and choice: People as politicians. *Theory and Psychology, 1*, 451–475.

Thaler, R. (1980). Toward a positive theory of consumer choice. *Journal of Economic Behavior and Organization, 1*, 39–60.

Thaler, R. (1985). Mental accounting and consumer choice. *Marketing Science, 4*, 199–214.

Thaler, R. H., & Johnson, E. J. (1990). Gambling with the house money and trying to break even: The effects of prior outcomes on risky choice. *Management Science, 36*, 643–660.

Thorndike, E. L., & Woodworth, R. S. (1901). The influence of improvement in one mental function upon the efficiency of other functions. *Psychological Review, 8*, 247–261.

Thrall, R. M., Coombs, C. H., & Davis, R. L. (Eds.). (1954). *Decision processes*. New York: Wiley.

Thurstone, L. L. (1927). A law of comparative judgment. *Psychological Review, 34*, 273–286.

Thurstone, L. L. (1959). *The measurement of values*. Chicago: University of Chicago Press.

Titchener, E. B. (1909). *A textbook of psychology*. New York: Macmillan.

Trabasso, T., & van den Broek, P. (1985). Causal thinking and the representation of narrative events. *Journal of Memory and Language, 24*, 612–630.

Tulving, E. (1972). Episodic and semantic memory. In E. Tulving & W. Donaldson (Eds.), *Organization of memory* (pp. 381–403). New York: Academic Press.

Tversky, A., & Gati, I. (1978). Studies of similarity. In E. Rosch & B. B. Lloyd (Eds.), *Cognition and categorization* (pp. 79–98). Hillsdale, NJ: Erlbaum.

Tversky, A., & Kahneman, D. (1971). The belief in the "law of small numbers." *Psychological Bulletin, 76*, 105–110.

Tversky, A., & Kahneman, D. (1973). Availability: A heuristic for judging frequency and probability. *Cognitive Psychology, 5*, 207–232.

Tversky, A., & Kahneman, D. (1974). Judgment under uncertainty: Heuristics and biases. *Science, 185*, 1124–1131.

Tversky, A., & Kahneman, D. (1980). Causal schemas in judgments under uncertainty. In M. Fishbein (Ed.), *Progress in social psychology* (Vol. 1, pp. 49–72). Hillsdale, NJ: Erlbaum.

Tversky, A., & Kahneman, D. (1981). The framing of decisions and the psychology of choice. *Science, 211*, 453–458.

Tversky, A., & Kahneman, D. (1986). Rational choice and the framing of decisions. *Journal of Business, 59* (No. 4, Pt. 2), S251–S278.

Tversky, A., & Kahneman, D. (1991). Loss aversion in riskless choice: A reference-dependent model. *Quarterly Journal of Economics*, *107*(4, November), 1039–1061.

Tversky, A., & Shafir, E. (1992). Choice under conflict: The dynamics of deferred decision. *Psychological Science*, *3*, 358–361.

Valentine, C. W. (1930). The innate bases of fear. *Journal of Genetic Psychology*, *37*, 394–419.

Verhave, T., & van Hoorn, W. (1987). The winds of doctrine: Ebbinghaus and his reputation in America. In D. S. Gorfein & R. R. Hoffman (Eds.), *Memory and learning: The Ebbinghaus centennial conference* (pp. 89–102). Hillsdale, NJ: Erlbaum.

von Neumann, J., & Morgenstern, O. (1944, 1947, 1953). *Theory of games and economic behavior* (three editions). Princeton, NJ: Princeton University Press.

Wagenaar, W. A., Keren, G., & Lichtenstein, S. (1988). Islanders and hostages: Deep and surface structures of decision problems. *Acta Psychologica*, *67*, 175–189.

Wason, P. C. (1966). Reasoning. In B. M. Foss (Ed.), *New horizons in psychology*. Harmondsworth, UK: Penguin.

Wason, P. C., & Johnson-Laird, P. N. (1972). *Psychology of reasoning: Structure and content*. London: B. T. Batsford.

Wason, P. C., & Shapiro, D. (1971). Natural and contrived experience in a reasoning problem. *Quarterly Journal of Experimental Psychology*, *23*, 63–71.

Wattenmaker, W. D., Dewey, G. I., Murphy, T. D., & Medin, D. L. (1986). Linear separability and concept learning: Context, relational properties, and concept naturalness. *Cognitive Psychology*, *18*, 158–194.

Wattenmaker, W. D., Nakamura, G. V., & Medin, D. L. (1988). Relationships between similarity-based and explanation-based categorization. In D. J. Hilton (Ed.), *Contemporary science and natural explanation* (pp. 204–240). New York: New York University Press.

Weber, E. U., Bockenholt, U., Hilton, D. J., & Wallace, B. (1993). Determinants of diagnostic hypothesis generation: Effects of information, base rates, and experience. *Journal of Experimental Psychology: Learning, Memory, and Cognition*, *19*, 1151–1164.

Weber, E. U., Goldstein, W. M., & Barlas, S. (1995). And let us not forget memory: The role of memory processes and techniques in the study of judgment and choice. In J. R. Busemeyer, R. Hastie, & D. L. Medin (Eds.), *The Psychology of Learning and Motivation: Vol. 32. Decision Making from a Cognitive Perspective* (pp. 33–81). San Diego: Academic Press.

Weber, E. U., Goldstein, W. M., & Busemeyer, J. R. (1991). Beyond strategies: Implications of memory representation and memory processes for models of judgment and decision making. In W. E. Hockley & S. Lewandowsky (Eds.), *Relating theory and data: Essays on human memory in honor of Bennet B. Murdock* (pp. 75–100). Hillsdale, NJ: Erlbaum.

Wellman, H. M., & Gelman, S. A. (1992). Cognitive development: Foundational theories of core domains. *Annual Review of Psychology*, *43*, 337–375.

Wilkins, M. C. (1928). The effect of changed material on ability to do formal syllogistic reasoning. *Archives of Psychology*, *16*, No. 102.

Wright, J. C., & Murphy, G. L. (1984). The utility of theories in intuitive statistics: The robustness of theory-based judgments. *Journal of Experimental Psychology: General*, *113*, 301–322.

Yamagishi, T., & Hill, C. T. (1983). Initial impression versus missing information as explanations of the set-size effect. *Journal of Personality and Social Psychology, 44,* 942–951.

Yates, J. F., Jagacinski, C. M., & Faber, M. D. (1978). Evaluation of partially described multiattribute options. *Organizational Behavior and Human Performance, 21,* 240–251.

22   The case for rules in reasoning

Edward E. Smith, Christopher Langston, and Richard E. Nisbett

One of the oldest views about the nature of thought is that reasoning is guided by abstract rules of inference. This view has its origins in Plato's theories of reasoning and education, and was the rationale behind "formal discipline" approaches to education ranging from the medieval scholastics' teaching of the syllogism to the English "public school" curriculum of Latin and mathematics. In modern times, abstract inferential rules have played important roles in some of the most influential theories of cognition, including those of Newell and Simon (e.g., 1972) and Piaget and Inhelder (e.g., 1958). This blue-blood intellectual history notwithstanding, the role of abstract rules has recently come under attack from a variety of sources.

Part of the attack stems from the development of alternatives to rule-based models of thought. One class of alternatives is *instance* models, which assume that solving a problem involves the retrieval of specific instances from memory, one or more of which is then used as an analog for the current problem. Sophisticated instance models were first developed in the study of categorization, and the key ideas of the approach have been extended to reasoning (see Medin & Ross, 1989, for a review). Thus, numerous researchers contend that deductive reasoning is more a matter of retrieving examples than of applying rules (e.g., Griggs & Cox, 1982; Manktelow & Evans, 1979; Reich & Ruth, 1982). A related development in artificial intelligence is the

This chapter originally appeared in *Cognitive Science*, 1992, *16*, 1–40. Copyright © 1992 by Ablex Publishing Corporation. Reprinted by permission.

The research reported here was supported by a grant from the National Science Foundation (BNS–8705444) to Edward E. Smith and by grants from the National Science Foundation (BNS–8709892 and SES–8507342), the Sloan and Russell Sage Foundations, and the Army Research Institute (MDA 903–89–C–022) to Richard E. Nisbett.

We are indebted to Keith Holyoak, Michael Morris, Steven Pinker, Zenon Pylyshyn, Lance Rips, Steven Sloman, an anonymous reviewer, members of the Wednesday night seminars at the University of Michigan, and especially Douglas Medin for critiques of earlier versions of this article.

emergence of *case-based* reasoning models. These models assume that knowledge about a topic is partly represented by particular cases, which are stored with a relevant generalization, and which figure centrally in reasoning processes (e.g., Kolodner, 1983; Schank, 1982). Still another theoretical development that eschews rules is *connectionism*. Connectionist models contain only simple processing units, each of which sends excitatory and inhibitory signals to other units, with nothing like a rule in sight. Yet these neural-like models can often produce the same behavior as rule models (e.g., McClelland & Rumelhart, 1986).

In addition to the challenge of rival models, the rule-based approach to reasoning is at odds with certain broad intellectual movements that affect psychology. One is the evolutionary approach to behavior, which holds that much of cognition may be attributable to specific mechanisms rather than to general purpose ones like applying abstract inferential rules (e.g., Buss, 1991). Along different lines, the heuristic approach to choice and decision making that is gaining strength in decision theory and economics contends that people lack the rules necessary for normatively correct reasoning, such as the base-rate and regression principles (e.g., Kahneman & Tversky, 1973; Nisbett & Ross, 1980; Tversky & Kahneman, 1971, 1986). Work in this tradition shows, for example, that people often substitute judgments about similarity for normatively required rule-based reasoning. Although these broad trends lack the "bite" of alternative models, they have contributed to the tarnishing of the rule-based approach to reasoning.

The case for abstract rules, then, appears debatable. In this article, we try to give some direction to the debate. We propose eight criteria for deciding whether a given abstract rule is applied, where each criterion essentially embodies a phenomenon that is more readily explained by a rule-based approach than by an alternative model. We argue that use of these criteria indicates there is substantial evidence for people's use of several deductive and inductive inferential rules, all of which have in common that they are widely considered to be normatively required for correct reasoning.

Two controversial issues about rule following

Abstraction and application

To appreciate what is involved in the debate about rules, we need to say what it means to claim that a person is following a rule. Note first that our interest is in a person *following* a rule, not in a person's behavior merely *conforming* to a rule. When we fall down, for example, our behavior conforms to certain rules of physics, but no one would want to claim that we are actually following these rules. For rule following to occur, there must be a correspondence between the rule and a mental event; indeed, there should be a one-to-one correspondence between the symbols of the rule and the components of a mental event (Pylyshyn, 1990).

As a paradigm case of following an abstract rule, consider the situation where a reasoner is presented with the statements, "If Abner is over 18, then he can vote; Abner is over 18," and tries to determine what follows from these statements by using the propositional logic rule *modus ponens – If p then q; p; therefore q* (quotation marks indicate specific statements, italics indicate rules). To say that the reasoner "follows" or "uses" modus ponens requires that the reasoner:

1. Recognize that the input is of a certain abstract kind (the input is of the form *If p then q*), and as a consequence it is subsumed by a certain rule (modus ponens); and
2. Applies the rule to the input (instantiates *If p then q* with "If Abner is over 18 then he can vote," *p* with "Abner is over 18," and concludes *q*, that "Abner can vote").

Step 1 establishes that *the input can be coded as an instantiation of an abstraction*. Step 2 establishes that *the rule itself is applied*; that is, variables stated in the rule (*p* and *q*) are instantiated with constants from the input (such as, "Abner is over 18"), and then another process inspects this instantiated representation and draws the appropriate conclusions. Some opponents of rules have taken issue with the claim about abstraction, whereas others are troubled by the claims about applying a rule.

Consider first the abstraction issue. A code or representation can be abstract in several different senses. It can

- contain relatively few meaning components (this is the sense in which *color* is more abstract than *red*),
- contain variables (such as *p* and *q* in modus ponens),
- have a high degree of generality,
- be relatively nonperceptual.

The four meanings are clearly interrelated. In particular, a rule that contains variables must contain relatively few meaning components (because the variables have replaced some components), and must have some degree of generality (because the variables range over certain values). In this article, we generally use the term *abstract* to mean *contains variables*, with the other three meanings typically being implied as well (exceptions to this usage will be explicitly noted).

Given this interpretation of abstraction, we note that many of those who favor instance models, and some who champion case-based models (e.g., Lewis, 1988), object to the claim that inputs are coded and processed as instantiations of abstract structures. They would not, for example, believe that our miniproblem about Abner is ever coded in terms of anything as abstract as modus ponens. And if the problem is not coded abstractly, it cannot be assimilated to an abstract rule. Hence, the contrast between rules on the one hand versus instances and cases on the other, comes down, in large part, to the question of how abstractly we represent problems (see Barsalou, 1990).

We can further illustrate this contrast with a task that has been widely used in reasoning research and that will figure prominently in this article, Wason's (1966) four-card problem (also known as the "selection" task). In the standard version of the problem, four cards are laid out displaying the symbols "E," "K," "4," and "7." Each card has a letter on one side and a number on the other. The task is to determine which of these cards needs to be turned over to determine the truth or falsity of the hypothesis: "If a card has a vowel on one side, then it has an even number on the other." In another version of the problem, the four cards read "beer," "coke," "22," and "16," and the hypothesis to be tested is: "If a person is drinking beer, s/he must be over 18." Though the two versions are formally identical, people do much better on the drinking version than on the standard version. (The correct answers are "E" and "7" in the standard version, and "beer" and "16" in the drinking version.) According to proponents of abstract rules, people solve the four-card problem by applying rules that, though less general than propositional logic rules, still are general enough to cover various kinds of relations; in this case, the rules concern the relations involved in *permission*. Because rules concerned with permission are likely to apply to drinking but not to alphanumeric symbols, people do better on the drinking version than on the standard version of the problem (Cheng & Holyoak, 1985). In contrast, according to the proponents of instance models, people solve the four-card problem by retrieving from memory either specific episodes or domain-specific rules (like rules about drinking in particular bars) that are applicable to the problem. The drinking version of the problem is likely to retrieve either a domain-specific rule that is applicable to the current problem or a specific episode that can be analogized to the current problem, whereas the standard version is not likely to do so. That is why the drinking version leads to better performance (Griggs, 1983; Manktelow & Evans, 1979).

Unlike instance models, connectionist models are not hostile to the notion of stored abstractions per se. Some connectionist models (e.g., Hinton & Sejnowski, 1984) include units that represent entities like *animate* and *metallic*, which are abstract in the senses of containing few meaning components, being very general, and being relatively nonperceptual. Other connectionist models embrace abstractions in that they deal with the representation of variables and variable binding (e.g., Smolensky, 1988). However, connectionist models are incompatible with the claims that a rule can be represented *explicitly* as a separate structure, and that this structure is inspected by distinct processes. This seems to be the most widely held interpretation of rule following, and it is the one we will pursue for most of this article.

Thus, the two major issues that fuel the antirule movement concern how abstractly we represent problems, and whether we process explicitly represented rules. At this time, there is comparatively little empirical data on reasoning that can be brought to bear on the rule-application issue. The abstraction issue is a different story; in this case there is a large body of relevant data on reasoning. The bulk of this article is concerned with these data, in particular with determining how well the data line up with a set of proposed criteria that can be used to distinguish abstract representations from concrete, specific ones. In the final section we return to the rule-application issue.

Need for criteria in dealing with the debate

Many researchers would agree that people can reason both ways: by applying abstract rules and by analogizing to stored instances. But to go beyond this bland and uninformative generalization we need to know how to determine when people reason in each way. That is, we need agreement about what counts as evidence for abstract-rule use and what counts as evidence for instance use. In this article we will propose eight such criteria and apply them to proposals about rule systems in deductive and inductive reasoning. We claim that the criteria taken together will often suffice to resolve controversy about a given case of reasoning concerning whether abstract rules are or are not being used. Furthermore, we will argue that the existing evidence concerning these criteria establishes that people often use abstract rules when reasoning about everyday problems. Before considering the criteria, however, several constraints on the scope of the discussion and several ground rules need to be spelled out.

First, we are concerned with the use of rules in *reasoning* (i.e., evaluating a hypothesis in light of evidence). Many arguments have already been advanced for the use of abstract rules in language comprehension and production (e.g., Chomsky, 1985; Pinker & Prince, 1988), but in view of the possibility that language may be a special skill, we cannot generalize this evidence to the case of reasoning.

Another constraint is that, within the realm of reasoning, we are concerned with *inferential* rules, which, by definition, apply to multiple content domains (where content domains are different areas of knowledge that have specific properties, areas like chess or physics or adult social relations). Rules at this level include logical rules, rules for causal deduction dealing with necessity and sufficiency, contractual rules including rules for permission and obligation, statistical rules such as the law of large numbers, and decision rules such as cost–benefit rules. They are to be distinguished from empirical rules, no matter how general, that describe events in some content domain. Inferential rules are also to be distinguished from *operating principles* (Holland, Holyoak, Nisbett, & Thagard, 1986), which are immutable principles that work automatically in running the cognitive system. An example is the similarity principle, which holds that objects sharing known properties tend to share unknown ones as well. This principle plays a substantial role in reasoning but it is not clear that use of the principle involves following an explicit rule (for contrasting views on this, though, see Collins & Michalski, 1989; Smith, Lopez, & Osherson, 1992). Throughout the rest of this article, when we refer to "abstract rules" we mean "abstract inferential rules."

A related constraint is that most of the abstract rules of interest are, in some sense, *natural* ones. We have in mind the kind of rule that *could* be induced by any cognitively mature human given normal experience with the environment. That is, exemplars of the rule are plentiful in everyday experience, and inducing the rule from these exemplars would require neither excessive demands on any relevant processing mechanism (e.g., short-term memory) nor coding of events in ways that are uncongenial (e.g., disjunctions, as in "a red circle or a loud tone"). Furthermore, natural rules are such that they lead to many pragmatically useful inferences. We realize that all this does not amount to a definition, but we take comfort in the fact that the notion of a natural rule, or the related notion of a natural concept, has proven exceptionally difficult to characterize formally (see, e.g., Goodman, 1955; Murphy & Medin, 1985).

Another ground rule is that we do not assume that there is always conscious awareness of the use of inferential rules. Some inferential rules may be applied only unconsciously (Nisbett & Wilson, 1977). Others may be applied some of the time with a concomitant recognition that the rule is being used.

In our discussion, we will make no attempt to distinguish a specific instance ("Abner being told that he must be over 21 to drink at Joe's Bar") from an instance-specific rule (*If Abner wants to drink at Joe's bar, he must be over 21*). We neglect this distinction in part because our concern for most of this article is with the abstraction issue, not the rule-application issue, and in part because it is not clear what empirical evidence could be brought to bear on the distinction.

Our final ground rule concerns the criteria themselves. We do not believe that any single criterion provides iron-clad evidence for the use of an abstract rule (nor does negative evidence for a single criterion establish that the rule does not operate). Rather, it is the use of multiple criteria in converging operations that can make a strong case for or against the use of a particular rule. We also make no claim that the criteria are exhaustive of those that would provide evidence for or against the assertion that an abstract rule is used for some task. They exhaust only our knowledge of criteria that actually have been examined.

Evidence for criteria of rule following

In this section we will defend the use of eight different criteria for establishing whether reasoning makes use of abstract rules and apply each criterion to relevant evidence. Three of the criteria derive from psycholinguistics, where more than in any other area an effort has been made to establish that behavior is based on rule following. Three of the other criteria involve the performance measures of speed, accuracy, and verbal report that are routinely used by experimental psychologists to examine cognitive processes. The remaining two criteria make use of training procedures to establish that highly general rules can be "inserted" by abstract training methods. We list the criteria, and then present a rationale for each of them and a discussion of its use to date.

Eight criteria for rule use

Criteria stemming from linguistics

1. Performance on rule-governed items is as accurate with unfamiliar as with familiar material.
2. Performance on rule-governed items is as accurate with abstract as with concrete material.
3. Early in acquisition, a rule may be applied to an exception (the rule is overextended).

Performance Criteria

4. Performance on a rule-governed item or problem deteriorates as a function of the number of rules that are required for solving the problem.
5. Performance on a rule-governed item is facilitated when preceded by another item based on the same rule (application of a rule primes its subsequent use).
6. A rule, or components of it, may be mentioned in a verbal protocol.

Training Criteria

7. Performance on a specific rule-governed problem is improved by training on abstract versions of the rule.
8. Performance on problems in a particular domain is improved as much by training on problems outside the domain as on problems within it, as long as the problems are based on the same rule.

We note in advance that the criteria vary among themselves with respect to the strength of evidence they provide for rule use. This variation will become evident as we discuss the criteria. We note further that the criteria also vary with respect to how many different abstract rules they have been applied to. Consequently, for some criteria, such as Criterion 1, we will consider numerous rules, whereas for other criteria we will discuss but a single rule.

Criterion 1: Performance on rule-governed items is as accurate with unfamiliar as with familiar items

Rationale. The logic behind Criterion 1 stems from the idea that an abstract rule is applicable to a specific item because the item can be represented by some *special abstract structure* that also defines the rule (the special structure is the antecedent part of the rule). Because even novel items can possess this special structure, they can be assimilated to the rule (see Rips, 1990). Consider the phonological rules for forming plurals of English nouns. One of the rules is (roughly) of the form, *If the final phoneme of a singular noun is voiced, then add the phoneme |z| to it.* This rule identifies the special structure, *singular noun whose final phoneme is voiced,* and any noun – familiar, unfamiliar, or nonsense – that can be represented by this structure can be assimilated to the rule. This is why the fact that any English speaker can tell you the plural of the nonsense item "zig" is "zigz" (as in "cows") has been taken by many psycholinguists as evidence that people do indeed possess the phonological rule in question (e.g., Berko, 1958).

To see how this criterion can be applied to reasoning rules, consider again modus ponens (*If p then q; p; therefore q*). Clearly, this rule can be applied to novel items, even nonsense ones. If someone tells you that "If gork then flum, and gork is the case," you no doubt will conclude that "flum" follows. To the extent you can draw this conclusion as readily as you can with familiar material, the rule should be attributed to your repertoire.

To make the argument for rule following even stronger, it is useful to consider a sketch of a prototypical rule model (which is just an amplification of our previous comments about rule following):

When a test item or problem is presented, it is coded in a form that is *sufficiently abstract* to lead to access of an abstract rule: Once accessed, if need be, the rule can be used for further abstract coding of the test item. The next stage is to instantiate, or bind, the variables in the rule with entities from the input. Finally, the rule is applied to yield the desired answer; that is, inspection of the instantiated representation reveals that the antecedent of the rule has been satisfied, thereby licensing the conclusion. There are therefore four stages: coding, access, instantiation (variable binding), and application.

We can illustrate the model with our "If gork then flum; gork?" example. When presented with this item, you might code it, in part, as an "If X, then Y" type item. This would suffice to access modus ponens. Next, you would instantiate *p* with "gork" and *q* with "flum." Then you would apply the rule and derive "flum" as an answer. Note that had you initially coded the item more superficially – say, as an "If-then claim" – this might still have sufficed to activate modus ponens, which could then have been used to elaborate the abstract coding. Though this is merely a sketch of a model, it is compatible with the general structure of rule-based models of deductive and inductive reasoning (e.g., Collins & Michalski, 1989; Rips, 1983).

With this sketch in hand we can be more explicit about how our criterion of equivalent accuracy for familiar and unfamiliar items fits with rule following. If we assume that there is no effect of familiarity on the likelihood of coding an item sufficiently abstractly, then there will be no effect of familiarity on the likelihood of accessing an abstract rule. Similarly, if we assume there is no effect of familiarity on instantiating a rule or inspecting an instantiated representation, there will be no effect of familiarity on applying a rule. Both assumptions seem plausible, which makes the criterion plausible (i.e., familiar items should not lead to greater accuracy). Indeed, if anything, the more familiar an item is, the *less* likely it is to be coded abstractly. This is because familiarity often rests on frequency, and frequent presentations of an item might lead one to represent it in terms of its specific content.

For a criterion to be truly useful, of course, the phenomenon it describes must also be difficult to account for by a nonrule-based explanation. The major alternatives to rule models are instance models, and Criterion 1 is indeed hard to explain in terms of instances. To appreciate this point, consider a rough sketch of a prototypical instance model:

When a test item or problem is presented, it is first coded, and this representation serves to activate stored instances from memory. The basis for access is the similarity of the test item and stored instances. One or more of the stored instances then serve as an analog for the test item. More specifically, a mapping is made between certain aspects of the retrieved instance and known aspects of the test item; this mapping then licenses the transfer of other aspects of the retrieved instance to unknown aspects of the test item. There are, therefore, three major stages: coding, access, and mapping.

This sketch of a model captures the general structure of current analogy models (e.g., Gentner, 1983; Holyoak, 1984; Holyoak & Thagard, 1989). In applying the sketch to the phenomenon captured by Criterion 1, two critical questions arise. The first is whether the representation of an instance codes the special structure of the rule, or is instead restricted to more concrete information. To illustrate, suppose you have stored an instance of the statement, "If you drive a motorcycle in Michigan, then you must be over 17"; the question of interest amounts to whether your stored instance includes information equivalent to *If p implies q; p; therefore q*. If an instance representation does include such information, then it essentially includes the rule. This strikes us not only as implausible, but also as contrary to the intended meaning of "instance." In particular, one does not think of an instance as containing variables. In what follows, then, we will assume that instances do not encode the abstraction they instantiate, though often they may encode features that are correlated with the abstraction. Thus, instance models differ from rule models not just in whether the test item accesses an instance or a rule, but also in how abstractly the test item is coded to begin with. (A possible exception to this principle arises when people are explicitly encouraged to process the instances deeply. In experimental situations like this, there is evidence that abstractions are indeed coded, though the abstractions that have been studied are different from the inferential rules that we discuss; see Hammond, Seifert, & Gray, 1991.)

The second critical question for an instance model is how to compute the similarity between the test item and the stored instance. If the similarity is computed over all features, then the model cannot explain the phenomenon of equal accuracy for familiar and unfamiliar items, because there is no guarantee that the stored instances most similar to "gork implies flum" will be useful in dealing with the test item. Perhaps "glory and fame" will be retrieved, and this conjunction is of no use in dealing with the test item. A comparable story holds for our phonological example. If overall similarity is what matters, "zig" may retrieve "zip" from memory, and the latter's plural will not work for the test item.

To salvage an instance model we must assume that the similarity between the test item and stored instance is computed over very restricted features, namely, those correlated with the special structure of the rule. Consider again a stored instance of the regulation, "If you drive a motorcycle in Michigan, then you must be over 17." The representation of this instance may well contain features corresponding to the concepts *if* and *then*, where these features are correlated with modus ponens. If such features were given great weight in the similarity calculation, a useful analog might be retrieved. There are, however, three problems with the assumption of differential weighting. First, it is ad hoc. Second, it may be wrong, as a growing body of evidence indicates that the retrieval of analogs is influenced more by concrete features, like appearance and taxonomic category, than abstract ones (e.g., Gentner & Toupin, 1986; Holyoak & Koh, 1987; Ross, 1987). Third, for some rules there may be no obvious features correlated with the rule's special structure (a good example is the law of large numbers, as we will see later). In short, when it comes to explaining the phenomenon that accuracy is as high for novel rule-based items as for familiar ones, an instance model seems to be either wrong or ad hoc. As we will see, the same conclusion holds for many of the other phenomena we consider.

Evidence about modus ponens. Criterion 1 supports the hypothesis that people use modus ponens. Our "if gork then flum" example suggests that we can perform extremely well on unfamiliar rule-based items.

Surprisingly, we have had difficulty locating a published experimental report that permits a comparison between performance with familiar and unfamiliar instances of modus ponens. Perhaps the closest to the mark is a study by Byrne (1989, Experiment 1). In this study, subjects were given statements of the form, If p then q and p, and had to decide which of three possible conclusions was correct, one of them of course being q. Subjects' performance – which was extremely close to perfect – showed no difference between the very familiar item, "If it is raining, then we'll get wet. It is raining.?", and the seemingly less familiar item, "If she meets her friend, then she will go to a play. She meets her friend.?" For these data, modus ponens passes Criterion 1.

Evidence about modus tollens. Modus tollens is a rule in propositional logic that states, *If p then q; not q; therefore not p.* Unlike modus ponens, subjects seem to have more difficulty in applying modus tollens to unfamiliar than to familiar items. Some critical evidence comes from a study by Cheng and Holyoak (1985), which used the four-card problem described earlier. Recall that in this paradigm subjects decide which of four cases must be checked to determine the truth or falsity of a hypothesis. Cheng and Holyoak used the hypothesis, "If a letter is sealed, then it must carry a 20-cent stamp," along with four cards corresponding to "sealed," "unsealed," "20-cent," and "10-cent." Note that the hypothesis has (part of) the special structure of modus tollens with the "10-cent" card instantiating the role of *not q*. Cheng and Holyoak presented the hypothesis and choices to two groups of subjects, with one group being familiar with the hypothesized regulation and the other group not being familiar with the regulation. There were more choices of the *not q* card in the group familiar with the hypothesized regulation than in the group that was not. Hence, modus tollens fails Criterion 1, suggesting that it is not a rule that most people naturally follow.

Evidence about contractual rules. Cheng and Holyoak (1985) and their colleagues (Cheng, Holyoak, Nisbett, & Oliver, 1986) proposed that people have sets of abstract rules (often referred to as "schemas") that characterize contractual relations of various types. Thus, people have a set of abstract *permission* rules, which they use to understand that a certain action may be carried out only when a precondition of some kind is established. The permission rules include:

1. If action A is taken, precondition P must be satisfied.
2. If action A is not taken, precondition P need not be satisfied.
3. If precondition P is satisfied, action A can be taken.
4. If precondition P is not satisfied, action A must not be taken.

Note that this set of rules carries with it an indication of the checking procedures necessary to establish whether a permission contract has been violated: Examine cases where an action has been carried out (to establish that the precondition obtained, Rule 1), and cases where the precondition does not obtain (to establish that the action was not carried out, Rule 4). Presumably people also have a set of abstract *obligation* rules, which they use to understand that when a certain precondition obtains, a particular action must be carried out. The rules include:

1'. If precondition P is satisfied, action A must be taken.
2'. If precondition P is not satisfied, action A may be taken.
3'. If action A is taken, precondition P may or may not be satisfied.
4'. If action A is not taken, precondition P must not be satisfied.

Again, the rules specify checking procedures to establish whether violations of an obligation contract has occurred (see Rules 1' and 4').

The major line of evidence establishing that people use such abstract rules comes from studies using the four-card problem. One important finding is that as long as the hypothesis being tested can be assimilated to the permission rules, the familiarity of the hypothesis has no effect on performance. For example, Cheng et al. (1986) presented subjects with the relatively unfamiliar hypothesis, "If a passenger wishes to enter the country, then he or she must have had an inoculation against cholera," along with the choices "entering," "not entering," "inoculated," and "not inoculated"; subjects were also presented with the relatively familiar hypothesis, "If a customer is drinking an alcoholic beverage, then he or she must be over 21," along with the choices "drinking," "not drinking," "over 21," and "under 21." Subjects performed as well with the unfamiliar hypothesis as the familiar one. Subjects correctly identified which cases must be checked ("entering," "not inoculated," "drinking," "under 21") and avoided checking the other cases that could not establish a violation of the hypothesis, and did so to the same extent whether the rule was familiar or not. (Note that selecting "not inoculated" or "under 18" counts as evidence for a permission rule but not for modus tollens, because other items that fit modus tollens but not the permission rule were handled poorly.)

There is similar evidence for the use of obligation rules. Again using the four-card problem, Cheng et al. (1986) presented subjects with relatively unfamiliar hypotheses that could be assimiliated to the obligation rules, such as, "If one works for the armed forces, then one must vote in the elections," along with choices like "armed forces," "not armed forces," "vote," and "not vote." They also presented subjects with somewhat more familiar hypotheses that could be assimilated to obligation, such as "If any miner gets lung cancer, then the company will pay the miner a sickness pension," along with choices like "lung cancer," "not lung cancer," "pension," and "no pension." Again, subjects performed as well with the unfamiliar hypothesis as with the familiar one.

The evidence just cited has some weaknesses. There was no independent check on the variation in familiarity, and very few items were used. Still, the evidence is suggestive. Furthermore, as noted earlier, it is difficult to construct an account of these results in terms of an instance model. Such an account has to explain why it is that whatever instances are dredged up from memory by the intersection of events like "entering a country" and "having an inoculation" are just as likely to key the appropriate checking procedures as the direct memory of actual cases of drinking though less than 21 years old, not being able to drink because of being less than 21 years old, and so on.

Evidence about causal rules. Morris, Cheng, and Nisbett (1991) have investigated a version of Kelley's (1972) causal schema theory. Kelley's theory assumes that people have different rule sets (often referred to as "schemas") for causal situations that differ with respect to the necessity and sufficiency of the causes involved. For example, people understand that some types of causes are both necessary and sufficient (e.g., 100°C temperature causes water to boil); some types are necessary but not sufficient (exposure to the

Hong Kong flu virus, together with other preconditions, causes Hong Kong flu); some types are sufficient but not necessary (lack of fuel, among other factors, causes a car to be inoperable); and some types are neither necessary nor sufficient (smoking, together with other preconditions, and among other factors, causes lung cancer).

Using the four-card problem and related paradigms, Morris et al. (1991) provided evidence that people follow such causal rules. They showed that subjects usually performed appropriate checking procedures to establish whether a given case could overturn a particular causal hypothesis. Moreover, this was true even when the hypothesis was an unfamiliar one, involving entities never encountered before by the subjects. For example, for the hypothesis, "Temperature above 1500°C causes the element Floridium to turn into a gas," most subjects understood that all four possible events ("temperature above 1500°C," "temperature below 1500°C," "Floridium in gaseous form," "Floridium in liquid form") should be checked in order to see whether the hypothesis was overturned. If we focus on the data from the more sophisticated subjects (advanced graduate students), more than 70% of their tests of unfamiliar hypotheses were completely correct, whereas only 6% of the tests would be expected to be completely correct by chance alone. Although the study lacks a comparison with the testing of familiar hypotheses, the obtained level of performance is sufficiently high to suggest that subjects (particularly sophisticated ones) were using the rules.

Evidence about the law of large numbers. Nisbett, Krantz, Jepson, and Kunda (1983) argued that people have an intuitive appreciation of the law of large numbers and an ability to apply it to real-world situations. The central notion in the law of large numbers is that sample parameters approach population parameters as a direct function of the number of cases in the sample, and as an inverse function of the degree of variability associated with the parameter. In the limiting case of no variability for the parameter, a sample of one case is adequate for an induction to the population value.

To show that people appreciate these notions as an abstract rule, Nisbett et al. (1983) asked subjects to imagine that they were visitors to a South Pacific island who were being introduced to a range of local phenomena they had never seen before. They were to imagine that they saw an unusual bird called a "shreeble," which was blue in color, and asked to estimate what percent of shreebles on the island were blue. Other subjects were asked the same question after being told to imagine they had seen either 3 or 20 shreebles, all of which were blue. Subjects' estimates were systematically affected by the number of cases. They believed that a higher fraction of shreebles were blue when examining 20 cases than when examining 3 cases, and believed that a higher fraction were blue when examining 3 cases than 1 case. In contrast, the number of cases did not affect the percentage estimates when the entities in question were members of the "Barratos" tribe and the parameter was skin color. (The modal estimated percentage to the skin-color question was 100%, even with only one case.) This pattern of findings is consistent with subjects' reports of their assumptions about variability, as they generally assumed that bird kinds are variable with respect to color, whereas isolated tribes are uniform with respect to color. Again, we see a high level of performance with relatively unfamiliar material, so high as to suggest the use of rules even though the study lacks an explicit comparison with familiar material.

Finally, it should be noted that it is difficult to explain the high level of performance by direct application of an instance model. Presumably, such a model would assume that, when told about shreebles, subjects retrieve similar instances, some particular tropical birds, for example, examine their variability with respect to color, and qualify their generalizations as a function of the presumed variability. This still leaves unexplained, however, why subjects recognize that they have to qualify generalizations more for small samples than for large ones. And it is extremely unlikely that subjects retrieve a prior problem that they had solved by applying the law of large numbers, because there are no obvious features of the shreeble problem that are correlated with that rule.

Criterion 2: Performance with rule-governed items is as accurate with abstract as with concrete materials

Rationale. This criterion is similar to our first one. However, whereas Criterion 1 was concerned with unfamiliar or nonsensical items, Criterion 2 is concerned with abstract items that may in fact be very familiar. To appreciate Criterion 2, note that intuition suggests that the rule modus ponens can readily be applied to a totally abstract item, such as "If A then B; A; therefore B." (This item is abstract in the sense of containing few features, and, possibly, in the sense of containing variables.) Good performance on this item fits with the sketch of a rule model we presented earlier, because there is no reason to expect that abstract items are less likely than concrete ones to access the modus ponens rule, and no reason to expect abstract items to fare less well than concrete ones in instantiating the rule or inspecting an instantiated representation. If anything, we might expect abstract items to be both more likely to access the rule and easier to instantiate, because abstract items are more similar to the rule than are concrete items. Note further that good performance on abstract items is quite difficult to explain in terms of an instance model, because the only thing that an abstract item and a retrieved instance can possibly have in common is the special structure of the rule. That is, the use of abstract items allows one to strip away all content but the special structure, and consequently, performance must be based on the special structure alone (Rips, 1990). For these reasons, Criterion 2 is among the most diagnostic ones we will consider.

Evidence about modus ponens. As for Criterion 1, intuitive evidence alone makes it plausible that modus ponens passes Criterion 2. But it is worth considering some experimental results. Evans (1977) presented each of 16 subjects four modus ponens problems of the following abstract sort:

> If the letter is L, then the number is 5
> The letter is L
> _____
> Therefore the number is 5.

The task was to decide whether the conclusion (the statement below the line) was valid or invalid. Performance was perfect: all 16 subjects got all four questions right. Modus ponens passes Criterion 2 with flying colors.

Evidence about modus tollens. Comparable research shows poor performance on modus tollens using abstract material. This was the striking finding of the classic Wason (1966) article that introduced the four-card problem. Given cards labeled "A," "B," "4," and "7," and asked to turn over enough cards to test the hypothesis, "If there is an A on the front, then there is a 4 on the back," even highly intelligent subjects rarely turn over the "7" card (finding an "A" on the other side would establish the falsity of the hypothesis). This is the chief evidence against people using modus tollens.

We note in passing that this sort of negative evidence was overgeneralized by many to become evidence against formal rule systems in general, and is another component in the current popularity of instance models. The studies on contractual and causal schemas by Cheng and her colleagues amount to a demonstration that there has been such an overgeneralization. Subjects solve problems that are syntactically identical to the Wason four-card problem so long as the content of the problem suggests a contractual or causal interpretation allowing an appropriate, abstract rule to be applied.

Evidence about contractual rules. Some of Cheng's work just alluded to shows good performance on the permission rule using abstract materials. In the four-card problem, Cheng and Holyoak (1985) presented subjects with the hypothesis, "If one is to take action A, then one must first satisfy precondition P," along with choices like "A," "not A," "P," and "not P." Performance on this abstract problem (61% correct) far exceeded performance on a control problem ("If a card has an A on one side, it must have a 4 on the other") that could not be assimilated to the permission rule (19% correct). Although the study lacked a direct comparison with concrete materials, the level of performance was sufficiently high to suggest the use of a rule. (See, also, Cheng & Holyoak's 1989 study of an abstract precaution rule.)

Evidence about causal rules. Morris et al. (1991) provided some evidence that people can accurately apply causal rules to purely abstract material. They presented subjects with causal hypotheses that were qualified with respect to necessity and sufficiency, and asked subjects to indicate whether particular states of affairs could overturn the hypotheses. For example, subjects were told that a scientist believes that "Event A causes event B," and further believes that "The occurrence of event A is the only cause of event B, and that event A only sometimes causes event B." When presented with possible patterns of events – namely, "A and B," "A and not B," "not A and B," and "not A and not B" – subjects were highly accurate in selecting those patterns that could refute the hypotheses ("not A and B"). Furthermore, a change in the causal hypothesis – say, "A causes B, but A is not the only cause of B, and A always causes B" – led to marked changes in the subjects' choice of a refuting pattern ("A and not B"). Although the study again lacked an explicit comparison to concrete materials, the high level of performance seems difficult to account for by an instance model: Over 60% of the tests of abstract hypotheses were completely correct, whereas the percentage expected by chance is only 6%.

Criterion 3: Early in acquisition, a rule may be applied to an exception (a rule is overextended)

Rationale. In psycholinguistics, this criterion has figured prominently in studies of how children master the regular past-tense form of English verbs. The relevant rule is to add "ed" to the stem of verbs to form the past tense, such as "cook–cooked." A finding that has been taken as evidence for following this rule is the tendency of young children to overextend the rule to irregular forms, such as "go–goed," even though they had previously used the irregular form correctly (Ervin, 1964). The rule specifies a special structure – the stem of a verb – and the phenomenon arises because children apply the rule to items containing the special structure even though the items should have been marked as exceptions. In terms of our sketch of a rule model, early in acquisition, exceptional verbs are likely to be represented in a way that accesses the relevant rule, and once the rule is accessed it is instantiated and applied.

Perhaps for more than any other criterion, there has been a concerted effort to formulate nonrule-based accounts of overextension. Thus, Rumelhart and McClelland (1987) offered a connectionist account of the overextension of the past-tense "rule," and others offered instance-based accounts of apparent overextensions of classification rules (see, e.g., Medin & Smith, 1981). In general, then, this criterion seems less diagnostic than the previous two we considered. We include it, though, because it may prove to be diagnostic in specific cases. Indeed, with regard to overextension of the past-tense rule, critiques of the Rumelhart and McClelland proposal by Pinker and Prince (1988) and Marcus et al. (1990) suggest that a rule-based theory still provides the fullest account of the data. The critics noted, for example, that children are no more likely to overgeneralize an irregular verb that is similar to many regular ones than to overgeneralize an irregular verb that is similar to few regular ones. Yet, in most connectionist models, as in instance models, generalization is based on similarity. The lack of similarity effects fits perfectly with a rule-based account, of course. Thus, in situations where the likelihood of overgeneralizing an exception does not depend on the similarity of the exception to the regular cases, the criterion is indeed diagnostic.

Evidence about the law of large numbers. The overextension criterion has rarely been applied to abstract rules. An exception is the law of large numbers. Fong, Krantz, and Nisbett (1986) trained subjects on this rule, and found they sometimes applied it to cases where it was inappropriate. For example, in one problem presented after training, subjects were told about a basketball talent scout who watched a particular prospect through two games and concluded that he had excellent skills but a tendency to misplay under extreme pressure. The former inference was based on nearly 2 hours of play, the latter on a single episode. Trained subjects were more likely than controls to assert correctly that the "pressure" diagnosis was based on too little evidence, but were also more likely to assert incorrectly that the global judgment of excellent skills was similarly based on too little evidence. Thus, trained subjects sometimes overextended the rule to cases where it was not appropriate. The fact that this kind of overextension occurred lends credibility to the claim that a rule corresponding to the law of large numbers was indeed being followed, especially because virtually no control (untrained) subjects expressed the view that a larger sample would have been helpful in assessing the prospect's skills.

An instance model has difficulty explaining this specific phenomenon. According to such a model, an overextension would occur whenever the basketball problem retrieves a stored problem that just happened to utilize the law of large numbers. But such problems might be very diverse, with few if any sharing content with the basketball problem. Therefore, the only way to insure that the basketball problem retrieves a useful analog is to make the problematic assumption that retrieval is heavily based on the features correlated with the special structure of the rule.

> *Criterion 4: Performance on a rule-governed problem deteriorates as a function of the number of rules that are required to solve the problem*

Rationale. Criterion 4 essentially holds that rules provide the appropriate unit for measuring the complexity of a problem. We can illustrate the criterion by considering problems that vary in the number of times they require application of the rule modus ponens. Even after equating for reading time, deciding that Argument 2 is valid presumably would take longer and be more error prone than deciding that Argument 1 is valid, because Argument 2 requires one more application of modus ponens:

1. If it's raining, I'll take an umbrella
   It's raining
   _____
   I'll take an umbrella

2. If it's raining, I'll take an umbrella
   If I take an umbrella, I'll lose it.
   It's raining
   _____
   I'll lose an umbrella

(Our example might suggest that the phenomenon is an artifact of the premises being more complex in Argument 2 than in Argument 1; however, using correlational techniques, Rips, 1983, found no evidence that premise complexity per se affects the accuracy of reasoning.)

The phenomenon of interest follows from our sketch of a rule model as long as one or more of the stages involved – coding, access, instantiation, and application – is executed less efficiently when it has to do $n + 1$ things than just n things. As many theorists have pointed out, this vulnerability to sheer number may disappear with extended practice. In Anderson's (1982) rule-based model of cognitive skills, for example, rules that are frequently applied in succession come to be "compiled" or chunked into a single rule; in such a case, performance would be rule-based yet fail to meet Criterion 4. The diagnosticity of this criterion is further reduced by the fact that the basic phenomenon involved seems roughly compatible with an instance model: What needs to be assumed is that problems that supposedly require more rules are really just problems that generally have fewer or less accessible analogs in memory. Again, though, we include the criterion because it may prove very diagnostic in certain cases, for example, in cases where there is a *linear* relation between the number of rules that a problem requires and the reaction time needed to solve the problem. Also, the criterion has a history of use in evaluating rule-based hypotheses. For example, in psycholinguistics, it figured centrally in testing the hypothesis that the complexity of a sentence was an increasing function of the number of transformational rules needed to derive the surface form of the sentence (Miller, 1962).

Evidence about modus ponens. We know of no direct application of Criterion 4 like our double modus ponens example. Rather than being applied to a single rule used a varying number of times, the criterion has been applied to a set of rules. Osherson (1975), Rips (1983), and Braine, Reiser, and Rumain (1984) all applied the criterion to proposed sets of logical rules that include modus ponens along with a dozen or so other rules from propositional logic (such sets are capable of determining the validity of most arguments in propositional logic and, hence, constitute relatively complete theories of people's logical capabilities). The work of these investigators shows that there is a monotonic relation – and sometimes a linear one – between the number of rules needed to determine whether an argument is valid and the reaction time and accuracy of the final response. Insofar as modus ponens is a rule in the systems of all three investigators, there is indirect evidence for the use of modus ponens.

Criterion 5: Performance on a rule-based item is facilitated when preceded by another item based on the same rule (application of a rule primes its subsequent use)

Rationale. The rationale for this criterion is that, once used, a mental structure remains active for a brief time period and during this period the structure is more accessible than usual. In terms of our rule model, the access stage has been facilitated. (Anderson, 1982, made a similar assumption relating recency of rule use to ease of subsequent access.) Our sketch of an instance model would be able to account for the phenomenon to the extent that successively presented rule-based items are also similar in content; but as we will see, the plausibility of this account depends on the specific findings involved.

Evidence about contractual rules. As far as we know, the priming criterion has been applied only to contractual rules. In a study we performed recently (Langston, Nisbett, & Smith, 1991), subjects were presented on each trial with a different version of the four-card problem. Sometimes the version conformed to a permission rule (*If precondition P is satisfied, action A can be taken*), whereas other times it conformed to an obligation rule (*If precondition P is satisfied, action A must be taken*). It was therefore possible to have successive trials in which the permission rule would be used twice, as illustrated in Argument 3 below, as well as successive trials in which the permission rule is used only once, as in Argument 4:

3a. If a journalist has a press pass, she can cross a police line
 b. If a journalist gets a statement on the record, she can quote her source
4a. If a journalist is a member of the union, she must pay dues
 b. If a journalist gets a statement on the record, she can quote her source

Subjects made more correct responses in testing the rule in 3b than in 4b. The same permission rule was involved in both cases, but was primed only in 3b. (Repetition of the rule was confounded with repetition of the word "can," but as we will see later, repetition of "can" alone has no effect.)

It might seem that an instance model can readily explain these results. All that need be hypothesized is that subjects use the previous item as an analog for the current problem they are working on. This would lead to a correct response for 3b and an incorrect one for 4b. This predicts, however, that errors on permission (obligation) problems would be correct responses, had the problems in fact been obligation (permission) problems. This prediction was not supported. There is, however, another aspect of the Langston et al. results that does suggest a role for instances. Langston et al. found priming effects only for items similar in content (as in 3). If the priming item shared little content with the target item, there was no improvement in either accuracy or latency (even though the word "can" was repeated). Nisbett (1991) found a similar failure of semantically unrelated items to produce priming of the law of large numbers in an untimed problem-solving situation. The fact that rule-priming depends on the similarity of the prime and target items suggests that both rules and instances may be involved in these tasks (hence, the criterion is not very diagnostic). We return to this issue in the final section.

Criterion 6: A verbal protocol may mention a rule or its components

Rationale. The rationale for this criterion is based on the standard interpretation of protocol analysis. Presumably, the protocol is a direct reflection of what is active in the subject's short-term or working memory (Ericsson & Simon, 1984), and if a particular rule has been in working memory, then it may have been recently used. Or, to put it in terms of our sketch of a rule model, the products of the access, instantiation, or application stages may reside (perhaps only briefly) in working memory, which makes them accessible to report. There is no reason to expect an instance model to yield such reports. However, the protocol criterion is still of limited diagnosticity, given that there are cases of apparent rule following in which the rules cannot be reported (namely, in language), as well as cases of reported rules for tasks for which there is independent evidence that the rules were not followed (Nisbett & Wilson, 1977).

Evidence about modus ponens. In Rips' (1983) studies of deductive reasoning, he had subjects talk aloud while solving some problems. Rips found some clear parallels between the successive statements in a protocol and the sequence of propositional rules needed to solve the problem. Because one of these rules is modus ponens, these findings provide some indirect evidence for modus ponens meeting our protocol criterion. Similarly, Galotti, Baron, and Sabini (1986) collected verbal protocols while subjects tried to generate conclusions to syllogistic arguments. They concluded that the protocols "provide direct evidence of the existence of deduction rules" (p. 19; the protocols also provide evidence of the existence of nonrule-like entities).

Evidence about the law of large numbers. In Piaget and Inhelder's (1951/1975) classic study of the child's conception of chance, they found surprisingly clear paraphrases of the law of large numbers even from children aged 10 to

12. For example, in one situation a child is presented with a pointer that could stop on one of eight different colored locations, and is asked if there is more likely to be an equal number of stops on each color if the pointer is spun 15 times or 800 times. One child replied:

It will be more regular with 800 because that's larger. For a small number [of chances] [the outcome] changes each time and it depends on the number of times, but with a larger number of tries it has more chances of being more regular. (p. 89)

Although this protocol provides some prima facie evidence for the use of the law of large numbers, a skeptic could easily claim that the reasoning revealed in the protocol is not what is actually mediating the problem solving, and that people are merely inventing plausible stories to explain their behavior. What is needed to strengthen protocol evidence is a linking of it to performance measures. This is exactly what Nisbett and his colleagues have done. They found evidence that some people can articulate an abstract version of the law of large numbers, and that those who invoke it in justification of their answers to problems covered by the rule are in fact more likely to give correct answers. For example, in the isolated-island problem discussed earlier, Nisbett et al. (1983) found that subjects often justified their willingness to make strong generalizations from a single case on the basis of assumptions about low variability and the resulting generalizability even from small samples. Subjects who explicitly gave such justifications were more likely to reason in accordance with the law of large numbers in general. Similarly, Jepson, Krantz, and Nisbett (1983), and Fong et al. (1986) found that some subjects often articulated quite general versions of the rule in justifying answers to specific problems. For example, it was common for subjects to say things like, "The more examples you have, the better the conclusion you can draw." Subjects who provided such articulations of the rule gave answers in accordance with the rule on a higher proportion of problems than did other subjects.

> *Criterion 7: Performance on a specific rule-based problem is improved by training on an abstract version of the rule*

Rationale. The idea behind this criterion is that, because rule following is presumably what underlies performance on specific problems, practice on an abstract version of the rule (abstract in all senses we have considered) can improve performance on specific problems. In part, this should be true because training improves the rule – clarifies it, renders it more precise, and even changes its nature so as to make it more valid. From the perspective of our sketch of a rule model, practice on the rule in the abstract could also benefit performance by increasing the accessibility of the rule and perhaps also by facilitating the application of the rule. (To the extent that there were *any* examples in the training, there could be a facilitation of the instantiation stage as well.) From the perspective of an instance model, there is no obvious reason why such abstract training should have any effect on performance. Criterion 7 is therefore quite diagnostic.

Evidence about modus tollens. Cheng et al. (1986) showed that training on rules from propositional logic, particularly modus tollens, did not lead to any improvement in performance on the four-card problem, specifically on selection of the choice corresponding to *not q*. Training was of two forms. One form was an extensive laboratory session describing the rule and its application in Venn diagrams, truth tables, and an illustrative conditional statement. The other was an entire course in introductory logic that was centered on conditional logic, including the modus tollens rule. Criterion 7, therefore, speaks against the use of modus tollens. (Abstract instruction also did not improve performance on the component of the four-card problem that could be solved by application of modus ponens – selection of the *p* choice – but errors were sufficiently infrequent for ponens as to raise the possibility that there was a ceiling effect.)

Evidence about contractual rules. In another study, Cheng et al. (1986) showed that comparable training on an abstract statement of the obligation rule ("If precondition P is satisfied, action A must be taken") did improve performance on the four-card problem. Training included drill in the checking procedures required to establish whether an obligation had been violated. Subjects were then asked to solve various versions of the four-card problem, including versions to which an obligation interpretation could be applied relatively easily, and arbitrary versions, such as the original Wason (1966) letter-and-number problem. We performed a reanalysis of the Cheng et al. results and found that the abstract training improved performance on those versions of the problem that could possibly be interpreted in obligation terms ("If a house was built before 1979, then it has a fireplace"), and did not improve performance on problems for which an obligation interpretation seemed out of the question (such as the original Wason problem).

We mentioned earlier that there is no obvious way in which an instance model can handle these results, but a nonobvious way might proceed as follows: Although the training involved only abstractions, subjects may have generated their own examples and subsequently retrieved those examples during the four-card problem. What is wrong with this account is the usual set of difficulties. It seems most unlikely that the examples generated during training would have anything in common with the test items in the four-card problem, other than that they involved the notion of obligation. Again, the account rests on the ad hoc assumption that retrieval is primarily based on whatever is correlated with the special structure of the rule.

Evidence about the law of large numbers. Fong et al. (1986) showed that training on the law of large numbers affects the way people reason about a wide range of problems involving variability and uncertainty. They taught their subjects about the law of large numbers using purely abstract concepts and procedures. They defined for them the notions of *sample, population, parameter*, and *variability*, and showed by urn-problem demonstrations that larger samples are more likely to capture population parameters than smaller samples. (These demonstrations, according to our sketch of a rule model, might have influenced the instantiation stage.) Subjects were then asked to solve problems involving random generating devices, such as slot machines and lotteries, problems dealing with objective, quantifiable behavior, such as athletic and academic performances, and problems dealing with subjective judgments or social behaviors that are not normally coded in quantifiable terms. For example, one objective problem referred to earlier required subjects to recognize that a basketball talent scout's assessment of a potential player was based on a relatively small sample of behavior and might be mistaken. A subjective problem described a head nurse's assertion that the most compassionate nurses, as judged from the first few days on the job, generally turn out to be no more concerned than the others, together with her attribution that this was probably the case because the most caring nurses build up a shell to protect themselves. A statistical answer to this problem recognized that a few days' observation of nurses' behavior might not be a large enough sample for a stable estimate of an attribute like compassion. In line with a rule model, the abstract rule training produced a substantial increase in the number and quality of statistical answers, and did so to about the same degree for all three problem types.

Further evidence on the law of large numbers and other rules. An extensive set of studies by Nisbett and his colleagues on the effects of undergraduate and graduate training on reasoning is relevant to Criterion 7. They found that undergraduate training in psychology and the social sciences (Lehman & Nisbett, 1990) and graduate training in psychology (Lehman, Lempert, & Nisbett, 1988) markedly increased the degree to which students call on statistical principles (like the law of large numbers) in reasoning about everyday events involving uncertainty. Fong et al. (1986) found that a single course in statistics had a marked effect on the way students reason about sports. These results speak to Criterion 7 to the extent that statistics is typically taught as a highly abstract set of rules.

Similarly, Morris et al. (1991) found that graduate training in psychology improved students' abilities to apply causal rules to both unfamiliar and purely abstract material. In contrast, training in philosophy or chemistry had no effect on students' causal reasoning, presumably because neither of these fields emphasizes the reasoning required for inferences about various types of causality. Again, the work is relevant to Criterion 7 to the extent that instruction about causality in psychology is quite formal and owes little to detailed work with concrete examples.

Finally, work by Larrick, Morgan, and Nisbett (1990; Larrick, Nisbett, & Morgan, 1993) shows that formal training in cost–benefit rules affects people's reasoning about an indefinitely large number of problems involving choice in everyday life.

> *Criterion 8: Performance on problems in a particular domain is improved as much by training on problems outside the domain as on problems within it, as long as the problems are based on the same rule*

Rationale. If a major product of training is an abstract rule that is as applicable to problems from one domain as to those from another, then subjects taught how to use the rule in a given content domain should readily transfer what they have learned to other domains. To put it in terms of our sketch of a rule model: The major products of training are increases in the accessibility of the rule and in the consequent ease with which the rule can be instantiated and applied, and all of these benefits should readily transfer to domains other than those of the training problems. The upshot is that domain-specificity effects of training might be relatively slight. To the extent such effects are slight, instance models are embarrassed because they naturally predict better performance for test problems that resemble training ones. Hence, Criterion 8 is very diagnostic of rule following.

Evidence about the law of large numbers. This criterion has thus far been applied only to the law of large numbers. Fong et al. (1986) trained subjects in one of three domains: random generating devices, objectively measurable abilities and achievements, or subjective judgments. Then subjects worked on test problems from all three domains. Performance on the test problems – as measured by the frequency of mention of statistical concepts and laws, and by the quality of the answers – was improved by the training. Most importantly, the degree of improvement for problems in the untrained domains was as great as for problems in the trained domain. For example, training on probabilistic device problems improved performance on objective and subjective test problems as much as it did for probabilistic device test problems.

The domains employed by Fong et al. (1986) are very broad ones, leaving open the possibility that two problems from the same domain shared very little in the way of content, perhaps little more, in fact, than two problems from different domains. But this possibility is ruled out by a more recent study. Fong and Nisbett (1991) examined two different objective attribute domains: athletic contests and ability tests. They taught some of their subjects to apply the law of large numbers to one domain, and some to apply this rule to the other domain. When subjects were tested immediately, again, there was no effect at all of training domain on performance. This is strong evidence for rule following. When subjects were tested after 2 weeks, however, there was some effect of domain on performance, although there was still a significant training effect across domains as well. The domain-specificity effect after a delay should probably not be attributed too quickly to retrieval of examples from memory. Performance at the later testing time was unrelated to the ability to recall details of examples, but was related to the ability to recall the abstract rule. The latter findings suggest that, during training, subjects may have learned how to code the elements of a given domain in terms of the rule, which could result in domain-specific coding and access processes. Such processes would lead to an advantage for problems in the trained domain after a delay when access was more problematic.

It is worth emphasizing that the utter lack of domain-specificity effects, when testing takes place immediately, is particularly problematic for an instance model. Such a model requires that the more similar the content of the test and training problems, the more likely a test problem will retrieve a training problem, which will culminate in better performance when the test and training problems are from the same domain. The only way to salvage the model is to posit that retrieval is heavily based on only those features correlated with the special structure of the rule. Yet, it is not even clear that there are any content features of a problem that are correlated with the law of large numbers. As usual, then, the assumption in question seems ad hoc, and likely wrong.

A possible ninth criterion

Criterion 8 says that after training, performance on a rule-governed item is unaffected by its similarity to items encountered during training. A generalization of this phenomenon yields a new criterion: *Performance on a rule-governed item is unaffected by its degree of similarity to previously encountered items.* This is a very diagnostic criterion, because the hallmark of instance models is their sensitivity to similar items stored in memory.

We have not included the preceding as one of our criteria because we have not been able to find a study in which it has been successfully used to bolster the case for abstract rules in reasoning. Perhaps one reason the proposed similarity criterion has not been used is that it is exceptionally sensitive to any use of instances whatsoever. But we may be being too pessimistic here, because there are psycholinguistic studies where the proposed similarity criterion has been met, thereby providing very strong evidence for rule use. Consider again research on phonological rules showing that people can supply the plurals of nonsense nouns. The fact that people can as readily supply the plural for "zamph" as for "zig" – even though "zamph" does not rhyme with any English word and hence is not very similar to any known instance – is an indication that performance is unaffected by the similarity of the test item to previous instances (Pinker & Prince, 1988). A comparable story holds for the rule for forming the past tense of regular verbs. Young children are no more likely to produce the correct past tense for regular verbs that are similar to many other regular verbs, than they are to produce the correct past tense for regular verbs that are similar to few other regular verbs

(Marcus et al., 1990). Perhaps this kind of evidence can be obtained with abstract reasoning rules.

General discussion

In this final section, we begin by summarizing our results, and then take up a number of outstanding issues. One such issue concerns reasoning mechanisms that involve both rules and instances; a second issue concerns the possibility of a type of rule following other than the explicit sort we have considered thus far; the final issue deals with the implications of our findings and arguments for connectionist models of reasoning.

Summary

Throughout most of this article we have been concerned with two interrelated matters: possible criteria for rule following and possible rules that are followed. Let us first summarize our progress regarding the possible criteria, then turn to what we have found out about rules.

Criteria. We have presented and defended a set of criteria for establishing whether or not a rule is used for solving a given problem. Satisfaction of the less diagnostic of these criteria – those concerned with overextension, number of rules, priming, and protocols – adds something to the case that a given rule is used for solving a given problem. Satisfaction of the more diagnostic criteria – those concerned with familiarity, abstractness, abstract training effects, and domain independence in training – adds even more to the case for rule following. And satisfaction of most or all of these criteria adds greatly to the case for rule following. These criteria can serve to put the debate between abstraction-based and instance-based reasoning into clearer perspective.

Table 22.1 presents each of the eight criteria crossed with the five different rule systems we have examined in detail; broken lines indicate that the rule system failed the criterion of interest. Table 22.1 makes it easy to see a pair of points concerning the criteria. One is that most of the criteria have been underused. It is clear that application of the criteria has been relatively haphazard, with many tests of a particular criterion for some rules and only one or two tests of a smattering of the other criteria. We suspect that the criteria used have been chosen relatively arbitrarily, and that investigators often have tested less powerful criteria than they might have, simply because they were not aware of the existence of other, more powerful ones. Our overview of criteria and the rationales behind them should help to organize and direct research on the use of rules.

The other point about the criteria that is readily apparent from Table 22.1 is that the criteria converge. That is, if a rule passes one criterion it generally passes any other criterion that has been applied. Conversely, if a rule fails

Table 22.1. *Criteria for use of abstract rules for reasoning and evidence base relating to them*

Criteria	Rule types				
	Modus ponens	Modus tollens	Contractual (permissions & obligations)	Causal	Law of large numbers
1. Good performance on unfamiliar items	Bryne (1989)	Cheng & Holyoak (1985) Numerous others ///	Cheng et al. (1986) Cheng & Holyoak (1985)	Morris et al. (1991)	Nisbett et al. (1983)
2. Good performance on abstract items	Evans (1977)	Wason (1966) Numerous others //	Cheng & Holyoak (1985)		
3. Overextension early in training					Fong et al. (1986)
4. Number of rules and performance	Osherson (1975) Rips (1983) Braine et al. (1984)				
5. Priming effects			Langston et al. (1991)		Piaget & Inhelder (1951/1975) Jepson et al. (1983) Nisbett et al. (1983) Fong et al. (1986)
6. Protocols identify rules	Rips (1983)				
7. Abstract training effects	/// Cheng et al. (1986) ///	/// Cheng et al. (1986) ///	Cheng et al. (1986)	Morris et al. (1991)	Fong et al. (1986) Lehman & Nisbett (1990) Lehman et al. (1988)
8. Domain independence of training					Fong et al. (1986) Fong & Nisbett (1991)

Note: Broken lines indicate rule system failed the criterion of interest.

one criterion it generally fails other criteria that have been applied. We have only one case of this convergence of failures – modus tollens – because our main concern has been with abstract rules that are likely to be in people's repertoires. If we turn our attention to unnatural rules, which are unlikely to be in people's repertoires, we should see other failures to satisfy the criteria. Consider, for example, work by Ross (1987), in which people are taught relatively unnatural rules from probability theory, such as the rule that specifies the expected number of trials to wait for a particular probabilistic event to occur (the "waiting time" rule). Ross observed a strong violation of our domain-independence-of-training criterion, that is, performance on a test problem markedly depended on its similarity to a training problem. Recent results by Allen and Brooks (1991), who taught subjects artificial rules, makes exactly the same point. These failures of unnatural rules to pass the criterion attest to the validity of the criteria.

Three qualifications of the criteria are also worth mentioning. First, for purposes of clarity we have stated some of our criteria in an absolute or all-or-none fashion, but probably it would be more useful to treat each criterion in a relative fashion. We can illustrate this point with Criterion 1, *performance on rule-governed items is as accurate with unfamiliar as familiar items.* Taking the criterion literally, there is evidence for rule following only when there is absolutely *no* difference between unfamiliar and familiar items. But surely the phenomenon that underlies the criterion admits of degrees, perhaps because of moment-to-moment variations in whether an individual uses a rule. Given this, Criterion 1 is better stated as *the less the difference in perform-ance between unfamiliar and familiar rule-governed items, the greater the use of rules.* Similar remarks apply to Criterion 2 (good performance on abstract items), Criterion 7 (abstract training effects), and Criterion 8 (domain inde-pendence of training). It is noteworthy that actual uses of these criteria tend to employ the relative interpretation (see, e.g., the Allen & Brooks, 1991, use of domain-independence-of-training effects).

A second qualification of the criteria stems from the fact that their diagnosticity has been measured in terms of how difficult they are to explain by models based on *stored* instances. But Johnson-Laird (1983) has champi-oned a theoretical approach which holds that people reason by generating *novel* instances (in his terms, "reasoning by means of mental models"). To illustrate, suppose someone is told, "If gork then flum." They would repre-sent this conditional in terms of the following sort of mental model:

gork1 = flum 1
gork2 = flum 2
        (flum 3).

The equals sign indicates that the same instance is involved, and the paren-theses indicate that the instance is optional. If now told there exists a gork, one can use this mental model to conclude there also exists a flum, and in this way implement modus ponens. What is important about this for our purposes is that a theory based on such novel instances seems more compatible with our criteria than theories based on stored instances. For example, there is no obvious reason why one cannot construct a mental model as readily for an unfamiliar item as for a familiar one, or as readily for an abstract item as a concrete one.

The final qualification is simply that the application of our criteria does not provide as definitive data on the rule-versus-instance issue as does a contrast of detailed models. Our criteria are needed mainly in situations where detailed reasoning models have not been developed: the usual case as far as we can tell. (An exception is Nosofsky, Clark, & Shin, 1989, who did contrast detailed rule and instance models, but who considered rules that are not abstract by our definitions.) Our criteria also provide useful constraints in developing detailed rule models, for example, any rule model that is concerned only with abstract rules ought to produce comparable perform-ance for unfamiliar and familiar items, for abstract and concrete items, and so on.

Rules. Table 22.1 also tells us about what rules are followed. We believe that the applications of the criteria to date serve to establish that people make use of a number of abstract rules in solving problems of a sort that occur frequently in everyday life. In particular, there is substantial evidence for at least three sorts of rule systems.

For modus ponens, there is evidence that people: (a) perform as well – that is, make inferences in accordance with the rule – on unfamiliar as on familiar material; (b) perform as well on abstract as on concrete material; (c) perform better if they must invoke the rule fewer rather than more times; and (d) sometimes provide protocols suggesting that they have used the rule. (On the other hand, there is some evidence that the rule cannot be trained by abstract techniques, but this evidence may merely indicate that the rule is already asymptotic.)

For contractual rules, namely permission and obligation rules, there is evidence that people: (a) perform as well on unfamiliar as on familiar mate-rial; (b) perform as well on abstract as on concrete material; (c) show priming effects of the rule, at least within a content domain; and (d) benefit from training in their ability to apply the rule to any material that can plausibly be interpreted in terms of it. There is also some evidence of a comparable kind for formally similar causal rules.

For the system of statistical rules under the rubric of the law of large numbers, it has been shown that people: (a) perform well with unfamiliar material; (b) overextend the rule early in training; (c) often mention the rule in relatively abstract form in justification of their answers for particular problems; (d) improve in their ability to apply the rule across a wide number of domains by purely abstract training on the rule; and (e) improve their performance on problems outside the domain of training as much as on problems within it.

The demonstrations that people follow modus ponens and the law of large numbers are of particular interest in view of the fact that these two rules are normative and promote optimal inferential performance. Evidence for people following certain abstract inferential rules thus amounts to evidence for people manifesting aspects of rationality. Although there is less data about causal rules, what evidence there is suggests that people also follow these rules (see Table 22.1), which again are normative. And there is some recent evidence for the use of still another set of normative rules, those governing economic choices (Larrick et al., 1990; 1993).

In contrast to the positive evidence summarized before, there are three lines of negative evidence on the question of whether people use modus tollens. It has been shown that people perform poorly: (a) with unfamiliar items; (b) with abstract items; and (c) even after formal training in the rule. We therefore believe that the consensus among students of the problem that most people do not use modus tollens is justified in terms of the criteria studied to date. This demonstration indicates that application of our criteria can cut both ways: Negative evidence relating to the criteria can cast substantial doubt on the use of a rule, just as positive evidence can buttress the case for its use.

Of course modus ponens, modus tollens, contractual rules, and the law of large numbers are just a handful of the many possible seemingly natural rules that people may follow in reasoning about everyday problems. There are, for example, numerous rules in propositional logic other than ponens and tollens that have been proposed as psychologically real (see, for instance, Braine et al., 1984). One such rule is *and-introduction*, which states *If p is the case and if q is the case then p and q is the case*. The obvious question is: How does and-introduction stack up against our eight criteria? The same question applies to other rules from propositional logic, and to rules that have figured in Piagetian-type research (including transitivity, commutativity, and associativity), as well as to rules that come from other bodies of work. The point is that all we have done in this article is sample a rule or two from a few major branches of reasoning – deduction, statistics, and causality – and there are other rules of interest in these and other branches of reasoning.

A final point to note about the evidence for rules is that the work to date shows not merely that people *can* follow rules when instructed to do so in artificial problem-solving situations, but that they *do* follow quite abstract inferential rules when solving ordinary, everyday problems. For example, in their studies of the law of large numbers, Fong et al. (1986) performed not merely laboratory experiments, but field studies in which subjects did not even know they were being tested. In one study, male subjects were called in the context of an alleged "survey on sports opinions." Subjects were enrolled in introductory statistics courses and were called either at the beginning of the course or at the end. After being asked a few questions about NBA salaries and NCAA rules, it was pointed out to them that although many batters often finish the first 2 weeks of the baseball season with averages of .450 or higher, no one has ever finished the season with such an average. They were asked why they thought this was the case. Most subjects responded with causal hypotheses such as, "the pitchers make the necessary adjustments." Some, however, responded with statistical answers such as, "there are not many at-bats in 2 weeks, so unusually high (or low) averages would be more likely; over the long haul nobody is really that good." There were twice as many statistical answers from subjects tested at the end of the term as from subjects tested at the beginning.

Similarly, Larrick et al. (1990) found that subjects who were taught cost–benefit rules came to apply them in all sorts of life contexts, from consumer decisions about whether to finish a bad meal or bad movie, to professional decisions about whether to pursue a line of work that was turning out to be disappointing, to hypothetical questions about institutional policy and international relations.

Thus, the work reviewed here establishes not merely that people can follow abstract rules self-consciously in appropriate educational, experimental, or professional settings, but that such rules play at least a limited role in ordinary inference.

Combining rule and instance mechanisms

Our review indicates that pure instance models of reasoning and problem solving are not viable. There is too much evidence, stemming from the application of too many criteria, indicating that people use abstract rules in reasoning. On the other hand, there is also abundant evidence that reasoning and problem solving often proceed via the retrieval of instances (e.g., Allen & Brooks, 1991; Kaiser, Jonides, & Alexander, 1986; Medin & Ross, 1989; Ross, 1987). At a minimum, then, we need to posit two qualitatively different mechanisms of reasoning. Whereas some situations may involve only one of the mechanisms, others may involve both.

In addition to *pure-rule* and *pure-instance* mechanisms, hybrid mechanisms may be needed as well. In particular, hybrid mechanisms may be needed to account for the situations noted earlier in which people process instances deeply enough to encode some information about the relevant abstraction as well as about the concrete aspects of the instance. These are the situations that are the concern of most case-based reasoning models (e.g., Hammond et al., 1991; Kolodner, 1983; Schank, 1982). In such situations, people have essentially encoded both an instance and a rule, so a hybrid mechanism must specify how the two representational aspects are connected. We consider two possibilities.

One possibility is that a retrieved instance provides access to a rule. That is, when an item is presented, it first accesses similar instances from memory that the reasoner can use to access a rule. Then, the final stages of rule processing – instantiation and application – ensue, though the instance may serve as a guide for these two stages. We can illustrate this mechanism with the drinking version of the four-card problem. When presented the problem, presumably a subject uses this item to retrieve from memory an episode of a drinking event; this representation may contain the information that people below the drinking age are in violation of the law, and the concept of *violation* may be used to access the permission rule; from here on, processing would continue as specified in our sketch of a rule model except that the retrieved instance can be used to guide the instantiation and application stages. This hybrid process, which we will refer to as *instance-rule mechanism*, captures the intuition that we often understand an abstract rule in terms of a specific example.

The other possibility is that a rule provides access to a relevant instance (a *rule-instance* mechanism). That is, when an item is presented it is coded abstractly, and this abstraction accesses the appropriate rule (these are the first two stages of our sketch of a rule model). The rule then provides access to some typical examples, and these instances control further processing. Again, we can illustrate with the drinking version of the four-card problem. When presented the problem, a subject codes the item in terms of *permission*, and uses this code to access the permission rules. Associated with these rules are typical examples of *permission* situations, and one or more of these instances is used as an analog for the present problem (that is, it is used for the mapping stage).

A few comments are in order about these mechanisms. Note that we are not proposing the two hybrid mechanisms as alternatives to the two pure mechanisms (rule and instance). Rather, we suspect that all four mechanisms can be used, albeit with different situations recruiting different mechanisms. (The experimental situations we reviewed in this article likely involved either the *pure-rule* or the *rule-instance* mechanism.) In situations where more than one mechanism is involved, presumably the processes operate simultaneously and independently of one another. Thus, the final answer may be determined by a kind of "horse race" between the operative mechanisms, with the mechanism that finishes first determining the final judgment.

Note further that our hybrid mechanisms allow room for instance-type effects should they occur. Consider again Criterion 1, that novel rule-based items are treated as accurately as familiar ones. The available evidence is consistent with this criterion, but the criterion deals only with accuracy. Perhaps if one were to measure reaction times, familiar rule-based items might be processed faster than novel ones. Such a result could be handled easily by our *instance-rule* mechanism. Familiar items should be faster in accessing a relevant instance because familiar items are themselves likely to be instances. In addition, we have already seen an indication of instance effects even for accuracy. Such an effect appeared in connection with Criterion 5, that application of a rule primes its subsequent use. Recall that in the four-card problem, Langston et al. (1991) found evidence for priming of contractual rules only when the prime and target were similar in content.

This pattern of results also fits nicely with the *instance-rule* mechanism. Only when the target and prime are similar in content does the target retrieve the prime instance, and only when the prime is retrieved does one gain access to the relevant rule. Thus, instance-type effects do not imply that rules were not involved.

Finally, another case of instance-type effects during rule use is provided by Ross (1987). Ross trained subjects on the waiting-time rule of probability theory and then had them solve new test problems with the rule present. Even though the rule was present, subjects appeared to rely on training problems when determining how to instantiate the rule. These results indicate that instances are used not just to access a rule but also to help instantiate it, as in the instance-rule mechanism. (These results, however, may depend in part on the fact that the rule involved was not a natural one.)

In short, the dichotomy between pure rules and pure instances is too simple. Hybrid mechanisms seem plausible, particularly in light of the role they play in current versions of case-based reasoning.

Two kinds of rule following

Until now we have acted as if explicit rule following is the only kind of rule following. But a critical observation suggests the need to consider a second kind. The observation (due to Douglas Medin, personal communication, April 1991) is that, when *linguistic* rules are stacked up against our eight criteria they seem to consistently fail three of them, namely verbal protocols, abstract training effects, and context independence in training. That is, people are notoriously unable to verbalize the linguistic rules they purportedly use, and they fail to benefit much from explicit (school) instructions on these rules. If linguistic rules meet only five of our criteria whereas reasoning rules (generally) meet all eight, perhaps the kind of rule followed involved in language is different from that involved in reasoning.

Presumably there is a kind of rule following that is *implicit* rather than *explicit*; that is, the rule is never explicitly represented, which accounts for why it can neither be reported nor affected by explicit instruction. The rule might be implemented in the hardware, and is essentially a description of how some built-in processor works (see Pinker & Prince, 1988, Section 8.2). Implicit rules are close to what we earlier characterized as operating principles of a system, and rules like this may be part of our basic cognitive architecture. Such notions fit nicely with Pylyshyn's (1984) concept of *cognitive penetrability*. His basic idea is that anything that is part of the fixed cognitive architecture cannot be altered (penetrated) by goals, context, or instruction. If some linguistic rules are part of our basic architecture, they should not be affected by instruction, which means that our two instructional criteria should fail, as they in fact do. (The seeming imperviousness of modus ponens to instruction leaves open the possibility that this rule too may be represented implicitly.)

Implications for connectionist models

Although we know of no limit, in principle, on the ability of connectionist models to code abstractions, the evidence we have presented for abstract rules does not fit well with the connectionist program.

For one thing, what seems to be the most straightforward account of much of the evidence involves concepts that are anathema to connectionism. The account we have in mind is that of explicit rule following: The rule and input are mentally represented explicitly, and application of the rule to the input involves an inspection of the input to determine whether the antecedent of the rule has been satisfied. Notions of *explicit data structures* and *inspection of explicit structures* simply lie outside the ontology of connectionism. Of course, connectionists may be able to develop alternative accounts of the data, but there is no reason to believe the resulting connectionist models will be as parsimonious as the sort of rule-based model we advocate. This is particularly the case given that the abstract rules that have to be modeled all involve variable bindings, which remains a difficult issue in connectionist work (for discussion, see Holyoak, 1991). In short, rule-based models provide a simple account of the data, and no comparable connectionist alternatives are thus far in sight.

In constructing alternative models of the evidence, connectionists face another difficulty. The evidence indicates that people can use two qualitatively different mechanisms in reasoning, which we have termed "rules" and "instances," whereas connectionist models endorse a uniform representation. Connectionist models can either blur the rule-instance distinction, in which case they are simply failing to capture a major generalization about human cognition, or they can somehow mark the distinction, in which case they may be merely implementing a rule-based model in a connectionist net. We say "merely" because it is not clear that such an implementation will yield any new important insights about reasoning.

The preceding points have been programmatic, but the remaining one is more substantive. According to rule models, the rationale for some rules hinges on a *constituency relation* – like that which holds between *If p then q* and *p* – but most current connectionist models lack true constituency relations. In discussing this issue, we need to keep separate *localist* connectionist models, in which a concept can be represented by a single node, and *distributed* models, in which a concept is represented by a set of nodes. We consider localist models first.

To understand the constituency issue, consider modus ponens. Given *If p then q* and *p*, the fact that the latter is a constituent of the former is part of why we can conclude *q*. To take an even simpler example, consider again and-introduction: *If p is the case and if q is the case then p and q is the case*. Here, it is clear that the basis of the rule is a constituency relation; the rule essentially states, *if each of its constituents is the case, then a conjunction is the case*. In contrast, localist connectionist models lack constituency relations, so such relations can never serve as the bases for rules.

The reason localist connectionist models lack constituency relations is that their nodes (their representations) lack any internal structure, including a part–whole structure. In a localist model for and-introduction, for example, there might be separate nodes for p, q, and p and q, which are connected in such a way that whenever the nodes for p and q are both activated, the node for p and q is activated. Importantly, the node for p and q has no internal structure, and in no sense contains the node for p or that for q. Hence, the relation between the p and q nodes on the one hand, and the p and q node on the other, is strictly causal (as opposed to constituency). That is, activation of p and q causes activation of p and q in exactly the same way that activation of a node for *fire* might cause activation of a node for *smoke*. Although we know of no data on whether constituency relations are perceived as the bases of some rules, our intuitions suggest they are, which favors the rule account. (For a fuller discussion of these issues, see Fodor and Pylyshyn, 1988.)

Distributed connectionist models seem better able to accommodate constituency relations because they at least have a part–whole structure. Thus, if p and q is represented by a set of nodes, then some part of that set can, in principle, represent p and another part q. However, current distributed connectionist models still have trouble capturing constituent structure, as Fodor and McLaughlin (1990) pointed out. The latter authors take up a proposal of Smolensky's (1988), in which a concept (rule) is represented in terms of a vector whose components represent the activity levels of the members of the relevant set of nodes. According to Smolensky, vector a is a constituent of vector b if there exists a third vector – call it x – such that $a + x = b$; a is a part of b because b is derivable from $a(+x)$. But this proposal permits the possibility that b may be activated without a being activated. In the case of and-introduction, this means that p and q could be activated without p being activated. Such a thing should be impossible if p is a true constituent of p and q. Again, to the extent some rules are based on constituent structure, the rule account is favored over current connectionist rivals.

None of this is to suggest that connectionist models do not have an important role to play – they have been very successful in capturing aspects of perception, memory, and categorization, for example – but rather to suggest that some aspects of reasoning may be inherently rule based, and hence, not naturally captured by connectionist models. Of course, a rule-based model, unlike a connectionist one, will not look like a biological model. Thus, to pursue rule-based models of reasoning is to give up the wish that all mental phenomena be expressive of biological phenomena rather than merely emergent on them. It has always been hard to make the leap from mere neural connections to abstract rules that seem metaphorically to sit astride the hustle and bustle of biological activity in the brain, altering and managing the results of such activity, and being modified by the mere words of outsiders and the ministrations of educators. We do not pretend to be able to make the leap from the known facts of the behavior of the nervous system to a plausible, emergent set of highly modifiable abstract rules. We claim merely that a correct theory of mind may have to do so.

References

Allen, S. W., & Brooks, L. R. (1991). Specializing the operation of an explicit rule. *Journal of Experimental Psychology: General, 120,* 278–287.

Anderson, J. R. (1982). Acquisition of cognitive skill. *Psychological Review, 89,* 369–406.

Barsalou, L. W. (1990). On the indistinguishability of exemplar memory and abstraction in category representation. In T. K. Srull & R. S. Wyer (Eds.), *Advances in social cognition* (Vol. 3). Hillsdale. NJ: Erlbaum.

Berko, J. (1958). The child's learning of English morphology. *Word, 14,* 150–177.

Braine, M. D. S., Reiser, B. J., & Rumain, B. (1984). Some empirical justification for a theory of natural propositional logic. In G. H. Brown (Ed.), *Psychology of learning and motivation.* Orlando, FL: Academic.

Buss, D. (1991). Evolutionary personality psychology. *Annual Review of Psychology, 42,* 459–491.

Byrne, R. M. J. (1989). Suppressing valid inferences with conditionals. *Cognition, 31,* 61–83.

Cheng, P. W., & Holyoak, K. J. (1985). Pragmatic reasoning schemas. *Cognitive Psychology, 17,* 391–416.

Cheng, P. W., & Holyoak, K. J. (1989). On the natural selection of reasoning theories. *Cognition, 33,* 285–314.

Cheng, P. W., Holyoak, K. J., Nisbett, R. E., & Oliver, L. M. (1986). Pragmatic versus syntactic approaches to training deductive reasoning. *Cognitive Psychology, 18,* 293–328.

Chomsky, N. (1985). *Knowledge of language.* New York: Praeger.

Collins, A. M., & Michalski, R. (1989). The logic of plausible reasoning: A core theory. *Cognitive Science, 13,* 1–50.

Ericsson, K. A., & Simon, H. A. (1984). *Protocol analysis: Verbal reports as data.* Cambridge, MA: MIT Press.

Ervin, S. M. (1964). Imitation and structural change in children's language. In E. H. Lenneberg (Ed.), *New directions in the study of language.* Cambridge, MA: MIT Press.

Evans, J. St. B. T. (1977). Linguistic factors in reasoning. *Quarterly Journal of Experimental Psychology, 29,* 297–306.

Fodor, J. A., & McLaughlin, B. P. (1990). Connectionism and the problem of systematicity: Why Smolensky's solution doesn't work. *Cognition, 35,* 183–204.

Fodor, J. A., & Pylyshyn, Z. (1988). Connectionism and cognitive architecture: A critical analysis. *Cognition, 28,* 3–72.

Fong, G. T., Krantz, D. H., & Nisbett, R. E. (1986). The effects of statistical training on thinking about everyday problems. *Cognitive Psychology, 18,* 253–292.

Fong, G. T., & Nisbett, R. E. (1991). Immediate and delayed transfer of training effects in statistical reasoning. *Journal of Experimental Psychology: General, 120,* 34–45.

Galotti, K. M., Baron, J., & Sabini, J. (1986). Individual differences in syllogistic reasoning: Deduction rules or mental models? *Journal of Experimental Psychology: General, 115,* 16–25.

Gentner, D. (1983). Structure mapping: A theoretical framework for analogy. *Cognitive Science, 7,* 155–170.

Gentner, D., & Toupin, C. (1986). Systematicity and surface similarity in the development of analogy. *Cognitive Science, 10,* 277–300.

Goodman, N. (1955). *Fact, fiction and forecast* (chap. 3). Cambridge, MA: Harvard University Press.

Griggs, R. A. (1983). The role of problem content in the selection task and the THOG problem. In J. St. B. T. Evans (Ed.), *Thinking and reasoning.* London: Routledge & Kegan Paul.

Griggs, R. A., & Cox, J. R. (1982). The elusive thematic-materials effect in Wason's selection task. *British Journal of Psychology, 73,* 407–420.

Hammond, K. J., Siefert, C. M., & Gray, K. C. (1991). Functionality in analogical transfer: A hard match is good to find. *The Journal of the Learning Sciences, 1,* 111–152.

Hinton, G. E., & Sejnowski, T. J. (1984). Learning semantic features. *Proceedings of the Sixth Annual Conference of the Cognitive Science Society* (pp. 63–70). Boulder, CO.

Holland, J. H., Holyoak, K. J., Nisbett, R. E., & Thagard, P. T. (1986). *Induction: Processes of inference, learning, and discovery.* Cambridge, MA: Bradford Books/ MIT Press.

Holyoak, K. J. (1984). Analogical thinking and human intelligence. In R. J. Sternberg (Ed.), *Advances in the psychology of human intelligence* (Vol. 2). Hillsdale, NJ: Erlbaum.

Holyoak, K. J. (1991). Symbolic connectionism: Toward third-generation theories of expertise. In K. A. Ericsson & J. Smith (Eds.), *Toward a general theory of expertise: Prospects and limits.* Cambridge, MA: Cambridge University Press.

Holyoak, K. J., & Koh, K. (1987). Surface and structural similarity in analogical transfer. *Memory & Cognition, 15,* 332–340.

Holyoak, K. J., & Thagard, P. T. (1989). Analogical mapping by constraint satisfaction. *Cognitive Science, 13,* 295–355.

Jepson, C., Krantz, D. H., & Nisbett, R. E. (1983). Inductive reasoning: Competence or skill? *Behavioral and Brain Sciences, 6,* 494–501.

Johnson-Laird, P. N. (1983). *Mental models.* Cambridge, MA: Harvard University Press.

Kahneman, D., & Tversky, A. (1973). On the psychology of prediction. *Psychological Review, 80,* 237–251.

Kaiser, M. K., Jonides, J., & Alexander, J. (1986). Intuitive reasoning on abstract and familiar physics problems. *Memory and Cognition, 14,* 308–312.

Kelley, H. H. (1972). Causal schemata and the attribution process. In E. E. Jones, D. E. Kanouse, H. H. Kelley, R. E. Nisbett, S. Valins, & B. Weiner (Eds.), *Attribution: Perceiving the causes of behavior.* Morristown, NJ: General Learning Press.

Kolodner, J. L. (1983). Reconstructive memory: A computer model. *Cognitive Science, 7,* 281–328.

Langston, C., Nisbett, R., & Smith , E. E. (1991). *Priming contractual rules.* Unpublished manuscript, University of Michigan, Department of Psychology, Ann Arbor.

Larrick, R. P., Morgan, J. N., & Nisbett, R. E. (1990). Teaching the use of cost-benefit reasoning in everyday life. *Psychological Science, 1,* 362–370.

Larrick, R. P., Nisbett, R. E., & Morgan, J. N. (1993). Who uses the cost-benefit rules of choice? Implications for the normative status of microeconomic theory. *Organizational Behavior and Human Decision Processes, 56*, 331–347.

Lehman, D. R., Lempert, R. O., & Nisbett, R. E. (1988). The effects of graduate training on reasoning: Formal discipline and thinking about everyday life events. *American Psychologist, 43*, 431–443.

Lehman, D., & Nisbett, R. E. (1990). A longitudinal study of the effects of undergraduate education on reasoning. *Developmental Psychology, 26*, 952–960.

Lewis, C. (1988). Why and how to learn: Analysis-based generalization of procedures. *Cognitive Science, 12*, 211–256.

Manktelow, K. I., & Evans, J. St. B. T. (1979). Facilitation of reasoning by realism: Effect or noneffect? *British Journal of Psychology, 70*, 477–488.

Marcus, G. F., Ullman, M., Pinker, S., Hollander, M., Rosen, T. J., & Xu, F. (1990). *Overextensions* (Occasional Paper No. 41). MIT, Center for Cognitive Science.

McClelland, J. L., & Rumelhart, D. E. (1986). *Parallel distributed processing* (Vol. 1). Cambridge, MA: MIT Press.

Medin, D. L., & Ross, B. H. (1989). The specific character of abstract thought: Categorization, problem solving, and induction. In R. J. Sternberg (Ed.), *Advances in the psychology of human intelligence* (Vol. 5). Hillsdale, NJ: Erlbaum.

Medin, D. L., & Smith, E. E. (1981). Strategies and classification learning. *Journal of Experimental Psychology: Human Learning and Memory, 7*, 241–253.

Miller, G. A. (1962). Some psychological studies of grammar. *American Psychologist, 7*, 748–762.

Morris, M. W., Cheng, P., & Nisbett, R. E. (1991). *Causal reasoning schemas*. Unpublished manuscript, University of California, Department of Psychology, Los Angeles.

Murphy, G. L., & Medin, D. L. (1985). The role of theories in conceptual coherence. *Psychological Review, 92*, 289–317.

Newell, A., & Simon, H. A. (1972). *Human problem solving*. Englewood Cliffs, NJ: Prentice-Hall.

Nisbett, R. E., (1991). Priming the law of large numbers. Unpublished manuscript, University of Michigan, Department of Psychology, Ann Arbor.

Nisbett, R. E., Krantz, D. H., Jepson, D., & Kunda, Z. (1983). The use of statistical heuristics in everyday inductive reasoning. *Psychological Review, 90*, 339–363.

Nisbett, R. E., & Ross, L. (1980). *Human inference: Strategies and shortcomings of social judgment*. Englewood Cliffs, NJ: Prentice-Hall.

Nisbett, R. E., & Wilson, T. D. (1977). Telling more than we can know: Verbal reports on mental processes. *Psychological Review, 8*, 231–259.

Nosofsky, R. M., Clark, S. E., & Shin, H. J. (1989). Rules and exemplars in categorization, identification, and recognition. *Journal of Experimental Psychology: Learning, Memory, and Cognition, 15*, 282–304.

Osherson, D. (1975). Logic and logical models of thinking. In R. Falmagne (Ed.), *Reasoning: Representation and process*. New York: Wiley.

Piaget, J., & Inhelder, B. (1958). *The growth of logical thinking from childhood to adolescence*. New York: Basic Books.

Piaget, J., & Inhelder, B. (1975). *The origin of the idea of chance in children*. New York: Norton. (Original work published 1951)

Pinker, S., & Prince, A. (1988). On language and connectionism: Analysis of a parallel distributed processing model of language acquisition. *Cognition, 28*, 73–194.

Pylyshyn, Z. (1984). *Computation and cognition: Toward a foundation for cognitive science.* Cambridge, MA: MIT Press.

Pylyshyn, Z. (1990). Rules and representations: Chomsky and representational realism. In A. Kasher (Ed.), *The Chomskyian turn.* Cambridge, MA: Blackwell.

Reich, S. S., & Ruth, P. (1982). Wason's selection task: Verification, falsification and matching. *British Journal of Psychology, 73,* 395–405.

Rips, L. J. (1983). Cognitive processes in propositional reasoning. *Psychological Review, 90,* 38–71.

Rips, L. J. (1990). Reasoning. *Annual Review of Psychology, 41,* 321–353.

Ross, B. H. (1987). This is like that: The use of earlier problems and the separation of similarity effects. *Journal of Experimental Psychology: Learning, Memory, and Cognition, 13,* 629–639.

Rumelhart, D. E., & McClelland, J. L. (1987). Learning the past tenses of English verbs: Implicit rules or parallel distributed processing. In B. MacWhinney (Ed.), *Mechanisms of language acquisition.* Hillsdale, NJ: Erlbaum.

Schank, R. C. (1982). *Dynamic memory: A theory of learning in people and computers.* Cambridge, England: Cambridge University Press.

Smith, E. E., Lopez, A., & Osherson, D. N. (1992). Category membership, similarity, and naive induction. In A. F. Healy, S. M. Kosslyn, & R. M. Shiffrin (Eds.), *Essays in honor of William K. Estes: Vol. 2. From learning processes to cognitive processes* (pp. 181–206). Hillsdale, NJ: Erlbaum.

Smolensky, P. (1988). On the proper treatment of connectionism. *Behavioral and Brain Sciences, 11,* 1–23.

Tversky, A., & Kahneman, D. (1971). Belief in the law of small numbers. *Psychological Bulletin, 2,* 105–110.

Tversky, A., & Kahneman, D. (1986). Rational choice and the framing of decisions. *Journal of Business, 59,* S251–S278.

Wason, P. (1966). Reasoning. In B. Foss (Ed.), *New horizons in psychology.* Harmondsworth, England: Penguin.

23 An alternative metaphor in the study of judgment and choice: People as politicians

Philip E. Tetlock

Our initial assumptions about human nature profoundly influence how we design, execute, and interpret research in the psychological and social sciences. Lakatos's (1970) concept of the research program offers a useful framework for thinking about the influence of these underlying assumptions. He argues that underlying all research programs are "hard-core" assumptions that alternatively inspire and inhibit theoretical creativity. Hard-core assumptions inspire creativity by highlighting phenomena that otherwise would have been neglected and by pointing to ways of articulating middle-range theories that are sufficiently specific and falsifiable to guide actual empirical work. Lakatos calls this function the "positive heuristic" of a research program. Hard-core assumptions can also inhibit creativity by limiting the range of research questions that investigators pose and by encouraging a rigid, defensive attitude toward research findings that challenge hard-core assumptions. Lakatos calls this function the negative heuristic of a research program. The negative heuristic directs researchers to develop a protective belt of auxiliary hypotheses that shelters the hard-core from refutation.

Although the research literatures on judgment and choice are voluminous and in some cases forbiddingly technical, these literatures have not outgrown their roots in hard-core assumptions. Implicitly or explicitly, researchers still make assumptions about the underlying goals or functions of judgment and choice. One influential hard-core metaphor has been that of the social perceiver as intuitive psychologist whose primary goal is to achieve cognitive mastery of the causal structure of the environment (Kelley,

Reprinted with permission from P. E. Tetlock, "An alternative metaphor in the study of judgment and choice: People as politicians," *Theory and Psychology*, 1991, 1(4), 451–475. Copyright © 1991 Sage. Reprinted by permission of Sage Publications Ltd.

   I very much appreciate the thoughtful comments on this article by Gerd Gigerenzer, Klaus Fiedler, and Randall Peterson.

1967). This metaphor contains the seeds of an ambitious research agenda as well as a set of normative criteria for evaluating judgment and choice. The key question becomes: What kind of intuitive psychologist is the average perceiver? How good a job does the intuitive psychologist do in generating hypotheses about the causes of behavior, testing hypotheses dispassionately against the evidence, and abandoning favorite hypotheses in the face of contradictory evidence? The psychologist metaphor should not, of course, be confused with the theories derived from it. It is possible to spin out many testable middle-range theories of our competence as intuitive psychologists. The most optimistic middle-range theorists depict people who rely on lay versions of formal logical and statistical procedures to arrive at conclusions (Kelley, 1967). The most pessimistic theories depict people as "cognitive misers" who are prone to a variety of judgmental failings (Nisbett & Ross, 1980). There are also middle-range theories near the midpoint of the optimism–pessimism continuum – theories that emphasize people's capacity to shift from simpler to more complex cognitive strategies in response to situational demands (Fiske & Taylor, 1991; Kruglanski, 1990; Petty & Cacioppo, 1986).

Another metaphor has profoundly shaped the development of the decision-making literature: that of the intuitive economist whose primary goal in life is to maximize subjective expected utility. Once again, the hard-core metaphor highlights an ambitious research agenda as well as a set of normative criteria for evaluating the quality of judgment and choice. The key question becomes: How effective or ineffective are people as intuitive economists? Working from this metaphorical premise, it is again possible to articulate and refine many testable middle-range theories of the intuitive economist – some more optimistic (neoclassical theory is predicated on optimism), and some more pessimistic (Kahneman & Tversky, 1979). The optimists downplay the frequency and severity of violations of the normative axioms of rational choice theory (sometimes even by reformulating the axioms); the pessimists stress the robustness of the violations, even when people are making high-stakes decisions in competitive market environments.

The preponderance of the current evidence favors a moderately pessimistic assessment of our skills as both intuitive psychologists and economists. As intuitive psychologists, we appear to be too quick to draw strong conclusions about others' personalities from fragmentary and unrepresentative evidence (Jones, 1979), too slow to revise our hypotheses in response to new evidence (Nisbett & Ross, 1980), too confident in the correctness of our judgments in many settings (Fischhoff, 1982), and too quick to lose faith in genuinely diagnostic evidence when that evidence is embedded among irrelevant or distractor variables (Nisbett, Zukier, & Lemley, 1981). Our record as intuitive economists is hardly more impressive. We try to avoid the painful value trade-offs that expected utility maximization demands we confront. We give far too much weight to considerations that normative theory says we should ignore. Far from ignoring sunk costs, for example, we often escalate our commitments to failing policies. And we often ignore variables to which normative theories say we should attend. In many situations, people appear as oblivious to opportunity costs as they are attentive to sunk costs.

There is substantial convergence in the theoretical explanations advanced for our shortcomings as intuitive psychologists and economists. People, it is widely agreed, are limited-capacity information processors who rely on inferential shortcuts to help them make sense of an otherwise impossibly complex environment and to make otherwise hopelessly difficult decisions. We rely on the availability, representativeness, anchoring, and simulation heuristics to make inferences about causality and probability; we rely on noncompensatory choice rules to escape dissonant trade-offs; and we rely upon our preconceptions ("existing knowledge structures") in interpreting new evidence. The price of cognitive economy, in this view, is increased susceptibility to error and bias.

The political research program

Although the psychologist and economist metaphors have stimulated important discoveries, both research programs are seriously incomplete.[1] In the pursuit of general laws of thought, the psychologist and economist research programs have largely ignored the social environments in which people make most decisions. Subjects in laboratory studies of cognitive processes rarely feel accountable to others for the positions they take. They function in a social vacuum (or as close an approximation as can be achieved) in which they do not need to worry about the interpersonal consequences of their conduct. Such issues are simply irrelevant to the explanatory goals of these research programs.

Such issues are absolutely central, however, to the politician research program, which picks up where the cognitive research programs leave off. The starting point for analysis is the information processor – with whatever general cognitive limitations he or she may possess – in a complex social-institutional environment. Whereas the central objective of the cognitive research programs is to identify fundamental laws of thought, the central objective of the political research program is to identify the strategies that people have developed for coping with fundamental features of their every-day social world.

Like the psychologist and economist research programs, the politician program rests on hard-core assumptions. And like the other metaphors, the politician metaphor contains the intellectual seeds of a research agenda. The key questions become as follows. What kind of intuitive politician is the average person? How well do people do in placating the constituencies to whom they feel accountable? And what strategies do people use in coping with accountability demands? This shift in questions posed proves to be profoundly consequential from both a descriptive and a normative perspective. At a descriptive level, the politician metaphor stimulates middle-range theorizing that stimulates experimental work that leads to new insights into the social and political boundary conditions on particular response tendencies. It turns out that many well-replicated effects interact in complex ways with accountability manipulations. Whether people deny trade-offs, jump to conclusions from fragmentary evidence, persist with first impressions despite contradictory evidence, or display overconfidence in their predictions depends critically on whether they expect to justify their views to others, the identity of those others, and when they learn of the need to justify their views.

At a normative level, the politician metaphor highlights an alternative set of criteria for judging effects to be errors or biases. Response tendencies that look like judgmental flaws from one metaphorical perspective frequently look quite prudent from another perspective. In this paper, we note five effects that look like errors within the psychologist or economist research programs but that look quite reasonable within the politician research program. To be sure, it is possible to extend this line of argument too far and to search for a political rationale for every judgmental shortcoming in the literature. One can push Quine's "principle of charity" to the point of absurdity. Ultimately the reader must judge whether we have struck a reasonable balance among competing metaphorically grounded conceptions of rationality.

The hard core of the politician research program

Given the crucial role that underlying assumptions play in guiding empirical work, these assumptions deserve to be spelled out in detail. The first assumption deals with the nature of the social world in which people make up their minds; the second, with the goals and motives that drive judgment and choice.

Assumption 1: Accountability of conduct as a universal feature of the natural decision environment

In everyday life, people are presumed to be agents of their actions who can be held responsible for what they do. It makes sense to ask people for the reasons underlying their actions because it is assumed that people can monitor and control their conduct in accord with self-generated plans of action (a once heretical idea that is now widely accepted – Bandura, 1977).

The accountability of conduct is a social-cultural adaptation to the problem of how to co-ordinate relationships among self-regulating agents. As such, accountability is a key component of the solution to the original Hobbesian riddle of how society is even possible (cf. Scott & Lyman, 1968). Organized social life cannot exist without regularity. This regularity is provided by shared norms and social practices. Accountability is a critical rule and norm enforcement mechanism – the social psychological link between individual decision-makers and the social systems to which they belong. Expectations of accountability are an implicit or explicit constraint on virtually everything people do (If I do this, how will others react?). Failure to act in ways for which one can construct acceptable accounts leads to varying degrees of censure, depending on the gravity of the offense and the norms of the society.

Assumption 2: People as approval-and-status-seekers

People seek the approval and respect of those to whom they are accountable for many reasons, including:

1. *The motivation to protect and enhance one's social image or identity.* One of the most influential assumptions in social science is that people seek approval and respect as ends-in-themselves. Indeed, Zetterberg (1957, p. 189) has gone so far as to propose that "the maximization of favorable attitudes from others is the counterpart in sociological theory to the maximization of profit in economic theory." A warehouse of findings in social psychology attests to the influence of this view of human nature, including work on ingratiation, conformity, and strategic attitude shifts (Jones & Wortman, 1973; Tetlock, 1983a, 1983b).

2. *The motivation to protect and enhance one's self-image.* This assumption has an equally venerable status in psychology (Sherif & Cantril, 1947). From this perspective, people do not seek approval as an end-in-itself, but rather as a means of bolstering their own self-worth. A substantial literature exists on the ego-defensive tactics that people use to dissociate themselves from negative outcomes and to associate themselves with positive outcomes (Tetlock & Levi, 1982).

3. *The motivation to acquire power and wealth.* Social exchange theorists (e.g., Blau, 1964) have emphasized a third motive for seeking approval and respect: the quest for material resources. Researchers in organizational behavior have been most sensitive to this motivational dimension of human nature: people can be fruitfully viewed as rational actors who compete for scarce resources within rule-governed political contests for power (Pfeffer, 1981).

Strategies for coping with accountability

To summarize, the politician research program rests on two hard-core assumptions: the first posits that accountability of conduct is a universal problem of social life; the second posits that people seek the approval and respect of those to whom they are accountable. These postulates direct empirical work in radically new directions.

Just as there are middle-range theories that depict people as more or less effective intuitive psychologists and economists, so one can imagine theories that depict people as more or less effective politicians. At one end of the effectiveness continuum would be theories that posit Machiavellian levels of political cunning. People, in this view, are incessant schemers who actively seek out information about the expectations of others, carefully calculate the impact of their decisions, anticipate potential objections, and craft accounts to pre-empt these objections (Snyder's high self-monitors). At the other end of the effectiveness continuum would be theories that portray people as hopelessly inept politicians who may try to maintain good relations with important constituencies, but who instead frequently antagonize them. Indeed, it may be reasonable to extrapolate from work within the economist and psychologist traditions that people often are poor politicians. Insofar as people fail on cognitive tasks critical for "good judgment" defined within a psychological or economic framework, there is a good chance they will also fail on cognitive tasks critical for skillful political maneuvering.

The social contingency model of judgment and choice falls near the midpoint of the effectiveness continuum. The model is an eclectic creation that borrows from a number of theoretical traditions. The model posits, for instance, that the cognitive miser image of the information processor provides a useful first approximation for predicting how people cope with accountability. All other things being equal, people prefer least effort solutions. They adopt positions likely to gain the favor of those to whom they feel accountable. The social contingency model also posits, however, that the solutions to accountability predicaments are not always so straightforward. The model predicts that, when people do not know the views of the prospective audience and are not under pressure to justify past actions, accountability will motivate them to abandon their cognitive-miserly ways and to become relatively flexible, and self-critical thinkers. Finally, the model identifies a third coping strategy. When people have irrevocably committed themselves to a course of action, accountability will again motivate cognitive effort. This time, however, the result will be not self-critical thought, but instead rigid, defensive, and evaluatively consistent thought. Accountability will prompt people to generate as many reasons as they can why they are right and potential critics wrong.

The acceptability heuristic: The cognitive miser in social context

The simplest strategy for coping with accountability is to make decisions that one is confident others will accept. This coping strategy is compatible with the view of people as cognitively lazy. Often the socially acceptable option is obvious, likely to come to mind quickly, and to be bolstered by supportive arguments readily available in the environment (especially true in group polarization and groupthink situations). The acceptability heuristic allows one to avoid "unnecessary" cognitive work (analyzing the pros and cons of courses of actions, interpreting contradictory evidence, making trade-offs). All one needs to do is to adopt the salient acceptable option.

People frequently do exactly that. For instance, several experiments have found that negotiators who expect to justify bargaining outcomes to the groups they represent have much more difficulty arriving at mutually beneficial compromise agreements than do negotiators who are not under such pressure (Pruitt, 1981). The most plausible explanation is that accountability to constituents (who presumably favor tough stands) induces concern for appearing strong by refusing to make concessions. Negotiators respond by employing competitive tactics that, while obstacles to resolving conflicts of interest, are effective in protecting their images in the eyes of constituents.

In our own experimental work, subjects who know the views of the audience and do not feel locked into any prior attitudinal commitment tend to shift their views toward those of the prospective audience (Tetlock, 1983b; Tetlock, Skitka, & Boettger, 1989). Subjects who feel accountable to a liberal audience report substantially more liberal attitudes than do subjects who feel accountable to a conservative audience. Moreover, most subjects do not internalize these attitude shifts. When we content analyze confidential thought protocols, accountability to a known audience affects neither the number nor the self-rated importance of the liberal and conservative thoughts. When we have assessed attitudes in a follow-up interview, these strategic attitude shifts quickly disappear. Consistent with Cialdini, Petty, and Cacioppo (1981), most people quickly revert back to their original positions.

The acceptability heuristic is not limited to laboratory experiments; it operates in high-level policy-making settings. The political necessity of defending one's conduct is a key constraint on how policy-makers make choices. Historical case studies of government decisions abound with references to policy-makers assessing possible lines of defense against critics and opponents (Anderson, 1981; Graber, 1976).

In the same spirit, Pfeffer (1981) stresses the importance of justifiability in managerial decision-making. He argues that the primary task of managers is to make what is going on in the organization meaningful to the participants and to develop a consensus around key activities. A critical determinant of managerial success is the ability to convince both internal (within the organization) and external observers that the operations of the organization are consonant with prevailing systemic values.

In overview, the acceptability heuristic complements and fleshes out the cognitive miser characterization of the decision-maker. The most salient consideration in many decisions is the justifiability of policy options. The cognitive research program tells us that people use few items of information in making up their minds; the social contingency model tells us that subjective estimates of the reactions of those to whom they are accountable will be prominent among those few items of information considered. The cognitive research program focuses on process (how people think), the social contingency model focuses on content (what people think). Although this may seem a natural division of labor, the distinction is far from airtight. Demands for accountability not only affect what people think, they also affect how people think.

Motivating cognitive misers to be thoughtful. Although the acceptability heuristic is a cognitively economical and socially adaptive strategy, its usefulness is limited to settings in which one can easily discern the expectations of those to whom one is accountable. The question arises: How do people cope with accountability in normatively ambiguous situations in which they do not know what the audience wants and they are not locked into any prior commitments?

Under these conditions, accountability can indeed induce people to abandon their cognitive miserly ways. Predecisional accountability to unknown audiences has been found in numerous studies to motivate vigilant, complex, and self-critical thought (for reviews, see McAllister, Mitchell, & Beach, 1979; Tetlock, 1985).

In one series of studies, Tetlock (1983a, 1983b) and Tetlock et al. (1989) hypothesized that when people know the views of those to whom they are accountable they rely on the acceptability heuristic and shift their views toward the anticipated audience. By contrast, when people do not know the views of the prospective audience, they think through the issue much more carefully to arrive at a defensible position. Accountability to unknown others motivates people to consider arguments on both sides in order to prepare themselves for a wide variety of critical reactions to their views. To test these hypotheses, we asked subjects to report their positions on controversial issues (capital punishment, affirmative action) under one of four conditions: expecting their positions to be confidential or expecting to justify their positions to an individual with liberal, conservative, or unknown views. In addition, subjects were asked to report their thoughts (confidentiality always guaranteed) on each issue prior to committing themselves to a position. These thought protocols were then subjected to detailed content-analysis to assess the "integrative complexity" of subjects' thinking on the issues. (How many aspects of each issue did they distinguish? Did they interpret issues in dichotomous, good–bad terms, or did they recognize arguments of both sides?)

Subjects coped with pressures to justify their opinions in two qualitatively distinct ways: strategically shifting their public positions (thus making the task of justification easier) and thinking about issues in more multidimensional ways (thus preparing themselves for possible arguments that could be raised against their positions). Subjects relied on strategic attitude shifts when accountable to an audience with well-defined liberal or conservative views. Not surprisingly, subjects accountable to a liberal expressed more liberal views whereas subjects accountable to a conservative expressed more conservative views. Accountability to an audience with well-defined views had no impact on the complexity of private thoughts on the policy issues. The reverse pattern of findings emerged among subjects who felt accountable to an individual with unknown views. Here accountability had no impact on the liberalism/conservatism of the public stands taken, but had a pronounced impact on the complexity of private thoughts on the issues. Subjects displayed much more tolerance for cognitive inconsistency (recognizing good features of rejected policies and bad features of accepted ones) and much more recognition of value trade-offs (e.g., the need to deter crime and protect the lives of the innocent, the need to remedy past racial injustices without creating new ones). Subjects accountable to an unknown audience appeared to engage in pre-emptive self-criticism. They attempted to anticipate arguments that critics might raise. This cognitive reaction can be viewed as an adaptive strategy to protect one's self- and social-image. Expecting to justify one's views to an unknown audience raised the prospect of failure: the other person might find serious flaws in the positions taken. To reduce the likelihood of such an esteem-threatening and embarrassing event, subjects demonstrated their awareness of alternative perspectives on the issues. The implicit message was: "You can see I'm no fool. I may believe this, but I understand the counterarguments."

The rationalization heuristic: The cognitive miser on the defensive

The previous section focused on situations in which the desire for approval and respect motivated integratively complex thought. In all these situations, people had no basis for confidently inferring the policy preferences of those to whom they were accountable, thus reducing the usefulness of the acceptability heuristic. Another critical ingredient was also present. People realized that they had to explain their conduct before they had committed themselves to a course of action. Pre-decisional accountability – combined with normative ambiguity – promoted thoughtful analysis of options.

Other circumstances can trigger very different coping responses. For instance, imagine that people are accountable not for decisions they have yet to make, but for decisions they have already made. Imaging, moreover, that these decisions have led to questionable or undesirable consequences (lower profits, employee dissatisfaction, etc.). Under these conditions, the same motive – the desire for approval and respect – is likely to lead not to a forward-looking rationality, but rather to a backward-looking rationality: a defensive search for ways of rationalizing past conduct. The primary concern of decision-makers will be with portraying earlier actions in the best possible light.

Tetlock et al. (1989) showed how a minor variation in the timing of an accountability manipulation can dramatically influence the coping strategies activated. In this study, subjects reported their thoughts on four controversial issues either before or after they had made a commitment to attitudinal stands. Some subjects believed their stands were private; others believed that they would later be asked to justify their stands to an audience with unknown, liberal, or conservative views. Subjects who felt accountable and reported their thoughts after making attitudinal commitments became much less integratively complex than unaccountable subjects who reported their thoughts after making the attitudinal commitment and than either unaccountable or accountable subjects who reported their thoughts prior to taking a stand. Once accountable subjects had publicly committed themselves, the major function of thought became the generation of as many justifications for those stands as they could. As a result, the integrative complexity of the thoughts reported plunged (subjects were far less likely to see the other point of view), and the number of pro-attitudinal thoughts increased (subjects generated thoughts that were evaluatively consistent with their public attitudinal stands).

There is also considerable evidence that post-decisional accounting goes beyond mere verbal rationalizations (Festinger, 1964; Staw, 1980). In a variety of experimental paradigms (The Dollar Auction, The Waiting Game, Business Simulations) investigators have demonstrated that the need to justify policies that have worked out badly places great pressure on decision-makers to increase their commitments to these failing policies.

Normative assessments of coping strategies

Thus far, we have considered three strategies people use to cope with accountability. We turn now to an explicitly normative issue: To what extent, and under what conditions, do these coping strategies enhance or degrade the quality of judgment and choice?

The acceptability heuristic

This strategy has obvious adaptive value for the individual decision-maker. People, quite correctly, view opinion conformity as a reliable means of gaining the approval and respect of others. Although limiting conditions exist (one should not be too sycophantic), we generally evaluate others more positively to the degree their attitudes are similar to our own.

The acceptability heuristic also has adaptive value for groups and organizations. To the degree group members practice this heuristic, it will be easy to reach consensus. And, to the degree group members feel accountable to constituencies who have a good understanding of the issues, decision-makers who take the views of these constituencies into account are likely to do a better job than decision-makers who ignore them. Under such conditions, the acceptability heuristic may check judgmental fallacies that decision-makers never would have corrected on their own.

The acceptability heuristic can, of course, also be highly dysfunctional. From the standpoint of maximizing individual career prospects, a decision-maker who relies solely on the acceptability heuristic runs the risk of appearing uncreative, unnecessary, or spineless. Decision-making groups that consist solely of practitioners of the acceptability heuristic are likely candidates for groupthink (Janis, 1989). If no one is willing to voice unpopular doubts, the likelihood of serious miscalculations may increase dramatically. Finally, just as decision-makers can recommend the right solution because they are accountable to a wise audience, they can also recommend the wrong solution because they are accountable to a short-sighted audience. The acceptability heuristic may cause doctors to over-prescribe drugs and tests for their patients (because they expect to be accountable to judges and juries who are prone to certainty-of-hindsight) or it may cause the chief financial officers of corporations to argue against costly long-term modernization programs (because they are accountable to an investment community that focuses on maximizing quarterly returns). The acceptability heuristic implies that decision-makers can be no better as well as no worse than the constituencies to whom they are accountable.

Several experiments have illustrated the dysfunctional effects of the acceptability heuristic. In a simulation of Food and Drug Administration decisions to admit or ban particular drugs on the U.S. pharmaceuticals market, Tetlock and Boettger (1991a) found that accountable subjects were much more responsive to the level of risk posed by the drug even when the predicted benefits substantially outweighed the predicted risks. We also demonstrated that accountable subjects were much more influenced by the knowledge that the drug either already was or was not on the U.S. market. Accountable subjects became especially risk-averse when considering a drug that had not yet been allowed into the market. They were also more likely to try to escape the decisional dilemma that had been created for them (cf. Janis, 1989, on defensive avoidance). Accountable subjects confronted by close-call cost–benefit decisions were more likely to procrastinate (by deferring the decision until further research had been done, although many people would die in the interim and there was little prospect of more conclusive evidence from the further work) and to buckpass (to refer the decision to another government agency). One can, of course, attach very different normative labels to these effects. From a harsh perspective, accountability encourages political cowardice that results in unnecessary deaths; from a more charitable perspective, accountable subjects were appropriately circumspect about their qualifications to make decisions that would profoundly affect the well-being of others.

In short, simple normative generalizations about the acceptability heuristic fail us. Whether one applauds the results of the heuristic depends critically on whether one approves of the priorities of the relevant audience.

Pre-emptive self-criticism

Pre-decisional accountability to unknown audiences often motivates people to anticipate objections that others might raise to their views and to incorporate those objections into their own attitudinal position. The result is more flexible and multidimensional patterns of thinking.

Once again, a highly conditional normative assessment is in order. Considerable evidence now indicates that encouraging pre-emptive self-criticism attenuates, sometimes even eliminates, certain judgmental biases (belief perseverance, the fundamental attribution error and overconfidence). Sometimes, however, encouraging complex, self-critical thought leads to judgments that many normative observers decry (the dilution effect, the tendency to pay undue attention to worst case scenarios, and the tendency to take weak initial negotiating stands). In short, from one normative perspective, pre-emptive self-criticism represents a laudable movement toward open-mindedness and complexity. From another normative perspective, pre-emptive self-criticism looks like confusion, vacillation and weakness.

The benefits of complexity

Inducing pre-emptive self-criticism has proven to be a powerful method of eliminating judgmental biases that other types of incentives appear to have limited effects on. I consider three such examples here: belief perseverance, the fundamental attribution error, and overconfidence.

Reducing belief perseverance. The prevailing view of the person within the cognitive research program has been that of a theory-driven thinker who relies heavily on initial impressions in integrating new evidence. Belief perseverance is not, however, an immutable law of human thought. Tetlock (1983b) found that accountability could – under certain conditions – prevent first impressions from dominating final judgments (although it could not reverse the effect once it had occurred). Subjects were presented with arguments from a murder trial: half of the arguments cast doubt on the defendant's guilt and half suggested that the defendant was indeed guilty. Subjects also received the evidence, in one of three orders: an exonerating/incriminating, an incriminating/exonerating, and a randomly alternating order of presentation. Unaccountable subjects showed a substantial primacy effect: early evidence had greater impact on subjective probability ratings of guilt than later evidence. Subjects who expected to justify their judgments of the defendant's guilt before viewing the evidence were, however, immune to the primacy effect. Moreover, accountability did not eliminate the primacy effect by merely affecting the types of judgments subjects were willing to express (e.g., by turning people into fence-sitters). Two lines of evidence argued strongly against such a response bias artifact. First, accountability per se was not sufficient to eliminate the primacy effect. Subjects who realized they were accountable only after exposure to the evidence displayed primacy effects comparable in magnitude to those of unaccountable subjects. Only accountability prior to the evidence destroyed the primacy effect. Second, subjects who realized they had to justify their views prior to the evidence recalled more case information than subjects who felt unaccountable or accountable only after exposure to the evidence. A response bias interpretation cannot explain these effects on memory. Taken as a whole, the data strongly suggest that pre-exposure accountability induced people to become more vigilant information processors who were willing to revise initial impressions in response to changing evidence.

A social check on the fundamental attribution error.   An extensive body of work now points to the existence of a systematic bias in person perception: a pervasive tendency among observers to overestimate dispositional causes of behavior and to underestimate situational constraints on behavior (Jones, 1979; Nisbett & Ross, 1980). Indeed Ross (1977) was sufficiently confident in the robustness of the phenomenon to label it the fundamental attribution error.

The most widely accepted explanation for the effect emphasizes people's reliance on simple heuristics in social perception. Behavior, it is argued, engulfs the "perceptual field." The person and his or her behavior form a natural perceptual-cognitive gestalt. What could be more obvious than the palpable fact that without the actor there can be no act? And what could be simpler than to ascribe dispositions to the actor that render the actor–act linkage intelligible (aggressive people behave aggressively, intelligent ones intelligently . . .)? Nisbett and Ross (1980) noted that personality dispositions are generally the most available and representative explanations for behavior. People prefer dispositional explanations because such explanations typically come first to mind, and people rarely consider less obvious situational ones.

The most widely cited evidence for the fundamental attribution error comes from the attitude-attribution paradigm (Jones, 1979) in which subjects are presented with written or spoken statements of opinion that a target person allegedly made under conditions of high or low choice. The task is to infer the "true" attitude of the target person.

Tetlock (1985) conducted an essay attribution experiment that explicitly manipulated whether subjects felt accountable for their attributional judgments and when they learned of being accountable. Subjects were sometimes confronted by an essay that advocated a minority quota system for college admissions and sometimes by an essay that opposed such a system. In addition, subjects sometimes learned that the essay writer did not choose the position advocated (it was a requirement for participating in the experiment) or sometimes learned that the writer had freely chosen to take the position advocated. The final independent variable was accountability. Subjects either did not feel accountable for their causal attributions, learned they were accountable prior to exposure to the evidence on which they would be basing their judgments, or learned of being accountable only after exposure to the evidence.

Several findings stand out. First, the classic overattribution effect was replicated when subjects did not feel accountable for their attributional judgments or when subjects learned of being accountable only after all the evidence. Although these subjects made less confident inferences about the writer's attitudes in the low choice than in the high choice conditions, they still made quite strong inferences about underlying attitudes in the low choice conditions. Second, subjects who learned of being accountable prior to the evidence did not "overattribute." When these subjects learned that the writer had not chosen the position, they refrained from drawing strong inferences about the writer's underlying attitudes from the essay. It is also worth noting that pre-exposure accountability did not make subjects indiscriminately cautious. Pre-exposure accountability subjects drew every bit as extreme inferences about the writer's underlying attitudes in the high choice condition as did unaccountable or post-exposure accountability subjects.

These results are difficult to reconcile with a response bias interpretation. If accountability merely transformed people into fence-sitters, it should not have mattered when subjects learned of being accountable or whether subjects made inferences about low vs. high choice writers. The specificity of the effects on attributional judgments suggests that accountability did not just shift response thresholds; rather, it encouraged people to become more differentiated and circumspect thinkers about the causes of behavior.

Inducing appropriate confidence. People are often excessively confident in the correctness of their factual judgments and predictions (Fischhoff, 1982). Tetlock and Kim (1987) investigated the impact of accountability on cognitive processing in a personality prediction task. They presented the subjects with the responses of actual test takers to 16 items drawn from a widely used personality test and then asked subjects to perform three tasks: (a) to form written impressions of each test taker; (b) to predict how each individual responded to an additional 16 items; and (c) to assign confidence ratings to their predictions.

Three experimental conditions were of special interest: no accountability (subjects learned all responses would be anonymous), pre-exposure accountability (subjects learned of the need to justify their predictions prior to forming impressions of the test takers), and post-exposure accountability (subjects learned of being accountable only after forming impressions and reporting them).

Several effects emerged. First, pre-exposure accountability subjects formed more integratively complex impressions of the test takers. They were more likely to recognize contradictory evidence on the test taker's standing on personality dimensions (e.g. needs for achievement and affiliation) and to offer multidimensional trait characterizations of the test takers. Pre-exposure accountability subjects were more likely to say things like: "This person is friendly and outgoing in some situations, but not in others," or: "This person likes the company of others, but will give priority to his work when push comes to shove."

Second, pre-exposure accountability subjects made more accurate predictions of the actual responses of the test takers to the remainder of the tests. Few people have such extreme scores on the Affiliation or Achievement scales that one can do a good job predicting their responses to individual items from undifferentiated trait labels. It helps, in most cases, to be more integratively complex.

Third, pre-exposure accountability subjects reported more realistic levels of confidence than no-accountability and post-exposure accountability subjects. Moreover, this accountability did not merely make people more cautious or socially risk-averse. Three aspects of evidence allowed us to eliminate this interpretation:

1. Post-exposure accountability subjects did not display a reduction in the overconfidence effect. Post-exposure accountability subjects reported confidence ratings that were virtually identical to unaccountable subjects.
2. The confidence ratings of pre-exposure accountability subjects were not just lower, they were also better calibrated.
3. The superior calibration was not achieved at a cost in resolution (another sign that accountability subjects were not just indiscriminately bunching up all of their confidence ratings at the low end of the probability scale).

A final result is worth noting. Analysis of covariance indicated that when we controlled for the effects of pre-exposure accountability on the complexity of the initial impressions subjects formed of the test takers, the improvements in both accuracy and calibration were substantially reduced. Pre-exposure accountability may be an effective debiasing manipulation, at least in part, because it motivates complex, self-critical thought.

Potential dysfunctional effects of motivating integrative complexity

Motivating integrative complexity and improving judgment and choice are not synonymous. Sometimes encouraging integrative complexity, far from debiasing judgment, may make matters worse. Tetlock and Boettger (1989), for instance, have shown that pre-exposure accountability to an unknown audience motivates integrative complexity, but also increases the magnitude of an effect often viewed as a judgmental bias – the tendency to make increasingly regressive predictions when diagnostic evidence is accompanied by non-diagnostic information (what Nisbett et al., 1981, have called the dilution effect). In one experimental scenario, we asked subjects to predict the grade-point averages of target students. Subjects received either only diagnostic evidence (e.g., a student studies 3 or 31 hours per week) or diagnostic evidence plus irrelevant information (e.g., the student is a cheerful person, plays tennis three or four times a month, and has never dated anyone for longer than two months). This information had been carefully selected from pre-testing; pre-test subjects were virtually unanimous that the information was useless. Nonetheless, this "useless" information caused subjects to be less confident in their predictions. Moreover, accountability exacerbated this dilution effect. Accountable subjects tried to be "good" complex thinkers and to integrate both diagnostic and non-diagnostic evidence in making predictions about grade-point average. By motivating integrative complexity, the accountability manipulation sent our subjects off on inferential wild goose chases. One accountable subject concluded that because the student is cheerful he is well-adjusted and likely to be doing well in school; another concluded from the fact the student occasionally plays tennis that he has a high activity level and is likely to be successful. In short, pre-exposure accountability to an unknown audience motivated subjects to be more integratively complex, but it did not make them more discriminating consumers of the information at their disposal.

Another example of the arguably maladaptive effects of integrative complexity comes from the Tetlock and Boettger (1991a) study that examined judgments of the acceptability of a drug on the U.S. pharmaceutical market. As noted earlier, accountable subjects were more responsive to the level of risk posed by the drug, and especially so when they believed the drug had not yet been admitted into the market. Analysis of covariance indicated that subjects who thought in more integratively complex ways were largely responsible for this three-way interaction between the status quo manipulation, the accountability manipulation, and the level of risk manipulation. Examination of the thought protocols revealed a preoccupation with worst-case-scenario thinking and explicit concern for what they would say to those who might be injured by their decisions. There is, of course, nothing immoral or irrational about such concerns. It is noteworthy, however, that these subjects were much more tolerant of risk created by a drug that was already on the market (the status quo condition). Removing a drug with a high benefit–cost ratio from the market would antagonize those constituencies that are currently using it. Introducing a drug with an equally positive benefit–cost ratio focuses attention on those constituencies who would be hurt. In short, there are some settings in which accountability pressures that motivate integrative complexity also increase reluctance to make decisions that involve painful trade-offs. The Tetlock and Boettger (1991a) study, for instance, found that accountable subjects (especially in the non-status-quo conditions) were not only more hesitant to accept levels of risk from the new drug, they were also more likely to search for ways of passing responsibility for making the decision to others and to defer making the decision until later.

The rationalization heuristic

Post-decisional accountability often triggers defensive bolstering. The normative costs and benefits of this coping strategy look like mirror images of those for pre-emptive self-criticism. The danger of defensive bolstering is that one will rigidly persevere with a failing policy in a vain effort to recoup sunk costs. By generating supportive cognitions, decision-makers who practice defensive bolstering blind themselves to changing policy in ways that would better promote their long-term values. Of course, it is not always a good idea to abandon a policy at the first sign of trouble. Decision-makers who practice defensive bolstering are more likely to stick with a fundamentally good policy that has recently run into short-term difficulty. There is a fine line between principled determination "to stay the course" and stubborn refusal "to acknowledge the facts."

Another look at normative issues

From a social contingency perspective, each of the three major coping responses to accountability is appropriate under some circumstances and inappropriate under others. An Aristotelian golden mean is lurking here. One should be sensitive to the views of important constituencies, but avoid appearing so chameleonic that one loses their trust and confidence. One should be self-critical, but not to the point of paralysis. And one should stick by one's principles but not to the point of dogmatism and self-righteousness.

In discussing the normative pros and cons of different coping strategies, I have implicitly accepted the characterization of certain effects as errors or biases within the cognitive research programs. The social contingency model of judgment and choice reminds us, however, that response tendencies that look like errors and biases given one set of functionalist assumptions often look prudent given another set of functionalist assumptions. Before labelling an effect an error or bias, one should consider: (a) the interpersonal and political goals that people are trying to achieve by making judgments of a particular type; (b) whether cognitive strategies that serve people well in everyday life lead them seriously astray in laboratory experiments on judgment and choice.

(a) The fundamental attribution error

The tendency to overestimate dispositional causes and to underestimate situational ones looks like an error within the intuitive psychologist framework. If we assume, however, that people are intuitive politicians who have incentives to hold others strictly accountable for their conduct, the same judgment policy takes on a different normative complexion. One way of pressuring other people to behave is by indicating to them that one has a low tolerance for justifications or excuses and that one will treat their behavior as automatically diagnostic of underlying intentions.

In one study discussed earlier, Tetlock (1985) found that accountable subjects were more resistant to the overattribution effect. The interpretation was that accountability had improved the quality of attributional judgment by motivating subjects to be more discriminating and thoughtful information processors. The social contingency model warns us, however, not to assume: (a) that accountability will always have such an effect; (b) that the preference for dispositional explanations is always best viewed as an error. In some situations, accountability may make people into more thoughtful, intuitive scientists; in other situations, accountability may transform people into more punitive, intuitive lawyers or politicians. Much hinges on exactly how subjects define the experimental situation (is the experimenter interested in my ability to make subtle causal distinctions, or in the moral and political soundness of my judgment?). A testable hypothesis is that when subjects feel their moral judgment is of primary interest, accountability demands will motivate them to hold people more rigorously responsible for their actions. As Axelrod (1984) notes, people are not only expected to act in accord with prevailing norms, they are also expected to censure those who violate norms (a norm to enforce norms or a metanorm). Insofar as accountable subjects feel that their moral mettle is being tested (their willingness to apply metanorms), they may be more motivated to hold others responsible and to reject situational explanations or excuses.

(b) The dilution effect

From a purely cognitive standpoint there is little justification for reducing one's confidence in the diagnosticity of a cue when that cue is accompanied by irrelevant information. From the perspective of the social contingency model, however, this erosion of confidence may be fully justified. Far from representing bias, the dilution effect may be a rational response to the interpersonal and institutional demands on individual perceivers. The presentation of information in dilution experiments can be likened to a conversation between the researcher and the subject – an interaction in which subjects assume, following Grice's (1975) "axioms of conversation," that the information presented is indeed relevant to the task at hand. This assumption is hardly unreasonable. In most contexts, people refrain from making statements that are utterly irrelevant to the interaction. Given that the experimenters deemed it appropriate to include an assortment of evidence in their communications to subjects, one would expect a good Bayesian to attach a high prior probability to the evidence being relevant to the task. The dilution effect – and its magnification in the accountability conditions – may be as much an expression of demand characteristics (the experimenter expects me to use all the evidence in preparation for the conversation) as of judgmental heuristics.

In a recent experiment, we disentangled these diverging normative interpretations of the dilution effect by presenting information in ways that were more or less likely to evoke a conversational mental set (Tetlock & Boettger, 1991b). The experiment replicated the work of Tetlock and Boettger (1989), with the addition of one major independent variable: whether subjects were told that the information had been screened for relevance (explicit priming of conversational axioms), whether subjects had been told that all of the information was not relevant for this prediction task (explicit de-activation of conversational axioms), and whether subjects were given no explicit guidance one way or the other with respect to the relevance of the information. This experiment revealed that accountability magnified the dilution effect, as before, in the no-priming condition and, to a lesser extent, in the explicit-priming-of-conversational-axioms condition. Accountability did not, however, magnify the dilution effect when subjects were warned that all the information was not relevant. These results suggest that accountability motivated subjects to integrate the information at their disposal only when there was a reasonable presumption of relevance. When that presumption was removed, accountable subjects became somewhat more resistant to the dilution effect than unaccountable subjects.

(c) Ambiguity aversion

Ellsberg (1961) notes that one or more axioms of utility theory are violated whenever choices are made on the basis of avoidance of ambiguity. Ambiguity about probabilities, even when expressed as second-order probabilities, are formally irrelevant in decision analysis but play a large role in everyday decision-making. There is considerable evidence, however, that avoidance of ambiguity affects public policy. Insurers are unwilling to cover chemical and waste-processing firms because it is so difficult to specify the distribution of anticipated claims (Kunreuther, 1987). Einhorn and Hogarth (1981) have also suggested that ambiguity aversion explains why some technologies are feared more than their first-order probabilities of failure or accident warrant.

One interpretation is that dislike of ambiguity is simply a pure preference, like the preference for a "fair" coin over a coin biased in some unknown way. Another interpretation is suggested by Loomes and Sugden (1982), who argue that people sacrifice transitivity to accommodate feelings of regret. In this scheme, people avoid ambiguity because they anticipate the deep regret they would feel if a worst-case scenario materialized (if they bet on a coin that was severely biased against them).

It should not be surprising from a social contingency model perspective that accountability exacerbates ambiguity avoidance (as Curley, Yates, & Abrams, 1986, found). Accountable decision-makers are more likely to anticipate how difficult it would be to justify choosing an option that led to a worst-case outcome. One would stand accused of recklessness.

(d) The attraction effect

Imagine a choice between two major alternatives, A and B. A is superior to B on one major dimension of evaluation (say, less expensive) whereas B is superior to A on the other major dimension of evaluation (say, quality). One confronts a trade-off, a difficult one because the options have been carefully preselected to have approximately equal offsetting strengths and weaknesses. People find the choice much easier, however, if one introduces (a logically irrelevant) third option, C, that is inferior in *both* cost and quality to B, but inferior in only one respect to A. B becomes more attractive vis-à-vis A by virtue of being the dominant option with respect to C.

From a rigorous rational actor perspective, people who fall prey to the attraction effect have committed an error (violation of Luce's principle of regularity). Why should a difficult trade-off become easier by adding an inferior third option? From a social contingency perspective, subjects' behavior makes a good deal of sense. As Simonson (1989) notes, it is now easier to justify selecting B than A. B "dominates" C whereas A does not. Simonson shows that holding subjects accountable for their choices magnifies the attraction effect. A kind of social rationality is at work. People seem to reason "I'm less likely to be blamed if I choose the option that dominates at least one option than if I choose the option that requires trade-offs no matter what comparison I make. In justifying B, I can point to its unequivocal superiority over C." From social experience in both giving and receiving accounts, people have learned that one is less likely to be blamed when one can offer a clear-cut, sensible-sounding set of reasons for one's conduct.

(e) The status quo effect

Standard models of rational choice posit that individuals select one of a known set of alternative choices with certain outcomes. People possess preferences that satisfy the basic choice axioms – that is, they have a transitive ranking of these alternatives. Rational choice simply means that they select their most preferred alternative in this ranking. If we know the decision-maker's ranking, we can predict his/her choice infallibly. For instance, an individual's choice should not be affected by removing or adding an irrelevant (i.e., not top ranked) alternative. Conversely, when we observe his/her actual choice, we know it was his/her top ranked alternative.

A fundamental property of the rational choice model, under certainty or uncertainty, is that only preference-relevant features of the alternative should influence the individual's decision (Luce, 1977). Thus, neither the order in which the alternatives are presented nor any arbitrary labels they may carry should affect the individual's choice. Of course, in real world decision-problems the alternatives often come with influential labels. Indeed one alternative inevitably carries the label status quo – that is, doing nothing or maintaining one's current or previous decision is almost always a possibility.

In a series of experimental studies, Samuelson and Zeckhauser (1987) have shown that, faced with new options, decision-makers often stick disproportionately with the status quo alternative. This preference for the status quo is not, of course, automatic evidence of irrationality. Decision-makers might prefer the status quo in order to avoid transaction costs or uncertainty. Samuelson and Zeckhauser, however, eliminated these alternative explanations experimentally.

From the perspective of the social contingency model, the preference for the status quo has a number of additional "rational" sources. Decision-makers may prefer to persist with current policy in order to justify the sacrifices that they have already made on behalf of that policy. Such retrospective rationality is highly consistent with the defensive bolstering strategy of coping with anticipated accountability demands. Another factor contributing to commitment to the status quo is regret avoidance. Occasionally people find themselves in the unpleasant position of regretting the consequences of previous decisions. These "lessons of experience" teach people to avoid, if possible, regrettable consequences. Indeed, there is substantial evidence that regret avoidance influences decision-making. For instance, people tend to avoid decisions in which they could appear after the fact to have made the wrong choice, even if in advance the decision appeared correct given the information available at the time (see earlier discussion of ambiguity aversion). And, as Kahneman and Tversky (1982) argue in their discussion of the simulation heuristic, people feel greater regret for bad outcomes that are the result of new actions than for similar outcomes resulting from inaction. Avoidance of decision regret is therefore one additional cause of status quo bias. It favors adherence to status quo norms or routine behavior at the expense of innovation, and it reinforces the inclination to conform to social norms.

This reasoning suggests that, if anything, accountability demands will magnify rather than attenuate the status quo effect. This prediction is consistent with what Tetlock and Boettger (1991a) found in their simulation of decisions to admit or reject particular drugs from the U.S. pharmaceutical market.

Concluding thoughts

The major theme of this paper can be stated simply: experimental research on judgment and decision-making has adopted a misleadingly narrow focus on its subject-matter. It needs to be broadened to take into consideration the impact of social and institutional context. Enormous room exists for an expansion of theoretical and empirical work on the role of contextual variables – in particular, accountability – in shaping both what and how people think. People are in a fundamental sense politicians who depend on the good will of the constituencies to whom they are accountable. The strategies people develop for coping with this ubiquitous problem of social existence merit much more systematic attention than has thus far been accorded them.

Note

1 One could argue that the psychologist and economist metaphors are best thought of as special cases of the more general metaphor of the person as statistician (Gerd Gigerenzer, personal correspondence). Psychologists draw on methods of statistical inference such as analysis of variance and Bayes' theorem to set normative standards for good judgment; economists draw on probability theory and differential calculus to characterize rational choice. This common denominator helps to explain the emphasis in both metaphorical frameworks on formal models, the interest in deviations from the predictions of formal models, and the relative neglect of both content and context.

References

Anderson, P. A. (1981). Justifications and precedents as constraints in foreign policy decision-making. *American Journal of Political Science, 25*, 738–761.

Axelrod, R. (1984). *The evolution of cooperation*. New York: Basic Books.

Bandura, A. (1977). Self-efficacy: Toward a unifying theory of behavioral change. *Psychological Review, 84*, 191–215.

Blau, P. (1964). *Exchange and power in social life*. New York: Wiley.

Cialdini, R. B., Petty, R. E., & Cacioppo, J. T. (1981). Attitude and attitude change. *Annual Review of Psychology, 32*, 357–404.

Curley, S. P., Yates, J. F., & Abrams, R. A. (1986). Psychological sources of ambiguity avoidance. *Organizational Behavior and Human Decision Processes, 38*, 220–256.

Einhorn, H., & Hogarth, R. M. (1981). Behavioral decision theory. *Annual Review of Psychology, 31*, 53–88.

Ellsberg, D. (1961). Risk, ambiguity and the Savage axioms. *Quarterly Journal of Economics, 75*, 643–669.

Festinger, L. (Ed.). (1964). *Conflicts, decision, and dissonance*. Stanford, CA: Stanford University Press.

Fischhoff, B. (1982). Debiasing. In D. Kahneman, P. Slovic, & A. Tversky (Eds.), *Judgment under uncertainty: Heuristics and biases* (pp. 422–444). New York: Cambridge University Press.

Fiske, S., & Taylor, S. (1991). *Social cognition* (2nd ed.). Reading, MA: Addison-Wesley.

Graber, D. (1976). *Verbal behavior and politics*. Urbana, IL: University of Illinois Press.

Grice, H. P. (1975). Logic and conversation. In P. Cole & J. L. Morgan (Eds.), *Syntax and semantics, 3: Speech acts* (pp. 41–58). New York: Academic Press.

Janis, I. L. (1989). *Crucial decisions*. New York: Free Press.

Jones, E. E. (1979). The rocky road from acts to dispositions. *American Psychologist, 34*(2), 107–117.

Jones, E. E., & Wortman, C. (1973). *Ingratiation: An attributional approach*. Morristown, NJ: General Learning Press.

Kahneman, D. & Tversky, A. (1979). Prospect theory: An analysis of decision under risk. *Econometrica, 47*, 263–291.

Kahneman, D., & Tversky, A. (1982). The simulation heuristic. In D. Kahneman, P. Slovic, & A. Tversky (Eds.), *Judgment under uncertainty: Heuristics and biases* (pp. 201–208). New York: Cambridge University Press.

Kahneman, D., & Tversky, A. (1984). Choice, values, and frames. *American Psychologist, 39*, 341–350.

Kelley, H. H. (1967). Attribution theory in social psychology. In D. Levine (Ed.), *Nebraska symposium on motivation*. Omaha, NE: University of Nebraska Press.

Kruglanski, A. (1990). Lay epistemic theory in social-cognitive psychology. *Psychological Inquiry, 1,* 202–246.

Kunreuther, H. (1987). The failure of EIL coverage: Gridlock in environmental insurance. *Environment, 29*(1), 18–20, 31–34.

Lakatos, I. (1970). Falsification and the methodology of scientific research programmes. In I. Lakatos & A. Musgrave (Eds.), *Criticism and the growth of knowledge*. Cambridge: Cambridge University Press.

Loomes, G., & Sugden, R. (1982). Regret Theory: An alternative theory of rational choice under uncertainty. *Economic Journal, 92,* 805–824.

Luce, R. D. (1977). The choice axiom after twenty years. *Journal of Mathematical Psychology, 15,* 215–233.

McAllister, P. W., Mitchell, T. R., & Beach, L. R. (1979). The contingency model for the selection of decision strategies: An empirical test of the effects of significance, accountability, and reversibility. *Organizational Behavior and Human Peformance, 24,* 228–244.

Nisbett, R. E., & Ross, L. (1980). *Human inference: Strategies and shortcomings of social judgment*. Englewood Cliffs, NJ: Prentice-Hall.

Nisbett, R. E., Zukier, H., & Lemley, R. (1981). The dilution effect: Nondiagnostic information. *Cognitive Psychology, 13,* 248–277.

Petty, R. E., & Cacioppo, J. T. (1986). The elaboration likelihood model of persuasion. In L. Berkowitz (Ed.), *Advances in experimental social psychology, Vol. 19.* New York: Academic Press.

Pfeffer, J. (1981). Management as symbolic action: The creation and maintenance of organizational paradigms. In B. M. Staw & L. Cummings (Eds.), *Research in organizational behavior, Vol. 3.* Greenwich, CT: JAI Press.

Pruitt, D. (1981). *Negotiation behavior*. New York: Academic Press.

Ross, L. (1977). The intuitive psychologist and his shortcomings: Distortions in the attribution process. In L. Berkowitz (Ed.), *Advances in experimental social psychology, 10,* 174–221. New York: Academic Press.

Samuelson, W., & Zeckhauser, R. (1987). Status quo bias in decision making. *Journal of Risk and Uncertainty, 1,* 7–59.

Scott, M., & Lyman, S. (1968). Accounts. *American Sociological Review, 33,* 46–62.

Sherif, M., & Cantril, H. (1947). *The psychology of ego-involvements*. New York: Wiley.

Simonson, I. (1989). Choice based on reasons: The case of attraction and compromise effects. *Journal of Consumer Research, 16,* 158–174.

Staw, B. M. (1980). Rationality and justification in organizational life. In B. M. Staw & L. Cummings (Eds.), *Research in organizational behavior, Vol. 2.* Greenwich, CT: JAI Press.

Tetlock, P. E. (1983a). Accountability and the complexity of thought. *Journal of Personality and Social Psychology, 45,* 74–83.

Tetlock, P. E. (1983b). Accountability and the perseverance of first impressions. *Social Psychology Quarterly, 46,* 285–292.

Tetlock, P. E. (1985). Accountability: A social check on the fundamental attribution error. *Social Psychology Quarterly, 48,* 227–236.

Tetlock, P. E., & Boettger, R. (1989). Accountability: A social magnifier of the dilution effect. *Journal of Personality and Social Psychology, 57,* 388–398.

Tetlock, P. E., & Boettger, R. (1991a). *Accountability, anticipatory regret, and worst case scenarios*. Unpublished manuscript. University of California.

Tetlock, P. E., & Boettger, R. (1991b). *The dilution effect: Judgmental bias or conversational convention*. Unpublished manuscript. University of California.

Tetlock, P. E., & Kim, J. (1987). Accountability and overconfidence in a personality prediction task. *Journal of Personality and Social Psychology, 52,* 700–709.

Tetlock, P. E., & Levi, A. (1982). Attribution bias: On the inconclusiveness of the cognition-motivation debate. *Journal of Experimental Social Psychology, 18,* 68–88.

Tetlock, P. E., Skitka, L., & Boettger, R. (1989). Social and cognitive strategies of coping with accountability: Conformity, complexity, and bolstering. *Journal of Personality and Social Psychology, 57,* 632–641.

Zetterberg, H. L. (1957). Compliant actions. *Acta Sociologica, 2,* 188–199.

24 Between hope and fear: The psychology of risk

Lola L. Lopes

I. Introduction

Most things begin to look a little funny if you stare at them long enough. So too the psychology of risk. What is most disconcerting is that there is so much theory for so little substance. Countless hours have been spent by psychologists and economists alike in trying to explain theoretically why people buy both lottery tickets and insurance. Lottery tickets cost a dollar. One. We buy insurance (when we can afford it) so that we can sleep better. Is it really so strange that we should want to buy both?

This chapter is about risk: what risk is (if it is any *thing* at all), how people think about it, what they feel about it, and what they do about it. The chapter is also about how *psychologists* think about risk: how they study it, what tasks they use, what factors they vary, and what models they build (or borrow) to describe risk-taking behavior.

Technically, the word *risk* refers to situations in which a decision is made whose consequences depend on the outcomes of future events having known probabilities. Choices among the different kinds of bets in games like roulette and craps are good examples of choices make under risk. Insurance companies also operate under risk when they set the premiums for ordinary life insurance. But most of the time our knowledge of probabilities is not so exact. Sometimes it's pretty good (as with the weather tomorrow or the going rates for auto loans just now); other times it's pretty awful (as with

This chapter originally appeared in L. Berkowitz (Ed.), *Advances in Experimental Social Psychology, Volume 20* (pp. 255–295). San Diego: Academic Press, 1987. Copyright © 1987 by Academic Press, Inc. Reprinted by permission.

The writing of this article and the research reported in it were facilitated by Office of Naval Research contract N00014-84-K-0065, NR 197-079. I am grateful to Leonard Berkowitz, Patricia Devine, Mary Douglas, Robin Keller, David Messick, Gregg Oden, Sandra Schneider, and Alex Wearing for their helpful criticism and comments and (again) to Gregg Oden for his MacWonderful help with the graphics.

whether a wedding reception should be held indoors or outdoors several months hence or whether the fixed-rate mortgage that's offered today is going to feel like a bargain or a burden 10 years down the road). When our knowledge of probabilities is very inexact (or lacking entirely) we say that decisions are make under uncertainty or ignorance. Obviously, risk shades into ignorance and most important decisions are made part way between the poles.

Psychological studies of risky choice (which is the term used conventionally to refer to all but the most extreme instances of ignorance or ambiguity) fall into two groups. At one extreme are the studies run by mathematically inclined experimental psychologists in which subjects make decisions about gambles described in terms of amounts and probabilities. At the other extreme are studies run by personality psychologists who are mostly interested in individual differences in risk taking. Their tasks tend to be closer to everyday experience and they often involve elements both of chance and skill.

A. The experimentalists' view

A good example of an experimental task comes from Kahneman and Tversky (1979), who asked subjects questions similar to this: which would you rather have, $3000 for sure or an 80% chance of winning $4000? Most subjects prefer the $3000 for sure even though the expected value of the gamble is higher, .80 × $4000 = $3200. Such preferences are conventionally labeled "risk averse," as are preferences favoring a 90% chance of winning $3000 over a 45% chance of winning $6000.

Experimental psychologists tend to explain risk-averse behavior in one of two ways. Some theories of risky choice see the subject as trading off potential return with "risk," a construct that is most often identified with variability in the outcome distribution. For example, Coombs's (1975) "portfolio theory" is based on the premise that choices among risks reflect a compromise between maximizing expected value and achieving an individually determined ideal level of risk. Thus, investors who prefer low risk must accept the lower but safer returns associated with bonds, whereas investors who prefer more risk can opt for the higher but less safe returns of stocks and commodities.

Theories that consider risk to be a function of the variability among potential outcomes are intuitively appealing, but they are less commonly held than alternative theories based on weighted-value models, the best known of which is expected utility theory. In expected utility theory, subjects are assumed to "compute" something similar to an expected value, but instead of using the objective dollar amounts, they operate on subjective amounts (or utilities) which are usually nonlinearly related to dollar amounts.

The first use of the utility concept was made by Daniel Bernoulli in 1738.

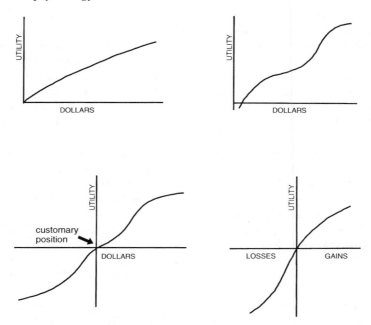

Figure 24.1. Examples of utility functions with four different shapes. The Bernoullian function (upper left) is uniformly risk averse (negatively accelerated). The functions in the upper right, lower left, and lower right (suggested by Friedman & Savage, 1948; Markowitz, 1952; and Kahneman & Tversky, 1979, respectively) have regions of risk aversion (negative acceleration) and risk seeking (positive acceleration). The upper two functions range from zero assets to large positive assets. The lower two functions range about a customary asset level (e.g., the status quo).

He argued that the value of money is not absolute, but depends on how much one has already: "Any increase in wealth, no matter how insignificant, will always result in an increase in utility which is inversely proportionate to the quantity of goods already possessed" (Bernoulli, 1967, p. 25). This view implies that a constant gain, say $1000, will be worth more subjectively to a poor person than a rich person. It also implies that subjective differences between amounts of money that differ by a constant get smaller as the absolute magnitudes of the amounts get larger. In other words, there's more difference psychologically between $1000 and $2000, say, than between $10,000 and $11,000. In Bernoullian terms, money has *marginally decreasing utility* (which is short for saying that the subjective value of constant increments gets smaller and smaller). In mathematical terms, the utility function (which relates the objective value of money to its subjective value) is negatively accelerated. An example of a negatively accelerated utility function is shown in the upper left quadrant of Figure 24.1.

Bernoulli's utility theory predicts risk aversion. This is easy to understand intuitively. Consider a gamble that offers a .5 chance of winning $2000 and a .5 chance of winning nothing. The expected value of the gamble is $1000, but it is worth less subjectively to anyone having a Bernoullian utility function. This is because the subjective value of $1000 is more than half the distance between nothing and $2000. Thus, the utility of $1000 for sure must be greater than the *average* of the utility of nothing and the utility of $2000 (which is all that the expected utility is – an average in which utilities are weighted by their probability of occurrence).

A problem, however, is that people are not always risk averse. For example, they buy lottery tickets even though it is well known that, on average, lotteries are mathematically unfair (which doesn't mean, of course, that they are crooked, but only that the price of the ticket is more than the expected value). People are also sometimes "risk seeking" (as it is conventional to say) when choosing among risks that have negative consequences (Markowitz, 1959; Williams, 1966; Kahneman & Tversky, 1979). For example, many people would prefer to face an 80% chance of losing $4000 than to lose $3000 for sure even though the expected value of the risky loss ($3200) is greater than the sure loss.

Risk-seeking choices can be explained by weighted-value theories in two different ways. One way is to say that the utility function is not always negatively accelerated, but instead has one or more regions of positive acceleration. Three examples of such kinky utility functions are shown in Figure 24.1. The function in the upper right quadrant was proposed by Friedman and Savage (1948), that in the lower left by Markowitz (1952), and that in the lower right by Kahneman and Tversky (1979).[1] Each of these functions has one or more regions of negative acceleration (which predict risk-averse behavior such as the purchase of insurance and the rejection of gambles) and one or more regions of positive acceleration (which predict risk-seeking behavior such as the purchase of gambles, notably long shots that offer very large prizes at very small probabilities).

Another way to explain risk-seeking choices is to suppose that the weights people use in evaluating gambles are not identical to the objective probabilities. Thus, people may purchase lottery tickets because they (optimistically) assign more weight to the probability of winning than is justified objectively. This notion that subjective probabilities may differ from stated probabilities is consistent with subjectively expected utility theory (Savage, 1954). It is also consistent with more general weighted utility models (Edwards, 1962; Karmarkar, 1978; Kahneman & Tversky, 1979) in which the subjective values attached to probabilities do not even act like probabilities mathematically.

To sum up, then, most experimentalists explain risky choice by positing an internal process for evaluating gambles that is structurally similar to computing expected values. However, the objective values are replaced by

subjective values such as utilities and probability weights that differ quantitatively from their objective counterparts.

B. The personologists' view

A good example of a task used by personality psychologists is the "ring toss"
game originally used by McClelland (1958) in his studies of achievement
motivation. In this task, subjects throw rings onto a peg from a distance that
they are allowed to choose themselves. At one extreme, they can stand so
near the peg that success is virtually certain. At the other extreme, they can
stand so far away that success is virtually impossible. The variable of interest, therefore, is not how well they do objectively, but rather where they
stand.

This is a task in risky choice (even though the probabilities are only
roughly known) because subjects are choosing among alternative actions
that have the character of gambles. One can choose (and some do) to stand
near the peg, in which case the probability of success is high, but the personal
satisfaction in getting the ring over the peg is small. Alternatively, one can
stand further back, in which case the probability of success is smaller, but the
satisfaction is greater. One can even choose a long shot (literally), in which
the probability of success is virtually nil, but the potential satisfaction is
enormous. (Consider the heady burst of satisfaction that comes in basketball
when a desperation shot, tossed the full length of the court, drops neatly
through the net. It helps, of course, if it is one's own team that has made
the shot.)

Personologists explain people's choices in the ring toss game in terms of
their motivations (McClelland, 1961; J. Atkinson, 1983). People who have
high motivation to succeed (M_s) tend to pick intermediate distances (particularly if they are also low in the motive to avoid failure, M_{af}). The theoretical
rationale for this is that there is a three-way multiplicative relation between
motivation, probability, and incentive (J. Atkinson, 1957). Since probability
of success (closeness to the peg) and incentive value (anticipated satisfaction
from making the particular shot) are inversely related to one another, the
attractiveness of the task for the person with high M_s and low M_{af} is least
when the probability of succeeding is either very small or very large, and it
is maximum when probability is at an intermediate value.[2]

People who are low in M_s, however, especially if they are also high in M_{af},
more often stand either very near or very far from the peg. Either way, these
people reduce their performance anxiety by virtually guaranteeing that they
will experience either the tepid success of a trivial accomplishment or the
denatured failure of not doing something that cannot be done anyway except
by sheer good luck.

Thus, personologists focus on the similarities and differences between
different people's needs and on the various options that people pursue for

meeting their needs. They also stress the often competitive nature of needs and the resulting compromises that must be made between certainty and incentive, for instance, or between the motive to achieve success and the motive to avoid failure (both of which can exist in the same person at the same time).

II. Psychophysical versus motivational theories of risk

The gamble task and the ring toss task appear to have little in common, but they are alike structurally. In each case the subject chooses among alternative options, each of which can be characterized by the probabilities and values that are attached to uncertain outcomes. In fact, one can with some justice interpret subjects' choices in the ring-toss task as maximizing expected utility (cf. J. Atkinson, 1958). But there are profound differences in the theoretical mechanisms that have been used to explain subjects' choices in these two tasks.

Bernoullian explanations are *psychophysical* in exactly the sense of ordinary sensory psychophysics. In fact, the quantitative function that Bernoulli suggested for utility reappeared more than 100 years later as Fechner's general psychophysical law. But this means that in Bernoullian theory risk-averse *behavior* has neither to do with *risk* nor with *aversion*. Instead, it has only to do with the way we experience quantity. The person who turns down an 80% chance of winning $4000 in favor of a sure $3000 is *not*, therefore, avoiding risk, nor even experiencing risk in any theoretically relevant way, but is only responding to the same sorts of factors that make the difference in heaviness between 1 pound and 2 pounds seem greater than the difference between 10 pounds and 11 pounds.

The same can be said for explanations in which objective probabilities are replaced by subjective probabilities or by probability weights. In fact, Kahneman and Tversky (1984) have referred to their decision-weight function as reflecting the "psychophysics of chances" (p. 344). Their decision weights are assumed to differ from objective probabilities due to factors that are like those found in perception. For example, category-boundary effects make a change from impossibility to possibility (or from possibility to certainty) seem larger than a comparable change in the middle of the scale. This is the same sort of thing that happens in the "categorical perception" of human speech. Sounds that actually change in equal acoustic increments from an ideal "ba" to an ideal "da" are perceived to shift abruptly from sounding like clear ba's to sounding like clear da's (Liberman, Harris, Hoffman, & Griffith, 1957).

Motivational explanations, on the other hand, construe the decision maker as analyzing possible outcomes and assessing risks (by which is usually meant simply the probability of achieving some goal). For example, McClelland (1961) gave the following account of how children who are high in achievement motivation decide where to stand:

If they stand too close to the peg, they are much more likely to throw the ring on . . . but they are less likely to get any feelings of achievement satisfaction from doing so. If they stand too far away, they are both much less likely to succeed and more likely to regard success as "luck," than if they stand a moderate distance from the peg. In fact, they are behaving like the businessman who acts neither traditionally (no risk) nor like a gambler (extreme risk), but who chooses to operate in a way in which he is most likely to get achievement satisfaction (moderate risk, in this case about one chance in three of succeeding). (p. 212)

There are many places in McClelland's account where one could evoke psychophysical mechanisms to explain why different children make different choices: they might attach different subjective values to success at different distances; or they might assign different probabilities to succeeding at a given distance; they might even differ in the way they perceive distances. But this is not how achievement theorists explain things. McClelland is careful to rule out such factors. For example, he acknowledges that children who are high in achievement motivation tend to perceive their probability of success more favorably than children with low achievement motivation, particularly when there is no evidence one way or the other. However, when they have reasonable knowledge based on past performance, they use that knowledge appropriately and do not display a greater perceived probability of success than children who are low in achievement motivation. In his words, achievement-motivated children "are not impractical 'dreamers' overestimating their success at everything; instead they rely on facts so far as they are available, and then fall back on generalized self-confidence" (McClelland, 1961, p. 223).

One can also examine the possibility that achievement-motivated children simply place higher subjective value on success by looking at their preferences in games of pure chance. In this situation they clearly prefer the shortest odds they can get (the safest bets) followed by intermediate values. Children with low achievement motivation, on the other hand, tend to like long shots that offer large prizes, but at small probability (McClelland, 1961).

A. The role of cognition

We have, then, two different approaches to explaining risky choice, one primarily psychophysical and the other primarily motivational. The theories differ also in the degree to which they are *cognitive*. The motivational theories have strong cognitive components. In order to choose appropriately, task difficulty must be analyzed for the relative contributions of skill and chance, past experience must be marshalled and used to assess probabilities, goals must be set and future feelings predicted about what will be satisfying and what not. Thus, it is motivation that incites action and gives it direction (i.e., approach or avoidance), but it is cognition that guides action to its intended goal.

Psychophysical theories, on the other hand, have not been couched in cognitive terms, although they certainly might be. One could, for example, justify a Bernoullian utility function in terms of Maslow's (1954) notion of a need hierarchy. On this view, $1000 really *is* worth more to a poor person than to a rich person because the poor person will spend the money to satisfy more basic needs (food, shelter) whereas the rich person will spend it on more transcendent needs (operas, electronic running shoes). Likewise, people's tendency to treat small probabilities as zero might be justified cognitively in terms of the degree to which small probabilities can be expected to produce discernible impacts on how we choose to live our daily lives. This was done, in fact, by the early probabilist, Buffon, who urged that all probabilities less than .0001 be treated as "morally" (which is to say, psychologically) equal to zero (Daston, 1980).

This is not, however, how psychophysical theories are justified. Indeed, they tend most often not to be justified at all. But Kahneman and Tversky (1979) have been refreshingly clear about their theoretical foundations. They say of their value (or utility) function,

Our perceptual apparatus is attuned to the evaluation of changes of differences rather than to the evaluation of absolute magnitudes. When we respond to attributes such as brightness, loudness, or temperature, the past and present context of experience defines an adaptation level, or reference point, and stimuli are perceived in relation to this reference point. . . . Many sensory and perceptual dimensions share the property that the psychological response is a concave function of the magnitude of physical change. . . . We propose that this principle applies in particular to the evaluation of monetary changes. (pp. 278–279)

Likewise, their description of probability weighting, while less clearly articulated, seems to rest primarily on perceptual and attentional metaphors.

B. Risk-taking reconsidered

Personality psychologists and experimental psychologists tend to have very different goals. Personologists, at least traditionally (i.e., pre-Mischel, 1968), have taken an idiographic approach to explaining behavior. Thus, they have been concerned with the things that make us *different* from one another. Since these are necessarily attached to the individual and not to the situation (which is held constant), the theoretical emphasis has fallen on the structures and dynamics of the inner person. Experimentalists, on the other hand, have typically taken the nomothetic approach, which is aimed at understanding Everyman and the ways in which we are all alike. This approach puts the emphasis on the commonly experienced environment which, in the context of the laboratory, reduces to the *stimulus*. Experimental theories, whether they are behavioral or cognitive, tend to revolve around the transformation of the stimulus into the response. If this can be done without invoking individual differences or higher-level cognition, all the better. Hence the appeal of the psychophysical metaphor for explaining risky choice (or more properly, for explaining the most common choice pattern while ignoring entirely the patterns of a substantial minority of subjects).

When the scientific paths of personologists and experimentalists cross as they have in the area of risky choice, the weaknesses of each tradition are illuminated by the strengths of the other. Personality theorists paint with a broad brush and a richly hued palette, at least compared to their monochromatic experimental colleagues. McClelland's (1961) *The Achieving Society* is breathtaking in its scope and intent, ranging methodologically from the laboratory to the field and substantively from history to economics and from psychology to sociology. But the experimental evidence tends to be unsystematic and unconvincing, at least for the experimentalist schooled in the parametric (if you can vary it, vary it) tradition. Thus, although the motivational approach is appealing for its whole-person flavor (with motivation and emotion and cognition all having their place), the actual experiments are scattered far too sparingly over the conceptual domain. In particular, the motivational treatment of risk taking in the domain of pure chance is disappointing, especially when one considers that we regularly deal with risks (e.g., farmers planting crops, investors choosing a stock) whose outcomes are largely out of our personal control.

Experimentalists, on the other hand, tend to explore their domain more thoroughly, not necessarily because they are better scientists, but because the tradition of looking for "critical tests" keeps the experimental stimulus changing in interesting ways. Thus, the history of thought in risky choice has proceeded in relatively discrete steps as paradoxical results posed initially as challenges to the theory eventually became accommodated via theoretical elaboration. (A comparison with Ptolemaic astronomy would not be unwarranted after 250 years of elaboration on a theory that has remained essentially unchanged structurally.) But in the service of the detailed view, the big picture tends to be lost. So it is with risky choice; after all the study and all the clever theorizing, we are left with a theory of risk taking that fails to mention risk. It also fails to consider (much less explain) the motivational and emotional factors that give risky choice its experiential texture: the hopes and fears that give us in due measure both purpose and pause.

In the remainder of this chapter, I present a theory of risky choice that attempts to meld the strengths of both approaches. Empirically and methodologically it is tied to the experimental approach to risky choice. But theoretically it is more strongly tied to motivational approaches, particularly those of McClelland (1961) and J. Atkinson (1983). Nevertheless, the theory was developed independently of the latter theories and has at least some formal roots in economics (see Lopes, 1984). Although the basic theoretical constructs of the new theory are quite similar to those found in the achievement literature, I will make no particular attempt to bring the two approaches into tighter theoretical alignment since that could (and probably would) do disservice to the fact that the task domains have important differences, particularly those involving the skill/chance dimension. However, the strong theoretical similarities increase my confidence in both approaches.

III. The task and the representation of the stimulus

The term "risky choice" can be read two ways. Risky choices are choices that have an element of danger. They are risky and may come to a bad end. Losses may be sustained, hopes may be shattered, or opportunities wasted. Risky choices are also choices among risks or between risks and sure things. In this sense, risks are gambles. Most research on risk has concentrated on gambles in which there are only two possible outcomes. In fact, a not inconsiderable part of this research has dealt with what might be called one-outcome gambles, in which one outcome represents a change (e. g., winning $4000) and the other represents the *status quo*. The focus on two-outcome gambles seems reasonable to most researchers in part because such gambles lend themselves well to parametric manipulation in the laboratory. In addition, two-outcome gambles are conceptually simple, a fact of at least some consequence given the known limitations in human beings' ability to process information.[3]

Real-world risks, on the other hand, hardly ever have just two outcomes. More often they range essentially continuously over the outcome variable. (Consider interest rates on Individual Retirement Accounts. As I write, they are averaging from around 7.5% for short-term investments up to around 9.5% for long-term investments. Is 9.5% enough to tie up funds for a long period, or will we have another bout of high interest rates? And if so, how high will they go?) In fact, two-outcome gambles occur mostly in the context of formal gambling (and psychology experiments). A $2 bet on red in roulette, for example, will either win $2 or lose $2. Likewise, a horse player betting $2 at odds of 5 to 1 will either win $8 or lose $2. In either case, it seems unlikely that players will make a separate decision each time they place a bet. Instead, the decision to play usually entails placing a series of bets, with resulting net outcomes that range in principle from all losses to all wins.

The experiments described in this chapter have investigated how people chose among multioutcome gambles (or "lotteries" as we refer to them with subjects). Figure 24.2 gives six examples of these lotteries listed in the order in which they are preferred by risk-averse subjects (Schneider & Lopes, 1986): riskless > short shot > peaked > rectangular > bimodal > long shot. Each of the lotteries has 100 lottery tickets (represented by tally marks) and each has an expected value of approximately $100. The lotteries differ, however, in how the prizes are distributed. The long shot, for example, has 31 tickets that each win nothing, 22 tickets that each win $49, and so forth up to a single ticket that wins $439. In contrast, the short shot has only 1 ticket that wins nothing, 2 tickets that each win $13, and so forth up to 31 tickets that each win $130. (Note that the riskless lottery is so named because it has a

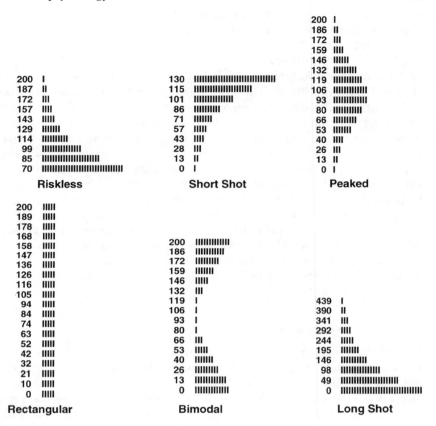

Figure 24.2. Examples of stimulus lotteries for gains. Each lottery has 100 tickets (represented by tally marks) and each has an expected value of approximately $100. The values at the left give the prizes that are won by tickets in that row. The lotteries are ordered from the upper left to the lower right in the order that they are preferred by risk-averse subjects.

riskless, i.e., sure, component that guarantees, in this case, a minimum win of $70.)

All the lotteries in the figure are "gain" lotteries, which means that their prizes are all ≥ 0. Loss lotteries were also used in some of the experiments. Loss lotteries are just like gain lotteries except that their outcomes are negative. Thus, for example, the long shot for losses has 31 tickets that each lose zero, 22 tickets that each lose $49, and so forth down to 1 ticket that loses $439. Likewise, the riskless loss lottery guarantees a riskless (sure) loss of at least $70.

Three kinds of task have been used. In the most common task subjects were shown pairs of lotteries in all possible combinations and asked which they would prefer if they were allowed a free draw from either (Lopes, 1984, Experiments 1 and 2; Schneider & Lopes, 1986). Pair-preference data can be used to infer preference orders over the entire set of stimuli. The second kind of task involved judgments of riskiness also expressed in pair-choices (Lopes, 1984, Experiments 3 through 6). These can be used to infer risk orders (which are not the same as preference orders except for risk-averse people). The third kind of task (Lopes, 1987) was embedded in a standard pair-preference task. Subjects were shown pairs of lotteries and asked to express their preferences for each. For a subset, however, they were also asked to explain their preferences in writing. These written protocols were collected for a group of 14 graduate students from a variety of departments. In order to avoid the known pitfalls of retrospective reports (Ericsson & Simon, 1980), the protocols were obtained directly at the point of choice.

This chapter focuses primarily on preference data from Lopes (1984) and Schneider and Lopes (1986). Examples of the verbal protocols are used throughout, however, for illustration. In the protocols, lotteries are referenced by the names listed in Figure 24.2. These names were not, however, used by the subjects.

A. How can we represent risks?

One of the most important steps in psychological theorizing is to find a representation of the stimulus that has psychological fidelity, by which I mean a representation that highlights the stimulus features that actually affect behavior. For the most part, two-outcome gambles have been treated as though the functional stimulus is identical with the presented stimulus: a pair of outcomes each associated with a probability of occurrence. For lotteries like those in Figure 24.2, however, we seem to respond more to the *shapes* of lotteries than to the amounts and probabilities of individual outcomes.

The idea that risk is a function of shape has been proposed both for theories of risk perception (Luce, 1980; Pollatsek & Tversky, 1970) and for theories of risk preference (Allais, 1979; Coombs, 1975; Hagen, 1969; Markowitz, 1959). In these theories, shape is identified with the statistical moments of the distribution, particularly mean, variance, and skewness.[4] Variance is generally considered to be bad (i.e., risky), whereas positive skewness (a predominance of low outcomes with a few high outcomes) has been identified with hope and negative skewness (a predominance of high outcomes with a few low outcomes) has been identified with fear (Hagen, 1969). In this view preference for the short shot over the long shot would be interpreted as due to the short shot's much lower variance. Likewise, preference for the riskless lottery over the short shot would be interpreted as a preference for positive skewness since these lotteries have equal variance.

Moments models have several virtues, not the least of which is that any distribution can be described, in principle, to any desired level of precision by a sufficiently large set of its moments. But they also have major difficulties. Some of these are technical as, for instance, the fact that, subjectively speaking, risk does not really act like variance.[5] More serious, however, is the fact that such theories implicitly assume that moments have independent psychological reality. That seems doubtful except for the simplest comparisons. It is not all that easy to intuit the relative variance of lotteries that differ in skewness (e.g., the peaked lottery versus the short shot) except when the differences are very great (e.g., the peaked lottery versus the long shot).

In the present theory, lotteries are represented by cumulative graphs called Lorenz curves that are used in economics to show how wealth is distributed among people. Welfare economists find them useful for saying things like "The poorest 20% of the population in Country X have less of their country's wealth than the poorest 20% in Country Y." What is relevant for us is that subjects tend to talk as though they also view lotteries in cumulative terms. Here, for example, are reasons given by three typically risk-averse subjects for why, in a forced choice between the short shot and the long shot, they prefer the short shot (Lopes, 1987).

I'd rather have greater chances of winning a little something than greater chances for nothing. The triple jackpot [in the long shot] doesn't make me want to go for it cuz the odds are too great. (Subject #10)

I choose the [short shot] because there is only one chance of me losing and the best odds indicate a good chance of winning $71 or more. The [long shot] has too many opportunities to lose – it is too risky. (Subject #7)

In the [long shot], 32% do better than the best in the [short shot], but 31% get nothing at all. The [short shot] is the better risk. (Subject #14)

Notice the inequalities: the keynote of these protocols is the cumulative likelihood of meeting or exceeding a goal (e.g., "greater chances of winning a little something," "a good chance of winning $71 or more," "do better than the best"). The protocols also suggest that the subjects are mostly concerned about doing badly (getting zero or a small amount).

Here for comparison are protocols from three subjects who chose the long shot. These subjects were among the most risk seeking of the group. Note their clear focus on the long shot's large prizes.

The chance for winning nothing is small with the [short shot] but since the dollar amount in the [long shot] is attractive I run the risk of losing and go for the [long shot]. (Subject #12)

The top prize money of the [long shot] is better. You still have a good chance of winning some money in the [long shot] as well as having a shot at the top prize money. The in-between prize money in the [long shot] is not all that bad, and is greater than the top prize money of the [short shot]. (Subject #9)

I'll take the added risks of losing it all or getting a lower number for the chance of the higher prizes. Therefore I'll pick the [long shot]. (Subject #11)

PRIZES (P)	TICKETS (T)	PROB. (PR)	PxT	CUM PR.	CUM PxT	CUMPxT TOTPxT
0	1	.01	0	.01	0	.000
13	1	.01	13	.02	13	.001
26	3	.03	78	.05	91	.009
40	5	.05	200	.10	291	.029
53	7	.07	371	.17	662	.067
66	9	.09	594	.26	1256	.126
80	11	.11	880	.37	2136	.215
93	13	.13	1209	.50	3345	.337
106	13	.13	1378	.63	4723	.475
119	11	.11	1309	.74	6032	.607
132	9	.09	1188	.83	7220	.726
146	7	.07	1022	.90	8242	.829
159	5	.05	795	.95	9037	.909
172	3	.03	516	.98	9553	.961
186	1	.01	186	.99	9739	.980
200	1	.01	200	1.00	9939	1.000

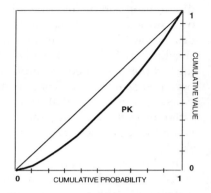

Figure 24.3. Demonstration of how to draw the Lorenz curve for a lottery. The left part of the figure shows how probabilities and relative gains can be cumulated for the peaked lottery. The graph on the right gives the Lorenz curve. This plots the cumulative probability on the abscissa and the cumulative proportion of the winnings on the ordinate.

B. How to draw a Lorenz curve (and why)

Lorenz curves are convenient for looking at lotteries cumulatively and for comparing lotteries selectively on either low outcomes or high outcomes. They also highlight differences and similarities among lotteries that are not immediately apparent by direct inspection of the lotteries. Figure 24.3 shows how a Lorenz curve is graphed. Column 1 at the left shows the prizes for the peaked lottery ordered from the least (at the top) to the most (at the bottom). Column 2 gives the number of tickets at each level and column 3 converts these into probabilities. Column 4 is the product of columns 1 and 2 (which is the total prize money at each level). Columns 5 and 6 are running sums of columns 3 and 4, respectively, and column 7 is column 6 divided by the total prize money. This gives the cumulative proportion of prize money at each level.[6]

The Lorenz curve is plotted at the right. The abscissa gives the cumulative probability (column 5) and the ordinate gives the cumulative proportion of prize money (column 7). Notice that the Lorenz curve runs from the lower left (the low or "bad" end of the curve representing tickets with small prizes) to the upper right (the high or "good" end of the curve representing tickets with big prizes). If every ticket in the lottery were a $100 sure thing, the Lorenz curve would fall on the diagonal. To the extent that the tickets have unequal prizes, the Lorenz curve bows away from the diagonal.

Figure 24.4 gives the Lorenz curves for the long shot and the short shot. Notice that the curve for the long shot lies everywhere *below* the curve for the short shot. This is the sign of large relative dispersion. The long shot's several large outcomes (indicated by the steepness of the curve at the upper end) must be paid for by its many zero and small outcomes (indicated by the

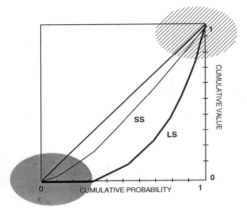

Figure 24.4. Comparison of the Lorenz curves of the long shot (LS) and the short shot (SS). Lorenz curves that lie near the diagonal at the low end (stippled area) have relatively few small outcomes. Lorenz curves that lie far from the diagonal at the high end (striped area) have a few extremely large outcomes or relatively many moderately large outcomes.

flatness of the curve at the lower end). The Lorenz curve for the short shot, on the other hand, lies nearer the diagonal since it has no really large outcomes and only a few small outcomes. These considerations lead directly to a simple rule for choosing between lotteries: people who want to avoid the *worst* outcomes should prefer lotteries whose Lorenz curves lie *near* the diagonal at the *low* end (stippled area at lower left), and people who want to have a go at the *best* outcomes (at least as good a go as can be gotten) should prefer lotteries whose Lorenz curves lie *far* from the diagonal at the *high* end (striped area at upper right).

Figure 24.5 shows the Lorenz curves for the short shot and the riskless lottery. These make an interesting comparison because their Lorenz curves cross one another: the curve for the riskless lottery is nearer the diagonal at the low end (stippled area lower left) but further away at the high end (striped area upper right). Thus, the riskless lottery offers both higher minima *and* higher maxima. Not surprisingly, it appeals to both kinds of subjects. Here are Subject #10 (risk averse) and Subject #11 (risk seeking) from Lopes (1987) explaining why they chose the riskless lottery.

The [riskless lottery] has (1) a higher jackpot (2) greater chance of winning a larger amount *under* $100. I look at the highest amount I could lose rather than the highest amount I could win. (Subject #10)

I picked the [riskless lottery] because both the minimum and the maximum amounts are more, and because for both there's a good chance of getting around $100. (Subject #11)

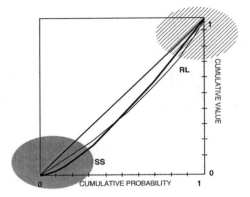

Figure 24.5. Comparison of the Lorenz curves for the riskless lottery (RL) and the short shot (SS). The fact that the curves cross one another indicates that RL is good both for avoiding small outcomes (stippled area) and for approaching large outcomes (striped area).

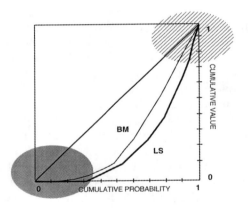

Figure 24.6. Comparison of Lorenz curves for the bimodal lottery (BM) and the long shot (LS). These lotteries are very similar at their low ends (stippled area) but very different at their high ends (striped area).

Figure 24.6 gives Lorenz curves for the bimodal lottery and the long shot. These lotteries (which look very different superficially) are similar at their low ends (lots of small outcomes) but differ markedly at their high ends (lots of moderately large outcomes versus a few *really* large outcomes). People who want to avoid low outcomes should have a mild preference for the bimodal lottery since it lies a little nearer to the diagonal at the low end.

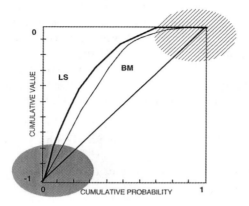

Figure 24.7. Comparison of Lorenz curves for the bimodal (BM) and long-shot (LS) *loss* lotteries. These lotteries are very different at their low ends (stippled area) but very similar at their high ends (striped area).

People who want to win large outcomes, however, should have a relatively strong preference for the long shot since its Lorenz curve lies quite a bit further from the diagonal at the high end. This is exactly what happens (Lopes, 1984; Schneider & Lopes, 1986). The pattern is illustrated by the following two protocols from Lopes (1987), the former expressing a mild preference for the bimodal lottery and the latter expressing a stronger preference for the long shot.

I chose the [bimodal lottery], because there seems to be twice as much chance to get nothing in the [long shot]. Unfortunately, there's a 50% chance of getting less than $100 in the [bimodal lottery]. The [long shot] also has higher stakes. However, all those zeros worry me. (Subject #5)

[Took long shot] because (1) very hi win possible, (2) chance of winning ≥ $100 about same as for other distribution. [The bimodal lottery] has too little possible gain for the hi risk of winning nothing. (Subject #6)

Lorenz curves can also be used to describe loss lotteries. The only thing that needs to be remembered is that for losses, the *best* (biggest) outcome is zero. (Not hard to remember when real losses are being considered!) Figure 24.7 gives the Lorenz curves for the bimodal loss lottery and the long-shot loss lottery. Although they look a little different than Lorenz curves for gain lotteries (the curves now being *above* the diagonal), they are read in exactly the same way. Cumulative probability still runs from 0 at the left to 1 at the right and cumulative proportion of value still runs from the smallest value at the bottom (*minus* 1) to the largest value at the top (zero). The worst outcomes are still in the lower left corner and the best outcomes are still in the upper right corner. If all the tickets were for a $100 loss, the Lorenz curve would fall on the diagonal.

The rule for choosing also stays the same: people who want to avoid the worst outcomes (big losses) should prefer lotteries whose Lorenz curves lie *near* the diagonal at the low (bad) end (stippled area); people who want to obtain the best outcomes (small losses) should prefer lotteries whose Lorenz curves lie *far* from the diagonal at the high (good) end (striped area).

These different reasoning patterns can be seen clearly in subjects' protocols. Here, for example, are two typically risk-averse subjects from Lopes (1987) explaining why they prefer the bimodal loss lottery to the long-shot loss lottery:

With the [bimodal lottery], the most that I can lose is $200. With the [long shot], I could lose $439. (Subject #2)

I would not risk losing $439, or even $292 and up. (Subject #3)

In contrast, here is a subject who chooses the long shot:

I choose the [long shot] because there is a preponderance of tickets that can incur no loss, and a fair number of other tickets that could lose less than $98. In the [bimodal lottery] 50% of the tickets do stand to lose $93 or less but there are fewer that can promise to cause no financial loss. I notice that there are large amounts to be lost if one is unlucky, but the chances of being unlucky are somewhat slimmer in the [long shot]. (Subject #1)

Negative lotteries are particularly interesting because they often present difficult choices. Here, for example, is a subject who has chosen the peaked loss lottery over the rectangular loss lottery:

I go back and forth on this, the gain on improving the chances on a low loss increases the chance of a higher loss. I pick the [peaked lottery] to try to reduce the higher loss. (Subject #11)

Another subject, however, chooses to gamble on the long shot rather than take a sure $100 loss.

In the [sure thing] no way could I lose more than $100. But no way could I lose less, either. In the [long shot] there are enough chances to lose less than $100 to justify losing a lot more. I'll go ahead and see if I can get less than $100 loss – maybe even zero loss – rather than accept a sure loss of $100. If I lose $100 I might as well lose $439. I don't like it either way. However, the [chances] of losing $439 or $390 or $341 – etc. down to $146 are quite high. But so are zero, $49, or $98, or $146. So I'll take the chance. I don't feel great about it, though. (Subject #13)

Conflicts such as these are relatively common for loss lotteries. This is important because it suggests the existence of an additional factor in risky choice that is not captured by the Lorenz curve analysis. This factor will be discussed below.

Finally, Lorenz curves for loss lotteries can also cross one another, producing agreement in choice between risk-averse and risk-seeking individuals. Figure 24.8 shows the Lorenz curves for the riskless loss lottery and the short-shot loss lottery. Below are protocols from the same two subjects (the former risk averse and the latter risk seeking) who previously defended their

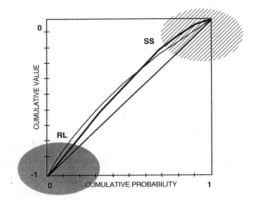

Figure 24.8. Comparison of Lorenz curves for the riskless (RL) and the short-shot (SS) *loss* lotteries. The fact that the curves cross one another indicates that SS is good both for avoiding large losses (stippled area) and for approaching small or zero losses (striped area).

choice of the riskless lottery over the short shot for gains. Below they tell why they *reject* the riskless lottery for losses.

[Took short shot because] (1) there is a greater chance of losing $130 or more with the [riskless lottery]. (2) There is a greater chance of losing less than $70 in the [short shot]. (Subject #10)

I pick the [short shot] because the maximum loss is less and because you may be able to hit as low as zero loss. No matter what, you lose $70 and possibly $200 in the [riskless lottery] – too much risk. (Subject #11)

To sum up, Lorenz curves have at least four virtues for representing lotteries. First, being cumulative, they reflect the fact that subjects tend to evaluate lotteries in terms of inequalities. Second, they facilitate comparison of the particular regions in lotteries that appear to be salient to people with different goals. Third, they suggest similarities and differences among lotteries that, although they may seem obvious in retrospect, do not easily come to mind from inspection of the lotteries themselves. Fourth, they predict when people having different goals will agree (or disagree) about lotteries and when differences will be relatively large (or small). These are no small virtues for a stimulus representation. But that is all that Lorenz curves are: a way of representing lotteries. It is not to be supposed that people convert risks into "mental Lorenz curves." Clearly, they do not. The purpose of the Lorenz curve representation is to deepen understanding of the functional stimulus and to help us psychologists see (literally) what it is that people focus on when they compare lotteries.

IV. A two-factor theory for risky choice

Until fairly recently, personologists focused largely on variables inside the skin, leaving experimentalists to deal with situational variables. Lately, however, personologists have come to agree with Mischel's judgment that "traditional trait-state conceptualizations of personality, while often paying lip service to man's complexity and to the uniqueness of each person, in fact lead to a grossly oversimplified view that misses both the richness and the uniqueness of individual lives" (Mischel, 1968, p. 301). Nevertheless, it is clear that "while stimuli or situations come to evoke and maintain behavior patterns, they do not respond by themselves" (Mischel, 1968, p. 295). Behavior has sources, both inner and outer. We are disposed by our unique constitutions and histories to behave in certain ways, but it is "situational stimuli that evoke [our responses], and it is changes in conditions that alter them" (Mischel, 1968, p. 296).

The present theory uses both a dispositional factor and a situational factor to explain risky choice. The dispositional factor describes the underlying motives that dispose people to be generally oriented to achieving security (i.e., risk averse in conventional terminology) or to exploiting potential (i.e., risk seeking in conventional terminology). The situational factor describes people's responses to immediate needs and opportunities. As will be shown, these factors are sometimes in conflict and sometimes in concert, producing complex patterns of behavior in which risk-averse choices and risk-seeking choices exist side by side in the same individual's behavior.

A. Factor 1: Security versus potential

In an earlier article (Lopes, 1984), I argued that risk-averse and risk-seeking individuals differ in whether they pay most attention to the worst outcomes in a distribution or the best outcomes. Risk-averse people appear to be motivated by a desire for *security*, whereas risk-seeking people appear to be motivated by a desire for *potential*. The former motive values safety and the latter, opportunity.

In mathematical terms, security motivation corresponds to weighting the worst outcomes in a lottery more heavily than the best outcomes, and potential motivation corresponds to the opposite. Such processes could be modeled mathematically by applying appropriate weights to the cumulative functions that constitute the data for Lorenz curves. Indeed, there are several functions currently in use by welfare economists that could be used to quantify risk-averse and risk-seeking preferences (A. Atkinson, 1970; Dahlby, 1985). Describing these functions will not be necessary at present, however, since raw Lorenz curves show all we need to know.

There are, however, two general points that should be made about weighting. First, weights in the theory are joint functions of the magnitudes of probabilities *and* the magnitudes of the outcomes to which they are attached. This is a fundamental departure from the family of weighted-value models since, in those models, probability and value are independent. Second, weights reflect individuals' *goals* and not their perception of probabilities or values. Thus, the fact that a person chooses, for example, to minimize the likelihood of a bad outcome does not imply either that (subjectively) he underestimates the value of good outcomes or that he overestimates the probability of bad outcomes. Although psychophysical effects may occur in either the money or the probability domain, these are considered to be of secondary importance in determining risky choice.

The security/potential factor is conceived to be a dispositional variable, reflecting the way individuals typically respond to risks. Not surprisingly, security motivation (risk aversion) is the far more common pattern (see Lopes, 1984; Schneider & Lopes, 1986), so common, in fact, that economists have considered it to be the pattern for Everyman (Arrow, 1971; Pratt, 1964). This is probably not due to chance. Standards of prudence are passed from parent to child in the normal course of growing up. If that is not enough, hard experience informs us in no uncertain terms that, as Damon Runyan said, "the race is not always to the swift nor the battle to the strong, but that's the way to bet" (cited in Ellsberg, 1961, p. 644). Risk seekers, on the other hand, may dog the long shots, waiting (as a famous risk seeker once said) for "that one streak of luck, properly ridden and encouraged," to compensate them for all the bad times (Thackrey, 1968, p. 67, quoting Nick the Greek).

It should also be noted that the fact that someone is primarily motivated by one of the poles of the security/potential factor does not imply that he or she is unaware of the other pole. It is better to think of these opposing tendencies as existing in some strength in everyone (as do M_s and M_{af} in Atkinson's 1983, theory), but with potential much less important than security and aspiration for risk-averse people and security much less important than potential and aspiration for risk-seeking people. Such weak motives would tend to come into play primarily when the stronger motives are insufficient to determine choice.

B. Factor 2: Aspiration level

The security/potential factor reflects the way that a person usually looks at risks. Risk-averse people look more at the downside and risk seekers more at the upside. But risk seekers may play it safe from time to time, and even the most risk-averse person will take chances – even big chances – when necessary. Aspiration level (Lopes, 1983; Siegel, 1957; Simon, 1955) is a situational variable that reflects the opportunities at hand ("What can I get?") as well as the constraints imposed by the environment ("What do I need?").

The aspiration level that functions in any given situation (including the present task situation) can reflect at least three different sources. The first is the direct assessment of what is reasonable or safe to hope for. For illustration, here is a subject from Lopes (1987) who has rejected the short shot in favor of the peaked lottery:

The chances are in the [peaked] lottery that I will get something close to $100, and I might get much more. I don't know why [I should] let $130 be the top limit when there's a reasonable chance of nearing $100 and a possibility for more. (Subject #3)

The next subject has chosen the riskless lottery in preference to a $100 sure thing.

Since I am assured of winning something I am willing to risk a moderate amount for the possibility of a substantially greater amount. (Subject #4)

In both these cases, the subjects have taken the riskier option, but not before assuring themselves that it is prudent to shoot for its somewhat higher prizes.

The second source of aspiration levels is the direct contextual influence of the other alternatives in the choice set. Here, for example, is a subject choosing between the short shot and the riskless lottery:

I chose the [riskless lottery] because I am assured of winning at least $70. In addition, I have a better than even chance of winning more than $70. It is the assurance of winning $70 that appeals to me. (Subject #7)

Based on this rationale, the subject's aspiration level appears to be no higher than $70. However, when the same subject is given a choice between a sure $100 (the sure thing) and the riskless lottery, she says,

I chose the [sure thing] because I would rather take the $100 as a sure thing than risk winning less. The other lottery also offers a sure thing ($70 at the least); however, the chances of winning less than $100 are about 50-50 in that lottery, so I opt for the safe bet of $100, a sure thing. (Subject #7)

The same shifting of aspiration level also occurs for losses. Here are two more protocols from the previous subject. In the first she rejects the long-shot loss lottery in favor of the short shot. In the second she accepts the long shot in favor of a sure $100 loss.

I chose the [short shot] because the most I could lose would be $130 and that seems safer than the [long shot]. Also the odds in both lotteries seem to favor a loss of between $50–$150, so I figure the lottery which has the lowest ceiling on a possible loss is the safest risk. (Subject #7)

A $100 loss up front is too hard for me to swallow – I chose the [long shot] as it allows for many chances to lose *less* than $100. True, the maximum loss could be as high as $439, but it is still a risk I am willing to take. (Subject #7)

Notice that the subject seems to switch from considering a $130 loss to be acceptable to considering a $100 loss to be unacceptable. Statements like these make it clear that sure things have a powerful influence in organizing choice, and the same seems to be true of values that are highly likely, though not certain.

The seemingly special status of certainty in risky choice has received a prominent role in several theories (Allais, 1979; Kahneman & Tversky, 1979; Machina, 1982), but the mechanism through which certainty effects operate is as yet unclear. One possibility (Kahneman & Tversky, 1979) is that they are instances of subjective category-boundary effects in the perception of probability (see Section II). Another possibility, however, is that certainty *is* objectively special since it permits planning to proceed unimpeded by uncertainty about outcomes that may not be resolved in the near future (see Section VI,C).

The third way that aspiration levels get set is by outside influence. For example, a recent study by Lopes and Casey (1994) looked at the role of necessity in a competitive game in which players attempted to take or defend territory on a game board by choosing among moves having distributions of possible outcomes similar to the lotteries in Figure 24.2. The data revealed a tendency for subjects to prefer riskier moves when they were in a bad position near the end of a round. This is quite sensible: if there is little or no chance that the safer option will yield sufficient territory for a win within the number of moves remaining, the riskier option may be the probabilistically better choice (i.e., more likely to yield a winning outcome).[7]

Finally, it should be noted that, although aspiration level is situational, it probably interacts with the security/potential factor, with security-motivated people tending to set more modest aspiration levels than potential-motivated people for both gains and losses. This possible interaction necessarily complicates the independent assessment of the contributions of security/potential and aspiration to risky choice. Nevertheless, support for the conceptual distinction between the two factors exists in the fact that, as will be seen, the factors often act in opposition to one another.

C. Conflict between security/potential and aspiration

Conflict arises in two places in the present theory. One, obviously, is the conflict between security and potential. It is a truism in the investment world that risk and return go together. If you want safety, you pay for it in yield; if you want yield, you pay for it in worry. To say that security/potential defines a dispositional variable is to say that people typically choose one way or the other between avoiding bad outcomes and approaching good outcomes. But this does not mean that people do not *see* what they do not *choose*. In making a clear decision for, say, security, a person may acknowledge regretfully the loss of opportunity. People also are quick to notice the special benefits of choices such as the riskless lottery that allow them to have their cake and eat it too.[8]

The second form of conflict is both more interesting and less obvious. These are the conflicts that can be created as different situations induce different patterns of agreement and disagreement between dispositional

Table 24.1. *Hypothetical preferences for risk-averse and risk-seeking individuals for gain and loss lotteries*

Risk-averse individual

	Gain lotteries				Loss lotteries			
LOT[a]	AL	SEC	SEC × AL	REL PREF	AL	SEC	SEC × AL	REL PREF
ST	1.00	1.00	1.000	.310	.00	1.00	.000	.000
RL	1.00	.83	.830	.257	.00	.58	.000	.000
SS	.90	.58	.522	.162	.10	.83	.083	.284
PK	.90	.58	.522	.162	.10	.58	.058	.199
RC	.75	.33	.248	.077	.25	.33	.083	.284
BM	.60	.17	.102	.032	.40	.17	.068	.223
LS	.47	.00	.000	.000	.53	.00	.000	.000

Risk-seeking individual

	Gain lotteries				Loss lotteries			
LOT	AL	POT	POT × AL	REL PREF	AL	POT	POT × AL	REL PREF
ST	1.00	.00	.000	.000	.00	.00	.000	.000
RL	.69	.42	.290	.143	.00	.17	.000	.000
SS	.78	.17	.133	.065	.03	.42	.013	.022
PK	.74	.42	.311	.153	.02	.42	.008	.013
RC	.60	.66	.396	.195	.10	.66	.066	.111
BM	.52	.83	.432	.213	.24	.83	.199	.333
LS	.47	1.00	.470	.231	.31	1.00	.310	.520

[a] Abbreviations: ST, sure thing; RL, riskless lottery; SS, short shot; PK, peaked lottery; RC, rectangular lottery; BM, bimodal lottery; and LS, long shot. AL is probability of achieving the aspiration level. SEC is security and POT is potential. REL PREF is relative preference.

motives toward security or potential and the immediate needs and opportunities affecting aspiration level.

Consider someone who is dispositionally motivated to achieve security and suppose that, in the present task situation, the person has a modest aspiration level, say $50. Faced with the choice between the short shot and the long shot, the person would tend to reject the long shot on both counts: it is clearly less secure in Lorenz curve terms and it is also less likely to satisfy the aspiration level. The same would be true for almost any pair of gain lotteries. This is because there is a positive correlation between the ordering of the lotteries in terms of security and the ordering of the lotteries in terms of the probability that they will achieve the aspiration level.

For losses, however, there is a conflict between security and aspiration. Consider the same person choosing between the same two lotteries, but this time for losses, and suppose that the aspiration level is to lose no more than $50. The short shot is obviously more secure since its losses are capped at

$130, but it is much less likely to yield a loss of $50 or less. This would be true for almost any pair of loss lotteries: the ordering on security runs essentially opposite to the ordering on aspiration level.

For a potential-motivated person, the situation would be just reversed. For losses, potential and aspiration level are positively correlated, but for gains they are quite likely to be negatively correlated.

Conflict between security/potential and aspiration can produce quite complex patterns of data (see Coombs & Avrunin, 1983, for a general discussion of data patterns produced by conflict). Table 24.1 gives some values for illustration. The top of the table is for a risk-averse individual and the bottom is for a risk seeker. Gain choices are on the left and loss choices on the right. The aspiration level of the risk-averse person is assumed to be $50 for both gains and losses, whereas the aspiration level of the risk seeker is assumed to be $80 for gains and $20 for losses. These values are purely hypothetical, but they accord with our intuition that risk-averse people probably have more modest aspiration levels than risk seekers.

Let's begin with the risk-averse person. Column 1 lists the six lotteries from Figure 24.2 plus a $100 sure thing. Columns 2 and 6 (AL) give the probabilities that the lotteries will yield the aspiration level: $50 or more for gains and $50 or less for losses. Columns 3 and 7 (SEC) give hypothetical values on security. (Keep in mind that the riskless lottery and the short shot change places as one goes from gains to losses.) These values range evenly between 1 for the sure thing and 0 for the long shot except for a tie in each ordering. (For gains, the worst outcomes in the short shot and the peaked lottery are almost identical in probability and value. Their Lorenz curves would be essentially superimposed at the low end. In the same way, for losses, the worst outcomes for the riskless lottery and the peaked lottery are almost identical. Their Lorenz curves would also be superimposed at the low end.)

Columns 4 and 8 (SEC × AL) show how security and aspiration are integrated. A multiplying rule is used because the choice is *conjunctive*. A lottery lacking good values on either security or aspiration will be rejected. The final two columns (REL PREF) simply normalize the products to a common base (by dividing by the sum of products) in order to allow an easier comparison of relative preference.

A similar analysis is given in the bottom of the table for the risk-seeking person. Values for potential (POT) have replaced values for security, and the aspiration levels are now $80 or more for gains and $20 or less for losses. Note here that the ties in potential are now between the riskless lottery and the peaked lottery for gains and the short shot and the peaked lottery for losses.

Starting first with the risk-averse person, note that relative preferences for gain lotteries tend to decrease from the sure thing to the long shot. This reflects the strong positive correlation between SEC and AL for gains ($r = .97$). For losses, however, there is an inverse U pattern: preferences are low at the extremes but higher in the middle. This reflects the strong negative correlation between AL and SEC for losses ($r = -.91$).

For the risk seeker, the simple pattern occurs for losses: preferences tend to increase from the sure thing to the long shot, reflecting the strong positive correlation between POT and AL for losses ($r = .92$). For gains, however, the pattern is complex. The least preferred lotteries are the sure thing and the short shot, and the most preferred are the bimodal, the rectangular, and the long shot. This complexity reflects the negative correlation between POT and AL for gains ($r = -.97$).

To sum up, the present two-factor theory integrates a dispositional tendency to seek either security or potential with situationally driven aspiration levels. Security motivation captures the Bernoullian (1967) intuition that people are generally disposed to prefer sure things and gambles without large chances of bad outcomes. However, the theory handles equally directly the less prevalent tendency of some people to approach long shots and other gambles offering the unlikely possibility of large outcomes. In addition, the theory deals directly with situational circumstances that may cause a person to experience conflict between dispositionally driven preferences and externally driven goals. Thus, the theory explains how the person can be risk averse in the economic sense (i.e., typically preferring sure things) but sometimes make the same choices as someone who is ordinarily risk seeking.

V. Evidence for the two-factor theory

A. Riskiness is the absence of security

The first bit of support for the present theory comes from judgments of riskiness. In Experiments 3 and 4 of Lopes (1984), subjects were shown pairs of gain lotteries and were asked to say which was the riskier. In virtually every case, the lottery judged to be the riskier was the one whose Lorenz curve lay further from the diagonal at the low end. The only exceptions involved the relative riskiness of riskless lotteries and short shots. (There were three examples of each.) About half the subjects judged the riskless lotteries to be the riskier (contrary to the original expectation) and about half judged the opposite.

Experiments 5 and 6 of the same study suggested why this was so. In the former experiments, the term "risk" was left vague so that subjects could supply their own meanings. In the latter experiments, however, subjects were asked to select the lottery for which it would be riskier to pay $100. Under this condition, judgments for the other lotteries were virtually unchanged, but subjects were now nearly unanimous that the (so-called) riskless lotteries were the risker, a judgment that makes objective sense because there is a good chance that riskless lotteries will yield substantially less than $100 (e.g., $70). Apparently in the original experiment subjects adopted different aspiration levels. For most lotteries, riskiness does not depend on whether the aspiration level is low ($50) or high ($100), but for the riskless lotteries the shift in aspiration is crucial.

The ability of the present theory to account for judgments of riskiness is a point in its favor, particularly as contrasted with psychophysical models. In the latter models, there is no such thing as risk. Although they predict risky choice, they are silent on judgments of risk. Intuitively, however, risk plays a role in risky choice. Risk is the absence of security; security is the absence of risk. Seems simple enough.

B. Risk attitude is more than the psychophysics of money

The second bit of support for the theory is that it can predict the preferences of both risk-averse and risk-seeking people. In experiments 1 and 2 of Lopes (1984), subjects were shown various pairs of lotteries and asked to say which they would prefer to play. The subjects were then divided according to whether or not they tended to take the sure thing when it was offered. Risk-averse subjects (i.e., those subjects who took the sure thing 8 or more times out of 10) had preferences that were essentially perfectly predicted by security motivation (i.e., they preferred lotteries whose Lorenz curves lay near the diagonal at the low end). Risk-seeking subjects (i.e., those who took the sure thing 3 or fewer times out of 10) had preferences that were for the most part predicted by potential motivation (i.e., they preferred lotteries whose Lorenz curves lay far from the diagonal at the high end).

The ability to account for people whose choices are primarily risk seeking is another benefit of the present theory. Psychophysical theories and moments theories are theories of Everyman because they are based mechanistically on principles that should hold for us all: "our perceptual apparatus is attuned to the evaluation of changes or differences" (Kahneman & Tversky, 1979, p. 278); "uncertainty . . . has a disutility growing worse with increasing speed when [the] standard deviation [of utilities] increases" (Hagen, 1979, p. 274). But Everyman is risk averse for gains even though every man (or woman) is not.[9] The two-factor theory puts risk seekers and risk-averse people on equal footing. Although their choices may differ profoundly, their choice *processes* have more similarities than differences. They understand risks in the same way (cumulatively) and they trade off the same factors. Their goals may differ, but they have the same conceptual equipment.

C. Risky choice is not conflict free

The best evidence for the two-factor theory comes from a recent study of the preferences of preselected risk-averse and risk-seeking subjects for gain and loss lotteries (Schneider & Lopes, 1986). Subjects were selected from a large group of undergraduates who had filled out a brief questionnaire asking for their preferences in five choice pairs. Each pair contained a positive two-

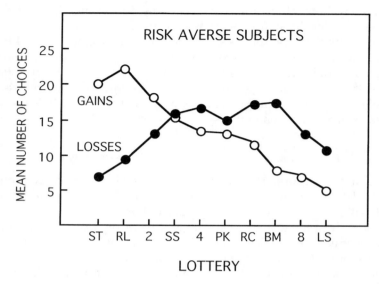

Figure 24.9. Mean preference data for risk-averse subjects for gain lotteries (open symbols) and loss lotteries (filled symbols). Data are the number of times a subject chose a lottery out of the total number of times the lottery was available for choice. (From "Reflection in preferences under risk: Who and when may suggest why" by S. L. Schneider and L. L. Lopes, *Journal of Experimental Psychology: Human Perception and Performance*, 1986. Copyright 1986 by The American Psychological Association. Reprinted by permission.)

outcome gamble and a sure thing of equal expected value. In accord with conventional usage, risk-averse subjects were defined as those who selected the sure thing every time, and risk-seeking subjects were defined as those who selected the gamble at least four times. Thirty subjects were selected from each group.

The 10 stimuli in the experiment included the 6 stimuli in Figure 24.2 plus a $100 sure thing. Subjects were given the stimuli in all possible pairs and asked for their preferences. The pooled data are in Figures 24.9 and 24.10 for risk-averse and risk-seeking subjects, respectively. The stimuli from Figure 24.2 and the sure thing are listed on the abscissa by letter codes (ST = sure thing, RL = riskless, SS = short shot, PK = peaked, RC = rectangular, BM = bimodal, LS = long shot). The lotteries identified by number were an additional riskless lottery (2), an additional short shot (4), and an additional long shot (8). The open symbols are for gain lotteries and the filled symbols are for loss lotteries.

Looking first at the risk-averse subjects, it is clear that their preferences for gains decrease essentially monotonically from the sure thing to the long shot. Their preferences for losses, however, have an inverse U pattern, being low for the sure thing and the riskless lotteries (at the left) as well as for the long

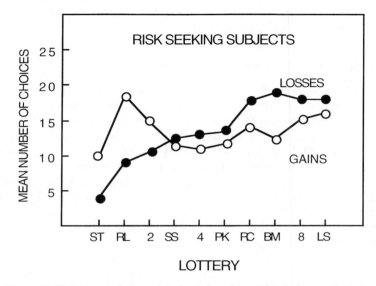

Figure 24.10. Mean preference data for risk-seeking subjects for gain lotteries (open symbols) and loss lotteries (filled symbols). Data are the number of times a subject chose a lottery out of the total number of times the lottery was available for choice. (From "Reflection in preferences under risk: Who and when may suggest why" by S. L. Schneider and L. L. Lopes, *Journal of Experimental Psychology: Human Perception and Performance*, 1986. Copyright 1986 by The American Psychological Association. Reprinted by permission.)

shots (at the right). These qualitative patterns (which were highly reliable statistically) are exactly what the present theory predicts (cf. Table 24.1). For gain lotteries, security and aspiration support the same choices, producing monotonicity. For losses, however, security and aspiration conflict, producing nonmonotonicity.

The risk-seeking subjects also follow the pattern predicted by the two-factor theory. Their preferences are essentially monotonically increasing from the sure thing to the long shot for losses, but vary complexly for gains. Worst liked are the sure thing, the short shots, and the peaked lottery; long shots and riskless lotteries are better liked. These patterns were also highly reliable statistically.

Considering the crudeness of the estimates used in Table 24.1, the fit is remarkably good. Both groups like RL a little better than they should for gains, and risk seekers like long shots a little less well than they should for losses, but the overall picture is as it should be. The presence of nonmonotonicity in both data sets confirms the existence of conflicting factors in risky choice. And the mirror symmetry between the two subject groups confirms their structural similarity. They are basically doing the same thing, but their values differ at least on the security/potential factor, and probably on aspiration level as well.

VI. The things we don't talk about

Psychologists who study risky choice *don't* talk about a surprisingly large number of factors that are psychologically relevant in choosing among risks. Given the poverty of our theoretical language, it is, perhaps, surprising that we manage to talk at all. Here are some words that are not to be found in the theoretical vocabulary: fear, hope, safety, danger, fun, plan, conflict, time, duty, custom. Nor can these words be given meaning in psychophysical theories. The language of psychophysics is the language of perceptual distortion. It has room neither for the experience of emotion (fear, hope, fun), nor for the physical context in which risks occur (safety, danger), nor for the social constraints on individual action (custom, duty), nor for the cognitive activity of the chooser (plan, conflict).

Distributional theories, on the other hand, can express these meanings easily. Oddly, however, it was an economist (Hagen, 1969) who identified skewness with hope and fear, whereas psychologists working with similar theories (Coombs, 1975; Coombs & Lehner, 1981; Luce, 1980; Pollatsek & Tversky, 1970) have shied away from using such language.

Queasiness about the ordinary language of emotion and intention goes back in psychology at least to Watson's behaviorist manifesto and in the area of risky choice has been amplified by exposure to a similar movement in economics termed *positive economics* (Friedman, 1953). In fact, modern economic expected utility theory (von Neumann & Morgenstern, 1947) has relegated even the classical psychophysical concept of utility to the status of an epiphenomenon. In the modern view, utility does not precede and cause preferences; it is, instead, merely a convenient fiction that can be used by the practitioner to summarize the preferences of those who, by choice or chance, follow the dictates of the von Neumann and Morgenstern axiom system.

If, however, hope and fear and plans are necessary ingredients in risky choice, then it is not unscientific to talk about them. Many social scientists working outside the narrow confines of the laboratory or the mathematical proof treat these terms casually, like old friends. In the remainder of this chapter I draw on these broader approaches to risk and show their relation to the present theory.

A. Fear and the safety-first principle

Psychophysical theories of risky choice do without a psychological concept of risk, but people cannot. Risk is a fact of our physical and social environments. This is nowhere more clear than in agriculture, particularly subsistence agriculture in which one's livelihood can be literally threatened from all sides (by floods, by pests, by invading armies). Agricultural economists look at risk quite differently than the axiomatically minded economists who have influenced psychology most strongly in recent years. For the agricultural economist, both risk and risk aversion are real, with behavior connected to need by a simple rule called the safety-first principle.

The subsistence farmer is in a difficult position. Food crops provide food for the table and have low variance of return, but their expected return is also low. Cash crops are more variable but have higher expected return. The problem is how much of each crop to plant. Although many different models of farmers' choice processes have been developed (Anderson, 1979), they all boil down to a simple rule: first take care of subsistence needs (food for the larder and seed for the coming season) and then plant cash crops. Although the farmer's world may be risky, the farmer does not view himself as gambling. In Ortiz's (1979) words, "The peasant's preference for subsistence over starvation cannot be rephrased into a preference for X chance of Y income over $X - n$ chance of $Y - m$ income; such paraphrasing totally misrepresents his options and it is unnecessary" (p. 235).

It should also be noted that, although fear feeds risk aversion, risk taking can be fed either by hope or by necessity (see Section IV,B). Conventional economic theory treats risk taking as a luxury. Neither individuals nor firms are supposed to indulge in it unless they can afford it. Kunreuther and Wright (1979), however, have pointed out that sometimes the poorest farmers devote as large a proportion of their land to cash crops as the richest farmers. Likewise, Bowman (1982) has demonstrated that economically troubled firms often engage in riskier behavior than economically sound firms. In both these cases, risk-seeking behavior is interpreted as arising from necessity. If there is not enough safety even when safety is put first, the risky choice may be the only choice.

The connections between the safety-first principle and the two-factor theory are obvious. The safety-first principle aims at security. A target level is set and choices are made so as to maximize the probability of achieving the target. The resulting choices are "cautiously suboptimal" (Day, 1979). However, risk-taking behavior may predominate when the aspiration level cannot be achieved safely. In neither case do the choices reflect the psychophysics of money or of chances. Nor are they merely the signs of pessimistic or optimistic world views. Farmers who follow the principle want (and need) to accept the risks of cash cropping, but they can do so only up to a point. Their choices reflect the planful activities of intelligent, though unsophisticated, people who know the odds and bet that way.

B. Planning is applied hoping

The flip side of the safety-first principle is entrepreneurship, in which safety takes second place to opportunity. McClelland (1961) described entrepreneurs as people who display a willingness to take risks in situations in which their skills and effort can make a difference. The issue of control appears to be particularly important. Although spectators may judge that entrepreneurs take more risks than the average person, entrepreneurs see themselves as not being particularly risk prone (Keyes, 1985, pp. 207–209; McClelland, 1961, p. 222). This is also true of people who engage in physically risky professions or hobbies: "First they challenge fate, and then they try to bullwhip fate to its knees by making their adventure as predictable as possible. In fact, it's not adventure they're after. It's mastery" (Keyes, 1985, p. 115). Even in casino gambling, where outcomes cannot be controlled, high-stakes gamblers take pride in the control of their emotions (see for example, Alvarez, 1983, pp. 47, 169; Thackrey, 1968, pp. 62–63).

A lot has been written about control in recent years. Langer (1977) has synthesized an impressive body of experimental evidence documenting the fact that people behave as though they believe that chance events can be controlled. In her view, the illusion of control comes about for several good reasons: (1) people are motivated to master their environment; (2) it is unpleasant to believe that one has no control; (3) chance and skill elements coexist in many situations; and (4) the illusion can help us emotionally more than it can harm us practically.

One might suppose (as Langer has *not*) that risk-taking behavior is caused by the optimistic illusion that outcomes are more controllable than they really are. McClelland (1961), however, has argued that entrepreneurship is independent of optimism. He presents evidence from four different countries that school boys who are high in optimism are "conscientious, efficient, forward-looking, *managerial* types [who work] hard and efficiently at everything more or less indiscriminately" (pp. 227–228), but they are not necessarily high in achievement motivation. A student who is high in achievement motivation works hard only on those things that can give a sense of personal responsibility. "If there is no challenge, he doesn't work so hard: in this sense he would make a poor bureaucrat" (p. 228).

The belief that one can control one's fate appears to be necessary to good mental health (Abramson, Seligman, & Teasdale, 1978). When highly desired outcomes are believed to be unlikely or when highly undesirable outcomes are believed to be likely, and when the individual believes that nothing can be done to change these likelihoods, depression results, causing attendant motivational and affective deficits.

Beliefs about control and motivation feed back on one another. When aversive events occur despite one's efforts to prevent them, motivation to control events is reduced both in animals (Maier & Seligman, 1976) and in humans (Hiroto, 1974; Hiroto & Seligman, 1975). When control is later made possible, the motivational deficit prevents learning from occurring. Responses that are not made cannot be reinforced. A vicious cycle results.

Feedback between control and motivation can also be positive. Sawyer (cited in McClelland, 1961, p. 222) has argued that self-confidence in individuals can lead to the very circumstances that are necessary to achieve success. He gives as an example the settling of the American West in the

19th century. Had not so many people behaved as though it was possible, it would *not* have been possible. Although individuals failed in large numbers, sufficiently many survived that settlement was collectively accomplished.

In the present theory, people may be motivated by achievement (potential) as well as by security. McClelland (1961) stressed in his work that people who are high in achievement motivation do not like to gamble. That may be so in the narrow confines of two-outcome gambles presented in the laboratory. In the real world it seems unlikely that achievement-motivated people could be obsessed by security. Although one cannot control the actual outcome in chance situations, one can control the likely outcome. This is what portfolio managers do in the investment field. Maximum return and maximum safety cannot both be had, but one can assemble portfolios that trade a little risk for an acceptable return. Balancing the unavoidable risks in one's personal portfolio is a skillful activity that should appeal to achievement-motivated individuals.

C. Anticipation and imagination

Uncertainty is embedded in time. There is a now in which some things are true, a future in which other things may be true, and a still farther future in which we may reflect on the past. At the point of choice we look forward along this track, and we also anticipate looking back. The temporal element is what gives risk both savor and sting.

Pope (1983) has criticized expected utility theory for having ignored the time between the decision and the resolution of the uncertainty, what she calls the pre-outcome period, during which fear and hope operate. She points out that the period can be long not only for long-term decisions such as individuals choosing careers, governments embarking on social programs, and businesses making major capital investments, but also for repeat short-term decisions: "after deciding to devote a fraction of the housekeeping funds to a weekly lottery ticket, housekeepers can dream from age nineteen to ninety-nine that they will become millionaires after the next drawing" (p. 156).

Uncertainty in the pre-outcome period can be pleasurable or unpleasurable. A traveler to Las Vegas may pay an extra fee to avoid the worrisome uncertainty of the $1000 deductible on a rental car and then proceed at all speed to a casino in order to purchase the delightful uncertainty of gambling. Insurance cannot stop disaster from happening, but it can stop worry. Gambling cannot guarantee future bliss, but it can give hope. For small amounts of money we can enjoy the current psychological benefits of either in the same way that we enjoy other psychological commodities such as entertainment and convenience.

Decisions involving larger amounts of money and other sorts of serious consequences require us to extend our analysis beyond the time in which the uncertainty is resolved. Fears and hopes are then no longer relevant, but regret and disappointment are. Bell (1982, 1985) has argued that if we experience regret over decisions that turned out badly or disappointment over outcomes that fail to match up to expectations, these factors are as important to consider as more tangible monetary benefits and losses. "Psychological satisfaction, as opposed to the satisfaction derived from consumption, is an appropriate objective that should be included in any decision analysis if the decision maker regards it as a criterion for decision" (Bell, 1985, p. 26).

Decision makers also look to a future in which their preferences may change (March, 1978) and in which options not currently imagined may have become possible. Day (1979) has pointed out that farmers and business managers alike resist procedural changes that put them too far from current practice. This is a sensible rule for adapting to dynamic environments (both internal and external) since it leaves the old practice available as a fallback position should the new policy not produce the expected effects.

The importance of having safe fallback positions in real life may account for the fact that the perceived riskiness of technological hazards is not solely related to estimates of annual fatalities but also reflects dread of outcomes that are perceived to be uncontrollable, catastrophic, not easily reversed, and of high risk to future generations. Thus, intelligent but technically unsophisticated raters (students and members of the League of Women Voters) estimate fewer annual deaths from nuclear power than from home appliances but nevertheless consider nuclear power to be much more risky (Slovic, Fischhoff, & Lichtenstein, 1980, Tables 2 and 3).

Psychophysical theories of risk do not consider time, although one might conceive a psychophysics of future events. Economists use a similar notion (time preference rates) to handle the fact that money now is generally worth more than money later. But as Pope (1983) has argued, such a concept would deal only with changes in the worth of the final outcomes and not with the emotions that one experiences in the interim. Theories (such as the present theory) that recognize planning and conflict resolution as an integral part of risky choice can deal more naturally with such temporal factors both as they affect changes in the aspiration level and as they affect position on the security/potential dimension.

D. Sherpas and other high rollers

All life chooses among risks, though we do not ordinarily think of trees choosing how to gamble their seed or amoebas choosing whether to approach or avoid possible prey. For the lowest organisms, evolution has done the choosing and equipped them with prewired choices. For higher organisms, however, cognition increasingly intervenes, allowing learning and reason to override rote instinct. Humans are the most complex cognitively and exhibit responses to risk that sometimes have little to do with the satisfaction of immediate wants or needs. Among these are the responses of our social selves.

High-standard mountaineering is incredibly risky. The chances of being killed on a Himalayan climb are about 1 in 10. Why is it done? What is there on the top of such mountains that anyone might want? Obviously, the answer is aesthetic, not practical, at least for the recreational climber (if such a word can be applied to so hazardous an avocation), who must expend considerable personal resources and obtain even more considerable institutional resources just to make the attempt.

But the Sherpas who carry the loads also share in the risks. Why do the Sherpas climb? The conventional view is that they climb out of economic necessity. Michael Thompson (1980), however, himself an Everest climber, disputes this distinction between Sherpa and non-Sherpa. In Thompson's view, risks that are pursued for practical purposes become tame in the process as has commercial air travel. But risks that are pursued for themselves do not become tame. Thus, for aesthetic purposes a proposed Everest route "is only felt to be worthwhile if there is considerable uncertainty as to its outcome" (p. 278). Sherpas also take this view and refer scornfully to the route that Hillary and Tenzing followed, the easiest of the routes for obvious reasons, as "the Yak route" – a small joke among those who share a common aesthetic.

Risk taking is one of the ways we define ourselves psychologically and socially (Douglas & Wildavsky, 1982). It is a mistake to suppose even in the realm of financial risks that choice is a purely monetary matter. For entrepreneurs and high-stakes gamblers alike, money is not the main thing. It is a way of measuring results, a way of keeping score (cf. Alvarez, 1983, p. 42; McClelland, 1961, p. 237; Thackrey, 1968, pp. 57–58). In the same way, many currently well-to-do people who grew up in the Great Depression continue to value security in a way that their more fortunate children cannot understand. A penny saved is not a penny saved; it is security in the bank.

Nor should custom and duty be forgotten in their effects on risk taking. Consider the story of the *Reindeer* and the *Montcalm* (Mowat, 1982). In March of 1932 the salvage tug *Reindeer* set to sea carrying 28 men in a furious storm to rescue a damaged freighter. *Reindeer* was not designed for such work and was old and ill-equipped. Within hours the tug was foundering 60 miles from land. The vessel *Montcalm*, meanwhile, had been damaged also by the storm and was running for harbor. When it became clear that no other ship could reach *Reindeer* in time, the master of *Montcalm*, Captain Rothwell, turned his ship back to sea. "It had been no easy decision. *Montcalm* carried sixty passengers and a crew of fifty, and their lives were all in Rothwell's care. The risk to them was real enough, but the death of *Reindeer*'s men was sure unless that risk was taken" (Mowat, 1982, p. 46). Although *Reindeer* sank, all were saved, even the ship's dog.

To understand such events requires a more comprehensive view than can be provided by the simple psychophysics of lives saved or lives lost (cf.

Tversky & Kahneman, 1981) or even by the machinery of hope and fear. *Reindeer* was there because risk is the essence of salvage work. Rothwell was captain of *Montcalm* because he was capable of exercising the traditional duty that sailors bear to other sailors. Theories that attempt to explain all of risky choice in the narrow terms of purely perceptual or purely cognitive or purely motivational mechanisms will necessarily miss much of what impels people toward or away from particular risks. The factors that influence human risk taking range from psychophysics to society and from fear to fun. So too should the psychology of risk.

Notes

1 Kahneman and Tversky (1979) call their function a "value function" to distinguish it from the utility function of modern expected utility theory (von Neumann & Morgenstern, 1947). Because this article deals primarily with the psychophysical or classical interpretation of utility, the single word "utility" is used throughout to refer to the subjective value of money or other commodities.

2 Originally the value was assumed to be .50, but now it is believed to be nearer .35 (J. Atkinson, 1983).

3 Researchers presumably also have limitations in their ability to process information. This might be an additional reason for preferring two-outcome gambles, though it does not get mentioned.

4 Hagen's (1969) theory is expressed in terms of the moments of the distribution of psychological or subjective values. In the present case, however, the relations among the moments of the objective distributions are similar to those that would obtain for the subjective distributions.

5 The variance is unchanged when a positive constant is added to each outcome in the distribution. Risk, however, decreases (Keller, Sarin, & Weber, 1986). For example, if $1,000,000 were added to each of the outcomes in the various lotteries in Figure 24.2, their variances would be unchanged, but they would have become much more similar in terms of perceived riskiness.

6 The graphical analyses that are used in this chapter apply only to lotteries having equal expected value. Although Lorenz curves can be drawn for lotteries that differ in expected value (by omitting the normalization step in column 7), comparisons of such Lorenz curves would need to take this into account. In such cases, comparison by means of a mathematical index of security or potential would probably be preferable (see Section IV,A).

7 It is worth noting that strategies that involve maximizing the probability of meeting a goal or aspiration level are fundamentally different from strategies of maximizing expected utility. In the utility formulation, necessity can only be captured by assuming that the utility function temporarily becomes positively accelerated in the region of the target value (see, e.g., Kahneman & Tversky, 1979, p. 279). Such explanations are obviously ad hoc since they can be called into play anytime the standard psychophysics of the situation cannot explain the preference. The alternative view that subjects sometimes attempt to maximize the probability of achieving aspiration levels has been taken by Allais (1979) and by Lopes (1981). Although this view seems to make intuitive sense, it violates the axioms of expected utility theory and has been considered to be irrational for that reason (see, e.g., Samuelson, 1977, p. 48).

8 In cases of strong conflict involving extremely important outcomes (e.g., health issues, large financial transactions, career changes, etc.) conflict may be reduced by various psychological bolstering processes (Festinger, 1957; Janis & Mann, 1977). Whether these entail distortion of values and probabilities during the choice process or selectional mechanisms operating in the construction of a postdecisional rationalization for the chosen alternative is an important question, but not one to which the present experiments can speak. Nevertheless, even if there is considerable distortion predecisionally, security/potential and aspiration level would still function in people's deliberations about the presumably distorted distributions.

9 One could, of course, explain individual differences within a psychophysical theory by supposing that people with different preferences have different utility and probability functions. This would, however, vitiate the claim that risky choices can be explained by basic perceptual processes. At the limit, the functions would become a means for summarizing

preferences after the fact (as is the case for the von Neumann & Morgenstern, 1947, utility function), but such functions would lack predictive and explanatory power.

References

Abramson, L. Y., Seligman, M. P., & Teasdale, J. D. (1978). Learned helplessness in humans: Critique and reformulation. *Journal of Abnormal Psychology, 87,* 49–74.

Allais, M. (1979). The foundations of a positive theory of choice involving risk and a criticism of the postulates and axioms of the American School. In M. Allais & O. Hagen (Eds.), *Expected utility hypotheses and the Allais Paradox* (pp. 27–145). Dordrecht: Reidel (original work published 1952).

Alvarez, A. (1983). *The biggest game in town.* Boston: Houghton Mifflin.

Anderson, J. R. (1979). Perspective on models of uncertain decisions. In J. A. Roumasset, J.-M. Boussard, & I. Singh (Eds.), *Risk, uncertainty, and agricultural development* (pp. 39–62). New York: Agricultural Development Council.

Arrow, K. J. (1971). *Essays in the theory of risk-bearing.* Chicago: Markham.

Atkinson, A. B. (1970). On the measurement of inequality. *Journal of Economic Theory, 2,* 244–263.

Atkinson, J. W. (1957). Motivational determinants of risk-taking behavior. *Psychological Reivew, 64,* 359–372.

Atkinson, J. W. (1958). Towards experimental analysis of human motivation in terms of motives, expectancies, and incentives. In J. W. Atkinson (Ed.), *Motives in fantasy, action, and society* (pp. 288–305). Princeton, NJ: Van Nostrand.

Atkinson, J. W. (1983). *Personality, motivation, and action.* New York: Praeger.

Bell, D. E. (1982). Regret in decision making under uncertainty. *Operations Research, 30,* 961–981.

Bell, D. E. (1985). Disappointment in decision making under uncertainty. *Operations Research, 33,* 1–27.

Bernoulli, D. (1967). *Exposition of a new theory on the measurement of risk.* Farnsborough Hants, England: Gregg Press (original work published in 1738).

Bowman, E. H. (1982). Risk seeking by troubled firms. *Sloan Management Review, 23,* 33–42.

Coombs, C. H. (1975). Portfolio theory and the measurement of risk. In M. F. Kaplan & S. Schwartz (Eds.), *Human judgment and decision processes.* New York: Academic Press.

Coombs, C. H., & Avrunin, G. S. (1983). Single-peaked functions and the theory of preference. *Psychological Review, 84,* 216–230.

Coombs, C. H., & Lehner, P. E. (1981). Evaluation of two alternative models of a theory of risk: I. Are moments of distributions useful in assessing risk? *Journal of Experimental Psychology: Human Perception and Performance, 7,* 1110–1123.

Dahlby, B. G. (1985). *Ranking income distributions in a Harsanyi framework.* Research paper 85-12, Department of Economics, University of Alberta.

Daston, L. J. (1980). Probabilistic expectation and rationality in classical probability theory. *Historia Mathematica, 7,* 234–260.

Day, R. H. (1979). Cautious suboptimizing. In J. A. Roumasset, J.-M. Boussard, & I. Singh (Eds.), *Risk, uncertainty, and agricultural development* (pp. 115–130). New York: Agricultural Development Council.

Douglas, M., & Wildavsky, A. (1982). *Risk and culture*. Berkeley, CA: University of California.

Edwards, W. (1962). Subjective probabilities inferred from decisions. *Psychological Review, 69*, 109–135.

Ellsberg, D. (1961). Risk, ambiguity, and the Savage axioms. *Quarterly Journal of Economics, 75*, 643–669.

Ericsson, K. A., & Simon, H. A. (1980). Verbal reports as data. *Psychological Review, 87*, 215–251.

Festinger, L. (1957). *A theory of cognitive dissonance*. Evanston, IL: Row Peterson.

Friedman, M. (1953). *Essays in positive economics*. Chicago: University of Chicago.

Friedman, M., & Savage, L. J. (1948). The utility analysis of choices involving risk. *Journal of Political Economy, 56*, 279–304.

Hagen, O. (1969). Separation of cardinal utility and specific utility of risk in theory of choices under uncertainty. *Saertrykk av Statsokonomisk Tidsskrift, 3*, 81–107.

Hagen, O. (1979). Towards a positive theory of preferences under risk. In M. Allais & O. Hagen (Eds.), *Expected utility hypotheses and the Allais Paradox* (pp. 271–302). Dordrecht: Reidel.

Hiroto, D. S. (1974). Locus of control and learned helplessness. *Journal of Experimental Psychology, 102*, 187–193.

Hiroto, D. S., & Seligman, M. E. P. (1975). Generality of learned helplessness in man. *Journal of Personality and Social Psychology, 31*, 311–327.

Janis, I. L., & Mann, L. (1977). *Decision making: A psychological analysis of conflict, choice, and commitment*. New York: Free Press.

Kahneman, D., & Tversky, A. (1979). Prospect theory: An analysis of decision under risk. *Econometrica, 47*, 263–291.

Kahneman, D., & Tversky, A. (1984). Choices, values, and frames. *American Psychologist, 39*, 341–350.

Karmarkar, U. S. (1978). Subjectively weighted utility: A descriptive extension of the expected utility model. *Organizational Behavior and Human Performance, 21*, 61–82.

Keller, L. R., Sarin, R. K., & Weber, M. (1986). Empirical investigation of some properties of the perceived riskiness of gambles. *Organizational Behavior and Human Decision Processes, 38*, 114–130.

Keyes, R. (1985). *Chancing it*. Boston: Little, Brown.

Kunreuther, H., & Wright, G. (1979). Safety-first, gambling, and the subsistence farmer. In J. A. Roumasset, J.-M. Boussard, & I. Singh (Eds.), *Risk, uncertainty, and agricultural development* (pp. 213–230). New York: Agricultural Development Council.

Langer, E. J. (1977). The psychology of chance. *Journal for the Theory of Social Behavior, 7*, 185–207.

Liberman, A. M., Harris, K. S., Hoffman, H. S., & Griffith, B. C. (1957). The discrimination of speech sounds within and across phoneme boundaries. *Journal of Experimental Psychology, 54*, 358–368.

Lopes, L. L. (1981). Decision making in the short run. *Journal of Experimental Psychology: Human Learning and Memory, 7*, 377–385.

Lopes, L. L. (1983). Some thoughts on the psychological concept of risk. *Journal of Experimental Psychology: Human Perception and Performance, 9*, 137–144.

Lopes, L. L. (1984). Risk and distributional inequality. *Journal of Experimental Psychology: Human Perception and Performance, 10*, 465–485.

Lopes, L. L. (1987). *Reasoning and risk aversion*. In preparation.

Lopes, L. L., & Casey, J. T. (1994). Tactical and strategic responsiveness in a competitive risk-taking game. *Acta Psychologica, 85*, 39–60.

Luce, R. D. (1980). Several possible measures of risk. *Theory and Decision, 12*, 217–228.

Machina, M. J. (1982). "Expected utility" analysis without the independence axiom. *Econometrica, 50*, 277–323.

Maier, S. F., & Seligman, M. E. P. (1976). Learned helplessness: Theory and evidence. *Journal of Experimental Psychology: General, 105*, 3–46.

March, J. G. (1978). Bounded rationality, ambiguity, and the engineering of choice. *Bell Journal of Economics, 9*, 587–608.

Markowitz, H. (1952). The utility of wealth. *Journal of Political Economy, 60*, 151–158.

Markowitz, H. M. (1959). *Portfolio selection: Efficient diversification of investments*. New York: Wiley.

Maslow, A. H. (1954). *Motivation and personality*. New York: Harper.

McClelland, D. C. (1958). Risk-taking in children with high and low need for achievement. In J. W. Atkinson (Ed.), *Motives in fantasy, action, and society* (pp. 306–321). Princeton, NJ: Van Nostrand.

McClelland, D. C. (1961). *The achieving society*. Princeton, NJ: Van Nostrand.

Mischel, W. (1968). *Personality and assessment*. New York: Wiley.

Mowat, F. (1982). *Grey seas under*. New York: Bantam.

Ortiz, S. (1979). The effect of risk aversion strategies on subsistence and cash crop decisions. In J. A. Roumasset, J.-M. Bousard, & I. Singh (Eds.), *Risk, uncertainty, and agricultural development* (pp. 231–246). New York: Agricultural Development Council.

Pollatsek, A., & Tversky, A. (1970). A theory of risk. *Journal of Mathematical Psychology, 7*, 540–553.

Pope, R. (1983). The pre-outcome period and the utility of gambling. In B. P. Stigum & F. Wenstøp (Eds.), *Foundations of utility and risk theory with applications* (pp. 137–177). Dordrecht: Reidel.

Pratt, J. W. (1964). Risk aversion in the small and in the large. *Econometrica, 32*, 122–135.

Samuelson, P. A. (1977). St. Petersburg paradoxes: Defanged, dissected, and historically described. *Journal of Economic Literature, 15*, 24–55.

Savage, L. J. (1954). *The foundations of statistics*. New York: Wiley.

Schneider, S. L., & Lopes, L. L. (1986). Reflection in preferences under risk: Who and when may suggest why. *Journal of Experimental Psychology: Human Perception and Performance, 12*, 535–548.

Siegel, S. (1957). Level of aspiration and decision making. *Psychological Review, 64*, 253–262.

Simon, H. A. (1955). A behavioral model of rational choice. *Quarterly Journal of Economics, 69*, 99–118.

Slovic, P., Fischhoff, B., & Lichtenstein, S. (1980). Facts and fears: Understanding perceived risk. In R. C. Schwing & W. A. Albers, Jr. (Eds.), *Societal risk assessment: How safe is safe enough?* New York: Plenum.

Thackrey, T. (1968). *Gambling secrets of Nick the Greek*. Chicago: Rand McNally.

Thompson, M. (1980). Aesthetics of risk: Culture or context. In R. C. Schwing & W. A. Albers, Jr. (Eds.), *Societal risk assessment: How safe is safe enough?* New York: Plenum.

Tversky, A., & Kahneman, D. (1981). The framing of decisions and the psychology of choice. *Science, 211*, 453–458.

von Neumann, J., & Morgenstern, O. (1947). *Theory of games and economic behavior*. Princeton NJ: Princeton University (2nd ed.).

Williams, A. C. (1966). Attitudes toward speculative risks as an indicator of attitudes toward pure risks. *Journal of Risk and Insurance, 33*, 577–586.

Author index

Subject index

person impression (cont.)
  judgment relationship, 432–3
  on-line versus memory-based, 438–48
  and positive affect, 514
  primacy effects, 432
  social goals in, 441
  spontaneous inferences, 440–2
  two-memory hypothesis, 434–5
personality; *see also* dispositions
  and positive test strategies, 227–8
  versus psychophysical factors, 686–90
  and risk choices, 685–710
  two-factor theory, risk decisions, 700–10
perspective effects
  content-domain influences on, 582–3
  and incomplete information, 583
persuasion research, 8
phonological rules, 625
physician protocols, *see* medical judgments
Piagetian developmental theory, 580
Poisson process models, 458
policy models, 543–7
political research program, 657–80; *see also*
    accountability
"portfolio theory," 682
positive affect, 509–34
  asymmetric influence of, 510–11
  capacity-reduction hypothesis, 527–9
  cognitive flexibility stimulus, 513–16,
    527–9
  complex decision-making influence, 524–6
  context interactions, 512, 518
  helping behavior stimulus, 519, 521
  and heuristic strategies, 526–9
  and motivation, 519–21
  versus negative affect, memory, 510
  problem-solving facilitation, 517–18
  and risk preference, 522–4
  systematic cognitive processing
    interference, 527–9
positive economics movement, 710
positive expectations, 422–3
positive feedback
  and exactingness, 249–51, 277
  incentives interaction, 264–7
  response strategy consistency role, 256–7,
    275
positive test strategy, 205–43
  in concept identification paradigm, 225
  conditions favoring use of, 214–24
  confirmation bias relationship, 209
  contingency judgments advantages, 229–
    32
  definition, 206, 209
  four-card problem application, 226–7
  and intuitive personality testing, 227–8
  and outcome feedback, 228–9
  in probabilistic environments, 221–4
  in rule-discovery tasks, 209–24
post-decisional accounting, 665–6, 672–3

pragmatic reasoning schemas, 578
predicted utility, 394–410
  accuracy, 396–408
  experienced utility relationship, 393–410
  stereotypes in, 400, 406
preemptive self-criticism, 667–8
preference reversal paradigm, 201
preferential choice
  and accountability, 676–7
  anticipatory motivation, 713–14
  content effects, 581–91
  disjunctive reasons, 84–8
  domain specificity, 566–605
  early research, 4–6, 9–11, 14–19
  gambling paradigm, critique of, 566–605
  information processing approach, 18–19
  and organism–environment relationships,
    23–4
  prior knowledge effects, 593–601
  reason-based model, 72–89
  and risk, lottery paradigm, 690–710
  surface task structure role, 552–64
preparedness, 576
primacy effects
  and jury decisions, 475–6
  rule-based reasoning, 636–7
prisoner's dilemma game
  iterated format, 381–2, 391n1
  methodological weaknesses, 381–2
  uncertainty conditions effect on, 88
Probabilistic Functionalism, 27
probabilistic judgments, 24–34, 95–143
  ANOVA model modification, 294–300
  Brunswikian theory, 7–8, 95–143
  in causal inference, 285–321
  confidence framework, 95–143
  and conjunctive causes, 300–1
  content-dependent tasks, 601–2
  contrast effects model, 285–321
  early research, 7–8
  frequency versus confidence tasks, 102–38
  heuristics and biases in, 24–6, 135–7
  linear heuristics, 301–7
  and main effect contrasts, 290–1
  mental models, 95–143; predictions, 104–9
  motivational versus mental models, 124–5
  normality criterion, 309–11
  paradigm shift in research, 25–6
  personality perspective, 685–8
  psychophysical perspective, 686–8
  and risk decisions, weighted values, 682–4
  subjectivity influences, 9–11
probability cues, 99–103
  representative sampling, 103–24, 133–5
  vicarious functioning of, 100–1
problem solving
  content-dependent reasoning in, 578–80
  and positive affect, 517–18
procedural memory
  in nondeliberative decision making, 584